Why You Need this New Edition

If you're wondering why you should buy this new edition of _Women's Lives: A Psychological Exploration_, here are 7 good reasons!

- The section on adolescence contains **new data** on the "menstrual suppression" debate, factors affecting "loss of voice" in adolescence, and the sexualization of young girls.

- **New material** in the education chapter includes expanded coverage of factors related to girls' and women's math and science performance, **new research** on stereotype threat, and the thought-provoking debate on the alleged "boy crisis" in education.

- The sexuality chapter includes **new findings** on the fluidity of female sexual orientation and **updated information** on same-sex marriages and civil unions in the U.S. and abroad.

- The much-admired chapter on Balancing Work and Family (Chapter 11) is **expanded** and includes **new coverage** of the controversy concerning whether professional women are "opting out" of the labor force to stay home with their children.

- The health chapters contain **updated** and **expanded coverage** of ethnicity, poverty and healthcare, the global AIDS epidemic, the debate surrounding the new vaccine against the human papillomavirus, and **new material** on eating disorders across the lifespan.

- **Expanded coverage** of violence against women includes updated information on the horrors of human trafficking, women in war zones, and honor killings.

- Nearly 1,200 **new** references from 2005 on, give students insights into cutting-edge developments.

SECOND EDITION

Women's Lives

A Psychological Exploration

Claire A. Etaugh
Bradley University

Judith S. Bridges
University of Connecticut at Hartford, Emerita

Allyn & Bacon

Boston   New York   San Francisco
Mexico City   Montreal   Toronto   London   Madrid   Munich   Paris
Hong Kong   Singapore   Tokyo   Cape Town   Sydney

Acquisitions Editor: Michelle Limoges
Editorial Assistant: Paige Clunie
Marketing Manager: Nicole Kunzmann
Production Supervisor: Roberta Sherman
Editorial Production Service: TexTech, Inc.
Manufacturing Buyer: JoAnne Sweeney
Electronic Composition: TexTech, Inc.
Photo Researcher: Martha Shethar
Cover Administrator: Kristina Mose-Libon

Library of Congress Cataloging-in-Publication Data

Etaugh, Claire.
    Women's lives : a psychological exploration / Claire A. Etaugh, Judith S. Bridges. — 2nd ed.
        p. cm.
    Includes bibliographical references and index.
    ISBN-13: 978-0-205-59418-4
    ISBN-10: 0-205-59418-2
    1. Women—Psychology.   2. Women—North America—Social conditions.
I. Bridges, Judith S.   II.   Title.
HQ1206.E883 2010
155.3'33—dc22   2008043566

10 9 8 7 6 5 4   HAM 13 12 11

Allyn & Bacon
is an imprint of

www.pearsonhighered.com

ISBN-10: 0-205-59418-2
ISBN-13: 978-0-205-59418-4

DEDICATION

To Andi: my daughter, my friend.

—C.E.

To my husband, Barry, my life partner and best friend,
who is always there for me and to my children, Rachel and Jason,
and their spouses, Gray and Nora, who reflect the promise
of a more gender-equal tomorrow.

—J.S.B.

CONTENTS

PREFACE   xix

1 INTRODUCTION TO THE PSYCHOLOGY OF WOMEN: HISTORY AND RESEARCH   1

  Definitions: Sex and Gender   2

  Women and Men: Similar or Different?   3
    Similarities Approach   3
    Differences Approach   3

  Feminism   4

  History of Women in Psychology   6
    Women and the American Psychological Association   7
    Women's Contributions   8

  History of the Psychology of Women   8
    The Early Years   8
    The Recent Years   9

  Studying the Psychology of Women   10
    Bias in Psychological Research   10
    Feminist Research Methods   17
    Drawing Conclusions from Multiple Studies   18

  Themes in the Text   20
    Theme 1: Diversity of Women's Experiences   20
    Theme 2: Gender Differences in Power   21
    Theme 3: Social Construction of Gender   22

2 CULTURAL REPRESENTATION OF GENDER   26

  Stereotypes of Females and Males   28
    The Content of Gender Stereotypes   28
    The Perceiver's Ethnicity and Gender Stereotypes   30
    The Target's Characteristics and Gender Stereotypes   31
    Stereotypes of Girls and Boys   34
    Bases for Gender Stereotypes   34
    Stereotypes Based on Identity Labels   36

Sexism   37

Ambivalent Sexism   37

Changes in Sexist Attitudes over Time   38

Modern Sexism   38

Experiences with Sexism   40

Representation of Gender in the Media   41

Pattern 1: Underrepresentation of Females   42

Pattern 2: Underrepresentation of Specific Groups of Females   43

Pattern 3: Portrayal of Gender-Based Social Roles   46

Pattern 4: Depiction of Female Communion and Male Agency   48

Pattern 5: Emphasis on Female Attractiveness and Sexuality   49

Significance of Gender-Role Media Images   51

Representation of Gender in the English Language   52

Language Practices Based on the Assumption That Male
Is Normative   52

Negative Terms for Females   55

Significance of the Differential Treatment of Females and Males
in Language   57

3   GENDER SELF-CONCEPT: DEVELOPMENTAL PROCESSES AND INDIVIDUAL DIFFERENCES   60

Gender Self-Concept   61

Prenatal Development   62

Stages of Prenatal Sex Differentiation   62

Intersexuality   64

Case Studies   66

Theories of Gender Typing   68

Psychoanalytic Theory   68

Social Learning Theory   70

Cognitive Developmental Theory   72

Gender Schema Theory   74

Gender-Related Traits   76

Changes in Gender-Related Traits over Time   77

Gender-Related Traits and Psychological Adjustment   79

Evaluation of the Concept of Androgyny   80

Gender Attitudes   80

Individual Differences in Gender-Related Attitudes   83

Perceived Value of Female versus Male Gender-Related Attributes   86

4 INFANCY, CHILDHOOD, AND ADOLESCENCE   92

Children's Knowledge and Beliefs about Gender   93
Distinguishing between Females and Males   94
Gender Identity and Self-Perceptions   94
Gender Stereotypes   95

Gender-Related Activities and Interests   96
Physical Performance and Sports   97
Toys and Play   98
Gender Segregation   100

Influences on Gender Development   103
Parents   103
Siblings   108
School   108
Peers   109
Media   109

Puberty   109
Events of Puberty   110
Menarche   112
Gender Differences in Puberty   113
Early and Late Maturation in Girls   114

Psychosocial Development in Adolescence   115
Identity   116
Self-Esteem   116
Gender Intensification   118
Body Image   119

5 GENDER COMPARISONS: SOCIAL BEHAVIOR, PERSONALITY, COMMUNICATION, AND COGNITION   127

Gender-Related Social Behaviors and Personality Traits   128
Aggression   128
Prosocial Behavior   130
Influenceability   130
Emotionality   131
Moral Reasoning   132

Communication Style   133
  Verbal Communication   133
  Nonverbal Communication   137

Gender Comparison of Cognitive Abilities   138
  Verbal Ability   139
  Visual–Spatial Ability   140
  Mathematics Ability   143

6   SEXUALITY   153

Sexuality   154
  Sexual Anatomy and Sexual Response   154
  Sexual Attitudes   156
  Sexual Behaviors   157
  Sexual Problems   159

Lesbians and Bisexual Women   163
  Bisexual Women   164
  Attitudes Towards Lesbians   165
  Explanations of Sexual Orientation   168

Sexual Activity During Adolescence   169
  Frequency of Sexual Activity   170
  Factors Associated with Sexual Activity   171
  The Double Standard   172
  Sexual Desire   172

Sexual Activity in Midlife   173
  Physical Changes   173
  Patterns of Sexual Activity   173

Sexual Activity in Later Life   174
  Benefits of Sexual Activity in Later Life   175
  Sexual Behavior of the Elderly   176
  Factors Affecting Sexual Behavior   176
  Enhancing Sexuality in Later Life   177

7   REPRODUCTIVE SYSTEM AND CHILDBEARING   181

Menstruation   182
  The Menstrual Cycle   182
  Menstrual Pain   184
  Attitudes toward Menstruation   184

Menstrual Joy   185
Premenstrual Syndrome   185

Contraception   188
Contraception in Adolescence   188
Methods of Contraception   189

Abortion   191
Incidence   191
Methods   192
Consequences of Abortion   192

Pregnancy   194
Pregnancy: Physical and Psychological Changes   195
Miscarriage   197
Teenage Pregnancy   198

Childbirth   200
Stages of Childbirth   200
Methods of Childbirth   201
Childbearing after 40   202
Childbearing in the Later Years   203
Postpartum Distress   205
Infertility and Assisted Reproductive Technology   205

Reproductive Functioning in Midlife and Beyond   208
Menopause   208
Hormone Replacement Therapy   210

8 RELATIONSHIPS   216

Friendships   217
Friendship in Adolescence   217
Friendship in Adulthood   218
Friendship in Later Life   219

Romantic Relationships   220
Importance of Physical Attractiveness   220
Perception of Sexual Interest   223
Dating   223
Recent Trends in Dating   226

Committed Relationships   227
Marriage   227
Cohabitation   229
Lesbian Relationships   230

Single Women   232
Divorced Women   232
Never-Married Women   235
Widowed Women   236
Women Who Have Lost a Same-Sex Partner   238

Motherhood   238
Stereotypes of Mothers   239
Single Mothers   240
Lesbian Mothers   242
Mothers with Disabilities   243
The "Empty Nest" Period   243

Relationships in the Later Years   246
Siblings   246
Adult Children   247
Grandchildren   248
Parents   252

9   EDUCATION AND ACHIEVEMENT   258

Women's Educational Values, Attainment, and Campus Experience   259
Educational Values   260
Educational Attainment   260
Campus Climate   263

Women's Work-Related Goals   267
Career Aspirations   268
Career Counseling   269
Work–Family Expectations   270
Work–Family Outcomes   272
Salary Expectations   273

Influences on Women's Achievement Level and Career Decisions   273
Orientation to Achievement   274
Personality Characteristics   276
Sexual Orientation   277
Social and Cultural Factors   277
Job-Related Characteristics   279

Entering the Workplace   280

10 EMPLOYMENT   283

Women's Employment Rates and Occupational Choices   285
Employment Rates   285
Occupational Choices   286

Gender Differences in Leadership and Job Advancement   288
Leadership Positions   288
Barriers That Hinder Women's Advancement   289
Women as Leaders   293

Gender Differences in Salaries   293
Comparative Salaries   293
Reasons for Differences in Salaries   295

Women's Job Satisfaction   299
Gender Differences in Satisfaction   300
Factor Influencing Lesbians' Job Satisfaction   301

The Older Woman Worker   302
Employment Rates   302
Why Do Older Women Work?   302
Entering the Workforce in Later Life   303
Age Discrimination in the Workplace   303

Changing the Workplace   304
Organizational Procedures and Policies   304
Strategies for Women   305

Retirement   307
The Retirement Decision   307
Adjustment to Retirement   309
Leisure Activities in Retirement   311

Economic Issues in Later Life   314
Poverty   314
Retirement Income: Planning Ahead   315

11 BALANCING FAMILY AND WORK   323

Attitudes toward Women's Family and Employment Roles   326
Role of Ethnicity   326
Role of Motherhood   326
Personal Aspirations   326

Division of Household Labor   329

Importance of Work and Family Roles for Women and Men   329

Housework and Child Care   329

Caring for Aging Parents   330

Leisure Time   331

Women's Perceptions of the Division of Family Labor   331

Explanations of the Division of Family Labor   332

Family–Work Coordination   333

Parental Leave   333

Balancing Family and Work   335

Effects of Mothers' Employment on Children   340

Effects of Women's Employment on the Marital Relationship   341

Solutions to Family–Work Balancing Difficulties   342

Midlife Transitions in Family and Work Roles   347

Satisfaction with Life Roles   347

Regrets about Life Direction   348

Making Changes   348

Midlife Transitions: A Cautionary Note   349

12   PHYSICAL HEALTH   353

Health Services   354

The Physician–Patient Relationship   355

Type and Quality of Care   356

Ethnicity, Poverty, and Health Care   357

Lesbian Health and Health Care   358

Health Insurance   359

Sexually Transmitted Infections (STIs)   360

Overview of STIs   360

AIDS   362

Reproductive System Disorders   366

Benign Conditions   367

Cancers   367

Hysterectomy   368

Osteoporosis   369

Risk Factors   370

Prevention and Treatment   370

Heart Disease   372

Gender Differences   372

Risk Factors   372

Diagnosis and Treatment   374
Psychological Impact   375

Breast Cancer   375
Risk Factors   376
Detection   377
Treatment   379
Psychological Impact   380

Physical Health in Later Life   381
Gender Differences in Mortality   381
Social Class and Ethnic Differences   384
Gender Differences in Illness   385
Disability   385

Promoting Good Health   386
Physical Activity and Exercise   386
Nutrition   389

13   MENTAL HEALTH   393

Factors Promoting Mental Health   395
Social Support   395
Optimism: "The Power of Positive Thinking"   395

Mental Health in Childhood and Adolescence   396
Internalizing Disorders in Girls   397
Externalizing Disorders in Girls   397

Eating Disorders   397
Types of Eating Disorders   397
Causes of Eating Disorders   400
Treatment of Eating Disorders   401

Substance Use and Abuse   402
Alcohol   402
Illegal Substances   404

Anxiety Disorders and Depression   405
Anxiety Disorders   405
Depression   406
Suicide   408

Mental Health of Lesbians   411
Stresses and Problems   412
Coping Mechanisms   412

Mental Health of Older Women   412
Gender Differences   413
The Vital Older Woman   413

Diagnosis and Treatment of Psychological Disorders   414
Gender Bias in Diagnosis   414
Gender Bias in Psychotherapy   415
Therapy Issues for Women of Color and Poor Women   416
Types of Therapy   416

14   VIOLENCE AGAINST GIRLS AND WOMEN   421

Sexual Harassment at School   423
Elementary and Secondary School   423
The College Campus   423

Sexual Harassment in the Workplace   426
Incidence   427
Consequences   430
Explanations   430
Women's Responses   431

Violence against Girls   432
Child Sexual Abuse   432
Infanticide and Neglect   435

Dating Violence   437
Incidence of Dating Violence   437
Who Engages in Dating Violence?   438

Rape   438
Incidence   439
Acquaintance Rape   439
Factors Associated with Acquaintance Rape   440
Effects of Rape   443
Rape Prevention   445
Theories of Rape   445

Intimate Partner Violence   447
Incidence   448
Role of Disability, Social Class, and Ethnicity   448
Risk Factors   449
Effects of Intimate Partner Violence   450
Leaving the Abusive Relationship   451
Theories of Intimate Partner Violence   451
Interventions   451

Elder Abuse   452
Types of Abuse   452
Who Is Abused and Who Abuses?   454
What Can Be Done?   454

15 **A FEMINIST FUTURE: GOALS, ACTIONS, AND ATTITUDES   459**

    Feminist Goals   460

        Goal One: Gender Equality in Organizational Power   460
        Goal Two: Gender Equality in Relationship Power   461
        Goal Three: Gender Equality in Power for All Groups of Women   461
        Goal Four: Greater Flexibility in the Social Construction of Gender   461

    Actions to Achieve These Goals   462

        Research and Teaching   462
        Socialization of Children   464
        Institutional Procedures   465
        Individual Actions   467
        Collective Action   467

    Feminist Beliefs   470

        Feminist Identification   471
        Emergence of Feminist Beliefs   474
        Men and Feminism   475

    Postscript   475

    REFERENCES   479

    NAME INDEX   575

    SUBJECT INDEX   592

    PHOTO CREDITS   600

PREFACE

Over the last few decades, the burgeoning interest in the psychology of women has been reflected in a rapidly expanding body of research and a growing number of college-level courses in the psychology of women or gender. *Women's Lives: A Psychological Exploration* draws on this rich literature to present a broad range of experiences and issues of relevance to girls and women. Because it does not presuppose any background in psychology, this book can be used as the sole or primary text in introductory-level psychology of women courses and, with other books, in psychology of gender or interdisciplinary women's studies courses. Additionally, its presentation of both current and classical research and theory make it a suitable choice, along with supplementary materials, for more advanced courses focused on the psychology of women or gender.

Every chapter reflects substantial changes in this field during the past few years. We have made several changes based on the extremely helpful comments from reviewers and the many students and faculty who have used the two lifespan editions and the first topical edition of this book. This new topical revision includes the following highlights:

- Over 2,700 twenty-first-century references emphasize the latest research and theories, with 1,130 new to this edition.
- *Explore Other Cultures*, a boxed feature in each chapter, provides students with an understanding of the role of cultural, social, and economic factors in shaping women's lives around the world.
- The unique lifespan approach of two previous editions is embedded within topical chapters on sexuality, reproduction and childbearing, education and achievement, employment, physical health, mental health, and violence against girls and women.
- Coverage of the lives of women in the middle and later years is far more extensive than in any other textbook in the field.
- An updated list of Web sites and current books at the end of each chapter provides students with resources for additional study and research.
- Expanded use of vignettes and quotes from women add richness to the data and help students personally connect with the material.
- Expanded coverage of many topics reflects scientific and social developments of the new millenium.

These changes are broken down by chapter and include:

- Chapter 1: Updated information on women in psychology.
- Chapter 2: Expanded section on representation of women in the media.
- Chapter 3: Current information on intersexuality.

- Chapter 4: New data on women in sports, the "menstrual suppression" debate, factors affecting "loss of voice" in adolescence, and the sexualization of young girls.
- Chapter 5: Expanded section on factors related to girls' and women's math and science performance, including new research on stereotype threat.
- Chapter 6: New findings on the fluidity of female sexual orientation.
- Chapter 7: Current trends in the medicalization of childbirth, assisted reproductive technology, childbirth in women over 40, and the latest data on the effects of hormone replacement therapy.
- Chapter 8: Expanded coverage of trends in cosmetic surgery (including the "mommy makeover"), the increasing acceptance of single lifestyles, and current data on same-sex marriages and civil unions in the United States and abroad.
- Chapter 9: Current information on women's educational aspirations and attainments, and discussion of the debate on the alleged "boy crisis" in education.
- Chapter 10: Expanded coverage of women in the global factory, and updated information on women leaders around the world.
- Chapter 11: Discussion of the disputed claim that professional women are "opting out" of the labor force to stay home with their young children.
- Chapter 12: Update on ethnicity, poverty, and health care; the global AIDS epidemic; and coverage of the debate about the new vaccine against human papillomavirus.
- Chapter 13: Expanded coverage of eating disorders across the lifespan.
- Chapter 14: Updated information on human trafficking, women in war zones, and honor killings.
- Chapter 15: Current information on women's movements worldwide and on factors related to the emergence of feminist beliefs.

Special Features Related to Content and Organization

Lifespan Approach Embedded within Topical Chapters.   Almost all textbooks in this field use a topical approach and also include two or three chronological chapters. Typically, there is a chapter or two on childhood and adolescence and one on women in the middle and later years. Almost all coverage of midlife and older women is contained in that one chapter. The result is that many of the issues and experiences relating to women in midlife and beyond are barely touched on or simply are not covered at all. These older women remain relatively invisible.

Our approach is different. We have taken the unique lifespan approach of our two earlier chronologically focused texts and have embedded this approach within almost all chapters, including topical chapters on sexuality, reproduction and childbearing, education and achievement, employment, physical health, mental health, and violence against girls and women. Midlife and older women are discussed in all chapters except the one on infancy, childhood, and adolescence.

Integration of Women's Diversity throughout the Text.   The text provides extensive coverage of women of color, women in other cultures around the world, and lesbian and bisexual women. Although there is less information available, we also include material on poor women and women with disabilities whenever possible. We chose to integrate women's diversity throughout each chapter rather than in separate chapters on subgroups of women. An integrated approach demonstrates similarities and differences in life-stage experiences of diverse groups of women without creating the impression that certain groups of women are treated separately because they deviate from the norm.

Thorough Examination of Balancing Family and Work.   It is clear that at this point in our history, the balancing of family and work is a major issue facing North American families. We devote an entire chapter to this timely topic in order to thoroughly explore the theories, challenges, benefits, and solutions associated with this great challenge of the twenty-first century.

Pedagogical Features

Introductory Outline.   Each chapter begins with an outline of the material, thus providing an organizational framework for reading the material.

Opening Vignettes.   In order to grab students' attention and connect the material to real life, each chapter begins with one or two actual or hypothetical experiences illustrating one or more issues discussed in the chapter.

What Do You Think? Questions.   The text includes critical-thinking questions in every chapter. The end-of-the-chapter What Do You Think? questions foster skills in synthesis and evaluation by asking the student to apply course material or personal experiences to provocative issues from the chapter.

Get Involved Exercises.   As a means of providing firsthand involvement in the material, each chapter contains a number of student activities. Some require collecting data on a small number of respondents and others focus solely on the student. Furthermore, each exercise is accompanied by critical-thinking What Does It Mean? questions that focus on explanations and implications of the activity's findings.

The active learning involved in these activities serves several purposes. First, it reinforces the material learned in the text. Second, those exercises that involve surveys of other people or analyses of societal artifacts introduce students to the research process, which, in turn, can stimulate interest in research, increase familiarity with a variety of assessment techniques, and provoke critical evaluation of research techniques. Third, the Get Involved activities demonstrate the relevance of the course material to students' experiences or to the experiences of important people in their lives.

Explore Other Cultures.   In order to provide students with a deeper appreciation of women in a global context, each chapter contains between one and five boxed features highlighting the role of cultural, social, and economic factors in shaping women's lives around the world.

Learn about the Research.   To stimulate student interest in and appreciation of research as a source of knowledge about girls and women, each chapter has one or two boxed sections that focus on research. These Learn about the Research sections either highlight an interesting current study or present an overview of recent findings in an intriguing research area. We expose students to a variety of research techniques (content analysis, interviews, questionnaires) without requiring that they have any background in psychological research methods. Furthermore, to highlight the importance of diversity in research samples, our selections include studies of underrepresented populations.

Following the research presentation are What Does It Mean? questions. These provoke more critical thinking by asking the student to consider a variety of issues related to the research, such as explanations and implications of the findings.

Key Terms.   Bolded terms and italicized definitions within the text help students preview, understand, and review important concepts.

Summary.   The point-by-point end-of-the-chapter summary helps the student synthesize the material.

If You Want to Know More.   Recommended readings at the end of each chapter facilitate more extensive examination of the material. This edition includes 81 new recommended books to stimulate students to expand their knowledge.

Web sites.   An updated list of Web sites at the end of each chapter provides students with additional resources.

Writing Style

In order to engage the student and construct a nonhierarchical relationship between ourselves and the student, we use a nonpedantic first-person writing style. To reinforce this relationship in some of the opening vignettes and within the text, we also present our own experiences or those of our friends and families.

Ancillary Materials

Instructor's Manual and Test Bank.   The Instructor's Manual and the Test Bank contain a variety of activities to stimulate active learning. The Instructor's Manual includes critical thinking discussion topics and offers exercises that the instructor can use instead of, or supplementary to, the Get Involved activities incorporated within the text. In addition, the manual includes film and video listings as well as additional Internet Websites. Finally, it contains multiple-choice and essay questions for each chapter.

PowerPoint Presentations.   The PowerPoint presentation contains outlines of key topics for each text chapter, presented in a clear and visually attractive format.

Acknowledgments

We owe a great deal to the many reviewers whose expert suggestions and insights were invaluable in the development of this book. Our sincere thanks to all of you who reviewed the text for this second edition: Veanne Anderson, Indiana State University; Kim Dielmann, University of Central Arkansas; Carol Miller, Anne Arundel Community College; Nancy Rogers, University of Cincinnati; and Barbara Winstead, Old Dominion University. Our thanks also go out to the reviewers of the first edition: Jill Johnson, Carl Sandburg College; Barbara A. Rienzo, University of Florida; Harriet Amster, University of Texas at Arlington; Judith LeMaster, Scripps College; Susan K. Johnson, University of North Carolina—Charlotte; Maria Lavooy, University of Central Florida; Leslee Koritzke, Los Angeles Trade Tech College; Jo-Ellen Asbury, Bethany College; Laura Madson, New Mexico State University; Sandra Harris, Troy State University; Kristen Kling, St. Cloud State University; Wendy Bartkus, Pennsylvania State University—Schuylkill Campus.

It has been a pleasure to work with the publishing professionals at Allyn & Bacon. In particular, we acknowledge the invaluable support and assistance of Michelle Limoges, our editor for this book. We also are deeply indebted to Pat Campbell and Maggie Koehler, who flawlessly and cheerfully carried out the mind-boggling tasks of locating and keeping track of over 1,100 new references, securing permissions, revising the indexes, proofreading, and carrying out numerous other tasks essential to the production of this book.

Thanks also to the students in our Psychology of Women courses who provided excellent editorial suggestions on earlier versions of the manuscript and for whom, ultimately, this book is written.

Finally, the book could not have been completed without the loving support of our families. Judith thanks her mother, Ruth; mother-in-law, Hilde; and children, Rachel and Jason, and their spouses, Gray and Nora, for providing support and inspiration throughout this project. Also, her deepest appreciation goes to her husband Barry for his unwavering patience, understanding, and encouragement. Claire's heartfelt thanks go to the women and men who have enriched her life and have been an endless source of encouragement and support throughout this project: her late parents, Martha and Lou; siblings, Paula, Bonnie, and Howard; children, Andi and Adam; grandchildren, Anthony and Isabel; and "extended family" of friends, Peggy, Pat, Par, Barbara, Michael, Kevin, Pam, Holly, Linda, and Colleen.

CHAPTER

1

Introduction to the Psychology of Women

History and Research

Definitions: Sex and Gender

Women and Men: Similar or Different?
Similarities Approach
Differences Approach

Feminism

History of Women in Psychology
Women and the American Psychological
Association
Women's Contributions

History of the Psychology of Women
The Early Years
The Recent Years

Studying the Psychology of Women
Bias in Psychological Research
Feminist Research Methods
Drawing Conclusions from Multiple Studies

Themes in the Text
Theme 1: Diversity of Women's Experiences
Theme 2: Gender Differences in Power
Theme 3: Social Construction of Gender

In 1965 when I (Judith) was applying to graduate schools, the chair of one psychology department informed me that my college grades met the criterion for male, but not female, admission into the program. That department (and others) had two sets of standards and, obviously, fewer women than men were admitted. When I look back at that time it is amazing to me to realize that I quietly accepted this pronouncement. I was disappointed but not outraged. I rejoiced at my acceptance by a comparable department but never thought to protest discriminatory admission policies (which were not unique to that department). A generation ago I did not identify this issue or any other gender inequality in institutional, legal, or interpersonal practices as a problem. However, over the last several decades my awareness and concern about these issues dramatically changed. Claire and I are deeply committed to gender equality in all areas of life and hope that this text will help illuminate both the progress women have made and the challenges that remain in the attainment of this important goal.

In this chapter we set the groundwork for the study of the psychology of women. We present major definitions, explore relevant history, examine research issues, and discuss the themes of the book. We begin with a look at the difference between sex and gender.

Definitions: Sex and Gender

Psychologists do not agree completely on the definitions of the words *sex* and *gender*. *Sex* is used to refer either to whether a person is female or male, or to sexual behavior. This ambiguity of definition sometimes can cause confusion. For example, Claire offered a course several years ago entitled "The Psychology of Sex Differences." The course dealt with behavioral similarities and differences of females and males. After the first day of class, some students approached her with a puzzled look on their faces. The course title had led them to believe that the subject matter of the course was human sexuality.

The words *sex* and *gender* have often been used interchangeably to describe the differences in the behaviors of women and men. One example is the term *sex roles*, which is sometimes used to refer to culturally prescribed sets of behaviors for men and women. *Sex Roles* is even the name of a highly respected journal. Yet many psychologists believe that the term *gender roles* is more appropriate to describe the concept of culturally assigned roles.

To avoid confusion, we use the term **sex** to refer to *the classification of individuals as female or male based on their genetic makeup, anatomy, and reproductive functions.* Even these definitions may be too simple: Recent research on intersexed individuals has led to the suggestion that there are more than two sexes (Fausto-Sterling, 2000; Russo & Tartaro, 2008). See Chapter 3 for further discussion of that issue. We will use **gender** to refer to *the meanings that societies and individuals give to female and male categories* (Golden, 2008).

Women and Men: Similar or Different?

Scholars who study sex and gender issues usually take one of two approaches. Either they emphasize the similarities between women and men or they focus on the differences between them.

Similarities Approach

Those who adhere to the similarities viewpoint seek to show that *men and women are basically alike in their intellectual and social behaviors. Any differences that do occur are produced by socialization, not biology* (Bohan, 2002; Eagly et al., 2004). This approach, also called the **beta bias,** has its origins in the work of early twentieth-century women psychologists. As we shall see later in the chapter, a number of these psychologists carried out research that challenged the prevailing belief that women were different from (and inferior to) men. Most feminist theory and research dealing with gender differences has retained this similarities approach (Bohan, 2002).

Differences Approach

The differences viewpoint, also known as the **alpha bias,** *emphasizes the differences between women and men.* Historically, these differences have been thought to arise from *essential qualities within the individual that are rooted in biology* (Bohan, 2002; Prentice & Miller, 2006; Wood & Eagly, 2002). This concept is known as **essentialism.**

The differences perspective has ancient origins in both Western and Eastern philosophies, which associate men with reason and civilization and women with emotion and nature (Hare-Mustin & Marecek, 1990). As we have seen, early psychologists often equated women's differences from men with inferiority and "otherness." Men set the standard while women were seen as deviations from that standard (Strickland, 2000). For example, Sigmund Freud stated that because women do not have a penis, they suffer from penis envy. Using the same logic, one could argue just as persuasively that men experience uterus envy because they cannot bear children. (Karen Horney [1926/1974], a psychoanalyst who challenged many of Freud's views, made this very proposal.)

Contemporary feminists regard female–male differences as arising from a culture's expectations of how individuals should behave. In other words, any behavioral differences between the genders are not inborn but are socially constructed (Bohan, 2002; Eagly et al., 2004; Marecek et al., 2004). As we shall see at the end of the chapter, the social construction of gender is one of the three major themes of this book.

Some feminists have added still another twist to the differences approach. They embrace cultural feminism, a view that celebrates those positive qualities historically associated with women, such as a sense of human connection and concern for other people (Bohan, 2002; Jordan et al., 2003; Miller & Stiver, 1997). The theories of Nancy Chodorow (1990) and Carol Gilligan (1982, 1993) illustrate the cultural feminist approach. According to Chodorow, early childhood experiences forever set females and males down different paths in their development of identity, personality, and emotional needs. Girls develop an early attachment to their mother, whom they perceive as similar to themselves. This leads girls to develop relational skills and a desire for close emotional connections. Boys, on the other hand, reject their emotional attachment to their mother, who is perceived as dissimilar. Boys instead identify with male figures who are often more distant. In the process, they become more invested in separation and independence and develop a more abstract and impersonal style (Basow & Rubin, 1999). Gilligan (1982, 1993) also sees women's identity as based on connections and relationships to others. She believes that women reason and make moral judgments in a "different voice," a voice concerned with caring and responsibility. Men, on the other hand, are more concerned with abstract rights and justice. These different patterns of reasoning are equally valid and sophisticated, according to Gilligan. We shall discuss moral reasoning in females and males in greater detail in Chapter 5.

Regardless of one's approach to gender comparisons, the study of gender and the psychology of women is rooted in a feminist perspective. Therefore, let's now examine the meaning of feminism.

Feminism

"Feminism . . . means you promote that men and women should have equal rights—economic, political, and with health care" (Meghann McCluskey, college sophomore, quoted in Dube, 2004, p. B5). "Feminists are . . . bra-burning, hairy-legged, man-hating lesbians. They constantly look for sexism and find it everywhere . . ." (Dube, 2004, p. B5, describing how another of her college students views feminism). Do either of these definitions reflect your own view of feminism? Although the term *feminism* is frequently used by the media, in opinion polls, and in casual conversation, people obviously differ in their conceptions of its meaning. There is even diversity among feminists. Although united in their belief that women are disadvantaged relative to men (Worell, 1996), feminists differ in their beliefs about the sources of this inequality and the ways to enhance women's status. Let's examine five different types of feminism embraced by feminist scholars.

Liberal feminism is *the belief that women and men should have the same political, legal, economic, and educational rights and opportunities* (Ens & Sinacore, 2001; Henley et al., 1998). Liberal feminists advocate reform; their goals are to change attitudes and laws that are unfair to women and to equalize educational, employment, and political opportunities. For example, they seek the creation of an educational environment that encourages women's growth in all academic fields, removal of barriers to full participation and advancement in the workplace, and more political leadership positions for women. Liberal feminists stress the similarities between females and males and contend that gender differences are a function of unequal opportunities.

In contrast, **cultural feminism** reflects *the belief that women and men are different and that more respect should be given to women's special qualities, such as nurturance, concern about others, and cooperativeness* (Ens & Sinacore, 2001; Henley et al., 1998). Cultural feminists are concerned about destructive outcomes related to masculine traits, such as aggressiveness and lack of emotional expressiveness, and want to empower women by elevating the value attached to their interpersonal orientation.

Another type of feminism, **socialist feminism,** reflects *the attitude that gender inequality is rooted in economic inequality* (Ens & Sinacore, 2001; Henley et al., 1998). Socialist feminists believe that various inequalities based on gender, ethnicity, and social class interact with one another and cannot be eliminated until the capitalistic structure of North American society is changed.

Radical feminism, on the other hand, is *the belief that gender inequality is based on male oppression of women* (Ens & Sinacore, 2001; Henley et al., 1998). Radical feminists contend that **patriarchy,** *male control over and dominance of women*, has existed throughout history and must be eliminated to achieve gender equality. In other words, different from socialist feminists, radical feminists see men, rather than capitalism, as the source of women's oppression. Consequently, they are concerned not only about inequality in societal institutions, such as the workplace, but also about power differential in the family and other types of intimate relationships.

Many women of color have argued that the feminist movement is concerned primarily about issues that confront White women. Consequently, they often embrace **women of color feminism** (also known as womanism), which is *the belief that both* **racism,** *bias against people because of their ethnicity, and* **classism,** *bias based on social class, must be recognized as being as important as* **sexism,** *gender-based bias* (Boisnier, 2003; Ens & Sinacore, 2001; Henley et al., 1998).

Clearly, there is no reason why a feminist perspective has to be limited to one viewpoint. Many individuals combine two or more into their personal definition of feminism. Now, perform the exercise in Get Involved 1.1 to more closely examine each of these types of feminism.

GET INVOLVED **1.1**
How Do People View Feminism?

Answer the following questions and then ask several female and male acquaintances to do the same. Save your own answers but do not refer back to them after completing this chapter.

First, indicate which of the following categories best characterizes your identity as a feminist:

1. consider myself a feminist and am currently involved in the Women's Movement
2. consider myself a feminist but am not involved in the Women's Movement
3. do not consider myself a feminist but agree with at least some of the objectives of feminism

4. do not consider myself a feminist and disagree with the objectives of feminism

Second, on a scale from 1 (strongly disagree) to 6 (strongly agree), indicate the extent to which you disagree or agree with each of the following statements.

1. Women should be considered as seriously as men as candidates for the presidency of the United States.
2. Although women can be good leaders, men make better leaders.
3. A woman should have the same job opportunities as a man.
4. Men should respect women more than they currently do.

5. Many women in the workforce are taking jobs away from men who need the jobs more.
6. Doctors need to take women's health concerns more seriously.
7. Women have been treated unfairly on the basis of their gender throughout most of human history.
8. Women are already given equal opportunities with men in all important sectors of their lives.
9. Women in the United States are treated as second-class citizens.
10. Women can best overcome discrimination by doing the best they can at their jobs, not by wasting time with political activity.

What Does It Mean?

Before computing your scores for the 10 items, reverse the points for statements 2, 5, 8, and 10. That is, for a rating of 1 (strongly disagree), give 6 points, for a rating of 2, give 5 points, and so on. Then sum the points for the 10 items. Higher scores reflect greater agreement with feminist beliefs.

1. Are there differences in the feminist labels and/or feminist attitude scores between your female and male respondents?
2. For each respondent, including yourself, compare the feminist attitude score to the selected feminist category. Did you find

that individuals who gave themselves a feminist label (i.e., placed themselves in category 1 or 2) generally agreed with the feminist statements and obtained a score of 40 or higher? Similarly, did the individuals who did not label themselves as feminists (e.g., category 3 or 4) tend to disagree with the feminist statements and receive a score below 40? If there was no correspondence between the feminist identity label and the feminist beliefs, give possible reasons.
3. Do you think that individuals who vary in ethnicity and social class might hold different attitudes about feminism? If yes, explain.

Source: Reprinted with permission from Plenum Publishing Corp. from Morgan (1996).

History of Women in Psychology

The first women in psychology faced a number of obstacles, especially in establishing their credentials, since many universities in the late 1800s and early 1900s did not welcome women who sought advanced degrees (Hogan & Sexton, 1991; Milar, 2000). Judith's experience described at the beginning of this chapter indicates that overt sexist policies toward women in psychology continued well into the twentieth century. Nevertheless, several women overcame the odds to become pioneers in the field (Kimmel & Crawford, 2001). Margaret Floy Washburn was the first woman to receive a Ph.D. in psychology in America in 1894. It took another 40 years before doctorates in psychology were awarded to Black women—Inez Beverly Prosser and Ruth Winifred Howard ("February Is Black History Month," 2004).

Women and the American Psychological Association

One year after the founding of the American Psychological Association (APA) in 1892, 2 of the 14 new members admitted were women: Mary Whiton Calkins and Christine Ladd-Franklin (Hogan & Sexton, 1991). Calkins went on to become the first woman president of the APA in 1905. Margaret Floy Washburn was elected the second woman president in 1921. It would be 51 years before the APA had another female leader.

Since the early 1970s, the number of women in APA leadership roles has increased notably and 11 women have become president (Brehm, 2007). In 2005, women represented 53 percent of the APA members, 49 percent of the council of representatives, and 38 percent of the board of directors, although only 26 percent of APA fellows, the most prestigious membership category. More than one-third of the reviewers and nearly half of the associate editors of APA journals (but only 28 percent of the editors) are women (American Psychological Association, 2006).

Eleven women have been elected president of the American Psychological Association. In chronological order, they are Mary Whiton Calkins, Margaret Floy Washburn, Anne Anastasi, Leona Tyler, Florence Denmark, Janet Spence, Bonnie Strickland, Dorothy Cantor, Norine Johnson, Diane Halpern, and 2007 president Sharon Stephens Brehm (shown here).

Women's Contributions

Women have been relatively invisible in psychology; their contributions to the field have often been overlooked or ignored (Scarborough, 2005). Coverage of gender-related topics has also been limited. However, the situation is improving. Florence Denmark (1994) examined undergraduate psychology textbooks from 1982 and 1993 for the inclusion of women's contributions and of gender-related topics. The more recent books showed progress in both areas. Claire and her students (Etaugh et al., 1995) similarly found that coverage of gender-related topics in introductory psychology textbooks increased by nearly 40 percent between the early 1970s and the early 1990s.

Even when the works of women psychologists are cited, they may still be overlooked. There are two related reasons for this apparent invisibility of many women psychologists. First, the long-standing practice in psychology books and journal articles is to refer to authors by their last name and first initials only. (Ironically, even if this practice were to change, some women authors still might choose to use their initials in order to avoid possible gender-biased devaluation of their scholarly work [Walsh-Bowers, 1999].) Second, in the absence of gender-identifying information, people tend to assume that the important contributions included in psychology books and articles have been carried out by men. When Claire learned about the Ladd-Franklin theory of color vision in introductory psychology, she assumed that two men named Ladd and Franklin had developed the theory. Only later did she discover that it was the work of Christine Ladd-Franklin. Similarly, most people assume that it was *Harry* Harlow who established the importance of touch in the development of attachment. How many individuals know that his wife, psychologist Margaret Kuenne Harlow, was his research partner and a codeveloper of their groundbreaking theory? In order to make the contributions of women psychologists more visible in this book, we frequently use first names when identifying important researchers and theorists.

History of the Psychology of Women

Ignorance about women pervades academic disciplines in higher education, where the requirements for the degree seldom include thoughtful inquiry into the status of women as part of the human condition.(Carolyn Sherif, cited in Denmark et al., 2000, p. 1)

How has the psychology of women developed as a field since Carolyn Sherif wrote that sentence about 30 years ago? Let us turn to a brief history of the feminist approach to the study of gender.

The Early Years

Rachel Hare-Mustin and Jeanne Marecek (1990) call the early years of psychology "womanless" psychology. Not only were there few women psychologists, but also women's experiences were not deemed important enough to study. Concepts in psychology were based on the male experience. For example, as we shall see in Chapter 3,

Sigmund Freud formulated his views of the Oedipus complex and penis envy from a male perspective but applied them to both genders. The same is true of Erik Erikson's notion of the development of identity during adolescence, as we shall see in Chapter 6.

In addition, early psychologists viewed women as different from and inferior to men (Denmark et al., 2008). For example, to explain their premise that women are less intelligent than men and thus unfit for higher education, male psychologists claimed that women's brains were smaller than men's (Bem, 2008; Hines, 2007; see Gould, 1981, for a historical review). This theory seemed to be discredited by the discovery that *relative* brain size—the weight of the brain relative to the weight of the body—is actually greater in women than in men. But stereotypes are not that easily erased. Scientists began comparing various segments of the brain in the two genders in an attempt to find the cause of women's purported inferior intelligence. No differences were found (Caplan & Caplan, 1999). Yet the search continued. In 1982, the prestigious journal *Science* published a study claiming that the corpus callosum (the connection between the two hemispheres of the brain) is larger in women than in men. The researchers stated that this difference might account for women's supposedly inferior spatial skills. (See Chapter 6 for a detailed discussion of this topic.) The study had many flaws, including the fact that only nine males' brains and five females' brains had been examined. Ruth Bleier, a neuroanatomist, and her colleagues did a study that corrected the flaws and used a much larger number of brains. They found no gender differences. Yet *Science* refused to publish their findings on the grounds that they were too "political" (Caplan & Caplan, 1999; Spanier, 1997).

The first generation of women psychologists carried out research that challenged assumptions of female inferiority (Bem, 2008). Helen Thompson Woolley found little difference in the intellectual abilities of women and men. Leta Stetter Hollingworth tackled the prevailing notion that women's menstrual cycles were debilitating, rendering women unfit to hold positions of responsibility. She demonstrated that intellectual and sensory-motor skills did not systematically vary across the menstrual cycle (Denmark et al., 2008).

The Recent Years

A number of events in the 1960s signaled the beginning of the modern feminist movement in the United States, including the publication of Betty Friedan's (1963) book *The Feminine Mystique*, the passage of the Equal Pay Act (see Chapters 9 and 14), and the formation of the National Organization for Women (NOW). In each case, the spotlight turned on glaring economic, social, and political inequities between women and men.

During these years, the psychology of women emerged as a separate field of study. In 1969, the Association for Women in Psychology was founded, followed in 1973 by the APA Division (now Society) of the Psychology of Women. Several textbooks on the psychology of women were written, journals such as *Psychology of Women Quarterly* and *Sex Roles* were established, and college courses on the topic began to appear. Feminist theorists and researchers demonstrated the sexist bias of much psychology theory, research, and practice. They set about expanding knowledge about women and correcting erroneous misinformation from the past (Bohan, 2002; Denmark et al., 2008). Today, women make up nearly half of the psychologists in the workforce. This percentage is very likely to increase because two-thirds of doctoral degrees in psychology now are awarded to women (American Psychological Association, 2006; Cynkar, 2007).

Studying the Psychology of Women

With a basic understanding of the history of the psychology of women, we now turn to an examination of issues involved in performing psychological research. As you probably learned in introductory psychology, our understanding of human behavior stems from research conducted by psychologists and other scientists who use the scientific method to answer research questions. Although you might have learned that this method is value–free, that it is not shaped by researchers' personal values, feminist scholars (Sechzer & Rabinowitz, 2008) argue that values can influence every step of the research process. Let's turn now to a brief discussion of these steps to see how researchers' own ideas about human behavior can influence our understanding of the psychology of women.

Bias in Psychological Research

Selecting the Research Topic.   The first step in any scientific investigation is selecting the topic that will be examined. Just as your personal preferences lead you to choose one term paper topic over another, scientists' personal interests influence the topics they decide to investigate. Throughout the history of psychology, most psychologists have been male; thus, for many years, topics related to girls and women were rarely investigated (Sechzer & Rabinowitz, 2008). Since 1970, however, the increasing number of female psychologists and the growth of the psychology of women as a discipline have been accompanied by steadily increasing research attention to topics of importance to women. This progression of interest has been documented by Judith Worell (1996), who notes a dramatic increase in publications on issues of importance to women between 1974 and 1993. For instance, she reports that, while no studies on female achievement were published in 1974, 161 were published in 1993, and published investigations of rape increased from 35 to 306 during the same period.

Another influence on topic selection is the researcher's assumptions about gender characteristics. For example, a psychologist who believes leadership is primarily a male trait is not likely to investigate the leadership styles of women. To give another example, aggressive behavior typically is associated with males. Consequently, relatively little is known about aggressive behavior in girls and women (Cummings & Leschied, 2002).

Bias in topic selection is even more evident when we focus on women of color. Not only is there a limited number of psychologists of color (Feldman, 1998) but researchers, influenced by the biased assumption that people of color are deviant, deficient, and helpless, have also examined ethnic minority women in relation to only a narrow range of topics (Kimmel & Crawford, 2001; Tucker & Herman, 2002). For example, women of color are more likely to be included in examinations of poverty and teen pregnancy than in investigations of other topics (Reid, 1999). The tendency to treat women of color as helpless deviates substantiates a negative image of ethnic minority females and denies their full personhood as women with a wide breadth of concerns and experiences.

Formulating the Hypothesis.   Once the topic is selected, the researcher generally formulates a hypothesis (a prediction) based on a particular theoretical perspective. Consequently, the researcher's orientation toward one theory or another has a major influence on the direction of the research. To better understand this effect, we look at the link between two theories of rape and related research hypotheses. One theory proposes that rape has evolved through natural selection, which leads to the hypothesis that rape is present in nonhuman animals (e.g., Thornhill & Palmer, 2000). A very different theory contends that rape stems from a power imbalance between women and men. One hypothesis stemming from this theory is that regions of the country with more gender inequality of power should have higher rates of rape than regions with less power imbalance (e.g., Whaley, 2001). As we see in the next section, these different hypotheses lead to very different kinds of research on rape.

Theoretical perspectives about ethnicity can similarly influence the hypotheses and direction of research. As Pamela Trotman Reid and Elizabeth Kelly (1994) noted, many studies on women of color are designed to "illuminate deficits and deviance from White norms" (p. 483). Rather than examining strengths of women of color, this deviance perspective leads to research that focuses on ethnic minority women as powerless victims.

Designing the Study.   Because the methods used to gather data stem from the underlying predictions, hypotheses based on disparate theories lead to different procedures. This, in turn, affects the type of knowledge we gain about the topic under investigation. Returning to our rape example, the hypothesis that rape is not unique to humans has led to investigations of forced copulation in nonhuman species (Thornhill & Palmer, 2000), research which would not be appropriate to the investigation of a power hypothesis. The prediction that rape is linked to the degree of gender inequality in society has led to studies of the relationship between a city's rape rate and its occupational and educational gender inequality (e.g., Whaley, 2001). Each of these procedures provides very different kinds of information about rape that can lay the foundation for different attitudes about this form of violence (see Chapter 11). Examining specific aspects of research design will show us the ways bias can also affect the choice of procedures.

Selecting Research Participants.   One of the consistent problems in psychological research has been the use of samples that do not adequately represent the general population. A **sample** refers to *the individuals who are investigated in order to reach conclusions about the entire group of interest to the researcher* (i.e., the **population**). For example, a researcher might be interested in understanding the emotional experiences of first-time mothers in the first months following childbirth. It would be impossible, however, to assess the experiences of all new mothers (*population*). Instead, the investigator might seek 100 volunteers from among mothers who gave birth in any one of three hospitals in a specific geographical area (*sample*).

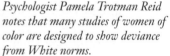

Psychologist Pamela Trotman Reid notes that many studies of women of color are designed to show deviance from White norms.

Unfortunately, research participants are not always representative of the larger population. Throughout most of the history of psychology, psychologists have focused primarily on White, middle-class, heterosexual, able-bodied males (Kimmel & Crawford, 2001; Unger, 2001). This procedure can lead to unfortunate and incorrect generalizations about excluded groups. It would be inappropriate, for example, to draw conclusions about women's leadership styles by examining male managers. Furthermore, focusing on selected groups can lead to the disregard of excluded groups.

A related issue is whether and how researchers specify the gender composition of their samples. One problem is that a sizable minority of authors have not reported this information. For example, between 30 percent and 40 percent of studies published in 1990 in a large variety of major psychology journals failed to mention the gender makeup of their participants (Ader & Johnson, 1994; Zalk, 1991). Therefore, the reader does not know whether the findings are applicable to both genders. Interestingly, the failure to report gender in the title of the article or to provide a rationale for sampling only one gender was more common in studies with male-only participants than in studies with female-only participants. Furthermore, discussions based on male participants were more likely to be written in general terms, whereas those based on only female participants were likely to be restricted to conclusions about females. According to Deborah Ader and Suzanne Johnson (1994, pp. 217–218), these practices suggest that "there remains a significant tendency to consider male participants 'normative,' and results obtained from them generally applicable, whereas female participants are somehow 'different.'" That is, it appears that males are considered to be the standard against which all behavior is measured.

Although there has been improvement in the gender balance of participants in psychological research, samples have been limited in other ways. One problem is the relative invisibility of people of color (Russo & Vaz, 2001; Williams et al., 2002). Even psychologists critical of the male bias in traditional psychology have erred by using primarily White samples (Hall, 2003; Reid & Kelly, 1994). For example, between 1989 and 1991, only about 10 percent of the articles published in journals that focus on women and gender roles examined the ethnicity of the participants (Reid & Kelly, 1994). A positive development is that these journals now require a description of the ethnicity of the sample even if it is restricted to typically studied White participants. However, it should be noted that specifying the ethnic composition of the sample does not imply that the researcher actually examined the relationship between the participant's ethnicity and the behavior under investigation.

Samples have been restricted, additionally, in their socioeconomic status: Most participants have been middle class, and poor women are nearly invisible (Heppner & O'Brien, 2006; Lott & Bullock, 2007). As a result, problems that have a much greater impact on poor women than on middle-class women are rarely studied. For example, very little is known about the sexual harassment of low-income women by their landlords, even though this is unfortunately a common occurrence (Reed et al., 2005). In addition, most studies of employed women have focused on those in professional and managerial jobs. Unfortunately, we know relatively little about women in blue-collar jobs (Nelson et al., 2002). Moreover, when researchers do study poor and working-class individuals, they tend to focus on people of color (Reid, 1999), perpetuating a biased assumption about ethnicity and social class as well as limiting our understanding of both poor White women and middle-class women of color.

It should also be noted that many of the middle-class individuals who serve as research participants are college students (Sears, 1997). Because this group is restricted in age, education, and life experiences compared to the general population, there are numerous findings based on these samples that cannot be generalized to other types of people.

Other groups, such as lesbian, gay, and bisexual individuals and people with disabilities, have rarely been studied in psychological research, and less research has focused on older women than on younger women or girls (Garnets, 2008; Gergen, 2008; Olkin, 2008). What can explain researchers' narrow focus on White, middle-class, heterosexual, able-bodied, younger individuals? One possibility is that psychologists are more interested in understanding the experiences of people like themselves, and the majority of investigators fit the characteristics of the typical participants. Another possibility is that psychologists might use these individuals in their research because it is easier to recruit them. These are the people most likely to be located within the situational contexts—such as academic or professional environments— inhabited by researchers. Also, due to cross-group mistrust and/or misunderstanding, it is sometimes more difficult for nonminority investigators to recruit minority individuals (Russo & Vaz, 2001). Whatever the causes, the exclusion of certain groups of people from psychological examination not only devalues their experiences but can also lead to inaccurate conclusions about them based on faulty generalizations. To get firsthand knowledge about the extent of biased samples in recent psychological research, complete the exercise in Get Involved 1.2.

GET INVOLVED 1.2
Are Samples in Psychological Research Biased?

In this exercise you are to evaluate samples used in recent psychological studies and to compare descriptions of samples published in journals oriented toward women or gender to mainstream psychological journals. At your campus library select one recent issue of *Psychology of Women Quarterly* or *Sex Roles*. Also, select a recent issue of one of the following: *Journal of Personality and Social Psychology, Journal of Experimental Social Psychology, Developmental Psychology, Child Development,* or *Journal of Consulting and Clinical Psychology*. For each article in these issues, read the brief section that describes the participants. This is found in the Method section of the article and is usually labeled Participants, Sample, or Subjects. As you read these sections, make note of the following information:

1. a. Is the gender of the participants specified?
   b. If yes, does the sample include females only, males only, or both females and males?
2. a. Is the ethnicity of the participants specified?

b. If yes, does the sample include predominantly or exclusively Whites, predominantly or exclusively individuals of another single ethnic group, or a balanced mixture of individuals from two or more ethnic groups?
3. a. Is the social class of the participants specified?
   b. If yes, is the sample predominantly or exclusively middle class, predominantly or exclusively working class or poor, or a mixture of social classes?
4. a. Are any other characteristics of the participants (e.g., sexual orientation, presence of a disability, etc.) given?
   b. If yes, specify.

After recording the information for each article from one journal, add up the number of articles that specified the gender of the sample, the number that specified ethnicity, and so on. Similarly, sum the articles that included both genders, those that included more than one ethnic group, and so forth. Follow the same procedure for the other journal.

What Does It Mean?

1. Which participant characteristic was described most frequently? Explain why.
2. Which participant characteristic was represented in the most balanced way? Explain why.
3. Which participant characteristic was specified least often? Explain why.
4. Did the two journals differ in their descriptions of their samples? If yes, explain any observed differences.
5. What are the implications of your findings?

Source: Reprinted with permission from Plenum Publishing Corp. from Morgan (1996).

Women with disabilities rarely are included in psychological research.

Selecting the Measures.   Another step in the design of a study is the selection of procedures to measure the behaviors or characteristics under investigation. These procedures can determine the results that we find. For example, in their comparison of female and male aggression, Mary Harris and Kelly Knight-Bohnhoff (1996) obtained different findings depending on how they measured aggressive behavior. When participants were asked to indicate their physical aggression, males reported more aggression than females; however, when asked about their verbal aggression, there was no gender difference. As you can see, relying on only one of these measures would have distorted the conclusion.

Analyzing and Interpreting the Findings.   Once the data have been collected, the researcher performs statistical analyses to discover whether the findings support the hypotheses. Although there are numerous types of statistical tests, they all provide information about the **statistical significance** of the results, which means that *the findings are not due to chance alone*. For example, in a study of college students' perceptions of rape, Judith asked respondents to rate the degree to which a specific rape was due to the victim's failure to control the situation, from 0 (not at all) to 10 (to a great extent) (Bridges, 1991). The findings showed that females had an average rating of 2.75 and males had a rating of 4.59. These numbers have no meaning in themselves. However, a statistical analysis applied to these data indicated that the difference of 1.84 between the male and female averages was not due to chance alone; males, more than females, believed the victim failed to adequately control the situation.

   Once statistical tests have been applied to the data, the researcher must interpret the findings. Statistical analyses inform us only about the likelihood that the data could have been produced by chance alone. Now, the researchers must discuss explanations and implications of the findings. One type of bias occurring at this stage is interpreting the findings in a way that suggests a female weakness or inferiority. For example, studies have shown that females use more tentative speech than males do (see Chapter 11). They are more likely than men to say, "I *sort of* think she would be a good governor" or "She *seems* to be a strong candidate." Some researchers (e.g., Lakoff, 1990) have suggested this is an indication of females' lack of confidence—an interpretation pointing to a female deficit. Another equally plausible and more positive interpretation is that females use more tentative speech as a means of encouraging other people to express their opinions (e.g., Wood, 1994). Susan Fiske, past president of the Association for Psychological Sciences, offers another example of how a trait can be labeled to suggest female inferiority. She cites the "field independence–field dependence" continuum. Men have been described as "field independent" (not being influenced by a surrounding context), considered a favorable attribute, whereas "field *de*pendence was this disease women had" (Wargo, 2007, p. 17). What about being labeled field *sensitive,* clearly a more positive term, she asks?

A second problem related to the interpretation of findings is generalizing results based on one group to other groups. As discussed earlier in this chapter, psychologists frequently examine narrowly defined samples, such as White male college students, and sometimes they generalize their findings to other people, including females, people of color, and non–middle-class individuals. Linda Gannon and her associates (1992) examined evidence of generalization from one gender to the other found in several major psychology journals published from 1970 to 1990. Although there has been improvement since the 1970s, when inappropriate gender generalizations occurred in 19 percent to 76 percent of the articles, these researchers found that even in 1990 percentages ranged from 13 percent to 41 percent.

A third bias in the interpretation of data has been the assumption that the presence of gender differences implies biological causes (Hines, 2007). For example, Camilla Benbow and Julian Stanley (1980) found more males than females among the mathematically gifted. Although these investigators did not examine biological factors, they interpreted their findings to suggest that the difference was based on biological factors rather than on differing life experiences.

Communicating the Findings

Publishing.   The primary way that psychologists communicate their research findings to others is by publishing their studies, usually in psychological journals. Unfortunately, there is a publication bias. Editors and reviewers who make decisions about which studies are worthy of publication tend to favor those that report statistical significance over those that do not. This publication bias can affect the body of our knowledge about gender. Studies that show a statistically significant gender difference are more likely to be published than those that do not and can lead to exaggerated conclusions about the differences between females and males (Hyde & Mezulis, 2001).

Another type of publication bias exists as well. Victoria Brescoll and Marianne LaFrance (2004) found that politically conservative newspapers were more likely than liberal newspapers to use biological explanations for gender differences. Moreover, readers tended to believe whatever bias was represented in these news stories. Let the reader beware!

Gender-Biased Language.   The language that researchers use in their research papers is another possible source of gender bias in the communication of findings. Gender-biased language, such as the use of the male pronoun to refer to both genders, can lead to serious misinterpretation. As is discussed in Chapter 2, the male pronoun tends to be interpreted as males only, not as males and females (Crawford, 2001). Fortunately, although this practice was prevalent in the 1970s and 1980s, the *Publication Manual of the American Psychological Association* (American Psychological Association, 2001) now specifies that gender-biased language must be avoided. Research is now more likely to be reported using nonsexist language (Sechzer & Rabinowitz, 2008).

Another, more subtle type of biased language is the use of nonparallel terms when writing about comparable female and male behaviors, thus implying an essential difference between the genders. For example, much of the research on gender and employment refers to women who work outside the home as "employed mothers" but refers to men who work outside the home as simply "employed" (Gilbert, 1994). This distinction carries the implicit assumption that the primary role for women is motherhood whereas the primary role for men is the provider role.

Conclusion.   Although it is unlikely that most researchers attempt to influence the research process in order to support their preconceived ideas about a topic, the biases they bring to the research endeavor can affect their choice of topic, hypotheses, research design, interpretation of findings, and communication about the study. Given that researchers have very human personal interests, values, and theoretical perspectives, they do not fit the image of the objective scientist (Caplan & Caplan, 1999).

Despite these inherent biases, we do not want to give the impression that psychological research is unduly value-laden or that it provides no useful information about the psychology of women. Most researchers make a concerted attempt to be as unbiased as possible, and research from psychology and other social scientific disciplines has provided a rich body of knowledge about females' experiences. However, we must read this research critically, with an understanding of its possible limitations—especially its failure to focus on the diversity of girls and women. For a look at doing gender research around the world, see Explore Other Cultures 1.1.

Feminist Research Methods

Traditional psychological research emphasizes objectivity, control, and quantitative measures as a means of understanding human behavior, and some feminist psychologists advocate adherence to this general methodology. Others, however, contend that more accurate representations of women's lives are achieved with subjective procedures, such as women's qualitative accounts of their experiences (Jarviluoma et al., 2003; Naples, 2003; Sechzer & Rabinowitz, 2008). For example, a subjective investigation of women's friendships might ask participants to describe, in their own words, the most important friendships they have had. In contrast, an objective measure might ask them to complete a questionnaire written by the researcher in which they indicate how often they have experienced a variety of feelings and interactions in their most important friendships. Whereas the subjective approach attempts to capture each participant's

Doing Cross-Cultural Research on Gender

Cross-cultural research has made important contributions to our understanding of gender development (Best & Thomas, 2004). Nevertheless, there are methodological pitfalls that need to be avoided in order to draw meaningful conclusions from such research. Judith Gibbons (2000) gives an example of how similar findings may have different meanings depending upon the culture being studied. She and her colleagues studied adolescents' drawings of the ideal woman. In a variety of cultures, many adolescents drew the ideal woman as working in an office. However, when the drawings were then presented to peers in the same culture for interpretation, adolescents gave responses that were both similar across cultures, but also culturally specific. For instance, in all countries studied, women working in offices were described as hardworking. However, Guatemalan adolescents also viewed them as working for the betterment of their families, Filipino teenagers described them as adventurous and sexy, and U.S. teens saw them as bored with the routine of office work.

Another formidable methodological challenge in cross-cultural research is the issue of sampling. In studying gender issues, samples often are drawn in a certain setting, such as colleges and universities, as a way to ensure equivalent samples. But college or university students do not reflect the population similarly in different countries because the proportion of the population attending university differs widely internationally.

unique perspective, the objective approach compares participants' responses to a standard situation. For a more detailed examination of principles of feminist research, look at Learn about the Research 1.1.

Drawing Conclusions from Multiple Studies

Researchers use one of two procedures to draw conclusions about gender differences on the basis of large numbers of published studies. This section examines these two techniques.

Narrative Approach.   The traditional way of examining psychological gender differences has been to sift through dozens or even hundreds of studies on a particular topic and to form an impression of the general trends in their results. The first major attempt to synthesize the research on gender differences in this narrative fashion was carried out by Eleanor Maccoby and Carol Nagy Jacklin in 1974. In this massive undertaking, they tallied the results of over 1,600 published and unpublished studies appearing in the 10 years prior to 1974. Gender differences were declared to exist when a large number of studies on a given topic found differences in the same direction. Although the contribution of this pioneering work is enormous, a major drawback is its use of a simple "voting" or "box-score" method, which gave each study the same weight regardless of sample size or magnitude of the reported difference (Eagly et al., 1995). In addition, the possibility of subtle biases is always present in any narrative review.

Meta-Analysis.   A more sophisticated and objective technique of summarizing data has been developed in recent years. **Meta-analysis** is *a statistical method of integrating*

LEARN ABOUT THE RESEARCH 1.1

Principles of Feminist Research

Although feminists have a variety of opinions about the most effective methods for studying girls and women, they agree that such research should increase our understanding of females and help change the world for them (Kimmel & Crawford, 2001; Sechzer & Rabinowitz, 2008). Thus, feminists, like all researchers, bring a set of values to the research process, values that can direct the nature and interpretation of the research. An important assumption of the feminist approach to knowledge is that research cannot be value free (Weatherall, 1999). Accordingly, Claire and her colleague, Judith Worell (Worell & Etaugh, 1994), have articulated a set of principles that are based on the values of feminist research. These are summarized as follows:

1. Challenging the traditional scientific method.
   a. Correcting bias in the research process.
   b. Expanding samples beyond White middle-class participants.
   c. Acknowledging the legitimacy of both quantitative and qualitative methods.
2. Focusing on the experiences of women.

   a. Examining diverse categories of women.
   b. Investigating topics relevant to women's lives.
   c. Attending to women's strengths as well as their concerns.
3. Considering gender imbalances in power.
   a. Recognizing that women's subordinate status is a sign of power imbalance, not deficiency.
   b. Attempting to empower women.
4. Recognizing gender as an important category for investigation.
   a. Understanding that a person's gender can influence expectations about and responses to that person.
5. Recognizing the importance of language.
   a. Changing language to be inclusive of women.
   b. Understanding that language can both influence thought and be influenced by thought.
6. Promoting social change.
   a. Creating a science that benefits women.
   b. Guiding action that will lead to justice for women.

What Does It Mean?

1. Assume you are a feminist researcher interested in examining how women handle their paid employment and family obligations. Using the feminist principles outlined above, describe the characteristics of the sample you might wish to study and the research methods you would use in collecting your data.
2. A hypothetical study of the educational expectations of White, Mexican American, and Vietnamese American eighth-grade girls found that the White girls expect to complete more years of schooling than the other groups. The researcher concluded that Latina and Asian American girls have lower educational expectations than White girls. Critique this conclusion, using feminist research principles.

Source: Based on Worell and Etaugh (1994).

the results of several studies on the same topic. It provides a measure of the magnitude, or size, of a given gender difference rather than simply counting the number of studies finding a difference (Hyde, 2007; Hyde & Grabe, 2008).

Gender researchers using meta-analysis first locate all studies on the topic of interest. Then they do a statistical analysis of each study that measures the size of the difference between the average of the men's scores and the average of the women's scores. This difference is divided by the standard deviation of the two sets of scores. The standard deviation measures the variability or range of the scores. For example, scores ranging from 1 to 100 have high variability, while scores ranging from 50 to 53 show low variability. Dividing the difference between men's and women's scores by the standard deviation produces a *d* statistic. Finally, the researchers calculate the average of the *d* statistics from all the studies they located. The resulting *d* is called the **effect size.** *It indicates not only whether females or males score higher but also how large the difference is.* This is one of the major advantages of meta-analysis over the traditional narrative method of summarizing research (Hyde & Grabe, 2008).

The value of *d* is large when the difference between means is large and the variability within each group is small. It is small when the difference between means is small and the variability within each group is large (Halpern, 2000). Generally a *d* of 0.20 is considered small, 0.50 is moderate, and 0.80 is large. However, these guidelines still do not settle the debate of whether a particular difference is *meaningful* or important (Hyde & Grabe, 2008). In cancer research, for example, even a very small effect size can have powerful consequences. Suppose a treatment was discovered that completely cured a small number of women with a highly lethal form of cancer. Although the effect size might be quite small, this discovery would be hailed as a major medical breakthrough. As we discuss later in the book, the effect sizes for some psychological gender differences are greater than those found in most psychological research (Halpern, 2000) while others are close to zero.

Now that we have explored the historical and methodological framework for understanding the psychology of women, we focus on the major themes that characterize this book.

Themes in the Text

Science is not value free. As we have seen, the evolving belief about the importance of women has had a powerful impact on topics and methods of psychological research. Similarly, this text is not value neutral. It is firmly rooted in a feminist belief system, which contends (1) that the diversity of women's experiences should be recognized and celebrated; (2) that men hold more power than women; and (3) that gender is shaped by social, cultural, and societal influences. These beliefs are shared by many feminist psychologists and are reflected throughout this book.

Theme 1: Diversity of Women's Experiences

As we saw in the discussion of research biases, minimal attention given to females throughout most of the history of psychology not only devalues women's experiences but also often leads to incorrectly generalizing men's experiences to include women. Similarly, a psychology of women restricted to White, middle-class, heterosexual, able-bodied, young females in North America minimizes the importance of women of color, poor and working-class women, lesbian and bisexual women, women with disabilities, older women, and women in other cultures, and it can lead to the false conclusion that the experiences of the majority are applicable to all.

Consequently, this text examines the heterogeneity of females' experiences. We discuss both similarities and differences in the attitudes, emotions, relationships, goals, and behaviors of girls and women who have a diversity of backgrounds. For example, we explore interpersonal relationships of heterosexual and lesbian women (Chapter 8), physical and mental health concerns of White women and women of color (Chapters 12 and 13), problems on campus and in the workplace faced by women with disabilities (Chapters 8 and 9), and health, employment, and interpersonal issues of older women (Chapters 8, 10, and 12). However, because most of the research to date on the psychology of women has been based on restricted samples, it is important to note that our presentation includes a disproportionate amount of information about middle-class, heterosexual, able-bodied White women and girls.

When referring to cultural variations among people we use the term *ethnicity* or *ethnic group* rather than *race*. **Race** is *a biological concept that refers to physical characteristics of people* (Feldman, 1998). However, experts disagree about what constitutes a single race (Feldman, 1998), and there is considerable genetic variation among people designated as a single race. **Ethnicity,** on the other hand, refers to *variations in cultural background, nationality, religion, and/or language* (Feldman, 1998), a term more closely associated with the variations in attitudes, behaviors, and roles that we discuss in this book.

Unfortunately, there are no universally acceptable labels that identify a person's ethnicity. Some terms are based on geographical origin as in *African American* and *Euro-American* whereas others are based on color, such as *Black* and *White*. Furthermore, each major ethnic category encompasses a diversity of ethnic subtypes. For example, Americans with Asian ancestry, regardless of their specific origin (e.g., Japan, China, Korea, Vietnam) are generally grouped into a single category of Asian Americans. Similarly, Whites from countries as diverse as Ireland, Germany, and Russia are combined into one ethnic group. With the hope that our usage does not inadvertently offend anyone, ethnic group labels used in this book are Asian American, Black, Latina/o, Native American, and White, recognizing that each of these broad ethnic categories actually encompasses a diversity of cultures.

Theme 2: Gender Differences in Power

In no known societies do women dominate men. . . . Men, on average, enjoy more power than women, on average, and this appears to have been true throughout human history.(Pratto & Walker, 2004, p. 242)

Two interlocking ideas characterize our power theme. One is that the experiences of women in virtually all cultures are shaped by both **organizational power,** *the ability to use valuable resources to dominate and control others,* and **interpersonal power,** *the ability* *to influence one's partner within a specific relationship.* The greater organizational power of males compared to that of females is evident in our discussion of numerous topics, including gender differences in salary (Chapter 10), the underrepresentation of women in high-status occupations (Chapter 10), and sexual harassment (Chapter 14). Additionally, gender differences in interpersonal power are clearly reflected in our discussions of interpersonal violence (Chapter 14), rape (Chapter 14), and the allocation of household responsibilities (Chapter 11).

Both of these power differentials reflect an undesirable imbalance in a form of power, called **power-over,** *a person's or group's control of another person or group.* This type of power is distinguished from **power-to,** *the empowerment of self and others to accomplish tasks* (Chrisler, 2008c). Whereas the former is a negative type of power that restricts opportunities and choices of members of the less powerful group, the latter allows for personal growth for all. Thus, feminist psychologists want to eliminate the former and increase the latter (Denmark & Klara, 2007).

A second component of our theme of power differences is that many women experience more than one type of power imbalance. In addition to a gender difference in power, women can experience power inequities as a function of their ethnicity, social class, sexual preference, age, and physical ability (Ostenson, 2008). Furthermore, the effects of these imbalances are cumulative. For example, women of color experience greater discrimination in the workplace than do White women (Chapter 10). As bell hooks (1990) stated, "By calling attention to interlocking systems of domination—sex, race, and class—Black women and many other groups of women acknowledge the diversity and complexity of female experience, of our relationship to power and domination" (p. 187).

One consequence of gender differences in power is that women and women's issues receive less emphasis and visibility than men and men's issues. In this chapter, for example, we saw that women's contributions to psychology have often been overlooked. We examine other instances of this problem in our discussion of specific topics, such as the underrepresentation of females in the media (Chapter 2) and the exclusion of women from major studies of medical and health issues (Chapter 12).

Theme 3: Social Construction of Gender

As indicated at the beginning of this chapter, social scientists differentiate between sex, the biological aspects of femaleness and maleness, and gender, the nonbiological components. Our third theme, the **social construction of gender,** points out that *the traits, behaviors, and roles that we associate with females and males are not inherent in one's sex; they are shaped by numerous interpersonal, cultural, and societal forces.* Even if some aspects of being a female or a male are biologically based, we live in a society that emphasizes gender, and our development as women and men—as well as our conceptions of what it means to be a female or a male—is significantly influenced by cultural and societal values (Denmark et al., 2008; Epstein, 2007). We do not exist in a sterile laboratory; instead, we are continually affected by an interlocking set of expectations, pressures, and rewards that guide our development as women and men.

Furthermore, our experience and conceptions of femaleness and maleness cannot be viewed as separate from our ethnicity and social class (hooks, 1990) or from our sexual orientation and physical ability/disability. Each of these identities is also socially constructed. Lesbian women, for example, are affected not only by societal expectations about what women are like, but also by people's beliefs about and attitudes toward lesbianism.

The social construction of gender is discussed in relation to several topics in the text. For example, we examine theories that explain how children develop their ideas about gender (Chapter 3); we explore the processes of instilling a child with expectations about what it means to be a girl or boy (Chapter 4); and we examine social influences on gender in our discussion of gender differences in self-esteem (Chapter 5), friendship (Chapter 8), and the division of household labor (Chapter 11).

SUMMARY

Definitions: Sex and Gender

- Sex refers to the classification of females and males based on biological factors. Gender refers to social expectations of roles and behaviors for females and males.

Women and Men: Similar or Different?

- The similarities approach (beta bias) argues that women and men are basically alike in their behaviors and that any differences are a product of socialization.
- The differences approach (alpha bias) emphasizes that women and men are different and that these differences are biologically based.

Feminism

- Liberal, cultural, socialist, radical, and women of color feminism all posit that women are disadvantaged relative to men. They differ in their assumptions about the sources of this inequality.

History of Women in Psychology

- For many years, women attained few leadership positions and awards in the APA, but gains have been made in recent years.
- Women's contributions to psychology have often been overlooked or ignored, but that situation is improving.

History of the Psychology of Women

- In the early years of psychology, women were viewed as inferior to men and their experiences were rarely studied.
- Early women psychologists carried out research that challenged the assumptions of female inferiority.
- In the 1970s, the psychology of women emerged as a separate field of study.

Studying the Psychology of Women

- Psychological research is not value free. Throughout most of its history, psychology did not pay much attention to the experiences of girls and women in either the topics investigated or the participants studied.
- Since 1970 there has been an increase in research focus on females; however, most of this research has been focused on White, middle-class, heterosexual, able-bodied women.
- Generalizing results based on one type of participant to other types of people can lead to inaccurate conclusions.
- The researcher's theoretical perspective influences the hypothesis examined in the research, which in turn affects the type of information learned from the research.
- The measures used to study the research topic can influence the findings of the research.
- Due to a publication bias, published studies are more likely to present gender differences than gender similarities.

- Very few studies use blatantly biased gender language, but a more subtle bias can be detected in the use of nonparallel terms for comparable female and male behaviors.
- Some feminists advocate the use of traditional objective, quantitative research methods.
- Others favor the use of subjective, qualitative procedures.
- There are several principles that characterize most feminist research.
- The narrative approach and meta-analysis are two methods of integrating results of several studies on the same topic.
- Meta-analysis is a statistical method that provides a measure of the magnitude of a given difference, known as the effect size.

Themes in the Text

- Three themes are prominent in this text.
- First, psychology must examine the experiences of diverse groups of women.
- Second, the greater organizational and interpersonal power of men compared to women negatively shapes and limits their experiences. Women of color, poor and working-class women, lesbian women, and women with disabilities experience additional power inequities, with cumulative effects.
- Third, gender is socially constructed; it is shaped by social, cultural, and societal values.

KEY TERMS

sex	patriarchy	effect size
gender	women of color feminism	race
beta bias	racism	ethnicity
alpha bias	classism	organizational power
essentialism	sexism	interpersonal power
liberal feminism	sample	power-over
cultural feminism	population	power-to
socialist feminism	statistical significance	social construction of gender
radical feminism	meta-analysis	

WHAT DO YOU THINK?

1. Do you prefer the similarities approach or the differences approach to the study of gender issues? Why?

2. Which definition of feminism or combination of definitions best reflects your own view of feminism? Why?

3. Do you think it would be desirable for women and/or men if more people identified themselves as feminists? Explain your answer.

4. We noted a few experiences of women that are influenced by a gender imbalance in power, and we will cover other examples throughout the text. However, can you now identify any behaviors or concerns of women that you think are influenced by a power imbalance?

IF YOU WANT TO LEARN MORE

Calasanti, T. M., & Slevin, K. F. (Eds.). (2006). *Age matters: Realigning feminist thinking.* New York: Routledge.

Caplan, P. J., & Caplan, J. B. (1999). *Thinking critically about research on sex and gender* (2nd ed.). New York: HarperCollins.

Collins, L. H., Dunlap, M. R., & Chrisler, J. C. (Eds.). (2002). *Charting a new course for feminist psychology.* Westport, CT: Praeger.

Darlington, P. S. E., & Mulvaney, B. M. (2003). *Women, power, and ethnicity: Working toward reciprocal empowerment.* New York: Haworth.

Fenstermaker, S., & West, C. (2002). *Doing gender, doing difference: Social inequality, power, and resistance.* New York: Routledge.

Hill Collins, P. (2000). *Black feminist thought: Knowledge, consciousness, and the politics of empowerment.* New York: Routledge.

Jarviluoma, H., Moisala, P., & Vilkko, A. (2003). *Gender and qualitative methods.* Thousand Oaks, CA: Sage.

Jordan, J. V., Walker, M., & Hartling, L. M. (Eds.). (2004). *The complexity of connection: Writings from the Stone Center's Jean Baker Miller Training Institute.* New York: Guilford.

Meezan, W., & Martin, J. I. (Eds.). (2004). *Research methods with gay, lesbian, bisexual, and transgender populations.* Binghamton, NY: Harrington Park Press.

Naples, N. A. (2003). *Feminism and method: Ethnography, discourse analysis and activist research.* New York: Routledge.

O'Connell, A. N. (2001). *Models of achievement: Reflections of eminent women in psychology* (Vol. 3). Mahwah, NJ: Erlbaum.

Pilcher, J., & Whelehan, I. (2004). *50 key concepts in gender studies.* London: Sage.

Rothenberg, P. S. (2003). *Race, class, and gender in the United States* (6th ed.). New York: Freeman.

Shaw, S. M., & Lee, J. (Eds.). (2001). *Women's voices, feminist visions.* Mountain View, CA: Mayfield.

WEBSITES

Feminism

Feminist Utopia
http://www.amazoncastle.com/feminism/feminism.htm

Cultural Representation of Gender

VICTORIA'S SECRET
New York Chicago Los Angeles

Stereotypes of Females and Males
  The Content of Gender Stereotypes
  The Perceiver's Ethnicity and Gender
    Stereotypes
  The Target's Characteristics and Gender
    Stereotypes
  Stereotypes of Girls and Boys

  Bases for Gender Stereotypes
  Stereotypes Based on Identity Labels
Sexism
  Ambivalent Sexism
  Changes in Sexist Attitudes over Time
  Modern Sexism
  Experiences with Sexism

Representation of Gender in the Media
    Pattern 1: Underrepresentation of Females
    Pattern 2: Underrepresentation of Specific
       Groups of Females
    Pattern 3: Portrayal of Gender-Based Social
       Roles
    Pattern 4: Depiction of Female Communion
       and Male Agency
    Pattern 5: Emphasis on Female
       Attractiveness and Sexuality
Significance of Gender-Role Media Images

Representation of Gender in the English Language
    Language Practices Based on the
       Assumption That Male Is Normative
    Negative Terms for Females
    Significance of the Differential Treatment
       of Females and Males in Language

In September 1970, on the day I (Judith) enthusiastically (but somewhat nervously) began my academic career, there was a meeting of the faculty at my small campus. As is generally the custom, the campus director took this opportunity to introduce me and another new professor to the rest of the faculty and staff. His introduction of my male colleague in the physics department was both unsurprising and appropriate; he identified him as "Dr. Lantry Brooks" and then provided his academic credentials. Although my educational background was also given, the director introduced me, quite awkwardly, as "Dr., Mrs. Judith Bridges."

What images of women's and men's roles does this dual title suggest? Is there a power difference implied by the different forms of address used for my male colleague and me?

Leap ahead to 2008. At that time, a colleague of Claire's went through a lengthy decision-making process about the surname she would use after her forthcoming marriage. She knew her fiancé was not going to change his name, and she considered taking his name, retaining her birth name, or hyphenating their names. She decided to hyphenate.

Does this colleague's decision have any effect on people's impressions of her? When students read her name in the course schedule, when she applies for grants, when she is introduced to new acquaintances, does her hyphenated name suggest a different image than her alternative choices would have? Why do we associate different characteristics with different surname choices; that is, what social experiences help shape these images?

In this chapter, we explore these issues and similar ones as we examine stereotypes of females and males, the nature of sexism, and the representations of gender in the media and in language.

Stereotypes of Females and Males

Before we begin, think about your conception of the *typical* adult woman and the *typical* adult man. Then indicate your ideas in Get Involved 2.1.

The Content of Gender Stereotypes

The characteristics shown in Get Involved 2.1 reflect **gender stereotypes,** that is, *widely shared beliefs about the attributes of females and males.* These views are present in virtually all cultures that have been studied (Désert & Leyens, 2006). As this sample of traits indicates, *personality characteristics associated with women, such as sympathy and warmth, reflect a concern about other people.* Social scientists call this cluster of attributes **communion.** *The group of traits associated with men, including achievement orientation and ambitiousness,* on the other hand, *reflects a concern about accomplishing tasks* and is called **agency** (Abele & Wojciszke, 2007).

Consistent with the tendency to associate communal traits with females and agentic traits with males is people's tendency to expect different roles for women and men (Kite et al., 2008). For example, although most women are employed (U.S. Census Bureau, 2007c), many individuals continue to expect that women will be the primary caregivers of both children and elderly parents and that men will be the primary providers (Steinberg et al., 2008).

Interestingly, some of these stereotypes have remained relatively unchanged since the 1970s, especially those involving experiencing and expressing emotion and caring as more typical of women and those involving assertiveness, independence, and activity as more typical of men (Kite et al., 2008; Nesbitt & Penn, 2000; Pierce et al., 2003). However, the typical woman is no longer considered to be less logical, direct, ambitious, or objective than the typical man or to have greater difficulty in making decisions or separating ideas from feelings. These traits represent a cluster of agentic characteristics having to do with competence and the capacity to be effective (Nesbitt & Penn, 2000).

You might have noted that the attributes comprising the male stereotype are more highly regarded in North American society and are more consistent with a powerful image than those comprising the female cluster (Fiske & Cuddy, 2006). In Western culture, with its strong emphasis on the value of hard work and achievement, we tend to associate agentic qualities, such as ambition and independence, with power and prestige and to evaluate these traits more positively than communal attributes, such as gentleness and emotionality. On the other hand, highly competent and agentic women often are disliked, especially by men (Masser & Abrams, 2004). Thus, gender stereotypes are the first indication of the power imbalance discussed in Chapter 1.

Gender stereotypes are relevant to another theme introduced in Chapter 1, the social construction of gender. Regardless of their accuracy, gender-related beliefs serve as lenses that guide our expectations and interpretations of other people. They can elicit stereotypic behaviors from others. For example, a high school teacher who believes that females are more nurturant than males might ask female students to volunteer in a daycare center run by the school. This would provide females but not males the opportunity

GET INVOLVED 2.1

How Do You View Typical Females and Males?

Indicate which of the following characteristics reflect your conception of a *typical* adult woman and a *typical* adult man. Write W next to each characteristic you associate with women and M next to each characteristic you associate with men. If you think a particular trait is representative of both women and men, write W and M next to that trait.

_____ achievement oriented	_____ emotional
_____ active	_____ gentle
_____ adventurous	_____ independent
_____ affectionate	_____ kind
_____ aggressive	_____ people oriented
_____ ambitious	_____ pleasant
_____ boastful	_____ rational
_____ charming	_____ softhearted
_____ daring	_____ sympathetic
_____ dominant	_____ warm

What Does It Mean?

Did your conceptions of a typical woman and a typical man match those reported by samples of university students from the United States and 28 other countries? These students described the typical woman with traits including affectionate, charming, emotional, gentle, kind, people oriented, softhearted, sympathetic, and warm; they described the typical man with characteristics such as achievement oriented, active, adventurous, ambitious, boastful, daring, independent, rational, and showing initiative.

1. If your impressions of the typical woman and the typical man did not agree with the descriptions reported by these samples of college students, give possible reasons.

2. What was the ethnic identity of the typical woman and man that you considered when performing this activity? If you thought about a White woman and man, do you think your conceptions would have varied had you been asked to specifically consider Blacks, Latinas/os, Asian Americans, or Native Americans? If yes, what are those differences and what can explain them?

3. Similarly, did you think of a middle-class woman and man? Would your impressions have varied had you thought about working-class or poor females and males? Explain any possible differences in gender stereotypes based on social class.

Source: Based on De Lisi and Soundranayagam (1990) and Williams and Best (1990).

to develop their caregiving traits. Thus, the teacher's stereotype about the communal characteristics of girls and women might actually contribute to the construction of female-related traits in her female students.

The importance of gender stereotypes in the social construction of gender is also evident in the choices individuals make about their own behavior. For example, based on gender-related beliefs, more adolescent females than males might be likely to seek out babysitting experiences and, thus, more strongly develop traits such as nurturance and compassion.

The traits we have examined thus far are those that North Americans see as *representative* of most women and men. However, an examination of the characteristics people view as *ideal* for each gender indicates some discrepancy between people's stereotypes about most women and men and their conceptions of what women and men should be like. Sue Street and her colleagues (Street, Kromrey et al., 1995; Street, Kimmel et al., 1995) studied college students' and faculty's conceptions about the *ideal woman* and the *ideal* man as well as beliefs about *most* women and *most* men. Their findings showed that both students and faculty perceived most women as communal and most men as agentic. However, they viewed the ideal woman as very high in both female-related and male-related traits; that is, they believed she should be caring, sensitive, gentle, and compassionate as well as logical, intelligent, achievement oriented, and assertive. Additionally, although these respondents saw the ideal man as highest in agentic traits, they believed he should be relatively high in compassion as well. Thus, both students and faculty believe ideal persons of both genders should have both types of characteristics.

The Perceiver's Ethnicity and Gender Stereotypes

When you performed Get Involved 2.1, did your selection of traits for females and males match those found in previous research? Alternatively, did you find that you either were less restrictive than the samples investigated in these studies or that you used different stereotypes? Possibly you indicated that some of these characteristics were reflective of both females and males or that some were more representative of the gender not usually associated with the stereotype. Although there is considerable consistency among people in their gender stereotypes, all individuals do not think alike.

In fact, there is evidence that people from different ethnic backgrounds vary in the degree to which they believe the ideal characteristics for females are different from the ideal traits for males, with Blacks less stereotypic in their views than Latinas/os or Whites (Kane, 2000; Leaper, 2002). For example, Allen Harris (1994) asked 500 female and 500 male shopping-mall patrons from each of these three ethnic groups to rate the desirability of personality traits for either a woman or a man in their culture. The Blacks were less likely than the Whites or Latinas/os to associate specific characteristics with each gender; instead they considered a larger variety of traits as desirable for both females and males. For example, Blacks rated assertiveness, independence, and self-reliance as equally desirable for Black women and men, whereas the other two ethnic groups evaluated these traits as more desirable for men than women in their cultural groups. Also, Blacks viewed eagerness to soothe hurt feelings as equally desirable for individuals of both genders, but Whites and Latinas/ós perceived it as more desirable for women than men. The results of this and other studies indicate that among these three ethnic groups, Blacks are the least likely to adhere to rigid gender stereotypes for women and men.

The Target's Characteristics and Gender Stereotypes

We have seen that people with diverse ethnic backgrounds differ somewhat in their perception of stereotypes of women and men. Now let's examine how these stereotypes vary as a function of the characteristics of the person who is the object, or target, of the stereotype. These characteristics include a woman's age, ethnicity, social class, sexual orientation, and ableness.

Age.   One of the challenges facing older people in North America and many other parts of the world is the presence of stereotypes (mostly negative) that many people hold about the elderly (Cuddy et al., 2005). Both children and adults express stereotyped views about older people, some positive (warm kind, friendly, wise) and others negative (incompetent, unhealthy, inactive, unattractive, feeble) (Cuddy et al., 2005; Kite et al., 2005; Montepare & Zebrowitz, 2002). Such stereotypes are part of a concept known as **ageism.** This term refers to *bias against people on the basis of their age* (Nelson, 2005). Ageism can be targeted toward any age group ("Children don't respect their elders"; "Teenagers are rebellious"). But ageism is usually directed at people in later life. Ageism resembles sexism and racism in that all are forms of prejudice that limit people who are the object of that prejudice. Unlike sexism and racism, however, everyone will confront ageism if they live long enough (Martens et al., 2005).

Ageism seems to be more strongly directed toward women than men. For centuries, unflattering terms have been used to describe middle-aged and older women: crone, hag, wicked old witch, old maid, dreaded mother-in-law (Have you ever heard any jokes about fathers-in-law?) (American Psychological Association, 2007a; Bugental & Hehman, 2007; Markson, 2001; Sherman, 2001). Another example of negative attitudes toward older women is the double standard of aging that we will examine later in the chapter.

Still another example is the relative invisibility of middle-aged and older women in the media. Joan Chrisler (2007) notes that the scarcity of images of women over 50 in the media conveys the message that women should either hide the signs of aging or stay hidden. The few older women who appear on television shows are portrayed less favorably than older men. They are often depicted as comic or eccentric figures, asexual, marginal, passive, unsuccessful, or downright villainous (Palmore, 2001; Sherman, 2001; Wilkinson & Ferraro, 2002; Zebrowitz & Montepare, 2000). Whereas prime-time male characters age 65 and older are depicted as active, middle-aged mature adults, women of that age are more likely to be designated as elderly (Signorielli & Bacue, 1999).

Psychologists seem to share society's negative views of older women. They are more likely to rate older women of both races as less assertive, less willing to take risks, and less competent than younger women (American Psychological Association, 2007a).

Negative attitudes toward the elderly are far from universal, however. For a look at some of the factors that influence views of older individuals, turn to Learn about the Research 2.1.

Although aging women have traditionally been viewed less positively than aging men, there is some indication that attitudes toward older women may be improving. One positive sign is what psychologist Margaret Matlin (2001) calls the "Wise and Wonderful Movement." In the 21st century, there has been an explosion of books on women who discover themselves in middle or old age. The books present a positive picture of the challenges and opportunities for women in their later years. Two of these books, by Pamela Blair (2005) and Suzanne Levine (2004), are listed as recommended readings at the end of this chapter.

LEARN ABOUT THE RESEARCH 2.1

Who Is Ageist?

Many factors are related to attitudes toward the elderly. Two of these are age and ethnicity. Older adults have more positive attitudes toward aging and the elderly than do younger adults (Chasteen, 1998; Harris et al., 1988). In a 1993 *New Woman* magazine survey of over 6,000 of its readers, younger women were more fearful of growing old than older women. Among women in their twenties, 54 percent expressed such a fear compared with only 23 percent of those over 60. Women over age 50 expressed positive views of older women. Half reported that the best part of aging is feeling a firm sense of self. Older women were more satisfied with their lives than younger women. In response to the question "How do you feel about life as a whole?" 26 percent of women over 50 were "delighted, pleased" and 37 percent were "mostly satisfied," as compared with only 17 percent and 28 percent, respectively, of women under 30 (Perlmutter et al., 1994). Among younger adults, those with positive, supportive relationships with their grandparents have less negative stereotypes and more positive feelings about older adults (Mitchell & Stricker, 1998).

Views toward older adults also vary among ethnic groups. Whites generally show less favorable attitudes than do ethnic minority groups. In research by Mary Harris and her colleagues (Harris et al., 1988), for example, Whites were less likely to enjoy spending time with the elderly than were Latinos and Native Americans. Other studies (e.g., Boduroglu et al., 2002) show that views of the elderly are more positive in China than in the United States.

What Does It Mean?

1. Why do you think young women are more afraid of growing old than are older women?
2. Why do you think members of ethnic minority groups hold more positive views of the elderly than Whites do?
3. What are some factors, other than age and ethnicity, that might be related to attitudes toward the elderly?

Ethnicity.　　Studies find both commonalities and differences in stereotypes of individuals who vary in ethnicity. In one investigation, Yolanda Niemann and her colleagues (Niemann et al., 1994) asked a multiethnic sample of college students to list adjectives that came to mind when they thought of individuals in each of eight different ethnic and gender groups: White, Black, Mexican American, and Asian American females and males. Examination of the most frequently mentioned traits showed that all women, regardless of their ethnicity, were seen as pleasant. However, other traits varied as a function of ethnic identification. For example, whereas Black women were viewed as speaking loudly, Asian American women were seen as speaking softly. Further, only Mexican Americans were characterized as family oriented and only Blacks were described as antagonistic.

Unfortunately, in this study and others (Donovan et al., 2005), college students viewed Black women in terms of the cultural matriarchal stereotype: tough, direct, aggressive, dominant, and strong. This somewhat negative stereotype indicates that White individuals may overlook the harsh realities of racial and gender oppression in the lives of many Black women and may perceive Black women through a racist lens, a problem experienced by other ethnic minority women as well (Chisholm & Greene, 2008).

Social Class.　　Studies have found that individuals of lower socioeconomic status are typically characterized as dishonest, dependent, lazy, stupid, uneducated, promiscuous, drug using, and violent (Bullock et al., 2001; Cozzarelli et al., 2001). One study (Lott & Saxon, 2002) found that a working-class woman was judged as more crude and irresponsible than a middle-class woman, even when she was running for PTO president in her child's school.

Sexual Orientation.　　Some heterosexual people believe that in lesbian relationships one partner consistently assumes the masculine role in sexual relations as well as in other behaviors and dress, the so-called butch role, while the other partner assumes the femme, or traditional feminine, role. Contrary to popular assumptions, sexual and other behaviors of lesbians seldom reflect butch–femme gender roles. Many gays and lesbians claim that the labels "masculine" and "feminine" represent efforts of the heterosexual community to pigeonhole them in traditional ways (Rathus et al., 2008).

Ableness.　　Although there has been little research on this topic, there is some evidence that people attribute more negative characteristics to women with disabilities than to able-bodied women. Such *biases against people because of their disability* is known as **ableism** (Chisholm & Greene, 2008). Women with disabilities, unlike able-bodied women, are not assumed to be wives and mothers. Rather than expecting these women to function as nurturers, stereotypical images of women with disabilities emphasize their dependence on others (Olkin, 2008).

In summary, we can see that gender stereotypes are not applied uniformly to all women. A woman's age, ethnicity, social class, sexual orientation, and ableness influence stereotypes of her.

Stereotypes of Girls and Boys

We have seen that people have different expectations of the traits and behaviors of adult females and males. Now let's examine adults' gender-stereotypic expectations of children.

As early as the first few days of life, newborn girls and boys are perceived differently. Parents rate newborn daughters as finer featured, less strong, and more delicate than newborn sons, despite medical evidence of no physical differences between them (Karraker et al., 1995). Thus, it is apparent that adults hold gender stereotypes of the physical characteristics of children immediately after the child's birth.

Adults' stereotypes of children are not restricted to early infancy. In one study (Martin, 1995), Canadian college students were asked to rate the typical characteristics of 4- to 7-year-old girls and boys. The evidence for gender stereotypes was quite clear. Out of 25 traits, these young adults rated 24 as being more typical for one gender than the other. Additionally, the traits seen as typical for girls versus boys reflected the communion–agency stereotypes evident in gender stereotypes of adults. For example, these students rated girls, compared to boys, as more gentle, sympathetic, and helpful around the house, and they rated boys as more self-reliant, dominant, and competitive than girls.

Bases for Gender Stereotypes

Our exploration of the origins of gender stereotypes focuses on two related issues: (1) the reasons why people stereotype on the basis of gender and (2) the reasons why these stereotypes center on communal traits for females and agentic attributes for males. In other words, we will consider explanations for both the *process* and the *content* of gender stereotyping.

Social Categorization. Because we are bombarded daily with diverse types of people, behaviors, situations, and so on, we simplify our social perceptions by *sorting individuals into categories*, a process called **social categorization.** We focus on the characteristics people share with other members of that category. As an example, in a hospital we might categorize the health professionals we encounter as doctors and nurses. Then, the differential set of characteristics we associate with physicians versus nurses serves as a behavior guide when we interact with them, enabling us to ask questions appropriate to each of their skills and knowledge.

Although we make use of a variety of cues for the sorting process, social categorization is frequently based on easily identified characteristics, such as ethnicity, age, and gender (Baker, 2001). This makes sense because these attributes are usually the first that we observe and provide an easy basis on which to sort people. Thus, the process of gender stereotyping begins with the categorization of individuals as females or males with the implicit assumption that the members of each gender share certain attributes. Then, when we meet a new individual, we attribute these characteristics to this person.

Although the social categorization and stereotyping processes help simplify our understanding of and interactions with people, they can lead us astray: Neither all females nor all males are alike. We are most likely to rely on stereotypes when we have little differentiating information about the person. Once more details about a person are available, we use that information in addition to the person's gender to form our impression and guide our interactions (Kite et al., 2008). For example, when evaluating an individual's level of ambition, we might make use of the person's gender if no other information were available. However, this information would be much less important if we knew the individual was the CEO of a major corporation.

Social Role Theory.   Given that people naturally divide others into gender categories and attribute similar characteristics to all members of a category, we turn now to the question of why people associate communion with females and agency with males. One possibility is that these stereotypes stem from our observations of the types of behaviors individuals typically perform in their social roles. According to **social role theory** (Eagly & Diekman, 2006), *stereotypes of women and men stem from the association of women with the domestic role and men with the employee role*. This theory contends that because we have observed women primarily in the domestic role, we assume women have the nurturing traits characteristic of that role. Similarly, because more men than women have traditionally been seen in the employment role, we perceive men as having the agentic traits displayed in the workplace.

Support for this theory of gender stereotypes comes from numerous studies that show the influence of a person's social role on the application of gender-related traits to her/him. For example, there is evidence that social roles can override gender when assigning communal or agentic characteristics to others. Specifically, when participants are asked to describe a woman and a man who are homemakers, they view them as equally communal. Similarly, when asked to describe a full-time female and male employee, they perceive both as agentic. In addition, women and men who are employed are viewed as more agentic than those who are not (Mueller & Yoder, 1997; Riggs, 1997), mothers are seen as more communal than nonmothers (Bridges et al., 2000; Etaugh & Poertner, 1992), and married women are perceived as more communal than unmarried women (Etaugh & Nekolny, 1990; Etaugh & Poertner, 1991). Clearly, when people are aware of an individual's social role, their stereotypes of the person are influenced by that role information.

The influence of social roles on gender stereotypes is evident even when people are asked to describe women and men in both the past and the future. When both college and noncollege adults were asked to rate the average woman and the average man in 1950, 1975, 2025, and 2050, they viewed females as becoming dramatically more masculine over time and males as becoming somewhat more feminine (Diekman & Eagly, 1997). What accounts for these perceptions? In support of social role theory, the researchers found that the decreasing degree of gender stereotyping was related to the belief that the occupational and domestic roles of women and men during this time period have become and will continue to become increasingly similar.

Keep in mind, however, the evidence presented earlier in this chapter—that stereotypes have remained relatively constant, at least since the 1970s. What can explain the discrepancy between the increased participation of women in the labor force and the consistency of gender stereotypes over time? Although a greater number of women are now employed than was the case in the past, the proportion of women in the paid workforce continues to be lower than the corresponding proportion of men. Also, regardless of their employment role, women still have the primary caregiving responsibility in their families and are more likely than men to be employed in caregiving occupations, such as nursing and early childhood education. Although social roles are gradually changing, women remain the primary nurturers and men the primary providers. Consequently, it is not surprising that our stereotypes of females and males have been resistant to change.

Stereotypes Based on Identity Labels

Recall the experience Judith described at the beginning of the chapter when she was introduced as "Dr., Mrs. Bridges." The fact that the campus director introduced her this way but did not present her male colleague as "Dr. Lantry Brooks who happens to be married" implies he believed that a woman's identity, more than a man's, is shaped by her marital role. Although his use of a dual title was highly unusual, his belief about a woman's identity is consistent with the long-standing cultural norm that a woman is defined in terms of her relationship to a man (e.g., Lakoff, 1990). Given that a woman's title of address can signify her marital role and that her marital status has been viewed as an important aspect of her identity, we might expect different stereotypes of women who use different titles for themselves. Consider the woman who chooses not to use the conventional "Miss" versus "Mrs." labels that inform about her marital status but instead identifies herself with the neutral "Ms." Kelly Malcolmson and Lisa Sinclair (2007) recently replicated 10-year-old studies that had found that women who prefer the title Ms. are perceived as more agentic but less communal than traditionally titled women. Thus, the Ms. title remains a powerful cue eliciting a stereotype consistent with male gender-related traits and inconsistent with female gender-related traits. Other recent research by Carol Lawton and her colleagues (Lawton et al., 2003) found that Ms. was often defined as a title for unmarried women, especially by younger adults. Older unmarried women were more likely to prefer Ms. as their own title than were younger unmarried women, while married women overwhelmingly preferred the use of Mrs.

Given that our impressions of a woman are influenced by her preferred title, a related question is whether these stereotypes vary according to another identity label, a woman's choice of surname after marriage. Similar to the preference for Ms. as a title of address, a woman's choice of a surname other than her husband's, such as her birth name or a hyphenated name, is a nontraditional practice that separates the woman's personal identity from her identity as a wife. Nowadays, about 20 percent of college-educated brides do not take their husband's last name, compared with only 4 percent in 1975 (Grossman, 2007). Thus, it is not surprising that studies by Claire, Judith, and their students (Etaugh et al., 1999; Etaugh & Conrad, 2004; Etaugh & Roe, 2002) showed that college women and men view married women who use a nontraditional surname as more agentic and less communal than women who follow the patriarchal practice of taking their husband's name after marriage.

Why do a woman's preferred title and surname influence the characteristics attributed to her? One possibility is that individuals have observed more women with nontraditional forms of address (i.e., title and/or surname) in the workplace than in the domestic role and, thus, attribute her with more agentic traits. For example, there is evidence that married women who use nonconventional surnames are highly educated and have prestigious occupations (Guzman, 2002; Johnson & Scheuble, 1995). Thus, consistent with social role theory (Eagly & Diekman, 2006), stereotypes of women who prefer nontraditional forms of address might be due to the belief that they are in nontraditional roles.

Sexism

The definition of sexism as bias against people because of their gender can be directed at either females or males. However, women have a power disadvantage relative to men and are, therefore, more likely to be targets of sexism (Glick & Fiske, 2007). Therefore, our discussion focuses on the more specific definition of sexism as *stereotypes and/or discriminatory behaviors that serve to restrict women's roles and maintain male dominance.* For example, stereotypes such as "women are dependent and passive," "women should be the primary caregivers," and "women are not competent to be police officers or university presidents" serve to shape women's role choices. *Violating these gender stereotypes can result in social and economic reprisals*—a phenomenon referred to as the **backlash effect** (Rudman & Fairchild, 2004). For example, a highly qualified female job applicant may be viewed as socially deficient, leading to hiring discrimination and ultimately the maintenance of male dominance in the culture at large.

Consider the real-life case of Ann Hopkins, a high-achieving professional at Price Waterhouse, one of the country's most prestigious accounting firms. In 1982, Hopkins was one of 88 candidates for partner and the only female candidate. At that time she had more billable hours than any other contenders. Additionally, she had brought in $25 million worth of business and was highly esteemed by her clients. However, Ann Hopkins was turned down for the partnership. She was criticized for her "macho" style and was advised to "walk more femininely, talk more femininely, dress more femininely, wear makeup and jewelry" (Hopkins, 2007, p. 62).

Ms. Hopkins filed a lawsuit, asserting that her promotion had been denied on the basis of her gender. Although she won this suit, her employer appealed the decision all the way up to the Supreme Court. The Court decided in Ann Hopkins's favor and, in 1990, a federal district court judge concluded that gender-based stereotyping had played a role in the firm's refusal to promote Ms. Hopkins to partner. After this decision, Ann Hopkins did become a partner and was awarded financial compensation for her lost earnings (Hopkins, 2007).

Ambivalent Sexism

Generally, we consider sexism to comprise *negative* stereotypes about women, such as the beliefs that women are fragile, submissive, and less competent than men. And, of course, we can see how stereotypes such as these are detrimental to women. Interestingly, however, Peter Glick and Susan Fiske (2007) have proposed that sexism can be

ambivalent, encompassing both **hostile sexism,** or negative stereotypes of women, and **benevolent sexism,** or positive characterizations such as "women are pure" and "women should be protected."

Although hostile sexist beliefs are overtly demeaning, benevolent sexist views are usually accompanied by genuine affection, and the holder of these attitudes might be unaware of their implicit sexist bias. For example, a husband who shields his wife from the family's financial difficulties because he believes she would be unable to cope might be unaware of the biased assumptions implicit in his desire to protect her. According to Glick and Fiske (2007), hostile and benevolent sexism both imply that women are weak and best suited for traditional gender roles. Both serve to justify and maintain patriarchal social structures. In other words, ambivalent sexism includes both positive and negative beliefs about women, but both serve to maintain the power imbalance between women and men. In support of this view, research shows that individuals who endorse benevolent sexism also endorse the concept of "paternalistic chivalry," that is, being courteous and considerate to women but at the same time favoring traditional courtship behaviors for women (Viki et al., 2003). Some aspects of benevolent sexism may appeal to some women. For example, beliefs that women are less physically strong or more emotionally sensitive allow women to not engage in distasteful activities ranging from taking out the garbage to fighting in wars (Goodwin & Fiske, 2001). However, recent research shows that benevolent sexism actually has a more harmful effect on women's performance on cognitive tasks than has hostile sexism (Dardenne et al., 2007). In one study, patronizing statements read before task performance led to feelings of self-doubt and decreased self-esteem, which undermined performance. Hostile sexist statements did not have this negative effect. For a look at ambivalent sexism around the world, see Explore Other Cultures 2.1.

Changes in Sexist Attitudes over Time

Since 1970, the United States has experienced a significant decrease in overt sexism. For example, in 1970, 48 percent of a sample of college students expressed the belief that married women with children should stay home (Twenge, 1997a); however, only 20 percent expressed agreement with this belief in 2005 (Pryor et al., 2005). Similarly, 74 percent of men surveyed in 1977 felt that women should tend the home and children while men earn money, whereas only 42 percent expressed this view in 2002 (Barnett, 2004). Further, a meta-analysis of 71 undergraduate samples from 1970 to 1995 (Twenge, 1997a) showed a steadily decreasing adherence to overt sexism by both females and males. Unfortunately, little is known about the sexist beliefs of noncollege adults, such as working- or middle-class women and men or adults on welfare.

Modern Sexism

It is likely that the reduction in sexism is due, in part, to legislative actions (e.g., 1960s legislation prohibiting education and workplace discrimination on the basis of sex) and other social changes (e.g., the significant influx of married women into the workplace in the last few decades). However, some of the decline in overt sexism might actually

EXPLORE OTHER CULTURES 2.1
Benevolent Sexism Is a Global Phenomenon

Peter Glick, Susan Fiske, and their colleagues (2000) measured ambivalent sexism in over 15,000 participants in 19 countries in Africa, Asia, Europe, the Americas, and Australia. While both hostile and benevolent sexism were prevalent in all cultures, these attitudes were strongest in Africa and Latin America and weakest in Northern Europe and Australia. Without exception, men showed more hostile sexism than women. In contrast, women in about half the countries endorsed benevolent sexism as much as or even more than men did (Figure 2.1). What accounts for these cross-cultural differences? The key factor appears to be the degree to which gender inequality exists in the various nations. Gender inequality is measured by such things as women's (relative to men's) participation in a country's economy and political system, their life expectancy, educational level, and standard of living. In countries with the greatest gender inequality (i.e., in Africa and Latin America), both men's and women's sexism scores were highest. Furthermore, the more hostile sexism the men showed, the more likely women were to embrace benevolent sexism, even to the point of endorsing it more strongly than men. How can this be explained? According to Glick and Fiske (2007), the greater the threat of hostile sexism from a society's men, the stronger the incentive for women to adopt benevolent sexism's protective nature.

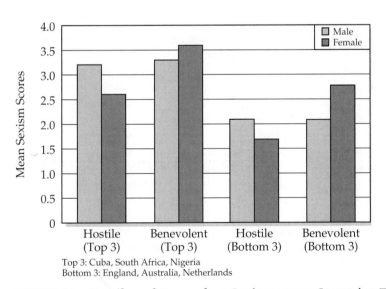

Top 3: Cuba, South Africa, Nigeria
Bottom 3: England, Australia, Netherlands

FIGURE 2.1   Hostile and Benevolent Sexism across Countries: The Top Three versus the Bottom Three

reflect the decreased social acceptability of blatantly sexist views, rather than a real weakening of beliefs that serve to maintain traditional roles and power differences. Several theorists have suggested that a more subtle type of sexism has emerged in North America. This ideology, called **modern sexism** (Swim et al., 2005), is based on the coexistence of conflicting attitudes. According to this perspective, some people hold egalitarian values but, at the same time, harbor negative feelings toward women. The resulting ideology is *characterized by the belief that gender discrimination is no longer a problem in society and is manifested by harmful treatment of women in ways that appear to be socially acceptable*. For example, a modern sexist might argue that policies that foster gender equality, such as affirmative action, should not be implemented. Thus, it is possible for a person to espouse sexist beliefs such as these but not appear to be prejudiced against women.

Do you know anyone who endorses modern sexism? See Get Involved 2.2 for examples of modern sexist beliefs.

Experiences with Sexism

Sadly, most girls and women experience sexism at one time or another. In a recent study of 600 teenage girls of varied socioeconomic and ethnic backgrounds (Leaper & Brown, 2008), half of the girls reported hearing discouraging, sexist comments about their abilities in science, math, or computers. Three-fourths had received disparaging comments about their athletic abilities and sports involvement. Male peers were the most common perpetrators of academic and athletic sexist remarks. Such disapproval may lead some girls to downplay their interests and competencies in sports or academic areas, which can ultimately diminish later achievements in these areas. Even more troubling, perhaps, teachers were a frequent source of discouraging remarks about girls' academic abilities, as were fathers. (More about this in Chapter 4.)

Have you ever experienced unfair treatment by teachers, employers, strangers, romantic partners, and others because of your gender? Have you ever been the target of inappropriate or unwanted sexual advances or sexist name calling? Have you ever been forced to listen to sexist jokes? Elizabeth Klonoff and Hope Landrine (1995) asked 631 culturally diverse college and noncollege women how often incidents like these had happened to them. All except 6 women (99 percent) reported experiencing sexist discrimination at least once in their lives. Among the most commonly experienced events, reported by more than 80 percent of the women, were being forced to listen to sexist jokes, being sexually harassed, and experiencing a lack of respect. Although less common, 40 percent of the women reported some type of employment discrimination and 19 percent indicated they had taken legal or institutional action to pursue discrimination on the basis of gender.

The perception of sexism is dependent, in part, on a woman's interpretation. To one woman a joke that sexually degrades women is sexist, but to another woman that joke is simply funny. Not only do women vary in their interpretation of sexist incidents, but they also differ from one another in their willingness to acknowledge their own experience with discrimination. In a study of college students, Kobrynowicz and Branscombe (1997) found that women who have a strong desire for social approval are

GET INVOLVED 2.2
Who Holds Modern Sexist Beliefs?

On a scale from 1 (strongly disagree) to 7 (strongly agree), indicate the extent to which you disagree or agree with each of the following statements. Also, ask several female and male acquaintances who vary in age to respond to these statements.

1. It is rare to see women treated in a sexist manner on television.
2. Society has reached the point where women and men have equal opportunities for achievement.
3. Over the past few years, the government and news media have been showing more concern about the treatment of women than is warranted by women's actual experiences.
4. Discrimination against women is no longer a problem in the United States.
5. Women's requests in terms of equality between the sexes are simply exaggerated.
6. Universities are wrong to admit women in costly programs such as medicine, when in fact, a large number will leave their jobs after a few years to raise their children.
7. Due to social pressures, firms frequently have to hire underqualified women.

What Does It Mean?

Sum the ratings you gave to these seven statements. Do the same for each of your respondents. Note that each statement reflects a sexist belief; therefore, the higher the score, the greater the sexism.

1. Are there differences between the views of your female and male respondents? Explain your finding.
2. Are there differences between the views of respondents who vary in age? Explain your finding.
3. Do you think it is possible that a person could endorse one or more of these beliefs but not be supportive of traditional roles and male dominance? Why or why not?

Source: Based on Swim et al. (1995) and Tougas et al. (1995).

---

less likely to acknowledge they had experienced discrimination than are those willing to risk disapproval. According to these researchers, claiming sexism might be perceived as socially undesirable for women who are greatly concerned about the amount of approval they receive from others.

Representation of Gender in the Media

We have seen that North American adults have different conceptions of females and males. We turn now to the depiction of these stereotypes in the media. On a daily basis we are bombarded with differential images of females and males on television, in the movies, in books, and in magazines. Are these images consistent with gender stereo-typing? Try the exercise in Get Involved 2.3 to examine television portrayals of gender.

Numerous investigations of the depiction of females and males in both electronic and print media have revealed several consistent patterns: the under representation of females, the underrepresentation of specific groups of females, the portrayal of gender-based social roles, the depiction of female communion and male agency, and the emphasis on female attractiveness and sexuality. Our first task is to examine these patterns. Then we consider the effects of media images on gender stereotypes and attitudes.

Pattern 1: Underrepresentation of Females

As we have previously seen, women are perceived as less powerful than men; men's roles are viewed as more important. This imbalance of power and value is reflected in the media's underrepresentation of females. Although the percentage of female characters in television shows increased from 28 percent in the 1970s to 39 percent in the 1990s (Signorielli & Bacue, 1999), it is clear that the proportion of females continues to be low. Similarly, the percentage of female characters in TV commercials (Bartsch et al., 2000; Ganahl et al., 2003) and movies (American Psychological Association Task Force, 2007; Lauzen, 2003) ranges from approximately 20 to 45 percent. One recent study of 101 G-rated films found that three out of four characters were male (Lamb, 2006). This underrepresentation is also mirrored in children's television programs (APA Task Force, 2007), video games and video game covers (Burgess et al., 2007), Sunday morning news analysis shows (Brazile, 2007), and even in computer clipart images (Milburn et al., 2001).

This situation has improved in recent years in certain types of children's reading material. For example, picture books of the 1990s featured males and females equally in titles, as central characters, and in pictures (Gooden & Gooden, 2001; Lane & Etaugh, 2001). Children's school textbooks are less gender biased then they were 30 years ago, but male characters continue to outnumber female ones in basic readers and math materials (Meece & Scantlebury, 2006).

GET INVOLVED 2.3

How Are Females and Males Portrayed on Prime-Time Television?

Watch five different prime-time shows and record the following information: (1) the number of major female and male characters; (2) the ethnicity of these characters; (3) the employment status and occupation, if employed, of each major female and male character; (4) the marital and parental status of these characters; (5) the approximate age of each of these characters (e.g., 20s, 30s); and (6) whether or not each character's physical appearance was mentioned or otherwise appeared to be an important characteristic of that person. After recording this information, examine commonalities and differences in the depiction of females and males and in the portrayal of different age groups. Also, if these shows featured women and/or men of color, compare portrayals of characters of varying ethnicities.

What Does It Mean?

1. Are your findings consistent with those presented in this chapter? If not, what do you think might explain any differences you observed?
2. Do your findings indicate that members of each gender are depicted similarly, regardless of their ethnicity or age? If you

found differences related to ethnicity or age, explain them.
3. Do you think that media images of gender, as described in this chapter and as shown by your analysis, help shape our construction of gender? Explain your answer.

Pattern 2: Underrepresentation of Specific Groups of Females

Ethnicity.   The invisibility of females is most evident when considering females in less powerful social categories. Women and girls of color, especially Latinas, Asian Americans, and Native Americans, are featured very infrequently in children's and adult's television shows, commercials (Coltrane & Messineo, 2000; Van Evra, 2004), and movies (Lauzen, 2003). When they do appear, they are highly stereotyped (Berry, 2007). For example, Latina characters are often shown in low-status occupations such as maids (Navarro, 2002). On prime-time television shows, Black women and men, compared to Whites, are portrayed as more provocative and less professional in dress and to be more passive, and are judged to be the laziest and least respected ethnic group (Mastro & Greenberg, 2000). Ethnic minority women are also underrepresented

The media often depict Latina characters in low-status occupations, as in the movie Maid in Manhattan.

in advertisements in a wide variety of periodicals (Sengupta, 2006; Taylor et al., 1995) and are nearly invisible in fiction stories in large-circulation women's magazines (Peirce, 1997).

Age.   Another seriously underrepresented group is older women. In television shows (Fouts & Burggraf, 1999; Signorielli & Bacue, 1999), television commercials (Ganahl et al., 2003), and movies (Lauzen, 2003), female characters are younger than male characters, with most women under age 35. In fact, women over 50 are portrayed in only 12 percent of the roles in popular movies, and among the top actors aged 50 or older, only 20 percent are women (Haskell & Harmetz, 1998). Older women of color are rarely seen (Robinson et al., 2004).

Print media are no exception. In magazines geared toward 40- and 50-year-old women, for example, most of the models are in their 20s and early 30's (Bessenoff & Del Priore, 2007). Those older women who do appear in the media are praised for their youthful appearance and for hiding the signs of aging. In the words of Susan Bordo,

> *I'm 56. The magazines tell me that at this age, a woman can still be beautiful. But they don't mean me. They mean Cher, Goldie, Faye, Candace. Women whose jowls have disappeared as they've aged, whose eyes have become less droopy, lips grown plumper, foreheads smoother with the passing years. "Aging beautifully" used to mean wearing one's years with style, confidence, and vitality. Today, it means not appearing to age at all.*(2004, p. 246)

In our youth-oriented society, the prospect of getting older is generally not relished by either sex. For women, however, *the stigma of aging is much greater than it is for men.* Susan Sontag (1979) has labeled this phenomenon the **double standard of aging.** The same gray hair and wrinkles that enhance the perceived status and attractiveness of an older man diminish the attractiveness and desirability of an older woman. Some researchers account for this by noting that a woman's most socially valued qualities—her ability to provide sex and bear children—are associated with the physical beauty and fertility of youth. As she ages, she is seen as less attractive because her years of social usefulness as childbearer are behind her. Men, however, are seen as possessing qualities—competence, autonomy, and power—that are not associated with youth but rather increase with age (Etaugh, 2008).

Older women in popular films are portrayed as more unfriendly, unintelligent, unattractive, and wicked (Bazzini et al., 1997). Attractive actresses such as Meryl Streep, Jessica Lange, and Diane Keaton are labeled "geezer babes"—and thus too old for romantic parts—while male actors many years their senior are paired with young ingenues (Chrisler, 2007; Genzlinger, 2004; Haskell, 1998). Along the same lines, an analysis of Academy Award nominations for Best Actress and Best Actor from 1927–28 to 1990 found that women over the age of 39 accounted for only 27 percent of all winners for Best Actress, while men in the same age category won 67 percent of Best Actor awards (Markson & Taylor, 1993). Hollywood's long-standing tendency to add years to actresses and subtract them from actors has led to some interesting—and biologically impossible—movie relationships. For example, 29-year-old Angelina Jolie

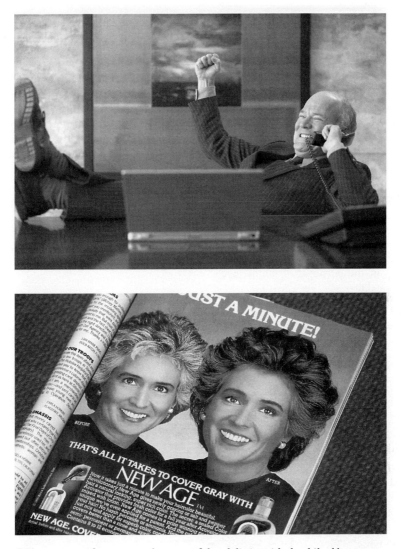

Older men are often portrayed as powerful and distinguished, while older women are perceived as losing their attractiveness.

played the mother of 28-year-old Colin Farrell in the 2004 film *Alexander* (Beumont, 2005). Before going further, try Get Involved 2.4.

Sexual Orientation. Lesbians and gay men have been another underrepresented group in the media. As recently as 20 years ago, there were few visible gay characters, and they were usually portrayed as psychopaths, suicidal, unattractive, or isolated (D'Erasmo, 2004; Stanley, 2004; Weinraub & Rutenberg, 2003; Wloszczyna, 2003). But as gays and lesbians have become more accepted in recent years, gay characters are

GET INVOLVED 2.4

Media Advertisements and the Double Standard of Aging

Look through newspapers and magazines for advertisements that include middle-aged adults. Then answer the following questions:

1. Are there differences in the appearance of the women and the men?

2. Do females and males advertise different products?
3. In advertisements with two or more people, what is the role of the principal male or female in relationship to others?

What Does It Mean?

1. Do the advertisements show evidence of a double standard of aging?
2. What can advertisers do to minimize differences in the portrayal of middle-aged females and males?

3. How do media images of midlife adults help shape our perceptions of middle-aged women and men?

Source: Berk et al. (1998).

Angelina Jolie (left), age 29, plays the mother of 28-year-old Colin Farrell (right) in the film Alexander.

increasingly featured in mainstream television shows, films, and theater. Television shows such as *Will and Grace* (a straight woman and a gay man are best friends), *Queer Eye for the Straight Guy* (gay experts in fashion, food, and interior design do a makeover on "aesthetically challenged" straight men), and *Queer as Folk* (a portrayal of gay men's lives) are mainstream hits. The year 2004 saw the debut of *It's All Relative*, featuring a woman raised by two liberal gay men who is engaged to the son of Irish-Catholic conservatives, and *The L-Word*, the first lesbian-focused series. In 2005, a long-time character on *The Simpsons* came out of the closet and Homer Simpson conducted dozens of same-sex weddings to boost tourism in his town (Waxman, 2005). Also in that year, MTV started the first cable television channel directed at gay and lesbian viewers (Carter & Elliott, 2004). The trend-setting *New York Times* began publishing same-sex wedding and commitment ceremony announcements in 2002. And a 2003 issue of the popular magazine *Brides* had a feature on what to wear to a same-sex wedding (Toussaint, 2003).

Pattern 3: Portrayal of Gender-Based Social Roles

Females and males are portrayed differently in the media not only in terms of their numbers but also in relation to their social roles. Over the last few decades there has been an increase in the percentage of prime-time TV shows that feature female characters who are employed, with 60 percent of female characters depicted as working in the 1990s (Signorielli & Bacue, 1999). Furthermore, their range of jobs has broadened; in the 1990s only one quarter were shown in traditional female jobs, such as secretary or nurse (Signorielli & Bacue, 1999). But although women lawyers, doctors, and police officers appear on television, many of these depictions are unrealistic. For example, not all women in these professions are young and beautiful (Van Evra, 2004)!

On the other hand, consistent with the stereotypical association of men in the worker role and women in the family role, popular television shows (National Partnership for Women & Families, 1998; Signorielli & Bacue, 1999), commercials (Furnham & Saar, 2005; Robinson & Hunter, 2007; Royo-Vela et al., 2008; Valls-Hernandez & Martinez-Vicente, 2007), and movies (Signorielli, 1997) still show more men than women with jobs and more women than men in traditional family roles. In the movies, women are more likely than men to hold powerless occupations, such as retail clerk, and they rarely are shown in leadership roles (Lauzen, 2003). Even in movies with a strong, successful, independent woman character, the woman's life is more constrained than the man's and traditional cultural patterns triumph in the end (Dowd, 2007). Also, although most married men in TV shows are employed, there are few married working women in these shows (Signorielli, 1997). Thus, despite the presence of several positive employed-female role models on television and the fact that the majority of American married women are employed (U.S. Census Bureau, 2007c), there is little depiction of women who successfully combine a career and marriage. Television seems to be saying that successful women professionals cannot have rewarding home lives, if indeed they have any at all (Garfinkel, 2002).

Similarly, the Sunday comics feature more women than men at home and fewer women than men in career activities (Brabant & Mooney, 1997; LaRossa et al.,

2001). Children's picture books also reflect this role difference by depicting women as homemakers and nurturers (Etaugh et al., 2007; Lehr, 2001). In addition, when females are portrayed as working, children's readers (Purcell & Stewart, 1990) and cartoons (Spicher & Hudak, 1997) show them in a smaller variety of occupations. Furthermore, the majority of feature articles in the leading teen magazine for girls, *Seventeen*, focus on traditional topics, such as appearance and relationships (Schlenker et al., 1998). Only 40 percent address more feminist themes, such as self- and career development. The world of work is dominated by powerful men, and fashion modeling is presented as the pinnacle of "women's work" (Massoni, 2004). Moreover, stereotyped depictions of women in both general interest and fashion magazine advertisements have decreased only slightly over the past 50 years (Lindner, 2004).

Despite the increasing participation of women in sports, female athletes continue to be underrepresented in the media (Zill et al., 2004). Moreover, those who participate in traditional feminine sports such as tennis, golf, or gymnastics get more coverage than women who compete in more masculine team sports such as basketball or softball (Fink & Kensicki, 2002; Tuggle et al., 2002). In the 2000 Olympics, women who competed in sports involving power or hard physical contact—discus throw, javelin throw, shot put, weightlifting, martial arts—received almost no television coverage (Tuggle et al., 2002). Moreover, the athleticism of female athletes tends to be underplayed. For example, in the official media guide of the National Collegiate Athletic Association, female athletes are more likely than male athletes to be shown in passive and nonathletic poses (Buysse & Embser-Herbert, 2004). In addition, sports announcers highlight female athletes' femininity, minimize their athletic ability, and use comments that imply that female athletes are less respectable than their male counterparts (Parker & Fink, 2008).

Pattern 4: Depiction of Female Communion and Male Agency

Consistent with the depiction of females and males in different social roles, the communion stereotype for females and the agency stereotype for males are both evident in the media. Despite the growing body of movies and TV shows featuring women fighting and committing mayhem—*Survivor, Fear Factor, Buffy the Vampire Slayer, Kill Bill, Charlie's Angels,* and others (Greenwood, 2007; Solomon, 2005)—boys and men are depicted as more assertive, aggressive, and powerful than females in a range of media (Basow, 2008). These include adult films (Hedley, 1994), children's cartoons (APA Task Force, 2007), Disney films (Levant, 1997), children's literature (Etaugh et al., 2003; Louie, 2001), and even coloring books (McPherson et al., 2007). Furthermore, consistent with their greater power, males are presented as narrators in approximately 70 to 90 percent of commercials that use voice-overs (e.g., Bartsch et al., 2000; Valls-Fernández & Martinez-Vicente, 2007), thus projecting an image of authority and expertise.

The media also feature females as communal, as oriented toward other people. For example, even when a woman is depicted as an action hero—such as Xena the Warrior princess—she is liked best when she embodies traditionally valued feminine traits such as nurturance, compassion, and using the mind over the sword (Calvert et al., 2001). In both television and movies, women are more likely than men to focus on their romantic relationships (Signorielli, 1997). Most mothers in children's literature are nurturers. Many are homemakers, while others are in traditional female nurturing occupations such as teaching, nursing, or social work (Lehr, 2001).

Pattern 5: Emphasis on Female Attractiveness and Sexuality

The media define females, more than males, by their looks and sexuality. For example, commercials show more women than men in suggestive clothing (APA Task Force, 2007). Women are depicted as sex objects in two-thirds of the ads appearing in women's fashion magazines and in magazines for teen girls (Stankiewicz & Rosselli, 2008). In addition, commercials, television shows, and movies portray women as more likely than men to receive comments about their appearance (Lauzen & Dozier, 2002; Signorielli, 1997). In pursuit of physical perfection, women routinely risk their health to undergo extensive plastic surgery on TV reality shows such as *Extreme Makeover* and *The Swan* (Orenstein, 2004; Pozner, 2004).

The lyrics to popular music frequently contain explicit sexual references, which are often degrading to women (Martino et al., 2006). Moreover, music videos emphasize women's sexuality rather than their musical talent (Van Evra, 2004). In the words of one researcher (Arnett, 2002, p. 256), ". . . a typical music video. . . features one or more men performing while beautiful, scantily clad young women dance and writhe lasciviously." Sports announcers and writers frequently refer to a female athlete's attractiveness, emotionality, femininity, and heterosexuality, thus conveying to the audience that her stereotypical gender role is more salient than her athletic role (APA Task Force, 2007; Billings et al., 2002; Fink & Kensicki, 2004; Knight & Giuliano, 2001).

This emphasis on female appearance and sex appeal is apparent in print as well as electronic media. Mainstream magazines targeted at teenagers and young women stress the importance of improving one's physical attractiveness through diet, exercise, fashion, and use of beauty products (APA Task Force, 2007). Similarly, popular women's magazines prey on women's insecurities to get them to buy the advertisers' wares (Blyth, 2004). Kate Peirce (1997) contends that magazines targeted at working women focus as much on appearance as beauty and fashion magazines do. She notes that in one 1995 issue of *New Woman*, 12 pages of makeup ads preceded the table of contents. Even popular children's fairy tales, such as Cinderella, Snow White, and Sleeping Beauty, highlight youthful feminine beauty, which often is associated with being White, virtuous, and economically privileged (Baker-Sperry & Grauerholz, 2003). Moreover, the depiction of women is more sexualized than that of men. Sexual imagery in women's magazine advertising has, in fact, increased in recent years (Frith et al., 2005; Nelson & Paek, 2005; Reichert & Carpenter, 2004). Sexualized images of female athletes abound in women's sports and fitness magazines (Hardin et al., 2005). A typical example is a photograph from *Shape* magazine showing four women members of the U.S. Olympic swim team standing naked behind a strategically draped American flag.

Not only is a woman's attractiveness portrayed as highly important but that attractiveness is also depicted as overly thin (Grabe et al., 2008; Lorch, 2007). For example,

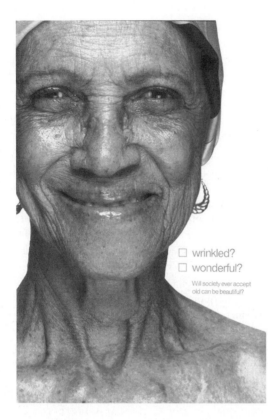

☐ wrinkled?
☐ wonderful?

Will society ever accept
old can be beautiful?

*Irene Sinclair, age 96, in a Dove
commercial challenging traditional
stereotypes of beauty.*

most *Playboy* centerfolds are underweight, and approximately one-third are so thin that
they meet the World Health Organization's standard for anorexia nervosa, a severe eating disorder (see Chapter 13) (Spitzer et al., 1999). Magazines focusing on sports that
emphasize thinness—gymnastics, ice skating, dancing—are more likely to feature overly
thin cover models than are magazines dealing with sports such as running, tennis, and
swimming (Ginsberg & Gray, 2006). Gregory Fouts and Kimberley Burggraf (1999,
2000) found that the number of below-average-weight female characters in Canadian
situation comedies was greater than that found in the general population. Additionally,
they observed that the thinner the female, the more positive comments she received
from male characters and the heavier the woman, the more derogatory remarks she got.
On the show *America's Next Top Models*, dangerously underweight young women reaped
praise for their looks, while normal-weight contestants at 5 feet 8 inches and 130 lbs
were mocked as "plus-sized" (Pozner, 2004). Overweight women not only are underrepresented on television and considered less attractive, but they are also less likely to interact with romantic partners (Greenberg et al., 2003).

   Thus, the media still portray appearance and sexuality as two highly valued
aspects of a woman's identity. More specifically, they present the message that it is
White beauty that is valued (Baker, 2005; Pacheco & Hurtado, 2001). Black actresses
and models who are depicted as physically desirable are likely to be light-skinned and

to possess White facial features (Perkins, 1996), thus informing the Black viewer that not just beauty but White beauty is important.

The media's portrayal of women's appearance does have some recent bright spots. In 2004, for example, Dove launched "The Dove Campaign for Real Beauty," a global effort intended to act as a catalyst for widening the definition and discussion of beauty. The campaign targeted the United States and Great Britain and featured billboard images of six women of various ages, sizes, types, and shapes (Hoggard, 2005). Each photograph showed a woman whose appearance challenges traditional stereotypes of beauty and asked viewers to judge her looks by casting votes and joining a discussion of beauty issues at the campaign's Website. For example, "Oversized? Outstanding?" were the choices next to Tabatha Roman, 34, a plus-size woman, and "Wrinkled? Wonderful?" appear next to the photo of Irene Sinclair, 96.

Significance of Gender-Role Media Images

As this discussion indicates, despite the nearly equal numbers of North American females and males, the media portray a world more heavily populated by males than by females, a world in which males are more likely than females to have jobs and be active and assertive and where beauty and romantic relationships are central to females' identity. Research shows that media not only reflect and transmit existing stereotypes but also have a socializing effect (APA Task Force, 2007; Pecora et al., 2007; Reichert & Lambiase, 2006). For example, exposure to music videos leads to and is associated with stronger endorsement of traditional gender roles and greater acceptance of dating violence (Ward, 2002; Ward et al., 2005). Thus, the media can play an important role in shaping our construction of gender and in providing us with expectations of what females and males are like—their personality traits, social roles, and value to society. In addition, the very limited depiction of non-White or older females can reinforce perceptions of the powerlessness of these groups and communicate that their experiences are not important (Van Evra, 2004).

Consider other types of media that might portray females and males stereotypically. See, for example, Learn about the Research 2.2 to find out about stereotypes in greeting cards.

LEARN ABOUT THE RESEARCH 2.2

Are Babies Portrayed Stereotypically in Birth Congratulations Cards?

We have seen that girls and boys are portrayed stereotypically in virtually all media. To explore how infant girls and boys are portrayed, Judith and her students examined the visual images and verbal messages present in 61 birth congratulations cards for girls and 61 cards for boys.

Not surprisingly, pink was the most common color used on the cards for girls and blue on the cards for boys. Boys were more likely to be shown performing physical activities, such as walking or building, whereas girls were pictured passively sitting or lying down. Similarly, more of the cards for boys featured toys, such as sports equipment and vehicles, that require considerable action, whereas girls were pictured with baby toys, such as rattles and mobiles, that required less physical involvement. Larger animals, including bears and dogs, were more common on the cards for boys and smaller, less aggressive birds and rabbits were shown on the cards for girls.

What Does It Mean?

Answer these questions before reading the remaining part of the research description.

1. The pictures on the cards for girls and boys differed in terms of the types of activities the children were doing and the types of toys and animals presented. How do these differential images fit in with gender stereotypes of females and males as discussed in this chapter?
2. Do any of the study's findings suggest that one gender is more culturally valued than the other? Explain your answer.
3. If you were buying a birth congratulations card for a friend or relative, would you look for a gender-stereotypic or a nonstereotypic card? Why?

Source: Bridges (1993).

Although there were few gender-specific verbal messages in the cards, there were several interesting differences. Girls, more than boys, were described as "little" and "sweet," while the happiness of parents or the child was included more often in the verbal message to boys than in the message to girls.

One conclusion of this study was that birth congratulations cards do portray newborns in gender-stereotypic ways. In keeping with the stereotypical conception that males are more active than females, the types of activities, toys, and animals shown on the cards portrayed boys as more active than girls. Similarly, the tendency to characterize girls more than boys as "little" and "sweet" is consistent with the stereotypic conception of more passive and less powerful females. It is possible that the more frequent reference to happiness on the cards for boys might reflect a greater societal value placed on males than on females and/or it might be indicative of a stronger preference for a son than for a daughter.

Representation of Gender in the English Language

The last section demonstrated how communication via the mass media, such as television and magazines, portrays different images of females and males. This section examines language itself: the different ways females and males are depicted in the English language and how this differential portrayal can shape our conceptions of gender. *Language that unnecessarily differentiates between females and males or excludes and trivializes members of either sex* is called **sexist language.** Let's examine different types of sexist language.

Language Practices Based on the Assumption That Male Is Normative

Numerous language practices reflect the assumption that **male is normative;** that is, that *male behaviors, roles, and experiences are the standards (i.e., norms) for society.* Integral to this perspective are the assumptions that males are more important than females and that female behaviors, roles, and experiences are deviant, that is, different from the norm (Wood, 1994). One indication of this assumption is that adults tend to think of males as persons, as standard or normative individuals in society. For example, Mykol Hamilton (1991) found that college students were more apt to describe typical persons as males than as females and to refer to a male as a *person* but a female as a *woman*. Try Get Involved 2.5 and see if your findings match those reported by Hamilton. Even animals, flowers, and inanimate objects tend to be conceived as male when their sex is unspecified (Lambdin et al., 2003).

Now let's examine some of the language practices that reflect this belief of male as normative.

Masculine Generic Language.   Consider the following situation:

> *At the first session of a training program called "Reducing Man's Addictions" the program's director informed participants that they would be divided into small groups for discussion of the material and that each group should appoint a chairman to facilitate its discussion. Also, the director indicated that at the end of the training program each participant would have sufficient knowledge so that he could work at a drug rehabilitation center.*

GET INVOLVED 2.5

Are Both Women and Men Persons?

Ask two acquaintances of each gender to help you with this activity. Tell them you are studying people's choices about grammatical structure; that is, you are examining students' selections of specific words in a sentence. Therefore, you would like them to fill in the blank in each of the following:

1. Debra Cook won the raffle at the charity fund-raising event. The event organizers will send the prize to this _____ in two weeks.

    person   woman

2. Dave Sherman moved to a new town and went to the Town Hall to register to vote. The registrar of voters gave this _____ the application form.

    person   man

What Does It Mean?

Examine the selections made by your respondents.

1. Did they select different terms depending on the gender of the person?
2. Were there any differences between the answers of the females and males?

3. Did these answers correspond to the findings of Hamilton, as discussed in this chapter?
4. What interpretation can you offer for your findings?

Source: Based on Hamilton (1991).

Describe your image of this event. Does the program deal with addiction problems of both women and men or men only? Will the chairs of the groups be men or women? What is the gender of the participants? Are these gender images clear?

Now substitute *woman's* for *man's*, *chairwoman* for *chairman*, and *she* for *he*. Ask yourself the same questions.

Regardless of your own interpretations of these two verbal descriptions, note that the latter was written using gender-specific (i.e., female) terms whereas the former was written in **masculine generic language,** which is *language that uses male terms but purports to be inclusive of females and males.* Both male pronouns, such as *he* and *his*, and male nouns, such as *chairman, freshman, businessman, man-hours, and forefathers*, are used not only in reference to males but also as inclusive of both genders (reflecting the assumption that male is standard).

Are these masculine generic terms actually interpreted as gender neutral; that is, are they as likely to elicit images of females as males? An abundance of research suggests they are not. Far from communicating gender-neutral images, these terms tend to be exclusionary, connoting just what they directly indicate, that is, men and boys (Conkright et al., 2000; Crawford, 2001; Klein & Larson, 2004). For example, in one study (Switzer, 1990), first- and seventh-grade children listened to the following story:

> Pretend that [teacher's name] told you that a new student is coming to be a part of your class. Tomorrow will be _____ first day. Describe how you think _____ will feel on the first day. (p. 74)

Students heard the story with one of the following pronouns inserted in the blanks: *he, he or she,* or *they*. The results clearly showed that *he* is not assumed to mean both females and males. Its exculsionary interpretation was demonstrated by the finding that 93 percent of the children who heard the *he* story, wrote that the student was a boy. On the other hand, when the pronouns were the inclusive *he or she* or *they*, the girls were more apt to write about a girl than a boy and the boys were more likely to write about a boy than a girl.

Given that male pronouns are evidently not gender neutral, it is not surprising that the use of male nouns as gender neutral similarly connotes male images. In one study (McConnell & Fazio, 1996), college students rated a *chairman* as more masculine than either a *chair* or a *chairperson*, suggesting that the former leads to more male-related mental imagery than the other two. Therefore, it is not surprising that the newer, gender-neutral terms, chair and chairperson, are more likely used in reference to women whereas the traditional term, chairman, is more often used to indicate a man (Romaine, 1999).

Spotlighting.   **Spotlighting** refers to *the practice of emphasizing an individual's gender,* as in *"Female* professor receives prestigious grant" or, as in a recent headline about a spy who for decades had handed British atomic secrets to Russia, "Grandma led two lives" (Knightley, 1999). Consistent with the male as normative perspective, this practice of highlighting a woman's gender serves to reinforce the notion that males are the standard (Bem, 2008). That is, although spotlighting does give recognition to specific females, at the same time, it conveys the message that these females are exceptions.

One investigation of gendered spotlighting involved the examination of televised broadcasts of the 1989 women's and men's National Collegiate Athletic Association final four basketball tournaments (Messner et al., 1993). The researchers observed spotlighting an average of 26 times per game during the women's tournament with commentary, such as ". . . is a legend in *women's* basketball" or "this NCAA *women's* semifinal is brought to you by . . ." (p. 125). However, there was no evidence of spotlighting during the men's games.

Diminutive Suffixes for Female Terms.   The English language sometimes differentiates genders by using a root word to designate a male and an added suffix to specify a female. This language feature, like others discussed in this section, is based on the assumption of the male as the standard. A suffix is needed to indicate the nonnormative exception, the female. Examples of this include *actor/actress*, *poet/poetess*, and *author/authoress*. In fact, according to Suzanne Romaine (1999), the only English words where the female term is the root word with a male suffix added are *widower* and *bridegroom*. Why do these words have female roots? Perhaps the term *widower* reflects the fact that women generally outlive men and *bridegroom* might be based on the traditional expectation that women's roles are linked to marriage and the family.

Romaine (1999) contends that this practice of marking the female with a suffix added to the male root is one way the English language signifies that a woman is a "lesser man" (p. 140). Similarly, Casey Miller and Kate Swift state, "the significance of a word like authoress is not that it identifies a female but that it indicates deviation from what is consciously or unconsciously considered the standard" (1991, p. 171).

Negative Terms for Females

Another language practice that reflects the differential treatment of females and males is the greater number of negative terms depicting women than men.

Parallel Terms.   There are numerous pairs of words in the English language in which the objective meanings of the female and male terms are comparable, but the female word has a negative connotation. Consider, for example, *bachelor* and *spinster* or *old maid*. All three refer to unmarried persons, but the female terms connote an undesirable state reflecting rejection and old age. Another example is *master* versus *mistress*. Originally these referred to a man and woman in charge of a household, a usage that still pertains to *master*. *Mistress*, however, has developed a sexual connotation with negative overtones (Romaine, 1999).

Childlike Terms.   Have you ever heard the term *girl* in reference to an adult woman? Perhaps you have noted a male manager say something like the following to one of his associates: "I'll have my *girl* phone your *girl* to schedule a lunch meeting for us." Given that neither of the secretaries to whom he is referring is likely to be "a female child," a dictionary definition of girl, the term *girl* is not appropriate. However, it is more common for people to refer to adult women as *girls* than to adult men as *boys* (Basow, 2001). For example, in the investigation (Messner et al., 1993) of televised commentary

Tide twists Vols' title plans

Disappearing act won't help Vols' status

TUSCALOOSA, Ala.

If you're a Tennessee men's basketball fan, you can rest easy today.

You no longer have to fret about those whispers concerning the possibility of one or more Vols jumping to the NBA early.

Let's just put it this way: junior Tony Harris and sophomore Vincent Yarbrough should be thankful there was only one NBA scout in the building to witness the second half of UT's 80-75 loss to Alabama on Saturday.

"Both of those Tennessee guys have a tremendous future," Seattle SuperSonics regional scout Yvan K. Kelly said diplomatically.

Note: The key word is "future."

As for the present, that's another story. Harris was 1 for 9 against Alabama and scored four points.

"It's going to be a big transition for Tony to play the point in the pros, and size (under 6 feet) is going to be more of a problem in the pros than in college," Kelly said.

GARY LUNDY

Hot second half helps Alabama ambush No. 7 UT

By Mike Strange
News-Sentinel sportswriter

TUSCALOOSA, Ala. — Among the several costly turnovers Tennessee fumbled away in the closing minutes Saturday, the biggest was this: the chance to control its own destiny.

The SEC men's basketball championship the Vols covet hasn't fallen completely out of reach, but now it also will be decided in places such as Gainesville and Lexington.

"We just put the ball in somebody else's hands," said UT's Vincent Yarbrough, assessing the damage after No. 7-ranked Tennessee was upset by Alabama 80-75.

UT arrived at Coleman Coliseum in the driver's seat of a tight SEC race. However, the Vols got unseated by a young Alabama team that rose to the occasion, cheered on by a crowd of 9,053.

The Crimson Tide (13-13, 6-8 SEC) overturned a 10-point Tennessee lead early in the second half and held the cold-shooting, fumble-fingered Vols at bay down the stretch.

The intensity Tennessee showed in its victory over Kentucky three days earlier was nowhere to be found.

"We came in thinking because we're Tennessee, they'd lay down for us," senior C.J. Black said, searching for an explanation.

"You look at our defense against Kentucky," UT coach Jerry Green said, "and our offense and how much enthusiasm and energy we've got to expend."

Lady Vols seek a repeat defense against LSU

Today's probable starters

LSU

Lady Volunteers

LSU (20-4, 9-2)				Tennessee (22-3, 10-1)		
Coach: Sue Gunter (35th year)				Coach: Pat Summitt (26th year)		
	Ht.	Yr.	Avg.		Ht.	Yr.	Avg.
Katrina Hibbert f	5-11	Sr.	12.2	T. Catchings f	6-1	Jr.	15.2
April Brown f	5-11	Jr.	10.2	Semeka Randall f	5-10	Jr.	14.0
DeTrina White f	5-11	So.	10.9	Michelle Snow c	6-5	So.	12.4
Marie Ferdinand g	5-9	Jr.	16.0	Kristen Clement g	5-11	Jr.	6.4
Angela Crockett g	5-10	Jr.	4.1	Kara Lawson g	5-9	Fr.	14.9

Time: 3 p.m.   Radio: Lady Vols Network   Series: UT leads 25-5.

By Dan Fleser
News-Sentinel sportswriter

A visit from LSU today recalls the finest hour for Tennessee's defense.

The 3 o'clock tip-off at Thompson-Boling Arena is the second regular-season meeting for these SEC rivals. The first game, Jan. 6 in Baton Rouge, La., probably was second to none for the Lady Vols.

"That could've been our best game of the year," UT coach Pat Summitt said of the 86-50 victory.

One of the biggest reasons for the one-sided result was Tennessee's defenders helping limit the Tigers to 36.8 percent shooting from the floor. They also played a part in 25 LSU turnovers.

Striving for a repeat performance would be a noble quest, but probably not realistic. Summitt conceded to the one-of-those-nights nature of the first encounter.

"We were on a roll," she said. "They couldn't get on track. It snowballs."

Nonetheless, taking a stab at better defensive consistency would be a useful objective. Before the first LSU-Tennessee game, the defense was viewed as good but not great. Thirteen games later, the same perspective applies.

The Lady Vols are more apt to have their moments on defense.

Obviously they've had their share, as evidenced by their record (22-3, 10-1 SEC) and their national ranking (2nd). A nine-game winning streak adds to their stature.

"I believe we can get a (defensive) stop against any team in the country at any time," freshman guard Kara Lawson said.

She offered this assessment after UT's defenders held Mississippi State scoreless during the final 2:35 of last Thursday's 79-75 comeback victory. This work was a crucial accompaniment to the Lady Vols' 11-point finishing kick across the same time span.

The defensive stand was a

Please see LADY VOLS, page C7

Highlighting the female gender but not the male gender reinforces the assumption that males are the standard and females are the exception.

of women's and men's sports discussed above, the researchers found that, although the female athletes were not younger than their male counterparts, the broadcasters referred to female basketball and tennis players as *girls* but never called the male athletes *boys*.

Other childlike terms that are applied more to women than to men include *baby*, *babe*, and *sweetie*. Although these terms might be perceived as signs of affection in an intimate relationship, their use by nonintimates reflects the childlike quality of many terms used to identify women.

Is the use of these terms detrimental to women? Research suggests that it might be. For example, when female and male respondents in a study were asked about their impressions of adult women, they described women who were referred to as *girls* as being less responsible than women who were labeled *women* (Kitto, 1989). Such a negative depiction could clearly apply to other childlike terms.

Animal and Food Terms.   Researchers of the gender biases of language (e.g., Wood, 1994) point to the heavy use of animal names and food products in reference to women as another example of the negative depiction of females. Examples of these include the animal labels *fox*, *chick*, *bitch*, and *cow*, and the food-related terms *honey*, *cookie*, *dish*, and *feast for the eyes*.

Sexualization of Women.   As discussed earlier in this chapter, the media treat a woman's sexuality as an important aspect of her identity. American English also places a strong emphasis on a woman's sexuality. In one study (Grossman & Tucker, 1997), college students were asked to list all of the slang words they could think of for either a woman or a man. Although there was no difference in the number of terms associated with each gender, approximately 50 percent of the terms used for females were sexual (e.g., *slut*), whereas less than 25 percent of those used for males were. Furthermore, there are far more negative sexual terms for women than for men (Crawford, 2001).

In Grossman and Tucker's study of slang, the terms used for women were more negative than those used for men. For example, among the most frequently listed terms were *bitch* and *slut* for women but *guy* and *dude* for men.

Significance of the Differential Treatment of Females and Males in Language

We have examined several indications that English depicts males as the societal standard and that many language conventions portray females in negative terms. Do these practices matter? According to Janet Swim and her colleagues (Swim et al., 2003, 2004), they certainly do. Sexist language reinforces and perpetuates gender stereotypes and status differences between women and men. Whether or not the speaker or writer intends harm, sexist language can have a negative effect on how girls and women perceive themselves.

The words of Jessica, a 25-year-old college senior, make this point vividly:

> *Using animal and food terms to refer to women is obviously degrading, and hazardous to a woman's self-esteem. If a woman hears herself being called a cow or bitch enough, she will believe that she is one. I didn't think it could happen if you were a strong person; I mean, I know I'm not a bitch, right? Wrong. After five years of hearing it from a significant other, I actually found myself calling myself these names aloud! It's powerful.*

SUMMARY

Stereotypes of Females and Males

- Based on the tendency to sort others into gender categories, we assume that certain characteristics, behaviors, and roles are more representative of females and others of males. These are called gender stereotypes.
- Stereotypes vary according to the ethnicity of the person holding the stereotype and the ethnicity and social class of the target person.

- Stereotypes of women with disabilities differ from stereotypes of able-bodied women.
- According to social role theory, because we associate females with the domestic role and males with the employment role, our female stereotype tends to center on communion and our male stereotype on agency.
- Women who choose to be called "Ms." or who use a nontraditional name after marriage are

perceived as more agentic and less communal than women who prefer conventional titles of address.

Sexism

- Several different forms of sexism have been proposed by scholars. Ambivalent sexism includes both hostile and benevolent attitudes. Modern sexism is a subtle form of sexism, based on egalitarian values combined with underlying negative feelings toward women.
- Large numbers of women have experienced either minor or major sexist incidents.

Representation of Gender in the Media

- Females are underrepresented in the media.
- Certain groups of women are particularly underrepresented, including ethnic minority women, older women, and lesbians.
- The stigma of aging is greater for women than men. This double standard is based on society's emphasis on youthful physical beauty for women.
- Although the media do depict women in occupational roles, TV features few women who combine family and work roles.

- Similarly, the Sunday comics, children's books, and teen magazines present messages consistent with the importance of the domestic role for women and the provider role for men.
- Many forms of media portray males as more agentic than females and show females as being relationship oriented.
- Media images emphasize the importance to females of physical attractiveness and sexuality.
- The media both reinforce and contribute to our stereotypes of gender.

Representation of Gender in the English Language

- Numerous English language practices, including the use of the masculine generic, spotlighting, and diminutive suffixes for female terms, are based on the assumption that the male is normative.
- Other practices that deprecate women include the use of parallel terms, childlike terms, animal and food terms, sexual terms, and negative slang.
- The differential treatment of females and males in language both reflects and helps shape our gender images.

KEY TERMS

gender stereotypes	social role theory	double standard of aging
communion	backlash effect	sexist language
agency	ambivalent sexism	male is normative
ageism	hostile sexism	masculine generic language
ableism	benevolent sexism	spotlighting
social categorization	modern sexism	

WHAT DO YOU THINK?

1. We have seen that women who use the title Ms. or who do not take their husband's surname after marriage are perceived as more agentic and less communal than women who use Miss or Mrs. or who take their husband's name. One explanation for this is provided by social role theory. Can you think of any other possible explanations?

2. Consider the work by Glick and Fiske on ambivalent sexism.

    a. Do you agree that positive stereotypes of women can serve to maintain patriarchal roles and relationships? Why or why not?

    b. Do you believe that benevolent and hostile sexism are equally detrimental to women? Why or why not?

3. We have examined numerous sources of societal representations of gender, such as greeting cards, children's books, and televi-sion commercials. What other types of media might reflect gender stereotypes?

4. Which of the various language features that treat females and males differently do you think has the most detrimental effect on girls and women? Why?

5. Provide evidence, from the chapter or from your own experience, that language influences our perceptions of gender.

IF YOU WANT TO LEARN MORE

Black, P. (2004). *The beauty industry: Gender, culture, pleasure*. New York: Routledge.

Blair, P. D. (2005). *The next fifty years: A guide for women at midlife and beyond*. Charlottesville, VA: Hampton Roads.

Cole, E., & Daniels, J. H. (Eds.). (2005). *Featuring females: Feminist analyses of media*. Washington, DC: American Psychological Association.

Cortese, A. J. (2004). *Provocateur: Images of women and minorities in advertising*. (2nd ed.). Lanham, MD: Rowman & Littlefield.

Gill, R. (2007). *Gender and the media*. Cambridge, England: Polity Press.

Halmlund, C. (2002). *Impossible bodies: Femininity and masculinity at the movies*. New York: Routledge.

Kilbourne, J. (2000). *Can't buy my love: How advertising changes the way we think and feel*. New York: Touchstone Books.

Lamb, S. (2006). *Packaging girlhood: Rescuing our daughters from marketers' schemes*. New York: St. Martin's Press.

Lehr, S. (Ed.). (2001). *Beauty, brains, and brawn: The construction of gender in children's literature*. Portsmouth, NH: Heinemann.

Levine, S. B. (2004). *Inventing the rest of our lives: Women in second adulthood*. New York: Viking Press.

Reichert, T., & Lambiase, J. J. (Eds.). (2005). *Sex in consumer culture: The erotic content of media and marketing*. Mahwah, NJ: Erlbaum.

Van Evra, J. (2004). *Television and child development* (3rd ed.). Mahwah, NJ: Erlbaum.

Wilson, C. C., Gutierrez, F., & Chao, L. (2004). *Racism, sexism, and the media* (3rd ed.). Thousand Oaks, CA: Sage.

WEBSITES

The Media

Media Watch
http://www.mediawatch.com

Representation of Gender in Language

Gender Neutral Language
http://dir.yahoo.com/society_and_culture/gender/gender_neutral_language/

Gender Self-Concept

Developmental Processes
and Individual Differences

Gender Self-Concept

Prenatal Development
  Stages of Prenatal Sex Differentiation
  Intersexuality
  Case Studies

Theories of Gender Typing
  Psychoanalytic Theory
  Social Learning Theory
  Cognitive Developmental Theory
  Gender Schema Theory

Gender-Related Traits
  Changes in Gender-Related Traits over
    Time

  Gender-Related Traits and Psychological
    Adjustment
  Evaluation of the Concept of Androgyny

Gender Attitudes
  Individual Differences in Gender-Related
    Attitudes
  Perceived Value of Female versus Male
    Gender-Related Attributes

In 1965, shortly after starting graduate school, Judith participated in a discussion about graduate student issues with her eight male classmates. During this conversation, much to her surprise and dismay, one of the men offered his impression of her lack of femininity. When asked for clarification, he said without hesitation, "Judith is too highly achievement oriented to be feminine."

Now consider the lighthearted mockery of gender-expected behaviors shown by Judith's daughter and son-in-law during their wedding ceremony. On the one hand, the setting was traditional with the bride in a long white gown, the groom in a formal tuxedo, and an entourage of bridesmaids and ushers. On the other hand, inconsistent with traditional expectations, at the end of a beautiful and serious service celebrating the bride and groom's love for each other, the officiate concluded with "Now you may kiss the groom!"

The comment by Judith's classmate suggests that, in his mind, people cannot combine female-stereotypic and male-stereotypic characteristics. Do you see problems with this type of thinking?

Do you know people who, like Judith's daughter and son-in-law, believe our behaviors should not be dictated by our gender? Do you know others who see value in separate roles for women and men? In this chapter we focus on issues like these as we examine the integration of gender into one's personal identity. After a brief look at the components of gender self-concept, we look at prenatal sex development and its influence on these gender concepts. Then we explore theoretical perspectives of gender learning and conclude with an examination of variations among people in their gender self-concepts.

Gender Self-Concept

One component of gender self-concept is **gender identity:** *one's self-definition as a female or male.* This identity generally develops between the ages of 2 and 3. Most individuals establish a gender identity in accordance with their external reproductive organs. **Transgendered individuals,** however, do not. They have a *gender identity inconsistent with their reproductive organs.* They firmly believe they were born with the body of the wrong sex and really feel that they are the other sex (Rosenberg, 2007).

Despite the usual consistency between anatomy and gender identity, there are variations in the degree to which people incorporate gender stereotypes into their own personalities and attitudes. As we saw in Chapter 2, there are numerous commonly held expectations about the appropriate traits and roles for females and males. However, these gender stereotypes reflect *beliefs* about individuals; they do not tell us what anyone is *actually* like. Although these stereotypes are descriptive of some people, they are not representative of all. Instead, individuals differ from one another in their adherence to cultural stereotypes about gender. That is, they differ in the extent to which their traits, behaviors, interests, and roles conform to those expected for their gender. Moreover, they differ in their **gender attitudes,** their *beliefs about the appropriate traits, interests, behaviors, and roles of females and males.*

Are various domains of an individual's gender self-concept associated with one another? Although most people's gender identity is consistent with their anatomy, that does not imply a connection between gender identity and gender-related attributes. A person can feel that she is a female but have male-related traits, such as ambition and independence, or engage in roles generally associated with men, such as construction worker or engineer. Furthermore, a person's gender-related attributes are not linked to her or his **sexual orientation.** *Preference for a same- or other-gender sexual partner* does not reflect the individual's gender-related traits, behaviors, interests, or roles (Zucker, 2001).

Prenatal Development

Our journey toward understanding the development of a personal sense of gender begins with an examination of **prenatal sex differentiation,** that is, *the biological processes that influence the making of our physical sex.* As we shall see, prenatal sex differentiation consists of a highly complex set of processes. The first step, the joining of the sex chromosomes in the fertilized egg, is followed by several other prenatal events that collectively contribute to the determination of sex (see Table 3.1). Furthermore, not only is the biological process highly complex, but also the meaning of biological sex is multidimensional; it is defined by our chromosomes, hormones, reproductive organs, and brain organization (Hines, 2004b; Tobach, 2001).

Stages of Prenatal Sex Differentiation

The stages of prenatal sex differentiation begin with the sex chromosomes, followed by the development of the gonads and hormones, internal reproductive organs, and external genitalia and differentiations of the brain. Let us examine each of these steps in greater detail.

TABLE 3.1   **Stages of Prenatal Sex Differentiation of Females and Males**

Stages	Females	Males
1. Chromosomes	XX	XY
2. Gonads and hormones	Ovaries (estrogens)	Testes (androgens)
3. Internal reproductive organs	Uterus, fallopian tubes, and upper vagina	Vas deferens, seminal vesicles, and prostate
4. External genitalia	Clitoris, labia, and vaginal opening	Penis and scrotum
5. Brain	Female differentiation of the hypothalamus	Male differentiation of the hypothalamus

Chromosomes.   Sex differentiation begins with the combining of the sex chromosomes at conception. Normally individuals inherit 23 pairs of chromosomes from their parents. Twenty-two of these pairs contain genes that determine the general nature of the human species and the individual's specific characteristics (e.g., eye color), and one pair consists of the sex chromosomes, containing the genetic material that begins the process of sex differentiation. Genetic females have two X chromosomes, one received from each parent, and genetic males have one X chromosome received from their mother and one Y from their father.

Gonadal Development.   Until the sixth week of development there are no anatomical differences between XX and XY embryos. In fact, all embryos contain the same undifferentiated tissue that will later develop along sexual lines (Biason-Lauber et al., 2004). However, at that point in time, the Y chromosome in XY embryos directs the previously undifferentiated gonadal tissue to develop into testes, the male sex glands. In XX embryos, gonadal development begins at approximately the twelfth week after conception; the previously undifferentiated gonadal tissue develops into ovaries, the female sex glands. Recent evidence suggests that the X chromosome might direct this development (Tobach, 2001).

   Once the gonads develop, the remaining process of sex differentiation is regulated by the sex hormones. Most research has examined XY development, and we know that prenatal male differentiation requires the presence of the *male sex hormones,* collectively known as **androgens.** Until recently, it was believed that no gonadal hormones were necessary for female development; differentiation of female sex organs would proceed in the absence of androgens (Hughes, 2004). Now there is evidence that the *female sex hormones,* collectively known as **estrogens,** play a more active role in female development than previously believed (Tobach, 2001).

Development of Internal Reproductive Organs.   The female and male internal reproductive organs develop from the same previously undifferentiated tissue. Both XX and XY fetuses contain two sets of tissues, the Müllerian ducts and the Wolffian ducts. The **Müllerian ducts** are *the foundation for female structures.* The **Wolffian ducts** serve as *the basis for male internal reproductive structures.* In XX individuals, the Müllerian ducts differentiate into the uterus, fallopian tubes, and upper vagina and the Wolffian tissue degenerates. In XY development, two substances produced by the testes govern the process of developing male internal reproductive structures. **Testosterone,** an androgen, is necessary for the transformation of the Wolffian ducts into the male organs, including the vas deferens, seminal vesicles, and prostate; and the **Müllerian-inhibiting substance** is necessary for the degeneration of the Müllerian ducts (Hughes, 2004).

External Genitalia.   Similar to the development of the internal reproductive structures, the external structures develop from previously undifferentiated tissue present in both XX and XY individuals. In XX fetuses, estrogen differentiates this tissue as the clitoris, labia, and vaginal opening. In XY development, testosterone transforms the tissue into the penis and the scrotum (Tobach, 2001).

Brain Differentiation.   Sex differences in the brain are less observable and, predictably, more controversial than sex differences in reproductive organs. However, experimentation on lower animals and case histories of humans whose prenatal exposure to androgens was abnormal for their genetic sex shows that there is a critical period of time during which exposure to sex hormones can affect the hypothalamus and, thereby, influence the threshold for subsequent behaviors. For example, in both animals and humans, this early exposure to androgens organizes the hypothalamus so that it becomes insensitive to estrogen (Rathus et al., 2005). The result is the elimination of the normal hormonal cyclical pattern associated with the menstrual cycle. We explore behavioral and sexual effects in humans in the next section as we examine the outcomes of certain variations in prenatal sex differentiation.

Intersexuality

The pattern of sex differentiation just described is the typical one that characterizes the prenatal development of most individuals. However, several variations can occur, and an examination of these can help us understand the role of the chromosomes and hormones in gender identity and gender-related attributes.

Intersexuality, *the intermingling of female and male sexual characteristics,* occurs in as many as 1.7 percent of births (Golden, 2008). In some cases, the baby has ambiguous genitalia that look like an enlarged clitoris or a mini-penis. In other cases, the external genitalia are at odds with the baby's gonads (Lee et al., 2006). In Western cultures, which recognize only two genders, the typical course of action has been early genital surgery, coupled with gender reassignment (Navarro, 2004). (See Explore Other Cultures 3.1 for a different view.) But genital surgery can lead to loss of fertility, reduced sexual functioning, urinary difficulties, and psychological problems, without providing the individual with any firmer sense of gender identity or increased quality of life (Golden, 2008; Lerner, 2003; Minto et al., 2003). The Intersex Society of North America (ISNA), along with an increasing number of researchers, recommend that any surgery be postponed until adolescence, when the individual can make an informed choice (Gorman & Cole, 2004; Navarro, 2004; Pinholster, 2005). Let us take a closer look at some of the varieties of intersexuality.

Turner Syndrome.   **Turner syndrome** is *a condition in which the individual has a single X chromosome rather than a pair of sex chromosomes.* The missing chromosome could have been an X or a Y but is defective or lost. Because two chromosomes are necessary for the development of the gonads, the individual has neither ovaries nor testes. Externally, the genitalia are female and the individual is reared as a girl. Estrogen therapy at puberty enables girls with Turner syndrome to develop female secondary sex characteristics, such as breasts and pubic hair (Hines, 2004b; Sybert & McCauley, 2004).

Congenital Adrenal Hyperplasia (CAH).   **Congenital adrenal hyperplasia** is *an inherited disorder in which the adrenal glands of a genetic female malfunction and produce abnormally high levels of androgens* (Berenbaum & Resnick, 2007). Because this hormone is not produced until after the internal reproductive organs develop, these individuals have a uterus. However, the disorder causes either a partial or complete masculinization of the external genitals with the formation of an enlarged clitoris or a penis. Usually CAH is diagnosed at birth and the baby is reared as a girl, receiving some degree of surgical feminization of the genitals. Additionally, because this condition does not cease at birth, the individual generally receives hormonal therapy to prevent continued masculinization of her body.

Androgen-Insensitivity Syndrome.   The **androgen-insensitivity syndrome** is *an inherited disorder in which the body of a genetic male cannot utilize androgen* (Hines, 2004b). Analogous to CAH, in which prenatal exposure to androgen masculinizes the external genitals of a genetic female, this inability of body tissue to respond to androgen feminizes the external genitals of a genetic male. Usually, the feminization of the external genitalia is complete and there is no suspicion that the baby is a genetic male (see photograph on p. 66). Similarly, the inability of the body to respond to androgen prevents the Wolffian ducts from differentiating into the internal male reproductive structures. However, because of the presence of the Müllerian-inhibiting substance, the Müllerian ducts do not develop into the internal female organs. Consequently, the individual has no internal reproductive organs.

EXPLORE OTHER CULTURES 3.1
Multiple Genders

All societies recognize female and male genders and roles, although there is considerable cross-cultural variability in how these roles are expressed. The United States and virtually all Western nations formally recognize only two genders, and any variations from these are considered abnormal. Recent efforts to be more flexible in recognizing additional gender categories (e.g., Fausto-Sterling, 2000; Parker, 2007) are highly controversial. A number of non-Western cultures, however, recognize third and fourth genders. These are women and men who do not fit typical gender identities and roles. Often, these individuals are considered spiritually enlightened by having an alternative gender, and they may be respected and accepted (Kimmel, 2002; Whelehan, 2001). The Hijras of India are hermaphrodites or castrated men who are viewed as a third gender embodying the spirits of both females and males. Frequently called upon to bless new babies, they dress as females, live in Hijra communities, and some maintain a monogamous relationship with a man (Mahalingam, 2003). In Indonesia, transvestites known as "waria"—a combination of the words for woman and man—have been welcomed for centuries as entertainers and beauticians (Perlez, 2003). Many Native North American societies recognized so-called "two-spirit" individuals (Balsam et al., 2004; Walters et al., 2006). Biological female two-spirits typically were found west of the Rockies among the Apache, Cheyenne, Mohave, Navajo, and Tlingit. The "manly hearted woman," for example, wore men's clothes, led war parties, and was completely accepted in that role. As native societies assimilated European beliefs, however, third- and fourth-gender roles often disappeared, changed, or came to be viewed negatively (Balsam et al., 2004; Walters et al., 2006).

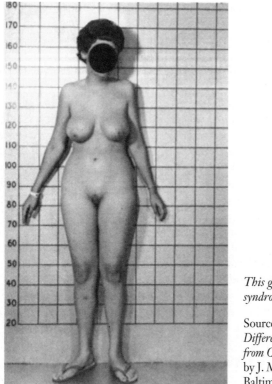

This genetic male has androgen-insensitivity syndrome.

Source: *From Man & Woman, Boy & Girl: The Differentiation and Dimorphism of Gender Identity from Conception to Maturity* (p. 116, Figure 6.4), by J. Money and A. A. Ehrhardt 1972, Baltimore: John Hopkins.

5 Alpha-Reductase Deficiency.   The **5 alpha-reductase deficiency** is *an inherited condition in a genetic male that prevents the prenatal differentiation of the external genital tissue into a penis* (Zucker, 2001). In other ways, prenatal development follows a male blueprint; testes and male internal reproductive organs develop. At birth, these genetic males appear to be girls and are labeled as such. However, the surge of testosterone at puberty causes a belated masculinization of the external genitals and the development of male secondary sex characteristics, such as a deepening voice and facial hair. Thus, these genetic males, generally raised as girls, now develop the body of a male. In the Dominican Republic, where certain communities have a high frequency of the disorder, it is known as *guevdoces*, or "eggs (i.e., testicles) at twelve" (Lippa, 2005).

Case Studies

The relative influence of prenatal and postnatal experiences on gender-related development has been the focus of considerable controversy. Case histories of intersexuals have examined the role of prenatal hormones in the development of nonsexual gender-related attributes, gender identity, and sexual orientation and have produced inconsistent findings. Several researchers contend that prenatal biological factors are highly influential, whereas others conclude that experiences after birth play the most significant role in shaping individuals' gender-related attributes.

First, let's examine the effects of prenatal hormones on gender-related interests and activities. On the one hand, higher levels of testosterone in pregnant women are related to more masculine-typed toy choices and activities in their daughters at age 3.5 years (Hines et al., 2002). In addition, girls with CAH, who were exposed to androgens prenatally, show stronger-than-average preferences for boys' toys and activities and for boys as playmates (Berenbaum & Bryk, 2008; Berenbaum & Resnick, 2007). They report themselves to be more aggressive and less maternal. Most of the affected women are heterosexual, and their sexual and gender identity is almost always female (Cohen-Bendahan et al., 2005).

Investigations on the effects of prenatal estrogen suggest that it might not be necessary for the development of female gender-related interests or role expectations. For example, girls with Turner syndrome, who lack prenatal estrogen, are similar to matched controls in their preferences for female playmates and female-style clothing, satisfaction with the female gender role, and interest in marriage and motherhood. Similarly, androgen-insensitive (XY) individuals raised as females tend to have female-related interests, although they too lack prenatal estrogen. Such individuals are generally romantically and sexually attracted to males. On tests of verbal and spatial skills, they also perform more like females than males (Lippa, 2005; Sybert & McCauley, 2004).

Turning to the development of gender identity, research similarly provides inconsistent findings. Some investigators have pointed to the importance of the gender of rearing, that is, experiences after birth, in gender identity (Zucker et al., 1996). Others, such as Milton Diamond (1997), contend that prenatal experiences predispose individuals toward a female or male identity. He suggests, for example, that prenatal processes influence some intersexuals to switch from the gender of rearing to an identity with the other gender. One recent study examined genetic males with normal male hormones but who were born without a penis and subsequent underwent early sex-reassignment surgery and were raised as girls. Nearly half still developed male gender identity by adolescence (Reiner & Gearhart, 2004).

There is some evidence that cultural values also play a role in the development of gender identity. Consider, for example, studies of individuals who have experienced the female-to-male body change caused by 5 alpha-reductase deficiency. In the Dominican Republic, 16 of 18 who were raised as girls elected to reverse their gender identity at puberty and become males (Imperato-McGinley and colleagues, cited in Deaux & Stewart, 2001). Another study in New Guinea found that some changed and some did not, but that those who did switch from a female to a male identity did so as a result of social pressure stemming from their inability to fulfill their female role (Herdt & Davidson, 1988). Although there might be a variety of explanations for these cultural differences, the researchers suggest that cultural expectations have some influence in shaping gender identity, at least for individuals with conflicting body signals.

Last, in examining influences on sexual orientation, case studies of intersexual individuals have led some researchers to contend that sexual orientation has its origins in prenatal development. Melissa Hines (2004a), for example, points to an increased lesbian or bisexual orientation among women with CAH and suggests that prenatal exposure to androgen may serve as one influence on sexual orientation. However, based on their review of research on the topic, Amy Banks and Nanette Gartrell (1995) conclude that atypical prenatal hormone exposure is not related to increased same-gender sexual orientation.

What can we conclude about this controversial issue? Unfortunately, it is difficult to evaluate the relative contribution of biological and postnatal factors because case studies do not allow for adequate control (Berenbaum & Bryk, 2008). For example, CAH girls have somewhat masculinized genitalia. Consequently, it is difficult to separate effects of their atypical exposure to prenatal hormones from the psychological and interpersonal reactions they might experience after birth. Both CAH girls and their parents are aware of their masculinization, and this knowledge might serve as a powerful influence on the girls' gender-related self-concept and on their parents' treatment of them (Berenbaum & Bryk, 2008). At this time, the most accurate conclusion to be drawn appears to be that gender is both a biological and a social phenomenon. The challenge for researchers is to examine how biological processes interact with social influences from the earliest years onward (Berenbaum & Bryk, 2008).

Theories of Gender Typing

Now we turn to an exploration of the major theories that attempt to explain *the acquisition of the traits, behaviors, and roles that are generally associated with one's gender,* a process known as **gender typing.** Although these theories propose different processes involved in the learning of gender, only one (psychoanalytic theory) contends that the development of gender-related attributes is rooted in biological sex differences. The other perspectives share the assumption that gender traits, behaviors, and roles are socially constructed, that they develop from children's interactions with others and are not inherent in our biology. Furthermore, even psychoanalytic theory emphasizes the perceived significance of anatomical differences, rather than the effect of hormonal or other biological sex differences on gender development. For a summary of the major theories of gender typing, see Table 3.2.

Psychoanalytic Theory

We begin our theoretical exploration with an examination of psychoanalytic theory, developed by Sigmund Freud. **Psychoanalytic theory** proposes that *gender typing stems from children's awareness of anatomical differences between females and males combined with their strong inborn sexual urges.* According to this theory, during the so-called phallic stage of development (between ages 3 and 6 years) two experiences occur that have dramatic consequences for gender-related development. The first is the child's discovery of the anatomical differences between females and males and the second is the child's love for the parent of the other gender.

The boy's sexual attraction for his mother, known as the **Oedipus complex,** is accompanied by a belief that his father is a rival for his mother's affections and that his father, similarly, perceives him as a competitor. The boy's growing awareness of the anatomical differences between males and females leads him to assume that females have been

TABLE 3.2   Theories of Gender Typing

Theory	Major Theorist	Sources of Learning	Motive	Sequence of Events
Psychoanalytic theory	Sigmund Freud	Parents; emotional bond with same-sex parent is critical	Internal: reduce fear and anxiety; no reinforcement necessary	(Same-sex) parental attachment → identification (modeling) → gender identity
Social learning theory	Walter Mischel	Parents, larger social system provide models; child is relatively passive	External: reinforcements. Internal: Expected reinforcements. "I want rewards. I am rewarded for doing girl things. Therefore, I want to be a girl."	(Same-sex) parental attachment (due to rewards) → modeling (identification) → gender identify
Social cognitive theory	Albert Bandura	Parents, larger social system provide models; child is more active than in social learning theory in evaluating social standards; cognition plays a greater role	Similar to social learning theory	Similar to social learning theory
Cognitive–Developmental Theory	Lawrence Kohlberg	Parents and larger social system interacting with child's cognitive system	Internal: desire for competence. "I am a girl. Therefore, I want to do girls things. Therefore, doing girl things is rewarding."	Gender identity → modeling (same-sex parent) → (same-sex) parental attachment
Gender-Schema Theory	Sandra Bem	Parents and larger social system interacting with child's cognitive system. Society dictates that gender is an important schema, so child organizes information around this schema.	Similar to cognitive-developmental theory	Because child learns that gender is an important schema, child develops gender identity. Sequence then proceeds as in cognitive-developmental theory.

castrated, and that he, too, will be castrated by his powerful rival, his father. The boy's *fear of castration by his father,* called **castration anxiety,** induces him to give up his Oedipal feelings for his mother. When he does so, he forms *a close emotional bond* with his father, called **identification.** Through this identification process, the boy adopts his father's masculine behaviors and traits and incorporates his father's values into his superego (the moral component of personality), thus developing a strong sense of morality.

The phallic stage follows a different course for the little girl. Her discovery of the anatomical distinction between females and males does not resolve the Oedipus complex as in boys but rather sets it in motion. Sometimes referred to as the Electra complex, the girl develops **penis envy,** *a desire to possess the male genitals,* and blames the mother for her castrated state. Her desire for a penis is replaced by a desire for a child and she turns to her father to fulfill that wish. Because the girl lacks the fear of castration (having already been castrated), the chief motive for resolving the Oedipus complex is absent. However, with the realization that she will never possess her father, the girl gradually gives up her Oedipal feelings, identifies with her mother, and begins the acquisition of her mother's feminine traits and behaviors. Although she, too, begins superego development, this development is weak because it is not driven by the powerful motivator of castration anxiety. Freud further believed that the girl's continuing wish for a penis into adulthood contributes to the woman's sense of inferiority.

Evaluation.   First, Freud's theory clearly is highly male-biased as shown by his use of the male term *phallic* to label the critical stage of gender development, his emphasis on the superiority of the male organ, and his assumption that females are doomed to feelings of inferiority because they lack a penis. For these reasons, psychoanalytic theory is not widely embraced by feminist scholars (Bem, 2008). Second, key psychoanalytic concepts, such as penis envy and castration anxiety, are conceptualized as unconscious; thus, they cannot be measured empirically. Third, Freud has been criticized for his emphasis on the anatomical foundations of gender development to the virtual exclusion of societal influences. From Freud's perspective, gender is constructed from the presence or absence of a penis and not the societal value attached to males. Subsequent psychoanalytic thinkers have placed greater emphasis on the psychological and sociocultural aspects of gender development. Others, including Karen Horney, Clara Thompson, Nancy Chodorow, Jessica Benjamin, and Ellen Kaschak, have proposed psychoanalytic views that minimize the masculine orientation of Freud's theory (Bell, 2004; Casey, 2002; Denmark et al., 2008).

Social Learning Theory

Whereas psychoanalytic theory envisions the growing child as pushed around by her/his inborn desires, **social learning theory,** originally proposed by Walter Mischel (1966), views *gender development as influenced by the social environment.* Based on learning theory principles, this perspective proposes that *children acquire behaviors associated with their gender because those behaviors are more likely to be imitated and to be associated with positive reinforcement.*

Observational Learning.   One mechanism through which gender-related behaviors are acquired is **observational learning** (also called imitation or modeling); that is, *the* *acquisition of behaviors via the observation of role models.* Children are continually exposed to both real-life and media models who engage in gender-stereotypic behaviors. Because they are more likely to emulate similar models than to emulate dissimilar models, they are more likely to observe and imitate same-gender individuals rather than other-gender individuals (Bussey & Bandura, 2004). Through the observation of these models, children learn which behaviors are considered appropriate for someone of their gender. For example, 5-year-old Jenny sees her mother bake cookies and then uses her play kitchen to pretend she is baking. And, because the nurses in her pediatrician's office are females, Jenny believes that only women can be nurses. Jenny also learns that it is important for women to be pretty because she sees televised female role models who are frequently concerned about their appearance.

Reinforcement and Punishment. Social learning theory maintains that even though children sometimes engage in cross-gender observational learning in addition to same-gender imitation, they are likely to perform primarily gender-appropriate behaviors. The mechanisms that explain this phenomenon are reinforcement and punishment. If people expect a positive reinforcement (reward) for performing the behavior, it is likely they will engage in that behavior. On the other hand, if they anticipate a negative consequence (punishment), they are not likely to perform that act. Thus, girls and boys learn, both through observing the consequences to models and as a result of the outcomes received for their own behaviors, that girls are more likely to be rewarded for certain actions and boys for others. For example, a girl playing "dress-up" might be praised for her beauty as she parades around wearing her mother's old dress and high heels. If her brother wears the same outfit, however, his parents might tell him to take off the clothes.

Cognition. A modification of social learning theory, known as **social cognitive theory,** states that *observational learning and rewards and punishments following behavior cannot alone account for gender typing; thought processes (cognitions) also play a role.* As children develop, they not only receive rewards and punishments from others but also begin to internalize standards about appropriate gender-related behavior (Bussey & Bandura, 2004; Olson & Dweck, 2008). Consequently, children initially engage in gender-appropriate behaviors because of the anticipation of rewards from others. However, as they gain experience and maturity, they develop internal standards about gender-related behavior, which motivates them to engage in gender-appropriate activities in order to gain self-satisfaction and avoid self-censure. For example, Pablo might refuse to play with his sister's dolls because playing with them would violate his personal standard of appropriate behavior for boys.

Evaluation. Unlike psychoanalytic theory, the concepts of the social learning perspective are clear and observable. Therefore, numerous studies have examined the theory's assumptions. These studies have provided support for some aspects of the theory and are inconclusive about others.

One assumption of social learning theory is that girls and boys receive encouragement and reinforcement for different behaviors. In support of this perspective, several studies show that parents do treat their daughters and sons differently, at least in regard to some behaviors. For example, mothers encourage their preschool daughters more than their sons to talk about interactions with other people, thus fostering a greater interpersonal interest and concern (Flannagan et al., 1995). In addition, parents buy their daughters and sons different types of toys, encourage different play activities, and assign them different chores (see Chapter 4).

According to social learning theory, the other process in gender typing is observational learning. Although children do imitate same-gender role models, observational learning is not restricted to the behaviors of individuals of the same gender as the child (Martin et al., 2002). Other characteristics, such as a model's power, can influence the selection of role models. Thus, while children no doubt learn from the behaviors of important adults in their lives, including parents and teachers, this learning is not restricted to adults of the same gender as the child.

Cognitive Developmental Theory

Cognitive developmental theory, originally formulated by Lawrence Kohlberg (1966), contends that *children are neither pushed by their biological desires nor pulled by external rewards and punishments. Instead, children are active learners, attempting to make sense of the social environment.* They actively search for patterns and rules that govern the functioning of females and males and then follow these in an attempt to best adapt to social demands.

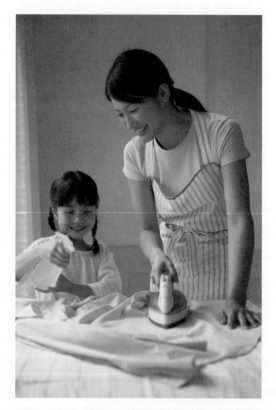

According to social learning theory, children acquire gender roles by imitating same-gender models and receiving reinforcement for doing so.

By approximately 3 years of age, children can correctly label their own gender (that is, they have gender identity). However, they do not yet know that gender is unchangeable, that neither time nor behavioral and appearance modifications can alter one's gender. For example, Kohlberg (1966) reported that most 4-year-olds believe that a girl could become a boy if she wanted to if she engaged in boy-related activities, or if she wore a boy's clothes. As an example of this thinking, he reported the following conversation between two preschool children (p. 95):

JOHNNY: I'm going to be a airplane builder when I grow up.

JIMMY: When I grow up, I'll be a Mommy.

JOHNNY: No, you can't be a Mommy. You have to be a Daddy.

JIMMY: No, I'm going to be a Mommy.

JOHNNY: No, you're not a girl, you can't be a Mommy.

JIMMY: Yes, I can.

It appears that Johnny, but not Jimmy, has developed the concept of **gender constancy,** *the belief that gender is permanent regardless of changes in age, behavior, or appearance,* a belief that generally develops between the ages of 4 and 7 years.

According to Kohlberg (1966), the absence of gender constancy in young children is not a function of their lack of knowledge of genital differences. Even children who have this awareness at an early age do not conclude that gender cannot be altered. Instead, the absence of gender constancy is due to the young child's reliance on superficial physical characteristics, such as clothing or hair length. Preschool children do not recognize that changes in any object's visible characteristics do not necessarily alter its quality. For example, Kohlberg (1966) writes that most 4-year-olds believe a cat would become a dog if its whiskers were cut off.

Cognitive developmental theory contends that gender typing cannot take place until children understand that their gender is unchangeable. Once they acquire that understanding, they begin to behave in gender-appropriate ways, which enables them to effectively adapt to the social world. To learn which behaviors are performed by females and which are performed by males, children actively observe parents and other role models. In this process they seek out information about which behaviors are gender-appropriate and which are not. Then they engage in the gender-appropriate behaviors because behaving in a gender-consistent manner is, in itself, rewarding.

The cognitive developmental view of children's use of the social environment is very different from the social learning perspective. According to social learning theory, rewards for gender-appropriate behavior lead to the development of gender-appropriate behaviors and attitudes. Cognitive developmental theory, on the other hand, argues that rewards for gender-consistent behavior merely inform the child what is gender appropriate and that children engage in these behaviors because acting in a gender-consistent manner is, in itself, rewarding. Let's look at an example to help clarify the distinction. Six-year-old Caitlin has been praised for helping her mother cook dinner. According to social learning theory, she then wants to cook again because she anticipates positive reinforcement from others (and possibly from herself) for cooking.

The attainment of gender constancy would not be necessary because her desire to cook stems from her expectation of positive reinforcement, not because cooking is defined as a female activity. According to cognitive developmental theory, on the other hand, the praise received by Caitlin serves as information that cooking dinner is a female activity. If she has attained gender constancy, she now wants to cook because behaving in a gender-consistent manner is, in itself, rewarding.

Evaluation.   The concepts of cognitive developmental theory, like those of social learning theory, are clearly defined and easily measured and have generated consider-able research. One important assumption of this perspective is that gender typing is dependent on an awareness of the unchangeability of gender. Examination of this assumption has provided mixed results (Martin et al., 2002; Ruble et al., 2007). Some, but not all, studies have shown that children who have achieved gender constancy are more likely than their peers to select gender-appropriate activities and to have knowl-edge of gender stereotypes (Evans et al., 2003).

A second assumption of cognitive developmental theory is that children tend to value same-gender activities once they attain gender constancy. On this point the theory receives considerable support; numerous studies show that children value their own gender more highly than they value the other gender (e.g., Powlishta, 2001).

A major criticism of cognitive developmental theory is that it does not specify why children use gender as a classifying concept. Kohlberg (1966) asserts that children want to adhere to social rules so as to best master the social environment, but his theory does not explain why these rules are structured around gender. As Bem (1983, p. 601) stated, "The theory fails to explicate why sex will have primacy over other potential categories of the self such as race, religion, or even eye color."

Gender Schema Theory

Gender schema theory, proposed by Sandra Bem (1983), incorporates elements of cog-nitive developmental and social learning theories. Like the first, it proposes that *children develop an interrelated set of ideas, or schema, about gender that guides their social perceptions and actions.* However, unlike cognitive developmental theory, gender schema theory postu-lates that the use of gender as an organizing principle is not inevitable; it does not natu-rally stem from the minds of children. Similar to social learning theory, it assumes that *gender schema development stems from learning the gender norms and practices of society.*

The theory proposes that children formulate conceptions of the traits and roles associated with females and males on the basis of societal expectations. They then use this information to regulate their own behavior, and their self-esteem becomes contin-gent on their adherence to these gender schemas (Bem, 1981).

A significant difference between gender schema and cognitive developmental theories lies in the basis for gender schema development. Whereas Kohlberg (1966) assumes that the development of cognitive conceptualizations about gender is a natural process, Bem (1981) contends that the use of gender as a way of processing social infor-mation occurs because societal norms and practices emphasize its importance. Thus, children do not organize the social environment on the basis of physical attributes, such as eye color or hair color, because society does not give these characteristics the same significance it applies to gender. Bem argues that children cannot avoid noticing that different toys, activities, jobs, and chores are deemed acceptable for girls and boys by their parents, peers, and teachers. As one illustration, Bem (1983) points out that elementary school teachers do not line up children separately by race because they do not want to emphasize race as a distinguishing characteristic. They might, however, group children by sex, thus increasing its perceived importance as a distinguishing characteristic.

Bem (1983) claims that individuals vary in the degree to which they use gender schemas to understand and evaluate others and to guide their own behavior. According to Bem, people who have strong gender schemas consider a narrower range of activities as acceptable for individuals of each gender, including themselves. For example, boys have more powerful gender schemas than girls (Gelman et al., 2004). This finding is consistent with research showing that boys are more likely than girls to maintain gender boundaries (see Leaper, 2000, for a review).

Even within a given sex, some individuals have stronger, less flexible gender schemas than do others. Bem suggests that variations among people might be influenced by individual differences in exposure to gender as an organizing characteristic. Consequently, she proposes several strategies parents can use for minimizing the development of gender schemas and, consequently, for reducing the development of gender-stereotypic attitudes and behavior. Can you think of parental practices that might be effective? Read Get Involved 3.1 and answer the questions to learn about Bem's proposal.

GET INVOLVED **3.1**

Parental Strategies for Minimizing Gender Schemas in Children

Bem (1983) suggests that the following parental practices might help reduce gender schema development in children:

1. Elimination of gender stereotyping from parental behavior. For example, parents could share household duties instead of dividing them along gender lines.
2. Elimination of gender stereotyping from the choices parents present their children. That is, they could offer toys, activities, and clothing associated with both females and males.
3. Definition of femaleness and maleness along anatomical and reproductive lines only. That is, parents could reduce children's tendency to organize the social world according to gender by teaching their children that one's sex is relevant only for

reproduction. Bem offers the following anecdote about her four-year-old son Jeremy and his nursery school classmate as an illustration of the limiting outcomes of a cultural definition of gender and the greater flexibility of a biological definition:

One day Jeremy decided to wear barrettes to school. Several times that day, another little boy told Jeremy that he, Jeremy, must be a girl because "only girls wear barrettes." After trying to explain to this child that "wearing barrettes doesn't matter" and that "being a boy means having a penis and testicles," Jeremy finally pulled down his pants as a way of making his point more convincingly. The other child was not impressed. He simply said, "Everybody has a penis; only girls wear barrettes." (p. 612)

What Does It Mean?

1. Do you agree that each of the practices proposed by Bem could help reduce gender schema development? Why or why not?
2. Which of these, if any, do you think you would use, or are using, in raising your own children? Explain your answer.
3. According to gender schema theory, minimizing the use of gender schemas for perceiving the social world should reduce the development of gender stereotypes. Are there other practices that might help reduce gender stereotyping?
4. What advantages and/or disadvantages might result if all children were raised to restrict their definition of gender to reproductive characteristics only?

Evaluation.   Kohlberg's (1966) cognitive developmental theory does not explain why children structure their social perceptions around gender. One strength of gender schema theory, on the other hand, is that it illustrates how societal messages can influence the formation of gender schemas.

In addition, there is considerable research support for the theory (Casey, 2002; Martin & Dinella, 2001). For example, one of its assumptions is that gender schemas help individuals organize their memories, thus facilitating the recollection of gender-consistent information. Consistent with this view, research shows that individuals remember material consistent with their own gender better than they remember material consistent with the other gender (Ganske & Hebl, 2001; Martin et al., 2002; Susskind, 2003). For example, Isabelle Cherney and Brigette Ryalls (1999) asked adults to recall items that were located in a room where they were waiting for an experiment to begin. Females were better able to remember female-related items, such as a makeup kit, a cookbook, and a purse, whereas males were better at recalling male-related objects, including aftershave, a sports video, and a necktie.

Gender-Related Traits

We have explored a variety of theories that explain gender typing. Now let's examine variations in individuals' conformity to stereotyped expectations about their gender. As mentioned previously, people differ in the degree to which their own traits, behaviors, interests, and roles are consistent with gender stereotypes.

The most commonly measured variation has been in the gender-related traits individuals ascribe to themselves, that is, in their personal identification with female-related and male-related characteristics. Historically, these two sets of traits were viewed as bipolar, that is, as opposite extremes of a single continuum. In the chapter opening vignette, we saw that Judith's classmate believed she could not be both feminine and achievement oriented. This belief reflects the bipolar view that a person cannot have characteristics stereotypically associated with both females and males.

In the 1970s, there was a change in this characterization of female-related and male-related traits. At that time, psychologists began to conceptualize the two dimensions as independent, rather than opposite, of one another. Unlike a bipolar dimension, such as tall–short, in which it is impossible to be described by both traits, the new perspective posited that individuals can exhibit any combination of female-stereotypic and male-stereotypic characteristics. That is, a high degree of one does not imply a low degree of the other.

In 1974 Sandra Bem proposed that femininity and masculinity should be assessed independently and developed the Bem Sex Role Inventory (BSRI) to accomplish that goal. The BSRI includes one set of traits viewed as more desirable for females than for males and another set of items seen as more desirable for males than for females. At approximately the same time, Janet Spence, Robert Helmreich, and Joy Stapp (1974) published the Personal Attributes Questionnaire (PAQ), which also has two separate dimensions to measure gender-related personality characteristics. On the PAQ these two scales comprise personality characteristics seen as desirable for both females and males but viewed as more representative of one gender than the other. On both instruments the female-related scale comprises communal traits and the male-related scale reflects agentic traits (see Chapter 2); however, when used as measures of gender-related trait identification, they have typically been labeled either "femininity" and "masculinity" or "expressiveness" and "instrumentality."

The scoring of the BSRI and the PAQ reflects the goal of each to evaluate femininity/expressiveness and masculinity/instrumentality as independent dimensions. Thus, respondents receive a score on each dimension, and the combination of the two indicates which of four categories best describes their gender-related traits. These categories are (1) **femininity,** *a high score on the femininity/expressiveness scale and a low score on the scale for masculinity/instrumentality*; (2) **masculinity,** *a high score on the masculinity/instrumentality scale and a low score on the femininity/expressiveness scale*; (3) **androgyny** (derived from the ancient Greek words for male—*andro*—and female—*gyn*), *high scores on both scales*; and (4) **undifferentiation,** *low scores on both scales*. Any individual, regardless of gender, can be characterized by any of these categories.

Although most investigations of gender-related traits have focused on White college students, a few have examined college and/or noncollege women with diverse ethnic backgrounds. These have shown that Black college women often report high levels of masculinity and androgyny (e.g., Buckley & Carter, 2005). To assess your own gender-related traits, try Get Involved 3.2.

Changes in Gender-Related Traits over Time

> *College women and high school girls' . . . assertiveness . . . increased from 1931 to 1945, decreased from 1946 to 1967 and increased from 1968 to 1993. . . . Why did women's assertiveness scores switch twice over the century?* (Twenge, 2001, pp. 133, 141)

In the 1970s, studies showed that more female than male college students scored high on femininity, whereas more males than females scored high on masculinity and approximately one-third of both genders were androgynous (e.g., Spence & Helmreich, 1978). To determine whether there has been any change over time, Jean Twenge (1997b) performed a meta-analysis of femininity and masculinity scores based on samples from over 50 different college campuses since the 1970s. Interestingly, the most notable

GET INVOLVED **3.2**

What Are Your Gender-Related Traits?

The following is a partial set of characteristics from the Personal Attributes Questionnaire. For each item, choose the letter that best describes where you fall on the scale. Choose **A** if you feel the characteristic on the left strongly describes you and choose **E** if the trait on the right is strongly descriptive of you. Choose **C** if you are in the middle, and so on. Also, ask a friend to rate you on these characteristics.

1. Not at all independent	A. B. C. D. E	Very independent
2. Not at all emotional	A. B. C. D. E	Very emotional
3. Very rough	A. B. C. D. E	Very gentle
4. Not at all competitive	A. B. C. D. E	Very competitive
5. Not at all helpful to others	A. B. C. D. E	Very helpful to others
6. Not at all kind	A. B. C. D. E	Very kind
7. Not at all self-confident	A. B. C. D. E	Very self-confident
8. Gives up very easily	A. B. C. D. E	Never gives up easily
9. Not at all understanding of others	A. B. C. D. E	Very understanding of others
10. Goes to pieces under pressure	A. B. C. D. E	Stands up well under pressure

What Does It Mean?

To score yourself, give 0 points to a response of **A,** 1 point to **B,** and so on. Then add up your points for items 2, 3, 5, 6, and 9; this comprises your femininity/expressiveness score. Similarly, sum your points for items 1, 4, 7, 8, and 10; this comprises your masculinity/instrumentality score. Use the same procedure to score your friend's ratings of you.

1. Are your two scores similar to each other or is one much higher than the other? Does your pattern of scores reflect the gender-related trait category you think best describes you? Why or why not?

2. Is your pattern of scores similar to the pattern based on your friend's ratings? If not, describe the differences. Also, explain why your friend views your gender-related traits differently than the way you perceive them.

3. Although the Personal Attributes Questionnaire is widely used today, it was based on 1970s' perceptions of traits more typical of either females or males. Are there any characteristics presented here that no longer seem to be more representative of one gender than the other? Which ones? What evidence do you have for the gender similarity on those traits?

Source: From *Masculinity and Femininity: Their Psychological Dimensions, Correlates and Antecedents* by Janet T. Spence and Robert L. Helmreich, Copyright © 1978. By permission of the University of Texas Press.

change found by Twenge was the dramatic increase in masculinity scores of women. Also, there was a significant increase in androgyny among women and a weaker increase among men. Other research (Harper & Schoeman, 2003; Spence & Buckner, 2000; Twenge, 2001) has found that women and men no longer differ on a number of items long considered to be masculine. These include being active, independent, self-reliant, ambitious, assertive, acting as a leader, and defending one's beliefs. When compared to their own mothers, today's college women show more masculine-typed and less feminine-typed behaviors (Guastello & Guastello, 2003).

Jean Twenge, Janet Spence, and Camille Buckner suggest that these changes in gender-related traits may be accounted for by societal changes that have occurred in recent years. Girls have been encouraged to become more assertive, to stand up for their rights, to be independent rather than helpless, and to have high occupational aspirations. They have been given more opportunities to develop their agentic skills, especially in the educational, vocational, and sports arenas.

Similarly, women were expected to be self-sufficient during the Great Depression and World War II, in the early-to-middle years of the twentieth century, whereas passive domesticity was encouraged in the 1950s and early 1960s. These shifts in women's status and roles closely parallel the changes in women's assertiveness over the course of the century (Twenge, 2001).

Thus, today's young women are more likely than their counterparts in the seventies to have witnessed or experienced roles that involve male-stereotypic characteristics. This could have contributed to the development of their greater masculinity and, in turn, their greater androgyny. Thus, consistent with the view that gender is socially constructed, changes in women's personal sense of gender seem to be related to their social experiences.

Gender-Related Traits and Psychological Adjustment

Once psychologists started to conceptualize gender-related traits as being more complex than a single dimension of femininity–masculinity, they began to examine the psychological well-being of individuals who varied in their pattern of gender-stereotypic traits. For example, Bem (1975) hypothesized that because androgynous individuals are comfortable engaging in both feminine and masculine behaviors, they can adapt more adequately to various situational demands and should report greater well-being than nonandrogynous individuals. Research shows, however, that it is high masculinity, and not the specific combination of high masculinity and high femininity, that is strongly related to well-being and self-esteem (D. Moore, 2007; Russo & Tartaro, 2008; Saunders & Kashubeck, 2002; Ward, 2000). Predictably, it is the positive aspects of masculinity (e.g., independence, mastery), not its negative components (e.g., aggressiveness, selfishness), that are linked with psychological health (Woodhill & Samuels, 2003).

What can explain the positive relationship between masculinity and psychological adjustment? As we saw in Chapter 2, male-related traits are more highly valued in North America than female-related traits. Therefore, people with male-stereotypic traits feel better about their ability to function effectively. Derek Grimmell and Gary Stern (1992) found support for this explanation in college students' BSRI self-ratings, their BSRI ratings of the ideal person, and their psychological well-being. These investigators found that students' masculinity score was related to their psychological adjustment. Moreover, respondents' adjustment was predicted by the difference between their self-reported masculinity and their ratings of masculinity for the ideal person. The higher their own masculinity in relation to their perception of ideal masculinity, the higher their own self-esteem and the lower their anxiety and depression. Thus, it appears that the degree to which we feel we possess highly valued masculine traits is a good predictor of our psychological adjustment.

However, before we conclude that androgyny is not related to psychological well-being, let's consider a different conceptualization of androgyny. See Learn about the Research 3.1 for a newer approach to androgyny measurement and its psychological benefits.

Evaluation of the Concept of Androgyny

When the psychological measurement of androgyny was introduced in the 1970s, it was received enthusiastically by feminist scholars. It replaced the notion that psychological health required that females be feminine and males be masculine. By embodying socially desirable traits for both females and males, androgyny seemed to imply the absence of gender stereotyping. Furthermore, by incorporating both feminine and masculine behaviors it appeared to broaden the scope of behaviors that can be used to handle different situations and, thus, lead to more flexible and adaptive behaviors.

Although androgyny continues to be viewed by feminist scholars as more positive than restrictions to either femininity or masculinity, several feminist criticisms have been leveled against this concept. One is that the notion of androgyny, similar to the bipolar differentiation of femininity–masculinity, is based on the division of gender into female-stereotypic and male-stereotypic characteristics (Bem, 1993; Hoffman & Youngblade, 2001). Rather than making traits *gender-neutral*, androgyny involves the combination of *gender-specific* orientations. A second concern is that androgyny might be erecting unrealistic goals for individuals—the requirement that people be competent in both the communal and agentic domains. Third, according to Bem (1993), the concept of androgyny does not deal with masculinity and femininity in their unequal cultural context. It neither acknowledges nor attempts to eliminate the greater cultural value placed on male activities. Last, Bem is concerned that androgyny will not lead to the elimination of gender inequality, a goal that requires *societal* rather than *personal* change. That is, the mere existence of individuals with both feminine and masculine traits does not alter the patriarchal power structure in society.

Gender Attitudes

Let's turn now to an examination of variations in gender attitudes. People differ in the degree to which they believe that gender should dictate females' and males' roles. Some individuals hold a **traditional gender attitude,** *the belief that females should engage in communal behaviors and roles and males should engage in agentic behaviors and roles.* They might believe, for example, that women should be the primary rearers of children whereas men should be the primary financial providers or that women are better suited than men to nursing whereas men are better suited than women to corporate management. Others adhere to a **nontraditional or egalitarian gender attitude,**

LEARN ABOUT THE RESEARCH 3.1

A Real-Life Approach to Androgyny

Examination of gender-related traits indicates that masculinity, and not the coexistence of masculinity and femininity, best predicts psychological adjustment. Recently, however, Jayne Stake argued that the psychological benefits of androgyny should not be dismissed on the basis of measuring individuals' ratings of their gender-related traits. Instead, she suggested we consider androgyny as the integration of communal and agentic behaviors given in response to expectations demanded by specific life situations. That is, measurement of these behaviors must be grounded in situational contexts.

Stake focused on work-related expectations because job settings tend to require a wide range of behaviors from the worker. Her specific interest was in individuals' responses to demands on the job that required both communal and agentic behaviors. She wanted to discover whether people who use both types of behaviors when they respond to these situations experience any benefits compared to those who rely on one type or neither type. Accordingly, in individual interviews, 194 undergraduate students were asked to describe a work situation in which they were expected to behave with both "sensitivity and caring" (e.g., "Be sensitive to the needs of others," "Show others you care about them") and

"mastery and independence" (e.g., "Always show that you can handle things on your own—without the help of others," "Show you have technical know-how"). Then they were asked to describe the behaviors they used to cope with these dual expectations. Similarly, they were asked to consider the overall expectations in their job and to describe what they usually did to respond to these expectations. These coping strategies in both the specific situation as well as in the job setting overall were coded into one of the four categories generally used to classify gender-related traits. In addition, students indicated to what extent their well-being was affected by work situations that expected both types of behaviors.

The results showed that androgynous coping behaviors used in response to dual expectations in specific job situations and dual expectations in the job overall were related to the highest level of well-being. Individuals who used both communal and agentic behaviors experienced more rewards and fewer negative outcomes than those using other types of strategies. Thus, it is possible that examining gender-related attributes as behavioral responses to specific situations rather than as general personality traits might be a fruitful approach to understanding the beneficial effects of various gender-related orientations.

What Does It Mean?

1. Stake examined expectations for communal and agentic behaviors in the workplace. Can you think of other situations that might make simultaneous demands?
2. Identify a job experience you had where both types of demands were made. Describe

how you handled it and how you felt in this situation. Was your experience consistent with the results reported here?

Source: Stake (1997).

the belief that behaviors and roles should not be gender specific. To get more familiar with the meaning of gender attitudes, take the test in Get Involved 3.3.

The Sex-Role Egalitarianism Scale (King & King, 1990), which is shown in part in Get Involved 3.3, illustrates the multidimensional nature of gender attitudes. This scale comprises beliefs about appropriate roles within five life domains: marital, parental, employment, social–interpersonal–heterosexual, and educational. There is

GET INVOLVED 3.3
What Are Your Gender Attitudes?

On a scale from 1 (strongly agree) to 7 (strongly disagree), indicate the degree to which you agree or disagree with each of the following statements:

1. The husband should be the head of the family.
2. Keeping track of a child's out-of-school activities should be mostly the mother's responsibility.
3. Home economics courses should be as acceptable for male students as for female students.

4. A person should generally be more polite to a woman than to a man.
5. It is more appropriate for a mother rather than a father to change their baby's diaper.
6. It is wrong for a man to enter a traditionally female career.
7. Things work out best in a marriage if a husband leaves his hands off domestic tasks.
8. Women can handle pressures from their jobs as well as men can.
9. Choice of college is not as important for women as for men.

What Does It Mean?

Before computing your score, reverse the points for statements 3 and 8. That is, if you answered "1" (strongly agree) to these two questions, give yourself 7 points, if you answered "2," give yourself 6 points, and so on. Then sum the points for the 9 items. Note that higher scores reflect more nontraditional or egalitarian gender attitudes.

1. These statements come from the Sex-Role Egalitarianism Scale, developed in the 1980s. Are there any questions that you think are no longer adequate measures of egalitarian gender beliefs? If yes, give your reasons.
2. Look at your answers to Get Involved 3.2. Is there any consistency in the extent to which you describe yourself as communal

and/or agentic and your beliefs about appropriate gender-related behaviors and roles? For example, if you received high scores on both communion and agency, reflecting an androgynous identity, did your answers to the questions in this activity indicate egalitarian beliefs? Can you explain why a person's gender-related traits might not be associated with her or his gender attitudes?
3. If most North Americans were to endorse egalitarian gender beliefs, what positive outcomes might be experienced by women and girls? By men and boys? Would there be any negative consequences for either gender? Explain.

Source: Reproduced by permission of Sigma Assessment Systems, Inc., P.O. Box 610984, Port Huron, MI 48061-0984. Tel: (800) 265-1285.

Gender Attitudes in Global Context

Deborah Best and her colleagues (Best, 2001; Best & Thomas, 2004) have conducted studies of the gender attitudes of university students in 14 different countries. Their research indicates that gender attitudes range from traditional to more egalitarian both across and within cultures. For example, the most egalitarian attitudes were found in northern European countries (the Netherlands, Germany, Finland, England). The United States was in the middle of the distribution, and the most traditional attitudes were found in Africa and in Asian countries (Nigeria, Pakistan, India, Japan, Malaysia). Other studies have found that Muslim nations in the Middle East and North Africa are the least likely of all nations to endorse gender equality (Norris & Inglehart, 2004). Across countries, women hold more egalitarian views than men. Within a given country, however, the gender attitudes of women and men correspond highly (Best & Thomas, 2004; Olson et al., 2007). Now go back to Chapter 2, and compare these results with those of Glick and Fiske on hostile and benevolent sexism across cultures.

considerable evidence that gender attitudes are not uniform across these dimensions. Instead, North American college students tend to have more nontraditional beliefs about women's employment roles than they do about women's combined family and work roles (Anderson & Johnson, 2003; Holland & Andre, 1992; Powell & Yanico, 1991). For example, Holland and Andre found that approximately 84 percent of a college student sample disagreed with the statement that it is more important for a wife to help her husband with his career than for her to have a career of her own. However, only 42 percent believed a woman should accept an employment opportunity if it meant her husband would have to find another job and her family would have to move. For a look at gender–role attitudes in other countries, read Explore Other Cultures 3.2.

Individual Differences in Gender-Related Attitudes

As we have seen, gender attitudes can vary from traditional to egalitarian. Now let's examine demographic and personality characteristics that are related to differences in gender attitudes.

Gender. Not surprisingly, one characteristic is gender. Dozens of studies using predominantly White samples have shown that males have more traditional beliefs about the appropriate roles for women than females (e.g., Anderson & Johnson, 2003; Aosved & Long, 2006; Corrigal & Konrad, 2007; Eagly & Diekman, 2006; Levant et al., 2007; Nierman et al., 2007; Riggio & Desrochers, 2005; Robinson et al., 2004). Similarly, Black men (Kane, 2000) and Asian men (Anderson & Johnson, 2003; Ui & Matsui, 2008) hold more traditional gender-role attitudes than their female counterparts.

Ethnicity.   Another demographic characteristic that is related to gender attitudes is ethnicity. As we saw in Chapter 2, Black women are less likely than White or Latina women to adhere to gender stereotypes. Thus, we might think their attitudes about gender-related behaviors and roles would be uniformly more egalitarian.

Interestingly, research comparing Black and White views about gender roles shows a complex pattern. On the one hand, Black women seem to hold more traditional views about the domestic domain. They have more stereotypical views about children's domestic roles (Dugger, 1988) and women's responsibilities for housework and child care (Binion, 1990). According to Dugger (p. 439), this traditional view might reflect a defensive reaction against the "labeling of Black women as 'matriarchs' . . . who rob their sons and men in general of their manhood." On the other hand, there is some evidence that Black women hold more egalitarian views about women's employment and political roles than White women do (Harris & Firestone, 1998). Also, Black college women, compared to White college women, perceive less conflict in the combination of the provider and domestic roles (e.g., Bridges & Etaugh, 1996), a difference possibly due to Black women's longer history of combining work and family roles.

What about gender attitudes of Latinas? Traditionally, Latina/o families have been characterized as patriarchal, with a dominant, powerful husband/father and a submissive, self-sacrificing wife/mother. Thus, it is not surprising that Latina women have been found to hold more traditional views about women's employment and political roles than either Black or White women (Harris & Firestone, 1998). However, there is evidence that the views held by Latina women are becoming less traditional, over time. The Latina/o family has been undergoing many changes related to gender (Castaneda, 1996). They have been experiencing an increasingly greater flexibility in the division of household responsibilities and a more egalitarian approach to family decision making (Gonzalez & Espin, 1996). For example, Donna Castaneda (1996) notes that second- and third-generation Latinas/os are less likely than first-generation women and men to believe that the husband should be the sole provider and decision maker within the family and that females should do all of the housework and obey the husband's/father's demands. Thus, the degree of acculturation of Latina women and Latino men seems to be strongly related to their gender attitudes.

Research on Native Americans has focused on their actual gender-related behaviors and roles rather than on their attitudes and has shown great variations over time and across tribal groups. According to scholars such as Theresa LaFromboise and her associates (LaFromboise et al., 1999), women's behaviors and roles in traditional Native American life included caregiving, spiritual continuation of their people, and transmission of cultural knowledge. Many Native American societies were characterized by complementary but equally powerful roles for some women and men while other groups institutionalized alternative female roles. For example, within several Plains tribes, women's roles included masculine ones, such as the "warrior woman" and the "manly-hearted woman" (aggressive and independent) in addition to the traditional role of the submissive, hard working wife. Other tribes, such as the Navajo and Iroquois, were matrilineal; women owned the material goods and passed these on to their daughters and sisters and played important economic, political, and spiritual roles.

In traditional Navajo and Iroquois culture, women played important economic, political, and spiritual roles.

Interestingly, LaFromboise and her colleagues (1999) contend that colonization by Europeans and the continuing acculturation process by which Native Americans have become more involved in the dominant White culture have contributed in several Native American societies to a breakdown in complementary female–male roles and to an increase in male dominance and the subjugation of women. However, in many tribes, women continue to experience considerable political power because of their traditional roles of caretakers for the community and transmitters of the culture. In order to learn more directly about the gender attitudes of women of different ethnicities, perform the interviews described in Get Involved 3.4.

Other Factors.   There is some evidence that gender attitudes are related to religious factors. Among college students, Jews tend to have less traditional gender beliefs than Protestants (Lottes & Kuriloff, 1992; Willetts-Bloom & Nock, 1994), and Catholics fall somewhere in between (Harville & Rienzi, 2000). Moreover, the more strongly individuals embrace religion in their lives, the more traditional their gender attitudes are (Bang et al., 2005; Brewster & Padavic, 2002; D. Robinson et al., 2004).

Other demographic characteristics related to gender attitudes are social class, political ideology, age, year in college, academic performance, and college major.

GET INVOLVED **3.4**

Ethnic Variations in Gender Attitudes

Interview two college women of approximately the same age (i.e., both traditional-age students or both older adults), from each of two different ethnic groups. Ask the following questions:

1. Do you think there should be different roles for women and men in the family? In dating relationships? In the workplace? If your respondent answered "yes" to any of these, ask her to be specific.
2. What is your career goal?

3. How important is your future/current career to your personal identity?
4. Do you want to get married and have children? If yes, do you think you will have any difficulty balancing your family and work roles?
5. Who do you think should be the primary provider in your family?
6. How do you think you and your spouse/partner will divide up the household responsibilities, including child care?

What Does It Mean?

1. Although your sample is very small, did you observe any ethnic differences? Did these differences match those discussed in the text? If yes, show the connections. If no, explain why your results might differ from those reported in past research.

2. You interviewed college women. Do you think your findings might have been different had your respondents been college graduates? Working-class or poor women without a college education? Explain your answers.

Specifically, nontraditional views about gender tend to be associated with higher social and educational level (Brewster & Padavic, 2002), having liberal political views (Apparala et al., 2003; Cichy et al., 2007), being a young, rather than an older, adult (Apparala et al., 2003), being a senior in college as opposed to a first-year student (Bryant, 2003), having a high GPA (Ahrens & O'Brien, 1996; Bryant, 2003), and, for women, majoring in a male-dominated field (Karpiak et al., 2007).

In addition, gender attitudes are related to a personality characteristic known as authoritarianism, which is characterized by intolerance of ambiguity and is strongly related to prejudice toward members of perceived outgroups such as Blacks, Jews, gays, and disabled people. As you might guess, both women and men who are high in authoritarianism endorse traditional societal roles for women and men (Duncan et al., 2003). Traditional attitudes about gender are also associated with the belief that gender differences are caused by biological or religious (divine) causes as opposed to differences in socialization or opportunities (Neff & Terry-Schmitt, 2002).

Perceived Value of Female versus Male Gender-Related Attributes

Derek Grimmell and Gary Stern (1992) found that college students value masculinity more strongly than femininity. This is consistent with our previous discussion of the greater power held by males in North American society. Is it, therefore, more advantageous to be a male than to be a female? Alternatively, are gender-related advantages and disadvantages equally distributed between the genders or, perhaps, balanced in favor of females? To examine this question, try the exercises in Get Involved 3.5.

When Arnie Cann and Elizabeth Vann (1995) asked college students to list as many advantages and disadvantages as they could associate with being the other gender, they found that, overall, both women and men associated more advantages with being male. Specifically, these students considered differences in physical appearance requirements and actual physical differences as more disadvantageous to females than to males. For example, they believed that more females than males must be concerned about their appearance and that biological differences, such as pregnancy and menstruation, are disadvantageous to females. Interestingly, these students did not perceive males to have more social-role advantages than females. Although females were seen to be limited by workplace discrimination and the expectation to be subordinate

---

GET INVOLVED **3.5**

Would You Rather Be a Female or a Male?

Have you ever considered what life would be like if you were the other gender? Think about what it is like to be a female or male. Then think about any advantages and/or disadvantages that would occur if you were the other gender. For each of the following three categories, list any advantages and/or disadvantages of being the other gender: (1) *social roles*, that is, opportunities that are not equally available to the two genders and/or behaviors that are considered more appropriate for one gender than the other; (2) *physical appearance expectations;* and (3) *physical differences*, for example, reproductive, size, or strength differences. Also, ask an other-gender friend to perform the same exercise. Discuss your answers with your friend.

What Does It Mean?

1. Did you imagine more advantages and/ or disadvantages in one category than the others? If yes, how can you explain the pattern of perceived advantages and disadvantages?
2. Are the responses of your other-gender friend complementary to your own responses? In other words, are your friend's perceptions of the advantages of being your gender consistent with your perceptions of the disadvantages of being your friend's gender? Why or why not?
3. Examine the number of advantages relative to disadvantages that you associated with being the other gender and consider the relative importance of each. Do the same for your friend's responses. Do you and/or your friend attach greater value to one gender or the other? If yes, how can you explain this?
4. If you or your friend perceive a relative advantage of one gender over the other, discuss some societal changes that would have to occur to reduce this discrepancy?

Source: Cann and Vann (1995).

in their relationships, males were viewed as hurt by the social pressure on them to be successful and to play a leadership role. Thus, these students seemed to be aware that the gender imbalance in power puts women at a disadvantage and that the social construction of the agentic, achievement-oriented male role establishes potentially difficult expectations for men.

Given the evidence that males are seen as having more advantages than females, it is not surprising that people evaluate males more negatively than they do females who violate gender expectations (Ruble & Martin, 1998). Scholars have proposed two possible explanations for this difference. The **social status hypothesis** contends that *because the male gender role is more highly valued than the female role is, a male is seen as lowering his social status by engaging in female-stereotypic behaviors, whereas a female performing male-stereotypic behaviors is perceived as raising her status* (e.g., McCreary, 1994). Consequently, males who engage in cross-gender behaviors are viewed more negatively than are females who deviate from gender expectations. As stated by Bem (1993), our society so thoroughly devalues whatever thoughts, feelings, and behaviors are culturally defined as feminine that crossing the gender boundary has a more negative cultural meaning for men than it has for women—which means, in turn, that male gender-boundary-crossers are much more culturally stigmatized than female gender-boundary-crossers (pp. 149–150).

The social status hypothesis receives some support from the finding that people believe that occupations with higher prestige require skills associated with masculine characteristics and that these jobs should pay more than those requiring feminine characteristics (Kite, 2001).

The other explanation of the more negative evaluation of male gender-role violation is the **sexual orientation hypothesis** (e.g., McCreary, 1994). This perspective argues that *cross-gender behavior in boys but not girls is considered a sign of actual or potential same-sex sexual orientation*. Several investigations have provided support for this perspective. For example when Donald McCreary (1994) asked college students to evaluate either a child or an adult who had cross-gender traits and interests, he found they considered it more likely that the feminine male was or would become a gay man than that the masculine female was or would become a lesbian.

SUMMARY

Gender Self-Concept

- Gender self-concept includes gender identity and gender attitudes.

Prenatal Development

- Prenatal sex differentiation is a multistage process. The joining of the sex chromosomes at conception is followed by the differentiation of the gonads, the development of the internal and external reproductive organs, and the organization of the hypothalamus.

- After the gonads develop, the presence or absence of androgens influences the development of the reproductive organs and the brain.
- Estrogens appear to play a role in female development.
- Some individuals experience variations in their prenatal development known as intersexuality.
- Turner syndrome is a chromosomal disorder in which the individual has a single X chromosome. These individuals are raised as girls and have female gender expectations, although they have no sex glands and no prenatal estrogen.

- Genetic females with CAH are usually reared as girls, although they have a partial or complete masculinization of their external genitals.
- Genetic males with the androgen-insensitivity syndrome have feminized external genitals and are reared as girls.
- Genetic males with a 5 alpha-reductase deficiency experience a female-to-male body transformation at puberty.
- Case studies of intersexuals provide mixed evidence regarding the influence of prenatal biological factors on nonsexual gender-related attributes, gender identity, and sexual orientation. Some researchers claim that gender-related development is dependent on prenatal factors, and others point to the importance of the gender of rearing.

Theories of Gender Typing

- Psychoanalytic theory proposes that gender typing stems from the child's identification with the same-gender parent, a process that occurs when the child resolves the Oedipus complex.
- For the boy the resolution stems from fear of castration by the father. For the girl it stems from the realization that she will never possess her father.
- Because the girl's desire for a penis continues, she experiences inferiority feelings throughout her life.
- Social learning theory proposes that children acquire gender behaviors via imitation of same-gender models and positive reinforcement of their own gender-consistent behaviors. Social cognitive theory stresses the added role of cognition.
- Cognitive developmental theory contends that once children attain gender constancy, they are motivated to behave in gender-appropriate ways. Thus, they actively seek out the rules that characterize female behavior and male behavior. They then engage in gender-consistent behaviors because it enables them to competently adjust to the social environment.
- Gender schema theory proposes that children develop an interrelated set of ideas about gender. They learn the societal norms and practices that signify the importance of gender.

They then organize the social world on the basis of gender and guide their own actions accordingly.

Gender-Related Traits

- On the basis of their gender-related traits, individuals can be categorized as feminine, masculine, androgynous, or undifferentiated.
- Research has shown an increase in masculinity and androgyny in women over time.
- Masculinity is related to psychological adjustment.
- Androgyny was once considered to be highly desirable, but recently feminist scholars have criticized it.

Gender Attitudes

- Gender attitudes are multidimensional.
- College students have less traditional beliefs about the value of the employment role for women but more-traditional views about the combination of women's employment and family roles.
- Among Whites, women are generally more nontraditional in their beliefs than men are.
- Among women, Blacks hold more traditional views about domestic responsibilities than Whites, but they have more nontraditional views about the combination of women's employment and family roles.
- The roles of Latina/o women and men have become more egalitarian over time, but Latinas have more traditional views than Black and White women.
- The gender-related behaviors and roles of Native American women vary greatly across tribes and in several societies increased acculturation has been accompanied by greater male dominance.
- Traditional gender attitudes are linked to being older, more religious, less educated, of lower social class, politically conservative, and authoritarian.
- College women and men associate more advantages with being male than with being female.
- Males, compared to females, are more negatively evaluated for engaging in cross-gender behavior.

KEY TERMS

gender identity
transgendered individuals
gender attitudes
sexual orientation
prenatal sex differentiation
androgens
estrogens
Müllerian ducts
Wolffian ducts
testosterone
Müllerian-inhibiting substance
intersexuality
Turner syndrome

congenital adrenal hyperplasia
androgen-insensitivity
   syndrome
5 alpha-reductase deficiency
gender typing
psychoanalytic theory
Oedipus complex
castration anxiety
identification
penis envy
social learning theory
observational learning
social cognitive theory

cognitive developmental
   theory
gender constancy
gender schema theory
femininity
masculinity
androgyny
undifferentiation
traditional gender attitude
nontraditional or egalitarian
   gender attitude
social status hypothesis
sexual orientation hypothesis

WHAT DO YOU THINK?

1. If you gave birth to an intersexual child, would you decide on surgerical restructuring of the child's reproductive system and genitalia early in life, or would you wait until closer to puberty when your child could participate in the decision? Give reasons for your answer.

2. Evidence indicates that boys, more than girls, select role models who are powerful. Explain this finding.

3. As discussed in Chapter 2, it is possible that the media not only reflect gender stereotypes but also help shape them. Now that you are familiar with theories of gender typing, use one of these theories to explain how the media might contribute to an individual's acquisition of gender stereotypes.

4. Which gender-typing theory or theories best explain(s) the development of gender-related traits, behaviors, and roles? Explain.

To help you develop your reasons, critically think about the evaluations presented in the text. Indicate why you believe that some of the evaluative comments seem to be more credible than others. Additionally, if you have had any contact with young children, try to provide anecdotal support for some of the theoretical concepts.

5. Discuss the advantages and disadvantages to girls/women and boys/men of gender-related trait identifications consistent with stereotypes, that is, femininity in females and masculinity in males. Can you think of the advantages and disadvantages of an androgynous identity?

6. There is some evidence that individuals who internalize their religious beliefs and attempt to live by them hold more traditional gender attitudes than individuals who do not. Consider possible explanations for this finding.

IF YOU WANT TO LEARN MORE

Anselmi, D. L., & Law, A. L. (1998). *Questions of gender: Perspectives and paradoxes*. Boston: McGraw Hill.

Bem, S. L. (1993). *The lenses of gender: Transforming the debate on sexual inequality*. New Haven, CT: Yale University Press.

Blakemore, J. E. O., Berenbaum, S. A., Liben, L. S. (2005). *Gender development.* New York: Psychology Press.

Colapinto, J. (2000). *As nature made him: The boy who was raised as a girl.* New York: HarperCollins.

Fausto-Sterling, A. (2000). *Sexing the body: Gender politics and the construction of sexuality.* New York: Basic Books.

Hines, M. (2004). *Brain gender.* New York: Oxford University Press.

Preves, S. (2003). *Intersex and identity: The contested self.* Rutgers, NJ: Rutgers University Press.

White, J. W. (2009). Taking sides: *Clashing views in gender* (4th ed.). New York: McGraw-Hill.

WEBSITES

Gender Identity

Border Crossings
http://www.uiowa.edu/-commstud/resources/bordercrossings/

Women's Studies Links

http://dir.yahoo.com/health/diseases_and_conditions/intersexuality

Infancy, Childhood, and Adolescence

Children's Knowledge and Beliefs about Gender
    Distinguishing between Females and Males
    Gender Identity and Self-Perceptions
    Gender Stereotypes

Gender-Related Activities and Interests
    Physical Performance and Sports
    Toys and Play
    Gender Segregation

Influences on Gender Development
    Parents
    Siblings
    School

    Peers
    Media

Puberty
    Events of Puberty
    Menarche
    Gender Differences in Puberty
    Early and Late Maturation in Girls

Psychosocial Development in Adolescence
    Identity
    Self-Esteem
    Gender Intensification
    Body Image

I was 6 when I realized there were different expectations for boys and girls. My brother and I used to play dress up at home all the time. It was an Easter Sunday and I wanted to wear the tie and my brother wanted to wear the dress. My father got really mad and my mom told us that since we were going to church I had to wear the dress and my brother had to wear the suit. I had a fit about the hose itching and my father told me to get used to it because girls were supposed to dress like girls and boys like boys. (Traci, 23-year-old college senior)

My mom wanted me to wear pink and my brother blue. At Christmas all of the granddaughters were given make-up and Barbie dolls whereas the boys were given GI Joe or hunting gear. My mother raised me to know how to cook, clean, budget, and do all of the work to take care of children and a household. However, my brother has never even washed a dish. (Jamie, 20-year-old college junior)

Both my parents encouraged me to do well in school, but while my brother was signed up for karate lessons at the YMCA I was signed up for things like jazz dance. When I joined girls' football in high school, my mother cringed every time I left the house in a jersey or came back with a bloody lip. She kept telling me she would "never understand." I was teased constantly, mostly by boys. They told me I would never be good enough at football, but I kept my head high and ignored them. (Erika, 20-year-old college junior)

An old nursery rhyme declares that little girls are made of "sugar and spice and everything nice," while little boys are made of "frogs and snails and puppy dogs' tails."

Are girls and boys really as different as the nursery rhyme suggests? Is there even a kernel of truth in these age-old stereotypes? And if so, what factors might be responsible? The childhood recollections of Traci, Jamie, and Erika indicate the important contributions made by family members. In this chapter, we focus on the development of girls in infancy, childhood, and adolescence and examine both similarities and differences between girls and boys during these years. We also explore factors that influence gender development, including the roles played by parents, schools, peers, and the media. We then look at the physical transformations of adolescence, examining puberty and individual differences in rates of physical maturation. Finally, we turn to psychosocial development in adolescence, exploring identity, self-esteem, gender, intensification, and body image.

Children's Knowledge and Beliefs about Gender

Early childhood is a time when much of the social construction of gender takes place. Let's examine some of these processes more closely. For a summary of the major milestones of gender stereotyping and gender-role adoption, see Table 4.1.

TABLE 4.1   Milestones of Gender Typing

Age	Gender Stereotyping and Gender-Role Adoption	Gender Identity
1–5 years	• "Gender-appropriate" toy preferences emerge. • Gender stereotyping of activities, occupations, and behaviors appears. • Gender segregation in peer interaction emerges and strengthens. • Girls' preference for play in pairs, boys' for play in larger groups, appears.	• Gender constancy develops in a three-stage sequence: gender labeling, gender stability, and gender consistency.
6–11 years	• Gender segregation reaches a peak. • Gender-stereotyped knowledge expands, especially for personality traits and achievement areas. • Gender stereotyping peaks between ages 5 and 7, then becomes more flexible.	• "Masculine" gender identity strengthens among boys; girls' gender identity becomes more androgynous.
12–20 years	• Gender-role conformity increases in early adolescence and then declines. • Gender segregation becomes less pronounced.	• Gender identity becomes more traditional in early adolescence ("gender intensification"), after which highly stereotypic self-perceptions decline.

Note: These milestones represent overall age trends. Individual differences exist in the precise age at which each milestone is attained and in the extent of gender typing.
Source: Adapted from Berk (2003).

Distinguishing between Females and Males

From birth, infants are surrounded by abundant cues signifying gender. They are given gender labels and are outfitted in color-coded clothing, diapers, and blankets (Eisenberg et al., 1996). It is not surprising that children learn to differentiate between females and males at an early age. Infants as young as 3–4 months of age can tell the difference between pictures of adult female and male faces, and 6-month-olds are able to distinguish between their voices. By the age of 12 months, children can match the face and voice of men and women (Zosuls et al., 2008). Between the ages of 2 and 2½ years, they can accurately label pictures of girls and boys (Etaugh & Duits, 1990; Etaugh et al., 1989). Young children who learn to identify females and males early show more gender-typical preferences for toys and peers than children of the same age who do not make this distinction (Martin, 1999).

Gender Identity and Self-Perceptions

As we saw in Chapter 3, children develop gender identity between 2 and 3 years of age. By that time they can accurately label their own gender and place a picture of themselves with other same-gender children (Campbell et al., 2002; Zosuls et al., 2008). As children grow aware of their membership in a particular gender category, they begin to view their own gender more favorably than the other gender (Powlishta, 2001; Ruble & Martin, 1998; Susskind et al., 2005). In one study of children in second through tenth grade, for example, girls believed that girls were nicer, harder workers, and less selfish than boys. Boys, on the other hand, felt that *they* were nicer, harder workers, and less selfish than girls (Etaugh et al., 1984).

Gender Stereotypes

In Chapter 2, we discussed how gender stereotypes are formed. This process begins early in life. Rudimentary knowledge about gender-typical objects and activities develops during the second year. Children as young as 24 months know that certain objects (e.g., ribbon, dress, purse) and activities (e.g., putting on makeup, rocking a baby, vacuuming) are associated with females and that other objects (e.g., gun, truck, screwdriver) and activities (e.g., fixing a car, shaving) are associated with males (Levy et al., 1998; Poulin-Dubois et al., 2002). By age 3, they display knowledge of gender stereotypes for toys, clothing, occupations, and activities (Campbell et al., 2004; Fagot et al., 1992; Zosuls et al., 2008). For example, children of this age generally agree that boys play with cars and trucks whereas girls play with dolls. Gender-stereotyped knowledge of activities and occupations increases rapidly between ages 3 and 5 and is mastered by age 6 or 7 (Leaper & Friedman, 2007; C. F. Miller et al., 2006; Zosuls et al., 2008). For a closer look at how occupational stereotypes develop throughout childhood, read Learn about the Research 4.1.

In addition, preschoolers demonstrate a rudimentary awareness of gender stereotypes for personality traits. Traits such as "cries a lot," "gets feelings hurt easily," "needs help," "likes to give hugs and kisses," and "can't fix things" are applied to girls, while "hits people," "likes to win at playing games," "is not afraid of scary things," and "fixes things" are seen as characteristics of boys (Bauer et al., 1998; Ruble & Martin, 1998). Preschoolers are also more likely to label an ambiguous emotional display by boys as anger, but as sadness when displayed by girls (Parmley & Cunningham, 2008). In general, knowledge of gender-typical personality traits emerges later than other stereotype information (Eisenberg et al., 1996) and increases throughout elementary school (Best & Williams, 1993).

The gender stereotypes learned in the toddler and preschool years become quite rigid between 5 and 7 years of age. They then become more flexible until early adolescence when they begin to become more traditional again (Crouter et al., 2007; Liben & Bigler, 2002; Martin et al., 2002; Martin & Ruble, 2004; Trautner et al., 2005). For example, Thomas Alfieri and his colleagues (Alfieri et al., 1996) presented 12 trait-related terms, half of them feminine and half masculine, to children ranging in age from 9 to 16 years. The children were asked whether the items described males, females, or both. Gender-trait flexibility, indicated by choosing the "both" option, peaked at ages 11 and 12 and declined thereafter. Boys showed less flexibility than girls, particularly regarding masculine traits. Similarly, research by Elaine Blakemore (2003) and by Lisa Serbin and her colleagues (Serbin et al., 1993) has found that 11-year-olds know more about stereotypes than younger children but

LEARN ABOUT THE RESEARCH 4.1
Gender Stereotypes about Occupations

The stereotype that certain occupations are more appropriate for one gender than the other emerges early in childhood (Helwig, 1998). Even children as young as 2 and 3 years of age make a distinction between "women's jobs" and "men's jobs" (Betz, 2006). Girls generally are less rigid in their occupational stereotypes than boys (Helwig, 1998; Jessell & Beymer, 1992). In addition, girls are more likely to have nonstereotyped career aspirations for themselves (Belansky et al., 1993; Fulcher, 2005). In one study (Etaugh & Liss, 1992), kindergarten through eighth-grade children were asked about their occupational aspirations. Through the third grade, most girls chose traditional feminine occupations, such as nurse and teacher. About 25 percent listed

traditionally male occupations, such as doctor and pilot. Older girls, however, were more likely than younger ones to choose a traditionally masculine career and were less likely to pick a feminine one. Boys, on the other hand, aspired to masculine careers at all ages and *never* chose a feminine occupation. The results for females may be related to the finding that, by fourth grade, children view stereotypical feminine occupations less favorably than masculine occupations (Bukatko & Shedd, 1999). In studies done in the early 1970s, boys aspired to a wider variety of occupations than did girls. However, more recent studies report that girls are now selecting more varied occupations than boys (Helwig, 1998; Phipps, 1995; Trice et al., 1995).

What Does It Mean?

1. Why are girls more flexible in their career aspirations than boys?
2. Why are male-dominated careers more attractive to both girls and boys than are female-dominated careers?

3. What are some ways that gender stereotypes about occupations can be reduced?

---

are also more aware of gender-role exceptions, such as girls using tools and sports equipment, and boys engaging in domestic chores. While these older children retain the broad stereotypes, their increasing cognitive maturity allows them to recognize the arbitrary aspects of gender categories, and they are more willing to accept and even try behaviors that are typical of the other gender (Etaugh & Rathus, 1995; Katz & Walsh, 1991). How do gender stereotypes develop in other cultures? Read Explore Other Cultures 4.1.

Gender-Related Activities and Interests

We have seen that children acquire gender stereotypes at an early age. Are these stereotypes reflected in the interests children develop and the play activities they choose? Let's now examine this question.

EXPLORE OTHER CULTURES 4.1
How Do Children Develop Gender Stereotypes in Other Cultures?

Deborah Best and John Williams (described in Best & Thomas, 2004) developed a Sex Stereotype Measure to assess children's knowledge of gender stereotypes. When they gave it to 5-, 8-, and 11-year-olds in 25 countries, they found that stereotype learning in all countries accelerated during the early school years and was completed during adolescence. Girls and boys learned thestereotypes at the same rate. There was a tendency for male-typed traits to be learned somewhat earlier than female-typed traits. However, female-typed traits were learned earlier than male traits in Latin/Catholic cultures (Brazil, Chile, Portugal, Venezuela) where, according to Best and Williams, the female stereotype is more positive than the male stereotype. In predominantly Muslim countries, children learned the stereotypes at an earlier age than in non-Muslim countries, perhaps reflecting the greater divide between female and male roles in Muslim cultures.

Physical Performance and Sports

In the preschool and elementary school years, girls and boys are fairly similar in their motor skills. Boys are slightly stronger, and they can typically run faster, throw a ball farther, and jump higher (Mondschein et al., 2000). Their activity levels also tend to be greater, at least in some settings (Danner et al., 1991). Girls are better at tasks requiring overall flexibility, precise movement, and coordination of their arms and legs. This gives them an edge in activities such as jumping jacks, balancing on one foot, and gymnastics (Etaugh & Rathus, 1995).

Gender differences in motor skills favoring boys become increasingly pronounced from childhood through adolescence (Small & Schultz, 1990; Thomas & French, 1985). What might account for this change? Thomas and French suggest that childhood gender differences in motor skills (with the exception of throwing) are more likely a result of environmental factors than biological ones. Ruth Hall (2008) points out that boys receive more opportunities, encouragement, and support for participating in sports. It is not surprising that by middle childhood, boys in most cultures spend more time than girls in vigorous, competitive, athletic activities, particularly in team sports (Colley et al., 2005).

During puberty, hormonal changes increase muscle mass for boys and fat for girls, giving boys an advantage in strength, size, and power. But hormones are only part of the story. Social pressures on girls to act more feminine and less "tomboyish" intensify during adolescence, contributing to girls' declining interest and participation in athletic activities (Colley et al., 2005; McHale, Shanahan et al., 2004; Vilhjalmsson & Kristjansdottir, 2003). This trend is troubling, given that involvement in sports is associated with a number of positive traits in girls and women, including higher self-esteem, better body image, enhanced sense of competence and control, reduced stress and depression, delayed sexual activity, lessened likelihood of substance abuse, better academic performance, and

Girls are better than boys at tasks requiring flexibility and precise movement.

higher college graduation rates (Daniels & Leaper, 2006; Fredricks & Eccles, 2006; Kulig et al., 2003; Pate et al., 2000; Shaffer & Wittes, 2006; Smolak, 2006; Troutman & Dufur, 2007). The good news is that the participation of girls and young women in sports has increased dramatically since the passage in 1972 of Title IX of the Education Amendments Act. This federal legislation bars discrimination in all educational programs, including athletics. The number of girls and women in high school and college athletic programs is at least 10 times greater now than before Title IX (Acosta & Carpenter, 2008). Currently, 42 percent of U.S. college athletes are women, with the percentage being highest in larger institutions (Women's Sports Foundation, 2007). Canada has seen a similar rise in female student athletes (Hoeber, 2008). The bad news is that schools still spend disproportionately more money on scholarships, recruiting, and operating expenses for men's sports and on the salaries of coaches (mostly White males) of men's teams (Cunningham, 2008; Lipka, 2007; Suggs, 2005; Wolverton, 2006). Moreover, since the passage of Title IX, the percentage of college women's teams coached by female head coaches has dropped from 90 percent to 43 percent (Acosta & Carpenter, 2008). Only 8 percent of Division I college programs have women as athletic directors (Acosta & Carpenter, 2008). Furthermore, Black women have made fewer gains than White women, both as players and coaches (R. L. Hall, 2008; Smith, 2007; Suggs, 2005a, 2005b).

Toys and Play

Gender differences in children's play activities and interests are more evident than they are in other areas such as personality qualities or attitudes (McHale et al., 1999). Girls and boys begin to differ in their preference for certain toys and play activities

Participation of girls and women in sports has increased dramatically since Title IX, but men's sports are better funded.

early in life, and at times these interests are quite intense (DeLoache et al., 2007). By the time they are 12 to 18 months old, girls prefer to play with dolls, cooking sets, dress-up clothes, and soft toys, while boys choose vehicles, sports equipment, and tools (Campbell et al., 2000; Leaper & Friedman, 2007; Serbin et al., 2001). By 3 years of age, gender-typical toy choices are well established and these differences persist throughout childhood (Cherney & London, 2006; McHale, Kim et al., 2004; McHale, Shanahan et al., 2004). However, girls are more likely than boys to display neutral or cross-gender toy choices and activities (Cherney & London, 2006; Green et al., 2004; McHale, Kim et al., 2004; Wood et al., 2002). For example, girls are more likely to request transportation toys and sports equipment as gifts than boys are to ask for dolls (Etaugh & Liss, 1992).

Why are girls more likely to depart from the stereotype? In most cultures, masculine activities have greater prestige than feminine ones. Thus, according to the social status hypothesis (see Chapter 3), a girl who plays with "boys'" toys will be viewed more positively than a boy who plays with "girls'" toys, who will be seen as lowering his status. As we shall see later, girls who prefer boys' company and activities do, in fact, receive more peer and parental acceptance than boys who prefer the company and activity of girls (Carr, 2007). Moreover, children generally find boys' toys more interesting and appealing than girls' toys (Blakemore & Centers, 2005; Rosenblum, 1991). You can do lots more fun and exciting things with Legos than with a tea set!

Because of their preferences, girls and boys experience very different play environments (Edwards et al., 2001). During the preschool and elementary school years, boys spend more time than girls in vigorous physical outdoor activities such as playing with large vehicles, climbing, exploratory play, sports, and **rough-and-tumble play,** which consists of *playful chasing, tumbling, hitting and wrestling, often accompanied by laughter and screaming* (Lindsey & Mize, 2001; Pellegrini et al., 2002; Rose & Rudolph, 2006). Boys are more likely to engage in competitive activities, to play in large groups of five or more children, and to take more physical risks in their play (Rose & Rudolph, 2006, Ruble et al., 2006; Weinberger & Stein, 2007). Their fantasy play focuses on action and adventure themes (Leaper & Friedman, 2007). In conflict situations with other children, they are more likely to use powerful, controlling strategies (Sims et al., 1998). Girls' play preferences, on the other hand, include dolls, domestic play, reading, and arts and crafts. They also engage in more symbolic (i.e., "pretend") play than boys (Edwards et al., 2001; McHale, Gouter & Tucker, 2001). Girls' play is more sedentary, more cooperative, more socially competent, and more supervised and structured by adults. Also, girls are more likely than boys to play with a small group of children or just one other child (Rose & Rudolph, 2006; Rubin et al., 2006; Ruble et al., 2006). To take a closer look at play patterns of girls and boys, try Get Involved 4.1.

Gender Segregation

By 3 years of age, children prefer playing with children of the same gender, with girls showing this preference somewhat earlier than boys (A. Campbell et al., 2004; Hay et al., 2004; Martin & Fabes, 2001). Gender segregation increases during childhood and is especially strong in the elementary school years (Maccoby, 2002; Rose & Rudolph, 2006). Even when children choose seats in the lunchroom or get into line, they frequently arrange themselves in same-gender groups. Peer pressure can be a powerful motivator, as illustrated in Barrie Thorne's (1993) observation of second graders seating themselves in the lunchroom. One table was filling with both boys and girls, when a high-status second-grade boy walked by. He commented loudly, "Too many girls," and headed for a seat at another table. The boys at the first table picked up their trays and moved, leaving no boys at the first table, which had now been declared taboo. Children who cross the "gender boundary" are unpopular with their peers, although there are certain conditions under which contact with the other gender is permissible. Often these overtures involve playful teasing, pushing, and grabbing (Pellegrini, 2001), as seen in Table 4.2.

Why do children play primarily with children of their own gender? According to Eleanor Maccoby (1998), there are two reasons why girls may avoid boys. One is that they don't like the rough, aggressive, dominant play style of boys. A second is that boys

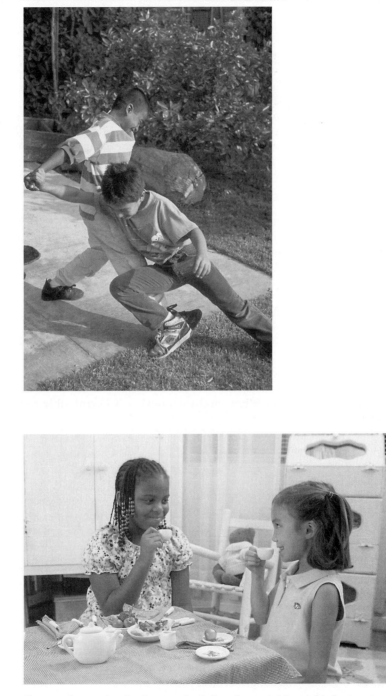

Boys spend more time in vigorous physical outdoor activities; girls' play is quieter, more symbolic, and more socially competent.

GET INVOLVED 4.1

Play Patterns of Girls and Boys

Observe preschool-aged children in a day-care center or preschool during a free-play session. Keep a record of the following behaviors:

1. The toys that girls choose and those that boys choose.

2. The activities girls engage in and those that boys engage in.
3. How often (a) girls play with other girls; (b) boys play with other boys; (c) girls and boys play with each other.

What Does It Mean?

1. Did boys and girls show different patterns of toy choice and activity preference? If so, describe these patterns. How do you account for the differences you observed (if any)?
2. Which toys in general were most in demand? Were these "girl" toys, "boy" toys, or gender-neutral toys?

3. Did boys prefer to play with same-gender peers more than girls did, was it the other way around, or were there no differences? How do you account for the differences you observed (if any)?

TABLE 4.2   Knowing the Rules: Under What Circumstances Is It Permissible to Have Contact with the Other Gender in Grade School?

Rule:	The contact is accidental.
Example:	You're not looking where you are going, and you bump into someone.
Rule:	The contact is incidental.
Example:	You go to get some lemonade and wait while two children of the other gender get some. (There should be no conversation.)
Rule:	The contact is in the guise of some clear and necessary purpose.
Example:	You may say "pass the lemonade" to persons of the other gender at the next table. No interest in them is expressed.
Rule:	An adult compels you to have contact.
Example:	"Go get that map from X and Y and bring it to me."
Rule:	You are accompanied by someone of your own gender.
Example:	Two girls may talk to two boys though physical closeness with your own partner must be maintained and intimacy with the others is disallowed.
Rule:	The interaction or contact is accompanied by disavowal.
Example:	You say someone is ugly or hurl some other insult or (more commonly for boys) push or throw something at them as you pass by.

Source: From Sroufe et al. (1993). Reproduced with permission of the Society for Research in Child Development, Inc.

are unresponsive to their polite suggestions. Analogously, boys may avoid girls because girls are not responsive to their rough play (Eisenberg et al., 1996). An alternative view is that rather than actively trying to avoid children of the other gender, children simply prefer the company of their own gender because they share a preference for gender-typed toys and activities (Zosuls et al., 2008).

Influences on Gender Development

Socialization refers to *the process by which each generation passes along to children the knowledge, beliefs, and skills that constitute the culture of the social group.* Since societies prescribe somewhat different social roles for adult females and males, girls and boys are typically socialized differently in order to prepare them for the adult roles they will play (Basow, 2008; Reid et al., 2008). This is a restatement of the third theme of our book; namely, that much of gender is socially constructed. A variety of sources help shape the behaviors and interests of boys and girls. These include parents, teachers, peers, and the media. In Chapter 3, we briefly mentioned the role of these influences when we discussed theories of gender typing. In this section, we examine these factors in greater detail.

Parents

When I was 4 or 5, my father asked me what I wanted to be when I grew up.

ME: *I'll be a carpenter and make furniture.*
HIM: *Oh, no, Holly, girls can't be carpenters. Only boys can.*
ME: *Okay, then I'll be a fisherman.*
HIM: *No, girls can't be fishermen either. They aren't strong enough.*

(Holly, 45-year-old middle-school teacher)

Children's gender-typed views about themselves and others are closely linked to the gender self-concepts and attitudes of their parents (Mendelsohn & Perry-Jenkins, 2007; Tenenbaum & Leaper, 2002). How do parents transmit their views on gender to their children? One of the most obvious ways in which parents influence gender development is by providing their sons and daughters with distinctive clothing, room furnishings, and toys. Infant girls are likely to be dressed in a ruffled pink outfit (sometimes with a bow attached to wisps of hair), whereas baby boys typically wear blue (Pomerleau et al., 1990; Shakin et al., 1985). The bedrooms of infant and toddler girls contain dolls, dollhouses, and domestic items and are decorated in pastel colors, frills, and flowery patterns. Baby boys' rooms feature animal themes, sturdy furniture, blue bedding, and a variety of sports equipment, vehicles, military toys, and educational materials (Basow, 2008). Clearly, infants are too young to express their preference in these matters.

Could it be that infant girls and boys give off subtle cues that influence their parents' gender-typed behavior? Research suggests that this is not the case. For example, in some studies, adults are asked to play with an unfamiliar infant who has a girl's name and is dressed in girls' clothing. Other adults play with an infant who wears boys' clothes and has a boy's name. (In fact, it is actually the same baby, who is dressed and named according to whether it is introduced as one gender or another.) Adults who believe the child is a boy are more likely to offer "him" a football or hammer and to encourage physical activity. Those who think the baby is a girl are more apt to offer a doll (Etaugh & Rathus, 1995; Stern & Karraker, 1989).

Parents and other adults are less likely to purchase cross-gender toys than to purchase gender-typical toys for children, even when children request the cross-gender toy (Etaugh & Liss, 1992; Karraker & Hartley, 2007). Boys are even less likely than girls to receive such toys (Fisher-Thompson et al., 1995). Parents, especially fathers, also tend to offer gender-typical toys to children during free play and are more supportive when children engage in gender-typical activities than in cross-gender activities (Basow, 2008; Blakemore & Hill, 2008). Both mothers and fathers play more roughly with little boys than with little girls, and fathers in particular roughhouse with their young sons (Bronstein, 2006; Lindsey & Mize, 2001). Given that fathers treat children in more gender-typical ways than mothers do, it is not surprising that children's gender-typical activity preferences are more closely linked to their father's gender-related attitudes than to their mother's (McHale et al., 1999).

One way in which parents foster gender stereotypes in their children is through conversation. Susan Gelman and her colleagues (Gelman et al., 2004) videotaped mothers and their daughters or sons (ages 2, 4, or 6) discussing a picture book that focused on gender. Although mothers rarely expressed gender stereotypes directly, they emphasized gender concepts indirectly. For example, they provided gender labels (e.g., "That's a policeman"), contrasted males and females (e.g., "Is that a girl job or a boy job?"), and gave approval to their children's stereotyped statements (e.g., "Ballet dancers are girls!").

Parents also shape their children's environment by assigning chores based on gender (Cunningham, 2001; Dodson & Dickert, 2004). In many cultures around the world, girls are more likely to be given domestic and child-care tasks centered around the home, whereas boys typically are assigned outside chores such as yard work and taking out trash (Eisenberg et al., 1996; Larson & Verma, 1999). For a closer look at the relationship between toy giving, chore assignments, and children's gender-related development, read Learn about the Research 4.2.

Parents treat daughters and sons differently in other ways than encouraging activities or assigning chores. For example mothers talk more to their daughters than to their sons as early as 6 months of age (Clearfield & Nelson, 2006). They also use warmer, more supportive speech with daughters than with sons (Gleason & Ely, 2002). Earlier, we saw that mothers also talk more about emotions with their daughters. Parents also emphasize prosocial behaviors and politeness more with their daughters than their sons (Eisenberg & Fabes, 1998) and act more warmly toward their daughters (Zhou et al., 2002). Furthermore, cross-cultural research in Argentina, Italy, and the United States shows that mothers are more emotionally involved with their toddler daughters than with their toddler sons, and that daughters, in turn, are more responsive than sons (Bornstein et al., 2008; Lovas, 2005). In addition, parents control their daughters more than their sons, while granting their sons greater autonomy and greater opportunities to

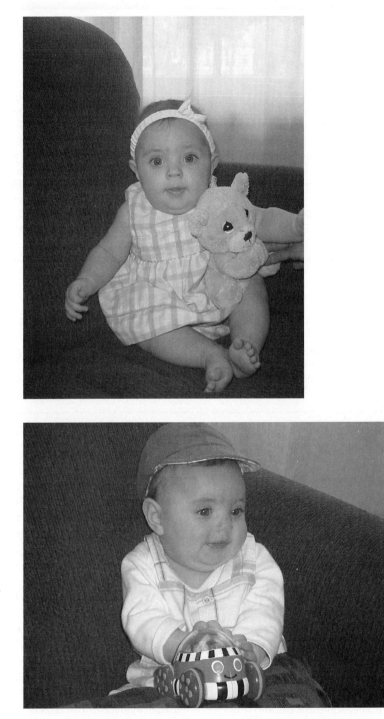

Isabel or Isaac? Adults are more likely to offer a doll to "Isabel" and a football to "Isaac." (In fact, both babies are Claire's granddaughter, Isabel.)

LEARN ABOUT THE RESEARCH **4.2**

Learning Gender-Related Roles at Home and at Play

Are the toys children request and receive and the chores adults assign them related to gender differences in play activities and occupational goals? To study this question, Claire Etaugh and Marsha Liss (1992) gave questionnaires to 245 5- to 13-year-olds before and after Christmas, asking which gifts they requested and which ones they received.

The children also were asked to name their friends, play activities, assigned chores, and occupational aspirations. Children generally requested and received gender-typical toys. They were less likely to receive requested cross-gender toys (such as a girl asking for a baseball glove). Children who wanted and received gender-typical toys were also more likely to be assigned gender-typical chores (such as yard work and taking out the garbage for boys, and kitchen work and dusting for girls), to engage in gender-typical play activities, and to have same-gender friends. Girls preferred masculine toys and jobs more than boys preferred feminine ones. As they got older, both girls and boys increasingly preferred masculine toys, and girls increasingly chose masculine occupations.

What Does It Mean?

1. Why do you think parents and other adults are more likely to give children a requested gender-typical toy than a requested cross-gender toy? What message does this send? Did you ever ask for a gender-atypical toy? Did you get it?

2. Why do girls prefer masculine toys and jobs more than boys like feminine ones? Explain.
3. How might the assignment of gender-typical chores help influence the formation of gender roles?

take risks (Leaper & Friedman, 2007; Morrongiello & Hogg, 2004; Smetana & Daddis, 2002). For example, parents are more likely to make decisions for girls and to give them help even if it is not requested. Boys, on the other hand, are encouraged to make their own decisions and to solve problems on their own (Pomerantz & Ruble, 1998). Moreover, mothers expect more risky behaviors from sons than from daughters and consequently intervene less frequently to stop boys' injury-risk behavior in play settings (Morrongiello & Dawber, 2000; Morrongiello & Hogg, 2004).

Parents serve as role models for their children's development of gender concepts (Sutfin et al., 2008). Take the case of maternal employment. More mothers work outside the home today than ever before. Also, although to a lesser degree, more fathers are participating in child care and household chores (see Chapter 11). Not surprisingly, researchers have found that maternal employment is associated with less stereotyped gender-related concepts and preferences in boys and girls (Hoffman & Youngblade, 2001; Lewis, 2007; Riggio & Desrochers, 2005). Children also show less stereotyping in their activity preferences if their fathers are highly involved in sharing child care and housework and if their mothers frequently engage in traditional "masculine" household tasks such as washing the car and doing yard work (Etaugh & O'Brien, 2003; Murray & Steil, 2000; Serbin et al., 1993).

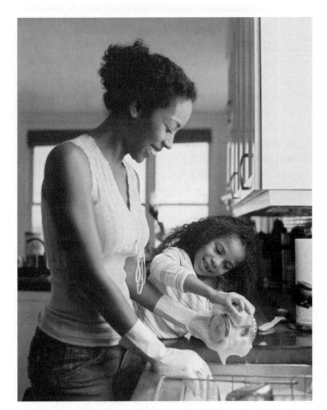

In many cultures, girls are more likely than boys to be assigned domestic chores in the home.

Children growing up in single-parent homes tend to be less traditional in their gender stereotypes and activities than those from two-parent homes (Leaper, 2000). One reason for this is that a single parent engages in activities normally carried out by both parents, such as housework, child care, home repairs, and going to work. In addition, the absent parent is most often the father, who usually encourages children's adherence to gender norms more strongly than the mother does (Etaugh & Rathus, 1995; Katz, 1987).

Parents in both North America and Europe react negatively to children who do not adhere to traditional gender roles. As we saw in Chapter 2, this is especially true for boys (Blakemore & Hill, 2008; Iervolino et al., 2005). In one study (Sandnabba & Ahlberg, 1999), for example, Finnish parents expected cross-gender boys to be less well adjusted psychologically and more likely to become gay than cross-gender girls.

Young children whose parents strongly encourage gender-typical play learn gender labels at an earlier age than other children (Fagot & Leinbach, 1993). Moreover, preschool boys choose more stereotyped toys when they believe that their fathers think cross-gender play is "bad" (Raag & Rackliff, 1998). More than one male college student has confided to Claire that as a child he longed to play with his sister's Barbie dolls but would do so only when no one else was home.

Siblings

The role of siblings in gender role socialization has received less attention than that of parents and peers. Yet siblings are the most frequent out-of-school companions for children and young adolescents (Parke & Buriel, 2006). Not surprisingly, siblings make significant contributions to each other's development (Kim et al., 2006, 2007; Parke & Buriel, 2006). Consistent with social-learning predictions about the importance of role models (see Chapter 3), older siblings appear to play a role in the gender socialization of their younger siblings (Crouter et al., 2007; McHale et al., 2003). For example, a large-scale longitudinal study in England (Rust et al., 2000) found that both girls with older sisters and boys with older brothers were more gender-typed than only children of their gender. These only children, in turn, were more gender-typed than children with other-gender older siblings.

School

Schools convey powerful messages to children about gender typing. For one thing, the school social structure is biased. Women hold most of the low-paying elementary school teaching positions, while males occupy more than half of the higher-paying high school teaching jobs. Additionally, men are more often in the leadership positions of principal and superintendent (Meece & Scantlebury, 2006). This sends a clear signal that men hold more power than women, one of the themes of this book.

In the classroom, girls are often treated unequally by their teachers. That was the conclusion of the American Association of University Women (AAUW) (AAUW, 1992) in a report reviewing over 1,000 publications about girls and education. Both the AAUW report and a more recent meta-analysis of empirical studies (Jones & Dindia, 2004) showed that teachers pay far less attention to girls than to boys. This finding is strikingly documented by Myra and David Sadker (1994) in their book *Failing at Fairness*. The Sadkers found that teachers call on boys more often and give them more time to answer questions. Boys are more likely to be praised, corrected, helped, and criticized constructively, all of which promote student learning. Girls are more likely to receive a bland and ambiguous "okay" response. Black girls are the least likely to be given clear feedback. Teachers are more likely to accept calling out from boys, while girls are reprimanded for the same behavior. Boys are rewarded for being smart, while girls are rewarded for being neat, pretty, and compliant. In addition, teachers are likely to give girls the answer when they ask for help but tend to help boys use strategies to figure out the answer themselves (DeZolt & Hull, 2001; Meece & Scantlebury, 2006). Unfortunately, teachers are generally unaware that they are treating boys and girls differently. Later in the chapter, we will see how such unequal treatment may contribute to the declining self-esteem of adolescent girls.

African American girls may encounter unique educational perceptions and obstacles. A recent two-year study at a predominantly Black and Latino middle school found that Black girls performed well academically, but that teachers often questioned their manners and behavior. Many teachers perceived the Black girls as "loud and confrontational" and tried to mold them into displaying more "lady-like" behaviors, such as being quieter and more passive (Morris, 2007).

Peers

Children exert strong pressures on each other to engage in gender-appropriate behavior. As early as the preschool years, they modify their activity and toy preferences to conform to the patterns their peers reward. The mere presence of other children inhibits gender-inappropriate play (Eisenberg et al., 1996; Lott & Maluso, 2001). Children who show gender-typical behavior are accepted by their peers (Yunger et al., 2004). Boys who display traditionally feminine activities are teased, rejected, and disliked by both boys and girls, whereas girls who engage in traditionally masculine activities generally are accepted by children of both sexes (Rubin et al., 2006). Even the label given to boys who show cross-gender behavior—"sissy"—has negative overtones, whereas the term used for girls who display cross-gender behavior—"tomboy"—does not. It is thus not surprising that gender-atypical boys have more social adjustment problems than gender-atypical girls (Kreiger, 2005).

Media

We saw in Chapter 2 that females are underrepresented in the media and that females and males are portrayed in stereotyped ways. What is the impact of these media messages on children's gender-related learning? Most of the research has focused on television. Children's television viewing averages 2–5 hours a day for preschoolers and peaks at about 4 hours a day at age 11 (Fabes & Martin, 2003), but there are large individual differences in viewing. Children who are heavy viewers have greater knowledge of gender stereotypes (Van Evra, 2004; Ward & Harrison, 2005; L. M. Ward, 2007). In these correlational studies, it is difficult to know the direction of influence. Television may cause children to develop stronger stereotypes. On the other hand, children with stronger stereotypes may choose to watch more television because it shows images that are consistent with their beliefs (Van Evra, 2004). A third alternative is that both factors are involved.

Stronger evidence of the impact of television comes from experiments that examined whether television can undo or counter the stereotypic messages. These studies found that exposure to characters who engage in nontraditional behaviors and roles (nurturing boys and girl auto mechanics, for example) reduced children's gender stereotypes about activities, domestic roles, and occupations (Ward & Harrison, 2005).

For a closer and more personal look at influences on gender role development, try the exercise in Get Involved 4.2.

Puberty

I think what is happening to me is so wonderful, and not only what can be seen on my body, but all that is taking place inside [. . .] Each time I have a period (and that has only been three times) I have the feeling that in spite of all the pain, discomfort, and mess, I have a sweet secret, and that is why, although it is nothing but a nuisance to me in a way, I always long for the time that I shall feel that secret within me again. (Frank, 1995, pp. 158–159)

GET INVOLVED 4.2

Influences on Gender Development

Describe your own gender socialization. Focus on specific things that were said, done, or modeled by (a) your parents and other family members; (b) your teachers; (c) your peers; (d) television, books, and other media. Then ask two female friends and two male friends to do the same.

What Does It Mean?

Include your own responses when answering the following questions:

1. Did the females and the males you interviewed describe different kinds of socialization experiences? If so, what were they?
2. Identify aspects of your own socialization and that of your friends that are consistent with the material presented in the chapter.

3. When did you realize there were social expectations for your gender?
4. What happened in situations when you crossed gender lines?
5. How have your socialization experiences affected your current choices in activities friends, major, career, etc.?

Source: Based on Gilbert and Scher (1999).

One of the most moving accounts of a young woman's entry into adolescence was written by Anne Frank, a Jewish girl who lived in Nazi-occupied Holland in World War II. Anne kept a diary during the two years she and her family hid from the Germans in an attic. Anne wrote about her sudden physical growth, commenting on the shoes that no longer fit her and the undershirts that became "so small that they don't even cover my stomach" (Frank, 1995, p. 101). She also grew concerned about her appearance and asked her sister "if she thought I was very ugly" (p. 55). A few months before she and her family were discovered and sent to die in a concentration camp, Anne wrote the above entry about the "wonders that are happening to [my] body."

In this section we will explore the physical transformations of adolescence. First we describe the events of puberty. We then discuss gender differences in these events. Finally, we examine individual differences in rates of physical maturation.

Events of Puberty

Puberty is the *period of life during which sexual organs mature and the ability to reproduce emerges*. Increasing levels of sex hormones stimulate the development of primary and secondary sex characteristics. **Primary sex characteristics**—in girls, the ovaries, fallopian tubes, uterus, and vagina—*are structures that make reproduction possible*. **Secondary sex characteristics** are *visible signs of sexual maturity that are not directly involved in reproduction*, such as breast development and the appearance of pubic and underarm hair (Rathus et al., 2008). Table 4.3 summarizes these changes.

TABLE 4.3   Stages of Pubertal Development in Females

Beginning sometime between ages 8 and 11

Pituitary hormones stimulate ovaries to increase production of estrogen.
Internal reproductive organs begin to grow.
Pubic hair begins to appear.
Breast development begins.

Beginning sometime between ages 9 and 15

First the areola (the darker area around the nipple) and then the breasts increase
   in size and become more rounded.
Pubic hair becomes darker and coarser.
Growth in height continues.
Body fat continues to round body contours.
A normal vaginal discharge becomes noticeable.
Sweat and oil glands increase in activity, and acne may appear.
Internal and external reproductive organs and genitals grow, which makes the
   vagina longer and the labia more pronounced.

Beginning sometime between ages 10 and 16

Areola and nipples grow, often forming a second mound sticking out from the
   rounded breast mound.
Pubic hair begins to grow in a triangular shape and to cover the center of the mons.
Underarm hair appears.
Menarche occurs.
Internal reproductive organs continue to develop.
Ovaries may begin to release mature eggs capable of being fertilized.
Growth in height slows.

Beginning sometime between ages 12 and 19

Breasts near adult size and shape.
Pubic hair fully covers the mons and spreads to the top of the thighs.
The voice may deepen slightly (but not as much as in males).
Menstrual cycles gradually become more regular.
Some further changes in body shape may occur into the early 20s.

Note: This table is a general guideline. Changes may appear sooner or later than shown, and not always
in the indicated sequence.
Source: Rathus et al. (2008), p. 422. Reprinted with permission from Allyn & Bacon.

Most White girls begin to show signs of puberty by the age of 10, and Black girls do so about a year earlier (DeRose & Brooks-Gunn, 2006). Other studies confirm that feelings of sexual attraction, one of the behavioral hallmarks of puberty, also first appear between the ages of 9 and 10 (Marano, 1997). However, recent research shows that many girls start puberty far earlier than previously thought. For example, Marcia Herman-Giddens and her colleagues (1997, 2004) found that by the age of 8, more than 10 percent of White girls and about one-third of Black girls have some breast development, pubic hair, or both.

Menarche

Menarche, *the first menstrual period,* is a dramatic and meaningful event in women's lives. Many women have vivid memories of their first menstrual period and, even years later, can describe details of the experience (Chrisler, 2008a). (If you, the reader, are female, can you?)

The average age of menarche in the United States is about 12.2 years for Black girls and 12.5 years for White girls, although it is quite normal for a girl to begin to menstruate any time between 9 and 16 (DeRose & Brooks-Gunn, 2006; McDowell et al., 2007). *Over the past 150 years, the onset of puberty and the attainment of adult height and weight have occurred at progressively earlier ages in the United States and western Europe* (Posner, 2006). This **secular trend** is most likely a result of better nutrition and medical care. The onset of puberty seems to be triggered when individuals reach a certain body weight. Improved nutrition, health, and living conditions have led to the achievement of that weight at a younger age (DeRose & Brooks-Gunn, 2006). The rise in obesity among American children may play a role as well, since girls with a high percentage of body fat in early childhood show more advanced pubertal development at age 9 (Lee et al., 2007).

Environmental stress is also linked to an earlier onset of puberty (Ellis, 2004). Research has found that girls from divorced families or families high in parental conflict begin to menstruate earlier than girls whose parents are married or have lower levels of conflict (DeRose & Brooks-Gunn, 2006; Mendle et al., 2006). One explanation for these findings is that stress may lead to overeating, which increases body weight, which then triggers the onset of puberty. Alternatively, we know that early-maturing mothers tend to have early-maturing daughters, possibly because of genetic factors (Belsky et al., 2007; Ellis & Essex, 2007). Early maturers become sexually active, marry, and give birth at younger ages than others. But early marriages are more likely to end in divorce. So, girls whose parents divorce may reach puberty early not because of parental conflict and divorce, but simply because their own mothers matured early (Mustanski et al., 2004).

In North America, girls have mixed feelings about starting to menstruate, with Black and Latina girls reporting more negative attitudes than White girls (Chrisler, 2008a). On the one hand, menstruation is an eagerly awaited sign of growing up (Fingerson, 2006). In the words of one adolescent girl, "It's a great feeling knowing that one day when you want to have a baby, that you can do it. To me that's just amazing" (Commonwealth Fund, 1997, p. 39). Still, some girls also believe that menstruation is embarrassing, frightening, or disgusting (Chrisler, 2008a; Kissling, 2006). Young adolescent girls also worry about having an "accident" and about someone knowing they have their menstrual period. "When you're in middle school and you're getting your period, you don't want to tell anyone. I was ashamed when I got my period," (Commonwealth Fund, 1997, p. 39).

Feminine hygiene advertisements reflect and reinforce these concerns by focusing on the discomfort and messiness of menstrual periods and the potential embarrassment of "showing" (Chrisler, 2008a). Women are taught to conceal the fact that they are menstruating. Even within the family household, menstruation often is not openly discussed. One of Claire's students shared the following experience: "When I started my period, I didn't tell a soul. I wrote down 'pads' on my parents' grocery list and they showed up in the bathroom closet. That was the extent of the 'birds and bees' talk in my family." Cultural pressure to hide menstrual cycles and marketing pitches for products that keep a woman clean and deodorized during her menstrual cycles send a clear message to women that their bodies are unacceptable in their natural state. Moreover, with the recent availability of contraceptives that eliminate menstrual periods, ads for these drugs emphasize the debilitating effects of periods and the joys of menstrual suppression (Houppert, 2007). Not surprisingly women who place a great deal of emphasis on their appearance and body image have more negative attitudes and emotions, including disgust and shame, toward their menstrual cycles (Roberts, 2004).

A negative attitude toward menstruation before menarche is associated with greater menstrual discomfort (Yeung, Tang, & Lee, 2005). For example, girls whose mothers lead them to believe that menstruation will be uncomfortable or unpleasant later report more severe menstrual symptoms. Moreover, girls who begin to menstruate earlier than their peers, or who are otherwise unprepared and uninformed about pubertal changes, find menarche especially distressing (American Psychological Association, 2002; Reid et al., 2008). When 14- and 15-year-old girls were asked what advice they would give to younger girls about menarche, they recommended emphasizing the normalcy of menstruation, providing practical information on handling menstrual periods, and discussing what menarche actually feels like (American Psychological Association, 2002).

Gender Differences in Puberty

Besides the obvious differences in secondary sex characteristics, girls and boys differ in other ways as they move through puberty. For one thing, girls begin and finish puberty about two years before boys, on average (DeRose & Brooks-Gunn, 2006). The **adolescent growth spurt,** *a rapid increase in height and weight,* also starts earlier in girls, at about age 9, while boys start their spurt at about age 11. The period of peak growth occurs at age 12 for girls and 14 for boys, on average, and then tapers off for two years or so. Boys grow more than girls during their spurt, adding an average of 12 inches to their height, while girls grow slightly over 11 inches. Boys also gain more weight than girls do during their growth spurt (Susman & Rogol, 2004).

Body shape changes in puberty as well. Girls gain twice as much fatty tissue as boys, largely in the breasts, hips, and buttocks, while boys gain almost twice as much muscle tissue as girls (DeRose & Brooks-Gunn, 2006). These changes produce the more rounded shape of women as compared to men.

As the growth spurt begins to slow down, adolescents reach sexual maturity. In girls, the most obvious sign is menarche. We shall discuss other aspects of menstruation in Chapter 7.

Early and Late Maturation in Girls

> *I remember when I got my first period. It was the summer between fourth and fifth grades—I guess I was 10 . . . By sixth and seventh grades, I had this intense desire to hang out with older kids, usually older boys. I tried pot for the first time when I was 12. I could usually convince people I was 15 when I was in seventh grade and I started hanging out with other girls who looked older . . . Sometimes we would go off with older boys. Often we were drinking or smoking pot . . . Overall, I was pretty unhappy during the teen years; at times, I guess, depressed. I had a hard time fitting in at school even though I got good grades. I was always looking for a group where I belonged. It wasn't until college that I really found my niche.* (Graber & Brooks-Gunn, 2002, p. 35)

The timing of the events of puberty vary considerably from one girl to another (DeRose & Brooks-Gunn, 2006), as shown in Table 4.3. Early-maturing girls may feel awkward and self-conscious because they begin the physical changes of puberty earlier than their peers. Boys may tease them about their height and developing breasts, which can lead to feelings of body shame (Lindberg et al., 2007; Summers-Effler, 2004). In addition, because they look older than they actually are, others may place sexual and other expectations on them that are difficult to meet. No wonder that early maturers tend to have lower self-esteem, higher levels of depression and anxiety, and a poorer body image than girls who mature later (Collins & Steinberg, 2006; Ellis, 2004; Harter, 2006; Posner, 2006; Yuan, 2007).

Early-maturing girls tend to associate with older peers (Poulin & Pedersen, 2007). This may explain why they begin sexual activity at an earlier age and are more likely to engage in risky behavior such as smoking, drinking, substance abuse, and delinquent behavior (Biehl et al., 2007; Ellis, 2004; Posner, 2006). But not all early-maturing girls

The timing of puberty varies considerably from one girl to another.

suffer negative consequences. Instead, early maturation seems to accentuate behavioral problems in girls who had already shown adjustment difficulties earlier in childhood (Weichold et al., 2003).

Once early-maturing girls reach high school, they come into their own socially. They may serve as advisors to their later-maturing girlfriends on such increasingly important topics as makeup, dating, and sex. By the end of high school, early-maturing girls seem to be as well adjusted as other girls (Brody, 1999b). By age 30, they appear to be more self-possessed and self-directed than their later-maturing peers. Perhaps learning to cope with the stresses of puberty at an early age prepares early-maturing girls to deal effectively with later stressful events (Weichold et al., 2003).

Late-maturing girls may have relatively low social status during the middle school and junior high school years. They look and are treated like "little girls" and are often excluded from boy–girl social activities. Late-maturing girls often are dissatisfied with their appearance and lack of popularity. By tenth grade, however, they are noticeably showing the physical signs of puberty. They often wind up more popular and more satisfied with their appearance than early-maturing girls (Simmons & Blyth, 1987). One reason for this may be that late maturers are more likely to develop the culturally valued slender body shape than early maturers, who tend to be somewhat heavier.

Psychosocial Development in Adolescence

How much do I like the kind of person I am? Well, I like some things about me, but I don't like others. I'm glad that I'm popular since it's really important to me to have friends. But in school I don't do as well as the really smart kids. That's OK, because if you're too smart you'll lose your friends. So being smart is just not that important. But what's really important to me is how I look. If I like the way I look, then I really like the kind of person I am. I've also changed. It started when I went to junior high school. I got really depressed. There was this one day when I hated the way I looked, and I didn't get invited to this really important party, and then I got an awful report card, so for a couple of days I thought it would be best to just end it all. I was letting my parents down, I wasn't good-looking anymore, and I wasn't that popular and things were never going to get better. I talked to Sheryl, my best friend, and that helped some. (adapted from Harter, 1990, pp. 364–365)

This self-description from a 15-year-old girl illustrates some of the psychological characteristics of adolescent females. Notice how important physical appearance is to her self-esteem. Note also that she discloses her private thoughts to her best friend. Can you recall what was important to you at age 15?

Adolescence is a time of learning more about oneself and others. Two key issues are developing a sense of who you are and how you feel about yourself. Adherence to traditional gender roles often becomes stronger and girls begin to focus a great deal on their appearance. In this section we explore four aspects of psychosocial development in the adolescent girl: identity formation, self-esteem, gender intensification, and body image.

Identity

One of the most important tasks of adolescence is to develop a sense of **identity,** that is, *deciding who we are and what we want to make of our lives*. According to Erik Erikson (1968, 1980), adolescent identity formation involves commitment to a vocation and a philosophy of life. In order to do so, adolescents must **individuate,** that is, *see themselves as separate and unique*. Carol Gilligan (1982), Sally Archer (1992), Ruthellen Josselson (1994), and others maintain that this model describes the traditional identity development of males better than that of females. They believe that achieving identity for both female and male adolescents requires an interplay between separateness (meeting one's own needs) and connectedness (satisfying the needs of those one cares for) (Jaffe, 1998).

Research supports the view that adolescent females and males take similar paths in their quest for identity. Elements of career choice, personal competence, and interpersonal relationships are central to the identity of both genders (Archer, 1992; Giesbrecht, 1998; Murray, 1998). For one thing, adolescent girls' educational and career aspirations have increased in recent years and now parallel those of boys (Denmark, 1999). In addition, an increasing number of teenagers (83 percent of females and 72 percent of males) say that having a good marriage and family life is extremely important to them as a life goal (Popenoe & Whitehead, 1999). However, whereas most adolescent girls see interconnections between their career goals and family goals, most adolescent boys perceive no connection between the two. For example, young women place greater emphasis than young men do on flexible working hours that facilitate the coordination of employment and childrearing (see Chapter 11). Still, it appears that, nowadays, individual differences in identity development may be more important than gender differences (Archer, 1993; Marcia, 1993).

Unfortunately, little research has been conducted on the identity formation of ethnic minority adolescent girls. The few studies that have been done find that one key factor in this process is the family unit, often an extended kinship network, which is a highly valued part of life among Asian Americans, Blacks, Latinas/os, and Native Americans. Identity with the family and community seems to provide strength and resources for adolescent girls of color as they strive to integrate their ethnicity and their femaleness within a larger society that devalues both (de las Fuentes & Vasquez, 1999; Vasquez & de las Fuentes, 1999).

Self-Esteem

The two really blonde girls in our class dressed better than the rest of the girls, and I always felt like I couldn't compete with them. This feeling carried on throughout high school. Even though I felt like I was smarter than the boys, I didn't feel better because I didn't look nice enough to impress them. Basically, I grew up not really caring for boys and thinking that they were stupid, but that it was important to impress them by looking nice. I was so confused. I felt superior, but not. And I felt anxious around both males and females, but probably more anxious around males. (Jamie, 25-year-old college senior)

Self-esteem is *the sense of worth or value that people attach to themselves.* High self-esteem has long been associated with healthy psychological adjustment and good physical health (Baumeister et al., 2003; Stinson et al., 2008; Trzesniewski et al., 2006). Beginning in early adolescence, self-esteem diminishes for both genders, with girls showing lower self-esteem than boys (Cambron et al., 2008; Frost & McKelvie, 2004; Hoffmann et al., 2004; Major et al., 1999; Malanchuk & Eccles, 2006). A meta-analysis of over 97,000 respondents by Kristen Kling and her colleagues (1999) shows that this gender gap becomes greatest in late adolescence, with a small-to-moderate effect size of 0.33 (see Chapter 1). This gender difference continues throughout adulthood, narrowing only in old age (Malanchuk & Eccles, 2006). Black girls have higher self-esteem than White, Latina, and Asian American girls during late adolescence (Gray-Little & Hafdahl, 2000; Greene & Way, 2005; Gutman & Eccles, 2007; Twenge & Crocker, 2002). Compared to White adolescent girls, Black girls have more confidence in their physical attractiveness, sports ability, femininity, popularity, and social relations (Malanchuk & Eccles, 2006).

What causes girls' self-esteem to decline in adolescence and why do Black girls remain more self-confident than others? For one thing, perceived physical appearance is closely linked to self-esteem (Barker & Bornstein, 2007; Fingeret & Gleaves, 2004; Klomsten et al., 2004; Mercurio & Landry, 2008). Girls are more dissatisfied with their appearance than boys, a difference that increases during adolescence (Harter, 1998; Klomsten et al., 2004). But Black girls, as we shall see, are less concerned about body shape and size than White girls, and physical appearance is less important to their sense of self-worth (Buckley & Carter, 2005; Malanchuk & Eccles, 2006). Upon entering adolescence, for example, the self-esteem of obese Latina and White girls drops more than that of nonobese girls, but obese Black girls do not show this decline (Strauss, 2000).

In addition, we saw earlier in this chapter that schools shortchange girls in ways that undermine girls' perceptions of their competence and importance (AAUW, 1992; Sadker & Sadker, 1994). Black girls, however, seem less dependent on school achievement for their self-esteem. Their view of themselves is more influenced by their community, family, and sense of ethnic identity (American Psychological Association, 2002; Tolman & Brown, 2001). Some researchers believe that Black females are socialized early in life by their mothers and other female relatives and mentors to be strong, independent women who can cope with a society in which racism, sexism, and classism can be barriers to the development of a positive identity (Costigan et al., 2007; Rhodes et al., 2007; Ward, 2007; Way, 1995). In one study of African American female college students, for example, over 75 percent mentioned a sense of strength as a key component of their sense of identity (Shorter-Gooden & Washington, 1996).

Several theorists, including Carol Gilligan (1993, 2002) and scholars at the Stone Center (e.g., Jordan, 1997), maintain that as girls make the transition to adolescence, they become aware of growing up in a patriarchal society that devalues women and that views the desirable stereotype of the "good woman" as being nice, pleasing to others, and unassertive. This places girls in conflict with their view of themselves as self-sufficient, independent, and outspoken. Many girls respond to this conflict by losing confidence in themselves and by suppressing their thoughts, opinions, and feelings, that is, by "losing their voice."

However, research by Susan Harter and her colleagues (Harter, 1998, 1999) found that adolescent boys and girls did not differ with respect to the loss of voice. About a third of young people of both genders said they disguised their true feelings and thoughts in dealing with certain categories of individuals, but a large majority of these females and males did not report doing so. Harter and her colleagues found that *gender role identity*, not gender itself, predicted the level of voice, a finding since confirmed by other researchers (e.g., Smolak & Munstertieger, 2002). Masculine and androgynous adolescents of both genders reported higher levels of voice and higher self-esteem than those with a feminine orientation. Although the feminine girls in Harter's study reported loss of voice in public contexts, such as school and group social situations, this did not occur with parents or close friends. Support, approval, and acceptance from parents and teachers appear critical to the development of high esteem and to the expression of one's thoughts and feelings (Harter, 1998).

Gender Intensification

All through grade school, I had been very active in sports. Basketball was my favorite and I was really good at it. Basketball gave me self-esteem. When I was 13, I set my life's goal—to one day coach the Boston Celtics. I will never forget the reactions I got when I told people this. Everyone—my friends, my parents' friends, other adults—all said the same thing: A girl could never coach a professional men's team. Until then, it hadn't occurred to me that gender mattered. I just thought you needed talent and desire, which I had. I was totally heartbroken. Then I began to question whether women were as good as men in basketball. If not, why was I playing? I didn't ever again want people to tell me I couldn't do something because I was a girl. So I quit basketball and became a cheerleader. I didn't really want to, but I felt people wouldn't like me unless I became a "complete and total girl." (Liz, 21-year-old college senior)

Gender differences in value orientation become pronounced at the onset of adolescence. For example, a study by Kimberly Badger and her colleagues (1998) of geographically diverse American adolescents found that as early as sixth grade, girls were more likely than boys to place a high value on (1) compromising; (2) being kind and forgiving; (3) expressing feelings; (4) wanting to know what people are like inside; (5) enjoying people; (6) getting along with others; and (7) having friends, cooperating, and helping. Early adolescence is also marked by an increase in the rigidity of gender-role stereotypes, although girls continue to remain more flexible than their male peers (Bartini, 2006; Basow, 2006). This *increasing divergence in gender-related behaviors and attitudes of girls and boys that emerges in early adolescence* is known as **gender intensification** (Galambos, 2004). At this age, perceiving yourself to be a typical member of your same-sex peer group is important to a sense of psychological well-being (Carver et al., 2003; Yunger et al., 2004).

Several factors contribute to the development of gender intensification. For one thing, the physical changes of puberty accentuate gender differences in appearance. Peers, parents, and other adults, especially those with traditional views of gender, apply increasing pressure on girls to display "feminine" behaviors (Carr, 2007; Crouter et al., 2007; Raffaelli & Ontai, 2004), as illustrated poignantly by Liz's experience. This magnification of traditional gender expectations is stronger for girls than for boys, probably because girls have been given more latitude than boys have to display cross-gender behaviors in middle childhood (Crockett, 1991). In addition, when adolescents begin to date and enter romantic relationships, they may increase their gender-stereotypical behavior in order to enhance their appeal to the other gender. For example, girls become intensely interested in appearing physically attractive to boys and spend long hours focusing on their clothes, hairstyles, complexions, and weight (Hilbrecht et al., 2008; Maccoby, 1998). Furthermore, cognitive changes make adolescents more aware of gender expectations and more concerned about what others think of them (Crockett, 1991). The resulting adherence to a traditional construction of gender seems at least partly responsible for the gender differences in self-esteem, friendship patterns, dating behaviors, and cognitive skills that we discuss in this chapter and in Chapters 5 and 8.

Gender intensification starts to decrease by middle to late adolescence. Gender-related occupational stereotypes (see earlier in this chapter) become more flexible, and sexist attitudes (see Chapter 2) become less pronounced. Also, the understanding that gender-related traits, behaviors, and roles are culturally created and modifiable increases (Crockett, 1991).

Body Image

> I was always heavier than other females my age, but was very healthy and athletic as a child and into high school. I played basketball, soccer, tennis, and softball. My weight was never an issue for me until I reached adolescence. I suddenly became very conscious of my weight. Boys in my class would make comments. It took me several years before I could become comfortable with my weight and grow to like my body. (Becky, 22-year-old senior)

The weight gain associated with puberty occurs within a cultural context that emphasizes a female beauty ideal of extreme thinness (Smith, 2008). According to some feminist theorists (Fingeret & Gleaves, 2004; Grabe et al., 2007), girls and women in Western culture internalize society's view of the body as a sexualized object to be looked at and evaluated, a process termed *self-objectification*. As girls internalize the "thin ideal" body image of Western society, which is unattainable for most women, they become intensely dissatisfied with their weight and shape (Chrisler, 2008c; Muehlenkamp et al., 2005; Paxton et al., 2006). Interestingly, preschool girls are more positive about their appearance than boys are about theirs (Marsh et al., 2002). But girls' body image starts to decrease in the early grade-school years, and substantial numbers of preteen girls diet to control their weight (Colton et al., 2007; Smolak, 2006). By adolescence, girls are much more concerned with body weight and appearance than are males of the same age. They have a less positive body image, are less satisfied with their weight, and are more likely to be dieting (Centers for Disease Control and Prevention, 2007; Frederick et al., 2007; Gadbois & Bowker, 2007; Gillen & Lefkowitz, 2006; Markey & Markey, 2005; Peterson et al., 2007; Yates et al., 2004). American adolescent girls and women often view themselves as too heavy even at average weight levels, and many of them have a negative view of their overall appearance (Markey et al., 2004; Sarwer et al., 2005; Yuan, 2007). Similarly, a recent body image survey conducted by a British teen magazine found that only 8 percent of the teenage girls responding were happy with their body. Even though 58 percent said they were of normal weight, two-thirds of the entire sample thought they needed to lose weight. A quarter of the respondents admitted that they already suffered from an eating disorder (Barton, 2005).

The importance of body image to adolescent females is indicated by the close association between teenage girls' body image and their self-esteem. The more negative their body image is, the lower their self-esteem. For adolescent boys, however, the relationship is minimal or nonexistent (Dohnt & Tiggemann, 2006; Kashubeck-West et al., 2005; Kelly et al., 2004; McHale, Corneal et al., 2001; Siegel, 2002). Being heavier is associated with having a poorer self-image and greater body image dissatisfaction with one's body in girls as young as age 6 (Stephens et al., 2007; Stice, 2002).

Gender differences in body image have grown since the middle of the twentieth century according to a meta-analysis of 222 studies by Alan Feingold and Ronald Mazzella (1998). Their analysis showed a dramatic increase in the number of women with a poor body image, particularly during the adolescent years. Men's body image, however, has remained relatively stable over time (Cash et al., 2004). Along these

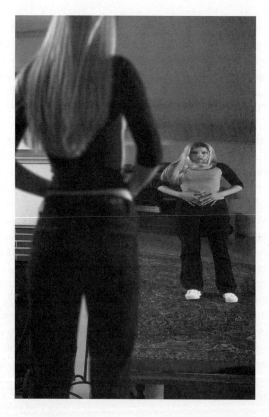

Many adolescent girls are dissatisfied with their weight and shape.

same lines, Joan Jacobs Brumberg (1997), after reviewing 150 years of girls' diaries, concluded that the focus of adolescent girls has shifted from developing their talents, interests, character, and contributions to society to worrying about their weight, shape, and appearance. According to one therapist who works with teenage girls, (Netburn, 2002, pp. ST1, ST7), "'Who am I?' has been replaced by 'What image should I project?' and part of that image involves for many girls engaging in unhealthy behaviors: dieting, tanning, smoking to keep your weight down." We will discuss the unhealthy weight control behaviors known as eating disorders in Chapter 13.

A major factor contributing to the increase in poor body image is the increasing emphasis in Western culture on thinness as the ideal female body shape (Bordo, 2004; Rubin et al., 2004). Studies of *Playboy* centerfolds, Miss America contestants, and fashion models over the last few decades have found that the average size and shape of the idealized woman has become thinner and more boyish (Rubinstein & Caballero, 2000; Smith, 2008; Spitzer et al., 1999; Voracek & Fisher, 2002). For example, the average fashion model in 1985 was a size 8, while today she is a size 0 or 2 (Betts, 2002). Magazines designed for an audience of women or girls are far more likely than magazines aimed at men or boys to focus on becoming slim, trim, and beautiful through diet, exercise, and cosmetic surgery (APA Task Force, 2007). Furthermore, as mentioned in Chapter 2, thin central women characters are overrepresented in television situation comedies and receive more positive comments from male characters the thinner they are (Fouts & Burggraf, 1999). So powerful is the cultural emphasis on slenderness in adolescent girls and young women that simply viewing photographs or media images of physically attractive women with idealized physiques is associated with diminished self-evaluations of attractiveness, less body-image satisfaction, lower self-esteem, increased anger, anxiety, depressed mood, eating disorder symptoms, and approval of surgical body alteration (Birkeland et al., 2005; Brown et al., 2007; Durkin et al., 2007; Grabe et al., 2008; E. A. Hamilton et al., 2007; Harper & Tiggemann, 2008; Smolak, 2006; Vaughan & Fouts, 2003). Even girls as young as 5 experience heightened body dissatisfaction after exposure to Barbie doll images (Dittmar et al., 2006). In addition, adolescent girls who read beauty and fashion magazines and articles about dieting are more likely to use unhealthy dieting methods (Utter et al., 2003; Van den Berg et al., 2007). In the words of one adolescent girl:

> *There's such pressure. I look at movie stars and I'm like, "Oh, my God. She's so pretty. She's so thin. I want to look like that." I'm not a small person. I am never going to be like a size 2. I should be happy with what I am and just accept that. But inside I'm freaking out because I can't eat.* (Commonwealth Fund, 1997, p. 67)

Pressure from family and friends to be thin and to look good can undermine girls' body images (Ata et al., 2007; Dohnt & Tiggemann, 2006; McCabe et al., 2006; Peterson et al., 2007; Puhl & Latner, 2007). Overweight teenagers are more likely than normal-weight children to be physically bullied by their peers or excluded from social activities (Janssen et al., 2004). Furthermore, girls whose peers tease them about their weight and pressure them to lose weight have poorer body esteem and engage in more disordered eating behaviors (Puhl & Latner, 2007). Even simply having conversations with peers about appearance lowers body satisfaction in girls (Jones, 2004). Mothers are three times as likely to identify weight as a problem in girls than in boys. In some cases, parents will talk in their daughter's presence about her need to lose weight (Cox et al., 2006; Goode, 2003). Teasing—especially by girls' fathers and brothers—is also emerging as a powerful influence on those who feel bad about their bodies (Eisenberg et al., 2003; Thompson, in Berger, 2000). Marla Eisenberg and her colleagues (2003) found that adolescents who were teased by family members or peers about their weight were more likely than other teenagers to be depressed and to think about or attempt suicide.

In their search for the "perfect look," more teenage girls are choosing to undergo cosmetic surgery (APA Task Force on the Sexualization of Girls, 2007). Moreover, the procedures requested are changing from a generation ago. While nose reshaping still is the most popular surgery, girls are increasingly choosing breast augmentation, liposuction, and tummy tucks (DeAngelis, 2005; Dittmann, 2005). Preteen girls, or "tweens" as they are now called, get manicures, pedicures, and facials (Tyre & Pierce, 2003). More than half of 5- to 9-year-old girls report using lipstick or lip gloss, and nearly two-thirds use nail polish (Sweeney, 2008). It's not unusual to see girls age 12 or younger trying to look like Britney Spears or Christina Aguilera, with pierced bellybuttons, skimpy tube tops, strappy high-heeled shoes, and revealing shorts. Marketers call it K.G.O.Y., or Kids Getting Older Younger (Trebay, 2003).

Black women are more satisfied with their bodies and are less concerned about weight loss and dieting than are White females (Breitkopf et al., 2007; Frederick et al., 2007; Grabe & Hyde, 2006; Kelly et al., 2004; Mack et al., 2004; Wardle et al., 2004). Standards of beauty and attractiveness in Black culture place less emphasis on thinness than in White culture (Omari & Mitchell, 2003; Sherry et al., 2004). However, even though females of color may be more satisfied with their bodies than their White counterparts, they still have concerns about weight and are more likely than males of color to be dieting (Cash & Pruzinsky, 2002; Eaton et al., 2006; Grunbaum, 2004). Moreover, cosmetic surgery is gaining in popularity among Black women, with the most popular procedures being tummy tucks, breast reduction, and liposuction compared to nose reshaping, liposuction, and breast augmentation in White women (Samuels, 2004). Both body dissatisfaction and eating disorders have been reported among Asian, Black, Latina, and Native American girls and women, and among the urban poor as well as the suburban middle class (Bisage et al., 2005; Brodey, 2005; Forbes & Frederick, 2008; Franko et al., 2007; Franzoi & Chang, 2002; Regan & Cachelin, 2006). The more that American ethnic minority women and non-Western women have adopted the values of mainstream U.S. society, the more likely they are to suffer from eating problems (Stark-Wroblewski et al., 2005). Try Get Involved 4.3 for a closer look at the body images of Black and White women.

Lesbians are less preoccupied with weight and dieting and have higher levels of body self-esteem than heterosexual women, but they have still more weight concerns than heterosexual men (Lakkis et al., 1999; Morrison et al., 2004; Rothblum, 2002; Share & Mintz, 2002). Why are lesbians more comfortable with their bodies? According to Judith Daniluk (1998), lesbians are branded by society as sexually unappealing because of their sexual orientation, no matter how slender and beautiful they might be. This decoupling of physical attractiveness and sexual appeal may help protect lesbians from developing a negative body image. Another explanation (Hefferman, 1999) is that lesbians may be less likely than heterosexual women to base romantic relationships on physical appearance (see Chapter 8).

GET INVOLVED 4.3

Perceptions of Actual and Desirable Physique

For this exercise, survey four young adult females, two Black and two White. Show each woman the following nine figure drawings and ask her the following questions:

1. Using the numbers under the figures, which represents your perception of *your current body*?

2. Which represents your perception of *your ideal body*?

3. Which is the body you feel *men find the most attractive*?

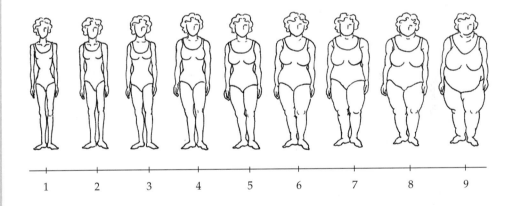

1 2 3 4 5 6 7 8 9

What Does It Mean?

1. How did the women's perceptions of their current body compare with their perception of their ideal body?

2. How did women's perceptions of their current body compare with what they feel men find most attractive?

3. Were there any differences in the perceptions of Black and White women?

SUMMARY

Children's Knowledge and Beliefs about Gender

- Children are able to distinguish females and males as early as 3–4 months of age.
- By age 2 or 3 years, they can label their own gender and they show some awareness of gender-typical objects, activities, and occupations.
- Awareness of gender stereotypes for personality traits emerges later in the preschool years.
- Stereotypes become more flexible after age 7.

Gender-Related Activities and Interests

- Preschool girls and boys are similar in their motor skills.
- Differences favoring boys become more pronounced in adolescence as a result of both environmental and biological factors.
- Participation in sports is associated with positive traits in females. Their participation has soared since the passage of Title IX.
- By age 3, gender differences in toy choices and activities are well established.
- Gender segregation, the preference for same-gender children, emerges by age 3 and increases during childhood.

Influences on Gender Development

- Both parents, but fathers more than mothers, encourage gender-typical toys, play activities, and chore assignments for their children.
- Parents talk more to their daughters, give them less autonomy, and encourage their prosocial behaviors.
- Maternal employment is associated with less stereotyped gender-related concepts and preferences in sons and daughters.
- Older siblings influence the gender development of younger siblings.

- Boys receive more attention from teachers than girls do. They are more likely to be called on, praised, and criticized constructively.
- Girls are also shortchanged in school textbooks.
- Children exert strong pressures on each other to engage in gender-typical behavior.
- Boys are viewed more negatively than girls when they engage in cross-gender activity.
- Children who are heavy TV viewers are more aware of gender stereotypes.
- Exposure to characters who show nontraditional behaviors reduces children's gender stereotypes.

Puberty

- During puberty, sexual organs mature and secondary sex characteristics appear.
- Menarche is a major event of puberty.
- Girls who mature early tend to adjust less easily than late-maturing girls.

Psychosocial Development in Adolescence

- Adolescent girls and boys show similar patterns of identity development, focusing both on occupational choices and interpersonal relationships.
- Girls begin to show lower self-esteem than boys in early adolescence, and the gender gap widens during adolescence. Explanations include girls' dissatisfaction with their physical appearance, shortchanging of girls in school, and girls' "losing their voice."
- Early adolescents show an increasing divergence in gender-related behaviors and attitudes, known as gender intensification.
- Adolescent girls, compared to boys, have a more negative body image and are more likely to diet. Cultural pressures for slimness are partly responsible.

KEY TERMS

rough-and-tumble play	puberty	secondary sex characteristics
socialization	primary sex characteristics	menarche

secular trend   identity   self-esteem
adolescent growth spurt   individuate   gender intensification

WHAT DO YOU THINK?

1. Should parents attempt to raise their children in gender-neutral ways? If so, why? What would be the advantages? What would be the disadvantages? Incorporate material from Chapters 2 and 3 into your answers.

2. Why do you think teachers pay more attention to boys than to girls? What can be done to ensure more equal treatment of girls in the classroom?

3. In your opinion, why are boys who engage in feminine activities viewed more negatively than girls who engage in masculine activities?

4. Lois Gould (1990), in her fictional *X: A Fabulous Child's Story*, wrote about Baby X, whose gender was concealed from everyone except its parents. This created considerable consternation among relatives and family friends. Why do you think that was?

5. The earlier onset of puberty in the United States and western Europe has not been accompanied by earlier gains in social and emotional development that would help children successfully manage their sexuality. What are the implications for individual adolescents and for society?

6. Using what you know about gender-role identity, explain why masculine and androgynous adolescents have higher self-esteem than feminine adolescents.

7. What actions can parents and teachers take to help enhance the self-esteem of adolescent girls?

8. How does the social construction of gender influence women's body images versus men's body images?

IF YOU WANT TO LEARN MORE

Bettis, P. J., & Adams, N. G. (2005). *Geographies of girlhood: Identities in-between*. Mahwah, NJ: Erlbaum.

Bordo, S. (2004). *Unbearable weight: Feminism, western culture and the body*. Los Angeles: University of California Press.

Cash, T. F., & Pruzinsky, T. (Eds.). (2002). *Body image: A handbook of theory, research and practice*. New York: Guilford.

Denner, J., & Guzman, B. L. (Eds.). (2006). *Latina girls: Voices of adolescent strength in the United States*. New York: New York University Press.

Edut, O. (Ed.). (2003). *Body outlaws: Rewriting the rules of beauty and body image* (2nd ed.). Emeryville, CA: Seal Press.

Fingerson, L. (2006). *Girls in power: Gender, body, and menstruation in adolescence*. Albany: State University of New York Press.

Haag, P. (1999). *Voices of a generation: Teenage girls on sex, schools, and self*. Washington, DC: American Association of University Women.

Harris, A. (Ed.). (2004). *All about the girl: Culture, power, and identity*. New York: Routledge.

Johnson, N. G., Roberts, M. C., & Worell, J. (Eds.). (1999). *Beyond appearance: A new look at adolescent girls*. Washington, DC: American Psychological Association.

Laflamme, L. M. (2001). *Rites of passage: A celebration of menarche*. New York: Synchronicity Press.

Leadbeater, B. J. R., & Way, N. (Eds.). (2007). *Urban girls revisited: Building strengths*. New York: New York University Press.

McDonagh, E., & Pappano, L. (2007). *Playing with the boys: Why separate is not equal in sports*. Oxford, England: Oxford University Press.

Roan, S. L. (2001). *Our daughters' health: Practical and invaluable advice for raising confident girls ages 6–16*. New York: Hyperion.

Sadker, M., & Sadker, D. (1994). *Failing at fairness: How America's schools cheat girls*. New York: Scribner.

Zager, K., & Rubenstein, A. (2002). *The inside story on teen girls*. Washington, DC: American Psychological Association.

Zimmerman, T. S. (2002). *Integrating gender and culture in parenting*. New York: Haworth.

WEBSITES

Sports

Empowering Women in Sports
http://www.feminist.org/sports

http://www.girlpower.gov/
http://www.girlsinc.org/
http://www.nedic.ca/

5

Gender Comparisons

Social Behavior, Personality, Communication, and Cognition

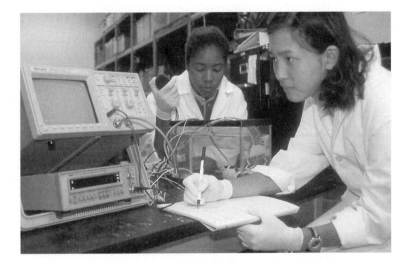

Gender-Related Social Behaviors and Personality Traits
    Aggression
    Prosocial Behavior
    Influenceability
    Emotionality
    Moral Reasoning

Communication Style
    Verbal Communication
    Nonverbal Communication

Gender Comparison of Cognitive Abilities
    Verbal Ability
    Visual–Spatial Ability
    Mathematics Ability

In high school, I once struggled with some concepts in my advanced algebra class. My teacher did not help me much. He kept telling me not to worry about it; that I would not be using algebra in my future. I excelled in that class, and kept taking math courses, which surprised him. (Nathalie, 22-year-old college senior)

Gender-Related Social Behaviors and Personality Traits

In Chapter 2, we examined numerous gender stereotypes. How accurately do these stereotypes reflect actual differences in the social behaviors, personality characteristics, communication style, and cognitive abilities of females and males? In this chapter, we review all four of these areas. As we shall see, some stereotypes have at least a grain (or more) of truth to them, whereas others are not supported by the evidence. Two cautionary notes: First, even when gender differences are found, they are typically small. Second, there is considerable overlap in the characteristics of females and males (Halpern, 2004a; Hyde, 2005). For example, girls are generally more nurturant toward younger children than boys are, but some boys show greater nurturance than some girls.

Aggression

She talks about you.
You talk about her.
She glares at you.
You stare at her.
Is it a rumor, or is it the truth?
She lies to you, you lie right back.
You need a friend, but for sure not her.
She takes your guy.
You want him back.
Too much stress, too much pressure.
But I guess this is life.
(Kelsey, 12 years old)

Aggression is behavior that is intended to hurt someone, either physically or verbally. By age 2, boys show higher levels of physical aggression than girls, and during the preschool period, the differences become striking (Alink et al., 2006; Baillargeon et al., 2007; Miner & Clarke-Stewart, 2008; NICHD, 2004). Boys continue to be more physically aggressive than girls into adulthood (Archer, 2004; Card et al., 2008; Dodge et al., 2006; Frieze, 2005; Herrenkohl et al., 2007;). The differences hold across socioeconomic groups and across cultures (Archer, 2004; Hines, 2004a). Girls, however, are slightly more likely than boys to use **relational aggression,** which involves *harming others through nonphysical hurtful manipulation of their peer relationships.* For example, girls might exclude a peer from their play group, or spread malicious rumors and gossip about her, as illustrated in Kelsey's poem in the beginning of this section and in the 2004 movie *Mean Girls* (Herrenkohl et al., 2007; Pepler et al., 2008; Susman et al., 2007). Girls are also more likely than boys to be victims of relational aggression (Cummings & Leschied, 2002; French et al., 2002). This gender difference in how children display aggression is so striking that even preschool children are aware of it (Giles & Heyman, 2005).

Interestingly, although aggression is typically associated with rejection by peers, girls who use relational aggression tend to be both popular and powerful within their peer group (Cillessen & Mayeux, 2004; Rose et al., 2004). What might account for this unexpected finding? According to Suzanna Rose and her colleagues (2004), strategic use of relational aggression may serve to maintain social dominance as well as to display superiority.

Both biological and environmental influences may contribute to gender differences in aggression (Brendgen et al., 2005). On the biological side, it has been noted that the gender difference emerges early and appears across most cultures. In addition, the sex hormone testosterone appears to play a role, at least in animal aggression. Research on the relationship between aggressive behavior and testosterone in humans, however, has produced mixed results (Frieze, 2005; Ramirez, 2003). A meta-analysis by Angela Book and her colleagues (2001) yielded a weak, positive correlation between testosterone and aggressive behavior in humans. However, this correlation is difficult to interpret, since the causal direction can go either way. That is, increasing testosterone levels can lead to aggression, but it is also the case that acting aggressively (such

Girls are more likely than boys to use relational aggression.

as winning a wrestling match) leads to a rise in testosterone levels (Dodge et al., 2006; Frieze, 2005). Jacquelyn White and Robin Kowalski (1994) suggest that studies showing a connection between aggression and testosterone may be unduly emphasized because they are consistent with the stereotype of the aggressive male and the submissive female.

Environmental factors are probably even more important than biological ones in producing gender differences in aggression. For one thing, parents, teachers, and peers are less tolerant of aggressive acting-out behaviors in girls (Chaplin et al., 2005; Martin & Ross, 2005; White, 2001). Consequently, girls expect more guilt, more peer and parental disapproval, and fewer material gains for aggression than boys do (Eisenberg et al., 1996). In addition, parents' encouragement of boys' physical play and the use of gender-typical toys such as guns may serve to promote aggression. Furthermore, the rougher, dominance-oriented play of boys' groups may contribute to the maintenance of higher aggression levels in boys (Coie & Dodge, 1998).

Prosocial Behavior

Prosocial behavior is *voluntary behavior intended to benefit someone else*. It includes helping, comforting and caring for others, sharing, and cooperating (Eisenberg et al., 2006). The stereotype is that females are more nurturant, supportive, and helpful than males (Cole et al., 2007). Are they?

Some studies of children have found no gender differences in prosocial behavior, but when differences are found they favor girls (Knafo & Plomin, 2006; Zakriski et al., 2005). For example, toddler girls under the age of 2 years are more likely than boys to comfort someone in distress (Kiang et al., 2004). Girls also help others more than boys do (Caprara et al., 2001; Eisenberg et al., 2006). This tendency of girls to be more prosocial has been found in a variety of cultures (Eisenberg et al., 2006). Studies with adults, however, paint a different picture, with men helping more than women. This is partly because studies with adults frequently involve instrumental and chivalrous assistance, such as rescuing strangers, sometimes in potentially dangerous situations (e.g., helping to change a tire or picking up a hitchhiker). Women, on the other hand, are more likely to offer psychological support and help to friends and family members (Barry & Wentzel, 2006; Eisenberg & Morris, 2004; Sprecher et al., 2007). Unfortunately, this aspect of helpfulness has largely been overlooked by researchers.

Gender differences in helping styles are consistent with stereotyped expectations for males and females. How do the differences arise? In many societies, girls are expected to be more nurturant, kind, and emotionally supportive than boys, and they are rewarded for these behaviors. Boys, meanwhile, are more often rewarded for helping behaviors that involve rescuing, risk taking, and chivalry (Becker & Eagly, 2004; Eisenberg et al., 2006).

Influenceability

Females tend to be stereotyped as more easily influenced and more conforming than males. Is there any evidence to support this view? Again, the answer depends on several

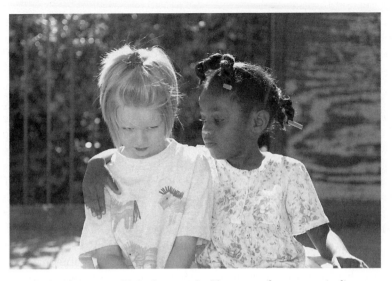

Preschool girls are more likely than preschool boys to comfort someone in distress.

factors, such as the type of measure used and even the gender of the researcher. The two major types of tasks used to measure the ability to influence are persuasion studies and group pressure conformity studies. In **persuasion studies,** *participants indicate their position on a controversial topic. A different position supported by arguments is presented by another individual and the participant's position is again measured.* **Group pressure conformity studies** are similar, except that *a group of people, not just one individual, supports a position discrepant with the participant's.*

Alice Eagly and Linda Carli (1981) performed a meta-analysis on both kinds of studies and found that women were more easily influenced than men. The gender difference was greater for the conformity studies, but all differences were small. Females were influenced more when masculine topics, such as technology or sports, were used. The gender difference was also greater when the researchers were male.

Several factors may account for these findings. For one thing, females are socialized to yield to social influence, while males are trained to do the influencing. Remember also that from an early age, females show more cooperation and less conflict in group settings. Accepting the views of others can be viewed as a mechanism for maintaining social harmony and avoiding conflict. In addition, consistent with our theme that females have less power than males, women are accorded a lower status than men in most societies. Individuals of lower status generally learn to conform to the wishes of higher-status individuals (Eagly et al., 2000).

Emotionality

Females are thought to be more emotional than males: more fearful, anxious, easily upset, and emotionally expressive. Males are viewed as more likely to express anger and pride and to hide or deny their emotions (Dittmann, 2003; Plant et al., 2004; Simon & Nath, 2004). Even preschool children, when read stories in an emotionally ambiguous context, are more likely to perceive boys as angry and girls as sad (Parmley & Cunningham, 2008). Is there any truth to these stereotypes?

Preschool girls express less anger and more fearfulness than boys. They are also better at labeling emotions and understanding complex emotions such as pride (Bosacki & Moore, 2004). In elementary school, boys start to hide negative emotions such as sadness, while girls begin to hide negative emotions, such as disappointment, that might hurt others' feelings. By adolescence, girls report more sadness, shame, and guilt, whereas boys deny experiencing these feelings. Girls and women also report experiencing emotions more intensely and more readily than boys and men (Eisenberg et al., 1996; Polce-Lynch et al., 1998; Simon & Nath, 2004). Note that these findings do not answer the question of whether females are actually more emotional than males or whether they simply are more likely to report their feelings.

Another aspect of emotionality is **empathy,** which involves *feeling the same emotion that someone else is feeling.* The stereotype is that women are more empathic than men. Are they in reality? The answer depends on how you measure empathy. When individuals are asked to report how they feel in certain situations (e.g., "Does seeing people cry upset you?"), females show more empathy than males (Eisenberg & Morris, 2004; Wentzel et al., 2007). However, when individuals' behaviors are observed unobtrusively or when their physiological reactions are measured, no gender differences in empathy are found (Eisenberg et al., 1996). These findings suggest that when people know what is being measured and can control their reactions, they may act in the socially acceptable gender-typical manner.

Socialization seems to be an important factor in the development of differences in emotionality (or in the willingness to report emotions). Parents report being more accepting of fear in girls and anger in boys. Mothers focus more on emotions, particularly sad emotions, when talking to their daughters (Fivush et al., 2000; Gleason & Ely, 2002). In addition, parents put more pressure on sons to control their emotions, while encouraging their daughters to be emotionally expressive (DeAngelis, 2001). Parents emphasize closer emotional relationships with daughters than with sons. As early as preschool, mothers and daughters already are closer emotionally than mothers and sons (Benenson et al., 1998).

A series of studies by Penelope Davis (1999) on adults' memories of childhood events provides an interesting illustration of the apparent social construction of gender differences in emotionality. She found that, in general, females and males did not differ either in the number of memories recalled or in how quickly they recalled them. However, females consistently recalled more childhood memories of events associated with emotion and were faster in accessing these memories. Furthermore, this difference was observed across a wide range of emotions experienced by both the individuals and others.

Moral Reasoning

Are there gender differences in moral reasoning? The question has been hotly debated ever since Lawrence Kohlberg (1985) proposed that males show higher levels of moral reasoning than females. In his research, Kohlberg asked individuals to respond to moral dilemmas. In one dilemma, a druggist refuses to lower the price of an expensive drug that could save the life of a dying woman. Her husband, who cannot afford the drug, then steals it. Was he right or wrong in doing so, and why? Kohlberg reported that males' answers emphasized abstract justice and "law and order," which he believed to be more advanced than the emphasis on caring and concern for others expressed by females. As we saw in Chapter 1, Carol Gilligan (1982, 1993) argued that females' moral reasoning is just as advanced as that of males, but that females speak "in a different voice" that emphasizes personal connections rather than abstract legalities.

Research, however, generally fails to support Kohlberg's and Gilligan's view that there are gender differences in the underlying basis of moral reasoning (Turiel, 2006). For example, a meta-analysis of 113 studies by Sara Jaffee and Janet Hyde (2000) found only slight differences in the care orientation favoring females and in the justice orientation favoring males. In some studies, in fact, women are more likely than men to show both a care response *and* a justice response (Mainiero et al., 2008). In addition, an extensive review by Lawrence Walker (1991) revealed that females score as high as males on Kohlberg's measure of moral reasoning. And, among college students in the United States, women are more concerned with moral issues than are men (Skoe et al., 2002).

Moral reasoning appears to be more dependent on the context of the situation than on the gender of the individual (Turiel, 2006). For example, both women and men are more likely to use a care-based approach when interacting with a friend than with a stranger, or when interacting with a member of their in group as opposed to someone outside their group (Ryan et al., 2004).

Communication Style

> *In short, feminine talk is a lot of polite talk about silly things; whereas masculine talk is a little blunt talk about important things.* (Spender, 1979, quoted in Popp et al., 2003)

People believe that men have demanding voices, swear, are straight to the point, forceful, and boastful. Women, on the other hand, are thought to talk a lot, speak politely and emotionally, enunciate clearly, use good grammar, talk about trivia, and gossip (Popp et al., 2003). According to a bestselling book, women and men are so different in their communication styles that it is as if *Men Are from Mars, Women Are from Venus* (Gray, 1992). What does research tell us about differences between the communication styles of females and males?

Verbal Communication

Evidence supports a number of gender differences, and one of these is, indeed, a difference in talkativeness. Interestingly, however, the talking behavior of females and males is the opposite of the stereotype. In many situations studied by researchers, including online discussion groups, males talk more than females, speak more frequently, and for longer periods of time. Furthermore, this gender difference is apparent as early as the preschool years and continues throughout adulthood (Cameron, 2007; Carli & Bukatko, 2000; Gleason & Ely, 2002; Kramarae, 2001).

Given the gender difference in talkativeness, we might expect that males also interrupt others more than females do. Research indicates that gender differences in the number of interruptions depend on the situations and also that women and men have different goals when they interrupt others (Gleason & Ely, 2002). One purpose of an interruption is *to show interest and affirm what the other is saying*—an **affiliative interruption**—for example, by saying "uh-huh." A second reason for interrupting is *to usurp the floor and control the conversation*—an **intrusive interruption.** This might be accomplished by taking over the conversation even though the previous speaker shows no signs of relinquishing the floor. It might not surprise you to learn that females are more likely to engage in affiliative interruption and males, in intrusive interruption (Athenstaedt et al., 2004; Eckert & McConnell-Ginet, 2003; Leman et al., 2005). These differences are consistent with both the social construction of females as other-directed and caring and the gender inequality in power. Affiliative interruptions are one way to express an interest in other people, and females might have learned through their socialization that this was one means of showing concern about and reinforcing others. On the other hand, both intrusive interruptions and talkativeness are associated with the desire to maintain dominance and with the power to do so. More powerful individuals are seen as having the right to dominate the conversation and to usurp the floor. This connection between power and communication behavior is illustrated in a study by Elizabeth Cashdan (1998), who observed female and male college students in group discussions and asked them to rate their housemates on characteristics of power. Her findings showed that the more powerful students were the ones who talked the most.

Gender differences have also been found in conversational style. Consistent with communal and agentic stereotypes, studies show that females use more emotional, polite, soothing, and supportive speech, while males use more direct, goal-oriented, and abrupt speech (Kramarae, 2001; Leaper, 2004; Leaper & Smith, 2004; Mulac et al., 2001). For example, women are more likely than men to refer to emotions and use intensive adverbs ("She is *really* friendly"), whereas men tend to use directives ("Think about this") and judgmental adjectives ("Working can be a drag") more than women do. Women also are more apt to use personal pronouns (Brownlow et al., 2003; Pennebaker et al., 2003).

Another gender difference in conversational style is that females use speech that is sometimes referred to as more tentative. Such speech may contain uncertainty verbs (e.g., "It *seems* that the class will be interesting"), hedges (e.g., "*I kind of feel* you should not be too upset about this"), tag questions ("It's hot in here, *don't you think?*"), and disclaimers of expertise ("*I may be wrong, but . . .*") (Carli & Bukatko, 2000; Goldshmidt & Weller, 2000; Mulac, 1998).

One explanation for this gender difference in speech is that females have lower self-esteem than males and, consequently, speak more tentatively (Lakoff, 1990). Another interpretation is that women's tentativeness results not from their uncertainty but from their lower status (Weatherall, 2002). Less powerful individuals are more likely to use more tentative speech, regardless of their own confidence in what they are saying, and, as we have noted throughout this text, women have less power than men. In support of this explanation, research suggests that females use more tentative language in their conversations with men but not in their interactions with other women (Carli & Bukatko, 2000).

Still another perspective on this gender difference in conversational style is that the language features used by women do not reflect tentativeness at all but instead are due to women's communal orientation—their desire to leave open the lines of communication and encourage the participation of others (Weatherall, 2002). Research has found that tag questions in fact serve a variety of functions depending on the situation. For example, in one study (Cameron, in LaFrance, 2001a), both women and men in powerful roles used tag questions to generate talk from other participants. However, women and men in less powerful roles used them to seek reassurance for their opinions. This finding indicates that gender differences in verbal communication depend in part on the situation. For example, conversational style is generally more gender-stereotyped in same-sex groups than in mixed-sex groups (Athenstaedt et al., 2004; Leaper, 2004). In the latter groups, women and men tend to adjust their behaviors to each other. Whatever the explanation for women's greater use of so-called tentative speech, such speech makes people seem less credible, powerful, or persuasive (Brownlow et al., 2003). Can you think of how this perception might be problematic for women in leadership positions?

Another aspect of conversational style is the way people respond to a friend's troubles. Shari Michaud and Rebecca Warner (1997) found that women were more likely than men to offer sympathy in response to a friend's problems, whereas men were more likely to change the subject. In addition, women were more likely than men to appreciate receiving advice or sympathy, whereas men were more likely to resent it. On the other hand, recent research by Erina MacGeorge and her colleagues (2004) found only slight differences in the way women and men responded. Both sexes preferred to listen, sympathize, and give thoughtful advice. Men were only slightly more likely to give advice, and women were slightly more likely to provide support. Similarly, both women and men appreciated advice that was relevant to their problems and was given in a respectful, kind manner. MacGeorge and her colleagues concluded that women and men do not come from two different communication cultures but are instead from the same "planet." Do Get Involved 5.1 to see whether your findings support the view of Gray or MacGeorge.

Like Erina MacGeorge, Anthony Mulac (1998) argues that gender differences in communication style are subtle and that it is difficult to identify the gender of speakers simply from their words. Mulac and his colleagues performed several studies in which college students were asked to determine the gender of a communicator after reading a written communication, such as a transcription of a speech from a public speaking class or an essay describing landscape photos. In none of these situations were respondents able to guess accurately the gender of the communicator. Mulac concluded that, "spoken and written language used in everyday communication by women and men, as well as girls and boys, displays a high degree of similarity" (p. 131).

Similar to conversational style, the actual content of females' and males' conversations, at least with their same-gender friends, is characterized by both gender similarities and differences. In an attempt to learn what young adult women and men talk about with their friends, Ruth Anne Clark (1998) asked college students to list all the topics discussed in a recent conversation with a same-gender close friend and to indicate the dominant topic. Not surprisingly, given the importance of romantic relationships to young adults, both females and males talked about the other gender. However, women's conversations more than men's were dominated by interpersonal issues. Whereas 64 percent of the women reported that other people (both male and female) were the dominant topic of their conversations, this was true for only 40 percent of the men. Furthermore, 36 percent of the men said that sports and other leisure activities were their primary focus. Another difference in content was the type of discussion about other people, with women more likely than men to discuss the nature of their relationships or problems in these relationships. Despite these gender differences, it is important to keep in mind that this study was done with college students and tells us little about the topics of interest to older women and men or to girls and boys.

GET INVOLVED **5.1**

"Troubles Talk": Effects of Gender on Communication Styles

Give the following two-part survey to two female and two male traditional-aged college students.

PART I. Imagine your friend is upset because of having one of the PROBLEMS listed below. For each problem, indicate how likely you would be to make each of the listed RESPONSES.

PROBLEM A: Your friend says "I'm upset because I may be breaking up with my dating partner." What do you do?

| Offer sympathy | very unlikely | 1 | 2 | 3 | 4 | 5 | very likely |
| Change the subject | very unlikely | 1 | 2 | 3 | 4 | 5 | very likely |

PROBLEM B: Your friend says "I'm upset because I may fail a course." What do you do?

| Offer sympathy | very unlikely | 1 | 2 | 3 | 4 | 5 | very likely |
| Change the subject | very unlikely | 1 | 2 | 3 | 4 | 5 | very likely |

PART II. Now imagine that you have each of the problems cited above. Indicate how you FEEL when your friend makes the indicated RESPONSES.

PROBLEM A: You tell your friend "I'm upset because I may be breaking up with my dating partner." Your friend offers SYMPATHY. How much do you feel the following?

| Grateful | not at all | 1 | 2 | 3 | 4 | a lot |
| Resentful | not at all | 1 | 2 | 3 | 4 | a lot |

PROBLEM B: You tell your friend "I'm upset because I may fail a course." Your friend gives ADVICE on solving the problem. How much do you feel the following?

| Grateful | not at all | 1 | 2 | 3 | 4 | a lot |
| Resentful | not at all | 1 | 2 | 3 | 4 | a lot |

Source: Adapted from Michaud and Warner (1997).

What Does It Mean?

For Part I, compare the scores of your female and male respondents on the "sympathy" scale of the two problems. Do the same for the "change the subject" scale. For Part II, compare the female and male respondents in terms of how grateful or resentful they are for receiving sympathy (Problem A), and how grateful or resentful they are for receiving advice (Problem B).

1. Did you find the same results as Michaud and Warner (1997) for Parts I and II of the survey? If not, give reasons.
2. As described in the chapter, John Gray theorizes that women and men come from

two different cultures of communication, whereas Erina MacGeorge disagrees. Do your findings support the view of Gray or MacGeorge? Explain.

3. Your data, like those of Michaud and Warner (1997), were collected from traditional-aged college students. Do you think that middle-aged women and men would respond differently? (You would, of course, have to make the problems age-appropriate by, for example, substituting "spouse" for "dating partner," and "get a poor job performance evaluation" instead of "fail a course.") Explain your answer.

Nonverbal Communication

Consistent with the communal stereotype, people believe that females are more likely than males to engage in nonverbal behaviors that demonstrate interpersonal interest and warmth. Are these beliefs accurate? Considerable evidence shows that they are. For one thing, girls and women are more likely than boys and men to engage in mutual eye contact with another individual for longer periods of time, particularly if that individual is female (Goldshmidt & Weller, 2000; Hall et al., 2000). This gender difference in gazing behavior is not present at birth but appears as early as 13 weeks of age and continues through adulthood (Leeb & Rejskind, 2004). Females also smile, lean forward more, and approach others more closely (Hall et al., 2000; 2001; LaFrance et al., 2003). Girls and women also are more sensitive to the meanings of nonverbal messages portrayed by others and more accurately interpret their emotions (Brody & Hall, 2000). In addition, research on interpersonal sensitivity indicates that females are better than males at initially getting to know the personality traits, emotional states, and behavioral tendencies of other people. They are also more accurate at recalling the appearance of social targets (Horgan et al., 2004).

One explanation for these gender differences is the differential socialization of females and males, with females receiving greater societal encouragement for being socially concerned (McClure, 2000). Smiling and gazing communicate interest and involvement in another person. In addition, women's ability to accurately decipher other people's emotional states might stem from their greater interest in others and their more extensive experience with emotional communication.

A different explanation of females' superior sensitivity skills lies in their subordinate status within society. In order to adapt best socially—to know how to respond appropriately and to structure their own action—less powerful individuals must be good interpreters of the nonverbal cues of more powerful people (LaFrance, 2001a). They must be able to anticipate the reactions of those with power. In other words, the ability to decipher the nonverbal behavior of others might serve as a protective mechanism that guides the interpersonal relationships of all lower-status individuals, including women.

Touch is another form of nonverbal communication. Nancy Henley (1995) proposed a framework for understanding gender differences in tactile communication. She contended that there is an unwritten societal rule that high-status individuals can touch low-status individuals, but those of low status cannot touch those of high status. For example, it is more likely that the president of a corporation will pat a janitor on the back than the reverse. Based on this assumption, Henley asserted that because males in North America have a greater degree of power than females, there is more male-to-female touching than the reverse. Despite the logic of this perspective, research on gender differences in touching has provided mixed findings, with no overall gender differences in touching (Hall, 1996).

Of course, tactile communication can vary widely—from hugs that show affection, to inappropriate sexual touching that is harassing, to formal handshakes that communicate respect. Given the complexity of the types of touch and the nature of relationships in which touching can take place, it is not surprising that researchers have failed to observe any overall gender differences in touching (Hall, 1996). One investigation, however, suggests an interesting relationship among gender, status, and touching. Judith Hall (1996) trained college students to unobtrusively observe and record touching behavior that occurred among professionals attending either a psychology or a philosophy convention. Her results indicated no overall tendency for one gender to touch the other gender more nor for more touching to be initiated by higher-status professionals (based on factors such as the prestige of their university or the academic rank of the individual) than by lower-status professionals. However, when the toucher and recipient were of similar status, males were more likely to touch females than vice versa. Hall suggested that when individuals are similar in professional status, gender serves as a status cue that can dictate rules about touching. Obviously, gender and status differences in touching are more complex than were originally believed. Additional variables, such as age and type of relationship, also can affect who touches whom (Hall & Veccia, 1992).

Gender Comparison of Cognitive Abilities

Research into questions about sex differences and similarities in intelligence is fraught with political minefields and emotional rhetoric from all ends of the political spectrum. But research is the only way we can distinguish between those stereotypes that have some basis in fact and those that don't. (Diane Halpern, president-elect of the American Psychological Association, cited in Kersting, 2003a)

Although females and males do not differ in general intelligence, they do vary in certain cognitive skills. Some differences emerge in childhood while others do not appear until adolescence (Halpern, 2007; Hines, 2007). No doubt some of these differences have a bearing on the career choices made by females and males. Remember our cautionary notes from the beginning of this chapter. Gender differences, where they exist, are generally small. Females and males are much more alike in cognitive abilities than they are different. Even when there is a small average difference favoring one gender on a test of a particular cognitive skill, many individuals of the other gender will score well above the average. Also recall from Chapter 1 that the presence of a gender difference does not tell us anything about the causes of the difference. Finally, keep in mind that cognitive skills, like the social behaviors and personality traits we discussed earlier in this chapter, develop within a social context. As we shall see throughout this section, attitudes and expectations about the cognitive performance of females and males play an important role in socially constructing that performance.

Verbal Ability

Verbal abilities include a variety of language skills such as vocabulary, reading comprehension, writing, spelling, grammar, and word fluency. Females show superior performance on most verbal tasks, although the differences are small (Halpern, et al., 2007; Hines, 2007; Hyde, 2007). Gender differences in verbal ability appear earlier than other cognitive gender differences. Girls are more vocal than boys during infancy, talk at an earlier age, produce longer utterances, have larger vocabularies, and are more fluent (Karass et al., 2002; Leaper & Smith, 2004; Statistics Canada, 2006; Stoner et al., 2005; Tamis-LeMonda et al., 2004). They also are less likely to have developmental delays involving language (Sices et al., 2004).

Girls continue to show an edge in verbal skills throughout the grade school years (Leventhal & Brooks-Gunn, 2004). They achieve higher scores on tests of reading comprehension and are less likely to display reading problems such as reading disability (dyslexia) and reading below grade level (Mullis et al., 2007; Rutter et al., 2004; U.S. Department of Education, 2007a,b). In adolescence, girls continue to outperform boys in reading, writing, and speech production (Halpern, 2007; Programme for International Student Assessment, 2004; U.S. Department of Education, 2007a,b).

Some researchers have suggested that gender differences in verbal skills and other cognitive abilities are becoming smaller (Feingold, 1988; Hyde & Linn, 1988). More recent reviews, however, have concluded that these differences are not diminishing and have remained relatively stable for decades (Nowell & Hedges, 1998; Voyer et al., 1995).

What might account for the greater verbal ability of girls? In Chapter 4, we saw that parents vocalize more to their infant daughters than to their infant sons (Clearfield & Nelson, 2006). This may lead to increased vocalization by female infants, which may in turn encourage parents to talk even more to their young daughters. Girls' early advantage with language may lead them to rely more on verbal approaches in their interactions with others, further enhancing their verbal ability (Halpern, 2000). In addition, playing with stereotypically feminine toys such as dolls and stuffed animals may encourage pretend play and the development of verbal skills (Cherney & London, 2006).

Parental expectations also may play a role in girls' superior verbal skills. Studies in Finland, Japan, Taiwan, and the United States find that as early as first grade, children and their mothers generally believe that girls are better than boys at language and reading (Lummis & Stevenson, 1990; Räty & Kasanen, 2007; Räty et al., 2006). In addition, girls whose mothers think that girls are better readers receive higher scores on reading comprehension and vocabulary than girls whose mothers think girls and boys read equally well.

Visual–Spatial Ability

Visual–spatial ability refers to skill in visualizing objects or shapes and in mentally rotating and manipulating them. Visual–spatial skills are used extensively in engineering, architecture, and navigation and in everyday activities such as doing jigsaw puzzles or reading maps.

Types of Visual–Spatial Ability.   Gender differences in visual–spatial ability are larger and more consistent than in other cognitive skills, with males outperforming females in many, although not all, areas (Halpern, 2004a; Voyer et al., 2000). The pattern of differences depends on the spatial ability being measured. For example, females consistently excel in remembering the spatial location of objects (Halpern, 2007). Three other facets of visual–spatial ability have been identified by Marcia Linn and Anne Petersen (1985). Tasks used to measure these three components are shown in Figure 5.1.

Mental rotation involves *the ability to rapidly manipulate two- or three-dimensional figures* (See Figure 5.1a). Meta-analyses (see Chapter 1) show that the largest gender difference in spatial skills occurs on tests of this ability, with an overall *d* value of 0.60 (Voyer et al., 1995). Boys begin to outperform girls as early as age 4 (Ehrlich et al., 2005; Levine et al., 1999), consistently do so by age 9, and the gender difference increases into adolescence and adulthood (Cherney & Collaer, 2005; Hines, 2007; Voyer et al., 1995).

Tests of **spatial perception** involve the *ability to locate the vertical or the horizontal while ignoring distracting information.* For example, individuals may be asked to identify a horizontal water line in a tilted bottle (see Figure 5.1b). Gender differences on spatial perception tests like this are smaller than those found on mental rotation tasks (overall *d* = 0.40) (Hines, 2007; Voyer et al., 1995). Boys begin to perform better than girls by age 9, and this difference gets larger during the adolescent and adult years.

Tasks measuring **spatial visualization** include *finding simple shapes hidden within larger, complex shapes* (see Figure 5.1c). Gender differences favoring males are much smaller or absent on these tasks (overall *d* = 0.20) (Voyer et al., 1995).

The size of gender differences on spatial visualization and spatial perception tasks has been decreasing over time (Feingold, 1993; Voyer et al., 1995). Differences on mental rotation tests, however, have remained stable or even increased (Ruble & Martin, 1998; Voyer et al., 1995).

Explanations of Gender Differences.   Several biological and environmental theories have been proposed to account for gender differences in visual–spatial abilities.

a. **Mental Rotation**
Choose the responses that show the standard in a different orientation.

Standard   Responses

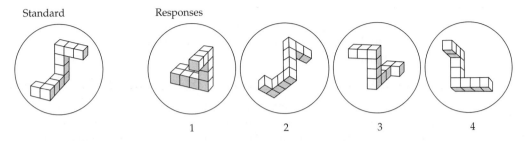

                             1   2   3   4

b. **Spatial Perception**
Pick the tilted bottle that has a horizontal water line.

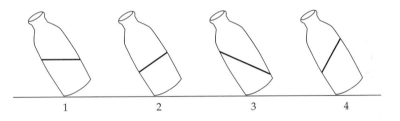

               1   2   3   4

c. **Spatial Visualization**
Find the figure embedded in the complex shape below.

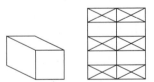

FIGURE 5.1   Types of spatial tasks. Large sex differences favoring males appear on mental rotation, and males also do better than females on spatial perception. In contrast, sex differences on spatial visualization are weak or nonexistent.

Source: From "Emergence and Characterization of Sex Differences in Spacial Ability:
A Meta-Analysis," M. C. Linn and A. C. Peterson, 1985, *Child Development, 56.* © The Society for Research in Child Development, Inc. Reprinted by permission.

Biological theories focus on genes, hormones, or the organization of the brain. According to one theory, visual–spatial ability is influenced by sex-linked recessive genes on the X chromosome. Research does not support this view, however (Newcombe, 2007a).

Another biological theory is that sex hormone levels affect visual–spatial skills in either of two ways (Halpern, 2007; Hines, 2007). One possibility is that hormones circulating in the bloodstream might directly affect visual–spatial performance (Halpern et al., 2007). Studies have shown that women with higher testosterone levels achieve better spatial scores than women with lower testosterone levels, whereas the reverse is true in men (Moffat & Hampson, 1996). Keeping in mind that women's testosterone levels, on average, are lower than those of men, these findings suggest that the optimal level of testosterone for certain spatial skills is in the low male range (Hampson & Moffat, 2004). Other research, however, finds that actively circulating sex hormones do not affect spatial performance in adolescent girls and boys (Liben et al., 2002).

Another possibility is that prenatal sex hormones might irreversibly organize the brain to enhance certain spatial functions. Evidence for this view comes from studies of girls with congenital adrenal hyperplasia (CAH) (see Chapter 3), which exposes them to high levels of prenatal androgens. At birth, the hormone imbalance is corrected and they are raised as girls. Some studies find that CAH girls display better visual–spatial skills than unaffected girls, but others do not (Berenbaum & Resnick, 2007). Some psychologists (e.g., Hines, 2004a), however, point out that parents' awareness of the possible masculinizing effects of androgens may influence their treatment of and expectations for their daughters.

Some theorists have attributed gender differences in visual–spatial skills to differences in the lateralization of female and male brains. **Lateralization** refers to the *specialization of the cerebral hemispheres of the brain to perform different cognitive functions.* For most of us, the left hemisphere is involved in language and mathematical computation, whereas the right hemisphere is more involved in processing visual and spatial information (Halpern, 2000). Some evidence suggests that male brains may be more completely lateralized or specialized than female brains (Halpern, 2000), but it is not clear that lateralization leads to better performance in visual–spatial or other cognitive skills (Newcombe, 2007a).

Numerous environmental theories have been proposed to explain gender differences in visual–spatial skills. Most of these focus on the impact of cultural gender stereotypes, observational learning, and encouragement of gender-typed activities and interests on shaping the experiences and attitudes of females and males. Participation in spatial activities fosters the development of spatial abilities in both girls and boys (Caldera et al., 1999; Halpern, 2000; Robert & Héroux, 2004), yet females engage in fewer spatial activities than males. Why is this? For one thing, gender-stereotyped "boys'" toys, such as blocks, Erector sets, Legos, and model planes and cars, provide more practice with visual–spatial skills than gender-stereotyped "girls'" toys (Cherney & London, 2006). Boys also are encouraged more than girls to participate in sports, which often involves moving balls and other objects through space (Etaugh & Rathus, 1995). Action video games, which are especially popular with boys, also appear to develop spatial skills (Cherney & London, 2006; Feng et al., 2007; Terlecki & Newcombe, 2005). If experience enhances the development of visual–spatial skills, then appropriate training ought to improve these skills. Research indicates that it does, for both females and males (Halpern et al., 2007). Some training procedures have reduced or eliminated gender differences (Feng et al., 2007; Marulis et al., 2005; Vasta et al., 1996; Voyer et al., 2000).

The stereotyping of visual–spatial activities as masculine also influences performance. Studies have found that females and males with more masculine self-concepts perform better on visual–spatial tasks than those with less masculine self-concepts (Halpern, 2000). For example, college men and women who describe themselves as having few stereotypical feminine traits or many stereotypical masculine traits get better scores on visual–spatial tests than students who show the reverse pattern (Signorella & Frieze, 1989). Simply changing the mindset of students before taking the spatial test also has a marked effect on the performance of females and males. In one study (McGlone & Aronson, 2006), college students were asked one of three sets of questions before performing a mental rotation test. One group of students was asked about living in a single-sex or coed dorm. This question has been shown to activate gender stereotypes. A second group was asked why they chose to attend a selective private college. This primes students to focus on their intellectual talent. The control group was asked an irrelevant question about living in the northeastern United States. In the control group, men outperformed women on the spatial test, as in prior research. In the group primed to focus on gender, the women did even worse, and the men did better. In the group cued to think about their status as students at a selective college, however, the gender gap closed dramatically. Women's scores increased while men's stayed the same, wiping out the gender difference in performance.

Mathematics Ability

In the most comprehensive review to date of gender differences in mathematics performance, Janet Hyde and her colleagues (1990) did a meta-analysis of 100 studies involving more than 3 million individuals. They found a small difference in computation skills favoring girls up to age 15. Girls and boys did equally well at understanding mathematical concepts at all ages. In tests of problem solving, boys began to do better than girls starting at age 15. In studies that sampled from the general population, overall gender differences were smallest, with females showing a slight edge over males. However, in highly select samples (for instance, college students or mathematically precocious youth), differences in mathematics performance were larger and favored males and now are fairly small (Else-Quest & Hyde, 2008).

Gender differences in mathematics performance have decreased over time. One striking example is the change in the number of mathematically gifted girls and boys who score 700 on the math section of the SAT exam at age 13. Twenty-five years ago, there were 13 boys for every girl at that high level, achieved by only 1 out of every 10,000 students. Now, the ratio is only 2.8 to 1 (Valian, 2007). In addition, gender differences in mathematics performance no longer exist among U.S. elementary school students, although they still are present in high school (Mullis et al., 2004). The magnitude of the gender difference in mathematics is not the same in all cultures, however, as shown in Explore Other Cultures 5.1. A recent international study of 15-year-olds (Baldi et al., 2007) found no gender differences in scientific literacy in 22 out of 30 countries. When gender differences are found in science performance, they are typically greatest in physics, and favoring males, and small or nonexistent in the life sciences (Martin et al., 2004).

When we shift from scores on standardized tests to grades in mathematics classrooms, a different picture emerges. Girls receive higher grades than boys (Halpern, 2007; Kenney-Benson et al., 2006), even in samples of mathematically precocious youth, where the male advantage on standardized tests is greatest (Lubinski & Benbow,

EXPLORE OTHER CULTURES 5.1

Gender Differences in Mathematics Achievement around the World

Cross-cultural studies have generally found that males outperform females in mathematics and have higher mathematics self-efficacy (Halpern, 2004a; Martin et al., 2004; Penner, 2003; Programme for International Student Assessment, 2004). Of particular interest, however, is the finding that the size of the gender difference varies with the status of women in the countries studied (Else-Quest & Hyde, 2008; Riegle-Crumb, 2000, cited in Penner, 2003). One key factor appears to be the role of women in the workforce. According to Riegle-Crumb, female students are aware of the opportunities available to them, which then influences the amount of effort they invest in their education. The greater the percentage of women in a nation's labor force and the more opportunities they have to enter high-status occupations, the more positive

are girls' attitudes toward math, and the smaller is the gender gap in mathematics test scores (Baker & Jones, 1993). Even though much has been written about the gender gap in math in the United States, the gap is larger in East Asian countries such as Japan and Taiwan, with their greater emphasis on traditional gender roles (Evans et al., 2002). One particularly interesting finding is that East Asian girls, although they lag behind boys in their own countries, still score higher in math than boys of many other nations, including the United States (Valian, 2007). In Iceland, girls contradict the gender stereotype completely, habitually outperforming Icelandic boys on all parts of their national math exams (Angier & Chang, 2005). These results suggest the powerful role of culture in the social construction of math performance.

2007). When female and male college students in the same mathematics courses are compared, females earn the same or higher grades than males who have received higher scores on the mathematics portion of the SAT (Wainer & Steinberg, 1992). (This finding applies to other academic subjects as well. In other words, women receive higher grades in college than their SAT scores would predict [Leonard & Jiang, 1999]. Thus, of the women and men who would receive the *same grades* in college, fewer of the women are admitted because of their lower SAT scores.) Let us now examine more closely some of the factors associated with women's math performance.

Factors Associated with Math Performance. The single best predictor of scores on mathematics achievement tests is the number of mathematics courses an individual has taken. High school girls are now as likely as boys to take advanced mathematics and advanced biology and chemistry courses (National Science Foundation, 2008; Planty et al., 2007).

In college, however, many women avoid choosing math and science courses and careers even when they are gifted in mathematics (Ashcraft, 2002; Watt, 2008a). This is troubling, since mathematics is a critical factor in career development, paving the way to high-status and high-salary careers in the sciences, medicine, engineering, and business (Dey & Hill, 2007; Shapka et al., 2008). Why, then, do many young women begin to avoid math and science in college?

One important clue is found in the attitudes and feelings that females and males develop toward mathematics. Nancy Betz (2008) and her colleagues have examined the concept of **mathematics self-efficacy,** *a person's beliefs concerning her or his ability to successfully perform mathematical tasks.* They and other researchers around the world show that males have greater mathematics self-efficacy than females (Crombie et al., 2005; Kurman, 2004; Nagy et al., 2008; Programme for International Student Assessment, 2004; Simpkins et al., 2006; Watt, 2008b). Compared to males, females are more anxious about math and have less confidence in their ability to learn it, despite their equal or superior performance on tests and in the classroom. This self-perception emerges as early as elementary school, when girls begin to view math and science as part of the male domain (Ashcraft, 2002; Clewell & Campbell, 2002), and it continues into adolescence (Beyer, 2006; Lips, 2004; Watt, 2008b; Wigfield & Eccles, 2002). The more that girls endorse this stereotype, and the lower their self-confidence in math, the poorer their math performance (Crombie et al., 2005; Pietsch et al., 2003), and the less interest they have in continuing math studies (Crombie et al., 2005; Denissen et al., 2007; Kiefer & Sekaquaptewa, 2007; Schmader et al., 2004). Adolescent girls are also less likely than adolescent boys to view mathematics and science as interesting and valuable for their future careers (Leahy & Guo, 2001; Marsh et al., 2005). These negative attitudes have been found in Black, Latina, and White girls (Catsambis, 1999). Keep in mind, however, that many girls and women have positive views about math. For a more detailed look at factors that are associated with women's perspectives on math, see Learn about the Research 5.1.

Explanations of Gender Differences. Several theories have been proposed to account for gender differences in math performance and attitudes. One viewpoint is

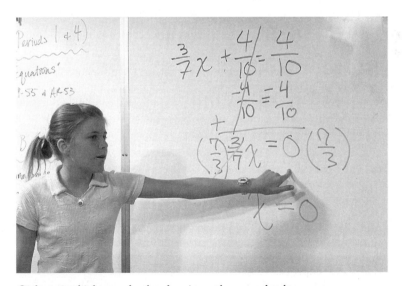

Girls receive higher grades than boys in math courses, but lower scores on standardized math tests such as the SAT. Why the discrepancy?

LEARN ABOUT THE RESEARCH 5.1
Factors Linked to Women's Perspectives on Math

Women's experiences with math and their attitudes toward it differ greatly. Debra Oswald and Richard Harvey (2003) set out to identify college women's differing perspectives on and experiences regarding math. They used a technique called the Q-method, which is considered a useful tool for feminist research (Kitzinger, 1999). In the first phase of the Q-method, women are interviewed about their thoughts, experiences, and attitudes regarding a topic, in this case, math. Researchers then select a large number of statements, called Q-sort items, and ask a new group of women to sort the items on a scale ranging from *strongly disagree* to *strongly agree*. Finally, participants with shared viewpoints are grouped together. Oswald and Harvey identified three groups of college women who differed in their experiences, attitudes, and awareness of stereotypes about math. Over half the women, labeled the Successfully Encouraged group, had high self-perceived math ability, found math to be personally relevant, and had positive attitudes toward it. They had been encouraged by parents and teachers and were relatively unaware of negative stereotypes. About

20 percent of women were in the Mathematically Aversive group. They did not like math, had negative perceptions of their ability, and were somewhat aware of negative stereotypes about women and math. Although not directly discouraged in math, neither were they encouraged to pursue it. Nearly 20 percent of women belong to the Stereotypically Discouraged group, consisting of women who were very aware of negative gender stereotypes regarding math, lacked parental and teacher support, and had negative experiences in math. These women were fairly neutral in their attitudes toward math and in their own math abilities.

This study clearly shows that a number of variables, including self-perceived ability, experience with math, encouragement (or discouragement), and degree of awareness of stereotypes, are key factors linked to women's perspectives on mathematics. The authors were encouraged that their largest group consisted of Successfully Encouraged women. They saw this as a possible indicator that women may become better represented in math-related fields in the future.

What Does It Mean?

1. The Stereotypically Discouraged group was keenly aware of gender stereotypes about math. Do you think these women might be experiencing *stereotype threat?* (See p. 147.) Explain your answer.
2. Do you think the results of this study would have been different if the participants had

been a group of noncollege women? Explain your answer.
3. Into which of the three groups would you place yourself? Explain your answer.

that genetic, hormonal, and/or structural brain differences underlie gender differences in mathematical ability (Geary, 2007; Kimura, 2007). Critics have argued that research fails to support this interpretation (Halpern, 2000; Newcombe, 2007a; Spelke, 2005), and the biological approach remains controversial.

Most researchers who study gender differences assert that whatever biological factors might exist are dwarfed by social forces that steer girls and young women away from mathematics. For starters, parents and peers give less encouragement and support to girls than to boys for studying math (Clewell and Campbell, 2002; Simpkins et al., 2005). As early as first grade, parents in the United States, Japan, China, Finland, and Great Britain believe that boys are better than girls in mathematics (Furnham et al., 2002; Lummis & Stevenson, 1990; Räty & Kasanen, 2007; Räty et al., 2006). These beliefs and expectations influence parents' perceptions and behaviors toward their children and also the children's own perceptions and behaviors (Tiedemann, 2000). For example, a series of studies by Jacquelynne Eccles and her colleagues (e.g., Eccles et al., 2000) found that parents with stronger stereotypes about the abilities of girls and boys in math, English, and sports had different expectations of their own daughters' and sons' abilities in these areas. These expectations, in turn, were linked to their children's performance and self-perceptions of competence regardless of their actual ability levels.

How are parents' expectations transmitted to their children? Among other things, parents provide different experiences for their daughters and sons. For example, they are more likely to buy their sons science-related toys and computer materials (Bleeker, 2003; Simpkins et al., 2005) and to enroll them in summer computer camps (D'Amico et al., 1995). (See Learn about the Research 5.2 for a discussion of gender, computers, and video games.) In addition, when parents take their young children to interactive science exhibits at museums, they are more likely to explain the science to their sons than to their daughters (Crowley et al., 2001). Similarly, both mothers and fathers are more likely to use scientific concepts and vocabulary when explaining a physics task to a son than to a daughter (Tenenbaum & Leaper, 2003; Tenenbaum et al., 2005).

Children receive the same message in the math and science classroom, as illustrated in Nathalie's comments at the start of the chapter. High school math and science teachers believe boys to be more interested, more confident, and higher achievers in these school subjects than girls (Plucker, 1996). Teachers not only expect boys to do better, but they also overrate male students' capacity to do math (Halpern, 2000; Li, 1999). Since expectations often guide behavior, it is not surprising to find that math teachers spend more time instructing, interacting with, and giving feedback to boys than to girls (AAUW, 1992; Jovanovic & Dreves, 1997). Even the president of Harvard University, Lawrence Summers, recently asserted that women may be innately inferior to men in mathematics (Angier & Chang, 2005). These remarks highlight the prejudices women scientists face at every stage of their careers (Kantrowitz, 2005). And who knows how many young women are discouraged by such remarks from pursuing such careers in the first place? Recent research (Beilock et al., 2007; National Academies of Sciences, 2007) indicates that negative stereotypes continue to discourage women from entering math and science careers and interfere with retention and advancement in these areas.

These prejudices provide another explanation for the poorer math performance of females, namely, the concept of **stereotype threat.** According to this view, developed by Claude Steele and his colleagues, *members of stereotyped groups (e.g., women and ethnic minorities) sometimes perform more poorly on tests because they are distracted and anxious about whether their performance will confirm a negative stereotype held about the group's ability* (Cadinu et al., 2005; Dar-Nimrod & Heine, 2006; Huguet & Régner,

2007; Jaffe, 2004; Kersting, 2003b; C. M. Steele, et al., 2002). Picture, for example, two college-bound straight-A high school students, one a girl and one a boy, taking the math portion of the SAT or ACT exam. While both experience frustration and difficulty with some of the problems, she has the additional performance-impairing stress of knowing that her performance may confirm the stereotype of female inferiority in math (Quinn & Spencer, 2001). Stereotype threat theory further predicts that performance suffers only when stereotype threat is activated but not when it is reduced or removed.

LEARN ABOUT THE RESEARCH 5.2
Gender, Computers, and Video Games

Girls and boys both like to play video games, but boys spend more time playing them (Brener et al., 2007; Dill & Thill, 2007; Hilbrecht et al., 2008; Ogletree & Drake, 2007; Willoughby, 2008). Why is this? One major reason is the content of video games, most of which have violent themes (Tafalla, 2007). The few females who appear in the games are often portrayed as "Barbies in sexy combat gear" (Vogt, 1997, p. 6). They are more likely than male characters to be shown partially nude or engaging in sexual behaviors (Burgess et al., 2005; Dill & Thill, 2007; Jansz & Martis, 2007; Miller & Summers, 2007; Ogletree & Drake, 2007). Feminist critics, such as bell hooks, challenge the notion that video-game portrayals of hypersexualized women as heartless killers represent an advance for women (Marriott, 2003). In fact, presenting women in this negative manner may decrease the attractiveness of many video games for girls and thus their time commitment. Girls and women prefer educational, action and adventure-type games, and have less interest in violence and sports themes (Cherney & London, 2006; Hafner, 2004; Wartella et al., 2004). Since 1995, the number of games designed for girls has increased sharply, but girls' games are as stereotyped as those designed for boys, featuring Barbies, makeovers, jewelry, and cooking (Rabasca, 2000; Seedyk & de Laet, 2005; Van Evra, 2004). In 1999, Mattel released the Barbie PC, a pink Barbie-themed computer for girls. But

to the dismay of several critics, the Barbie PC comes with just a little more than half of the educational software found on Mattel's companion computer for boys (blue, of course), the Hot Wheels PC. Omitted were programs dealing with logic, human anatomy, and spatial visualization (Headlam, 2000).

The gender gap in video-game usage has important implications for girls' experience with computers, since video games often provide a child's introduction to the computer. By the time children enter school, and well into adulthood, males have more positive attitudes toward computers than females and have greater confidence in their computer skills (Beyer, 2006; Johnson et al., 2008; Van Evra, 2004). Boys are more likely than girls to attend summer computer camps and clubs and to enroll in computer programming courses in high school and college (AAUW, 1998; Levesque 2003; Morahan-Martin & Schumacher, 1998). Although overall computer and Internet use rates for girls and boys are now about the same, boys are using computers to program, create Web pages, and solve problems, whereas girls' computer use tends to focus on verbal activities such as word processing, sending e-mail, or visiting chat rooms (DeBell & Chapman, 2004; Stabiner, 2003; Wartella et al., 2004).

How can girls' attitudes toward computing be improved? Video games and educational software should be less gender-biased instead of being

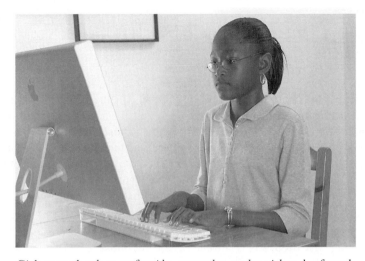

Girls, more than boys, prefer video games that are less violent, less focused on sports, and that emphasize intellectual challenge.

constructed around male themes of violence and adventure (Sheldon, 2004). Here are some other suggestions (AAUW, 2000; Burlingame-Lee & Canetto, 2005):

- Teachers should use computers throughout the curriculum, including areas in which girls excel.

- Efforts should be made to combat girls' popular stereotype that computer work is masculine and antisocial.
- Computer clubs and summer computer classes for girls should be encouraged.

What Does It Mean?

1. Why are most video games and educational software dominated by themes of violence and adventure?
2. What do you think accounts for gender differences in computer-related attitudes?

3. What can be done to minimize or eliminate these differences?
4. Why are positive attitudes toward computers important in today's society?

To test this prediction, Claude Steele and his colleagues (Spencer et al., 1999) gave mathematically skilled students two math tests. Before the tests, students were told that, in the past, men had done better than women on one test but not the other. On the test in which men supposedly outperformed women (thus activating stereotype threat), the women did worse than the men. But on the test in which women and men supposedly performed at the same level (thus eliminating the threat), women performed as well as men. Similar results have been found in many academic settings, from elementary school through college, using various manipulations to either activate or minimize stereotype threat (Davies et al., 2005; Ford et al., 2004; Johns et al., 2005; Keller & Dauenheimer, 2003; Lesko & Corpus, 2006; Muzzatti & Agnoli, 2007). The good news is that the pressures associated with negative stereotypes can be overcome by teaching students ways to reduce stereotype threat. For example, Catherine Good and her colleagues (Good, 2003) assigned college students to mentor seventh graders in a low-income ethnically diverse school district. Some children were told that intelligence developed over time, and that they could overcome challenges and achieve academic success. Others were given unrelated information about drug use. Girls given the positive message about their academic skills scored higher on a standardized math test than girls given the unrelated message. Similarly, minority and low-income students given the positive academic message did better on a standardized reading test than those in the unrelated message group.

Gender Equity in Science and Math Education. In the past decade, increasing emphasis has been given to establishing gender equity in the fields of science, mathematics, and engineering education. The National Science Foundation and the AAUW Educational Foundation alone have spent almost $90 million to fund over 400 projects aimed at increasing the participation of girls and women in these fields. The publication Under the Microscope (AAUW, 2004) provides an outstanding summary of these efforts. About two-thirds of the funded projects involve extracurricular activities such as field trips and museums; a large number include mentoring activities; and others provide workshops for teachers. Most projects, however, have occurred outside the regular school curriculum, rather than focusing on changing the formal school curriculum and the classroom environment.

What are some things teachers can do to make the math and science classroom more "girl friendly"? Females respond more positively to math and science instruction if they are taught in a cooperative, group-oriented manner, using an applied perspective and a hands-on approach rather than in the traditional competitive manner using a theoretical perspective and a book-learning approach (Hartman & Hartman, 2008). When the former practices are used, both girls and boys are more likely to continue taking courses in math and science and to consider future careers in these fields (Eccles & Roeser, 1999). In addition, having one or more faculty mentors is a key factor in attracting high school and college women to science careers (Downing et al., 2005).

SUMMARY

Gender-Related Social Behaviors and Personality Traits

- Girls and boys are more alike than different in their social behaviors and personality traits. Gender differences, when found, are generally small.
- Boys are more physically aggressive than girls, whereas girls are more likely to use relational aggression.

- Girls and boys are similar in prosocial behavior, but the few observed differences favor girls.
- Females are somewhat more easily influenced than males in certain situations.
- Girls are more likely than boys to express their emotions and report feeling empathy. Whether this reflects actual differences in emotionality or in the willingness to report feelings remains an open question.

- Research does not support Kohlberg's and Gilligan's claim of gender differences in the underlying basis of moral reasoning. Both females and males show caring and justice concerns in resolving moral conflicts.

Communication Style

- Gender differences in verbal communication include males' greater talkativeness and intrusive interruptions and females' greater affiliative interruptions and their use of speech characterized as tentative. When responding to friends' troubles, women are more likely than men to give support and less likely to give advice.
- Both college women and men like to talk to their friends about the other gender. However, women's conversations focus on interpersonal issues more than do men's.
- Females smile and gaze at their conversational partner more than males do. They are also better able to interpret nonverbal messages. These differences might reflect the communal socialization of females. Another possibility is that women's ability to understand others is an adaptive mechanism that stems from their lower societal status.
- Explanations for these gender differences focus on females' interpersonal orientation and the gender imbalance in power.

Gender Comparison of Cognitive Abilities

- Females and males do not differ in general intelligence but show some differences in certain cognitive skills.
- Girls have a slight advantage in verbal skills beginning in infancy. Girls outperform boys in reading, writing, and speech production and are less likely to have reading problems.
- On visual–spatial tests, gender differences favoring boys are greatest in mental rotation, less in spatial perception, and smaller or absent in spatial visualization.
- Girls are better than boys in mathematics computation skills and get better grades in mathematics courses. Boys are better at problem solving starting in mid-adolescence and perform better on standardized mathematics tests.
- Biological explanations for gender differences in cognitive skills focus on genetics, hormones, and brain structure or organization.
- Environmental explanations include differential socialization of girls and boys by parents and teachers, gender typing of activities as feminine or masculine, gender differences in attitudes toward various cognitive skills, and stereotype threat.

KEY TERMS

relational aggression
prosocial behavior
persuasion studies
group pressure conformity
    studies

empathy
affiliative interruption
intrusive interruption
mental rotation
spatial perception

spatial visualization
lateralization
mathematics self-efficacy
stereotype threat

WHAT DO YOU THINK?

1. Why do you think girls are more likely than boys to engage in relational aggression?

2. Adolescent girls report feeling more sadness, shame, and guilt than adolescent boys do. Do you think that females are actually

more emotional than males or are simply more likely to report their feelings? Explain your answer.

3. Explanations for gender differences in verbal communication style focus on females'

interpersonal orientation and the gender imbalance in power. Which of these explanations do you favor? Explain your answer.

4. What can parents do to maximize girls' potential for learning and liking math?

IF YOU WANT TO LEARN MORE

Cameron, D. (2007). *The myth of Mars and Venus: Do men and women really speak different languages?* New York: Oxford University Press.

Canary, D. J., & Dindia, K. (Eds.). (2006). *Sex differences and similarities in communication* (2nd ed.). Mahwah, NJ: Erlbaum.

Cooper, J., & Weaver, K. D. (2003). *Gender and computers: Understanding the digital divide.* Mahwah, NJ: Erlbaum.

Halpern, D. F. (2000). *Sex differences in cognitive abilities* (3rd ed.). Mahwah, NJ: Erlbaum.

Howes, E. V. (2002). *Connecting girls and science: Constructivism, feminism, and science education reform.* New York: Teachers College Press.

Margolis, J., & Fisher, A. (2002). *Unlocking the clubhouse: Women in computing.* Cambridge, MA: MIT Press.

Putallaz, M., & Bierman, K. L. (Eds.). (2004). *Aggression, anti-social behavior, and violence among girls.* New York: Guilford.

Shields, S. A. (2002). *Speaking from the heart: Gender and the social meaning of emotion.* Cambridge: Cambridge University Press.

Underwood, M. K. (2003). *Social aggression among girls.* New York: Guilford.

Xie, Y., & Shauman, K. A. (2003). *Women in science: Career processes and outcomes.* Cambridge, MA: Harvard University Press.

WEBSITES

Association for Women in Mathematics

http://www.awm-math.org/

Girl Tech: Getting Girls Interested in Computers

http://math.rice.edu/~lanius/club/girls.html

Women in Engineering: Programs and Advocates Network

http://wepan.cecs.ucf.edu

6 Sexuality

Sexuality
Sexual Anatomy and Sexual Response
Sexual Attitudes
Sexual Behaviors
Sexual Problems
Lesbians and Bisexual Women
Bisexual Women

Attitudes Towards Lesbians
Explanations of Sexual Orientation
Sexual Activity During Adolescence
Frequency of Sexual Activity
Factors Associated with Sexual Activity
The Double Standard
Sexual Desire

Sexual Activity in Midlife
   Physical Changes
   Patterns of Sexual Activity
Sexual Activity in Later Life
   Benefits of Sexual Activity in Later Life

Sexual Behavior of the Elderly
   Factors Affecting Sexual Behavior
   Enhancing Sexuality in Later Life

I don't want to be forced to take care of a child that I'm not ready for or get an S.T.D . . . As for sex, it'll happen someday, but just not today. (17-year-old female high school senior; in Villarosa, 2003, p. D6)

   We didn't have the choice of time when the kids were young. Now we have time during the day. We seldom make love at nighttime. Now we can choose. It might be 10 A.M. or 2 P.M.—whenever we're feeling turned on. (65-year-old woman; in Doress-Worters & Siegal, 1994, p. 85)

Did these opening vignettes surprise you? Both of them run counter to the popular stereotypes of the hormonally driven, sexually active teenager, on the one hand, and the sexually disinterested older woman, on the other. In this chapter, we explore the fascinating diversity of women's sexuality throughout the lifespan, including sexual attitudes, behaviors, problems, and orientations.

Sexuality

We start with a discussion of women's sexual anatomy and sexual response. Then we look at sexual attitudes, behaviors, and problems.

Sexual Anatomy and Sexual Response

External Female Sexual Anatomy.   The *external female sexual organs*, collectively called the **vulva**, are shown in Figure 6.1. Women can get a clear view of their own vulva by squatting and looking into a hand mirror. The **mons pubis** (also *mons veneris*, mountain of Venus) is *a pad of fatty tissue covering the pubic bone*. During puberty, it becomes covered with coarse hair. The hair continues between the legs and around the anus, the opening of the large intestine. The *fatty hair-covered area between the legs forms flaps called* the **labia majora** (outer lips). They surround *soft hairless flaps of skin*, the **labia minora** (inner lips). Between the inner lips and the anus lies the perineum (Rathus et al., 2008). Spreading the inner lips apart reveals that they join at the upper

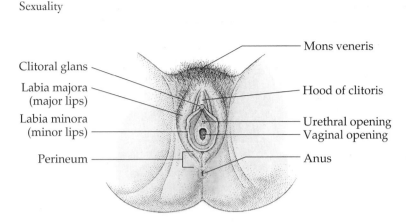

Clitoral glans

Labia majora
(major lips)

Labia minora
(minor lips)

Perineum

Mons veneris

Hood of clitoris

Urethral opening
Vaginal opening

Anus

FIGURE 6.1   Female External Sex Organs

Source: Rathus et al. (2008, p. 69, Fig. 3.5). Reprinted with permission from Allyn & Bacon.

end to form a fold of skin, or *hood* over the **clitoris.** *This highly sensitive organ, whose only known function is sexual pleasure, consists of erectile tissue that swells during sexual stimulation* (somewhat like the penis). Although smaller than the penis, the clitoris has more than twice as many nerve fibers (Schulman, 2003). Right below the clitoris is the urethral opening, through which urine passes. Below that is the larger vaginal opening. The **vagina** is *the canal leading to the uterus*. The menstrual blood passes through it and it is the birth canal during childbirth (Rathus et al., 2008).

The Sexual Response Cycle.   William Masters and Virginia Johnson (1966) first described the **sexual response cycle,** *the physiological responses of women and men to sexual stimulation from any source* (sexual intercourse, masturbation, etc.). They pointed out that women and men respond similarly during the four phases of the cycle. Here we discuss women's responses.

In the *excitement phase*, a major response is **vasocongestion,** *the swelling of genital tissues with blood*. Vasocongestion produces vaginal lubrication within 30 seconds after stimulation. The clitoris and labia swell with blood. The inner two-thirds of the vagina expand, the uterus elevates, the breasts enlarge, the nipples become erect, and the skin becomes flushed. Heart rate, breathing rate, and muscle tension increase.

During the *plateau phase*, the clitoris, now extremely sensitive, shortens and withdraws under the clitoral hood. *The low third of the vagina becomes engorged with blood, forming* the **orgasmic platform.** Heart rate, blood pressure, and breathing rate continue to rise.

In the *orgasmic phase*, the orgasmic platform, uterus, and anal sphincters contract strongly between 3 and 15 times, at intervals of less than a second. These contractions constitute the orgasm.

During the *resolution* phase, the *body returns to its pre-arousal state* within 15 to 30 minutes. Blood is released from engorged areas, the clitoris, vagina, uterus, and labia return to normal size, and muscle tension dissipates. Heart rate and breathing rate return to pre-arousal levels.

Multiple Orgasms.   Alfred Kinsey and his colleagues (Kinsey et al., 1953) reported that 14 percent of the women they interviewed experienced multiple orgasms. Although a few studies have reported higher percentages, most report figures of about 5 percent, in line with Kinsey's research ("Women Can Have," 2007). Unlike women, few, if any, men are physiologically capable of multiple orgasms. This is one of the major gender differences in sexual response, the other being that men but not women ejaculate during orgasm. While having multiple orgasms can be a good thing, some women now feel that they are sexually inadequate if they don't. One orgasm can be quite satisfying, as can sex that does not culminate in orgasm.

One or Two Kinds of Orgasm?   Freud (1938) proposed that there were two types of female orgasm: clitoral and vaginal. Clitoral orgasms were achieved through clitoral stimulation during masturbation. This form of orgasm, practiced by young girls, was considered immature and sexually inadequate in adult women. Women were expected to shift to vaginal orgasms, brought on by sexual intercourse. Masters and Johnson (1966), however, demonstrated that there is only one kind of orgasm, physiologically, whether it is brought on by clitoral or vaginal stimulation. Furthermore, the clitoris is indirectly stimulated even in vaginal intercourse. While orgasms resulting from clitoral and vaginal stimulation are physiologically the same, there may be psychological or subjective differences. For example, the context of sexual intercourse includes a partner to whom one may be emotionally attached, whereas masturbation is often (but not always) done without the presence of a partner.

Sexual Attitudes

The Sexual Double Standard.   Historically, women's sexuality was discouraged and denied, especially outside of marriage. The social construction of norms about female and male sexuality is nowhere seen more clearly than in this **sexual double standard,** *which allowed and even encouraged premarital sex for men, but not for women.* As premarital sex became more acceptable, the double standard has evolved into a belief that casual sexual activity is acceptable for men, but that women's sexual experiences should occur only in the context of a serious relationship (O'Sullivan et al., 2006). As examples of the double standard, young women are judged more negatively than young men when they provide a condom for protection (Fassinger & Arseneau, 2008) or when they have a sexually transmitted illness (Smith et al., 2008).

Gender Differences in Attitudes.   Women generally have less permissive attitudes toward sexual behavior than men (Kennedy & Gorzalka, 2002). In a review of a large number of studies on sexual attitudes and behavior, Mary Oliver and Janet Hyde (1993) found that women reported much more negative attitudes than men about casual premarital sex. Women were moderately less approving than men of extramarital sex and of premarital sex when couples are committed or engaged. They were somewhat more likely to feel anxious or guilty about sex and to endorse the double standard. No gender differences were found in attitudes toward masturbation, however. In general, gender differences in attitudes toward sexual behavior overall narrowed as people got older. These differences also diminished from the 1960s through the 1990s. Another consistent gender difference in attitudes is women's tendency to emphasize relationships and commitment as a context for sex (Tiegs et al., 2007). This difference has been widely documented among heterosexuals, lesbians, and gay men. Finally, men from countries around the world are more likely than women to rate sex as important and to report greater physical and emotional pleasure from it (Angier, 2007).

Attitudes Toward Women with Disabilities. Girls and young women with disabilities may face particular challenges in developing a healthy sexuality (APA Task Force, 2007). A common assumption is that women with disabilities are asexual beings who have no sex life and who are unsuitable as romantic partners (Crawford & Ostrove, 2003; Dotson et al., 2003; Nosek et al., 2006; Olkin, 2008). Many women with disabilities have spoken out about the unavailability of adequate counseling on sexuality, birth control, pregnancy, and childbirth. Women with disabilities are less satisfied with their sex lives than able-bodied women and report that they do not get enough touching in their lives (Mestel, 2000; Nosek et al., 2008). While able-bodied women often resent being treated as sex objects, some women with disabilities resent being treated as asexual objects (Lisi, 1993). The view of women with disabilities as asexual is based on misconceptions about the sexual desires and abilities of women with disabilities. Most individuals with disabilities have the same sexual desires as able-bodied persons. Their ability to perform sexually depends on their adjustment to the physical limitations of their disability and the availability of a helpful partner (Rathus et al., 2008).

Sexual Behaviors

There is considerable consistency between sexual attitudes and sexual behaviors. Those with more permissive attitudes toward premarital, extramarital, or homosexual relations are more likely to have engaged in those behaviors. For example, 75 percent of women and men who say extramarital relations are not at all wrong have had such relations, whereas only 10 percent of those who believe extramarital relations are always wrong have been unfaithful (Smith, 1994). The consistency between sexual attitudes and behaviors may mean that people act in accordance with their attitudes, but it can also mean that people rationalize their sexual activity by adopting matching attitudes. Both may be involved.

In the National Health and Social Life Survey (NHSLS), the most comprehensive study of sexuality in America in the 1990s, researchers surveyed a representative sample of over 3,400 Americans from ages 18 to 59 (Laumann et al., 1994). They found that the vast majority of married Americans reported having sexual relations either a few times per month or two to three times a week, with an average of seven times a month. The frequency of sexual relations declined gradually with age, with 50- to 59-year-olds reporting an average of four to five times a month. The most sexually active women were those ages 25 to 29, 96 percent of whom reported sexual activity during the past year as compared to 59 percent of the 55- to 59-year-old women. Both women and men expressed fairly high levels of satisfaction with marital sex, although women were slightly less satisfied.

Gender Differences.   A number of gender differences in sexual activity have been reported, largely corresponding to gender differences in attitudes toward sexuality. Men, compared to women, have a higher incidence of intercourse and oral sex, more frequent intercourse, a greater number of partners, and a younger age at first intercourse (AARP, 2005c; Mosher et al., 2005; Oliver & Hyde, 1993). Interestingly, the largest gender difference is in the incidence of masturbation, even though attitudes toward masturbation are about the same. The size of this difference is shown in the NHSLS study which found that 7 percent of women, but 28 percent of men, reported masturbating at least once a week (Laumann et al., 1994). Also, while the great majority of married individuals reported being faithful to their spouses, more men than women said they had engaged in extramarital sex (D. Smith, 2002). This gender gap is closing, however. In a nationwide survey in 1991, 10 percent of women reported being unfaithful. This figure jumped to 15 percent in 2002, while the percentage for men remained at 22 percent over the same time period (Ali & Miller, 2004).

Letitia Anne Peplau (2002) sums up these differences as indicating that men are more interested in sex than are women. She also contends that assertiveness and dominance are more closely linked to male sexuality than to female sexuality. For example, she notes that men tend to initiate sex in heterosexual relationships and that men are more likely than women to use intimidation or physical force to get an unwilling partner to engage in sex (see Chapter 14). Another, more controversial, gender difference proposed by Peplau (2002) and by Roy Baumeister (2000) is that women have greater sexual plasticity, that is, that their sexual beliefs and behaviors are more capable of being shaped and changed by cultural, social, and situational factors. For example, women are more likely than men to engage in sexual behavior that runs counter to their established pattern of sexual desire, that is, heterosexual women having sex with women and lesbians engaging in sex with men (Diamond, 2003b). Women's sexual attitudes and behaviors also seem to be affected more by their education level and by the views of their culture than are men's attitudes and behaviors (Fassinger & Arseneau, 2008; Peplau, 2002).

Although gender differences in sexuality are well documented, we also must keep in mind that there are tremendous variations in sexual expression among women of different ages, marital statuses, educational levels, religions, and races/ethnicities. Women who are younger, White, well educated, and have no religious affiliation have more varied sexual practices than other women. For example, they are more likely to have experienced oral and anal sex and to find these acts appealing (Laumann & Mahay, 2002).

Two limitations of research on sexual attitudes and behaviors must be kept in mind. One is the problem of volunteer bias. Many people refuse to participate in surveys of their sexual views and practices. Thus, samples are biased because they include the responses only of those individuals who are willing to discuss their intimate behavior. Such individuals tend to be more sexually permissive and to have more liberal attitudes toward sexuality than nonvolunteers. Therefore, survey results based on volunteer samples may not be representative of the population at large (Rathus et al., 2008).

A second problem is that all the results are based on self-reports, not on direct observations of behavior. It is possible that there are gender differences in reporting behaviors, but few, if any, differences in sexual behaviors or attitudes. Women may underreport their sexual experiences and men may exaggerate theirs (Oliver & Hyde, 1993). As a result of these two problems, we must take findings regarding gender differences in sexuality with a grain of salt.

Sexual Problems

What constitutes a sexual problem or dysfunction for women? How frequently do such problems occur? These issues are currently topics of vigorous debate among researchers. The research of Masters and Johnson described earlier in the chapter focused on the physiology of sexual response, culminating in orgasm. Anything interfering with this outcome was defined as a sexual problem. Some psychologists argue that emphasizing orgasm reflects the male perspective that sex ends with ejaculation, whereas for many women, orgasm is not the goal or the most important part of sexual activity (Fassinger & Arseneau, 2008; Tolman et al., 2003). In this section, we examine changing views of women's sexual problems.

The University of Chicago Study.   In a frequently cited survey of American adults, ages 18 to 59, by University of Chicago psychologists (Laumann et al., 1999), 43 percent of women and 31 percent of men reported experiencing sexual dysfunction. The researchers employed the widely used system for classifying sexual dysfunction in women and men that appears in the Diagnostic and Statistical Manual of the American Psychiatric Association (1994). Four categories are recognized: sexual desire disorders, sexual arousal disorders, orgasmic disorders, and sexual pain disorders. Feminist scholars have criticized this categorization, as we shall see shortly, because it is overly genital and neglects issues of relationships and social context (Hartley & Tiefer, 2003).

In the study by Laumann and his colleagues, the most frequent sexual problem among women was *a lack of desire for sexual activity*, or **inhibited sexual desire.** About one in four women reported having this problem. (Persons who have little interest in sex, but are not concerned by it, are not considered to have the disorder.) About one in seven women reported **sexual arousal disorder,** which involves *insufficient lubrication or a failure to be aroused.* Most women with the disorder also had problems with desire and/or orgasm as well (Williams & Leiblum, 2002). Nearly one in four women reported **female orgasmic disorder,** defined as *experiencing the excitement phase of the sexual response cycle but not achieving orgasm.* If a woman is satisfied with this situation, she is not considered to have an orgasmic disorder. About 7 percent of women reported **dyspareunia,** or *painful intercourse.* Often a physical condition, such as a vaginal infection, sexually transmitted disease, lack of lubrication, or a structural problem, is involved. Psychological factors such as anxiety about sex or prior sexual trauma also may be responsible (Rathus et al., 2008). Another sexual pain disorder documented by Laumann and his colleagues is **vaginismus,** the *involuntary contraction of vaginal muscles,* making intercourse painful or impossible. Vaginismus is often caused by factors such as childhood sexual abuse, rape, a family upbringing that included negative attitudes toward sex, and a history of painful intercourse (Rathus et al., 2008).

The researchers found that factors such as age, marital status, ethnicity, education, and economic status were related to the incidence of sexual dysfunction. For women, the prevalence of sexual problems declined as they got older, except for those who reported trouble lubricating. Men, on the other hand, had more problems with age, such as trouble achieving and maintaining an erection and lack of interest in sex. Single, divorced, separated, and widowed individuals showed an elevated risk of sexual problems. Formerly married women, for example, were more likely than married women to experience sexual anxiety and have trouble reaching orgasm. Ethnicity also was associated with sexual problems. White women were more likely to report sexual pain, while Black women more often experienced low levels of desire and pleasure. Latinas, on the other hand, reported lower rates of sexual problems than other women.

Women and men with less education and lower income reported more sexual problems than more highly educated and affluent individuals. For example, women without high school diplomas were twice as likely as college educated women to experience low desire, problems achieving orgasm, sexual pain, and sexual anxiety. Lower levels of household income were associated with an increase in all categories of sexual dysfunction for women, but only in erectile dysfunction (impotence) for men. What might account for this social class difference in sexual problems? Poorer physical and mental health in individuals of lower social status may be a factor, since diminished health is related to problems with sex (AARP, 2005c; Wenzel et al., 2004). Underlying physical conditions that can cause sexual dysfunction include diabetes, heart disease, neurological disorders, side effects of medications, alcoholism and drug abuse, or heavy smoking. Psychological causes of sexual problems include stress or anxiety from work, concern about poor sexual performance, marital discord, or depression. Some of these problems are all too common in the lives of poor women and men (Brill, 2004; DeUgarte et al., 2004; Tiefer, 2001). Unfortunately, the sociocultural predictors of sexual problems studied by Laumann and his associates were given little attention in the popular and professional media. Instead, they focused on the high incidence of physiological problems, and the need for drug companies to develop medical treatments, such as female Viagra, to treat women's sexual "illnesses" (Driscoll & Groskop, 2003; Hankin, 2004; Hartley & Tiefer, 2003).

In the years since the University of Chicago study, increasing attention has been focused on sociocultural factors in women's sexual problems. For example, a recent telephone survey of women ages 20–65 who were in a heterosexual relationship found that only 24.4 percent reported "marked distress" about their sexual relationship, their own sexuality, or both (Bancroft et al., 2003). This figure was considerably lower than the 43 percent reported by Laumann and his colleagues. Why the striking difference? One possibility is that the telephone study excluded women who did not have a sexual partner, potentially eliminating women with serious sexual problems. But another reason is that this study focused more on psychological than on physical aspects of sex. The researchers found that the best predictors of a woman's sexual satisfaction were her general emotional well-being and her emotional relationship with her partner. Physical aspects of sexual response in women, such as arousal, vaginal lubrication, and orgasm, were poor predictors.

A New View of Women's Sexual Problems.   Along these same lines, a group of therapists and sex researchers has developed a new view of women's sexual problems that identifies the sociocultural, political, psychological, social, and relational bases of women's sexual problems (O'Sullivan et al., 2006; Tiefer, 2006). These researchers define sexual problems as discontent or dissatisfaction with any emotional, physical, or relational aspect of sexual experiences that may arise in one or more of four interrelated aspects of women's sexual lives (see Table 6.1). This view focuses on the *prevention* of women's sexual problems through tackling the economic, political, and sociocultural root causes of the problems, and not on medical treatment alone (McHugh, 2007; Tiefer, 2006).

TABLE 6.1   Women's Sexual Problems: A New Classification

Sexual problems, defined as discontent or dissatisfaction with any emotional, physical, or relational aspect of sexual experience, may arise in one or more of the following four interrelated aspects of women's sexual lives.

I. Sexual Problems Due to Sociocultural, Political, or Economic Factors

A. Ignorance or anxiety due to inadequate sex education, lack of access to health services, or other social constraints:
   1. Lack of vocabulary to describe physical or subjective experience.
   2. Lack of information about sexual biology and life-stage changes.
   3. Lack of information about how gender roles influence men's and women's sexual expectations, beliefs, and behaviors.
   4. Inadequate access to information and services that could provide contraception and abortion, sexually transmitted disease (STD) prevention and treatment, counseling for sexual trauma and domestic violence.
B. Sexual avoidance or distress due to perceived inability to meet cultural norms regarding correct or ideal sexuality, including:
   1. Anxiety or shame about one's body, sexual attractiveness, or sexual responses.
   2. Confusion or shame about one's sexual orientation or identity, or about sexual fantasies and desires.
C. Inhibitions due to conflict between the sexual norms of one's subculture or culture of origin and those of the dominant culture.
D. Lack of interest, fatigue, or lack of time due to family and work obligations.

II. Sexual Problems Relating to Partner and Relationship

A. Inhibition, avoidance, or distress arising from betrayal, dislike, or fear of partner, partner's abuse or couple's unequal power, or arising from partner's negative patterns of communication.
B. Discrepancies in desire for sexual activity or in preferences for various sexual activites.
C. Ignorance or inhibition about communicating preferences or initiating, pacing, or shaping sexual activities.
D. Loss of sexual interest and reciprocity as a result of conflicts over commonplace issues such as money, schedules, or relatives, or resulting from traumatic experiences, such as infertility or the death of a child.
E. Inhibitions in arousal or spontaneity due to partner's health status or sexual problems.

III. Sexual Problems Due to Psychological Factors

A. Sexual aversion, mistrust, or inhibition of sexual pleasure due to:
    1. Past experiences of physical, sexual, or emotional abuse.
    2. General personality problems with attachment, rejection, cooperation, or entitlement.
    3. Depression or anxiety.
B. Sexual inhibition due to fear of sexual acts or of their possible consequences, such as pain during intercourse, pregnancy, sexually transmitted disease (STD), loss of partner, loss of reputation.

IV. Sexual Problems Due to Medical Factors

A. Pain or lack of physical response during sexual activity despite a supportive and safe interpersonal situation, adequate sexual knowledge, and positive sexual attitudes. Such problems can arise from:
    1. Numerous local or systemic medical conditions affecting neurological, neurovascular, circulatory, endocrine, or other systems of the body.
    2. Pregnancy, sexually transmitted diseases, or other sex-related conditions.
    3. Side effects of many drugs, medications, or medical treatments.
    4. A medical treatment or diagnostic procedure, such as a hysterectomy or other necessary procedure.

Source: New View of Women's Sexual Problems. (See Hartley and Tiefer, 2003.)

Women's sexual problems may stem from sociocultural, psychological, and relational factors, as well as medical conditions.

Lesbians and Bisexual Women

Before reading this section, try the exercise in Get Involved 6.1. Compare your findings with the information that follows.

Sexual orientation consists of three components: sexual/romantic attraction, sexual behavior, and sexual identity (Savin-Williams, 2006). In the past, women's sexual orientation was divided into two categories: lesbian and heterosexual. Later, the bisexual category was added. Recently, a "mostly straight" identity has been proposed to describe women who fall between homosexuality and heterosexuality (Thompson & Morgan, 2008). A **lesbian** is a woman who is *emotionally and sexually attracted to other women*, a **gay male** is *attracted to other men*, and a **bisexual** person is *attracted to both men and women* (Frankowski, 2004). It is difficult to estimate the number of women who are lesbian and bisexual because negative attitudes toward homosexuality discourage some individuals from reporting this behavior. In addition, the sexual identities of women may change over time. Whereas many gay men recall their same-sex attraction

---

GET INVOLVED 6.1

Attitudes Towards Lesbians

Ask two female and two male friends to complete the following exercise:

Our society views some groups of unmarried women as having higher social status or acceptability than other groups of unmarried women. Give each group below a Social Status Score based on how you think these groups are viewed in our society. Assign each group a score ranging from 1 to 100, with *high* scores indicating *high* status and *low* scores indicating *low* status.

Social Status Score

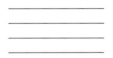

divorced heterosexual women	_____
never-married homosexual women	_____
widowed heterosexual women	_____
never-married heterosexual women	_____

What Does It Mean?

1. In what ways are your female and male respondents' answers alike? In what ways are they different? Explain the differences and similarities.
2. How does the social status of lesbians compare to that of the three groups of heterosexual women?
3. How would you account for the differences in social status of these four groups of women?

Source: Etaugh and Fulton (1995).

as beginning before puberty, many lesbians report not feeling same-sex attractions until adulthood (Diamond, 2007). In the NHSLS mentioned earlier, 2 percent of American women *identified* themselves as having a lesbian sexual orientation; 2 to 4 percent reported *engaging in sexual behavior* with women in the past five years; and 8 to 12 percent reported some *sexual attraction* to other women, but no sexual interaction since age 15. About 1 percent of women reported having a bisexual identity, and 1.4 percent reporting having both female and male partners (Laumann et al., 1994). However, a ten-year longitudinal study of lesbian and bisexual women found that two-thirds of the participants had changed sexual-minority identities at least once in their lives and over one-third had done so more than once (Diamond, 2008). In addition, the comprehensive National Longitudinal Study of Adolescent Health found a great deal of fluidity in romantic attractions and relationships over an 18-month period. For example, of the 4 percent of girls who reported bisexual attraction at the beginning of the study, only one-fourth did so 18 months later; the majority of them now reported attraction to and relationships with males (Russell & Seif, 2002). Findings like these suggest that female sexual orientation is more "fluid" than that of males, meaning that it is more sensitive to situational and contextual factors (Diamond, 2007).

Bisexual Women

Because most people view sexual orientation as consisting of two categories—heterosexual and homosexual—bisexual individuals tend to be either invisible (Macalister, 2003) or viewed as merely going through a transitional stage between heterosexuality and homosexuality (Diamond, 2008). Women who claim to be bisexual are often told that they are denying their true sexuality, and bisexuality sometimes is seen as a cop-out from commitment to a particular lifestyle or partner (Rust, 2000). Furthermore, bisexuality is often criticized by both heterosexuals and homosexuals as indicating promiscuity, indecisiveness, or immaturity (Morgan, 2002; Mulick & Wright, 2002). The dilemma faced by a bisexual woman was expressed this way:

> *Invisibility is a problem. Few people know we exist because we don't "fit" into either the heterosexual or the lesbian world. When we are open, both worlds judge us.* (Boston Women's Health Book Collective, 1992, p. 214)

One of Claire's students described the following experience in her journal:

> *If I hear "The lesbian's dating a boy?!" one more time . . . So I met a boy and we've started dating, not a big deal to me but obviously to others. My main issue here is pigeon-holing. "I thought you were supposed to be gay," as if I have become a caricature of a human.* (Angelique, age 22)

However, recent research shows that some women and men feel attracted to both sexes simultaneously and may carry on relationships with both men and women at the same time (Reinhardt, 2002). Large-scale surveys have found that among women, bisexual attractions are much more common than exclusive attractions to women, and many bisexuals are more attracted to one gender than the other (Rust, 2001). Currently, more women are experimenting with bisexuality or at least feel more comfortable reporting same-sex encounters than was the case in the early 1990s: 12 percent in 2005 versus 4 percent in 1998 (Mosher et al., 2005).

Same-sex sexuality thus is a matter of degree for many women, who do not clearly fit into any one category. In the words of Susan:

> *I'm in a physical/sexual sense 60 percent heterosexual and 40 percent gay . . . My sexual fantasies are often with a man but my romantic ones are with a woman . . . In the emotional realm I'm 30 percent heterosexual and 70 percent gay. I can't imagine spending my life with a guy! Sex wouldn't be enough. I want to take long trips with girls. I want to exchange lipstick colors and compare Hillary [Clinton] stories . . . I'm attracted to certain types of males, both the really femme girly boys and the really masculine studs . . . and the really feminine girls with powdered faces. The butch ones can be a Friday night fantasy. Don't think about writing down that I'm a lesbian, or even bisexual. I hate both words!* (Savin-Williams, 2006, p. 316)

Attitudes Towards Lesbians

Heterosexism is *the view that heterosexuality is the norm and that homosexuality is abnormal.* Sexual minority individuals may themselves internalize heterosexist attitudes (Szymanski & Owens, 2008). This view often leads to **homophobia,** *negative reactions to homosexuality and irrational fear of homosexuals.* Such reactions are pervasive not only in American society (Harper et al., 2004; Whitley, 2001a), but also in many other parts of the world (see Explore Other Cultures 6.1). In a 2002 survey of American adults, for example, 53 percent felt that sex between adults of the same sex is always wrong,

---

EXPLORE OTHER CULTURES 6.1
Lesbianism around the World

Lesbians and gay men are discriminated against in varying degrees by laws and social policies around the world. Same-gender sexual behavior still is illegal in 45 countries, including many African and predominantly Muslim nations. In these countries, homosexuality may be punishable with prison sentences (for example, in Nicaragua), beatings (Malaysia), and death (Afghanistan, Iran, Sudan, and Yemen [Burn, 2005]). Even where homosexuality is not illegal, lesbians and gays often do not "come out" for fear of losing their children, jobs, and social status, or becoming the target of physical or verbal attack (Burn, 2005).

While Americans have become more accepting of homosexuality in the past few decades, they are less tolerant than citizens of most other advanced democracies in Europe and North America. In France, Britain, Italy, Germany, Czech Republic, and Canada, 75 percent or more believe society should accept homosexuality. Americans, by comparison, are evenly divided on this issue, similar to the views in Latin American countries.

Lesbianism was acceptable in a number of Native American cultures before Western colonization. For instance, women from the Mohave,

Maricopa, Cocopa, Klamath, and Kaska tribes could marry other women and make love with other women without stigma (Burn, 2005). However, contemporary attitudes of Native Americans, which have been influenced by the dominant American culture, may be less accepting (Amaro et al., 2002). In the African country of Lesotho, it is not unusual for women to have romantic relationships with each other before and even during heterosexual marriage (Burn, 2005). However, these relationships occur less often in Lesotho women exposed to Western ideas.

Lesbian experiences vary not only among countries, but also within them. San Francisco,

for example, has an active lesbian community, but in most places in the United States, lesbians remain closeted. In countries such as Estonia, where it is acceptable for women to be unmarried, lesbians are more readily tolerated. Similarly, Thai culture allows two women to live together for extended periods of time, be publicly affectionate and even raise a child together, without assuming their relationship is sexual. This makes it possible for lesbians to live together as long as they keep the sexual aspect of their relationship hidden (Burn, 2005).

---

although on a positive note, this was down from 74 percent 15 years earlier (Pew Research Center, 2003). A recent survey of nearly 300,000 first-year college students found that 24 percent believed there should be laws banning homosexual relationships. Interestingly, 32 percent of male students but only 18 percent of females endorsed this statement ("This year's freshmen at 4-year colleges: A statistical profile," 2008). Similarly, a poll found that over one-third of Americans oppose gay marriage or civil unions (Nagourney & Thee, 2007). This view is especially strong among males, Republicans, people with a high degree of religious commitment, older individuals, and those with less education (Pew Research Center, 2003). Another poll found that nearly half of Americans opposed adoption rights for lesbian and gay couples. On the other hand, about 75 percent felt homosexuals should have equal rights in employment and housing, and supported health insurance and inheritance rights for gay spouses (Kaiser Family Foundation, 2001). Similar attitudes exist in the United Kingdom (Ellis, 2002). Those who believe that homosexuality is biologically based are more accepting of homosexuals than those who see it as a choice (Boysen & Vogel, 2007). For a look at a number of factors that influence attitudes toward lesbians and gay men, turn to Learn about the Research 6.1.

Women of Color.   People of color hold somewhat more negative attitudes toward homosexuality than do Whites (Schiffman et al., 2005; Whitley, 2001b). Thus, according to Ruth Hall and Beverly Greene (2002), lesbian women of color are in triple jeopardy. They face societal barriers of sexism, racism, and homophobia. In ethnic minority cultures, women who do not adhere to traditional gender roles or who are not subordinate to men are often ostracized. Lesbian members of these communities may be more reluctant to "come out," choosing to remain invisible rather than be rejected (Castañeda, 2008; Cole & Guy-Sheftall, 2003; Parks et al., 2004).

Discrimination.   Discrimination against lesbians can take many forms. The most virulent form of homophobia is expressed in violent "hate crimes" often committed against gay males by groups of adolescent or young adult males (Federal Bureau of Investigation, 2002; Herek, 2007; Mason, 2002). The most frequent forms of harassment experienced by gay, lesbian, bisexual, and transgender youth in school are being

Lesbian relationships are more accepted in Europe and Canada than in the United States.

LEARN ABOUT THE RESEARCH 6.1

Who Is Homophobic?

Although negative attitudes toward lesbians and gays are prevalent in American society, the degree of homophobia varies markedly from one individual to another and some people are not homophobic at all. Homophobic attitudes are more likely to be found among individuals who are older, less well educated, politically conservative, and from the Midwest, South, and rural areas. Those who hold traditional gender-role attitudes, fundamentalist religious beliefs, and authoritarian right-wing views also have more negative attitudes toward lesbians and gays (Nagoshi et al., 2008; Pew Research Center, 2003; Whitley, 2002, 2007). Men are more homophobic than women (remember the study of the first-year college students?), particularly toward gay men (I. Anderson, 2004; Nierman et al., 2007; Roper & Halloran, 2007). Gender differences in attitudes toward lesbians are generally small or absent (Herek, 2000).

What Does It Mean?

1. Individuals with traditional gender-role attitudes are also more likely to have negative attitudes toward gays and lesbians. Propose a possible connection between these two sets of attitudes.

2. Why do you think men are more homophobic than women?

3. What steps can be taken by individuals and communities to ensure more equal treatment of lesbians and gays?

called names and being ridiculed in front of others (Beemyn, 2005; Rivers, 2002). One survey of community college students by Karen Franklin (1998) found that nearly one-quarter admitted to verbally harassing people they thought were gay or lesbian. Among men, 18 percent said they had physically assaulted or threatened to assault gays or lesbians. In a nationwide survey of more than 2,200 lesbians, gays, and bisexuals, three-quarters of the sample reported having experienced prejudice and discrimination based on their sexual orientation. About 75 percent had been verbally attacked and one-third had been the target of physical violence against their person or property (Kaiser Family Foundation, 2001). Lesbian and bisexual women are at greater risk of experiencing sexual and physical abuse than are heterosexual women (Moracco et al., 2007). One analysis of seven adolescent health surveys in Canada and the United States found that up to two in five lesbian and bisexual girls and one in three gay and bisexual boys reported abuse (Saewyc et al., 2004). Even at colleges with strong support groups for gay, lesbian, bisexual, and transgender students, more than one-third of these students say they have been harassed within the previous year, primarily by other students (Rankin, 2003).

Home may not be a safe haven either. Lesbian, gay, and bisexual teens and adults who "come out"—that is, declare their sexual orientation to others—may be rejected by their families. In some cases, they are compelled to leave home and seek survival in the streets (Herek & Garnets, 2007; Markowe, 2002; Rivers, 2002; Rostosky et al., 2004; Savin-Williams & Ream, 2003). Such experiences, not surprisingly, can lead to a reluctance to reveal one's sexual orientation (Fassinger & Arseneau, 2008) and to increased levels of emotional stress and psychological problems among harassed individuals (Marsh, 2006; Thompson & Johnston, 2004). We shall explore some of these problems more fully in Chapter 13. Despite the stresses faced by many lesbian, gay, and bisexual youth, the good news is that most display strength and resiliency and are often involved in antihomophobia advocacy efforts (Holmes & Cahill, 2004).

Although some states have laws that ban discrimination on the basis of sexual orientation in employment, credit, housing, and public accommodation, many do not. Only one-quarter of employers offer domestic partner health benefits ("Gays Win," 2003). Same-sex marriage is specifically banned in most states; as of this writing it is legal only in Massachusetts, Connecticut, and California, although, Hawaii, Maine, New Jersey, New Hampshire, Oregon Vermont, and Washington give same-sex couples spousal rights (Liptak, 2008; McFadden, 2008; "Ruling allows legal status for partners of same-sex," 2008). The Netherlands, Spain, Belgium, South Africa, and Canada allow same-sex marriages, and several other countries permit same-sex couples to register as partners (Garrow, 2004; Hoge, 2002; Liptak, 2008; Lyall, 2005; McLean, 2005). Courts in about half the states in the United States allow lesbian or gay individuals to adopt their partner's child (Liptak, 2005). This right was recently endorsed by the American Academy of Pediatrics (Belluck & Liptak, 2004).

Explanations of Sexual Orientation

The origins of homosexuality are complex and controversial (Diamond, 2007). A number of psychological and biological theories have been proposed. According to Sigmund Freud (1925/1989), all individuals are initially bisexual. The mother is the original love object for both girls and boys. In heterosexual development, the father becomes the girl's love object, and she substitutes other males for him as she gets older. When the mother remains the love object, lesbian development occurs. Little evidence exists in support of this theory, however. From a learning theory point of view, early positive sexual activity with members of one's own gender or negative sexual experiences with members of the other gender could lead to homosexuality. However, many lesbians and gay males are aware of their sexual orientation before they have engaged in any sexual activity (Carver et al., 2004).

Biological theories focus on genetic or hormonal factors. In one study, 48 percent of identical twin sisters of lesbians were also lesbians, compared with just 16 percent of fraternal twin sisters, and 6 percent of adopted sisters (Bailey et al., 1993). So, sexual orientation appears to be at least partly genetic. But if genetics were the whole story, 100 percent of the identical twin sisters would be lesbian.

Is sexual orientation influenced by sex hormones? In adulthood, there is no link between levels of female and male sex hormones and sexual orientation (Veniegas & Conley, 2000). *Prenatal* sex hormones may be a factor, however. Studies of intersexuality discussed in Chapter 3 pointed to the prenatal influence of androgen on the development of females' sexual orientation. For example, the inner ears of lesbians function more like the inner ears of men than those of heterosexual women (McFadden, 2002). Similarly, the finger-length patterns and the brain responses to sex hormones in lesbians resemble those of men more than those of heterosexual women (Berglund et al., 2006; Brown et al., 2002; Williams et al., 2000). These findings suggest that high levels of androgens (male sex hormones) during the prenatal period may partially masculinize certain physiological and anatomical characteristics of lesbians, including the brain structures responsible for sexual orientation (Lalumiére et al., 2000; Rahman et al., 2003).

Most likely, complex interactions among genetic, hormonal, and environmental factors determine sexual orientation, and different causal mechanisms may operate for different individuals (Rivers, 2002).

Sexual Activity during Adolescence

Why does it seem that all boys want is sex? (Brenda, age 14)

What happens when I have a boyfriend who wants to have sex and I don't? (Ruth, age 13)

Why is it that when a guy has sex with a girl, he is called a "stud," but the girl is considered a "slut"? (Veronica, age 13; all in Zager & Rubenstein, 2002)

Sex and pregnancy are the number one issues facing teenage girls today, according to a nationwide survey of girls, ages 11 to 17, by the American Association of University Women (Haag, 1999). As early as age 12, girls reported being pressured to have sex. This pressure comes not just from boys but also from their girlfriends and the media. Let's take a closer look at sexual activity during adolescence. We'll discuss teenage pregnancy in Chapter 7.

Frequency of Sexual Activity

Most adolescents begin having sexual intercourse in their mid- to late teens. Males become sexually active at younger ages than females and Black female teens typically become sexually active before other female teens (Federal Interagency Forum on Child and Family Statistics, 2007). In addition, adolescent boys, compared to girls, have more sex (including same-sex behavior) and have more sex partners (Fergus et al., 2007; Savin-Williams & Diamond, 2004). Rates of teenage sexuality reached near-record highs in the late 1980s, but have declined since the early 1990s. For example, the percentage of high school students who had intercourse decreased from 54 percent in 1991 to 47 percent in 2005 (Eaton et al., 2006). The decline has been most noticeable among Black females and among males of all ethnicities (Risman & Schwartz, 2002). Efforts to educate young people about safe sex and about the risks of pregnancy and sexually transmitted infections such as AIDS have played a key role in reducing these numbers (Bernstein, 2004; Villarosa, 2003). Still, by the time they graduate from high school, about two-thirds of girls will have engaged in sex (Impett & Tolman, 2006).

Many college students have casual sexual encounters ("hook-ups"), often following alcohol consumption.

Among both female and male college students and young adults, an increasingly common form of sexual activity is the **hook-up,** a *one-time casual unplanned sexual encounter that can range anywhere from kissing to intercourse* (McGinn, 2004; Williams, 2005). Elizabeth Paul and her colleagues (e.g., Paul & Hayes, 2002), for example, found that nearly 80 percent of the students they surveyed had hooked up, usually after consuming alcohol. On average, students had hooked up with 11 different partners during their college years.

Another trend in teenage sexuality involves using the Internet to interact with others (Denizet-Lewis, 2004). The term **cybersex** has several meanings but is often defined as a *social interaction between at least two persons who exchange computer messages for purposes of sexual arousal and satisfaction* (Döring, 2000). There are two feminist views of cybersex, quite different from each other. The victimization perspective focuses on how women and girls as individuals and as a group are harmed by online harassment and virtual rape. In contrast, the liberation perspective argues that cybersex benefits girls and women by allowing them to explore their sexuality freely and more safely (Döring, 2000). Which view do you agree with, and why?

Factors Associated with Sexual Activity

Many factors affect the onset of sexual activity and the risk of becoming pregnant or causing a pregnancy. These include the effects of puberty, family, and peers, as well as individual characteristics. Hormone levels do not predict the onset of sexual behavior in girls, but the observable level of pubertal development—whether they look mature to peers—does (Savin-Williams & Diamond, 2004). One likely reason for this is that the development of breasts, curves, and other secondary sex characteristics may attract sexual attention from males (Zabin & Cardona, 2002).

A recent survey (National Campaign to Prevent Teen Pregnancy, 2003) found that parents are the biggest influence on teenagers' decisions about whether to have sex and friends are next. Parents, however, underestimate their own influence and believe that teenagers' friends play a more important role. Unfortunately, only half of older teen women and just over a third of men this age say that they talked with a parent about birth control before they turned 18 (U.S. Department of Health and Human Services, 2004a).

Teenagers who delay the onset of sexual activity and who are at lower risk of pregnancy are close to their parents and communicate well with them (Fisher, 2004; Hutchinson et al., 2003; Parera & Surís, 2004; Roche et al., 2005). Their parents are more likely to be married, better educated, have a higher income level, and use firm, consistent discipline (Abma et al., 2004; East et al., 2006; McNeeley et al., 2002; Woodward et al., 2006; Zabin & Cardona, 2002). Teenagers who begin sexual activity at a later age are also more apt to be religious, have better grades in school, higher educational aspirations, greater social maturity, lower levels of alcohol, cigarette, and drug use, and, in the case of girls, be more apt to participate in sports (Beadnell et al., 2007; Collins & Steinberg, 2006; Hellerstedt et al., 2006; Santelli et al., 2003; Stueve & O'Donnell, 2005; Tucker et al., 2006; Vesely et al., 2004).

An early onset of sexual activity and increased risk of pregnancy are linked to having sexually active or pregnant siblings and peers, having had a single teenage mother, having parents with permissive values about sex and a preference for early marriage, and being in a committed dating relationship (Beadnell et al., 2007; Bersamin et al., 2008; Bonell et al., 2006; Collins & Steinberg, 2006; East et al., 2006; Reynolds-Repetti, 2006; Siebenbruner et al., 2007; Sieving et al., 2006). Girls who have sexual intercourse at an early age, as well as those who fail to use contraceptives, tend to have low self-esteem, negative body image, and little sense of control over their lives (APA Task Force, 2007; Meier, 2007; Spencer et al., 2002; Townsend, 2002; Zabin & Cardona, 2002). Sexual and physical abuse in childhood, which may contribute to these negative feelings about oneself, also increase the likelihood of both early sexual activity and early pregnancy (Elliott et al., 2002; Hendrick & Reddy, 2007; Hillis et al., 2004; Tyler & Johnson, 2006).

The Double Standard

Despite the relaxing of sexual prohibitions over the past few decades, the double standard of sexuality in our society—acceptable for boys, but not girls—remains alive and well (Ott et al., 2006). Parents may be willing to condone sexual experimentation in their sons ("Boys will be boys") but rarely sanction it in their daughters. Girls, more than boys, are encouraged to express their sexuality only within the context of a committed, socially approved relationship (Diamond, 2004). Consequently, it is not surprising to find that adolescent girls are more likely than adolescent boys to focus on the emotional aspect of sex (Tiegs et al., 2007) and to consider affection a prerequisite for sexual intimacy (Hyde & Durik, 2000). For example, the recent survey of nearly 300,000 first-year college students discussed earlier found that 60 percent of males, but only 35 percent of females agreed with the statement, "If two people really like each other, it's all right for them to have sex even if they've known each other for only a very short time" ("This Year's Freshman," 2005). In addition, there is a positive correlation between expectations for sexual intercourse and the length of the relationship for adolescent boys, but not for girls (Werner-Wilson, 1998). Girls' primary reason for having their first sexual intercourse is affection for their partner, whereas boys' main reason is curiosity (Hyde & Durik, 2000).

Sexual Desire

One rarely studied topic in the realm of adolescent sexuality is the sexual desire of teenage girls. When Deborah Tolman (2002) interviewed urban and suburban high school girls, all reported feelings of powerful sexual desire. At the same time, the girls feared the potential of negative consequences of expressing these desires: pregnancy, sexually transmitted infections (STIs), losing respect and reputation, and limiting educational opportunities. Individual girls resolved these "dilemmas of desire" in different ways. Some suppressed their sexual desires, others avoided situations that could arouse sexual feelings, and still others arranged conditions in which they could safely express desire.

Sexual Activity in Midlife

Sexual activity and satisfaction vary among midlife women just as they do among young women. Women who in their earlier years found sexual expression to be fulfilling typically continue to enjoy sex in their middle years and beyond. Other women, whose sexual desires were not strong earlier, may find that their interest diminishes further during middle age. In this section, we examine the sexuality of women in midlife.

Physical Changes

Most women experience a number of physical changes as they enter menopause, some of which may affect sexual activity (O'Sullivan, 2006; Torpy, 2007c). Decline in the production of estrogen is responsible for many of these changes. The vaginal walls become less elastic, thinner, and more easily irritated, causing pain and bleeding during intercourse. Decreases in vaginal lubrication can also lead to painful intercourse. Normal acidic vaginal secretions become less acidic, increasing the likelihood of yeast infections.

Various lubricants and moisturizers can ease vaginal dryness. Paradoxically, one of the best remedies is to have more sex! Sexual activity increases blood flow to the vagina, which makes the tissues fuller, and also triggers lubrication (Wingert & O'Sullivan, 2006). Signs of sexual arousal—clitoral, labial, and breast engorgement and nipple erection—become less intense in midlife, and sexual arousal is slower. Most menopausal women, however, experience little or no change in *subjective* arousal. Although the number and intensity of orgasmic contractions are reduced, few women either notice or complain about these changes. Furthermore, slower arousal time for both women and men may lengthen the time of pleasurable sexual activity (Etaugh, 2008).

Patterns of Sexual Activity

While some midlife women report a decline in sexual desire and the capacity for orgasm during these years, others report the opposite pattern (Birnbaum et al., 2007; Tracy & Junginger, 2007; Wingert & Kantrowitz, 2007) some women report an increased desire for nongenital sexual expression such as cuddling, hugging, and kissing (Mansfield et al., 1998). The extent of sexual activity in middle-aged women is strongly influenced by past sexual enjoyment and experience. Years of sexual experience can more than make up for any decrease in physical responsiveness (Rathus et al., 2008). Women who have been sexually responsive during young adulthood are most likely to be sexually active as they get older (Etaugh, 2008). In addition, both heterosexual and lesbian women who communicate openly with their partners and make changes in their sexual activities to adapt to menopausal changes are more likely than other women to report active and satisfying sex lives (Winterich, 2003).

Many postmenopausal women find that their sexual interest and pleasure are heightened. Recent books such as *Sex and the seasoned woman* (Sheehy, 2005) and *Prime*

(Schwartz, 2007) sing the praises of the sexual passions of midlife women. What are some possible reasons for this renewed sexual interest? One is freedom from worries about pregnancy (Torpy, 2007c). This factor may be especially relevant for older cohorts of women for whom highly effective birth control methods were unavailable during their childbearing years. A second reason is the increase in marital satisfaction which often develops during the postparental ("empty nest") years (Etaugh, 2008).

Sexual activity decreases only slightly and gradually for women in their forties and fifties. Greater declines in activity and in sexual satisfaction may result from physical or psychological changes, however. Physical causes include various medical conditions, certain medications, and heavy drinking (AARP, 2005b; Brody, 2007c). Hysterectomy does not impair sexual functioning. In fact, many women experience improved sexual function, including greater sexual desire, an increase in orgasms, and a drop in painful intercourse following a hysterectomy (Hartmann et al., 2004; Roovers et al., 2003). For those women who feel that their ability to enjoy sex after a hysterectomy is diminished, counseling can be helpful. Similarly, mastectomy does not interfere with sexual responsiveness, but a woman may lose her sexual desire or her sense of being desired. Talking with other women who have had a mastectomy often helps. One resource is the American Cancer Society's Reach to Recovery program (American Cancer Society, 2008a).

Sexual activity and contentment during middle age are more likely to diminish for individuals who have lost their partners (Henig, 2004a). For example, in a recent nationally representative study of sexuality in Americans age 45 and over, just over half of those polled, but two-thirds of those with sexual partners, were satisfied with their sex lives (AARP, 2005c). While women in their forties and fifties are nearly as likely as men to have a sexual partner (78 percent compared to 84 percent), the "partner gap" between women and men grows in the later years. Among individuals age 75 and older, 58 percent of men but only 21 percent of women have a partner.

Sexual Activity in Later Life

Before reading this section, try Get Involved 6.2. See how your attitudes and those of friends compare to the information in the chapter.

Sexual activity can be as gratifying in the later years as in the younger years (Butler & Lewis, 2002). Unfortunately, as Get Involved 6.2 demonstrates, there are a number of myths and stereotypes about sexuality in later life. Most of today's older Americans grew up at a time when attitudes toward sexuality were more restrictive than they are today, particularly for women (Leiblum & Sachs, 2002; Mares & Fitzpatrick, 2004). Unlike men, many women were taught that they should not enjoy sex and should not initiate it. This "double standard" of sexuality for women and men mentioned earlier in the chapter exists for adults of all ages. Older women also are subjected to the "double standard" of aging discussed in Chapter 2. Thus, compared to older men, women in their later years are perceived as sexually inactive and sexually unattractive (Tariq & Morley, 2003). In a special issue of the *Journal of Social Issues* devoted entirely to sexuality a few years ago, there was not a single word about the sexuality of older women (Goodchilds, 2000). Many older women themselves are

GET INVOLVED **6.2**

Attitudes Toward Sexuality in Later Life

On a scale from 1 (strongly disagree) to 7 (strongly agree) indicate the extent to which you disagree or agree with each of the following statements. Also, ask three female and three male acquaintances who vary in age to respond to these statements.

1. Older people lose their interest in sex and no longer engage in sexual activity.
2. Changes in hormone levels that occur during and after menopause cause women to find sex unsatisfying and unpleasant.

3. Women who are beyond the childbearing years lose their sexual desire and their sexual desirability.
4. In order to have a full and satisfying sex life, a woman must have a male partner.
5. Older women who still enjoy sex were probably nymphomaniacs when they were younger.
6. Older people with chronic illness or physical disabilities should cease sexual activity completely.

What Does It Mean?

Add up the ratings you gave to these six statements. Do the same for each of your respondents. Note that each statement reflects a myth based on folklore and misconceptions. Therefore, the higher the score, the more the respondent holds unfounded beliefs about sexuality in later life.

1. Are there differences between the views of your female and male respondents? Explain your answer.

2. Are there differences between the views of respondents who vary in age? Explain your answer.
3. Could society's attitudes toward aging and the elderly be related to the persistence of these myths about sexuality in later life? Explain your answer.

Source: Doress-Worters and Siegal (1994); Gibson (1996).

self-conscious about their aging bodies (Henig, 2004a). Men tend to choose younger women or women who look young as their sexual partners and mates (Daniluk, 1998; Rathus et al., 2005). Let us examine older women's sexuality—the benefits of sexual activity in later life, sexual behaviors and the factors affecting them, and enhancement of sexual experience in the later years.

Benefits of Sexual Activity in Later Life

Sexual activity can have physical, psychological, and emotional benefits for the elderly (Burgess, 2004; Malatesta, 2007). The physical benefits include improving circulation, maintaining a greater range and motion of joints and limbs in arthritic persons, and controlling weight gain (Butler & Lewis, 2002; Leitner & Leitner, 2004). In one study of adults ranging from 60 to 91 years of age, others reported physical benefits of sex included reducing tension and helping one sleep (Doress-Worters & Siegal, 1994). Sexual activity among the elderly has psychological and emotional benefits as well. It can improve one's sense of well-being, increase life satisfaction, enhance a woman's feeling of femininity and desirability, offer an outlet for emotions, and provide a shared pleasurable experience (Leitner & Leitner, 2004). In the later years, sexual activities other than intercourse—oral sex, manual stimulation, caressing—bring pleasure with or without orgasm (Burgess, 2004; Rathus et al., 2008).

Sexual Behavior of the Elderly

Interest in sexual activity remains fairly high throughout adult life, declining only gradually in the later years (AARP, 2005c; Bancroft, 2007; Lindau et al., 2007). In a Duke University longitudinal study of adults ages 60 to 94, 50 percent of individuals 80 years and older reported still having sexual desires (Leitner & Leitner, 2004).

Some women find sex more satisfying and their attitudes toward sex more positive and open in later life. In one nationwide survey of Americans over age 60, 70 percent of sexually active women said they were as satisfied, or even more satisfied, with their sex lives than they were in their forties (Leary, 1998). Once grown children have left the nest, couples may experience a "second honeymoon" as marital satisfaction increases (Aubin & Heiman, 2004). (See the second vignette at the beginning of the chapter.)

In a recent U.S. survey (Lindau et al., 2007), nearly three-fourths of people aged 57–64, over half of those aged 64–75 and more than one quarter between 75 and 85 had engaged in sexual behavior within the past year. Many of them had done so two or three times a month. Women at all ages were less likely than men to be sexually active, in part because more of them lacked a partner. Decreased sexual desire of one's partner is another reason for a decline in sexual activity among the elderly (McHugh, 2007). It is probably no coincidence that while the incidence of masturbation peaks in the teenage years for males and then declines, the opposite trend applies to women. The lack of available partners for elderly women is a likely explanation for these findings (Belsky, 1999).

Factors Affecting Sexual Behavior

A number of both physical and psychological factors influence sexual behavior in older women.

Physical Factors.   The physical changes in the reproductive system that begin in midlife (see Chapter 7) become more pronounced in the later years, as estrogen levels continue to decline gradually. Physical changes, illness, chronic disabilities, and medication can affect sexuality in later life (Kuehn, 2008; Lindau et al., 2007; Tariq & Morley, 2003). However, even the most serious conditions should not stop women and men from engaging in satisfying sexual activity (Butler & Lewis, 2002). Heart disease, especially if one has had a heart attack, leads many older adults to give up sex, fearing it will cause another attack. But the risk of this is low. Most people can resume sexual activity in 12 to 16 weeks. Stroke rarely damages sexual function and it is unlikely that sexual exertion will cause another stroke. Arthritis, the most common chronic disability, causes joint pain that can limit sexual activity (Read, 2004). Surgery and drugs can relieve the pain, but in some cases the medications decrease sexual desire. Exercise, rest, warm baths, and changing the positions or timing of sexual activity can be helpful. Medications such as certain antidepressants and tranquilizers also can reduce a woman's sexual desire. However, a physician can often prescribe a different medication without this side effect.

Psychosocial Factors. A person's attitudes toward sex-related physical changes can interfere with sexual activity more than the actual changes themselves. A major psychosocial constraint is the societal view that sexual desire in the elderly, especially elderly women, is abnormal (McGinn & Skipp, 2002; Read, 2004). As a result, older adults who want to fulfill their sexual desires may feel apprehensive and guilty. In addition, many older women feel unattractive and thus may avoid sexual activity with a partner or decide not to seek a new partner if they become widowed or divorced (Burgess, 2004).

Another constraint for residents of nursing homes is that the attitudes of nursing home staff are often not supportive of sexual behavior. Although more nurses are respecting the wishes of their clients for sexual freedom and privacy (Johnson & Scelfo, 2003), many nursing home administrators feel that sexual activity on the part of residents "causes problems," even if the individuals are married. Even masturbation may be strongly discouraged (Beers & Jones, 2004; Butler & Lewis, 2002; Villarosa, 2002).

Enhancing Sexuality in Later Life

Sexual activity can be more rewarding for older adults if people come to realize that sexual expression is a normal part of life regardless of age. Sex counseling can help

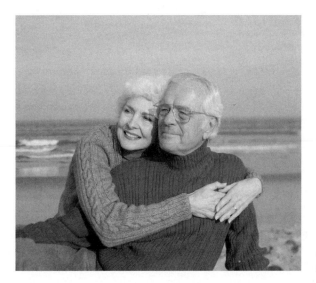

Sexual activity can be as gratifying in later life as in the younger years.

remove inhibitions restricting an older person's sexual behavior. Emphasizing the quality of the sexual relationship rather than performance can make sexual experiences more enjoyable for the elderly (Hillman & Stricker, 1994; Leitner & Leitner, 2004). Elderly people who are in supervised living arrangements need to be given opportunities to have private time together for intimate contact (Butler & Lewis, 2002). Healthcare professionals should provide information and counseling to the elderly regarding the impact of both normal physical changes and medical conditions on sexual functioning (Richardson & Lazur, 1995).

The many older women who are not in an ongoing physical relationship need to feel it is permissible to express their sexuality in whatever way is comfortable for them, whether it be enjoying their fantasies, engaging in masturbation, using a vibrator, or accepting an asexual lifestyle (Butler & Lewis, 2002; Read, 2004). While some older women are celibate because they lack the opportunity to meet partners, others choose to be celibate but still enjoy sensuous experiences:

> *In Colette's novel, Break of Day, I discovered celibacy as a strategy for older women who too often see themselves as stripped of identity without a partner. Colette sees age fifty-five as the end of having lovers, but the beginning of an aloneness that is joyous and drenched in sensuality—particularly for the artist in all of us. It is a great gift to be one's self at last.* (Marilyn Zuckerman, a poet in her sixties, in Doress-Worters & Siegal, 1994, p. 88)

SUMMARY

Sexuality

- The external female organs (vulva) consist of the mons pubis, labia majora, labia minora, and clitoris.
- The four phases of the sexual response cycle are excitement, plateau, orgasm, and resolution.
- Women, unlike men, are capable of multiple orgasms.
- Orgasms resulting from clitoral and vaginal orgasm are physiologically the same.
- The sexual double standard condones casual sexual activity for men, but not for women.
- Women have less permissive attitudes toward sexual behavior than men and emphasize relationships as a context for sex.
- There is considerable consistency between sexual attitudes and sexual behaviors.
- Women are less likely than men to engage in most sexual behaviors and to have extramarital sex.

- The four major types of sexual dysfunction are sexual desire disorders, sexual arousal disorders, orgasm disorders, and sexual pain disorders.
- The new view of women's sexual problems focuses on sociocultural, psychological, and relational factors.

Lesbians and Bisexual Women

- Lesbians and gays are attracted to same-sex persons; bisexuals are attracted to both sexes.
- Sexual identities of some sexual minority individuals change over time.
- Homophobia is pervasive in American society. It is most commonly found in older, less educated, politically conservative males who hold traditional gender-related attitudes and fundamentalist religious beliefs.
- Complex interactions among genetic, hormonal, and environmental factors appear to determine sexual orientation.

Sexual Activity during Adolescence

- Rates of teenage sexuality have been decreasing.
- The onset of sexual activity is influenced by pubertal development and individual characteristics as well as by family and peers.

Sexual Activity in Midlife

- Postmenopausal physical changes can lead to painful intercourse.
- Some women show a decline in sexual interest and capacity for orgasm, while others show the opposite pattern.

Sexual Activity in Later Life

- Sexual activity can have physical, psychological, and emotional benefits for the elderly.

- Interest in sexual activity remains fairly high throughout adulthood, declining gradually in the later years.
- Sexual interest in the elderly is greater than sexual activity. One reason, especially for women, is the lack of a partner.
- Physical changes, illness, disability, and psychosocial factors influence sexual behavior in older women.
- Sexuality may be enhanced through counseling, changes in societal attitudes, and greater opportunities for intimate contact.

KEY TERMS

vulva	orgasmic platform	gay male
mons pubis	sexual double standard	bisexual
labia majora	inhibited sexual desire	heterosexism
labia minora	sexual arousal disorder	homophobia
clitoris	female orgasmic disorder	hook-up
vagina	dyspareunia	cybersex
sexual response cycle	vaginismus	
vasocongestion	lesbian	

WHAT DO YOU THINK?

1. Why do you think women generally have less permissive attitudes toward sexual behavior than men do?

2. Why do you think that our society holds negative attitudes toward gays and lesbians?

3. If you were to design a school-based or community-based sex education program, what would you include?

4. What is your position on programs that provide contraceptives to teenagers?

IF YOU WANT TO LEARN MORE

Balsam, K. F. (Ed.). (2004). *Trauma, stress, and resilience among sexual minority women: Rising like the phoenix*. Binghamton, NY: Harrington Park Press.

Bogle, K. (2008). *Hooking up: Sex, dating, and relationships on campus*. New York: New York University Press.

Carpenter, L. M. (2005). *Virginity lost: An intimate portrait of first sexual experiences*. New York: New York University Press.

Cramer, E. P. (Eds.). (2003). *Addressing homophobia and heterosexism on college campuses*. Binghamton, NY: Harrington Park Press.

Daniluk, J. C. (2003). *Women's sexuality across the life span: Challenging myths, creating meanings*. New York: Guilford.

Diamond, L. (2008). *Sexual fluidity: Understanding women's love and desire*. Cambridge, MA: Harvard University Press.

Galupo, M. P. (Ed.). (2007). *Bisexual women: Friendship and social organization*. Binghamton, NY: Harrington Park Press.

Harvey, J. H., Wenzel, A., & Sprecher, S. (Eds.). (2004). *The handbook of sexuality in close relationships*. Mahwah, NJ: Erlbaum.

Kaschak, E., & Tiefer, L. (Eds.). (2002). *A new view of women's sexual problems*. New York: Haworth.

Lind, A., & Brzuzy, S. (Eds.). (2007). *Battleground: Women, gender, and sexuality*. Westport, CT: Green-wood Press.

Moore, S., & Rosenthal, D. (2006). *Sexuality in adolescence: Current trends* (2nd ed.). New York: Psychology Press.

Rathus, S. A., Nevid, J. S., & Fichner-Rathus, L. (2008). *Human sexuality in a world of diversity*. Boston: Allyn & Bacon.

Rose, T. (2003). *Longing to tell: Black women talk about sexuality and intimacy*. New York: Picador.

Schwartz, P. (2007). *Prime: Adventures and advice on sex, love, and the sensual years*. New York: HarperCollins.

Sheehy, G. (2006). *Sex and the seasoned woman: Pursuing the passionate life*. New York: Ballantine.

Tolman, D. L. (2002). *Dilemmas of desire: Teenage girls talk about sexuality*. Cambridge, MA: Harvard University Press.

Travis, C. B., & White, J. W. (Eds.). (2000). *Sexuality, society, and feminism*. Washington, DC: American Psychological Association.

WEBSITES

Disability

Disabled People's International
http://www.dpi.org

Lesbians

Gay/Lesbian Issues
http://gaylesissues.about.com/culture/gayleissues/

CHAPTER

7 Reproductive System and Childbearing

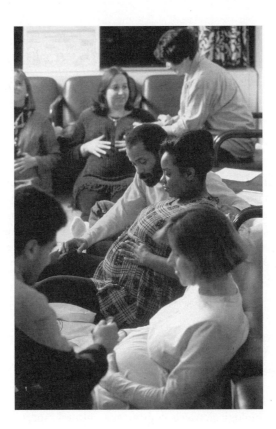

Menstruation
The Menstrual Cycle
Menstrual Pain
Attitudes toward Menstruation
Menstrual Joy
Premenstrual Syndrome (PMS)

Contraception
Contraception in Adolescence

Methods of Contraception
Abortion
Incidence
Methods
Consequences of Abortion

Pregnancy
Pregnancy: Physical and Psychological
Changes

Miscarriage
Teenage Pregnancy
Childbirth
Stages of Childbirth
Methods of Childbirth
Childbearing after 40
Childbearing in the Later Years

Postpartum Distress
Infertility and Assisted Reproductive
    Technology
**Reproductive Functioning in Midlife
and Beyond**
Menopause
Hormone Replacement Therapy

I felt godlike—a miracle worker. It was the best moment of my life. I felt my baby's head, then saw his face—I got to cut his cord and put him to my breast. I felt like I did the impossible. I couldn't believe he was finally out into the light. I felt holy. (Boston Women's Health Book Collective, 1992, p. 447)

Giving birth to a child can be one of the major events of a woman's life. Childbirth typically (although not exclusively) occurs during young adulthood, the years from about 20 to 40. In this chapter, we focus on women's reproductive system functioning throughout the lifespan, including menstruation, contraception, abortion, pregnancy, and childbirth. We conclude with an exploration of reproductive functioning in midlife and beyond, looking at menopause and hormone replacement therapy.

Menstruation

The menstrual cycle involves the release of a mature egg or ovum from its surrounding capsule or follicle. The cycle, which occurs in four phases, averages 28 days in length. (*Menstruation* is derived from the Latin word for *month*.) The menstrual cycle is governed by a feedback loop involving two brain structures—the hypothalamus and the pituitary gland—and the ovaries and uterus (Chrisler, 2008a). In this section we explore the biological, psychological, and cultural aspects of menstruation.

The Menstrual Cycle

In the *follicular* phase of the menstrual cycle, Days 4 to 14, low levels of estrogen and progesterone cause the hypothalamus to stimulate the pituitary gland to secrete follicle-stimulating hormone (FSH). This causes the ovaries to increase estrogen production and bring several follicles and their eggs to maturity. Estrogen stimulates development of the endometrium (uterine lining) in order to receive a fertilized egg. Estrogen also signals the pituitary to stop producing FSH and to start producing luteinizing hormone (LH). The LH suppresses development of all but one follicle and egg.

In the second or *ovulatory* phase, about Day 14, LH levels peaks, causing rupture of the follicle and release of the egg near a fallopian tube. During ovulation, some women experience *mittelschmerz* ("middle pain") on the side of the abdomen where the egg has been released (Chrisler, 2008a).

During the *luteal* phase, LH stimulates the follicle to form a yellowish group of cells called the *corpus luteum* ("yellow body"), which produces large amounts of progesterone and estrogen. These hormones, which reach their peak around Day 20 or 21 of the cycle, cause the endometrium to secrete nourishing substances in the event an egg is fertilized and implanted in the uterine lining. If fertilization does not occur, high progesterone levels cause the hypothalamus to stop the pituitary's production of LH. This causes decomposition of the corpus luteum and a sharp drop in levels of estrogen and progesterone through Day 28.

The fourth phase, *menstruation* (Days 1 to 4), occurs when the low levels of estrogen and progesterone can no longer maintain the uterine lining, which is shed and exits through the cervix (the lower end of the uterus) and vagina as menstrual flow. The low hormone levels trigger the beginning of another cycle. Should the egg be fertilized, however, the hormone levels remain high and a new cycle does not occur (Chrisler, 2008a).

Changes in the levels of the ovarian and pituitary hormones over the menstrual cycle are shown in Figure 7.1.

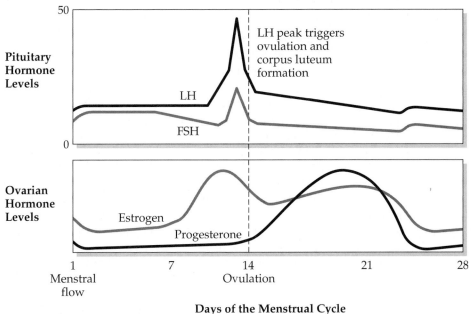

FIGURE 7.1 **Changes in hormone levels during the menstrual cycle.**

Source: Donatelle and Davis (1998), p. 190. Reprinted with permission from Allyn & Bacon.

CHAPTER 7

Menstrual Pain

Menstrual pain, or **dysmenorrhea,** includes painful abdominal cramps and lower back pain during menstruation. About 55 to 73 percent of women report experiencing menstrual pain each month (Hourani et al., 2004). Women who report higher levels of menstrual pain and discomfort are also more likely to report high levels of psychological stress in their lives, and poorer health. They also are more like to smoke and to be heavy drinkers (Gold et al., 2007; Hourani et al., 2004; Strine et al., 2005; Wang et al., 2004).

After the mid-twenties, the prevalence of reported pain declines, perhaps because of changes brought about by pregnancy (Parent-Stevens & Burns, 2000). The cause of this discomfort is thought to be **prostaglandins,** *hormonelike chemicals secreted by the uterine lining and other tissues as menstruation approaches.* These substances cause uterine contractions, decreased blood flow, and increased sensitivity to pain, which lead to cramping. Adolescents and women who suffer from severe menstrual pain have unusually high levels of prostaglandins (Boston Women's Health Collective, 2005). Over-the-counter antiprostaglandin drugs such as ibuprofen and aspirin help relieve menstrual pain in many women (Chrisler, 2008a). Also helpful is a low-fat vegetarian vegan diet, which includes grains, legumes, vegetables, and fruits, but no eggs or dairy products (Barnard et al., 2000).

Attitudes toward Menstruation

On a recent TV show, the plot involved a man intent on killing a group of female medical students. He wore a T-shirt that read "Don't trust anybody who bleeds for five days and doesn't die." That chilling statement said volumes about a mind-set going back millennia. (Pam, 49-year-old school teacher)

Throughout history, menstruation has had "bad press." Menstrual blood has been viewed as having magical and often poisonous powers. Menstruating women have been isolated and forbidden to prepare food or to engage in sexual activity (Kowalski & Chapple, 2000). Menstrual myths and taboos still exist, although in a somewhat less extreme form. For example, some adolescent girls and women believe that menstruating women should not exercise, swim, or wash their hair (Chrisler, 2008a). In addition, many euphemistic terms are used to avoid the word *menstruation:* "period," "that time of the month," "I've got my friend," "she's on the rag," "the curse," "Aunt FLO is visiting" (Costos et al., 2002; Fingerson, 2006). Have you heard or used other expressions? How many are positive? Many Americans believe that a woman cannot function normally when menstruating, but there is little evidence that athletic performance, academic performance, problem solving, memory, or creative thinking show meaningful fluctuations over the menstrual cycle (Chrisler, 2008b).

One recent study by Gordon Forbes and his colleagues (2003) illustrates that negative attitudes toward the menstruating woman remain strong. College men and women both perceived a menstruating woman, compared to the "average woman," as being more irritable, angry, and sad, and as less energized and less sexy. Men, but not women, also saw her as annoying, unreasonable, "spacey," less nurturing, less reliable and dependable, less creative and intellectually curious, and as more disagreeable and spiteful than other women. Women found some redeeming features in the menstruating woman, viewing her as more maternal, strong, and trustworthy than the average women.

Menstrual Joy

Despite the prevalence of negative attitudes toward menstruation, some women experience their menstrual periods as self-affirming, creative, and pleasurable, and as signifying femininity and fertility (Boston Women's Health Book Collective, 2005; Kissling, 2006; Lee, 2002). Negative expectations about menstruation may influence many women to focus more on its associated unpleasant symptoms. But what would happen if menstruation were portrayed in a more positive light? Researchers in the United States (Chrisler et al., 1994) and in Great Britain (Aubeeluck & Maguire, 2002) studied the effects of presenting positive and negative views on women's reported responses to menstruation. The researchers administered both the Menstrual Joy Questionnaire (MJQ) and the Menstrual Distress Questionnaire (MDQ) to college women (see Get Involved 7.1). The MJQ lists positive feelings that might be experienced before or during menstruation, such as self-confidence, creativity, and power. The MDQ lists negative feelings that might occur at these times, such as irritability, anxiety, and fatigue. The researchers found that women who completed the MJQ before they were given the MDQ reported less menstrual distress and more favorable attitudes toward menstruation than those who received the questionnaires in reverse order. It appears that the way menstruation is portrayed can affect the way women react to their menstrual cycles. Try the questionnaires in Get Involved 7.1 and see whether you find the same results.

Interestingly, the findings that menstruation actually has some positive aspects did not generate a lot of media publicity or subsequent research. According to Margaret Matlin (2003), this illustrates the **women-as-problem bias,** that is, *psychologists' preference for studying negative aspects of women's lives rather than positive ones.*

Premenstrual Syndrome

For me, menstrual distress is very real. Every month, the week before my period started, I became a different person. I felt such rage and could not control it. My husband and children suffered verbal and physical abuse for years. I thought I was going insane. In the last 3 years, I have been taking medication and am doing better. I feel like I can take back my life. (Sharah, 35 years old)

For most women, mild to moderate physical and emotional fluctuations are part of the normal menstrual cycle experience. Women may experience breast tenderness, bloating, anxiety, or mood swings that may be annoying but do not disrupt their daily lives (Parent-Stevens & Burns, 2000). A small minority of women, about 3 to 9 percent, experience *symptoms so severe that their normal functioning is impaired for the week of each*

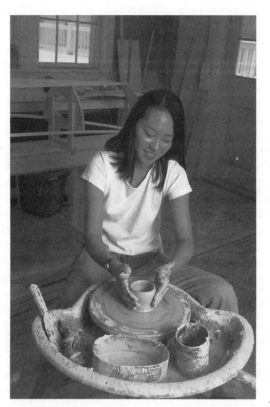

During their menstrual periods, some women experience "menstrual joy," a feeling of enhanced creativity and energy.

month preceding menstruation, as illustrated in Sharah's comments. These women are considered to suffer from **premenstrual syndrome (PMS).** No marked ethnic differences in the prevalence of PMS have been identified (Daw, 2002; Mortola, 2000).

What Is PMS? For years, controversy has swirled around the validity of PMS as a disorder because scientists have not agreed upon its definition. Since 1987, the American Psychiatric Association has included PMS in its diagnostic handbook, labeling it **Premenstrual Dysphoric Disorder (PMDD).** To be diagnosed with PMDD, *a woman must experience multiple symptoms during the week before her menstrual period, including depression, anxiety, mood swings, or anger/irritability. The symptoms must interfere markedly with work or social relationships and must be present only in the premenstrual phase of the cycle* (Chrisler, 2008b). Some women physicians feel that the diagnosis of PMDD validates the experiences of a group of women and is thus empowering (Hirshbein, 2003). But other theorists object to treating normal reproductive system functioning in women as a disease. Feminist psychologists such as Joan Chrisler, Paula Caplan, and others believe that PMDD's classification as a psychiatric disorder stigmatizes women as mentally ill, undermines their self-esteem, and feeds into socially constructed stereotypes about women (Caplan, 2008; Chrisler, 2008b; Chrisler et al., 2006; Cosgrove & Riddle, 2003; Daw, 2002).

For example, a widely held stereotype in North America is that women experience negative moods before their menstrual periods (Chrisler et al., 2007). Thus, if a woman feels anxious, sad, irritable, or moody and believes she is in the premenstrual phase of her cycle, she may attribute her feelings to PMS. The role of cultural factors in determining one's reaction to menstruation is further illustrated in a study of Samoan women who were exposed to modern Western culture and subsequently reported increased numbers of menstrual symptoms (Fitzgerald, 1990). Even within the same culture, differences in the life circumstances of individual women may influence their experiences with menstrual symptoms. For example, women who acknowledge high levels of stress related to work, family, or finances report increased severity of PMS (Gallant & Derry, 1995). Biological factors may also be involved. For instance, the brain of women with and without PMS react differently to normal fluctuating levels of estrogen and progesterone (Brody, 1998). It is unclear, however, whether these differences contribute to the development of PMS or result from it.

Treating PMS.   Whether PMS/PMDD is a mental disorder or not, it is important to give help to women who seek it (Daw, 2002). Various treatments for PMS have been tried. While some women report that dietary changes or progesterone supplements provide some relief, these approaches have generally been shown to be ineffective (Gold et al., 2007). Taking daily 1,200-milligram doses of calcium along with vitamin D, however, reduces the symptoms of PMS in many women. Vitamin B6 also may provide relief (Bertone-Johnson et al., 2005; Daw, 2002). The anti-anxiety drug Xanax and antidepressants that raise levels of the substance serotonin in the brain—including Prozac, Paxil, and Zoloft—relieve emotional and often physical symptoms in over 70 percent of women with PMS (Mortola, 2000; Steiner & Born, 2002).

Contraception

The typical American woman marries at age 25 and achieves her desired family size of two children by age 31. She then spends the next 20 years until menopause trying to avoid an unintended pregnancy (Dailard, 2003a). In this section, we look at the use of contraception, starting with the teen years.

Contraception in Adolescence

> *Girls make the decision [to use condoms] because males don't really care if you have a condom or not. . . . Just as long as he gets to [do] it. . . . He doesn't get pregnant.* (Sexually active teenage girl, in Denner and Coyle, 2006, p. 290).

The use of contraceptives, both condoms and long-acting hormonal methods, has increased among sexually active adolescents, especially girls, in recent years, due in part to the growing awareness of the danger of AIDS and other sexually transmitted infections (Santelli, J.S., Morrow, B., & Carter, M., 2004). Still, a substantial number of adolescents use contraceptives inconsistently or not at all. About one-fifth of girls ages 15 to 19 and their partners do not use contraceptives the first time they have sexual intercourse (Grunbaum, 2004). Many adolescent females wait a year or more after becoming sexually active to seek medical services for contraception. Unfortunately, about half of all adolescent pregnancies occur within 6 months after the onset of sexual activity (American Academy of Pediatrics, 2005).

Many adolescent girls and women resist initiating use of condoms or other contraceptives. There are several reasons for this. Some women do not have enough power and control in their relationship with a male partner to be able to persuade him to wear a condom, particularly if he is reluctant to do so (Stevens & Galvao, 2007; Woolf & Maisto, 2008). Also, women may reject condom use because it diminishes their sexual pleasure and disrupts intimacy (Bowleg, L., Lucas, 2004). For some women, sexual intercourse without condoms may symbolize feelings of trust, commitment, and "true love" in the relationship. For others, taking control of a sexual situation—even if just to introduce a condom—may disrupt their feminine sexual identity and threaten potential rewards they expect in the form of love and protection (Gavey & McPhillips, 1999). Other factors that contribute to lack of contraceptive use in women include reluctance to acknowledge one's own sexual activity, a sense of invincibility ("*I* won't get pregnant"), and misconceptions regarding use of contraception (Ayoola et al., 2007).

Which individuals are most likely to practice contraception? The older teenagers are when they begin sexual activity, the more likely they are to use contraception. Other factors associated with contraceptive use in high school and college students include being in a committed relationship, having high educational aspirations and achievement, having knowledge about sex and contraception, fearing HIV infection, having good communication and a supportive relationship with parents, discussing contraceptive use with parents and with one's partner, having friends who use contraceptives, waiting a longer time between the start of a relationship and having sex with that partner, and having high self-esteem and feelings of control over one's life (Henry et al., 2007; Manlove et al., 2003; Miller et al., 1998; Sheeran et al., 1999).

Teenagers who attend schools that distribute condoms, compared to teens in schools that don't, are less likely to have ever had sex, or to have had sex recently. Moreover, sexually active youth whose schools give out condoms are twice as likely to use condoms as those who can't get condoms at school (Blake et al., 2003). Unfortunately, however, few high schools in the United States make contraceptives available (Santelli et al., 2003).

Methods of Contraception

The one totally foolproof method of contraception is abstinence. Today, increasing numbers of teenagers are pledging not to have sex before marriage. However, a majority of those who take this virginity pledge do not live up to their vows (Brody, 2004a). Moreover, those teenagers who have taken a virginity pledge are *less* likely to use contraception when they do engage in sexual activity (Bearman, 2004; Manlove et al., 2003). In addition, sex education programs based on abstinence do not delay the onset of sexual activity nor decrease the number of teenagers having sex (Beil, 2007; Trenholm et al., 2007).

A wide variety of contraceptive choices are available in addition to abstinence (see Table 7.1). As women's reproductive goals change during their childbearing years, the type of contraception they choose also changes. Birth control pills are most often used by women in their twenties, by unmarried women, and by those with some college education. Tubal ligation is more commonly used by women who are over 34, have previously been married, have no more than a high school education, or who are poor. Tubal ligation for women has become far more common than vasectomy has for

TABLE 7.1   **Effectiveness Rates of Contraceptive Methods**

Method	Percent Effectiveness		Disadvantages
	Correct Use	Typical Use	
Birth control pills (combined hormones)	99.9	92.0	Risk of blood clots in smokers over 35
Norplant (implant)	99.9	99.0	Menstrual bleeding
Depo-Provera (injection)	99.7	97.0	Menstrual bleeding
Intrauterine device (placed in uterus)	99.4	99.0	Heavy menstrual flow; cramps; pelvic infections
Diaphragm (cup placed in vagina)	94.0	84.0	Need to insert before intercourse; genital irritation
Cervical cap (cup placed over cervix)	92.0	82.0	Urinary tract infection; high failure rate
Sponge (placed in vagina)	85.0	70.0	Need to insert before intercourse; high failure rate
Spermicide	94.0	71.0	Need to insert before intercourse; genital irritation
Condom (sheath placed over penis)	97.0	85.0	Need to put on before intercourse; may lessen male's sensations; may tear, slip off
Withdrawal (of penis before ejaculation)	96.0	77.0	High failure rate
Rhythm method (fertility awareness)	91.0	75.0	High failure rate
Tubal ligation (cutting and tying fallopian tubes)	99.5	99.3	Slight surgical risk
Vasectomy (cutting and tying sperm-carrying ducts)	99.9	99.8	Slight surgical risk

Source: Adapted from Alan Guttmacher Institute (2004a); and Rathus et al. (2008, p. 390 Table 12.1).

their male sexual partners (Alan Guttmacher Institute, 2005; Centers for Disease Control and Prevention, 2005). Of all these methods, the condom is the only one providing any protection against sexually transmitted infections. In addition to these methods, emergency contraception, or the so-called "morning after pill," is also available. This method, known as Plan B, is typically used when regular contraception ("Plan A") either fails or is skipped. It involves taking high doses of birth control pills within 72 hours after having sex, and then again 12 hours later. This procedure works by delaying ovulation or blocking fertilization of the egg (Hampton, 2007; Harris, 2006b). Contrary to popular belief, providing emergency contraception in advance to teenagers does not result in riskier sex practices or in decreased use of condoms or hormonal contraceptives (Gold et al., 2004).

Abortion

Abortion is one of the most commonly performed medical procedures and also one of the most controversial. In the United States, the debate over abortion centers around two opposing views: Abortion as a right and a means for attaining individual freedom and equity for women versus abortion as a threat to morality, the family, and society. These differing attitudes toward abortion in turn stem from different socially constructed beliefs, attitudes, and values about gender roles and female sexuality (Anleu, 2006; Beckman, 2006).

The 1973 landmark Supreme Court decision in *Roe v. Wade* gave women the legal right to terminate pregnancy by abortion during the first trimester (three months) of pregnancy. It allowed individual states to set conditions for second-trimester abortions and ruled third-trimester abortions illegal except when the mother's life was endangered (Rathus et al., 2008). Since then, a number of restrictions on abortion have been enacted (Annas, 2007; Donohoe, 2005; Miller, 2004). For example, nearly 90 percent of the states in the United States require parental consent or notification for minors seeking abortion (Adler et al., 2003; Miller, 2004). The United States Congress has barred the use of federal Medicaid funds to pay for abortion except when the mother's life is endangered or in cases of rape or incest. Since poor families rely on Medicaid for health care and few have private health insurance, low-income women now are less able to afford abortion (Donohoe, 2005). In addition, the U.S. Supreme Court recently upheld a congressional ban of a specific type of late-term abortion known as dilation and extraction and referred to by critics as "partial birth" abortion (Annas, 2007).

Nationwide polls conducted 30 years after the *Roe v. Wade* ruling have found that public opinion has shifted away from general acceptance of legal abortion toward a more ambivalent acceptance, favoring choice but only under certain conditions (Boonstra, 2007; Nagourney & Thee, 2007). The proportion of first-year college students believing that abortion should be legal was 57 percent in 2006, a drop of 6 percentage points since 1990 ("This Year's Freshmen," 2007).

Incidence

Half of the pregnancies among American women are unplanned and half of these are terminated by abortion (Russo & Tartaro, 2008). In 2004, nearly 840,000 women in the United States had abortions (Strauss et al., 2007). Not surprisingly, almost 90 percent of abortions take place within the first trimester (Strauss et al., 2007). In recent years, the abortion rate has steadily been declining. Teens have shown the most dramatic drop: a 25 percent decrease between 1985 and 2000.

Three-fourths of women obtaining abortions are under 30. Four out of five are unmarried, over half are already mothers, and about half have had a previous abortion. White women account for 53 percent of all abortions, but their abortion *rate* is below that of women of color. Black women are three times as likely as White women to have an abortion (Cohen, 2007; Strauss et al., 2007). Why are abortion rates higher for women of color? Research suggests that they are more likely than White women to become pregnant unwillingly. Cultural pressures may disadvantage minority women in negotiating sexual and contraceptive choices with their male partners (Travis & Compton, 2001).

A recent comprehensive global study of abortion found that abortion rates are similar in countries where it is legal and in those where it is outlawed (Sedgh et al., 2007). This suggests that banning abortion does not deter women who seek the procedure (Rosenthal, 2007). In addition, the study revealed that abortion is safe in countries where it is legal, but more dangerous in nations where it is illegal and often performed under unsafe conditions.

Methods

The safest and most common method of abortion is **vacuum aspiration,** in which *the contents of the uterus are removed by suction* (Strauss et al., 2007). While most American women prefer this surgical procedure, those up to nine weeks pregnant can choose to take certain drugs to induce abortion. Women take mifepristone, the French abortion pill known as RU-486, and two days later take the drug misoprostol. This procedure, known as a medical abortion, is highly effective when used within the first 49 days of pregnancy (Harris, 2006a). Women who choose medical abortion prefer its privacy, naturalness, and avoidance of surgery (Fielding et al., 2002). Currently, more than half of the early abortions in France, Scotland, and Sweden, but only 14 percent in the United States, are done with pills rather than surgically (Finer & Henshaw, 2003; Kolata, 2002, 2003; Strauss et al., 2007).

Consequences of Abortion

Abortion is one of the safest medical procedures available. The risk of death from childbirth (1 in 10,000) is about ten times higher than the risk of abortion performed within the first 12 weeks by a health professional (1 in more than 100,000) (David & Lee, 2001; Donohoe, 2005). What about the psychological consequences of abortion? Since abortion is a planned response to an unwanted pregnancy, the woman may experience positive emotions to it, such as feelings of relief or of having made a good decision. On the other hand, negative emotions such as anxiety, regret, or guilt may also arise because of moral and social sanctions against abortion (Bradshaw & Slade, 2003). Brenda Major and her colleagues (Major et al., 2000) found that a woman's reaction to abortion is affected by her particular circumstances, including her coping skills and the degree of social support she has. For example, a woman is more likely to experience postabortion stress if she has little social support from her partner, family, and friends; poorer coping skills; if she blames herself for the pregnancy; and if she has a prior history of depression. The most negative feelings occur *before* the abortion. While some women report mild distress afterward—guilt, anxiety, and regrets—the strongest feeling is one of relief (Adler & Smith, 1998). Research on the long-term psychological aftereffects of abortion has found no link between abortion and subsequent poor mental health, especially when the abortion is conducted during the first trimester (Donohoe, 2005; Russo, 2008). When women seek but are *denied* abortions (as was the case in some eastern European countries), their children are more likely than children of mothers who did not seek abortion to feel neglected or rejected, to drop out of school, and to have social problems at work and with friends (David & Lee, 2001).

So far in this chapter, we have focused on the reproductive lives of young women in the United States. For a more global picture, turn to Explore Other Cultures 7.1 and 7.2.

EXPLORE OTHER CULTURES **7.1**

Young Women's Reproductive Lives around the World

In order for young women throughout the world to best fulfill their future roles as mothers, workers, and leaders, they need improved access to education and to reproductive health services. How are their reproductive health needs currently being met? (We look at education in Chapter 9.) Reports by the Alan Guttmacher Institute (1998, 2002b; Singh et al., 2003) gathered information on this question from 49 developing and 6 developed countries around the globe. Here are some of the key findings:

• Up to 60 percent of adolescent births throughout the world are unplanned.

• Contraceptive use by married and unmarried adolescents is greater than in the past, but in most of the world is still low. Among married adolescents, for example, contraceptive use is less than 5 percent in India and Pakistan and under 30 percent in Africa and the Middle East.

• Adolescent childbearing is declining in countries where it had been common, as access to education increases and the advantages of delayed childbearing are recognized. Still, in many parts of the developing world, 40 to 60 percent of women—especially rural adolescents and those with little education—have their first child before age 20. In the developed world, by contrast, fewer than 1 in 10 have an early first birth.

- Sexually transmitted infections that threaten the lives and health of young women and their newborns are on the rise, particularly in the developing world. For example, in some parts of Africa, nearly 40 percent of pregnant women test positive for HIV (see Chapter 12).
- Sexual relationships that result from force, coercion, and abuse, and cultural practices such as female genital mutilation (see Explore Other Cultures 7.2), and sexual

exploitation of young girls and adolescents for commercial gain, endanger the reproductive and mental health of young women.

In most countries, the poorest young women are at greatest risk of poor sexual and reproductive health. A recent study from 12 developing countries in Asia, sub-Saharan Africa, and Latin America found that poor women are more likely than wealthier women to be married and have a child by age 18 and are less likely to use contraceptives, use maternal health services, or know how to protect themselves from HIV (Rani & Lule, 2004).

EXPLORE OTHER CULTURES 7.2
Female Genital Mutilation

Female genital mutilation (FGM), *the surgical removal of parts of the external female genitalia*, is a major source of reproductive health problems for girls and women in 27 African countries, parts of the Middle East, and East Asia, as well as for immigrants of those nations who live in Europe and North America (Burn, 2005; Elmusharaf et al., 2006). An estimated 2 million girls and women per year undergo this procedure, usually in early childhood or adolescence. The mildest and most common form of FGM involves removing the clitoris, but usually both the clitoris and labia minora are removed. The most extreme form, known as **infibulation** or pharaonic circumcision, consists of *removing the clitoris, labia minora, and the inner two-thirds of the labia majora, which are then sewn together*. A tiny pencil-sized hole is left for the passage of urine and menstrual flow (Corbett, 2008). The procedure usually is performed by women, often

using crude, unsterilized instruments and without anesthesia. Resulting medical problems range from pain and infection through long-term difficulties with urination, menstruation, sexual intercourse, and giving birth (Burn, 2005).

Why does this practice persist when it is so obviously harmful to women? Girls in these cultures are considered unmarriageable without undergoing FGM. Some people mistakenly believe that the Islamic religion requires it. Others argue that eliminating the source of women's sexual sensations ensures female chastity (Rosenberg, 2004). A 1996 federal law has banned the practice in the United States, and it is condemned by the United Nations and World Health Organization. Women's organizations in Africa are actively involved in efforts to eradicate FGM, which is now outlawed in 15 African nations (Rosenberg, 2004; Corbett, 2008).

Pregnancy

For much of history, a woman's life was dominated by pregnancy and childbirth. A hundred years ago, death associated with pregnancy and childbirth was a serious threat for women around the globe. In the twentieth century, the risk dropped significantly for women in developed nations, but it continues to pose a major risk for those in developing countries (Maine & Chavkin, 2002; United Nations Population Fund, 2004). For a closer look at this issue, see Explore Other Cultures 7.3.

In the past several decades, the advent of the birth control pill, widespread contraceptive use, and legalized abortion have allowed individuals to plan and control the size of their families (Propp, 2003). The marvels of modern technology make it possible to monitor pregnancy virtually from the moment of conception and render it possible for infertile couples to bear children. In this section, we explore pregnancy, miscarriage, and pregnancy in teenagers.

Pregnancy: Physical and Psychological Changes

Pregnancy begins when an egg and sperm cell unite in the fallopian tube. The fertilized egg begins to divide as it travels toward the uterus, a three- or four-day journey. When it arrives, it implants itself into the thick lining of the uterus. Pregnancy

EXPLORE OTHER CULTURES 7.3
Pregnancy-Related Deaths around the World

Women in developed countries rarely die of complications of pregnancy nowadays, but these complications remain the number one cause of death and disability of young women in less-developed parts of the world (Kantrowitz, 2007b; Save the Children, 2007). For example, the maternal mortality rate is 46 times higher for sub-Saharan Africa than for industrialized nations (920 maternal deaths for every 100,000 live births versus only 20 for industrialized nations) (United Nations Population Fund, 2004; World Health Organization, 2004). Even within the same geographic area, striking differences exist. Haitian women, for instance, are nearly ten times more likely to die in pregnancy than Dominican women, who live on the same island. And the maternal mortality rate for Russian women is eight times higher than that of their Finnish neighbors (Save the Children, 2007). Women at greatest risk around the world are those who are poor, live in rural areas, and are members of minority groups. For example, Black women in the United States are four times more likely to die of pregnancy complications than are White women. In Canada,

Native women are at greater risk than White women (Maine & Chavkin, 2002). A key factor in these differences in maternal mortality is access to good-quality health care. Black Americans receive poorer health care than White Americans, even when they are of the same socioeconomic status (Saftlas et al., 2000). In developing countries, the low social status of women hampers their access to existing health care services (Save the Children, 2007). Women's lack of power in families and communities gives them little say over decisions that could save their lives (Murphy, 2003; UNIFEM, 2008). For example, even where low-cost transportation has been arranged by charitable organizations to increase access to emergency facilities, some husbands refuse to spend scarce resources on their wives, even though they would do so for themselves or their sons (Liljestrand & Gryboski, 2002).

Women in war zones are at especially high risk. In Afghanistan, for example, one woman dies out of every six who give birth. Currently, this is the highest rate in the world (Kantrowitz, 2007b; Save the Children, 2007).

typically lasts 40 weeks and is divided into three trimesters of three months each. A missed menstrual period is often the first indication of pregnancy although simple tests which are available in any drugstore can detect pregnancy within days after conception (Carlson et al., 2004).

Physical Changes.   During pregnancy, the blood volume in the body doubles and the breasts generally increase two bra sizes. The most dramatic change occurs in the uterus, which grows from two ounces to two pounds, not including the placenta or the baby (Curtis & Schuler, 2004; Schulman, 2003). Early signs of pregnancy include breast tenderness, more frequent urination, fatigue, and nausea. Nausea and vomiting usually are confined to the first trimester and, despite being called "morning sickness," they can occur anytime during the day (Brody, 2006b). Claire and Judith can vouch for the value of eating crackers or toast slowly in the morning before getting up. Ginger and vitamin B6 are also good for reducing nausea (Brody, 2006b). Food aversions and cravings also may develop (Curtis & Schuler, 2004). For example, Claire couldn't stand coffee or onions, which she normally loved. Many women describe the second trimester as the easiest stage of pregnancy (Carlson et al., 2004). During this phase, most of the nausea and fatigue disappear. By the end of the fifth month, women begin to feel fetal movements ("quickening"). During the third trimester, weight gain and protrusion of the abdomen become quite noticeable. Some of the activities of daily living, such as tying one's shoes, may become a challenge. The expanding uterus exerts increasing pressure on the other internal organs, which may lead to breathlessness, heartburn, and a need for frequent urination (Carlson et al., 2004).

In the past, pregnancy was viewed as an illness, but that is less true today. Most women feel that their pregnancy is a normal and healthy—if somewhat inconvenient—experience. Regular exercise along with good nutrition reduces or eliminates many discomforts (Boston Women's Health Book Collective, 2005). Claire played pool well into her first pregnancy, until her bulging abdomen made it too difficult to bend over the pool table. During her pregnancy with her second child, a summer baby, she swam until the day she gave birth.

Psychological Changes during Pregnancy.   A woman's feelings during pregnancy vary tremendously depending on such factors as her economic circumstances, her desire to be pregnant, her physical condition, and her childhood experiences (Carlson et al., 2004; Halbreich, 2005). At each stage, women sometimes feel positive and sometimes negative. Feelings of being more sensual, potent, creative, and loving may occur. Negative feelings include loss of individuality, worries about whether the baby will be normal, distress at gaining weight and looking awkward, concerns about changes in the couple's relationship, and anxieties about coping with the responsibilities of parenting (Boston Women's Health Collective, 2005; Ohye et al., 2003; Read, 2004).

Reactions to Pregnant Women.   A pregnant woman elicits a variety of reactions from those around her. Many women have had the experience of having their pregnant abdomen patted by people who would not consider such a gesture with a nonpregnant woman (Neiterman, 2007). Research by Hilary Lips (1997) shows that young adults perceive pregnant women as irritable, emotional, and suffering from physical maladies. In addition, pregnant women in the workplace may face discrimination in the job interview and are perceived as less competent workers than other women (Bragger et al., 2002; Eastman & Utley, 2004). Recent studies have found that even when viewed as equally qualified, dependable, committed, and fit for the position, a pregnant applicant received lower hiring recommendations than a nonpregnant candidate from both female and male raters (Cunningham & Macan, 2007; Masser et al., 2007). The discomfort some people feel around pregnant women was made abundantly clear to Claire in the end-of-semester course evaluations filled out by students when she was seven months pregnant. Some made negative comments about her teaching while pregnant; one said "Go home and have your baby." More recently, Claire's daughter-in-law Jen, who worked at a restaurant, told her supervisor that she was pregnant. Over her objections, he promptly reduced her hours (and thus her income) and assigned her to a less desirable shift.

Miscarriage

Miscarriage is the *spontaneous loss of a pregnancy during the first 28 weeks of gestation* (Krakovsky, 2006). At least one in seven known pregnancies results in miscarriage. However, the actual rate is considerably higher because about half of very early pregnancies are lost before a woman realizes that she is even pregnant (Brody, 2008b).

Most miscarriages are a result of major genetic defects in the embryo or fetus. Others are caused by hormonal imbalances in the mother, structural problems in the uterus or cervix, or diseases of the immune system (Daly, 2005; Grady, 2008a). Following one miscarriage, a woman's chances of having a subsequent normal pregnancy remain quite high. Even after three miscarriages, her chances of maintaining the next pregnancy are still about 65 percent (Brody, 2008b).

Until recently, it was assumed that miscarriages were not very stressful to the parents because the embryo or fetus was not yet a "real child." Well-meaning friends and relatives, even to this day, say things such as "It was meant to be" or "You can always have another child." Worse yet, others may say nothing, as though the event had not happened (Brier, 2008; Leon, 2001). But, in fact, parents start anticipating the birth of their child very early in pregnancy, and so a miscarriage produces grieving and a sense of loss (Daly, 2005; Moss, 2008; Sanderson, 2004). In addition, women may feel guilty and somehow responsible for the pregnancy loss. They also may feel angry and jealous toward other pregnant women. These feelings may be mingled with anxiety about the possibility of problems occurring in a future pregnancy (Carlson et al., 2004). Women who have been struggling for years with infertility problems, and women who have delayed parenthood into their thirties may be especially devastated when they experience a miscarriage. Fathers grieve too, of course, but their grief typically is of shorter duration and less intense than that of mothers (Brier, 2008; Diamond et al., 2005; Krakovsky, 2006).

Listening and responding supportively to the grieving parents can be very helpful (Springen, 2005). Speaking with others who have been through the same experience is often beneficial for the parents. For example, when Claire's daughter Andi miscarried during her first pregnancy at age 39, she found it comforting to talk to her cousin, who had had two consecutive miscarriages before giving birth to a healthy baby.

Teenage Pregnancy

In an AAUW survey of teenage girls, Blacks and Latinas mentioned pregnancy as an issue in their lives more than White and Asian American girls and did so at a younger age. Black and Latina girls described pregnancy as a "choice," which they counseled their peers not to make at an early age. Asian American and White girls described pregnancy as an "accident" and cautioned against the "risks" and "dangers" of sex (Haag, 1999).

Nevertheless, over 800,000 American girls age 15 to 19 become pregnant each year, and most of these pregnancies are unplanned (Alan Guttmacher Institute, 2004b). Substantial ethnic disparities exist among birth rates for adolescents. In 2005, the birth rate per 1,000 females, ages 15–17, was 8 for Asian Americans, 12 for Whites, 31 for Native Americans, 36 for Blacks, and 49 for Latinas (Martin et al., 2007). Between 1991 and 2005, the birth rate among teenagers declined, with a bigger decrease among the youngest teenagers (ages 10–14) and an especially big drop among Black adolescents (Federal Interagency Forum, 2007; Hamilton et al., 2007). Among those teens who do have babies, however, the proportion that is unmarried has jumped from 15 percent in 1960 to 84 percent in 2006 (Hamilton, Martin & Ventura, 2007). The decrease in teenage births is not a result of abortion, which has declined among teenagers starting in the 1990s. Rather, young people are delaying sex until they are older, having sex less frequently, and using birth control, especially condoms, more often and more responsibly. They are also choosing more effective contraceptive methods, such as long-lasting hormonal implants (Boonstra, 2002; Dailard, 2003b; Santelli et al., 2007; Ventura et al., 2003). How do pregnancy rates in the United States compare to those in other industrialized nations? For the answer, see Explore Other Cultures 7.4.

Consequences of Teenage Pregnancy. The consequences of unplanned teenage pregnancy are often grim. Teenage mothers are likely to live in poverty and to suffer from a lack of psychological and social support. In addition, they typically drop out of school, have less stable employment patterns, and are more likely to be on welfare. Their marriages are less apt to be stable, they are more depressed, and they are more likely to have additional children out of wedlock (Coley & Chase-Lansdale, 1998; Hofferth & Reid, 2002; Kalil & Kunz, 2002; Zabin & Cardona, 2002).

Children born to teenagers have an increased risk of prematurity, birth complications, and death within the first year (Federal Interagency Forum, 2007), which may result partly from the young age of the mother and partly from inadequate prenatal care. Pregnant teenagers and mothers are more likely than other women to engage in behaviors which put their unborn babies and young infants at risk. For example, they are more likely to smoke during pregnancy and are less likely to put their infants in the back sleep position, which helps prevent sudden infant death syndrome (Phares et al., 2004). The children of young mothers are also more apt to have emotional, behavioral, and cognitive difficulties, most likely as a result of their impoverished caregiving environment (Federal Interagency Forum, 2007; Hofferth & Reid, 2002), and they are more likely to

Most teenage pregnancies in the United States are unplanned, often with negative consequences for both mother and child.

EXPLORE OTHER CULTURES 7.4

Why Is the Teen Pregnancy Rate So High in the United States?

Despite the decline in births among American teenagers, the United States still has one of the highest teen pregnancy rates among industrialized nations. The U.S. rate is nearly twice that of Great Britain and Canada, and at least four times the rates of France, Germany, and Japan (Boonstra, 2002; Darroch et al., 2001). What could account for this big difference? Are U.S. teenagers more sexually active? Do they begin having sex at an earlier age? Research by Jacqueline Darroch and her associates (2001) found that levels of sexual activity and the age at which teenagers initiated sex did not, in fact, vary appreciably across the countries. The major reason that teen pregnancy is higher in the United States, they found, is that teens' use of contracep-

tives is higher in other countries, where teenage sexual activity is more accepted and contraceptive services are much more widely available (Alan Guttmacher Institute, 2002a). The differing attitudes toward teenage sexuality in the United States and Europe are reflected in their sex education policies. An "abstinence-only" policy is often emphasized in sex education in the United States, whereas Europeans emphasize informed choice and responsibility (National Campaign, 2003; Roth, 2003). Many European countries have provided comprehensive sex education to all school children for many years. These programs encourage abstinence but also provide information about birth control methods and provide free access to contraceptives (Papalia, 2005).

be abused or neglected (Annie E. Casey Foundation, 1999). In adolescence, children of teenagers show higher rates of school failure, delinquency, and earlier sexual activity and pregnancy than teens born to older mothers (Coley & Chase-Lansdale, 1998).

Support for Pregnant Teenagers.   Support programs for pregnant teenagers have met with some success in improving the lives of teenage parents and their children (Kaufmann, 1996; Reichman & McLanahan, 2001; Seitz, 1996). Programs include one or more of the following components: family planning services, child-care provisions, education about parenting and job skills, and welfare reform incentives. Teenage mothers who participate in comprehensive programs have fewer children in the long run and are more likely to complete high school and become economically self-sufficient. Their children are healthier, suffer less abuse, have fewer developmental problems, and do better in school (Chira, 1994; Gennetian & Miller, 2002; Seitz, 1996).

Preventing Teenage Pregnancy.   Programs aimed at preventing teen pregnancy have taken various approaches: providing knowledge of sexuality and contraception, teaching abstinence, building decision-making job and social skills, enhancing gender and ethnic pride, and discussing life options (Daniluk & Towill, 2001; DiClemente et al., 2004; Lewin, 2001a). Programs that combine elements of these approaches are the most successful in delaying sexual activity, increasing contraceptive use, and reducing pregnancy (Dailard, 2002; DiClemente et al., 2004; Robin et al., 2004; Schemo, 2000a; Zabin & Cardona, 2002). While an overwhelming majority of American parents favor sex education in school, there is considerable debate on what should be taught, when, and by whom. In recent years, many school-based programs have increasingly focused only on abstinence because they are prohibited from mentioning contraception as they receive federal funding (Ali & Scelfo, 2002; Lindberg et al., 2006). Unfortunately, as we saw earlier, this approach has little effect on reducing sexual activity or pregnancy (Beil, 2007; Lewin, 2001b; Risman & Schwartz, 2002; Trenholm et al., 2007).

Childbirth

Women describe the birth of their first child as a physically and psychologically transforming experience (DiMatteo & Kahn, 1997; also see the vignette at the beginning of the chapter). In Chapter 8, we will examine some of the psychological aspects involved in making the transition to motherhood. In this section, we focus on the biological aspects of childbirth. We also examine postpartum distress, infertility, and assisted reproductive technology.

Stages of Childbirth

In the first stage, the cervix becomes dilated to 10 centimeters (about 5 inches) in diameter, a process that may last from a few hours to a day or more. In the second stage, which lasts from a few minutes to several hours, uterine contractions move the baby through the vagina. At the end of this stage, the baby is born. During the third stage, which lasts from a few minutes to an hour, the placenta detaches from the uterine wall and is expelled. Progesterone and estrogen levels drop dramatically during the second and third stages (Rathus et al., 2008).

Methods of Childbirth

Throughout most of the twentieth century, women gave birth in hospitals, attended by obstetricians using surgical instruments and anesthetics. While use of these medical procedures has saved lives and reduced pain, it also has depersonalized childbearing. Feminists argue that it has taken from women control over their own bodies and, through drugs, denied many women the experience of giving birth (Anleu, 2006; Rathus et al., 2008).

One example of the "medicalization" of the birth process is the **cesarean section** (or C-section). *Incisions are made in the abdomen and uterus and the baby is surgically removed*. C-sections are performed if vaginal delivery is expected to be difficult or threatens the health of the mother or baby—as when the mother's pelvis is small or misshapen, the baby is very large, or the baby is not in the normal birth position. But more pregnant women in the United States and Canada are choosing to deliver this way when there is no medical need (Barrett, 2006; Ecker & Frigoletto, 2007). In the United States, the rate rose from 5 percent in 1970 to a record high of 31 percent of all births (Hamilton, Martin & Ventura, 2007). This increase in unnecessary C-sections may be driven in part by busy mothers wanting to schedule their deliveries (Yabroff, 2008), as well as by obstetricians seeking to avoid potential malpractice suits (Declerq et al., 2006).

Another example of the medicalization of childbirth is the induction of labor for practical (rather than medical) reasons, such as the convenience of the doctor, hospital, or parents. While the procedure is relatively safe, it increases the risk of C-sections, especially in first-time mothers. The reason is that the cervix may not dilate quickly enough. In the United States, the rate of labor-induced births doubled from 10 percent in 1990 to 22 percent by 2005, causing some experts to speak out against the practice (Ecker & Frigoletto, 2007; Martin et al., 2007).

Parents now can choose among more family-centered approaches to childbearing. The most popular method in the United States is prepared child birth, or the **Lamaze method.** *Prelabor classes teach the mother to control her pain through relaxation, breathing techniques, and focusing exercises*. A labor coach (usually the husband or partner) provides moral support and coaches techniques of breathing and relaxation during childbirth (Donatelle & Davis, 1998; Torpy, 2002). Others also may serve as a labor coach: a woman's mother, sister, friend, or *an experienced and knowledgeable female labor and birth coach* known as a **doula.** Doula comes from the Greek word meaning "woman caregiver of a woman." Studies have found that women who are randomly assigned a doula during labor have less pain and anxiety during labor, need less medication, have fewer C-sections, and have shorter labors and less postpartum depression than women without a doula (Boston Women's Health Collective, 2005; Wilgoren, 2005). In addition, women assigned doulas are found to be more sensitive, loving, and responsive to their infants two months later (Gilbert, 1998).

Home birth also has increased in recent years, providing families with familiar settings and enhancing the feeling that the woman and her family are in control. More women are also choosing to deliver in homelike birthing centers outside a hospital. Family members and friends may be present during labor and delivery. Many hospitals now provide similar family-friendly birthing rooms (Carmichael, 2004). Other aspects of family-centered birth include minimizing the use of anesthesia, using the more natural (and gravity-assisted) sitting position to give birth and eliminating practices such as enemas, shaving of the genital area, and performing an episiotomy, an incision that widens the vaginal opening to allow passage of the baby's head (Kuhn, 2005; Tarkan, 2002).

Using certified nurse-midwives for prenatal care and delivery has also become increasingly popular in the United States. Certified nurse-midwives attended only 1 percent of births in 1975 but now perform about 10 percent of vaginal deliveries (Carmichael, 2004; Pérez-Peña, 2004). Mortality rates are lower and birth weights are higher for infants delivered by nurse-midwives than for those delivered by physicians even though nurse-midwives tend to serve traditionally higher-risk women such as teenage mothers and those with lower income and less education (Lydon-Rochelle, 2004). The most likely explanation for this is that nurse-midwives, compared to physicians, spend more time with patients during prenatal visits, provide more patient education and counseling, and are with their patients throughout labor and delivery (Strong, 2000).

Childbearing after 40

A growing number of women are having children after the age of 40 (Martin et al., 2007). In 2003, over 103,000 U.S. women between 40 and 44, and nearly 6,000 women between 45 and 49 gave birth, a record high. But because fertility begins to decline after age 27, older women have a harder time conceiving. Among women over 40, half will require medical assistance in order to conceive (Brody, 2004b). About 15 to 20 percent of women aged 40 to 42 can become pregnant using their own eggs, compared with fewer than 3 percent of women over 44, as an increasing percentage of their eggs become abnormal (Gibbs, 2002; St. John, 2002). Women over 40 have more miscarriages than younger women, more preterm, low-birth-weight and stillborn babies, higher levels of complications during pregnancy, more chromosomal abnormalities (such as Down syndrome), and are more likely to have cesarean sections (Ananth et al., 2005; Brody, 2004b; Cleary-Goldman et al., 2005; Jacobsson et al., 2004; Yang et al., 2006). The good news is that almost all older mothers, like their younger counterparts, have healthy babies, and that infant mortality rates are comparable for the two groups (Berkowitz et al., 2006; Etaugh, 2008).

A lesser-known fact about midlife pregnancy is that about half of the pregnancies of women over 40 are unintended—a rate second only to teenagers. During perimenopause, the years prior to the end of menstruation, women may grow lax about birth control because they think there is little risk of pregnancy and may believe they have reached menopause. However, a woman's menstrual cycle becomes less regular in perimenopause and she may go several months without a period before having one (Goldberg, 2003).

To find out more about individual women's experiences with pregnancy and childbirth, try Get Involved 7.2.

Childbearing in the Later Years

Claire remembers seeing an amusing comic strip several years ago that featured an elderly couple sitting in rocking chairs. The woman, knitting a tiny sweater, was obviously pregnant. Looking at her husband with an irritated expression on her face, she exclaimed "You and your 'once more for old times' sake!'" The humor of the situation was based on the impossibility of an elderly woman's becoming pregnant. But this is no longer a laughing matter.

Late in 2006, Carmen Bousada gave birth in Spain to healthy twin boys. News of the event spread like wildfire around the globe. What made this birth so special? Carmen Bousada was 67 years old (James, 2007). Donated sperm fertilized a young woman's donor eggs in a test tube, and the resulting embryos were implanted in Bousada's hormonally readied uterus. Most fertility clinics set an age limit of 50 to 55 for a woman seeking in vitro fertilization, but Bousada lied about her age. Recent breakthroughs in transplanting ovarian tissue and in freezing eggs and embryos further raise the possibility that women may be able to bear children well into their golden years (Grady, 2004; Kalb, 2004a).

GET INVOLVED 7.2

Pregnancy and Childbirth Experiences

1. Briefly interview two women in their twenties, two middle-aged women, and two older women about their experiences with pregnancy and childbirth. It is helpful, but not essential, if you know your respondents fairly well. You may interview your sisters, cousins, friends, mother, aunts, grandmothers, and so on. Keep a record of your respondents' comments.

2. Compare and contrast the responses of the women in the three age groups.

What Does It Mean?

1. In what ways are the pregnancy experiences of the three groups of women different? In what ways are they alike?

2. In what ways are the childbirth experiences of the three groups different? In what ways are they alike?

3. What social and historical conditions may have influenced the pregnancy and childbirth experiences of these three generations of women?

Carmen Bousada (shown at left, walking with her infants and a babysitter) recently gave birth at the age of 67 to the healthy twins in the stroller. Why was this controversial?

Controversy swirls around the issue of whether postmenopausal women should be denied help in becoming pregnant (Budd, 2002; "Donor-Egg," 2002; James, 2007; Newman, 2000; Thomas, 2005). Those who support this view cite several reasons: (1) Such pregnancies risk the mother's health; (2) an older mother is less likely than a younger one to live long enough to raise her child to adulthood; (3) it is unnatural and a perverse use of technology that has been widely accepted for younger women for nearly 30 years.

These arguments have been rebutted by others who claim that (1) The complications that could affect the older mother's health also occur in younger women, although less frequently, and are treatable ("Donor-Egg," 2002); (2) Any responsible mother, regardless of age, should make provisions for the care of her child in the event that she dies before the child is grown. Some younger women with severe medical conditions have babies. Should they also be barred from reproducing? (3) If the reproductive technology exists, why shouldn't an older woman take advantage of it? Should older women be denied other medical advances such as coronary bypass surgery? (Claire's mother-in-law had this procedure when she was in her early eighties and lived another twenty years in robust health. She did not, however, contemplate having another child.)

Marcia Angell, a physician and former executive editor of the *New England Journal of Medicine*, believes that both age discrimination and gender discrimination are at the root of society's discomfort about older women's having babies (Angell, 1997). Think of people's reactions to the news of men becoming fathers in their seventies and eighties: comedian Charlie Chaplin, actor Tony Randall, and former U.S. Senator Strom Thurmond, to mention but a few. Rather than disapproval, there is acceptance and even admiration of the sexual prowess of these older men.

Postpartum Distress

During the postpartum period, the first weeks after birth, many women experience some psychological distress. Postpartum distress is widely reported in countries around the world, although it is not universally perceived as an illness requiring the intervention of health professionals (Oates et al., 2004). The mildest and most common form, called **maternity blues** or baby blues, is experienced by up to 75 percent of new mothers. *This mood state, characterized by crying, anxiety, and irritability, typically begins three to four days after childbirth and lasts about two to four days.* Maternity blues are more common following a first birth and may reflect the mother's adjustment to parenthood (Beckman, 2006).

One out of eight women have *severe feelings of depression that last for weeks or months after delivery.* These changes, called **postpartum depression,** are characterized by anxiety or panic attacks, loss of interest in daily activities, despair, feelings of worthlessness and guilt, sleep and appetite disturbances, fatigue, difficulty in concentrating, and thoughts of harming oneself or the baby. One or 2 in 1,000 women experience postpartum psychosis, a serious condition that often includes delusions, hallucinations, and thoughts (or deeds) of hurting oneself or the infant (Carlson et al., 2004; Marsh, 2006; Sit et al., 2006). Andrea Yates, the woman convicted of drowning her five young children in the bathtub, suffered from postpartum psychosis. She explained that Satan told her this was the only way to save the children, because she was a "bad mother" (Johnson & Rust, 2005).

Women are more likely to develop postpartum depression if they are young, poor, less educated, and first-time mothers. Risk factors also include a history of mental illness, previous depression, marital difficulties or other stressful life events, and lack of support from family and friends (American Psychological Association, 2007b; Beckman, 2006; Brett et al., 2008). In interviews with 35 British and American mothers with postpartum depression, Natasha Mauthner (2002) found that many of the women held idealized cultural constructions of the "perfect mother" that contrasted sharply with their perception that they were not measuring up. It is unclear whether the drastic drop in levels of estrogen and progesterone after birth also plays a role, since symptoms of postpartum depression also occur in mothers of newly adopted children, (Boston Women's Health Collective, 2005; Whiffen, 2001).

Social support and various psychological interventions play an important role in reducing the risk of postpartum depression (Marsh, 2006). While support and therapy clearly help prevent and treat postpartum depression, the great majority of women recover from the condition within three to six months without any treatment (Cuijpers et al., 2008; Steiner et al., 2003).

Infertility and Assisted Reproductive Technology

Infertility is *the failure to conceive a child after a year of trying* (Clay, 2006). About one in ten Americans in their reproductive years experiences infertility and the likelihood of being infertile increases with age for both women and men. In 35–40 percent of the cases, the difficulty is traced to the woman, in 35–40 percent of the cases, the problem originates with the man, and in the remaining cases, the origin is combined or unknown (Clay, 2006). Causes of infertility in women include blockage of the fallopian tubes, failure of the ovaries to produce eggs, uterine fibroids, and **endometriosis,** *the presence of uterine lining tissue in abnormal locations* (Centers for Disease Control and Prevention, 2003). A leading cause of infertility in women is polycystic ovary syndrome (PCOS), in which high levels of the hormone testosterone interfere with ovulation. Clues that a woman may have PCOS are the presence of facial hair, acne, obesity, and infrequent or irregular periods (Torpy, 2007b). Lifestyle factors also play a role in infertility. If a woman is a heavy smoker, consumes large amounts of caffeine, or she or her partner drink heavily, the risk of infertility increases (Hassan & Killick, 2004).

About 15 percent of infertile couples have tried recently developed assisted reproductive technologies (Rebar & DeCherney, 2004). In 74 percent of those cases, couples use IVF or **in vitro fertilization** in which *the couple's own sperm and egg are fertilized in a glass laboratory dish ("in vitro" means "in glass") and the resulting embryo is transferred into the woman's uterus* (Wright et al., 2007). Louise Brown, born in England in 1978 as a result of IVF, was the first of these so-called test-tube babies, now numbering over one million strong worldwide (Berger, 2007; Mundy, 2007). In 15 percent of infertility treatments, the couples' frozen embryos are used, and in 12 percent, donor eggs are used. Donated eggs typically are used for older women who do not produce eggs or whose eggs are damaged (Wright et al., 2007). Older women who use donor eggs from young women can have successful pregnancies at least until their mid-fifties (Heffner, 2004; Orenstein, 2007). In the United States, egg selling is big business. So-called "Ivy League eggs" are in great demand, and ads in campus newspapers offer tens of thousands of dollars for the eggs of college women (Rabin, 2007a; Spar, 2007). On rare occasions, a "donor uterus" is used when a woman can produce eggs but cannot carry a pregnancy to full term. An embryo is produced by IVF using the couple's egg and sperm and is then placed in the donor's uterus. In one recent case, a 43-year-old woman carried twins for her daughter, who had no uterus, and gave birth to her own grandchildren ("Twins," 2004).

The "success rate," that is, the percentage of times a live birth results, is about 28 percent for the patient's frozen embryos, 34 percent for IVF, 51 percent for freshly fertilized embryos from donor eggs, and 31 percent for frozen embryos from donor eggs (Wright et al., 2007). Babies born after fertility treatments have higher rates of stillbirth, prematurity, low birth weight, and birth defects (Jackson et al., 2004). Depending on the procedure used, anywhere from about 25 percent to 40 percent are multiple births (Wright et al., 2007). In addition, the treatments are expensive. For example, the average cost of a single IVF effort in the United States is about $12,400, but insurance usually covers little or nothing of the procedure (Jain & Gupta, 2007; Petersen, 2006).

Another more controversial approach to infertility, **surrogate motherhood,** involves *paying a woman to be implanted with the embryo of another couple and give birth to the child.* About 1,000 infants are born through surrogacy every year in the United States (Ali & Kelley, 2008; Markens, 2007). This practice raises a number of social, legal, and financial questions (Beckman, 2006). Can a contract signed before a baby's conception be legally binding after birth? Who are the legal parents? Should the surrogate mother be paid for her services? Some critics are concerned about the potential economic exploitation of poor women as surrogate mothers. Yet most surrogates are married with children of their own and have a desire to help an infertile couple become parents (Ali & Kelly, 2008; Beckman, 2006). Overall, surrogacy appears to be a positive experience for surrogate mothers. These women have often completed a family of their own and wish to help an infertile couple become parents. They generally have a good relationship with the commissioning couple, have few problems handing over the baby, and many maintain contact with the couple and the child (Beckman, 2006; Jadva et al., 2003).

In addition, fears about the impact of surrogacy on the well-being of children and families appear to be unfounded (Golombok et al., 2004). In fact, mothers of children born via a surrogacy arrangement show more warmth towards their babies and are more emotionally involved than in families where the child is conceived naturally. Both the mother and father have better parenting skills than do the parents in nonsurrogate families, and the babies themselves show no differences in their temperament and behavior, when compared with nonsurrogate babies. Nor do there seem to be problems when the surrogate mothers hand over the babies to the mothers who have commissioned the surrogacy.

While some couples wish to have children but cannot, others make a choice not to have children. For a fuller discussion of this issue, see Learn about the Research 7.1.

LEARN ABOUT THE RESEARCH 7.1
Childfree by Choice

My husband and I told family and friends when we married that we didn't want to have children. They kept saying we would change our minds. My parents begged me to change my mind. When I was told at 25 years old during a cancer scare that I was sterile, . . . I joyfully announced to my hubby that we would no longer have to use birth control. I thought that the announcement of my "God"-given sterility would end the baby nag . . . but no— people began to tell me it was my duty to adopt, encouraged me to get on the fertility treatment treadmill, said they would pray for me, told me miracle baby stories or looked at me with pity. (40-year-old woman, in *Ms.*, 2004, p. 6)

More than at any other time in history, women and men in the industrialized world are deciding not to have children. Europe's population has been falling since 1998 as the birth rate there has continued to decline. At this rate, Europe will have 90 million fewer people by 2050 (Elder, 2003). Among U.S. women 40–44 years old in 2004, nearly one in five had no children, compared with one in ten three decades earlier (Dye, 2005). Although some of these women ultimately will have a child, most will not.

The decision to not have children is facilitated by the availability and legality of effective forms of birth control, the women's movement's emphasis on women's right to make choices in their lives, and the wider participation of women in the labor force (Koropeckyj-Cox, Romano, & Moras, 2007). However, the decision not to have children—to be childless or "childfree"—goes against the traditional gender norms of almost all cultures. Women who make this choice are often criticized as shallow, selfish, deviant, and unfeminine (Else-Quest, 2006; Gillespie, 2003; D. M. Hall, 2008). They may be marginalized, pitied, given unsolicited advice, and pressured by others to have children (Mollen, 2005).

Why do women choose not to have children? The reasons are many. Some women want autonomy, economic independence, and increased career prospects. Other women simply do not enjoy children, believe that they would not make good parents, or want a flexible lifestyle that would be hampered by children. Still others perceive motherhood to be a sacrifice and a burden, involving loss of time, energy, and ultimately, identity (Dierbeck, 2003; Gillespie, 2003; Park, 2005; Westcott, 2006).

One recent study by Debra Mollen Baker (2003) of intentionally childfree women found that several had shown a resistance to traditional gender roles while growing up, with half describing themselves as tomboys. While most of these women did not experience abusive or neglectful childhoods, some detected that their mothers were dissatisfied or ambivalent about their parental role. These women tended to value at least some traditionally masculine activities and values and felt more supported by their fathers than their mothers in their decision to not have children.

What Does It Mean?

1. Are the terms "childless" and "childfree" exact synonyms? In what ways do they differ in meaning?
2. In what way could a mother's dissatisfaction or ambivalence about parenting influence her daughter's decision about whether to have children?
3. What can be done to increase society's acceptance of women who decide not to have children?

Reproductive Functioning in Midlife and Beyond

Declining estrogen production results in menopause, one of the most obvious biological events of women's middle years, and also hastens the development of osteoporosis.

Menopause

Menopause is the *cessation of menstrual periods for a full year*. For most American women, menopause occurs between the ages of 45 and 55, with an average age of 51. Smokers reach menopause up to 2 years earlier than nonsmokers (Dunivin, 2006; Mikkelsen et al., 2007). Menopause occurs because of the decline in the number of ovarian follicles (egg-producing cells), which results in a decline in the production of both estrogen and progesterone. Some estrogen continues to be produced after menopause by the adrenal glands and fat cells (Sherwin, 2007). *The five to seven years preceding the beginning of menopause*, known as the **perimenopause,** are marked by increasing irregularity of the menstrual cycle and variations in the amount of menstrual flow (Chrisler, 2008b). As we shall see, the way in which a woman experiences menopause reflects a host of physiological, psychological, and cultural factors (Rossi, 2004).

Physical Symptoms. The frequency and severity of physical symptoms associated with menopause vary widely among women. In fact, the *only* symptom that all menopausal women experience is the end of menstruation. In North America, the most commonly reported symptom is the **hot flash**, *a sudden feeling of heat that spreads over the body with mild or profuse sweating, that usually lasts one to five minutes, and may occur several times daily* (Lamberg, 2007). Surveys report that anywhere between 50 and 80 percent of menopausal women experience hot flashes (Grady, 2006; Lamberg, 2007). For example, in a nationwide study of adult Americans by the MacArthur Foundation, half of the post-menopausal women surveyed reported having no hot flashes at all, only 25 percent said they had hot flashes at least once a month, and 12 percent reported having them almost daily (Rossi, 2004). Some women will have hot flashes for a few months, some for a few years, and many not at all. Hot flashes at night (sometimes called *"night sweats"*) can interfere with the sleep of some menopausal women, but most women find hot flashes to be only a minor inconvenience (Grady, 2006; Lamberg, 2007).

Loss of estrogen also causes thinning of the vaginal lining and decreased vaginal lubrication. These changes can lead to painful sexual intercourse and also make the vagina more prone to infection. Headaches, joint and muscle pains, and tingling sensations are other physical symptoms that are occasionally reported (Chrisler, 2008b; Dennerstein et al., 2007; Torpy, 2007c). Women who smoke experience more severe symptoms (Gold et al., 2006; Tice & Grady, 2006). The most serious physical consequence of menopause, osteoporosis, is discussed in Chapter 12.

Women in different ethnic and cultural groups vary in the kinds and degree of menopausal symptoms they report. For example, hot flashes are more prevalent in Black and Latina women than in white women and are least common in Asian American women (Appling et al., 2007).

Psychological Reactions. It is popularly believed that menopausal women are more likely to display such psychological symptoms as depression, irritability, or mood swings. There is no evidence, however, that these or other psychological symptoms are more prevalent among menopausal women (H. Roberts, 2007). Some women may feel irritable or tired, but these feelings may be linked to disruptions in sleep caused by hot flashes (Chrisler, 2008a).

Even if some women do show heightened psychological distress during the menopausal years, this cannot be attributed solely to biological processes. Changes in social roles that occur in midlife (see Chapter 11) may be largely responsible for increased distress. Women not only are confronting their own aging during this time but may also be coping with stressful changes in the family: the illness or death of a spouse, divorce or separation, difficult teenagers, children who are preparing to leave home, and/or aging parents who require care (Lamberg, 2007).

Attitudes toward Menopause. Popular images and stereotypes of menopausal women are overwhelmingly negative in North America. Menopause continues to be described in the medical literature (Derry, 2006; Dillaway, 2005). The popular press reinforces the notion of menopause as a condition of disease and deterioration that requires treatment by drugs (Anleu, 2006; Voda & Ashton, 2006).

Many women, however, view menopause as a positive or central transition (Dillaway, 2005). In fact, most middle-aged American women, however, minimize the significance of menopause as only a temporary inconvenience. Many look forward to menopause as marking the end of menstruation and childbearing (Chrisler, 2008a). In the MacArthur Foundation survey mentioned earlier, the majority of postmenopausal women reported feeling "only relief" when their menstrual periods stopped, while only 2 percent said they experienced "only regret" (Rossi, 2004).

Not surprisingly, women express more positive attitudes toward menopause when it is described as a normal life transition than when it is described as a medical problem (Gannon & Ekstrom, 1993). A woman who expects menopause to be unpleasant is apt to focus on its negative aspects. For example, women with a negative attitude toward menopause are more likely to report vaginal dryness, decreased sexual interest, and negative mood (Collins, 1997).

Attitudes toward menopause also differ according to a woman's ethnic and cultural background. For example, one study of over 16,000 Asian American, Black, Latina, and White women found that Black women had the most positive attitudes toward menopause whereas Asian American women were least positive (Sommer et al., 1999). Across ethnic groups, better-educated women held more positive views.

What are women's experiences with and attitudes toward menopause in non-Western societies? Take a look at Explore Other Cultures 7.5.

Hormone Replacement Therapy

Hormone replacement therapy (HRT) is *a medical treatment that replaces hormones whose levels drop after menopause*. Women who have had their uterus removed can take

---

EXPLORE OTHER CULTURES 7.5
Menopause: Symbol of Decline or of Higher Status?

Women in non-Western cultures often have menopausal experiences and attitudes very different from those reported by Western women, indicating that menopausal symptoms are at least in part socially constructed (Winterich, 2007). For example, Japanese and Indonesian women are much less likely than women in Western cultures to report hot flashes or other physical symptoms (Sowers, 2000; Steiner et al., 2003), and among Mayan women, hot flashes are virtually unknown (Feldman, 2000). Women of high social castes in India and Lakota Sioux women in the United States report very few negative symptoms, and menopause is in fact an eagerly anticipated event. Why might that be? When these women reach menopause, they are freed from menstrual taboos and are able to participate more fully in society (Feldman, 2000; Sherwin, 2001; Winterich, 2003). No wonder they experience few negative menopausal symptoms! In Western cultures, on the other hand, aging does not confer higher status on a woman but rather lowers it. It is thus not surprising that there are more complaints about "symptoms" in such a youth-oriented culture (Godfrey & LowDog, 2008).

Women of high social castes in India look forward to menopause which frees them from menstrual taboos and allows them full participation in society.

estrogen alone, while those who still have their uterus are advised to take a combination of estrogen and synthetic progesterone (progestin) in order to protect against uterine cancer (American Cancer Society, 2008b).

The combined estrogen–progestin pill relieves the menopausal symptoms of hot flashes, night sweats, insomnia, and vaginal dryness. It helps prevent osteoporosis and reduces the risk of colon cancer. However, recent large-scale studies in the United States and the United Kingdom found that it also increases the risk of heart attack, stroke, blood clots, breast and ovarian cancer, gallbladder disease, and dementia (Heiss et al., 2008; Lamberg, 2007; Schneider, 2004; Vickers et al., 2007). The use of estrogen alone also increases the risk of stroke and dementia and fails to protect against heart disease, although it does not increase the risk of breast cancer and protects against hip fractures (Stefanick et al., 2006). Recent studies indicate that women who started HRT early in menopause are less likely to have these risks than women who began the therapy 10–15 years later (Goldberg, 2008).

Which women should use HRT after menopause? That decision must be based on each woman's evaluation of the benefits and risks to herself (see Table 7.2) given her personal and family medical history. Some women whose quality of life suffers because of extreme hot flashes or vaginal atrophy elect to use HRT. However, they are now advised to take the lowest dose that provides relief, and for the shortest time possible

TABLE 7.2   Benefits and Risks of Combined Hormone Replacement Therapy

Benefits	Risks
Ends hot flashes	Increases risk of heart attack and stroke
Relieves vaginal dryness and atrophy	Increases risk of ovarian cancer
Delays bone loss	Increases risk of uterine cancer if estrogen
Increases bone density	is taken without progesterone
Decreases risk of colon cancer	Increases risk of gallbladder disease
May decrease risk of parkinson's disease	Increases risk of breast cancer
May delay cognitive decline if given	Increases risk of urinary incontinence
at menopause	

Sources: Goldberg (2008); Grodstein et al. (2003); Million Women Study Collaborators (2007); H. Roberts (2007); Sherwin (2007).

(Goldberg, 2008; Manson & Bassuk, 2007). Women should definitely *not* use hormones if they have a history of, or are at a higher risk for, heart disease, stroke, cancer of the breast or uterus, chronic liver disease, or diabetes. Women should *consider* avoiding hormones if they have migraine headaches, gallbladder disease, uterine fibroid tumors, high blood pressure, seizure disorders, or blood clots (Deborah Grady, 2006; Manson & Bassuk, 2007; "New Risks," 2004).

Alternatives to Standard Hormone Replacement Therapy. The usual dose of estrogen given in HRT is 0.625 milligram. However, lower doses may confer similar benefits in building bones and relieving hot flashes and vaginal dryness, while lowering risks (Manson & Bassuk 2007; Rabin, 2007b; Tice & Grady, 2006). An alternative approach is the use of synthetic estrogens that have some of the benefits but fewer of the risks of natural estrogen. One such hormone, raloxifene, appears to offer some protection against heart disease among women with elevated risk of the disease (Barrett-Connor et al., 2002). It also *reduces* the risk of breast cancer and bone loss (Springen, 2007). Antidepressants also reduce hot flashes in recently menopausal women (Parker-Pope, 2007).

Lifestyle modifications, especially those involving regular exercise and dietary modifications appear to be beneficial in reducing menopausal symptoms. Limiting or eliminating caffeine, alcohol, cigarettes, and spicy foods also reduces the frequency of hot flashes (Brody, 2006a; Manson & Bassuk, 2007; H. Roberts, 2007). Consuming foods and herbs that contain estrogen-like substances, such as soy products, wild yams, flaxseed, and black cohosh may be helpful as well (Krebs et al., 2004; "Menopause Herb Garden," 2008; Welty et al., 2007a), although the evidence is mixed. Known as **phyto-estrogens,** these *plant foods do not contain estrogen but affect the body in a similar manner*. Phyto-estrogens are many times weaker than pharmaceutical estrogens and may not help women experiencing severe effects of menopause. Furthermore, there is as yet no evidence that these estrogen substitutes provide the same long-term benefits against osteoporosis that estrogen provides (North American Menopause Society, 2003).

S U M M A R Y

Menstruation

- The menstrual cycle is regulated by hormones, brain structures, and reproductive organs.
- Attitudes toward menstruation remain somewhat negative, despite evidence that physical and psychological performance does not change meaningfully over the menstrual cycle.
- Some women experience menstrual joy, a feeling of heightened creativity and energy.
- Only a small minority of women experience the symptoms of premenstrual syndrome (PMS). However, a majority believe they suffer from the disorder.

Contraception

- Contraceptive use has increased among adolescents, but many use contraceptives sporadically or not at all.
- The type of contraception chosen by women changes as their reproductive goals change.

Abortion

- Most abortions occur within the first trimester by means of the vacuum aspiration method.
- Early abortion is physically safe and generally has no negative psychological aftereffects.

Pregnancy

- Physical effects of pregnancy include nausea, fatigue, and weight gain.
- Women have both positive and negative feelings during pregnancy.
- People may react negatively to a pregnant woman.
- Most miscarriages result from genetic defects in the embryo or fetus.
- The teenage pregnancy rate is higher in the United States than in most industrialized nations, but the teenage birth rate is declining, probably due to increased condom use.
- Teen pregnancy has serious economic, social, and medical costs.

- Programs stressing abstinence, contraception, and life skills can delay sexual activity and reduce pregnancy rates.

Childbirth

- The three stages of childbirth are dilation of the cervix, birth of the baby, and expulsion of the placenta.
- Rates of cesarean delivery and induction of labor are high in the United States.
- Family-centered approaches to childbearing include the Lamaze method, home birth, birthing rooms and centers, and use of midwives.
- Older women have more difficulty conceiving but generally have healthy babies.
- Many women experience maternity blues shortly after giving birth. A small percentage experience the more severe postpartum depression and postpartum psychosis.
- About 15 percent of infertile couples have tried reproductive technologies, such as in vitro fertilization, frozen embryos, donor eggs, and surrogate motherhood.

Reproductive Functioning in Midlife and Beyond

- Menopause, caused by a decrease in estrogen production, causes hot flashes and vaginal dryness but is not linked to heightened psychological distress.
- Menopausal experiences and attitudes differ across ethnic and cultural groups.
- Middle-aged women usually have positive attitudes toward menopause.
- Benefits of hormone replacement therapy (HRT) include decrease in menopausal symptoms and decrease in the risk of osteoporosis and colon cancer.
- Risks of HRT include increased risk of heart attack, stroke, breast cancer, ovarian cancer, gall bladder disease, and dementia.
- Alternatives to HRT include synthetic estrogens and phyto-estrogens.

KEY TERMS

dysmenorrhea	infibulation	endometriosis
prostaglandins	miscarriage	in vitro fertilization
women-as-problem bias	cesarean section	surrogate motherhood
premenstrual syndrome (PMS)	Lamaze method	menopause
premenstrual dysphoric	doula	perimenopause
disorder (PMDD)	maternity blues	hot flash
vacuum aspiration	postpartum depression	hormone replacement therapy
female genital mutilation	infertility	phyto-estrogens

WHAT DO YOU THINK?

1. If a friend of yours unexpectedly became pregnant, what factors might influence her decision about whether or not to terminate the pregnancy?

2. Why do you think that even though many college students have heard about the risks of sexually transmitted diseases, including HIV infection, they fail to use condoms regularly or to engage in other self-protecting behaviors? What actions could be taken to make more of your friends engage in "safer sex" practices?

3. Do you favor or oppose school-based education programs that provide contraceptives to teenagers? Support your answer.

4. Who is the baby's real mother—the surrogate mother who conceived and carried the baby or the wife of the man who fathers the baby? Is motherhood primarily a biological or psychological concept? Explain your answers.

5. Should women in their fifties and sixties have babies? Why or why not?

6. In your opinion, why do young women have more negative views of menopause than middle-aged women?

IF YOU WANT TO LEARN MORE

Chrisler, J. C. (Ed.). (2004). *From menarche to menopause: The female body in feminist therapy.* New York: Haworth.

Kissling, E. A. (2006). *Capitalizing on the curse: The business of menstruation.* Boulder, CO: Lynne Rienner.

Love, S. (1998). *Dr. Susan Love's hormone book: Making informed choices about menopause.* New York: Random House.

Markens, S. (2007). *Surrogate motherhood and the politics of reproduction.* Berkeley, CA: University of California Press.

Mauthner, N. S. (2002). *The darkest days of my life: Stories of postpartum depression.* Cambridge, MA: Harvard University Press.

North American Menopause Society. (2006). *Menopause guidebook: Helping women make informed healthcare decisions around menopause and beyond* (6th ed.). Cleveland, OH: Author.

Thacker, H. L. (2007). *Women's health: Your body, your hormones, your choices.* Cleveland, OH: Cleveland Clinic Press.

Turkington, C., & Alper, M. M. (2003). *Understanding fertility and infertility: The sourcebook for reproductive problems, treatments, and issues.* New York: Checkmark Books.

Ussher, J. M. (2005). *Managing the monstrous feminine: Regulating the reproductive body.* Hampshire, UK: Psychology Press.

Wingood, G. M., & DiClemente, R. J. (Eds.). (2002). *Handbook of women's sexual and reproductive health.* New York: Kluwer Academic/Plenum.

WEBSITES

Sexuality & Reproductive Health

About Go Ask Alice!
http://www.goaskalice.columbia.edu/

Contraception

About Go Ask Alice!
http://www.goaskalice.columbia.edu/
Planned Parenthood: Your Contraceptive Choices
http://www.plannedparenthood.org/pp2/portal/medicalinfo/birthcontrol/

Pregnancy and Childbirth

Reproductive Health
http://www.cdc.gov/reproductivehealth/index.htm

Childbirth
http://www.childbirth.org
Pregnancy & Child Health Resource Centers
http://www.mayoclinic.com/findinformation/healthylivingcenter/index.cfm

Infertility

Infertility Resources
http://www.ihr.com/infertility

Menopause

North American Menopause Society
http://www.menopause.org

CHAPTER

8 Relationships

Friendships
   Friendship in Adolescence
   Friendship in Adulthood
   Friendship in Later Life

Romantic Relationships
   Importance of Physical Attractiveness
   Perception of Sexual Interest
   Dating
   Recent Trends in Dating

Committed Relationships
   Marriage
   Cohabitation
   Lesbian Relationships

Single Women
   Divorced Women

Never-Married Women
Widowed Women
Women Who Have Lost a Same-Sex
   Partner

Motherhood
   Stereotypes of Mothers
   Single Mothers
   Lesbian Mothers
   Mothers with Disabilities
   The "Empty Nest" Period

Relationships in the Later Years
   Siblings
   Adult Children
   Grandchildren
   Parents

A middle-aged lesbian couple had been together for 15 years when their daughter was born. To celebrate the joyous occasion, they held a naming ceremony attended by their closest friends. The nonbiological mother held the baby and presented her with her full name consisting of her given name and each of her parents' surnames. Then each parent lit a candle and made a wish for their baby girl. Following this, they expressed their feelings for one another and for the new family they had created. (Muzio, 1996)

Last Sunday, Ashley and I went over to my mom's house and we made applesauce together. It was really fun because it was all three of us and I used to do that with my mom when I was a kid ... And we were just working together doing all the different parts of the applesauce and conversing. And it was just a real regular time. We were all acting like friends, but at the same time there was that bond there— that grandmom, mom, daughter thing. It was neat. (Denise, age 38, in Fingerman, 2001, p. 66)

These vignettes portray women's experiences with interpersonal relationships in different parts of the life cycle. In this chapter, we explore the nature of women's close relationships—including friendships, romantic relationships, marriage and other long-term relationships, unattached lifestyles, and motherhood. We end the chapter by examining women's relationships in the later years with their siblings, adult children, grandchildren, and parents.

Friendships

Close relationships are essential to good mental health and well-being. Friends, in particular, are a major source of support and self-esteem throughout our lives (Castañeda & Burns-Glover, 2008; Worell, 2006). Let's take a closer look at gender differences in friendships, starting in adolescence and moving through the adult lifespan.

Friendship in Adolescence

Starting in childhood and throughout life, our closest friends tend to be people of our own gender. Even though romantic attachments increase during adolescence, in general, most teenagers still choose members of their own gender as friends and as best friends (Ruble et al., 2006). Starting in early adolescence, girls report greater satisfaction with their same-gender friendships than do boys (Thomas & Daubman, 2001). They also report more positive friendship quality, trust, security, and closeness (Rose & Rudolph, 2006; Valkenburg & Peter, 2007).

Intimacy, the sharing of thoughts and feelings with someone else, is a key characteristic of adolescent friendships, especially those of girls (Reynolds & Repetti, 2006; Rubin et al., 2006). Girls show greater increases in intimacy from early to late adolescence, they report more self-disclosure and emotional support, and they spend more time with their friends than do boys (Collins & Steinberg, 2006; Rose & Rudolph, 2006).

Girls tend to have a few very close friends, and their friendships are characterized by self-disclosure and emotional support. Boys are more likely to have larger, less intimate friendship groups that focus on shared group activities, mostly sports and competitive games (de Guzman et al., 2004). In the words of one adolescent girl,

> *I've had a best friend for about five years now, and she pretty much knows everything about me. I'd probably turn to her for all of my problems because she's always helped me out and always gave me the right answers for everything.* (Commonwealth Fund, 1997, p. 19)

Studies of ethnically and socioeconomically diverse adolescents have found friendship patterns that differ somewhat from those commonly seen among White, middle-class adolescents (Brown et al., 1999). For example, Julia Duff (1996) found differences in how upper- and middle-class suburban White girls and poor and working-class urban girls of color describe their closest friendships with other girls. Whereas 95 percent of the White girls reported competition as an aspect of their friendships, only 38 percent of girls of color did so. Similarly, the White girls were five times as likely to report feeling "used" by a close friend and were nearly three times as likely to indicate that jealousy was an issue. Other research suggests that differences in adolescent girls' friendship patterns may be more strongly related to social class than to ethnicity. In one study (Gallagher & Busch-Rossnagal, 1991), for example, middle-class Black and White girls were more likely to disclose beliefs and attitudes to their friends than were Black and White girls of lower socioeconomic status.

Friendship in Adulthood

Both women and men highly value their friendships. These close relationships provide mutual support and encouragement as well as interpersonal intimacy. However, it seems clear that, as in adolescence, women's friendships are more intimate and supportive than men's (Rose, 2007). Furthermore, women and men achieve closeness with their friends somewhat differently. Women are described as operating "face to face," by sharing thoughts and feelings, whereas men develop closeness "side by side," by sharing activities with their friends (Sanchez-Hucles, 2003).

The greater emphasis on emotional expressiveness shown by women is reflected in several ways. Both adult and adolescent females disclose more to their friends and reveal more intimate information than males do (Castañeda & Burns-Glover, 2008; Rose, 2007). When helping a friend with a problem, women are also more likely than men to express greater empathic understanding of their friend's problem (George et al., 1998).

The emotional support shown in heterosexual female friendships is a particularly important quality of lesbian friendships as well, since lesbians are frequently subjected to antagonism in their social environment. The reinforcement and empathy that are part of close relationships in this "family of choice" can help lesbians cope with prejudice from the broader society (Clunis et al., 2005; Galupo, 2007; Green, 2004). Social support can also help them develop and maintain their lesbian identity (Stanley, 2002).

How can we account for gender differences in emotional intimacy and expressiveness in friendships? Consistent with our assumption that gender is socially constructed, experiences and attitudes shape orientations toward friendship. As we saw in Chapter 4, parents are more likely to encourage emotional expression in their daughters and discourage it in their sons, and females and males carry these messages into their peer relationships. Furthermore, because emotional expression is viewed as a female trait and many males think of gay men as having feminine traits, males might associate emotional closeness between males with homosexuality, a perceived connection that can be threatening and might steer men away from expressing emotions to their male friends (Castañeda & Burns-Glover, 2008).

Although most of the research on adult friendship has focused on same-sex friends, some recent studies have examined cross-sex friendships (Monsour, 2002). These friendships are similar in many ways to same-sex friendships but also offer some unique benefits. Female–male friends provide each other with insider perspectives and other-sex companionship and also sensitize each other to gender differences in communication style. Feminine men have more cross-sex friendships than masculine men, and masculine women have more cross-sex friendships than feminine women (Reeder, 2003).

Friendship in Later Life

Friends provide the emotional support and companionship that sustain women as they meet the challenges, changes, and losses of later life. Because so many married women eventually lose their spouses through death or divorce, most women grow old in the company of other women (Monsour, 2002). In later life, women are more engaged with friendships and social networks than are men and are more likely both to give and to receive emotional support (Arber, 2004; Canetto, 2003). Friendships among older women enhance physical and mental health and contribute to continued psychological growth (Gergen & Gergen, 2006; Moremen, 2008). Older women's close friends tend to be about the same age and socioeconomic status, have the same social and ethnic background, and live close to each other (Rawlins, 2004).

Social class influences the way in which friendships are made and maintained. Elderly middle-class women often make friends through membership in an association. The main basis of such friendships is shared interest of the group and its activities. Working-class and poor women are more likely to choose relatives as close friends and to provide concrete and practical assistance to each other (Moreman, 2008; Sanchez-Hucles, 2003).

Women's social involvement with their friends includes both home- and community-based activities. The most common social activity of older women and their close friends is getting together for conversation. Frequent topics of discussion include reminiscing about memorable events involving their spouses, children, and careers (Rawlins, 2004).

Women and their friends also help one another with transportation, shopping, and running errands (Adams, 1997). Those who perceive an equal give-and-take in their relationships with friends are more content and happy with the friendships (Roberto, 2001). Long-term friends contribute to a sense of continuity and connection

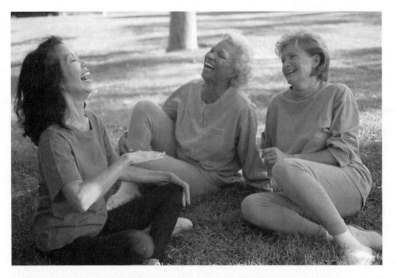

Friends provide emotional support and companionship for women as they grow older.

with the past. Over time, friends can come to be considered as family, further increasing one's sense of connectedness (Hall, 2007).

For some lesbians, friendships function as an extended family (Knickmeyer et al., 2002). Many midlife and older lesbians who came out during a period that was more hostile toward lesbianism than is true today were not accepted by their families. For them, and for other lesbians who have been rejected by their families of origin, friendships serve this familial role (Herek, 2006). And because most lesbians have not been married and have not created a traditional family, these social networks of friends can be an important source of support to midlife and older women (Grossman et al., 2000; Rose, 2007).

Romantic Relationships

The process of looking for a suitable partner preoccupies many of us during our teen and young adult years. In this section, we look at some features of this process. What qualities do women and men look for in a potential partner? How do they act in dating situations? How do they gauge their partner's interest in having sex?

Importance of Physical Attractiveness

What do females and males look for in a romantic partner or mate? People are often attracted to potential mates whom they perceive as loving, supportive, and secure in their relationships (Klohnen & Luo, 2003). Women prefer men who display self-assurance and stand up for themselves with other men, but who also exhibit warmth and agreeableness (Gangestad et al., 2004). Although both genders also value physical attractiveness, men put more emphasis on looks than women do, whereas women put a higher priority on status and resources (Brabeck & Brabeck, 2006; Eastwick & Finkel, 2008; Kenrick, 2006; Sheldon, 2007). Personal advertisements written by women and men are good illustrations of this gender difference. Consider this hypothetical ad: "Attractive, slender blonde seeking financially stable partner." Who comes to mind, a woman or a man? Studies show that heterosexual women's and men's ads complement one another. Women are more likely to offer physical attractiveness and ask for financial stability. On the other hand, men are more apt to ask for physical attractiveness, including specific facial and bodily features (e.g., blue eyes, long legs, thin) and offer financial security (e.g., Gonzalez & Meyers, 1993; Sears-Roberts Alterovitz & Mendelsohn, 2008; Willis & Carlson, 1993). The personal ads of gays and lesbians similarly show that gay men are more interested in the attractiveness of their partners than are lesbian women (Hatala & Prehodka, 1996). Lesbians also are less likely than heterosexual females to offer attractiveness as an attribute, perhaps because they are less likely to base their relationships on physical appearance (Kimmel, 2002; Smith & Stillman, 2002b).

This great value placed on physical appearance has unfortunate consequences for heterosexual women. Not only can it contribute to a distorted body image and eating disorders (see Chapters 4 and 13), but it also denigrates women by placing more importance on superficial characteristics than on behaviors and accomplishments. Best-selling books such as *How Not to Look Old* (Krupp, 2008) play on women's fears of losing not only their sexual allure, but their edge in the workforce as well.

Because of the double standard of aging (see Chapter 2), midlife women are more dissatisfied with their appearance than midlife men (Donaghue & Smith, 2008). Consequently, they are more likely than men to use age concealment techniques, such as liposuction, face lifts, tummy tucks, and injectable wrinkle fillers such as Botox (Cognard-Black, 2007; Singer, 2006). In addition, the demand for cosmetic genital surgery is increasing in the United States and the United Kingdom, as more women seek to have "designer vaginas" (Liao & Creighton, 2007). Even young mothers are increasingly getting "mommy makeovers"—including a breast lift, tummy tuck, and liposuction—intended to reduce postpartum stretch marks and abdominal fat (Singer, 2007). Moreover, women feel pressured to seek out surgery at younger ages than a decade ago, often beginning with their eyelids in their mid- or late thirties, and moving through a series of cosmetic surgeries over the next few decades (Merkin, 2004). While the vast majority of cosmetic surgeries are performed on White women, ethnic minority women are increasingly seeking these procedures.

The emphasis on physical appearance has a particularly negative impact on women with disabilities. These women are less likely than nondisabled women to be perceived as attractive and desirable and may even evoke reactions of repulsion and rejection. Not surprisingly, the resulting poor self-image and fear of rejection can lead women with disabilities to avoid social and intimate relationships (Crawford & Ostrove, 2003; Olkin, 2008).

The results reported in this section were based on U.S. samples. What do females and males in other cultures look for in a romantic partner or prospective mate? See Explore Other Cultures 8.1.

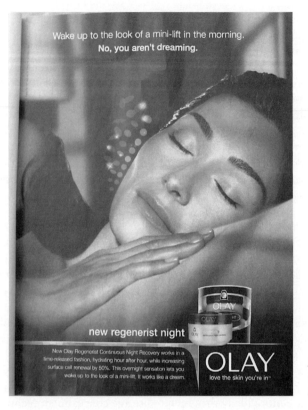

Midlife women are more likely than midlife men to use age-concealment techniques.

EXPLORE OTHER CULTURES 8.1
What Do People in Other Cultures Look for in a Mate?

David Buss (1994) and his colleagues have studied the characteristics that adults in 37 cultures prefer in potential mates. In all cultures, men valued physical attractiveness more highly than did women. They also preferred younger mates and mates with housekeeping and cooking skills. Women in 36 of 37 cultures, however, valued "good earning capacity" more than men did and they preferred older mates. Still, there was a great degree of consistency in the preferences of women and men. Both ranked "kind and understanding" as most important, followed by "intelligent," "exciting personality," and "healthy." Despite these overall similarities, cultural differences occurred on almost all items. The largest cultural difference was found for chastity, which was considered to be unimportant by northern Europeans, but very important in China, India, and Iran. What might account for these cultural differences? Alice Eagly and her colleagues (Eastwick, Eagly et al., 2004) reexamined the 37 cultures as well as a subset of 9 of these cultures. They found that women's preference for older mates with resources and men's preference for younger women with domestic skills and intact virginity were most pronounced in societies in which women's status was low. These differences decreased as societies became more egalitarian. In other words, gender differences in the characteristics that people prefer in mates reflect the extent to which women and men occupy different roles in a given society.

Perception of Sexual Interest

How do young adults determine sexual interest of their partner? In heterosexual relationships, both males and females interpret certain nonsexual behaviors as cues that one's partner is interested in sex. For example, some young adults believe that asking someone out on a date indicates the requester is interested in having sex (Mongeau et al., 1998). Also, some assume that how much a partner spends on a date influences how far things go sexually (Ross & Davis, 1996).

In general, men are more likely than women to perceive sexual interest in nonsexual behaviors (Lindgren et al., 2007). For example, college men are more likely than college women to misperceive flirting (Henningsen, 2004), friendliness (Farris et al., 2008), or even a brief conversation (Henningsen et al., 2006; Levesque et al., 2006) as indicating sexual interest. Explanations of these gender differences range from differential socialization to greater readiness toward sexual arousal in men (Levesque et al., 2006). Whatever the cause, can you identify problems stemming from the cues men use to perceive sexual interest? Unfortunately, the sexual meaning men give to many nonsexual behaviors can lead to a misunderstanding of women's desires and to possible sexual aggression.

Almost all of the research on dating has focused on able-bodied women and men. Persons with disabilities face other issues in dating relationships. To examine some of these issues for women with disabilities, see Learn about the Research 8.1.

Dating

Onset of Dating.   Mixed-gender peer groups start to form during early adolescence. These groups are central to the emergence of dating and romantic relationships that begin to blossom at this time (Rubin et al., 2006). Dating serves a variety of purposes apart from its obvious role as a courting ritual that can lead to serious commitment and marriage. Dating can help one learn how to establish intimacy with other individuals. It can develop new interests in sports or hobbies, serve as an opportunity for sexual experimentation, enhance a teenager's social status and popularity, and help forge a sense of identity (Gallagher, 2001; Sanchez-Hucles, 2003).

Since the beginning of the century, the age when U.S. adolescents start dating has decreased. Many girls now begin to date at age 12 or 13, and many boys at 13 or 14. Some children start as early as age 10 (Jarrell, 2000). About one-quarter of 12-year-olds have been involved in a romantic relationship, compared to 70 percent of 18-year-olds (Rubin et al., 2006).

You will recall from Chapter 6 that the age when sexual activity begins depends on a number of factors. Many of these same factors are related to the age at onset of dating. For example, Black teenagers begin both dating and sexual activity earlier than White and Latina/o adolescents. Other factors related to early dating include early age at puberty, being poor, and not having a strong religious identity (Bingham et al., 1990; Compian & Hayward, 2003; Miller & Moore, 1990). Girls from divorced or stepparent families initiate dating and sexual activity earlier than girls whose parents are married.

Young people usually bring to their early dating encounters a set of beliefs regarding how they should behave in order to appeal to the other gender and maintain

LEARN ABOUT THE RESEARCH 8.1
Dating Issues for Women with Physical Disabilities

Because previous research had shown that women with physical disabilities are considered asexual and not acceptable as romantic partners, Diana Rintala and her colleagues examined dating issues experienced by women with and without disabilities. Their national sample included 475 women with disabilities (average age, 41.5) and 425 able-bodied women (average age, 38). These women responded to mailed questionnaires.

There were some differences in the dating histories of these groups of women. Women who were disabled before their first date began dating approximately two and one-half years later than nondisabled women. However, there was no difference in the percentage of women with or without disabilities who had ever had sex with a man, although somewhat fewer women with disabilities reported having had sex with a woman.

The findings indicated several differences between these two groups of women in issues related to dating. Compared to nondisabled women, the women with disabilities were less satisfied about their dating frequency and perceived more problems trying to attract dating partners. They were also more concerned about both physical obstacles in the environment and societal barriers to dating, including people's assumptions that women with disabilities are uninterested in or unable to have sexual intimacy. Last, women with disabilities experienced more personal barriers to dating, such as pressure from family members not to date and low frequency of getting out of the house to socialize.

Based on these findings, the authors suggest several interventions that might improve the dating experiences of women with disabilities. Some of these are (1) removal of physical barriers in public places, (2) educating the public about disability and sexuality, and (3) educating families about the appropriateness of dating for women with disabilities.

What Does It Mean?

1. Rintala and her colleagues offered some general forms of intervention. What specific strategies could be used to educate the public about disability and sexuality and to change families' feelings about the appropriateness of dating? What solutions other than those presented here might improve the dating situation for women with disabilities?

2. This investigation focused on women only. Do you think men with disabilities experience similar problems? Explain your answer.

Source: Rintala et al. (1997).

---

the relationship. The advice passed along to girls by girlfriends, mothers, older siblings, and the media frequently includes such helpful hints as massaging the boy's ego, bringing up subjects that he enjoys talking about, admiring his accomplishments (but not mentioning yours), and being understanding, but not too assertive or confrontational. A boy, on the other hand, learns to "take care" of a girl he dates by making the arrangements, being chivalrous (opening the door, helping her put her coat on), paying for the date, and taking her home (Boynton, 2003; Maccoby, 1998; Rose, 2000). Notice how traditionally gender-typed these dating expectations are.

Dating Scripts.   Suzanna Rose and Irene Hanson Frieze (1993) explored this subject in greater detail by studying the expected **dating scripts** and actual dating behavior of college students on a first date. A dating script is a *culturally developed sequence of expected events that guides an individual's behavior while on a date.* (The task they used is described in Get Involved 8.1. Try it with some of your friends.) Students' expected dating behaviors and their actual behaviors were very similar. Some aspects of the dating script were the same for females and males. These included worrying about one's appearance, talking, going to a show, eating, and kissing goodnight. Many of the elements of the date, however, were strongly gender-stereotypical. Males were the initiators. They asked for and planned the date, drove the car and opened doors, and started sexual interaction. Females, on the other hand, reacted to what men did: being picked up, having doors opened, and responding to sexual overtures. They also focused more on the private domain, such as concern about appearance and enjoying the date (Rose & Frieze, 1993). More recent research has confirmed that these dating scripts continue to operate in the twenty-first century (Lane & Pool, 2005; Serewicz & Gale, 2008). Dating scripts of lesbians and gay males are similar in many respects to those of heterosexuals, but they are not as strongly gender-typed (Rose & Zand, 2002).

GET INVOLVED 8.1

Dating Scripts of Women and Men

Complete the following task from the study by Rose and Frieze (1993, p. 502). Then ask two unmarried female and two unmarried male undergraduates to do the same.

From the perspective of your own gender, list the actions which a woman (use the word

"man" for male participants) would typically do as she (he) prepared for a first date with someone new, then met her (his) date, spent time during the date, and ended the date. Include at least 20 actions or events which would occur in a routine first date, putting them in the order in which they would occur.

What Does It Mean?

1. What elements of a dating script were shared by your female and male respondents?
2. In what ways were the dating scripts gender-stereotypical?
3. How do your results compare to those of Rose and Frieze (1993) described in the text?
4. Based on your knowledge of gender stereotypes, gender-related attitudes, and

   socialization experiences, what might account for the differences in the dating scripts of females and males?
5. Do you think that the degree of traditional gender-stereotypical behavior in dating scripts would be the same on a fifth date as on a first date? Explain your answer.

Dating scripts reflect not only the stereotype of the communal female and the agentic male but also suggest that heterosexual romantic relationships are characterized by a continuing power imbalance between women and men (Laner & Ventrone, 1998). Does research evidence support this assumption of greater male power? Studies of late adolescents and young adults report wide variations in respondents' perceptions of the distribution of power in their heterosexual relationships. Judgments of equality were found in 29 to 79 percent of samples (Galliher et al., 1999; Sprecher & Felmlee, 1997) with variations reflecting the gender of the perceiver, differences among the samples in different studies, and types of power examined. Thus, some dating couples view their relationships as egalitarian, at least in terms of certain types of power, whereas others perceive a power imbalance. When there is inequality, who is seen as having more control? Consistent with males' greater power in society, couples are more likely to view males than females as the powerful partner (Sprecher & Felmlee, 1997). The status and value attached to males in North America might provide men with interpersonal resources to control outcomes in their romantic relationships with women. Moreover, men are more likely than women to view the male as the more powerful partner, possibly reflecting men's greater endorsement of a masculine power ideology (Sprecher & Felmlee, 1997).

Recent Trends in Dating

As more individuals remain single for longer periods of time, or become single as a result of divorce, elaborate partnering "markets" to help people in their quest for companionship and sex have developed in major cities, according to research by Edward Laumann and his colleagues (2004). His research team interviewed over 2,000 adults in four Chicago neighborhoods, including those with largely Black, Hispanic, or gay populations. They found that the partnering markets operate differently for women and men. Women, for example, were less likely than men to meet a partner through institutions such as work or church as they got older, making it harder to find someone. One reason for this is that men in their forties often sought women who were at least five to eight years younger. Neighborhoods and cultures also influenced the ways in which people found partners. In Hispanic neighborhoods, for example, family, friends, and the church played a more important role in meeting partners than in other areas. Young, upper-income individuals on the city's north side were more apt to find partners at school or work. Gay men surveyed were more likely to look for short-term relationships, while lesbians usually sought long-term partners.

Another contemporary way to meet a potential partner is to visit online dating sites. A growing number of singles—over 45 million in 2002—now subscribe to these services (Harmon, 2003; Mahoney, 2003). As of 2004, more than 800 dating sites were available (Williams, 2004). Online dating is rapidly shedding its image as a last resort for losers or a meeting ground for casual sex, as word spreads of successful long-term relationships that began online. Not surprisingly, traditional "dating scripts" still apply, at least in the sense that men almost always send the first e-mail message and rarely respond when a woman does so (Harmon, 2003).

Not only are there more single Americans than ever before, but more of them are middle-aged or elderly. Many older singles are either dating or looking for someone to date, according to a recent survey by AARP (2003). Interestingly, one-third of the women (like most men) prefer to date younger individuals. Older singles have more realistic dating expectations than younger ones. Few of them expect or want dating to lead to marriage. Instead they are looking for someone to talk to and do things with. And, like their younger single counterparts, many older adults are looking for partners or companions online (Sidener, 2004).

On the other hand, some singles report that the increased pressure to date encouraged by the barrage of Web sites, matchmaking services, books on attracting a mate, and reality television shows (*The Bachlorette*, *Average Joe*) is leading to "dating fatigue" (Zernike, 2003a). More people are dropping out of dating services, spending less time compulsively looking for people to date, and becoming more comfortable with not being part of a couple.

Committed Relationships

Committed relationships can take several different forms. Among heterosexuals, the most common type of committed relationship by far is marriage. Cohabitation (i.e., living together) has increased in recent years, often as a prelude to marriage. Lesbians and gay men also form committed relationships, although they are unable to legally marry in most of the United States. In this section, we examine these forms of committed relationships.

Marriage

Although nearly all Americans hold marriage as a deal, powerful social and cultural forces have made marriage increasingly optional in the twenty-first century (Cherlin, 2005; Nock, 2005). Most women view marriage positively, although some variation occurs across ethnic groups. Latinas place a higher value on marriage than other groups (Kaufman & Goldscheider, 2007). Latina women's commitment to marriage might reflect the strong value placed on family in Latina/o culture (Tucker & Mitchell-Kernan, 1995). Black women show less interest in marriage than do women of other ethnic groups, perhaps because they see marriage as less important to their individual success (Kaufman & Goldscheider, 2007). How can these differences be explained?

Marriage Rates.   High marriage rates indicate the continuing value placed on marriage in our society. In 2005, 81 percent of White, 74 percent of Latina, 80 percent of Asian American, and 61 percent of Black women 18 years or older were married or had been married at some point, with percentages for men at 74, 63, 70, and 58, respectively (U.S. Census Bureau, 2007c). The median age at first marriage has been increasing. In 2003, it was 25.3 for women and 27.1 for men, an increase of approximately four years since 1970 (Fields, 2004). This increase in age of marriage is due in part to changes in economic conditions, leading both women and men to desire some degree of financial security before embarking on a long-term commitment. In addition, as more women pursue higher education and careers, they tend to marry later (Kaufman & Goldscheider, 2007). For women with a bachelor's degree, the average age at first marriage is over 27, and for those with a master's or professional degree, it is 30 (Coontz, 2006). Women with disabilities are less likely to marry and are more likely to marry later in life than men with disabilities or nondisabled women (Olkin, 2008). The vast majority of Americans marry individuals of their own race. However, during the past 25 years the number of interracial marriages has increased, comprising 3.8 percent of all married couples in 2003 (U.S. Census Bureau, 2006).

Nature of the Relationship.   Not surprisingly, emotional expressiveness is very important for marital satisfaction. Disclosure of personal information to one's spouse and a willingness to express positive feelings about him or her lead to happier marriages (Culp & Beach, 1998; Vangelisti & Daly, 1997). Wives also tend to be happier and more satisfied when their husbands are emotionally engaged and spend time with them (Wilcox & Nock, 2007).

Consistent with the social construction of females as emotionally expressive and concerned about the feelings of others, women are more involved than men in maintaining this important emotional communication (e.g., Steil, 2001). They are more likely to try to listen to their spouses and make them feel loved (Lynch, 1998). In addition, wives provide better support on days when their husbands experience greater stress than they do. By contrast, when wives experience more stress, their husbands display a mixture of support and negativity (Neff & Karney, 2005).

Based on these gender differences in social-emotional involvement, one might expect that women's marital outcomes would be less positive than men's. In fact, several studies do show that men experience greater marital satisfaction than women (e.g., Lasswell, 2002; Steil, 2001); however, other research shows no gender difference in marital satisfaction (e.g., Lucas et al., 2003). Further research is needed before firm conclusions can be drawn.

Whether or not men experience more satisfaction from their marriages than women do, it is clear that marriage provides women and men with many benefits. Both married women and men are happier than their unmarried counterparts, a relationship found around the globe (Diener et al., 2000; Joutsenniemi et al., 2006). Moreover, married individuals, especially those in good relationships are mentally and physically healthier and better able to deal with work-related stress (Holt-Lunstad et al., 2008; Kiecolt-Glaser & Newton, 2001; Lee & Gramotnev, 2007; Proulx et al., 2007; Saxbe et al., 2008). They show a lower incidence of risky and antisocial behavior and greater financial success and stability (Johnson et al., 2004). This "marriage benefit" is smaller for women than for men, however, and is possibly even nonexistent, according to some researchers (Felder, 2006). People in strained, unhappy relationships usually fare worse medically than happily married individuals. Furthermore, marital stress affects women's health and sense of well-being more than men's (Lerner, 2002; Proulx et al., 2007).

Why are people in good marriages happier and healthier than single individuals? One obvious answer is the care and support they receive from their spouse, although, as we have seen, women provide more care and support than they receive. Second, married couples often benefit financially because they have a combined household and, frequently, two incomes. Third, spouses tend to encourage health-promoting behaviors in one another (DiMatteo, 2004; He et al., 2005; Jin & Christakis, 2007). It is also possible, of course, that individuals with positive personality traits and healthier lifestyles are more likely to attract a mate in the first place (Johnson et al., 2004).

Marriage in Later Life. As life expectancy has increased, so has the incidence of long-term marriages. About one marriage in five now lasts at least 50 years (Birchler & Fals-Stewart, 1998). Since women typically marry older men and outlive them and since men are more likely to remarry following widowhood or divorce, many more men than women are married in later life. Among Americans aged 75 to 84, only one-third of women are married, compared with 70 percent of men. For people 85 and over, the percentages are much lower, especially for women: Only 13 percent of women and 56 percent of men are married (He et al., 2005).

Marriage appears to provide numerous benefits in later life, particularly for men. Married people, especially men, live longer. As noted above, they also have better mental and physical health and more economic resources than unmarried people (Kinsella & Velkoff, 2001). The majority of older people rate their marriages as happy or very happy, with men more satisfied than women. In one longitudinal study of couples married between 50 and 69 years (Field & Weishaus, 1992), many respondents reported increased satisfaction and feelings of closeness in old age. In part, marital satisfaction in later life probably reflects the selective survival of marriages that did not end in divorce (Huyck, 1995).

Cohabitation

Cohabitation, *the state in which an unmarried couple lives together,* has dramatically increased in the United States over the last several decades. An estimated 50 percent or more of couples in the United States Cohabitation is even more common in Europe (Popanoe, 2008) live together before marriage (Stanley et al., 2006).

For many couples, cohabitation serves as a trial marriage. In fact, the majority of first marriages and remarriages follow a period of cohabitation (Smock & Manning, 2004). Most high school seniors now view cohabitation as a desirable way for couples to determine before marriage whether they are compatible (Smock & Manning, 2004). At least half of U.S. teenagers expect to cohabit before marriage (Manning et al., 2007). For some couples, especially divorced or widowed persons, cohabitation is seen as an alternative to marriage and may involve having children (Popanoe, 2008; Raley & Wildsmith, 2004). Some cohabiting women mention finances, convenience, and housing needs as the main reasons for moving in with a partner (Sassler, 2004).

Despite its popularity, not all people are in favor of cohabitation. Not surprisingly, middle-aged and older adults are more opposed than are young adults (S. Roberts, 2007). Another major factor related to a willingness to cohabit is lower religiosity

(Rhoades et al., 2006; Smock & Manning, 2004), perhaps because cohabitation is counter to the teachings of many religions. Furthermore, women who hold more liberal sexual views and less traditional gender attitudes have more positive views of cohabitation (Huffman et al., 1994). Clearly, this lifestyle is inconsistent with traditional views about premarital chastity for women and is less likely than marriage to enable fulfillment of traditional gender roles.

How happy are cohabiting couples and how do they feel about their relationship? Cohabitors tend to be happier than single individuals who are not living with a partner, but not as happy as married couples (DeKlyen et al., 2006; Stack & Eshleman, 1998). In addition, cohabitors who do not expect to marry report less emotional commitment to their partner and feel less positive about their relationship than engaged or married cohabitors (Brown & Booth, 1996; Kline et al., 2004; Nock, 1995). Interestingly, there is some evidence that the differences between married and cohabiting couples' satisfaction and level of commitment are greater among Latinas/os than Blacks or Whites (Nock, 1995). Perhaps the strong value on family within Latina/o culture creates greater problems for Latina/o cohabiting couples.

Other comparisons show that married individuals who previously cohabited, compared to those who did not, have lower marital satisfaction, higher levels of domestic violence, and are more likely to get divorced (Rhoades et al., 2006; Stanley et al., 2006). This does not necessarily mean that cohabitation fosters marital instability. Possibly, these findings result from a **selection effect** whereby *the attitudes of individuals who cohabit are more accepting of divorce and less committed to marriage than the attitudes of noncohabitors* (Stanley et al., 2006).

Lesbian Relationships

Contrary to popular stereotypes, lesbians and gay men are as likely as heterosexuals to be part of a couple. Lesbian couples are more likely than gay men to be in a lasting, marriage-like relationship (Peplau & Fingerhut, 2007). For example, nearly two-thirds of the gay couples who have married in Massachusetts have been women (Bellafante, 2005).

In mid-twentieth century, some lesbians adopted rigid male (butch) and female (femme) gender-related behaviors and roles (Classen et al., 2005). These roles were criticized during the feminist movement of the 1960s, based on concerns about sexism inherent in traditional gender expectations (Peplau & Beals, 2001; Smith & Stillman, 2002a). The last 20 years has seen a reemergence of the butch and femme experience for some lesbian women (Levitt & Hiestand, 2004). Even so, lesbian relationships tend to be egalitarian, with household activities, decision-making tasks, and other relationship behaviors based more on individual skills and interests than on rigid gendered conceptions of appropriate behaviors. In fact, lesbian relationships are characterized by more equality of power and a more equal division of paid and unpaid labor than are either heterosexual or gay relationships (Clunis et al., 2005; Khor, 2007; Kurdek, 2005; Rothblum, 2007). Interestingly, bisexual women who have had relationships with partners of both genders report more conflicts over power in their heterosexual

Lesbian couples are more likely than gay men to be in a lasting, marriage-like relationship.

than in their same-gender relationships, in part because of dissatisfaction with the power balance in heterosexual relationships (Weinberg et al., 1994).

Most lesbians are involved in sexually exclusive relationships (Peplau & Beals, 2001). Although they may engage in less frequent sex than either heterosexuals or gays (Herek, 2006), they engage in considerable nongenital physical expression, such as hugging and cuddling, and are as satisfied with their sexual relationships as are heterosexual and gay couples (Littlefield et al., 2000; Patterson, 2000).

Although lesbians are generally satisfied with their relationships, lesbian couples experience a variety of unique stressors. First, the coming-out process can be problematic (Patterson, 2000). Conflicts can arise when one partner is more open about her sexual orientation than the other partner. Second, lesbians must cope with the frequent lack of societal acceptance of their relationship (Kurdek, 2005). Third, lesbian couples frequently face economic difficulties, in part because their income is based on the earnings of two women and women tend to earn less than men (see Chapter 10) and because many lesbian couples are denied domestic partner insurance benefits typically awarded to married individuals ("Gays Win," 2003). Finally, lesbian women are often denied custody of their children and may be prohibited from adopting their partner's child (Belluck & Liptak, 2004; Rothblum, 2007).

On a more positive note, lesbian couples report feeling less lonely than heterosexual married women (Grossman et al., 2001). Some writers suggest that lesbian couples are advantaged compared with heterosexual wives because they are more likely to have a partner with whom they expect to grow old, to share similar life expectancy, to be less threatened by changes in physical appearance, and to have accumulated their own financial resources through employment (Huyck, 1995).

Choosing to be in a relationship or to start a family can be especially problematic for disabled lesbians. They must deal with double stereotypes that do not see them as either possible partners or parents (O'Toole & Bregante, 1993).

Like heterosexual couples, same-sex partners form emotional attachments and commitments, and are usually satisfied with their relationships (Herek, 2006; Kurdek, 2005; Patterson, 2000; Peplau & Fingerhut, 2007; Roisman et al., 2008), and their satisfaction is based on similar factors. For example, both lesbians and heterosexuals feel better about their relationships when they and their partners share equal power and decision making, equal commitment to the relationship, and similar interests and backgrounds (Peplau & Beals, 2001). In addition, the quality of lesbians' relationships is dependent on their degree of openness about their sexual orientation. Lesbians who are open, especially to family and friends, tend to perceive their relationship more positively than those who are not in part because approval from one's family is highly related to relationship satisfaction (Caron & Ulin, 1997). Perhaps not surprisingly, lesbian couples who chose civil unions in Vermont when that option became available recently are more open about their sexual orientation than those not seeking that option (Balsam et al., 2008).

Aging lesbians must confront the triple obstacles of sexism, ageism, and homophobia (Jones, 2001). Older lesbians who faced prejudice and discrimination during more hostile times often hid their identities and their relationships with other women (Butler, 2004). Even now, because of social constraints, they may not openly acknowledge the nature of their relationship. Unfortunately, this secrecy has led to the near invisibility of the elder lesbian and gay population, and to reduced access to health services.

Elderly lesbians in long-term committed relationships typically provide each other with a mutual support system and the economic benefits of sharing resources and a home (Roberto, 2001). Having had to cope with the social stigma of homosexuality, many lesbians and gays may be better prepared than heterosexuals to cope with the stigma of aging (Kimmel, 2002).

Single Women

When people marry, they don't always live happily ever after. Some divorce, others lose their spouses or same-sex partners through death. A small percentage of women never marry at all. In this section, we examine women who are divorced, never married, widowed, or who have lost a same-sex partner.

Divorced Women

Most couples do not walk down the aisle with expectations of splitting up. Nevertheless, approximately 40 percent of all American marriages end in divorce, although divorce rates have decreased somewhat in recent years (Hurley, 2005). Although first marriages that end in divorce last about eight years, marriages can dissolve at any point in the life cycle (U.S. Census Bureau, 2007b). Marriages end for numerous reasons—including incompatibility, communication problems, infidelity, substance abuse, and physical violence.

While divorce occurs throughout the population, divorce rates differ depending on one's ethnic group, educational level, and age at marriage. Asian Americans have the lowest divorce rates in the United States and Native Americans have the highest. Black and Latina women are more likely to be separated than other women (Kreider & Simmons, 2003). College-educated individuals are less likely to divorce than those without college degrees (U.S. Census Bureau, 2006). In addition, the divorce rate falls as the age of marriage rises through the late 20s, then levels off (Shellenbarger, 2008).

Women with disabilities are more likely than nondisabled women or men with disabilities to be divorced (Olkin, 2008). Not surprisingly, both financial pressure and interpersonal problems can be contributing factors. If the spouse with a disability is unable to continue working, or if the nondisabled partner must quit work to care for her or his spouse, the couple might experience considerable financial strain. In addition, psychological reactions, such as anger or moodiness, on the part of either spouse or stress stemming from an overload of responsibilities for the able-bodied partner can damage the quality of the relationship. Consistent with the social construction of females as caregivers and the resultant socialization of girls to be responsive to the emotional needs within a relationship, wives are less likely than husbands to leave a spouse who has a disability (Etaugh, 2008).

Effects of Divorce on Women and Their Children.   Although divorced mothers view themselves as better parents than do mothers in high-conflict marriages, single parenting after a divorce can be highly stressful (Hetherington & Kelly, 2002). The breakup of a marriage produces numerous stressors for custodial parents and their children. Not only must both deal with strong emotional reactions, such as grief, anger, and guilt, but also their daily routines often involve major adjustment. Financial pressures can require the mother to begin or extend her employment, there can be major modifications in household responsibilities, and the family might have to change residence.

Given these and other stressors associated with parental divorce, children tend to experience a variety of emotional and behavioral problems in the immediate aftermath (Hetherington, 2004; Hetherington & Kelly, 2002; Wolchik et al., 2002), but most rebound within two years and are as psychologically healthy as children from two-parent homes. In fact, a meta-analysis comparing children from divorced and nondivorced families concluded that differences are very small and that children in conflict-ridden intact families experience lower levels of psychological well-being than do children in divorced families (Amato, 2005). Another recent meta-analysis found that children in joint-custody arrangements following divorce are as well-adjusted as children in two-parent families (Bauserman, 2002).

Divorced women also experience initial problems followed by satisfactory adjustment. Immediately following the breakup, it is common for divorced women to experience higher levels of depression and distress than married women. These negative reactions are greatest in the first few years after the divorce and decline over time (Lasswell, 2002), with few long-term effects on women's psychological adjustment (Etaugh, 2008; Lee & Gramotnev, 2007). Not surprisingly, other life conditions can affect a woman's adjustment to divorce. For example, studies suggest that Latinas experience more distress than White women, perhaps due to the triple burdens stemming from racism, sexism, and economic hardship (Parra et al., 1995). However, Black mothers show a greater sense of personal mastery following divorce than White mothers (McKelvey & McKenry, 2000), possibly because African American culture provides these women with greater coping skills to deal with the adversities of divorce.

Many women experience a dramatic decline in family income after divorce, which places them in a significantly worse financial situation than divorced men (Rice & Else-Quest, 2006). Divorced mothers are nearly twice as likely as divorced fathers to live in poverty. Fewer than two-thirds of divorced mothers with children under 21 are awarded child support, and less than half of these receive full child support on a regular basis (U.S. Census Bureau, 2003a). White mothers are more likely than other groups to receive child support and other assets (Steil, 2001). But regardless of ethnicity, divorced women with low income and low occupational status are at risk for distress and depression (Etaugh, 2008).

Despite the problems resulting from a breakup, divorce can represent a positive means of reacting to a neglectful, conflict-ridden, or abusive relationship, and women do not feel more upset after a divorce than they did in their high-conflict marriages. Although initially they experience depression and distress, women tend to be happier two years postdivorce than they were during the last year of their marriage. Further, divorced women are likely to be less depressed than women in unhappy marriages (Hetherington & Kelly, 2002).

In addition to relief from leaving a conflict-laden marriage, many women report a variety of positive psychological outcomes—greater feelings of independence and freedom, the ability to meet the challenges of living without a spouse; and to function as a single parent, which can produce a new sense of competence (Hetherington & Kelly, 2002). Moreover, they report greater life satisfaction than women who have never married (Etaugh, 2008).

Coping with Divorce.   What factors help women cope with the strains of divorce? Employment is one factor that can facilitate adjustment (Amato, 2000). It provides an identity outside of women's marital role, is an avenue for productivity and a source of positive distraction and social support for divorced women. A divorced teacher, commenting on how helpful it was to have the distraction of her job, stated, "Work filled my time and diverted my mind . . . I was very busy with my job. It kept my mind off things for a while" (Bisagni & Eckenrode, 1995, p. 581). And a clerical worker described the social support she received from her job: "My coworkers really do care. Like when I was going through the divorce, they really wanted to know if I was okay, without trying to pry . . . If I wasn't working here, if I couldn't talk to my coworkers, I probably would've gone to professional help a lot longer" (Bisagni & Eckenrode, p. 580).

Social support from family and friends is also vitally important in helping divorced women cope (Pinquart, 2003). Women who have a social network of friends and relatives to help them deal with the ramifications of divorce are less depressed and show more positive adjustment in the years following the marital breakup (Jenkins, 2003; Krumrei et al., 2007). Having a stable, new partner is another source of support that can have beneficial effects in postdivorce adjustment (Rice & Else-Quest, 2006).

Never-Married Women

Although some women become single at least for a period of time as a result of the end of a marriage, others never marry. Approximately 4 percent of women and 4% for men in the United States age 75 and over have never married (He et al., 2005). Women with disabilities are more likely than nondisabled women or men with disabilities to remain single (Olkin, 2008).

While marriage is still viewed as the expected lifestyle, today there is more freedom in, acceptance of, and support for single lifestyles than in the past. In a recent survey, 19 percent of Americans said a woman can lead a complete and happy life if she is single. The comparable figure for men was 67 percent (S. Roberts, 2007). Still, single women continue to be portrayed negatively in the media and are widely perceived as odd, social outcasts who lead barren, disappointing lives (Byrne & Carr, 2005; DePaulo & Morris, 2006; Reynolds et al., 2007). How do never-married heterosexual women feel about being single today? Evidence shows that many are ambivalent about their marital status. On the one hand, they miss the benefits of steady companionship and feel sad about growing old alone, but at the same time, they enjoy their freedom, independence, and opportunities for personal growth (AARP, 2003; DePaulo, 2006; Sharp & Ganong, 2007; Trimberger, 2005). Increasing numbers of single women are signing up for housewarming and birthday registries, having decided not to wait for marriage to request the china, crystal, and appliances they wish to own (Zernike, 2003a). Others are not only purchasing a home instead of renting but also buying a second, vacation home (Cohen, 2003). A new Website, SingleEdition.com, celebrates singlehood and offers shopping, financial, and other advice to singles (Newman, 2007).

The absence of a marital partner does not mean that single women are lacking social relationships. As we have seen, some date (AARP, 2003) or are in committed romantic relationships and many have strong ties to their extended families, network of friends, and community (DePaolo et al., 2007; Pinquart, 2003; Zernike, 2003a). Moreover, an increasing number of middle-aged never-married women are choosing to become mothers via adoption or sperm donation (Etaugh, 2008). In the words of one woman: "It would be nice to be in a relationship, but I don't really need that. My life is fine the way it is. And my life is full of love" (Boston Women's Health Book Collective, 1998, p. 187).

One disadvantage of being a single woman in midlife is that single women are expected, more so than their married sisters, to provide caregiving for aging parents, even at the expense of their own careers. Moreover, the single woman is less apt to have a caregiver for herself when this is needed, and as a result she is more likely to be institutionalized (Gottlieb, 1989).

On the plus side, never-married women typically have developed skills in independent living and in building support systems that stand them in good stead as they get older (Newtson & Keith, 2001). Compared with married women, the never-married older woman is better educated, in better health, places a great deal of importance on her job, is less likely to be depressed and commit suicide, values her freedom and autonomy, and has close connections with both siblings and other interpersonal supports (Etaugh, 2008). The workplace is a significant source of friends for single women, and in retirement these women go on to form new friendships with neighbors or members of organizations to which they belong (Doress-Worters & Siegal, 1994). Single older women have also learned to cope in their earlier years with the "stigma" of not being married and so are better able to deal with the effects of ageism in their later years. Most older, single women are satisfied with their lives and seem at least as happy as married women (Newtson & Keith, 2001; Paradise, 1993).

Widowed Women

Despite the increasing divorce rate, most marriages are terminated not by divorce, but by the death of a spouse. In most countries of the world, women are much more likely to become widowed than men, since women not only have a longer life expectancy but also tend to marry men older than themselves (Kinsella & Velkoff, 2001). In the United States, women 65 years and older are three times as likely as men of the same age to be widowed: 44 percent versus 4 percent. Black women are more likely than other women to be widowed (He et al., 2005).

Remarriage rates are much higher for widowers than for widows in many countries of the world (Kinsella & Velkoff, 2001; Walter, 2003). In the United States, for example, by two years after the death of a spouse, 61 percent of men are in a new romantic relationship, and 25 percent are remarried. The figures for women, on the other hand, are only 19 percent and 5 percent, respectively (Wortman et al., 2004). Consequently, older women are twice as likely as older men to live alone (He et al., 2005).

One obvious reason for the much lower remarriage rate of women is that unmarried older women greatly outnumber unmarried older men. In 2002, for instance, unmarried women aged 65 and over in the United States outnumbered unmarried men in that age category by more than 2 to 1 (He et al., 2005). Furthermore, since men tend to marry women younger than themselves, the pool of potential mates expands for an older man but shrinks for an older woman. In addition, widowed women are much less likely than widowed men to be interested in forming a new relationship. Widows point out that they value their independence and enjoy their freedom. Moreover, they are not eager to resume the domestic responsibilities of a long-term relationship. Many do not relish the idea of becoming a caregiver for an older man, having, in some cases, already experienced the stresses of caring for a terminally ill partner (Beers & Jones, 2004; Wortman et al., 2004). Widowers, on the other hand, typically want someone to organize their households and social lives and provide companionship (Olson, 2006).

> *Four months after her husband of 42 years died, Verna hit an emotional low. "I told myself I have two choices. I can sit home, mourn, complain and cry, or make a new life in which I would learn to smile and be happy again in my own activities such as volunteering and starting a social life with new friends who aren't couples.* (Arney, 2001)

Reaction and Adjustment to Widowhood.   Widowhood is one of the most stressful of all life events. The surviving spouse must not only cope with the loss of one's life partner but also adjust to a new status as a widowed person (Whitbourne & Skultety, 2006). During the first year after their husband's death, widows show poorer mental and physical health than longer term widows (Manzoli et al., 2007; Wilcox et al., 2003). Most elderly widowed individuals adjust to their spouse's death within two to four years, although feelings of loneliness, yearning, missing their partner, and lowered life satisfaction remain for extended periods of time (Lucas et al., 2003). As many as 10 to 20 percent of widows, however, experience long-term problems, including clinical depression, abuse of alcohol and prescription drugs, and increased susceptibility to physical illness. Among these are women with a prior history of depression, those whose marriages were less satisfactory, those whose husbands' deaths followed the deaths of other close relatives and friends, and those who depended on their husbands for most social contacts (Etaugh, 2008).

Other factors—age, the degree of forewarning of the spouse's death, and financial, social, and personal resources—also affect a woman's reaction to widowhood (Bradsher, 2001; Michael et al., 2003). Studies comparing the mental and physical health of older widows and older married women generally have not found any differences between these groups (Etaugh, 2008). Younger widows, on the other hand, initially experience greater difficulties in coping with their situation (Michael et al., 2003). One reason for the greater distress experienced by young widows may be the greater likelihood that the husband's death was unexpected. Although younger individuals experience greater distress following their partner's death, the length of recovery is greater for older people (Michael et al., 2003).

Widowhood often results in a substantial reduction in financial resources for women, not only because the husband's income ceases, but also because considerable expenses may be incurred during the husband's final illness (Carr & Ha, 2006; McGarry & Schoeni, 2003). Loneliness is another problem faced by widows. About 70 percent of elderly widows live alone (Fields & Casper, 2001). Having the social support of family, friends, and neighbors to stave off loneliness helps to alleviate the psychological and physical effects of loss-related stress (Guiaux et al., 2007; Laditka & Laditka, 2003; Pinquart, 2003; Zettel & Rook, 2004). Interestingly, research has found more loneliness among women who have lived with a spouse for many years than among women who live alone (Etaugh, 2008).

The death of a spouse takes a heavier toll on men than on women. Widowed men suffer more psychological depression, psychiatric disorders, physical illnesses, and have higher death rates and suicide rates than widowed women (Canetto, 2003; Christakis & Allison, 2006; Elwert & Christakis, 2008; Manzoli et al., 2007; Ray, 2004; Wisocki & Skowron, 2000). This may be due to the fact that women are more apt than men to admit a need for social support, to benefit from that support, and to have broad social networks with relatives and friends, including other widows (Antonucci et al., 2001; Carr & Ha, 2006; Ray, 2004).

The experiences of widowhood are vividly portrayed in a recent longitudinal study of over 4,300 older Australian widows by Susan Feldman and her colleagues (2000). The concerns of the widows were not restricted just to the experience of bereavement and loss but also involved the challenges of daily life, including financial and social matters. Recent widows worried about managing their personal finances and coping with financial hardship. Another common theme was the need to keep busy. Relationships to family, friends, neighbors, and social groups became especially important. Many women displayed an attitude of courage, strength, and resilience as they coped with the challenges of their new life. In the words of one woman, who had been widowed for four years,

> *I felt desolate and despairing [when he died] . . . I have managed to survive and lead a comfortable and quite interesting (albeit at times a rather lonely) life. I am pleased that I have adjusted, and I handle all of my affairs. I shall never get over the loss, but I have lived to see the day.* (Feldman et al., 2000, p. 164)

This realization that they have withstood an event that seemed insurmountable appears to enhance the self-esteem of widowed women (Carr, 2004a).

Keep in mind that our knowledge of widows has been obtained primarily from older women, most of whom had traditional marriages. When the young women of today become widows, they will be more likely than the current population of widows to have had a different set of life experiences, including a college education and a job or career that will better prepare them for a healthy adjustment to widowhood (Etaugh, 2008).

Women Who Have Lost a Same-Sex Partner

Lesbians and gay men may encounter unique problems when their partner dies. They may not be eligible for survivor benefits and in the absence of a will, they may have no claim to the partner's estate that they have helped to build (Carr & Ha, 2006; Whipple, 2005). Loss of a same-sex partner is especially stressful if the relationship was not publicly acknowledged, but even when the relationship is open, friends, family, and work colleagues may not comprehend the severity and nature of the loss (Walter, 2003; Whipple, 2005).

> *Recently, I vacationed with friends who had been friends also with my deceased partner-in-life. A guest arrived with slides of earlier vacations, including pictures of my lover. I objected that if I had been a man who had been recently widowed, they surely would have asked if I would object to showing the pictures. One friend responded she wanted very much to see them. She blanched when I suggested that she might feel differently after the death of her husband. Clearly, she thought that my relationship to Karen differed from her marriage; she evidently also thought my love differed from her friendship with Karen only by degree. Heterosexuals really do not understand what lesbians feel for their partners, even when they know us well. All of these friends had known Karen and me as lovers and had sent me bereavement condolences when Karen died.* (Doress-Worters & Siegal, 1994, p. 145)

Motherhood

One of the most intimate relationships a woman can experience is her relationship with her child. Consistent with the assumption that motherhood serves as a major source of fulfillment for women, many women view bearing and/or rearing their children as the most meaningful experience of their lives (Josselson, 1996). In the words of one mother, "For the first time I cared about somebody else more than myself, and I would do anything to nurture and protect her" (Boston Women's Health Book Collective, 1992, p. 488).

This does not mean, however, that parenting leads exclusively to positive emotions. Instead, mothers experience a swirl of opposing emotions. Motherhood can bring a great sense of love, connection, and joy accompanied by a tremendous burden of responsibility and guilt (Brabeck & Brabeck, 2006). As one woman said, "The first month was awful. I loved my baby but felt apprehensive about my ability to satisfy this totally dependent tiny creature. Every time she cried I could feel myself tense up and panic" (Boston Women's Health Book Collective, 1998, p. 511). Motherhood can produce an expansion of personal identity as well as the loss of self. Mothers can feel exhilarated by their new role yet resent or mourn the loss of other aspects of their lives that might now diminish, such as involvement in work or community activities, or even commitments to friendships, which necessarily change (Brabeck & Brabeck, 2006; Johnson & Rodgers, 2006). In addition, the transition to parenthood often has a negative impact on marital satisfaction (Lawrence et al., 2007; Twenge et al., 2003).

Stereotypes of Mothers

Despite the multidimensionality of women's actual experiences of motherhood, people tend to impose a "good mother" stereotype on them. The good mother stereotype is socially constructed as a warm, forgiving, generous, nurturing, person who easily is able to meet all her children's needs and who puts their needs before her own (Chrisler, 2008c; Douglas & Michaels, 2004; Rice & Else-Quest, 2006). Unfortunately, no mother is able to consistently meet either her own standards or the standards of others, and all suffer at least occasionally because of this idealized image (Chrisler, 2008). One mother complained, "I didn't know how to change a diaper any more than my husband did. In fact, I may have been more nervous about it, since I was 'supposed' to know how" (Boston Women's Health Book Collective, 1998, p. 511). Popular childrearing books do little to dispel this notion. One recent study examined the degree to which 23 current popular childrearing books portrayed the "new image" of the involved father (Fleming & Tobin, 2005). Only 4 percent of paragraphs mentioned fathers. In addition, the father's role was portrayed as predominantly ancillary to the mother's and was often depicted as voluntary and negotiable.

The good-mother image perpetuates feelings of inadequacy and guilt in women as they strive to achieve "perfect motherhood" (Warner, 2005). It also can lead people to blame mothers for their children's problems (Douglas & Michaels, 2004; Hall, 2008; Miller-Day, 2004; Rice & Else-Quest, 2006) because the social construction of the mother role, more than the father role, assumes an all-knowing, self-sacrificing, always-caring parent. This may explain why a man who harms or even kills his own children barely makes the local news, whereas when Andrea Yates drowned her five children (see Chapter 7), she received international attention (Barash, 2002). Moreover, mothers of murdered or missing children who do not act exactly as the public thinks they should lead to media speculation that they are murderers. The tears of

Patsy Ramsey, mother of murdered Jon Benet Ramsey, were labeled "an act," while Kate McCann was criticized for seeming too cool and composed about the disappearance of her young daughter in 2007 (Yabroff, 2007).

The good mother stereotype illustrates the **motherhood mandate,** *the societal belief that women should have children and that they should be physically available at all times to tend to their young children's needs* (Russo, 1979). This view of motherhood was very evident in North America before the women's movement in the 1960s and 1970s, but recent decades have seen a dramatic increase in the employment of women, including those with children (see Chapter 11). Does this mean that the motherhood mandate has waned? Many researchers believe it has come back in a different form. According to Betty Holcomb (1998), an editor of *Working Mother*, the 1990s witnessed "the birth of a new mystique about motherhood" (p. 48), evidenced by the media's glorification of middle-class mothers who leave the workplace to become full-time homemakers, combined with the contradictory denigration of women on welfare who stay home with their children. Susan Douglas and Meredith Michaels (2004) criticize the "new momism" in which the mother is expected to devote her entire being, all the time, to her children.

In addition to communal qualities, there are numerous demographic characteristics included in the societal image of the good mother (Johnston & Swanson, 2006; Rice & Else-Quest, 2006). She is expected to be middle-class, heterosexual, married, not too old, and to have a job that does not prevent her from spending "adequate" time with her children. The more a mother deviates from this image, the more devalued she is and the less likely her own mothering practices and experiences are seen as valid. Many mothers who are employed full-time struggle with tension between their worker identity and acceptance of intensive mothering expectations (Johnston & Swanson, 2007).

A recent content analysis of contemporary women's magazines by Deirdre Johnston and Debra Swanson (2003) found mixed messages that could undermine the confidence of both employed and stay-at-home mothers. Women were almost always portrayed as full-time homemakers, but these women were frequently shown as overwhelmed, confused, and interested only in superficial topics. When employed mothers were shown, their focus was on whether employment jeopardized family relationships.

Single Mothers

In the last several decades there has been a significant increase in the percentage of single-parent, mother-headed families. The proportion of infants born to unmarried women rose to 37 percent in 2005 (Martin et al., 2007). Whereas in 1970 approximately 12 percent of families were maintained by a mother only, this figure increased to 26 percent in 2003, including 47 percent of Black, 25 percent of Latina, 14 percent of White, and 13 percent of Asian families. By comparison, only 6 percent of households are maintained by a single father (Fields, 2004). Who are these single mothers? Approximately two-thirds are White, and most have one or two children. Furthermore, they tend to be very poor. Nearly half of all households below the poverty line are headed by single mothers (Bridges, 2003/2004). As Table 8.1 shows, about one-third of female-headed families with dependent children live in poverty, and this

TABLE 8.1   Poverty Status of Single-Parent Families in 2002

Ethnicity	Single-Mother Families % Below the Poverty Level	Single-Father Families % Below the Poverty Level
All ethnic groups	32	16
Black	40	26
Latina/o	40	22
White	26	11

Source: Fields (2004).

number is significantly greater among Black and Latina families than White families. Note that single-father families of all ethnicities are much less likely to be poor. *The increasing percentage of women living below the poverty line* is referred to as the **feminization of poverty** (Burn, 2005).

What are some of the problems experienced by single mothers? Given the high proportion of single mothers living in poverty and the lower earnings of women compared to men (see Chapter 10), it is not surprising that financial problems are a major source of stress. Also, because they are frequently juggling housekeeping, childrearing, and employment responsibilities, single mothers have to deal with problems involving time and the coordination of activities (Hertz & Ferguson, 1998).

How do women cope with the responsibilities of single motherhood? One important factor is social support. Studies of both White middle-class (Hertz & Ferguson, 1998) and Black Latina, and White low-income mothers (Olson & Ceballo, 1996; Shanok & Miller, 2007) found that support from family and friends is crucial. This support can be both emotional as well as instrumental, such as helping when there is an emergency, assisting with transportation to and from day care, and caring for a child while the mother is at work.

Suzanne Randolph (1995) discusses several strengths of Black families and communities that help Black single mothers cope more effectively. Because Blacks have a long history of maternal employment, single mothers have numerous role models for managing the stressors of coordinating these roles. **Extended families,** in which *at least one other adult family member resides in the same household as the mother and her children* and **augmented families,** in which *adult nonrelatives live with the mother and her children* are family structures in the Black community that can be helpful to single mothers. These families offer additional role models for the children and provide substitute caregivers when the mother is at work or is tending to other responsibilities outside of the home. Because extended families are frequently involved in childrearing in Latina/o and Native American as well as Black families (Coll et al., 1995), they can be helpful to single mothers in these communities as well.

Social support is one of the factors that is critical in promoting positive educational performance and behavior in children of single mothers. A recent study found that in the presence of favorable maternal characteristics, such as education and positive expectations of the child, along with social and economic resources supportive of parenting, children of single mothers did as well behaviorally and academically as children in two-parent homes (Ricciuti, 2004b). The findings were similar for Black, Latina, and White children. Unfortunately, many single mothers lack the social, economic, or parenting resources that promote good parenting.

Lesbian Mothers

Although North American society tends to think of families from a heterosexual perspective, a lesbian sexual orientation is not inconsistent with motherhood. In fact, it is estimated that up to 10 million children in the United States are raised by lesbian or gay parents (Pawelski et al., 2006). The majority of these children were born into previous heterosexual marriages; however, a growing number of lesbians choose to involve children in their lives after they have identified as lesbians. These women make use of artificial insemination, maternal surrogacy, adoption, or foster care (Henehan et al., 2007; Mitchell & Green, 2008; Pawelski et al., 2006; Peplau & Fingerhut, 2007).

Because custody battles involving lesbian mothers frequently focus on the psychological adjustment and parenting styles of lesbian mothers, numerous studies have examined lesbians in their motherhood role. These studies show that lesbian mothers are similar to heterosexual mothers in self-esteem and psychological adjustment (Golombok et al., 2003; Pawelski et al., 2006). This similarity between lesbian and heterosexual mothers is particularly noteworthy when we consider that lesbian mothers face stressors such as social disapproval not experienced by heterosexual parents. In addition, some lesbians face rejection by their families of origin when they decide to parent (Dominus, 2004; Gartrell et al., 2000; Johnson & O'Connor, 2002). Support can come from gay parents' groups that meet regularly to trade parenting tips and share information about gay-friendly schools and doctors (Dingfelder, 2005).

While lesbian women do not differ from heterosexual women in nurturance or commitment to their children, they do raise their daughters and sons in a less gender-stereotypic manner (Patterson, 2006; Sutfin et al., 2008). As models of gender-related behavior, they are less traditional than heterosexual mothers (Carrington, 2002). For example, partners are more likely to equally share financial and family responsibilities and be involved in feminist activities. Lesbian mothers also are less likely to purchase gender-stereotyped toys for their children and have less traditional gender-related expectations for their daughters.

Recent research on lesbian donor insemination families shows that the quality of children's relationship with the social mother is comparable to that with the biological mother (Vanfraussen et al., 2003). Moreover, unlike fathers in heterosexual families, the social mother is as involved in the child's activities as is the biological mother.

Just as the research on lesbian mothers finds few differences from heterosexual mothers, scores of studies show few differences between children raised by lesbian mothers and those raised by heterosexual mothers. Reviews of this research conclude that children from lesbian and heterosexual families are similar in psychological adjustment, self-esteem, moral adjustment, relationships with their peers, and cognitive functioning (Bos et al., 2006; Patterson, 2006; Rivers et al., 2008; Wainright & Patterson, 2006, 2008). Lesbian mothers raise their children in a less gender-stereotypic manner than heterosexual parents, and thus their children, especially daughters, are less likely to have stereotyped notions of masculine and feminine behavior. They also are more likely to aspire to occupations that cross traditional gender lines (Bos et al., 2006; Fulcher et al., 2003; Stacey & Biblarz, 2001). Also, adult children of lesbian parents, like those of heterosexual parents, have a gender identity and sex-typed behaviors and preferences consistent with their biological sex. They are not more likely than the adult children of heterosexual parents to have a lesbian, gay, or bisexual orientation (Dominus, 2004; Fulcher et al., 2008; Tasker, 2005; Wainright et al., 2004). See Learn about the Research 8.2 to examine the psychological and social outcomes of adults raised by lesbian mothers.

Mothers with Disabilities

The traditional view held by society is that women with disabilities are psychologically unable to cope with the demands of pregnancy, childbirth, and childrearing (Olkin, 2008). However, there is no evidence that disabled mothers are less capable parents than nondisabled women. In fact, studies have demonstrated the ingenuity of mothers with disabilities in developing their own adaptive methods of baby care and mothering (Olkin, 2008). Through the Looking Glass (TLG) is a non-profit organization that provides services and training to prospective and new parents with disabilities.

The "Empty Nest" Period

Since my boys left, I have started dedicating my time to worthy causes that I enjoy. I volunteer at the hospital, spend a few hours a week at a retirement home, and I joined a women's group. My husband and I also are planning a vacation. We haven't done that— just the two of us—in a long time. These changes are good for me. Sure I still miss the boys, but they're growing up now. It's part of life, so you make the best of it. (55-year-old woman)

Motherhood, as we have seen, is an important aspect of identity for most women. How do mothers experience the **empty nest period,** that is, *the period of a parent's life when children no longer live in the parent's home?* Considerable evidence indicates most women react quite positively and seek new opportunities for self-development (Whitbourne & Skultety, 2006). Some women pursue new careers, others further their education, and others provide service to their communities. And, because children can be a source of tension in any marriage, women often report higher marital satisfaction once their children have left home (Etaugh, 2008).

The empty nest period is not experienced the same way by all women. Some women, who are reluctant to let go of their parenting role, may perceive this period as stressful and as a time of loss (Whitbourne & Skultety, 2006). However, mothers who are employed during the childrearing years establish an identity in addition to their motherhood role, and this can ease the difficulty of relinquishing parenting responsibilities.

LEARN ABOUT THE RESEARCH 8.2
Adult Children of Lesbian Mothers

Most of the research on the effects of lesbian mothers on children has focused on school-age children. Fiona Tasker and Susan Golombok expanded on this research by examining the experiences of young adults who had been raised by lesbian mothers and comparing these to the experiences of their counterparts reared by heterosexual mothers. The researchers restricted the heterosexual sample to adults whose mothers had been single for some period while raising them in order to compare two groups of children whose mothers differed in sexual orientation, but not in the presence of a man in the household. Twenty-five children of lesbian mothers and 21 children of heterosexual mothers were interviewed.

The findings showed no difference in the psychological well-being of the two groups of adult children. Moreover, adults raised by lesbian mothers were no more likely than those in heterosexual families to have experienced same-gender sexual attraction. However, there was a difference in sexual experimentation. Of those who reported some same-gender interest, children raised by lesbian mothers were more likely than children in heterosexual families to have been involved in a same-gender sexual relationship. These relationships ranged from a single incident of kissing to cohabitation. All of the respondents in both groups had also experienced at least one heterosexual relationship. Having a lesbian mother may thus broaden the adolescent's view of acceptable sexual behavior possibilities. However, the finding that 23 of the 25 young adults raised by lesbian mothers identified themselves as heterosexuals suggests that consideration of same-gender sexual relationships does not lead to a lesbian or gay sexual identity.

In regard to childhood peer relationships, slightly more of the adults raised in lesbian rather than heterosexual families recalled having been teased about their sexuality. However, the percentage who reported this teasing was low; it included 11 percent of the children of lesbian mothers compared to 4 percent of the children raised by heterosexual mothers.

What Does It Mean?

1. The respondents from heterosexual families had been raised by mothers who had been single for some period of time during the respondent's childhood. Do you think differences between the two groups would have been more pronounced if the adult children of heterosexual mothers had come from homes with both a mother and father? Explain your answer.

2. Prepare an argument in support of or in opposition to lesbian motherhood. Refer to the findings of this study, other material from this chapter, theories of gender typing (see Chapter 3), and any other information that you believe is relevant.

3. Do you think that adults raised by lesbian mothers, versus those reared by heterosexual mothers, differ in the way they raise their own children? Explain your answer.

Source: Tasker and Golombok (1997).

There is no evidence that disabled women are less capable mothers than other women.

Of course, mothers do not stop being parents when their children move out, but rather remain involved in their children's lives in somewhat different ways. While their contacts are generally less frequent, they continue to offer advice and encouragement and sometimes provide goal-directed help, such as financial assistance (Etaugh & Bridges, 2008). Although most mothers experience the departure of their children at some point during midlife, there are variations in children's age of departure, and a significant number return home for some period of time after leaving, for financial or personal reasons. Nearly half of the middle-aged parents with children over the age of 18 have an adult child living with them (Jennings, 2007; Kreider, 2007). Parents' reaction to their children's return is related to the degree to which the return is characterized by a continued dependence on the parents. Parents experience greater parent–child strain the greater the children's financial dependency and the lower their educational attainment. Furthermore, parents' satisfaction with the living arrangement is positively related to their child's self-esteem, possibly because low self-esteem signals difficulty in assuming independent adult roles. These findings suggest that parents are most satisfied with the parent–child relationship and experience the highest degree of well-being when they perceive their children as assuming the normative roles of adulthood (Etaugh, 2008). To find out more about experiences during the empty nest period, try Get Involved 8.2.

GET INVOLVED 8.2

Women's Experiences during the "Empty Nest" Period

Interview two midlife women whose children have left home. Choose any women available to you, such as relatives, neighbors, classmates, and the like. However, if possible, select one woman whose last child left home within the year and another whose children have been gone for several years. Ask each to identify (1) any positive and/or negative experiences. Also, ask each to indicate (2) any changes in her employment role (e.g., started a new job, increased her work hours), community service, and/or leisure activities as a result of her children's departure, and to indicate (3) whether she perceives these changes as primarily positive or primarily negative.

What Does It Mean?

1. How would you characterize the experiences of your two interviewees? Did they mention more positive or negative experiences? How do their experiences compare to the postparental outcomes reported in the text?
2. What changes, if any, did they make in their life roles? How did they feel about these changes?
3. Were there any differences in the experiences of the woman whose children recently left home and the woman whose children left years earlier? If yes, how do you explain these differences?
4. Do you think the empty nest experiences of these midlife women will differ from the future experiences of today's young adults? Why or why not?

Relationships in the Later Years

As women get older, they experience several changes in their family relationships. Earlier in the chapter, we saw that marriages may end as a result of divorce or death. Bonds with siblings often become stronger as one gets older. In addition, new life enters the family in the form of grandchildren and great-grandchildren. Role reversal often occurs as aging women become caregivers for their even older parents. In this section, we will explore these changes.

Siblings

Sisters and brothers play a unique role in the lives of older people, drawing on the shared experiences of childhood and most of the lifespan (Noller, 2005). Feelings of closeness and compatibility among siblings increase throughout the course of adulthood and are generally strong in later life (Kim et al., 2006; Scharf et al., 2005). Sibling bonds vary across ethnic groups, with Blacks and Latinas/os relying more on siblings for assistance than do their White counterparts (Bedford, 1995). Relationships with sisters are emotionally closer than those with brothers, and the bond between sisters is particularly close (Carr & Ha, 2006; Kim et al., 2006; Spitze & Trent, 2006). The closer women and men over 65 are to their sisters, the fewer symptoms of depression they have. This is especially true for recently widowed women. For rural aged women, life satisfaction is higher if they simply have a sister living nearby, regardless of the amount of contact they have (Bedford, 1995).

The closeness of the sibling bond in later life is illustrated in the following comment:

> *I have two sisters who live upstairs. People are always surprised that we get along so well, living in the same house. My sisters never go out without coming by to ask me if they can get me anything. We weren't always like that. We were too busy with our own lives. Now we try hard to help each other.* (a 70-year-old widow, in Doress-Worters & Siegal, 1994, p. 134)

Adult Children

Women are typically described as the family "kinkeepers," maintaining the bonds between and within generations. They typically organize family communication and their children are more apt to confide in them than their fathers (Van Gaalen & Dykstra, 2006; Lefkowitz & Fingerman, 2003). Adult daughters maintain closer ties to their parents than do sons. During adolescence, the mother–daughter relationship is often characterized by both closeness and emotional conflict. Closeness typically increases once the daughter leaves home to attend college (Smetana et al., 2004). Adult daughters continue to have more harmonious relationships with their mothers than with their fathers (Bianchi, 2006; Van Gaalen & Dykstra, 2006). The positive link between grown daughters and their mothers can be enormously satisfying, as shown in recent surveys of older women and their middle-aged daughters (Fingerman, 2001; Miller-Day, 2004). Close mother–daughter ties are characterized by satisfying interactions, a history of little conflict, few control issues, and many opportunities for informal contact (Blieszner et al., 1996; Lefkowitz & Fingerman, 2003). In the words of four mothers;

> *She has been awfully good to me in every way, when I'm sick and when I'm well, when I'm in a good humor and when I'm in a bad humor.*

> *I can reason with [my daughter] and she understands me. We just sit down and talk it over. We never have an argument. Not that we're perfect, but it's just not necessary.*

> *We go for lunch. We go shopping . . . I may go three or four days or a week and not see her, but we talk. I feel like that starts my day.* (Blieszner et al., 1996, pp. 13–18)

> *She tells me about her work and sometimes her problems, which includes me in her world. It makes me happy.* (Fingerman, 2001, p. 60)

While some older women (and men) live with their adult children, this is the least preferred residential choice for elderly people (Bould & Longino, 2001). Elderly Americans strongly prefer living alone in their own home even when in declining health (Older Women's League, 2006). Most would rather have "intimacy at a distance" than live with relatives. Half of elderly parents do, however, live within 10 miles of an adult child (Usdansky, 2000). Elderly women who live alone report high levels of psychological well-being and appear to be doing as well as, or even better than, older women who live with a spouse (Michael et al., 2001). Informal and formal caregiving systems in the community contribute to this well-being by enabling older persons to remain at home longer. The elderly usually first seek care from the informal system of family, friends, and neighbors (Family Caregiver Alliance, 2003). When informal sources cannot meet their needs, older individuals turn to the services of organizations and professionals, such as Meals on Wheels, van service for the disabled, home aides, and visiting nurses (Older Women's League, 2006).

Nearly one in ten elderly men and two in ten elderly women reside with their adult children, siblings, or other relatives (Etaugh, 2008), usually because of increasing infirmity. Living with an adult child is more prevalent among ethnic minority elderly than among Whites in the United States, and this living arrangement is also common in developing countries (Bongaarts & Zimmer, 2002; Kinsella & Velkoff, 2001). (For a closer look see Explore Other Cultures 8.2.)

In the United States, older Asian Americans are most likely to live with their children. Blacks and Latinas/os are less likely to live with their children than Asian Americans, and Whites are least likely to do so (Federal Interagency Forum on Aging, 2004). As we saw earlier, older ethnic minority women play key roles in their family networks by providing economic, social, and emotional support to their adult children and grandchildren. Poor Black households are predominantly organized around women, with older women at the center. Males are more directly involved in Latina/o and Native American households and families. Still, women in these groups enjoy greater prestige, respect, and domestic authority as they grow older (Armstrong, 2001; Padgett, 1999).

Grandchildren

> *The greatest gift I ever received was my grandmother. My grandmother has been the backbone of my life since I was 18 months old, when I began living with her. My grandmother put her life on hold so that I could become the best I could be.* (Sharoia Taylor, age 16, in AARP, 2004, p. 11)

The stereotyped portrayal of a grandmother is often that of an elderly, white-haired woman providing treats for her young grandchildren. However, grandmothers do not fit into any one pattern. While more than 75 percent of Americans over age 65 are grandparents, some people become grandparents as early as their late twenties. About half of women experience this event by age 47, and some spend half of their lives as grandmothers (Etaugh, 2008; Sheehy, 2002). Nowadays, many middle-aged grandmothers are in the labor force and may also have responsibilities for caring for their elderly parents (Etaugh, 2008). Thus, they may have less time to devote to grandparenting activities. On the other hand, more grandmothers are taking on the responsibility of raising their grandchildren, as we will see later in the chapter. Grandmothers' involvement with their grandchildren depends on a number of factors,

EXPLORE OTHER CULTURES **8.2**

Living Arrangements for Elderly Women and Men

In the United States, nearly half of all women aged 75 and older live alone, in contrast to about one-fifth of men in the same age category. Looked at another way, close to 80 percent of all U.S. adults 75 and over who live by themselves are women (Fields, 2004; He et al., 2005). Figures for Canada and Great Britain are comparable to those for the United States, and a similar pattern is found in most other developed countries. In most Asian countries, however, the situation is quite different. About 75 percent of elderly women and men live with relatives, many of them in three-generation households (Ofstedal et al., 2003). Multigenerational families also remain common in rural parts of Eastern Europe, including Russia, Poland, and Romania. Even so, older women in these countries still are two to three times as likely as older men to live alone (Mercer et al., 2001).

In developing countries, relatively few older women and men live alone. In some of these countries, it is traditional for an older woman to live with her eldest son. This arrangement is commonly found in some African countries and in several Asian nations, including China, India, Pakistan, and Bangladesh (U.S. Census Bureau, International Database, 1995, 1997). You may recall from Chapter 4 that these Asian countries place a much higher value on sons than daughters, resulting in abortion of female fetuses and greater neglect of female children. Can you see the link between these practices and the sons' obligation to care for parents in their old age?

including geographical distance, the grandmother's relationship with her grandchild's parents, and the grandmother's physical and mental health (Roberto, 2001).

Earlier in the chapter, we noted that the ties between family generations are maintained largely by women. One example of this is that grandmothers tend to have warmer relationships with their grandchildren than do grandfathers. The maternal grandmother often has the most contact and the closest relationship with grandchildren (Walther-Lee & Stricker, 1998). Children living with a single mother tend to be especially close to their maternal grandmother (Bridges et al., 2007). In some parts of the world, in fact, the presence of a grandmother may spell the difference between life and death for her grandchildren (see Explore Other Cultures 8.3).

An old song proclaims, "Over the river and through the woods to grandmother's house we go." Nowadays this isn't always possible. As more parents separate and divorce, they may refuse to let grandparents see their grandchildren. An estranged parent may deny children access to their grandparents as a means of punishing the spouse. All 50 states once had laws allowing grandparents to petition courts to continue seeing their grandchildren if their child's marriage ended through divorce or death. Now, many states have made grandparent visitation laws invalid deciding that they go against the rights of the parent (AARP, 2005a).

Providing Care and Support for Grandchildren. During their grandchild's infancy and preschool years, nearly half of the grandmothers in the United States provide the children's parents with considerable emotional support, information, help with child

EXPLORE OTHER CULTURES **8.3**

Grandmothers: The Difference between Life and Death

According to anthropologist Kristen Hawkes and her colleagues (cited in Angier, 1999), post-menopausal women have helped ensure the survival and fitness of their grandchildren since prehistoric times. These women, no longer reproductively active themselves, are able to invest their energies in providing for the physical and psychological health of grandchildren and other young relatives. Hawkes and her colleagues studied the present-day Hadza hunter-gatherers of Northern Tanzania and found that older women gather more edible plant foods than any other members of the group. Nursing Hadza women, unable to provide for their older children while tending their infants, rely not on their mates but on these postmenopausal women relatives—their mothers, aunts, or elderly cousins—to make sure that the

older children are well fed. The presence or absence of a grandmother often makes the difference between life or death for grandchildren in other subsistence cultures as well. Recently, anthropologists Ruth Mace and Rebecca Sear (cited in Angier, 2002) found that in rural Gambia, the presence of a maternal grandmother doubled the survival rate of her toddler grandchildren. However, the presence of a paternal grandmother (the father's mother) made no difference in the children's survival. Even more surprisingly, the presence of the father didn't either! Similar results have been found in parts of rural India and Japan as well (Angier, 2002). Why do you think the role of the maternal grandmother is especially important?

care and household chores, and to a lesser degree, financial support (Black et al., 2002; Etaugh, 2008). For example, almost one-third of all preschoolers whose mothers work or are in school are looked after by their grandparents, usually a grandmother (U.S. Census Bureau, 2007a). Some baby-boomer grandmothers (such as Claire and her sister) are retiring or taking time off from their careers to become nannies for their grandchildren (Alexander, 2004; Lee, 2007). The grandmother's role in lending economic, social, and emotional support for her children and grandchildren is more active in many ethnic minority groups than among Whites. For example, Asian American grandparents are more likely than other groups to care for their grandchildren whose mothers are employed (K. Smith, 2002). Latina women are an important source of social support for their young adult daughters with children (Ginorio et al., 1995) and their advice is often sought in major family decisions (Facio, 2001). Both Native American and Black grandmothers are significant figures in the stability and continuity of the family (John et al., 2001; Johnson et al., 2003; Pittman, 2007). In one study of low-income multiracial Hawaiian children who had an absent or incapacitated parent, the nurturance and guidance of grandparents was a key factor in the children's well-being as they grew to adulthood (Werner, 2004; Werner & Smith, 2001). Similarly, a recent nationwide study in the United States found that close, supportive relationships with grandparents was linked with better mental health in adolescents and young adults raised in single-parent families (Ruiz & Silverstein, 2007).

For some children, grandparents are part of the family household. The number of grandparents living in homes with grandchildren has doubled since 1970 to 5.7 million

In some parts of the world, grandmothers spell the difference between life and death for their grandchildren.

in 2005 (Simmons & Dye, 2003; U.S. Census Bureau, 2007a), including 8 percent of Black, Native American, and Latina/o adults, 6.4 percent of Asian American adults, and 2.5 percent of White adults. Some of the increase results from an uncertain economy and the growing number of single mothers, which has sent young adults and their children back to the parental nest (Navarro, 2006). In other cases, elderly adults are moving in with their adult children's families when they can no longer live on their own. New immigrants with a tradition of multigenerational households have also swelled the number of such living arrangements (Navarro, 2006). The arrangement benefits all parties. Grandparents and their grandchildren are able to interact on a daily basis. The grandparents often assume some parenting responsibilities, which makes it possible for young single mothers to stay in school (Gordon et al., 2004; Navarro, 2006) In some cases, living with a single mother and a grandmother is associated with improved cognitive outcomes for the child (Dunifon & Kowaleski-Jones, 2007).

Raising Grandchildren. Increasing numbers of grandparents now find themselves raising their grandchildren on their own. Of the 5.7 million grandparents living in a household with a grandchild, over 40 percent *are raising their grandchildren without a parent present.* Nearly 80 percent of these **skip-generation parents** are grandmothers (Wang & Marcotte, 2007). Grandparents become full-time caregivers for their grandchildren for a number of reasons: parental illness, child abuse, substance abuse, psychological or financial problems, and military deployment (Goyer, 2005; Pittman, 2007). In some developing countries, parents migrate to urban areas to work, while grandparents remain behind and raise the grandchildren (Yardley, 2004). The AIDS epidemic has also increased the number of grandparents who are raising grandchildren in many nations, including the United States (Altman, 2006; Knodel et al., 2003; UNAIDS, 2004). Children reared by their grandparents fare well relative to children in families with one biological parent. They also show little difference in health and academic performance relative to children raised in traditional families (Thomas et al., 2000).

The belief that caregiving grandmothers are primarily poor ethnic women of color is a myth. Parenting grandmothers can be found across racial and socioeconomic lines (Harm, 2001). About half the grandparents raising grandchildren are White, 29 percent are Black, 17 percent are Latina/o, 3 percent are Asian American, and 2 percent are Native American. Black women who are raising their grandchildren, compared to White women, report feeling less burdened and more satisfied in their caregiving role, even though they are generally in poorer health, dealing with more difficult situations, and dealing with them more often alone (Pruchno, 1999).

Rearing a grandchild is full of both rewards and challenges (Waldrop, 2004). While parenting a grandchild is an emotionally fulfilling experience, there are psychological, health, and economic costs. A grandmother raising the young child of her drug-addicted adult daughter may concurrently feel ashamed of her daughter; anxious about her own future, health, and finances; angry at the loss of retirement leisure; and guilt about her own parenting skills (Harm, 2001; Williamson et al., 2001). Moreover, grandparents primarily responsible for rearing grandchildren are more likely than other grandparents to suffer from a variety of health problems, including depression, diabetes, high blood pressure, heart disease, and a decline in self-rated physical and emotional health. Furthermore, they tend to delay seeking help for their own medical problems (Gibbons & Jones, 2003; "Grandmother Caregivers," 2005; Lee et al., 2003; Oburu, 2005; Ruiz et al., 2003).

Grandparents raising grandchildren are often stymied by existing laws that give them no legal status unless they gain custody of the grandchild or become the child's foster parents. Each of these procedures involves considerable time, effort, and expense. Yet without custody or foster parent rights, grandparents may encounter difficulties in obtaining the child's medical records, enrolling the child in school, or becoming eligible for certain forms of financial assistance (Beltran, 2004; Haskell, 2003; Sumberg, 2007). For example, the welfare grant that a low-income grandmother collects on her grandchild's behalf is only a fraction of what she would receive if she were to become the child's foster parent (Bernstein, 2002). In most instances, grandchildren are ineligible for coverage under grandparents' medical insurance, even if they have custody (Ellin, 2004a). In some cases, states ignore the significant expenditures made by caretaker grandparents when calculating the grandparents' eligibility for Medicaid ("Grandparents Raising Grandchildren," 2002). Consequently, many grandparent caregivers face significant financial challenges (Wang & Marcotte, 2007).

Parents

While more women are becoming caregivers of their grandchildren, others are providing care for their aging parents, spouses, or other relatives. Nearly half of all caregivers of the elderly are daughters. Daughters-in-law and granddaughters play a substantial role as well (Katz et al., 2000; National Alliance for Caregiving, 2004).

The elderly caregiver may herself have some health problems (Carey, 2006; "Characteristics and Health," 2007; Older Women's League, 2006; Vitaliano et al., 2004) and is facing her own aging. The sight of her parent becoming more frail and dependent may conjure up a frightening and saddening vision of what is in store for her. Elderly daughters sometimes feel angry and guilty at the sacrifices involved in looking after a parent.

> *My grandmother lived to be almost one-hundred-and-two years old, and my mother cared for her until she was ninety-seven and had to go into a nursing home. Now my mother obviously feels it is her turn, which it is. I am the real problem here, for I have led a very active life and cannot seem to adjust to this demanding and devastating situation. I do not know what to hope for and am almost overcome with the inevitable guilt at my resentment and anger. I have no one to talk to.* (a 72-year-old woman, in Doress-Worters & Siegal, 1994, p. 208)

Ethnic minority groups provide more care for aging family members than Whites do, and they also feel more guilty about the amount of care given. Among Asian Americans, 42 percent help care for older relatives, compared to 34 percent of Latinos/as, 28 percent of Blacks, and 19 percent of Whites (AARP, 2001). One of Claire's Black students described how her family takes care of its sick or elderly members rather than putting them in nursing homes. Her widowed 76-year-old grandmother, for example, cared for her frail great-grandmother for many years until the older woman died at the age of 102.

We have been discussing older women's relationships with family and friends. To explore this topic on a more personal level, try Get Involved 8.3.

GET INVOLVED **8.3**
Interview with Older Women

Interview two women aged 65 or older. It is helpful, but not essential, if you know your respondents fairly well. You may interview your mother, grandmothers, great-aunts, great-grandmothers, and so on. Keep a record of your respondents' answers to the questions below. Compare and contrast the responses of the two women.

1. What is one of the nicest things to happen to you recently?
2. How would you describe your relationship with your children?
3. Do you have any sisters and brothers? How would you describe your relationship with them?
4. What do you like about being a grandparent? (if applicable)
5. What types of activities do (did) you enjoy with your grandchildren?
6. Tell me about your best friends and the kinds of things you enjoy doing together.
7. What do you like about your current living situation?
8. What do you dislike about it?

9. In general, what are your feelings on nursing homes?
10. How do you feel about the life you've led?

What Does It Mean?

1. How would you characterize the relationships of your interviewees with their adult children? Do they appear to be closer to their daughters than to their sons? If so, why?
2. What kinds of relationships do your interviewees have with their grandchildren? Have either or both participated in childcare activities with their grandchildren? How do their experiences compare to those reported in the text?

11. As an experienced woman, what tidbit of wisdom could you pass on to me?

3. Were there any differences in the relationships of these women with their sisters as compared to their brothers? If yes, how do you explain these differences?
4. How does the discussion in this chapter help you understand your respondents' attitudes toward their current living situation and toward nursing homes?

SUMMARY

Friendships

- Girls' friendships are more intimate than those of boys. Girls tend to have a few close friendships whereas boys have larger, less intimate friendship groups.
- Both college women and men like to talk to their friends about the other gender. However, women's conversations more than men's focus on interpersonal issues.
- Emotional closeness is important to the friendships of both heterosexual and lesbian women but is more central to women's than men's friendships.
- Gender socialization and heterosexual males' perceived connection between emotional closeness and homosexuality are two explanations for the gender difference.
- Friendships among older women enhance physical and mental health.

Romantic Relationships

- Heterosexual women are more likely than heterosexual men to value a romantic partner's financial stability and less likely to place importance on physical attractiveness. Similarly, lesbian women put less emphasis on physical attractiveness than gay men do.
- Heterosexual and gay men put more emphasis on the physical attractiveness of a potential partner than heterosexual and lesbian women.
- Middle-aged women are more likely than middle-aged men to use age-concealment techniques.
- Romantic relationships are commonly characterized by traditional gender-related behaviors and roles. When there is a power imbalance, the male is generally viewed as the more powerful partner.
- The age when adolescents start to date has decreased.
- Many dating behaviors are strongly gender-stereotypical.
- Men are more likely than women to perceive nonsexual behaviors, such as a female asking out a male, as indicative of sexual interest.
- Current dating trends include development of urban "partnering markets," online dating services, dating among older singles, and resisting pressures to date.

Committed Relationships

- Most women and men marry, but the age of marriage has gone up in recent years.
- Emotional expressiveness contributes to marital well-being, and wives are more involved than husbands in maintaining this emotional communication.
- Women and men who are married are happier and healthier than their unmarried counterparts.
- More men than women are married in later life. Couples often report increased marital satisfaction with age.
- Cohabitors who do not intend to marry tend to be less satisfied with their relationships than married individuals, in part because of the absence of legal commitment.
- Married couples who previously cohabited are more likely to get divorced. This might be accounted for by a selection effect.
- Most lesbians are in committed, egalitarian, sexually exclusive relationships. Although many experience stressors not encountered by heterosexuals, they are similar to their heterosexual counterparts in their relationship satisfaction.
- Older lesbians in committed relationships provide each other with a mutual support system and shared economic benefits.

Unattached Lifestyles

- About 40 percent of U.S. marriages end in divorce.
- Divorce is associated with stressors for both women and their children.
- Despite initial emotional problems, both women and children tend to effectively adjust.
- Divorced women are generally less depressed than those in unhappy marriages.
- Employment and social support help women cope during the postdivorce period.
- Single women report mixed feelings about being unattached. Some regret the absence of a steady partner, some are satisfied living alone, and some become involved in romantic relationships. Many are very involved in social networks of relatives, friends, and neighbors.

- Single women have skills in independent living and in building support systems.
- Women are more likely than men to be widowed but are much less likely to remarry.
- Reaction to widowhood depends on several factors including age, degree of forewarning of the spouse's death, and financial and social resources.
- Loss of a lesbian partner may be very stressful.

Motherhood

- Stereotypes of mothers, including the good mother stereotype, the matriarch, welfare mother, and superwoman images of Black mothers, can lead to blaming mothers and mothers' self-blame if something goes wrong or if the mothers deviate from the ideal stereotype.
- Two major challenges faced by single mothers are financial problems and numerous responsibilities. Social support, as well as extended and augmented families, can help single mothers cope.
- Lesbian and heterosexual mothers are similar in mothering style and adjustment. Children reared in lesbian and heterosexual families are similar in their psychological and social adjustment and their sexual orientation.
- Most women report positive feelings about the postparental period. Women who were employed during the childrearing years find it easier to relinquish the parental role.

Relationships in the Later Years

- Feelings of closeness among siblings increase during adulthood, and the sister-sister bond is especially strong.
- Older women generally have positive relationships with their adult daughters.
- Unmarried elderly adults, most of whom are women, prefer living alone. Living with an adult child is the least popular choice, especially among Whites.
- The closeness of the grandparent–grandchild relationship depends on many factors.
- Visitation rights for grandparents is a growing social issue.

- More grandparents than ever live in multigeneration households, particularly in ethnic minority groups.
- Increasing numbers of grandmothers are rearing their grandchildren.

- Growing numbers of elderly adults, especially women, are caregivers of their parents.

KEY TERMS

dating scripts
cohabitation
selection effect

motherhood mandate
feminization of poverty
extended families

augmented families
empty nest period
skip-generation parents

WHAT DO YOU THINK?

1. The text discusses several negative consequences of the strong emphasis placed by men on a romantic partner's appearance. Can you think of other negative ramifications of this strong value? What kind of societal changes might contribute to a de-emphasis on physical attractiveness in romantic attraction?

2. Letitia Peplau (1998) contends that research on lesbian and gay couples can help dispel biased stereotypes. What are some common stereotypes about lesbian couples? How can scientific research be made public and accessible so that these stereotypes can be altered? Do you think there should be an attempt to eradicate these stereotypes as well as other unfavorable attitudes? Explain your answer.

3. Do you agree with Holcomb's (1998) contention that there has been a resurgence of praise for women who give up their careers for full-time motherhood? If so, how can society reconcile the contradictory assumptions that full-time motherhood is desirable for middle-class mothers, but that poor mothers should combine employment with parenthood? How do you think people react to middle-class mothers who choose to continue their employment? How do they react to fathers who opt for full-time parenting? Explain each of your answers.

4. What are the advantages and disadvantages of grandparents rearing their grandchildren?

5. Are elderly widows better off living alone? With family members? In a retirement community? Why?

6. More single women are deliberately choosing to have and rear children on their own. Are they being selfish? Explain your answer.

IF YOU WANT TO KNOW MORE

Bigner, J. J. (Ed.). (2006). *An introduction to GLBT family studies*. Binghampton, NY: Haworth.

Clunis, D. M., Fredriksen-Goldsen, K. I., Freeman, P. A., & Mystrom, N. (2004). *Lives of lesbian elders: Looking back, looking forward*. Binghamton, NY: Harrington Park Press.

Coontz, S., Raley, G., & Parson, M. (Eds.). (2008). *American families: A multicultural reader* (2nd ed.). New York: Routledge.

DePaolo, B. (2006). *Singled out: How singles are stereotyped, stigmatized, and ignored, and still live happily ever after*. New York: St. Martin's Press.

Douglas, S., & Michaels, M. (2004). *The mommy myth: The idealization of motherhood and how it has undermined women*. New York: Free Press.

Florsheim, P. (2003). *Adolescent romantic relations and sexual behavior: Theory, research, and practical implications*. Mahwah, NJ: Erlbaum.

Ginsburg, G. D. (2000). *Widow to widow: Thoughtful, practical ideas for rebuilding your life*. New York: Perseus.

Laumann, E. O., et al. (2004). *The sexual organization of the city*. Chicago: University of Chicago Press.

Miller-Day, M. A. (2004). *Communication among grandmothers, mothers, and adult daughters: A qualitative study of maternal relationships*. Mahwah, NJ: Erlbaum.

Sidel, R. (2006). *Unsung heroines: Single mothers and the American dream*. Berkeley, CA: University of California Press.

Trimberger, E. K. (2005). *The new single woman*. Boston: Beacon.

Warner, J. (2005). *Perfect madness: Motherhood in the age of anxiety*. New York: Riverhead Books.

WEBSITES

Lesbian Mothers

Lesbian Mothers Support Society
http://www.lesbian.org/lesbian-moms/

Living Arrangements

Senior Living Alternatives
http://www.senioralternatives.com/

Caregiving

National Alliance for Caregiving
http://www.caregiving.org

Grandparents

http://www.aarp.org/grandparents

9 Education and Achievement

Women's Educational Values, Attainment, and Campus Experience
    Educational Values
    Educational Attainment
    Campus Climate

Women's Work-Related Goals
    Career Aspirations
    Career Counseling
    Work–Family Expectations
    Work–Family Outcomes
    Salary Expectations

Influences on Women's Achievement Level and Career Decisions
    Orientation to Achievement
    Personality Characteristics
    Sexual Orientation
    Social and Cultural Factors
    Job-Related Characteristics

Entering the Workplace

You might recall from the opening vignette in Chapter 1 that when Judith applied to graduate school in 1965 she was told that several psychology graduate programs had higher admission standards for female applicants than male applicants. The unofficial explanation for this discriminatory practice was the need to limit the number of female students because they were more likely than men to drop out of lengthy graduate programs for marriage and/or childrearing. This view that women would or should not pursue both family life and a career was evident, also, in the comment of a male graduate student who asked why Judith wanted a doctorate given that, at some point, she hoped to get married and have children. Similarly, when she did later get married, a female cousin suggested she now give up her Ph.D. aspirations and become a mother instead.

This perceived dichotomy between career and family might seem strange today. The cultural milieu has changed dramatically since the 1960s. Today the majority of college women want to have it all—both a career and a family (e.g., Davey, 1998; Hoffnung, 2004). On the other hand, some women today experience conflicts between their career goals and their commitment to relationships. As educational psychologist Sally Reis states:

Smart ambitious young women come to college with all these big plans, but then they fall in love, and all their priorities change. It happens during college, in terms of the workload they take. It happens as they graduate, and many put off graduate school to feed the relationship. Maybe they work to support their partners, or they follow them. Then once they have children, those original goals are pushed far off. (quoted in D'Arcy, 1998, p. F3)

In this chapter, we set the framework for understanding women's experiences in the workplace. First, we examine females' educational expectations, values, attainments, and college experiences. Next, we explore young women's career aspirations, issues related to career counseling, and their plans regarding coordination of their careers with family life. Then we turn to influences on their career choices and gender bias in the hiring process.

Women's Educational Values, Attainment, and Campus Experience

As we discuss in more detail in Chapter 10, men earn higher salaries than women (Institute for Women's Policy Research, 2007, April) and occupy higher positions in their jobs (Fassinger, 2001). Further, more men than women achieve prominence in domains such as politics, literature, and the professions. It has been suggested that these discrepancies indicate that women, compared to men, place a lower value on education and have a lower level of educational attainment. Does the evidence support these assumptions? In this section, we examine women's educational values, attainments, and experiences on the college campus.

Educational Values

To answer the question about values, Barbara Bank (1995) examined females' and males' reasons for seeking a bachelor's degree. Her results showed that female and male respondents placed a similar value on college education and reported similar explanations for desiring a degree. Both mentioned enjoyment, determination, and skill, as well as career plans, occupational prestige, and financial rewards. Furthermore, recent research has found no gender differences in the educational expectations of Asian American Black, Latino/a, Native American, and White adolescents and young adults (Mello, 2008; Simpkins et al., 2006). Thus, the evidence indicates that women and men have similar educational values and expectations. Now we turn to their actual educational experiences.

Educational Attainment

In the United States, 85 percent of females and 84 percent of males graduate from high school (U.S. Census Bureau, 2005). Until the mid-80s, men earned the majority of bachelor's degrees each year, but since 1985, women have surpassed men (U.S. Census Bureau, 2007c). Some critics view this situation as a "boy crisis" in education. For more on this issue, see Learn about the Research 9.1.

You can see in Table 9.1 that within each ethnic group, women obtain the majority of associate's, bachelor's, master's, and doctoral degrees. Asian American, Black, and Latina women also earn half or more of professional (e.g., medical, dental, law) degrees. Both doctoral and professional levels of education have experienced a dramatic change in the participation of women in the past few decades. For example, in 1965 women obtained only 12 percent of doctoral and 4 percent of professional degrees (U.S. Census Bureau, 2003b), compared to the 2006 figures of 49 percent and 50 percent, respectively. Today, women earn about three-fourths of degrees in veterinary medicine and two-thirds of degrees in pharmacy, formerly male-dominated fields. They also earn nearly half of the law and medical degrees ("The Nation: Students," 2007).

LEARN ABOUT THE RESEARCH 9.1

Is There a "Boy Crisis" in Education?

Girls, nowadays, are more likely than boys to do well in school, graduate high school, and get college degrees. Some critics suggest that as girls have progressed, boys have fallen behind (Basow, 2008). A few have even gone so far as to claim that there is a "boy crisis" or a "war against boys" in which resources have been lavished on female students at the expense of males (e.g. Sommers, 2000, Tyre, 2006). Some colleges are pushing hard to recruit more male students, even going so

far as giving men "special consideration." Jennifer Delahunty Britz, dean of admissions and financial aid at Kenyon College refers to this as "the dirty little secret of admissions." She and others note that some outstanding female applicants are being denied entrance to top colleges, while males with lesser credentials are admitted (Whitmire, 2007; Wilson, 2007a,b).

Two recent studies (AAUW, 2008b; Mead, 2006) cast serious doubt on the existence of a boy crisis in education. The studies used data from the National Assessment of Educational Progress, a federally funded survey of student achievement in the United States since 1971, as well as SAT and ACT college entrance exam scores, and other measures of educational achievement. Both studies find that, in the words of study-author Sara Mead, "the real story is not bad news about boys doing worse; it's good news about girls doing better" (Mead, 2006, p. 3). Boys actually are scoring higher on standardized tests and achieving more than ever before. But girls have improved their performance even more. The same is true of college enrollments, which are on the rise for both sexes. Once again, women's enrollment rates are increasing faster than men's.

Some groups of boys *are* falling behind, particularly African American and Latino boys and boys from low-income families. The gender gap is greatest among low-income students of all races but disappears among students whose families are at the top of the economic ladder (AAUW, 2008b; King 2006; Mead, 2006). In fact, a recent nation-wide study by the American Council of Education found that high-income men of all races are slightly *more* likely than high-income women to be in college (King, 2006). The results from all three studies suggest that social class is a better predictor of school success than is gender. Several writers note that the educational crisis among low-income, ethnic minority boys will not be solved by blaming the preponderance of female teachers at the lower grades, or a school climate that allegedly favors girls' learning styles. Smaller classes and better-trained teachers will help, as will teaching boys skills that will better prepare them for classroom success: learning to pay attention, listening, and cooperating with peers (Basow, 2008; Brown, 2006; Jacobson, 2006; Warner, 2006).

What Does It Mean?

1. Why do you think women's college-going rates have exceeded those of men in the past few years?
2. Sara Mead, author of one of the studies discussed above, states that "the idea that women might actually surpass men in some areas . . . seems hard for many people to swallow. Thus, boys are routinely characterized as falling behind even as they improve in absolute terms" (2006, p. 3). Do you agree or disagree with this statement? Support your answer.
3. What can be done to ensure that students of all genders and races have the education and opportunities they need to realize their potential?

TABLE 9.1   Degrees Conferred by Ethnicity and Gender, 2004–2005

Type of Degree	Ethnicity									
	Asian Americans		Blacks		Latinas/os		Native Americans		Whites	
	Women	Men	Women	Men	Women	Men	Women	Men	Women	Men
Associate's	59%	41%	69%	31%	62%	38%	67%	33%	60%	40%
Bachelor's	55	45	66	34	61	39	60	40	56	44
Master's	54	46	71	29	64	36	65	35	61	39
Doctorate	52	48	66	34	58	42	63	37	54	46
Professional	55	45	64	36	50	50	49	51	48	52

Source: "The Nation: Students" (2007, p. 16); U.S. Department of Education (2004).

This high level of educational attainment by women is, unfortunately, more true of able-bodied women than of women with disabilities. Women with disabilities also have less education than men with disabilities and are less likely to graduate from high school or attend college (Fuller-Thomson & Minkler, 2005; Olkin, 2006). Furthermore, they are less likely than males with disabilities to receive occupationally oriented vocational training that can provide them with the skills needed in the job market (Wagner, 1992).

So far, we have been discussing educational attainment of girls and women in the United States. In developing societies, many girls are unable to attend school at all, or attend for just a few years before they drop out (Epstein, 2007). For a closer look at this serious problem, see Explore Other Cultures 9.1 and 9.2.

EXPLORE OTHER CULTURES 9.1
Educating Girls Worldwide: Gender Gaps and Gains

What is the state of education for girls around the world? Studies of developing and developed nations (Haddock & Cincotta, 2006; United Nations Children's Fund, 2007) report both good news and bad news. The good news is that between 1985 and 2005, access to education improved worldwide, particularly for girls at the secondary (high school) level. More than half the countries studied now have no gender gap, including the United States, where 99 percent of girls and boys go to school.

The bad news is that dozens of countries still have serious gender gaps, with 75 million fewer girls than boys in school. Two out of every three children without even a primary school education are girls (Slaughter-Defoe et al., 2002). Gender disparities are greatest in South Asia, the Middle East, and sub-Saharan Africa, where, not surprisingly, male literacy rates far surpass those of females (United Nations Children's Fund, 2007). In most countries, girls from poor families are less likely to attend school than those from wealthier households (Rani & Lule, 2004). In Africa and Latin America, increasing numbers of unmarried girls are dropping out of school because of unplanned pregnancy. School policies often require the expulsion of pregnant girls. Another reason that girls leave school earlier than boys is to work the land. In Africa, girls and women do 80 percent of the agricultural work,

although they own just 1 percent of the farmland (Smith, 2005). Moreover, the AIDS epidemic in Africa is forcing many girls to leave school to support the family and care for the sick (see Chapter 12).

Educating girls has many benefits. The more years of education, the fewer, healthier, and better educated are their subsequent children. In addition, empowering women through literacy can enhance their voice in family affairs and reduce gender inequality in other areas (Ibrahim, 2004/2005; Larson & Wilson, 2004). How can girls' enrollment in school be increased? Strategies suggested by international organizations ("Gender Equality," 2003; United Nations Children's Fund, 2007) include

Build more schools, especially in rural areas of developing countries.
Lower the costs to families of educating their daughters.
Educate parents about the importance of educating daughters as well as sons.
Provide programs to prevent teenage pregnancy.
Encourage teen mothers to stay in school.
Attach day-care centers to schools to look after young children, allowing their older sisters to attend school.
Recruit more female teachers.

EXPLORE OTHER CULTURES **9.2**

The Oppressive Educational Climate under Taliban Rule

In 1996, the ultraconservative Islamic Taliban regime took over in Afghanistan. It promptly banned education for girls and women and fired the female teachers. This was a severe blow in a country where only 20 percent of women can read compared to a literacy rate of 50 percent for males (Fang, 2006). For the five years of Taliban rule, almost no females saw the inside of a classroom, although some courageous women secretly taught small groups of girls in their homes, and some girls were home-schooled by their parents (Dominus, 2002). With the end of Taliban rule, women and girls eagerly flocked back to the classroom, despite attempts by Islamic militants to damage or destroy some of their schools (Rohde, 2002). Hundreds of women's literacy classes formed in neighborhood houses as women gathered to learn to read and write (Gall, 2002). Yet even in the "new" Afghanistan, the educational picture still is far from rosy. In 2004, the Afghan Supreme Court banned married women from attending high school classes. Moreover, because a rise in banditry and rape has made roads unsafe even in daylight, many girls do not dare go to schools (Kristof, 2004a). This problem is particularly acute in rural areas, where only 31 percent of girls are enrolled in school, compared with 62 percent of boys (UNICEF, 2004). Taliban attacks on girls' schools have escalated and hundreds have been closed down (Moreau & Yousafzai, 2006; "Schoolgirls Under Fire," 2007).

Campus Climate

> *Julie Zeigler arrived at Duke University in 2003 to work on a doctorate in physics. Instead, she left in 2004 with only a master's because of a hostile atmosphere towards women that female graduate students and faculty say has existed for years. These women report that male physicists have kissed and grabbed them, ignored them, refused to take them seriously and greeted their comments and questions with hostility.* (Wilson, 2004a)

The gender biases in elementary and high school (Chapter 4) continue into college and graduate school. Female students often experience a **chilly climate** in the classroom and elsewhere on campus, in which *faculty members display different expectations for women students, or single them out or ignore them* (Allan & Madden, 2006; Betz, 2008; Sandler et al., 1996; Shepela & Levesque, 1998). Some faculty members use sexist language, tell sexist jokes, suggest that women are less able to learn the material, ignore women's comments, or focus on women's appearance and sexuality rather than their intellectual competence. Other biases include rarely covering material by female authors or theorists, seldom using examples containing women, and portraying women only in traditional roles (Myers & Dugan, 1996). Eventually, this chilly atmosphere can negatively affect women's feelings of self-worth and confidence. The impact may be even greater for ethnic minority women, lesbian and bisexual women, and women with disabilities. They may be the target of blatant sexist, racist, homophobic, and other prejudicial acts, such as placing signs on residence hall room doors that bar members of certain groups. Or they may experience more subtle humiliations, such as a professor's sexual or racial humor.

These Iranian girls gather around their teacher at a school near Tehran. They are among the fortunate, as nearly one-third of Iranian females are illiterate.

Female faculty members can also experience a chilly climate, especially when they become mothers. Many female professors report that they felt treated like valued colleagues until they had children. After that, they felt their colleagues' assessment of their competence and commitment began to decline. For example, when a male faculty member spends the day at home to do research, it's assumed he did just that. But the same action by a female faculty member may be construed as taking time off to be with the baby (Williams, 2002).

The chilly climate for women is another reflection of the gender inequality of power in North American society. Sexist treatment of women on campus, whether blatant or subtle, reflects a greater value attached to males and serves to maintain an already existing power imbalance. Furthermore, this treatment reinforces constructions of women as inferior or less valued than men.

Single-Sex Institutions.   Given the existence of an uncomfortable climate on some mixed-gender campuses, it is not surprising that several scholars (Creighton, 2007; Gross, 2004; Meece & Scantlebury, 2006; Watson et al., 2002) point out the benefits of single-sex high school and college environments for women's academic and personal development. Women's colleges provide more leadership opportunities for women students, higher achievement expectations for them, and more female role models within the faculty and administration (Reid & Zalk, 2001). Students at women's colleges participate more actively in class, collaborate more frequently with other students, both in and out of class, and report higher levels of support than women at co-educational schools (Kinzie et al., 2007). Other benefits of women's high schools and colleges are the greater likelihood of close student–faculty relations, increased self-confidence and self-esteem, and less sexism (Meece & Scantlebury, 2006; Salomone, 2007; Umbach et al., 2004).

Also, women's college graduates are more likely than graduates of mixed-gender institutions to pursue male-dominated fields, such as the physical sciences and mathematics, to reach high levels of achievement in their careers and, for both reasons, to earn higher salaries (Reid & Zalk, 2001; Wolf-Wendel et al., 2000).

The Academic Environment for Women of Color. Not surprisingly, the climate for female students of color on college campuses is more problematic than that for White women. Some women of color experience primarily White campuses as unwelcoming and unsupportive (Hackett et al., 1992), and Black students who drop out of college are more likely than Whites to attribute their college withdrawal to frustration and a lack of social and academic support (Allen, 1996). Moreover, some of the students examined in a study by Crawford and MacLeod (1990) reported instances of racist comments on the part of their professors. For example, one female student stated that a male "instructor makes sexual and racial 'jokes' and comments that I find offensive. There has {sic} been repeated allusions to the 'stupidity' of Native Americans and the inferiority of cultures other than his own" (Crawford & MacLeod, 1990, p. 119).

Claude Steele et al. (2002; Jaffe, 2004) suggests that "stereotype threat" (discussed in Chapter 5 in relation to women) can also seriously affect the college experience of students of color. He contends that Black students' awareness of the societal devaluation of Black people creates a pressure to defy negative stereotypes about ability. According to Steele, in addition to concern about their own academic performance, Black students must deal with the possibility that their poor performance will confirm the inferiority of their ethnic group in the eyes of others. In an attempt to feel less vulnerable, they may downplay the importance of achievement to their self-esteem.

Some educators believe that women's colleges provide a more effective educational environment for female students.

Another problem for some students of color is that they experience the individualism prominent in academic life as inconsistent with the collectivistic values of their culture. The individualistic value system of Western, primarily North American and European, cultures emphasizes personal achievement, independence, and individual uniqueness. The collectivistic values of Asian, Native American, and Latina/o cultures, on the other hand, stress the importance of the group, including the family, the community, and the work team. This competitive style of college education can be uncomfortable for these students. Native Americans, for example, have difficulties adjusting to the competitive climate (Canabal, 1995; LaFromboise et al., 1990). As one Native American senior stated, "When I was a child I was taught certain things, don't stand up to your elders, don't question authority, life is precious, the earth is precious, take it slowly, enjoy it. And then you go to college and you learn all these other things and it never fits" (Canabal, 1995, p. 456).

Although the clash between individualism and collectivism can produce conflicts for some students, Angela Lew and her colleagues (Lew et al., 1998) note that these value systems can coexist. These researchers examined the achievement values of Asian American students and found that some students adopted both sets of values; they saw individual achievement as a way to fulfill both personal and family goals. Lew and her associates suggest that internalization of both value systems can be helpful because it enables the student to function effectively in two different cultural environments. Of course, it may be easier for some students than for others to integrate and reconcile the disparate sets of values.

The Academic Environment for Working-Class and Poor Women.   Research on working-class and poor women's adjustment to college life is very limited. However, one interesting study (LePage-Lees, 1997) of high-achieving women from working-class or poor families found that many of these women felt they had to hide their backgrounds from others in order to achieve during undergraduate and graduate school. Also, they felt their socioeconomic backgrounds put them at an intellectual disadvantage, that other students were better prepared and more intelligent. One respondent said: "People now think the only issue is ethnicity, and I still think that economic level is an important issue regardless of ethnicity. Economics doesn't explain everything but it explains a lot" (p. 380).

Another type of poor woman with special needs and difficulties in the college environment is the woman on welfare. Those who decide to better themselves and their children through their own higher education anticipate and receive many benefits. However, they also face numerous obstacles. As Erika Kates (1996) points out, these women must cope with child-care responsibilities, transportation costs, reductions in federal assistance, and other difficulties. On the positive side, higher education is an important route to a reasonable income and greatly reduces reliance on federal aid (e.g., Kates, 1996). The story of Pauline illustrates the obstacles and benefits. This Black woman attended college at age 17 but dropped out after falling in love. She then had three children and was deserted by the children's father. Once her youngest child was in child care, she began community college as a welfare recipient. While in school she faced several obstacles; however, Pauline successfully completed college and then found a job in her town's school department (Kates, p. 550).

Women with Disabilities and the Physical Campus Environment.   The institutional environment we have discussed thus far focuses on behavioral issues. Women with disabilities face not only these issues but must also cope with challenges in bureaucracy and the physical environment. According to Lillian Holcomb and Carol Giesen (1995), women with disabilities on college campuses face obstacles such as inadequate funding of support services, old buildings not designed to be barrier-free, and campus grounds made inaccessible by not having curb cuts. In addition, they can experience increased burdens in the time needed to engage in activities such as traversing an inaccessible campus or using Braille to study.

Use the survey in Get Involved 9.1 to assess the academic climate on your campus.

Women's Work-Related Goals

In an address to the graduating class of a women's college, feminist author Gloria Steinem noted a major difference between the goals of her generation of female college

---

GET INVOLVED **9.1**

Does Your Campus Have a Hospitable Environment for Women?

Answer the questions presented below and ask three female students the same questions. If possible, select interviewees who vary in ethnicity, physical ability/disability, and/or sexual orientation.

1. Did you ever hear a professor tell a sexist or racist "joke" during or outside of class?
2. Did you ever hear a professor make a derogatory comment about a student's gender, ethnicity, physical disability, or sexual orientation? If yes, indicate the nature of that comment.

3. Do you feel that women and men receive the same degree of encouragement and support from their instructors? If not, explain.
4. Do you feel that women of color, women with disabilities, and lesbian women receive the same degree of encouragement and support from their instructors as White, nondisabled, heterosexual women? If not, explain.
5. Do you experience any conflict between the values that characterize this campus and the values of your cultural group?

What Does It Mean?

1. Did you find any evidence of sexism, racism, bias against women with disabilities, and/or prejudice against lesbians? If yes, do you think these experiences affect the educational process of students who are targets of these behaviors? Why or why not?
2. Did you find any evidence of differential support for students because of their

gender, ethnicity, physical ability, or sexual preference? If yes, do you think this can affect the educational process of students who receive less support? Why or why not?
3. Did you note any conflict between campus and cultural values? If yes, is this conflict similar to that described in the text?

graduates in 1956 and those of young women today: "I thought we had to marry what we wished to become. Now you are becoming the men you once would have wanted to marry" (Goldberg, 1999, p. G3). This quote suggests that college women are striving for—and attaining—high-achievement goals; they are no longer living vicariously through the accomplishments of their husbands. In the following discussion we see that women do, indeed, have high aspirations. However, we also see that there continue to be some differences in the career goals of females and males.

Career Aspirations

There are few differences in the career aspirations of women with and without disabilities (DeLoach, 1989) and among women of different ethnicities (Fouad & Byars-Winston, 2005). However, there is some evidence that Black college women expect success more than White women do (Ganong et al., 1996). In addition, Asian American college women are more likely than White college women to aspire toward male-dominated and more prestigious occupations (Leung et al., 1994). One explanation is that although Asian culture values traditional gender roles, Asian American families encourage their daughters to pursue nontraditional prestigious occupations associated with social recognition (Leung et al., 1994).

Research has shown that high school girls and boys generally aspire to careers that are equal in prestige (Watson et al., 2002) and that college women are as motivated as college men to pursue a career and to achieve success in their field (Hoffnung, 2004). During high school and college, however, women sometimes lower their aspirations, major in less prestigious, often female-dominated, career fields and, therefore, eventually end up in lower-level careers (Betz, 2008; Frome et al., 2008; Fulcher, 2007; Hoffnung, 2004; Lips, 2004; VanLeuvan, 2004). Let us take a closer look at factors that influence young women's career aspirations.

Women are more likely to seek and earn degrees in academic disciplines that focus on people, such as, education, psychology, and health sciences (Lips, 2004) (see Table 9.2). Interestingly, girls who believe in the altruistic value of math and science have more interest in, and more positive attitudes toward, these fields than do other girls (Weisgram & Bigler, 2006). What might account for this? One explanation is that, as we saw in Chapter 4, girls are socialized toward communal behaviors. Consistent with the social construction of women as caring and nurturant, they are encouraged to develop a strong interest in and concern for other people.

Table 9.2 also shows that relatively few female students aspire toward computer and information sciences, engineering, and physical sciences. Even those qualified college women who venture into the sciences and engineering are more likely than college men to drop out of these programs (Hartman & Hartman, 2008; Lips, 2004; J. Steele et al., 2002). For example, among biology majors with A averages, 80 percent of the women, compared to 60 percent of the men, change majors. In the physical sciences, these percentages are 69 percent of women versus only 1 percent of men, and in engineering 71 percent compared to 18 percent (Selingo, 1998). This is unfortunate, given the high status and high pay associated with these careers and given the need for additional qualified scientists (American Association of University Women, 2004).

TABLE 9.2   Bachelor's, Master's, and Doctoral Degrees, 2004–2005, in Selected Fields by Gender

Educational Field	Bachelor's Degree		Master's Degree		Doctorate	
	Women	Men	Women	Men	Women	Men
Biological/life sciences	62%	38%	60%	40%	49%	51%
Business & management	50	50	42	58	40	60
Computer & information sciences	22	78	29	71	19	81
Education	79	21	77	23	67	33
Engineering	20	80	22	78	19	81
English	68	32	69	31	59	41
Health professions	87	13	79	21	71	29
Mathematics	45	55	44	56	28	72
Physical sciences	42	58	39	61	28	72
Psychology	78	22	79	21	71	29
Social sciences & history	50	50	51	49	43	57
Visual & performing arts	61	39	57	43	54	46

Source: "The Nation: Students" (2007); U.S. Department of Education (2004).

What accounts for women's continued low participation rate in these academic areas? As we saw in Chapter 5, the possibility that females are less mathematically or scientifically skilled can be ruled out. We also noted in that chapter that parents and teachers are less likely to encourage the development of math or science skills in girls than boys. We saw that gender differences in attitudes toward and interest in science emerge as early as elementary school (AAUW, 2004), with girls becoming less confident of their ability to do well in math and science (Betz, 2008). In addition, stereotypes of scientists as "nerds" who are obsessed with technology, but who have little interest in people, conflict more with the gender roles of women than of men (Beyer, 2006; Selwyn, 2007). The dearth of female role models and insufficient faculty encouragement may be other factors that play an important role in steering women away from careers in the sciences (Beyer, 2006; VanLeuvan, 2004). In addition, female students who do choose to major in math, science, and engineering report higher levels of discrimination than either women in female-dominated majors—such as arts, education, humanities, and social sciences—or men in any major (J. Steele et al., 2002).

Career Counseling

During the 1950s and 1960s, women were largely invisible to career counselors because women were not viewed as pursuing careers (Betz, 2008). Starting in the 1960s and 1970s, career counselors tended to steer girls and women toward traditionally female careers (Farmer, 2006). Although there is now much greater acceptance of females' pursuit of traditionally male occupations, some counselors, teachers, and parents continue to show gender-biased attitudes toward career choices. Many girls are discouraged from taking advanced math and science courses or from choosing high-status professions dominated by males (Fassinger & Asay, 2006). Gender bias also permeates vocational interest inventories and aptitude testing (Lonborg & Hackett, 2006).

What can career counselors do to support, encourage, and expand the career aspirations of young women? Nancy Betz (2008) suggests that counselors should help women in the following areas: (1) advocating for family-friendly work policies, such as flex time; (2) locating support systems and mentors; (3) encouraging husbands or partners to participate fully in housework and child care; (4) developing effective cognitive and behavioral coping strategies; (5) obtaining necessary education, training, and job-hunting skills. Career counselors also need to become aware and understand that both women's and men's views and needs are shaped by culture, ethnicity, social class, sexual orientation, and ableness (Hook & Bowman, 2008; Lonborg & Hackett, 2006).

Work–Family Expectations

> *My plan is to get a job after graduate school and hopefully marry. After a few years of establishing myself in my career, I plan to have two children. After a short maternity leave, I plan to work part time, and hope my husband will too, so one of us can always be home. When I told my boyfriend this, he said he hasn't even considered how to balance work and family, and he was astonished that my plans for the future are all mapped out.* (Erika, 21-year-old college senior)

The vast majority of college women nowadays desire marriage, motherhood, and a career. For example, in Michele Hoffnung's (2004) survey of senior women at five different American colleges, 96 percent planned to have a career, 86 percent planned to marry, and 98 percent planned to have children. (See Learn about the Research 9.2 for a study of Canadian women's plans.) If you are interested in both employment and parenthood, have you considered how you would like to combine these? Research shows that most college women, like Erika, want to work before they have children and interrupt their employment for some period during their children's early years (e.g., Bridges & Etaugh, 1996). The majority of male students, however, are like Erika's boyfriend and are much less likely to think about connections between career and family goals (Friedman & Weisbrod, 2005; Konrad, 2003; Mahaffy & Ward, 2002).

Although most college women want to interrupt their employment for childrearing, Black college women want to discontinue their employment for a shorter period of time than White women do. For example, Judith and Claire found that Black women want to return to employment when their first child was approximately 2 years old, whereas White women want to delay employment until their child was approximately 4 (Bridges & Etaugh, 1996).

Why do Black college women prefer an earlier return to employment after childbirth? One factor is that White college women are more likely than their Black peers to believe that maternal employment is harmful to young children (Bridges & Etaugh, 1996; Murrell et al., 1991). For example, Whites are more likely than Blacks to think that continuous maternal employment produces negative outcomes for children, such as low self-esteem, feelings of neglect, and lack of maternal guidance (Bridges & Etaugh, 1996). The more positive attitude of young Black women might, in turn, be related to Black women's long history of combining the roles of mother and provider (Farmer, 2006). Audrey Murrell and her colleagues (Murrell et al., 1991) found that college-educated Black women had a stronger work orientation and a more intense commitment to professional goals than White women. Along these same lines, evidence suggests that college-educated Black women are more likely than their White counterparts to be encouraged by their parents to consider an occupation as essential to success (Higginbotham & Weber, 1996). Together, this body of research indicates that employment may be a more integral aspect of Blacks' construction of women's roles than it is for Whites.

L E A R N A B O U T T H E R E S E A R C H 9.2

Young Women's Preferred and Expected Patterns of Employment and Childrearing

E. Heather Davey (1998) assessed the views of Canadian college and noncollege young women regarding their preferences and expectations for combining employment and childrearing. Respondents were given a choice of three options: leaving work before the birth of the first child, working until the birth of the first child and working again after the youngest child reaches an age deemed appropriate by the respondent, or working continuously, with maternity leaves as needed.

She found that only a small minority either wanted or expected to leave employment before motherhood. Interestingly, there was a difference in preferences for and expectations about the other two options. Although 50 percent desired a long interruption of employment, only 29 percent expected to follow this pattern. Furthermore, whereas 46 percent wanted to work continuously, taking maternity leaves as needed, 59 percent expected to do so. The researcher points out that this last pattern more realistically conforms to current employment trends and she suggests that the more realistic expectations shown by these young women reflect their increasing awareness of economic realities.

What Does It Mean?

1. What are other explanations of the discrepancies between these women's preferred and expected employment-childrearing patterns?
2. Do you think there are differences between young men's preferred and expected employment–fatherhood patterns? Explain your answer.

3. Do you think it would be useful for young women thinking about their careers to have realistic expectations about how they will combine the employment and parenting roles? If yes, what can be done to guide young women toward a realistic appraisal of their future roles?

Source: Davey (1998).

Some educated women of color face another role-related problem: finding an appropriate mate within one's ethnic group. Evidence suggests that uneducated Native American men are reluctant to marry college-educated women (LaFromboise et al., 1990) and that Native American college women fear they will not be able to marry Native men (Medicine, 1988). Similarly, Black college women express the desire to marry a person of equal or greater educational and occupational status. However, because they earn a higher proportion of every type of higher education degree than Black men, they may be frustrated in this desire (Ganong et al., 1996).

Work–Family Outcomes

In the previous section, we saw that the great majority of college women expect to "have it all": career, marriage, and motherhood. How do these expectations relate to actual career and family outcomes? In order to explore this question, Michele Hoffnung (2004) surveyed women seniors at five northeastern colleges and then followed them up seven years later.

Career remained the major focus for the women throughout their twenties. Not quite half had married, and most had not yet started a family. Marital status was unrelated to educational attainment and career status seven years out from college graduation. The few women who had become mothers, however, had fewer advanced degrees and lower career status than other women. They typically chose more traditional careers that took less time to train for, such as teacher or physical therapist. These women also held more traditional attitudes towards women's rights, roles, and responsibilities and were more likely to come from families with lower socioeconomic status.

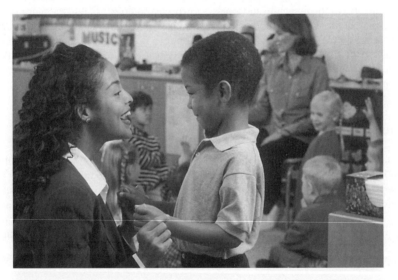

Black college women prefer an earlier return to employment after childbirth than do White women.

In college, women of color had lower expectations for marriage than White women did and, in fact, they were less likely to be married seven years later. Their educational attainments were equal to those of White women and their careers had higher status. These findings are consistent with research we looked at in the previous section suggesting that college-educated women of color have very high career motivation (Bridges & Etaugh, 1996; Murrell et al., 1991).

Salary Expectations

Consistent with a tendency to have less prestigious career aspirations than men do, women expect lower salaries in their jobs. Kenneth Sumner and Theresa Brown (1996) asked college students in a variety of majors to give their salary expectations. Students' assessments of their entry-level incomes were closely linked to their college major. Given that salaries tend to be higher in male-dominated occupations than in female-dominated occupations (Lipson, 2001), it is not surprising that students in male-dominated majors expected higher starting salaries than did those in female-dominated fields. However, when asked to indicate their peak salaries, students revealed large gender differences regardless of major. Males in male-dominated, female-dominated, and gender-neutral majors expected higher peak salaries than women in these fields did. For example, in male-dominated majors, males expected an average of $67,500 whereas females expected only $48,600, and in female-dominated majors, the averages were $55,600 for men and $34,000 for women.

Why do women expect lower salaries? One possibility is that women know that females earn lower salaries than males and base their own salary expectations accordingly (Heckert, 2002). Another possibility is that women lower their salary expectations because they place importance on making accommodations in their job to fulfill their family obligations (Heckert, 2002; Jackson et al., 1992). A third possibility is that women are more likely than men to believe they deserve less (Yoder, 2000) (see Chapter 10).

Influences on Women's Achievement Level and Career Decisions

Although this chapter focuses on education and achievement, it is essential to note that achievement goals can be satisfied in diverse ways. Raising a well-adjusted and loving child, providing emotional and physical support to a spouse recovering from a stroke, and helping the homeless in one's community are only a few of the numerous forms achievement can take that are independent of education and occupation. However, despite the diversity of achievement directions, researchers have focused primarily on the traditional areas of education and occupation, and if we define achievement in this manner, it appears that women have achieved less than men. As we noted at the beginning of this chapter, more men than women attain the highest educational levels, aspire to the most prestigious careers, and hold high positions within their occupational fields. Now we examine possible internal and external influences on women's achievement level and occupational decisions. First, we look at their orientation to achievement in general and the personality traits that might be related to their career decision making. Then, we explore social and cultural influences on young women's educational and occupational pursuits.

Orientation to Achievement

For several decades, psychologists attempted to explain women's lower achievement compared to men's as due, in part, to their orientation to achievement.

Achievement Motivation.   One explanation was that females' **achievement motivation,** that is, their *need to excel,* was lower than males'. However, early studies by David McClelland and others on which this conclusion was based used a male-biased theoretical framework. Achievement was defined primarily in ways applicable to men's lives and emphasized competition and mastery in such areas as school, jobs, and sports. But achievement can also occur in other domains, such as the personal or interpersonal areas (Mednick & Thomas, 2008).

At the present time, researchers believe that women and men are similarly motivated to achieve (Hyde & Kling, 2001). However, gender socialization practices of families, peers, teachers, and others teach youngsters not only the importance of achievement but also the "appropriate" direction it should take for their gender. For example, girls tend to learn that, if they have children, they should be the primary caregiver. Consequently, they may adjust their achievement goals in order to meet this expectation.

Fear of Success.   Another view of women's lower achievement in comparison to men's came from Matina Horner (1972), who proposed that women want to achieve but have a **fear of success,** that is, *a motive to avoid situations of high achievement.* Horner contended that women were concerned about the negative social consequences that can result from success, especially social rejection and loss of femininity. This suggestion might seem strange as you read this book at the beginning of the twenty-first century. However, in the 1970s and 1980s, this idea was embraced by many scholars who studied females' fear of success.

To test her concept of the fear of success, Horner devised the following statement: *After first-term finals, Anne/John finds herself/himself at the top of her/his medical school class.* She asked college women to write a paragraph about Anne and college men to write about John. Approximately two-thirds of the women wrote negative stories with themes such as Anne's physical unattractiveness, her inability to have romantic relationships, rejection by her peers, and her decision to transfer into a less prestigious occupation. Most of the stories told by the men about John, on the other hand, reflected positive outcomes.

Although Horner believed these results indicated a motive to avoid success on the part of women, subsequent research points to a different conclusion. It now appears that these stories did not reflect women's fear of high-achieving situations in general, but rather their awareness of negative consequences that can occur when individuals violate gender stereotypes. Medicine, especially in the 1970s when Horner performed her study, was strongly dominated by men. Thus it is likely that females' negative stories reflected their concern about the problems individuals face in gender-atypical occupations, rather than their desire to avoid a high level of achievement (Hyde & Kling, 2001). A subsequent study showed that both women and men wrote negative stories about a successful woman in medicine *and* a successful man in nursing (Cherry & Deaux, 1978). Years of subsequent research on this topic have failed to find reliable gender differences in fear of success (Mednick & Thomas, 2008). Consequently, psychologists today do not believe that women's lower level of educational or occupational achievement can be accounted for by their fear of success.

Achievement Attributions.   A third explanation given for gender differences in levels of achievement is that females and males make different **achievement attributions,** that is, *explanations about their good and poor performance.* In general, people are *more likely to attribute positive events to their own internal traits, such as their ability or effort, whereas they tend to attribute negative events to external causes such as task difficulty or bad luck.* This **self-serving attributional bias,** like self-esteem (see Chapter 4), is linked to healthy psychological adjustment and happiness (Mezulis et al., 2004). In other words, taking responsibility for good performance (e.g., "I did well on the test because I know the material"), but attributing poor performance to external factors (e.g., "I failed the test because it was unfair"), enables a person to maintain a good self-image. On the other hand, the reverse pattern—blaming yourself for failure while not taking credit for your successes—could lead to an unwillingness to persevere in a challenging situation and to low self-esteem.

      A recent meta-analysis by Amy Mezulis and her colleagues (2004) shows that females, but not males, show a marked decline in the self-serving attributional bias starting in early adolescence. (Reread the section on self-esteem in Chapter 4, and note the similar, and possibly related, decline.) These gender differences in attributions of performance are small, however (see review by Mednick & Thomas, 2008), and are associated with the type of performance situation. For example, in male-stereotyped domains, such as mathematics, males attribute success to ability more than do females, but in female-stereotyped domains, such as languages or English, the reverse pattern occurs (Beyer, 1997; Birenbaum & Kraemer, 1995). Similarly, women are more likely to attribute failure to lack of ability on a math test than on a verbal test, whereas men show the reverse tendency (Kiefer & Shih, 2004).

Achievement Self-Confidence.   Another internal barrier that has been used to explain women's lower achievement in comparison to men's is their lower self-confidence. Many studies show that males are more self-confident in academic situations than females. For example, girls tend to underestimate their grades, ability level, and class standing whereas boys tend to overestimate theirs (Furnham et al., 2006; Smith, 2006; Wigfield et al., 2006). Mary Crawford and Margo MacLeod (1990) also found that when asked why they don't participate in class discussion, college women's responses reflected questionable confidence in their abilities, such as "might appear unintelligent in the eyes of other students" and "ideas are not well enough formulated" (p. 116). Men's reasons, on the other hand, focused on external factors, as in "have not done the assigned reading" or participation might "negatively affect [their] grade" (p. 116). Other research suggests that even among high achievers in the sciences, fewer women than men believe their scientific ability to be above average (Sonnert & Holton, 1996).

Females do not show lower levels of confidence in all situations, however. Studies indicate that females' confidence is lower than males' in male-linked tasks, such as mathematics, but is higher in female-linked tasks, such as reading and English, arts and music, and social skills (Byrne, 2008; Jacobs et al., 2002; Nagy et al., 2008; Watt, 2004; Wigfield et al., 2006). Females' confidence is also higher when performance estimates are made privately rather than publicly (e.g., Daubman et al., 1992). Research by Kimberly Daubman and her colleagues (1997; Heatherington et al., 1993) suggests that in some situations, what appears to be lower self-confidence (e.g., publicly predicting lower grades for oneself) might really reflect women's desire to be liked or to protect others from negative feelings about themselves.

Conclusion. Early conclusions that women have lower aspirations than men because they are not as highly motivated to excel and because they fear the negative consequences of success have not been supported. Although some evidence exists for gender differences in achievement attributions and self-confidence, these differences are not observed in all situations. Furthermore, as is the case with all types of psychological gender differences, the differences are small and do not apply to all females and males. Thus, most social scientists point to other factors to help explain different career aspirations and attainment levels of women and men.

Personality Characteristics

Are personality characteristics related to women's career aspirations? The answer is "yes." For example, women who work full-time are more likely to support egalitarian roles for women than are women who work part-time (Cunningham et al., 2005). Also, women who choose male-dominated careers are more likely than those who pick female-dominated careers to be competitive, autonomous, and instrumental and to have less traditional gender attitudes (Betz, 2008; Hutson-Comeaux et al., 2002).

Another personality factor related to career choice is the individual's **self-efficacy,** that is, *the belief that one can successfully perform the tasks involved in a particular domain.* Individuals with high self-efficacy for a particular field are more likely to aspire toward that field as a career (Wigfield et al., 2006). For example, while females tend to have lower self-efficacy in mathematics and science than males (Betz, 2008) (see Chapter 5), those women who select and persist in careers in science or engineering have high self-efficacy for mathematics (Larose et al., 2008). Furthermore, females, compared to males, have higher self-efficacy for health-related professions and female-dominated skilled labor occupations. These gender differences, in turn, correspond to differences in occupational choice.

Sexual Orientation

Many lesbians become aware of their sexual identity during late adolescence or adulthood, at the same time that they are selecting a career. The overlap of these two processes can influence career development (Hook & Bowman, 2008; Lippa, 2008). Lesbians might put career selection on hold as they explore their sexuality and intimate relationships (Bieschke & Toepfer-Hendey, 2006). Also, as a result of coming out, many lose the family support that can be beneficial to the career-selection process.

In addition, lesbians' career choices might be directly affected by their perception of the occupational climate for lesbians and gays. Whereas some lesbians select occupations they perceive as employing large numbers of lesbians and gays in order to experience an environment in which there is safety in numbers, lesbians who are closeted or anxious about their sexual identity might avoid these occupations (Colgan et al., 2008; Hook & Bowman, 2008).

On the positive side, Fassinger (1995) notes that lesbians tend to be less traditional in their attitudes about gender than are heterosexual women. Consequently, they tend to consider a broader range of occupational options and are more likely to choose jobs in male-dominated fields. These jobs, as we shall see, pay more than jobs in the female-dominated areas (Peplau & Fingerhut, 2004).

Social and Cultural Factors

Although some internal characteristics are related to individuals' career choices, career decisions are made within a sociocultural context in which the attitudes of significant people and the values of one's culture contribute to career selection as well. Support and encouragement from parents are very important for women of all ethnicities (Betz, 2008; Li & Kerpelman, 2007). Parental support and availability influence career aspirations and achievements in Black (Fisher & Padmawidjaja, 1999; Pearson & Bieschke, 2001), Native American (Juntunen et al., 2001), and Latina (Fisher & Padmawidjaja, 1999) women. High-achieving Black and White women report receiving considerable family support for pursuing their highly prestigious careers and being strongly influenced by their families' values regarding the benefits of hard work (Richie et al., 1997; Simpson, 1996). For example, a Black female attorney whose father was a janitor, commented: "They wanted me to have a better life than they had. For all of us. And that's why they emphasized education and emphasized working relationships and how you get along with people and that kind of thing" (Higginbotham & Weber, 1996, p. 135). The same-sex parent appears to have the greatest effect on career expectations and outcome of adolescents (Whiston & Keller, 2004). One longitudinal study of female high school seniors, for example, found that attachment to the mother contributed to high career aspirations five years later (O'Brien et al., 2000). Another longitudinal study showed that mothers' high expectations for their 10-year-old daughters predicted the latter's earnings in adulthood (Flouri & Hawkes, 2008). Among female college students, those with plans for a nontraditional career are more likely than other women to have a mother with a nontraditional career and a father who supports their career choice (Whiston & Keller, 2004).

In addition to social support, cultural values play a role in women's career development. According to McAdoo (in Higginbotham & Weber, 1996), many Black families believe that college education and professional attainment are family, as well as individual, goals. Moreover, there is evidence that high-achieving Black women who move up from their working-class backgrounds feel a sense of obligation to their families. In one study (Higginbotham & Weber, 1996), almost twice as many Black as White upwardly mobile women expressed this sense of familial debt. A Black occupational therapist said: "I know the struggle that my parents have had to get me where I am. I know the energy they no longer have to put into the rest of the family even though they want to put it there and they're willing. I feel it is my responsibility to give back some of that energy they have given to me. It's self-directed, not required" (p. 139). In contrast, here is the comment of a White library administrator: "Growing up in a family, I don't think it's that kind of a relationship—that's their job. I feel that way with my son. I certainly love him but I don't want him ever to be in a position to think he owes me" (p. 140).

Another cultural value shown by Black women is their concern for their communities. Many successful Black women are committed to ending both sexism and racism in the workplace and community (Richie et al., 1997) and see their achievements as ways of uplifting Black people (Collins, in Higginbotham & Weber, 1996). As expressed by a high-ranking Black female city official: "Because I have more opportunities, I've got an obligation to give more back and to set a positive example for Black people and especially for Black women. I think we've got to do a tremendous job in building self-esteem and giving people the desire to achieve" (Higginbotham & Weber, 1996, p. 142). Similarly, many Latina adolescents from working-class families realize that their parents work long hours at multiple, dead-end jobs. They aspire to fulfilling careers that will allow them to create better lives for themselves and their families, and that will also enable them to make a positive contribution to their community (Marlino & Wilson, 2006). Many high-achieving Latina women receive family encouragement and have a supportive social network. However, some experience a conflict between traditional cultural values that guide them toward family-oriented goals and other socialization factors that encourage high educational and career attainment (Flores et al., 2006; Gomez et al., 2001; Kitano, 1998).

Conflicting values also are evident in the experiences of educated Native American women (McCloskey & Mintz, 2006). Although research on Native Americans' achievement goals is sparse, it suggests that family and community members often try to discourage Native women from attending college. Consequently, those that persist in seeking a college education feel they are going against their culture (Kidwell, in LaFromboise et al., 1990).

To more directly learn about family and cultural influences on women's career goals, perform the interviews described in Get Involved 9.2.

In addition to cultural variations across ethnic groups, values associated with social class can influence career decisions. According to Constance Flanagan (1993), working-class families, who hold more traditional gender attitudes than middle-class families, also see less value in academic achievement. Thus, working-class women who have an interest in school and a willingness to be independent of their families are

GET INVOLVED **9.2**

Family and Cultural Values about Education and Career Goals

Interview two female students who vary in ethnicity. Select your interviewees from any two of the following ethnic groups: Asian American, Black, Latina, Native American, and White. Inform them you are exploring connections between women's family and cultural values and their education and career goals.

First, ask each respondent to indicate her college major, career goal, and expected educational attainment (i.e., highest educational degree). Second, ask her to evaluate the degree to which her family's values support her specific educational aspirations and career goals. Third, ask her to evaluate the degree to which her specific educational aspirations and career goals were influenced by her ethnic or national cultural values.

What Does It Mean?

1. Did you find any differences among respondents in the extent to which they received support from their families? If yes, refer to information presented in the text or to your own ideas and explain these differences.

2. Did your respondents report that their goals were influenced by their values? Is the information you obtained consistent with the material presented in the text? If not, explain the discrepancies.

---

likely to become invested in employment immediately after high school, whereas middle-class women with those attributes are apt to seek higher education.

Job-Related Characteristics

Individuals vary in the benefits they want from working in a particular job, and these benefits can play a role in guiding career selections. Research shows that college women and men do not differ in the importance they place on pay, job qualities, or factors related to promotions and job perks (Heckert et al., 2002).

However, women and men differ in the importance they attach to other job-related attributes, which can account for some of the differences in their occupational choices. For both college students (Konrad et al., 2000) and successful women and men (Dyke & Murphy, 2006), differences are generally consistent with gender roles and stereotypes. For example, males are somewhat more likely to value material success, earnings, promotions, freedom, challenge, leadership, and power. Females are more apt to value interpersonal relationships, helping others, and striking a balance between professional achievement and personal relationships.

Another gender difference in job values is the greater emphasis women place on good, flexible working hours and ease of commuting especially if they had children (Corrigall & Konrad, 2006; Heckert et al., 2002; Konrad et al., 2000). This gender difference probably reflects women's belief that mothers should stay home and care for infants, a value that is expressed during many stages of females' lives. For example, twelfth-grade girls who place a high value on having a family-friendly job are more likely to change their career aspirations from male-dominated fields (e.g., science) to female-dominated occupations (Frome et al., 2008).

Regardless of the type of job, women's ratings of the importance of several job characteristics rose during the 1980s and 1990s. These include job security, power, prestige, feelings of accomplishment, task enjoyment, and using one's abilities. It is possible that as gender barriers to opportunity declined, women's aspirations rose to obtain previously unavailable job attributes (Konrad et al., 2000).

Entering the Workplace

We have seen that a variety of personal, social, and cultural factors contribute to women's career choices. Once they have made their selections, do women run into any obstacles in the workplace? In Chapter 10, we look into women's experiences on the job, but we begin here by examining the hiring process.

Antidiscrimination laws prohibit the use of gender (as well as ethnicity, national origin, or age) as a determinant in hiring or in other employment decisions. However, gender-based and other forms of discrimination still occur (Crosby et al., 2007). Both gender and ethnic discrimination in hiring have been reported in studies of Black and White female professionals and managers (Richie et al., 1997; Weber & Higginbotham, 1997). As an example of this bias, Rhea Steinpreis and her colleagues (1999) sent a job resume to psychology academicians and asked them to evaluate the quality of the work-related experience that was presented. Although the resumes were identical, those who were told the applicant was a man evaluated the credentials more positively and indicated a greater willingness to hire than did their colleagues who were told the applicant was a woman. Along the same lines, female job candidates or candidates described as having feminine traits (regardless of biological sex) are considered best suited for jobs dominated by women. Men, or applicants described as having masculine traits, are judged as best suited for male-dominated occupations (Kleyman et al., 2004). In addition, employers are less likely to hire mothers than equally qualified nonmothers. Fathers by contrast, are not disadvantaged in the hiring process (Correll et al., 2007).

Although gender discrimination can influence hiring decisions, it does not occur in all situations. Not surprisingly, one factor that influences evaluation of job applicants is the gender dominance of the occupation. A recent meta-analysis (Davison & Burke, 2000) found evidence of a promale bias for male-dominated jobs and a profemale bias for female-dominated jobs.

Another factor that affects bias in hiring decisions is the amount of information provided about the applicant. Gender bias is most likely when little information is provided about the candidate's qualifications. In this situation, the gender of the applicant is highly salient and can give rise to stereotyped impressions and decisions. On the other hand, when the candidate's academic and employment records are presented, her or his qualifications strongly influence the evaluator's impression (Davison & Burke, 2000).

SUMMARY

Women's Educational Values, Attainment, and Campus Experience

- College women and men have similar values and expectations about their educational attainment.
- Women obtain the majority of associate's and bachelor's degrees, whereas men earn the majority of doctoral and professional degrees.
- The campus climate can be problematic for some women. They may experience sexism in the classroom and many perceive the academic environment as hostile and demeaning.
- Women of color, poor women, and women with disabilities experience additional problems on campus.

Women's Work-Related Goals

- College women generally aspire to less prestigious careers than college men. Few women decide to enter the physical sciences or engineering.
- Career counselors can do several things to support and expand women's career aspirations.
- Most college women envision their futures as involving employment, marriage, and motherhood. Many plan to interrupt their employment for childrearing.
- Women have lower salary expectations than men. Possible explanations are women's knowledge that females earn less than males, their willingness to accommodate their jobs to their family life, and their belief that they deserve less.

Influences on Women's Achievement Level and Career Decisions

- There is no evidence that women have less motivation to achieve than men do or that

women stay away from high-achieving situations because they fear success.
- Gender differences in attributions for performance are very small and are more likely to occur when making attributions in gender-stereotypic domains.
- Women display less self-confidence than men, especially in relation to male-linked tasks and when estimates of one's performance are made publicly.
- Women with nontraditional gender-related traits or attitudes are more likely to aspire toward male-dominated careers.
- Women's feelings of self-efficacy for particular occupational fields are related to their aspirations for those fields.
- Lesbians' career decisions are sometimes influenced by their perceptions of the job climate for lesbians and gays.
- Family support and family and cultural values can influence women's career development.
- Job-related characteristics valued more highly by males include a good salary, promotions, and opportunity for advancement.
- Characteristics valued more strongly by females than males are interpersonal relationships and helping others. However, women in male-dominated occupations highly value masculine-typed job qualities.

Entering the Workplace

- There is some evidence of gender discrimination in hiring, especially when the job is dominated by the other gender.

KEY TERMS

chilly climate
achievement motivation

fear of success
achievement attributions

self-serving attributional bias
self-efficacy

WHAT DO YOU THINK?

1. Discuss your opinion about the relative advantages and disadvantages for women of attending a women's college versus a mixed-gender college.

2. This chapter discusses several issues faced by women of color and women with disabilities on college campuses. Select two or three of these concerns and suggest institutional procedures that could address these problems and improve the academic climate for these groups.

3. Many women who desire both employment and motherhood want to interrupt their employment for childrearing. What can explain this? As part of your answer, discuss the extent to which gender differences in power (see Chapter 1) and gender socialization (see Chapter 4) explain this.

4. The traditional conception of achievement as the attainment of high academic and occupational success has been criticized as reflecting the achievement domains of men more than of women. Do you agree with this criticism? Give a rationale for your answer. Also, if you agree, suggest other indices of success that would reflect women's achievement more accurately.

5. Discuss the relationship between gender stereotypes and common career choices of young women and men. Also, several changes have occurred in the educational attainment and career aspirations of women over time. Show how a changing social construction of gender has contributed to this.

IF YOU WANT TO LEARN MORE

American Council on Education. (2005). *Leadership through achievement: Women of color in higher education*. Washington, DC: Author.

Bonham, G. W. (Ed.). (2006). *Women on campus: The unfinished liberation*. Piscataway, NJ: Transaction.

Datnow, A., & Hubbard, L. (2002). *Gender, policy, and practice: Perspectives on single-sex and coeducational schooling*. New York: Routledge.

Howes, E. V. (2002). *Connecting girls and science: Constructivism, feminism, and science education reform*. New York: Teachers College Press.

Maslak, M. A. (Ed.). (2007). *The structure and agency of women's education*. Albany: State University of New York Press.

Sax, L. J. (2008). *The gender gap in college: Maximizing the developmental potential of women and men*. San Francisco, CA: Jossey-Bass.

Tolley, K. (2002). *The science education of American girls: A historical perspective*. New York: Routledge.

Walsh, W. B., & Heppner, M. J. (Eds.). (2006). *Handbook of career counseling for women* (2nd ed.). Mahwah, NJ: Erlbaum.

Watt, H. M. G., & Eccles, J. S. (Eds.). (2008). *Gender and occupational outcomes: Longitudinal assessment of individual, social, and cultural influences*. Washington, DC: American Psychological Association.

WEBSITES

Education

American Association of University Women
http://www.aauw.org

Women with Disabilities

Disabled People's International
http://www.dpi.org

CHAPTER

10 Employment

Women's Employment Rates and Occupational Choices
    Employment Rates
    Occupational Choices
Gender Differences in Leadership and Job Advancement
    Leadership Positions

Barriers That Hinder Women's
    Advancement
Women as Leaders
Gender Differences in Salaries
    Comparative Salaries
    Reasons for Differences in Salaries

Women's Job Satisfaction
Gender Differences in Satisfaction
Factor Influencing Lesbians' Job Satisfaction

The Older Woman Worker
Employment Rates
Why Do Older Women Work?
Entering the Workforce in Later Life
Age Discrimination in the Workplace

Changing the Workplace
Organizational Procedures and Policies
Strategies for Women

Retirement
The Retirement Decision
Adjustment to Retirement
Leisure Activities in Retirement

Economic Issues in Later Life
Poverty
Retirement Income: Planning Ahead

When I got my offer, I was so thrilled and honored, I accepted my job immediately. I didn't even think to bargain. Maybe we lack self-confidence, so we undersell ourselves. (Martha West, law professor, in Fogg, 2003, p. A14)

When a man leaves, he is getting the golden parachute to enjoy the good life. When a woman leaves of her own accord, they say 'Well, she couldn't take the pressure' . . . I'll say the unspoken: A lot of companies are still more comfortable with a White man in the job. (John Challenger, chief executive of Challenger, Gray, & Christman, a Chicago firm that tracks chief executives, in Stanley, A., 2002)

A couple of times in my career, someone would tell me that I couldn't do something. I would just tell myself that I wasn't going to talk to that person anymore, and I went ahead and did it anyway . . . I tell other women that persistence pays, and that if you can't work through a problem, to go around it. (Christine King, chief of AMI Semiconductor, in King & Olsen, 2002)

We're still climbing Mount Everest, and we're maybe halfway up . . . There are pockets [of success], and there always have been. And what's exciting is there are more pockets of success now. (Megan Smith, MIT graduate, former chief executive of a dot-com, now in business development at Google, in Hafner, 2003)

In this chapter, we examine the nature of women's employment. We begin with an overview of how many women work, what kinds of jobs they have, the challenges they face in job advancement and becoming leaders, the salaries they receive, and their job satisfaction. We then focus on the status of older women workers. Next, we consider procedures and policies that can improve the work environment for women. Finally, we turn to retirement and economic issues facing older women.

In our exploration of these topics, we use the terms *employment* and *work* interchangeably, so it is important that we clarify their meaning. According to Irene Padavic and Barbara Reskin (2002), the term *work* refers to activities that produce a good or a service. Thus, it includes all sorts of behaviors, such as cooking dinner, mowing the lawn, writing a term paper, teaching a class, fixing a car, volunteering in a nursing home, or running a corporation. The kind of work that we cover in this chapter is work for pay, a major focus of the lives of women (and men) in terms of both time and personal identity. However, our focus on paid employment does not imply that this form of work is more valuable than other types of productive activities. Our society would not function without the unpaid labor that contributes to family and community life.

Women's Employment Rates and Occupational Choices

What percentage of women are employed? What occupations do they choose? Let's discuss each of these issues.

Employment Rates

Women's labor force participation has increased dramatically in recent decades, especially among mothers of young children. Whereas in 1970 only 30 percent of married women with children under age 6 were in the labor force, by 2005 this number had increased to 60 percent (U.S. Census Bureau, 2007c). Among all individuals age 16 years and older, 59 percent of White women and 62 percent of Black women are employed compared to 74 percent of White men and 67 percent of Black men (U.S. Census Bureau, 2007c). Women with disabilities have lower employment rates than either men with disabilities or able-bodied women (Fassinger, 2008; Fuller-Thomson & Minkler, 2005; Olkin, 2008).

What accounts for the influx of women into the workplace? Several factors have contributed (DiNatale & Boraas, 2003). First, the women's movement provided encouragement for women to consider other role options in addition to the home-maker role. Second, women's current higher level of educational attainment (see Chapter 9) has better prepared them for careers that provide greater challenge, stimulation, and a sense of accomplishment. Women with higher levels of education are more likely to be employed and to return to work more rapidly after giving birth (Downs, 2003). Third, many women must work for financial reasons. Today, few middle-class families can afford home ownership, adequate health insurance, and a middle-class lifestyle on one income (Halpern, 2005). In working-class families, two incomes are often needed to remain above the poverty line (Casper & King, 2004). Nearly half of married working women earn half or more of their family's income (AFL-CIO, 2004). When single women with children are included, over 60 percent of working women earn at least half of the family income and about one-third earn virtually all of it. Economic necessity is particularly great for women who are single heads of households, since they comprise half of all families living in poverty in the

United States (Casper & King, 2004; Proctor & Dalaker, 2002). In 2002, 23 percent of all families with children were headed by an unmarried mother, and 73 percent of these mothers were employed (U.S. Census Bureau, 2003c). Unfortunately, for poor women who are heads of households, the employment opportunities are greatly limited, and numerous obstacles block the way to employment. Read Learn about the Research 10.1 for an exploration of employment issues for sheltered homeless and low-income women.

Occupational Choices

One way to examine the occupational choices of women and men is to look at the occupations that employ the fewest number of women and those that employ the greatest number of women. The 20 occupations with the lowest percentage of women are in just four major groups, sometimes called "hard hat" occupations: construction; installation, maintenance, and repair; production; and transportation and material moving. The 20 occupations with the greatest concentration of women are similarly clustered in just a few groups, principally health care, office and administrative work, teaching, and caring for young children (Weinberg, 2004).

Occupational segregation has declined considerably in the past 30 years (Ridgeway & England, 2007). Women have increased their numbers in both managerial and professional jobs, and now hold half of these positions. However, a closer look at the gender distribution within professions overall shows significant differences in the types of occupations pursued by women and men. In 2005, 95 percent of dietitians and nutritionists were women compared with only 14 percent of architects and engineers. In addition, although more women have entered the relatively high-paying skilled trades (e.g., as carpenters, plumbers, and electricians), they still comprise less than 3 percent of these workers (Crosby, 2008; U.S. Census Bureau, 2007c). Women remain segregated in so-called "pink-collar" fields. Nearly 30 percent of female employees work in just 10 occupations. Most of these are low-status, low-paying service jobs such as receptionist, cashier, restaurant server, nursing aide, and cook (AAUW Educational Foundation, 2003). Thus, the workplace continues to be characterized by significant sex segregation, with men tending to dominate the most prestigious occupations such as medicine, engineering, and banking (Cleveland et al., 2005). This situation persists all around the globe (Epstein, 2007).

Furthermore, more employers today are cutting costs by hiring part-time or temporary workers, who are paid less and have minimal or no benefits. Women are more likely than men to hold these jobs, whose flexibility may fit well with a woman's family obligations (American Psychological Association, 2004; Marler & Moen, 2005).

The workplace is segregated not only by gender but also by ethnicity. More Whites than Blacks and Latinas/os are employed in high-status and high-paying managerial or professional occupations and more ethnic minorities than Whites hold service jobs (U.S. Census Bureau, 2007c). However, the ethnic differences among women are not as great as the gender differences. For example, secretarial work and cashiering are among the four most common jobs for Asian American, Black, Latina, and White women (Padavic & Reskin, 2002).

LEARN ABOUT THE RESEARCH 10.1

Employment Decision Making of Sheltered Homeless and Low-Income Single Mothers

The passage of state and federal welfare reform programs in 1996 increased employment rates and reduced poverty rates among poor, single mothers. However, earning enough to support a family continues to be problematic for these women and their employment options remain very limited. A low-wage earner who has left the welfare system may earn too much to be eligible for benefits such as Medicaid and food stamps, yet be too poor to afford health insurance or adequate food. Thus, many former welfare recipients are more financially strapped than before (Clampet-Lundquist et al., 2004; Costello & Wight, 2003). In addition, much of the low-income work available occurs in evening or night shifts, creating scheduling and child-care problems for families (Hawkins & Whiteman, 2004).

In order to understand both the obstacles to and positive influences on the employment of poor mothers, Margaret Brooks and John Buckner (1996) interviewed 220 homeless mothers living in shelters and 216 housed mothers on welfare. Most of these women were White, Latina, or Black, the majority had never been married, and they had an average of two children.

Among those respondents who had been employed during the preceding five years, nearly 40 percent had worked in service occupations, primarily food service and cashier jobs. This figure is higher than the percentage of women in general who work in these occupations. Because these jobs are frequently of limited duration, pay low wages, provide little opportunity for advancement, and offer limited benefits, they do not readily lead to self-sufficiency.

Having a high school diploma or GED and a primary female caregiver who had been employed during the respondent's childhood were more common among women who had worked. On the other hand, one characteristic more prominent among women who did not work was difficulty speaking or understanding English.

Given their living and financial conditions, these women experienced numerous barriers to employment. The greatest were child care and family responsibilities. The majority of respondents reported the need for child-care assistance in order to be able to seek employment. In addition, more than one-quarter expressed the need for transportation and job training.

The authors concluded their study by stating:

> *Until work opportunities for low-skilled individuals are created, until women receive job training and education, and until affordable, quality child care is available, the task of becoming self-supporting will remain a daunting one for single mothers. Welfare reform that ignores these needs is fraught with peril for thousands of families and our society as a whole.* (p. 536)

What Does It Mean?

1. How can some of the problems raised by this study be addressed by government, the private sector, educational institutions, or other societal institutions? Be specific.
2. What can poor women do to ensure that their children have better opportunities?
3. Most of the research on women's achievement and career aspirations has focused on middle-class women. Which factors examined in Chapter 9 do not appear to be relevant to the lives of poor women? Explain your answer.

Source: Brooks and Buckner (1996).

Gender Differences in Leadership and Job Advancement

Nearly half of all law school graduates and nearly half of the new associates in law firms are women. Yet, women represent only 17 percent of partners at law firms. (O'Brien, 2006)

Half of the students in divinity school now are women. But in the mainline Protestant churches that have been ordaining women for decades, they account for just 3 percent of pastors of large congregations that average over 350 per service . . . Many women clergy call this the stained-glass ceiling. (Banerjee, 2006)

Women constitute only 17 percent of opinion writers at The New York Times, 10 percent at The Washington Post, 28 percent at U.S. News & World Report, 23 percent at Newsweek, and 13 percent at Time. Overall, only 24 percent of nationally syndicated columnists are women and they tend to be White and right wing. (Ashkinaze, 2005)

Leadership Positions

Women make up nearly half of the paid labor force of the United States and about half of those are in managerial positions. Yet the higher up one goes in an organization, the scarcer women become. For example, women constitute only 10 percent of Fortune 500 corporate officers, 15 percent of board directors of these companies, 17 percent of U.S. senators, 17 percent of congressional representatives, 16 percent of state governors, 23 percent of college and university presidents, and 2 percent of chief executives at Fortune 500 firms. The situation for women of color is even worse. Similar small proportions of women in high positions exist in other nations (Broadbridge & Hearn, 2008; Center for American Women and Politics, 2008; Creswell, 2006; Rosen, 2007; June, 2007). However, while the United States has yet to elect a woman as President, other countries such as Pakistan (Benazir Bhutto), Israel (Golda Meir), India (Indira Gandhi), and Great Britain (Margaret Thatcher) have been elevating women to the role of chief executive for decades (Kornblut, 2006). In the twenty-first century alone, several women have risen to lead their countries. These include Ellen Johnson Sirleaf of Liberia, Africa's first female president; Michelle Bachelet of Chile, the first woman to lead a major Latin American country; and Angela Merkel, the first female chancellor of Germany. Out of 184 countries, the United States ranks sixty-eighth—just above Turkmenistan—in women's participation in the lower or single legislative body of the country. Women make up just 16 percent of the U.S. House of Representatives. Sweden is near the top of the list, with 47 percent, while Saudi Arabia, Qatar, and Kyrgyzstan are at the bottom with 0 percent women (Inter-Parliamentary Union, 2007). Even in female-dominated fields, men dominate the top ranks. For example, about 97 percent of school superintendents are men (Fassinger, 2001).

The concept of the **glass ceiling** refers to *invisible but powerful barriers that prevent women from advancing beyond a certain level*. For ethnic minority women this barrier has been called a "concrete ceiling" because these women have even greater difficulties moving into higher positions (Russell, 2006). Some also suggest the existence of a **sticky floor** in traditional women's jobs, meaning *women have little or no job ladder, or path, to* *higher positions* (Sanchez et al., 2007). Clerical work is an example of an occupation with little room for growth. Furthermore, some women report experiencing a **maternal wall,** in which they *get less desirable assignments, lower salaries, and more limited advancement opportunities once they become mothers* (Rhode & Williams, 2007).

Barriers That Hinder Women's Advancement

What prevents women from reaching positions of leadership? We turn now to the role of mentors, social networks, and discrimination.

Mentors and Social Networks. A **mentor** *is a senior-level person who takes an active role in the career planning and development of junior employees.* Mentors help their mentees develop appropriate skills, learn the informal organizational structure, meet appropriate people, and have access to opportunities that enable them to advance. Consequently, mentoring has positive effects on job satisfaction, promotion, and career success (Eagly & Carli, 2007; Heyl, 2005; Settles et al., 2007).

Women employees may have difficulty in identifying an appropriate mentor. The limited number of women in senior-level positions makes it hard for a woman to find a female mentor. In addition, men may be reluctant to mentor young women (Foust-Cummings et al., 2008; McCann, 2004; Nolan et al., 2008) for fear of gossip about an affair or a possible sexual harassment suit (O'Brien, 2006).

A second vehicle for advancement that is limited for women and people of color is access to informal social networks. These networks can provide information about job opportunities as well as opportunities to meet important members of the organization. Furthermore, they offer social support and can serve as an important step in developing a mentoring relationship with a senior-level person. Networking is strongly related to women's jobs and life satisfaction (Auster, 2001). However, male reluctance to deal with

Liberian President Ellen Johnson Sirleaf, Africa's first female president, is shown shortly before receiving the 2007 U.S. Presidential Medal of Freedom in Washington, DC. More women around the world are assuming positions of political power, although their numbers remain small.

women means women are less likely than men to be invited to informal social events (e.g., golf outings, lunches) or to be included in informal communication networks (Eagly & Carli, 2007; Foust-Cummings et al., 2008). In addition, women are more likely to have child-care responsibilities right after work, which limits their opportunities for after-hours socializing with male colleagues (Allen, 2004). One way for women to become part of a network is to join local or national organizations such as the National Association for Female Executives and the American Association of University Women (AAUW), attend events, and meet people (Eddleman et al., 2003).

Discrimination. Another factor limiting the job advancement of women is sex discrimination, that is, unfavorable treatment based on gender. Recently settled lawsuits against major corporations and brokerage firms including Wal-Mart, Morgan Stanley, Merrill Lynch, Boeing, and Abercrombie & Fitch reveal major sex and ethnic inequities in pay and promotion (Anderson, 2006, 2007; Greenhouse, 2004; "Major Companies," 2004). For example, brokerage firms have been found to take away women's clients and commissions, give them pay cuts and demotions following maternity leave, and assign lucrative accounts to male cronies (Anderson, 2007).

Gender discrimination is alive and well in higher education as well. For example, the more prestigious the university, the fewer women it has on the faculty and in tenured positions (Wilson, 2004b). Those women who do get hired at major research universities often experience discrimination. At the Massachusetts Institute of Technology (MIT), the most prestigious science and engineering university in the United States, a study in the late 1990s found that women were disadvantaged not only in promotions and salary but also in research grants, appointments to important committees, types of teaching assignments, and even in the size of their research laboratories. Furthermore, not one woman had ever served as head of a science department (Rimer, 2005; Zernike, 2001). As a result of the report, several women scientists received salary increases, research funds, and larger or improved laboratories, but three years later, many women at MIT still felt marginalized (Smallwood, 2002). For example, in one engineering department, women were rarely asked to serve on search committees when new faculty were hired. The small inequities which may seem insignificant in isolation accumulate over time to create an unfair and hostile environment for women (Fassinger, 2008).

Experiences of gender discrimination at work are related to more negative relationships with supervisors, and coworkers, along with lower levels of organizational commitment and job satisfaction (Bond et al., 2004; Murray, 2003). Moreover, discrimination may affect women more negatively than men. For women, perceiving and experiencing discrimination is associated with negative psychological symptoms, such as increased anxiety and depression, and lowered self-esteem. Among men, however, the perception and experience of discrimination is unrelated to well-being (Schmitt et al., 2002). A more subtle form of discrimination is **patronizing behavior,** in which *supervisors give subordinates considerable praise while withholding valued resources such as raises and promotions.* Such behavior has a more negative effect on the performance of female workers than male workers (Vescio et al., 2005).

Let's now look at three factors that help explain why women experience discrimination in the workplace: stereotypes, cultural differences, and perceived threat.

Stereotypes. One important factor is the operation of gender stereotypes. The successful manager is seen as having male gender-stereotypic traits, such as ambition, decisiveness, self-reliance, ability to handle stress, and strong commitment to the work role. This "think manager–think male" mindset leads to the conclusion that a woman is less qualified (Cleveland et al., 2005; Diekman et al., 2004; Eagly, 2007; Ryan & Haslam, 2007). Across a wide variety of settings, women are presumed to be less competent than men and less worthy to hold leadership positions (Eagly & Carli, 2007; Mavin, 2008; Ridgeway & England, 2007). A review of studies in the United States, Germany, the United Kingdom, China, and Japan by Virginia Schein (2001) reveals that individuals in these nations, especially men, perceive men to be more qualified managers. Madeline Heilman's (2001) review of research on leadership in organizations shows that the success of female managers is devalued or is attributed to external factors rather than to the woman's competence. When women are perceived to be as competent as men, they are often viewed as violating gender stereotypes that require women to be communal. As a consequence, people, especially males, often dislike highly competent and agentic women and dismiss their contributions (Catalyst, 2007a; Eagly & Carli, 2001; Heilman et al., 2004; Masser & Abrams, 2004). Women also are more negatively evaluated when they adopt less pleasant aspects of masculine style of leadership, that is, an autocratic, angry, punitive, nonparticipative approach (Atwater et al., 2001; Brescoll & Uhlmann, 2008; Eagly & Carli, 2007; Tapia, 2008). In the words of a male corporate vice president "With a male executive there's no expectation to be nice. He has more permission to be an ass. But when women speak their minds, they're seen as harsh" (Banerjee, 2001). In order to be influential, women therefore must combine agentic qualities such as competence and directness with communal qualities such as friendliness and warmth (Eagly & Carli, 2007; Heilman & Okimoto, 2007).

Unfavorable gender stereotypes of women are most likely to operate when the evaluators are men (Duehr & Bono, 2006; Jackson et al., 2007; Uhlmann & Cohen, 2005). In one study, for example, female college students perceived female managers as high in agentic traits, but male college students did not (Deal & Stevenson, 1998). In fact, male respondents characterized female managers very negatively, viewing them as bitter, easily influenced, hasty, nervous, passive, and shy. Given that more than half of all managers and administrators are men and that men dominate higher-level management positions, many female workers are evaluated by men and, therefore, face the possibility of similar stereotype-based judgments and decisions.

Negative gender stereotypes also are more likely to operate when women perform in a male domain. In such settings, women are less likely than men to be selected as leaders, be promoted, receive positive evaluations for their leadership, or be liked (Eagly & Carli, 2007; Heilman & Haynes, 2005; Heilman & Okimoto, 2007; Kumra & Vinnicombe, 2008).

The operation of negative stereotyping when women work in male-related jobs or use masculine styles is clearly illustrated by the experience of Ann Hopkins (see Chapter 2). Ms. Hopkins was an extremely competent, high-achieving accountant who did not receive her earned promotion to partner because her employers claimed she was not sufficiently feminine. Apparently Ann Hopkins was punished for her masculine style in a male-dominated field. A recent study of thousands of women and men working in the fields of science, engineering, and technology portrays a pervasive macho culture where women are outsiders (Hewlett et al., 2008). The study reported that the culture within the fields of science, engineering, and computer science is at best unsupportive and at worst hostile to women. The statistics in the report paint a grim picture: nearly two-thirds of the women say they experienced sexual harassment on the job; over half said that in order to succeed, they had to "act like a man"; half of the women engineers lacked a mentor; and 40 percent of technology workers said they needed to be available "24/7," hours that put greater strain on working mothers than on working fathers. Given such a culture, it is not surprising that by age 40, half of the women respondents had left science, engineering, and technology for other fields, a rate twice that of their male colleagues.

Cultural Differences.   In addition to gender stereotypes, the perception of cultural differences between the evaluator and subordinate can influence discrimination in the workplace. Differences between White male managers and females or people of color can create tension that managers attempt to avoid. As one corporate manager stated: "What's important is comfort, chemistry, relationships, and collaborations. That's what makes a shop work. When we find minorities and women who think like we do, we snatch them up" (Federal Glass Ceiling Commission, 1995a, p. 28). His need to emphasize minorities and women suggests that he thinks achieving rapport with these groups is less likely to occur than rapport with other White men.

Perceived Threat.   A third factor influencing discrimination in the workplace is the perception of threat. Many White middle and upper-middle managers view the career progression of women or people of color as a direct threat to their own advancement. "If they are in, there's less of a chance for me. Why would I want a bigger pool? White men can only lose in this game. I'm endangered" (Federal Glass Ceiling Commission, 1995a, p. 31). In one study of a large Canadian federal agency, 126 male managers estimated the number of women at their level in their department and indicated their perception of whether men in management are disadvantaged relative to women (Beaton et al., 1996). As you might expect, the more women were estimated to be in a department, the greater the perception that women pose a threat to men. Similarly, women view women's gains in power more positively than men do (Diekman et al., 2004). Not surprisingly, groups that are disadvantaged by the present hierarchy are more likely to approve of social change.

What do all of the barriers against the advancement of women have in common? Consistent with one of our major themes, these obstacles are clear reflections of power differences in the workplace. Men have higher status and more resources; that is, they have higher organizational power. Although there has been progress in recent years, men continue to have the ability to control opportunities and decisions that have major impact on women (Epstein, 2007). On the positive side, however, as more and more women and people of color enter higher-status occupations and gradually advance within these fields, they will acquire greater organizational resources, thus contributing to a reduction in this power inequality.

Women as Leaders

We have seen that women face more barriers to becoming leaders than men do, especially in male-dominated fields (Eagly & Carli, 2007). How do women and men actually behave once they attain these positions? In other words, what are their leadership styles? And are women and men equally effective as leaders?

Alice Eagly (2007) has identified three types of leaderships styles: **transformational, transactional,** and **laissez-faire.** Transformational leaders *set high standards and serve as role models by mentoring and empowering their subordinates.* Transactional leaders *clarify workers' responsibilities, monitor their work, reward them for meeting objectives, and correct their mistakes.* Laissez-faire leaders *take little responsibility for managing* (Eagly, 2007).

Studies indicate that women are more transformational and that men are more transactional (Eagly & Johannesen-Schmidt, 2001; Eagly et al., 2003). Male managers are less likely than female managers to reward good performance and are more likely to pay attention to workers' mistakes, wait until problems become severe before attending to them, and be absent and uninvolved in critical times.

Recent research shows that women's more transformational style and greater use of rewards for good performance are linked to higher ratings of effectiveness (Eagly, 2007). For example, a five-year study of the leadership skills of over 2,400 female and male managers found that female managers were rated significantly better than their male counterparts by their supervisors, themselves, and the people who worked for them (Pfaff & Associates, 1999). These differences extended both to the communal skills of communication, feedback, and empowerment and to agentic skills such as decisiveness, planning, and setting standards.

Gender Differences in Salaries

> *Women, want to earn more than men? Here's how: Clean up hazardous waste! Install telecommunications lines! Otherwise, forget it.*

This clearly fictitious job ad is based on real data released recently by the U.S. Census Bureau on the salaries of hundreds of jobs (Weinberg, 2004). In the two jobs mentioned above, women earned slightly more than men, on average. For three other jobs, they earned the same: meeting planners, cafeteria workers, and construction helpers. In the other 500 jobs, women earned less.

In this section, we look at the gender gap in salaries and explore reasons for this difference.

Comparative Salaries

Although the earnings gap between women and men has declined over the last few decades, in 2006, women still earned only 77 cents for each dollar men earned

(DeNavas-Walt et al., 2007). Men who work full time earn a median annual salary of $41,386 compared with $31,858 for women (Institute for Women's Policy Research, 2008). Women of color fare even more poorly than White women (except for those with college degrees, as we'll see shortly). Among full-time workers, Black women earn 72 percent of what White men earn and Latinas earn just under 60 percent (AAUW, 2008a). Similarly, women with disabilities have lower earnings than their male counterparts and earn only 69 percent of what women in general earn (Yoder, 2000). In addition, the gender gap in pay increases with age. In 2003, women full-time workers age 55 to 64 earned 60 percent of the salary of men the same age. Women age 25 to 34, on the other hand, were paid 85 percent of the wages of men of comparable age (U.S. Census Bureau, 2006). Why are older women's earnings depressed? For one thing, older women have spent less time in the labor force than younger women. Also, many started working when employers were free to discriminate in pay between women and men doing the same work. Even now, more than 45 years after the passage of the 1963 Federal Equal Pay Act, the legacy of once-legal salary discrimination remains (Bosworth et al., 2001).

Although women of color make less than White women on average, Black women with bachelor's degrees earn slightly more than similarly educated White women (U.S. Census Bureau, 2005) What are possible reasons for these differences? For one thing, minority women, especially Blacks, are more likely to hold two jobs or work more than 40 hours per week. In addition, Black professional women tend to return to the work force earlier than others after having a child. Also, employers in some fields may give extra financial incentives to hire young Black professional women.

Given that the majority of employed women provide at least half of their families' income and that a sizable minority of families are headed by employed single women, the gender gap in wages has important implications for families. Not only is it detrimental to the financial well-being of many families, both two-parent and single-parent, but it also places more women than men at risk of poverty (AAUW, 2008a; DeNavas-Walt et al., 2004).

To get a more detailed picture of the gender gap, let's examine wage differentials within selected occupations. In 2004, the ratio of female-to-male earnings was 80 percent for software engineers, 73 percent for lawyers, 85 percent for pharmacists, and 52 percent for physicians (AAUW, 2008a; U.S. Bureau of Labor Statistics, 2005). Even in occupations that employ primarily women, women's salaries are lower than men's. In 2004, female nurses earned 87 percent as much as male nurses, and, among secretaries and administrative assistants, women earned 92 percent of what men earned (U.S. Bureau of Labor Statistics, 2005). As we saw earlier, these wage discrepancies are smaller for younger women than for older ones (Luciano, 2003).

What is the cumulative effect of the gender pay gap? Unfortunately, it is far from trivial. For the average woman with a bachelor's degree, the wage gap translates into $900,000 over her lifetime (Day & Newburger, 2002). For poor, single mothers, the earnings gap poses an additional set of problems. Many unmarried women who are employed do not earn enough to support their families. In fact, there is evidence that if single mothers were paid the same as men, who are comparable in education and number of hours worked, the poverty rate for their families would be reduced by 50 percent

(AFL-CIO & The Institute for Women's Policy Research, 1999). Instead, these women are at high risk for both welfare and homelessness.

Not surprisingly, most studies show that women believe their salaries are not commensurate with the value of their work or their abilities and experience. Regardless of their age, ethnicity, occupation, or income, women believe that the most necessary change in the workplace is better pay (Castro, 1997). Although most studies show that employed women tend to be dissatisfied with their salaries, recall that women have lower salary expectations than men do (see Chapter 9). Do you think these lower expectations can have an impact on satisfaction? Turn to Learn about the Research 10.2 for some intriguing perspectives on this question.

Reasons for Differences in Salaries

Several factors have been offered as explanations of the pay differential. In considering these reasons, keep in mind the societal power differential in the workplace.

Gender Differences in Investments in the Job.   According to the **human capital perspective,** *salaries reflect investments of human capital (e.g., education and work experience) and because of their family responsibilities, women, relative to men, reduce their investment in their education and jobs* (Bergmann, 2007). That is, women are paid less than men because they have less training and put less time into their careers. Does the evidence support this viewpoint?

We look first at the influence of educational background. If educational differences could explain salary differences, females and males with comparable levels of education should earn similar wages. The reality is that at every level of educational attainment, from high school to master's degree, Asian, Black, Latina, and White women earn less than men in the same ethnic group (U.S. Census Bureau, 2006). It is disheartening that male high school dropouts earn almost as much as women with some college experience, and that the average salary of women with a college degree is $25,000 less than the earnings of male college graduates (U.S. Census Bureau, 2006). College-educated Black women earn only $1,500 more than White male *high school* graduates (AAUW, 2002). Overall, a bachelor's degree increases a man's lifetime earnings by $1.1 million but adds only $600,000 to a woman's earnings (Day & Newburger, 2002).

What about investment of time on the job? Women spend an average of 39 hours per week at work compared to men's 41 hours (U.S. Census Bureau, 2006), and time at work does play some role in the wage gap (AAUW, 2007; Frieze et al., 2006). Another indicator of time investment is the interruption of employment. Because of their childbearing and childrearing responsibilities, women are more likely than men to temporarily leave employment (AAUW, 2008a). However, employment interruptions are becoming less common because there is a greater dependence on two incomes, thus shortening parental leaves, and because women are having fewer children. For example, a survey of senior managers (Korn/Ferry, in the Federal Glass Ceiling Commission, 1995a) found that only one-third of the women in their study had ever taken a leave, most leaves were for less than six months, and excluding interruptions for maternity, men took more leaves than women.

LEARN ABOUT THE RESEARCH 10.2

How Do Women Perceive Their Wages?

Salary expectations are closely related to perceptions of entitlement. That is, the higher the salary a person feels entitled to, the higher the salary the person expects. In addition, several scholars contend that salary satisfaction is influenced by the consistency between actual salary and salary believed to be deserved (Bylsma & Major, 1994; Jackson et al., 1992). One study (Bylsma & Major, 1994) showed that, women, compared to men, feel they deserve lower pay and are more likely to feel satisfied with objectively lower earnings. What could possibly explain women's feelings of lower pay entitlement?

According to Linda Jackson and her colleagues (1992), women perceive lower salaries as fair salaries. These researchers suggest that, as a result of differential socialization, women and men have different attitudes toward money, which affect their views of a fair wage.

Another explanation is that women and men have different perceptions of personal entitlement because they have different standards of comparison (Gutek, 2001; Hogue & Yoder, 2003). People tend to evaluate what they deserve by comparing themselves to similar others. Because women's salaries have historically been lower than men's, the standard women use to judge entitlement is lower than the standard used by men. This lower comparison standard then influences women to feel they deserve less than men feel they deserve. Consequently, they are satisfied with lower pay.

What Does It Mean?

1. Jackson and her colleagues suggest that women have lower standards than men for fair salaries. Additionally, they claim that this might be because women and men have different attitudes toward money. First, show how different views about money could lead to different perceptions of fair salaries. Then, use information from any chapters in the text to formulate an argument that either supports or refutes the assumptions of gender differences in perceived fairness and attitudes toward money.

2. Use material from any chapters in the text to frame an argument that either supports or refutes Bylsma and Major's claim that women and men have different perceptions of what they deserve and that these differences are due to different comparison standards.

3. Bylsma and Major contend that the lower comparison standards and feelings of entitlement are applicable to any less-powerful group. If this assumption is correct, can you suggest ways to counteract the influence of lower comparison standards?

So, do differences in investment help explain pay differences? According to Padavic and Reskin (2002), human capital differences were a major source of the gender wage gap in the 1970s but that influence is now less important. Studies that have taken into account all human capital differences show that these differences explain only 50 to 75 percent of the gender wage gap (AFL-CIO & The Institute for Women's Policy Research, 1999). In other words, 25 to 50 percent of the salary difference cannot be explained by differences in educational background and time commitment. Let's look at other possible factors.

Occupational Segregation.   A major factor contributing to both gender and ethnic differences in pay is the difference in jobs held by women and men and by individuals in
different ethnic groups (AAUW, 2008a; Bergmann, 2007). We saw earlier in this chapter
that women and people of color are less likely than White men to attain higher-level,
higher-paying positions. Women tend to be congregated in female-dominated occupations, and these occupations are at the low end of the salary scale. According to the
National Committee on Pay Equity, the greater the number of women or people of color
in an occupation, the lower the wages (Lipson, 2001). As an example, child-care workers
earn a lower hourly wage than car washers or parking lot attendants (Weinberg, 2004).

    Why do occupations employing mostly women pay less than those employing
mostly men? One answer is that women's occupations are devalued relative to men's
(Bergmann, 2007). In Chapter 3, we saw that people more highly value males and male-
related attributes. In the workplace this value difference gets translated into employers'
higher evaluation of male-dominated jobs and job-related skills associated with men
(Cohen & Huffman, 2003). For example, physical strength, which characterizes men
more than women, is highly valued and well compensated in metal-working jobs.
Nurturance, a trait associated with females, on the other hand, is not highly valued.
Consequently, occupations that rely on caregiving, such as child care, are on the low
end of the pay scale (Padavic & Reskin, 2002).

Salary Negotiations.   Another reason for the gender gap in salaries is that women
are less likely than men to initiate salary negotiations and are more willing to accept
whatever salary is offered by their employer (Babcock & Laschever, 2008; Williams-
Nickelson, 2007). For example, in Linda Babcock's survey of recent Carnegie Mellon
graduates who had master's degrees, only 7 percent of the women but 57 percent of the
men had negotiated their salaries. Moreover, those who negotiated raised their salaries
by an average of about $4,000 (Babcock & Laschever, 2008). Even when women do
negotiate, they don't fare as well as men. When negotiating a starting salary or a raise,
men receive an average of 4.3 percent more than the initial offer, whereas women
receive only 2.7 percent more (Eddleman et al., 2003). By failing to negotiate for their
starting salary, women will lose about $560 by age 60 (Babcock & Laschever, 2008).

    Why are women less likely to bargain when setting their starting salaries or raises?
One factor is that women are generally less comfortable than men with self-promotion.
Starting in childhood, boys are encouraged to talk about their achievements, whereas
girls are taught to be polite, compliant, modest, and not to brag (AAUW, 2007; Eagly &
Carli, 2007). This makes some women feel that negotiating brands them as overly
aggressive and pushy. In addition, women are more likely to believe that employers
will notice and reward good performance without being asked (Fogg, 2003; Katz &
Andronici, 2006). Another related factor, as we saw in Learn about the Research 10.2,
is that women often underestimate their worth. In addition, men may overestimate theirs
(Hogue et al., 2007). For example, a recent study of business students by Lisa Barron
(cited in Ellin, 2004b) found that 71 percent of the men indicated they were entitled to
more money than other job applicants, whereas 70 percent of women believed they were
entitled to a salary equal to that of other candidates. For tips on negotiating your salary,
see Table 10.1.

TABLE 10.1   Tips on Effectively Negotiating Salaries

1. Find out salary information for comparable jobs by using Websites, contacting professional associations, talking to colleagues, using your college's placement office.
2. Assess the value of your skills and work experience using the same resources mentioned in item 1.
3. During negotiations, indicate that salary is important to you.
4. Negotiate things other than salary: benefits, perks, job title, responsibilities, and so on.
5. Be persistent and willing to compromise. If the hiring individual says "no," don't simply accept this. Ask "How close can you come to my offer?"
6. Role-play salary negotiations with experienced colleagues, or job counselors at your college.

Sources: Ellin (2004b); Frankel (2004); Williams-Nickelson (2007).

Wage Discrimination.   One key factor in the gender gap in salaries is **wage discrimination,** *differential payment for work that has equal or substantially similar value to the employer* (AAUW, 2008a). Unequal pay scales were once considered justifiable by employers on the basis that women work only for "extras" or "pocket money" or that women can function with less money than men can (Padavic & Reskin, 2002). Since passage of the 1963 Federal Equal Pay Act, however, unequal pay for equal work has been illegal. Nevertheless, because wage discrimination laws are poorly enforced, equal pay legislation has not guaranteed equality (Burn, 2005). It should not be surprising, therefore, that thousands of women have filed discrimination claims (Padavic & Reskin, 2002), and settlements have been made for women employed in a range of occupations.

Another troubling finding is that *women with children earn significantly less than childless women, even when they have comparable education, work experience, and job characteristics.* This phenomenon, known as the **motherhood penalty** or maternal wall averages about a 5 percent reduction in salary per child (AAUW, 2007; Glauber, 2007; Ridgeway & England, 2007). What can account for the motherhood penalty? Researchers suggest two possibilities. One is that mothers may be less productive on the job than nonmothers because the latter can spend more of their nonemployment time in refreshing leisure, rather than in exhausting housework and child care. Alternatively, employers may discriminate against mothers in terms of job placement, promotion, or pay levels within jobs (Budig & England, 2001). In support of this view, outstanding employees who are mothers are perceived as less professionally competent than those who have no children (Cuddy et al., 2004). They also are viewed as less competent and committed than employed fathers and are held to higher performance and punctuality standards (Correll et al., 2007; Heilman & Okimoto, 2008). Once again, as we saw in Chapter 2, social roles influence gender stereotypes.

Discriminatory policies contribute to ethnic differences in pay as well as to gender differences. For example, a study conducted by the Fair Employment Council of Washington sent out pairs of Black and White women, matched in work experience and backgrounds, to apply for the same advertised jobs. Not only did more White than Black women receive job offers, but they were also more likely to be offered a higher starting salary (Bendick, in Frye, 1996). What are wages and working conditions like for women in developing nations? For a closer look, read Explore Other Cultures 10.1.

Now that you are familiar with some of the problems experienced by women in the workplace, perform the interviews in Get Involved 10.1 to gain firsthand knowledge about women's experiences with wage or promotion discrimination, and with other forms of gender-biased treatment.

Women's Job Satisfaction

Earlier in this chapter, we saw that women and men congregate in different jobs and that the most prestigious occupations employ more men than women. We also noted that women's job levels and salaries are generally lower than men's. Do these gender differences in occupational dimensions correspond to differences in job satisfaction?

EXPLORE OTHER CULTURES 10.1
Girls and Women in the Global Factory

The fact that women's work worldwide is frequently unpaid or underpaid is closely linked to women's lower power and status (Burn, 2005). In many developing countries in Africa, Central America, and Asia, thousands of women and girls as young as 8 work for low wages 15 or more hours a day, everyday, in **sweatshops**—*businesses that violate safety, wage, and child labor laws* (International Labour Organization, 2004). Health problems are common in these factories due to harsh working conditions such as poor ventilation, exposure to chemicals, and repetitive motion. Shawn Burn (2005) points out that most of the clothes, shoes, toys, and electronics purchased by North Americans were likely manufactured by women working in sweatshops in nations such as Bangladesh, Burma, China, the Dominican Republic, Haiti, Honduras, Indonesia, Guatemala, Malaysia, Mexico, Nicaragua, the Philippines, and Vietnam. In El Salvador, for example, the young female workers are paid an average of 18 cents for each $20 shirt that they sew for such companies as the Gap, J. Crew, and Eddie Bauer (Burn, 2005). In addition, thousands of women and girls are trafficked into the United States from other countries and are forced to work against their will in factories, restaurants, on farms, and in people's homes (Clarren, 2007). These women laborers seldom question their working conditions, having grown up in male-dominated households where they have learned to be subservient and dutiful (Cairoli, 2001). In addition, they often are unaware of their rights and are afraid of losing their jobs if they assert themselves. The efforts of the International Labour Organization, along with women's increasing union membership and the work of women activists around the world, have produced some progress in passing laws to improve women's work conditions, producing greater implementation of these laws, and educating women about their rights (Burn, 2005).

Gender Differences in Satisfaction

Given the existence of the glass ceiling, it is not surprising that women express less satisfaction than men about their promotional opportunities (Chiu, 1998; Lyness & Thompson, 1997). Surprisingly, however, research generally finds no gender differences in overall job satisfaction (Martinez, 2005). The fact that women are as satisfied as men suggests that many factors contribute to the overall satisfaction gained from one's job. Job and salary level are two sources. Social support from peers and supervisors is also strongly related to job satisfaction (Bond et al., 2004; Settles et al., 2007). Ellen Auster (2001) suggests that a number of other factors are associated with women's midcareer satisfaction:

1. having children, which seems to serve as a counterbalance to work pressures (see Chapter 11);
2. for ethnic minority women, developing a broad social network that crosses racial/ethnic boundaries;
3. having employment gaps (e.g. parental leave) that are voluntary and supported by the organization;
4. using flexible options, such as job-sharing and flextime (see Chapter 11);
5. having mentors in one's career;
6. networking (that is, developing relationships that have the potential to assist in one's career);
7. having balanced proportions of women and men within one's work unit;
8. experiencing lower levels of sex bias and discrimination;
9. having family-friendly organizational policies such as parental leave, day care, and fitness activities (see Chapter 11);

GET INVOLVED **10.1**
Gender-Based Treatment in the Workplace

Interview two employed women. If possible, select full-time employees, but if they are not available, include any working women, including students with part-time jobs. Ask each respondent to discuss her experiences with the following:

(1) discrimination in salary, (2) discrimination in promotion, (3) gender stereotyping by coworkers or supervisors, and (4) any other types of gender-based unfair treatment.

What Does It Mean?

1. Compare the reported experiences of your respondents with the information reported in the chapter. Describe both the differences and similarities between your findings and the material presented in the text. Give possible reasons for the differences, if any.

2. What kinds of changes do you think could be instituted so that the specific problems your respondents identified would be eliminated or greatly reduced?

Many of the clothes, shoes, toys, and electronics purchased by North Americans are manufactured by women working in Asian or Latin American sweatshops.

10. having opportunities for autonomy, creativity, training, development, and advancement within a context of job security;
11. having lower stress levels.

Factor Influencing Lesbians' Job Satisfaction

Increasing numbers of organizations have adopted antidiscrimination policies that include sexual orientation, although these are still in the minority (Button, 2001). Unfortunately, many lesbian, gay, and bisexual employees experience workplace discrimination based on their sexual orientation (Embrick et al., 2007; Ward & Winstanley, 2005). Such discrimination is related to lower levels of job satisfaction and organizational commitment and higher levels of psychological distress (Fassinger, 2008). Thus, the decision of whether or not to come out is a major concern for lesbian workers (Catalyst, 2007b). Potential benefits of coming out include the development of a positive identity, enhanced self-esteem, and self-acceptance (Kolchakian & Fassinger, 2003). On the negative side, lesbian and bisexual women fear that sexual identity disclosure might precipitate workplace discrimination. This fear is not without some basis in fact. Lesbian, gay, and bisexual individuals have been fired or passed over for promotion because of their sexual orientation (Harper et al., 2004). In fact, it is legal to do so in over 60 percent of the states in the United States (Fassinger, 2008). As one example, a college presidency offered to a woman was withdrawn when the board of trustees found out that she was a lesbian (Reid & Zalk, 2001). Lesbian women of color experience an extra burden because they risk adding homophobia to the gender or ethnic prejudice which they might already experience (Gallor, 2003). Given the possible risks of coming out in the workplace, it is not surprising that the majority of lesbians do not disclose their sexual identity at work (Ward & Winstanley, 2005).

The Older Woman Worker

After Helen Martinez's children were grown, she found employment as a secretary with a large corporation. Eventually, she was promoted to executive secretary, a position she held for several years. Helen decided to retire when her husband did. He was 65; she was 61. They did some traveling and joined a local senior citizens group. After 8 years, her husband died. Helen found that her Social Security benefits and the income from her pension were barely enough to support her. At the age of 70, she decided to go back to work for her old firm. She works 2½ days a week, running a job bank. Now 79, she does not plan to retire again unless forced to by poor health.

Dr. Marguerite Vogt, age 88, has been a dedicated molecular biologist for 70 years. Her many accomplishments include her groundbreaking research on the polio virus that led to the development of the polio vaccine. Dr. Vogt, who works at the Salk Institute in San Diego, continues to spend 10 hours a day, 7 days a week, in her laboratory. "I like it here," she says, "If I were to stay at home, I'd be bored." (Angier, 2001)

Helen Martinez is typical of many women workers who enter or reenter the labor force in later life. Marguerite Vogt, on the other hand, is an example of older women workers who have been employed continuously throughout their adult lives. In this section, we examine the varying experiences of older women workers.

Employment Rates

Labor force participation of middle-aged and older women has increased sharply over the past 35 years. Two-thirds of married women and more than 70 percent of unmarried women aged 45 to 64 now are in the labor force. Over the age of 65, about 16 percent of single women, 13 percent of married women, and 11 percent of widowed and divorced women are employed (U.S. Census Bureau, 2006). During the same 35-year period, by contrast, men have been retiring earlier. By 2005, only 84 percent of 45- to 64-year-old married men were in the workforce, compared to 91 percent in 1970. Similarly, the participation rate of married men 65 and over dropped from 30 to 21 percent (U.S. Census Bureau, 2006). As a consequence of these changes, which hold across all ethnic groups, the proportion of paid workers 45 and over who are women is higher than ever before.

Why Do Older Women Work?

Older women work for most of the same reasons as younger women. Economic necessity is a key factor at all ages. In addition, feeling challenged and productive and meeting new coworkers and friends give women a sense of personal satisfaction and recognition outside the family (Choi, 2000; Etaugh, 2008). Active involvement in work and outside interests in women's later years appear to promote physical and psychological well-being. Work-centered women broaden their interests as they grow older and become more satisfied with their lives. Employed older women have higher morale than women retirees, whereas women who have never been employed outside the home have the lowest (Perkins, 1992).

Entering the Workforce in Later Life

Many older women have been employed throughout adulthood. For some—working-class women, women of color, and single women—economic necessity has been the driving force. But for many women, a more typical pattern has been movement in and out of the labor force in response to changing family roles and responsibilities. Some women, for example, decide to reenter the labor force after their children are grown, or following divorce or the death of their spouse (Etaugh, 2008). The prospects of entering or reentering the labor force after 25 or 30 years may be daunting to some women who wonder if they have the skills to be hired. Older women should not overlook the wealth of relevant experience they have accumulated through their homemaking, childrearing, and volunteer activities.

Age Discrimination in the Workplace

Earlier in the chapter, we discussed gender discrimination in employment. As women get older, they, like men, also confront age discrimination in the workplace (Gordon & Arvey, 2004). The reasons for age discrimination and the age range during which it occurs differ for women and men. Women's complaints filed with the Equal Employment Opportunity

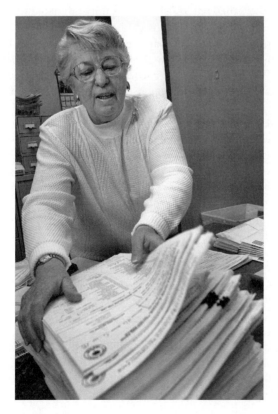

Many older women have been employed throughout adulthood, while others enter or reenter the labor force in later life.

Commission primarily concern hiring, promotion, wages, and fringe benefits. Men more often file on the basis of job termination and involuntary retirement (Etaugh, 2008).

Women also experience age discrimination at a younger age than men (Rife, 2001). This is another example of the "double standard of aging" discussed in Chapter 2. Women are seen as becoming older at an earlier age than men (Kite & Wagner, 2002; Sherman, 2001). Our society's emphasis on youthful sexual attractiveness for women and the stereotype of older women as powerless, weak, sick, helpless, and unproductive create obstacles for older women who are seeking employment or who wish to remain employed.

Changing the Workplace

We have seen that women continue to be more heavily congregated in lower-status occupations, to have limited opportunities for advancement, to earn lower salaries than men, and to be targets of biased behavior. What can be done to continue improvements in the work environment that have begun during the last few decades?

Organizational Procedures and Policies

Pay Equity.   We have seen that equal pay legislation has not eliminated the gender or ethnicity wage gaps. As long as women and men or Whites and people of color are segregated in different occupations, it is legal to pay them different wages. One way of narrowing these earnings gaps is **pay equity,** *pay policies based on workers' worth and not their gender or ethnicity* (AAUW, 2002). Pay equity would require that employees in different jobs that are similar in skill, effort, and responsibility receive comparable wages.

Affirmative Action.   Think of what affirmative action means to you. To what extent do you characterize affirmative action as a set of procedures that ensures equitable treatment of underrepresented individuals or, alternatively, as a policy that fosters preferential treatment and reverse discrimination? Affirmative action goals and procedures are highly misunderstood. Let's examine the legal conception of affirmative action as well as typical misconceptions of its meaning.

Affirmative action in employment refers to positive steps taken by a company, institution, or other type of employer to ensure that the workplace provides equal opportunity for all (Crosby, 2008). That is, affirmative action involves deliberate actions that facilitate the recruitment and advancement of historically underrepresented workers. To achieve equity, these procedures involve weighing candidates' qualifications as well as group membership. Is this definition consistent with your conception of affirmative action?

Perceptions of affirmative action are often unfavorable (Crosby, 2008). According to Jennifer Eberhardt and Susan Fiske (1998), many people attribute the achievements (e.g., job attainment, promotion) of less powerful individuals (e.g., women, people of color) to group-based preferential treatment but ascribe the accomplishments of more powerful individuals (e.g., White males) to merit. Consequently, they think that affirmative action results in reverse discrimination that hurts qualified White males in favor of unqualified women or people of color. Contrary to these misperceptions, Eberhardt and Fiske claim that the recruitment and promotion of unqualified individuals and the reliance on group membership only, without consideration of qualifications, are highly unusual and illegal practices. Furthermore, the U.S. Department of Labor (n.d.) reports that accusations of reverse discrimination comprised less than 2 percent of the 3,000 discrimination cases filed in federal court between 1990 and 1994 and that few of these were upheld as legitimate claims.

Despite criticisms of its practices, affirmative action has played an important role in reducing gender inequity in the workplace (Crosby, 2008), and there is evidence that it has done so without negatively affecting performance, productivity, or company profits (Murrell & Jones, 1996). Its success in bringing more women into the workplace and increasing the gender similarity in occupations, job levels, and salaries is likely to result in even further reductions in gender imbalances in the future.

What kind of actions would be most effective in improving the workplace for women? The exercise in Get Involved 10.2 explores this issue.

Other Organizational Procedures. Improvements for women and other underrepresented groups must also involve changes in the workplace itself. It is essential for employers to develop a work environment that values diversity and to back up this attitudinal climate with well-publicized antidiscrimination policies. Managers and other workers can be sensitized about both subtle and blatant forms of prejudice and discrimination in the work environment and can learn that the employer will not tolerate any form of discrimination. This can be accomplished through workshops aimed at increasing awareness of how stereotypes operate in evaluating and treating less powerful individuals, including women, people of color, lesbians and gays, and people with disabilities (Walsh & Heppner, 2006).

Another strategy, recommended by the Federal Glass Ceiling Commission (1995b), is for organizations to identify employees with high potential, including women and people of color, and provide them with career development opportunities, such as specialized training, employer-sponsored networks, and job assignments that expand their experience and organizational visibility. Equally important, the commission stresses, is that senior management clearly communicate throughout the organization its firm commitment to a diverse workforce.

In order to facilitate reporting of complaints, organizations also should make use of clear, well-publicized procedures for filing and evaluating claims of discrimination. Organizations that enact such procedures and ensure that claims can be filed without fear of recrimination produce more favorable work environments for women (Russell, 2006).

Strategies for Women

Although organizational efforts have more far-reaching effects, there are several actions that women can take as they either prepare themselves for employment or attempt to improve their own situation while in the workplace (Walsh & Heppner, 2006). Women can benefit from workshops or work-related social networks that arm

GET INVOLVED **10.2**

Ways to Make the Workplace Better for Women

Listed below are six factors that can contribute to an improvement in women's opportunities and experiences at work. Indicate how important you think each would be to making the workplace better for women in the future by rank ordering these from 1 to 6. Give a 1 to the factor you think would be most beneficial to improving future conditions for women, give a 2 to the factor you consider would be next most helpful, and so on. Also, ask a woman who differs from you in ethnicity to do the same.

__ 1. women's hard work
__ 2. the efforts of feminists to improve conditions for women
__ 3. women's past contributions that demonstrate their value as workers
__ 4. laws that make it less likely for employers to discriminate
__ 5. greater number of women who know how to succeed in the workplace
__ 6. a workplace that is more responsive to women's needs

What Does It Mean?

Factors 1, 3, and 5 (Set A) all point to actions on the part of working women. Factors 2, 4, and 6 (Set B) reflect adaptations resulting from political/social activism, legal mandates, and adaptations within the workplace. Determine the number of items in each set that you included among your top three items. Do the same for your other respondent.

Konek and her colleagues asked a large number of career women to rank these influences and found that these women ranked the items in Set A higher than those in Set B. The researchers interpreted this as an emphasis on individualism, a belief that one's success is due to one's own efforts.

1. Did your answers match the responses of the study's respondents? If yes, was the reason the same? That is, do you value self-reliance and hard work more than external changes that provide increased opportunities?

2. Make the same comparison for your other respondent. Do her answers reflect an emphasis on individualism?

3. Did you notice any differences between the answers given by you and your other respondent? If yes, is it possible that these differences reflect a different emphasis on individualism versus collectivism?

4. Which actions mentioned in the text but not included on this list would be effective? Additionally, are there other strategies that might be beneficial?

Source: Based on Konek et al. (1994).

them with information that can help them better understand and fight against discriminatory practices in the workplace.

A useful strategy for women who experience discrimination is to join together with others who are experiencing similar inequities. Reporting a shared problem can, in some situations, receive both attention and a commitment to institutional change. Remember how a collective effort by women in the School of Science at the Massachusetts Institute of Technology led to improvements in salary, research money, and laboratories.

Retirement

Much of what we know about the effects of retirement is based on studies of men, despite the steady increase in women in the workplace over the past 60 years. This bias reflects the assumption that retirement is a less critical event for women than for men because of women's lesser participation in the labor force and their greater involvement in family roles. But almost half of workers now are women, and retirement has equally important consequences for them (Kim & Moen, 2001b). In this section, we examine factors that influence women's decision to retire, their adjustment to retirement, and their leisure pursuits in retirement. Conduct the interviews in Get Involved 10.3 to learn about the work and retirement experiences of individual older women.

The Retirement Decision

The decision to retire depends upon many factors including health, income, occupational characteristics, and marital and family situations (Choi, 2000). When men retire,

---

GET INVOLVED **10.3**

Interview with Older Women: Work and Retirement

Interview two women, age 65 or older. It is helpful, but not essential, to know your interviewees fairly well. You may interview your mother, grandmothers, great-aunts, great-grandmothers, and so on. Keep a record of your interviewees' responses to the questions below. Compare and contrast the responses of the two women.

1. (If employed) How are things going in your job?
2. Have you reached most of the goals you set for yourself in your life?
3. When do you plan on retiring? (or when did you retire?)

4. What are some of the day-to-day activities that you look forward to after retirement (or that you've enjoyed since retirement)?
5. How will (did) retirement change you and your lifestyle?
6. How will you adjust (or how have you adjusted) to these changes?
7. In general, how would you describe your current financial situation?
8. What do you think of the Social Security system?

What Does It Mean?

1. How do the work and/or retirement experiences of these women compare with the experiences of older women reported in this book?

2. Are the financial situations of your respondents similar or different to those of older women described in the text? In what ways?

they are leaving a role that has typically dominated their adult years. They are more likely than women to retire for involuntary reasons, such as mandatory retirement, poor health, or age. Women, on the other hand, are more apt to retire for voluntary, family-related reasons, such as the retirement of one's husband or the ill health of a relative (Canetto, 2003; Hyde, 2003).

Compared to men, women arrive at the threshold of retirement with a different work and family history, less planning for retirement, and fewer financial resources (Butrica & Uccello, 2004; Carp, 2001b; Kim & Moen, 2001a, 2001b). As noted earlier, women typically experience greater job discontinuity. They may have had fewer opportunities to obtain personal career goals and may therefore be more reluctant to retire. Given their more discontinuous employment history and their employment in lower-paid jobs, women are not as likely as men to be covered by pension plans, and their Social Security benefits are lower (Hawthorne, 2007). Many older women workers with low salaries choose to continue to work as long as they can. These women may not be able to afford the luxury of retirement because of economic pressures, such as inadequate retirement income or sudden loss of a spouse. Widowed and divorced women are more apt than married women to report plans for postponed retirement or plans not to retire at all (Duenwald & Stamler, 2004). A growing number of women continue to work after their husbands retire. In 2000, 11 percent of all couples involving a man 55 or over consisted of a retired husband and an employed wife (Leland, 2004).

In addition, women who have strong work identities have more negative attitudes toward retiring than those with weaker work identities. Professional women and those who are self-employed, who presumably have strong work identities, are less likely than other women to retire early. Martha Graham, for example, danced until age 76 and then kept choreographing for another 20 years. Georgia O'Keeffe continued to paint into her nineties (Springen & Siebert, 2005). Older professional women do not often make systematic plans for their retirement, nor do they wish to do so (Etaugh, 2008; Heyl, 2004). Working-class women and men, on the other hand, are more likely to view retirement as a welcome relief from exhausting or boring labor (Gross, 2004).

We have seen why some women may delay their retirement. Why do others retire early? Poor health is one of the major determinants of early retirement. Since aging Black women and men tend to be in poorer health than aging Whites, they are likely to retire earlier (Bound et al., 1996). Health is a more important factor in the retirement decision for men than for women—especially unmarried women—among both Blacks and Whites (Etaugh, 2008). This gender difference may result from the fact that, unlike married men, married women in poor health may withdraw early from the labor force or do not enter it in the first place. Early withdrawal or nonparticipation in the workforce is enabled by having a provider husband and by societal expectations that employment is optional for women.

Women's role as primary caregiver is another factor contributing to their early retirement. Of the 2.2 million people who provide unpaid home care to frail elderly individuals, nearly three-quarters are women (Canetto, 2001). Elder care responsibilities often result in increased tardiness and absenteeism at work, as well as health problems for the caregiver (Mor-Barak & Tynan, 1995). Because most businesses do not offer work flexibility or support to workers who care for elderly relatives, more than 20 percent of women caregivers reduce their hours or take time off without pay. Of those who continue to work, more than 8 percent are forced to retire earlier than planned (Etaugh, 2008). Also, women whose husbands are in poor health are more likely to retire than women whose husbands enjoy good health (Talaga & Beehr, 1995).

Some women, of course, simply want to retire, whether to spend more time with a partner, family, or friends; to start one's own business; to pursue lifelong interests; or to develop new ones.

> *I haven't regretted retiring. I didn't quit my job through any dissatisfaction with the job or the people but I just felt that my life needed a change. I noticed that after working an eight-hour day I didn't have much steam left for a social life and fun. It's been pleasant spending these years doing what I want to do because I spent so many years accommodating myself to other people's needs and plans.* (a woman in her seventies, in Doress-Worters & Siegal, 1994, p. 183)

Adjustment to Retirement

Retirement has long been seen as an individual—primarily male—transition. But now, couples must increasingly deal with two retirements, according to Phyllis Moen and her colleagues (2001). In their study of 534 retired couples, these researchers found that retirement was a happy time for the couples. But the transition to retirement, defined as the first two years after leaving a job, was a time of marital conflict for both women and men. Wives and husbands who retired at the same time were happier than couples in which the spouses retired at different times. Marital conflict was highest when husbands retired first, perhaps because of uneasiness with the role reversal of a working wife and a stay-at-home husband. Not only does the situation pose a potential threat to the husband's role as provider, but it can also lead to disagreements over the division of household labor (Davey & Szinovacz, 2004; Mares & Fitzpatrick, 2004).

Although both genders typically adjust well to retirement, women may take longer to get adjusted (Etaugh, 2008). Newly retired women report lower morale and greater depression than newly retired men (Moen et al., 2001). Men seem to enjoy the freedom from work pressure when they retire whereas women appear to experience the retirement transition as a loss of roles. Because women are not under the same socially prescribed pressures to be employed as are men, those who *do* work, whether out of financial need or commitment to their job, may find it more difficult to stop working (Szinovacz, 1991).

For both men and women, a high level of life satisfaction in retirement is generally associated with having good health, adequate income, and a high activity level (Fitzpatrick & Vinick, 2005; Kim & Moen, 2001a,b). Financial factors may account for the fact that Black retirees have lower levels of life satisfaction than White retirees and that Black women are less satisfied than Black men (Krause, 1993). Marital status is a contributing factor as well. Married people have more positive retirement attitudes and higher retirement satisfaction than unmarried retirees. Retired women, particularly unmarried ones, are more involved with friends, family, organizations, and volunteer work than are retired men or lifelong housewives (Carp, 2001b; Dorfman, 1995; Etaugh, 2008). These social contacts are important for the life satisfaction of retired women, particularly those who are unmarried (Dorfman & Rubenstein, 1993; Reeves & Darville, 1994). For women who have never married, retirement can represent an especially significant transition. Although work assumes a greater importance in their lives than in the lives of never-married men and other women, most never-married women appear to be satisfied with retirement. Still, many develop second careers after retirement, or continue to work part-time (Rubinstein, 1994).

We shall see in Chapter 11 that multiple roles often have positive consequences for women who are employed. What is the effect of multiple role identities on older retired women? Pamela Adelmann (1993) compared Black and White women aged 60 and over who considered themselves retired only, homemakers only, or both. Women who called themselves both retired and homemakers had higher self-esteem and lower depression than women identified with only one role, especially the homemaker role. Apparently, multiple-role identities continue to benefit women even after retirement. For a closer look at the influence of major life changes such as illness, marital transition, and death of loved ones on adaptation to retirement, read Learn about the Research 10.3.

LEARN ABOUT THE RESEARCH **10.3**
Do Major Life Events Influence Adaptation to Retirement?

Many elderly adults are exposed to at least one of the following major life events requiring adjustment: divorce; major injury or illness experienced by oneself, the spouse, or other family members; the death of one's spouse, child, other family members, or friends; moving to another dwelling or another town; and moving in with a child, other family member, or friend. How do these events affect one's adaptation to retirement? Do women and men react differently to these events? To find out, Maximiliane Szinovacz and Christine Washo (1992) surveyed people who had retired from state jobs in Florida within a five-year period. Women reported experiencing more major life events than men, particularly during the period preceding retirement. Recent retirees who had been exposed to two or more major life events were found to be adapting less well to retirement. Women were much more adversely affected than men.

What Does It Mean?

1. Why do retired women experience more major life events than men?
2. Why do you think the women retirees were more affected by major life events than were men? Think about some of the factors that influence women to retire in the first place.

Leisure Activities in Retirement

Leisure or free time in later life is a fairly recent social phenomenon. In 1900, the average work week was over 70 hours. Most adults died by their mid-forties, and worked until their death. Until the Social Security Act of 1935, retirement was not a reality for most Americans. The economic safety net provided by Social Security, along with increased life expectancy, has given older Americans the opportunity for retirement and, consequently, an increased amount of free time (Stanley & Freysinger, 1995).

Gender Differences.   Women and men, regardless of age, vary in the nature of leisure activities they prefer. Elderly women are more likely than elderly men to participate regularly in social activities, baking and canning, sewing and quilting, collecting, and reading. Elderly males are more frequent participants in vigorous or moderate physical activity, yard work, spectator sports, hunting, and fishing. Elderly women and men show little difference in activities such as walking, crafts and painting, cards, and bingo (Mobily, 1992). In retirement, women are more likely than men to integrate their spheres of leisure activity, bringing together their worlds of friends, home, and hobbies (Hanson & Wapner, 1994).

Much of the research on leisure activities for the elderly has focused on middle-class Whites and has been studied largely from a male perspective. Very little is known about the context and meanings of leisure for aging, usually poor, minority women. Katherine Allen and Victoria Chin-Sang interviewed 30 retired Black women whose average age was 75. Work had largely dominated the lives of the women. Most of them had worked domestic and service jobs. When asked how their experience of leisure had

Women's leisure activities often bring together their worlds of friends, home, and hobbies.

changed since retirement, most women replied that they had none in the past. The women considered leisure time in older age to be time to relax or to work with and for others as they chose. The church and the senior center provided important contexts for their leisure activities (Allen & Chin-Sang, 1990).

Factors Affecting Leisure Activity.   One factor influencing participation in leisure activity is age. A longitudinal study of women and men at age 54 and again at 70 found that the frequency of women's leisure activity involvement was less likely than that of men to be affected by increasing age. Men's participation in all categories of leisure activity declined between the ages of 54 and 70. On the other hand, women's informal social, home, spectatorship, travel, and hobbies/crafts activities showed no change over the 16-year period. Only their participation in sports and volunteering/formal organizations declined (Stanley & Freysinger, 1995). For another look at the relationship between age and leisure activity, try the exercise in Get Involved 10.4.

Other variables affecting leisure involvement are the amount of free time, transportation, and information on and availability of leisure programs. Some elderly people (usually the poor, because they have to, and the more educated and affluent, because they want to) continue to work long after the age of 65. Additionally, caring for ill family members, a responsibility usually assumed by women, can severely curtail the amount of available free time. Women, more than men, may be affected by the availability of transportation services, information about recreational facilities and programs, and the availability of such programs. In one study, women were more likely to list the following as obstacles to recreation participation: lack of partners, family commitments, lack of information, lack of transportation, and physical difficulties (Riddick, 1993). The last of these obstacles is likely to become an even greater problem in the future. Because those over 85 (a majority of them women) are the fastest growing segment of the population, increasing emphasis will need to be given to providing and adapting leisure services for the moderately impaired or low-functioning elderly (Leitner & Leitner, 2004).

Varieties of Leisure Activity.   There are many paths to fulfilling leisure activities for women in later life. Some older women devote themselves to pursuits which they had little time for in their younger years. Think of Grandma Moses, for example, who took up painting late in life and became an internationally acclaimed artist. Then there are the increasing number of elderly adults who are taking college courses and participating in Elderhostels (Tyre, 2002). Other older women become volunteer workers in a wide variety of community settings: schools, hospitals, museums, churches, and service organizations, including the Peace Corps (Gross, 2004; Lowell, 2004). Devotion to volunteering remains strong until very old age. Twenty-three percent of people 75 and older are still volunteering, compared with only 4 percent who continue to be employed (Commonwealth Fund, 1993b). Volunteer service provides a number of benefits for the elderly, including increased life satisfaction (Beers & Jones, 2004; Morrow-Howell et al., 2003). In one recent study, older African American women who volunteered as tutors in elementary schools showed improved physical activity, social interaction, and cognitive stimulation compared to a control group of nonvolunteers (Fried et al., 2004).

GET INVOLVED 10.4

Leisure Activities of Elderly and Young Women

1. Make three columns with the following headings:

Young Women's Current Activities	Older Women's Current Activities	Older Women's Past Activities

2. Briefly interview three young adult females about their current leisure activities. List the most common activities in the first column.

3. Briefly interview three women ages 65 or older about their current leisure activities and about their leisure activities when they were in their early twenties. List their most common current activities in the second column, and their most common leisure activities when they were young adults in the third column.

What Does It Mean?

1. How do the leisure activities of the older women compare with the leisure activities of older women reported in this book?
2. How similar are the current leisure activities of the older women to those when they were young women?
3. Are the leisure activities of the older women when they were young adults more similar to their current activities, or to the activities of the young adult females you interviewed? In what way?
4. Based on this exercise, would you predict that young women's leisure activities in later life would be more similar to their present activities or to those of today's older women? Explain your answer.

Source: From Leitner and Leitner (2004). Reprinted with permission from The Haworth Press.

Whatever a woman's situation as she ages, there is usually some way in which she can serve as an **advocate,** *a person who plays an active role in making changes in her life, the lives of others, and in society* (Dowling, 2001). For example, women can and do join and actively participate in any of a number of organizations that advocate for the rights of older persons or specifically for older women. AARP (formerly The American Association of Retired Persons), with over 24 million members, is a powerful advocacy group. The Gray Panthers, a smaller, more activist group, was founded by Maggie Kuhn following her forced retirement at age 65. The Older Women's League (OWL) focuses on social policies affecting midlife and older women (Doress-Worters & Siegal, 1994). Some older women have been political and social activists for most of their lives and do not let their age slow them down. For example, Doris "Granny D" Haddock walked across the United States when she was 90 to raise awareness of finance reform. In 2004, at age 93, she undertook a 15,000 mile road trip to encourage working women to vote (Bridges et al., 2003/2004). Then there are sisters Carrie and Mary Dann, now in their 70s, who have fought for over 30 years to keep the U.S. government from seizing tribal lands (Bridges et al., 2003/2004).

Becoming an activist can transform the life of an older woman. Take the case of Rosemary Bizzell, a widow and grandmother of eight. Prior to joining OWL, she had never been involved in community affairs. Within three years, she had risen to prominence in the city council and in state government. In her words,

> *My self-image as an older woman has improved tremendously in spite of much rejection in job hunting. Apparently I was supposed to count my blessings and not expect to advance. Well, becoming involved in OWL has certainly challenged me. I cannot thank the OWLs enough for opening up a whole new world for older women. I am proud of the opportunity to be part of it.*(Doress-Worters & Siegel, 1994, p. 436)

Economic Issues in Later Life

> *After I've paid the rent, I pay the phone bill. My burial plot is all paid for, and I have just a little insurance for my grown children. Then there's my health. My doctor refused Medicaid—after 15 years—and now I have to pay him $27 out of every check. Then it takes $2.50 to do the laundry—you've got to keep your linens clean. I try to buy the cheapest things. I always make my own milk from powder. I only buy bread and chicken, and those no-name paper articles, but it still adds up. If I need clothes, I go across the street to the thrift shop. I watch for yard sales—if you see something for half a buck, there's a Christmas present. If I have 80 cents, I can go to the Council on Aging for a hot lunch. But the last two weeks of the month are always hard. You just can't make it. I'm down to my last $10, and I've got more than two weeks to go.* (a woman in her seventies, cited in Doress-Worters & Siegal, 1994, pp. 191–192)

At every age, women are more likely to live in poverty than men, and poverty rates are higher for ethnic-minority women than for their White counterparts (He et al., 2005; Lovell et al., 2008). But financial insecurity can be an even greater problem for older women, who are nearly twice as likely as older men to live in poverty (AARP, 2008; AAUW, 2006). In this section, we examine reasons for the precarious financial condition of many older women. We then turn to actions that young women can take to ensure a more secure financial future when they retire.

Poverty

What factors account for the relatively high poverty rates of older women? Their lower lifetime earnings and reduced time in the labor force adversely affect eligibility and benefits from Social Security and pensions (WISER, 2007). Women also are less likely to have accumulated income from savings and investments. The net result is that the income gap between women and men increases in retirement. U.S. women aged 65 and older have an average income of only a little more than half that of men the same age (AARP, 2008).

Another factor associated with poverty is marital status. Nearly one percent of single older women in the United States live in poverty and are poorer than their counterparts in other industrialized nations (Fleck, 2007; He et al., 2005). Formerly

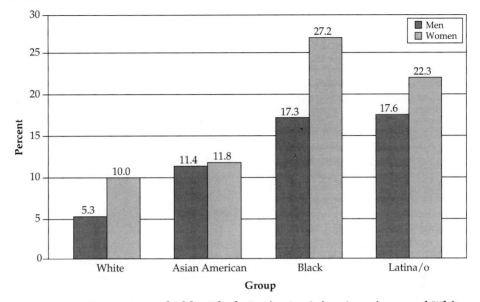

FIGURE 10.1   Percentage of Older Black, Latina/o, Asian American, and White Women and Men below the Poverty Level, 2002–2005.

Source: Institute for Women's Policy Research (2007, November).

married women (i.e., widows or divorced women) are worse off financially than older women who have never married (Arber, 2004; Canetto, 2003). Among married women, however, only 5 percent are below the poverty line (He et al., 2005; Lee & Shaw, 2008). But a married woman is just a heartbeat away from widowhood. The income from a husband's pension is usually reduced considerably or eliminated when he dies, greatly increasing his widow's risk of plunging into poverty. Since women usually marry older men and outlive them, there is a high likelihood that they will live alone on a meager income as they grow older. The costs of a husband's illness and burial may seriously deplete the couple's savings, leaving the widow in a precarious economic state (Canetto, 2003). The longer an older woman lives, the further her assets must stretch. This situation helps explain why the very oldest women have the highest poverty rates (WISER, 2002). Figure 10.1 illustrates a recent analysis of the percentage of older unmarried women and men who live below the poverty level.

For a closer look at the economic status of older women in other parts of the world, read Explore Other Cultures 10.2.

Retirement Income: Planning Ahead

It is difficult for young women to look ahead to their retirement years. However, information in this chapter makes it clear that women must take steps early in their adult life to make plans to improve their financial security in retirement. Until fairly recently,

TABLE 10.2   Retirement Planning for Women

1. Establish your own savings and checking accounts.
2. Learn about your payroll benefits, such as health insurance, pension plan, and Social Security.
3. Set up an emergency fund worth three to six months' salary.
4. Learn about financial planning by taking a course or finding a financial advisor.
5. Consider setting up an IRA.
6. Carry enough insurance to cover loss of life, health, home, and earning power.
7. Make a will.
8. Set up a **durable power of attorney,** *a document which authorizes someone to manage your financial affairs should you become incompetent.*

Sources: Fisher and Shelly (2002); Orman (2001); WISER (2007).

retirement planning and money management were thought to be best left to husbands (WISER, 2007). As a result, many women of all ages have relatively little understanding of what retirement planning entails. It is never too early to start thinking about the issues involved. See Table 10.2 for guidelines on how to start planning for retirement *now*.

First, you need to know that a secure retirement is based on a three-legged stool consisting of Social Security, pension income, and individual savings. As we have seen,

EXPLORE OTHER CULTURES 10.2

Economic Status of Older Women

In richer (i.e., developed) countries, the elderly can more easily afford to retire because of Social Security systems or pensions. In the United States and New Zealand, for example, only about 10 percent of women aged 65–69 are in the labor force (Kinsella & Velkoff, 2001). As in the United States, however, these benefits are often inadequate for women since they penalize the female-dominated activities of homemaker, part-time employee, domestic worker, and agricultural worker. In several countries, even women who have worked for much of their adult lives receive smaller pensions than men. In one study, women's benefits as a proportion of men's were 64 percent in the United States, 77 percent in France and Switzerland, and 85 percent in Sweden. However, at least five developed countries provide equal benefits for women and men: Australia, New Zealand, Great Britain, Germany, and the Netherlands (Mercer et al., 2001).

In developing nations, the economic situation for older women is much more grim than in developed countries. Social Security and pension plans are often nonexistent. Therefore, elderly women and men must continue working. In Rwanda, for example, nearly three-quarters of women between 65 and 69 remain economically active (Kinsella & Velkoff, 2001). The low status of women in developing countries can have devastating effects in later life. For example, in most of sub-Saharan Africa, women do not have land rights or property rights. A husband typically allocates his wife a plot of land to work on to produce food for the family. But if he dies, she no longer has the right to that land or even to the family's house. The land and house are taken over by the husband's family, and she often is evicted and left destitute ("Africa's Homeless Widows," 2004; LaFraniere, 2005a).

*In developing countries, elderly women and men must continue working
because there are no Social Security or pension benefits.*

all three are linked to a woman's lifetime earnings, work history, and marital status
(Lewis & Hounsell, 2007).

Social Security.   Social Security benefits are the major source of income for most
elderly women, especially those who are poor. Social Security provides more than half
of the income for women 65 years and older (AAUW, 2006) and keeps half of the
elderly women from sinking into poverty. Almost 25 percent of all older women rely
on Social Security as their *only* source of income (AAUW, 2008c). Heavy reliance on
Social Security can be a financial nightmare. For example, the average Social Security
benefit for retired women workers in 2005 was $86 a month, only slightly above the
federal poverty threshold for older adults (Lewis & Hounsell 2007).

The Social Security system, inaugurated in 1935, was designed to serve the traditional family of that time, which included a breadwinner father, a homemaker mother,
and children. Most of today's families do not fit that mold, since the majority of women
are in the labor force. Women's different work patterns mean that they are disadvantaged by a Social Security system designed to reward male work histories that often
include many uninterrupted years in a relatively high-paying job (Older Women's
League, 2002).

Ethnic minority women, who tend to be concentrated in lower-paying jobs and
to have higher unemployment rates, receive even lower benefits than White women
(Lewis & Hounsell, 2007). Because they are more likely than White women to be
employed "off the books" where benefits do not accrue, theirs are the lowest of all,
while those of White men are the highest. Moreover, many women apply for their
benefits early, at age 62, because they need the income. But doing so reduces benefits
to 80 percent of their normal amount (Feldstein, 1998).

Spousal Benefits.   A lifelong homemaker has no Social Security protection in her own name. She is eligible to receive a spousal benefit equal to half of her husband's benefit if they have been married for at least 10 years. A divorced woman is also eligible to receive half of her ex-husband's benefit if they were married for at least 10 years. If the marriage did not last 10 years, however, she receives no compensation. If a divorced woman remarries, she automatically forfeits her right to her former husband's spousal benefit. A widow receives 100 percent of her husband's benefit, although she is ineligible for any benefits until she is 60. If she applies for benefits at age 60 rather than waiting until age 65, however, her benefits are reduced (Social Security Administration, 2007).

Dual Entitlement.   Married women who are wage earners have **dual entitlement** but are, in effect, penalized as well. *They qualify for Social Security benefits based on both their own and their husband's work history.* But these women receive the higher of the two benefits to which they are entitled; they do not receive both. Dually entitled women often are eligible for higher benefits based on their husband's work record than on their own. Over 60 percent of retired, wage-earning wives draw benefits based on their husband's work records. They would have been entitled to these benefits even if they had never worked a day in their lives! Thus, the Social Security contributions that married women make as workers seem unnecessary and unfair (Feldstein, 1998; Institute for Women's Policy Research, 2005; Social Security Administration, 2007).

Pensions.   The second leg of the retirement stool—private pensions—can be an important source of income for women. But only about one-fourth of the older women have income from pensions compared with nearly half of the men (Kinsella & Velkoff, 2001). In addition, the average pension benefit paid to women is just slightly more than half that paid to men (Steinberg et al., 2008). Black and Latina women are less likely than White women to receive any pension income (Costello & Wight, 2003). Why do so few women receive pension benefits? Let us briefly examine some reasons for this.

Work Patterns.   As with Social Security, private pension plans are designed for employees who follow the traditional male work pattern of long continuous years of employment in higher-paying jobs. Women not only work less continuously and in lower-paying jobs, but they are also more likely to work at jobs that have low pension coverage (service jobs, nonunion jobs, small businesses). Moreover, women are much more likely than men to work in part-time or temporary jobs, which have little or no pension coverage (AARP, 2008; AAUW, 2008c; Warner, 2007).

Vesting.   Women's shorter job tenure also makes it more difficult for them to receive pensions because of a practice known as **vesting.** *The vesting period is the number of years of participation in a company plan that is required to be eligible for a pension.* The majority of plans require five years on the job in order to be vested. However, the average job tenure for a woman is only 4.8 years compared with 5.0 years for men (Hounsell, 2008).

Nonportability.   Women also are disadvantaged because of **nonportability** of pension plans. This means that *most traditional pension plans cannot be taken from one job to another.* This practice affects women more than men, since women are more likely to change jobs frequently. Even if a woman has worked enough years to be vested in a pension plan, she may lose a large portion of her pension benefits if she changes jobs. The reason is that the pension is based on her wages as of the date she leaves the plan. Inflation will severely reduce the value of her benefit by the time she reaches retirement age (Older Women's League, 1998).

Spousal Benefits.   As with Social Security benefits, a woman is more likely to receive spousal pension benefits as a wife, widow, or divorcée than she is from her own experience as a worker. A widow typically receives a benefit of half the amount the couple received when the husband was alive. A divorced woman, too, can receive similar survivor's pension benefits when her former husband dies. On the other hand, she does not automatically receive any of his pension benefits following divorce. Many women do not realize that if they divorce, the divorce settlement can be written to include a share of their husband's pension (Hoffman, 2002; Uchitelle, 2001).

Savings and Investments.   The third leg of the retirement stool is income from savings and investments. Today's older women have little income from savings, and their lower earnings leave them with few resources to invest (WISER, 2006b).

Women who do invest are much more cautious investors than men (Little, 2005) and are more likely to invest in conservative options such as bonds, certificates of deposit, and money-market accounts that pay lower returns than stocks. Although women tend to take fewer risks in the stock market, they do slightly better than men. Why? According to financial expert Jane Bryant Quinn (2001), women trade less, and those who trade less do better.

SUMMARY

Women's Employment Rates and Occupational Choices

- More than 60 percent of women 16 years and older, including those who are married and have young children, are employed. Economic necessity is a major reason for women's employment.
- Although the last several decades have seen a decrease, gender and ethnic segregation in the workplace continues to be highly prevalent. The most prestigious occupations are dominated by White men.

Gender Differences in Leadership and Job Advancement

- Women and people of color are less likely than White males to attain high positions in their occupations.

- Barriers that hinder women's advancement include the glass ceiling, shorter job ladders, limited availability of mentors, exclusion from informal social networks, and discrimination.
- Discriminatory treatment is due, in part, to the operation of gender stereotypes, cultural differences between managers and subordinates, and White males' perception of threat.
- Women are presumed to be less capable leaders than men. Males often express dislike for highly competent and agentic women.
- As leaders, women tend to be more transformational and less transactional than men.

Gender Differences in Salaries

- Women earn 80 percent of what men earn. The gender discrepancy is even greater between

women of color and White men. These income differences result from several factors, including gender differences in job investments, in occupations, in job levels, and in salary negotiation, as well as discrimination.
- Women tend to be dissatisfied with their incomes, although under some circumstances, they express less pay dissatisfaction than men.

Women's Job Satisfaction

- Findings regarding women's and men's overall satisfaction with their jobs are mixed, but women are less satisfied with their advancement opportunities than men are.
- One factor contributing to job satisfaction for lesbian women is the organizational climate for lesbians and gays.

The Older Woman Worker

- Increased numbers of middle-aged and older women are in the labor force. Economic necessity is a key reason.
- Employment among older women promotes physical and psychological well-being.
- Women face age discrimination in the workplace at a younger age than men.

Changing the Workplace

- Organizational strategies that can improve the workplace for women and people of color include implementation of pay equity, establishment of clearly defined affirmative action policies and procedures, and maintenance of an organizational environment characterized by sensitivity to diversity.

Retirement

- Women's retirement decisions depend on many factors.
- Women earning low wages tend to delay retirement, as do professional and self-employed women. Older women with caregiving responsibilities tend to retire early.
- The decision to retire is influenced by individual, family, economic, and occupational factors.
- The transition to retirement is a time of marital conflict, especially when husbands retire first.
- Satisfaction in retirement is associated with having good health, adequate income, high activity level, and contact with friends and relatives.
- Older women and men differ in the nature of their preferred leisure activities.

Economic Issues in Later Life

- Older women, especially minorities, are more likely than older men to be poor or near-poor.
- The poverty rate is greater for very old women and for unmarried women.
- Because women, compared with men, spend less continuous time in the workforce, and are in more low-paying jobs, their eligibility for and benefits from Social Security and pensions suffer. Women also have less income from savings and investments than do men.
- Preretirement planning in young adulthood can improve women's financial security during later life.

KEY TERMS

glass ceiling
sticky floor
maternal wall
mentor
patronizing behavior
transformational
transactional

laissez-faire
human capital perspective
wage discrimination
motherhood penalty
sweatshops
pay equity
affirmative action

advocate
durable power of attorney
dual entitlement
nonportability
vesting

WHAT DO YOU THINK?

1. The Families and Work Institute survey showed that approximately one-half of female respondents would like to work even if they had no financial need to work. What kinds of rewards, other than financial, are provided by employment? How does gender socialization affect the particular values women attach to work? Explain your answers.

2. Why do you think many people have negative impressions, including misconceptions, of affirmative action? Incorporate information about stereotypes, gender socialization, gender differences in power, and/or any other material related to this course.

3. This chapter discussed several procedures for improving the workplace for women and people of color. What other actions can be undertaken by employers or individuals in these groups to decrease gender and ethnicity inequities in the work environment?

4. How might greater gender equity in the workplace change the current social construction of gender? Would this, in turn, influence the gender acquisition of gender-related traits, behaviors, roles, and/or the career goals of future generations of females? Explain your answers.

5. Given the substantial influx of women into the labor force in the past several decades, the proportion of retired working women to life-long homemakers will continue to increase among elderly women. What are the implications of this?

6. What can be done to help ease the "feminization of poverty"?

7. What are some implications of the older woman's greater economic insecurity?

8. What is meant by the statement that elderly minority women are in "triple jeopardy." Provide and discuss examples.

IF YOU WANT TO KNOW MORE

AAUW Educational Foundation. (2003). *Women at work*. Washington, DC: Author.

Aitchison, C. (2004). *Gender and leisure: A social-cultural nexus*. New York: Routledge.

Babcock, L., & Laschever, S. (2008). *Ask for it: How women can use the power of negotiation to get what they really want*. New York: Bantam.

Ceci, S. J., & Williams, W. M. (Eds.). (2007). *Why aren't more women in science?* Washington, DC: American Psychological Association.

Chin, J. L., Lott, B., Rice, J. K., & Sanchez-Hucles, J. (Eds.). (2007). *Women and leadership: Transforming visions and diverse voices*. Malden, MA: Blackwell.

Crosby, F. J., Stockdale, M. S., & Ropp, S. A. (Eds.). (2007). *Sex discrimination in the workplace*. Malden, MA: Blackwell.

Eagly, A. H., & Carli, L. L. (2007). *Through the labyrinth: The truth about how women become leaders*. Boston, MA: Harvard Business School Press.

Hall, P. (2002). *The bonus years: Women and retirement*. New York: Miranda Press.

Hewlett, S. A. (2007). *Off-ramps and on-ramps: Keeping talented women on the road to success*. Boston, MA: Harvard Business School Press.

Johnson, J. (2002). *Getting by on the minimum: The lives of working-class women*. New York: Routledge.

Kellerman, B., & Rhode, D. L. (Eds.). (2007). *Women and leadership: The state of play and strategies for change*. San Francisco: Wiley.

Nelson, D. L., & Burke, R. J. (2003). *Gender, work, stress, and health*. Washington, DC: American Psychological Association.

Parker, P. S. (2005). *Race, gender, and leadership: Reenvisioning organizational leadership from the perspectives of African-American women executives*. Mahwah, NJ: Erlbaum.

WEBSITES

Women in the Workplace

Women's Bureau of the U.S. Department of Labor
http://www.dol.gov/wb/

Lesbians in the Workplace

Human Rights Campaign: Workplace
http://www.hrc.org/issues/workplace.asp

Pay Equity

AFL-CIO: Working Women Working Together
http://www.aflcio.org/women

Retirement and Economic Issues

AARP (formerly, American Association of Retired Persons)
http://www.aarp.org/
Gender and The Social Security System
http://www.socialsecuritymatters.org/

Balancing Family and Work

**Attitudes toward Women's Family
and Employment Roles**
    Role of Ethnicity
    Role of Motherhood
    Personal Aspirations

Division of Household Labor
    Importance of Work and Family Roles
      for Women and Men
    Housework and Child Care

Caring for Aging Parents
Leisure Time
Women's Perceptions of the Division
    of Family Labor
Explanations of the Division of Family
    Labor

Family–Work Coordination
    Parental Leave
    Balancing Family and Work

Effects of Mothers' Employment on
    Children
Effects of Women's Employment on the
    Marital Relationship
Solutions to Family–Work Balancing
    Difficulties

**Midlife Transitions in Family and Work
Roles**
    Satisfaction with Life Roles
    Regrets about Life Direction
    Making Changes
    Midlife Transitions: A Cautionary Note

The beginning of my academic career in the early 1970s coincided with early parenthood. My daughter was less than 1 year old when I started working as an assistant professor of psychology and my son was born two years later. Although I adored my children, loved being their mother, and got enormous satisfaction from my career, juggling the two roles was often stressful. To this day, I can vividly recall the anxiety and confusion that erupted when my daughter or son woke up too sick to go to their caregiver's home or when both were of school age and school was canceled because of snow (a frequent occurrence in our New England community). Also, I remember being plagued by worry that my commitment to my children was preventing me from devoting sufficient time and energy to my career and that my employment was somehow hurting my children. Interestingly, however, I don't recall ever feeling that my husband's job was damaging our children or that being a father was hindering his job advancement. (Judith Bridges)

Historically, women and men had different roles within the family. Men were the economic providers and women the caregivers and homemakers. However, the traditional family comprising children, a provider-father, and a stay-at-home mother is relatively rare today (American Psychological Association, 2004). Whereas 57 percent of children in 1960 were raised in this type of household, only about 14 percent of children are now at home full-time with their mothers (Hattery, 2001). As we saw in Chapter 10, the majority of women, including married women with children, are now employed. Not only are more married women working, but they are also working longer hours than women did a generation ago (Schnittker, 2007). Consequently, there has been a major transformation in women's roles.

Today's young women are involved in a challenging balancing act between the demands of completing their education, beginning their professional lives, finding a partner, and having children. Some women postpone or even forego marriage and/or children in favor of work or career, others leave the workplace or choose part-time employment while their children are young, and still others are combining family and full-time careers. Women balance these roles of worker, wife, and mother in different combinations over the course of their lives (Steinberg et al., 2008). Recent stories in high-profile media have asserted that highly educated mothers are "opting out" of careers to stay home with their children. In Learn about the Research 11.1, we examine the evidence for and against this assertion.

This chapter explores issues related to the coordination of women's multiple responsibilities in the domestic and employment domains. We begin with a look at attitudes toward their family and employment roles. Then we examine the impact of women's employment on the division of labor in the home as well as the challenges, costs, and benefits of balancing family and work. We explore employer resources that facilitate this coordination and consider strategies women use to manage family and work responsibilities. We conclude with a discussion of midlife transitions in family and work roles.

LEARN ABOUT THE RESEARCH 11.1

Are Women "Opting Out" of Careers?

In recent years, news headlines in national media such as the *New York Times*, the *Wall Street Journal, Newsweek*, and *Time* have claimed that mothers are increasingly "opting out" of their careers to stay home with their children (Boushey, 2005; Hewlett, 2007). Two highly visible *New York Times* articles in 2003 and 2005 making this claim used small, nonrandom samples of atypical women to prove their point. One was a group of Princeton graduates belonging to a book club, whose husbands' incomes were large enough to support them and their children. The other was a small sample of Yale first-year and senior students responding to an email survey about their future plans. Social scientists were highly critical of these anecdotal data, some of it collected from women who were years away from even joining the workforce (Barnett, 2007).

Studies based on large, representative samples show that women are, in fact, *not* opting out, and that working mothers are more likely than ever to pursue jobs and careers while raising

their families (Percheski, 2008). It is true that mothers' labor force participation rates declined between 2000 and 2004, but so did the rates of childless women, childless men, and fathers, due to a tight labor market (Boushey, 2005; Goldin, 2006). Highly educated women aged 25–45 are as likely to be in the labor force as women without children, a trend that started in the mid-1980s and continues to this day (Boushey, 2005; Percheski, 2008). In the face of this evidence, what might account for the myth that the best and brightest American women are dropping out of the workplace? Harvard economist Claudia Goldin (2006) offers the opinion that some people find it hard to believe that women can both contribute to their profession and participate meaningfully in raising children. Psychologist Rosalind Barnett (2007) similarly notes that the social construction of women as the primary caregivers seems to take precedence over the evidence that most women today intend to combine family and employment, and in fact thrive on it.

What Does It Mean?

1. How does the debate on whether women are opting out of the workforce illustrate how different research methods can lead to very different conclusions?
2. During an economic recession, women and men with and without children are more likely to leave the labor force. Why

has the focus been largely on *mothers* who leave the workforce?
3. What social and economic conditions of the past few decades have led to an increase in the percentage of women who are combining work and family roles?

Attitudes toward Women's Family and Employment Roles

Although the traditional view of the male provider–female homemaker was once seen as the expected and desirable family type, most adults today do not perceive it as ideal. In 1977, 66 percent of American adults believed that husbands should be providers and wives full-time homemakers. However, in the late 1990s, that figure dropped to 40 percent (Cherlin, 1998; Smith, 1999). In a recent nationwide survey of first-year college students, only 21 percent believed that married women should be full-time home-makers. Just 16 percent of the women endorsed that view, compared with 27 percent of the men ("This Year's Freshmen," 2005).

Role of Ethnicity

Individuals of diverse ethnic backgrounds support employment of women. In one large-scale survey (Taylor et al., 1999), Black, Mexican American, and White respondents all endorsed the belief that women and men should contribute to their family's finances. However, a sizable minority of the Black and Mexican American respondents, especially those who were recent immigrants, indicated that despite the expectation of joint financial contribution, men should maintain the primary financial responsibility for their family. Possibly, this belief is an attempt to maintain male dignity in a society that makes it difficult for ethnic minority men to fulfill their provider role responsibility (Taylor et al., 1999).

Role of Motherhood

Although North Americans tend to accept women's employment role, their approval of this role varies greatly depending on the presence and age of a woman's children. For example, a national survey (Smith, 1999) found that the overwhelming majority of adults from Canada and the United States approve of women working full-time if they have no children or if their children are gone from the home. However, they are much less supportive of full- or even part-time employment for mothers of preschoolers. Several polls in recent years have found that by ratios of 3 or 4 to 1, Americans believe that women with young children should stay at home with them (Lewin, 2001b; Sylvester, 2001). For a closer look at attitudes toward maternal employment in other industrialized nations, see Explore Other Cultures 11.1.

Personal Aspirations

As we saw in Chapter 9, most college women desire both a career and motherhood but want to discontinue their employment for a period of time during their children's early years (e.g., Bridges & Etaugh, 1996; Davey, 1998). These plans are consistent with college women's general attitudes about combining motherhood and employment. The majority of college women (and men) believe that mothers *should* stay home with their baby for at least the first few months (Novack & Novack, 1996), so it is not surprising that both college women and men evaluate mothers who resume full-time employment after a brief maternity leave more negatively than mothers who interrupt their employment until their children are in school (Bridges & Etaugh, 1995). Furthermore, college students and employed women perceive full-time employed mothers as less communal than mothers who reduce their work hours after their baby's birth (Etaugh & Folger, 1998; Etaugh & Moss, 2001).

In addition, mothers who are employed full-time are judged more harshly than nonmothers who are employed full-time. They are viewed as both less nurturing *and* less professionally competent (Etaugh & Folger, 1998). Along the same lines, mothers are judged as less likely to be hired than are nonmothers with the same credentials (an example of the "maternal wall"). Fathers, on the other hand, are judged to be as hireable as nonfathers (Fuegen et al., 2004).

Although college women tend to have negative attitudes toward early maternal employment, there is some variation in these beliefs. One key moderating factor is the employment history of young women's own mothers. White women's attitudes toward employed mothers are more positive the younger they were when their own mothers got involved in paid work (Novack & Novack, 1996), and the longer their mothers worked during their own childhood, the earlier they want to return to employment after childbearing (Bridges & Etaugh, 1996). Adolescent and young adult children

---

EXPLORE OTHER CULTURES 11.1

Attitudes toward Married Women's Employment: A Cross-cultural Perspective

Judith Treas and Eric Widmer (2000) examined attitudes toward married women's employment in 23 largely Western and industrial countries. Almost everyone agreed that married women should work, preferably full-time, before they had children. Support for full-time work was almost as high after children were grown. Mothers of preschoolers were expected either to stay home or work only part-time. Those with school-age children were expected to work only part-time. Despite this general consensus, nations also showed some difference in attitudes. Basically, three different nation clusters were identified: the "work-oriented," "family accommodating," and "motherhood-centered." The work-oriented cluster consisted of Canada, East Germany, Israel, the Netherlands, Norway, Sweden, and the United States. Whatever the life-course stage, this cluster's respondents were the least likely to recommend that married women stay home.

Unlike other clusters, they favored part-time employment for mothers of preschoolers. These countries had more egalitarian gender-role attitudes than the other nations in the study and perceived fewer conflicts between women's work and family roles. The "family accommodating" cluster (Australia, Austria, West Germany, Great Britian, Italy, Japan, New Zealand, Northern Ireland, and Russia) put less emphasis on maternal employment. They expected mothers to stay at home with preschoolers and work only part-time not only when their children reached school age, but even after they were grown. The "motherhood centered" cluster (Bulgaria, the Czech Republic, Hungary, Ireland, Poland, Slovenia, and Spain) endorsed full-time employment before and after marriage, but staying at home with preschoolers and, even to some extent, with school-age children. Not surprisingly, this group had the most traditional gender-role attitudes.

whose mothers were employed during their childhood do not feel they were neglected and actually appreciate the effort their mothers undertook to help provide for the family (Gerson, 1999). Consistent with the assumption that gender is constructed in part from interpersonal experiences, it seems likely that positive experiences with an employed mother early in their childhood lead women to consider the combination of motherhood and employment as acceptable female role choices that are not harmful to children. Try the Get Involved 11.1 activity to examine attitudes toward employed mothers at your college or university.

GET INVOLVED 11.1
How Do College Students Evaluate Employed Mothers?

For this activity, based on a study by Judith and Ann Marie Orza (1993), ask four traditional-aged (18–21-year-old) female students to read a brief description of a mother and indicate their impression of her on several rating scales. Give two participants Description A, followed by the rating scales, and two participants Description B, followed by the same scales.

Description A: Carol is a 34-year-old married woman with a 7-year-old child in second grade. Carol is employed full-time as a newspaper reporter. She worked as a reporter before her child was born and then resumed working full-time at the end of her six-week maternity leave.

Description B: Carol is a 34-year-old married woman with a 7-year-old child in second grade. Carol is employed full-time as a newspaper reporter. She worked as a reporter before her child was born and then resumed working full-time when her child was in first grade and thus in school all day.

Now indicate how much you like and respect Carol by completing the following two rating scales:

like her very little	1 2 3 4 5 6 7	like her very much
respect her very little	1 2 3 4 5 6 7	respect her very much

What Does It Mean?

Calculate the average rating for each respondent. A high score reflects a positive evaluation of the mother and a low score shows a negative evaluation. Next, average the responses given by the two respondents who read the description of the continuously employed mother (Description A) and average the scores of the two who read the paragraph about the mother who interrupted her employment (Description B).

1. As discussed in the text, this study found that mothers who take a brief maternity leave are more negatively evaluated than

those who interrupt their employment. Did you find the same results? If yes, give reasons for this finding.

2. Describe any socialization experiences that might be associated with young women's personal beliefs about a brief maternity leave versus interrupted employment.

3. This study on attitudes toward maternal employment and others presented in the text examined traditional-aged college students. Do you think that older women would have different impressions? Explain your answer.

Source: Based on Bridges and Orza (1993).

Division of Household Labor

Increasing numbers of women and men have substantial household obligations along with major work responsibilities. What is the relative importance of work and spousal and parental roles in the lives of women and men? Do the husbands of employed women contribute more to unpaid child care or housekeeping labor than the husbands of nonemployed women? Has this changed over time? Are women and men satisfied with this division of labor? We now explore these questions and others related to the division of family responsibilities.

Importance of Work and Family Roles for Women and Men

Rachel Cinamon and Yisrael Rich (2002) examined the importance of spousal, parental, and work roles for married and employed professional women and men. Among the women, 40 percent put equal emphasis on family and work, 44 percent put more emphasis on family, and just 16 percent put more emphasis on work. Men, on the other hand, were less likely to put equal emphasis on family and work (34 percent), or to put more emphasis on family (32 percent). They were more likely than women to place more emphasis on work (33 percent). Based on these results, what might you predict about the division of household labor between women and men? Read on to see if you were right.

Housework and Child Care

Studies published in the 1970s and the 1980s showed that husbands increased their household labor very little when their wives were employed. Although husbands have increased their housework participation somewhat since the 1970s and wives have reduced theirs, men's contribution to household labor in the United States, Canada, and Europe still does not equal that of women (Coyle, 2005; Hook, 2006; Thébaud, 2007; Treas & Tai, 2007).

In 1965, American women did 35 hours of housework a week, compared to 5 hours for men. By 2005, women averaged 19 hours and men averaged 11 hours (Eagly & Carli, 2007). The division of housework between women and men is more egalitarian in countries with progressive gender ideologies (Fuwa, 2004; Nordenmark, 2004). For example, men in Japan, which has relatively traditional gender attitudes, perform only 4 hours of housework a week, compared to 24 hours for men in Sweden, where gender ideologies are more egalitarian (Johnson, 2002). Among U.S. employed couples with no children, wives spend about 5 more hours per week performing housework than their husbands do, but among employed couples with children, the combined housework and child care gap jumps to 17 hours (Goldstein, 2000). Also, although research shows greater husband involvement in household and child-care duties in Black, compared to White, families (Coltrane, 2000; Lang & Risman, 2006; Sanderson & Thompson, 2002), employed women still perform a disproportionate share of these responsibilities in Black, Latina/o, and White families (Bureau of Labor Statistics, 2004). Women still assume the main responsibility for traditional female chores such as cooking, cleaning, and shopping, whereas men have more responsibility for traditional male chores such as yard work, repairs, and car maintenance (Bureau of Labor Statistics, 2004; Mannino & Deutsch, 2007). Note that the tasks done by women are generally performed one or more times per day or week, while those by men are done only periodically.

Regardless of their employment role, women continue to perform most child-care activities, including feeding and bathing young children, attending school conferences and sports events, helping with homework, disciplining, taking children to the doctor, and providing or arranging for substitute care when there is a school vacation or a child is sick (Institute for Women's Policy Research, 2007, February; Laflamme et al., 2002; Mannino & Deutsch, 2007; Maume, 2007; Milkie et al., 2002; Renk et al., 2003). In lesbian families, couples are likely to share both child care and household tasks (Bronstein, 2006; Goldberg & Perry-Jenkins, 2007).

Caring for Aging Parents

Increasing numbers of women currently fulfill another caregiving role in addition to raising their children. They provide care to aging parents and other relatives who need assistance with daily living tasks such as cooking, bathing, financial management, transportation to doctors, and shopping. As with child caregiving, women provide the majority of this care both in the United States and abroad (Broadbridge & Hearn, 2008; Brown, 2006; Hanratty et al., 2007; National Alliance for Caregiving, 2004). In fact, it has been estimated that women can expect to spend 18 years providing care to an elderly parent (Older Women's League, 2001), a period of time roughly comparable to that devoted to childrearing. Although men also provide assistance, female caregivers may spend as much as 50 percent more time providing care than male caregivers (Family Caregiver Alliance, 2003; Stephens et al., 2009).

Housework and child care are more equally shared in dual-career couples.

The average female caregiver is age 46, married, and works outside the home. We saw in Chapter 8 that she is likely to be a daughter, daughter-in-law, or granddaughter (National Alliance for Caregiving, 2004; Stephens et al., 2009). The financial impact of caring for elderly relatives is considerable. One national survey found that one-third of women decreased work hours, and nearly one-third passed up a job promotion, training, or assignment. Some women took a leave of absence or switched from full-time to part-time employment. Still others quit their jobs or retired early (Family Caregiver Alliance, 2003). Taking time out of the labor force for caregiving places an additional strain on women's retirement income. In addition, caregivers of elderly parents may also have less time for family and friends, further increasing emotional strain (National Alliance for Caregiving, 2004). No wonder caregivers of older relatives are more likely than noncaregivers to show higher levels of depression, anxiety, hostility, and stress ("Characteristics and Health," 2007; Michelson & Tepperman, 2003; Pinquart & Sörensen, 2006; Raschick & Ingersoll-Dayton, 2004).

Leisure Time

With all the time women are spending on child care, elder care, and employment, is there any time left for leisure? It is no surprise that employed mothers have less leisure time than nonemployed mothers (Bureau of Labor Statistics, 2004; Cherlin & Krishnamurthy, 2004). Feminists point out that the concept of leisure is different for women and men, with women experiencing less time for leisure in their lives than men. A common focus of women's leisure, according to this perspective, is the combining of family obligations with leisure opportunities. A woman may perceive the family's leisure as her leisure and vice versa. The home is the most common place in which women's leisure occurs. In this way, leisure can sometimes be combined with household chores. Women may often "double up" their activities and may be engaging in a leisure activity such as watching TV, while at the same time doing housework, such as cooking or mending. Thus, much of women's leisure time may be fragmented rather than occurring in large blocks of time (Bittman & Wajcman, 2000; Mattingly & Bianchi, 2003). Even after retirement, women have less time for leisure than men, since they continue to remain more occupied with domestic chores and family responsibilities (Bernard & Phillipson, 2004). For example, we saw in Chapter 8 that many older women have caregiving responsibilities for grandchildren, ailing spouses, or parents.

Women's Perceptions of the Division of Family Labor

Although women perform about two-thirds of the total household labor, only about one-third of them rate their division of labor as unfair (Wilcox & Nock, 2007). What might account for this apparent paradox between women's heavier workload and their sense of satisfaction about the allocation of domestic responsibilities? Possibly, women are satisfied because their gender socialization has led them to believe that both childrearing and household work are in women's domain. Based on this construction of the female role, there might not be any discrepancy between what they expected and what they experienced. Also, if women do not assume most of what they consider to be women's work, they might feel guilty (Mannino & Deutsch, 2007). Additionally, some women might compare their own household responsibility to that of other women, rather than to their husband's responsibility and, therefore, not see themselves as unfairly burdened.

For those women who feel that the division of domestic labor is unfair, the perceived inequity does not stem from the amount of time they spend on household tasks, but from their *share* of the total time spent by the couple (Coltrane, 2000). In research involving Asian American, Black, Latina, Middle Eastern American, and White wives, the more time wives spent relative to their husbands', the more likely they were to view the allocation of family responsibilities as unfair and to feel dissatisfied with it (Stohs, 2000; Van Willigen & Drentea, 2001). On the other hand, the more a wife believes she matters to her husband, the more likely she is to report that the division of housework is fair, regardless of the share of housework she performs (Kawamura & Brown, 2007).

Explanations of the Division of Family Labor

What factors account for women's disproportionate share of child care and housekeeping duties? This section considers three possible answers to this question.

Time Constraints.   One explanation for the unequal division of household labor is that domestic responsibilities are allocated on the basis of each spouse's time availability (Burn, 2005). Consistent with this view, full-time homemakers, who have more time available, spend more time in household tasks than do employed women (Coltrane, 2000). Furthermore, the more hours wives spend in paid work, the less time they expend in housework (Coltrane, 2000; Mannino & Deutsch, 2007).

Although spouses' time availability is to some extent related to the amount of time they invest in household labor, some patterns of domestic involvement are inconsistent with this explanation. First, even when comparing spouses with comparable work hours, mothers spend more time than fathers caring for their children (Institute for Women's Policy Research, 2007, February). Second, while researchers typically find that the more time fathers spend on their jobs, the less time they devote to parenting and housework, some studies find no relationship (Coltrane, 2000). Thus, it appears that time availability plays some role but cannot alone adequately explain the allocation of domestic responsibilities.

Relative Power.   Another possible answer to our question is that women's disproportionate share of household labor results from their lower degree of marital power (Burn, 2005; Hook, 2004). According to this view, power in marriage depends, in part, on work-related resources, such as income. The more resources one partner has in relation to the other, the greater that partner's influence (i.e., power) over the other. Because people tend to dislike household chores and to assign them little prestige, the person with the greater resources will use his or her power to limit engagement in these tasks.

Does research support this view? Evidence indicates that the discrepancy in husbands' and wives' income does not explain women's participation in household labor. Rather, what influences her share of housework is simply how much she earns herself (Gupta, 2007). For every $7,500 in additional income, a woman's share of housework declines by one hour per week. Yet, even when wives bring greater work resources to the marriage, the impact of our expectations about males' higher status, value, and power remain. For example, Veronica Tichenor (2005) found that among couples, when wives earned significantly more than their husbands, neither husbands nor wives evaluated the wife's career as more important than the husband's. Furthermore, despite their lower income, husbands maintained greater financial decision-making power. Marital power is apparently influenced by more than occupational resources; men's participation in housework doesn't increase when they have fewer occupational resources than their wives because they maintain other forms of power.

Gender Attitudes. A third explanation for the division of household labor is that the unequal distribution reflects spouses' personal beliefs about appropriate gender roles (Burn, 2005; Hook, 2004). People construct images of the roles expected for each gender, and this construction guides their own behavior. According to this view, many couples, including dual-income couples, have internalized the traditional gender beliefs that managing children and the home is *primarily* the wife's responsibility and that husbands should be the *main* financial providers. These views reflect strong societal norms, and many individuals who are socialized into these beliefs as a result of observation in the home, assigned chores, and media depictions of gender roles may be hard pressed to deviate from them.

Consistent with this explanation, men who have nontraditional attitudes about family roles spend more time doing housework than those with traditional views (Coltrane, 2000), whereas women with nontraditional beliefs spend less time in household labor than women who have traditional attitudes (Mannino & Deutsch, 2007). Moreover, college students with traditional gender-role attitudes are more likely to find it acceptable for a man to contribute less to household chores (Swearingen-Hilker & Yoder, 2002).

Family–Work Coordination

Parental Leave

Although we have seen that young college women would like to discontinue their employment for some period of time after the birth of their baby, most women do not follow that pattern. In 2005, 56 percent of married women with infants 1 year or under were employed (U.S. Census Bureau, 2007c).

The high employment rate of mothers with infants points to the importance of adequate parental leave policies, and three-quarters of Americans favor paid maternity leave (Smith, 1999). Parents would benefit from leave policies that provide sufficient time to adjust to parenthood and for biological mothers to recuperate from the physical stresses of pregnancy and birth. Incredibly, the United States is one of the few countries in the world without a national policy requiring paid parental leave. (See Explore Other Cultures 11.2.) In North America, there is a stark contrast between Canada, which provides 17 weeks of paid leave, and the United States, which has no federal legislation governing leave with pay. The only federal law mandating parental leave in the United States is the Family and Medical Leave Act, which is applicable only to workplaces with 50 or more employees, thus covering only about half of the workforce. It allows workers (women and men) who have been employed for a year in those companies to take up to 12 weeks of *unpaid* leave for medical conditions or family responsibilities, including the birth or adoption of a child (Rhode & Williams, 2007). Only 8 percent of American workers receive paid family leave benefits through policies of their employer or state (Lovell et al., 2007). Many women thus take shorter leaves than they would like to take because their families cannot afford their loss of income.

What other factors are related to the length of a woman's parental leave? Women with higher levels of education work later into their pregnancies, return to work more rapidly after giving birth, and are more likely to return to work full-time than women with less education (Downs, 2003; Johnson & Downs, 2005). Women with more nontraditional attitudes about combining employment and parenting also expect to resume working sooner (Lyness et al., 1999). In addition, pregnant women who perceive their employers as supportive of employees' family needs are more committed to their organizations and expect an earlier return to employment after childbirth (Lyness et al., 1999). Possibly, the belief that the employer is sensitive to work–family issues

EXPLORE OTHER CULTURES 11.2
Parental Leave Policies around the World

Paid and job-protected maternity leaves from work were first established over a century ago in Europe to protect the health of mothers and their newborn infants. Beginning in the 1960s, these policies have expanded to also cover paternity leaves in most industrialized nations and several developing countries (Heymann et al., 2007). The European Union adopted a minimum 14-week maternity leave in 1992 and a similar paternal leave in 1998. Most developed countries far exceed this minimum, however, providing an average of 10 months leave (Waldfogel, 2001). The Scandinavian countries have the most generous policies. In Sweden, which far outspends the United States on family benefits, parents receive 80 to 90 percent of their salary during a 14-month child-care leave (Burn, 2005). Germany provides a 14-week leave at full salary, another two years at a modest flat rate, and a third unpaid year. Of the 169 countries providing paid leaves, including many developing nations in Africa, Asia, and Latin America, 98 offer at least 14 weeks of paid leave (Heymann et al., 2007). The United States offers the briefest leave of any industrialized nation (12 weeks) and is among only four countries with an unpaid leave, the others being Liberia, Papua New Guinea, and Swaziland (Heymann et al., 2007). Why do you think the United States lags so far behind other nations?

contributes to a greater comfort at work and an expectation that family responsibilities will be accommodated.

The Wisconsin Maternity Leave and Health project (Petersen & Hyde, 2008) examined the relationship between the length of maternity leave and mothers' mental health. The researchers found that leave time was not related to psychological state unless the mother experienced other stressors, such as marital problems or an unrewarding job. If these difficulties were present, mothers with shorter leaves were more depressed 4 months after childbirth than those with longer leaves. However, by 12 months after the birth, this effect disappears (Klein et al., 1998).

How does parental leave affect women's experiences on the job? One survey of over 4,000 employed mothers (Marshall, 1998) found that more than two-thirds said their boss supported their taking time off after the birth of their baby and felt their leave did not negatively affect their career, while one-third felt they were treated less favorably after their leave and approximately half believed that people at their job view women who take maternity leave as less committed to their work. (Remember the chilly climate experienced by women faculty members with babies described in Chapter 9?) Although the evidence is mixed, it suggests that using family leave may, in fact, be harmful to one's career, and more so to the careers of men than women. Male employees who take leave for birth or care of a sick parent are viewed as less committed to the organization than men who do not take leave or women who take leave for the same reason (Wayne & Cordeiro, 2003). Stay-at-home fathers often find a stigma attached to their decision, especially when they return to the workforce after a period at home. Some employers, for example, question whether staying at home is a cover for "couldn't find work" (Dunham, 2003).

Balancing Family and Work

Do you think balancing family and work involves both costs and rewards? What kind of costs and rewards might stem from juggling these roles? Consider these questions, then try Get Involved 11.2 to explore your personal expectations of this issue.

When Judith and Claire (Bridges & Etaugh, 1996) asked White and Black college women to respond to the items presented in Get Involved 11.2, they found that these students estimated that the benefits would be greater than the costs (70 percent versus 55 percent). Although the White and Black students had similarly viewed the probability of benefits, the White students estimated a higher likelihood of negative outcomes from working during motherhood than did the Black students (58 percent versus 49 percent). The long history of Black women's employment (Hattery, 2001) may contribute to their more positive attitude toward maternal employment. These different views held by Black and White women show that these attitudes are socially constructed from individuals' experiences and do not inevitably arise from one's gender.

In actuality, the effects of performing family and work roles are complex and encompass both negative and positive aspects. Because of this, it is important to examine women's actual experiences associated with these roles as well as explanations of these outcomes.

Concerns. Previously we saw that employed women perform the bulk of child-care and housework duties. Understandably, one major concern expressed by these family–work jugglers is simply finding the time to adequately fulfill all their responsibilities (Cornelius & Skinner, 2008; DeGroot & Fine, 2003). Another primary issue is arranging for good child care. "If I did not find good care, I simply would not work"

GET INVOLVED **11.2**

What Psychological Experiences Do You Think You Will Have If You Combine Employment and Motherhood?

Pretend that you have two children and a spouse/partner employed full-time outside of the home. Given these circumstances think about the experience you might have if you, also, were employed full-time outside the home throughout your child-rearing years. For each of the following possible consequences of employment during parenthood, estimate the probability, from 0 percent to 100 percent, that you would experience that outcome.

__1. higher self-esteem
__2. more guilt feelings
__3. greater feeling of missing out on your children's developmental progress (e.g., first steps)
__4. greater self-fulfillment
__5. greater number of conflicting demands
__6. greater intellectual stimulation
__7. more resentment from spouse/partner
__8. more anxiety about your child
__9. more mental exhaustion
__10. greater degree of pride
__11. more social stimulation
__12. more irritability
__13. more conflict with your spouse/partner
__14. more approval from other people

What Does It Mean?

Items 2, 3, 5, 7, 8, 9, 12, and 13 are possible costs and items 1, 4, 6, 10, 11, and 14 are possible benefits of employment for mothers. For each of these two sets of outcomes, calculate the average probability that you reported. First, add up the eight probabilities you specified for the costs and divide that total by 8. Then, sum the probabilities you estimated for the six benefits and divide that total by 6. After calculating your averages, read the text's presentation of the findings of this study.

1. Compare your expectations to those reported in the text. Are they similar? If not, can you think of reasons for any observed differences?
2. Do you think your expectations will influence your decision about the timing of your employment and childbearing?
3. Do you think your answers would have differed if you were the other gender? Refer to material on gender attitudes and gender socialization to explain your answer.

Source: Based on Bridges and Etaugh (1996).

(Snyder, 1994, p. 166). "I honestly do think that if Lizzie hadn't been there to take her then things would have been different because I don't think I would have been able to leave her with somebody I didn't know" (Leach et al., 2006, p. 483). Comments like these illustrate the central importance that child care has for employed women. Not surprisingly, worries about child care can lead to high levels of stress for employed mothers (Leach et al., 2006; Press et al., 2006).

Costs.   As we saw earlier in this chapter, women carry most of the responsibility related to child care and housework. As might be expected, many women, especially mothers, experience **role strain,** that is, *stress stemming from one's roles.* In the words of one employed mother of an infant, "Everything was a compromise. When I went to work, I felt like I should be at home. And when I was at home, I thought I left in the middle—all of these management meetings would be going on and I'm like up and out of there. And everybody's looking around like, 'Where's she going?'" (Hattery, 2001, p. 58). Role strain can stem from **role overload,** *role demands that exceed one's available time and/or energy,* and/or **interrole conflict,** *incompatible demands stemming from two or more roles.* Role overload can occur, for example, when, after 9 hours of work and commuting, a mother does her family's laundry, cooks dinner, washes the dishes, and supervises her children's homework. Interrole conflict, on the other hand, would occur if a mother wants to attend her child's band concert at school but is expected to chair an important business meeting scheduled for the same time. Women in two-career families often experience the dual pressures of performing well in fast-paced demanding careers and performing well in their roles as mothers, increasing their risk of both physical and emotional exhaustion (Luthar & Sexton, 2004). As described by Florence Denmark and her colleagues (1996, p. 108): "Between work and family, women face competing demands on their attention. Some days they may feel they cannot accept one more demand on their time. Too much stress and they are like a balloon ready to pop." In fact, the more role strain women experience, the greater their depression and stress and the lower their job and life satisfaction (Bird & Rogers, 1998; Kossek & Ozeki, 1998).

What produces role strain? According to the **scarcity hypothesis,** *excessive role responsibilities deplete the individual's limited supply of time and energy and, consequently, can lead to stress.* When individuals have more responsibilities than they have time or energy for handling them, or when they are overwhelmed by conflicts between their role responsibilities, they can experience frustration, fatigue, or other indications of stress (Barnett, 2001; Stephens et al., 2009).

Estimates of the percentage of employed women who experience role strain vary from 40 percent (Galinsky & Bond, 1996) to over 80 percent (Carlisle, 1994). This large range is to be expected because experiences related to family–work balancing can be influenced by numerous factors, not the least of which is the presence of children. The wife and worker roles alone are not related to role overload or conflict. It is the addition of the mother role to the worker role that creates women's role strain (Evenson & Simon, 2005). Also, the less their husbands are involved in child care and domestic chores, the more likely it is that employed mothers experience stress or depression (Kiecolt-Glaser & Newton, 2001).

As we stated above, mothers' perceptions of the quality of their child-care arrangements are crucial to their level of role strain. One study showed that professional women were more likely than blue-collar or clerical women to report better child-care arrangements and to be able to forget about family issues while at work (Burris, 1991). Possibly, their greater comfort about their children's care enabled them to focus on work without the intrusion of family concerns.

Although men are not immune to either role overload or interrole conflict, considerable evidence demonstrates that employed married women are more likely than employed married men to experience both of these and that this gender difference holds across several ethnic groups, including Whites (e.g., Berger et al., 1994; Duxbury & Higgins, 1994), Blacks (McLoyd, 1993), and Latinas/os (Berger et al., 1994). The social construction of women as the major caregivers and homemakers and the construction of men as the primary providers means that women's family and work roles are parallel to one another whereas men's are simultaneous. Women's employment is seen as *additional to* their family role, whereas men's employment is viewed as *part of* their family role (Simon, 1995). This leads to greater role strain for women than for men (Kiecolt-Glaser & Newton, 2001; Sachs-Ericsson & Ciarlo, 2000).

In addition to role strain, lesbian role jugglers must face other problems as well. For example, their coworkers and/or supervisors might disapprove of their choice of intimate partner, making the work environment uncomfortable. Furthermore, the lack of insurance benefits available for lesbian families can produce economic pressures (Fassinger, 1995).

Benefits.   Juggling family and work can lead to role overload and interrole conflict, but it can also bring numerous rewards, including higher self-esteem, better physical health, greater respect from others, and greater economic security (Auster, 2001; McMunn et al., 2006; Steinberg et al., 2008). As one professional woman put it: "I feel that I would be a much better mother if I combined motherhood with employment. I think I would be more fulfilled and feel a sense of accomplishment about my life" (Granrose & Kaplan, 1996, p. 47). Indeed, even though employed mothers are more likely than unemployed mothers to report they "always feel rushed," they are also more likely to say that they get "a great deal" or "a very great deal" of satisfaction from their family lives (Cherlin & Krishnamurthy, 2004).

The benefits of multiple role coordination are explained by the **enhancement hypothesis** (Crosby & Sabbatini, 2006; Greenhaus & Powell, 2006). According to this perspective, *each additional role provides a new source of self-esteem, social approval, social status, and other benefits.* Successfully applying the different skills required by different roles can lead to achievements in many areas. Consequently, family–work balancers can develop competence in numerous domains and experience greater personal pride and fulfillment.

Aside from any rewards associated with managing several roles, women can benefit by using one role to buffer strains associated with another (Crosby & Sabbatini, 2006); that is, positive or neutral events in one role can reduce the psychological impact of negative events in another role. A 35-year-old professional woman describes it like this: "Sometimes I have a really rough day at work and then I come home and these two little kids run to the door. My older daughter says 'I'm really glad you got picked to be my mother.' Then, I forget the day at work" (Crosby, 1991, p. 103). Similarly, daughter caregivers who enjoy their jobs are less likely to feel stressed by the demands of caring for an ailing parent than are women whose work is less satisfying (Martire & Stephens, 2003).

Faye Crosby and Laura Sabbatini (2006) discuss three reasons why buffering helps psychological well-being. First, involvement in more than one role offers the opportunity for a time-out, giving the family–work juggler an opportunity to distance herself from the problems in one role while she engages in another role. For instance, a mother who is upset about her child's lack of achievement in school can put that worry aside while she focuses on her employment responsibilities.

Second, challenges in one role help put into perspective worries associated with another role. For example, a woman who is very bothered about interpersonal conflicts with her coworkers might view this problem as less important when faced with her husband's serious illness. When his health improves, she might continue to view the interpersonal tension at work as minor.

Third, buffering helps protect women's self-esteem. Positive or even neutral events in one role can help restore self-esteem that has been damaged by negative events in another role. Thus, the disappointment of not receiving a promotion at work can be mitigated by a mother's feelings of competence as she helps her child successfully cope with a bully at school.

In addition to benefits earned while juggling family and work roles, there is evidence of long-term positive outcomes. Longitudinal research shows that among women who graduated from college in the 1960s, those who combined family and employment roles in early adulthood have more positive role experiences in middle age and experience greater midlife well-being than do other women (Vandewater et al., 1997).

Gender Attitudes and Family–Work Balancing Experiences. The effects of women's employment on their well-being are related, in part, to their gender attitudes. Employed women with nontraditional attitudes report more benefits than women with traditional beliefs (Marshall & Barnett, 1993). In addition, nonemployed mothers with nontraditional views tend to be more stressed than those with traditional beliefs. For example, mothers who want to work outside the home but are full-time homemakers are more depressed than full-time homemakers who do not want to be employed (Aube et al., 2000). When women's roles are consistent with their attitudes about appropriate roles, they experience better psychological outcomes.

Ethnic Comparison of Family–Work Balancing Experiences. Few studies have examined the outcomes of family and work roles for women in different ethnic groups, but available limited research points to similar reactions in ethnically diverse women. Latina and White women managing multiple roles report comparable degrees of role overload and distress (Berger et al., 1994). A similar study of Black and White middle-class women found no ethnic differences in the personal costs or benefits related to respondents' family and work roles (Bridges & Orza, 1996).

Effects of Mothers' Employment on Children

Nearly two-thirds of infants and preschool children in the United States spend time in the care of nonparental caregivers (Federal Interagency Forum, 2007). Yet, as we have seen, most Americans do not favor employment for mothers with preschoolers. It is not scientific evidence, but rather the gender-role belief that mothers belong at home that seemingly fuels the argument against nonmaternal child care. Most researchers conclude that maternal employment and nonmaternal care are not harmful. Recent studies find no added risks for children's social, academic, or emotional development nor for their relationships with their mothers, even in infancy (Ahnert et al., 2006; Burchinal & Clarke-Stewart, 2007; Erel et al., 2000; Goldberg et al., 2008; NICHD Early Child Care Research Network, 2006; Parke & Buriel, 2006; Tran & Weinraub, 2006). Moreover, Ellen Galinsky's (2001) interviews with more than 1,000 children in grades three to twelve found that children's perceptions of their mothers' parenting abilities were not related to whether their mothers were employed.

In fact, children often benefit from maternal employment. For example, recent research found that preschoolers with employed mothers were more prosocial, less anxious, and less hyperactive than children whose mothers were not employed (Nomaguchi, 2006). Girls and boys whose mothers are employed develop less stereotypical attitudes about gender roles than children with nonemployed mothers (Goldberg & Lucas-Thompson, 2008; Riggio & Desrochers, 2005). Because the employment role is seen as an agentic role and because maternal employment frequently necessitates nonstereotypical structuring of household responsibilities among both parents and children, employed mothers often serve as less traditional role models than do full-time homemakers. Both female and male college students with employed mothers have more egalitarian views toward sharing household and child-care tasks than students with nonemployed mothers (Cunningham, 2001; Riggio & Desrochers, 2006; Treas & Tai, 2007). Moreover, sons of employed women, compared to sons of nonemployed women, perceive females as more competent, and view men as warmer and more expressive (Parke & Buriel, 2006). In addition, adolescent girls whose mothers are employed tend to have higher educational and career aspirations than their counterparts with nonemployed mothers.

High-quality child care as measured by characteristics such as appropriate group size, favorable staff-to-child ratio, teacher training, and caregivers' commitment to children provides significant emotional and intellectual benefits to children, especially those from economically disadvantaged homes (Clarke-Stewart & Miner, 2008; Fukkink & Lont, 2007; Loeb et al., 2004; Marshall, 2004; Montes et al., 2005; NICHD Early Child Care Research Network, 2004). Higher rates of educational attainment and employment, as well as lower rates of criminal offenses in adulthood, are associated with high-quality care for children from disadvantaged backgrounds (Reynolds, et al., 2007). Research also links the quality of child care to children's well-being, social-emotional development, cognitive growth, and subsequent adjustment (NICHD, Early Child Care Research Network, 2003; Phillips & Adams, 2001; Reynolds, A. J. et al., 2007; Votruba-Drzal et al., 2004).

Our exploration of the effects of maternal employment on children's development and our discussion of benefits that can result from this employment do not imply

High-quality day care provides significant emotional and intellectual benefits to children.

that full-time homemaking is detrimental to children's development. What is important is the consistency between a mother's role (employed or not employed) and her belief about the value of maternal employment for her children. Mothers whose roles match their own attitudes are likely to be more effective parents. A mother who is dissatisfied with her role is less likely to display the type of positive parenting characteristics that can lead to good outcomes for her children (Goldberg & Lucas-Thompson, 2008; Hoffman & Youngblade, 2001; Lerner et al., 2002).

Interestingly, most research on the effects of parental employment on children has focused on maternal employment. The social construction of gender leads us to conceptualize parenting within the female gender role and to frame child care as a women's issue rather than as a family issue (Newcombe, 2007b).

Effects of Women's Employment on the Marital Relationship

Since employment of wives and mothers represents a departure from traditional gender roles, does it have implications for the marital relationship? Research has produced inconsistent findings on this question. Some studies have found that women's employment increases the incidence of divorce, while others show no such effect (Sayer & Bianchi, 2000). Data from the comprehensive National Survey of Families and Households shed light on the reason for this discrepancy. Women's employment does not affect the likelihood of divorce among couples who are happily married. However, it is a factor in ending unhappy marriages (Schoen et al., 2002; Shellenbarger, 2008). Can you think of a reason for this? According to the economic opportunity hypothesis, employment gives women the resources to leave an unhappy marriage (Schoen et al., 2002). How about the alternative hypothesis that a woman's employment *causes* a rift in the marital relationship? Let us examine some of the research that relates women's employment to the marital satisfaction of both wives and husbands.

Does a man's sense of well-being depend on whether the wife views her employment as an essential aspect of her identity (as a career) versus as a means of earning a living (as a job)? Terri Orbuch and Lindsay Custer (1995) examined this question in study samples of Black and White men married to homemakers, career-oriented wives, or job-oriented wives. Their results showed that husbands of homemakers had the lowest well-being and husbands of women who viewed their employment as a job had the highest. How can these findings be explained? According to Orbuch and Custer, one possibility is that husbands of job-oriented wives benefited from the financial support of a working wife but didn't experience the potentially greater challenge to their traditional role associated with a career-oriented spouse. Consistent with this explanation, men experience a decline in well-being when their wives' share of the family household income increases (Rogers & DeBoer, 2001).

Turning to wives' feelings about their marriage, satisfaction is related, in part, to the consistency between wives' roles and their gender-related attitudes. In interviews with married women, Maureen Perry-Jenkins and her colleagues (1992) found that employed women who were uncomfortable about their work role experienced less marital satisfaction than those who wanted to work outside the home, and were less satisfied than full-time homemakers. It appears that positive outcomes can accrue from either full-time homemaking or from combining family and work. What is more important than the actual roles is the attitude toward those roles.

Studies of the relationship between women's employment and wives' and husbands' sexual satisfaction show parallel findings. Janet Shibley Hyde and her colleagues (2001) studied the association between employment and the sexual experiences of more than 500 heterosexual women and their husbands or intimate partners and found that neither women's employment status nor the number of hours they spent at work was related to their sexual frequency or enjoyment. What was important was the quality of their jobs. Both women and men reported greater sexual satisfaction when they had more rewarding work experiences. This could be because positive experiences in the workplace help couples more fully enjoy their sexual relationship or because a satisfactory sex life contributes to enjoyment on the job. Or, it may be that neither domain influences the other, but that well-adjusted adults lead lives that are satisfying in many domains, including work and sexual relationships.

Solutions to Family–Work Balancing Difficulties

As we have seen, the numerous rewards that can accrue from combining family and work roles do not eliminate the challenges jugglers face in managing their roles. What approaches can help reduce these difficulties?

Resources Offered by Employers.   Given the kinds of information we have examined in this chapter, it is not surprising that a 1999 national survey of workers in the United

States found that 97 percent said balancing family and work is their most important concern, taking precedence over issues such as job security and salary ("W/F Balance," 1999). Employers can play a key role in helping parents coordinate their family and work roles (Institute for Women's Policy Research, 2007, February). One way is by offering paid family leave, discussed earlier.

A second family-friendly benefit is flexible work hours (American Psychological Association, 2004). **Flextime,** *flexible work scheduling that allows the employee to choose the arrival and departure time within a set of possible options offered by the employer,* can enable parents to better accommodate their work hours to their children's regular child-care or school schedules and to deal with unforeseen and unscheduled family demands. One recent poll of over 750 organizations found that over half of them offered flextime and nearly one-third offered compressed work weeks (Taylor, 2001). Flexible benefits such as these are associated with increased employee retention and engagement, reduced work–family conflict, lower absenteeism, greater job satisfaction, and higher productivity (Crosby & Sabattini, 2006; Halpern, 2005; Hewitt Associates, 2008; Wang & Walumbwa, 2007), benefiting both employees and employers.

A third option that helps many workers is telecommuting. The increasing use of technology in the labor force makes this option to work from home attractive to certain types of workers (Steinberg et al., 2008). In 2006, 45 million Americans telecommuted at least some of the time. As with flextime, telecommuting is linked to greater job satisfaction, increased performance, and reduced work–family conflict (Gajendran & Harrison, 2007).

Fourth, employer help with child care would ease a major burden faced by employed parents. Child-care assistance programs can include referral services and day-care subsidies as well as on-site day care and backup day care when families have emergencies (Hartmann et al., 2007). Given that child care is one of employed parents' greatest worries, it is not surprising that workers who have child-care benefits show greater commitment to their employer (Wang & Walumbwa, 2007). Parents also need assistance with care of older children (Hartmann et al., 2007). School programs that provide before- and after-school care would not only provide safe and stimulating activities for children but would also reduce parental worry and eliminate the need for parents to coordinate multiple daily child-care arrangements.

Finally, elder-care benefits would help many of the millions of workers who provide care for older relatives. But very few companies in the United States provide such benefits, claiming that they are too costly (Gross, 2006).

Unfortunately, family-friendly benefits such as flexible hours, telecommuting, on-site child care, and elder-care benefits are offered primarily by large companies, yet the majority of workers are employed by small companies. Furthermore, companies that employ better-educated, highly skilled workers are more likely to offer these benefits than companies with a primarily unskilled labor force (AAUW Educational Foundation, 2003; Friedman, 2001; Stier, 2000).

Support from Other People.   Enlisting the aid of others to reduce their domestic burden can be effective for some family–work jugglers (Frone, 2003; Stuenkel, 2005). Women who have the financial resources can purchase services they would otherwise

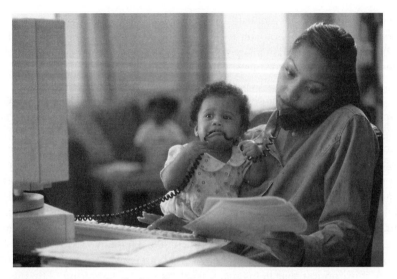

Telecommuting is a family-friendly option that allows employees to work from home.

perform, such as housecleaning and meal preparation. Other women rely on the assistance of friends, family, and neighbors (Gilbert & Kearney, 2006). Women's well-being is positively related to their husbands' greater participation in child care and housework (Galinsky & Bond, 1996; Ozer, 1995) as well as to husbands' emotional support (Matire et al., 1998). Keep in mind, however, that support from husbands or male partners is frequently construed as "help," not as a shared responsibility, underscoring the social construction of different and unequal roles for women and men.

Some employed couples work alternating shift schedules in order to share the child-care duties, thus reducing or eliminating the need for nonparental care. For a close look at the gender attitudes of some working-class couples who use this strategy, turn to Learn about the Research 11.2.

LEARN ABOUT THE RESEARCH 11.2

How Do Working-Class Couples with Alternating Shifts Reconcile Their Own Roles with Their Traditional Gender Attitudes?

We saw in Chapter 10 that nonstandard shift work often creates scheduling and logistical problems for families (Hawkins & Whiteman, 2004). Nonstandard schedules are linked with lower marital satisfaction and with marital instability, especially in families with children (Presser, 2004).

When two parents work different shifts, this creates transitions termed **tag-team parenting** (Daly, 2004), in which *parents hand off the child-care responsibilities to each other as they come and go from work.* This arrangement clearly represents a departure from traditional gender roles. How do working-class couples with alternating shifts reconcile these more fluid roles with their traditional gender attitudes?

Francine Deutsch and Susan Saxon (1998) interviewed 23 primarily White working-class couples who had traditional views about parental, marital, and employment roles. These couples alternated their work shifts, so that one parent would be able to take care of the children while the other parent worked outside the home. Husbands worked an average of 46 hours per week in blue-collar occupations, such as custodian or electrician, and wives worked an average of 33 hours per week in a variety of jobs, including clerical worker and food service worker.

Some of the couples handled the inconsistency between their gender attitudes and their own roles by modifying their traditional views. For example, one woman commented, "When we first married, Larry felt like I was there to be his wife, to do the dishes, to clean the house, to take care of the kids. Things have changed since then. We're more equals. It's more like I'm his wife, not his slave" (p. 344).

Other ways that these couples handled inconsistencies between their attitudes and roles was to maintain the belief that their family roles still reflected three core elements of traditional gender roles. First, they continued to hold the view that the husband was the primary provider.

As one husband said, "I have to work and I have to be the breadwinner" (p. 349). Second, these couples, especially the husbands, did not view the worker role as a primary aspect of the mother's identity. Instead they saw it as a financial necessity. One husband said, "I think it would be great if she could be home all the time. . . . Right now she's really got no choice because we need the money, but if it were her decision . . . and she wanted to stay home, hey great" (p. 350). Interestingly, however, many of the wives viewed their jobs as providing rewards beyond the financial one. As one woman said, "I look forward to 5:30 every night . . . taking off in the car by myself. . . . I love my job . . . I love doing the paperwork and working with numbers . . . anyone asks me a question, 9 out of 10 times I have an answer for them and it's wonderful. I feel very successful" (p. 351). Third, these mothers and fathers saw the mother as the primary caregiver. One mother stated it like this, "As much as we try to do everything 50/50, if Jimmy gets hurt and he cries, I think I'm the one that should take care of him" (p. 356).

The authors conclude that these couples were able to reconcile potentially discrepant attitudes and role behaviors by viewing their roles as constrained by financial considerations and maintaining their beliefs that the husband was still the primary breadwinner and the wife, the primary caregiver.

What Does It Mean?

1. The couples examined in this study were primarily White and working class. Do you think middle-class couples or couples with different ethnicities might reconcile their attitudes and roles in a different way? Give reasons for your answer.

2. What are the advantages and disadvantages to the children of parents who work alternating shifts?

3. What are the advantages and disadvantages to the marriage of alternating shifts?

Source: From Deutsch and Saxon (1998).

Personal Coping Strategies. Unfortunately, some women receive no support from others, or the help they do receive is insufficient. Under these circumstances, women use several personal strategies to manage their numerous role responsibilities. One is to negotiate with their employer about reduced hours (Hewlett, 2007). Women who reduce their work hours as a means of coping with family and work responsibilities report both benefits and costs. They experience greater satisfaction at home and less work–family conflict than women employed full-time. However, at work, they report less career opportunity and work success (Hewlett, 2007).

Another strategy for women is to change their perceptions of their responsibilities (Chrisler, 2008c). They might, for example, lower their standards for house-cleaning or accept the possibility that a promotion might take longer to achieve. Many employed women utilize this strategy at least to some extent. As we saw earlier in this chapter, employed mothers spend fewer hours doing housework than do stay-at-home mothers.

A third approach women use to coordinate family and work roles is to put in extra time in order to handle all role responsibilities (Chrisler, 2008c; Hewlett, 2007). This approach can be very difficult and exhausting, and women who use it are sometimes referred to as "superwomen." A fourth strategy used by college-educated women is to devote themselves to their careers and then take time off to be stay-at-home mothers while their children are young. This option, however, is seldom realistic for single mothers or for women whose husbands do not earn a sizable income (Hewlett, 2007). The exercise in Get Involved 11.3 will help you gain firsthand information about women's experiences in balancing family and work roles.

GET INVOLVED 11.3
Women's Experiences in Coordinating Family and Work Roles

Interview two employed mothers. If possible, select mothers who have children under 6. However, if not possible, interview mothers with children of any age. Ask each to talk about the following experiences: (1) time problems, if any, in performing all of their responsibilities; (2) conflicts, if any, between demands from different roles; (3) problems, if any, in arranging for child care; (4) psychological benefits they receive from their mother role; (5) psychological benefits they receive from their work role; (6) personal coping strategies and/or employer benefits that have helped them deal with any time problems, conflicts, or child-care difficulties; and (7) additional employer benefits they would find beneficial.

What Does It Mean?

1. What new information did you learn from these mothers' experiences that you did not learn from the text?
2. Did the responses of these women enhance your understanding of the costs and benefits of balancing motherhood and employment? Explain your answer.
3. Which solution do you think is the most effective for dealing with family–work balancing? Explain your answer.
4. Which family–work balancing hypothesis best accounts for these mothers' experiences? Explain your answer.

Midlife Transitions in Family and Work Roles

Many women who currently are in their middle adult years go through a process of life review, that is, an intensive self-evaluation of numerous aspects of their lives (Etaugh, 2008). They reexamine their family and occupational values and goals, evaluate their accomplishments, and sometimes consider new career directions. Some make transitions to different jobs during their middle adult years while others begin their paid work role at this point in their lives.

Because of the many societal gender-role messages encountered by the current cohort of midlife women, some have followed traditional roles early in adulthood and continued these roles at midlife while others began their adult lives committed to traditional roles but made changes in their middle adult years. Still others deviated from traditional expectations by committing themselves to careers in early adulthood. Because each of these patterns of choices can be fulfilling (Vandewater & Stewart, 1997), many women are satisfied with their life paths and, therefore, make no changes at midlife.

Given changing societal standards about appropriate roles for women, it is not surprising that one characteristic theme in the life reviews of midlife women today has been the search for an independent identity. Ravenna Helson (1992) has noted that for many women, the need to rewrite the life story in middle age is related to the lessening of the dependence and restriction associated with marriage and motherhood as children grow up. Thus, many heterosexual women attempt to affirm their own being, independent of their husbands, through graduate education, beginning a career, or switching careers (Burns & Leonard, 2005; Helson, 1992; Shellenbarger, 2004; Stewart & Vandewater, 1999). Lesbian midlife women, however, generally do not experience major transitions at midlife. Many are not mothers and have not experienced the role constraints characteristic of traditional heterosexual marriages. Therefore, they are not aiming to redefine themselves as separate from significant others. Furthermore, they already have a strong sense of self due to years of defining themselves independently of others' expectations and fighting hostility directed toward the lesbian community, and most have considered work an important part of their identity throughout their adult lives (Etaugh, 2008).

Satisfaction with Life Roles

For both young and midlife women, paid work is a significant predictor of psychological and physical well-being (Klumb & Lampert, 2004). Middle-aged women who are involved in either beginning or building their career are both psychologically and physically healthier than women who are maintaining or reducing their career involvement (Etaugh, 2008). Women who have attained the occupational goals they set for themselves in young adulthood also have a greater sense of life purpose and are less depressed in midlife than those who fall short of their expectations (Carr, 1997). Furthermore, satisfaction with work predicts a general sense of well-being: the more satisfied women are with their jobs, the better they feel in general (Vandewater et al., 1997).

For other women, being a full-time homemaker or student can be associated with the same degree of psychological well-being as that experienced by women who are employed (McQuaide, 1998). Midlife homemakers whose life goal was this domestic role have a comparable sense of purpose in life to women who aspired toward and achieved an occupational role. Not surprisingly, however, women who are involuntarily out of the workforce, due to forced early retirement or layoff, are not as satisfied with midlife as women with a chosen role (Etaugh, 2008). Thus, there are multiple routes to well-being in midlife, and it appears that a key factor influencing midlife role evaluation is not a woman's *role* per se but fulfillment of her *preferred role* (Carr, 1997).

Regrets about Life Direction

Although some midlife women are satisfied with traditional roles, others are distressed about missed educational or occupational opportunities. Some middle-class women, who as young adults devoted themselves solely to marriage and motherhood, in midlife voice regrets about their earlier traditional decisions. Abigail Stewart and Elizabeth Vandewater (1999) examined regrets experienced by women who graduated in the mid-1960s from either Radcliffe College or the University of Michigan. The concerns reported by these women centered on disappointment about not pursuing a more prestigious career, marrying before establishing a career, and not returning to work after having children. Stewart and Vandewater found that the experience of regret was not necessarily associated with reduced psychological adjustment. Instead, the crucial factor appeared to be acting on these regrets to effect life changes. The women who acknowledged their regrets and made modifications based on these regrets experienced greater psychological well-being at midlife than those who had regrets but did not use those as a basis for altering their life direction.

Why did some women have regrets but not act on them? Interestingly, it was not the presence of external constraints, such as the number of children they had, that seemed to prevent these women from making goal-related changes. Instead, it was the tendency to focus on negative life events; to engage in self-pity, moodiness, and negativism. These women seem to have been constrained by personality characteristics rather than external obstacles.

Making Changes

Pursuing a new direction at midlife involves making significant changes in one's life role during the middle adulthood years. A midlife woman who chooses to switch direction at this point must be willing to leave one long-term role (e.g., full-time homemaking or career) that has been a significant part of her identity and proceed down a new and as yet unfamiliar path. In so doing, she is leaving a role to which she has devoted considerable time and energy during her adult years. What are the psychological experiences of women who begin a work role or alter occupational directions in midlife?

Let's look at Stewart and Vandewater's (1999) sample of 1964 Radcliffe College graduates who made major work-related changes in midlife. After an earlier, full-time commitment to the traditional roles of wife and mother or to traditional female jobs, such as elementary or secondary school teaching, they realized there was a broader set of options available to them and decided to follow a new career interest or return to an earlier interest that they had never pursued. What precipitated their new directions? For many, the women's movement made a strong impact on their midlife development by raising their awareness of the increasing possibilities open for women and, consequently, changing the way they constructed the female role. As they described it: "[The] women's movement taught me that I could be a doer and not a helper" and "[The] women's movement and political activism of the '60s led me to law school" (p. 404). These women were happy about the changes they made and felt a sense of accomplishment and pride. However, despite new directions suggested by the increasing societal acceptance and encouragement of women's diverse roles, making these significant life changes was often difficult.

Midlife Transitions: A Cautionary Note

We saw in Chapter 1 that generalization on the basis of one type of respondent can lead to false conclusions about individuals who are not represented in the sample. For at least two reasons, the research findings presented here are relevant to a very specific group of midlife women and should not be extended to other females. First, the respondents in these studies reflect a homogeneous educational and socioeconomic group of women. They were primarily White, highly educated, middle-class women. The midlife experiences of women of color, less-educated women, and poor women are vastly different. Large variations in the options available to different groups of women can affect their aspirations and opportunities during both early adulthood and at midlife. For example, poor women may feel so constrained by poverty that significant change and growth at midlife appears outside the realm of possibility.

Second, the midlife experiences discussed here must be placed in their historical context. As social constructions of gender have evolved over time, women have experienced differing perceptions of their options. Women examined in the studies reported here were in their middle adult years at the beginning of the twenty-first century. Consequently, the gender-based social climate that shaped their development was different from the societal attitudes influencing the lives of future generations of midlife women. For example, today's midlife women were exposed to traditional and flexible gender role expectations at different points in their lives. Thus, it is likely that they experienced more regrets about previous traditional choices than future generations of midlife women will. Because there are greater options for young women today than there were in the 1960s and 1970s when current midlife women were making life choices, it is possible that fewer young women today will find the need to make significant revisions in their life paths during middle age (Stewart & Ostrove, 1998). Today's elderly women have also experienced different constructions of women's roles than have current midlife women. Because they were in midlife before the major societal role changes discussed here, they did not experience the career and role opportunities encountered by today's midlife women and, consequently, were not faced with decisions about major role changes.

SUMMARY

Attitudes toward Women's Family and Employment Roles

- The majority of North Americans approve of women's employment. However, only half believe mothers of preschool children should work.
- Most college women want to combine a career with motherhood. However, they would like to interrupt their employment for childrearing and believe mothers should stay home for a period of time.
- Students more negatively evaluate mothers who continue their employment after the birth of their baby than mothers who interrupt their employment for childrearing.

Division of Household Labor

- Women perform most of the child care and housekeeping duties in the family. This pattern exists across ethnic groups.
- Equal distribution of these responsibilities is more likely in dual-career than in dual-earner or traditional couples.
- Women provide the majority of care for aging parents and other elderly relatives.
- Much of women's leisure time is fragmented into small blocks of time.
- Women tend to be satisfied with the division of labor, although they perform the greater share.
- One reason may be that women have been socialized to view household duties as their domain. They might also view their obligations as fair compared to those of other women.
- Explanations for the unequal division of labor focus on time constraints, relative power, and gender attitudes. There is more support for the latter two than for the first.

Family–Work Coordination

- The United States is one of the few industrialized countries that does not have federal legislation mandating paid parental leave.
- Women take shorter parental leaves if they are more highly educated, have nontraditional

attitudes toward combining employment and parenting, and perceive their employers as family-friendly.
- Women across ethnic groups experience role strain as well as numerous benefits from multiple role juggling.
- Role strain can be explained by the scarcity hypothesis; benefits, such as self-esteem and approval from others, can be explained by the enhancement hypothesis.
- Another benefit of engaging in both family and work roles is that one role can buffer strains associated with the other.
- Most research shows no negative effects of maternal employment on children.
- Day care, even during infancy, does not hinder the child's social, academic, or emotional development. Furthermore, it can help improve school performance and reduce the social problems of children from low-income homes.
- Children with employed mothers have less stereotypical attitudes about gender roles than children of full-time homemakers.
- Positive psychological feelings, good parenting, and marital satisfaction are more likely when a woman feels comfortable about her role, whether as a full-time homemaker or employed wife and mother.
- Employer resources, such as flextime, telecommuting, and child-care assistance, and husbands' participation in family responsibilities and provision of emotional support can help women more effectively manage their multiple demands.
- Personal adjustments, such as altering one's role definitions, changing one's perceptions of responsibilities, and attempting to perform all role duties, are types of strategies women use to balance their family and work roles.

Midlife Transitions in Family and Work Roles

- Many women go through a life review during their middle adult years.
- Because those who are in midlife at the beginning of the twenty-first century were exposed to traditional gender-role expectations during

their early years and to flexible gender roles later, many women now seek an identity independent of their husband's.

■ Some midlife women are satisfied with either the career or traditional paths they have followed.

■ Other women experience regrets about previous traditional role choices, and some of these women choose to make significant changes in their life direction.

KEY TERMS

traditional couples
dual-career couples
dual-earner couples
role strain

role overload
interrole conflict
scarcity hypothesis
enhancement hypothesis

flextime
tag-team parenting

WHAT DO YOU THINK?

1. Use any theory of gender typing (see Chapter 3) to explain the current division of household labor as presented in the text. Would this theory predict a greater equality of child care and household responsibility in the future? Explain your answer.

2. Recall that women seem to be satisfied with an unequal division of household labor. Do you agree with the explanations given in the text? Are there other factors that can account for this phenomenon? Explain your answers.

3. Explain why young Black women, compared to White women, desire an earlier return to employment after they have children. Refer to material in previous chapters and any other information that addresses the question.

4. Women now experience more role strain than men. Do you think this will change in the future? Explain your answer.

5. Does any of the material in this chapter have public policy implications related to parental leave? That is, does it point to the need for new parental leave legislation? Explain your answer.

6. Discuss the origins and implications of the widespread conceptualization of parenting as a female role. What benefits to mothers, fathers, and children would stem from a more inclusive view of parenting?

IF YOU WANT TO KNOW MORE

Bianchi, S. M., Robinson, J. P., & Milkie, M. A. (2006). *Changing rhythms of American family life.* New York: Russell Sage.

Crouter, A. C., & Booth, A. (Eds.). (2004). *Work-family challenges for low-income parents and their children.* Mahwah, NJ: Erlbaum.

Dunne, G. A. (Ed.). (1998). *Living "difference": Lesbian perspectives on work and family life.* Binghamton, NY: Haworth Press.

Evans, C. (2006). *This is how we do it: The working mothers' manifesto.* New York: Hudson Street Press.

Halpern, D. F., & Murphy, S. E. (Eds.). (2004). *From work-family balance to work-family interaction: Changing the metaphor.* Mahwah, NJ: Erlbaum.

Jones, F., Burke, R., & Westman, M. (2005). *Work-life balance: A psychological perspective.* New York: Psychology Press.

Kossek, E. E., & Lambert, S. J. (2005). *Work and life integration: Organizational, cultural, and individual perspectives.* Mahwah, NJ: Erlbaum.

Mason, M. A., & Ekman, E. M. (2007). *Mothers on the fast track: How a new generation can balance family and careers.* New York: Oxford University Press.

Muhlbauer, V., & Chrisler, J. (Eds.). (2007). *Women over 50: Psychological perspectives.* New York: Springer.

Poelmans, S. A. Y. (2005). *Work and family: An international research perspective.* Mahwah, NJ: Erlbaum.

Schindler-Zimmerman, T. (Ed.). (2002). *Balancing family and work: Special considerations in feminist therapy.* New York: Haworth.

Schreider, B., & Waite, L. J. (2005). *Being together, working apart: Dual-career families and the work-life balance.* Cambridge, UK: Cambridge University Press.

Shifrin, K. (Ed.) (2009). *How caregiving affects development: Psychological implications for child, adolescent, and adult caregivers.* Washington, DC: American Psychological Association.

WEBSITES

Family–Work Coordination

Catalyst
http://www.catalystwomen.org/
Institute for Women's Policy Research
http://www.iwpr.org/
Work and Family: National Partnership
for Women and Family
http://www.nationalpartnership.org/

Work and Family Connection
http://www.workfamily.com
Sloan Work and Family Research Network
http://www.bc.edu/wfnetwork

12 Physical Health

Health Services
The Physician–Patient Relationship
Type and Quality of Care
Ethnicity, Poverty, and Health Care
Lesbian Health and Health Care
Health Insurance

Sexually Transmitted Infections (STIs)
Overview of STIs
AIDS

Reproductive System Disorders
Benign Conditions
Cancers
Hysterectomy

Osteoporosis
Risk Factors
Prevention and Treatment

Heart Disease
Gender Differences
Risk Factors
Diagnosis and Treatment
Psychological Impact

Breast Cancer
Risk Factors
Detection
Treatment
Psychological Impact

Physical Health in Later Life
  Gender Differences in Mortality
  Social Class and Ethnic Differences
  Gender Differences in Illness
  Disability

Promoting Good Health
  Physical Activity and Exercise
  Nutrition

Physical health is not just a biological phenomenon, but a social one as well. It involves both individual behaviors and lifestyles and societal systems. As viewed from a feminist perspective, women's health and health care are linked to inequalities in assessment, treatment and access to care, and lack of research on health topics relevant to women in general and to ethnic minority women (Boston Women's Health Book Collective, 2005; Moore, 2008; Robbins & Padavic, 2007; Travis & Meltzer, 2008).

In this chapter, we examine issues in women's health and health care. We start by focusing on health services. Next, we turn to sexually transmitted infections, including AIDS, which has become the scourge of adolescent and young women worldwide. We then explore disorders that tend to affect women in the middle and later years: reproductive system disorders, osteoporosis, heart disease, and breast cancer. We continue with a discussion of women's health later in life. We close by focusing on ways to promote good health.

Health Services

About 10 years ago, Dr. Annette Stanton, a professor of psychology at the University of Kansas, attended a university reception with a colleague. She reacted strongly when her colleague referred to a recent study concerning the connection between heart disease and caffeine consumption, which had received a great deal of media coverage. "I guess our hearts are safe if we have a cup of coffee," he said. "Your heart may be safe; I have no idea about the safety of my heart! That study was conducted on over 45,000 men," retorted Dr. Stanton. (adapted from Stanton, 1995, p. 3)

Only two decades or so ago, little was known about many aspects of women's health. Women were routinely excluded as research participants in large studies designed to examine risk factors and potential treatments for various diseases. Even the first clinical trials to examine the effects of estrogen on heart disease were conducted solely on men! Scientists gave two principal reasons for confining medical experiments to men. First, women's monthly hormonal fluctuations "complicated" research results. Second, potential ethical and legal problems might arise from experimenting on women who would later bear children. The "male is normative" assumption (see Chapter 2) played a role as well (Dunivin, 2006; Roth, 2003; World Health Organization, 2004).

In any case, the recognition that women have a number of poorly understood medical problems and that diseases sometimes affect women and men in radically different ways has increasingly led health researchers to include women in their studies (Pinn, 2003). Under the leadership of the first woman Director of the National Institutes of Health, Bernardine Healy, the federal government established an Office of Research on Women's Health, and the National Institutes of Health (NIH) now requires the inclusion of women in federally funded medical research (Sarto, 2004; Simon et al., 2005). However, although more women are being studied, men continue to be the focus for much of the research on the leading cause of death among both women and men: heart disease (Mikhail, 2005; Rosenfeld, 2006). Few studies include elderly women, even though heart disease is common in this group (Mosca et al., 2004). In addition, women, older people, and ethnic minorities are underrepresented in recent research on two of the leading causes of cancer death: lung cancer and colorectal cancer (Murthy et al., 2004). Other health issues of ethnic minority women also have not been sufficiently explored (Bowleg, 2008).

Basic research on the biomedical differences between women and men remains a low priority at NIH (Simon et al., 2005). Moreover, medical researchers often ignore the requirement that they analyze their data to see if women and men respond differently to a given treatment (Hayes et al., 2003). In addition, women are still underrepresented in studies to establish standard doses of new medications. This omission can have serious consequences, since women, especially older women, may have adverse effects from unnecessarily high drug doses, which have been established using male body weight as the standard (Anderson, 2005; Correa-de-Araujo, 2005).

In addition, gender biases still exist within the health-care delivery system, leading to differences in the way health professionals interact with women and men and to differences in the care women and men receive (Travis & Meltzer, 2008). In this section, we examine issues of gender discrimination in health services.

The Physician–Patient Relationship

Sexism in the physician–patient interaction is well documented. Feminist analyses describe the interaction between female patients and male physicians as paternalistic, with women patients treated as subordinates. Male physicians frequently trivialize women's experiences by interrupting female patients and making jokes in response to their concerns. Physicians may belittle women's health complaints by attributing them to psychosomatic factors (Canetto, 2003; Wilkinson & Ferraro, 2002). For example, women's pain reports are taken less seriously than men's and they receive less aggressive treatment for it. Women's pain reports are more likely to be dismissed as "emotional" and thus not "real" (Wartik, 2002). This stereotype may account for the fact that women consistently receive more prescriptions for tranquilizers, antidepressants, and anti-anxiety drugs than men (Canetto, 2003; Correa-de-Araujo et al., 2005; Curtis et al., 2004).

Sexist views of women are perpetuated in medical journal advertisements and medical textbooks as well. For example, anatomy and physical diagnosis textbooks have considerably fewer illustrations of women than men, and most of these are in the sections on reproduction (Mendelson, in Levison & Straumanis, 2002). Similarly, 80 percent of recent cardiovascular drug ads in medical journals feature men only, even though heart disease is the number one killer of both women and men. When women are included, they tend to be younger than the average age of women with heart disease. In addition, the women are predominantly White, even though the rate of heart disease for African American is 72 percent higher than for White women (Ahmed et al., 2004). Moreover, most physicians depicted in medical journal ads are White males while most of their patients are portrayed as White women. Female patients are also much more likely than male patients to be shown nude or provocatively dressed (Hawkins & Aber, 1993; Metzl, 2003). Elderly female patients often are portrayed as disheveled, disoriented, and needing medication for sleep or depression, thus perpetuating both ageist and sexist stereotypes (Hawkins & Aber, 1993).

A nationwide survey of women's health by the Commonwealth Fund (2003) found that women were twice as likely as men to report negative feelings about the patient–physician relationship. One-fourth of women (compared to 12 percent of men) reported that they were "talked down to" by a physician. Moreover, 17 percent of women (compared to 7 percent of men) have been told that a medical condition they felt they had was "all in their head." Female physicians are more likely than male physicians to establish interpersonal rapport with their patients and to provide them with information and preventive services (Bertakis & Azari, 2007; Roter et al., 2002; Street, 2002). They also spend more time with their patients and tend to focus on them as people rather than on the procedures they need (Brukner, 2003; Steinhauer, 1999). Patients of female physicians report a greater willingness to reveal personal problems such as family violence or sexual abuse (Clancy, 2000). Not surprisingly, both women and men express more satisfaction with women physicians (Bean-Mayberry et al., 2006; Bertakis et al., 2003; Coulter et al., 2000).

Type and Quality of Care

Discrimination based on gender affects not only interpersonal aspects of health care but also the type and quality of care that women receive. When we look at medical conditions that affect both women and men, women often receive less adequate care even when the severity of the condition is the same for both. As we shall see later in this chapter, women with heart disease receive less aggressive treatment than men (Chou et al., 2007; Correa-de-Araujo et al., 2006). Women are also not as likely as men to receive kidney dialysis, a kidney transplant, or knee replacement surgery (Borkhoff et al., 2008; Canetto, 2001; Clancy, 2000).

Biases exist even in childhood. For example, girls who are growing too slowly are referred to specialists only half as often as boys (Grimberg et al., 2005). While it is true that boys tend to suffer greater social consequences if they are short, slow growth may be a sign of underlying disease. The failure of doctors to send small girls for closer examination can mean that serious problems go undetected.

Ageism presents older women with a double whammy. For one thing, health-care professionals often emphasize older women's dependence, reinforcing women's perceptions of low self-efficacy and decreasing their active health-care behaviors

(Nussbaum et al., 2005). Moreover, older women are less likely than younger women to receive Pap smears, mammograms, or tests for colon cancer (Kosiak et al., 2006; "QuickStats," 2008). In addition, physicians often attribute an older woman's chronic ailments to natural aging and consequently they are less apt to treat her for these conditions. For example, despite the fact that urinary incontinence and arthritis, which affect more women than men, can be treated effectively using medical or behavioral means, many health professionals dismiss it as an inevitable part of the aging process (Nussbaum et al., 2005).

Ethnicity, Poverty, and Health Care

Women of color are more likely than White women to be poor and uninsured (DeNavas-Walt et al., 2007). Latinas have the highest uninsurance rate of any group of women (Travis & Meltzer, 2008). Because the lack of health insurance is often a financial barrier to seeking preventive health care, women of color and poor women are less likely to get the medical care they need (Halpern et al., 2008; Taylor et al., 2006). In particular, women of color have often lacked access to preventive health services such as Pap smears, mammograms, and cholesterol screening (Bolen et al., 2007; Kagay et al., 2006). Furthermore, experiences with prejudice, language barriers, or culturally inappropriate health care cause many women of color to visit the doctor less frequently than White women do (American Cancer Society, 2008b; Jacobs et al., 2005; Kilbourne et al., 2006). In the words of one lower-income Latina woman, "They don't understand my language, my culture, my issues" (Clemetson, 2002, p. A12). Breast cancer and cervical cancer screening rates are especially low among certain Latina subgroups, particularly poor Mexican and Dominican women. For many of these women, personal barriers such as fear, shame, and embarrassment prevent them from seeking screening (Behbakht et al., 2004; Garbers et al., 2003).

The good news is that the number of ethnic minority women receiving mammograms and Pap smears has risen substantially during the past decade (American Cancer Society, 2008a; Sassi et al., 2006). The bad news is that even when their insurance and income are the same, racial and ethnic minorities in the United States often receive health care of lower quality than Whites (Bowleg, 2008; Robbins & Padavic, 2007). In addition, poor women receiving Medicaid assistance have different reproductive health benefits than women with employment-based health insurance. Poor women on Medicaid receive mandated coverage of contraceptives, unlike working- and middle-class women. On the other hand, working- and middle-class women often have mandated coverage for infertility treatments which Medicaid does not cover. The result is a policy that discourages poor women from having children (Lott & Bullock, 2001).

White women use prescription medications at a somewhat higher level than women of color (National Center for Health Statistics, 2007). One possible reason for this is that ethnic minority women may be more likely to encounter special difficulties procuring and using medications. Language differences and cultural differences in perceptions of illness can make communicating with the doctor especially problematic. As a result, ethnic minority women and men may have greater difficulty following a prescribed regimen (Flores, 2006).

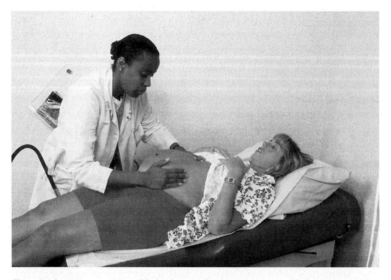

Female physicians are more likely than male physicians to establish rapport with their patients.

Lesbian Health and Health Care

There is some evidence that lesbian and bisexual women may be at increased risk for certain health problems. These risks do *not*, however, arise simply from having a particular sexual orientation. Rather, certain risks may be more prevalent among lesbians because of lifestyle factors. For example, lesbian and bisexual women may face heightened risks of breast and ovarian cancer because they are less likely than heterosexual women to experience the hormonal changes associated with pregnancy and because they are more likely to smoke and consume alcohol (Case et al., 2004; Mercer et al., 2007; Sandfort et al., 2006).

The social stigma attached to homosexuality also contributes to elevated health risks for lesbians by reducing access to health care (Bauer & Wayne, 2005; Corliss et al., 2007; Heck et al., 2006). Surveys have found that many lesbians avoid going to the doctor for routine checkups—especially gynecological exams—because they feel uncomfortable talking about issues that may reveal their sexual orientation and consequently elicit negative reactions from the physician (Clark et al., 2003; Marrazzo, 2004; Seaver et al., 2008). In the words of one young woman, "If you lie, then you may not get the information you need to take care of yourself. And if you come out, your doctor may become really uncomfortable with you" (Thompson, 1999, p. A25). Lesbians also tend to limit their visits to doctors because they are less likely to have health insurance, since lesbians often cannot share spousal benefits (Heck et al., 2006). Even for lesbians who do have coverage, managed health-care plans often limit women's ability to choose lesbian-friendly health-care providers. The reduced access to health care that results from fear of discrimination and from financial barriers puts lesbians at greater risk for preventable illnesses and makes them more likely to die from diseases that are treatable if detected early

(Bradford & White, 2000; "Lesbian Community," 2004; Mayer et al., 2008; Sved, 2001). Surveys of the health-care choices of lesbians have found preferences for care that is comprehensive, person-centered, and inclusive of them as lesbian (Seaver et al., 2008).

Health Insurance

We have seen that women of color are more likely than White women to lack health insurance. Another group with a high rate of uninsurance are women in their late fifties and early sixties. Millions of these midlife women do not receive employer-based health insurance and are not yet eligible for Medicare benefits, which begin at age 65. Currently, one in seven women age 60–64 has no health insurance (OWL, 2007).

Let us now look at the kinds of insurance programs available to U.S. adults and see how they affect women. These can be grouped into government plans (Medicare, Medicaid) and private plans (fee-for-service and managed care).

Government Plans. **Medicare,** established in 1965, is the *federal program designed to provide medical care for those who are over 65 or permanently disabled, regardless of income.* Medicare covers less than half of medical costs and it does not cover most long-term care, or home and supportive care. These limitations affect women disproportionately because they have more, and more complex, medical conditions than men. In addition, some physicians do not accept Medicare patients because the reimbursement is low (AARP, 2005b; Iglehart, 2002; Jacoby, 2002).

Medicaid, established the same year as Medicare, is a *combined state and federal program designed to provide medical care for the needy of any age.* As with Medicare, many health-care providers refuse to see Medicaid recipients because of low reimbursement rates (Iglehart, 2003). These patients have no choice but to rely on clinics and emergency rooms.

Individuals with high medical bills who do not qualify for Medicaid *ultimately become eligible once they have depleted most of their financial resources and assets.* This process, called **spending down,** is most common among residents of nursing homes, most of whom are women (Beers & Jones, 2004; Meyer & Bellas, 1995).

Women rely more heavily than men on both Medicaid and Medicare because they are more likely to be poor and because they live longer (Older Women's League, 2000). Women are less likely than men to have insurance through their own employer since they are more likely to work in temporary or part-time jobs or in occupations that do not provide health insurance benefits. A woman who is covered under a spouse's plan risks losing coverage in the event of divorce, death, or the spouse's retirement (Older Women's League, 2004).

Private Insurance Plans. The majority of Americans are covered by private health insurance provided by their own employer or the employer of a family member. One of the two types of private plans is **fee-for-service insurance** (also known as indemnity insurance). *The insurer pays part of the cost (usually 80 percent) for specified services, including hospitalization (up to a certain limit) and diagnostic services, but not preventive care.* The second type of private insurance is **managed care,** which has become the leading means of financing health care (AARP, 2002a,b). Managed care *provides services to members for a flat fee and emphasizes preventive care and early detection of disease more than fee-for-service plans do.* Health maintenance organizations (HMOs) and preferred provider organizations (PPOs) are the most common types of managed care (Torpy, 2007a). Providing inexpensive screening procedures such as mammograms and Pap tests makes the services affordable for many women. It is therefore not surprising that women in managed care are more likely than those in fee-for-service plans to receive Pap smears and colon cancer screening (Katzenstein, 1999). Moreover, women over 65 in HMOs are more likely than fee-for-service patients to have had their cancers diagnosed at an earlier stage (Riley et al., 1999). However, managed care often limits access to specialists and reduces treatment options for many women, particularly older women who frequently have many chronic ailments requiring treatment by different specialists. Limited finances often prevent elderly women from seeing the physicians or purchasing the medications not covered by their managed care insurance (AARP, 2002a,b; Older Women's League, 2004). Moreover, women enrolled in HMOs are more likely to report not getting needed care and having difficulties reaching their physician when needed. Women in HMOs are also less satisfied with their physicians than those not in HMOs (Collins & Simon, 1996).

Older women may view health and health care differently than younger women. To compare how these two groups view health issues, try Get Involved 12.1.

Sexually Transmitted Infections (STIs)

Sexually transmitted infections (STIs) have reached epidemic proportions, especially among young Americans ages 15–24. Of the more than 19 million new cases of STIs diagnosed in the United States each year, nearly 9 million occur in teens and young adults (National Institute of Child Health and Human Development, 2007). At least one in four teenage American girls and nearly half of teenage African-American girls are infected (Altman, 2008). We will first give an overview of STIs (see Table 12.1) and then turn to AIDS, the most life-threatening of the STIs.

Overview of STIs

If untreated, STIs can have serious consequences. The most common STI in the United States today, human papillomavirus (HPV), increases the risk of cervical cancer (Runowicz, 2007). About 45 percent of the women in America, ages 20–24, are infected with HPV (Gostin & DeAngelis, 2007). Chlamydia and gonorrhea can lead to chronic pain, pelvic inflammatory disease, stillbirth, infertility, and even death (National Institute of Allergy and Infectious Diseases, 2007). People with syphilis, gonorrhea, chlamydia, or herpes are more likely than others to become infected with the AIDS virus, in part because they have open sores that allow the virus to enter the body (National Institutes of Health, 2004).

STIs have a disproportionate impact on women. They are transmitted more easily to women than to men and are more difficult to diagnose in women (Madkan et al.,

GET INVOLVED 12.1
What Women Say about Their Health

Answer the following questions, which were included in a nationwide poll (Elder, 1997). Then ask two young adult women and two women age 65 or older to answer the same questions.

1. Whom would you trust more to be your doctor, a woman or a man, or would you trust them equally?
2. Which presents the more serious risk, heart disease or breast cancer?
3. How would you describe your health: excellent, good, fair, or poor?
4. In general, who has more health problems, men or women?

5. Who handles being sick better, women or men?
6. Whose complaints do doctors take more seriously: men's, women's, or about the same for both?
7. How often do doctors talk down to you? Most of the time, some of the time, hardly ever, or never?
8. Where do you get most of your medical information: doctors, television, newspapers and magazines, or the Internet?

What Does It Mean?

1. How do the responses of the older women compare with the information presented in the chapter?
2. How do the responses of the older women compare with the responses of your college-age friends? How can age account for these differences?

3. Can you think of any factors other than age that might account for any differences between the responses of the two groups of women?

2006; National Institute of Allergy and Infectious Diseases, 2007). In addition, women may be at high risk of STIs because of social and cultural norms that dictate that women do not decline sexual intercourse with their partners or insist on the use of condoms (Pettifor et al., 2004; Roberts & Kennedy, 2006). Factors that enhance a woman's risk for contracting STIs include being under 25, using condoms inconsistently, being sexually active at an early age, and having sex frequently and with multiple partners (National Institute of Child Health and Human Development, 2007). Because the risk of woman-to-woman sexual transmission of STIs is small, the prevalence of STIs in lesbians is fairly low (Wingood & DiClemente, 2002). It is not zero, however, contrary to the beliefs of many lesbian women (Marrazzo et al., 2005).

One factor behind the rapid increase in STIs is that the majority of American women have relatively little knowledge of STIs and even less concern about contracting one. In one poll, for example, women and men were asked to name the two most common STIs. Only 13 percent of women named HPV, the most common sexually transmitted infection in the United States (Altman, 2008; Dogar, 1999; Dunne et al.,

TABLE 12.1   Major Sexually Transmitted Infections (STIs)

STI	Mode of Transmission	Symptoms	Treatment
Gonorrhea	Vaginal, oral, or anal sex, or from mother to newborn during delivery	In women, vaginal discharge, burning urination, irregular menstrual periods	Antibiotics, e.g., ceftriaxone
Chlamydia	Vaginal, oral, or anal sex, or from mother to newborn during delivery	In women, painful urination, lower abdominal pain, vaginal discharge	Antibiotics, e.g., doxycycline azithromycin
Syphilis	Vaginal, oral, or anal sex, or touching an infectious chancre (sore)	Initially, hard, round painless chancre (sore)	Antibiotics, e.g., azithromycin, doxycycline
Genital herpes	Vaginal, oral, or anal sex; most contagious during active outbreaks	Painful sores around genitals, thighs, buttocks	No cure, but acyclovir (Zovirax) promotes healing
Trichomoniasis	Sexual contact	In women, yellowish odorous vaginal discharge; itching, burning in vulva. Often, no symptoms	Metronidazole (Flagyl)
HPV/Genital warts	Sexual and other contact, such as infected towels, clothing	Painless warts on genital area or anus, or in vagina, cervix, or rectum	Cryosurgery (freezing), burning, surgical removal, preventive vaccine
Acquired immune deficiency syndrome (AIDS)	Sexual contact; infected blood transfusions; mother to fetus during pregnancy or through childbirth or breastfeeding	Fever, weight loss, fatigue, opportunistic infections such as rare forms of cancer and pneumonia	No cure. Antiretroviral drugs like AZT may delay progress of the disease

Source: Rathus et al. (2008), pp. 513–516, Table 16.1. Reprinted with permission from Allyn & Bacon.

2007). Moreover, many women and adolescent girls are not very comfortable communicating with their partners or doctors about STIs (Ginty, 2000; Vastag, 2001). For more on this subject, see Learn about the Research 12.1.

AIDS

Acquired immunodeficiency syndrome (AIDS) is *caused by the human immunodeficiency virus (HIV)*. The most devastating of all the STIs, it is now the leading cause of death in Africa and the fourth leading cause of death worldwide (Bellamy, 2004). While the overall number of AIDS cases in the United States began to drop in the mid-90s, cases of HIV infection and AIDS among individuals of color have continued to increase. Women—particularly women of color—are the fastest-growing group of

Americans infected with HIV. Heterosexual sex has become the leading method of transmission for women both in the United States and abroad (Espinoza et al., 2007; "National Women and Girls HIV/AIDS Awareness Day," 2008). For a closer look at the global AIDS epidemic, see Explore Other Cultures 12.1.

AIDS is the sixth leading cause of death in America for women age 25 to 34, but the leading cause of death for Black women in that age group (Anderson & Smith, 2004; Bowleg, 2008). Women accounted for nearly 30 percent of new HIV infections in the United States in 2001–2004 ("Epidemiology of HIV/AIDS," 2006). While many are young, low-income women of color who live in urban areas, the incidence of HIV-infected rural White women is also on the rise (Wingood & DiClemente, 2002). Black women, who constitute just 13 percent of American women, make up more than two-thirds of women with AIDS in the United States (Bowleg, 2008). Poverty, inadequate health care, and a dearth of information about safe sex are major reasons (Kalb & Murr, 2006) Why are Black women at heightened risk for AIDS? Some researchers cite the lower number of economically viable and available Black men, which may lead Black women to take more sexual risks in order to attract a partner (Mays, cited in Chamberlin, 2007; Villarosa, 2004).

LEARN ABOUT THE RESEARCH 12.1
Knowledge and Communication about Sexually Transmitted Infections

In 1997, a telephone survey was conducted with a national sample of women from 18- to 44-years old who had been to a new gynecologist or obstetrician for the first time within the previous year (Lewin, 1997). Only 3 percent of the women believed they were at risk for sexually transmitted infections. When asked what STIs they were aware of, less than one-quarter could name chlamydia, one of the most common STI. Most of the women did not know that chlamydia and other STIs increased susceptibility to HIV infection. Only 15 percent of the women discussed STIs other than AIDS with their physician, and just 3 percent raised the topic themselves. HIV and AIDS were discussed in 21 percent of the visits, but only 2 percent of patients initiated the topic. Most women believed it was up to the physician to bring up the subject. Yet physicians are reluctant to broach the subject, for fear of offending their patients (Ginty, 2000). A recent survey found that fewer than one in 10 women ages 25–34 were advised by their gynecologist to get an STI test, despite the prevalence of many STIs in this age group (Salganicoff et al., 2003).

What Does It Mean?

1. Why do you think that most obstetricians and gynecologists do not discuss STIs with their patients?
2. What actions can be taken to better educate women about STIs? What do we need to teach young people in school on this topic?
3. What can be done to increase communication between a woman and her reproductive health-care provider?

Women, especially Black, are sicker at the time of diagnosis with HIV or AIDS and die more quickly than men with the disease (Espinoza et al., 2007). Why are women often diagnosed at a later stage of HIV than men? For one thing, women generally are viewed as being at low risk for the disease and so they and their physicians may overlook signs of HIV infection that they exhibit. Second, women usually serve as caregivers for family members and, increasingly, as breadwinners. As a result, they may delay seeking health care for themselves until they are very ill. Finally, as noted above, many HIV-infected women live in poverty and do not have access to health care (Kalb & Murr, 2006).

Decisions about childbearing can be difficult for HIV-infected women (Clark et al., 2004). Without any intervention, the chances of passing the virus to their children are 20 to 25 percent (Santora, 2005). In industrialized countries, an infected woman who takes antiretroviral drugs during pregnancy, has a cesarean delivery, and avoids breastfeeding has only about a 1 to 2 percent chance of infecting her child. But in developing countries, complex antiretroviral drug regimens often are unavailable, and avoidance of breastfeeding is not a realistic option for most women (Coovadia, 2004). Consequently, many women with HIV must wrestle with the fact that their children may be infected and may also be motherless at a young age (Ciambrone, 2003). It is helpful for HIV-infected women to share dilemmas such as this with a support group (Wingood & DiClemente, 2002). Many of these women feel isolated and have not disclosed their illness out of fear of rejection and ostracism (Feist-Price & Wright, 2003; Herbert & Bachanas, 2002). Often, a support group may be a woman's first opportunity to meet other women with HIV or AIDS and to receive help in locating government-subsidized sources of anti-HIV medication (Cowley & Murr, 2004).

The best way to prevent AIDS is to practice "safer sex," that is, avoid unprotected sex with multiple partners and always use latex condoms during sexual intercourse (Goldberg, 2008; Steiner & Cates, 2006). The good news is that in recent years, American teenagers have shown improvement in these HIV-related sexual risk behaviors (Smith, 2003). Unfortunately, many young people, including college students, still fail to engage in safer sex practices. Factors underlying these risky sexual behaviors include a perceived low risk of infection and negative attitudes toward condom use (Rathus et al., 2008).

AIDS in Older Women.   Whatever a woman's age, if she is sexually active, she is at risk for contracting sexually transmitted diseases, including HIV. Since older women are generally viewed as sexually disinterested and inactive, they are less likely to be given information about safer sex practices (Gearon, 2008). Few educational and prevention programs target this age group (Altschuler et al., 2004).

Today, however, about 1,300 new cases of HIV/AIDS among women age 55 and older are diagnosed each year, and this number is growing (Prejean et al., 2006). In the mid-1980s, most AIDS cases among women in that age group were caused by blood transfusions. Now, heterosexual contact is the leading cause (McNeil, 2004; Rathus et al., 2008). One factor putting older women at increased risk during heterosexual contact is the increased thinning of the vaginal tissues and the decrease in lubrication after menopause. These conditions can lead to small skin tears or abrasions during sexual activity that increase the chance of HIV entering the bloodstream (Levy et al.,

EXPLORE OTHER CULTURES **12.1**

The Global AIDS Epidemic

An estimated 40 million people worldwide, nearly half of them women, are infected with HIV (UNAIDS, 2007). Sub-Saharan Africa, with 10 percent of the world's population but over two-thirds of the world's HIV/AIDS sufferers, is the most severely affected region. There, 60 percent of those infected are women (UNAIDS, 2007). In Swaziland, one of the hardest hit countries, 40 percent of adults have the virus (Kristof, 2006).

Adolescent girls and young women of childbearing age in Africa are two to five times more likely to develop HIV/AIDS than their male counterparts for a variety of biological, social, and economic reasons (Marton, 2004; UNAIDS, 2004). Many adolescent women marry older men, who have likely had several previous sexual partners. At the same time, cultural resistance to condom use is high. Moreover, most adolescents in sub-Saharan Africa do not know how to prevent AIDS (Burn, 2005). These factors result in high rates of sexually transmitted infections, which increase chances of HIV transmission. In addition, the poverty, economic dependency, and low status of women render them powerless to protect themselves against unsafe or unwanted sex. In South Africa, for example, Kristin Dunkle and her colleagues (2004) found that women with violent or controlling male partners are at increased risk of HIV infection. Abusive men were more likely to be infected themselves and imposed risky sexual practices on their partners. Sadly, the proportion of infected women is rapidly expanding in other parts of the world as well, particularly Eastern Europe and Central and Southeast Asia ("A Global Menace," 2006; UNAIDS, 2007). In India, where the vast majority of females with HIV are infected by their husbands, women are not able to negotiate safe sex (Steinbrook, 2007). Those who challenge their spouses by asking them to use condoms risk domestic violence. Women who contract HIV from their husbands may be abandoned by their families. Some then become sex workers to survive, further spreading the disease (Marton, 2004). Even those girls and women who do not contract HIV are deeply affected by the epidemic, since the burden of caring for the sick usually falls on them. Girls are often withdrawn from school to care for ailing parents or younger siblings, or to earn an income (Kristof, 2006; United Nations Population Fund, 2004).

A handful of developing countries have had some success in slowing the spread of HIV through AIDS education and condom promotion, and in providing greater access to HIV treatment for those who are infected. In sub-Saharan Africa, for example, Uganda and Zimbabwe appear to be reversing their widespread epidemics (UNAIDS, 2007). Still, nine out of ten people who need HIV treatment are not being reached. Without treatment, 5 to 6 million people in developing countries will die of AIDS every two years (UNAIDS, 2004).

2003). Another factor in the rise of HIV in the elderly is the increase in sexual activity fueled by Viagra, but without a corresponding increase in condom use (Zablotsky & Kennedy, 2003). Many of today's aging baby boomers grew up before the HIV epidemic and didn't learn how to negotiate condom use with their partners. The result is that over 60 percent of sexually active older singles report having unprotected sex (Kantrowitz, 2006b).

Older women who have HIV infection may have a harder time than infected younger women in obtaining a correct diagnosis and treatment. Physicians do not

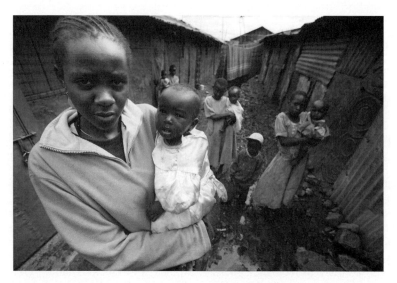

Adolescents and young women account for nearly 60 percent of Africans with HIV/AIDS. Pictured here are a group of young HIV-positive women living in Nairobi, Kenya.

expect to see AIDS in older women (McNeil, 2004), and therefore they are more likely to make a late diagnosis or a misdiagnosis. Symptoms of AIDS resemble those of various age-related diseases including Alzheimer's, which is one of the most common misdiagnoses (McNeil, 2004). Women of this age group are also less likely to think of themselves as being at risk for AIDS, and so they may not think to ask for an HIV test (Akers et al., 2007). Failure to diagnose HIV early can have serious consequences at any age since it is harder to arrest the disease when it becomes more advanced. But older adults with HIV are even more likely to deteriorate rapidly because of their already weakened immune system (Karpiak et al., 2006).

HIV infection takes an enormous emotional toll on older women, many of whom live alone and are already trying to cope with physical, economic, and personal losses. While today's younger women are used to talking more freely about sexual problems, this is difficult for many older women. They feel ashamed and may suffer alone, avoiding telling friends and family (Fowler, 2003). Some avoid intimate contact with grandchildren, such as kissing on the lips, for fear of endangering the youngsters. Those women who join therapy groups often find them to be a great source of emotional support (Ciambrone, 2003).

Reproductive System Disorders

Sexually transmitted infections are not the only diseases that can affect the reproductive system. We now turn to other disorders including benign (noncancerous) conditions such as endometriosis and fibroid tumors, as well as various cancers.

Benign Conditions

Endometriosis is a chronic and sometimes extremely painful condition in which the *lining of the uterus (endometrium) migrates and grows on pelvic structures, such as the ovaries, fallopian tubes, and bladder.* Over five million women in the United States are diagnosed with this condition each year. Endometriosis can cause pelvic and menstrual pain and heavy bleeding. Severe endometriosis is a major cause of infertility (Goldberg, 2008).

Up to three out of four women will develop **fibroid tumors,** which are *noncancerous growths of the uterus*, at some time in their lives. Fibroids are not dangerous, but they can cause severe pelvic pain, heavy bleeding, and possibly infertility and miscarriage. They occur more often in Black women than in White women (Goldberg, 2008).

Cancers

Endometrial or uterine cancer is the most common cancer of the female reproductive tract and is often characterized by vaginal bleeding. Risk factors include estrogen replacement therapy (without use of progestin), smoking, and obesity (American Cancer Society, 2008; Viswanathan et al., 2005). Although it is more common in White women than in Black women, Black women are more likely to die from it. Because most cases are detected early, this is one of the most curable cancers of the reproductive system, with a five-year survival rate of 95 percent for localized uterine cancer (American Cancer Society, 2008b).

Cancer of the **cervix,** *the lower end of the uterus,* is the third most common cancer of the female genital system, after uterine and ovarian cancer (American Cancer Society, 2008b). In the United States, it has a five-year survival rate of more than 90 percent in its early stages (American Cancer Society, 2008b). Black, Latina, and Native American women, however, have a much higher death rate, probably because their more limited access to medical care prevents early diagnosis and treatment (Ahmed et al., 2004). Factors that increase the risk of cervical cancer include smoking, obesity, early age at first intercourse, multiple sex partners, extended use of oral contraceptives, and infection with human papilloma virus (HPV), the common virus that causes genital warts (American Cancer Society, 2008b). The **Pap smear,** *an inexpensive and effective screening technique*, has been used for over 50 years to identify precancerous changes in the cervix. The test has slashed cervical cancer deaths by 75 percent and saved tens of thousands of lives (Runowicz, 2007). Of those women who develop cervical cancer in the United States, about 60 percent have never had a Pap smear (Runowicz, 2007). Women should start getting an annual Pap test by age 21 or three years after the onset of sexual activity, whichever comes first. If a woman 30 or older has had three normal test results in a row, the interval can increase to every two to three years (Popescu & Carmichael, 2008). Unfortunately, only 80 percent of women have Pap smears at least once every three years. Women who are poor, uninsured, less educated, and elderly are least likely to get regular Pap tests (Bolen et al., 2007; "QuickStats," 2008). The good news that a recently developed vaccine protects women against HPV and may virtually eliminate cervical cancer over the next several decades (American Cancer Society, 2008b).

Some parents, however, object to their daughters being given the preventive vaccine, fearing that doing so might send the subtle message that premarital sex is acceptable (Charo, 2007). What is your view of this issue?

Ovarian cancer received increased attention after the comedian Gilda Radner (1990) and the editor-in-chief of *Harper's Bazaar,* Liz Tilberis (1998), wrote books about their courageous fight against the disease, which ultimately killed them. Ovarian cancer is a major killer of women, causing more deaths than any other cancer of the female reproductive system. It is a so-called "silent killer" because its symptoms usually do not appear until the cancer is in an advanced stage. At that stage, the five-year survival rate is only 30 percent (American Cancer Society, 2008b). Risk factors include having immediate family members with ovarian, breast, or colon cancer; taking fertility drugs or hormone replacement therapy; being obese; and smoking. However, bearing children, breastfeeding, taking birth control pills, and eating a low-fat diet are protective factors (American Cancer Society, 2008b; Hannaford et al., 2007; Lacey et al., 2006; Prentice et al., 2007). Currently, there is no reliable means of early detection. However, certain symptoms are much more likely to occur in women with ovarian cancer: bloating, pelvic or abdominal pain, difficulty eating or feeling full quickly, and frequent or urgent urination. Women with these symptoms for more than a few weeks are advised to see their doctor ("Symptoms," 2007).

Hysterectomy

Each year, over 600,000 women in the United States undergo a **hysterectomy,** the *removal of the uterus* (Kuppermann et al., 2004). By age 60, more than one in three American women have had their uterus removed, one of the highest rates in the world (Goldberg, 2008). For years, many critics have questioned the high rate of hysterectomy in this country. While removal of the uterus is considered appropriate in cases of cancer of the uterus, cervix, or ovaries, these situations account for only a small fraction of the total. Endometriosis, heavy menstrual bleeding, and chronic pelvic pain are other common reasons for hysterectomy (Torpy et al., 2004). But the most common reason is the presence of fibroid tumors (Carlson et al., 2004). Because Black women are more likely than White women to have fibroid tumors, their hysterectomy rates also are higher (Keshavarz et al., 2002). Other less invasive procedures, such as *blocking blood flow to the fibroids* (a procedure called **fibroid embolization**), are now available to women (Goldberg, 2008).

These less invasive procedures may have fewer negative psychological effects than hysterectomy. For example, Jean Elson (2004) interviewed 44 women, ages 24 to 69, whose uterus had been removed for benign conditions. All the women reflected on their gender identity following surgery. Their reactions ranged all the way from "Now I feel like a fake woman" to "I have always been . . . the same person" (Ayoub, 2004, p. A18). Most of the women did not miss menstruation much, but they missed the potential to have children. This was true whether or not they already had children and even if they never intended to have them (Ayoub, 2004). In spite of feelings of loss, however, many women view their hysterectomy positively as relieving chronic pain and enabling them to regain control over their bodies (Markovic et al., 2008).

Another common practice, which has been heavily criticized, is the removal of the ovaries along with the uterus, even when the ovaries are normal and healthy. Physicians who carry out such surgery contend that when a women is in her mid-40s or older, the ovaries' major function is over and that removing them forestalls the possibility of ovarian cancer (Carlson et al., 2004). Can you see the sexist bias in this argument? Could one not equally argue that the prostate and testes of middle-aged men should be removed to prevent cancer of these organs?

Osteoporosis

Osteoporosis is an *excessive loss of bone tissue in older adults which results in the bones becoming thinner, brittle, and more porous.* Osteoporosis affects about 10 million Americans, 80 percent of them women (National Osteoporosis Foundation, 2008b; Zeller, 2007). But the seeds of osteoporosis are sown in adolescence, when bone building is most rapid. By their early 20s, women reach their peak bone mass (Kantrowitz, 2007a). At age 30, gradual bone loss begins. The rate of bone loss accelerates sharply for 10 years after the onset of menopause, as estrogen levels drop (Kantrowitz, 2007a). Each year, 1.5 million fractures related to osteoporosis occur in the United States. Half of all women over

Osteoporosis increases after menopause and can lead to disabling and even fatal fractures.

50 years of age will have a fracture during their lifetime because of osteoporosis (Baker, 2007). These fractures can be crippling and painful and can cause permanent loss of mobility. Moreover, 20 percent of patients with a hip fracture die of complications such as blood clots and pneumonia (Calis & Pucino, 2007; Wilson et al., 2006).

Risk Factors

Some women are more likely to develop osteoporosis than others. For a list of risk factors, see Table 12.2. Postmenopausal women with one or more of these risk factors, and all women over 65, should consider getting a bone density test, which can detect even a small loss of bone mass (Springen, 2007).

Prevention and Treatment

A look at Table 12.2 indicates some ways to build and keep as much bone as possible. Increasing calcium intake during childhood, adolescence, and young adulthood is the most effective way of building denser bones and reducing risk of bone fracture (Tang et al., 2007). In order to suppress bone loss, the National Institutes of Health

TABLE 12.2   Risk Factors for Osteoporosis

Biological Factors

- Gender: women's risk is greater because their bones are smaller and lighter
- Age: after age 30, bone loss begins
- Menopause: drop in estrogen levels increases bone loss
- Thin, small-framed body
- Ethnicity: Black women, who have heavier bone density, are at lower risk
- Family history of osteoporosis or older relatives with fractures

Lifestyle Factors

- Diet low in calcium and vitamin D
- High intake of sodium, protein, caffeine
- Lack of physical activity
- Smoking
- Alcohol intake of two or more drinks a day

Medical Factors

- History of rheumatoid arthritis, liver disease, thyroid disorder
- Eating disorders
- Certain medications: diuretics, steroids, anticonvulsants

Sources: Khosla and Melton (2007); National Osteoporosis Foundation (2008a,b); Zeller (2007).

recommends consumption of 1,300 milligrams of calcium per day for adolescents, 1,000 milligrams for women 19 to 50, and 1,200 milligrams for postmenopausal women. Good sources of calcium include low-fat and nonfat milk, cheese, and yogurt; tofu and other soy products, fruits and vegetables, especially dark-green leafy vegetables such as kale and turnip greens; and canned sardines and salmon (Kantrowitz, 2007a; Lanham-New, 2006; U.S. Department of Health and Human Services, 2004b).

Unfortunately, adolescents consume far less calcium than they should, and their calcium intake has been declining over the past 30 years. Teenage girls now drink 50 percent more soft drinks and one-third less milk than they did in 1977 (O'Neil, 2003). The result is that only 14 percent of adolescent girls consume adequate amounts of calcium (Brody, 2003a). In addition, most women consume only about half the daily amount of calcium they need. Calcium supplements are good additional sources, especially those containing calcium carbonate (found in Tums and Rolaids) or calcium citrate (found in Citracal). The body can absorb up to 500 milligrams of calcium at a time, so if a person takes 1,000 milligrams per day, it should be divided into two doses (Kantrowitz, 2006; U.S. Department of Health and Human Services, 2004b).

Calcium cannot be absorbed without vitamin D. Many women do not get the 800 international units of vitamin D per day shown to decrease the likelihood of osteoporosis and bone fractures (Tang et al., 2007). Milk fortified with vitamin D and sunlight are two of its best sources. While as little as 15 minutes per day in the sun helps the body produce Vitamin D, most adults may need dietary supplements in order to prevent vitamin D deficiency (Brody, 2008a).

Diet is only part of the equation, however. Exercise is very important in increasing bone mass during adolescence and young adulthood and in slowing bone loss after menopause (Springen, 2007). The exercise should be weightbearing, such as brisk walking, low-impact aerobics, or lifting weights. Even everyday activities such as climbing stairs, walking the dog, doing yard work, gardening, or playing with children can be beneficial. It is never too late to start exercising and a little bit of physical activity is better than none (Brender, 2006; Lee, 2007).

Decreasing or eliminating smoking and decreasing consumption of alcohol and most sources of caffeine are good not only for strong bones but may also confer many other health benefits, as we shall see later in the chapter. Drinking black or green tea, however, seems to strengthen bones (Wu et al., 2002).

Estrogen helps build and maintain strong bones. Estrogen replacement therapy starting in perimenopause and continuing after menopause slows bone loss, increases bone mass, and reduces the incidence of fractures (Khosla & Melton, 2007; Springen, 2007). However, because hormone replacement therapy now is known to increase the risk of heart attack, stroke, and breast cancer (see Chapter 7), it is no longer considered an option for preventing osteoporosis. Fortunately, other medications can help a woman strengthen her bones. Drugs called bisphosphonates (sold as Fosamax, Actonel, and Boniva) decrease the risk of hip and spinal fractures. **Raloxifene**, a *synthetic estrogen* marketed as Evista, decreases bone loss in post-menopausal women and reduces the risk of spinal fractures and also breast cancer (Colon-Emeric, 2006; National Osteoporosis Foundation, 2008a).

Heart Disease

Heart disease is the leading cause of death for both women and men around the world. More women in the United States die of heart disease than from all forms of cancer combined, including breast cancer (Mikhail, 2007; Wingert & Kantrowitz, 2007). Yet women show a devastating lack of awareness of the risks of heart disease. Most women perceive breast cancer as a far greater threat to their health than heart disease. Although nearly 30 percent of American women die from heart disease annually, only 10 percent fear it as their greatest health risk. Conversely, only 4 percent will die of breast cancer, even though 22 percent of women fear dying from it (Society for Women's Health Research, 2005). While awareness that heart disease is the top killer of women has grown since 2000, awareness of risk factors for the disease remains low, particularly for women younger than age 45 and for ethnic minority women (Christian et al., 2007; Fang et al., 2008).

Gender Differences

Heart disease in women becomes apparent about 10 years later than in men. Illness and death from heart disease increase dramatically in women after menopause, due partly to declining estrogen levels. By age 75, a woman has a greater risk of heart attack and heart disease than a man her age (Brody, 2005). Women are more likely than men to die after a heart attack (Davidson et al., 2008; Rosenfeld, 2006; Travis & Meltzer, 2008). If they survive, they are more likely to have a second attack (Hong et al., 2003). Since women are older than men when they develop heart disease, their prognosis is poorer. But women are more likely than men to die after treatment for heart disease, even when they are equally old and ill (Milcent et al., 2007).

Risk Factors

Some risk factors for heart disease are unchangeable. In addition to gender and age, these include ethnicity and family history. The death rate from heart attack is higher for Black women than White women, who, in turn, are much more likely to die from heart disease than are Latina, Native American, and Asian American women. In addition, the risk of heart disease and stroke increases if close family members have had these diseases ("Disparities in Premature Deaths," 2004; Jha et al., 2003; Lloyd-Jones et al., 2004).

Major risk factors over which women have control include physical inactivity, smoking, being overweight, having a poor diet, and using hormone replacement therapy (Ford et al., 2007; Travis & Meltzer, 2008). Women who have none of these factors have a much lower risk of heart disease than other women. Even young women, who have a low rate of heart disease, should begin controlling these risk factors early in life (Mitka, 2007).

Inactivity is a major risk factor in heart disease and stroke. Sedentary women are nine times more likely to die from cardiovascular disease than women who are very active. Women benefit from vigorous exercise such as aerobics, running, biking, or swimming for at least 30 minutes, three to four times a week. But even moderate everyday activities such as a brisk walk, gardening, household chores, and climbing stairs for a total of 30 minutes on most days provide health benefits (Beers & Jones, 2004; Lippert, 2008; Mora et al., 2006; Ogilvie et al., 2007). Unfortunately, more than 80 percent of American women are sedentary or do not engage in any regular physical activity. In addition, women become even less active as they get older, when they most need the cardiovascular benefits of exercise (U.S. Census Bureau, 2003c).

High blood pressure (hypertension) is another major risk factor for heart attack and the most important risk factor for stroke (Hong et al., 2003; Mikhail, 2007). By their sixties, at least half of all women have high blood pressure, with Black women having higher than average rates (Carlson et al., 2004). Reducing salt intake, losing weight (if overweight), exercising, eating a fiber-rich diet, and taking medication (if needed) can bring blood pressure under control (Carlson et al., 2004; Streppel et al., 2005). Best of all, eating one square of dark chocolate a day lowers blood pressure (Tonks, 2007). Who says if it's good for you it must taste bad?

Women with *diabetes* are more likely to have a heart attack or stroke than are nondiabetic women. Diabetes may be delayed by controlling blood sugar, eating less saturated fat, staying physically active, and maintaining a normal weight (Beers & Jones, 2004; Mosca et al., 2007). Being *overweight* also increases the risk of both heart attack and stroke (Weinstein et al., 2008). Overweight individuals are more likely to develop high blood pressure, high cholesterol levels, and diabetes (Flegal et al., 2007; Muennig et al., 2006). The good news is that dropping just 10 percent of one's body weight can lower cholesterol, blood pressure, and the risk of diabetes.

Smoking is a powerful risk factor for heart disease and stroke in women (Mosca et al., 2007). Smoking is especially harmful in women because it decreases estrogen's protective effects and can cause menopause to occur about two years early. The vast majority of women who develop heart disease before age 50 are smokers. The good news is that quitting smoking cuts heart attack risk by a third within two years (Wingert & Kantrowitz, 2007) and by nearly two-thirds within five years (Kenfield et al., 2008).

Diet also is important in reducing the risk of heart disease and stroke. A heart-healthy diet—sometimes called "the Mediterranean diet"—is rich in vegetables and fruits, whole grains, nuts, soy, monounsaturated oils (olive, canola), and protein derived from fish, beans, low-fat or nonfat dairy products, lean meats, and poultry (American Heart Association, 2007; Brody, 2007b; Welty et al., 2007b). Drinking tea appears to protect against heart disease as well, especially in women. In addition, women who consume one alcoholic drink per day are less likely to suffer a heart attack or stroke than women who do not drink (Dorn et al., 2007; King et al., 2008; Nagourney, 2007). Moreover, one baby aspirin (81 mg) per day lowers the risk of both heart disease and cancer in women (Chan et al., 2007).

Hormones also affect heart disease. *Birth control pills*, which contain estrogen and progestin, increase women's risk of heart disease and stroke (Baillargeon et al., 2005). As noted earlier in the chapter, *hormone replacement therapy* also increases the risk of heart disease.

Men and women with aspects of so-called Type A personality—particularly mistrust and hostility—are more prone to develop heart disease (Geipert, 2007;

Being overweight increases a woman's risk of heart attack, stroke, breast cancer, and diabetes.

Grady, 2006). In addition, depression is strongly associated with getting heart disease and with dying from it (Frasure-Smith & Lespérance, 2005; Glassman & Bigger, 2007). Since women are more likely than men to be depressed (see Chapter 13), this factor increases women's risk. In addition, women who are divorced, widowed, or unhappily married have a higher risk of heart disease than women who are satisfied with their marriages (Troxel et al., 2005).

Diagnosis and Treatment

The management, diagnosis, and treatment of heart disease in women are poorly understood and often carried out in an inconsistent manner. The result is that women receive poorer care (Bönte et al., 2008; Spurgeon, 2007; Travis & Meltzer, 2008). Women with heart disease often do not receive the aggressive treatment from physicians that men do (Rosenfeld, 2006; Vaccarino et al., 2005). For one thing, physicians often miss the signs of heart disease and heart attack in women because women are less likely to show the "classic" male symptom of crushing chest pain and are more apt than men to show symptoms such as nausea, dizziness, shortness of breath, sweating, chest pressure or heaviness, exhaustion, sleep disturbance, back or abdominal pain, heartburn, heart palpitations, or just an odd, unwell feeling. Women may be misdiagnosed as simply suffering from indigestion, muscle pain, stress, or anxiety (Rosenfeld, 2006; Skerrett & Leopald, 2008). In addition, it is often believed that women are less threatened by heart disease, which is untrue (Linn & Kessel, 2006; Travis & Meltzer, 2008). In one recent online survey of 500 randomly selected physicians, women at risk of developing heart disease were more likely than men to be assigned to a low-risk category. They were less likely to be advised to change their living habits and to take medications to help prevent heart attacks (Brody, 2005). Even when women experience the classic symptom of pain, they are more reluctant than men to seek medical care, believing that they would be "wasting the doctor's time" (Richards et al., 2002). Sometimes they ignore the symptoms because they are too busy taking care of everybody else (Schoenberg et al., 2003).

When women do show up at the emergency room with the classic heart attack symptoms, they are less likely than men to be admitted for evaluation (Washington & Bird, 2002). Furthermore, they are not as likely as men to receive one of the most important diagnostic heart tests, the angiogram, which can show blockage in coronary arteries. Women heart patients also are less likely to be treated by a specialist and are less likely to receive cholesterol-lowering drugs, devices such as pacemakers, stents (to open clogged arteries) and treatments such as angioplasty (also used to clear arteries), coronary bypass surgery, and implantable defibrillator. And in the critical hours following a heart attack, fewer women are given clot-dissolving drugs (Carlson et al., 2004; Redberg, 2007; Rosenfeld, 2006; Spurgeon, 2007) and they wait longer than men to receive an emergency angioplasty to open blocked arteries ("Women and Heart Health," 2005). Moreover, they are less often given aspirin, which aids in dissolving blood clots, or beta-blockers, which protect against future heart attacks (Cho et al., 2008; Correa-de-Araujo et al., 2006). Women also get fewer referrals for cardiac rehabilitation programs following heart attacks, even though they benefit from therapy at least as much as men do (Ayala et al., 2008; Krantz et al., 2004; "Women and Heart Health," 2005). In addition, women are often underrepresented in studies designed to test the effectiveness of such programs (Rosenfeld, 2006).

Psychological Impact

The psychosocial health of women following a heart attack or coronary bypass surgery is worse than that of men (Doering et al., 2007; Garavalia et al., 2007; Majerovitz, 2006). Women are more anxious and depressed, return to work less often, take longer to recuperate physically, and resume their sex lives later than men. In spite of their poorer heath, women resume household activities sooner than men and are more likely to feel guilty that they cannot quickly resume the chores they once did (Packard, 2005; Prentice, 2008). Women's poorer psychosocial functioning after heart attack and heart surgery can take a toll on their well-being, productivity, and quality of life. In addition, the greater depression experienced by women after heart attack or heart surgery is associated with a greater risk of death and of second heart attacks. Health-care providers need to become aware of the potential difficulties faced by women with heart disease and to take steps to enhance the recovery of their female patients (Carlson et al., 2004; Rosenfeld, 2006).

Breast Cancer

As we noted earlier, women fear breast cancer more than any other disease including heart disease, the top killer of women. Yet breast cancer is not even the number one cancer killer of women. That dubious distinction falls to lung cancer (American

Cancer Society 2008a; Grady, 2007). One out of every eight women will develop breast cancer at some time in her life. Although this statistic sounds frightening, it represents a lifetime risk. Before age 40, only 1 in 213 women develops breast cancer. Between ages 50 and 55, the risk increases to 1 in 26 women, and at age 70, it rises to 1 in 15. It is only for women who are 90 years and older that the risk is 1 in 8 (American Cancer Society, 2008a).

The majority of women in whom breast cancer is diagnosed—80 percent—do not die of the disease. Moreover, the death rate from breast cancer has been dropping in recent years as a result of earlier detection, improved treatments, and a decrease in the use of hormones to treat menopause (Grady, 2007). The five-year survival rate for women with localized breast cancer is 98 percent. Even if the cancer has spread to lymph nodes, 84 percent of women will be alive five years later. If it invades bones or other organs, the rate drops to 27 percent (American Cancer Society, 2008a).

Why is the prospect of getting breast cancer so terrifying? According to Jane Brody (1999a) and Ellen Ratner (1999), both breast cancer survivors and authors, the extensive publicity given to the disease in recent years in order to stimulate research and raise women's awareness has created the misleading impression that breast cancer is more common and more deadly than it actually is. In addition, while only a small number of women die of breast cancer in their 30s and 40s, their untimely deaths may trigger greater alarm than the heart attack deaths of a far greater number of women later in life.

Risk Factors

Age, as we have just seen, is the greatest risk factor for breast cancer. In fact, 70 percent of women who develop breast cancer have no risk factors other than age (Smith et al., 2000).

Ethnicity and *social class* are also risk factors. White women are slightly more likely than Black women to get breast cancer overall, but Black women are far more likely to die from it (American Cancer Society, 2008a; Grady, 2006). Part of the reason is that Black women are poorer. Low-income women, regardless of race, are diagnosed later, receive lower quality of care, and are more likely to die of breast cancer than other women (American Cancer Society, 2008a; Halpern et al., 2008). But in addition, the tumors of Black women appear to be faster growing and more malignant (Grady, 2007).

Family history of breast cancer—especially in one's mother, sister, or daughter—is another risk factor, accounting for 5 to 10 percent of breast cancers. A small percentage of women with a family history of breast cancer have unusually high risk—50 to 87 percent—as a result of inheriting one of two breast cancer genes, BRCA-1 and BRCA-2. Inherited breast cancer occurs at younger ages, is more likely to affect both breasts, and often appears in multiple family members, including men, over several generations. The genes are more common in Jewish women of Eastern European origin than in other groups (Brandt-Rauf et al., 2006; Weitzel et al., 2007).

Age, ethnicity, and family history are risk factors women cannot change. Other factors over which they have little or no control include *early age at menarche, late age at menopause, late age at first birth* (after 30), and *having no or few children*. All these events lengthen the amount of time women's breast tissue is exposed to high levels of estrogen, which can stimulate growth of breast cancer cells (Porter, 2008; Travis & Meltzer, 2008).

Women can reduce their risk of breast cancer by making certain lifestyle choices. One of these choices is not *smoking* (Al-Delaimy et al., 2004; Cerhan et al., 2004). Consumption of one or more *alcoholic* drinks per day also increases the risk of developing breast cancer (American Cancer Society, 2008a).

The role of *fat consumption* in breast cancer is controversial. Some studies have found a link between overall fat intake and incidence of breast cancer (Thiebaut et al., 2007). Other research, however, has shown that the *type* of fat is important ("Breast Cancer," 2003; Menendez et al., 2005; Wolk et al., 1998). Monounsaturated fat (olive oil, canola oil) may reduce the risk of breast cancer, whereas polyunsaturated fat (corn, safflower, and soybean oil) and animal fat may increase it. *High-carbohydrate diets*, especially those high in refined sugars, also are linked to greater risk of breast cancer (Cerhan et al., 2004; Romieu et al., 2004), as are diets low in calcium and vitamin D (Lin et al., 2007).

Being overweight after menopause increases a woman's chances of developing breast cancer (Porter, 2008). Body fat produces estrogen which can help breast cancer grow. One way to reduce fat is to engage in *physical activity*. Strenuous exercise in adolescence and young adulthood can delay onset of menstruation or interrupt it. This lowers a woman's overall exposure to estrogen, possibly inhibiting development of breast cancer (Maruti et al., 2008). Even among postmenopausal women, physical activity reduces breast cancer risk, most likely because it reduces body fat (Holmes et al., 2005; Porter, 2008). Recent use of *birth control pills* and *hormone replacement therapy* both increase risk of breast cancer (American Cancer Society, 2008a; Grady, 2007; Kahlenborn et al., 2006). To assess your risk of breast cancer, try Get Involved 12.2.

Detection

The American Cancer Society recommends that women age 20 and older do a monthly breast self-examination about a week after their menstrual period ends (during menstruation breasts have normal lumps) (Smith & Saslow, 2002). Figure 12.1 provides instructions. Many women do not examine their breasts, partly out of fear of finding a lump. (Keep in mind that most lumps are noncancerous.) This is unfortunate, because a substantial portion of breast cancers are found during self-examination, particularly among women under 40 (Ferraro, 2006). A major reason for this is that mammograms are less effective at detecting tumors in dense young breast tissue. Women with dense breast tissue and those with high risk of breast cancer are encouraged to use ultrasound, digital mammograms, or magnetic resonance imaging (MRI) to help find early breast cancer (Grady, 2008b; Susan G. Komen, 2008). All women should also have a clinical breast exam by a health professional every three years from ages 20 to 39 years and annually from age 40 onward (American Cancer Society, 2006).

How to Examine Your Breasts

Do you know that 95% of breast cancers are discovered first by women themselves? And that the earlier the breast cancer is detected, the better the chance for a complete cure? Of course, most lumps or changes are not cancer. But you can safeguard your health by making a habit of examining your breasts once a month – a day or two after your period or, if you're no longer menstruating, on any given day. And if you notice anything changed or unusual – a lump, thickening, or discharge – contact your doctor right away.

How to Look for Changes

Step 1
Sit or stand in front of a mirror with your arms at your side. Turning slowly from side to side, check your breasts for
• changes in size or shape
• puckering or dimpling of the skin
• changes in size or position of one nipple compared to the other

Step 2
Raise your arms above your head and repeat the examination in Step 1.

Step 3
Gently press each nipple with your fingertips to see if there is any discharge.

How to Feel for Changes

Step 1
using small circular motions to feel the inner, upper quarter of your left breast. Start at your breastbone and work toward the nipple. Also examine the area

Step 2
Imagine that your breast is divided into quarters.

Step 3
With the fingers of your right hand held together, press firmly but gently, using small circular motions to feel the inner, upper quarter of your left breast. Start at your breastbone and work toward the nipple. Also examine the area around the nipple. Now do the same for the lower, inner portion of your breast.

Step 4
Next, bring your arm to your side and feel under your left armpit for swelling.

Step 5
With your arm still down, feel the upper, outer part of your breast, starting with your nipple and working outwards. Examine the lower, outer quarter in the same way.

Step 6
Now place the pillow under your right shoulder and repeat all the steps using your left hand to examine your right breast.

FIGURE 12.1   Doing a Breast Self-Examination

Source: From American Cancer Society (2008a). Reprinted with permission.

A **mammogram,** *a low-dose X-ray picture of the breast,* detects small suspicious lumps up to two years before they are large enough to be felt. Major health organizations such as the American Cancer Society and the National Cancer Institute recommend a yearly mammogram for women over 40 (Elmore et al., 2005). Nationwide, the number of women who are screened has increased since 1990. Now, nearly 80 percent of eligible women have had a mammogram in the last two years (Bolen et al., 2007).

However, women with low income or less than a high school education, who have more limited access to affordable health care, are less likely to be screened (Bolen et al., 2007). In addition, women age 65 and older are screened less often than those ages 40–64 (Kosiak et al., 2006). Some women avoid mammograms because they fear the pain or discomfort of the procedure itself, while others fear receiving a breast cancer diagnosis (Consedine et al., 2004; Magai et al., 2007).

Since breast cancer typically strikes after age 50, some women and their doctors may ignore early warning signs, such as a self-detected small lump, assuming it's only a benign cyst. Consequently, young women tend to be diagnosed when their disease has progressed further (Leibson-Hawkins, 2004).

Treatment

When breast cancer is diagnosed, several treatment options are available. For many years, the standard treatment was **radical mastectomy,** *the removal of the breast, underlying chest wall, and underarm lymph nodes.* Because of disfigurement and side effects,

GET INVOLVED **12.2**

Assessing Your Risk Breast Cancer

Put a check mark next to each risk factor listed below. The total number of checks gives a general indication of your relative risk. Remember that some women have many risk factors but never get breast cancer. Others have few or no factors but do get the disease. Getting older increases one's risk.

After you assess your relative risk, give the questionnaire to female friends and relatives, including both young and older women.

Breast Cancer Risk Factors

- BRCA1 or BRCA2 gene mutation
- Family history of breast cancer
- High breast density
- Personal history of breast cancer
- Menopause after age 55
- Not having children
- Having first child after age 35

- Being overweight after menopause
- More than one alcoholic drink per day
- Younger than 12 at first period
- Postmenopausal HRT consisting of estrogen and progestin

Total: _____

What Does It Mean?

1. How did breast cancer risk vary with the age of your respondents??

2. What advice can you give to your respondents who have moderate to high risk of breast cancer?

Source: Susan G. Komen for the Cure. (2008). *Risk factors and prevention.* Dallas, TX: Author.

it now is rarely done. **Modified radical mastectomy** involves *removal of the breast and underarm lymph nodes* and **simple mastectomy,** *removal of the breast only.* In **lumpectomy,** also known as partial mastectomy or breast-conserving surgery, only *the lump and some surrounding tissue are removed.* Lumpectomy is almost always followed by several weeks of radiation. For small tumors in the early stages of disease, lumpectomy followed by radiation is as effective in terms of 20-year survival as mastectomy (American Cancer Society, 2008a; Punglia et al., 2007).

Chemotherapy may be used to kill cancer cells that the surgeon was not able to remove. Other drugs that cut rates of breast cancer occurrence include the estrogen blockers valoxifene and tamoxifen and drugs called aromatase inhibitors (Moore, 2007; Stefanick, 2006). Another drug, Herceptin, shrinks tumors in women who have a certain type of fast-growing cancer or whose advanced breast cancer is not responsive to other treatments (Pollack, 2007).

Psychological Impact

The diagnosis of breast cancer and the surgery that often follows causes depression, anxiety, and anger in many women (Burgess et al., 2005). If the cancer recurs at some point after treatment, women may experience even higher levels of distress. Concerns about bodily appearance can be substantial for women who have had breast surgery. Lumpectomy has a more positive effect on body image and sexual functioning than mastectomy (Compas & Luecken, 2002).

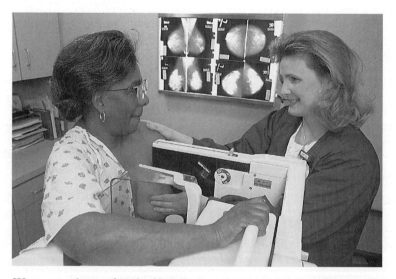

Women over the age of 40 should receive a yearly mammogram.

Individual differences in reactions to breast cancer vary considerably. Young women appear to be affected more negatively than middle-aged or older women. They are more likely to have to deal with disruptions in family life and careers, as well as problems with fertility and sexual functioning. Consequently, they show greater declines in social functioning, mental health, and quality of life (Kroenke et al., 2004). But regardless of age, women with a "fighting spirit," higher levels of hostility, and those who voice their fears and anxieties survive breast cancer longer than those who show passive acceptance, stoicism, emotional inhibition, feelings of hopelessness, or denial of facts about the cancer (Compas & Luecken, 2002; Ray, 2004; Revenson, 2001).

The importance of support groups in helping women cope with cancer cannot be underestimated. David Spiegel and his colleagues (2002) found that after attending weekly group therapy sessions for a year, women with advanced breast cancer showed less emotional distress and more adaptive coping responses than women who had been assigned to a control group. A 10-year follow-up found that the women in group therapy had lived on average twice as long (36.6 versus 18.9 months from entry in the study to death) as women in the control group. Similarly, breast cancer patients who have friends, close relatives, and adult children live longer than patients who lack these sources of social support (Kroenke et al., 2006). One reason for these results is that psychological intervention can increase levels of an antibody that fights breast cancer tumors (Andersen & Emery, 1999). While social support does not always improve survival rates, it can enhance quality of life, mood, energy levels, and tolerance of chemotherapy and reduce depression and pain (Andersen & Emery, 1999; Goodwin et al., 2001; Nagourney, 2004). Overall, psychosocial interventions that focus on reducing stress, increasing knowledge, and improving coping skills give breast cancer patients a greater sense of control, improved body image and sexual functioning, reduced distress, and greater adherence to their prescribed course of therapy (Dittmann, 2003; Smith & Saslow, 2002; Taylor et al., 2003).

Physical Health in Later Life

In this section, we examine factors contributing to women's health in later life. We also explore gender differences in **mortality** (*death rates*) and in **morbidity** (*illness*), look at disability in old age and, finally, discuss the conditions that promote good health.

Gender Differences in Mortality

Women are sicker; men die quicker. This old saying sums up what is often referred to as the **gender paradox:** *women live longer than men, but in poorer health* (Goldman & Hatch, 2000). Even in the poorest countries, women outlive men (Barford et al., 2007) but report poorer health (HSBC Insurance, 2007).

The female–male mortality gap begins before birth. While 115 males are conceived for every 100 females, the rate of miscarriage and stillbirth is higher for males.

Although about 105 live males are born for every 100 live females, more male babies die in infancy (Arias, 2004) and thereafter throughout life. Starting at age 42, women outnumber men (U.S. Census Bureau, 2008). Between ages 65 and 69, only 81 males survive for every 100 females. Between ages 80 and 84, the ratio is down to 53 to 100, and by age 100, women outnumber men four to one (Cavanaugh & Blanchard-Fields, 2006; Jones, 2003).

At the turn of the twentieth century, life expectancy in the United States was about 51 years for women and 48 years for men. Since then, the gender gap has widened. Life expectancy at birth now is about 80 for women and 5½ years less for men. The gender gap exists for both Blacks and Whites. White women tend to outlive White men by five years (80.8 versus 75.7) and Black women, on average, outlive Black men by seven years, 76.5 versus 69.5 (Kung et al., 2008). Why do women outlive men? Some explanations focus on biological factors, others on lifestyle behavioral differences.

Biology.   One biological explanation is that women's second X chromosome protects them against certain lethal diseases—such as hemophilia and some forms of muscular dystrophy—that are more apt to occur in individuals (i.e., men) who have only one X chromosome. Another biological reason for women's greater longevity is their higher estrogen levels, which seem to provide protection against fatal conditions such as heart disease (Kajantie, 2008). In addition, women have a lower rate of metabolism, which is linked to greater longevity. Another suggestion is that women's immune systems are more robust than men's, making men more susceptible to contracting certain fatal diseases (Gaylord, 2001; Perls & Fretts, 1998).

Lifestyle Behaviors.   One lifestyle factor accounting for the gender gap in mortality is that males are more likely than females to engage in potentially risky behaviors such as smoking, drinking, violence, and reckless driving. They also may be exposed to more hazardous workplace conditions (Bogg & Roberts, 2004; Federal Interagency Forum, 2007; Grunbaum et al., 2004; Vyrostek et al., 2004). Table 12.3 shows that accidents and unintentional injuries are the third leading cause of death of males, but the seventh leading cause for females. Men are twice as likely as women to die of cirrhosis, caused largely by excessive drinking. In addition, homicide claims the lives of nearly four times as many men as women (Miniño et al., 2007).

Smoking.   As women's lifestyles have become more similar to men's, so have some of their health behaviors. For example, while the frequency of men's smoking has declined over the past 40 years, that of women has increased since the 1930s and remains high among women aged 18–24 (Stewart et al., 2004). Nearly one in five women in the United States currently smoke. The prevalence of smoking varies widely across ethnic groups. Among women, Asian-Americans have the lowest rates (5 percent), followed by Latinas (10 percent), Blacks (19 percent), Whites (20 percent), and Native Americans (29 percent [Brener et al., 2007; Centers for Disease Control and Prevention, 2007])

The result of women's increase in smoking and men's decrease is that smoking-related deaths from lung cancer have declined for men but have soared for women

TABLE 12.3   Ten Leading Causes of Death for Females and Males in 2005

Rank	Women	Men
1	Heart disease	Heart disease
2	Cancer	Cancer
3	Cerebrovascular diseases (stroke)	Unintentional injuries
4	Chronic lung disease (asthma, bronchitis)	Chronic lung disease (asthma, bronchitis)
5	Alzheimer's disease	Cerebrovascular diseases (stroke)
6	Unintentional injuries	Diabetes
7	Diabetes	Pneumonia and influenza
8	Pneumonia and influenza	Suicide
9	Kidney disease	Kidney disease
10	Septicemia (infection of the blood)	Alzheimer's disease

Source: Heron (2007); National Center for Health Statistics (2007).

(Espey et al., 2007), surpassing breast cancer as the leading cause of cancer deaths among women. Smoking also is a key factor in the rise of chronic lung disease and stroke as a cause of death in women (American Cancer Society, 2008b).

Among high school students, girls are as likely to smoke as boys (Centers for Disease Control, 2007). Teenage girls are drawn to smoking for many reasons, including an attempt to express independence, curb appetite, reduce stress, and display "adult" behavior (Chesley et al., 2004; "Making the Grade," 2004; Maldonado-Molina et al., 2007). Young women are heavily targeted by the tobacco industry, which has intentionally designed cigarettes to promote smoking in women (Carpenter et al., 2005; Henningfield et al., 2005; Patel et al., 2004; Quindlen, 2007). In response to one advertiser's slogan, "You've come a long way baby," Claire reminds her students, "Yes, your rates of lung disease are getting closer to men's."

Another behavioral difference contributing to women's longevity is that women make greater use of preventive health services and are more likely to seek medical treatment when they are ill (Rabin, 2006). This may help explain why women live longer than men after the diagnosis of a potentially fatal disease. Women's greater tendency to visit the doctor's office suggests that they are more health conscious than men. Women generally know more than men about health, do more to prevent illness, are more aware of symptoms, are more likely to talk about their health concerns, and ask doctors more questions during visits (Elder, 1997; Levine, 2004; "Women Heed Warnings," 1998).

Women also outlive men because of their more extensive social support networks involving family, friends, and formal organizational memberships. Involvement in social relationships is related to living longer, perhaps because social ties reduce the impact of life stresses or convince us to increase our health-producing behaviors (Giles et al., 2005; Holt-Lunstad et al., 2008; McGinnis & Foege, 2004; Ray, 2004).

Social Class and Ethnic Differences

Women live longer than men regardless of social class and ethnic membership. Nevertheless, there are differences in longevity among women of different social classes and ethnic groups, as well as across cultures (see Explore Other Cultures 12.2).

Social Class.   Around the world, women and men with higher incomes and more education have longer life expectancies and better health (Lawlor & Sterne, 2007; Lawlor et al., 2006; Mannheim Research Institute, 2005; Schnittker, 2007). Some of this difference can be accounted for by a higher incidence of risk factors such as smoking, obesity, high blood pressure, and physical inactivity among the poor and working class. People with lower incomes are less able to afford decent medical care or even adequate food and experience higher levels of chronic stress as a result of such experiences as financial difficulties and job loss. The combination of all these factors shortens life expectancy and increases rates of illness and disease (Hill & Needham, 2006; Kivimäki et al., 2007; Sack, 2008; Singh & Siahpush, 2006).

Ethnicity.   Health risks and mortality rates for women vary by ethnic group (see Table 12.4). Mortality rates from all of the major causes of death (except car accidents, chronic lung disease, and suicide) are higher for Black women than for White women. Black, Latina, and Native American women are more likely than White women to die of diabetes. Asian American women, compared to White women, have lower mortality rates from heart disease; stroke; lung, breast and cervical cancer; cirrhosis; and chronic lung disease. Black women have the shortest life expectancy of any group and Asian Americans the longest (Heron, 2007). Differences in mortality rates for women of different ethnic groups are related to their economic status throughout their lives. Blacks

---

EXPLORE OTHER CULTURES **12.2**

Health Report Card for Women around the World

Women outlive men in almost every nation. In over half of developed countries, women's life expectancy is at least 80 years, an average of seven years more than men (Kinsella & Velkoff, 2001; National Center for Health Statistics, 2004). In developing countries, on the other hand, women outlive men by only three years. Women live longest in Japan—an average of 84 years—but live only until 43 years, on average, in Uganda. Longevity has increased for both sexes in almost all nations, with the exception of some African countries that have been devastated by HIV/AIDS (Mercer et al., 2001). Death in childbirth partially accounts for the smaller female advantage in longevity in developing countries, mostly in sub-saharan Africa and South Asia (World Health Organization, 2007). In some countries, however, the smaller difference also is a result of selective abortion and neglect of female children (see Chapter 14). Access to better health care helps account for the larger longevity differences between females and males in developed countries (Cavanaugh & Blanchard-Fields, 2006).

TABLE 12.4   Leading Causes of Death for Females by Ethnicity, 2005

Rank	White	Black	Native American	Asian/Pacific Islander	Latina
1	Heart disease	Heart disease	Heart disease	Cancer	Heart disease
2	Cancer	Cancer	Cancer	Heart disease	Cancer
3	Stroke	Stroke	Unintentional injuries	Stroke	Stroke
4	Chronic lung disease	Diabetes	Diabetes	Diabetes	Diabetes
5	Alzheimer's disease	Kidney disease	Stroke	Unintentional injuries	Unintentional injuries

Note: Native American includes American Indian and Alaskan Native females.
Source: Heron (2007); National Center for Health Statistics (2007).

and Native Americans, for example, have high mortality rates and low lifetime family incomes, while Asian Americans have some of the highest family incomes and lower mortality rates (Torrez, 2001).

Gender Differences in Illness

Although they live longer than men, women have more chronic conditions that cause suffering but do not kill. This is true in every country in which these statistics have been gathered, including developing nations (Beers & Jones, 2004; Mannheim Research Institute, 2005; Mathers et al., 2002). Women have higher rates of chronic fatigue syndrome, fibromyalgia, thyroid conditions, migraine headaches, anemia, urinary incontinence, and more than 80 autoimmune disorders such as rheumatoid arthritis, Crohn's disease, multiple sclerosis, and lupus (Carlson et al., 2004; Fairweather & Rose, 2004; Holroyd-Leduc & Straus, 2004; National Institutes of Health, 2004). American and Canadian women are less likely than their male counterparts to rate their health as excellent and more likely to describe it as good or fair (Adams et al.; 2008; Lawlor & Sterne, 2007; Quail et al., 2007; Sanmartin et al., 2004).

These statistics do not mean, however, that women are more likely than men to develop health problems. Women spend 71 of their years in good health and free of disability, compared with only 67 years for men. But because women live longer than men, it is women who more often live many years with chronic, often disabling illnesses (He et al., 2005). Keep in mind that a person may have one or more chronic diseases without being disabled. The key issue is whether the chronic condition restricts daily life or reduces the ability to take care of oneself (Bee, 2000).

Disability

As you might expect, the chance of developing a disability increases with age. About 18 percent of women ages 16 to 64 but 43 percent of women aged 65 and over have at least one functional limitation that affects basic physical activities such as walking, climbing stairs, lifting, or carrying ("Women and Disability," 2004). The degree of disability resulting from chronic conditions is assessed by measuring how well individuals can carry out two groups of activities: (1) **activities of daily living (ADLs),** which include *basic self-caring activities such as **eating**, bathing, toileting, walking, and getting in and out of a bed or chair*; and (2) **instrumental activities of daily living (IADLs),** which *go beyond personal care to include preparing meals, doing housework, shopping, doing laundry, attending social activities, using the telephone, taking medications, and managing money* (Majerovitz, 2006). Older women are more likely than older men to have functional limitations that affect both ADLs and IADLs (Adams et al., 2008; Minkler et al., 2006).

Among women age 65 to 74, 6 percent need help with ADLs such as bathing and dressing, while 18 percent need assistance with IADLs such as shopping and household chores (Campbell et al., 1999). In the 85 and over age group, 23 percent of women require help with ADLs, compared to only 12 percent of men ("How Healthy," 2003). African American women are more likely than other women to report chronic and/or disabling conditions, followed by Native American, Latina, and White women. Asian American women are only half as likely as other women to suffer from disabilities (Canetto, 2003; Carlson et al., 2004; He et al., 2005; Kelley-Moore & Ferraro, 2004). Life satisfaction is often lower for women who have disabilities than for other women. They are more likely to be depressed, to have elevated stress levels, and to rate their health as only fair or poor (Chevarley et al., 2006; Nosek et al., 2006). But chronic illness need not prevent a woman from enjoying her life. In the Women's Health and Aging study, 35 percent of women with moderate to severe disabilities reported a high sense of happiness and personal mastery and low levels of anxiety and depression (Unger & Seeman, 2000).

Promoting Good Health

It is a mistake simply to equate getting older with getting sicker. Throughout life, women can take active steps to maintain good health and decrease the impact of any health problems that develop. Lifestyle choices involving physical activity, good nutrition, not smoking, and moderate alcohol use can promote longevity and good health (He et al., 2005; Majerovitz, 2006).

In this section we examine practices that promote good health. For a closer look at some of these factors in elderly women, see Learn about the Research 12.2.

Physical Activity and Exercise

Most people are pantywaists. Exercise is good for you. (Emma "Grandma" Gatewood, age 67, the first person to hike the entire 2,170 miles of the Appalachian Trail three times, quoted in Snell, 2002.)

Physical Benefits.   The numerous health benefits of physical activity have been well documented. Regular physical exercise is linked with a reduction in the incidence of

LEARN ABOUT THE RESEARCH 12.2

Good Health Habits and Longevity

The relationship between good health habits and longevity was demonstrated dramatically in the Alameda County Study, a large-scale longitudinal investigation conducted in Alameda County, California (Breslow & Breslow, 1993; Kaplan, 1992). At the beginning of the study, the researchers asked each of the nearly 7,000 randomly chosen adults about their health practices. In a follow-up study done 18 years later, five good health behaviors were found to predict lower rates of death among the participants: keeping physically active, not smoking, drinking moderately, maintaining normal weight, and sleeping seven to eight hours a night. The most unexpected finding was that being involved in close relationships was as powerful a predictor of life expectancy as good health practices. Women and

men who followed the greatest number of good health practices and who were most involved in social networks were least likely to die over the 18 years of the study. Moreover, these individuals were only half as likely to develop disabilities.

Another more recent study suggests that both social activities and other nonstrenuous "productive" activities such as cooking, shopping, gardening, and volunteering may be just as important as physical activity in helping elderly people live longer (Glass et al., 1999). The findings, based on nearly 3,000 women and men age 65 and over living in New Haven, Connecticut, showed that physical, social, and productive activities produced similar benefits in increasing longevity.

What Does It Mean?

1. In this chapter, we have seen that women are more health conscious than men. Why do you think that is? What are the implications for women's greater longevity?
2. How can more women and men be encouraged to develop good health habits?
3. Teenagers and young adults are less likely to engage in good health practices than

are middle aged and older adults. What might account for this difference?
4. How would you explain the findings that social and productive activities increase longevity?

---

heart disease, stroke, breast cancer, colon cancer, ovarian cancer, hypertension, diabetes, and osteoporosis (Brody, 2008c; Goldberg, 2008; Ogilvie et al., 2007; "Prevalence," 2007). Even among individuals who cannot achieve ideal weight, exercise reduces the risk of health decline (Sui et al., 2007; Weinstein et al., 2008).

In the later years, physical activity enhances the range of motion of joints which can help arthritics maintain normal functioning. It also helps maintain the muscle strength, balance, and flexibility needed to perform activities of daily living (Hall, 2007). Exercise programs designed to improve balance and increase flexibility and strength in elderly women and men reduce the likelihood of falls, improve walking speed, and decrease reports of pain and disability (Chang et al., 2004). Even the very old can benefit from exercise. Maria Fiatarone and her colleagues (1994) conducted a study with 100 women and men whose average age was 87 (about one-third were in their 90s). Half worked out for 45 minutes three times a week on leg-strengthening machines. The program improved walking speed, stair-climbing ability, and overall level of physical activity. Four individuals were able to discard their walkers for canes.

Psychological Benefits. Women are more likely than men to exercise not only for physical fitness, but also for the psychological benefits it provides (AARP, 2002a). Regular exercise promotes a sense of well-being, feelings of accomplishment, happiness, and increased self-esteem. It also decreases tension, anxiety, depression, and anger (Carmichael, 2007; Menec, 2003; Nagourney, 2005; Netz et al., 2005; van Gool et al., 2006; Wilcox et al., 2006). Exercise improves physical appearance by developing and toning muscles and reducing body fat. Feeling good about personal appearance enhances self-esteem. Regular physical activity can develop increased abilities in one's favorite recreational activities, which also can improve self-esteem (Donatelle, 2009). Furthermore, physically active older adults outperform the sedentary elderly on tests of memory, reaction time, reasoning, attention, planning ability, mental speed, and mental flexibility. They also are less likely to develop dementia. These findings suggest that regular participation in exercise improves cognitive functioning in later life (Carmichael, 2007; Colcombe & Kramer, 2003; Majerovitz, 2006; Singh-Manoux et al., 2005; Weuve et al., 2004). An alternative explanation, of course, is that smart people may exercise more because they are aware of its benefits!

Factors Linked to Women's Activity Levels.   Although inactivity increases with age for both sexes, women of all ages are less apt to exercise than men (Brener et al., 2007; U.S. Census Bureau, 2007c). The proportion of American women who say they never exercise almost doubles, from 23 percent for those under 30 to 42 percent for those 75 and older. Only one-third of women over 75 show appropriate activity levels.

Latina, Native American, Asian American, and Black women and girls exercise less than White women and girls (Eaton et al., 2006; Kruger et al., 2005; Richmond et al., 2006). Much of this ethnic difference may be accounted for by differences in educational and income levels. Ethnic minority women are more likely to live in poverty and have lower income and educational levels than White women. Their neighborhoods often lack facilities that enable and promote physical activity (Powell et al., 2006). The proportion of women who engage in exercise rises as educational and income levels increase (Adams & Schoenborn, 2006; Cassetta et al., 2007).

One explanation for the low levels of physical activity among older women is the stereotype that exercise is increasingly seen as inappropriate as a person ages. This stereotype applies even more strongly to women than to men because of the societal expectation that at all ages, women are less physically active than men (Travis & Compton, 2001). In addition, the social construction of gender dictates that women are the primary caregivers and managers of home and family. Taking time away from domestic responsibilities to indulge in personal leisure may cause some women to feel selfish or guilty. In addition, the caregiving duties that many older women perform may sap their energy and make them too tired to be physically active (Hall, 2007; Reichert et al., 2007).

Older women must not only overcome sexist and ageist views about appropriate physical activity in later life but must also combat chronic health problems that inhibit many older people from exercising. Arthritic pain and urinary incontinence, chronic conditions that are much more prevalent in older women than in older men, may serve as deterrents to physical activity. Other barriers include the absence of a companion and the lack of convenient transportation to a safe and affordable exercise facility. In addition, some women feel that they are too old to improve their physical condition, fear that exercise may lead to injury or death, or believe that the declines of aging cannot be reversed (Markham, 2006; Nygaard et al., 2005; Reichert et al., 2007; Wilcox et al., 2003a). Unfortunately, older women are less likely than young women or older men to receive exercise counseling from their physicians ("Estimated percentage," 2007). Moreover, the issue of attractive exercise programming for older women has been largely overlooked by exercise specialists, yet another example of the relative invisibility and lack of power of older women (Travis & Compton, 2001).

Nutrition

As we have seen, good nutrition is a key factor in promoting health. Regardless of age, a healthful diet includes lots of vegetables, fruits, and whole grains; moderate amounts of protein; and sparing use of fats, oil, and sugar (Hall, 2007; Torpy, 2006).

But a woman's nutritional needs also vary over her lifespan. During puberty, for example, calorie requirements rise to at least 2,200 per day for the average girl, and more if she is physically active. Calcium intake is especially important to ensure maximum bone growth. Pregnant women need about 300 extra calories a day to attain the recommended weight gain of 22 to 27 pounds. Breastfeeding women require extra fluids, calcium, protein, and 500 more calories per day than prior to pregnancy. By menopause, women need only about two-thirds of the calories required when they were 20, plus increased consumption of calcium, vitamin B_{12}, and vitamin D (Carlson et al., 2004; Johnson, M.A. 2004; Lichtenstein et al., 2008).

Many older women who live independently do not consume sufficient amounts of one or more essential nutrients. The reasons for these deficiencies include difficulty getting to stores, insufficient income to buy wholesome foods, medications that interfere with absorption of nutrients, chronic conditions that restrict people to bland diets low in certain nutrients, problems with chewing, and loss of appetite. Poor appetite can result from illness, inactivity, diminished senses of taste and smell, depression, or eating alone (Brody, 2001; Wellman et al., 2007). Adequate intake of calcium and vitamin D is very important for older women in order to minimize the onset and severity of osteoporosis (Finkelstein, 2006; Houston et al., 2007). But few women consume the 1,200–1,500 milligrams of calcium recommended during the menopausal and postmenopausal years (North American Menopause Society, 2003). In addition, older people do not absorb vitamin D as readily as they did when younger. Thus, nutritionists recommend that elderly women take vitamin supplements to make sure that their dietary needs are met (Carlson et al., 2004; Johnson, M.A. 2004).

SUMMARY

Reproductive System Disorders

- Benign disorders of the reproductive system include endometriosis and fibroid tumors.
- Uterine and cervical cancers have higher survival rates than ovarian cancer.
- The Pap smear is an effective screening device for cervical cancer.
- American women have one of the highest hysterectomy rates in the world.

Osteoporosis

- Osteoporosis, the loss of bone tissue, increases after menopause and can lead to disabling and even fatal fractures.
- Building and maintaining bone mass is enhanced by increasing calcium intake; decreasing use of alcohol, caffeine, and tobacco; increasing physical activity; and taking estrogen or certain medications.

Heart Disease

- Heart disease, the leading killer of women, increases dramatically after menopause.
- Women develop heart disease later than men and are twice as likely to die of it.
- Risk factors for heart disease include gender, age, ethnicity, family history, smoking, physical inactivity, high cholesterol levels, high blood pressure, diabetes, and being overweight.

- Women with heart disease receive less aggressive treatment than men.

Breast Cancer

- One in eight women will develop breast cancer, but survival rates have been increasing.
- Risk factors include age, ethnicity, family history, drinking, smoking, weight gain, and inactivity.
- Many women do not do monthly breast self-exams or get regular mammograms.
- For small early tumors, lumpectomy with radiation is as effective as mastectomy.
- Support groups help women cope with cancer.

Physical Health in Later Life

- At every age, women report more illness and use of health-care services than men, yet women consistently outlive men.
- Both biological factors and lifestyle differences are responsible for women's greater longevity.
- Health risks and mortality rates for women differ by social class and ethnic group.
- Older women are more likely than older men to have some difficulty with various activities of daily living.

Promoting Good Health

- Practices that promote good health include physical activity and good nutrition.

KEY TERMS

Medicare
Medicaid
spending down
fee-for-service insurance
managed care
acquired immunodeficiency
    syndrome (AIDS)
endometriosis
fibroid tumors

cervix
Pap smear
osteoporosis
hysterectomy
fibroid embolization
raloxifene
mammogram
radical mastectomy
modified radical mastectomy

simple mastectomy
lumpectomy
mortality
morbidity
gender paradox
activities of daily living (ADLs)
instrumental activities of daily
    living (IADLs)

WHAT DO YOU THINK?

1. Why do you think women's heart disease risks were largely ignored until fairly recently? What actions can individuals take to help improve this situation? What actions can members of the medical community take?

2. How can knowledge of risk factors for diseases in older White women and older women of color help us in prevention and early detection of these diseases? How can high risk factors be reduced for both groups?

3. Why do you think there is a difference between mammogram screening rates for women who differ in socioeconomic status? What actions could be taken to change these disparities?

4. Of the health conditions mentioned in this chapter, which ones can you prevent? Which ones can you delay? What actions can you take now to protect yourself from these problems? Which of these are you currently doing, and why?

IF YOU WANT TO LEARN MORE

Alexander, L. L., LaRosa, J. H., Bader, H., & Garfield, S. (2006). *New dimensions in women's health* (4th ed.). Sudbury, MA: Jones and Bartlett.

Banks, M. E., & Kaschak, E. (Eds.). (2003). *Women with visible and invisible disabilities: Multiple intersections, multiple issues, multiple therapies.* New York: Haworth.

Bird, C. E, & Rieker, P. P. (2008) *Gender and health: The effects of constrained choices and social policies.* New York: Cambridge University Press.

Cartwright, E., & Allotey, P. (Eds.). (2007). *Women's health: New frontiers in advocacy and social justice research.* Binghampton, NY: Haworth.

Ciambrone, D. (2004). *Women's experiences with HIV/AIDS: Mending fractured selves.* New York: Haworth.

Goldberg, N. (2002). *Women are not small men: Strategies for preventing and healing heart disease in women.* New York: Ballantine.

Goldberg, N. (2008). *Dr. Nieca Goldberg's complete guide to women's health.* New York: Ballantine.

Kolander, C. A., Ballard, D. M., & Chandler, C. K. (2007). *Contemporary women's health: Issues for today and the future.* New York: McGraw-Hill.

Link, J. (2007). *Breast cancer survival manual: A step by step guide for the woman with newly diagnosed breast cancer* (4th ed.). New York: Owl Books.

Meyer, I., & Northridge, M. (Eds.). (2007). *The health of sexual minorities: Public health perspectives on lesbian, gay, bisexual and transgender populations.* New York: Springer.

Northrup, C. (2006). *Women's bodies, women's wisdom: Creating physical and emotional health and healing.* New York: Bantam Books.

WEBSITES

Health Care and Health Issues: General

The AMA Women's Health Information Centre
http://www.ama-assn.org/
New York Times articles on women's health and excerpts from the Harvard Guide to Women's Health and the American Medical Women's Association Women's Complete Health Book
http://www.nytimes.com/women

The National Women's Health Information Center
http://www.4woman.gov
Iris Cantor Women's Health Center
http://www.cornellwomenshealth.com
The Society for Women's Health Research
http://www.womenshealthresearch.org/
http://www.fda.gov/womens/tttc.html

http://www.womensorganizations.org/
http://www.nwhn.org/
http://www.cdc.gov/health/womensmenu.htm

Disability

Disabled People's International
http://www.dpi.org
National Organization on Disability
http://www.nod.org
American Association of Persons with Disabilities
http://www.aapd-dc.org

Heart Disease

American Heart Association
http://www.amhrt.org
American Heart Association
http://www.americanheart.org/

Cancer

American Cancer Society
http://www.cancer.org
National Ovarian Cancer Coalition (NOCC)

http://www.ovarian.org
The Susan G. Komen Breast Cancer
Foundation
http://www.komen.org

Arthritis

Arthritis Foundation
http://www.arthritis.org
National Institute of Arthritis and
Musculoskeletal and Skin Diseases
http://www.niams.nih.gov

Diabetes

American Association of Diabetes Educators
http://www.diabeteseducator.org
National Institute of Diabetes and Digestive
and Kidney Diseases
http://www.niddk.nih.gov

Lesbian Health

Lesbian Health Research Center
http://www.lesbianhealthinfo.org

Factors Promoting Mental Health
    Social Support
    Optimism: "The Power of Positive
      Thinking"

**Mental Health in Childhood and
Adolescence**
    Internalizing Disorders in Girls
    Externalizing Disorders in Girls

Eating Disorders
    Types of Eating Disorders
    Causes of Eating Disorders
    Treatment of Eating Disorders

Substance Use and Abuse
    Alcohol
    Illegal Substances

Anxiety Disorders and Depression
  Anxiety Disorders
  Depression
  Suicide
Mental Health of Lesbians
  Stresses and Problems
  Coping Mechanisms
Mental Health of Older Women
  Gender Differences
  The Vital Older Woman

Diagnosis and Treatment of Psychological Disorders
  Gender Bias in Diagnosis
  Gender Bias in Psychotherapy
  Therapy Issues for Women of Color and
    Poor Women
  Types of Therapy

I was diagnosed with anorexia nervosa in my sophomore year of high school. I was always the bigger one of my friends and my boyfriend at the time would always tell me he liked the fact that I was chubby. I would see all the stick-skinny models and actresses on TV and feel completely disgusted with myself. At one point during my fight with anorexia, I weighed about 35 pounds less than was healthy for my height and I was very sick. It is so scary to look in a mirror and see fat when you are actually skin and bones. It ruined my relationship with so many loved ones and I still don't have regular menstrual cycles. (Stephanie, college junior, age 20)

It happened one Saturday night [at] a Greek restaurant . . . Suddenly I began to feel as if the walls were edging in. My palms grew damp, my heart drummed, my stomach churned. I had only one thought: If you don't get out of this restaurant immediately, you are going to faint or die. I mumbled that I didn't feel well and raced for the door . . . I began to avoid restaurants, but then my panic [appeared] in other venues . . . My world shrank to a thin corridor of safe places. (Anndee Hochman, 2004, pp. 99–100)

Overall, rates of mental illness are almost identical for women and men. There are, however, striking gender differences in the prevalence of specific mental disorders. Women have higher rates of eating disorders, depression, and anxiety disorders. Men are more likely to have impulse-control, antisocial, and substance abuse disorders (DeAngelis & Glass, 2006; Marsh, 2006; Silverman & Carter, 2006). In this chapter, we focus not only on pathology, but also on mental *health* and the factors that promote it. We begin the chapter by looking at two key factors that are associated with good mental health: social support and optimism. We then explore mental health in childhood and adolescence, followed by a discussion of eating disorders and substance abuse. Next, we explore anxiety disorders, depression, and suicide. We then discuss mental health issues of lesbians and of older women. We close with a look at the diagnosis and treatment of psychological disorders.

Factors Promoting Mental Health

Social Support

A substantial body of research indicates that both receiving and giving social support plays an important role in maintaining good mental health and helping people cope with stressful life events (Brown et al., 2003; Diener & Seligman, 2004; Durden et al., 2007; Ellis, 2006; Väänänen et al., 2005). This association is especially strong for females. For example, girls are more likely than boys to seek social support following stressful events, and this support appears to play a more protective role for girls than for boys (Jackson & Warren, 2000; Llabre & Hadi, 1997; Rose & Rudolph, 2006). Similarly, recent studies have found that women who feel more loved and supported by their friends, relatives, and children are at less risk for major depression. Among men, however, level of social support is less strongly related to the risk of depression (Kendler et al., 2005; Wareham et al., 2007).

Tend and Befriend.   Women also use social support as a coping aid more readily than men do. Shelley Taylor and her colleagues (2000, 2002, 2003) have proposed that women often respond to stress by tending to themselves and their children and by forming ties with others (the "tend and befriend" response). Men, in contrast, are more likely to show aggression or escape. This so-called "fight or flight" response was proposed by psychologists 60 years ago to explain how both men and women react to stress. That view, however, was heavily based on studies of males (Azar, 2000; Goode, 2000) and was just assumed to apply to females (yet another example of the "male as normative"). But Taylor and her colleagues found many studies that supported their model. For example, Rena Repetti's research (cited in Taylor et al., 2000) showed that mothers returning home after a stressful day at the office were more caring and nurturant toward their children, while stressed fathers were more likely to withdraw from their families or incite conflict. What stimulates these different behaviors in females and males? Taylor and her colleagues suggest that hormonal differences are partly responsible, but they and others are quick to reject the idea that gender stereotypes are biologically hard-wired. Alice Eagly (cited in Goode, 2000), for example, points out that the gender difference could be a result of cultural conditioning that prepares females from an early age for the role of caregiver and nurturer.

Optimism: "The Power of Positive Thinking"

Question: "Do you know the difference between an optimist and a pessimist?"
Answer: The first one sees the glass as half full, while the second sees it as half empty.

You may have heard this saying before, but did you also know that optimism can actually be good for your health? An optimistic outlook—the expectation that good rather than bad things will happen—has been linked to a variety of positive mental and

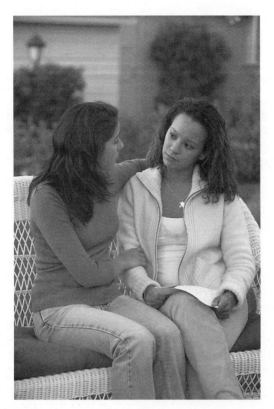

Women are more likely than men to use social support to cope with stress.

physical health outcomes (Giltay et al., 2004; Jones et al., 2004; Kivimäki et al., 2005; Schnieder, 2001). A recent study by Deborah Jones and her colleagues (2004), for example, found that optimism appeared to protect women from some of the health risks associated with depression. Another intriguing finding by Karen Matthews and her associates (2004) is that middle-aged women with an optimistic outlook on life are less likely to show the beginning of heart disease than are pessimists.

Mental Health in Childhood and Adolescence

Compared to boys, girls show fewer adjustment problems in childhood. Girls, however, are more likely than boys to first manifest psychological difficulties during the adolescent years (Blanchard et al., 2006; Costello et al., 2003; Federal Interagency Forum, 2007; Katz, 2008). Stress levels increase for both genders during these years. However, the patterns of stress girls encounter may leave them more vulnerable to emotional disorders, such as anxiety and depression, than do those experienced by boys (Broderick & Korteland, 2002; Costello et al., 2003; Rose & Rudolph, 2006). We shall explore these stresses later in the chapter.

Internalizing Disorders in Girls

Adjustment problems that are more common in girls and women, such as depression, anxiety, and social withdrawal, are often labeled "internalizing problems" (American Psychological Association, 2007a; Graber, 2004). Later in the chapter, we discuss these disorders in greater detail. Internalizing disorders are harder to detect and easier to overlook than the externalizing problems more often shown by boys and men: aggression, conduct disorders, antisocial behaviors, and attention deficit hyperactivity disorder (Hammarberg & Hagekull, 2006; Hill et al., 2006; Zhou et al., 2007). Early socialization of girls and boys into gender-typed behaviors may be responsible for these differences in the expression of distress (Andreasen, 2005; Hoffmann et al., 2004; Hoglund & Leadbeater, 2004).

Externalizing Disorders in Girls

Ironically, girls with externalizing disturbances are rarely studied because of the notion that these are "male" problems (Prinstein & La Greca, 2004; Serbin et al., 2004). This stereotype persists despite the fact that acts of violence by teenage girls are on the increase. Large national surveys show that 15 to 30 percent of girls have committed a serious violent offense, such as aggravated assault, by age 17 (Lamberg, 2002). Girls who show externalizing problems, compared to other girls, exhibit deficits in social, emotional, and communication skills and elevated rates of substance use, anxiety, and risky sexual behavior (Bierman et al., 2004; Prinstein & LaGreca, 2004; Wasserman et al., 2005; White, 2001). Moreover, these girls are more likely to have difficulties as adults. For example, longitudinal studies in Sweden (Wangby et al., 1999), New Zealand (Fergusson & Woodward, 2000), Canada (Serbin et al., 2004), and the United States (Molnar et al., 2005; Silver et al., 2007) found that girls with externalizing problems in childhood and early adolescence were at greater risks of all types of maladjustment in late adolescence and adulthood than were those without such problems. They had higher rates of educational failure, juvenile crime, substance abuse, mental health problems, pregnancy, and poor parenting skills. On the other hand, there was little or no relationship between having internalizing problems during adolescence and later maladjustment (Wangby et al., 1999).

Eating Disorders

The prevalence of eating disorders among women has increased dramatically since the 1980s in the United States and Western Europe, paralleling the increase in girls' and women's body dissatisfaction that we discussed in Chapter 4 (Neumark-Sztainer et al., 2006; Van Son et al., 2006). In this section, we examine types of eating disorders, their likely causes, and their treatment.

Types of Eating Disorders

Three major types of eating disorders have been identified. They are anorexia nervosa, bulimia nervosa, and binge eating disorder. Stephanie, one of Claire's students, described her battle with anorexia in the first vignette at the beginning of the chapter.

Anorexia Nervosa.   The defining characteristics of **anorexia nervosa** are *a refusal to maintain a minimal normal body weight (defined as 85 percent of ideal weight), intense fear of gaining weight, a distorted body image (feeling fat even when too thin), and amenorrhea* (lack of menstruation) in females. Anorexic individuals diet, fast, and exercise excessively in order to lose weight (Wonderlich et al., 2007). Unlike "normal" dieters, anorexics may lose 25 percent of their original body weight. Many of them share self-starvation tips and "thinspiration" messages on so-called "pro-ana" Websites (Carvajal, 2008; Nagourney, 2005; Norris et al., 2006). One recent survey of teens diagnosed with eating disorders at Stanford University's children's hospital found that 40 percent had visited "pro-ana" Websites (Irvine, 2005). Unfortunately, dramatic weight loss can cause osteoporosis, hormone abnormalities, dangerously low blood pressure, and damage to vital organs (Miller et al., 2005; Misra et al., 2004; Morris, 2004b). Anorexic individuals have a nearly 12-fold greater risk of death from all causes and a 57-fold greater risk of death by suicide than their peers (Zucker et al., 2007).

Girls and women account for more than 95 percent of cases of anorexia nervosa. About 1 percent of female adolescents and young adults suffer from the disorder in the United States and Western Europe (Berkman et al., 2007; Henig, 2004b). While anorexia is often thought of as a White, middle-class or upper-class disease, its incidence is increasing among women of color and poor women (Brodey, 2005; Franko et al., 2007; Jacobi et al., 2004). Although the peak period for anorexia is adolescence (Striegel-Moore & Bulik, 2007), females can become anorexic at virtually any age. It is no longer rare for 9- or 10-year-old girls to have the disorder (Tyre, 2005). In addition, a growing number of women in midlife and beyond are developing eating disorders. Many of these women have likely been overly concerned with weight and body image throughout their lives (Brandsma, 2007; Procapio et al., 2006). The midlife trigger for the eating disorder may be the 10- to 15-pound weight gain that typically occurs during menopause. Sometimes, losing a spouse, dealing with a troubled child, or even having a child leave for college can set off eating problems (Mangweth-Matzek et al., 2006; McKinley, 2006; Morris, 2004b).

Young women with physical disabilities also have an elevated risk of developing symptoms of eating disorders. These women may be more vulnerable because their disabilities often involve body-image disturbances, they feel lack of control resulting from needing assistance from others, and they may focus on weight maintenance to sustain mobility (Gross et al., 2000).

Bulimia Nervosa.   The primary features of **bulimia nervosa** are *recurrent episodes of uncontrolled binge eating, followed by purging activities aimed at controlling body weight.* Purging activities include self-induced vomiting, exercise, extreme dieting or fasting, and the abuse of laxatives, diuretics, or enemas (Shapiro et al., 2007). One young woman, bulimic since the age of 9, graphically describes her binge–purge cycles:

> *At my lunch break, I would eat a quarter-pounder with cheese, large fries, and a cherry pie. Then I would throw up in the antiseptic-scented bathroom, wash my face and go back on the floor, glassy-eyed and hyper. After work, I would buy a quarter-pounder with cheese, large fries, and a cherry pie, eat it on the way home from work, throw up at home*

Brazilian model Ana Carolina Reston is shown here in a fashion show a year before her death in 2006 from complications resulting from anorexia nervosa. She was just 21 years old when she died and weighed only 88 pounds.

with the bathtub running, eat dinner, throw up, go out with friends, eat, throw up, go home, pass out. (Hornbacher, 1998, p. 91)

Individuals with bulimia seem to be driven by an intense fear of weight gain and a distorted perception of body size similar to that seen in anorexics. Unlike anorexics, however, bulimics often maintain normal weight (Russo & Tartaro, 2008). Although usually not life-threatening, bulimia can cause intestinal and kidney problems, as well as extensive tooth decay because of gastric acid in the vomited food. Bulimia also may result in an imbalance of electrolytes, the chemicals necessary for the normal functioning of the heart (Alexander et al., 2000).

As with anorexia nervosa, young women account for more than 90 percent of the cases of bulimia. Across the United States and Western Europe, about 1 percent of females in late adolescence and early adulthood have bulimia (Shapiro et al., 2007). The typical onset is in late adolescence (Henig, 2004b).

Binge Eating Disorder.   This disorder is characterized by recurrent binge eating in the absence of compensatory weight-control efforts. It is the most common of the eating disorders, has a later onset, and is often associated with obesity (Berkman et al., 2007; Keel, 2005). Sex differences are far less pronounced for this disorder (Striegel-Moore & Bulik, 2007).

Causes of Eating Disorders

Biological, psychological, and cultural factors all seem to play a part in the development of eating disorders (Klump et al., 2007; Striegel-Moore & Bulik, 2007). Let us consider each of these in turn.

Biological Factors.   One line of biological evidence comes from comparing identical twins (who share the same genetic material) with fraternal twins (who share only half). An identical twin is much more likely than a fraternal twin to develop an eating disorder if her co-twin also has the disorder (Jacobi et al., 2004; Klump & Culbert, 2007). While this research suggests the existence of a genetic predisposition toward eating disorders, these findings could also reflect identical twins' highly similar social and cultural environments. Another biological consideration is that anorexics have disturbances in their levels of serotonin, a mood- and appetite-regulating chemical in the brain. However, these chemical imbalances may result *from* the eating disorder rather than cause it (Striegel-Moore & Bulik, 2007).

Psychological Factors.   Certain psychological characteristics also put young women at higher risk for eating disorders. These include low self-esteem, high levels of anxiety, depression, perfectionism, conscientiousness, competitiveness, obsessive-compulsive thoughts and behaviors, difficulty in separating from parents, strong need for approval from others, and perceived lack of control in one's life (Berkman et al., 2007; Cohen & Petrie, 2005; Jacobi et al., 2004; Keel, 2005; Mensinger et al., 2007). Eating disorders may also reflect family problems. For example, parents of anorexics are overly nurturant and overprotective and place undue emphasis on achievement and appearance. Families of bulimics are more hostile, conflicted, and disorganized, as well as less nurturant and supportive than families of anorexics or normal adolescents (Halmi, 2000). Another risk factor for eating disorders is sexual or physical abuse (Jacobi et al., 2004; Sanci et al., 2008).

Cultural Factors.   Some feminists view eating disorders as drastic attempts to attain the reed-thin ideal of beauty that has been socially constructed by a patriarchal society (e.g., Piran, 2001). The impact of the media in transmitting this message is illustrated dramatically in Anne Becker's study of adolescent girls living in Fiji (Becker et al., 2007). For details, read Explore Other Cultures 13.1.

In North America, the effect of cultural pressures to be thin is perhaps seen most vividly among girls and young women who are involved in sports. The incidence of disordered eating (ranging from excessive dieting to anorexia or bulimia) among female athletes is estimated to be as high as 62 percent, far greater than the estimate of 3 percent among the general population of girls and young women (Arnold, 2004). *The combination of disordered eating accompanied by amenorrhea and premature bone loss, or osteoporosis* (discussed in Chapter 12), is sometimes referred to as the **female athlete triad** (Longman, 2007). The prevalence of this condition appears to have grown along with girls' participation in dance and performance sports such as gymnastics and figure skating, in which a slim figure is considered ideal (Parsons & Betz, 2001; Powers,

2002). Athletes competing at an elite (that is, highly competitive national or international) level are at greatest risk (Smolak et al., 2000). Claire's student Betsy, who spent several years at a strict, elite ballet academy, described the pressure to stay thin:

> *Standing at the barre, the ballet master would poke and pull at your body. The professionals would stand outside between rehearsals always holding a cigarette. All the young students concluded that smoking, in replacement of food, made you thinner. Although I never started smoking, I started consuming orange juice . . . and that's all. At slumber parties on the weekends, I made sure that my friends thought I loved food, and saw me devour the pizza. I also made sure that they didn't see me get rid of it in the bathroom afterward.*

Treatment of Eating Disorders

Eating disorders are difficult to cure. Cognitive behavioral therapy, which helps people to change both their behaviors and the way they think about themselves and others, seems to be more effective than other forms of therapy for bulimia and binge-eating disorder. Antidepressants are also of use in treating these disorders (Chavez & Insel, 2007; Keel & Haedt, 2008; Mitchell et al., 2007; Wilson et al., 2007). Family therapy, which elicits the parents' aid in getting the client to eat and then gradually

---

EXPLORE OTHER CULTURES 13.1
Cultural Pressure to Be Thin

Numerous studies suggest that young women in populations undergoing Westernization and modernization may be at increased risk for disordered eating (Becker et al., 2007). A major reason for this association may be exposure to the modern Western cultural body ideal of thinness. In one striking example, Anne Becker interviewed girls in Fiji, a small Pacific island, just as television was introduced in 1995. Only 3 percent of girls reported they vomited to control their weight. In 1998, 15 percent reported the behavior. Similarly, 29 percent scored highly on a test of eating-disorder risk in 1998 compared with just 13 percent in 1995. The more television the girls watched, the more likely they were to diet and to report feeling "too big or fat." Several girls mentioned that they wanted to look like the Western women they saw on television shows (Becker et al., 2007). The study does not conclusively prove that television helps cause eating disorders. Still, Becker notes that the increases are dramatic in a culture that traditionally has equated a robust, nicely rounded body with health and that considers considerable weight loss ("going thin") a sign of illness.

A similar cultural shift is taking place in West and Central Africa where the big, voluptuous woman has been considered the ideal of female beauty. In Nigeria, for example, brides are sent to fattening farms before their weddings. But in 2001, tall, slim, Agbani Darego of Nigeria won the Miss World title. Since then, Nigerian girls and young women clamor to be thin (Onishi, 2002).

returns control of eating to the client, shows promise in the treatment of anorexia in adolescents (Bulik et al., 2007; Keel & Haedt, 2008; Wilson et al., 2007). Antidepressants sometimes help prevent relapse once the anorexic client returns to normal. They are not effective in reversing anorexic symptoms, however (Chavez & Insel, 2007; Crow, 2006).

Anorexia is particularly resistant to a wide range of interventions (Bulik et al., 2007). While long-term outcomes vary by study, typically fewer than half of the clients fully recover, about 25 to 30 percent show some improvement, approximately 20 percent remain chronically ill, and 5 to 10 percent are deceased (Fichter et al., 2006). In follow-up studies, up to two-thirds of treated anorexic patients continued to show disturbed attitudes toward food, weight, and body shape (Wentz et al., 2001). Treatment for bulimia tends to be more successful. About half of women diagnosed as bulimic show full recovery five to ten years later, while 30 percent show some symptoms and 20 percent still have the full-blown disorder (Keel, 2005). Binge-eating disorder has a more favorable prognosis than either anorexia or bulimia, with a recovery rate of about 80 percent five years after treatment and a low relapse rate (Russell & Carr, 2003).

Substance Use and Abuse

Until recently, substance use was considered primarily a male problem, and much of the research dealing with abuse of alcohol and other drugs was carried out on males. This oversight has led to inadequate diagnosis and treatment of women with substance abuse disorders (American Psychological Association, 2007; Russo & Tartaro, 2008). In this section, we concentrate on substance abuse issues in women.

Alcohol

Incidence.   Both in adolescence and adulthood, females are less likely than males to use alcohol and to be heavy drinkers (Adams & Schoenborn, 2006; Hasin et al., 2007; Johnston et al., 2007; Merrick et al., 2008). Overall, about 8 percent of women and 17 percent of men have been diagnosed with alcohol problems, a male-to-female ratio of over 2 to 1 (Greenfield, 2002). *However, while women's alcoholism starts later than men's alcoholism, it progresses more quickly*, a pattern called **telescoping** (Godfrey, 2007). White women have higher rates of alcohol use than women in other ethnic groups; they are followed by Native-American women, Black women, and Latinas. Asian American women have the lowest rates of alcohol use (Adams & Schoenborn, 2006).

Problem drinking in young women has been increasing at an alarming rate both in the United States and the United Kingdom (Eaton et al., 2008; Fletcher, 2005). For example, U.S. college women are now almost as likely as college men to engage in **binge drinking,** defined as *having five drinks in a row for men or four in a row for women at least once in the last two weeks.* Half of college men and 41 percent of college women are binge drinkers (Wechsler et al., 2002). Heavy drinking is especially prevalent among sorority women (Mohler-Kuo et al., 2004). Sadly, the gender gap in drinking has disappeared among young adolescents: Female and male high schoolers are equally likely to drink (both at 45 percent) and Females are almost as likely to binge drink (24 versus 28 percent) (Eaton et al., 2008). One possible explanation is an increase in alcohol advertising targeting teenage girls. In the past few years, advertising for low-alcohol drinks such as wine coolers and alcoholic iced teas has increased in national magazines, but especially in those read primarily by adolescent girls (Jernigan et al., 2004).

Health Consequences. Women have more body fat, less water, and less of the enzyme that breaks down alcohol than men do. As a result, they have higher levels of alcohol in their blood even when they consume the same amount of alcohol per unit of body weight (National Institutes of Health, 2005; Springen & Kantrowitz, 2004). For example, 3 ounces of alcohol consumed by a 120-pound woman has a greater effect on her than the equivalent 6 ounces of alcohol consumed by a 240-pound man has on him. As women age, they are subject to an even greater physiological susceptibility to alcohol's effect (Epstein et al., 2007). Thus, women experience impairment or intoxication after fewer drinks (APA, 2007a). Another consequence is that women develop cirrhosis of the liver, hepatitis, heart disease, and brain damage at lower levels of alcohol intake than men. Prolonged heavy drinking also increases the risk of breast cancer, osteoporosis, and infertility (National Institutes of Health, 2005; Prendergast, 2004; Springen & Kantrowitz, 2004). In addition, college women who drink heavily increase their risk of being sexually assaulted (Cole, 2006).

Drinking alcohol during pregnancy can lead to **fetal alcohol syndrome (FAS),** *a disorder characterized by mental retardation, growth deficiencies, facial deformities, and learning and behavioral problems* (O'Callaghan et al., 2007). FAS is the third most common birth defect and the leading preventable cause of mental retardation in the United States (Kvigne et al., 2004). Even light drinkers risk having children with **fetal alcohol effect (FAE),** *a milder but still serious form of FAS* (Sayal et al., 2007; "Surgeon General's Advisory," 2005). Unfortunately, more than half of the women of childbearing age drink occasionally, and 12 percent report that they binge drink at least once a month, potentially exposing fetuses early during the first trimester before the women realizes she is pregnant (Centers for Disease Control and Prevention, 2005). Sadly, a woman who binge drinks during pregnancy triples her child's odds of having drinking-related problems in young adulthood (Baer et al., 2003).

Risk Factors. Children of alcoholic parents or siblings have increased rates of alcoholism. Genetic factors may play about as strong a role for daughters as for sons, although findings are mixed (Bouchard, 2004; National Institute on Alcohol Abuse and Alcoholism, 2003). Adolescents whose parents and peers consume alcohol and tolerate its use are more likely to start drinking at an early age, which places them at higher risk for later alcohol-related problems (Jersild, 2002; Misra, 2001; National Institutes of Health, 2003). Women who were sexually abused in childhood or who had emotional or behavioral problems early in life are also at greater risk for later alcohol problems. Divorced and single women are more likely than married or widowed women to drink heavily and to have alcohol-related problems (National Institutes of Health, 2003). Women who are heavy drinkers also are more likely than other women to be depressed and anxious and to report stressful life events (King et al., 2003; Springen & Kantrowitz, 2004).

Treatment.   Society has set up several double standards for women and men. The double standard of aging was described in Chapter 2 and the double standard of sexuality was discussed in Chapter 6. There is also a double standard with regard to drinking. Heavy drinking in men is often expected and seen as normal, whereas heavy drinking in women is strongly criticized. As a result, women tend to hide or deny their alcohol use, making them less likely to seek help and to be more seriously ill before the disease is diagnosed (National Institutes of Health, 2003). Moreover, physicians are less likely to counsel female patients than male patients on alcohol or drug use (Bertakis & Azari, 2007; Chan et al., 2006). One study (Brown et al., 1995), for example, found that only one-third of women who had a checkup during the past year were asked about their drinking patterns. For women over 65, the rate dropped to one-sixth. This is yet another example of the invisibility of older women. Twelve-step alcoholism treatment programs such as Alcoholics Anonymous have been criticized for being based exclusively on research with alcoholic men. Alternative programs, such as Women for Sobriety, focus on the special issues and needs of women with drinking problems (Canterbury, 2002; Wartik, 2001). Although these programs have shown some success in treating alcohol disorders in women, they are in short supply (Windle & Windle, 2002). Current treatment options for older women are especially limited (Epstein et al., 2007).

Illegal Substances

Incidence.   Use of illegal substances such as marijuana, cocaine, heroin, hallucinogens, and steroids varies by gender and ethnic group. Among women, use is highest among Native Americans, followed by White, Latina, Black, and Asian American women. Regardless of ethnicity, however, males have higher rates of illegal drug use than females both in adolescence and adulthood. Males also use illegal drugs more heavily than females do (Johnston et al., 2007; Eaton et al., 2008). One possible reason for the gender gap is that drug use among girls and women is less acceptable in our society. Recently, the gender gap in substance use has decreased as a result of a steeper decline in use among males than among females (Johnston et al., 2005). One disturbing trend, for example, is an increase in the use of anabolic (muscle-building) steroids by preteen and adolescent girls (Elliot et al., 2007; Johnston et al., 2007). According to health experts, some teenage girl athletes are moving away from a preoccupation with thinness toward a lean, more muscular look, a trend labeled "reverse anorexia" (Adler, 2004; Nyad, 2004). Unfortunately, not only does steroid use expose females to the same severe health risks as boys (e.g., heart, liver, kidney, and skin diseases), but it also may damage their ability to bear children (Adler, 2004; National Institute on Drug Abuse, 2007).

Typically, individuals who use illegal substances use more than one and also use or abuse alcohol. In girls and women, the problem is compounded because they are more likely than men to both use and misuse prescription drugs, such as tranquilizers, antidepressants, and sleeping pills (Marecek & Hare-Mustin, 1998; Merline et al., 2004).

Treatment.   As with treatment for alcohol problems, women in drug abuse treatment programs have different needs than men in treatment (Russo & Tartaro, 2008).

A successful program for women often depends on meeting these different needs, according to Christine Grella, who found that women in women-only drug treatment programs were more than twice as likely to complete treatment as women in mixed-gender programs ("UCLA Study," 2000).

Anxiety Disorders and Depression

More than one in four Americans will have an anxiety disorder in their lifetime and nearly one in five will develop major depression (Kessler et al., 2005). Women are at greater risk than men for both disorders. In this section, we first review anxiety disorders. We then turn to depression and its all-too-frequent outcome: suicide.

Anxiety Disorders

Almost everyone feels anxious now and again. When you have to give a speech in class, for instance, it is normal to feel anxious. But when anxiety is irrational, excessive, and persists over several months, it is called an anxiety disorder (Carlson et al., 2004). Most anxiety disorders occur two to three times as frequently in women as in men (American Psychological Association, 2007a; McHugh, 2008; Silverman & Carter, 2006).

Generalized anxiety disorder is characterized by *excessive worry and anxiety about a variety of life situations or events.* Many people experience physical symptoms as well. It is one of the most common anxiety disorders, with about 7 percent of women developing it at some time in their lives (Silverman & Carter, 2006). The difference between ordinary worrying and generalized anxiety disorder is that the level of concern is excessive, resulting in distress and interfering with everyday functioning (Mahler, 2003).

Panic disorder is marked by *sudden unpredictable attacks of intense anxiety accompanied by a pounding heart, dizziness, sweating, shortness of breath, and trembling.* A person having an attack has a sense of impending doom, losing control, or dying (Hanisch et al., 2008). About 5 percent of women and 2 percent of men will develop this disorder at some time (Russo & Tartaro, 2008). As shown in the second vignette at the beginning of the chapter, panic disorder can lead to **agoraphobia,** a *fear of being in public places where escape might be difficult if one were suddenly incapacitated* (*agora* is the Greek word for "marketplace") (Hanisch et al., 2008). Agoraphobia, the most common phobia, will be experienced by about 7 percent of women and 4 percent of men during their lifetimes (Russo & Tartaro, 2008).

Agoraphobia is just one of a group of anxiety disorders known as a **specific phobia,** a *fear of a specific object, such as a spider, or a specific situation, such as being in public places, or flying.* Roughly 14 percent of women develop a specific phobia at some time in their life (Pigott, 2002). Specific phobias usually start in childhood. Social construction of gender-specific attitudes and behaviors may account for the higher prevalance of these phobias in females than in males. Expression of fear and anxiety is more socially acceptable in girls and women than in boys and men, who are discouraged from displaying these emotions (McHugh, 2008; Silverman & Carter, 2006).

Depression

> *I have been immobilized, unable to formulate thought or action. Can't get out of bed most of the time. I feel terrible—hopeless, joyless, exhausted, lost.* (Sondra, age 48, cited in "Depression & Women," 2003, p. 1)

Incidence.   **Depression** is *characterized by prolonged* **sadness or irritability** *and loss of pleasure in most activities* (Belmaker & Agam, 2008). Higher rates of depression among females first appear in early adolescence and continue into adulthood (Brown et al., 2007; Gutman & Eccles, 2007; Williams et al., 2007). Women with disabilities have higher rates of depression than able-bodied women (Olkin, 2006). A recent longitudinal study of Canadian teenagers by Nancy Galambos and her colleagues (2004) found that by late adolescence, 25 percent of females had experienced an episode of major depression. Across many nations, cultures, and ethnicities, women are about twice as likely as men to suffer from depression (Eaton et al., 2008; Mannheim Research Institute, 2005; Nolen-Hoeksema & Keita, 2003). Moreover, women are more likely than men to suffer an anxiety disorder along with their depression (Russo & Tartaro, 2008).

What are the stresses of adolescence that are linked to higher rates of depression in girls than in boys? Karen Rudolph and Constance Hammen (1999) found that teenage boys were more likely to complain of stressful situations such as doing poorly in school, getting sick, moving to a new school, getting in trouble with the police, or other events unrelated to interpersonal problems. Girls, on the other hand, experienced most of their stress from relationship problems, including fights with peers, siblings, or friends. Girls reported more symptoms of depression in response to stress than boys did. Their symptoms included being sad, feeling like crying, and feeling alone and unloved. Because girls have closer, more intimate relationships with family and friends than boys do, disruptions and conflicts in these relationships can lead to depression and distress (Graber, 2004; Hankin et al., 2007; Kendler et al., 2005). Just being in a romantic relationship is associated with depression in early adolescent girls (Davila, 2008).

Theories.   Many theories have been offered to explain the gender difference in depression. Gender differences in help-seeking behavior or willingness to report symptoms have been ruled out as possible reasons (Hankin & Abramson, 2001). One explanation is biological, linking depression to hormonal changes that occur during the menstrual cycle, the postpartum period, and menopause. As we saw in Chapter 7, however, menopause is not associated with an increase in depression. In Chapter 7, we also noted that direct relationships between menstrual and postpartum hormonal changes and depression are weak, temporary, and far from universal (Nolen-Hoeksema, 2002). One biological factor that *is* strongly linked to depression is having a low level of the neurochemical serotonin. Men produce more serotonin than women do, possibly making women more susceptible to depression (Cahill, 2005).

A second possible explanation is that stressful life events may precipitate depression, and that women's lives are more stressful than men's. Women are more likely than men to have low social status, undergo economic hardship, face discrimination in the workplace, experience marital and family strains, and be subjected to intimate partner violence, sexual abuse, and sexual harassment (National Institute of Mental Health, 2008; Russo & Tartaro, 2008). Research has documented that economic hardship, family-based strains, childhood sexual abuse, intimate partner violence, sexist discrimination, and neighborhood violence are indeed contributing factors to depression in women (Bazargan et al., 2005; Boothroyd et al., 2006; Dambrun, 2007; Ewart & Suchday, 2002; Lennon et al., 2002; Paranjape et al., 2007; Schulz et al., 2006; Stoppard & McMullen, 2003).

A third proposed explanation is that the feminine role makes women more vulnerable to depression by making them feel helpless and powerless to control aspects of their lives (Russo & Tartaro, 2008). Females are expected to be less competent and more in need of help than males. Their efforts and achievements are more likely to be ignored or devalued. The sense that one's actions do not count can lead to a feeling of "learned helplessness," which in turn is linked to depression. In support of this view, girls and women with more masculine behavior traits are less likely to experience depression than those with more feminine traits (Lengua & Stormshok, 2000; Obeidallah et al., 1996).

A fourth theory known as *silencing the self* (Jack, 2003) is based on the assumption that women are socialized to place a high value on establishing and maintaining close relationships. According to this view, women defer to the needs of others, censor their self-expression, repress anger, and restrict their own initiatives, which increases their vulnerability to depression.

Susan Nolen-Hoeksema (2007; Nolen-Hoeksema et al., 2008) has proposed a fifth theory based on the way that females and males respond when they are depressed. She and other researchers (e.g., Grabe et al., 2007) have found that when adolescent girls and women are depressed, they focus on their inner feelings and try over and over again to analyze the causes and consequences of their depression. This so-called *ruminative style* leads to more severe and longer-lasting depressed moods. Adolescent boys and men, on the other hand, tend to engage in activities to distract themselves when they are depressed (Mor & Winquist, 2002; Nolen-Hoeksema, 2007; Rose, 2002). Try Get Involved 13.1 to see whether you find differences in the way women and men respond when they are depressed.

These explanations of depression are not mutually exclusive. Indeed, several of these factors most likely are involved (Russo & Tartaro, 2008). For example, one large-scale study of adults suggests that women are more likely than men to get caught in a cycle of despair and passivity because of a lower sense of control over important areas of life, compounded by more chronic strain caused by women's lesser social power. In the study, chronic strain led to more rumination, which in turn increased feelings of powerlessness and depression (Nolen-Hoeksema et al., 1999).

Depression in Later Life. Depression among the elderly can be the result of medical illness and disability and in turn can contribute to heart disease and earlier onset of death (Lyness, 2004; McGuire et al., 2008). Major clinical depression affects 10 percent of elderly adults in the United States (Kuchment, 2006). Higher rates of depression are found among medically ill, unmarried, socially isolated, homebound, or functionally impaired older adults (Ciechanowski et al., 2004; Mannheim Research Institute, 2005; Unützer, 2007).

These statistics may be underestimates, however, because most depressed elderly are undiagnosed and untreated (Brody, 2006; Unützer, 2007). Studies of older adults who committed suicide have found that over half had visited a doctor within a month before their deaths, and 20 percent saw the doctor on the same day as the suicide (Brody, 2007) Unfortunately, even when elderly patients clearly are depressed, most physicians do not adequately diagnose or treat the condition (Tai-Seale et al., 2007). Older adults do not always experience the classic symptoms of depression: sleepless-ness, fatigue, low energy, loss of appetite, guilt feelings, and depressed mood. Rather, depressed elderly individuals may show anxiety, confusion, and physical complaints (Brody, 2007a). Some symptoms, such as sudden irritability and fault finding, or pes-simism and little hope for the future, may be dismissed as typical personality changes that accompany aging. Even the classic symptoms of low energy, loss of appetite, or loss of interest in former sources of enjoyment may be seen by doctors simply as char-acteristics of a frail older person (American Psychological Association, 2004). Further-more, some health professionals may feel that depression in the elderly is "normal" because of medical, financial, or family difficulties or the losses that come with age (Brody, 2007a; Unützer, 2007). While it is true that health problems among older adults may contribute to symptoms of depression (Wrosch et al., 2004), most older people confront their problems without becoming clinically depressed. In fact, elderly adults have a lower prevalence of psychological disorders than younger adults (Ameri-can Psychological Association, 2004). Sometimes, depression in the elderly is a side effect of medications given for conditions such as heart disease. A change in medica-tion frequently gets rid of the depression (McCoy, 2002).

When depressed older adults are correctly diagnosed and treated, they improve as much as younger patients (Brody, 2007a). Unfortunately, older women are less likely than younger women to receive psychotherapy, and women 75 and over are more likely to receive no treatment at all (Glied, 1998).

Suicide

Incidence. Across all ages and ethnic groups in the United States, men are four times more likely than women to commit suicide, whereas women are two to three times more likely than men to attempt it (Eaton et al., 2008; Range, 2006; "Suicide Trends," 2007). White and Native-American women and men have higher suicide rates than individuals in other ethnic groups and Black women have the lowest. Elderly White males have the highest rate of all (Goldston et al., 2008). The lower suicide rates among Black women are thought to be related to the protective factors of extended family and community networks and religious faith (Chaudron & Caine, 2004; Goldston et al., 2008). For a look at gender differences in suicide across cultures, see Explore Other Cultures 13.2.

Suicide in Adolescence and Young Adulthood. Among adolescents and young adults aged 10–24 years, suicide is the third leading cause of death for both males and females

GET INVOLVED 13.1

How Do Women and Men Respond to Depression?

For this activity, ask one young adult woman, one young adult male, one middle-aged woman, and one middle-aged male to complete the following survey.

What Do You Do When You're Feeling Depressed?

Instructions: Everyone gets depressed—sad, blue, down in the dumps—some of the time. People deal with being depressed in many different ways. For each item, please circle the number that best describes what you *generally* do when you are *depressed*. Choose the most accurate response for *you*, not what you think "most people" would say or do. There are no right or wrong answers.

	Never or Almost Never	Sometimes	Often	Always or Almost Always
1. I try to figure out why I am depressed	1	2	3	4
2. I avoid thinking of reasons why I am depressed	1	2	3	4
3. I think about how sad I feel	1	2	3	4
4. I do something fun with a friend	1	2	3	4
5. I wonder why I have problems that others do not	1	2	3	4
6. I think about all my short-comings, faults, and mistakes	1	2	3	4
7. I think of something to make myself feel better	1	2	3	4
8. I go to a favorite place to distract myself	1	2	3	4
9. I think about why I can't handle things better	1	2	3	4
10. I do something that made me feel better before	1	2	3	4

What Does It Mean?

Before adding up each respondent's scores for the ten items, reverse the points for items 2, 4, 7, 8, and 10. That is, for a rating of 1 (never or almost never), give 4 points; for a rating of 2, give 3 points, and so on. Then sum the points for the ten items for each respondent. Higher scores reflect greater rumination.

1. Are there differences between your female and male respondents in how they react when they are depressed? If so, how do you account for differences?

2. Did your young adults respond differently from your middle-aged adults? Account for any differences.

3. Did your results support Susan Nolen-Hoeksema's findings regarding how women and men respond when they are depressed? Account for any differences.

Source: Adapted from Butler and Nolen-Hoeksema (1994).

(Goldston et al., 2008; "Suicide Trends," 2007). Basic risk factors for adolescent suicide in both sexes include depression, exposure to suicide or suicide attempts by family or friends, substance or alcohol abuse, and having guns in the home (Range, 2006). Social factors are more strongly associated with having suicidal thoughts for girls than for boys. In particular, girls who are socially isolated from peers are more likely to think about suicide than are girls with strong social networks (Bearman & Moody, 2004).

Suicide in Later Life.   Risk factors associated with suicide in the elderly are the death of a loved one; physical illness; uncontrollable pain; the specter of dying a prolonged death that harms family members emotionally and financially; fear of institutionalization, social isolation; loneliness; elder abuse; and major changes in social roles, such as retirement. As in adolescence, those who abuse alcohol and other drugs, are depressed,

EXPLORE OTHER CULTURES 13.2
Gender Differences in Suicide: A Global Phenomenon

In nearly all countries, men are more likely than women to commit suicide. In industrialized nations, the male-to-female suicide ratio ranges from 2:1 in the Netherlands to 5.4:1 in the Russian Federation (Chaudron & Caine, 2004). The ratio for the United States is about 4:1 (Range, 2006). China is the only country where more women commit suicide than men ("China's Seismic Shifts," 2007). In one study of 29 nations (Lester & Yang, 1998), higher divorce rates were associated with higher suicide rates. Interestingly, this association was stronger for men than for women, in line with findings that marriage seems more beneficial for men than for women (see Chapter 8). Across cultures, unemployment is also more strongly associated with suicide and acceptance of suicide among men than among women (Helgeson, 2002). For women, suicide is more closely linked to their social and economic status. In nations where women's status is low, such as Afghanistan, China, India, and parts of Turkey, their suicide rates are relatively high (Frantz, 2000; Raj et al., 2008; "Suicide," 2004). In fact, suicide rates for girls and women in rural areas of China, Singapore, and India and in Southeastern Turkey are as much as twice that of boys and men (Aaron et al., 2004; Frantz, 2000; Kim & Singh, 2004). One of the differences between women's suicide in the West and in developing countries is the method used. Women in Western countries usually swallow pills or slash their wrists, which are treatable events. In Asia, however, women ingest highly lethal insecticides, hang themselves, or set themselves on fire (Aaron et al., 2004; Raj et al., 2008).

Why are young Asian women committing suicide at such a high rate? A major factor seems to be cultural and gender conflicts that are made more intense as these traditional agricultural societies are transforming themselves into industrial societies. Many girls are still forbidden to go to school or to work and they are forced into arranged marriages which may be abusive or unhappy (Kristof, 2004b; Moreau & Yousafzai, 2004; Raj et al., 2008). At the same time, they are exposed through movies and television to a more prosperous, egalitarian life which is denied to them. Such lack of control of one's life may lead to despair and suicide (Frantz, 2000).

Maggie Kuhn, who founded the Gray Panthers after her forced retirement at age 65, illustrates the active role older women can play as advocates for social change.

or suffer from other mental disorders are also at high risk (Brody, 2007a; He et al., 2005; McCloud et al., 2004; Roscoe et al., 2003).

On a positive note, remember that most older people with health and other problems cope well with the changes of later life and do not become depressed or suicidal (Beers & Jones, 2004). Many continue to lead active and productive lives. In the words of Maggie Kuhn, an older-woman activist:

> *Old age is not a disaster. It is a triumph over disappointment, failure, loss, illness. When we reach this point in life, we have great experience with failure. I always know that if one of the things that I've initiated falters and fails, it won't be the end. I'll find a way to learn from it and begin again.* (Kuhn, 1991, p. 214)

Mental Health of Lesbians

Until 1973, the American Psychiatric Association (1994) classified homosexuality as a mental disorder. It took nearly another 30 years for the American Psychological Association to adopt Guidelines for Psychotherapy with Gay, Lesbian, and Bisexual Clients ("Guidelines," 2000). These guidelines urge psychologists to understand how prejudice, discrimination, and violence pose risks to the mental health and well-being of lesbian, gay, and bisexual clients. Let us look at stress-related difficulties faced by the LGBT community and some helpful coping mechanisms.

Stresses and Problems

In Chapter 6, we discussed the widespread nature of prejudice and discrimination against lesbians, gays, and bisexuals in the United States and other Western nations. Such homophobia can cause considerable stress in the lives of lesbians, gays, and bisexuals and increase the risk of physical and psychological problems (Herek & Garnets, 2007; Poteat & Espelage, 2007; Silverschanz et al., 2008).

Compared to heterosexual teens, lesbian, gay, and bisexual adolescents have higher rates of substance abuse, poor school performance, truancy, running away from home, risky sexual behavior, conflicts with the law, depression, and suicidal thoughts (Bos et al., 2008; Busseri et al., 2008; Goodman et al., 2005; Marsh, 2006; Saewyc et al., 2006). In addition, lesbians report higher rates of problem drinking than heterosexual women (Mercer et al., 2007; Sandfort et al., 2006). Several studies have found that compared to heterosexual individuals, lesbians, gays, and bisexuals show poorer mental health, and higher rates of anxiety disorder, depression, suicide attempts, and suicide (Case et al., 2004; Cochran & Mays, 2007; Sandfort et al., 2006; Silenzio et al., 2007; Warner et al., 2004).

Coping Mechanisms

On a more positive note, many lesbians, gays, and bisexuals develop effective coping responses which are linked to good mental health. These include accepting one's sexual orientation, having a good social support network, being in a satisfying relationship, and actively participating in the lesbian and gay community (Adams & Jordan, 2006; Bowleg et al., 2004; David & Knight, 2002; Meyer, 2003). Having family and friends who acknowledge and support their sexual identity is another key factor linked to the well-being of lesbians (Beals & Peplau, 2005). Lesbians, gays, and bisexuals are also more likely than heterosexuals to seek psychological counseling (Balsam et al., 2004; King, M. et al., 2003; Meyer, 2003). About three-quarters of lesbians have used mental health services compared with anywhere from 14 to 29 percent of heterosexual women (Morris, 1998; Solarz, 1999). Lesbians may be especially vulnerable to misdiagnosis and other forms of bias (American Psychological Association, 2007a). Not surprisingly, sexual minority individuals are more likely to seek counsel from therapists who have been trained to work with the needs of this population (Stevenson, 2005).

Mental Health of Older Women

As my hair grays, my skin wrinkles, and my fat redistributes, I can't take it all too sorrowfully. I have had a productive youth and have accomplished enough during it to provide a dozen people with material for my birthday roast. Milestone birthdays of middle age are wonderful when you have made positive choices, managed the unexpected, learned from the storms and sorrows, but still find yourself emotionally and physically whole. (Pam, on the occasion of her fiftieth birthday)

In this section, we look at the mental health of women as they get older. First we focus on gender differences. We then concentrate on the vital older woman.

Gender Differences

The psychological health of women tends to improve as they get older (Herman-Stahl et al., 2007; Jones & Meredith, 2000; Kessler et al., 2004; Mroczek, 2000). For example, in one study of African Americans, Chinese Americans, Norwegians, and American nuns (Gross et al., 1997), older women showed fewer negative emotions and more emotional control than younger women. Still, older women, compared to older men, report more frequent negative emotions, poorer mental health, and a lower sense of well-being (Canetto, 2001; Lawlor & Sterne, 2007; Steffens et al., 2000). However, gender differences in depression decline or even disappear by age 80 because men's depression rates increase sharply after age 60, while those of women remain the same or decrease (Barefoot et al., 2001; Canetto, 2001; Freeman et al., 2004; Kasen et al., 2003). Similarly, women's neurotic tendencies decline as they age, but this is not the case for men (Srivastava et al., 2003). In addition the gender difference in self-esteem that emerges in adolescence (boys are higher), narrows and perhaps disappears in old age (Robins & Trzesniewski, 2005).

The Vital Older Woman

In my sixties, I found my first taste of freedom. My earlier life was spent living according to other people's expectations of me: my parents, my husband, my family. When your family doesn't need you anymore, that's frightening, but freeing. There's time to explore and contemplate what you've learned so far. And there's a duty to send out some of those messages so that other people can benefit from all the difficult lessons you've learned. (Anna Kainen, 1995, age 82, writer)

Women, speak out. Stand up for what you believe. Go back to that teenage person you were, who wanted something very badly, then go out and get it. This is a time in your life when there's nothing and no one standing in your way. (Elizabeth Watson, 1995, age 82, theologian and environmental activist)

We have examined a number of challenges faced by many older women: declining health, financial problems, and the loss of loved ones. But this does not mean that the later years of a woman's life are filled with frustration and despair. Many older women cope successfully with the challenges that old age brings. They don't just *endure* old age; they *enjoy* it.

Most older women maintain a positive outlook and high levels of life satisfaction (Majerovitz, 2006). In some cases, positive changes in family or work situations occur as a result of women's actions. In other cases, stress relief comes about through role changes and the passage of time. Finally, some women continue to lead lives that have always been relatively satisfying (Burns & Leonard, 2005). Elderly Black women express significantly more contentment with their lives than elderly White women, even though Blacks are more disadvantaged socioeconomically and perceive their health as worse than Whites do (Johnson, 1994). How can we explain this? Many aging minority women are able to draw on psychological, social, and cultural strengths which ease their transition to old age. They have spent their lives marshaling scarce resources to cope with everyday demands and these coping strategies pay off later on as self-reliance. Strengths also arise from family, church, community networks, and shared ethnic identity (Mattis, 2002; Padgett, 1999; Yoon & Lee, 2004). In addition, White women may have expectations of life in the later years that are unrealistically high.

Diagnosis and Treatment of Psychological Disorders

The diagnosis and treatment of psychological disorders in women have often been topics of controversy. Feminist researchers and theorists point out that diagnosis and treatment are conducted by a predominantly male psychiatric culture, using a medical model of psychological illness and viewing many aspects of female behavior as pathological (Blehar & Norquist, 2002). In recent times, gender bias has become more covert, but still remains a powerful force in psychological practice (American Psychological Association, 2007a). Let's take a closer look at diagnosis and treatment of women's psychological disorders.

Gender Bias in Diagnosis

Is there a double standard of mental health for women and men? In a classic study, Inge Broverman and her colleagues (1970) reported that mental health professionals gave similar descriptions for a "healthy" adult (gender unspecified) and a "healthy" male. A "healthy" woman, however, was seen as less healthy in several ways: more submissive, more excitable in minor crises, more emotional, more illogical, more easily hurt, more sneaky, and less independent.

Over the years, other researchers have repeated this study with mixed results. One meta-analysis found less bias in later studies than in earlier ones (Smith, 1980). Others have found that gender bias in diagnosis is alive and well. A recent study found that counselors-in-training continue to have different standards of mental health for women and men, and that "healthy women" are viewed differently than "healthy adults" (Seem & Clark, 2006).

Other research has found that therapists are influenced by deviations from traditional gender roles (Russo & Tartaro, 2008). In one study (Waisberg & Page, 1988), for example, female patients who showed "masculine" symptoms (alcohol abuse or antisocial personality) were rated as more seriously disturbed than males with the same symptoms. Similarly, male patients with "feminine" symptoms (anxiety or depression) were viewed as more disturbed than females with these symptoms. Drug treatment was more likely to be recommended for females, especially by male therapists. In another study (Robertson & Fitzgerald, 1990), therapists viewed one of two videotapes in which the same male actor discussed having symptoms of depression such as sleeplessness, poor appetite, and boredom. In one video, the male was portrayed in the traditional role of sole breadwinner with a full-time homemaker wife. In the other video, the employment and domestic roles of the husband and wife were reversed. Therapists rated the nontraditional male as less masculine and, more importantly, as more depressed than the traditional male. A recent meta-analysis of 42 studies (McGorty et al., 2003) found that professionals were more likely to diagnose and treat anxiety when it occurred in women and were more likely to diagnose and treat antisocial behavior when it occurred in men. These results suggest that individuals are judged as more psychologically disturbed when they violate traditional gender expectations. For more about gender biases in diagnosis, see Learn about the Research 13.1.

Gender Bias in Psychotherapy

Gender bias also exists in psychotherapy. It may take the form of fostering traditional gender roles (e.g., "be a better wife"), telling sexist jokes, not taking violence against women seriously, and seducing female clients (American Psychological Association, 1975). In one study (Fowers et al., 1996), for example, over 200 clinical psychologists were asked to recommend strategies that would best help hypothetical females and males with identically described problems. The psychologists indicated that male clients could best be helped by increasing their instrumental (traditionally masculine) actions, whereas females could benefit more by enhancing their expressive

---

LEARN ABOUT THE RESEARCH 13.1

What Is "Normal"? Gender Biases in Diagnosis

Some psychologists (e.g., Worell & Johnson, 2001) argue that the definitions of "normal" that guide psychological diagnoses are socially constructed by the dominant cultural group (i.e., White heterosexual males) and reflect stereotypical notions of gender, race/ethnicity, and sexuality. To test this view, Jill Cermele and her colleagues (2001) analyzed the depiction of women and men in the Casebook that accompanies the **Diagnostic and Statistical Manual IV,** the *standard classification system used in the United States.* The researchers found that the Casebook (Spitzer et al., 1994), which provides case studies to guide the clinician, does indeed contain stereotyped descriptions of women and men.

Men's personality traits were much more likely to be described in positive ways (e.g., charming, friendly, engaging) than in negative ways, whereas females were more often described negatively (e.g., frightened, sad, helpless). In addition, there were more than three times as many negative physical descriptions of women (e.g., disheveled, pale, obese) than of men, who were more often described positively (e.g., tall, handsome, healthy). Women were also more apt to be infantilized (e.g., described as tiny, childlike, frail, and girlish). In addition, they were more often referred to in terms of sexual behavior (e.g., seductive, flirtatious), even when these behaviors had nothing to do with the diagnosis.

What Does It Mean?

1. How might constructing women as different from men influence clinicians in diagnosing mental illness?

2. What can psychologists do to address biases in their notions of what constitutes normalcy and mental illness?

(traditionally feminine) behaviors. Moreover, therapists are more likely to see women's emotional problems as internally caused (intrapsychic) than they are to regard men's emotional problems in this way, and they may fail to perceive the external stresses of women's lives (Marecek & Hare-Mustin, 1998; Worell, 2001).

Some therapists expect a more positive outcome with male clients than with female clients. These therapists may have even lower expectations of outcomes for ethnic minority women, lesbians, and women with disabilities (American Psychological Association, 2007a).

Therapy Issues for Women of Color and Poor Women

Women of color and poor women face a number of external stresses that can cause or intensify mental health problems: racism, poverty, culturally approved subordinate status, and living in contexts of violence and chronic strain (American Psychological Association, 2006; Herman-Stahl et al., 2007; Russo & Tartaro, 2008). Unfortunately, financial constraints and time and transportation problems prevent many poor women from seeking help (Wang et al., 2005). In addition, people of color are underrepresented in the mental health professions, so that members of these groups often have a therapist who does not know their culture or speak their language. Nonminority providers may apply racial stereotypes to their minority patients instead of seeing them as individuals. Moreover, they can be insensitive to the social and economic conditions in which women of color and poor women live (Bryant et al., 2005; Gilbert & Kearney, 2006; Smith, L. 2005). One reason for this is that clinical psychology literature does not contain adequate coverage of ethnically diverse populations. For example, a recent analysis of the leading scholarly clinical psychology journals found that only 29 percent of the articles included ethnic minority populations, and only 5 percent focused specifically on these populations (Iwamasa et al., 2002).

Types of Therapy

Traditional Therapies.   Traditional psychotherapies are based on a medical model in which emotional pain is viewed as a "disease" which must be "treated" by an expert. This leads to a therapeutic relationship marked by an imbalance of power between therapist (often male) and patient (often female). In addition, the individual's emotional problems are seen as having internal, not external, causes. The goal of therapy is to promote the person's adjustment to existing social conditions (Worell & Remer, 2003).

Nonsexist and Feminist Therapies.   According to **nonsexist therapy,** *women and men should be treated equally and viewed as individuals.* In addition, there is less of a power imbalance between therapist and client. Nonsexist therapy is similar to traditional therapies, however, in its focus on internal causes of psychological problems. **Feminist therapy,** on the other hand, *emphasizes the role of social, political, and economic stresses facing women as a major source of their psychological problems* (Gilbert & Kearney, 2006; Worell & Remer, 2003). Feminist therapists focus on issues of oppression, such as

Feminist therapy strives toward an egalitarian therapist–client relationship based on mutual respect.

sexism, racism, and heterosexism. They encourage women to become psychologically and economically independent and to try to change a sexist society rather than adjust to it. Another principle of feminist therapy is that therapists should not be more powerful than their clients but should build egalitarian relationships with them (Rader & Gilbert, 2005). One vehicle for doing so is **counselor self-disclosure,** *the imparting of personal information about the life experiences of the therapist to the client* (Remer & Oakley, 2005). In addition, feminist therapy stresses awareness of the ethnic and cultural differences between client and therapist (Gilbert & Kearney, 2006, Szymanski, 2003; Worell & Remer, 2003). Feminist therapy is a philosophy underlying therapy rather than a specific therapeutic technique, and it can be integrated with other treatment approaches (Marecek, 2001).

SUMMARY

Factors Promoting Mental Health

- Social support enhances mental health.
- Females seek and use social support more than males do.
- In reaction to stress, women more often show the "tend and befriend" response, whereas men are more likely to exhibit "fight or flight" behavior.
- Optimism is linked to positive mental and physical health.

Mental Health in Childhood and Adolescence

- Stress levels increase for girls and boys during adolescence. Much of girls' stress stems from relationship problems and is linked to higher rates of depression.
- Externalizing problems in girls are less common than internalizing problems, but are more likely to be associated with adult maladjustment.

Eating Disorders

- Anorexia nervosa is marked by severe weight loss and fear of being overweight.
- Bulimia nervosa is characterized by cycles of binging and purging.
- Biological, psychological, and cultural factors are involved in these disorders, which occur most often in adolescent girls.
- Adolescent girls are less likely than boys to use most illegal drugs.
- Stress levels increase for girls and boys during adolescence. Most of girls' stress stems from relationship problems and is linked to higher rates of depression.
- Externalizing problems in girls are less common than internalizing problems but are more likely to be associated with adult maladjustment.

Substance Use and Abuse

- Women are less likely to be heavy drinkers than men, but binge drinking is increasing in college women.
- Women's alcoholism starts later than men's, progresses more quickly, and is diagnosed at a more advanced stage.
- Drinking in pregnancy can cause FAS or FAE.
- Women are less likely than men to use most illegal drugs.

Anxiety Disorders and Depression

- Anxiety disorders are more common in women than men. These include panic disorders and specific phobias.
- Depression is twice as common in women as in men. Possible explanations for this difference include biological factors, stressful life events, learned helplessness, self-silencing, and women's ruminative style in responding to depression.

Mental Health of Lesbians

- Homophobia can cause considerable stress in the lives of lesbians, gays, and bisexuals, resulting in a variety of psychological problems.
- Effective coping mechanisms include accepting one's sexual orientation, having social support and a satisfying relationship, and participating in the LGBT community.

Mental Health of Older Women

- The psychological health of women improves as they get older.
- Older women who cope successfully with aging tend to integrate agency and communion.
- Some older women continue their careers; others become volunteers, or advocates for social causes.

Diagnosis and Treatment of Psychological Disorders

- Gender bias exists in diagnosis and treatment of psychological disorders.
- Women of color face external stresses, which can intensify mental health problems and prevent them from seeking help.
- Traditional psychotherapies are marked by a power imbalance between therapist and client, and focus on internal causes of emotional problems.
- Nonsexist therapy treats women and men equally.
- Feminist therapy is nonsexist, encourages equal power between therapist and client, and focuses on societal causes of women's problems.

KEY TERMS

anorexia nervosa
bulimia nervosa
female athlete triad
telescoping
binge drinking
fetal alcohol syndrome (FAS)

fetal alcohol effect (FAE)
generalized anxiety disorder
panic disorder
agoraphobia
specific phobia
depression

Diagnostic and Statistical
    Manual IV
nonsexist therapy
feminist therapy
counselor self-disclosure

WHAT DO YOU THINK?

1. If you became aware that a friend of yours had an eating disorder, what steps could you take to try to help?

2. Why do you think our society is less tolerant of drinking in women than in men?

3. In your opinion, why are women more likely than men to suffer from anxiety disorders and depression?

4. Why do you think that U.S. males are more likely to commit suicide than females, whereas females are more likely to attempt it?

5. How might stereotypes about women and men affect the way psychotherapists work with female and male clients?

IF YOU WANT TO LEARN MORE

Bieschke, K. J., Perez, R. M., & DeBord, K. A. (Eds.) (2007). *Handbook of counseling and phychotherapy with lesbian, gay, bisexual, and transgender clients* (2nd ed.), Washington, DC: American Psychological Association.

Brown, D. R., & Keith, V. M. (Eds.). (2003). *In and out of our right minds: The mental health of African American women.* New York: Columbia University Press.

Bryant-Davis (2005). *Thriving in the wake of trauma: A multicultural guide.* Westport, CT: Praeger.

Enns, C. Z. (2004). *Feminist theories and feminist psychotherapies: Origins, themes, and diversity* (2d ed). New York: Haworth.

Gillem, A. R. (2004). *Biracial women in therapy: Between the rock of gender and the hard place of race.* New York: Haworth.

Levine, M. P., & Smolak, L. (2005). *The prevention of eating problems and eating disorders: Theory, research, and practice.* Mahwah, NJ: Erlbaum.

Liu, A. (2008). *Gaining: The truth about life after eating disorders.* New York: Hachette Book Group.

Malatesta, V. (Ed.). (2007). *Mental health issues of older women: A comprehensive review.* Binghampton, NY: Sage.

Mathy, R. M., & Kerr, S. K. (Eds.). (2005). *Lesbian and bisexual women's mental health.* New York: Taylor & Francis.

Mazure, C. M., & Keita, G. P. (Eds.). (2006). *Understanding depression in women: Applying empirical research to practice and policy.* Washington, DC: American Psychological Association.

Mendelsohn, S. J. (2007). *It's not about the weight: Attacking eating disorders from the inside out.* Lincoln, NE: iUniverse.

Mirkin, M. P., Suyemoto, K. L., & Okun, B. F. (Eds.). (2005). *Psychotherapy with women: Exploring diverse contexts and identities.* New York: Guilford.

Pope-Davis, D. B., Coleman, H. L. K., Liu, W. M., & Topoerk, R. L. (Eds.). (2003). *Handbook of multicultural competencies in counseling and psychology.* Thousand Oaks, CA: Sage.

Slater, L., Daniel, J. H., & Banks, A. E. (2003). *The complete guide to mental health for women.* Boston: Beacon Press.

Worell, J., & Goodheart, C. (Eds.). (2006). *Handbook of girls' and women's psychological health.* New York: Oxford University Press.

Worell, J., & Remer, P. (2003). *Feminist perspectives in therapy: Empowering diverse women.* Hoboken, NJ: Wiley.

WEBSITES

Mental Health

Mental Health Net: Self-help Resources Index
http://www.cmhc.com/

National Mental Health Association
http://www.nmha.org
Suicide Prevention Action Network
http://www.spanusa.org

Eating Disorders

http://www.mirror-mirror.org/

Alcohol and Substance Abuse

National Institute on Drug Abuse
http://www.nida.nih.gov

Vital Older Women

Older Women's League—OWL
http://www.owl-national.org/
Older Adult Consumer Mental Health
Alliance
http://www.oacmha.com

14 Violence against Girls and Women

Sexual Harassment at School
  Elementary and Secondary School
  The College Campus
Sexual Harassment in the Workplace
  Incidence
  Consequences

Explanations
Women's Responses
Violence against Girls
  Child Sexual Abuse
  Infanticide and Neglect

Dating Violence
  Incidence of Dating Violence
  Who Engages in Dating Violence?

Rape
  Incidence
  Acquaintance Rape
  Factors Associated with Acquaintance Rape
  Effects of Rape
  Rape Prevention
  Theories of Rape

Intimate Partner Violence
  Incidence

  Role of Disability, Social Class, and Ethnicity
  Risk Factors
  Effects of Intimate Partner Violence
  Leaving the Abusive Relationship
  Theories of Intimate Partner Violence
  Interventions

Elder Abuse
  Types of Abuse
  Who Is Abused and Who Abuses?
  What Can Be Done?

Ronnie Falco, a computer science graduate of the prestigious Stanford University, began a successful career as a software designer, work that she loved. Unfortunately, however, due to the frustrating interactions she had with her male colleagues, her computer career was short-lived. Her coworkers did not look at her when they spoke to her, directed questions at male colleagues even when she had greater expertise, and seemed to resent her successful solutions to problems. Consequently, after 10 years in the computer industry, Ronnie Falco left and went into the health field. (Piller, 1998)

I suffered at home for over 20 years watching my father try to kill my mother. It was unbelievably frightening to me, and I feel it's taken a terrible toll on me which is still going on. I'm talking about depression, relationship problems, you name it, my life feels like a mess. Living in that situation was horrific. I used to see the carving knife on the landing, and my father would chase my mother upstairs with it. I would hide her in my bedroom and put the chest of drawers against the door, and I'd tell her to get into my bed. Then I'd go out of my bedroom to take the knife off him. That happened dozens and dozens of times in my life. It's beyond words to describe this situation. My father never actually killed my mother, but the constant threat was almost as bad because I never knew what he'd do. I felt I could never go out—that I had to stay at home with my mother because who knew what would happen if I went out and left her alone. To put this on a child destroys you. (Susan, mid-thirties, in Russell, 2001, p. 132)

In this chapter, we focus on negative experiences that girls and women can encounter in personal relationships at school and on the job. We start with sexual harassment at school and in the workplace. We then turn to a bleak aspect of childhood for all too many girls: sexual abuse and others forms of violence and neglect. Next, we look at the disturbing violent side of some relationships, with an examination of dating violence, rape (including date rape), and intimate partner violence. We conclude with an examination of elder abuse.

Sexual Harassment at School

Sexual harassment in an educational setting includes unwelcome verbal or physical behavior of a sexual nature when (a) submission to or rejection of the behavior forms the basis for decisions about the student (e.g., admission, grades); or (b) the behavior creates an intimidating, hostile, or offensive study environment. Sexual harassment at school unfortunately is widespread around the globe (DeSouza, 2003; Shute et al., 2008). In most cases, boys harass girls, rather than the other way around. Ethnic minority girls, students with disabilities, and lesbian, gay, and bisexual students are more likely to be sexually harassed than their peers (Hill & Silva, 2005; Reid & Zalk, 2001; Wessler & De Andrade, 2006). Sexual harassment by peers is much more common than sexual harassment committed by teachers, but students are much more distressed when the harasser is a teacher (Hill & Silva 2005; Timmerman, 2003).

Elementary and Secondary School

Reports of student sexual harassment are on the rise among junior and senior high school students. In a 2001 survey by the American Association of University Women (AAUW), about half of the girls said they had received sexual comments or looks (see Figure 14.1). Nearly half reported being touched, grabbed, or pinched in a sexual way. Two-thirds of girls, but less than one-third of boys, said they were upset after being harassed. Nearly one-third of the girls reported that the unwanted activity made them not want to go to school or talk in class. Girls who are harassed are also more likely to experience academic difficulties, physical symptoms (e.g., headache, digestive upset), interpersonal relationship problems, and negative psychological outcomes such as feeling self-conscious, embarrassed, anxious, afraid, less confident, confused about who they are, and unpopular (Duffy et al., 2004; Felix & McMahon, 2006; Murnen & Smolak, 2000; Nishina & Juvonen, 2005; Timmerman, 2003). A troublesome finding is that teachers rarely intervene, even when they are aware of serious incidents of sexual harassment. Instead of considering sexual harassment to be serious misconduct, school authorities too often treat it as harmless instances of "boys will be boys" (AAUW, 2001).

A more recent study (Ormerod et al., 2008) found that girls still experience high rates of peer sexual harassment in high school and somewhat lower rates of harassment from school personnel. These experiences continue to be more stressful for girls than for boys. Just as disturbing, however, was the finding that harassment has damaging effects even on those who do not directly experience it, by creating a school climate which appears to tolerate harassment. Those girls and boys who perceived that sexual harassment was accepted at school also felt unsafe at school, tended to withdraw from school, and had lower self-esteem. Later in the chapter, we shall examine a closely related phenomenon, organizational tolerance of harassment, which has a similar chilling effect on women in the workplace.

The College Campus

Although sexual harassment was legally defined earlier in the chapter, there are wide variations in people's conceptions of harassing behaviors. Before reading this section,

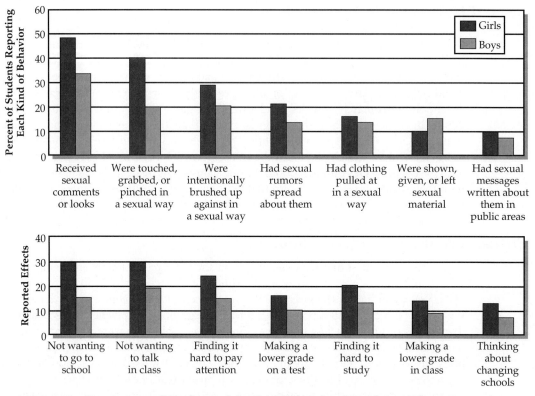

FIGURE 14.1   Percentage of Junior and Senior High School Students Who Reported Experiencing Unwelcomed Sexual Behavior at School "Often" or "Occasionally," and Its Effects

Source: American Association of University Women (AAUW, 2001).

perform the exercise in Get Involved 14.1 to examine the behaviors and situations that you and your acquaintances classify as sexual harassment.

Research shows there are gender differences in the tendency to classify behaviors such as those listed in Get Involved 14.1 as sexual harassment. Women perceive more situations as harassing than men do (Isbell et al., 2005; Lonsway et al., 2008; Rotundo et al., 2001; Smirles, 2004), and they are harsher in their judgments of the harasser (Sigal et al., 2005). Whether an individual perceives a behavior as harassment also depends, in part, on the role relationship between the harasser and target. When students are targets, behaviors are more likely to be seen as harassment if they are performed by a professor than by another student (e.g., Bursik, 1992). Did you find these two patterns when you performed the Get Involved activity?

The questions in Get Involved 14.1 raise two controversial issues related to power. One is whether sexual harassment, by definition, is restricted to behaviors performed by a person with authority (e.g., a professor) over a target (e.g., a student). The

GET INVOLVED 14.1

What Constitutes Sexual Harassment on Campus?

Check each of the following items that you believe is a form of sexual harassment if experienced by a student. Then ask one female student and one male student to do the same.

_____ comments on personal appearance by a student

_____ comments on personal appearance by a professor

_____ unwanted letters or phone calls of a sexual nature from a student

_____ unwanted letters or phone calls of a sexual nature from a faculty member

_____ unwanted sexually suggestive looks or gestures from a student

_____ unwanted sexually suggestive looks or gestures from a faculty member

_____ offensive sexually suggestive stories or jokes told by a student

_____ offensive sexually suggestive stories or jokes told by a faculty member

_____ inappropriate staring by a student that causes discomfort

_____ inappropriate staring by a faculty member that causes discomfort

_____ unwelcome seductive remarks or questions by a student

_____ unwelcome seductive remarks or questions by a faculty member

_____ unwanted pressure for dates by a student

_____ unwanted pressure for dates by a faculty member

_____ unwanted leaning, touching, or pinching by a student

_____ unwanted leaning, touching, or pinching by a faculty member

_____ unwanted pressure for sexual favors by a student

_____ unwanted pressure for sexual favors by a faculty member

_____ nonforced sexual relationship between a faculty member and a student

_____ nonforced sexual relationship between two students

_____ forced sexual intercourse by a student

_____ forced sexual intercourse by a faculty member

What Does It Mean?

Separately sum the behaviors you classified as sexual harassment if performed by a student and those seen as sexual harassment if performed by a faculty member. Do the same for each of your respondents.

1. Compare the number of behaviors seen as harassment if performed by a student to those if performed by a faculty member. Is there a difference in your answers or in those of your respondents? Try to explain any differences you might have found. Are these differences consistent with the evidence presented in the text?

2. Is there any difference in the number of behaviors seen as harassment by your female and male respondents? If yes, does it match the difference presented in the text? What do you think can explain this?

Source: Based on Shepela and Levesque (1998).

other is whether a sexual relationship between individuals who differ in power, as in a professor–student relationship, constitutes sexual harassment even if the student gives consent. In the first issue, the crucial criteria are (1) the target perceives the behavior as unwelcome, and (2) the unwanted behavior creates a hostile or offensive atmosphere for the target. If these conditions are met, it is not necessary that the perpetrator have power over the target (e.g., Fitzgerald, 1996).

There is greater controversy surrounding the second issue. Does a romantic relationship between a professor and student constitute sexual harassment, regardless of whether it is consensual? One view is that as long as the student is an adult and expresses willingness to enter into a sexual relationship with a professor, that relationship is acceptable. Male students are more likely than female students to subscribe to this view (L'Armand et al., 2002). Another perspective is that whenever a formal power differential between two people is present, a sexual relationship involves some degree of coercion because the target is not really in a position to freely consent or refuse. According to this viewpoint, *any* sexual behavior directed at a student by a professor is harassment (Fitzgerald, 1996). Some schools have gone so far as to forbid any consensual sexual relationship between students and faculty, while others merely suggest that such relationships are a bad idea (Bartlett, 2002). What is the policy at your school?

Incidence of Sexual Harassment.   The frequency of sexual harassment on college campuses is hard to assess for a number of reasons. Not only do few students submit formal complaints of harassment, but surveys of harassment experiences also show that the incidence varies from campus to campus. Also, the frequency of sexual harassment varies according to the specific type of unwanted conduct and the nature of the power relationship between the harasser and the target. Despite these problems, however, we can draw certain conclusions from recent surveys. First, most students indicate that females are more likely than males to be sexually harassed (Banyard et al., 2007; Hill & Silva, 2005). Second, women are more likely to experience subtle forms of harassment, such as unwanted sexually suggestive jokes or body language, than they are to encounter more blatant forms, such as unwanted sexual advances, although the latter do occur (Hill & Silva, 2005). Third, students are more likely to experience unwanted sexual behaviors by other students than by faculty members (Hill & Silva, 2005). Fourth, lesbian and bisexual women are more likely than heterosexual women to experience sexual harassment (Hill & Silva, 2005).

Responses to Sexual Harassment.   What do college students do when they experience sexual harassment? The most common response is to ignore the behavior. Avoidance of the harasser and talking to others about the harassment are other common reactions. Few file a formal complaint (Hill & Silva, 2005). Unfortunately, this lack of formal response hinders attempts to reduce the frequency of harassment. See Table 14.1 for recommended ways to reduce sexual harassment on campus.

Sexual Harassment in the Workplace

Analogous to the definition of sexual harassment in academic settings, the legal definition of **sexual harassment in the workplace** is *unwelcome verbal or physical behavior*

TABLE 14.1   Recommended Procedures for Reducing Sexual Harassment on Campus

Michele Paludi (1996) has made several recommendations about actions students can take to ensure that a campus environment is free of sexual harassment. Here is a sampling of these.

1. Find out whether your campus has policies and procedures for dealing with sexual harassment.
2. Establish a Sexual Harassment Awareness Week during which campuswide activities related to sexual harassment take place. These events can include activities such as plays, movies, and group discussions about sexual harassment.
3. Establish a peer educators program. Peer educators can provide both information to the campus community at large and support to those who have been harassed.

Source: Based on Paludi (1996).

when (a) submission to or rejection of the behavior forms the basis for work-related decisions (**quid pro quo harassment**), *or (b) the behavior creates an intimidating, hostile, or offensive work environment* (**hostile environment**) (Crosby, 2008; Rhode & Williams, 2007). Examples of quid pro quo harassment would be the offer of a promotion in exchange for sex and the threat of a layoff if sex were refused. The hostile environment form of harassment is illustrated by the experience of Ronnie Falco, the software engineer described in the vignette at the beginning of the chapter. In Louise Fitzgerald's widely used three-part model of sexual harassment, *quid pro quo* harassment is labeled **sexual coercion.** She divides the *hostile environment* category into two types of behavior: **Gender harassment** is insulting, hostile, and degrading behavior, but not for the purpose of sexual activity (i.e., "the put down"); **unwanted sexual attention** is unwelcome and offensive behavior of a sexual nature (i.e., "the come on") (Street et al., 2003).

Incidence

How common is sexual harassment in the workplace? Although few incidents reach the legal standard of harassment (Fitzgerald et al., 2001), unwanted sexual behaviors in the workplace are commonplace. Virtually all large-scale studies of sexual harassment conducted around the world have concluded that a large proportion of women experience some form of sexual harassment in the workplace (Cleveland et al., 2005; Ilies et al., 2003; Sigal & Annan, 2008). Most commonly, harassment takes the form of sexual remarks and jokes (Auster, 2001; Bell et al., 2002). Although sexual coercion is relatively rare, it does occur. Frequently, the victims are relatively uneducated, and desperately in need of work. Several particularly disturbing cases have involved Latina immigrant farm workers and food packers in the United States who have been forced to have sex with their supervisors or risk being fired, deported, given more physically demanding work, or receiving a cut in pay (Clarren, 2005; Simon, 1998).

Although any woman in any work situation might experience harassment, there are certain factors associated with the greater likelihood of its occurrence. We now turn to an examination of these.

Occupational Characteristics Related to Sexual Harassment.   Sexual harassment is more common in male-dominated blue-collar occupations, such as auto work, manufacturing, firefighting, law enforcement, custodial work, skilled repair, construction, and transit, than in other male-dominated, female-dominated, or gender-balanced jobs (Bell et al., 2002; Berdahl, 2007; Fassinger, 2001; Sadler et al., 2004).

To investigate the job climate for women in different occupations, Phyllis Mansfield and her colleagues (1991) examined female workers in two male-dominated (blue-collar) jobs and one traditional female-dominated job (school secretary). Among their respondents, 60 percent of the tradeswomen and 36 percent of the transit workers, compared to only 6 percent of the school secretaries, reported experiencing sexual harassment (Mansfield et al., 1991). Moreover, the blue-collar workers were more likely than the clerical employees to feel isolated and to perceive their supervisors and coworkers as sexist and disrespectful. Also, not surprisingly, they expressed less job satisfaction.

In another study of women in blue-collar occupations, Janice Yoder and Patricia Aniakudo interviewed Black female firefighters about their experiences on the job. The researchers found that nearly all these women were subjected to unwanted sexual behaviors including teasing and jokes, suggestive looks, deliberate touching, and unwelcome pressure for dates. In addition to sexual harassment, they reported isolation, lack of support, hostility, and hypercritical training, as well as racism. Consider one woman's experience: "No one really talked to me. It was difficult the first, I'd say, 6 months, because I was basically alone. I'd walk in and everything would get quiet. I'd go to eat; everybody leaves the room . . . I've been on the job now 7 years, and there're still guys that don't talk to me" (Yoder & Aniakudo, 1999, p. 141). Another woman described her first interaction with her White male captain as follows: "The first day I came on, the first day I was in the field, the guy told me he didn't like me. And then he said: 'I'm gonna tell you why I don't like you. Number one, I don't like you cuz you're Black. And number two, cuz you're a woman'" (Yoder & Aniakudo, 1999, p. 140).

Another historically male-dominated field associated with a high incidence of sexual harassment and sexual abuse is the military (Clapp & Chrisler 2008; Department of Defense, 2008; Ilies et al., 2003). In one glaring example, almost a quarter of the female cadets who graduated from the U.S. Air Force Academy in 2003 were sexually assaulted at the academy and 12 percent were victims of attempted rape. In addition, nearly 70 percent of female cadets reported experiencing sexual harassment at the academy. Many cadets did not initially report the incidents because they feared ostracism, humiliation, and reprisals (Young, 2003). Female cadets, who make up about 18 percent of the student body, report being warned by older students about a culture of rape and harassment that victims must accept without complaint if they want to remain at the academy. In the words of one student, "They tell you to expect getting raped, and if it doesn't happen to you, you're one of the rare ones. They say . . . if you want to graduate, you don't tell" (Janofsky & Schemo, 2003, p. YT 1). Recent studies report that 20 to 30 percent of women soldiers are raped while serving in the military (Benedict, 2008). In one 18-month period, over 100 servicewomen in Iraq, Kuwait, and Afghanistan reported being sexually assaulted or raped by fellow troops (Schmitt, 2004).

Sexual harassment in the workplace can take many forms.

Why is sexual harassment of women more common in male-dominated blue-collar occupations and the military than in other jobs? One possibility is that because these fields are strongly associated with the male gender stereotype, male-related physical attributes and skills are highly salient in the performance of these jobs. For example, the investigation of the Air Force Academy scandal suggests that male cadets felt that women slowed them down and were bad for morale (Janofsky & Schemo, 2003).

Target Characteristics Related to Sexual Harassment. Sexual harassment tends to target certain groups more than others. One key characteristic is gender. Women are far more likely than men to be targets and are more likely to report finding these experiences distressing (Ménard et al., 2003; Street et al., 2003). Women are more likely than men to feel frightened and degraded, whereas men are more likely to feel flattered by these behaviors (Berdahl & Moore, 2006; Magley & Shupe, 2005).

Age and marital status are two other target characteristics associated with harassment. Younger or unmarried women are more likely than older or married females to be harassed (Gutek & Done, 2001). This is possibly because younger and single women are seen as more powerless and vulnerable than their older or married counterparts.

Lesbian women are another group at higher risk (Bowleg et al., 2008; Silverschanz, et al., 2008). If their sexual identity is not known, they are seen as single women; thus, their risk goes up for that reason. Alternatively, if they are open about their identity, antilesbian prejudice can increase the likelihood that they will be targets of harassment.

Studies of women in the military have found that White women report the fewest harassment experiences followed by Asian American women, Latinas, and Black women. Native American women report the highest levels of harassment (Bergman & Drasgow, 2003). The marginalization of women of color within the work environment can lower their perceived power, further increasing their risk for harassment.

Characteristics of Offenders.   The picture that emerges from research on harassers is that the way these men construct gender might serve as a foundation for their harassing behaviors. Specifically, harassers tend to have negative attitudes toward women, hold traditional gender attitudes, and perceive sexual relationships as manipulative and exploitative (Gutek & Done, 2001; Lonsway et al., 2008; Ménard et al., 2003). That is, the most likely offenders appear to be traditional men who do not view women as equals.

Consequences

There is considerable evidence that serious psychological and physical consequences for women can result from sexual harassment, including decreased self-esteem, lowered life satisfaction, anger, fear, depression, anxiety, interpersonal difficulties, headaches, gastrointestinal problems, sleep disturbances, high blood pressure, disordered eating, substance abuse, and sexual problems. Additionally, women can experience undesirable job-related outcomes, including reduced job satisfaction, decreased morale, increased absenteeism, and a decline in organizational commitment (Bond et al., 2004; Cleveland et al., 2005; Lapierre et al., 2005; Lim & Cortina, 2005; Willness et al., 2007). Even if a woman has not experienced sexual harassment herself, just working in an organizational environment that is hostile toward women can have negative effects on her sense of well-being (Miner-Rubino & Cortina, 2004). As you might expect, the more frequent and ongoing the sexual harassment, the more distressing it is (Langhout et al., 2005).

Do women who acknowledge they have been harassed have more negative outcomes than those who do not? Studies have found that women who were targeted with unwelcome sexual behaviors had negative psychological and physical reactions, whether or not they labeled their experience as harassment (Magley et al., 1999; Munson 2001; Woodzicka & LaFrance, 2005). The authors note that women might not realize certain behaviors fit the definition of harassment or, alternatively, they might want to avoid the label of victim. The lack of labeling unwanted sexual acts as harassment does not, however, affect the consequences of those behaviors. It is the experiencing of these behaviors on the job, and not the labeling of them as harassment, that leads to unpleasant psychological and physical outcomes (Magley & Shupe, 2005).

Explanations

How can we account for the occurrence of sexual harassment in the workplace? According to **sex-role spillover theory** (Eagly & Carli, 2007), *in workplaces with unequal concentrations of women and men, gender is a highly salient attribute. Consequently, in these environments men respond to female employees more as women than as workers. That is, they allow gender roles to spill over into the workplace and to influence their interactions with female workers.* The high incidence of sexual harassment among blue-collar workers supports this theory and points to the importance of an employment context in which male-related physical attributes are very prominent (Ragins & Scandura, 1995). In this type of situation harassment reflects a restrictive construction of gender that specifies separate behaviors and roles for women and men. This inflexibility results in viewing women not as competent workers but as targets of male–female interactions.

The **power theory** of sexual harassment states that *sexual harassment is seen as an abuse of power to gain sexual favors or to reinforce the imbalance in power.* Because society accords greater power to men than to women, men generally have more power in the workplace, and some men abuse this power for sexual ends (Buchanan & Bruce, 2004/2005; Uggen & Blackstone, 2004). Consistent with this theory, women are more upset by unwanted sexual advances from high-status men than from low-status men (Bourgeois & Perkins, 2003). The male-dominated blue-collar occupations, where sexual harassment is most frequent, provides a good example of power theory. According to Fiske and Glick (1995), men in these occupations hold most of the power for several reasons. First, men historically view the blue-collar workplace as their own territory. Second, they are in the majority. Third, they view the few women who enter these occupations as being on probation. Fourth, the generally male supervisors support male workers' power. Fifth, men's overall greater physical strength is an important attribute for most blue-collar jobs. Sixth, men have higher status in society in general.

These factors not only maintain a power imbalance in which men are more likely to harass but also contribute to an **organizational tolerance** in which the negative effects of sexual harassment tend to be minimized and complaints about harassment are not taken seriously (Burn, 2005).

Women's Responses

> *After we, a mostly female staff, facilitated the removal of our harassing principal, we had a long group lunch together. We all shared our personal experiences with that man. The shocking thing was that most of the staff had been targeted at one time or another over an 18-year period, and that each of us thought we were the only one and that it was our fault.* (Holly, 50-year-old school teacher)

How do women respond to sexual harassment? Louise Fitzgerald and her colleagues (2001) propose a two-category framework that classifies the large variety of responses to sexual harassment as either internally focused or externally focused. **Internally focused responses** are *responses that attempt to manage the emotions and cognitions associated with the incident(s).* For example, ignoring the situation, minimizing the event, or blaming oneself are adjustments that aim to reduce negative emotions or thoughts about the situation. **Externally focused responses,** on the other hand, are *responses that attempt to solve the problem.* Examples are avoiding the harasser, asking him to stop, or seeking organizational assistance. Filing a complaint or lawsuit are rare responses (Beiner & O'Connor, 2007).

Most women who are sexually harassed do not confront the perpetrator or report the event, as in Holly's example at the beginning of this section. Why is this? For one thing, sexually harassed women frequently experience guilt, shame, and embarrassment as a result of their harassment (Beiner & O'Connor, 2007), and fear retaliation or humiliation. They also desire to maintain harmony in the workplace (Yagil et al., 2006). In addition, there are social costs to confronting the perpetrator, including fear of retaliation (Shelton & Stewart, 2004). These fears are often justified. Women who report their harassment often experience negative outcomes, such as lowered job evaluations, humiliation, and both physical and psychological health problems (Beiner & O'Connor, 2007; Cortina & Magley, 2003).

Latina women are more likely than White women to avoid or not report the harasser. This may stem from several elements in Hispanic culture, including respect for individuals of higher status, emphasis on harmonious ingroup relations, and a greater adherence to traditional gender roles, which fosters more tolerance of sexual harassment and discourages women from discussing sexual topics (Cortina, 2004; Wasti & Cortina, 2002).

Violence against Girls

Violence against women is a problem that encompasses physical and sexual abuse perpetrated against a woman or female child by persons known or unknown to her, such as spouses, partners, boyfriends, fathers, brothers, acquaintances, or strangers. . . . At least one woman in three globally is beaten, coerced into sex, or otherwise abused in her lifetime. . . . Because women represent 85% of the victims of incidents of nonfatal intimate assaults that occur each year in the U.S. . . . violence is a women's health concern, a human rights issue, and a major public health problem. (Herrera et al., 2006, p. 458)

Tragically, both girls and women are victims of violence around the globe. In this section, we focus on two forms of violence that are especially likely to be perpetrated against girls: child sexual abuse, and infanticide or neglect.

Child Sexual Abuse

Sexual abuse of children is viewed by many as among the most heinous of crimes (Rathus et al., 2008). While definitions vary, a typical definition of **child sexual abuse** *includes both contact and noncontact sexual experiences in which the victim is below the age of consent and the abuser is significantly older or in a position of power over the child* (Barnett et al., 2005). Sexually suggestive language or exhibitionism are examples of noncontact experience, while contact abuse may range from kissing, fondling, and sexual touching to oral sex and vaginal or anal intercourse. The most recent development in child sexual abuse is exploitation through the Internet. Children may be propositioned online for sexual activity, exposed to various forms of sexually explicit material, or experience online harassment (Barnett et al., 2005).

Incest is a form of child abuse. **Incest** *may be defined narrowly as sexual contact between a child and a close blood relative or other family member.* Incest may be particularly devastating emotionally to a child. It involves a loss of trust in and deep sense of betrayal by the abuser and perhaps other family members—especially the mother—whom the child may perceive as failing to provide protection (Rathus et al., 2008).

Incidence.   The incidence of child sexual abuse is difficult to pinpoint precisely. In the United States, approximately 240,000 children annually are victims of *substantiated* sexual abuse (Barnett et al., 2005). Because many cases of abuse are never reported, this figure is unfortunately quite conservative. An estimated 20 percent of girls and 5 percent of boys are abused during childhood (Villarosa, 2002). Asian American, Black, Latina, Native American, and White women report similar rates of child sexual abuse (Elliott & Urquiza, 2006; White & Frabutt, 2006). Children with disabilities are more likely to be sexual and physically abused than able-bodied children (Olkin, 2008).

For both females and males, most sexual abuse is committed by a family member or a family friend, takes place at home, and occurs more than once. The large majority of cases involve a female victim and a male perpetrator (Freyd et al., 2005; Hamby, 2005; White & Frabutt, 2006), a blatant illustration of the power differential between females and males. In the recent scandal involving child sexual abuse by Catholic clergy, the focus has been on priests who abused boys (Banerjee, 2005). But in fact it is far more common for priests to commit sexual acts with girls and women then with boys and men (Dillon, 2002).

The most frequently reported and publicized type of incest is between a daughter and her father or stepfather, but surveys indicate that brother–sister incest may actually be more common (Rathus et al., 2008). In one study of college students, for instance, 39 percent of the women and 21 percent of the men reported an incestuous relationship with a sibling of the other gender, while just 4 percent reported such a relationship with their father (Finkelhor, 1990). These figures for sibling incest are much higher than the reported incidence of sexual abuse mentioned above. Perhaps brother–sister incest is less likely to be perceived or reported as sexual abuse.

Few children tell anyone about being sexually abused. When they talk to anyone about it, they are most likely to confide in a friend or a parent (Bottoms et al., 2007; London et al., 2007). Why do so few children talk about being sexually abused? For one thing, they are relatively powerless, and they may fear retaliation from the abuser. Second, the offender is often a trusted and beloved adult whom the youngster may be reluctant to accuse. In addition, the child may feel embarrassed, humiliated, and responsible for encouraging or allowing the abusive behavior to occur (Freyd et al., 2005). Claire knows this from personal experience. As she walked home from school one day at age 12, a nicely dressed man who introduced himself as a doctor began chatting with her about the possibility of baby-sitting for his two young sons. He became increasingly graphic about the details of bathing them. When they reached her apartment building, he began fondling her breasts ("My boys don't have anything like this") until she broke away and ran upstairs, flushed with shame and guilt. It was days before she was able to tell her best friend and weeks before she told her mother. Until writing this book she had told no one else, and even decades after the incident, it was difficult for her to write these words.

Consequences. Sexual abuse can result in devastating consequences for children, not only in the short term, but throughout their adult lives (Draper et al., 2008; Russo & Tartaro, 2008; Sachs-Ericsson et al., 2005). Girls are more likely than boys to be sexually abused and they are more adversely affected by it (Long et al., 2005; Olff et al., 2007; Runyon et al., 2006; Tolin & Foa, 2006). Sexually abused children are more likely than other children to be depressed, anxious, or angry, to have behavioral and school problems, to show aggression and bullying, to feel ashamed, and to have low self-esteem (Barnett et al., 2005; Feiring et al., 2002; Spataro et al., 2004; Trickett & Gordis, 2004). Many sexually abused children show symptoms of posttraumatic stress disorder (PTSD) including fears, nightmares and sleep disturbances, and "flashbacks" of the traumatic event (Frieze, 2005; Margolin & Gordis, 2004; Olff et al., 2007; Tolin & Foa, 2006). Inappropriate sexual behavior directed toward themselves or other children and adults is also a common childhood reaction to sexual abuse (LeTourneau et al., 2004; Margolin & Gordis, 2004).

Adolescents who were sexually abused in childhood show earlier sexual activity, have more sex partners, and are more likely to engage in risky sexual behaviors and to become pregnant (Hendrick & Reddy, 2007; Koenig et al., 2004; Lemieux & Byers, 2008; Noll et al., 2003; Tyler & Johnson, 2006; Vigil et al., 2005; Wilson & Widom, 2008). They are also more likely than other teenagers to have eating disorders, be depressed, use drugs and alcohol, begin drug use at an early age, and try to injure themselves or commit suicide (Barnett et al., 2005; Ompad et al., 2005; Tyler, 2002).

In adulthood, victims of child sexual abuse continue to be more anxious, depressed, and angry; to have relationship and marital problems, and impaired self-concept; to feel isolated, stigmatized, and distrustful; to have sexual and substance-abuse problems; to have medical problems such as chronic pelvic pain, chronic headaches, and gastrointestinal problems; and to be more suicidal. They also are more likely to have experienced further sexual assault or physical abuse as adults (Classen et al., 2005; Freyd et al., 2005; Kimerling et al., 2007; Messman-Moore & Long, 2003; Ullman & Brecklin, 2003; Whiffen & MacIntosh, 2005; Whisman, 2006; Widom et al., 2007). Childhood abuse also is associated with violent criminal behavior in adulthood. For example, up to 75 percent of incarcerated women have been sexually or physically abused as children (Herrera et al., 2006). The effects of sexual abuse are greatest when the abuser was someone close to the child; when the abuse was frequent, severe, and continued over a long period of time; when force was used; when vaginal, oral, or anal penetration occurred; and when little social support was available after disclosure of the abuse (Barnett et al., 2005; Hulme & Agrawal, 2004; Runyon et al., 2006).

Treatment.   Healing from childhood incest and other forms of sexual abuse is a long and arduous process (Faria & Belohlavek, 1995; Godbey & Hutchinson, 1996). Group or individual psychotherapy helps women break their silence, gain perspective and realize they are not alone, relinquish feelings of responsibility for the abuse, and grieve for what they have lost (Bass & Davis, 1994; Boston Women's Health Book Collective, 2005; Price et al., 2001). Ultimately, therapy can improve survivors' self-esteem and their ability to have intimate relationships.

The effectiveness of treatment for victims of child sexual abuse depends on several factors (Barnett et al., 2005). For example, one study evaluated the outcome of group therapy for 65 women who had been sexually abused by their fathers, stepfathers, or another close male relative (Follette et al., 1991). Women with the best treatment outcomes were those who had more education, had experienced only fondling and not oral sex or intercourse, and had lower levels of distress and depression prior to treatment.

Therapy programs for sexually abused children and adolescents are also available. A comprehensive approach is usually recommended. This may involve play therapy or art therapy for very young children; group therapy for adolescents; individual therapy for the child and each parent; marital therapy for the parents; and family therapy (Cohen & Mannarino, 1998; Lutzker et al., 1999; Rathus et al., 2008). Cognitive behavioral therapy that specifically focuses on the abuse appears more effective than other treatments (Cohen et al., 2006).

Prevention.   Increasing numbers of schools are offering sexual-abuse prevention programs. According to one survey, about two-thirds of children in the United States have participated in such programs (Davis & Gidycz, 2000). The programs help children learn what sexual abuse is, how they can protect themselves from it, and what they should do if they experience actual or potential abuse (Chaffin & Schmidt, 2006; White & Frabutt, 2006). Children are taught to distinguish between "good" touching, such as an affectionate pat on the back, and "bad" touching. They are also encouraged to tell someone about any abuse that does occur. Children who participate in comprehensive school-based programs are more likely to use effective strategies such as refusing, running away, or yelling when confronted by a potential abuser, and they are more apt to report incidents to adults (Davis & Gidycz, 2000; Rathus et al., 2005).

In addition, all 50 states have enacted laws designed to inform communities of the presence of known sex offenders who have been released from prison. These laws are collectively referred to as Megan's Law, after a 7-year-old girl who was raped and murdered in 1994 by a male neighbor who had recently completed a prison sentence for child sexual abuse (Frieze, 2005; Trivits & Repucci, 2002).

Infanticide and Neglect

Sadly, cultural attitudes that devalue females in many parts of the world lead to practices that have harmful and even deadly effects on female infants and girls. To learn more, see Explore Other Cultures 14.1 and 14.2. You also may wish to reread Explore Other Cultures 7.2 on female genital mutilation.

EXPLORE OTHER CULTURES **14.1**
Where Are the Missing Girls in Asia?

Women around the world normally give birth to about 105 boys for every 100 girls. But according to recent census figures, there are 119 boys born in China for every 100 girls. In some Chinese villages, as many as 134 boys are born for every 100 girls (Yardley, 2005). In India, the ratio is 113 boys for every 100 girls from birth to age 6. In some areas, there are over 150 boys for every 100 girls (Hudson & den Boer, 2004). An estimated 100 million girls and women who should be alive in these two countries today are simply "missing" (Glenn, 2004; Kristof, 2002). In societies where the preference for sons is strong, such as China, India, and Pakistan, discrimination and abuse toward female children can take extreme forms such as infanticide, in which the newborn girl is suffocated, drowned, poisoned, or abandoned (Carmichael, 2004; Lee, 2004; Walia, 2005). In addition, girls in India, Pakistan, and China are often victims of neglect, not fed as well, vaccinated as often, or taken to the doctor as quickly when ill (Baghdadi, 2005; Kristof, 2002). Poor families in China and India often view their daughters as a burden, leading them to sell their baby girls for as little as $20 (Bonner, 2003; Kennedy, 2004; Rosenthal, 2003). With the advent of ultrasound, abortion rates of female fetuses have soared in both India and rural China (Grady, 2007; Jha et al., 2006).

The extreme preference for sons in these countries stems from the tradition that sons, not daughters, care for aging parents, perform religious rituals, and carry on the family name and occupation (Burn, 2005; Sang-Hun, 2007). In China, the pressure for sons is intensified by family planning laws that limit couples to one or two children (Yardley, 2005). In India, a girl is viewed as a burden who requires a costly dowry when she marries, leaving her parents in debt (Sheth, 2006).

What are the consequences of having a disproportionate number of males in the population? Scholars in both Asia and the West are concerned that the surplus of unattached men could trigger sex-related crimes such as rape, prostitution, abduction of women, and forced marriages as well as other violent crimes and social disorder (Hudson & den Boer, 2004; Tai, 2004). As a result, the Chinese government recently made selective sex abortions a criminal offense (Yardley, 2005).

EXPLORE OTHER CULTURES 14.2
Girls for Sale: The Horrors of Human Trafficking

About 1 million women and girls worldwide are lured into leaving their homeland each year and forced into prostitution or menial work in other nations (Pinheiro, 2006). Many are duped with the promise of good jobs in wealthier countries, only to find themselves bound by contracts that immediately place them in enormous debt. Some are forced into unpaid and often inhumane servitude as domestics or nannies (Ehrenreich & Hochschild, 2002; Perlez, 2004). But most are forced to work as prostitutes, literally as sexual slaves, in order to pay off their debt (Burn, 2005; Rafferty, 2008). Countries that are poor, have high unemployment, and lack women's rights show the most human trafficking, defined as the practice of buying and selling people for profit. Heavy trafficking occurs in East Asia, Africa, Central and Eastern Europe, and Latin America (Herman & West, 2003; "Putting the Sex Trade on Notice," 2004). Sex trafficking is not just a problem of poor countries, however. The United States has become a major importer of sex slaves. It is estimated that there are between 30,000 to 50,000 sex slaves in captivity in the United States at any given time, many from Thailand, India, Cambodia, Russia, and Ukraine (Landesman, 2004). Up to one-third of sex-trafficking victims from Russia and Ukraine are college students, often responding to ads for work abroad as a nanny, a model, or an exotic dancer (MacWilliams, 2003). But the typical age of trafficking victims is dropping. It is not uncommon to find girls as young as 13—or even 8 or 9—caught in the tragic net of sexual slavery (Herman & West, 2003; Landesman, 2004). One reason for this is that men who seek out prostitutes are looking for young girls in order to minimize their risk of exposure to HIV (McNeil, 2007). Sadly, child prostitution exists in virtually all countries (Robinson, 2007).

Dating Violence

A darker and rarely mentioned side of high school dating relationships is physical aggression toward a dating partner. Dating violence among high school students cuts across socioeconomic boundaries and is occuring with alarming frequency.

Incidence of Dating Violence

Studies show that anywhere from 9 percent to 65 percent of adolescents report having had at least one experience of physical aggression in a dating relationship, ranging from being hit, shoved, and slapped to being punched, choked, threatened with a weapon, and forced to engage in sexual activity (Barnett et al., 2005; Eaton et al., 2008). Females typically engage in the milder forms of violence, such as hitting and slapping, whereas boys engage in more serious acts of violence (Hickman et al., 2004; Noland et al., 2004). Most studies, perhaps surprisingly, find that males are more likely than females to report being victims of dating aggression (Hickman et al., 2004; Lichter & McCloskey, 2004; Noland et al., 2004).

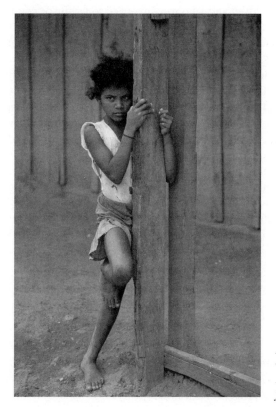

Many girls and young women around the world have been lured into sexual slavery. Pictured here is a child prostitute in a frontier Brazilian gold-mining town.

One possible explanation of these findings is that females underreport aggression and/or that males overreport it. Males might overreport their victimization in order to rationalize their own aggression (e.g., "She hits me, so I hit her back"). Another possibility is that females *are* actually more aggressive in their dating relationships. Girls are more likely than boys to report using violence as self-defense, or in retaliation for sexual assault, which is more commonly committed by males (Hickman et al., 2004; White, Donat et al., 2001).

Who Engages in Dating Violence?

Certain factors increase the likelihood that high school students will inflict dating violence. One of the strongest predictors of dating aggression for both girls and boys is being the recipient of dating violence (Fitzpatrick et al., 2004; Hendy et al., 2003; White, Donat et al., 2001). This finding supports the self-defense explanation. Believing that dating violence is justifiable is another strong predictor for both females and males. (Interestingly, both genders are more accepting of dating violence in females.) Holding traditional gender-role attitudes is also linked to dating violence for both sexes (Fitzpatrick et al., 2004; Lichter & McCloskey, 2004; Vézina & Hébert, 2007; White & Frabutt, 2006). In addition, dating violence is more prevalent among adolescents who were abused as children and who were exposed to family or community violence (Noland et al., 2004; Raiford et al., 2007).

Moreover, female victims of dating violence are more likely than nonvictims to show risky sexual behavior, depression, low self-esteem, attempted suicide, disordered eating behavior, and substance abuse (Eaton et al., 2007; Olshen et al., 2007; Raiford et al., 2007; Roberts et al., 2006). Other warning signals that a young couple's relationship may turn violent include possessiveness, controlling behavior, unpredictable mood swings, humiliating one's partner, and antisocial behavior (Bentley, 2007; Furman, 2002; Kelley, 2000). Sadly, these factors continue to be involved in violent adult relationships (Schumacher & Leonard, 2005), as we shall see later in the chapter. The fact that young women who experience dating violence in high school are at greater risk for sexual victimization during the college years and beyond highlights the need to implement programs early in the teen years to curtail such violence (Black et al., 2006; Vézina & Hébert, 2007). High school interventions such as the Safe Dates program reduce the incidence and severity of dating violence (Foshee et al., 2004).

Rape

During spring break of my senior year in high school, I went to San Padre Island with my girlfriends. One night, we went to a bar and somehow got split up. I had no money and didn't know the way back. Some guys said they'd take a cab with me. They got off at their hotel and told me to come to their room while they called my friends. I was scared to go in but I did. One big guy started to force himself on me. I fought him off and he finally stopped. He didn't actually rape me but he violated my body and my trust. He walked me to my hotel acting like nothing had happened. I never told anyone what went on. I felt people would blame me for losing my friends at the bar and being stupid. (Melinda, 20-year-old college junior)

The definition of **rape** varies across states. However, a common legal definition is *sexual penetration of any bodily orifice against the victim's will, obtained by physical force, the threat of force, or while the victim is incapable of giving consent because of mental illness, mental disability, or intoxication* (Bachar & Koss, 2001). The incident described above by Melinda fits the definition of an attempted rape. First, this student clearly communicated her nonconsent and, second, the size differential between the female student and the perpetrator provided him with the physical force necessary to proceed against her will.

Incidence

In the United States, a woman is raped every two minutes (Buddie & Miller, 2001). Between 15 and 25 percent of women will be raped during their lifetime and the prevalence of rape or attempted rape is highest among teenagers and young women under age 25 (Ahrens et al., 2008; Cole, 2006). Women with disabilities also have an elevated risk of being sexually assaulted (Martin, S.L. et al., 2004). One of the difficulties in obtaining a "true" rate of rape is that the measurement of sexual victimization is not consistent. For example, questionnaires often use terms such as *unwanted, nonvoluntary, forced,* and *coerced* as though they were synonyms, when in fact these terms have different meanings (Hamby & Koss, 2003).

Few studies have included large numbers of people of color. Furthermore, methodological problems, such as ethnic differences in willingness to report rape, make ethnic comparisons difficult. Given these limitations, the available evidence suggests that the rape rate is very high among Native Americans (Evans-Campbell et al., 2006) and is more prevalent among Whites than among Latinas/os or Asian Americans, who have the lowest (Herrera et al., 2006). Comparisons of Blacks and Whites, however, show inconsistent findings. Some indicate a higher prevalence of rape among Black than White women (Grunbaum et al., 2004; Rozee & Koss, 2001), whereas others suggest either the reverse pattern or no ethnic difference. Regardless of ethnic variations in the prevalence of rape, however, perpetrators tend to be of the same ethnicity and social class as their victims (George & Martinez, 2002).

Acquaintance Rape

Often he would rape me while I was still sleeping in my bedroom (Peacock, 1998). *I would wake with him inside me. He wouldn't stop even after I asked him to* (p. 229).

Numerous studies have shown that the most frequent form of rape differs from the type of incident typically conceptualized as rape. Many people view "real rape" as being committed by a stranger in a dark alley. But, in fact, 8 out of 10 cases of rape are **acquaintance rape,** in which *the perpetrator and victim know each other* (National Center for Injury Prevention and Control, 2005; "Sexual Assault Awareness," 2005). An estimated 8–14 percent of women have been raped by a spouse or cohabiting partner (Bennice & Resick, 2003), with the reported frequency of sexual aggression highest in Black couples, followed by Latina/o and White couples (Ramisetty-Mikler et al., 2007).

Although a large proportion of women have had incidents consistent with the legal definition, few actually label their experience as rape, especially if they are raped by an acquaintance (Abbey et al., 2005; Flack et al., 2007; Hammond & Calhoun, 2007; Kahn, 2004). How can this be explained? According to Mary Koss and Hobart Cleveland (1997), women believe that rape is rare, whereas sexual aggression is common and therefore harmless. Thus, women downplay the negative aspects of their experience by emphasizing what they view as relatively normal sexual aggression, or what some people refer to as "seductive behavior." In fact, there is a good deal of overlap in students' definitions of "rape" and "seduction" (Littleton & Axsom, 2003). Another view (Phillips, 2000) is that the woman blames herself for the experience, and at the same time feels responsible for protecting her partner and the relationship. She therefore reframes the situation as being not violent or abusive. Many women (as well as men) are not aware of the broad range of behaviors that constitute rape. Thus, not surprisingly, victims of acquaintance rape who do not acknowledge they have been raped have a narrower definition of rape than those who do acknowledge their victimization. When the assault involves a boyfriend, if the woman is impaired by alcohol or drugs, if the act involves oral or manual sex, or if the woman is verbally rather than physically coerced, she is unlikely to label the situation as rape (Abbey et al., 2004a; Kahn, 2004; Peterson & Muehlenhard, 2004).

Like Melinda, in the vignette opening this section, few victims of acquaintance rape report their assault to the police (Buddie & Miller, 2001; Cole, 2006; Flack et al., 2007). One reason is that they frequently engage in self-blame for putting themselves into a risky situation or for failing to communicate their intentions more clearly. They might also not want to go through the highly embarrassing procedures involved in a police investigation and might be aware of widespread lack of support for rape victims (Ahrens et al., 2008; Cole, 2006).

Factors Associated with Acquaintance Rape

What accounts for the high incidence of acquaintance rape?

Sexual Script.   Koss and her colleague (1997) contend that the social construction of the roles of men and women in male–female sexual situations provides a social context in which acquaintance rape can occur. This traditional **sexual script** is *a socialized set of expected behaviors characterized by an aggressive male who initiates and pushes for sexual activity and a gatekeeping female who sets the limits.* That is, instead of encouraging similar behaviors and goals, gender socialization teaches males to use any strategy in their pursuit of sexual intercourse and teaches females they are supposed to control men's sexual impulses.

Interpreting roles in this sexual script can lead to rape for a number of reasons. First, some men take the initiator role to the extreme and engage in sexual aggression. Second, as discussed in Chapter 8, men frequently infer sexual interest when it is not intended (Farris et al., 2008; Lindgren et al., 2007). As sexual initiator, a man's misperception of his partner's nonsexual behaviors as sexual interest can fuel his sexual aggressiveness (Bondurant & Donat, 1999). Third, the differing roles within the sexual script can set the framework for misunderstanding because the male assumes the female will attempt to limit sexual activity as part of her role. If a woman does not resist a man's sexual advances, both women and men assume that she is agreeing to have sex (Anderson et al., 2004). But if she says "no," a man may misinterpret this response as token resistance that really means "yes," leading him to disregard her objections to sex (Clark & Carroll, 2008).

To examine the actual frequency of token resistance to sex, Charlene Muehlenhard and Carie Rodgers (1998) asked college women and men to describe real situations, if any, in which they told a sexually willing partner that they didn't want to have sex although, in actuality, they intended to have sexual intercourse with that partner. Only 14 percent of the women respondents described situations that reflected token resistance to a man who had been a previous sexual partner and less than 2 percent reported token resistance to a man with whom they had never had intercourse. It appears that, although women sometimes engage in token resistance to sex, most do not. Thus, all refusals should be taken seriously.

Characteristics of Sexually Aggressive Men. Sexually aggressive men, including both rapists and those who use verbal coercion to gain sexual activity, are more likely than nonaggressive men to have witnessed or experienced family violence (Chapple, 2003). Furthermore, they are more likely to hold stereotypical attitudes about gender roles, feel hostility toward women, and be physically aggressive in other situations. They are also more likely to believe in **rape myths** (Ben-David & Schneider, 2005; Mosher & Danoff-Burg, 2005; Murnen et al., 2002; Warkentrin & Gidycz, 2007). These are *false beliefs about rape that are widely held and that serve to justify male sexual aggression against women* ("Sexual Assault Awareness," 2005). Some of the most prevalent rape myths are that women lead men on and therefore deserve to be raped, that women often make false accusations of rape, and that no woman can be raped against her will.

As might be expected, men tend to endorse these myths more than women do (e.g., Aosved & Long, 2006; Kennedy & Gorzalka, 2002; Nunes et al., 2004; White & Robinson Kurpius, 2002). Moreover, college men who participate in athletics or belong to fraternities are more likely to have rape-supportive attitudes than other college men (Murnen & Kohlman, 2007). Also, Black (Johnson et al., 1997), Latino (Cowan, 2000), and Asian American (Kennedy & Gorzalka, 2002) men more strongly believe rape myths than do White men. Black men's greater acceptance of beliefs supportive of rape might be related to a long history of racist law enforcement, which has made it even more difficult for Black women than for White women to report rape or to obtain legal justice (Bryant-Davis, 2003). The endorsement of these beliefs by Latino and Asian American men, on the other hand, may be due to the strong commitment to patriarchy in these cultures (Cowan, 2000; Mori et al., 1995). Among both women and men, rape myth acceptance is associated with greater sexism, racism, homophobia, ageism, classism, and religious intolerance (Aosved & Long, 2006; Chapleau et al., 2007). To get firsthand knowledge about rape myth acceptance, try

GET INVOLVED **14.2**
Gender and Rape Myths

Ask two female and two male acquaintances to indicate their degree of agreement with each of the following four statements about rape, from *strongly disagree* (1) to *strongly agree* (7). If possible, select participants from different ethnic groups.

_____1. Women often provoke rape.
_____2. Women enjoy rape.
_____3. Women frequently falsely claim they have been raped.
_____4. Only men who are psychologically disturbed engage in rape.

What Does It Mean?

Sum the four ratings for each respondent. The scores can range from 4 to 28, with higher scores reflecting greater acceptance of rape myths. After scoring each person's answers, average the scores of the two females and those of the two males.

1. Compare the scores of the females and males. Did your male respondents express greater acceptance of rape myths than your female respondents did? If yes, explain. If no, indicate possible reasons why your respondents did not reflect the typically found gender difference.
2. If you tested men of different ethnicities, did you note any difference in their scores?

If yes, is this difference consistent with that presented in the text? Was there a difference between women respondents of different ethnicities?
3. Which of these four statements received the greatest degree of agreement from your respondents and which received the least agreement? Give possible reasons for these findings.
4. What do you think influences the development of these rape myths?
5. How do you think rape myth acceptance can be reduced?

Get Involved 14.2. Then, to learn more about attitudes toward rape victims in other cultures, read Explore Other Cultures 14.3.

Characteristics of Victims.   Any woman can be sexually assaulted, but some are especially vulnerable, such as adolescents and young women, those with disabilities, poor and homeless women, and those living in war (Welch & Mason, 2007). Moreover, as we saw earlier in this chapter, women who are raped are more likely than nonvictimized women to have been sexually abused in childhood and/or adolescence (Söchting et al., 2004), possibly because early victimization can contribute to feelings of self-blame and powerlessness. Victims of domestic violence are also more likely than other women to suffer forced sexual activity (Campbell et al., 2007; Welch & Mason, 2007).

Alcohol Consumption.   There is considerable evidence that alcohol consumption by the perpetrator and the victim increases the risk of rape or attempted rape (Cole, 2006; Lacasse & Mendelson, 2007; Livingston et al., 2007; Welch & Mason, 2007). In part,

EXPLORE OTHER CULTURES 14.3
Attitudes toward Rape Victims around the World

How are rape victims viewed in cultures outside the United States? Madhabika Nayak and her colleagues (2003) and researchers led by Colleen Ward (cited in Best, 2001) examined cross-cultural attitudes toward rape victims by interviewing university students from 17 countries. Relatively favorable attitudes were found in the United Kingdom, the United States, Germany, and New Zealand, while less favorable views were expressed in Turkey, Mexico, Zimbabwe, India, Japan, Kuwait, and Malaysia. Having read Chapters 2 and 3 about cross-cultural differences in gender-role attitudes, can you see a recurring pattern in these findings regarding attitudes toward rape victims? In those countries with more egalitarian views of women, attitudes toward rape victims are more positive, whereas rape victims are more likely to be stigmatized in countries where women's status is much lower than that of

men. Some cultures have social and legal customs that sanction severe punishment of women in response to infractions of family "honor" (Vandello & Cohen, 2004). For example, under Muslim law, victims of rape are subjected to severe punishments, including imprisonment, public flogging, and death. Little distinction is made between forced and consensual sex. Men are rarely convicted in rape cases, but women who report a rape are often charged with adultery, which is considered a crime more serious than murder (Burn, 2005). Each year, hundreds of "honor killings" occur in Islamic cultures, in which girls or women are killed, often by male members of their own families, for perceived breaches of chastity (Arsu, 2005; Epstein, 2007). In Turkey, girls who have allegedly dishonored the family are pressured to commit suicide, in order to spare her family from having to murder her (Bilefsky, 2006).

---

this is because alcohol impairs the perpetrator's judgment and lowers the victim's resistance (Ahrens et al., 2008; Flack et al., 2007). Furthermore, when men drink, they may be more likely to misperceive women's drinking as a sign of sexual interest (Cole, 2006).

Effects of Rape

The psychological impact of rape can be profound. Whether they are victims of acquaintance rape or stranger rape, survivors may be plagued by anxiety, self-blame, shame, humiliation, powerlessness, depression, and suicidal thoughts (Polusny & Arbisi 2006; Welch & Mason, 2007). Some symptoms, such as self-blame and powerlessness, may be more common among acquaintance victims. As shown in one college student's emotional reaction to rape by her resident advisor, "I wouldn't even admit it to myself until about 4 months later when the guilt and fear that had been eating at me became too much to hide and I came very close to a complete nervous breakdown. I tried to kill myself, but fortunately I chickened out at the last minute" (Warshaw, 1988, pp. 67–68). Women with a prior history of emotional and behavioral problems have greater difficulty than other women in recovering from rape (Koss & Figueredo, 2004). Women who are victims of gang rape, which involve multiple perpetrators, also have more severe physical and emotional consequences than women who experience a single rape (Sadler et al., 2005).

Alcohol consumption increases the risk of sexual coercion and rape.

Amina Lawal, with her baby, is pictured in 2002 shortly after an Islamic court sentenced her to death by stoning for committing adultery. After a two-year appeal process that received international attention, she was pardoned.

Some rape victims also develop physical health problems, such as chronic headaches, pain, fatigue, and sleep disturbances (Crofford, 2007). Some may experience sexual problems, including diminished sexual activity, interest, and enjoyment (Ahrens et al., 2008; Welch & Mason, 2007). Some rape survivors, especially those who were assaulted by someone they knew, show increases in risky sexual behavior (Campbell et al., 2004). Others abuse drugs and alcohol or attempt suicide (Sturza & Campbell, 2005; Welch & Mason, 2007). Rebecca Campbell and her colleagues (2004) point out that many rape survivors are further victimized by insensitive treatment from police, prosecuting attorney, doctors, and mental health personnel. Placing unnecessary blame on rape survivors adds to the trauma of the original sexual assault and may hamper recovery.

Despite the many negative effects of rape, many survivors report positive life changes following sexual assault that help them cope with the event. For a closer look, see Learn about the Research 14.1.

Rape Prevention

Many rape education programs exist, most of them focusing on changing attitudes such as rape myths or increasing women's self-protection (Ahrens et al., 2008; Anderson & Whiston, 2005; Söchting et al., 2004). While education can help women learn how to communicate better with male partners or how to avoid high-risk situations, it is basically men's behaviors that must be changed if rape is to be prevented (Ahrens et al., 2008). Because attitudes supportive of rape and the sexual script are learned at a young age, rape education programs should also begin early (Cole, 2006).

In addition to rape education, institutions must develop effective procedures for dealing with complaints. Women who report a rape must be assured that their claim will be fairly investigated and that if guilt is determined, the perpetrator will receive appropriate sanctions (Ahrens et al., 2008).

Theories of Rape

How can rape be explained? Our examination focuses on three theories that posit different mechanisms to account for rape.

Evolutionary Theory. **Evolutionary theory** applies the principles of natural selection and its goal of reproductive survival to understand social behavior, including rape. According to this theory, rape evolved because in ancestral environments it was a strategy males could use to ensure their genes would be passed on to future generations. From an evolutionary view, it is to males' reproductive advantage to mate often and with numerous partners because they have abundant sperm, do not have to spend time gestating offspring, and cannot be sure of paternity of offspring. Thus, although evolutionary theorists believe that rape is inappropriate, they argue it has evolved as one method for achieving reproductive success (Thornhill & Palmer, 2000). To support this view, they note that forced copulations have been observed in a variety of animal species, and that females of childbearing age are the most likely rape victims (Thornhill & Palmer, 2000).

LEARN ABOUT THE RESEARCH 14.1
Positive Life Changes Following Sexual Assault

In the aftermath of traumatic events, some individuals may experience positive as well as negative life changes as a result of trying to come to terms with these events (Tedeschi & Calhoun, 2004). Patricia Frazier and her colleagues (2004) have been doing a longitudinal study of 171 women who experienced sexual assault, in order to assess the factors which best predicted positive life changes during the women's recovery process. Positive life change was measured by asking participants to rate the extent to which specific aspects of their lives had changed since the assault. Items dealt with one's self (e.g., "My ability to take care of myself"); relationships (e.g., "My relationships with family"); life philosophy or spirituality (e.g., "My sense of purpose in life"); and empathy (e.g., "My concern for others in my similar situation"). Participants rated each item on a 5-point scale ranging from "much worse

now" to "much better now." Higher scores indicated positive change. The participants, who were between 16 and 52 years old (mean age, 27), filled out questionnaires at two weeks, two months, six months, and one year after the assault.

One of the factors most strongly related to positive change was social support, which, as we have seen, is related to good mental health. A second factor related to positive change, called "approach coping," involved trying to view the stressful event differently and expressing emotions about it (as opposed to avoiding people and acting as if nothing had happened). In addition, those who relied on their religious faith to cope reported more positive change. Finally, survivors who perceived that they had control over their recovery process were more likely to show positive life changes.

What Does It Mean?

1. Based on these results, what suggestions could you offer to a friend of yours who had just experienced sexual assault?
2. This study focused on women only. Do you think that the results would be similar for

men who are survivors of sexual assault? Explain your answer.

Some critics, on the other hand, contend that it is not appropriate to draw conclusions about rape by observing nonhuman species because human behavior is more complexly determined (LaFrance, 2001b). Furthermore, Anne Fausto-Sterling (1992) argues that when the term "rape" is applied to other species, its meaning is altered; it no longer reflects a violation of the victim's will because will is an essentially human construct. She also maintains that so-called rape in animals does not have the same implications for females of these species as it does for human females for whom rape arouses fear and influences behavioral choices.

Others question the basic tenet of the theory that frequent copulation with multiple partners is reproductively effective for men. Natalie Angier (1999) argues that a continuous relationship with one woman might be as reproductively successful as promiscuous mating. Marianne LaFrance (2001b) notes that although the majority of rape victims are young women of childbearing age, there are numerous rapes of young children. Furthermore, the fact that some men rape wives and dating partners with whom they have also had consensual sex and that most men do not rape are not consistent with this assumption that the purpose of rape is reproduction (de Waal, 2002). Finally, evolutionary theorists ignore instances of rape that are inconsistent with the theory, such as homosexual rape or rape in the context of war (Ahrens et al., 2008).

Feminist Theory. A different perspective is offered by **feminist theory,** *which contends that rape is rooted in the longstanding and pervasive power imbalance between women and men* (Rozee, 2008). Men have greater legal, economic, and political power, which provides them with more power in interpersonal situations. Men use rape as one mechanism to control women and maintain their dominance.

Support for feminist theory at the societal level is provided by evidence that urban areas with greater gender equality in economic, legal, and political power have lower rape rates than do urban areas with less gender equality (Whaley, 2001). Moreover, a man's endorsement of male dominance and restricted rights for women is strongly connected to his acceptance of rape myths (Ahrens et al., 2008).

Social Learning Theory. **Social learning theory** provides a third perspective to the phenomenon of rape. As discussed in Chapter 3, this theory *contends that social behaviors are learned through observation and reinforcement. This includes learning both attitudes supportive of rape and sexually aggressive behaviors* (Frieze, 2005). The theory assumes, for example, that men can develop attitudes supportive of rape or sexually aggressive behaviors via media depictions of sexuality and violence. The theory further holds that their sexual aggressiveness can be reinforced by the widespread acceptance of rape myths which blame the victim and excuse the perpetrator, and by the traditional sexual script which encourages males to be aggressive in sexual situations.

Both of these assumptions have received some support from research. Consistent with the hypothesized influence of observational learning, Barongan and Hall (1995) found that, for some men, exposure to misogynous rap music increases their aggressive feelings toward women. Several studies have also shown that experience with pornography is related to greater sexual aggressiveness (Frieze, 2005). However, this relationship could reflect either an effect of pornography on sexual aggressiveness or the possibility that sexually aggressive men choose to view violent pornography. In support of the importance of reinforcement, men who more strongly accept rape myths tend to be more sexually aggressive (e.g., Malamuth et al., 1991).

Intimate Partner Violence

> *I have had glasses thrown at me. I have been kicked in the abdomen, kicked off the bed, and hit while lying on the floor—while I was pregnant. I have been whipped, kicked, and thrown, picked up and thrown down again.* (Boston Women's Health Book Collective, 1998, p. 162)

I was pretty much in a cage . . . He didn't let me use the phone . . . didn't let me go out . . . took away all of my freedom. (Zink & Sill, 2004, p. 33)

Acts of violence against women, sad to say, are usually committed by their male partner (Campbell et al., 2007). **Intimate partner violence,** also known as battering, or domestic violence, refers to *physical and psychological abuse committed by an intimate partner, that is, a spouse, romantic partner, or a former spouse/partner.* As illustrated in the first vignette of this section, intimate partner violence can range from moderate forms of physical abuse, such as slapping or throwing objects at the victim, to severe forms, including beating and using a weapon (Frieze, 2005). Psychological abuse includes overt attempts to dominate, isolate, and control, as well as more subtle actions that undermine the victim's self-esteem (Arias & Ikeda 2006; McHugh et al., 2008). This type of abuse is depicted in the second vignette that opened this section. Men's attacks on women are likely to be more severe than women's attacks on men (McHugh et al., 2008), resulting in 2 million injuries and 1,200 deaths each year (Black & Breiding, 2008). Over one-third of all murders of American women are committed by intimate partners, compared to only 4 percent of men's murders (Rothman et al., 2005).

Incidence

As with dating violence, women are somewhat more likely than men to commit violence against their partner, sometimes in self-defense (Serran & Firestone, 2004). Like rape, intimate partner violence is an underreported crime, but it is estimated that at least 2 to 3 million women are assaulted by their male partners in the United States each year (White & Frabutt, 2006). In one recent study, about half of women seeking health care at emergency departments or primary care clinics in the Midwest reported having experienced physical and/or emotional abuse at some point in their lives. One in four women reported severe physical or sexual abuse. Only one-quarter of the women had ever been asked about abuse by a health-care provider. Most, however, said they would reveal abuse if asked in a nonhurried, concerned manner (Kramer et al., 2004). Sadly, many doctors say that they don't ask such questions because of a lack of time, training, and easy access to services that help these patients (Marcus, 2008).

Violence in lesbian and gay relationships occurs about as often as in heterosexual couples (McHugh et al., 2008; Peterman & Dixon, 2003; Potoczniak et al., 2003; Rohrbaugh, 2004). Similar to violence in heterosexual relationships, this abuse can be both physical and emotional (Verni & Rinsky, 2006).

Role of Disability, Social Class, and Ethnicity

Disability, poverty, and ethnicity are all factors in intimate partner violence. Women with disabilities experience abuse at a somewhat high rate as able-bodied women, and their abusive relationships continue for a longer period of time (Brownridge, 2006; "Health and Wellness," 2004; Olkin, 2003). They are also abused by a greater number of people, including health-care providers or attendants, in addition to partners or family members. Poorer women and those with less education report the highest rates of physical abuse (Black & Breiding, 2008; Lown et al., 2006; Thompson et al., 2006). Black women are more likely than White women to be victims of domestic violence (Weston et al., 2005) and they are more severely abused (West, 2002). Black women, however, are more likely than other women to fight back against sexual assault. In one study of poor, urban women (Fine & Weis, cited in Fine & Carney, 2001), abused Black women were more likely than abused White women to secure orders of protection, call the police, go to a shelter, throw the batterer out of the house, or report the incident to brothers and fathers who might confront the abuser.

The Asian American community has the lowest reported rates of intimate partner violence of any other ethnic group (Black & Breiding, 2008), but this could be an underestimate of its actual occurrence. Asian Americans emphasize the family over the individual, the strong value placed on the male as the authority in the family, and the belief that family affairs must be kept private. These reasons may keep Asian American women from seeking assistance for their abuse, and those who do report it are likely to meet with considerable disapproval in their communities (Ho, 1990).

The incidence of domestic violence among Latinas/os in the United States have produced a mixed picture. Some studies show a high incidence of violent spousal behavior compared to other ethnic groups, while others do not (Castañeda, 2008; Cebello et al., 2004). Methodological problems, such as lumping together all Latina/o subgroups and not considering the influence of acculturation into U.S. society, may be responsible for these inconsistencies.

The limited research on abuse of Native American women indicates that their rate of intimate partner violence is the highest of all ethnic groups (Black & Breiding, 2008). This may be related to both alcohol abuse and patriarchal beliefs introduced by the Westernization of Native peoples (Allen, 1990).

Things are no better in other parts of the world, as you'll see in Explore Other Cultures 14.4.

Risk Factors

The need for power and control and the belief that men have the right to punish their female partners play an important role in men's intimate partner violence (Stahly, 2008; White & Frabutt, 2006). Alcohol and drug abuse by batterers in both heterosexual and lesbian relationships is also common (Boles & Miotto, 2003; Glass et al, 2008; Snow et al., 2006; White & Frabutt, 2006). Violent husbands are more likely than other husbands to display poor problem-solving and communication skills, high levels of anger and hostility, antisocial behavior, and low self-esteem. Occupational and marital stresses are also associated with intimate partner violence (Arias & Ikeda, 2006; Barnett et al., 2005; Hilton & Harris, 2005; Stith et al., 2004). Not surprisingly, male batterers and abused women are more likely than other men and women to have witnessed violence between their parents or experienced physical or sexual abuse in childhood (Arias & Ikeda, 2006; McHugh et al., 2008; Schafer et al., 2004; Taft et al., 2006; White & Frabutt, 2006). This does not mean that all adults with a history of violence will be involved in an abusive relationship, or that all those involved in domestic violence have a history of family battering (Hines & Saudino, 2002). However, these

EXPLORE OTHER CULTURES **14.4**
Intimate Partner Violence Around the World

Sadly, violence against women by their male partners occurs in all countries, regardless of economic class and religion (Burn, 2005; Malley-Morrison, 2004; Sigal & Annan, 2008). Recent data from Australia, the United States, Canada, Israel, and South Africa, for example, show that one-third to 70 percent of female murder victims are killed by their husbands or boyfriends (HELP Network, 2003; World Health Organization, 2002). In addition, thousands of women each year are victims of dowry-related killings or are disfigured by acid thrown in their faces by rejected suitors in Bangladesh, Colombia, India, Nigeria, and Pakistan (UNIFEM, 2003). In sub-Saharan Africa and in the patriarchal Arab societies of the Middle East, women themselves often consider wife beating to be justified under certain circumstances, such as

disobeying one's husband. Furthermore, they blame women for the beating, believe that women benefit from the violence, and oppose assistance for battered women from governmental agencies (Amowitz et al., 2004; Haj-Yahia, 2002; LaFraniere, 2005b).

To make matters worse, the criminal justice system may take crimes of violence against ethnic minority or immigrant women less seriously than those committed against majority women. For example, the longstanding ill treatment of the Roma (formerly called Gypsy) people in the Czech Republic and Croatia have made Roma women reluctant to report crimes of violence to the police. In some countries, the legal system downplays attacks on minority women, attributing them as part of the group's culture (UNIFEM, 2003).

---

findings do suggest that observing a parent commit violence gives boys the message that violence is a means for handling anger and conflict and influences the development of negative attitudes toward women. For women, the early experience of family violence can provide a similar message that aggression is a "normal" aspect of close relationships. It can also make it more difficult for the abused girl to learn how to accurately screen people and situations for danger (Koss et al., 1994).

Effects of Intimate Partner Violence

The effects of abuse include a wide variety of both physical and psychological problems. Health problems include physical injuries and reproductive difficulties. Abused women may also suffer psychological problems such as lower self-esteem, depression, anxiety, drug and alcohol abuse, sexual risk-taking behavior, eating disorders, posttraumatic stress disorder, and suicide attempts (Bonomi et al., 2006, 2007; Coker, 2007; Franco, 2007; Krahé et al., 2005; Pimlott-Kubiak & Cortina, 2003; Taft et al., 2006, 2007; Williams & Frieze, 2005). Furthermore, psychological abuse has as great an effect on women's physical and mental health as does physical violence (Arias & Ikeda, 2006), perhaps because it involves continual humiliation and the destruction of one's identity. Moreover, the health problems caused by physical and psychological abuse may keep women from obtaining or keeping employment, which can keep them financially dependent on the abuser (Riger & Staggs, 2004). Children who observe parental violence also suffer psychological trauma, as illustrated by Susan's anguished comments at the beginning of the chapter.

Leaving the Abusive Relationship

Many people wonder why abused women don't leave their batterer. One of the greatest barriers to leaving is financial concern, as many women do not have the economic resources to provide for their family (Bornstein, 2006; Koepsell et al., 2006). Another major obstacle is fear of retaliation (Chantler, 2006; Panchanadeswaran & McClosky, 2007, Stahly, 2008). Batterers can interpret women's attempt to leave as a loss of control and their violence can accelerate. As one battered woman reported, "The very first time that I attempted to leave he tried to choke me with the sheets to the point where I turned blue" (Sorenson, 1996, p. 129). Many older women have stayed in abusive marriages because they were socialized to remain with their husbands regardless of circumstances (Zink et al., 2004). Women with disabilities may also be more likely than other women to stay in an abusive relationship, especially if their job or transportation opportunities are limited, or if their only alternative living arrangement is in an institution (Olkin, 2008). In addition, women with more conservative religious beliefs tend to stay in abusive relationships longer than other women. Very religious strains of Judaism, Christianity, and Islam sometimes make it difficult for women to escape such relationships. In addition, both the batterer and the victim may misinterpret religious texts to justify the abuse. Muslim American women have been faced with an increase in domestic violence since the terrorist attacks on September 11, 2001. This abuse has largely been unreported in the past, but women are even more hesitant to come forth than before September 11 because of fear of deportation (Childress, 2003). Other immigrant women, similarly, may be reluctant to inform authorities about domestic violence because of fear of discrimination and anti-immigrant sentiment (Kasturirangan et al., 2004).

Theories of Intimate Partner Violence

Two theories presented as explanations of rape are also useful in understanding intimate partner violence. As discussed previously, feminist theory emphasizes gender power imbalance as a destructive factor in men's interactions with women. When applied to battering, it contends that men use violence against women as a means to maintain their power and status (McHugh et al., 2008; Stahly, 2008). Social learning theory, with its focus on observation and reinforcement, posits that domestic violence is a learned behavior that can develop from observing violence within the family and from receiving reinforcement for aggressive acts (Barnett et al., 2005).

Interventions

In the past 30 years, a body of laws has developed concerning domestic violence. These include mandatory arrest of the abuser (Iyengar, 2007) and orders of protection that prohibit the abuser from coming near or contacting the woman (Barnett et al.,

2005). The development of shelters and transitional housing programs for abused women have been other key interventions (McHugh et al., 2008; Sullivan, 2006). Feminist therapy (discussed in Chapter 13) is a useful tool for helping to reempower the battered woman. Another helpful intervention for battered women suffering from posttraumatic stress disorder (PTSD) is cognitive trauma therapy (Kubany et al., 2004). This treatment includes exploring the trauma; PTSD education; stress management; exposure to reminders of the abuse and abuser; self-monitoring of negative self-talk; cognitive therapy for guilt; and modules on self-advocacy, assertiveness, and how to identify perpetrators. Women receiving this therapy show large reductions in PTSD symptoms, depression, and guilt and substantial increases in self-esteem (Kubany et al., 2004). Programs also have been designed to treat the batterer either alone or with his partner. They deal with attitudes toward women and toward violence against women, as well as anger management (Frieze, 2005; McHugh et al., 2008; Wathen & MacMillan, 2003). Unfortunately, the effects of such programs in preventing further violence are modest (Babcock et al., 2004; Cattaneo & Goodman, 2005; Ferris, 2004; Gondolf, 2004).

Elder Abuse

> *A handyman befriends his elderly customer and gets her to pay his bills and deed her home to him.* (Sklar, 2000)
>> *A woman withdraws large sums from her ailing great-aunt's bank account to pay for her own expenses, including cars, furniture, and jewelry.* (Edwards, 2007)
>> *A crack-addicted man physically batters his elderly aunts if they do not give him money for his next fix. Eventually, they lose their savings and their home and are reduced to begging in the streets.* (Kleinfield, 2004)

Abuse of older adults is an alarming global phenomenon that has received increasing media attention in recent years. At least 4 percent of older adults—over 2 million people in the United States—experience moderate to severe abuse each year (Collins et al., 2000; Voelker, 2002). Patterns of abuse vary little among Blacks, Latinas/os, and Whites (Cavanaugh & Blanchard-Fields, 2006). Older Black women, however, have lower rates of reported sexual abuse than do Latinas and White women (Grossman & Lundy, 2003). Asian Americans are less likely than other groups to perceive situations as abusive and are less likely to seek help (Barnett et al., 2005). For a look at elder abuse in other countries, see Explore Other Cultures 14.5.

Types of Abuse

Elder abuse refers to physical, psychological, financial, and neglectful acts that harm the health or welfare of an older adult, and that occur within a relationship of trust (Centers for Disease Control and Prevention, 2003; see Table 14.2). Neglect and financial exploitation are the most commonly reported types of abuse (Bugental & Hehman,

TABLE 14.2   Types of Elder Abuse

Type of Abuse	Description
Physical and sexual abuse	Hitting, choking, hair pulling, kicking, sexually molesting, confining the person against her or his will
Psychological abuse	Threatening, humiliating, insulting, intimidating the person, forcing the person to do degrading things, treating the person like a child
Financial abuse	Destroying property or possessions, stealing the person's money, denying the person access to his or her money
Neglect	Depriving the person of items needed for daily living (food, warmth, shelter, glasses, dentures, money), inattention, isolation

Sources: Beers and Jones (2004); Collins et al. (2000).

2007). Most of these crimes are committed by family members and paid household workers or caregivers, as shown in the vignettes at the beginning of this section.

All states now have laws against elder mistreatment, with most mandating that abuse be reported. Yet various studies estimate that only one in every five or more cases is reported (Centers for Disease Control and Prevention, 2003; Hurme, 2002). One obstacle is denial of the problem. In addition, elderly persons themselves may lack the opportunity and the physical and mental ability to report abuse. They often fear not being believed, reprisal, abandonment, and institutionalization. Also, the victimized elderly may wish to protect the abuser, who is most often an adult child or a spouse (Beers & Jones, 2004; Edwards, 2007; Wei & Herbers, 2004).

EXPLORE OTHER CULTURES 14.5

A Global View of Elder Abuse

Unfortunately, elder abuse exists around the world (Malley-Morrison, 2004). Recent interviews with elderly people in Argentina, Austria, Brazil, Canada, India, Kenya, Lebanon, and Sweden (World Health Organization, 2002) indicate that while forms of abuse vary across countries, the most common victims are the elderly poor, widows, and childless older women. In Austria, India, Japan, Korea, Lebanon, and Taiwan, elderly women report that family conflict and jealousy lead to neglect and abuse by their daughters-in-law (Malley-Morrison, 2004; World Health Organization, 2002). In Kenya and Brazil, one serious form of abuse is the practice of abandoning older family members in hospitals, especially during times of drought, poor crop yields, or even holidays. A common theme across many cultures is a pervasive lack of respect for the elderly, whether in health, governmental, and commercial institutions or in personal interactions.

Who Is Abused and Who Abuses?

The typical victim of elder abuse is a woman over age 75. She often lives at home with adult caregivers but is isolated and fearful. Frequently, she is physically and/or mentally frail and may suffer from cognitive impairments. She is often widowed or divorced (Tolan et al., 2006; Wei & Herbers, 2004).

Over two-thirds of the abuse is inflicted by children, spouses, or other relatives. The typical abuser is a middle-aged son of the victim. Adult children with mental, alcohol, or drug problems are among the most likely to be abusers. Often, the abuser is the caregiver of the victim and may also be financially dependent upon the victim (Barnett et al., 2005; Hurme, 2002; Tolan et al., 2006; Wei & Herbers, 2004).

The stress of providing care for an ill relative may contribute to the problem of elder abuse. Some caregivers for an older person who is physically ill or suffers from dementia may express their frustration by becoming abusive (Hurme, 2002). The caregiver may be someone who neither chose to do so nor is able to cope with the financial, interpersonal, and time demands placed on him or her (Barnett et al., 2005).

While acknowledging that caring for an elderly relative can be stressful, one must be careful not to simply "blame the victim" for being abused. (Notice the parallel with inappropriately blaming a woman who has been raped.) The feminist perspective puts elder abuse in a larger social context. From this point of view, elder abuse is part of a spectrum of male violence against women (White & Frabutt, 2006) that reflects a social context in which men wield more power and dominance over women.

What Can Be Done?

Some of the options that are available to the younger abused woman—deciding to leave a relationship or going to a shelter—are impractical or virtually impossible for most abused elderly. Awareness of the problem is the first step. One encouraging sign is that in 2002, the United Nations recognized for the first time the need to eliminate violence against the elderly, especially women, around the world ("U.N. Offers," 2002). Education and training are essential to alert the general public and professional service providers to the prevalence of elder abuse and neglect. Professionals must learn to recognize the symptoms of abuse, understand the victim's denial, and strengthen the victim's resolve to end the abuse. The public should be encouraged to report any known or suspected case of abuse. Both the public and the victim must know where to turn for help. New laws have been passed in recent years governing the treatment of victims, especially women, that focus on the need for safety, assistance in accessing the courts, and information about the progress of the proceedings. This emphasis on victims' rights should be ensured by legislation at the state and federal levels. Support groups for victims help validate the victims' experiences and provide a sense of empowerment that may enable them to change the power structure of the abusive relationship (Barnett et al., 2005; Edwards, 2007; Schewe, 2002; Voelker, 2002; Wolf, 2001).

SUMMARY

Sexual Harassment at School

- Reports of sexual harassment are increasing among junior and senior high school students.
- Girls are more likely than boys to be sexually harassed by their schoolmates and they are more upset by it.
- Schools are now legally obligated to protect students from severe and pervasive harassment by other students.
- More female than male students experience sexual harassment on campus. Most incidents involve subtle forms of harassment, and most are perpetrated by other students.
- Ethnic and sexual minority students are more likely to experience harassment than are other students.

Sexual Harassment in the Workplace

- It is estimated that up to half of employed women will experience sexual harassment. Sexist remarks and jokes are common forms of harassment; sexual coercion is relatively rare.
- Women in blue-collar occupations and the military are more likely to be targets of harassment than other women.
- This might be due to the high prevalence of both the male gender stereotype and male-related physical traits in these fields.
- According to sex-role spillover theory, sexual harassment occurs because men respond to females in the workplace as women rather than workers. Power theory states that harassment is used by more powerful individuals either to gain sexual favors or to reinforce their position of greater power.
- Most targets of sexual harassment use informal strategies for dealing with the harassment, such as ignoring it or asking the harasser to stop. They rarely file formal complaints or seek legal redress.
- Numerous negative outcomes can stem from sexual harassment.

Violence against Girls

- The incidence of child sexual abuse may run as high as 20 percent of females and 5 percent of males. Most abuse is committed by a relative or family friend (usually male).
- Sexual abuse can have a devastating impact on the physical and mental health of children, both immediately and in the long term.
- School-based sexual-abuse prevention programs may help children avoid and report abuse. Psychotherapy can help abused children and women heal.
- Countries with strong preferences for boys show elevated rates of abortion, infanticide, and neglect of female children.
- Many girls and young women around the world have been lured into sexual slavery.

Dating Violence

- Substantial numbers of teenagers experience violence in their dating relationships. More males than females report being victims of such violence.

Rape

- An estimated one-quarter of women experience rape, much of it perpetrated by acquaintances.
- Physical aggressiveness, hostility toward women, gender-stereotypical attitudes, and a history of family violence differentiate sexually aggressive men from other men.
- Alcohol consumption increases the risk of sexual coercion and rape.
- Rape victims can experience a variety of emotional and health problems.
- Evolutionary, feminist, and social learning theories attempt to account for rape. Although some support for all three has been reported, there are many criticisms of evolutionary theory.

Intimate Partner Violence

- At least 2.5 million women are victims of domestic violence each year.
- Battering occurs in both lesbian and heterosexual relationships and across ethnic groups, although it is more frequent among Blacks than Whites.

- Major risk factors for both perpetrators and victims of domestic violence are a history of family violence and alcohol and drug abuse.
- Numerous physical and psychological problems can result from victimization, including physical injuries, reproductive difficulties, lower self-esteem, anxiety, and depression.
- Financial problems and fear of the perpetrator are the primary reasons for remaining in an abusive relationship.
- Feminist and social learning theories help explain domestic violence.

Elder Abuse

- Elder abuse can have physical, psychological, financial, and neglect dimensions. At least 4 percent of older adults in the United States are affected, but few cases are reported.
- The typical victim is a woman age 75 or older who lives with a caregiver. The typical abuser is a middle-aged son who has mental, alcohol, or drug problems.
- The following are essential in order to combat elder abuse: educating professionals and the public; reporting abuse cases; passing victims' rights laws; and forming support groups.

KEY TERMS

sexual harassment in an
   educational setting
sexual harassment in the
   workplace
quid pro quo harassment
hostile environment
sexual coercion
gender harassment
unwanted sexual attention

sex-role spillover theory
power theory
organizational tolerance
internally focused responses
externally focused responses
child sexual abuse
incest
rape
acquaintance rape

sexual script
rape myths
evolutionary theory
feminist theory
social learning theory
intimate partner violence
elder abuse

WHAT DO YOU THINK?

1. Some people have criticized the recent U.S. Supreme Court ruling that obligates schools to protect students from severe and pervasive sexual harassment by other students. Some argue that sexual taunting and even touching is a normal rite of adolescence. Others contend that even such apparently innocent gestures as the exchange of Valentine's Day cards by first graders will now be classified as sexual harassment and thus forbidden. What is your position on this issue, and why?

2. Which of the recommended procedures for reducing sexual harassment on campus do

you think would be particularly effective at your school? Can you think of other activities that might be beneficial on your campus?

3. Why are family members often the perpetrators of child sexual abuse? What actions can be taken to prevent such behaviors?

4. Using either the feminist or social learning theory as a framework, discuss societal changes that might lead to a reduction in both rape and intimate partner violence.

5. How can public awareness of elder abuse be increased?

IF YOU WANT TO LEARN MORE

American Association of University Women. (2001). *Hostile hallways: Bullying, teasing, and sexual harassment in school.* Washington, DC: AAUW Educational Foundation.

Anderson, I., & Doherty, K. (2008). *Accounting for rape: Psychology, Feminism, and discourse analysis in the study of sexual violence.* New York: Routledge.

Barnett, O., Miller-Perrin, C. L., & Perrin, R. D. (2005). *Family violence across the lifespan: An introduction* (2d ed.). Thousand Oaks, CA: Sage.

Denmark, F. L., Krauss, H. H., Halpern, E., & Sechzer, J. (Eds.). (2006). *Violence and exploitation against women and girls.* Boston, MA: Blackwell.

Frieze, I. H. (2005). *Hurting the one you love: Violence in relationships.* Belmont, CA: Thomson Wadsworth.

Kilmartin, C., & Allison, J. (2007). *Men's violence against women: Theory, research, and activism.* Mahwah, NJ: Erlbaum.

Lalumiere, M. L., Harris, G. T., Quinsey, W. L., & Rice, M. E. (2005). *The causes of rape: Understanding individual differences in male propensity for sexual aggression.* Washington, DC: American Psychological Association.

Levenkron, S., & Levenkron, A. (2007). *Stolen tomorrows: Understanding and treating women's childhood sexual abuse.* New York: W. W. Norton.

Lloyd, S. A., & Emery, B. C. (2000). *The dark side of courtship: Physical and sexual aggression.* Thousand Oaks, CA: Sage.

Logan, T. K., Cole, J., Shannon, L., & Walker, R. (2006). *Partner stalking: How women respond, cope, and survive.* New York: Springer.

Malley-Morrison, K. (Ed.). (2004). *International perspectives on family violence and abuse: A cognitive-ecological approach.* Mahwah, NJ: Erlbaum.

Mather, C. L., & Debye, K. E. (2004). *How long does it hurt: A guide to recovering from incest and sexual abuse for teenagers, their friends, and their families.* San Francisco: Jossey-Bass.

Ottens, A. J., & Hotelling, K. (Eds.). (2001). *Sexual violence on campus: Policies, programs, and perspectives.* New York: Springer.

Parrot, A., & Cummings, N. (2006). *Forsaken females: The global brutalization of women.* Lanham, MD: Rowman & Littlefield.

Pierce-Baker, C. (2000). *Surviving the silence: Black women's stories of rape.* New York: W. W. Norton.

Roberts, A. R. (Ed.) (2007). *Battered women and their Families* (3rd ed). New York: Springer.

Sokoloff, N. J., & Pratt, C. (Eds.). (2005). *Domestic violence at the margins: Readings on race, class, gender, and culture.* Rutgers, NJ: Rutgers University Press.

WEBSITES

Education

American Association of University Women
http://www.aauw.org

Sexual Harassment

Feminist Majority Foundation: Sexual Harassment Hotline Resource List
http://www.feminist.org/911/harass.html

Violence against Girls

Abuse/Incest Support
http://www.incestabuse.about.com/health/incestabuse/

Rape

National Clearinghouse on Marital and Date Rape
http://members.aol.com/ncmdr/index.html

Intimate Partner Violence

American Bar Association Commission on Domestic Violence
http://www.abanet.org/domviol/home.html
National Center for Injury Prevention and Control
http://www.cdc.gov/ncipc
Family Violence Prevention Fund
http://endabuse.org
Same-Sex Domestic Violence
http://www.xq.com/cuav/domviol.htm

State Reporting Requirements
http://endabuse.org/statereport/list.php3
Stop Abuse For Everyone (SAFE)
http://www.safe4all.org
U.S. Department of Justice
http://www.ojp.usdoj.gov/vawo

Elder Abuse

National Center on Elder Abuse
http://www.elderabusecenter.org

CHAPTER

15

A Feminist Future
Goals, Actions, and Attitudes

Feminist Goals
  Goal One: Gender Equality in
    Organizational Power
  Goal Two: Gender Equality in Relationship
    Power
  Goal Three: Gender Equality in Power for
    All Groups of Women
  Goal Four: Greater Flexibility in the Social
    Construction of Gender

Actions to Achieve These Goals
  Research and Teaching

  Socialization of Children
  Institutional Procedures
  Individual Actions
  Collective Action

Feminist Beliefs
  Feminist Identification
  Emergence of Feminist Beliefs
  Men and Feminism

Postscript

Several years ago, before my (Judith's) daughter left for college, I offered advice about her first-semester courses. Although Rachel accepted a few of my recommendations, she rejected my suggestion of a women's studies course, stating that gender was not an important issue. At age 17, she certainly had no idea the route her academic career would eventually take. Despite her initial protestations, Rachel ultimately registered for a women's studies course in order to fulfill a multicultural curriculum requirement, and this course proved to be a transforming experience. It exposed Rachel to research, theory, and ideology that dramatically affected her attitudes and interests. In fact, this course was the basis for her academic journey that began with a double major in sociology and women studies and culminated in a feminist doctoral dissertation in sociology.

We saw in Chapter 1 that science is not value free, and as Rachel's experience illustrates, neither is teaching. "The process of education is political" (Wyche & Crosby, 1996, p. 5); that is, both subject matter and teaching methods are influenced by the value system of the instructor and the academic community. Applying this to the field of psychology, Kimberly Kinsler and Sue Rosenberg Zalk (1996) contend that "the greatest value of psychology lies in the field's ability to reveal the psychological processes perpetuating social injustices and to correct the social systems that have an unjust impact on the quality of people's lives" (p. 35). Given this political dimension of teaching, we end this textbook with a look at feminist goals for the future.

In Chapter 1, we presented three feminist themes that have recurred throughout this book: gender inequality of power, diversity of women, and the social construction of gender. In this chapter, we return to these themes and translate them into goals for the future, consider actions for achieving these aims, and, because these goals have their root in feminist thought, explore the prevalence of feminist beliefs among North American women.

Feminist Goals

Based on the themes in this book, we have chosen four feminist goals for the future. Do you have others that you would add?

Goal One: Gender Equality in Organizational Power

Despite legislation that prohibits gender discrimination in employment (Title VII of the Civil Rights Act of 1964) and educational programs (Title IX, 1972), gender differences in organizational and interpersonal power continue to limit women's advancement in the workplace. Antidiscrimination legislation alone cannot change attitudes, and discriminatory policies are hard to monitor. Therefore, as has been noted throughout this text, men, especially White men, continue to have greater access to economic and political resources than women do. They continue to greatly outnumber women at high levels of management and in political office and to own most of the wealth (Chapter 10).

To combat this inequity, we choose as our first goal for the future greater equality of organizational power. A strong commitment from an organization's top management can help create a culture that promotes the advancement of young women (Costello & Wight, 2003). As more and more women attain levels of power currently held by men, gender equality will begin to affect other areas. Women's accessibility to important mentors and social networks will increase, providing even more promotion opportunities for women. And because job level is one factor determining salaries, women's wages will rise and become more similar to those of men. The close association between sexual harassment and the power imbalance also suggests that a greater power equality will mean less harassment of women.

Goal Two: Gender Equality in Relationship Power

In addition to greater organizational power, men continue to hold more interpersonal power relative to women. For instance, they tend to have more control over a couple's activities on dates and more influence in marriage (Chapter 8). A second goal, therefore, is greater equality in relationship power. Women would benefit by having a greater voice in dating decision making and a more balanced division of household labor. The latter, in turn, could reduce women's role overload and interrole conflict. Furthermore, because both rape and domestic violence are due, at least in part, to male dominance, shared interpersonal power would go a long way in reducing intimate violence against women.

Goal Three: Gender Equality in Power for All Groups of Women

Women are disadvantaged due not only to the gender inequality of power but also to differences within genders that add extra burdens to the lives of many women. White women are advantaged compared to women of color; middle-class women have more power than working-class or poor women; heterosexual women are privileged in comparison to lesbian women; able-bodied women are more advantaged than women with disabilities; and younger women have more power than their older counterparts. We have seen that ethnic minority women and women with disabilities experience even greater wage inequities than White and able-bodied women (Chapter 10). Furthermore, women of color and lesbian women experience more job discrimination and sexual harassment than White and heterosexual women (Chapters 10 and 14). Thus, a third power goal is to ensure that increases in female power benefit all women, regardless of ethnicity, class, disability/ability, sexual orientation, or age.

Goal Four: Greater Flexibility in the Social Construction of Gender

We have noted throughout the text that gender is socially constructed, that most gender behaviors and roles—such as career choice (Chapter 9), friendship behaviors (Chapter 8), and contribution to household labor (Chapter 11)—are shaped by interpersonal, societal, and cultural expectations and are not constrained by biological sex. In examining some of the mechanisms that influence this construction of gender, we explored stereotypes that reflect societal gender expectations (Chapter 3), theoretical perspectives about the mechanisms whereby children learn the behaviors and roles expected for their gender (Chapter 3), and parental shaping of the behaviors and interests of girls and boys (Chapter 4). We saw that it is not the biological nature of females and males that serves as the major foundation for people's view of gender or their gender-related activities and preferences, but their conception of what it means to be a female or a male in our society today.

Additionally we have seen that power, or rather the imbalance of power, also guides the social construction of gender (Howard & Hollander, 1997). People with more power, who are in dominant positions, are likely to acquire and use different traits and behaviors than people in subordinate positions. Individuals in high-status positions are more likely to display independence, a male gender-related trait that is difficult to embrace if one lacks access to necessary resources in the home, workplace, or social environment. People lacking powerful resources, on the other hand, are more likely to rely instead on emotional connections between people and, consequently, to develop female gender-related traits, such as compassion. Thus, females' and males' development of gender-related traits, behaviors, and roles is constructed via stereotype-based expectations; socialization by parents, peers, and others; and hierarchical status within society.

Unfortunately, a rigid construction of gender is damaging to human potential (Howard & Hollander, 1997; Katz, 1996). It hinders development of our unique talents and interests by guiding us in directions dictated by the social constructs of our biological sex. Judith recalls her days as a new bride when she refused to allow her husband to share the housecleaning, although both she and her husband were employed full-time. Her insistence was based on her traditional conception of the "wife" role, a perception that was constructed from television and magazine images and from the roles of many married couples at that time (the 1960s). Her "wife role" behaviors were not based on her own interests, her time availability, or her husband's desires, but solely on her construction of this role from the societal images and social behaviors she observed around her.

A fourth goal for women, then, is greater flexibility in the construction of gender. Flexibility can lead to an expansion in career options, more flexible decisions about work and family dilemmas, greater sexual equality, and numerous other reductions in gender-constrained behaviors that limit choices made by both women and men. Flexibility of gender-related behaviors and roles also has the potential to reduce the prevalence of sexual harassment and acquaintance rape (Chapter 14), both of which are fostered, at least in part, by traditional constructions of the behaviors of men and women. Further, it can enhance communication within heterosexual couples by freeing each partner from constraints expected for her or his gender.

Actions to Achieve These Goals

Research and Teaching

Research and teaching about the psychology of women can play a significant role in achieving feminist goals for several reasons. First, greater knowledge of gender differences in interpersonal and societal power can help clarify the role that power imbalance plays in women's lives. Understanding the extent to which male power influences rape and battering (Chapter 14), serves as the basis for the division of household labor (Chapter 11), and contributes to wage inequities (Chapter 10) means that both female and male students will be aware of the prevalence of male power. A reduction in male privilege cannot occur until people recognize that it exists (Case, 2007). Exposure to this issue within the classroom can increase awareness that can spark the motivation and action necessary for change. The more we (psychologists and students) understand the dynamics and the effects of power differentials, the better armed we are to reduce privilege and its negative consequences for the less powerful.

Second, research and teaching on the psychology of women enlightens us about the way we construct gender in our lives. Scientific investigation gives us a better understanding of the influences on this construction and of the effects our personal images of gender have on our experiences as females or males. Similarly, exploration of these issues in the classroom has the potential to transform. As both women and men learn about the social basis for gender behaviors and roles, they might feel freer to experiment and to make choices that are less traditional but more personally appropriate (Paludi et al., 2008).

Third, research and teaching about the experiences of diverse women can dispel myths and stereotypes that distort our understanding and reduce tolerance. These activities also foster greater understanding, appreciation, and celebration of our similarities and differences and can empower all females, not only those in the most privileged group. Although recent years have brought a greater inclusion of underrepresented groups in both research and educational curricula to achieve these diversity goals, the field must continue to expand the diversity of its research participants. A more representative body of knowledge can ensure that researchers, instructors, and students do not generalize from one narrow group of females, carrying the implicit message that people in this group are "normal" and any discrepant behaviors, attitudes, or roles on the part of other individuals are "abnormal" (Enns & Forrest, 2005).

Consideration of diverse women's experiences must include a broader scope of topics as well. Research and teaching must address previously underexamined issues, such as employment obstacles for poor women, dating concerns of women with disabilities, experiences of lesbian mothers, outcomes of living in an extended family, and achievement goals of working-class and poor young women. A broader conceptualization of research and teaching topics not only facilitates understanding but can also inform policy interventions. For example, although company-supplied day care might ease the work-family burden of women in white-collar and professional jobs, free temporary child care might be a better resource for women on welfare who are seeking job training. Similarly, principles guiding custody decisions for divorced heterosexual women might not apply to divorced lesbian women. It is only through an examination of questions relevant to all types of women that societal interventions can best address the diversity of women's needs.

Although there is much less information available about ethnic minority women, working-class and poor women, women with disabilities, lesbian and bisexual women, and older women, it is essential that we incorporate the knowledge base that does exist into our teaching (Lorber, 2005; Zack, 2005). Without this diversity focus in our teaching, students' "educational experience does not reflect social reality and is therefore derelict in preparing them, regardless of race, culture, ethnicity, sexual orientation, and gender, to function in a culturally pluralistic and global society" (Sue et al., 1999, p. 1066).

Socialization of Children

Another approach to developing greater flexibility in gender construction is the feminist socialization of children. Parents can bring up their children so that preferences and skills, rather than gender, are the defining characteristics that guide development. How can this be achieved? Read Learn about the Research 15.1 to examine Phyllis Katz's perspective on this topic (1996).

What would be the outcomes of gender-flexible upbringing? First, it would expand the range of activities, behaviors, and roles from which the child and, later, the adult could choose. Instead of assuming, for example, that males make dating decisions, pay for dates, and initiate sex (Chapter 8), whichever dating partner was more comfortable with these behaviors could select them. Furthermore, these might vary depending on the circumstances. This, in turn, could lead to more egalitarian relationships because decision making and instrumental behaviors would not be relegated specifically to males. Similarly, women and men would make occupational choices on the basis of skills, interests, and personal needs without consideration of the gender appropriateness of the field (Chapter 10), a process that might lead to greater occupational prestige and salaries for women and to greater job satisfaction for both genders.

Second, given the higher status of the male role in North American society, gender flexibility would lead boys to develop a greater understanding and respect for behaviors and roles traditionally associated with females. If boys observe their fathers and other influential adult men performing traditional female behaviors, such as washing the dishes and caring for young children, and if boys are required to perform these chores, they will be more apt to view the traditional female role as worthy and dignified. The far-reaching implications are, of course, that when these boys grow up to be men the values instilled in them in childhood will influence their own involvement in traditional female activities and increase their respect for others who perform such activities. This greater respect could, in turn, carry over to the workplace, where more familiarity with family-related activities might encourage the initiation and support of additional family-friendly policies.

Third, gender flexibility would minimize the extent to which people view and evaluate others on the basis of a rigid construction of gender. For example, girls who play sports would receive the same degree of encouragement as sports-oriented boys (Chapter 4) and women in blue-collar trades would be accepted rather than harassed by their coworkers (Chapter 14). We would evaluate mothers who voluntarily stay home to care for their children or those who elect to work full-time in the same way as we would evaluate fathers in these roles. We would have the same reaction to women and men who are fiercely independent and to those who are highly dependent. That is, if our children were brought up with a feminist perspective of equality, their impressions of others would be influenced by their behaviors and roles rather than by the

---

L E A R N   A B O U T   T H E   R E S E A R C H   15.1

Why and How Should We Raise Feminist Children?

Phyllis Katz asks what it means to raise a feminist child. One answer is the elimination of all gender-related traits, behaviors, and roles, that is, raising children so that gender is irrelevant. Katz contends, however, that this would not be possible. Children are exposed to influences beyond the home. Consequently, even if parents were to treat their daughters and sons identically, these children would continue to be exposed to other people for whom gender would be important.

Instead, Katz advocates raising children to be gender flexible, that is, to select activities and behaviors on the basis of "individual likes and skills rather than being bogged down by gender stereotypes" (pp. 333–334). She notes that because much gender learning takes place during

the preschool years, several actions by the parents can play an important role. One is role modeling. For example, maternal employment and nontraditional division of household labor by parents can help develop less stereotypic expectations and behaviors in children. Furthermore, the kinds of activities and goals encouraged by the parents can be instrumental. As examples, discouragement of gender stereotypic activities, toys, and future aspirations can be effective. Also, Katz notes that limiting the amount of television their children can watch might be beneficial because there is some evidence that children who watch less television have less stereotypic conceptions of gender.

What Does It Mean?

1. Do you think that the development of gender flexibility is a positive goal? Explain your answer.
2. Katz suggests it might not be possible to eliminate all gender-stereotypic influences on children. Do you agree or disagree? Explain your answer.

3. Regardless of your own opinion about gender flexibility, use the knowledge you have gained from this course to suggest other factors besides parental behaviors that might facilitate its development in children and adolescents.

Source: Katz (1996).

---

perceived suitability of those behaviors for individuals of one gender or the other, and the choice of roles, for everyone, would be limitless.

Institutional Procedures

Another route for attaining our goals is for institutions to initiate practices that reduce gender inequality and that create hospitable environments for both women and men. In Chapters 10 and 11, we examined organizational procedures that improve working conditions for women (e.g., pay equity, affirmative action) or that facilitate balancing of family and work (e.g., flextime, child-care assistance programs). Institutional initiatives can enhance the quality of life for women in other ways as well. Raising public awareness of women's issues on a community-wide basis, with stakeholders including

When children observe their parents performing nonstereotypic behaviors, they are likely to develop a less rigid construction of gender.

educators, religious organizations, media, and health-care institutions among others, is critical (APA Task Force, 2007). For example, Mary Koss and her colleagues (1994) propose several institutional interventions that can lower the risk of rape and domestic violence by reducing gender inequality and enhancing flexibility of gender-related behaviors and roles.

First, Koss and her associates emphasize the importance of education. They recommend that violence prevention begin in elementary school, when values about females' and males' roles are beginning to form, and continue through college. Although different topics would be appropriate at various educational levels, the curriculum should include an examination and reconceptualization of gender roles, prevention of substance abuse, and exploration of rape myths. This type of curriculum would expose children, adolescents, and young adults to problems inherent in traditional gender-related behaviors and roles, would make them more sensitive to the experiences and pressures of the other gender, and would make them aware of the nature of and influences on violence against women.

Second, these researchers suggest that the church can be involved in reduction of intimate violence. Because some people acquire their view of marital relationships through religious doctrine, programs aimed at reducing domestic violence can be particularly effective for these individuals, if associated with the church.

Third, Koss and her colleagues point to the need for change in media images. Researchers should advance our understanding about how the media contribute to violence against women and about ways they can be used to reduce this violence.

In addition to the prevention of violence against women, Koss and her colleagues address ways that health-care institutions can more effectively treat women who have been victimized. They stress the importance for health-care providers to have adequate training in treating the physical and mental health problems that arise from rape and battering. Providers must be sensitive to victims' needs and be able to offer effective medical treatment as well as appropriate referrals for psychological counseling or assistance with lifestyle changes, such as leaving their violent relationship.

Individual Actions

Many women seek to achieve success and better their own lives through individual efforts. In fact, consistent with a traditional North American value system that applauds individualism, many American women place greater emphasis on their own hard work in improving their lives than on women's collective efforts (Boxer, 1997; Konek et al., 1994). These women think that women's personal effort and success today, more than changes in organizational or governmental policies and practices, will lead to better opportunities for future generations of women (Konek et al., 1994), and they are willing to work hard, assert their rights, seek out opportunities for advancement, and make sacrifices if necessary.

Collective Action

Contrary to the individual approach, many feminist psychologists contend that collective action is necessary in order to achieve significant improvement in women's lives (White, Russo, & Travis, 2001; Worell, 2001). This does not imply that women should not work hard to attain personal goals. However, it does mean that women, both individually and in groups, should strive to empower all women, not just themselves; they should advocate for social change, not just personal betterment. Furthermore, these collective efforts should address the concerns of diverse groups of women.

One woman who has made a difference in the lives of many other women is Catherine Hamlin, an Australian-born surgeon who has spent over 40 years in Ethiopia repairing fistulas, which are seriously ripped tissues resulting from female genital mutilation. She and her husband founded a fistula hospital which has treated thousands of women. In 2003, Dr. Hamlin was named an honorary fellow in the American College of Surgeons (Bridges et al., 2003–2004).

Two other wonderful examples of women who have made a difference are the winners of the Nobel Peace Prize in 2003 and 2004. The 2003 winner is Shirin Ebadi, an Iranian lawyer, judge, writer, and university lecturer who has spent three decades advancing human rights in her country. While many professional women left Iran after the 1979 Islamic revolution, she stayed and became one of Iran's outspoken advocates for the rights of women and children (Alvarez, 2003; Sciolino, 2003). Wangari Maathai, the 2004 Nobel Peace Prize winner, is the first Black African woman to receive the award. She won for her work as the founder and leader of an organization that has fought deforestation of the land and has improved women's lives through education, family planning, and better nutrition (Maliti, 2004).

Girls and women also work together in groups to advocate for social change. One recent example of this type of activism is the work of a group of girls, ages 13 to 16, who

Wangari Maathai (left) and Shirin Ebadi (right), winners of the Nobel Peace Prize in 2004 and 2003, respectively, were honored for advancing human rights in their countries.

protested against Abercrombie and Fitch (A&F) tee shirts printed with demeaning slogans such as "Who needs a brain when you have these?" The girls worked with the Women and Girls Foundation of Southern Pennsylvania to organize a "girlcott" of A&F that drew national media attention and led A&F to withdraw the shirts from stores (APA Task Force, 2007).

The feminist movement in the United States, a collective movement aimed at enhancing women's lives, has unfortunately been focused primarily on the needs of White middle-class heterosexual women and has been criticized for failing to address racism, classism, and heterosexism. It seriously lags behind in dealing with unique problems faced by women of color, poor and working-class women, and sexual minority women (Green, 2006; Henry, 2004; Mankiller, 2004; Poo & Tang, 2004; White, Russo, & Travis, 2001). In the words of a Black college instructor and administrator, "Until very recently I did not call myself a feminist . . . even academic feminism did not include me until the 1980s. Feminism in the United States was pretty monolithic, pretty homogeneous . . . and these groups were very, very exclusive in terms of what they considered to be priorities . . . and so until recently, America did not embrace my experiences" (Kmiec et al., 1996, p. 58).

As bell hooks (1990) contends, women who differ in ethnicity and class have certain experiences in common by virtue of their gender. However, racism, classism,

EXPLORE OTHER CULTURES 15.1

Women's Movements Worldwide

Until recently, feminist academics from the Western world focused on the largely middle-class women's movements in the United States and Europe. However, women in the non-Western world, many of them poor, have also had a long history of battling for women's rights (Burn, 2005; Fraser & Tinker, 2004). Because cultures differ, the struggle does not always focus on the same set of issues. For example, family-planning agendas have helped to mobilize Western feminists but may be viewed skeptically by women in developing nations, where having many children confers status or provides a source of family labor (Burn, 2005). The Afghan Women's Bill of Rights, crafted by a group of Afghan women in 2003, has as its first priority the guarantee of an education. Then come health-care, personal security, and support of widows, with freedom of speech taking up fifth place. Even these basic rights are still in jeopardy in Afghanistan ("Afghan Women's Rights," 2003). In addition to women's movements that exist in individual countries,

there is also an international women's movement, sometimes called global feminism. This movement advocates the idea that all humans share the same rights, while at the same time it recognizes the diversity of women's lives and cultures. The global feminist movement is working to challenge violence against women, expand the education of girls, support women's reproductive and sexual freedom, increase women's political power, and champion women's access to economic independence (Fraser & Tinker, 2004; Paxton, P. et al., 2006). The United Nations has attempted to play a leadership role in this effort. In 1979, it issued a treaty known as the Convention on the Elimination of All Forms of Discrimination against Women. Out of 191 nations, 174 have ratified the treaty ("Gender Equality," 2003), although about one-third of the ratifiers listed reservations. The nonratifying countries include several from the Middle East and sub-Saharan Africa—as well as the "enlightened" United States! (Burn, 2005).

These Pakistani women are demonstrating against a government leader who tore up copies of women's rights laws in Pakistan's National Assembly in 2006.

heterosexism, and ableism contribute to double and triple jeopardies experienced by women who are not in the privileged group. Fortunately, the efforts of women of color, poor women, and lesbian women have gradually expanded the feminist movement's perspective, and participation by previously excluded groups has increased (Labaton & Martin, 2004). But this expansion of goals and inclusive participation must continue to grow. Attempts to achieve gender equality should concurrently strive to eradicate inequalities based on ethnicity, class, sexual orientation, physical disability/ability, and age. Only the collective efforts of diverse groups of women working together for the elimination of all types of power inequality can provide a brighter future for all girls and women. For a look at women's movements worldwide, see Explore Other Cultures 15.1.

Given that some women ascribe to beliefs in equality but are not oriented toward working for change for others, are there ways to enhance these women's motivation for social activism? Judith Worell (2001) suggests that communication with other women, learning about the experiences and problems of other women, and exposure to varied situations that involve gender discrimination can broaden one's understanding of women's issues and encourage individuals' greater involvement in advocating for women's rights. Taking women's studies courses, experiencing discrimination firsthand, and having a mother who is a feminist are linked to students' participation in collective action (Liss et al., 2004).

The Internet has revolutionized the way women organize and act collectively. The use of e-mail, Websites, Listservs, and search engines has improved communication for virtually all groups but has been especially important in linking women's groups, which tend to be small and often isolated from each other (Lee, S. 2004). One example of the effectiveness of the Internet in bringing women into the political process occurred when President George W. Bush cut off government funding to family planning programs outside the United States even if the money was not going to be used for abortion. *Los Angeles Times* writer Patt Morrison denounced the decision in her column and publicly made a donation to Planned Parenthood in Bush's name. The news spread rapidly via e-mail, and donations totaling half a million dollars poured into Planned Parenthood in the president's name (Lee, S. 2004).

Do our feminist goals for the future coincide with your perspectives and those of your acquaintances? Try Get Involved 15.1 to explore students' fantasies about their ideal futures.

Feminist Beliefs

We began the text with a discussion of the meaning of feminism, and now we come full circle, back to this topic. Because the goals we have presented and many of the actions taken to achieve these goals are rooted in a feminist perspective, it is important to explore the prevalence and accuracy of feminist beliefs.

Although most North Americans believe that feminism has had a positive impact on women's attainment of greater economic, political, and legal opportunities (Boxer, 1997), a relatively small number have argued that feminists are the root of numerous personal and social problems, and are especially responsible for the decline in the

GET INVOLVED 15.1

A Perfect Future Day

Imagine what you would like your life to be like ten years in the future. Write a paragraph describing what your ideal typical day would be like. Also, ask one same-gender and two other-gender students to perform the same exercise.

What Does It Mean?

Read through the four descriptions and record similarities and differences about the following: (1) marital status, (2) presence of children, (3) if married, family responsibilities of each spouse, (4) employment status, (5) if employed, gender dominance of the occupation, and (6) leisure activities.

1. Do the descriptions written by the women differ from those written by the men in relation to these or any other topics? If yes, use information learned in this course to explain these differences.

2. Are there any current gender-based expectations about interpersonal or societal roles and behaviors that might hinder your own ideal life from becoming a reality? If yes, what kinds of changes do you think would reduce this impediment? Would you be interested in working for this change?

Source: Based on Kerr (1999).

"traditional" North American family (Faludi, 2007; Huddy et al., 2000). Many feminists are, indeed, disturbed about the subordination of women within *patriarchal* families where husbands hold the power and dictate the activities of wives and children (Johnson, 1997), but they are supportive of egalitarian families in which husbands and wives share power and respect. It is untrue to say that most feminists oppose the notion of the family—they oppose the notion of an unequal family.

Another accusation made by some antifeminists is that feminists hate men. While it is true that many feminists object to male power which has oppressed women in the workplace, government, education, and the home (Johnson, 1997), an objection to male *privilege* should not be confused with an objection to men per se.

Sadly, these antifeminist beliefs not only dangerously distort the truth but also discredit feminist ideology. Given that most North Americans are strongly profamily and that males have high status and respect within society, the depiction of feminists as antifamily male-bashers sets them up for ridicule and makes it easier to dismiss their beliefs as extremist. What are your thoughts on feminism? Perform Get Involved 15.2 to reassess your views.

Feminist Identification

Although support for the women's movement has increased steadily since the mid-1970s, the proportion of American women who identify themselves as feminists remains low (Reid & Purcell, 2004; Rudman & Fairchild, 2007).

GET INVOLVED **15.2**
How Do You View Feminism?

Answer the following questions without looking back at the answers you gave in Chapter 1. First, indicate which of the following categories best characterizes your identity as a feminist.

  a. consider myself a feminist and am currently involved in the Women's Movement
  b. consider myself a feminist but am not involved in the Women's Movement
  c. do not consider myself a feminist but agree with at least some of the objectives of feminism
  c. do not consider myself a feminist and disagree with the objectives of feminism

Second, on a scale from 1 (strongly disagree) to 6 (strongly agree), indicate the extent to which you disagree or agree with each of the following statements.

  1. Women should be considered as seriously as men as candidates for the presidency of the United States.

2. Although women can be good leaders, men make better leaders.
3. A woman should have the same job opportunities as a man.
4. Men should respect women more than they currently do.
5. Many women in the workforce are taking jobs away from men who need the jobs more.
6. Doctors need to take women's health concerns more seriously.
7. Women have been treated unfairly on the basis of their gender throughout most of human history.
8. Women are already given equal opportunities with men in all important sectors of their lives.
9. Women in the United States are treated as second-class citizens.
10. Women can best overcome discrimination by doing the best they can at their jobs, not by wasting time with political activity.

What Does It Mean?

Before computing your score for the ten items, reverse the points for statements 2, 5, 8, and 10. That is, for a rating of "1" (strongly disagree), give 6 points, for a rating of "2," give 5 points, and so on. Then sum the points for the ten items. Note that higher scores reflect greater agreement with feminist beliefs.

  1. Compare your feminist identification (Part I) here with your feminist identifica-

tion at the beginning of the course (see Get Involved 1.1). If there has been a change, explain why.
  2. Compare your feminist beliefs at the two points in time. If there has been a change, explain why. What specific course material, if any, contributed to this change?

Source: Based on Morgan (1996).

According to recent nationwide polls and studies of college students (Breen & Karpinski, 2008; Henderson-King & Zhermer, 2003; Ramsey et al., 2007) only about 25 percent of American women label themselves as feminists, and the percentage of men is even lower. Furthermore, college women of color and working-class White women are less likely than middle-class White college women to label themselves as feminists (Aronson, 2003; Myaskovsky & Wittig, 1997). As stated earlier, the feminist movement has been dominated by White women, and many women of color feel that feminists do not have an interest in their unique experiences and concerns (Myaskovsky & Wittig, 1997). Some women of color, therefore, have embraced women of color feminism, a form of feminism that addresses racism and other issues of importance to ethnic minority females (see Chapter 1). Rachel Williams and Michele Wittig (1997) see another problem for some women of color—the perception of conflict between the values embraced by their ethnic group and values associated with feminist ideology. These scholars suggest that Asian American and Latina women may feel torn between the more patriarchal belief system of their cultures and the feminist value of egalitarianism.

Interestingly, many women who reject the feminist label support the goals of feminism (Aronson, 2003; Breen & Karpinski, 2008; Ramsey et al., 2007). Alyssa Zucker (2004; Bay-Cheng & Zucker, 2007) refers to this group of women as "egalitarians." How can these discrepancies between a feminist identification and views about feminist goals be explained? First, women may be concerned about negative images that some people attach to feminism and feminists. At a personal level, they might want to avoid a negative self-image which they believe would result from identifying themselves with a term that has negative connotations. At a public level, they might fear the social disapproval that could follow from their identification as a feminist (Quinn & Radtke, 2006; Ramsey et al., 2007). Some of these negative images are illustrated by the following definitions of feminists offered by college students. One negative image, that of feminists as man-haters, is illustrated by a student's definition of feminism as "opposing the male sex and it's usually rude and crude sarcastic remarks, papers, or books" (Jackson et al., 1996, p. 690). Still others appear to equate feminism with being unfeminine and physically unattractive (Rudman & Fairchild, 2007). In support of this view, women who rate themselves high in femininity are more likely to reject the "feminist" label than women who rate themselves high in masculinity (Toller et al., 2004). Thus, it is not surprising to find that college students respond more favorably to a profeminist message when it is presented by a feminine-appearing speaker than by a masculine-appearing speaker (Bullock & Fernald, 2003), a phenomenon referred to as "feminism lite."

A second reason that some women refuse to identify as feminists despite their agreement with many feminist goals is that they do not believe women are oppressed or that economic and political systems need to be changed (Nelson et al., 1997). Although they value equality of power and opportunity, they believe women have already attained this equality. One study of college women (Foster, 1999) found an association between students' belief that women are disadvantaged relative to men and their participation in activities that enhance the status of women (e.g., talking about women's issues with others, attending talks on women's issues, joining protests).

Women who perceived fewer gender differences in social conditions were less likely to be involved in activism.

A third reason some women do not label themselves as feminists is because they believe that a feminist identification implies collective action, but they favor individual efforts, rather than group-based actions, for achieving greater power (Rudman & Phelan, 2007).

Emergence of Feminist Beliefs

During this class, I feel my eyes have been opened to what not just women in general, but ethnic, young, old, and disabled women go through every day. . . . Before I took this class, I thought I was aware of all the issues women face. Boy, was I wrong! (Shawna, 21-year-old senior)

Before this course, I thought some women made too big a deal over women's rights issues. My eyes have been so opened, and now I am extremely sensitized to gender issues in society. I actively try to educate people on gender inequality of power and social construction of gender. I am really going to try to raise very gender-flexible children. In a way, I feel like I stepped out of the dark into the light. (Jessica, 25-year-old senior)

It has become customary for the three of us [friends taking Claire's Psychology of Women course] to discuss women's issues at a local coffee shop on Tuesday evenings, not just among ourselves, but our friends as well . . . I have never taken a class that has caused me to engage in so much conversation outside of the classroom. The biggest success of your class is that regardless of how people feel about a certain issue, your class is causing people to talk and more people are becoming aware of issues that wouldn't be discussed otherwise. . . . I feel that my eyes have been opened to a world of issues that have always been right in front of me. (Julie, 22-year-old senior)

One important route to feminist consciousness is enrollment in women's studies courses (Case, 2007; Paludi et al., 2008; Reid & Purcell, 2004; Stake & Malkin, 2003). Women's Studies programs (some are now called Gender Studies) have proliferated since the early 1970s, and about half of all universities in the United States currently offer a course on the Psychology of Women (Yoder, 2005). These courses help foster feminist goals by providing students with the knowledge to transform society (Case, 2007). Similar to the experiences of Shawna, Jessica, Julie (above), and Rachel (chapter-opening vignette), studies have shown that women's studies courses are instrumental in decreasing gender-stereotypic attitudes (Bryant, 2003; Case, 2007; Harris et al., 1999; Lovejoy, 1998; Wilson, 1997) and increasing commitment to feminism (Cole et al., 2001; Katz et al., 2004; Nelson et al., 2008; Yoder et al., 2007). Furthermore, Jayne Stake and her colleagues (see Stake, 2007) have found that women's studies and gender studies courses can encourage activism. Their investigations show that students who take such courses, compared to those who do not, become more active in feminist activities and make more changes in their own roles and/or ways of interacting with others. Moreover, these changes last over time. Exposure to feminism in other ways can also give rise to feminist identity. For example, feminists are more likely than other women to have feminists in their family of origin, such as their mother or sister (Nelson et al., 2008; Zucker, 2004). But even simply reading a paragraph containing positive statements about feminists increases the likelihood that women will identify themselves as feminist (Roy et al., 2007).

A second route toward feminism involves personal experiences women have that make them painfully aware that they live in a sexist society. For example, experiencing sexual harassment or rape is associated with increased support for feminism and women's rights activism (Cole et al., 2001; Livosky et al., 2008; Nelson et al., 2008; Zucker, 2004). For some women, social or historical events such as the *Roe v. Wade* Supreme Court decision on abortion rights, attending NOW meetings, or reading Betty Friedan's book *The Feminine Mystique* (1963) shaped their feminist identity.

Whatever a woman's route to feminism, studies show that women who identify as feminists have greater psychological well-being than other women (Eisele & Stake, 2000; Saunders & Kashubeck-West, 2006; Yakushko, 2007). This may result from a sense of greater independence and personal empowerment on the part of feminist women.

To assess your own involvement in feminist activism, try Get Involved 15.3.

Men and Feminism

Various men's movements have developed in recent years, partly as a response to the women's movement. The mythopoetic movement started by Robert Bly (1990) emphasizes men reconnecting with each other through rituals and retreats. Two religiously based movements of the late 1990s are the Promise Keepers, a Christian fundamentalist group, and the Million Man March, a Black men's group. Both of these movements seek to bring men back into the family, certainly a desirable objective. However, the underlying theme is a return to the traditional roles of men as leaders and women as followers (Kimmel, 2001).

Profeminism is another movement consisting of men who support equality of women and men in all spheres of life, both professional and personal. Profeminist men have organized several campus groups in addition to the National Organization for Men Against Sexism, which includes female as well as male members (Kimmel, 2001). One of the most successful profeminist organizations is the White Ribbon Campaign, which began in Canada in 1991 in response to the mass killing of 14 women engineering students at the University of Montreal by a deranged man. The campaign, whose slogan is "Men, working to end men's violence against women" has now spread to over 55 countries (United Nations, 2007).

Postscript

We end this exploration of women's lives with two cautionary notes. First, when thinking about the material in this text, keep in mind that the knowledge we have about the psychology of women is situated in a particular time in history. It is strongly connected to existing societal attitudes and to current political, economic, and legal events. As a result of economic and attitudinal changes in the last decades of the twentieth century, for example, a major concern for many married mothers in the new millenium is the

GET INVOLVED 15.3
How Involved in Feminist Activism Are You?

Check each of the following eight activities you engaged in during the six months before the beginning of this semester. Then check each activity you engaged in during this semester.

Before
___ kept informed on women's rights issues
___ talked with others to influence their attitudes about women's rights issues
___ signed a petition related to women's rights
___ attended a march, rally, or protest related to women's rights
___ wrote letters to politicians or newspapers about women's rights issues
___ contributed money to a women's rights cause or to politicians who supported such causes
___ circulated a petition about a women's rights cause
___ worked for a phone bank, letter writing campaign, or political campaign in the cause of women's rights
___ participated in other activity related to women's rights

During
___
___

___
___

___

___

___

___

___

What Does It Mean?

1. Has there been an increase in your feminist activities due to this course? If yes, indicate some of the information you learned that contributed to this change.
2. Which of the following types of activities do you believe is the preferable route toward increased rights and opportunities for women: individual effort alone or individual effort combined with collective action? Explain your answer.

Source: Based on Stake et al. (1994).

---

balancing of work and family, but this issue would have been irrelevant to stay-at-home mothers in the 1960s. We can expect that some of the information presented here will become obsolete over time. In fact, if women are successful in their efforts, if legislative initiatives and workplace policies address gender inequities in power and opportunities, and if gender roles become more flexible, some current problems, such as wage differentials and sexual harassment, will, we hope, be eliminated.

Second, as discussed in Chapter 1, teaching does not take place in an ideological vacuum. Even if not explicitly stated, a particular set of values underlies all scholarly research, textbooks, and course content, and this book is no exception. Our feminist values served as the basis for our examination of the lives of girls and women. Regardless of your own commitment to these beliefs, we hope your exploration of the psychology of women has been an enriching experience and that you have achieved an increased understanding of the negative effects of male privilege, a greater appreciation of women's diversity, and a greater awareness of the role interpersonal and societal forces play in shaping gender-based attitudes, behaviors, and goals. And, we sincerely hope you apply what you have learned from this text and course to other academic interests, career pursuits, your own experiences, and perhaps to societal change.

SUMMARY

Feminist Goals

- Greater gender equality of organizational and interpersonal power would benefit women in several ways by increasing opportunities in the workplace, giving women a greater voice in dating relationships, creating a more equitable division of household labor, and reducing intimate violence. It is essential that increases in women's power benefit all women, regardless of ethnicity, class, disability/ability, sexual orientation, or age.
- The benefits of a flexible construction of gender include behavior and role choices that reflect individual preferences instead of social expectations, as well as a reduction in sexual harassment and acquaintance rape.

Actions to Achieve These Goals

- Several actions can facilitate the achievement of these goals including a diversity-oriented psychology of women that can inform about the role of male privilege and the constraints of rigid gender roles and enhance our understanding of diversity and increase tolerance.
- Raising gender-flexible children would free people to make personally appropriate choices, rather than those based on gender-role expectations. Additionally, it would help foster greater appreciation of women's traditional roles and lessen the tendency to evaluate others on the basis of their conformity to gender expectations.
- Interventions by educational, religious, and health-care institutions, as well as the media, can address violence against women.

- Some women believe that they can enhance their own lives more through their individual efforts than as a result of collective action.
- Many feminists believe that improvement of the lives of women requires collective action. However, the feminist movement has been focused more on the lives of privileged women than on those who experience double and triple jeopardies stemming from racism, classism, homophobia, and/or ableism.

Feminist Beliefs

- North Americans have mixed views about the value of feminism. Some believe it has helped women. Others believe that feminists are responsible for many personal and social problems.
- Only 25 percent of North American women label themselves as feminists. Some of the women who do not identify themselves as feminists support the goals of feminism. Reasons for this discrepancy include negative images of feminists, the assumption that women have already attained power equality, and the belief that feminism implies collective action.
- Women's studies courses tend to decrease students' gender-stereotypic attitudes and increase their commitment to feminism and activism.
- Various men's movements have developed in recent years, including the mythopoetic movement, Promise Keepers, Million Man March, and profeminism.

WHAT DO YOU THINK?

1. The text presented greater equality of power and greater flexibility in the construction of gender as beneficial to girls and women. Do you think there are any disadvantages for females associated with these goals? In what ways would these goals benefit males? In what ways might they be detrimental to males?

2. Which one or more of the various strategies for improving women's lives do you think would be most effective? Explain your answer.

IF YOU WANT TO KNOW MORE

Bravo, E. (2007). *Taking on the big boys: Or why feminism is good for families, business, and the nation.* New York: Feminist Press.

Burn, S. M. (2005). *Women across cultures: A global perspective.* New York: McGraw-Hill.

Ens, C. Z., & Sinacore, A. L. (Eds.). (2005). *Teaching and social justice: Integrating multicultural and feminist theories in the classroom.* Washington, DC: American Psychological Association.

Ferree, M. M., & Tripp, A. M. (Eds.). (2006). *Global feminism: Transnational women's activism, organizing, and human rights.* New York: New York University Press.

Fraser, A. S., & Tinker, I. (Eds.). (2004). *Developing power: How women transformed international development.* New York: Feminist Press.

Henry, A. (2004). *Not my mother's sister: Generational conflict and third-wave feminism.* Bloomington, IN: Indiana University Press.

Kirk, G., & Okazawa-Rey, M. (2007). *Women's lives: Multicultural perspectives* (4th ed.). Mountain View, CA: Mayfield.

Labaton, V., & Martin, D. L. (Eds.). (2004). *The fire this time: Young activists and the new feminism.* New York: Anchor Books.

Naples, N. A., & Desai, M. (Eds.). (2002). *Women's activism and globalization: Linking local struggles and global politics.* New York: Routledge.

Seely, M. (2007). *Fight like a girl: How to be a fearless feminist.* New York: New York University Press.

Stetson, D. M. (2004). *Women's rights in the U.S.A.: Policy debates and gender roles* (3rd ed.). New York: Routledge.

Zack, N. (2005). *Inclusive feminism: A third wave theory of women's commonalty.* Lanham, MD: Rowman & Littlefield.

WEBSITES

Feminism

Feminist Utopia
http://www.amazoncastle.com/feminism/feminism.htm
Women of Color Web
http://www.hsph.harvard.edu/grhf/woc

Advocating for Change

Activist Web Sites for Women's Issues
http://www.research.umbc.ed/~korenman/wmst/links_actv.html
The Ethnic Woman International
http://www.ethnicwomanmagazinecable.com

REFERENCES

Aaron, R., et al. (2004, April 3). Suicides in young people in rural southern India. *Lancet, 363,* 1117–1118.

AARP. (2001). *In the middle: A report on multicultural boomers coping with family and aging issues.* Washington, DC: Author.

AARP. (2002a). *Global aging: Achieving its potential.* Washington, DC: Author.

AARP. (2002b). *Health insurance options for midlife adults.* Washington, DC: Author.

AARP. (2003). *Lifestyles, dating and romance: A study of midlife singles.* Washington, DC: Author.

AARP. (2004, Winter). *The GIC Voice,* p. 11.

AARP. (2005a). *Grandparent visitations rights.* Washington, DC: Author.

AARP. (2005b). *Sexuality at midlife and beyond: 2004 update of attitudes and behaviors.* Washington, DC: Author.

AARP. (2006). *Medicare at 40: Past accomplishments and future challenges.* Washington, DC: Author.

AARP International. (2008, March 10). *Financing for gender equality & empowerment of women: Are older women included?* Retrieved from http://www.aarpinternational.org/resource library/resourcelibrary_show.htm?doc_id=672892

AAUW. (1992). *How schools shortchange women: The AAUW report.* Washington, DC: AAUW Educational Foundation.

AAUW. (1998). *Gender gaps: Where schools still fail our children.* Washington, DC: AAUW Educational Foundation.

AAUW. (2000). *Tech-savvy: Educating girls in the new computer age.* Washington, DC: AAUW Educational Foundation.

AAUW. (2001). *Hostile hallways: Bullying, teasing, and sexual harassment in school.* Washington, DC: AAUW Educational Foundation.

AAUW. (2002). *Pay equity.* Washington, DC: AAUW Educational Foundation.

AAUW. (2003). *Women at work.* Washington, DC: AAUW Educational Foundation.

AAUW. (2004). *Under the microscope.* Washington, DC: AAUW Educational Foundation.

Abbey, A., et al. (2004a). Sexual assault and alcohol consumption: What do we know about their relationship and what types of research are still needed? *Aggression and Violent Behavior, 9,* 271–303.

Abbey, A., et al. (2004b). Similarities and differences in women's sexual assault experiences based on tactics used by the perpetrator. *Psychology of Women Quarterly, 28,* 323–332.

Abbey, A., Parkhill, M. R., & Koss, M. P. (2005). The effects of frame of reference on responses to questions about sexual assault victimization and perpetration. *Psychology of Women Quarterly, 29,* 364–373.

Abele, A. E., & Wojciszke, B. (2007). Agency and communion from the perspective of self versus others. *Journal of Personality and Social Psychology, 93,* 751–763.

Abma, J. C., Martinez, G. M., Mosher, W. D., & Dawson, B. S. (2004). Teenagers in the United States: Sexual activity, contraceptive use, and childbearing, 2002. National Center for Health Statistics. *Vital Health Statistics, 23*(24).

Acosta, R. V., & Carpenter, L. J. (2008). *Women in intercollegiate sport: A longitudinal, national study: thirty-one-year-update.* West Brookfield, MA: Acosta/Carpenter.

Adams, K. E. (2003). Patient choice of provider gender. *Journal of the American Medical Women's Association, 58,* 117–119.

Adams, L. L., & Jordan, V. B. (2006, August). *Factors contributing to resilience in LGB adolescents and young adults.* Poster presented at the annual meeting of the American Psychological Association, New Orleans, LA.

Adams, P. F., Lucas, J. W., & Barnes, P. M. (2008). *Summary health statistics for the U.S. population: National Health Interview Survey, 2006.* NCHS Vital Health Statistics 10(236). Washington, DC: U.S. Government Printing Office.

Adams, P. F., & Schoenborn, C. A. (2006). *Health behaviors of adults: United States, 2002–04.* NCHS Vital Health Statistics 10-230. Washington, DC: U.S. Government Printing Office.

Adams, R. G. (1997). Friendship patterns among older women. In J. M. Coyle (Ed.), *Handbook on women and aging* (pp. 400–417). Westport, CT: Greenwood.

Adelmann, P. K. (1993). Psychological well-being and homemaker vs. retiree identity among older women. *Sex Roles, 29,* 195–212.

Ader, D. N., & Johnson, S. B. (1994). Sample description, reporting, and analysis of sex in psychological research: A look at APA and APA division journals in 1990. *American Psychologist, 49,* 216–218.

Adler, J. (2004, December 20). Toxic strength. *Newsweek,* pp. 45–52.

Adler, N. E., Ozer, E. J., & Tschann, J. (2003). Abortion among adolescents. *American Psychologist, 58,* 211–217.

Adler, N. E., & Smith, L. B. (1998). Abortion. In E. A. Blechman & K. D. Brownell (Eds.), *Behavioral medicine and women: A comprehensive handbook* (pp. 510–514). New York: Guilford.

Adler, N. E., & Snibbe, A. C. (2003). The role of psychosocial processes in explaining the gradient between socioeconomic status and health. *Current Directions in Psychological Science, 12,* 119–123.

Afghan women's rights. (2003, September 24). *New York Times,* p. A26.

AFL-CIO. (2004). *Ask a working woman survey report.* Washington, DC: Author.

AFL-CIO & The Institute for Women's Policy Research. (1999). *Equal pay for working families: National and state data on the pay gap and its costs*. Washington, DC: Author.

Africa's homeless widows. (2004, June 16). *New York Times*, p. A18.

Ahmed, S. B., et al. (2004). Gender bias in cardiovascular advertisements. *Journal of Evaluation in Clinical Practice, 10*, 531.

Ahnert, L., Pinquart, M., & Lamb, M. E. (2006). Security of children's relationships with nonparental care providers: A meta-analysis. *Child Development, 74*, 664–679.

Ahrens, C. E., Dean, K., Rozee, P. D., & McKenzie, M. (2008). Understanding and preventing rape. In F. L. Denmark & M. A. Paludi (Eds.), *Psychology of women: A handbook of issues and theories* (2nd ed., pp. 509–554). Westport, CT: Praeger.

Ahrens, J. A., & O'Brien, K. M. (1996). Predicting gender-role attitudes in adolescent females: Ability, agency, and parental factors. *Psychology of Women Quarterly, 20*, 409–417.

Akers, A., Bernstein, L., Henderson, S., Doyle, J., & Corbie-Smith, G. (2007). Factors associated with lack of interest in HIV testing in older at-risk women. *Journal of Women's Health, 16*, 842–857.

Alan Guttmacher Institute. (1998). *Into a new world: Young women's sexual and reproductive lives*. New York: Author.

Alan Guttmacher Institute. (2002a). Teen pregnancy: Trends and lessons learned. *Issues in Brief, 2002 Series*, No. 3.

Alan Guttmacher Institute. (2002b). Women and societies benefit when childbearing is planned. *Issues in Brief, 2002 Series*, No. 1.

Alan Guttmacher Institute. (2004a). *Contraception use*. New York & Washington, DC: Author.

Alan Guttmacher Institute. (2004b). *U.S. teenage pregnancy statistics*. New York & Washington, DC: Author.

Alan Guttmacher Institute. (2005). *Contraceptive use*. New York & Washington, DC: Author.

Al-Delaimy, W. K., et al. (2004). A prospective study of smoking and risk of breast cancer in young adult women. *Cancer Epidemiology Biomarkers & Prevention, 13*, 398–404.

Alexander, E. A., Shimp, L. A., & Smith, M. A. (2000). Obesity and eating disorders. In M. A. Smith & L. A. Shimp (Eds.), *20 common problems in women's health care* (pp. 161–192). New York: McGraw-Hill.

Alexander, K. (2004, April 13). Grandma finds a job, looking after junior. *New York Times*, p. E2.

Alfieri, T., Ruble, D. N., & Higgins, E. T. (1996). Gender stereotypes during adolescence: Developmental changes and the transition to junior high school. *Developmental Psychology, 32*, 1129–1137.

Ali, L., & Kelley, R. (2008, April 7). The curious lives of surrogates. *Newsweek*, pp. 45–51.

Ali, L., & Miller, L. (2004, July 12). The secret lives of wives. *Newsweek*, pp. 47–54.

Ali, L., & Scelfo, J. (2002, December 9). Choosing virginity. *Newsweek*, pp. 61–65.

Alink, L. R. A., et al. (2006). The early childhood aggression curve: Development of physical aggression in 10- to 50-month-old children. *Child Development, 77*, 954–966.

Allan, E. J., & Madden, M. (2006). Chilly classrooms for female undergraduate students: A question of method? *The Journal of Higher Education, 77*, 684–711.

Allen, B. A. (1996). Staying within the academy. In K. F. Wyche & F. J. Crosby (Eds.), *Women's ethnicities: Journeys through psychology* (pp. 9–26). Boulder, CO: Westview.

Allen, K. R., & Chin-Sang, V. (1990). A lifetime of work: The context and meanings of leisure for aging black women. *Gerontologist, 30*, 734–740.

Allen, M. W. (2004). The role of laughter when discussing workplace barriers: Women in information technology jobs. *Sex Roles, 50*, 177–189.

Allen, P. G. (1990). *Violence and the American Indian woman. The speaking profits us: Violence in the lives of women of color.* Seattle, WA: SAFECO Insurance Company.

Altman, L. K. (2002, July 7). Drug reduces HIV rates in newborns, Thai study shows. *New York Times*, p. A3.

Altman, L. K. (2006, August 13). Grandmothers from Africa rally for AIDS orphans. *New York Times*, p. YT10.

Altman, L. K. (2008, March 12). Sex infections found in quarter of teenage girls. *New York Times*, pp. A1, A17.

Altschuler, J., Katz, A. D., & Tynan, M. (2004). Developing and implementing an HIV/AIDS educational curriculum for older adults. *The Gerontologist, 44*, 121–126.

Alvarez, L. (2003, October 11). Iranian lawyer, staunch fighter for human rights, wins Nobel. *New York Times*, pp. A1, A6.

Amaro, H., et al. (2002). Cultural influences on women's sexual health. In G. M. Wingood & R. J. DiClemente (Eds.), *Handbook of women's sexual and reproductive health* (pp. 71–92). New York: Kluwer Academic/Plenum.

Amato, P. R. (2000). The consequences of divorce for adults and children. *Journal of Marriage and the Family, 62*, 1269–1287.

Amato, P. R. (2005). The impact of family formation change on the cognitive, social, and emotional well-being of the next generation. *The Future of Children, 15*, 75–96.

American Academy of Pediatrics. (2005). Adolescent pregnancy: Current trends and issues. *Pediatrics, 116*, 281–286.

American Association of University Women. (2006). *Mom's retirement security*. Washington, DC: Author.

American Association of University Women. (2008a). *Pay equity: A simple matter of fairness*. Washington, DC: Author.

American Association of University Women. (2008b). *Where the girls are: The facts about gender equity in education*. Washington, DC: Author.

American Association of University Women. (2008c). *Women, retirement, and social security*. Washington, DC: Author.

American Cancer Society. (1997). *Cancer risk report*. Atlanta: Author.

American Cancer Society. (2003). *Breast cancer facts & figures 2003–2004*. Atlanta: Author.

American Cancer Society. (2008a). *Breast cancer resources*. Atlanta: Author.

American Cancer Society. (2008b). *Cancer facts & figures 2008*. Atlanta: Author.

American Heart Association. (2002). *2002 heart and stroke statistical update*. Dallas: Author.

American Heart Association. (2004). Evidence-based guidelines for cardiovascular disease prevention in women. *Circulation, 109*, 672–693.

American Heart Association. (2007). *Our 2006 diet and lifestyle recommendations*. Retrieved August 31, 2007, from http://www.americanheart.org/presenter.jhtml?identifier=851

American Psychiatric Association. (1994). *Diagnostic and statistical manual of mental disorders* (4th ed.). Washington, DC: Author.

American Psychological Association. (1975). Report of the task force on sex bias and sex-role stereotyping in psychotherapeutic practice. *American Psychologist, 30*, 1169–1175.

American Psychological Association. (2000). Guidelines for psychotherapy with lesbian, gay, and bisexual clients. *American Psychologist, 55*, 1440–1451.

American Psychological Association. (2001). *Publication manual of the American Psychological Association* (5th ed.). Washington, DC: Author.

American Psychological Association. (2002). *Developing adolescents: A reference for professionals*. Washington, DC: Author.

American Psychological Association. (2004). Guidelines for psychological practice with older adults. *American Psychologist, 59*, 236–260.

American Psychological Association. (2006). *Women in the American Psychological Association 2006*. Washington, DC: Author.

American Psychological Association. (2007a). Guidelines for psychological practice with girls and women. *American Psychologist, 62*, 949–979.

American Psychological Association. (2007b). *Postpartum depression*. Washington, DC: Author.

American Psychological Association Task Force on the Sexualization of Girls. (2007). *Report on the APA Task Force on the Sexualization of Girls*. Washington, DC: American Psychological Association.

Amowitz, L. L., et al. (2004). Human rights abuses and concerns about women's health and human rights in southern Iraq. *Journal of the American Medical Association, 291*, 1471–1479.

Ananth, C. V., Shiliang, L., Kinzler, W. L., & Kramer, M. S. (2005). Stillbirths in the United States, 1981–2000: An age, period, and cohort analysis. *American Journal of Public Health, 95*, 2213–2217.

Andersen, B. L. (2002). Biobehavioral outcomes following psychological interventions for cancer patients. *Journal of Consulting and Clinical Psychology, 70*, 590–610.

Andersen, B. L., & Emery, C. (1999, August). *Biobehavioral model of cancer stress: Psychological, behavioral, and biological responses*. Paper presented at the meeting of the American Psychological Association, Boston.

Anderson, G. D. (2005). Sex and racial differences in pharmacological response: Where is the evidence? Pharmacogenetics, pharmacokinetics, and pharmacodynamics. *Journal of Women's Health, 14*, 19–29.

Anderson, G. M. (2004). Making sense of rising caesarean section rates. *BMJ, 329*, 696–697.

Anderson, I. (2004). Explaining negative rape victim perception: Homophobia and the male rape victim. *Current Research in Social Psychology, 10*, 43–57.

Anderson, J. (2006, January 10). Six women at Dresdner file bias suit. *New York Times*, pp. C1, C4.

Anderson, J. (2007, April 25). Morgan Stanley to settle sex bias suit. *New York Times*, pp. C1, C18.

Anderson, L. A., & Whiston, S. C. (2005). Sexual assault education programs: A meta-analytic examination of their effectiveness. *Psychology of Women Quarterly, 29*, 374–388.

Anderson, R. N., & Smith, B. L. (2003). *Deaths: Leading causes for 2001*. National Vital Statistics Reports, 52(9). Hyattsville, MD: National Center for Health Statistics.

Anderson, R. N., & Smith, B. L. (2004). *Deaths: Leading causes for 2002*. National Vital Statistics Reports, 53. Hyattsville, MD: National Center for Health Statistics.

Anderson, S. E., Dallal, G. E., & Must, A. (2003). Relative weight and race influence average age at menarche: Results from two nationally representative surveys of U.S. girls studied 25 years apart. *Pediatrics, 111*, 844–850.

Anderson, S. J., & Johnson, J. T. (2003). The who and when of "gender-blind" attitudes: Predictors of gender-role egalitarianism in two different domains. *Sex Roles, 49*, 527–532.

Anderson, V. N., Simpson-Taylor, D., & Herrmann, D. J. (2004). Gender, age, and rape-supportive rules. *Sex Roles, 50*, 77–90.

Andreasen, N. C. (2005). Vulnerability to mental illnesses: Gender makes a difference, and so does providing good psychiatric care. *The American Journal of Psychiatry, 162*, 211–213.

Angel, J. L., & Angel, R. J. (2006). Minority group status and healthful aging: Social structure still matters. *American Journal of Public Health, 96*, 1152–1159.

Angell, M. (1997, April 25). Pregnant at 63? Why not? *New York Times*, p. A27.

Angier, N. (1999, February 21). Men, women, sex and Darwin. *New York Times Magazine*, pp. 48–53.

Angier, N. (2001, April 10). A lifetime later, still in love with the lab. *New York Times*, pp. D1, D6.

Angier, N. (2002, November 5). The importance of grandma. *New York Times*, pp. D1, D4.

Angier, N. (2007, April 10). Birds do it. Bees do it. People seek the keys to it. *New York Times*, pp. D1, D4.

Angier, N., & Chang, K. (2005, January 24). Gray matter and the sexes: Still a scientific gray area. *New York Times*, pp. A1, A15.

Anleu, S. R. (2006). Gendered bodies: Between conformity and autonomy. In K. Davis, M. Evans, & J. Lorber (Eds.), *Handbook of gender and women's studies* (pp. 357–375). London: SAGE Publications.

Annas, G. J. (2007). The Supreme Court and abortion rights. *New England Journal of Medicine, 356*, 2201–2206.

Annie E. Casey Foundation. (1999). *When teens have sex: Issues and trends*. Baltimore: Author.

Antonucci, T., et al. (2001). Widowhood and illness: A comparison of social network characteristics in France, Germany, Japan, and the United States. *Psychology and Aging, 16*, 655–665.

Aosved, A. C., & Long, P. J. (2006). Co-occurrence of rape myth acceptance and sexism, racism, homophobia, ageism, classism, and religious intolerance. *Sex Roles, 55*, 481–492.

Apparala, M. L., Reifman, A., & Munsch, J. (2003). Cross-national comparison of attitudes toward fathers' and mothers' participation in household tasks and childcare. *Sex Roles, 48,* 189–203.

Appling, S., Paez, K., & Allen, J. (2007). Ethnicity and vasomotor symptoms in postmenopausal women. *Journal of Women's Health, 16,* 1130–1138.

Arber, S. (2004). Gender, marital status, and ageing: Linking material, health, and social resources. *Journal of Aging Studies, 18,* 91–108.

Archer, J. (2000). Sex differences in aggression between heterosexual partners: A meta-analytic review. *Psychological Bulletin, 126,* 651–680.

Archer, J. (2002). Sex differences in physically aggressive acts between heterosexual partners. A meta-analytic review. *Aggression and Violent Behavior, 7,* 313–351.

Archer, J. (2004). Sex differences in aggression in real-world settings: A meta-analytic review. *Review of General Psychology, 8,* 291–322.

Archer, S. L. (1992). A feminist's approach to identity research. In G. R. Adams, T. P. Gullotta, & R. Montemayor (Eds.), *Adolescent identity formation* (pp. 25–49). Newberry Park, CA: Sage.

Archer, S. L. (1993). Identity in relational contexts: A methodological proposal. In J. Krogers (Ed.), *Discussion on ego identity* (pp. 75–99). Hillsdale, NJ: Erlbaum.

Arenson, K. W. (2002, July 4). More women taking leadership roles at colleges. *New York Times,* p. A1.

Arias, E. (2004). *United States life tables, 2002.* National Vital Statistics Reports, 53. Hyattsville, MD: National Center for Health Statistics.

Arias, I., & Ikeda, R. M. (2006). Etiology and surveillance of intimate partner violence. In J. R. Lutzker (Ed.), *Preventing violence: Research and evidence-based intervention strategies* (pp. 173–194). Washington, DC: American Psychological Association.

Armstrong, M. J. (2001). Ethnic minority women as they age. In J. D. Garner & S. O. Mercer (Eds.), *Women as they age,* 2nd ed. (pp. 97–114). New York: Haworth.

Arnett, J. J. (2002). The sounds of sex: Sex in teens' music and music videos. In J. Brown, K. Walsh-Childers, & J. Steele (Eds.), *Sexual teens, sexual media* (pp. 253–264). Hillsdale, NJ: Erlbaum.

Arney, H. T. (2001, May 23). Friends, active social life help turn widow's life around. *Peoria Times-Observer,* p. A8.

Arnold, K. D. (1993). Academically talented women in the 1970s: The Illinois valedictorian project. In K. D. Hulbert & D. Tickton (Eds.), *Women's lives through time* (pp. 393–414). San Francisco: Jossey-Bass.

Arnold, M. N. (2004, May). *Eating disorder symptomology in college athletes.* Poster presented at the meeting of the American Psychological Society, Chicago.

Aronson, P. (2003). Feminists or "postfeminists"? Young women's attitudes toward feminism and gender relations. *Gender & Society, 17,* 903–922.

Arriaga, X. B., & Foshee, V. A. (2004). Adolescent dating violence: Do adolescents follow in their friends', or their parents', footsteps? *Journal of Interpersonal Violence, 19,* 162–184.

Arsu, S. (2005, May 16). Turks to fight "honor killings" of women. *New York Times,* p. A10.

Ashcraft, M. H. (2002). Math anxiety: Personal, educational, and cognitive consequences. *Current Directions in Psychological Science, 11,* 181–185.

Ashkinaze, C. (2005, Summer). A matter of opinion. *Ms.,* p. 17.

Ata, R. N., Ludden, A. B., & Lally, M. M. (2007). The effects of gender and family, friend, and media influences on eating behaviors and body image during adolescence. *Journal of Youth and Adolescence, 36,* 1024–1037.

Athenstaedt, U., Haas, E., & Schwab, S. (2004). Gender role self-concept and gender-typed communication behavior in mixed-sex and same-sex dyads. *Sex Roles, 50,* 37–52.

Atwater, L., Carey, J., & Waldman, D. (2001). Gender and discipline in the workplace: Wait until your father gets home. *Journal of Management, 27,* 537–561.

Aube, J., Fleury, J., & Smetana, J. (2000). Changes in women's roles: Impact on and social policy implications for the mental health of women and children. *Development and Psychopathology, 12,* 633–656.

Aubeeluck, A., & Maguire, M. (2002). The Menstrual Joy Questionnaire alone can positively prime reporting of menstrual attitudes and symptoms. *Psychology of Women Quarterly, 26,* 160–162.

Aubin, S., & Heiman, J. R. (2004). Sexual dysfunction from a relationship perspective. In J. H. Harvey, A. Wenzel, & S. Sprecher (Eds.), *The handbook of sexuality in close relationships* (pp. 477–517). Mahwah, NJ: Erlbaum.

Auster, E. R. (2001). Professional women's midcareer satisfaction: Toward an explanatory framework. *Sex Roles, 44,* 719–750.

American Psychological Association 1997 awards. (1998). *American Psychologist, 53,* 365–372.

Ayala, C., Xie, J., McGruder, H. F., & Valderrama, A. L. (2008). Receipt of outpatient cardiac rehabilitation among heart attack survivors—United States, 2005. *Morbidity and Mortality Weekly Report, 57,* 89–94.

Ayoola, A. B., Nettleman, M., & Brewer, J. (2007). Reasons for unprotected intercourse in adult women. *Journal of Women's Health, 16,* 302–31 0.

Ayoub, N. C. (2004, April 2). Nota bene. *Chronicle of Higher Education,* p. A18.

Azar, B. (2000, July/August). A new stress paradigm for women. *Monitor on Psychology,* pp. 42–43.

Babcock, J. C., Green, C. E., & Robie, C. (2004). Does batterers' treatment work? A meta-analytic review of domestic violence treatment. *Clinical Psychology Review, 23,* 1023–1053.

Babcock, L., & Laschever, S. (2003). *Women don't ask: Negotiation and the gender divide.* Princeton, NJ: Princeton University Press.

Babcock, L., & Laschever, S. (2008). *Ask for it: How women can use the power of negotiation to get what they really want.* New York: Bantam.

Bachanas, P. J., et al. (2002). Psychological adjustment, substance use, HIV knowledge, and risky sexual behavior in at-risk minority females: Developmental differences during adolescence. *Journal of Pediatric Psychology, 27,* 373–384.

Bachar, K., & Koss, M. (2001). Rape. In J. Worell (Ed.), *Encyclopedia of women and gender* (pp. 893–903). San Diego: Academic Press.

Badger, K., Craft, R. C., & Jensen, L. (1998). Age and gender differences in value orientation among American adolescents. *Adolescence, 33,* 591–596.

Baer, J. S., et al. (2003). A 21-year longitudinal analysis of the effects of prenatal alcohol exposure on young adult drinking. *Archives of General Psychiatry, 60,* 377–385.

Baghdadi, G. (2005). Gender and medicines: An international public health perspective. *Journal of Women's Health, 14,* 82–86.

Bailey, J. M., Pillard, R. C., Neale, M. C., & Agyei, Y. (1993). Heritable factors influence sexual orientation in women. *Archives of General Psychiatry, 48,* 1089–1096.

Baillargeon, J.-P., McClish, D. K., Essah, P. A., & Nestler, J. E. (2005). Association between the current use of low-dose oral contraceptives and cardiovascular arterial disease: A meta-analysis. *The Journal of Clinical Endocrinology & Metabolism, 90,* 3863–3870.

Baillargeon, R. H., et al. (2007). Gender differences in physical aggression: A prospective population-based survey of children before and after 2 years of age. *Developmental Psychology, 43,* 13–26.

Bakalar, N. (2006, September 26). Despite equal cancer care, a racial disparity persists. *New York Times,* p. D7.

Bakalar, N. (2007, May 1). Wider screenings for H.I.V. are recommended. *New York Times,* p. H5.

Baker, B. (2007, Summer). Is bone testing all it's cracked up to be? *Ms.,* pp. 59–60.

Baker, C. N. (2005). Images of women's sexuality in advertisements: A content analysis of black- and white-oriented women's and men's magazines. *Sex Roles, 52,* 13–27.

Baker, D. M. (2003, August). *Childfree women's experience of gender.* Paper presented at the meeting of the American Psychology Association, Toronto.

Baker, D. P., & Jones, D. P. (1993). Creating gender equality: Cross-national gender stratification and mathematics performance. *Sociology of Education, 66,* 91–103.

Baker, N. L. (2001). Prejudice. In J. Worell (Ed.), *Encyclopedia of gender* (pp. 865–877). San Diego: Academic Press.

Baker-Sperry, L., & Grauerholz, L. (2003). The pervasiveness and persistence of the feminine beauty ideal in children's fairy tales. *Gender & Society, 15,* 711–726.

Baldi, S., Jin, Y., Skemer, M., Green, P. J., & Herget, D. (2007). *Highlights from PISA 2006: Performance of U.S. 15-year-old students in science and mathematics literacy in an international context.* Washington, DC: National Center for Education Statistics (NCES 2008-016).

Balsam, K. F., et al. (2004). Culture, trauma, and wellness: A comparison of heterosexual and lesbian, gay, bisexual, and two-spirit Native Americans. *Cultural Diversity and Ethnic Minority Psychology, 10,* 287–301.

Balsam, K. F., Beauchaine, T. P., Rothblum, E. D., & Solomon, S. E. (2008). Three-year follow-up of same-sex couples who had civil unions in Vermont, same-sex couples not in civil unions, and heterosexual married couples. *Developmental Psychology, 44,* 102–116.

Bancroft, J. H. J. (2007). Sex and aging. *New England Journal of Medicine, 357,* 820–822.

Bancroft, J., Loftus, J., & Long, J. S. (2003). Distress about sex: A national survey of women in heterosexual relationships. *Archives of Sexual Behavior, 32,* 193–208.

Banerjee, N. (2001, August 10). Some "bullies" seek ways to soften up. *New York Times,* pp. C1, C2.

Banerjee, N. (2005, February 19). Catholic group receives 1,092 new sex abuse reports. *New York Times,* p. A8.

Banerjee, N. (2006, August 26). Clergywomen find hard path to bigger pulpit. *New York Times,* pp. A1, A11.

Bang, E., Hall, M. E. L., Anderson, T. L., & Willingham, M. M. (2005). Ethnicity, acculturation, and religiosity as predictors of female college students' role expectations. *Sex Roles, 53,* 231–237.

Bank, B. J. (1995). Gendered accounts: Undergraduates explain why they seek their bachelor's degree. *Sex Roles, 32,* 527–544.

Banks, A., & Gartrell, N. K. (1995). Hormones and sexual orientation: A questionable link. *Journal of Homosexuality, 28,* 247–268.

Banyard, V. L., Ward, S., Cohn, E. S., Plante, E. G., Moorhead, C., & Walsh, W. (2007). Unwanted sexual contact on campus: A comparison of women's and men's experiences. *Violence and Victims, 22,* 52–70.

Barash, D. P. (2002, May 24). Evolution, males, and violence. *Chronicle of Higher Education,* pp. B7–B9.

Barash, D. P., & Lipton, J. E. (2002). *Gender gap: The biology of male-female differences.* New York: Transaction.

Barefoot, J. C., et al. (2001). A longitudinal study of gender differences in depressive symptoms from age 50 to 80. *Psychology and Aging, 16,* 342–345.

Barford, A., Dorling, D., Smith, G. D., & Shaw, M. (2006). Life expectancy: Women now on top everywhere. *BMJ, 332,* 808.

Barker, E. T., & Bornstein, M. H. (2007, March). *Temporal ordering of body dissatisfaction and self-esteem across early adolescence.* Poster presented at the meeting of the Society for Research in Child Development, Boston.

Barnard, N. D., Scialli, A. R., Hurlock, D., & Bertron, P. (2000). Diet and sex-hormone binding globulin, dysmenorrhea, and premenstrual symptoms. *Obstetrics & Gynecology, 95,* 240–244.

Barnett, O., Miller-Perrin, C. L., & Perrin, R. D. (2005). *Family violence across the lifespan: An introduction.* Thousand Oaks, CA: Sage Publications.

Barnett, R. C. (2001). Work-family balance. In J. Worell (Ed.), *Encyclopedia of women and gender* (pp. 1181–1190). San Diego: Academic Press.

Barnett, R. C. (2004). Preface: Women and work: Where are we, where did we come from, and where are we going? *Journal of Social Issues, 60,* 667–674.

Barnett, R. C. (2007). Women, leadership, and the natural order. In B. Kellerman & D. L. Rhode (Eds.), *Women & leadership: The state of play and strategies for change* (pp. 149–173). San Francisco: Jossey-Bass.

Barongan, C., & Hall, G. C. N. (1995). The influence of misogynous rap music on sexual aggression against women. *Psychology of Women Quarterly, 19,* 195–207.

Barrett, J. (2006, April 3). Special deliveries. *Newsweek*, p. 45.

Barrett-Connor, E., et al. (2002). Raloxifene and cardiovascular events in osteoporotic postmenopausal women. *Journal of the American Medical Association, 287*, 847–857.

Barry, C. M., & Wentzel, K. R. (2006). Friend influence on prosocial behavior: The role of motivational factors and friendship characteristics. *Developmental Psychology, 42*, 153–163.

Bartini, M. (2006). Gender role flexibility in early adolescence: Developmental change in attitudes, self-perception, and behaviors. *Sex Roles, 55*, 233–245.

Bartlett, T. (2002, April 5). The question of sex between professors and students. *Chronicle of Higher Education*, pp. A8, A9.

Barton, L. (2005, January 5). Celebrities distort girls' search for ideal shape. *The Guardian (London)*, p. 7.

Bartsch, R. A., Burnett, T., Diller, T. R., & Rankin-Williams, E. (2000). Gender representation in television commercials: Updating an update. *Sex Roles, 43*, 735–743.

Basow, S. A. (2001). Androcentrism. In J. Worell (Ed.), *Encyclopedia of women and gender* (pp. 125–135). San Diego: Academic Press.

Basow, S. A. (2006). Gender role and gender identity development. In J. Worell & C. D. Goodheart (Eds.), *Handbook of girls' and women's psychological health: Gender and well-being across the lifespan* (pp. 242–251). New York: Oxford University Press.

Basow, S. A. (2008). Gender socialization, or how long a way has baby come? In J. C. Chrisler, C. Golden, & P. D. Rozee (Eds.), *Lectures on the psychology of women* (pp. 80–95). New York: McGraw-Hill.

Basow, S. A., & Rubin, L. R. (1999). Gender influences on adolescent development. In N. G. Johnson, M. C. Roberts, & J. Worell (Eds.), *Beyond appearance: A new look at adolescent girls* (pp. 25–52). Washington, DC: American Psychological Association.

Bass, E., & Davis, L. (1994). *The courage to heal* (3rd ed.). New York: HarperCollins.

Bauer, G. R., & Wayne, L. D. (2005). Cultural sensitivity and research involving sexual minorities. *Perspectives on Sexual and Reproductive Health, 37*, 45–47.

Bauer, P. J., Liebl, M., & Stennes, L. (1998). Pretty is to dress as brave is to suitcoat: Gender-based property-to-property inferences by 4-year-old children. *Merrill-Palmer Quarterly, 44*, 355–377.

Baumeister, R. F. (2000). Gender differences in erotic plasticity: The female sex drive as socially flexible and responsive. *Psychological Bulletin, 126*, 347–374.

Baumeister, R. F., Campbell, J. D., Krueger, J. I., & Vohs, K. D. (2003). Does high self-esteem cause better performance, interpersonal success, happiness, or healthier lifestyles? *Psychological Science in the Public Interest, 4*, 1–44.

Bauserman, R. (2002). Child adjustment in joint-custody versus sole-custody arrangements: A meta-analytic review. *Journal of Family Psychology, 16*, 91–102.

Bay-Cheng, L. Y., & Zucker, A. N. (2007). Feminism between the sheets: Sexual attitudes among feminists, nonfeminists, and egalitarians. *Psychology of Women Quarterly, 31*, 157–163.

Bay-Cheng, L. Y., Zucker, A. N., Stewart, A. J., & Pomerleau, C. S. (2002). Linking femininity, weight concern and mental health among Latina, Black and White women. *Psychology of Women Quarterly, 26*, 36–45.

Bayley, T. M., et al. (2002). Food cravings and aversions during pregnancy: Relationships with nausea and vomiting. *Appetite, 38*, 45–51.

Bazargan, M., Bazargan-Hejazi, S., & Baker, R. S. (2005). Treatment of self-reported depression among Hispanics and African Americans. *Journal of Health Care of the Poor and Underserved, 16*, 328–344.

Bazzini, D. G., McIntosh, W. D., Smith, S. M., Cook, S., & Harris, C. (1997). The aging woman in popular film: Underrepresented, unattractive, unfriendly, and unintelligent. *Sex Roles, 36*, 531–543.

Beadnell, B., Wilsdon, A., Wells, E. A., Morison, D. M., Gillmore, M. R., & Hoppe, M. (2007). Intrapersonal and interpersonal factors influencing adolescents' decisions about having sex: A test of sufficiency of the theory of planned behavior. *Journal of Applied Social Psychology, 37*, 2840–2876.

Beals, K. P., & Peplau, L. A. (2005). Identity support, identity devaluation, and well-being among lesbians. *Psychology of Women Quarterly, 29*, 140–148.

Bean-Mayberry, B. A., Chang, C. H., McNeil, M. A., & Scholle, S. H. (2006). Ensuring high quality primary care for women: Predictors of success. *Women's Health Issues, 16*, 22–29.

Bearman, P. (2004, March). *Rules, behaviors, and networks that influence STD prevention among adolescents*. Paper presented at the meeting of the National STD Prevention Conference, Philadelphia.

Bearman, P. S., & Moody, J. (2004). Suicide and friendships among American adolescents. *American Journal of Public Health, 94*, 89–96.

Beaton, A. M., Tougas, F., & Joly, S. (1996). Neosexism among male managers: Is it a matter of numbers? *Journal of Applied Social Psychology, 26*, 2189–2203.

Becker, A. E., Fay, K., Gilman, S. E., & Striegel-Moore, R. (2007). Facets of acculturation and their diverse relations to body shape concern in Fiji. *International Journal of Eating Disorders, 40*, 42–50.

Becker, S. W., & Eagly, A. H. (2004). The heroism of women and men. *American Psychologist, 59*, 163–178.

Beckman, L. J. (2006). Women's reproductive health: Issues, findings, and controversies. In J. Worell & C. D. Goodheart (Eds.), *Handbook of girls' and women's psychological health: Gender and well-being across the lifespan* (pp. 330–338). New York: Oxford University Press.

Bedford, V. H. (1995). Sibling relationships in middle and old age. In R. Blieszner & V. H. Bedford (Eds.), *Handbook of aging and the family* (pp. 201–222). Westport, CT: Greenwood.

Bee, H. L. (2000). *The journey of adulthood* (4th ed.). Upper Saddle River, NJ: Prentice Hall.

Beemyn, B. G. (2005, Spring). Trans on campus: Measuring and improving the climate for transgender students. *Association of American Colleges and Universities, On Campus with Women, 34*(3), 1–5.

Beers, M. H., & Jones, T. V. (2004). *The Merck manual of health and aging*. Whitehouse Station, NJ: Merck Research Laboratories.

Behbakht, K., et al. (2004). Social and cultural barriers to Papanicolaou test screening in an urban population. *Obstetrics & Gynecology, 104*, 1355–1361.

Beil, L. (2007, July 18). Abstinence education faces an uncertain future. *New York Times*, pp. A1, A12.

Beilock, S., Rydell, R., & McConnell, A. R. (2007). Stereotype threat and working memory: Mechanisms, alleviation, and spillover. *Journal of Experimental Psychology: General, 136*, 256–276.

Beiner, T. M., & O'Connor, M. (2007). When an individual finds herself to be the victim of sex discrimination. In F. J. Crosby, M. S. Stockdale, & S. A. Ropp (Eds.), *Sex discrimination in the workplace* (pp. 19–56). Malden, MA: Blackwell.

Belansky, E. S., Early, D. M., & Eccles, J. S. (1993, March). *The impact of mothers and peers on adolescents' gender role traditionality and plans for the future*. Paper presented at the meeting of the Society for Research in Child Development, New Orleans.

Bellamy, C. (2004). Globalization and infectious diseases in women. *Emerging Infectious Diseases, 10*, 2022–2024.

Bell, L. C. (2004). Psychoanalytic theories of gender. In A. H. Eagly, A. E. Beall, & R. J. Sternberg (Eds.), *The psychology of gender* (pp. 145–168). New York: Guilford.

Bell, M. P., Cycyota, C. S., & Quick, J. C. (2002). An affirmative defense: The preventive management of sexual harassment. In R. J. Burke & D. L. Nelson (Eds.), *Gender, work stress and health*. Washington, DC: American Psychological Association.

Bellafante, G. (2005, May 8). Even in gay circles, women want the ring. *New York Times*, pp. ST1, ST7.

Belluck, P., & Liptak, A. (2004, March 24). Gay parents find big legal hurdles in custody cases. *New York Times*, pp. A1, A14.

Belmaker, R. H., & Agam, G. (2008). Major depressive disorder. *New England Journal of Medicine, 358*, 55–68.

Belsky, G. (Ed.). (2007). *Over the hill and between the sheets: Sex, love, and lust in middle age*. New York: Springboard.

Belsky, J. K. (1999). *The psychology of aging: Theory, research and interventions*. Pacific Grove, CA: Brooks-Cole.

Belsky, J. K. (2001). Aging. In J. Worell (Ed.), *Encyclopedia of women and gender* (pp. 95–107). San Diego: Academic Press.

Belsky, J., et al. (2007). Family rearing antecedents of pubertal timing. *Child Development, 78*, 1302–1321.

Beltran, A. (2004, Spring). Grandparents raising grandchildren face difficult legal decisions. *AARP: The GIC Voice*, pp. 1, 10.

Bem, S. L. (1974). The measurement of psychological androgyny. *Journal of Consulting and Clinical Psychology, 42*, 155–162.

Bem, S. L. (1975). Sex role adaptability: One consequence of psychological androgyny. *Journal of Personality and Social Psychology, 31*, 634–643.

Bem, S. L. (1981). Gender schema theory: A cognitive account of sex typing. *Psychological Review, 88*, 354–364.

Bem, S. L. (1983). Gender schema theory and its implications for child development: Raising gender-aschematic children in a gender-schematic society. *Signs, 8*, 598–616.

Bem, S. L. (1993). *The lenses of gender: Transforming the debate on sexual inequality*. New Haven, CT: Yale University Press.

Bem S. L. (2008). Transforming the debate on sexual inequality: From biological difference to institutionalized androcentrism. In J. C. Chrisler, C. Golden, & P. D. Rozee (Eds.), *Lectures on the psychology of women* (pp. 2–15). New York: McGraw-Hill.

Benbow, C. P., & Stanley, J. C. (1980). Sex differences in mathematical ability: Fact or artifact? *Science, 210*, 1262–1264.

Ben-David, S., & Schneider, O. (2005). Rape perceptions, gender role attitudes, and victim-perpetrator acquaintance. *Sex Roles, 53*, 385–399.

Benedict, H. (2008, Fall). The scandal of military rape. *Ms.*, 41–45.

Benefits of regular physical activity. (2000). *Journal of the American Medical Association, 283*, 3030.

Benenson, J. F., Morash D., & Petrakos, H. (1998). Gender differences in emotional closeness between preschool children and their mothers. *Sex Roles, 38*, 975–985.

Bennice, J. A., & Resick, P. A. (2003). Marital rape. *Trauma, Violence, & Abuse, 4*, 228–245.

Bensyl, D. M., Luliano, A. D., Carter, M., Santelli, J., & Gilbert, B. C. (2005). Contraceptive use—United States and Territories, Behavioral Risk Factor Surveillance System, 2002. *Morbidity and Mortality Weekly Report, 54*(SS-6).

Bentley, C. G., Galliher, R. V., & Ferguson, T. J. (2007). Associations among aspects of interpersonal power and relationship functioning in adolescent romantic couples. *Sex Roles, 57*, 483–496.

Beral, V., et al. (2007). Ovarian cancer and hormone replacement therapy in the Million Women Study. *Lancet, 369*, 1703–1710.

Berdahl, J. L. (2007). The sexual harassment of uppity women. *Journal of Applied Psychology, 92*, 425–437.

Berdahl, J. L., & Moore, C. (2006). Workplace harassment: Double jeopardy for minority women. *Journal of Applied Psychology, 91*, 426–436.

Bereczkei, T., Voros, S., Gal, A., & Bernath, L. (1997). Resources, attractiveness, family commitment: Reproductive decisions in human mate choice. *Ethology, 104*, 681–699.

Berenbaum, S. A., & Bryk, K. L. K. (2008). Biological contributors to gendered occupational outcome: Prenatal androgen effects on predictors of outcome. In H. M. G. Watt & J. S. Eccles (Eds.), *Gender and occupational outcomes: Longitudinal assessments of individual, social, and cultural influences* (pp. 235–264). Washington, DC: American Psychological Association.

Berenbaum, S. A., & Resnick, S. (2007). The seeds of career choices: Prenatal sex hormone effects on psychological sex differences. In S. J. Ceci & W. M. Williams (Eds.), *Why aren't more women in science? Top researchers debate the evidence* (pp. 147–157). Washington, DC: American Psychological Association.

Berger, L. (2000, July 18). A new body politic: Learning to like the way we look. *New York Times*, p. D7.

Berger, L. (2007, December 12). Racing to beat the clock. *New York Times*. Retrieved from http://health.nytimes.com/ref/health/healthguide/esn-infertilitywomeness.html

Berger, P. S., Cook, A. S., DelCampo, R. L., Herrera, R. S., & Weigel, R. R. (1994). Family/work roles' relation to perceived stress: Do gender and ethnicity matter? *Journal of Family and Economic Issues, 15*, 223–241.

Berglund, H., Lindstrom, P., & Savic, I. (2006). Brain response to putative pheromones in lesbian women. *Proceedings of the National Academy of Sciences, 103*, 8269–8274.

Bergman, M. E., & Drasgow, F. (2003). Race as a moderator in a model of sexual harassment: An empirical test. *Journal of Occupational Health Psychology, 8*(2), 131–145.

Bergmann, B. R. (2007). Discrimination through the economist's eye. In F. J. Crosby, M. S. Stockdale, & S. A. Ropp (Eds.), *Sex discrimination in the workplace* (pp. 213–234). Malden, MA: Blackwell.

Berk, L. E. (2003). *Child development* (6th ed.). Boston: Allyn & Bacon.

Berk, L. E., Wholeben, B. M., & Bouchey, H. A. (1998). *Instructors resource manual for Berk, L. E. (1998): Development through the lifespan.* Boston: Allyn & Bacon.

Berkman, N. D., Lohr, K. N., & Bulik, C. M. (2007). Outcomes of eating disorders: A systematic review of the literature. *International Journal of Eating Disorders, 40*, 293–309.

Berkowitz, R. L., Roberts, J., & Minkoff, H. (2006). Challenging the strategy of maternal age-based prenatal genetic counseling. *Journal of the American Medical Association, 295*, 1446–1448.

Bernard, M., & Phillipson, C. (2004). Retirement and leisure. In J. F. Nussbaum & J. Coupland (Eds.), *Handbook of communication and aging research* (2nd ed., pp. 353–382). Mahwah, NJ: Erlbaum.

Bernhard, L. A., & Birch, R. W. (2000). Sexuality. In M. A. Smith & L. A. Shimp (Eds.), *20 common problems in women's health care* (pp. 135–160). New York: McGraw-Hill.

Bernstein, N. (2002, August 14). Child-only cases grow on welfare. *New York Times*, pp. A1, A21.

Bernstein, N. (2004, March 7). In a culture of sex, more teenagers are striving for restraint. *New York Times*, pp. A1, A22, A23.

Berry, G. L. (2007). Television, social roles, and marginality: Portrayals of the past and images for the future. In N. Pecora, J. P. Murray, & E. A. Wartella (Eds.), *Children and television: Fifty years of research* (pp. 85–107). Mahwah, NJ: Erlbaum.

Bersamin, M., Todd, M., Fisher, D. A., Hill, D. L., Grube, J. W., & Walker, S. (2008). Parenting practices and adolescent sexual behavior: A longitudinal study. *Journal of Marriage and Family, 70*, 97–112.

Bertakis, K. D., & Azari, R. (2007). Patient gender and physician practice style. *Journal of Women's Health, 16*, 859–868.

Bertakis, K. D., Franks, P., & Azari, R. (2003). Effects of physician gender on patient satisfaction. *Journal of the American Medical Women's Association, 58*, 69–75.

Bertone-Johnson, E. R., Hankinson, S. E., Bendich, A., Johnson, S. R., Willett, W. C., & Manson, J. E. (2005). Calcium and vitamin D intake and risk of incident premenstrual syndrome. *Archives of Internal Medicine, 165*, 1246–1252.

Bessenoff, G. R., & Del Priore, R. E. (2007). Women, weight, and age: Social comparison to magazine images across the lifespan. *Sex Roles, 56*, 215–222.

Best, D. L. (2001). Cross-cultural gender roles. In J. Worell (Ed.), *Encyclopedia of women and gender* (pp. 279–290). San Diego: Academic Press.

Best, D. L., & Thomas, J. J. (2004). Cultural diversity and cross-cultural perspectives. In A. H. Eagly, A. E. Beall, & R. J. Sternberg (Eds.), *The psychology of gender* (pp. 296–327). New York: Guilford.

Best, D. L., & Williams, J. E. (1993). A cross-cultural viewpoint. In A. E. Beall & R. J. Sternberg (Eds.), *The psychology of gender* (pp. 215–248). New York: Guilford.

Betts, K. (2002, March 21). The tyranny of skinny, fashion's insider secret. *New York Times*, p. ST18.

Betz, N. (2006). Pathways to healthy development: Women's career development. In J. Worell & C. D. Goodheart (Eds.), *Handbook of girls' and women's psychological health: Gender and well-being across the lifespan* (pp. 312–320). New York: Oxford University Press.

Betz, N. E. (1994). Basic issues and concepts in career counseling for women. In W. B. Walsh & S. H. Osipow (Eds.), *Career counseling for women* (pp. 1–41). Hillsdale, NJ: Erlbaum.

Betz, N. E. (2008). Women's career development. In F. L. Denmark & M. A. Paludi (Eds.), *Psychology of women: A handbook of issues and theories* (2nd ed., pp. 717–752). Westport, CT: Praeger.

Beumont, P. (2005, January 9). Alexander the turkey? *Observer (London)*, p. 22.

Beyer, S. (1997, June). *Gender differences in causal attributions of imagined performance on English, history, and math exams.* Paper presented at the meeting of the American Psychological Society, Washington, DC.

Beyer, S. (2006). Comparing gender differences in computer science and management information systems majors. In E. M. Trauth (Ed.), *Encyclopedia of gender and information technology* (pp. 109–115). Hershey, PA: Idea Group.

Bianchi, S. M. (2000). Maternal employment and time with children: Dramatic change or surprising continuity? *Demography, 47*, 401–414.

Bianchi, S. M. (2006). Mothers and daughters "do," fathers "don't do" family: Gender and generational bonds. *Journal of Marriage and Family, 68*, 812–816.

Bianchi, S. M., Robinson, J. P., & Milkie, M. A. (2006). *Changing rhythms of American family life.* New York: Russell Sage.

Biason-Lauber, A., Konrad, D., Navratil, F., & Schoenle, E. J. (2004). A WNT4 mutation associated with Müllerian-duct regression and virilization in a 46, xx woman. *New England Journal of Medicine, 351*, 792–798.

Biehl, M. C., Natsuaki, M. N., & Ge, X. (2007). The influence of pubertal timing on alcohol use and heavy drinking trajectories. *Journal of Youth and Adolescence, 36*, 153–167.

Bierman, K. L., et al. (2004). Early disruptive behaviors associated with emerging antisocial behavior among girls. In M. Putallaz & K. L. Bierman (Eds.), *Aggression, antisocial behavior, and violence among girls: A developmental perspective* (pp. 137–161). New York: Guilford.

Bieschke, K. J., & Toepfer-Hendey, E. (2006). Career counseling with lesbian clients. In W. B. Walsh & M. J. Heppner (Eds.),

Handbook of career counseling for women (2nd ed., pp. 351–386). Mahwah, NJ: Erlbaum.

Bilefsky, D. (2006, July 16). How to avoid jail for honor killing? Honor suicide. *New York Times*, p. A3.

Billings, A. C., Halone, K. K., & Denham, B. E. (2002). "Man, that was a pretty shot": An analysis of gendered broadcast commentary surrounding the 2000 men's and women's NCAA Final Four basketball championships. *Mass Communication & Society, 5*, 295–315.

Bingham, C. R., Miller, B. C., & Adams, G. R. (1990). Correlates of age at first sexual intercourse in a national sample of young women. *Journal of Adolescent Research, 5*, 18–33.

Binion, V. J. (1990). Psychological androgyny: A black female perspective. *Sex Roles, 22*, 487–507.

Birchler, G., & Fals-Stewart, W. (1998). Marriage and divorce. In M. Hersen & V. B. Van Hasselt (Eds.), *Handbook of clinical geropsychology* (pp. 449–467). New York: Plenum.

Bird, C. E., & Rieker, P. P. (2008). *Gender and health: The effects of constrained choices and social policies*. New York: Cambridge University Press.

Bird, C. E., & Rogers, M. L. (1998, November). *Does the presence of children in a household lead to increased depression? An examination of the effects of children on men's and women's depression levels*. Paper presented at the Conference on Work and Family: Today's Realities and Tomorrow's Visions, Boston.

Birenbaum, M., & Kraemer, R. (1995). Gender and ethnic-group differences in causal attributions for success and failure in mathematics and language examinations. *Journal of Cross-Cultural Psychology, 26*, 342–359.

Birkeland, R., Thompson, J., Herbozo, S., Roehrig, M., Cafri, G., & van den Berg, P. (2005). Media exposure, mood, and body image dissatisfaction: An experimental test of person versus product priming. *Body Image, 2*, 53–61.

Birnbaum, G. E., Cohen, O., & Wertheimer, V. (2007). Is it all about intimacy? Age, menopausal status, and women's sexuality. *Personal Relationships, 14*, 167–185.

Bisaga, K., Whitaker, A., Davies, M., Chuang, S., Feldman, J., & Walsh, B. T. (2005). Eating disorder and depressive symptoms in urban high school girls from different ethnic backgrounds. *Journal of Developmental & Behavioral Pediatrics, 26*, 257–266.

Bisagni, G. M., & Eckenrode, J. (1995). The role of work identity in women's adjustment to divorce. *American Journal of Orthopsychiatry, 65*, 574–583.

Bittman, M., & Wajcman, J. (2000, September). The rush hour: The character of leisure time and gender equity. *Social Forces, 79*, 165–189.

Black, M. C., & Breiding, M. J. (2008). Adverse health conditions and health risk behaviors associated with intimate partner violence—United States, 2005. *Morbidity and Mortality Weekly Report, 57*, 113–117.

Black, M. C., Noonan, R., Leggs, M., Eaton, D., & Breiding, M. J. (2006). Physical dating violence among high school students—United States, 2003. *Morbidity and Mortality Weekly Report, 55*, 532–535.

Black, M. M., et al. (2002). Behavior and development of preschool children born to adolescent mothers: Risk and 3-generation households. *Pediatrics, 109*, 573–580.

Blake, S. M., et al. (2003). Condom availability programs in Massachusetts high schools: Relationships with condom use and sexual behavior. *American Journal of Public Health, 93*, 955–962.

Blakemore, J. E. O. (2001, April). *Children's violations of gender norms: Which ones matter?* Paper presented at the meeting of the Society for Research in Child Development, Minneapolis, MN.

Blakemore, J. E. O. (2003). Children's beliefs about violating gender norms: Boys shouldn't look like girls, and girls shouldn't act like boys. *Sex Roles, 48*, 411–419.

Blakemore, J. E. O., & Centers, R. E. (2005). Characteristics of boys' and girls' toys. *Sex Roles, 53*, 619–633.

Blakemore, J. E. O., & Hill, C. A. (2008). The child gender socialization scale: A measure to compare traditional and feminist parents. *Sex Roles, 58*, 192–207.

Blanchard, L. T., Gurka, M. J., & Blackman, J. A. (2006). Emotional, developmental, and behavioral health of American children and their families: A report from the 2003 National Survey of Children's Health. *Pediatrics, 117*, 1202–1212.

Bleeker, M. M. (2003, April). *Children's attraction to math and science: The importance of parents' gender stereotypes and activities*. Paper presented at the meeting of the Society for Research in Child Development, Tampa, FL.

Bleeker, M. M., & Jacobs, J. E. (2004). Achievement in math and science: Do mothers' beliefs matter 12 years later? *Journal of Educational Psychology, 96*, 97–109.

Blehar, M. C., & Norquist, G. (2002). Mental health policy and women. In S. G. Kornstein & A. H. Clayton (Eds.), *Women's mental health: A comprehensive textbook* (pp. 613–627). New York: Guilford Press.

Blieszner, R., Vista, P. M., & Mancine, J. A. (1996). Diversity and dynamics in late-life mother–daughter relationships. *Journal of Women and Aging, 8*(3/4), 5–24.

Bly, R. (1990). *Iron John*. Reading, MA: Addison-Wesley.

Blyth, M. (2004). *Spin sisters: How the women of the media sell unhappiness and liberalism to the women of America*. New York: St. Martins Press.

Boduroglu, A., et al. (2002, August). *Stereotypes about young and old adults: A cross-cultural comparison*. Paper presented at the meeting of the American Psychological Association, Chicago.

Bogg, T., & Roberts, B. W. (2004). Conscientiousness and health-related behaviors: A meta-analysis of the leading behavioral contributors to mortality. *Psychological Bulletin, 130*, 887–919.

Bohan, J. S. (2002). Sex differences and/in the self: Classic themes, feminist variations, postmodern challenges. *Psychology of Women Quarterly, 26*, 74–88.

Boisnier, A. D. (2003). Race and women's identity development: Distinguishing between feminism and womanism among black and white women. *Sex Roles, 49*, 211–218.

Bolch, M. B., & Murdock, T. B. (2003, August). *The relationship between the school environment and the emotional adjustment of LGB youth*. Paper presented at the meeting of the American Psychology Association, Toronto.

Bolen, J., Adams, M., & Shenson, D. (2007). Routine preventive services for older women: A composite measure highlights gaps in delivery. *Journal of Women's Health, 16*, 583–593.

Boles, S. M., & Miotto, K. (2003). Substance abuse and violence: A review of the literature. *Aggression and Violent Behavior, 8*, 155–174.

Bond, M. A., et al. (2004). Gendered work conditions, health, and work outcomes. *Journal of Occupational Health Psychology, 9*, 28–45.

Bondurant, B., & Donat, P. L. N. (1999). Perceptions of women's sexual interest and acquaintance rape. *Psychology of Women Quarterly, 23*, 691–705.

Bonell, C., et al. (2006). Influence of family type and parenting behaviours on teenage sexual behaviour and conceptions. *Journal of Epidemiology and Community Health, 60*, 502–506.

Bongaarts, J., & Zimmer, Z. (2002). Living arrangements of older adults in the developing world: An analysis of demographic and health survey household surveys. *The Journals of Gerontology Services B: Psychological Sciences and Social Sciences, 57*, S145–S157.

Bonner, R. (2003, June 23). A challenge in India snarls foreign adoptions. *New York Times*, p. A3.

Bonomi, A. E., Anderson, M. L., Rivara, F. P., & Thompson, R. S. (2007). Health outcomes in women with physical and sexual intimate partner violence exposure. *Journal of Women's Health, 16*, 987–997.

Bonomi, A. E., et al. (2006). Intimate partner violence and women's physical, mental, and social functioning. *American Journal of Preventive Medicine, 30*, 458–466.

Bönte, M., et al. (2008). Women and men with coronary heart disease in three countries: Are they treated differently? *Women's Health Issues, 18*, 191–198.

Bontempo, D. E. (2001, August). *Family relationships and victimization of lesbian, gay, and bisexual adolescents.* Paper presented at the meeting of the American Psychological Association. San Francisco.

Book, A. S., Starzyk, K. B., & Quinsey, V. L. (2001). The relationship between testosterone and aggression: A meta-analysis. *Aggression and Violent Behavior, 6*, 579–599.

Boonstra, H. (2002, February). Teen pregnancy: Trends and lessons learned. *The Guttmacher Report on Public Policy, 5*, 7–10.

Boonstra, H. (2004, March). Comprehensive approach needed to combat sexually transmitted infections among youth. *The Guttmacher Report on Public Policy, 3–4*, 13.

Boonstra, H. D. (2007). The heart of the matter: Public funding of abortion for poor women in the United States. *Guttmacher Policy Review, 10*, 12–16.

Boothroyd, R. A., et al. (2006). Poor and depressed, the tip of the iceberg: The unmet needs of enrollees in an indigent health care plan. *Administration and Policy in Mental Health, 33*, 172–181.

Bordo, S. (2003, December 19). The empire of images in our world of bodies. *Chronicle of Higher Education*, pp. 86–89.

Bordo, S. (2004). *Unbearable weight: Feminism, Western culture, and the body.* Berkeley: University of California Press.

Borkhoff, C. M., Hawker, G. A., Kreder, H. J., Glazier, R. H., Mahomed, N. N., & Wright, J. G. (2008). The effect of patients' sex on physicians' recommendations for total knee arthroplasty. *Canadian Medical Association Journal, 178*, 681–687.

Bornstein, M. H., et al. (2008). Mother–child emotional availability in ecological perspective: Three countries, two regions, two genders. *Developmental Psychology, 44*, 666–680.

Bornstein, R. F. (2006). The complex relationship between dependency and domestic violence: Converging psychological factors and social forces. *American Psychologist, 61*, 595–606.

Bos, H. M. W., Sandfort, T. G. M., de Bruyn, E. H., & Hakvoort, E. M. (2008). Same-sex attraction, social relationships, psychosocial functioning, and school performance in early adolescence. *Developmental Psychology, 44*, 59–68.

Bos, H. M. W., Van Balen, F., Sandfort, T. M. G., & Van den Boom, D. C. (2006, August). *Children's gender development and psychosocial adjustment in planned lesbian and heterosexual families.* Paper presented at the annual meeting of the American Psychological Association, New Orleans, LA.

Bosacki, S. L., & Moore, C. (2004). Preschoolers' understanding of simple and complex emotions: Links with gender and language. *Sex Roles, 50*, 659–675.

Boston Women's Health Book Collective. (1992). *The new our bodies, ourselves: A book by and for women.* New York: Touchstone.

Boston Women's Health Book Collective. (1998). *Our bodies, ourselves for the new century: A book by and for women.* New York: Touchstone.

Boston Women's Health Book Collective. (2005). *Our bodies, ourselves: A new edition for a new era.* New York: Touchstone.

Bosworth, B., Burtless, G., & Sahm, C. (2001, August). *The trend in lifetime earnings inequality and its impact on the distribution of retirement income.* Chestnut Hill, MA: Center for Retirement Research at Boston College.

Botta, R. A. (2003). For your health? The relationship between magazine reading and adolescents' body image and eating disturbances. *Sex Roles, 48*, 389–399.

Bottoms, B. L., Quas, J. A., & Davis, S. L. (2007). The influence of interviewer-provided social support on children's suggestibility, memory, and disclosures. In M.-E. Pipe, M. E. Lamb, Y. Orbach, & A.-C. Cederborg (Eds.), *Child sexual abuse: Disclosure, delay, and denial* (pp. 135–158). Mahwah, NJ: Erlbaum.

Bouchard, T. J., Jr. (2004). Genetic influence on human psychological traits: A survey. *Current Direction in Psychological Science, 13*, 148–151.

Bould, S., & Longino, C. F. (2001). Women survivors: The oldest old. In J. M. Coyle (Ed.), *Handbook on women and aging* (pp. 210–222). Westport, CT: Greenwood.

Bound, J., Schoenbaum, M., & Waidmann, T. (1996). Race differences in labor force attachment and disability status. *Gerontologist, 36*, 311–321.

Bourgeois, M. J., & Perkins, J. (2003). A test of evolutionary and sociocultural explanations of reactions to sexual harassment. *Sex Roles, 49*, 343–351.

Boushey, H. (2005). *Are women opting out? Debunking the myth.* Chicago: Council on Contemporary Families.

Bowleg, L. (2008). The health risks of being Black, Latina, woman, and/or poor: Redefining women's health within the context of social inequality. In J. C. Chrisler, C. Golden, &

P. D. Rozee (Eds.), *Lectures on the psychology of women* (pp. 204–219). New York: McGraw-Hill.

Bowleg, L., Brooks, K., & Ritz, S. F. (2008). "Bringing home more than a paycheck": An exploratory analysis of Black lesbians' experiences of stress and coping in the workplace. *Journal of Lesbian Studies, 12,* 69–84.

Bowleg, L., Craig, M. L., & Burkholder, G. (2004). Rising and surviving: A conceptual model of active coping among black lesbians. *Cultural Diversity and Ethnic Minority Psychology, 10,* 229–240.

Bowleg, L., Lucas, K. J., & Tschann, J. M. (2004). "The ball was always in his court": An exploratory analysis of relationship scripts, sexual scripts, and condom use among African American women. *Psychology of Women Quarterly, 28,* 70–82.

Boxer, S. (1997, December 14). One casualty of the women's movement: Feminism. *New York Times,* p. WK3.

Boynton, P. (2003). Abiding by the rules: Instructing women in relationships. *Feminism & Psychology, 13,* 237–245.

Boysen, G. A., & Vogel, D. L. (2007). Biased assimilation and attitude polarization in response to learning about biological explanations of homosexuality. *Sex Roles, 57,* 755–762.

Brabant, S., & Mooney, L. A. (1997). Sex role stereotyping in the Sunday comics: A twenty year update. *Sex Roles, 37,* 269–281.

Brabeck, M. M., & Brabeck, K. M. (2006). Women and relationships. In J. Worell & C. D. Goodheart (Eds.), *Handbook of girls' and women's psychological health: Gender and well-being across the lifespan* (pp. 208–217). New York: Oxford University Press.

Bradford, J., & White, J. C. (2000). Lesbian health research. In M. B. Goldman & M. C. Hatch (Eds.), *Women & health* (pp. 64–78). New York: Academic Press.

Bradley, C. J., Given, C. W., & Roberts, C. (2002). Race, socioeconomic status, and breast cancer treatment and survival. *Journal of the National Cancer Institute, 94,* 490–496.

Bradshaw, Z., & Slade, P. (2003). The effects of induced abortion on emotional experiences and relationships: A critical review of the literature. *Clinical Psychology Review, 23,* 929–958.

Bradsher, J. E. (2001). Older women and widowhood. In J. M. Coyle (Ed.), *Handbook on women and aging* (pp. 112–128). Westport, CT: Greenwood.

Bragger, J. D., Kutcher, E., Morgan, J., & Firth, P. (2002). The effects of the structured interview on reducing biases against pregnant job applicants. *Sex Roles, 46,* 215–226.

Brandsma, L. (2007). Eating disorders across the lifespan. *Journal of Women & Aging, 19,* 155–172.

Brandt-Rauf, S., Raveis, V., Drummond, N., Conte, J., & Rothman, S. (2006). Ashkenazi Jews and breast cancer: The consequences of linking ethnic identity to genetic disease. *American Journal of Public Health, 96,* 1979–1988.

Brazile, D. (2007, Summer). The Imus effect. *Ms.,* p. 79.

Breast cancer: The year in review. (2003, 4th quarter). *Frontline: The Susan G. Komen Breast Cancer Foundation Newsletter,* p. 4.

Brechwald, W. A., Hoy, M. B., Quinlan, N. P., & Costanzo, P. R. (2007, March). *Awareness and internalization of the thin ideal in an overweight youth sample: Implications for self-evaluation and psychological well-being.* Poster presented at the meeting of the Society for Research in Child Development, Boston.

Breen, A. B., & Karpinski, A. (2008). What's in a name? Two approaches to evaluating the label feminist. *Sex Roles, 58,* 299–310.

Brehm, S. S. (2007, July/August). Some thoughts about women, leadership, and the future. *Monitor on Psychology, 38,* 5.

Breitkopf, C. R., Littleton, H., & Berenson, A. (2007). Body image: A study in a tri-ethnic sample of low-income women. *Sex Roles, 56,* 373–380.

Brender, E. (2006). Fitness for older adults. *Journal of the American Medical Association, 296,* 242.

Brendgen, M., et al. (2005). Examining genetic and environmental effects on social aggression: A study of 6-year-old twins. *Child Development, 76,* 930–946.

Brener, N. D., et al. (2007). Youth Risk Behavior Surveillance—selected steps communities, 2005. *Morbidity and Mortality Weekly Report, 56* (SS02), 1–16.

Brescoll, V., & LaFrance, M. (2004). The correlates and consequences of newspaper reports of research on sex differences. *Psychological Science, 15,* 515–520.

Brescoll, V. L., & Uhlmann, E. L. (2008). Can an angry woman get ahead? Status conferral, gender, and expression of emotion in the workplace. *Psychological Science, 19,* 268–275.

Breslow, L., & Breslow, N. (1993). Health practices and disability: Some evidence from Alameda County. *Preventative Medicine, 22,* 86–95.

Brett, K., Barfield, W., & Williams, C. (2008). Prevalence of self-reported postpartum depressive symptoms—17 states, 2004–2005. *Morbidity and Mortality Weekly Report, 57,* 361–366.

Brewster, K. L., & Padavic, I. (2002). Change in gender ideology, 1977–1996: The contributions of intracohort change and population turnover. *Journal of Marriage and the Family, 62,* 477–487.

Bridges, J. S. (1991). Perceptions of date and stranger rape: A difference in sex role expectations and rape-supportive beliefs. *Sex Roles, 24,* 291–307.

Bridges, J. S. (1993). Pink or blue: Gender-stereotypic perceptions of infants as conveyed by birth congratulations cards. *Psychology of Women Quarterly, 17,* 193–205.

Bridges, J. S., & Etaugh, C. (1995). College students' perceptions of mothers: Effects of maternal employment-childrearing pattern and motive for employment. *Sex Roles, 32,* 735–751.

Bridges, J. S., & Etaugh, C. (1996). Black and white college women's maternal employment outcome expectations and their desired timing of maternal employment. *Sex Roles, 35,* 543–562.

Bridges, J. S., & Orza, A. M. (1993). Effects of maternal employment-childrearing pattern on college students' perceptions of a mother and her child. *Psychology of Women Quarterly, 17,* 103–117.

Bridges, J. S., & Orza, A. M. (1996). Black and white employed mothers' role experiences. *Sex Roles, 35,* 377–385.

Bridges, L. J., Roe, A. E. C., Dunn, J., & O'Connor, T. G. (2007). Children's perspectives on their relationships with grandparents following parental separation: A longitudinal study. *Social Development, 16,* 539–554.

Bridges, M. (2003/2004, Winter). Poverty up, women still down. *Ms.,* p. 16.

Bridges, M., et al. (2003/2004, Winter). 50 women who made a difference. *Ms.*, pp. 53–66.

Bridges, S. K., Lease, S. H., & Ellison, C. R. (2000, August). *Predicting women's sexual satisfaction: Implications for the new millennium.* Paper presented at the meeting of the American Psychological Association, Washington, DC.

Brier, N. (2008). Grief following miscarriage: A comprehensive review of the literature. *Journal of Women's Health, 17,* 451–464.

Brill, M. (2004). Antidepressants and sexual dysfunction. *Sexuality, Reproduction & Menopause, 2,* 35–40.

Broadbridge, A., & Hearn, J. (2008). Gender and management: New directions in research and continuing patterns in practice. *British Journal of Management, 19,* S38–S49.

Broderick, P. C., & Korteland, C. (2002). Coping style and depression in early adolescence: Relationships to gender, gender role, and implicit beliefs. *Sex Roles, 46,* 201–213.

Brodey, D. (2005, September 20). Blacks join the eating-disorder mainstream. *New York Times,* pp. D5, D8.

Brody, J. E. (1998, January 22). Study challenges idea of PMS as emotional disorder. *New York Times,* pp. A1, A18.

Brody, J. E. (1999a, October 12). Coping with fear: Keeping breast cancer in perspective. *New York Times,* p. D7.

Brody, J. E. (1999b, November 30). Yesterday's precocious puberty is norm today. *New York Times,* p. D8.

Brody, J. E. (2001, August 21). Nutrition a key to better health for elderly. *New York Times,* p. D8.

Brody, J. E. (2004a, June 1). Abstinence-only: Does it work? *New York Times,* p. D7.

Brody, J. E. (2004b, May 11). The risks and demands of pregnancy after 20. *New York Times,* p. D8.

Brody, J. E. (2005, April 12). Women struggle for parity of the heart. *New York Times,* p. D7.

Brody, J. E. (2006a, March 28). A chance find, and voilà! Goodbye, hot flashes. Hello, sleep. *New York Times,* p. D6.

Brody, J. E. (2006b, October 24). Nausea? There's no need to suffer in silence. *New York Times,* p. D7.

Brody, J. E. (2007a, November 27). A common casualty of old age: The will to live. *New York Times,* p. F7.

Brody, J. E. (2007b, August 21). Cutting cholesterol, an uphill battle. *New York Times,* p. D7.

Brody, J. E. (2007c, April 10). A lively libido isn't reserved for the young. *New York Times,* p. D5.

Brody, J. E. (2008a, February 19). An oldie vies for nutrient of the decade. *New York Times,* p. D7.

Brody, J. E. (2008b, March 25). Trying again after recurrent miscarriages. *New York Times,* p. D7.

Brody, J. E. (2008c, April 29). You name it, and exercise helps it. *New York Times,* p. D7.

Brody, L. R., & Hall, J. A. (2000). Gender, emotion, and expression. In M. Lewis & J. Haviland-Jones (Eds.), *Handbook of emotions* (2nd ed., pp. 338–349). New York: Guilford.

Brogan, D. J., O'Hanlan, K. A., Elon, L., & Frank, E. (2003, Winter). The hormone therapy dilemma: Women respond. *Journal of the American Medical Women's Association, 58,* 10–19.

Bronner, E. (1998, February 25). U.S. 12th graders rank poorly in math and science, study says. *New York Times,* pp. A1, C20.

Bronstein, P. (2006). The family environment: Where gender role socialization begins. In J. Worell & C. D. Goodheart (Eds.), *Handbook of girls' and women's psychological health: Gender and well-being across the lifespan* (pp. 262–271). New York: Oxford University Press.

Brooks, M. G., & Buckner, J. C. (1996). Work and welfare: Job histories, barriers to employment, and predictors of work among low-income single mothers. *American Journal of Orthopsychiatry, 66,* 526–537.

Broverman, I. K., Broverman, D. M., Clarkson, F. E., Rosenkrantz, P. S., & Vogel, S. R. (1970). Sex-role stereotypes and clinical judgements of mental health. *Journal of Consulting Psychology, 34,* 1–7.

Brown, C. E. (2007, May). *Examining college women's body image using the body figure scale.* Poster presented at the annual meeting of the Midwestern Psychological Association, Chicago.

Brown, E. R., et al. (1995, October). *Women's health-related behaviors and use of clinical preventive services: A report to the Commonwealth Fund.* Los Angeles: UCLA Center for Health Policy Research.

Brown, J. S., Meadows, S. O., & Elder, G. H., Jr. (2007). Race-ethnic inequality and psychological distress: Depressive symptoms from adolescence to young adulthood. *Development Psychology, 43,* 1295–1311.

Brown, L. M. (2006, Spring). What about the boys? *The Feminist Psychologist,* p. 5.

Brown, L. M., Way, N., & Duff, J. L. (1999). The others in my I: Adolescent girls' friendships and peer relations. In N. G. Johnson, M. C. Roberts, & J. Worell (Eds.), *Beyond appearance: A new look at adolescent girls* (pp. 205–225). Washington, DC: American Psychological Association.

Brown, S. L., et al. (2003). Providing social support may be more beneficial than receiving it: Results from a prospective study of mortality. *Psychological Science, 14,* 320–327.

Brown, S. L., & Booth, A. (1996). Cohabitation versus marriage: A comparison of relationship quality. *Journal of Marriage and the Family, 58,* 668–678.

Brown, W. M., Finn, C. J., Cooke, B. M., & Breedlove, S. M. (2002). Differences in finger length between self-identified "butch" and "femme" lesbians. *Archives of Sexual Behavior, 31,* 123–128.

Brownlow, S., Rosamond, J. A., & Parker, J. A. (2003). Gender-linked linguistic behavior in television interviews. *Sex Roles, 49,* 121–132.

Brownridge, D. A. (2006). Partner violence against women with disabilities: Prevalence, risk, and explanations. *Violence against Women, 12,* 805–822.

Brumberg, J. J. (1997). *The body project: An intimate history of American girls.* New York: Random House.

Bryant, A. N. (2003). Changes in attitudes toward women's roles: Predicting gender-role traditionalism among college students. *Sex Roles, 48,* 131–142.

Bryant, R. M., et al. (2005). Having our say: African American women, diversity, and counseling. *Journal of Counseling and Development, 83,* 313–319.

Bryant-Davis, T. (2003). Sexual abuse and rape: Thriving after sexual assault. In L. Slater, J. H. Daniel, & A. E. Banks (Eds.), *The complete guide to mental health for women* (pp. 154–163). Boston: Beacon Press.

Buchanan, N. T., & Bruce, T. A. (2004/2005, Fall/Winter). Contrapower harassment and the professional archetype: Gender, race, and authority. *Association of American Colleges and Universities, On Campus with Women, 34*(1–2).

Buckley, T. R., & Carter, R. T. (2005). Black adolescent girls: Do gender role and racial identity: Impact their self-esteem? *Sex Roles, 53,* 647–661.

Budd, K. (2002, May/June). Eggbeaters. *AARP,* p. 15.

Buddie, A. M., & Miller, A. G. (2001). Beyond rape myths: A more complex view of perceptions of rape victims. *Sex Roles, 45,* 139–159.

Budig, M. J., & England, P. (2001). The wage penalty for motherhood. *American Sociological Review, 66,* 204–225.

Bugental, D. B., & Hehman, J. A. (2007). Ageism: A review of research and policy implications. *Social Issues and Policy Review, 1,* 173–216.

Bukatko, D., & Shedd, J. (1999, April). *Children's evaluations of gender-stereotyped traits, activities and occupations.* Poster presented at the meeting of the Society for Research in Child Development, Albuquerque, NM.

Bulik, C. M., Berkman, N. D., Brownley, K. A., Sedway, J. A., & Lohr, K. N. (2007). Anorexia nervosa treatment: A systematic review of randomized controlled trials. *International Journal of Eating Disorders, 40,* 310–320.

Bullock, H. E., & Fernald, J. L. (2003). "Feminism?" Feminist identification, speaker appearance, and perceptions of feminist and antifeminist messengers. *Psychology of Women Quarterly, 27,* 291–299.

Bullock, H. E., Wyche, K. F., & Williams, W. R. (2001). Media images of the poor. *Journal of Social Issues, 57,* 229–246.

Bumpass, M. F., Crouter, A. C., & McHale, S. M. (2001). Parental autonomy granting during adolescence: Exploring gender differences in context. *Developmental Psychology, 37,* 163–173.

Burchinal, M. R., & Clarke-Stewart, K. A. (2007). Maternal employment and child cognitive outcomes: The importance of analytic approach. *Developmental Psychology, 43,* 1140–1155.

Bureau of Labor Statistics. (2004). *American time-use survey.* Washington, DC: Author.

Burgess, C., et al. (2005). Depression and anxiety in women with early breast cancer: Five year observational cohort study. *BMJ, 330,* 702–705.

Burgess, E. O. (2004). Sexuality in midlife and later life couples. In J. H. Harvey, A. Wenzel, & S. Sprecher (Eds.), *The handbook of sexuality in close relationships* (pp. 437–454). Mahwah, NJ: Erlbaum.

Burgess, M. C. R., Stermer, S. P., & Burgess, S. R. (2007). Sex, lies, and video games: The portrayal of male and female characters on video game covers. *Sex Roles, 57,* 419–433.

Burlingame-Lee, L. J., & Canetto, S. S. (2005). Narratives of gender in computer advertisements. In E. Cole & J. H. Daniel (Eds.), *Featuring females: Feminist analyses of media* (pp. 85–99). Washington, DC: American Psychological Association.

Burn, S. M. (2005). *Women across cultures: A global perspective* (2nd ed.). New York: McGraw-Hill.

Burn, S. M., & Busso, J. (2005). Ambivalent sexism, scriptural literalism, and religiosity. *Psychology of Women Quarterly, 29,* 412–418.

Burns, A. (2004). Treating depression in later life. *BMJ, 329,* 181–182.

Burns, A., & Leonard, R. (2005). Chapters of our lives: Life narratives of midlife and older Australian women. *Sex Roles, 52,* 269–277.

Burris, B. H. (1991). Employed mothers: The impact of class and marital status on the prioritizing of family and work. *Social Science Quarterly, 72,* 50–66.

Bursik, K. (1992). Perceptions of sexual harassment in an academic context. *Sex Roles, 27,* 401–412.

Buss, D. M. (1994). *The evolution of desire: Strategies of human mating.* New York: Basic Books.

Busseri, M. A., Willoughby, T., Chalmers, H., & Bogaert, A. F. (2008). On the association between sexual attraction and adolescent risk behavior involvement: Examining mediation and moderation. *Developmental Psychology, 44,* 69–80.

Bussey, K., & Bandura, A. (2004). Social cognitive theory of gender development and functioning. In A. H. Eagly, A. E. Beall, & R. J. Sternberg (Eds.), *The psychology of gender* (2nd ed., pp. 92–119). New York: Guilford.

Butler, L. D., & Nolen-Hoeksema, S. (1994). Gender differences in responses to depressed mood in a college sample. *Sex Roles, 30,* 331–346.

Butler, R., & Lewis, M. I. (2002). *The new love and sex after 60.* New York: Ballantine.

Butler, S. S. (2004). Gay, lesbian, bisexual, and transgender (GLBT) elders: The challenges and resilience of this marginalized group! *Journal of Human Behavior and the Social Environment, 9,* 25–44.

Butrica, B., & Uccello, C. (2004). *How will boomers fare at retirement?* Washington, DC: AARP.

Button, S. B. (2001). Organizational efforts to affirm sexual diversity: A cross-level examination. *Journal of Applied Psychology, 86,* 17–28.

Buysse, J. M., & Embser-Herbert, M. S. (2004). Constructions of gender in sport: An analysis of intercollegiate media guide cover photographs. *Gender & Society, 18,* 66–81.

Bylsma, W. H., & Major, B. (1994). Social comparisons and contentment: Exploring the psychological costs of the gender wage gap. *Psychology of Women Quarterly, 18,* 241–249.

Byrne, A., & Carr, D. (2005). Caught in the cultural lag: The stigma of singlehood. *Psychological Inquiry, 16,* 84–91.

Byrne, B. M. (2008). Testing for time-invariant and time-varying predictors of self-perceived ability in math, language arts, and science: A look at the gender factor. In H. M. G. Watt & J. S. Eccles (Eds.), *Gender and occupational outcomes: Longitudinal assessments of individual, social, and cultural influences* (pp. 145–170). Washington, DC: American Psychological Association.

Cadinu, M., Maass, A., Rosabianca, A., & Klesner, J. (2005). Why do women underperform under stereotype threat? Evidence for the role of negative thinking. *Psychological Science, 16,* 572–578.

Cahill, L. (2005, May). His brain, her brain. *Scientific American*, *292*, 40–47.

Caiazza, A., Shaw, A., & Werschkul, M. (2004). *The status of women in the states: Wide disparities by race, ethnicity, and region*. Washington, DC: Institute for Women's Policy Research.

Cairoli, M. Z. (2001). Factory as home and family: Female workers in the Moroccan garment industry. In C. B. Brettell & C. F. Sargent (Eds.), *Gender in cross-cultural perspective* (3rd ed., pp. 551–564). Upper Saddle River, NJ: Prentice Hall.

Caldera, Y. M., et al. (1999). Children's play preferences, construction play with blocks, and visual-spatial skills: Are they related? *International Journal of Behavioral Development*, *23*, 855–872.

Calis, K. A., & Pucino, F. (2007). Zoledronic acid and secondary prevention of fractures. *New England Journal of Medicine*, *357*, 1861–1862.

Calvert, S. L., Kondla, T. A., Ertel, K. A., & Meisel, D. S. (2001). Young adults' perceptions and memories of a television woman hero. *Sex Roles*, *45*, 31–52.

Cambron, M. J., Branum-Martin, L., Acitelli, L. K., & Stuebing, K. K. (2008). *What do we really know about gender differences in developmental self-esteem during adolescence?* Manuscript under review, University of Houston.

Cameron, D. (2007). *The myth of Mars and Venus: Do men and women really speak different languages?* Oxford, UK: Oxford University Press.

Campbell, A., Shirley, L., & Candy, J. (2004). A longitudinal study of gender-related cognition and behaviour. *Developmental Science*, *7*, 1–9.

Campbell, A., Shirley, L., & Caygill, L. (2002). Sex-typed preferences in three domains: Do two-year-olds need cognitive variables? *British Journal of Psychology*, *93*, 203–217.

Campbell, A., Shirley, L., Heywood, C., & Crook, C. (2000). Infants' visual preference for sex-congruent babies, children, toys, and activities: A longitudinal study. *British Journal of Developmental Psychology*, *18*, 479–498.

Campbell, J. C., Glass, N., Sharps, P. W., Laughon, K., & Bloom, T. (2007). Intimate partner homicide. *Trauma, Violence, & Abuse*, *8*, 246–269.

Campbell, R., Sefl, T., & Ahrens, C. E. (2003). The physical health consequences of rape: Assessing survivors' somatic symptoms in a racially diverse population. *Women's Studies Quarterly*, *31*, 90–104.

Campbell, R., Sefl, T., & Ahrens, C. E. (2004). The impact of rape on women's sexual health risk behaviors. *Health Psychology*, *23*, 67–74.

Campbell, V. A., et al. (1999). Surveillance for sensory impairment, activity, limitation, and health-related quality of life among older adults—United States, 1993–1997. *Morbidity and Mortality Weekly Report*, *48*(SS08), 131–156.

Campo-Flores, A. (2002, July 1). "Macho" or "sweetness"? *Newsweek*, p. 51.

Canabal, M. E. (1995). Native Americans in higher education. *College Student Journal*, *29*, 455–457.

Canetto, S. S. (2001). Older adult women: Issues, resources, and challenges. In R. K. Unger (Ed.), *Handbook of the psychology of women and gender* (pp. 183–197). New York: Wiley.

Canetto, S. S. (2003). Older adulthood. In L. Slater, J. H. Daniel, & A. E. Banks (Eds.), *The complete guide to mental health for women* (pp. 56–64). Boston: Beacon Press.

Cann, A., & Vann, E. D. (1995). Implications of sex and gender differences for self: Perceived advantages and disadvantages of being the other gender. *Sex Roles*, *33*, 531–541.

Canterbury, R. J. (2002). Alcohol and other substance abuse. In S. G. Kornstein & A. H. Clayton (Eds.), *Women's mental health: A comprehensive textbook* (pp. 222–243). New York: Guilford.

Capaldi, D. M., Kim, H. K., & Shortt, J. W. (2004). Women's involvement in aggression in young adult romantic relationships: A developmental systems model. In M. Putallaz & K. L. Bierman (Eds.), *Aggression, antisocial behavior, and violence among girls: A developmental perspective* (pp. 223–241). New York: Guilford.

Caplan, P. J. (2001). Motherhood: Its changing face. In J. Worell (Ed.), *Encyclopedia of women and gender* (pp. 783–794). San Diego: Academic Press.

Caplan, P. J., & Caplan, J. B. (1999). *Thinking critically about research on sex and gender* (2nd ed.). New York: HarperCollins.

Caplan, P. J. (2008, Summer). Pathologizing your period. *Ms.*, 63–64.

Caprara, G. V., Barbaranelli, C., & Pastorelli, C. (2001). Prosocial behavior and aggression in childhood and pre-adolescence. In A. C. Bohart & D. J. Stipek (Eds.), *Constructive and destructive behavior: Implications for family, school, and society* (pp. 187–203). Washington, DC: American Psychological Association.

Card, N. A., Stucky, B. D., Sawalani, G. M., & Little, T. D. (2008). Direct and indirect aggression during childhood and adolescence: A meta-analytic review of gender differences, intercorrelations, and relations to maladjustment. *Child Development*, *79*, 1185–1229.

Carey, B. (2006, February 16). Study details risk of caring for elderly spouses. *New York Times*, p. A27.

Carli, L. L., & Bukatko, D. (2000). Gender, communication, and social-influence: A development perspective. In T. Eckes & H. M. Trautner (Eds.), *The developmental social psychology of gender* (pp. 295–332). Mahwah, NJ: Erlbaum.

Carlisle, W. (1994). Sharing home responsibilities: Women in dual-career marriages. In C. W. Konek & S. L. Kitch (Eds.), *Women and careers: Issues and challenges* (pp. 140–152). Thousand Oaks, CA: Sage.

Carlson, K. J., Eisenstat, S. A., & Ziporyn, T. (2004). *The new Harvard guide to women's health*. Cambridge, MA: Harvard University Press.

Carmichael, M. (2004, January 26). No girls, please. *Newsweek*, p. 50.

Carmichael, M. (2004, May 10). Have it your way: Redesigning birth. *Newsweek*, pp. 70, 72.

Carmichael, M. (2007, March 26). Stronger, faster, smarter. *Newsweek*, pp. 38–46.

Caron, S. L., & Ulin, M. (1997). Closeting and the quality of lesbian relationships. *The Journal of Contemporary Human Services*, *78*, 413–419.

Carp, F. M. (2001a). Living arrangements for midlife and older women. In J. M. Coyle (Ed.), *Handbook on women and aging* (pp. 253–270). Westport, CT: Greenwood.

Carp, F. M. (2001b). Retirement and women. In J. M. Coyle (Ed.), *Handbook on women and aging* (pp. 112–128). Westport, CT: Greenwood.

Carpenter, C. M., Wayne, G. F., & Connolly, G. N. (2005). Designing cigarettes for women: New findings from the tobacco industry documents. *Addiction, 100*, 837–851.

Carpenter, L. J., & Acosta, R. V. (2008). *Women in intercollegiate sport: A longitudinal, national study: Thirty-one-year-update.* West Brookfield, MA: Acosta/Carpenter.

Carpenter, S. (2000, October). Strengthening the voices of women psychologists. *Monitor on Psychology*, p. 57.

Carr, C. L. (2007). Where have all the tomboys gone? Women's accounts of gender in adolescence. *Sex Roles, 56*, 439–448.

Carr, D. (1997). The fulfillment of career dreams at midlife: Does it matter for women's mental health? *Journal of Health and Social Behavior, 38*, 331–344.

Carr, D. (2004a). Gender, preloss marital dependence, and older adults' adjustment to widowhood. *Journal of Marriage and Family, 66*, 220–235.

Carr, D. (2004b). Psychological well-being across three cohorts: A response to shifting work-family opportunities and expectations? In O. G. Brim, C. D. Ryff, & R. C. Kessler (Eds.), *How healthy are we? A national study of well-being at midlife* (pp. 452–484). Chicago: University of Chicago Press.

Carr, D., & Ha, J.-H. (2006). Bereavement. In J. Worell & C. D. Goodheart (Eds.), *Handbook of girls' and women's psychological health: Gender and well-being across the lifespan* (pp. 397–405). New York: Oxford University Press.

Carr, J. G., Gilroy, F. D., & Sherman, M. F. (1996). Silencing the self and depression among women. *Psychology of Women Quarterly, 20*, 375–392.

Carrington, C. (2002). *No place like home: Relationships and family life among lesbians and gay men.* Chicago: University of Chicago Press.

Carter, B., & Elliott, S. (2004, May 26). MTV to start first network aimed at gays. *New York Times*, pp. C1, C8.

Carvajal, D. (2008, April 16). French bill takes chic out of being too thin. *New York Times*, p. A6.

Carver, P. R., Egan, S. K., & Perry, D. G. (2004). Children who question their heterosexuality. *Developmental Psychology, 40*, 43–53.

Carver, P. R., Yunger, J. L., & Perry, D. G. (2003). Gender identity and adjustment in middle childhood. *Sex Roles, 49*, 95–109.

Case, K. A. (2007). Raising male privilege awareness and reducing sexism: An evaluation of diversity courses. *Psychology of Women Quarterly, 31*, 426–435.

Case, P., et al. (2004). Sexual orientation, health risk factors, and physical functioning in the Nurses' Health Study II. *Journal of Women's Health, 13*, 1033–1047.

Casey, M. B. (2002). Developmental perspectives on gender. In S. G. Kornstein & A. H. Clayton (Eds.), *Women's mental health: A comprehensive textbook* (pp. 499–514). New York: Guilford.

Cash, T. F., Morrow, J. A., Hrabosky, J. I., & Perry, A. A. (2004). How has body image changed? A cross-sectional investigation of college women and men from 1983 to 2001. *Journal of Consulting and Clinical Psychology, 72*, 1081–1089.

Cash, T. F., & Pruzinsky, T. (Eds.). (2002). *Body image: A handbook of theory, research, and clinical practice.* New York: Guilford.

Cashdan, E. (1998). Smiles, speech, and body posture: How women and men display sociometric status and power. *Journal of Nonverbal Behavior, 22*, 209–228.

Casper, L. M., & King, R. B. (2004). Changing families, shifting economic fortunes, and meeting basic needs. In A. C. Crouter & A. Booth (Eds.), *Work-family challenges for low-income parents and their children* (pp. 55–79). Mahwah, NJ: Erlbaum.

Cassell, J., & Jenkins, H. (Eds.) (1998). *From Barbie to Mortal Kombat: Gender and computer games.* Cambridge, MA: MIT Press.

Cassetta, J. A., Boden-Albala, B., Sciacca, R. R., & Giardina, E. V. (2007). Association of education and race/ethnicity with physical activity in insured urban women. *Journal of Women's Health, 16*, 902–908.

Cassidy, T. (2006, March 26). Birth, controlled. *New York Times Magazine*, p. 20.

Castañeda, D. (1996). Gender issues among Latinas. In J. C. Chrisler, C. Golden, & P. D. Rozee (Eds.), *Lectures on the psychology of women* (pp. 167–181). New York: McGraw-Hill.

Castañeda, D. (2008). Gender issues among Latinas. In J. C. Chrisler, C. Golden, & P. D. Rozee (Eds.), *Lectures on the psychology of women* (pp. 250–267). New York: McGraw-Hill.

Castañeda, D., & Burns-Glover, A. L. (2008). Women's friendships and romantic relationships. In F. L. Denmark & M. A. Paludi (Eds.), *Psychology of women: A handbook of issues and theories* (2nd ed., pp. 332–350). Westport, CT: Praeger.

Castro, I. L. (1997, Spring). Worth more than we earn: Fair pay as a step toward gender equity. *National Forum, 77*, 17–21.

Catalyst. (2007a, July 17). Damned or doomed—Catalyst study on gender stereotyping at work uncovers double-bind dilemmas for women. Retrieved from http://www.catalyst.org/pressroom/pressdoublebind.shtml

Catalyst. (2007b, May 29). Initial report on LGBT (Lesbian, Gay, Bisexual, and Transgender) inclusion in the workplace. Retrieved from http://www.catalyst.org/pressroom/press_releases/LGBT_Release.pdf

Catalyst. (2008, February 14). High-tech industry making progress at building more inclusive environments but barriers still face women working in technology. Retrieved from http://www.catalyst.org/pressroom/press_2008_high_tech.shtml

Catsambis, S. (1999). The path to math: Gender and racial-ethnic differences in mathematics participation from middle school to high school. In L. A. Peplau, S. C. DeBro, R. C. Veniegas, & P. L. Taylor (Eds.), *Gender, culture, and ethnicity: Current research about women and men* (pp. 102–120). Mountain View, CA: Mayfield.

Cattaneo, L. B., & Goodman, L. A. (2005). Risk factors for reabuse in intimate partner violence: A cross-disciplinary critical review. *Trauma, Violence, & Abuse, 6*, 141–175.

Cavanaugh, J. C., & Blanchard-Fields, F. (2006). *Adult development and aging* (5th ed.). Belmont, CA: Wadsworth.

Cebello, R., et al. (2004). Domestic violence and women's mental health in Chile. *Psychology of Women Quarterly, 28*, 298–308.

Ceci, S. J., & Williams, W. M. (Eds.). (2007). *Why aren't more women in science? Top researchers debate the evidence*. Washington, DC: American Psychological Association.

Center for American Women and Politics. (2005). *Women in elected office 2005*. Retrieved from http://www.cawp.rutgers.edu

Center for American Women and Politics. (2008). *Record number of Women to serve in Senate and House*. New Brunswick, NJ: Rutgers University.

Centers for Disease Control and Prevention. (2000). *All the stages of our lives*. Atlanta: Author.

Centers for Disease Control and Prevention. (2002a). Annual smoking—attributable mortality, years of potential life lost, and economic costs—United States, 1995–1999. *Morbidity and Mortality Weekly Report, 51*, 300–303.

Centers for Disease Control and Prevention. (2002b). Trends in sexual risk behaviors among high school students—United States, 1991–2001. *Morbidity and Mortality Weekly Report, 51*, 856–858.

Centers for Disease Control and Prevention. (2003). Nonfatal physical assault-related injuries among persons aged ≥60 years treated in hospital emergency departments—United States, 2001. *Morbidity and Mortality Weekly Report, 52*, 812–816.

Centers for Disease Control and Prevention. (2007). Cigarette smoking among adults—United States, 2006. *Morbidity and Mortality Weekly Report, 56*, 1157–1161.

Centers for Disease Control and Prevention. (2005). Guidelines for identifying and referring persons with fetal alcohol syndrome. *Morbidity and Mortality Weekly Report, 54*(RR-11), 1–14.

Cerhan, J. R., et al. (2004). Adherence to the AICR cancer prevention recommendations and subsequent morbidity and mortality in the Iowa women's health study cohort. *Cancer Epidemiology Biomarkers & Prevention, 13*, 1114–1120.

Cermele, J. A., Daniels, S., & Anderson, K. L. (2001). Defining normal: Constructions of race and gender in the DSM-IV casebook. *Feminism & Psychology, 11*, 229–247.

Cesarean delivery. (2002). *Journal of the American Medical Association, 287*, 2738.

Chaffin, M. (2006). The changing focus of child maltreatment research and practice within psychology. *Journal of Social Issues, 62*, 663–684.

Chaffin, M., & Schmidt, S. (2006). An evidence-based perspective on interventions to stop or prevent child abuse. In J. R. Lutzker (Ed.), *Preventing violence: Research and evidence-based intervention strategies* (pp. 49–68). Washington, DC: American Psychological Association.

Chamberlin, J. (2007, October). Deep trouble in the Deep South. *Monitor on Psychology, 38*, 32–33.

Chan, A. T., Manson, J. E., Feskanich, D., Stampfer, M. J., Colditz, G. A., & Fuchs, C. S. (2007). Long-term aspirin use and mortality in women. *Archives of Internal Medicine, 167*, 562–572.

Chan, K. S., Bird, C. E., Weiss, R., Duan, N., Meredith, L. S., & Sherbourne, C. D. (2006). Does patient-provider gender concordance affect mental health care received by primary care patients with major depression? *Women's Health Issues, 16*, 122–132.

Chang, J. T., et al. (2004). Interventions for the prevention of falls in older adults: Systematic review and meta-analysis of randomised clinical trials. *BMJ, 328*, 680–683.

Chantler, K. (2006). Independence, dependence and interdependence: Struggles and resistances of minoritized women within and on leaving violent relationships. *Feminist Review, 82*, 27–49.

Chapleau, K. M., Oswald, D. L., & Russell, B. L. (2007). How ambivalent sexism toward women and men support rape myth acceptance. *Sex Roles, 57*, 131–136.

Chaplin, T. M., Cole, P. M., & Zahn-Waxler, C. (2005). Parental socialization of emotion expression: Gender differences and relations to child adjustment. *Emotion, 5*, 80–88.

Chapple, C. L. (2003). Examining intergenerational violence: Violent role modeling or weak parental controls? *Violence and Victims, 18*, 142–162.

Characteristics and health of caregivers and care recipients—North Carolina, 2005. (2007). *Morbidity and Mortality Weekly Report, 56*, 529–532.

Charo, R. A. (2007). Politics, parents, and prophylaxis—mandating HPV vaccination in the United States. *New England Journal of Medicine, 356*, 1905–1908.

Chasteen, A. L. (1998, August). *The role of age and age-related attitudes in perceptions of elderly individuals*. Paper presented at the meeting of the American Psychological Association, San Francisco.

Chaudron, L. H., & Caine, E. D. (2004). Suicide among women: A critical review. *Journal of the American Medical Women's Association, 59*, 125–134.

Chavez, M., & Insel, T. R. (2007). Eating disorders: National Institute of Mental Health's perspective. *American Psychologist, 62*, 159–166.

Cherlin, A. J. (1998, April 5). By the numbers. *New York Times Magazine*, pp. 39–41.

Cherlin, A. J. (2005). American marriage in the early twenty-first century. *The Future of Children, 15*, 33–55.

Cherlin, A. J., & Krishnamurthy, P. (2004, May 9). What works for mom. *New York Times*, p. WK13.

Cherney, I. D., & Collaer, M. L. (2005). Sex differences in line judgment: Relation to mathematics preparation and strategy use. *Perceptual and Motor Skills, 100*, 615–627.

Cherney, I. D., & London, K. (2006). Gender-linked differences in the toys, television shows, computer games, and outdoor activities of 5- to 13-year-old children. *Sex Roles, 54*, 717–726.

Cherney, I. D., & Ryalls, B. O. (1999). Gender-linked differences in the incidental memory of children and adults. *Journal of Experimental Child Psychology, 72*, 305–328.

Cherry, F., & Deaux, K. (1978). Fear of success versus fear of gender-inappropriate behavior. *Sex Roles, 4*, 97–101.

Chesley, E. B., et al. (2004). Longitudinal impact of weight-related intentions with the initiation and maintenance of smoking among adolescents. *Journal of Adolescent Health, 34*, 130.

Chevarley, F. M., Thierry, J. M., Gill, C. J., Ryerson, A. B., & Nosek, M. A. (2006). Health, preventive health care, and health care access among women with disabilities in the

1994–1995 National Health Interview Survey, Supplement on Disability. *Women's Health Issues, 16,* 297–312.

Chhin, C. S., Bleeker, M. M., & Jacobs, J. E. (2008). Gender-typed occupational choices: The long-term impact of parents' beliefs and expectations. In H. M. G. Watt & J. S. Eccles (Eds.), *Gender and occupational outcomes: Longitudinal assessments of individual, social, and cultural influences* (pp. 215–234). Washington, DC: American Psychological Association.

Childress, S. (2003, August 4). 9/11's hidden toll. *Newsweek,* p. 37.

China's seismic shifts: Gender, suicide, sex. (2007, Summer). *Ms.,* p. 26.

Chira, S. (1994, September 20). Teen-age mothers helped by Ohio plan, study finds. *New York Times,* p. A12.

Chisholm, J., & Greene, B. (2008). Women of color: Perspectives on "multiple identities" in psychological theory, research, and practice. In F. L. Denmark & M. A. Paludi (Eds.), *Psychology of women: A handbook of issues and theories* (2nd ed., pp. 40–69). Westport, CT: Praeger.

Chiu, C. (1998). Do professional women have lower job satisfaction than professional men? Lawyers as a case study. *Sex Roles, 38,* 521–537.

Chodorow, N. J. (1990). *Feminism and the psychoanalytic theory.* New Haven, CT: Yale University Press.

Cho, L., Hoogwerf, B., Huang, J., Brennan, D. M., & Hazen, S. L. (2008). Gender differences in utilization of effective cardiovascular secondary prevention: A Cleveland clinic prevention database study. *Journal of Women's Health, 17,* 515–521.

Choi, N. G. (2000). Determinants of engagement in paid work following Social Security benefit receipt among older women. *Journal of Women & Aging, 12,* 133–154.

Chou, A. F., et al. (2007). Gender disparities in cardiovascular disease care among commercial and Medicare managed care plans. *Women's Health Issues, 17,* 139–149.

Chrisler, J. C. (2007). Body image issues of women over 50. In V. Muhlbauer & J. C. Chrisler (Eds.), *Women over 50: Psychological perspectives* (pp. 6–25). New York: Springer.

Chrisler, J. C. (2008a). The menstrual cycle in a biopsychosocial context. In F. L. Denmark & M. A. Paludi (Eds.), *Psychology of women: A handbook of issues and theories* (2nd ed., pp. 400–439). Westport, CT: Praeger.

Chrisler, J. C. (2008b). PMS as a culture-bound syndrome. In J. C. Chrisler, C. Golden, & P. D. Rozee (Eds.), *Lectures on the psychology of women* (pp. 154–171). New York: McGraw-Hill.

Chrisler, J. C. (2008c). Presidential address: Fear of losing control: Power, perfectionism, and the psychology of women. *Psychology of Women Quarterly, 32,* 1–12.

Chrisler, J. C., Johnston, I. K., Champagne, N. M., & Preston K. E. (1994). Menstrual joy: The construct and its consequences. *Psychology of Women Quarterly, 18,* 347–387.

Chrisler, J. C., Rose, J. G., Dutch, S. E., Sklarsky, K. G., & Grant, M. C. (2006). The PMS illusion: Social cognition maintains social construction. *Sex Roles, 54,* 371–376.

Christakis, N. A., & Allison, P. D. (2006). Mortality after the hospitalization of a spouse. *New England Journal of Medicine, 354,* 719–730.

Christian, A. H., Rosamond, W., White, A. R., & Mosca, L. (2007). Nine-year trends and racial and ethnic disparities in women's awareness of heart disease and stroke: An American Heart Association national study. *Journal of Women's Health, 16,* 68–81.

Christopher, A. N., & Mull, M. S. (2006). Conservative ideology and ambivalent sexism. *Psychology of Women Quarterly, 30,* 223–230.

Ciambrone, D. (2003). *Women's experiences with HIV/AIDS: Mending fractured selves.* Binghamton, NY: Haworth Press.

Cichy, K. E., Lefkowitz, E. S., & Fingerman, K. L. (2007). Generational differences in gender attitudes between parents and grown offspring. *Sex Roles, 57,* 825–836.

Ciechanowski, P., et al. (2004). Community-integrated home-based depression treatment in older adults. *Journal of the American Medical Association, 291,* 1569–1577.

Cigarette smoking among adults—United States, 2006. (2007). *Morbidity and Mortality Weekly Report, 56,* 1157–1161.

Cillessen, A. H. N., & Mayeux, L. (2004). From censure to reinforcement: Developmental changes in the association between aggression and social status. *Child Development, 75,* 147–163.

Cinamon, R. G., & Rich, Y. (2002). Gender differences in the importance of work and family roles: Implications for work-family conflict. *Sex Roles, 47,* 531–541.

Clampet-Lundquist, S., et al. (2004). "Making a way out of no way": How mothers meet basic family needs while moving from welfare to work. In A. C. Crouter & A. Booth (Eds.), *Work-family challenges for low-income parents and their children* (pp. 203–241). Mahwah, NJ: Erlbaum.

Clancy, C. M. (2000). Gender issues in women's health care. In M. B. Goldman & M. C. Hatch (Eds.), *Women & health* (pp. 50–64). New York: Academic Press.

Clapp, S. K., & Chrisler, J. C. (2008, May). *Contrapower sexual harassment of military officers.* Poster presented at the meeting of the Association for Psychological Science, Chicago.

Clark, M. A., et al. (2003). The cancer screening project for women: Experiences of women who partner with women and women who partner with men. *Women & Health, 38,* 19–33.

Clark, M. D., & Carroll, M. H. (2008). Acquaintance rape scripts of women and men: Similarities and differences. *Sex Roles, 58,* 616–625.

Clark, R. A. (1998). A comparison of topics and objectives in a cross section of young men's and women's everyday conversations. In D. J. Canary & K. Dindia (Eds.), *Sex differences and similarities in communication: Critical essays and empirical investigations of sex and gender in interaction* (pp. 303–319). Mahwah, NJ: Erlbaum.

Clark, R. A., Maupin, R. T., Jr., & Hammer, J. H. (2004). *A woman's guide to living with H.I.V. infection.* Baltimore: John Hopkins University Press.

Clarke-Stewart, A., & Miner, J. L. (2008). Effects of child and day care. In M. M. Haith & J. B. Benson (Eds.), *Encyclopedia of infant and early childhood development* (Vol. 1, pp. 268–278). San Diego, CA: Academic Press.

Clarren, R. (2005, Summer). The green motel. *Ms.,* pp. 40–45.

Clarren, R. (2007, Summer). The invisible ones. *Ms.,* pp. 40–45.

Classen, C. C., Palesh, O. G., & Aggarwal, R. (2005). Sexual revictimization. *Trauma, Violence, & Abuse, 6*, 103–129.

Clay, R. A. (2006, September). Battling the self-blame of infertility. *Monitor on Psychology, 37*, 44–45.

Clearfield, M. W., & Nelson, N. M. (2006). Sex differences in mothers' speech and play behavior with 6-, 9-, and 14-month-old infants. *Sex Roles, 54*, 127–137.

Cleary-Goldman, J., et al. (2005). Impact of maternal age on obstetric outcome. *Obstetrics & Gynecology, 105*, 983–990.

Clemetson, L. (2002, October 7). A neighborhood clinic helps fill the gap for Latinos without health care. *New York Times*, p. A12.

Cleveland, J. N., Stockdale, M., & Murphy, K. R. (2000). *Women and men in organizations: Sex and gender issues at work.* Mahwah, NJ: Erlbaum.

Cleveland, J. N., Vescio, T. K., & Barnes-Farrell, J. L. (2005). Gender discrimination in organizations. In R. L. Dipboye & A. Colella (Eds.), *Discrimination at work: The psychological and organizational bases* (pp. 149–176). Mahwah, NJ: Erlbaum.

Clewell, B. C., & Campbell, P. B. (2002). Taking stock: Where we've been, where we are, where we're going. *Journal of Women and Minorities in Science and Engineering, 8*, 255–284.

Clunis, D. M., Fredriksen-Goldsen, K. I., Freeman, P. A., & Nystrom, N. (2005). *Lives of lesbian elders: Looking back, looking forward.* Binghamton, NY: Haworth Press.

Cochran, S. D. (2001). Emerging issues in research on lesbians' and gay men's mental health: Does sexual orientation really matter? *American Psychologist, 56*, 931–947.

Cochran, S. D., & Mays, V. M. (2007). Physical health complaints among lesbians, gay men, and bisexual and homosexually experienced heterosexual individuals: Results from the California Quality of Life Survey. *American Journal of Public Health, 97*, 2048–2055.

Cognard-Black, J. (2007, Summer). Extreme makeover: Feminist edition. *Ms.*, pp. 46–49.

Cohen, D. L., & Petrie, T. A. (2005). An examination of psychosocial correlates of disordered eating among undergraduate women. *Sex Roles, 52*, 29–42.

Cohen, J. A., & Mannarino, A. P. (1998). Factors that mediate treatment outcome of sexually abused preschool children: Six- and 12-month follow-up. *Journal of the American Academy of Child & Adolescent Psychiatry, 37*, 44–51.

Cohen, J. A., Mannarino, A. P., Murray, L. K., & Igelman, R. (2006). Psychosocial interventions for maltreated and violence-exposed children. *Journal of Social Issues, 62*, 737–766.

Cohen, P., et al. (2003). Variations in patterns of developmental transitions in the emerging adulthood period. *Developmental Psychology, 39*, 657–669.

Cohen, P. N., & Huffman, M. L. (2003). Occupational segregation and the devaluation of women's work across U.S. labor markets. *Social Forces, 81*, 881–908.

Cohen, R. (2004, November 28). In South Africa, denial is a form of protection. *New York Times*, p. WK3.

Cohen, S. A. (2007). Repeat abortion, repeat unintended pregnancy, repeated and misguided government policies. *Guttmacher Policy Review, 10*, 8–16.

Cohen-Bendahan, C. C. C., van de beek, C., & Berenbaum, S. A. (2005). Prenatal sex hormone effects on child and adult sex-typed behavior: Methods and findings. *Neuroscience and Biobehavioral Reviews, 29*, 353–384.

Coie, J. D., & Dodge, K. A. (1998). Aggression and antisocial behavior. In W. Damon (Series Ed.) & N. Eisenberg (Vol. Ed.), *Handbook of child psychology: Vol. 3. Social, emotional and personality development* (5th ed., pp. 779–862). New York: Wiley.

Coker, A. L. (2007). Does physical intimate partner violence affect sexual health? *Trauma, Violence, & Abuse, 8*, 149–177.

Colcombe, S., & Kramer, A. F. (2003). Fitness effects on the cognitive function of older adults: A meta-analytic study. *Psychological Science, 14*, 125–130.

Cole, E. R., Jayaratne, T. E., Cecchi, L. A., Feldbaum, M., & Petty, E. M. (2007). Vive la difference? Genetic explanations for perceived gender differences in nurturance. *Sex Roles, 57*, 211–222.

Cole, E. R., Zucker, A. N., & Duncan, L. E. (2001). Changing society, changing women (and men). In R. K. Unger (Ed.), *Handbook of the psychology of women and gender* (pp. 410–423). New York: Wiley.

Cole, J. B., & Guy-Sheftall, B. (2003). *Gender talk: The struggle for women's equality in African American communities.* New York: Random House.

Cole, T. B. (2006). Rape at U.S. colleges often fueled by alcohol. *Journal of the American Medical Association, 296*, 504–505.

Coley, R. L., & Chase-Lansdale, P. L. (1998). Adolescent pregnancy and parenthood: Recent evidence and future directions. *American Psychologist, 53*, 152–166.

Colgan, F., Creegan, C., McKearney, A., & Wright, T. (2008). Lesbian workers: Personal strategies amid changing organizational responses to 'sexual minorities' in UK workplaces. *Journal of Lesbian Studies, 12*, 31–45.

Coll, C. T. G., Meyer, E. C., & Brillon, L. (1995). Ethnic and minority parenting. In M. H. Bornstein (Ed.), *Handbook of parenting. Vol. 2. Biology and ecology of parenting* (pp. 189–209). Mahwah, NJ: Erlbaum.

Colley, A., Berman, E., & Van Millingen, L. (2005). Age and gender differences in young people's perceptions of sport participants. *Journal of Applied Social Psychology, 35*, 1440–1454.

Collins, A. (1997). A psychological approach to the management of menopause. In B. G. Wren (Ed.), *Progress in the management of the menopause* (pp. 94–98). Pearl River, NY: Parthenon.

Collins, K. A., Bennett, A. T., & Hanzlick, R. (2000). Elder abuse and neglect. *Archives of Internal Medicine, 160*, 1567–1568.

Collins, K. S., & Simon, L. J. (1996). Women's health and managed care: Promises and challenges. *Women's Health Issues, 6*(1), 39–44.

Collins, W. A., & Steinberg, L. (2006). Adolescent development in interpersonal context. In W. Damon, R. M. Lerner (Series Eds.) & N. Eisenberg (Vol. Ed.), *Handbook of child psychology: Vol. 3. Social, emotional, and personality development* (6th ed., pp. 1003–1067). Hoboken, NJ: Wiley.

Colón-Emeric, C. S. (2006). Ten vs five years of bisphosphonate treatment for postmenopausal osteoporosis. *Journal of the American Medical Association, 296*, 2968–2969.

Colton, P. A., Olmsted, M. P., & Rodin, G. M. (2007). Eating disturbances in a school population of preteen girls: Assessment and screening. *International Journal of Eating Disorders, 40*, 435–440.

Coltrane, S. (1997, Spring). Families and gender equity. *National Forum, 77*, 31–34.

Coltrane, S. (2000). Research on household labor: Modeling and measuring the social embeddedness of routine family work. *Journal of Marriage and the Family, 62*, 1208–1233.

Coltrane, S., & Messineo, M. (2000). The perpetuation of subtle prejudice: Race and gender imagery in 1990s television advertising. *Sex Roles, 42*, 363–389.

Commission on Women's Health. (2003). *The Commonwealth Fund Survey of women's health*. New York: Commonwealth Fund.

Commonwealth Fund. (1993). *The untapped resource: The final report of the Americans over 55 at Work program*. New York: Author.

Commonwealth Fund. (1997). *In their own words: Adolescent girls discuss health and health care issues*. New York: Author.

Commonwealth Fund. (1998). *The Commonwealth Fund 1998 survey of women's health*. New York: Author.

Compas, B. E., & Luecken, L. (2002). Psychological adjustment to breast cancer. *Current Directions in Psychological Science, 11*, 111–114.

Compian, L., & Hayward, C. (2003). Gender differences in opposite sex relationships: Interactions with puberty. In C. Hayward (Ed.), *Gender differences at puberty* (pp. 77–92). Cambridge: Cambridge University Press.

Comstock, G. (1991). *Television and the American child*. Orlando, FL: Academic Press.

Conkright, L., Flannagan, D., & Dykes, J. (2000). Effects of pronoun type and gender role consistency on children's recall and interpretation of stories. *Sex Roles, 43*, 481–497.

Conrad, C. (2005, July 22). The womanly art of negotiating. *Chronicle of Higher Education*, pp. C2–C3.

Considine, N. S., et al. (2004). Fear, anxiety, worry, and breast cancer screening behavior: A critical review. *Cancer Epidemiology, Biomarkers & Prevention, 13*, 501–510.

Coontz, S. (2006, June 5). Three 'rules' that don't apply. *Newsweek*, p. 49.

Coovadia, H. (2004). Antiretroviral agents—how best to protect infants from HIV and save their mothers from AIDS. *New England Journal of Medicine, 351*, 289–291.

Corbett, S. (2008, January 20). Inside a female-circumcision ceremony for young Muslim girls. *New York Times Magazine*, pp. 45–50.

Corcoran, K., & Ellin, A. (2003, August 3). Shattering ceilings. *New York Times*, p. BU12.

Corliss, H. L., Shankle, M. D., & Moyer, M. B. (2007). Research, curricula, and resources related to lesbian, gay, bisexual, and transgender health in U.S. schools of public health. *American Journal of Public Health, 97*, 1023–1027.

Cornelius, N., & Skinner, D. (2008). The careers of senior men and women—capabilities theory perspective. *British Journal of Management, 19*, S141–S149.

Correa-de-Araujo, R. (2005). It's your health: Use your medications safely. *Journal of Women's Health, 14*, 16–18.

Correa-de-Araujo, R., Miller, E., Banthin, J. S., & Trinh, Y. (2005). Gender differences in drug use and expenditures in a privately insured population of older adults. *Journal of Women's Health, 14*, 73–80.

Correa-de-Araujo, R., Stevens, B., Moy, E., Nilasena, D., Chesley, F., & McDermott, K. (2006). Gender differences across racial and ethnic groups in the quality of care for acute myocardial infarction and heart failure associated with comorbidities. *Women's Health Issues, 16*, 44–55.

Correll, S. J., Benard, S., & Paik, I. (2007). Getting a job: Is there a motherhood penalty? *American Journal of Sociology, 112*, 1297–1338.

Corrigall, E. A., & Konrad, A. M. (2006). The relationship of job attribute preferences to employment, hours of paid work, and family responsibilities: An analysis comparing women and men. *Sex Roles, 54*, 95–111.

Corrigall, E. A., & Konrad, A. M. (2007). Gender role attitudes and careers: A longitudinal study. *Sex Roles, 56*, 847–855.

Cortina, L. M. (2004). Hispanic perspectives on sexual harassment and social support. *Personality and Social Psychology Bulletin, 30*, 570–584.

Cortina, L. M., & Magley, V. J. (2003). Raising voice, risking retaliation: Events following interpersonal mistreatment in the workplace. *Journal of Occupational Health Psychology, 8*, 247–265.

Cosgrove, L., & Riddle, B. (2003). Constructions of femininity and experiences of menstrual distress. *Women & Health, 38*, 37–58.

Costello, C. B., & Stone, A. J. (Eds.). (2001). *The American woman 2001–2002*. New York: W. W. Norton.

Costello, C. B., & Wight, V. R. (2003). Taking it from here: Policies for the twenty-first century. In C. B. Costello, V. R. Wight, & A. J. Stone (Eds.), *The American woman 2003–2004: Daughters of a revolution—young women today* (pp. 127–142). New York: Palgrave Macmillan.

Costello, D., Swendsen, J., Rose, J., & Dierker, L. C. (2008). Risk and protective factors associated with trajectories of depressed mood from adolescence to early adulthood. *Journal of Consulting and Clinical Psychology, 76*, 173–183.

Costello, E. J., et al. (2003). Prevalence and development of psychiatric disorders in childhood and adolescence. *Archives of General Psychiatry, 60*, 837–844.

Costigan, C. L., Cauce, A. M., & Etchison, K. (2007). Changes in African American mother–daughter relationships during adolescence: Conflict, autonomy, and warmth. In B. J. R. Leadbeater & N. Way (Eds.), *Urban girls revisited: Building strengths* (pp. 177–201). New York: New York University Press.

Costos, D., Ackerman, R., & Paradis, L. (2002). Recollections of menarche: Communication between mothers and daughters regarding menstruation. *Sex Roles, 46*, 49–59.

Cotter, D. A., Hermsen, J. M., Ovadia, S., & Vanneman, R. (2001). The glass ceiling effect. *Social Forces, 80*, 655–681.

Coulter, I., Jacobson, P., & Parker, L. E. (2000). Sharing the mantle of primary female care: Physicians, nurse practitioners, and physician assistants. *Journal of the American Medical Women's Association*, 55, 100–103.

Cowan, G. (2000). Beliefs about the causes of four types of rape. *Sex Roles*, 42, 807–823.

Cowley, G., & Murr, A. (2004, December 6). The new face of AIDS. *Newsweek*, pp. 76–79.

Cox, D. L., et al. (2006, August). *Just between us: Mother-daughter relationships in the context of U.S. beauty culture*. Paper presented at the annual meeting of the American Psychological Association, New Orleans, LA.

Coyle, A. (2005). Changing times: Flexibilization and the re-organization of work in feminized labour markets. *The Sociological Review*, 53, 73–88.

Cozzarelli, C., Wilkinson, A. V., & Tagler, M. J. (2001). Attitudes toward the poor and attributions for poverty. *Journal of Social Issues*, 57, 207–228.

Crawford, D., & Ostrove, J. M. (2003). Representations of disability and the interpersonal relationships of women with disabilities. *Women & Therapy*, 26, 179–194.

Crawford, M. (2001). Gender and language. In R. K. Unger (Ed.), *Handbook of the psychology of women and gender* (pp. 228–244). New York: Wiley.

Crawford, M., & MacLeod, M. (1990). Gender in the college classroom: An assessment of the "chilly climate" for women. *Sex Roles*, 23, 101–122.

Creighton, J. V. (2007, May 21). Why we need women's colleges. *The Boston Globe*, p. A9.

Crenshaw, A. B. (2002, June 2). Her next stop? Growing numbers of American women face retirement financially poor. *Washington Post*, pp. H1, H3.

Creswell, J. (2006, December 17). How suite it isn't: A dearth of female bosses. *New York Times*, pp. BU9–BU11.

Crockett, L. J. (1991). Sex roles and sex-typing in adolescence. In R. M. Lerner, A. C. Petersen, & J. Brooks-Gunn (Eds.), *Encyclopedia of adolescence* (Vol. 2, pp. 1007–1017). New York: Garland.

Crofford, L. J. (2007). Violence, stress, and somatic syndromes. *Trauma, Violence, & Abuse*, 8, 299–313.

Crombie, G., et al. (2005). Predictors of young adolescents' math grades and course enrollment intentions: Gender similarities and difference. *Sex Roles*, 52, 351–367.

Crosby, F. J. (1991). *Juggling: The unexpected advantages of balancing career and home for women and their families*. New York: Free Press.

Crosby, F. J. (2008). Sex discrimination at work. In J. C. Chrisler, C. Golden, & P. D. Rozee (Eds.), *Lectures on the psychology of women* (pp. 42–57). New York: McGraw-Hill.

Crosby, F. J., & Sabattini, L. (2006). Family and work balance. In J. Worell & C. D. Goodheart (Eds.), *Handbook of girls' and women's psychological health: Gender and well-being across the life-span* (pp. 350–358). New York: Oxford University Press.

Crosby, F. J., Stockdale, M. S., & Ropp, S. A. (Eds.). (2007). *Sex discrimination in the workplace*. Malden, MA: Blackwell.

Crouter, A. C., Whiteman, S. D., McHale, S. M., & Osgood, D. W. (2007). Development of gender attitude traditionality across middle childhood and adolescence. *Child Development*, 78, 911–926.

Crow, S. J. (2006). Fluoxetine treatment of anorexia nervosa: Important but disappointing results. *Journal of the American Medical Association*, 295, 2659–2660.

Crowley, J. D. (2003). The anger of hope and the anger of despair: How anger relates to women's depression. In J. M. Stoppard & L. M. McMullen (Eds.), *Situating sadness: Women and depression in social context* (pp. 62–87). New York and London: New York University Press.

Crowley, K., Callanan, M. A., Tenenbaum, H. R., & Allen, E. (2001). Parents explain more often to boys than to girls during shared scientific thinking. *Psychological Science*, 12, 258–261.

Cuddy, A. J. C., Fiske, S. T., & Glick, P. (2004). When professionals become mothers, warmth doesn't cut the ice. *Journal of Social Issues*, 60, 701–718.

Cuddy, A. J. C., Norton, M. I., & Fiske, S. T. (2005). This old stereotype: The pervasiveness and persistence of the elderly stereotype. *Journal of Social Issues*, 61, 267–285.

Cuijpers, P., Brännmark, J. G., & van Straten, A. (2008). Psychological treatment of postpartum depression: A meta-analysis. *Journal of Clinical Psychology*, 64, 103–118.

Culp, L. N., & Beach, S. R. H. (1998). Marriage and depressive symptoms: The role and bases of self-esteem differ by gender. *Psychology of Women Quarterly*, 22, 647–663.

Cummings, A. L., & Leschied, A. W. (Eds.). (2002). *Research and treatment for aggression with adolescent girls*. In *Mellen studies in social work* (Vol. 5). Lewiston, NY: Edwin Mellen Press.

Cunningham, G. B. (2008). Creating and sustaining gender diversity in sport organizations. *Sex Roles*, 58, 136–145.

Cunningham, J., & Macan, T. (2007). Effects of applicant pregnancy on hiring decisions and interview ratings. *Sex Roles*, 57, 497–508.

Cunningham, M. (2001). The influence of parental attitudes and behaviors on children's attitudes toward gender and household labor in early adulthood. *Journal of Marriage and Family*, 63, 111–122.

Cunningham, M., Beutel, A. M., Barber, J. S., & Thornton, A. (2005). Reciprocal relationships between attitudes about gender and social contexts during young adulthood. *Social Science Research*, 34, 862–892.

Curtis, G., & Schuler, J. (2004). *Your pregnancy week by week* (5th ed.). Cambridge, MA: DaCapo Press.

Curtis, L. H., et al. (2004). Inappropriate prescribing for elderly Americans in a large outpatient population. *Archives of Internal Medicine*, 164, 1621–1625.

Cynkar, A. (2007, June). The changing gender composition of psychology. *Monitor on Psychology*, 38, 46–47.

Dailard, C. (2002). Abstinence promotion and teen family planning: The misguided move for equal funding. *The Guttmacher Report on Public Policy*, 5, 1–3.

Dailard, C. (2003a). Marriage is no immunity from problems with planning pregnancies. *The Guttmacher Report on Public Policy*, pp. 10–13.

Dailard, C. (2003b). Understanding "abstinence": Implications for individuals, programs and policies. *The Guttmacher Report on Public Policy*, pp. 4–6.

Daly, E. (2005, February 8). Specialists trying to unravel the mystery of miscarriage. *New York Times*, pp. D5, D8.

Daly, K. (2004). Exploring process and control in families working nonstandard schedules. In A. C. Crouter & A. Booth (Eds.), *Work-family challenges for low-income parents and their children* (pp. 117–125). Mahwah, NJ: Erlbaum.

Dambrun, M. (2007). Gender differences in mental health: The mediating role of perceived personal discrimination. *Journal of Applied Social Psychology, 37*, 1118–1129.

D'Amico, M., Baron, L. J., & Sissons, M. E. (1995). Gender differences in attributions about microcomputer learning in elementary school. *Sex Roles, 33*, 353–385.

Daniels, E., & Leaper, C. (2006). A longitudinal investigation of sport participation, peer acceptance, and self-esteem among adolescent girls and boys. *Sex Roles, 55*, 875–880.

Daniluk, J. C. (1998). *Women's sexuality across the life span: Challenging myths, creating meanings.* New York: Guilford.

Daniluk, J. C., & Towill, K. (2001). Sexuality education: What is it, who gets it, and does it work? In R. K. Unger (Ed.), *Handbook of the psychology of women and gender* (pp. 1023–1031). New York: Wiley.

Danner, F., Noland, F., McFadden, M., Dewalt, K., & Kotchen, J. M. (1991). Description of the physical activity of young children using movement sensor and observation methods. *Pediatric Exercise Science, 3*, 11–20.

D'Arcy, J. (1998, August 24). Marriage and family vs. career. *Hartford Courant*, pp. F1, F3.

Dardenne, B., Dumont, M., & Bollier, T. (2007). Insidious dangers of benevolent sexism: Consequences for women's performance. *Journal of Personality and Social Psychology, 93*, 764–779.

Dar-Nimrod, I., & Heine, S. J. (2006). Exposure to scientific theories affects women's math performance. *Science, 314*, 435.

Darroch, J. E., Frost, J. J., Singh, S., & the Study Team. (2001). *Teenage sexual and reproductive behavior in developed countries: Can more progress be made?* Occasional Report No. 3. New York: Alan Guttmacher Institute.

Daubman, K. A., Heatherington, L., & Ahn, A. (1992). Gender and the self-presentation of academic achievement. *Sex Roles, 27*, 187–204.

Daubman, K. A., & Sigall, H. (1997). Gender differences in perceptions of how others are affected by self-disclosure of achievement. *Sex Roles, 37*, 73–89.

Davey, A., & Szinovacz, M. E. (2004). Dimensions of marital quality and retirement. *Journal of Family Issues, 25*, 431–464.

Davey, E. H. (1998). Young women's expected and preferred patterns of employment and child care. *Sex Roles, 38*, 95–102.

David, H. P., & Lee, E. (2001). Abortion and its health effects. In J. Worell (Ed.), *Encyclopedia of women and gender* (pp. 1–14). San Diego: Academic Press.

David, S., & Knight, B. (2002, August). *Stress and coping among lesbian, gay, bisexual, and transgender older adults.* Paper presented at the meeting of the American Psychological Association, Chicago.

Davidson, P., et al. (2008). A cardiac rehabilitation program to improve psychosocial outcomes of women with heart disease. *Journal of Women's Health, 17*, 123–134.

Davies, P. G., Spencer, S. J., & Steele, C. M. (2005). Clearing the air: Identity safety moderates the effects of stereotype threat on women's leadership aspirations. *Journal of Personality and Social Psychology, 88*, 276–287.

Davies, P. T., Forman, E. M., Rasi, J. A., & Stevens, K. I. (2002). Assessing children's emotional security in the interparental relationship: The security in the interparental subsystem scales. *Child Development, 73*, 546–562.

Davila, J. (2008). Depressive symptoms and adolescent romance: Theory, research, and implications. *Child Development Perspectives, 2*, 26–31.

Davis, M. K., & Gidycz, C. A. (2000). Child sexual abuse prevention programs: A meta-analysis. *Journal of Clinical Child Psychology, 29*, 257–265.

Davis, P. J. (1999). Gender differences in autobiographical memory for childhood emotional experiences. *Journal of Personality and Social Psychology, 76*, 498–510.

Davis, S. D., Crawford, M., & Sebrechts, J. (Eds.). (1999). *Coming into her own: Educational success in girls and women.* San Francisco: Jossey-Bass.

Davison, H. K., & Burke, M. J. (2000). Sex discrimination in simulated employment contexts: A meta-analytic investigation. *Journal of Vocational Behavior, 56*, 225–248.

Daw, J. (2002, October). Is PMDD real? *Monitor on Psychology*, pp. 58–60.

Day, J. C., & Newburger, E. C. (2002). *The big payoff: Educational attainment and synthetic estimates of work-life earnings.* Current Population Reports P23–210. Washington, DC: U.S. Census Bureau.

Deal, J. J., & Stevenson, M. A. (1998). Perceptions of female and male managers in the 1990s: Plu ca change . . . . *Sex Roles, 38*, 287–300.

DeAngelis, C. D., & Glass, R. M. (2006). Women's health—advances in knowledge and understanding. *Journal of the American Medical Association, 295*, 1448–1450.

DeAngelis, T. (2001, December). Are men emotional mummies? *Monitor on Psychology*, pp. 40, 41.

DeAngelis, T. (2005, November). Cosmetic surgery's dark side. *Monitor on Pyschology, 36*, 41.

DeArmond, S., Tye, M., Chen, P. Y., Krauss, A., Rogers, D. A., & Sintek, E. (2006). Age and gender stereotypes: New challenges in a changing workplace and workforce. *Journal of Applied Social Psychology, 36*, 2184–2214.

Deaux, K., & Stewart, A. J. (2001). Framing gendered identities. In R. K. Unger (Ed.), *Handbook of the psychology of women and gender* (pp. 84–97). New York: Wiley.

DeBell, M., & Chapman, C. (2004). *Computer and Internet use by children and adolescents in 2001.* U.S. Department of Education, National Center for Education Statistics. NCES 2004-014. Washington, DC: U.S. Department of Education.

Declercq, E., Menacker, F., & MacDorman, M. (2006). Maternal risk profiles and the primary cesarean rate in the United States, 1991–2002. *American Journal of Public Health, 96*, 867–872.

DeGroot, J., & Fine, J. (2003). Integrating work and life: Young women forge new solutions. In C. B. Costello, V. R. Wight, & A. J. Stone (Eds.), *The American woman 2003–2004: Daughters of a revolution—young women today* (pp. 127–142). New York: Palgrave Macmillan.

de Guzman, M. R. T., Gustavo, C., Ontai, L. L., Koller, S. H., & Knight, G. P. (2004, August). Gender and age differences in Brazilian children's friendship nominations and peer sociometric ratings. *Sex Roles, 51*, 217–225.

DeJong Gierveld, J. (2004). Remarriage, unmarried cohabitation, living apart together: Partner relationships following bereavement or divorce. *Journal of Marriage and Family, 66*, 236–243.

Deklyen, M., Brooks-Gunn, J., Mclanahan, S., & Knab, J. (2006). The mental health of married, cohabiting, and non-coresident parents with infants. *American Journal of Public Health, 96*, 1836–1841.

Delaney, J., Lupton, M. J., & Toth, E. (1988). *The curse: A cultural history of menstruation* (Rev. ed.). Urbana: University of Illinois.

de las Fuentes, C., & Vasquez, M. J. T. (1999). Immigrant adolescent girls of color: Facing American challenges. In N. G. Johnson, M. C. Roberts, & J. Worell (Eds.), *Beyond appearance: A new look at adolescent girls* (pp. 131–150). Washington, DC: American Psychological Association.

De Lisi, R., & Soundranayagam, L. (1990). The conceptual structure of sex role stereotypes in college students. *Sex Roles, 23*, 593–611.

DeLoach, C. P. (1989). Gender, career choice and occupational outcomes among college alumni with disabilities. *Journal of Applied Rehabilitation Counseling, 20*, 8–12.

DeLoache, J. S., Simcock, G., & Macari, S. (2007). Planes, trains, automobiles—and tea sets: Extremely intense interests in very young children. *Developmental Psychology, 43*, 1579–1586.

DeNavas-Walt, C., Proctor, B. D., & Mills, R. J. (2004). *Income, poverty, and health insurance coverage in the United States: 2003.* Current Population Reports, P60–226. Washington, DC: U.S. Census Bureau.

DeNavas-Walt, C., Proctor, B. D., & Smith, J. (2007). *Income, poverty, and health insurance coverage in the United States: 2006.* Current Population Reports, P60–233. Washington, DC: U.S. Census Bureau.

Denissen, J. J. A., Zarrett, N. R., & Eccles, J. S. (2007). I like to do it, I'm able, and I know I am: Longitudinal couplings between domain-specific achievement, self-concept, and interest. *Child Development, 78*, 430–447.

Denizet-Lewis, B. (2004, May 30). Friends, friends with benefits and the benefits of the local mall. *New York Times Magazine*, pp. 30–35, 54–58.

Denmark, F. L. (1994). Engendering psychology. *American Psychologist, 49*, 329–334.

Denmark, F. L. (1999). Enhancing the development of adolescent girls. In N. G. Johnson, M. C. Roberts, & J. Worell (Eds.), *Beyond appearance: A new look at adolescent girls* (pp. 337–404). Washington, DC: American Psychological Association.

Denmark, F. L., & Klara, M. D. (2007). Empowerment: A prime time for women over 50. In V. Muhlbauer & J. C. Chrisler (Eds.), *Women over 50: Psychological perspectives* (pp. 182–203). New York: Springer.

Denmark, F. L., Klara, M. D., Baron, E., & Cambareri-Fernandez, L. (2008). Historical development of the psychology of women. In F. L. Denmark & M. A. Paludi (Eds.), *Psychology of women: A handbook of issues and theories* (2nd ed., pp. 3–39). Westport, CT: Praeger.

Denmark, F. L., Novick, K., & Pinto, A. (1996). Women, work, and family: Mental health issues. In J. E. Sechzer, S. M. Pfafflin, F. L. Denmark, A. Griffin, & S. J. Blumental (Eds.), *Women and mental health* (pp. 101–117). New York: Academy of Sciences.

Denmark, F. L., Rabinowitz, V., & Sechzer, J. (2000). *Engendering psychology.* Needham Heights, MA: Allyn & Bacon.

Denner, J., & Coyle, K. (2006). Condom use among sexually active Latina girls in alternative high schools. In B. J. R. Leadbeater & N. Way (Eds.), *Urban girls revisited: Building strengths* (pp. 281–300). New York: New York University Press.

Dennerstein, L., Lehert, P., Koochaki, P. E., Graziottin, A., Leiblum, S., & Alexander, J. L. (2007). A symptomatic approach to understanding women's health experiences: A cross-cultural comparison of women aged 20 to 70 years. *Menopause, 14*, 688–696.

Department of Defense. (2008). *FY07 report on sexual assault in the military.* Washington, DC: Author.

DePaulo, B. M., Moran, R. F., & Trimberger, E. K. (2007, September 28). Make room for singles in teaching and research. *The Chronicle of Higher Education*, pp. B44–B45.

DePaulo, B. M., & Morris, W. L. (2006). The unrecognized stereotyping and discrimination against singles. *Current Directions in Psychological Science, 15*, 251–254.

Depression across the lifespan. (2003, August). *National Women's Health Report, 25*, 6.

Depression & women. (2003, August). *National Women's Health Report, 25*, 1–4.

D'Erasmo, S. (2004, January 11). Lesbians on television: It's not easy being seen. *New York Times*, p. 1.

DeRose, L. M., & Brooks-Gunn, J. (2006). Transition into adolescence: The role of pubertal processes. In L. Balter & C. S. Tamis-LeMonda (Eds.), *Child psychology: A handbook of contemporary issues* (2nd ed., pp. 385–414). New York: Taylor & Francis.

Derry, P. S. (2006). A lifespan biological model of menopause. *Sex Roles, 54*, 393–399.

Désert, M., & Leyens, J.-P. (2006). Social comparison across cultures: I. Gender stereotypes in high and low power distance cultures. In S. Guimond (Ed.), *Social comparison and social psychology: Understanding cognition, intergroup relations and culture* (pp. 303–317). Cambridge: Cambridge University Press.

DeSouza, E. R. (2003, August). Antecedents and consequences of peer sexual harassment in Brazil. In E. R. DeSouza (Chair), *Sexual harassment of school-age students: A cross-cultural perspective.* Symposium presented at the meeting of the American Psychological Association, Toronto.

DeUgarte, C. M., et al. (2004). Female sexual dysfunction—from diagnosis to treatment. *Sexuality, Reproduction & Menopause, 2*, 139–145.

DeUgarte, C. M., Berman, L., & Berman, J. (2004). Female sexual dysfunction—from diagnosis to treatment. *Sexuality, Reproduction & Menopause, 2*, 139–145.

Deutsch, F. M., & Saxon, S. E. (1998). Traditional ideologies, nontraditional lives. *Sex Roles, 38,* 331–362.

de Waal, F. B. M. (2002). Evolutionary psychology: The wheat and the chaff. *Current Directions in Psychological Science, 11,* 187–191.

Dey, J. G., & Hill, C. (2007). *Behind the pay gap.* Washington, DC: American Association of University Women Educational Foundation.

DeZolt, D. M., & Hull, S. H. (2001). Classroom and social climate. In J. Worell (Ed.), *Encyclopedia of women and gender* (pp. 257–264). San Diego: Academic Press.

Diamond, D., Diamond, M., & Jaffe, J. (2005, August). *The psychology of reproductive traumas: Infertility and pregnancy loss.* Paper presented at the meeting of the American Psychological Association, San Diego, CA.

Diamond, L. M. (2003a). Was it a phase? Young women's relinquishment of lesbian/bisexual identities over a 5-year period. *Journal of Personality and Social Psychology, 84,* 352–364.

Diamond, L. M. (2003b). What does sexual orientation orient? A biobehavioral model distinguishing romantic love and sexual desire. *Psychological Review, 110,* 173–192.

Diamond, L. M. (2004). Emerging perspectives on distinctions between romantic love and sexual desire. *Current Directions in Psychological Science, 13,* 116–119.

Diamond, L. M. (2007). A dynamical systems approach to the development and expression of female same-sex sexuality. *Perspectives on Psychological Science, 2,* 142–161.

Diamond, L. M. (2008). Female bisexuality from adolescence to adulthood: Results from a 10-year longitudinal study. *Developmental Psychology, 44,* 5–14.

Diamond, M. (1997). Sexual identity and sexual orientation in children with traumatized or ambiguous genitalia. *Journal of Sex Research, 34,* 199–211.

Dickhäuser, O., & Stiensmeier-Pelster, J. (2002). Gender differences in computer work: Evidence for the model of achievement-related choices. *Contemporary Educational Psychology, 27,* 486–496.

DiClemente, R. J., et al. (2004). Efficacy of an HIV prevention intervention for African American adolescent girls: A randomized controlled trial. *Journal of the American Medical Association, 292,* 171–179.

Diekman, A. B., & Eagly, A. H. (1997, May). *Past, present, and future: Perceptions of change in women and men.* Paper presented at the meeting of the Midwestern Psychological Association, Chicago.

Diekman, A. B., Goodfriend, W., & Goodwin, S. (2004). Dynamic stereotypes of power: Perceptions of change and stability in gender hierarchies. *Sex Roles, 50,* 201–215.

Diener, E., Gohm, C. L., Suh, M., & Oishi, S. (2000). Similarity of the relation between marital status and subjective well-being across cultures. *Journal of Cross-Cultural Psychology, 31,* 419–436.

Diener, E., & Seligman, M. E. P. (2004). Beyond money: Toward an economy of well-being. *Psychological Science in the Public Interest, 5,* 1–31.

Dierbeck, L. (2003). Choosing childlessness. In L. Slater, J. H. Daniel, & A. E. Banks (Eds.), *The complete guide to mental health for women* (pp. 40–47). Boston: Beacon Press.

Dill, K. E., et al. (2001, August). *Violence, sex, race and age in popular video games: A content analysis.* Paper presented at the meeting of the American Psychological Association, San Francisco.

Dill, K. E., & Thill, K. P. (2007). Video game characters and the socialization of gender roles: Young people's perceptions mirror sexist media depictions. *Sex Roles, 57,* 851–864.

Dillaway, H. E. (2005). (Un)changing menopausal bodies: How women think and act in the face of a reproductive transition and gendered beauty ideals. *Sex Roles, 53,* 1–17.

Dillon, S. (2002, June 15). Women tell of priests' abusing them as girls. *New York Times,* p. A11.

DiMatteo, M. R. (2004). Social support and patient adherence to medical treatment: A meta-analysis. *Health Psychology, 23,* 207–218.

DiMatteo, M. R., & Kahn, K. L. (1997). Psychosocial aspects of childbirth. In S. J. Gallant, G. Puryear Keita, & R. Royak-Schaler (Eds.), *Health care for women: Psychological, social, and behavioral influences* (pp. 175–186). Washington, DC: American Psychological Association.

DiNatale, M., & Boraas, S. (2003). Young women, education, and employment. In C. B. Costello, V. R. Wight, & A. J. Stone (Eds.), *The American woman 2003–2004: Daughters of a revolution—young women today* (pp. 69–92). New York: Palgrave Macmillan.

Dingfelder, S. F. (2005, December). The kids are all right. *Monitor on Psychology, 36,* 66–67.

Dion, K. L., & Cota, A. A. (1991). The Ms. stereotype: Its domain and the role of explicitness in title preference. *Psychology of Women Quarterly, 15,* 403–410.

Dion, K. L., & Schuller, R. A. (1990). Ms. and the manager: A tale of two stereotypes. *Sex Roles, 22,* 569–577.

Disparities in premature deaths from heart disease—50 states and the District of Columbia, 2001. (2004, February 20). *Morbidity and Mortality Weekly Report, 53,* 121–125.

Dittmann, M. (2003, March). Coping with cancer through social connection. *Monitor on Psychology,* pp. 24–26.

Dittmann, M. (2005, September). Plastic surgery: Beauty or beast? *Monitor on Psychology, 36,* 30–32.

Dittmar, H., Halliwell, E., & Ive, S. (2006). Does Barbie make girls want to be thin? The effect of experimental exposure to images of dolls on the body image of 5- to 8-year-old girls. *Developmental Psychology, 42,* 283–292.

Dodge, K. A., Coie, J. D., & Lynam, D. (2006). Aggression and antisocial behavior in youth. In W. Damon, R. M. Lerner (Series Eds.), & N. Eisenberg (Vol. Ed.), *Handbook of child psychology: Vol. 3. Social, emotional, and personality development* (6th ed., pp. 719–788). Hoboken, NJ: Wiley.

Dodson, L., & Dickert, J. (2004). Girls' family labor in low-income households: A decade of qualitative research. *Journal of Marriage and Family, 66,* 318–332.

Doering, L. V., Cross, R., Magsarili, M. C., Howitt, L. Y., & Cowan, M. J. (2007). Utility of observer-rated and self-report instruments for detecting major depression in women after cardiac surgery: A pilot study. *American Journal of Critical Care, 16,* 260–269.

Dogar, R. (1999, Spring/Summer). STDs: Better safe than sorry. *Newsweek,* pp. 54–55.

Dohnt, H., & Tiggemann, M. (2006). The contribution of peer and media influences to the development of body satisfaction and self-esteem in young girls: A prospective study. *Developmental Psychology, 42,* 929–936.

Dominus, S. (2002, September 29). Shabana is late for school. *New York Times Magazine,* pp. 42–47, 56, 62–63, 118–120.

Dominus, S. (2004, October 24). Growing up with mom and mom. *New York Times Magazine,* pp. 68–75, 84, 143–144.

Donatelle, R. J. (2009). *Access to health, green edition* (11th ed.). San Francisco, CA: Benjamin Cummings.

Donatelle, R. J., & Davis, L. G. (1998). *Access to health* (5th ed.). Boston: Allyn & Bacon.

Donohoe, M. (2005). Increase in obstacles to abortion: The American perspective in 2004. *Journal of the American Medical Women's Association, 60,* 16–25.

Donor-egg pregnancies called safe after age 50. (2002, November 12). *New York Times,* p. A27.

Donovan, R. A., Sillice, M., & Masdea, J. R. (2005, March). *Have things changed? Contemporary images of Black and White women.* Paper presented at the annual meeting of the American Psychological Association, Washington, DC.

Doress-Worters, P. B., & Siegal, D. L. (1994). *The new ourselves growing older.* New York: Simon & Schuster.

Dorfman, L. T. (1995). Health, financial status, and social participation of retired rural men and women: Implications for educational intervention. *Educational Gerontology, 21,* 653–669.

Dorfman, L. T., & Rubenstein, L. M. (1993). Paid and unpaid activities and retirement satisfaction among rural seniors. *Physical & Occupational Therapy in Geriatrics, 12,* 45–63.

Döring, N. (2000). Feminist views of cybersex: Victimization, liberation, and empowerment. *Cyberpsychology & Behavior, 3,* 863–884.

Dorn, J. M., et al. (2007). Alcohol drinking pattern and non-fatal myocardial infarction in women. *Addiction, 102,* 730–739.

Dotson, L. A., Stinson, J., & Christian, L. (2003). "People tell me I can't have sex": Women with disabilities share their personal perspectives on health care, sexuality, and reproductive rights. *Women & Therapy, 26,* 195–209.

Douglas, S. J., & Michaels, M. (2004). *The mommy myth: The idealization of motherhood and how it has undermined women.* New York: Free Press.

Dowd, J. J. (2007, August). *The grip of tradition: Hollywood film and the reproduction of women's place.* Paper presented at the meeting of the American Sociological Association, New York.

Dowling, W. (2001). Volunteerism among older women. In J. M. Coyle (Ed.), *Handbook on women and aging* (pp. 242–252). Westport, CT: Greenwood.

Downing, R. A., Crosby, F. J., & Blake-Beard, S. (2005). The perceived importance of developmental relationships on women undergraduates' pursuit of science. *Psychology of Women Quarterly, 29,* 419–426.

Downs, B. (2003). *Fertility of American women: June 2002.* Current Population Reports, P20–548. Washington, DC: U.S. Census Bureau.

Draper, B., et al. (2008). Long-term effects of childhood abuse on the quality of life and health of older people: Results from the Depression and Early Prevention of Suicide in General Practice Project. *Journal of the American Geriatrics Society, 56,* 262–271.

Driscoll, M., & Groskop, V. (2003, January 5). Being a women isn't an illness. *Sun Times (London),* p. 14.

Dube, K. (2004, June 18). What feminism means to today's undergraduates. *Chronicle of Higher Education,* p. B5.

Duehr, E. E., & Bono, J. E. (2006). Men, women, and managers: Are stereotypes finally changing? *Personnel Psychology, 59,* 815–846.

Duenwald, M., & Stamler, B. (2004, April 13). On their own, in the same boat. *New York Times,* pp. E1, E13.

Duff, J. L. (1996). *The best of friends: Exploring the moral domain of adolescent friendship.* Unpublished doctoral dissertation, Stanford University.

Duffy, J., Wareham, S., & Walsh, M. (2004). Psychological consequences for high school students of having been sexually harassed. *Sex Roles, 50,* 811–821.

Dugger, K. (1988). Social location and gender-role attitudes: A comparison of black and white women. *Gender & Society, 2,* 425–448.

Duncan, L. E., Peterson, B. E., & Ax, E. E. (2003). Authoritarianism as an agent of status quo maintenance: Implications for women's careers and family lives. *Sex Roles, 49,* 619–630.

Dunham, K. J. (2003, August 26). Stay-at-home dads fight stigma. *New York Times,* pp. B1, B6.

Dunifon, R., & Kowaleski-Jones, L. (2007). The influence of grandparents in single-mother families. *Journal of Marriage and Family, 69,* 465–481.

Dunivin, D. L. (2006). Psychopharmacotherapy and women: Issues for consideration. In J. Worell & C. D. Goodheart (Eds.), *Handbook of girls' and women's psychological health: Gender and well-being across the lifespan* (pp. 447–454). New York: Oxford University Press.

Dunkle, K. L., Jewkes, R. K., Brown, H. C., Gray, G. E., McIntryre, J. A., & Harlow, S. D. (2004, May 1). Gender-based violence, relationship power, and risk of HIV infection in women attending antenatal clinics in South Africa. *Lancet, 363,* 1415–1421.

Dunne, E. F., et al. (2007). Prevalence of HPV infection among females in the United States. *Journal of the American Medical Association, 297,* 813–820.

Durden, E. D., Hill, T. D., & Angel, R. J. (2007). Social demands, social supports, and psychological distress among low-income women. *Journal of Social and Personal Relationships, 24,* 343–361.

Durkin, S. J., Paxton, S. J., & Sorbello, M. (2007). An integrative model of the impact of exposure to idealized female images on adolescent girls' body satisfaction. *Journal of Applied Social Psychology, 37,* 1092–1117.

Dush, C. M. K., Cohan, C., & Amato, P. (2003). Living together before marriage: Now common but still risky. *Journal of Marriage and the Family, 65,* 539–549.

Duxbury, L., & Higgins, C. (1994). Interference between work and family: A status report on dual-career and dual-earner mothers and fathers. *Employee Assistance Quarterly, 9,* 55–80.

Dye, J. L. (2005). *Fertility of American women: June 2004.* Current Population Reports, P20-555. Washington, DC: U.S. Census Bureau.

Dyke, L. S., & Murphy, S. A. (2006). How we define success: A qualitative study of what matters most to women and men. *Sex Roles, 55,* 357–371.

Eagly, A. H. (2007). Female leadership advantage and disadvantage: Resolving the contradictions. *Psychology of Women Quarterly, 31,* 1–12.

Eagly, A. H., & Carli, L. L. (1981). Sex of researchers and sex-typed communications as determinants of sex differences in influenceability: A meta-analysis of social influence studies. *Psychological Bulletin, 90,* 1–20.

Eagly, A. H., & Carli, L. L. (2007). *Through the labyrinth: The truth about how women become leaders.* Boston: Harvard Business School Press.

Eagly, A. H., & Diekman, A. B. (2006). III. Examining gender gaps in sociopolitical attitudes: It's not Mars and Venus. *Feminism & Psychology, 16,* 26–34.

Eagly, A. H., & Johannesen-Schmidt, M. C. (2001). The leadership styles of women and men. *Journal of Social Issues, 57,* 781–797.

Eagly, A. H., Johannesen-Schmidt, M. C., & van Engen, M. L. (2003). Transformational, transactional, and laissez-faire leadership styles: A meta-analysis comparing women and men. *Psychological Bulletin, 129,* 569–591.

Eagly, A. H., Karau, S. J., & Makhijani, M. G. (1995). Gender and the effectiveness of leaders: A meta-analysis. *Psychological Bulletin, 117,* 125–145.

Eagly, A. H., Makhijani, M. G., & Klonsky, B. G. (1992). Gender and the evaluation of leaders: A meta-analysis. *Psychological Bulletin, 111,* 3–22.

Eagly, A. H., Wood, W., & Diekman, A. B. (2000). Social role theory of sex differences and similarities: A current appraisal. In T. Eckes & H. M. Trautner (Eds.), *The developmental social psychology of gender* (pp. 123–174). Mahwah, NJ: Erlbaum.

Eagly, A. H., Wood, W., & Johannesen-Schmidt, M. (2004). Social role theory of sex differences and similarities: Implications for the partner preferences of women and men. In A. H. Eagly, A. E. Beall, & R. J. Sternberg (Eds.), *The psychology of gender* (pp. 269–295). New York: Guilford.

East, P. L., Khoo, S. T., & Reyes, B. T. (2006). Risk and protective factors predictive of adolescent pregnancy: A longitudinal, prospective study. *Applied Developmental Science, 10,* 188–199.

Eastman, V. J., & Utley, M. E. (2004, July). *Effect of pregnancy on judgments of a job applicant's qualifications.* Paper presented at the meeting of the American Psychological Association, Honolulu.

Eastwick, P. W., et al. (2006). Is traditional gender ideology associated with sex-typed mate preferences? A test in nine nations. *Sex Roles, 54,* 603–614.

Eastwick, P. W., & Finkel, E. J. (2008). Sex differences in mate preferences revisited: Do people know what they initially desire in a romantic partner? *Journal of Personality and Social Psychology, 94,* 245–264.

Eaton, D. K., Davis, K. S., Barrios, L., Brener, N. D., & Noonan, R. K. (2007). Associations of dating violence victimization with lifetime participation, co-occurrence, and early initiation of risk behaviors among U.S. high school students. *Journal of Interpersonal Violence, 22,* 585–602.

Eaton, D. K., et al. (2008). Youth Risk Behavior Surveillance— United States, 2007. *Morbidity and Mortality Weekly Report, 57*(SS-4), 1–131.

Eberhardt, J. L., & Fiske, S. T. (1998). Affirmative action in theory and practice: Issues of power, ambiguity, and gender versus race. In D. L. Anselmi & A. L. Law (Eds.), *Questions of gender: Perspectives and paradoxes* (pp. 629–641). Boston: McGraw-Hill.

Eccles, J. S., Freedman-Doan, C., Frome, P., Jacobs, J., & Yoon, K. S. (2000). Gender-role socialization in the family: A longitudinal approach. In T. Eckes & H. M. Trautner (Eds.), *The developmental social psychology of gender* (pp. 333–360). Mahwah, NJ: Erlbaum.

Eccles, J. S., & Roeser, R. W. (1999). School and community influences on human development. In M. H. Bornstein & M. E. Lamb (Eds.), *Developmental psychology: An advanced textbook* (4th ed., pp. 503–554). Mahwah, NJ: Erlbaum.

Ecker, J. L., & Frigoletto, F. D., Jr. (2007). Cesarean delivery and the risk-benefit calculus. *New England Journal of Medicine, 356,* 885–888.

Eckert, P., & McConnell-Ginet, S. (2003). *Language and gender.* Cambridge: Cambridge University Press.

Eddleman, J., Essien, L., & Pollak, L. (2003, Spring/ Summer). Success strategies. *AAUW Outlook,* p. 25.

Edwards, C. P., Knoche, L., & Kumru, A. (2001). Play patterns and gender. In J. Worell (Ed.), *Encyclopedia of women and gender* (pp. 809–815). San Diego: Academic Press.

Edwards, M. (2007, July–August). Protecting the vulnerable. *AARP Bulletin,* pp. 18–19.

Egan, J. (2006, March 19). Wanted: A few good sperm. *New York Times,* pp. 46–51, 66, 81, 98, 100.

Eggs shared, given, and sold. (2003). *Lancet, 362,* 413.

Ehrenreich, B., & Hochschild, A. R. (2002). *Global woman: Nannies, maids, and sex workers in the new economy.* New York: Henry Holt.

Ehrlich, S. B., Levine, S. C., & Goldin-Meadow, S. (2005, April). *Early sex differences in spatial skill: The implications of spoken and gestured strategies.* Paper presented at the meeting of the Society for Research in Child Development, Atlanta, GA.

Eisele, H., & Stake, J. (2008). The differential relationship of feminist attitudes and feminist identity to self-efficacy. *Psychology of Women Quarterly, 32,* 233–244.

Eisenberg, M. E., Neumark-Sztainer, D., & Story, M. (2003). Associations of weight-based teasing and emotional well-being among adolescents. *Archives of Pediatrics and Adolescent Medicine, 157,* 733–738.

Eisenberg, N. (2002). Prosocial development in early adulthood. *Journal of Personality and Social Psychology, 82,* 993–1006.

Eisenberg, N., & Fabes, R. A. (1998). Prosocial development. In W. Damon (Series Ed.) & N. Eisenberg (Vol. Ed.), *Handbook of child psychology. Vol. 3. Social, emotional and personality development* (5th ed., pp. 701–778). New York: Wiley.

Eisenberg, N., Fabes, R. A., & Spinrad, T. L. (2006). Prosocial development. In W. Damon, R. M. Lerner (Series Eds.), & N. Eisenberg (Vol. Ed.), *Handbook of child psychology: Vol. 3. Social, emotional, and personality development* (6th ed., pp. 646–718). Hoboken, NJ: Wiley.

Eisenberg, N., Martin, C. L., & Fabes, R. A. (1996). Gender development and gender effects. In D. C. Berliner & R. C. Calfee (Eds.), *The handbook of educational psychology* (pp. 358–396). New York: Simon & Schuster.

Eisenberg, N., & Morris, A. S. (2004). Moral cognitions and prosocial responding in adolescence. In R. M. Lerner & L. Steinberg (Eds.), *Handbook of adolescent psychology* (2nd ed., pp. 155–188). Hoboken, NJ: Wiley.

Elder, J. (1997, June 22). Poll finds women are the health-savvier sex, and the warier. *New York Times*, p. WH8.

Elder, S. (2003, September). Europe's baby bust. *National Geographic*, p.1.

Ellin, A. (2004a, October 17). Helping grandparents help the grandkids. *New York Times*, p. BU9.

Ellin, A. (2004b, February 29). When it comes to salary, many women don't push. *New York Times*, p. BU7.

Elliot, D. L., Cheong, J. W., Moe, E. L., & Goldberg, L. (2007). Cross-sectional study of female students reporting anabolic steroid use. *Archives of Pediatrics & Adolescent Medicine*, *161*, 572–577.

Elliott, G. C., Avery, R., Fishman, E., & Hoshiko, B. (2002). The encounter with family violence and risky sexual activity among young adolescent females. *Violence and Victims*, *17*, 569–592.

Elliott, K., & Urquiza, A. (2006). Ethnicity, culture, and child maltreatment. *Journal of Social Issues*, *62*, 787–809.

Elliott, N. (2004). Breast care should be better. *Women's Health in Primary Care*, *7*, 464–465.

Ellis, B. J. (2004). Timing of pubertal maturation in girls: An integrated life history approach. *Psychological Bulletin*, *130*, 920–958.

Ellis, B. J., & Essex, M. J. (2007). Family environments, adrenarche, and sexual maturation: A longitudinal test of a life history model. *Child Development*, *78*, 1799–1817.

Ellis, J. A. (2006). Social ties and health. *American Journal of Public Health*, *96*, 1341.

Ellis, S. J. (2002). Student support for lesbian and gay human rights: Findings from a large-scale questionnaire study. In A. Coyle & C. Kitzinger (Eds.), *Lesbian and gay psychology: New perspectives* (pp. 239–254). Oxford, UK: BPS Blackwell.

Elmore, J. G., Armstrong, K., Lehman, C. D., & Fletcher, S. W. (2005). Screening for breast cancer. *Journal of the American Medical Association*, *293*, 1245–1256.

Elmusharaf, S., Elhadi, N., & Almroth, L. (2006). Reliability of self reported form of female genital mutilation and WHO classification: Cross sectional study. *BMJ*, *333*, 124–127.

Else-Quest, N. W., & Hyde, J. S. (2008, May). *Cross-national gender differences in mathematics performance: A meta-analysis.*

Poster presented at the meeting of the Association for Psychological Science, Chicago.

Elson, J. (2004). *Am I still a woman?* Philadelphia: Temple University Press.

Embrick, D. G., Walther, C. S., & Wickens, C. M. (2007). Working class masculinity: Keeping gay men and lesbians out of the workplace. *Sex Roles*, *56*, 757–766.

Enns, C. Z., & Forrest, L. (2005). Toward defining and integrating multicultural and feminist pedagogies. In C. Z. Enns & A. L. Sinacore (Eds.), *Teaching and social justice: Integrating multicultural and feminist theories in the classroom* (pp. 1–23). Washington, DC: American Psychological Association Press.

Ens, C. Z., & Sinacore, A. (2001). Feminist theories. In J. Worell (Ed.), *Encyclopedia of women and gender* (pp. 469–480). San Diego: Academic Press.

Epidemiology of HIV/AIDS—United States, 1981–2005. (2006). *Morbidity and Mortality Weekly Report*, *55*, 589–592.

Epstein, C. F. (2007). Great divides: The cultural, cognitive, and social bases of the global subordination of women. *American Sociological Review*, *72*, 1–22.

Epstein, C. F., & Gambs, D. (2001). Sex segregation in education. In J. Worell (Ed.), *Encyclopedia of women and gender* (pp. 983–990). San Diego: Academic Press.

Epstein, E. E., Fischer-Elber, K., & Al-Otaiba, Z. (2007). Women, aging, and alcohol use disorders. *Journal of Women and Aging*, *19*, 31–48.

Erel, O., Oberman, Y., & Yirmiya, N. (2000). Maternal versus nonmaternal care and seven domains of children's development. *Psychological Bulletin*, *126*, 727–747.

Erikson, E. H. (1968). *Identity: Youth and crisis*. New York: Norton.

Erikson, E. H. (1980). *Identity and the life cycle*. New York: Norton.

Espey, D. K., et al. (2007). Annual report to the nation on the status of cancer, 1975–2004, featuring cancer in Natives. *Cancer*, *110*, 2119–2152.

Espinoza, L., Hall, H., Hardnett, F., Selik, R., Ling, Q., & Lee, L. (2007). Characteristics of persons with heterosexually acquired HIV infection, United States 1999–2004. *American Journal of Public Health*, *97*, 144–149.

Estimated percentage of patients aged ≥45 years who received exercise counseling from their primary-care physicians, by sex and age group—National Ambulatory Medical Care Survey and National Hospital Ambulatory Medical Care Survey, United States, 2003–2005. (2007). *Morbidity and Mortality Weekly Report*, *56*, 1142.

Etaugh, C. (1993). Maternal employment: Effects on children. In J. Frankel (Ed.), *The employed mother and the family context* (pp. 68–88). New York: Springer.

Etaugh, C. (2008). Women in the middle and later years. In F. L. Denmark & M. A. Paludi (Eds.), *Psychology of women: A handbook of issues and theories* (2nd ed., pp. 271–302). Westport, CT: Praeger.

Etaugh, C., Bridges, J. S., Cummings-Hill, M., & Cohen, J. (1999). "Names can never hurt me?" The effects of surname use on perceptions of married women. *Psychology of Women Quarterly*, *23*, 819–823.

Etaugh, C., & Conrad, M. (2004, July). *Perceptions of parents choosing traditional or nontraditional roles and surnames*. Poster presented at the meeting of the American Psychological Association, Honolulu, HI.

Etaugh, C., & Duits, T. (1990). Development of gender discrimination: Role of stereotypic and counter-stereotypic gender cues. *Sex Roles, 23*, 215–222.

Etaugh, C., & Folger, D. (1998). Perceptions of parents whose work and parenting behaviors deviate from role expectations. *Sex Roles, 39*, 215–223.

Etaugh, C., & Fulton, A. (1995, June). *Perceptions of unmarried adults: Gender and sexual orientation (not social attractiveness) matter*. Paper presented at the meeting of the American Psychological Association, New York.

Etaugh, C., Grinnell, K., & Etaugh, A. (1989). Development of gender labeling: Effect of age of pictured children. *Sex Roles, 21*, 769–773.

Etaugh, C., Jones, N. A., & Patterson, K. (1995, August). *Gender comparisons and stereotypes: Changing views in introductory psychology textbooks*. Paper presented at the meeting of the American Psychological Association, New York.

Etaugh, C., Levine, D., & Mennella, A. (1984). Development of sex biases in children: Forty years later. *Sex Roles, 10*, 913–924.

Etaugh, C., & Liss, M. B. (1992). Home, school, and playroom: Training grounds for adult gender roles. *Sex Roles, 26*, 129–146.

Etaugh, C., & Moss, C. (2001). Attitudes of employed women toward parents who choose full-time or part-time employment following their child's birth. *Sex Roles, 44*, 611–619.

Etaugh, C., & Nekolny, K. (1990). Effects of employment status and marital status on perceptions of mothers. *Sex Roles, 23*, 273–280.

Etaugh, C., & O'Brien, E. (2003, April). *Perceptions of parents' gender roles by preschoolers in traditional and egalitarian families*. Paper presented at the meeting of the Society for Research in Child Development, Tampa, FL.

Etaugh, C., & Poertner, P. (1991). Effects of occupational prestige, employment status, and mental status on perceptions of mothers. *Sex Roles, 24*, 345–353.

Etaugh, C., & Poertner, P. (1992). Perceptions of women: Influence of performance, marital, and parental variables. *Sex Roles, 26*, 311–321.

Etaugh, C., & Rathus, S. (1995). *The world of children*. Fort Worth, TX: Harcourt Brace.

Etaugh, C., & Roe, L. (2002, June). *"What's in a name?" Surname choice affects perceptions of women and men*. Poster presented at the meeting of the American Psychological Society, New Orleans.

Etaugh, C., Roe, L., & Zurek, R. (2003, July). *From "frogs and snails" to "Mr. Mom": Stereotypes of boys and men in children's books*. Poster presented at the European Congress of Psychology, Vienna.

Etaugh, C., & Spiller, B. (1989). Attitudes toward women: Comparison of traditional-aged and older college students. *Journal of College Student Development, 30*, 41–46.

Evans, E. M., Schweingruber, H., & Stevenson, H. W. (2002). Gender differences in interest and knowledge acquisition: The United States, Taiwan, and Japan. *Sex Roles, 47*, 153–168.

Evans, M. A., et al. (2003, April). *Gender constancy and sex-typed preferences: A meta-analytic integration*. Paper presented at the meeting of the Society for Research in Child Development, Tampa, FL.

Evans-Campbell, T., Lindhorst, T., Huang, B., & Walters, K. L. (2006). Interpersonal violence in the lives of urban American Indian and Alaska Native women: Implications for health, mental health, and help-seeking. *American Journal of Public Health, 96*, 1416–1422.

Evenson, R. J., & Simon, R. W. (2005). Clarifying the relationship between parenthood and depression. *Journal of Health and Social Behavior, 46*, 341–358.

Ewart, C. K., & Suchday, S. (2002). Discovering how urban poverty and violence affect health: Development and validation of a neighborhood stress index. *Health Psychology, 21*, 254–262.

Fabes, R. A., & Martin, C. L. (2003). *Exploring child development* (2nd ed.). Boston: Allyn & Bacon.

Facio, E. (2001). Chicanas and aging: Toward definitions of womanhood. In J. M. Coyle (Ed.), *Handbook on women and aging* (pp. 335–350). Westport, CT: Praeger.

Fagot, B. I., & Leinbach, M. D. (1993). Gender-role development in young children: From discrimination to labeling. *Developmental Review, 13*, 205–224.

Fagot, B. I., Leinbach, M. D., & O'Boyle, C. (1992). Gender labeling, gender stereotyping, and parenting behaviors. *Developmental Psychology, 28*, 225–230.

Fairweather, D., & Rose, N. R. (2004). Women and autoimmune diseases. *Emerging Infectious Diseases, 10*, 2005–2011.

Faludi, S. (1991). *Backlash: The undeclared war against women*. New York: Crown.

Faludi, S. (2007). *The terror dream: Fear and fantasy in post-9/11 America*. New York: Metropolitan Books.

Family Caregiver Alliance. (2003). *Women and caregiving: Facts and figures* [Fact sheet]. San Francisco: Author.

Fang, B. (2006, Fall). School's out. *Ms.*, pp. 24–25.

Fang, J., et al. (2008). Disparities in adult awareness of heart attack warning signs and symptoms—14 states, 2005. *Morbidity and Mortality Weekly Report, 57*, 175–179.

Faria, G., & Belohlavek, N. (1995). Treating female adult survivors of childhood incest. In F. J. Turner (Ed.), *Differential diagnosis and treatment in social work* (4th ed., pp. 744–753). New York: Free Press.

Farmer, A., & Tiefenthaler, J. (2004). *Domestic violence and its impact on women's economic status, employers, and the workplace*. San Francisco: Blue Shield of California Foundation.

Farmer, H. S. (2006). History of career counseling for women. In W. B. Walsh & M. J. Heppner (Eds.), *Handbook of career counseling for women* (2nd ed., pp. 1–44). Mahwah, NJ: Erlbaum.

Farris, C., Treat, T. A., Viken, R. J., & McFall, R. M. (2008). Perceptual mechanisms that characterize gender differences in decoding women's sexual intent. *Psychological Science, 19*, 348–354.

Fassinger, R. E. (1995). From invisibility to integration: Lesbian identity in the workplace. *The Career Development Quarterly, 44,* 148–167.

Fassinger, R. E. (2001). Women in nontraditional work fields. In J. Worell (Ed.), *Encyclopedia of women and gender* (pp. 1169–1180). San Diego: Academic Press.

Fassinger, R. E. (2008). Workplace diversity and public policy: Challenges and opportunities for psychology. *American Psychologist, 63,* 252–268.

Fassinger, R. E., & Arseneau, J. R. (2008). Diverse women's sexualities. In F. L. Denmark & M. A. Paludi (Eds.), *Psychology of women: A handbook of issues and theories* (2nd ed., pp. 484–505). Westport, CT: Praeger.

Fassinger, R. E., & Asay, P. A. (2006). Career counseling for women in science, technology, engineering, and mathematics (STEM) fields. In W. B. Walsh & M. J. Heppner (Eds.), *Handbook of career counseling for women* (2nd ed., pp. 427–452). Mahwah, NJ: Erlbaum.

Fausto-Sterling, A. (1992). *Myths of gender: Biological theories about women and men* (2nd ed.). New York: Basic Books.

Fausto-Sterling, A. (2000, July/August). The five sexes, revisited. *Sciences, 40,* 18–23.

February is black history month. (2004, February). *Women's Psych-E, 3*(2), 1.

Federal Bureau of Investigation. (2002). *Hate crime statistics, 2001.* Washington, DC: Author.

Federal Glass Ceiling Commission. (1995a, March). *Good for business: Making full use of the nation's human capital.* Washington, DC: Author.

Federal Glass Ceiling Commission. (1995b, November). *A solid investment: Making full use of the nation's human capital.* Washington, DC: Author.

Federal Interagency Forum on Child and Family Statistics. (2004). *Older Americans 2004: Key indicators of well-being.* Washington, DC: U.S. Government Printing Office.

Federal Interagency Forum on Child and Family Statistics. (2007). *American's children: Key national indicators of well-being, 2007.* Washington, DC: U.S. Government Printing Office.

Feigelson, H. S., et al. (2004). Weight gain, body mass index, hormone replacement therapy, and postmenopausal breast cancer in a large prospective study. *Cancer Epidemiology Biomarkers & Prevention, 13,* 220–224.

Feingold, A. (1988). Cognitive gender differences are disappearing. *American Psychologist, 43,* 95–103.

Feingold, A. (1993). Cognitive gender differences: A developmental perspective. *Sex Roles, 29,* 91–112.

Feingold, A., & Mazzella, R. (1998). Gender differences in body image are increasing. *Psychological Science, 9,* 32–37.

Feiring, C., Taska, L., & Lewis, M. (2002). Adjustment following sexual abuse discovery: The role of shame and attributional style. *Developmental Psychology, 38,* 79–92.

Feist-Price, S., & Wright, L. B. (2003). African American women living with HIV/AIDS: Mental health issues. *Women & Therapy, 26,* 27–44.

Felder, S. (2006). The gender longevity gap: Explaining the difference between singles and couples. *Journal of Population Economics, 19,* 543–557.

Feldman, R. S. (1998). *Social psychology* (2nd ed.). Upper Saddle River, NJ: Prentice Hall.

Feldman, R. S. (2000). *Development across the life span* (2nd ed.). Upper Saddle River, NJ: Prentice Hall.

Feldman, S., Byles, J. E., & Beaumont, R. (2000). "Is anybody listening?" The experiences of widowhood for older Australian women. *Journal of Women & Aging, 12,* 155–176.

Feldstein, K. (1998, April 13). Social Security's gender gap. *New York Times,* p. A27.

Felix, E. D., & McMahon, S. D. (2006). Gender and multiple forms of peer victimization: How do they influence adolescent psychosocial adjustment? *Violence and Victims, 21,* 707–724.

Feng, J., Spence, I., & Pratt, J. (2007). Playing an action video game reduces gender differences in spatial cognition. *Psychological Science, 18,* 850–855.

Fergus, S., Zimmerman, M., & Caldwell, C. (2007). Growth trajectories of sexual risk behavior in adolescence and young adulthood. *American Journal of Public Health, 97,* 1096–1101.

Fergusson, D. M., & Woodward, L. J. (2000). Educational, psychosocial, and sexual outcomes of girls with conduct problems in early adolescence. *Journal of Child Psychology and Psychiatry, 41,* 779–792.

Ferraro, S. (2006, December 26). Self-exams are passé? Believers beg to differ. *New York Times,* pp. D5, D8.

Ferris, L. E. (2004). Intimate partner violence. *BMJ, 328,* 595–596.

Fiatarone, M. A., et al. (1994). Exercise training and nutritional supplementation for physical frailty in very elderly people. *New England Journal of Medicine, 33,* 1769–1775.

Fichter, M. M., Quadflieg, N., & Hedlund, S. (2006). Twelve-year course and outcome predictors of anorexia nervosa. *International Journal of Eating Disorders, 39,* 87–100.

Field, D., & Weishaus, S. (1992). Marriage over half a century: A longitudinal study. In M. Bloom (Ed.), *Changing lives* (pp. 269–273). Columbia: University of South Carolina Press.

Fielding, S. L., Edmunds, E., & Schaff, E. A. (2002). Having an abortion using mifepristone and home misoprostol: A qualitative analysis of women's experiences. *Perspectives on Sexual and Reproductive Health, 34,* 34–40.

Fields, J. (2003, June). *Children's living arrangements and characteristics: March 2002.* Washington, DC: U.S. Census Bureau.

Fields, J. (2004). *America's families and living arrangements: 2003.* Current Population Reports, P20–553. Washington, DC: U.S. Census Bureau.

Fields, J., & Casper, L. M. (2001). *America's families and living arrangements: March 2000.* Current Population Reports, P20–537, Washington, DC: U.S. Census Bureau.

Fine, M., & Carney, S. (2001). Women, gender, and the law: Toward a feminist rethinking of responsibility. In R. K. Unger (Ed.), *Handbook of the psychology of women and gender* (pp. 388–409). New York: Wiley.

Finer, L. B., & Henshaw, S. K. (2003). Abortion incidence and services in the United States in 2000. *Perspectives on Sexual and Reproductive Health, 35,* 6–15.

Fingeret, M. C., & Gleaves, D. H. (2004). Sociocultural, feminist, and psychological influences on women's body satisfaction: A structural modeling analysis. *Psychology of Women Quarterly, 28,* 370–380.

Fingerman, K. L. (2001). *Aging mothers and their adult daughters: A study in mixed emotions.* New York: Springer.

Fingerson, L. (2006). *Girls in power: Gender, body, and menstruation in adolescence.* Albany: State University of New York Press.

Fink, J. S., & Kensicki, L. J. (2002). An imperceptible difference: Visual and textual constructions of femininity in Sports Illustrated and Sports Illustrated for Women. *Mass Communication & Society, 5,* 317–339.

Finkelhor, D. (1990). Early and long-term effects of child sexual abuse: An update. *Professional Psychology: Research and Practice, 21,* 325–330.

Finkelstein, J. S. (2006). Calcium plus vitamin D for postmenopausal women—bone appétit? *New England Journal of Medicine, 354,* 750–752.

Fisher, S. Y., & Shelly, S. (2002). *The complete idiot's guide to personal finance in your 40s and 50s.* Indianapolis, IN: Alpha Books.

Fisher, T. A., & Padmawidjaja, L. (1999). Parental influences on career development perceived by African American and Mexican American college students. *Journal of Multicultural Counseling and Development, 27,* 136–152.

Fisher, T. D. (2004). Family foundations of sexuality. In J. H. Harvey, A. Welzel, & S. Sprecher (Eds.), *The handbook of sexuality in close relationships* (pp. 385–409). Mahwah, NJ: Erlbaum.

Fisher-Thompson, D., Sausa, A. D., & Wright, T. F. (1995). Toy selection for children: Personality and toy request influences. *Sex Roles, 33,* 239–255.

Fiske, S. T., & Cuddy, A. J. C. (2006). Stereotype content across cultures as a function of group status. In S. Guimond (Ed.), *Social comparison and social psychology: Understanding cognition, intergroup relations and culture* (pp. 249–263). Cambridge: Cambridge University Press.

Fiske, S. T., & Glick, P. (1995). Ambivalence and stereotypes cause sexual harassment: A theory with implications for organizational change. *Journal of Social Issues, 51,* 97–115.

Fiske, S. T., & Stevens, L. A. (1993). What's so special about sex? Gender stereotyping and discrimination. In S. Oskamp & M. Costanzo (Eds.), *Gender issues in contemporary society* (pp. 173–196). Newbury Park, CA: Sage.

Fitzgerald, L., Collinsworth, L. L., & Harned, M. S. (2001). Sexual harassment. In J. Worell (Ed.), *Encyclopedia of women and gender* (pp. 991–1004). San Diego: Academic Press.

Fitzgerald, L. F. (1996). Sexual harassment: The definition and measurement of a construct. In M. A. Paludi (Ed.), *Sexual harassment on college campuses: Abusing the ivory power* (pp. 25–47). Albany, NY: SUNY.

Fitzgerald, L. F. (2003). Sexual harassment and social justice: Reflections on the distance yet to go. *American Psychologist, 58,* 915–924.

Fitzgerald, M. H. (1990). The interplay of culture and symptoms: Menstrual symptoms among Samoans. *Medical Anthropology, 12,* 145–167.

Fitzpatrick, M. K., et al. (2004). Associations of gender and gender-role ideology with behavioral and attitudinal features of intimate partner aggression. *Psychology of Men & Masculinity, 5,* 91–102.

Fitzpatrick, T. R., & Vinick, B. (2005). The impact of husbands' retirement on wives' marital quality. *Journal of Family Social Work, 7,* 83–90.

Fivush, R., Brotman, M. A., Buckner, J. P., & Goodman, S. H. (2000). Gender differences in parent–child emotion narratives. *Sex Roles, 42,* 233–253.

Flack, W. F., et al. (2007). Risk factors and consequences of unwanted sex among university students: Hooking up, alcohol, and stress response. *Journal of Interpersonal Violence, 22,* 139–157.

Flanagan, C. (1993). Gender and social class: Intersecting issues in women's achievement. *Educational Psychologist, 28,* 357–378.

Flannagan, D., Baker-Ward, L., & Graham, L. (1995). Talk about preschool: Patterns of topic discussion and elaboration related to gender and ethnicity. *Sex Roles, 32,* 1–15.

Fleck, C. (2007, October). Women and a secure retirement: Two steps forward, one step back. *AARP Bulletin,* pp. 1–2.

Flegal, K. M., Graubard, B. I., Williamson, D. F., & Gail, M. H. (2007). Cause-specific excess deaths associated with underweight, overweight, and obesity. *Journal of the American Medical Association, 298,* 2028–2037.

Fleming, L. M., & Tobin, D. J. (2005). Popular child-rearing books: Where is daddy? *Psychology of Men & Masculinity, 6,* 18–24.

Fletcher, V. (2005, January 14). Drunk girls under 14 ending up in hospital. *Daily Express (London),* p. 8.

Flores, G. (2006). Language barriers to health care in the United States. *New England Journal of Medicine, 355,* 229–231.

Flores, L., Navarro, R., & Ojeda, L. (2006). Career counseling with Latinas. In W. B. Walsh & M. J. Heppner (Eds.), *Handbook of career counseling with women* (2nd ed., pp. 271–314). Mahwah, NJ: Erlbaum.

Flouri, E., & Hawkes, D. (2008). Ambitious mothers-successful daughters: Mothers' early expectations for children's education and children's earnings and sense of control in adulthood. *British Journal of Educational Psychology, 78,* 411–433.

Fogg, P. (2003, April 18). The gap that won't go away: Women continue to lag behind men in pay; the reasons may have little to do with gender bias. *Chronicle of Higher Education,* pp. A12–A15.

Follette, V. M., Alexander, P. C., & Higgs, D. C. (1991). Individual predictors of outcome in group treatment for incest survivors. *Journal of Consulting and Clinical Psychology, 59,* 150–155.

Forbes, G. B., Adams-Curtis, L. E., White, K. B., & Holmgren, K. M. (2003). The role of hostile and benevolent sexism in women's and men's perceptions of the menstruating woman. *Psychology of Women Quarterly, 27,* 58–63.

Forbes, G. B., & Frederick, D. A. (2008). The UCLA Body Project II: Breast and body dissatisfaction among African, Asian, European, and Hispanic American college women. *Sex Roles, 58,* 449–457.

Ford, E. S., et al. (2007). Explaining the decrease in U.S. deaths from coronary disease, 1980–2000. *New England Journal of Medicine, 356,* 2388–2398.

Ford, T. E., Ferguson, M. A., Brooks, J. L., & Hagadone, K. M. (2004). Coping sense of humor reduces effects of stereotype threat on women's math performance. *Personality and Social Psychology Bulletin, 30,* 643–653.

Foshee, V. A., et al. (2004). Assessing the long-term effects of the safe dates program and a booster in preventing and reducing adolescent dating violence victimization and perpetration. *American Journal of Public Health, 94,* 619–624.

Foster, M. D. (1999). Acting out against gender discrimination: The effects of different social identities. *Sex Roles, 40,* 167–186.

Fouad, N. A., & Byars-Winston, A. M. (2005). Cultural context of career choice: Meta-analysis of race/ethnicity differences. *Career Development Quarterly, 53,* 223–233.

Foust-Cummings, H., Sabattini, L., & Carter, N. (2008). *Women in technology: Maximizing talent, minimizing barriers.* New York: Catalyst.

Fouts, G., & Burggraf, K. (1999). Television situation comedies: Female body images and verbal reinforcements. *Sex Roles, 40,* 473–481.

Fouts, G., & Burggraf, K. (2000). Television situation comedies: Female weight, male negative comments, and audience reactions. *Sex Roles, 42,* 925–932.

Fowers, B. J., Applegate, B., Tredinnick, M., & Slusher, J. (1996). His and her individualisms? Sex bias and individualism in psychologists' responses to case vignettes. *Journal of Psychology, 130,* 159–174.

Fowler, J. P. (2003). Aging with HIV: One woman's story. *Journal of Acquired Immune Deficiency Syndromes, 33,* S166–S168.

Franco, M. (2007). Posttraumatic stress disorder and older women. *Journal of Women & Aging, 19,* 103–117.

Frank, A. (1995). *The diary of a young girl: The definitive edition.* New York: Bantam Books.

Frankel, L. P. (2004). *Nice girls don't get the corner office 101: Unconscious mistakes women make that sabotage their careers.* New York: Warner.

Franklin, K. (1998, August). *Psychosocial motivations of hate crime perpetrators: Implications for educational interventions.* Paper presented at the meeting of the American Psychological Association, San Francisco.

Franko, D. L., Becker, A. E., Thomas, J. J., & Herzog, D. B. (2007). Cross-ethnic differences in eating disorder symptoms and related distress. *International Journal of Eating Disorders, 40,* 156–164.

Frankowski, B. L., & the Committee on Adolescence. (2004). Sexual orientation and adolescents. *Pediatrics, 113,* 1827–1832.

Frantz, D. (2000, November 3). Turkish women who see death as a way out. *New York Times,* p. A3.

Franzoi, S. L., & Chang, Z. (2002). The body esteem of Hmong and Caucasian young adults. *Psychology of Women Quarterly, 26,* 89–91.

Fraser, A. S., & Tinker, I. (2004). *Developing power: How women transformed international development.* New York: Feminist Press.

Fraser, M. B. (2002). *Solitaire: The intimate lives of single women.* New York: MacFarlane, Walter & Ross.

Frayne, S. M., et al. (2004). Effect of patient gender on late-life depression management. *Journal of Women's Health, 13,* 919–925.

Frazier, P., et al. (2004). Correlates of levels and patterns of positive life changes following sexual assault. *Journal of Consulting and Clinical Psychology, 72,* 19–30.

Frederick, D. A, Forbes, G. B., Grigorian, K. E., & Jarcho, J. M. (2007). The UCLA Body Project I: Gender and ethnic differences in self-objectification and body satisfaction among 2,206 undergraduates. *Sex Roles, 57,* 317–327.

Fredricks, J. A., & Eccles, J. S. (2006). Is extracurricular participation associated with beneficial outcomes? Concurrent and longitudinal relations. *Developmental Psychology, 42,* 698–713.

Freeman, E. W., et al. (2004). Hormones and menopausal status as predictors of depression in women in transition to menopause. *Archives of General Psychiatry, 61,* 62–70.

French, D. C., Jansen, E. A., & Pidada, S. (2002). United States and Indonesian children's and adolescents' reports of relational aggression by disliked peers. *Child Development, 73,* 1143–1150.

Freud, S. (1925/1989). Some psychological consequences of the anatomical distinction between the sexes. In P. Gay (Ed.), *The Freud reader* (pp. 670–678). New York: Norton.

Freud, S. (1938). The transformation of puberty. In A. A. Brill (Ed. and Trans.), *The basic writings of Sigmund Freud* (pp. 604–629). New York: Random House.

Freyd, J. J., et al. (2005). The science of child sexual abuse. *Science, 308,* 501.

Fried, L. P., et al. (2004, March). A social model for health promotion for an aging population: Initial evidence on the Experience Corps model. *Journal of Urban Health, 81,* 64–78.

Friedan, B. (1963). *The feminine mystique.* New York: Norton.

Friedan, B. (1993). *The fountain of age.* New York: Simon & Schuster.

Friedman, D. E. (2001). Employee supports for parents with young children. *The Future of Children, 11*(1), 63–71.

Friedman, S. R., & Weissbrod, C. S. (2005). Work and family commitment and decision making status among emerging adults. *Sex Roles, 53,* 317–325.

Frieze, I. H. (2005). *Hurting the one you love: Violence in relationships.* Belmont, CA: Thomson Wadsworth.

Frieze, I. H., et al. (2003). Gender-role attitudes in university students in the United States, Slovenia, and Croatia. *Psychology of Women Quarterly, 27,* 256–261.

Frieze, I. H., Olson, J. E., Murrell, A. J., & Seivan, M. S. (2006). Work values and their effect on work behavior and work outcomes in female and male managers. *Sex Roles, 54,* 83–93.

Frith, K. T., Cheng, H., & Shaw, P. (2005). The construction of beauty: A cross-cultural analysis of women's magazine advertising. *Journal of Communication, 55,* 56–70.

Frome, P. M., Alfeld, C. J., Eccles, J. S., & Barber, B. L. (2008). Is the desire for a family-flexible job keeping young women out of male-dominated occupations? In H. M. G. Watt & J. S. Eccles (Eds.), *Gender and occupational outcomes: Longitudinal assessments of individual, social, and cultural influences* (pp. 195–214). Washington, DC: American Psychological Association.

Frone, M. R. (2003). Work-family balance. In J. C. Quick & L. E. Tetrick (Eds.), *Handbook of occupational health psychology* (pp. 143–162). Washington DC: American Psychological Association.

Frost, J., & McKelvie, S. (2004). Self-esteem and body satisfaction in male and female elementary school, high school, and university students. *Sex Roles, 51*, 45–54.

Frye, J. C. (1996). Affirmative action: Understanding the past and present. In C. Costello & B. K. Krimgold (Eds.), *The American woman 1996–1997* (pp. 33–43). New York: Norton.

Fuegen, K., Biernat, M., Haines, E., & Deaux, K. (2004). Mothers and fathers in the workplace: How gender and parental status influence judgments of job-related competence. *Journal of Social Issues, 60*, 737–754.

Fukkink, R. G., & Lont, A. (2007). Does training matter? A meta-analysis and review of caregiver training studies. *Early Childhood Research Quarterly, 22*, 294–311.

Fulcher, M. (2005, April). *Individual differences in children's occupational aspirations as a function of parental traditionality.* Poster presented at the meeting of the Society for Research in Child Development, Atlanta, GA.

Fulcher, M. (2007, March). *Visions of future family roles in elementary school, high school, and college students.* Poster presented at the meeting of the Society for Research in Child Development, Boston.

Fulcher, M., Sutfin, E. L., & Patterson, C. J. (2003, April). *Parental sexual orientation, parental division of labor, and children's sex-typed occupational aspirations.* Paper presented at the meeting of the Society for Research in Child Development, Tampa, FL.

Fulcher, M., Sutfin, E. L., & Patterson, C. J. (2008). Individual differences in gender development: Associations with parental sexual orientation, attitudes, and division of labor. *Sex Roles, 58*, 330–341.

Fuller-Thomson, E., & Minkler, M. (2005). Functional limitations among older American Indians and Alaska Natives: Finding from the Census 2000 Supplementary Survey. *American Journal of Public Health, 95*, 1945–1948.

Fulton, S. A., & Sabornie, E. J. (1994). Evidence of employment inequality among females with disabilities. *Journal of Special Education, 28*, 149–165.

Fultz, N. H., & Herzog, A. (2000). Urinary incontinence. In M. B. Goldman & M. E. Hatch (Eds.), *Women & health* (pp. 1202–1212). San Diego: Academic Press.

Furman, W. (2002). The emerging field of adolescent romantic relationships. *Current Directions in Psychological Science, 11*, 177–180.

Furnham, A., Crawshaw, J., & Rawles, R. (2006). Sex differences in self-estimates on two validated IQ test subscale scores. *Journal of Applied Social Psychology, 36*, 417–440.

Furnham, A., Reeves, E., & Budhani, S. (2002). Parents think their sons are brighter than their daughters: Sex differences in parental self-estimations and estimations of their children's multiple intelligences. *Journal of Genetic Psychology, 163*, 24–39.

Furnham, A., & Saar, A. (2005). Gender-role stereotyping in adult and children's television advertisements: A two-study comparison between Great Britain and Poland. *Communications, 30*, 73–90.

Fuwa, M. (2004). Macro-level gender inequality and the division of household labor in 22 countries. *American Sociological Review, 69*, 751–767.

Gadbois, S., & Bowker, A. (2007). Gender differences in the relationships between extracurricular activities participation, self-description, and domain-specific and general self-esteem. *Sex Roles, 56*, 675–689.

Gajendran, R. S., & Harrison, D. A. (2007). The good, the bad, and the unknown about telecommuting: Meta-analysis of psychological mediators and individual consequences. *Journal of Applied Psychology, 92*, 1524–1541.

Galambos, N. L. (2004). Gender and gender role development in adolescence. In R. M. Lerner & L. Steinberg (Eds.), *Handbook of adolescent psychology* (2nd ed., pp. 233–262). Hoboken, NJ: Wiley.

Galambos, N. L., Leadbeater, B. J., & Barker, E. T. (2004). Gender differences in and risk factors for depression in adolescence: A 4-year longitudinal study. *International Journal of Behavioral Development, 28*, 16–25.

Galinsky, E. (2001, April). *Children's perspectives of employed mothers and fathers: Closing the gap between public debates and research findings.* Paper presented at the meeting of the Society for Research in Child Development, Minneapolis, MN.

Galinsky, E., & Bond, J. T. (1996). Work and family: The experiences of mothers and fathers in the U.S. labor force. In C. Costello & B. K. Krimgold (Eds.), *The American woman 1996–1997* (pp. 79–103). New York: Norton.

Gall, C. (2002, September 22). Long in dark, Afghan women say to read is finally to see. *New York Times*, pp. 1, 26.

Gallagher, C., & Busch-Rossnagal, N. A. (1991, March). *Self-disclosure and social support in the relationships of black and white female adolescents.* Poster presented at the Society for Research in Child Development, Seattle, WA.

Gallagher, W. (2001, November 13). Young love: The good, the bad, and the educational. *New York Times*, p. D6.

Gallant, S. J., & Derry, P. S. (1995). Menarche, menstruation, and menopause: Psychological research and future directions. In A. L. Stanton & S. J. Gallant (Eds.), *The psychology of women's health: Progress and challenges in research and application* (pp. 199–259). Washington, DC: American Psychological Association.

Galliher, R. V., Rostosky, S. S., Welsh, D. P., & Kawaguchi, M. C. (1999). Power and psychological well-being in late adolescent romantic relationships. *Sex Roles, 40*, 689–710.

Gallor, S. (2003, January). An exploration of social support in the lives of ethnic minority lesbians and gay men. In R. E. Fassinger (Chair), *Results of the National Gay and Lesbian Experiences Study.* Symposium presented at the meeting of the American Psychological Association Multicultural Summit, Los Angeles.

Galupo, M. P. (2007). Women's close friendships across sexual orientation: A comparative analysis of lesbian-heterosexual and bisexual-heterosexual women's friendships. *Sex Roles, 56*, 473–482.

Ganahl, D. J., Prinsen, T. J., & Netzley, S. B. (2003). A content analysis of prime time commercials: A contextual framework of gender representation. *Sex Roles, 49*, 545–551.

Gangestad, S. W., et al. (2004). Women's preferences for male behavioral displays change across the menstrual cycle. *Psychological Science, 15*, 203–207.

Gannon, L., & Ekstrom, B. (1993). Attitudes toward menopause: The influence of sociocultural paradigms. *Psychology of Women Quarterly, 17,* 275–288.

Gannon, L., Luchetta, T., Rhodes, K., Pardie, L., & Segrist, D. (1992). Sex bias in psychological research: Progress or complacency? *American Psychologist, 47,* 389–396.

Ganong, L. H., Coleman, M., Thompson, A., & Goodwin-Watkins, C. (1996). African American and European American college students' expectations for self and future partners. *Journal of Family Issues, 17,* 758–775.

Ganske, K. H., & Hebl, M. R. (2001). Once upon a time there was a math contest: Gender stereotyping and memory. *Teaching of Psychology, 28,* 266–268.

Garavalia, L. S., et al. (2007). Does health status differ between men and women in early recovery after myocardial infarction? *Journal of Women's Health, 16,* 93–101.

Garbers, S., et al. (2003). Barriers to breast cancer screening for low-income Mexican and Dominican women in New York City. *Journal of Urban Health, 80,* 81–91.

Garfinkel, P. (2002, February 24). As doctors on TV, women still battle the old clichés. *New York Times,* pp. AR17, AR50.

Garnets, L. D. (2008). Life as a lesbian: What does gender have to do with it? In J. C. Chrisler, C. Golden, & P. D. Rozee (Eds.), *Lectures on the psychology of women* (pp. 232–249). New York: McGraw-Hill.

Garrow, D. J. (2004, May 9). Toward a more perfect union. *New York Times Magazine,* pp. 52–57.

Gartrell, N., et al. (2000). The national lesbian family study: 3. Interviews with mothers of five-year-olds. *American Journal of Orthopsychiatry, 70,* 542–548.

Gavey, N., & McPhillips, K. (1999). Subject to romance: Heterosexual passivity as an obstacle to women initiating condom use. *Psychology of Women Quarterly, 23,* 349–367.

Gaylord, S. (2001). Women and aging: A psychological perspective. In J. D. Garner & S. O. Mercer (Eds.), *Women as they age* (2nd ed., pp. 49–68). New York: Haworth.

Gays win increasing protections in the workplace. (2003, Fall/Winter). *AAUW Outlook,* p. 6.

Gearon, C. J. (2008). HIV/AIDS prevention pushed for the 50+. *AARP.org.* Retrieved March 25, 2008, from http://www.aarp.org/family/love/articles/aids_prevention_for_50plus_pushed.html

Geary, D. C. (2007). An evolutionary perspective on sex differences in mathematics and the sciences. In S. J. Ceci & W. M. Williams (Eds.), *Why aren't more women in science? Top researchers debate the evidence* (pp. 173–188). Washington, DC: American Psychological Association.

Geckler, J., & Fox, L. (2005, May). *Midwestern regional college students attitudes toward homosexuality.* Poster presented at the meeting of the Midwestern Psychological Association, Chicago.

Geipert, N. (2007, January). Don't be mad. *Monitor on Psychology, 38,* 50–51.

Gelman, S. A., Taylor, M. G., & Nguyen, S. P. (2004). *Mother-child conversations about gender.* Boston: Blackwell Publishing.

Gender equality and the millennium development goals. (2003). Washington, DC: Gender and Development Group, World Bank.

Gennetian, L. A., & Miller, C. (2002). Children and welfare reform: A view from an experimental program in Minnesota. *Child Development, 73,* 601–620.

Genzlinger, N. (2004, January 20). An actress of a certain age eyes the beauty cult. *New York Times,* pp. B1, B5.

George, D., Carroll, P., Kersnick, R., & Calderon, K. (1998). Gender-related patterns of helping among friends. *Psychology of Women Quarterly, 22,* 685–704.

George, W. H., & Martinez, L. J. (2002). Victim blaming in rape: Effects of victim and perpetrator race, type of rape, and participant racism. *Psychology of Women Quarterly, 26,* 110–119.

Gergen, M. (2008). Positive aging for women. In J. C. Chrisler, C. Golden, & P. D. Rozee (Eds.), *Lectures on the psychology of women* (pp. 376–391). New York: McGraw-Hill.

Gergen, M. M., & Gergen, K. J. (2006). Positive aging: Reconstructing the life course. In J. Worell & C. D. Goodheart (Eds.), *Handbook of girls' and women's psychological health: Gender and well-being across the lifespan* (pp. 416–426). New York: Oxford University Press.

Gerson, K. (1999). *Children of the gender revolution: Some theoretical questions and preliminary notes from the field.* Boston: Boston College Center for Work & Family.

Gibbons, C., & Jones, T. C. (2003). Kinship care: Health profile of grandparents raising their grandchildren. *Journal of Family Social Work, 7*(1), 1–14.

Gibbons, J. L. (2000). Gender development in cross-cultural perspective. In T. Eckes & H. M. Trautner (Eds.), *The developmental social psychology of gender* (pp. 389–415). Mahwah, NJ: Erlbaum.

Gibbs, N. (2002, April 15). Making time for a baby. *Time,* pp. 49–54.

Gibson, H. B. (1996). Sexual functioning in later life. In R. T. Woods (Ed.), *Handbook of the clinical psychology of aging* (pp. 183–193). New York: Wiley.

Giesbrecht, N. (1998). Gender patterns of psychosocial development. *Sex Roles, 39,* 463–478.

Gilbert, L. A. (1994). Reclaiming and returning gender to context: Examples from studies of heterosexual dual-earner families. *Psychology of Women Quarterly, 18,* 539–558.

Gilbert, L. A., & Kearney, L. K. (2006a). Sex, gender, and dual-earner families: Implications and applications for career counseling for women. In W. B. Walsh & M. J. Heppner (Eds.), *Handbook of career counseling for women* (2nd ed., pp. 193–218). Mahwah, NJ: Erlbaum.

Gilbert, L. A., & Kearney, L. K. (2006b). The psychotherapeutic relationship as a positive and powerful resource for girls and women. In J. Worell & C. D. Goodheart (Eds.), *Handbook of girls' and women's psychological health: Gender and well-being across the lifespan* (pp. 229–238). New York: Oxford University Press.

Gilbert, L. A., & Scher, M. (1999). *Gender and sex in counseling and psychotherapy.* Boston: Allyn & Bacon.

Gilbert, S. (1998, May 19). Benefits of assistant for childbirth go far beyond the birthing room. *New York Times*, p. B17.

Gilbert, S. (1999, August 3). For some children, it's an after-school pressure cooker. *New York Times*, p. D7.

Gil-Burmann, C., Pelaez, F., & Sanchez, S. (2002). Mate choice differences according to sex and age: An analysis of personal advertisements in Spanish newspapers. *Human Nature, 13*, 493–508.

Giles, J. W., & Heyman, G. D. (2005). Young children's beliefs about the relationship between gender and aggressive behavior. *Child Development, 76*, 107–121.

Giles, L. C., Glonek, G. F. V., Luczcz, M. A., & Andrews, G. R. (2005). Effects of social networks on 10-year survival in very old Australians: The Australian longitudinal study of aging. *Journal of Epidemiological Community Health, 59*, 574–579.

Gillen, M. M., & Lefkowitz, E. S. (2006). Gender role development and body image among male and female first year college students. *Sex Roles, 55*, 25–37.

Gillespie, R. (2003, February). Childfree and feminine. Understanding the gender identity of voluntarily childless women. *Gender & Society, 17*, 122–136.

Gilligan, C. (1982). *In a different voice*. Cambridge, MA: Harvard University Press.

Gilligan, C. (1993). Joining the resistance: Psychology, politics, girls and women. In L. Weis & M. Fine (Eds.), *Beyond silenced voices* (pp. 143–168). Albany, NY: SUNY Press.

Gilligan, C. (2002). *Beyond pleasure*. New York: Knopf.

Giltay, E. J., et al. (2004). Dispositional optimism and all-cause and cardiovascular mortality in a prospective cohort of elderly Dutch men and women. *Archives of General Psychiatry, 61*, 1126–1135.

Ginorio, A. B., Gutiérrez, L., Cauce, A. M., & Acosta, M. (1995). Psychological issues for Latinas. In H. Landrine (Ed.), *Bringing cultural diversity to feminist psychology: Theory, research and practice* (pp. 241–263). Washington, DC: American Psychological Association.

Ginsberg, R. L., & Gray, J. J. (2006). The differential depiction of female athletes in judged and non-judged sport magazines. *Body Image, 3*, 365–373.

Ginty, M. M. (2000, August/September). What to ask your gynecologist. *Ms.*, pp. 64–68.

Giuliano, T. A., Popp, K. E., & Knight, J. L. (2000). Footballs versus Barbies: Childhood play activities as predictors of sport participation by women. *Sex Roles, 42*, 159–181.

Glass, N., Perrin, N., Hanson, G., Bloom, T., Gardner, E., & Campbell, J. C. (2008). Risk for reassault in abusive female same-sex relationships. *American Journal of Public Health, 98*, 1021–1027.

Glass, T. A., de Leon, C. M., Marottoli, R. A., & Berkman, L. F. (1999). Population based study of social and productive activities as predictors of survival among elderly Americans. *BMJ, 319*, 478–483.

Glassman, A. H., & Bigger, J. T., Jr. (2007). Antidepressants in coronary heart disease: SSRIs reduce depression, but do they save lives? *Journal of the American Medical Association, 297*, 411–412.

Glauber, R. (2007). Marriage and the motherhood wage penalty among African Americans, Hispanics, and whites. *Journal of Marriage and Family, 69*, 951–961.

Gleason, J. B., & Ely, R. (2002). Gender differences in language development. In A. McGillicuddy-DeLisi & R. DeLisi (Eds.), *Biology, society, and behavior: The development of sex differences in cognition. Advances in applied developmental psychology* (Vol. 21, pp. 127–154). Westport, CT: Ablex.

Glenn, D. (2004, April 30). A dangerous surplus of sons? *Chronicle of Higher Education*, pp. 14–18.

Glick, P., et al. (2000). Beyond prejudice as simple antipathy: Hostile and benevolent sexism across cultures. *Journal of Personality and Social Psychology, 79*, 763–775.

Glick, P., & Fiske, S. T. (2007). Sex discrimination: The psychological approach. In F. J. Crosby, M. S. Stockdale, & S. A. Ropp (Eds.), *Sex discrimination in the workplace* (pp. 155–188). Malden, MA: Blackwell.

Glied, S. (1998). The diagnosis and treatment of mental health problems among older women. *Journal of the American Medical Women's Association, 53*, 187–191.

A global menace. (2006, May 15). *Newsweek*, pp. 52–53.

Glud, E., et al. (2004). Hormone therapy and the impact of estrogen intake on the risk of ovarian cancer. *Archives Internal Medicine, 164*, 2253–2259.

Godbey, J. K., & Hutchinson, S. A. (1996). Healing from incest: Resurrecting the buried self. *Archives of Psychiatric Nursing, 10*, 304–310.

Godfrey, J. R. (2007). Toward optimal health: Kathleen Brady, Ph.D., M.D., discusses challenges of substance abuse in women. *Journal of Women's Health, 16*, 163–167.

Godfrey, J. R., & Low Dog, T. (2008). Toward optimal health: Menopause as a rite of passage. *Journal of Women's Health, 17*, 509–514.

Gold, E. B., et al. (2006). Longitudinal analysis of the association between vasomotor symptoms and race/ethnicity across the menopausal transition: Study of women's health across the nation. *American Journal of Public Health, 96*, 1226–1235.

Gold, E. B., et al. (2007). Diet and lifestyle factors associated with premenstrual symptoms in a racially diverse community sample: Study of women's health across the nation (SWAN). *Journal of Women's Health, 16*, 641–656.

Gold, M. A., Wolford, J. E., Smith, K. A., & Parker, A. M. (2004). The effects of advance provision of emergency contraception on adolescent women's sexual and contraceptive behaviors. *Journal of Pediatric and Adolescent Gynecology, 17*, 87–96.

Goldberg, A. E., & Perry-Jenkins, M. (2007). The division of labor and perceptions of parental roles: Lesbian couples across the transition to parenthood. *Journal of Social and Personal Relationships, 24*, 297–318.

Goldberg, C. (1999, May 16). Wellesley grads find delicate balance. *Hartford Courant*, p. G3.

Goldberg, C. (2003, September 30). Unexpectedly expecting: Pregnant after 40. *Boston Globe*. Retrieved from http://www.boston.com/news/globe/health_science/articles/2003/09/30/

Goldberg, N. (2008). *Dr. Nieca Goldberg's complete guide to women's health.* New York: Ballentine.

Goldberg, W. A., & Lucas-Thompson, R. (2008). Effects of maternal and paternal employment. In M. M. Haith & J. B. Benson (Eds.), *Encyclopedia of infant and early childhood development* (Vol. 2, pp. 268–279). San Diego, CA: Academic Press.

Goldberg, W. A., Prause, J., Lucas-Thompson, R., & Himsel, A. (2008). Maternal employment and children's achievement in context: A meta-analysis of four decades of research. *Psychological Bulletin, 134,* 77–108.

Golden, C. (2008). The intersexed and the transgendered: Rethinking sex/gender. In J. C. Chrisler, C. Golden, & P. D. Rozee (Eds.), *Lectures on the psychology of women* (pp. 136–152). New York: McGraw-Hill.

Goldfried, M. R. (2001). Integrating gay, lesbian and bisexual issues into mainstream psychology. *American Psychologist, 56,* 977–988.

Goldin, C. (2006, March 15). Working it out. *New York Times,* p. A27.

Goldman, M. B., & Hatch, M. C. (2000). An overview of women and health. In M. B. Goldman & M. C. Hatch (Eds.), *Women & health* (pp. 5–14). San Diego: Academic Press.

Goldshmidt, O. T., & Weller, L. (2000). "Talking emotions": Gender differences in a variety of conversational contexts. *Symbolic Interaction, 23,* 117–134.

Goldstein, A. (2000, February 29). Breadwinning wives are on the rise. *Hartford Courant,* pp. A1, A7.

Goldston, D. B., Molock, S. D., Whitbeck, L. B., Murakami, J. L., Zayas, L. H., & Hall, G. C. N. (2008). Cultural considerations in adolescent suicide prevention and psychosocial treatment. *American Psychologist, 63,* 14–31.

Golombok, S., et al. (2003). Children with lesbian parents: A community study. *Developmental Psychology, 39,* 20–33.

Golombok, S., et al. (2004). Families created through surrogacy arrangements: Parent–child relationships in the first year of life. *Developmental Psychology, 40,* 400–411.

Gomez, M. J., et al. (2001). Voces abriendo caminos (Voices forging paths): A qualitative study of the career development of notable Latinas. *Journal of Counseling Psychology, 48,* 286–300.

Gondolf, E. W. (2004). Evaluating batterer counseling programs: A difficult task showing some effects and implications. *Aggression and Violent Behavior, 9,* 605–631.

Gonzalez, F. J., & Espin, O. M. (1996). Latino men, Latina women, and homosexuality. In R. P. Cabaj & T. S. Stein (Eds.), *Textbook of homosexuality and mental health* (pp. 583–593). Washington, DC: American Psychiatric Press.

Gonzalez, M. H., & Meyers, S. A. (1993). "Your mother would like me.": Self-presentation in the personal ads of heterosexual and homosexual men and women. *Personality and Social Psychology Bulletin, 19,* 131–142.

Good, C., Aronson, J., & Inzlicht, M. (2003). Improving adolescents' standardized test performance: An intervention to reduce the effects of stereotype threat. *Personality and Social Psychology Bulletin, 24,* 645–662.

Goodchilds, J. D. (2000, Summer). Afterword. *Journal of Social Issues.* Retrieved from http://www.findarticles.com/cf_dls/m0341/2_56/66419872/print.jhtml

Goode, E. (2000, May 19). Scientists find a particularly female response to stress. *New York Times,* p. A20.

Goode, E. (2003, June 22). How to talk to teenage girls about weight? Very carefully. *New York Times,* p. WH8.

Gooden, A. M., & Gooden, M. A. (2001). Gender representation in notable children's picture books: 1995–1999. *Sex Roles, 45,* 89–101.

Goodman, M., et al. (2005, August). *Minority stress and psychological distress of lesbian and gay persons.* Poster presented at the meeting of the American Psychological Association, Washington, DC.

Goodwin, P. J., et al. (2001). The effect of group psychosocial support on survival in metastatic breast cancer. *New England Journal of Medicine, 345,* 1719–1726.

Goodwin, S. A., & Fiske, S. T. (2001). Power and gender: The double-edged sword of ambivalence. In R. K. Unger (Ed.), *Handbook of the psychology women and gender* (pp. 358–366). New York: Wiley.

Gordon, R. A., & Arvey, R. D. (2004). Age bias in laboratory and field settings: A meta-analytic investigation. *Journal of Applied Social Psychology, 34,* 468–492.

Gordon, R. A., Chase-Lansdale, P. L., & Brooks-Gunn, J. (2004). Extended households and the life course of young mothers: Understanding the associations using a sample of mothers with premature, low birth weight babies. *Child Development, 75,* 1013–1038.

Gorman, C., & Cole, W. (2004, March 1). Between the sexes. *Time,* pp. 54–56.

Gostin, L. O., & DeAngelis, C. D. (2007). Mandatory HPV vaccination: Public health vs private wealth. *Journal of the American Medical Association, 297,* 1921–1923.

Gottlieb, N. (1989). Families, work and the lives of older women. In J. D. Garner & S. O. Mercer (Eds.), *Women as they age: Challenge, opportunity, and triumph* (pp. 217–244). Binghamton, NY: Haworth.

Gould, L. (1990). X: A fabulous child's story. In A. G. Halberstadt & S. L. Ellyson (Eds.), *Social psychology readings: A century of research* (pp. 251–257). Boston: McGraw-Hill.

Gould, S. J. (1981). *The mismeasure of man.* New York: Norton.

Gowaty, P. A. (2001). Women, psychology and evolution. In R. K. Unger (Ed.), *Handbook of the psychology of women and gender* (pp. 53–65). New York: Wiley.

Goyer, A. (2005). *Intergenerational relationships: Grandparents raising grandchildren.* Washington, DC: AARP.

Grabe, S., & Hyde, J. S. (2006). Ethnicity and body dissatisfaction among women in the United States: A meta-analysis. *Psychological Bulletin, 132,* 622–640.

Grabe, S., Hyde, J. S., & Lindberg, S. M. (2007). Body objectification and depression in adolescents: The role of gender, shame, and rumination. *Psychology of Women Quarterly, 31,* 164–175.

Grabe, S., Ward, L. M., & Hyde, J. S. (2008). The role of the media in body image concerns among women: A meta-analysis of experimental and correlational studies. *Psychological Bulletin, 134,* 460–476.

Graber, J. A. (2004). Internalizing problems during adolescence. In R. M. Lerner & L. Steinberg (Eds.), *Handbook of adolescent psychology* (2nd ed., pp. 587–626). Hoboken, NJ: Wiley.

Graber, J. A., & Brooks-Gunn, J. (1998). Puberty. In E. A. Blechman & K. D. Brownell (Eds.), *Behavioral medicine and women: A comprehensive handbook* (pp. 51–58). New York: Guilford.

Graber, J. A., & Brooks-Gunn, J. (2002). Adolescent girls' sexual development. In G. M. Wingood & R. J. DiClemente (Eds.), *Handbook of women's sexual and reproductive health* (pp. 21–42). New York: Kluwer Academic/Plenum.

Grady, Deborah. (2006). Management of menopausal symptoms. *New England Journal of Medicine, 355,* 2338–2347.

Grady, Denise. (2002, September 3). Hot flashes: Exploring the mystery of women's thermal chaos. *New York Times,* p. D5.

Grady, D. (2004, September 24). Report of first birth for cancer survivor in a tissue implant. *New York Times,* pp. A1, A24.

Grady, D. (2006, April 18). In heart disease, the focus shifts to women. *New York Times,* pp. D1, D8.

Grady, D. (2007, February 6). Girl or boy? As fertility technology advances, so does an ethical debate. *New York Times,* pp. D5, D10.

Grady, D. (2008a, January 21). Pregnancy problems tied to caffeine. *New York Times,* p. A10.

Grady, D. (2008b, April 10). Sharper digital breast exams can add anxiety. *New York Times,* pp. A1, A16.

Grall, T. S. (2004). *The condition of education 2004.* NCES 2004-007. U.S. Department of Education, National Center for Education Statistics. Washington, DC: U.S. Government Printing Office.

Grandmother caregivers suffer more stress, depression. (2005, Summer). *AARP: The GIC Voice,* p. 15.

Grandparents raising grandchildren. (2002, June). *AARP Bulletin,* p. 27.

Granrose, C. S., & Kaplan, E. E. (1996). *Work-family role choices for women in their 20s and 30s: From college plans to life experiences.* Westport, CT: Praeger.

Gray, J. (1992). *Men are from Mars, women are from Venus.* New York: HarperCollins.

Gray-Little, B., & Hafdahl, A. R. (2000). Factors influencing racial comparisons of self-esteem: A quantitative review. *Psychological Bulletin, 126,* 26–54.

Green, B. L., & Russo, N. F. (1993). Work and family roles: Selected issues. In F. L. Denmark & M. A. Paludi (Eds.), *Psychology of women: A handbook of issues and theories* (pp. 685–719). Westport, CT: Greenwood.

Green, E. R. (2006). Debating trans inclusion in the feminist movement: A trans-positive analysis. *Journal of Lesbian Studies, 10,* 231–248.

Green, R. J. (2004). Risk and resilience in lesbian and gay couples: Comment on Solomon, Rothblum, and Balsam (2004). *Journal of Family Psychology, 18,* 290–292.

Green, V. A., Bigler, R., & Catherwood, D. (2004). The variability and flexibility of gender-typed toy play: A close look at children's behavioral responses to counterstereotypic models. *Sex Roles, 51,* 371–386.

Greenberg, B. S., et al. (2003). Portrayals of overweight and obese individuals on commercial television. *American Journal of Public Health, 93,* 1342–1348.

Greene, B. (2003). Women of color and relationships. In L. Slater, J. H. Daniel, & A. E. Banks (Eds.), *The complete guide to mental health for women* (pp. 100–103). Boston: Beacon Press.

Greene, M. L., & Way, N. (2005). Self-esteem trajectories among ethnic minority adolescents: A growth curve analysis of the patterns and predictors of change. *Journal of Research on Adolescence, 15,* 151–178.

Greenfield, S. F. (2002). Women and alcohol use disorders. *Harvard Review of Psychology, 10,* 76–85.

Greenhaus, J. H., & Powell, G. N. (2006). When work and family are allies: A theory of work-family enrichment. *Academy of Management Review, 31,* 72–92.

Greenhouse, S. (2004, November 17). Abercrombie & Fitch bias case is settled. *New York Times,* p. A16.

Greenwood, D. N. (2007). Are female action heroes risky role models? Character identification, idealization, and viewer aggression. *Sex Roles, 57,* 725–732.

Grimberg, A., Kutikov, J. K., & Cucchiara, A. J. (2005). Sex differences in patients referred for evaluation of poor growth. *Journal of Pediatrics, 146,* 212–216.

Grimmell, D., & Stern, G. S. (1992). The relationship between gender role ideals and psychological well-being. *Sex Roles, 27,* 487–497.

Grodstein, F., Clarkson, D. V. M., & Manson, J. E. (2003). Understanding the divergent data on postmenopausal hormone therapy. *New England Journal of Medicine, 348,* 645–650.

Groesz, L. M., Levine, M. P., & Murnen, S. K. (2002). The effect of experimental presentation of thin media images on body satisfaction: A meta-analytic review. *International Journal of Eating Disorders, 31,* 1–16.

Gross, J. (2004, April 23). Last hurdle for trailblazing women: The gold watch. Like men before them, professionals facing retirement ask what's next. *New York Times,* p. A19.

Gross, J. (2006, March 25). As parents age, baby boomers and business struggle to cope. *New York Times,* pp. A1, A10.

Gross, J. J., et al. (1997). Emotion and aging: Experience expression, and control. *Psychology and Aging, 12,* 590–599.

Gross, S. M., Ireys, H. T., & Kinsman, S. L. (2000). Young women with physical disabilities: Risk factors for symptoms of eating disorders. *Developmental and Behavioral Pediatrics, 21,* 87–96.

Grossman, A. H., D'Augelli, A. R., & Hersh-berger, S. L. (2000). Social support networks of lesbian, gay, and bisexual adults 60 years of age and older. *Journal of Gerontology: Psychological Sciences, 55B,* 171–179.

Grossman, A. H., D'Augelli, A. R., & O'Connel, T. S. (2001). Being lesbian, gay, bisexual, and 60 or older in North America. *Journal of Gay & Lesbian Social Services, 13,* 23–40.

Grossman, A. J. (2007, December 2). To be safe, call the bride by her first name. *New York Times,* p. ST22.

Grossman, A. L., & Tucker, J. S. (1997). Gender differences and sexism in the knowledge and use of slang. *Sex Roles, 37,* 101–110.

Grossman, S. E., & Lundy, M. (2003). Use of domestic violence services across race and ethnicity by women aged 55 and older. *Violence against Women, 9,* 1442–1452.

Grunbaum, J. A. (2004). Youth risk behavior surveillance—United States, 2003. *Morbidity and Mortality Weekly Report, 53*(SS-2).

Grundy, S. M. (2007). Should women be offered cholesterol lowering drugs to prevent cardiovascular disease? *BMJ, 334,* 982.

Guastello, D. D., & Guastello, S. J. (2003). Androgyny, gender role behavior, and emotional intelligence among college students and their parents. *Sex Roles, 49,* 663–673.

Guiaux, M., Van Tilburg, T., & Van Groenou, M. B. (2007). Changes in contact and support exchange in personal networks after widowhood. *Personal Relationships, 14,* 457–473.

Guidelines for psychotherapy with lesbian, gay, and bisexual clients. (2000). *American Psychologist, 55,* 1440–1451.

Gupta, S. (2007). Autonomy, dependence, or display? The relationship between married women's earnings and housework. *Journal of Marriage and Family, 69,* 399–417.

Gutek, B. A. (2001). Working environments. In J. Worell (Ed.), *Encyclopedia of women and gender* (pp. 1191–1204). San Diego: Academic Press.

Gutek, B. A., & Done, R. S. (2001). Sexual harassment. In R. K. Unger (Ed.), *Handbook of the psychology women and gender* (pp. 367–387). New York: Wiley.

Gutman, L. M., & Eccles, J. S. (2007). Stage-environment fit during adolescence: Trajectories of family relations and adolescent outcomes. *Developmental Psychology, 43,* 522–537.

Guzman, K. (2002, May 3). As wedding season looms, surname debate resumes. *Chicago Tribune,* pp. C1, C5.

Haag, P. (1999). *Voices of a generation: Teenage girls on sex, schools, and self.* Washington, DC: American Association of University Women.

Hackett, G., Betz, N. E., Casas, J. M., & Rocha-Singh, I. A. (1992). Gender, ethnicity, and social cognitive factors predicting the academic achievement of students in engineering. *Journal of Counseling Psychology, 39,* 527–538.

Haddock, S., & Cincotta, R. P. (2006). Closing the gender gap in education: Is there evidence of short-term declines in adolescent fertility? *Population Action International, 1,* 1–5.

Hafner, K. (2003, August 21). 3 women and 3 paths, 10 years later. *New York Times,* pp. E1, E7.

Hafner, K. (2004, October 14). What do women game designers want? *New York Times,* pp. E1, E4.

Haj-Yahia, M. M. (2002). Beliefs of Jordanian women about wife-beating. *Psychology of Women Quarterly, 26,* 282–291.

Halbreich, U. (2005). The association between pregnancy processes, preterm delivery, low birth weight, and postpartum depressions—the need for interdisciplinary integration. *American Journal of Obstetrics and Gynecology, 193,* 1312–1322.

Hall, D. M. (2008). Feminist perspectives on the personal and political aspects of mothering. In J. C. Chrisler, C. Golden, & P. D. Rozee (Eds.), *Lectures on the psychology of women* (pp. 58–79). New York: McGraw-Hill.

Hall, J. A. (1996). Touch, status, and gender at professional meetings. *Journal of Nonverbal Behavior, 20,* 23–44.

Hall, J. A., Carter, J. D., & Horgan, T. G. (2000). Gender differences in nonverbal communication of emotion. In A. H. Fischer (Ed.), *Gender and emotion: Social psychological perspectives* (pp. 97–117). Paris: Cambridge University Press.

Hall, J. A., LeBeau, L. S., Reinoso, J. G., & Thayer, F. (2001). Status, gender, and nonverbal behavior in candid and posed photographs: A study of conversations between university employees. *Sex Roles, 44,* 677–692.

Hall, J. A., & Veccia, E. M. (1992). Touch asymmetry between the sexes. In C. L. Ridgeway (Ed.), *Gender, interaction, and inequality* (pp. 81–96). New York: Springer.

Hall, R. E. (2003, June). Eurocentric bias in women's psychology journals: Resistance to issues significant to people of color. *European Psychologist, 8,* 117–122.

Hall, R. L. (2007). On the move: Exercise, leisure activities, and midlife women. In V. Muhlbauer & J. C. Chrisler (Eds.), *Women over 50: Psychological perspectives* (pp. 79–94). New York: Springer.

Hall, R. L. (2008). Sweating it out: The good news and the bad news about women and sport. In J. C. Chrisler, C. Golden, & P. D. Rozee (Eds.), *Lectures on the psychology of women* (pp. 96–115). New York: McGraw-Hill.

Hall, R. L., & Greene, B. (2002). Not any one thing: The complex legacy of social class on African American lesbian relationships. *Journal of Lesbian Studies, 6*(1), 85–109.

Hall, R. M., & Sandler, B. R. (1982). *The classroom climate: A chilly one for women?* Project on the Status and Education of Women. Washington, DC: Association of American Colleges.

Hall Smith, P., White, J. W., & Holland, L. J. (2003). A longitudinal perspective on dating violence among adolescent and college-age women. *American Journal of Public Health, 93,* 1104–1109.

Halmi, K. A. (2000). Eating disorder research in the past decade. *Women and Mental Health. Annals of the New York Academy of Sciences, 789,* 67–77.

Halpern, D. F. (2000). *Sex differences in cognitive abilities* (3rd ed.). Mahwah, NJ: Erlbaum.

Halpern, D. F. (2001). Sex difference research: Cognitive abilities. In J. Worell (Ed.), *Encyclopedia of women and gender* (pp. 963–971). San Diego: Academic Press.

Halpern, D. F. (2004a). A cognitive-process taxonomy for sex differences in cognitive abilities. *Current Directions in Psychological Science, 13,* 135–139.

Halpern, D. (2004b). Making it work: Recommendations for policies on working families. *Monitor on Psychology,* p. 5.

Halpern, D. (2004c). Transitions, reflections, resolutions. *Monitor on Psychology,* p. 5.

Halpern, D. (2005). Psychology at the intersection of work and family: Recommendations for employers, working families, and policymakers. *American Psychologist, 60,* 397–409.

Halpern, D. F. (2007). Science, sex, and good sense: Why women are underrepresented in some areas of science and math. In S. J. Ceci & W. M. Williams (Eds.), *Why aren't more women in science? Top researchers debate the evidence* (pp. 121–130). Washington, DC:. American Psychological Association.

Halpern, D. F., Benbow, C. P., Geary, D. C., Gur, R. C., Hyde, J. S., & Gernsbacher, M. A. (2007). The science of sex differences in science and mathematics. *Psychological Science in the Public Interest, 8,* 1–51.

Halpern, D. L. (2005). How time-flexible work policies can reduce stress, improve health, and save money. *Stress and Health, 21,* 157–168.

Halpern, M. T., Ward, E. M., Pavluck, A. L., Schrag, N. M., Bian, J., & Chen, A. Y. (2008). Association of insurance status and ethnicity with cancer stage at diagnosis for 12 cancer sites: A retrospective analysis. *Lancet Oncology, 9,* 222–231.

Hamby, S. L. (2005). Measuring gender differences in partner violence: Implications from research on other forms of violent and socially undesirable behavior. *Sex Roles, 52,* 725–742.

Hamby, S. L., & Koss, M. P. (2003). Shades of gray: A qualitative study of terms used in the measurement of sexual victimization. *Psychology of Women Quarterly, 27,* 243–255.

Hamilton, B. E., Martin, J. A., & Sutton, P. D. (2004). *Births: Preliminary data for 2003.* National Vital Statistics Reports, 53(9). Hyattsville, MD: National Center for Health Statistics.

Hamilton, B. E., Martin, J. A., & Ventura, S. J. (2007). *Births: Preliminary data for 2006.* National Vital Statistics Reports, 56(7). Hyattsville, MD: National Center for Health Statistics.

Hamilton, E. A., Mintz, L., & Kashubeck-West, S. (2007). Predictors of media effects on body dissatisfaction in European American women. *Sex Roles, 56,* 397–402.

Hamilton, M. C. (1991). Masculine bias in the attribution of personhood: People = male, male = people. *Psychology of Women Quarterly, 15,* 393–402.

Hamilton, M. C. (2001). Sex-related difference research: Personality. In J. Worell (Ed.), *Encyclopedia of women and gender* (pp. 973–981). San Diego: Academic Press.

Hammarberg, A., & Hagekull, B. (2006). Changes in externalizing and internalizing behaviours over a school-year: Differences between 6-year-old boys and girls. *Infant and Child Development, 15,* 123–137.

Hammond, C. B., & Calhoun, K. S. (2007). Labeling of abuse experiences and rates of victimization. *Psychology of Women Quarterly, 31,* 371–380.

Hampson, E., & Moffat, S. D. (2004). The psychobiology of gender: Cognitive effects of reproductive hormones in the adult nervous system. In A. H. Eagly, A. E. Beall, & R. J. Sternberg (Eds.), *The psychology of gender* (pp. 38–64). New York: Guilford.

Hampton, T. (2007). Study examines effects of advance access to emergency contraception. *Journal of the American Medical Association, 297,* 2067–2068.

Hanisch, L. J., Hantsoo, L., Freeman, E. W., Sullivan, G. M., & Coyne, J. C. (2008). Hot flashes and panic attacks: A comparison of symptomatology, neurobiology, treatment, and a role for cognition. *Psychological Bulletin, 134,* 247–269.

Hankin, B. L., & Abramson, L. Y. (2001). Development of gender differences in depression. *Psychological Bulletin, 127,* 773–796.

Hankin, B. L., Mermelstein, R., & Roesch, L. (2007). Sex differences in adolescent depression: Stress exposure and reactivity models. *Child Development, 78,* 279–295.

Hankin, S. (2004, Summer). Viagra or an Rx for sex? *Ms.,* p. 63.

Hanna, W. J., & Rogovsky, E. (1992). On the situation of African-American women with physical disabilities. *Journal of Applied Rehabilitation Counseling, 23,* 39–45.

Hannaford, P. C., Selvaraj, S., Elliott, A. M., Angus, V., Iversen, L., & Lee, A. J. (2007). Cancer risk among users of oral contraceptives: Cohort data from the Royal College of General Practitioner's oral contraception study. *BMJ, 335,* 651–654.

Hanratty, B., Drever, F., Jacoby, A., & Whitehead, M. (2007). Retirement age caregivers and deprivation of area of residence in England and Wales. *European Journal of Aging, 4,* 35–43.

Hanson, K., & Wapner, S. (1994). Transition to retirement: Gender differences. *International Journal of Aging and Human Development, 39,* 189–208.

Hanson, R. F., et al. (2001). Impact of childhood rape and aggravated assault on adult mental health. *American Journal of Orthopsychiatry, 71,* 108–119.

Hardin, M., Lynn, S., & Walsdorf, K. (2005). Challenge and conformity on "contested terrain": Images of women in four women's sport/fitness magazines. *Sex Roles, 53,* 105–117.

Hare-Mustin, R. T., & Marecek, J. (1990). On making a difference. In R. T. Hare-Mustin & J. Marecek (Eds.), *Making a difference: Psychology and the construction of gender* (pp. 1–21). New Haven, CT: Yale University Press.

Harm, N. J. (2001). Grandmothers raising grandchildren: Parenting the second time around. In J. D. Garner & S. O. Mercer (Eds.), *Women as they age* (2nd ed., pp. 131–146). New York: Haworth.

Harmon, A. (2003, June 29). Online dating sheds its stigma as losers.com. *New York Times,* pp. YT1, YT21.

Harper, B., & Tiggemann, M. (2008). The effect of thin ideal media images on women's self-objectification, mood, and body image. *Sex Roles, 58,* 649–657.

Harper, G. W., Jernewall, N., & Zea, M. C. (2004). Giving voice to emerging science and theory for lesbian, gay, and bisexual people of color. *Cultural Diversity and Ethnic Minority Psychology, 10,* 187–199.

Harper, M., & Schoeman, W. J. (2003). Influences of gender as a basic-level category in person perception on the gender belief system. *Sex Roles, 49,* 517–526.

Harris, A. C. (1994). Ethnicity as a determinant of sex role identity: A replication study of item selection for the Bem Sex Role Inventory. *Sex Roles, 31,* 241–273.

Harris, G. (2006a, March 18). After 2 more deaths, Planned Parenthood alters method for abortion pill. *New York Times,* p. A9.

Harris, G. (2006b, August 25). F.D.A. approves broader access to next-day pill. *New York Times,* p. A1.

Harris, K. L., Melaas, K., & Rodacker, E. (1999). The impact of women's studies courses on college students of the 1990s. *Sex Roles, 40,* 969–977.

Harris, M. B. (1994). Growing old gracefully: Age concealment and gender. *Journal of Gerontology: Psychological Sciences, 49,* 149–158.

Harris, M. B., & Knight-Bohnhoff, K. (1996). Gender and aggression II: Personal aggressiveness. *Sex Roles, 35,* 27–42.

Harris, M. B., Page, P., & Begay, C. (1988). Attitudes toward aging in a southwestern sample: Effects of ethnicity, age, and sex. *Psychological Reports, 62,* 735–746.

Harris, R. J., & Firestone, J. M. (1998). Changes in predictors of gender role ideologies among women: A multivariate analysis. *Sex Roles, 38*, 239–252.

Harter, S. (1990). Adolescent self and identity development. In S. S. Feldman & G. R. Elliot (Eds.), *At the threshold: The developing adolescent* (pp. 352–387). Cambridge, MA: Harvard University Press.

Harter, S. (1998). The development of self-representations. In W. Damon (Series Ed.) & N. Eisenberg (Vol. Ed.), *Handbook of child psychology. Vol. 3. Social, emotional and personality development* (5th ed., pp. 553–617). New York: Wiley.

Harter, S. (1999). *The construction of the self: A developmental perspective*. New York: Guilford.

Harter, S. (2006). The self. In W. Damon, R. M. Lerner (Series Eds.) & N. Eisenberg (Vol. Ed.), *Handbook of child psychology: Vol. 3. Social, emotional, and personality development* (6th ed., pp. 505–570). Hoboken, NJ: Wiley.

Hartley, H., & Tiefer, L. (2003, Spring/Summer). Taking a biological turn: The push for a "female Viagra" and the push for medicalization of women's sexual problems. *Women's Studies Quarterly, 31*, 42–54.

Hartman, H., & Hartman, M. (2008). How undergraduate engineering students perceive women's (and men's) problems in science, math and engineering. *Sex Roles, 58*, 251–265.

Hartmann, H., Hegewisch, A., & Lovell, V. (2007). *An economy that puts families first*. Washington, DC: Economic Policy Institute.

Hartman, K. E., et al. (2004). Quality of life and sexual function after hysterectomy in women with preoperative pain and depression. *Obstetrics & Gynecology, 104*, 701–709.

Harville, M. L., & Rienzi, B. M. (2000). Equal worth and gracious submission: Judeo-Christian attitudes toward employed women. *Psychology of Women Quarterly, 24*, 145–147.

Hasin, D. S., Stinson, F. S., Ogburn, E., & Grant, B. F. (2007). Prevalence, correlates, disability, and comorbidity of *DSM-IV* alcohol abuse and dependence in the United States. *Archives of General Psychiatry, 64*, 830–842.

Haskell, K. (2003, November 30). When grandparents step into the child care gap, money can be scarce. *New York Times*, p. YT 29.

Haskell, M. (1998, February 8). Where the old boy always get the girl. *New York Times*, p. AR11.

Haskell, M., & Harmetz, A. (1998, March–April). Star power. *Modern Maturity, 41*, 32–40.

Hass, N. (2002, June 16). Hey dads, thanks for the love and support (and the credit card). *New York Times*, pp. ST1, SP2.

Hassan, M. A. M., & Killick, S. R. (2004). Negative lifestyle is associated with a significant reduction in fecundity. *Fertility and Sterility, 81*, 384–392.

Hatala, M. N., & Prehodka, J. (1996). Content analysis of gay male and lesbian personal advertisements. *Psychological Reports, 78*, 371–374.

Hattery, A. (2001). *Women, work, and family: Balancing and weaving*. Thousand Oaks, CA: Sage.

Hawkins, D. N., & Whiteman, S. D. (2004). Balancing work and family: Problems and solutions for low-income families.

In A. C. Crouter and A. Booth (Eds.), *Work-family challenges for low-income parents and their children* (pp. 273–286). Mahwah, NJ: Erlbaum.

Hawkins, J. W., & Aber, C. S. (1993). Women in advertisements in medical journals. *Sex Roles, 28*, 233–244.

Hawthorne, F. (2007, October 23). Greater obstacles to retirement for women. *New York Times*, p. A13.

Hay, D. F., Payne, A., & Chadwick, A. (2004). Peer relations in childhood. *Journal of Child Psychology and Psychiatry, 45*, 84–108.

Hayes, S. N., Weisman, C. S., & Clark, A. (2003). The Jacobs Institute of Women's Health report on the prevention of heart disease in women: Findings and recommendations from the "Women and heart disease: Putting prevention into primary care" conference. *Women's Health Issues, 13*, 115–121.

Hayt, E. (2002, May 12). Admitting to mixed feelings about motherhood. *New York Times*, pp. ST1, ST2.

He, W., Sengupta, M., Velkoff, V. A., & DeBarros, K. A. (2005). *65+ in the United States: 2005*. Current Population Reports, P23–209. Washington, DC: U.S. Census Bureau.

Headlam, B. (2000, January 20). Barbie PC: Fashion over logic. *New York Times*, p. E4.

Health and wellness for women with disabilities. (2004, Winter). *Health Matters for Women Newsletter*, pp. 1, 4.

Heatherington, L., et al. (1993). Two investigations of "female modesty" in achievement situations. *Sex Roles, 29*, 739–754.

Heck, J., Sell, R., & Gorin, S. (2006). Health care access among individuals involved in same-sex relationships. *American Journal of Public Health, 96*, 1111–1118.

Heckert, T. M. (2002). Gender differences in anticipated salary: Role of salary estimates for others, job characteristics, career paths, and job inputs. *Sex Roles, 47*, 139–151.

Heckert, T. M., et al. (2002). Gender differences in anticipated salary: Role of salary estimates for others, job characteristics, career paths, and job inputs. *Sex Roles, 47*, 139–151.

Hedley, M. (1994). The presentation of gendered conflict in popular movies: Affective stereotypes, cultural sentiments, and men's motivation. *Sex Roles, 31*, 721–740.

Hefferman, K. (1999). Lesbians and the internalization of societal standards of weight and appearance. *Journal of Lesbian Studies, 3*(4), 121–127.

Heffner, L. J. (2004). Advanced maternal age—how old is too old? *New England Journal of Medicine, 351*, 1927–1929.

Heilman, M. E. (2001). Description and prescription: How gender stereotypes prevent women's ascent up the organizational ladder. *Journal of Social Issues, 57*, 657–674.

Heilman, M. E., & Haynes, M. C. (2005). No credit where credit is due: Attribution rationalization of women's success in male–female teams. *Journal of Applied Psychology, 90*, 905–916.

Heilman, M. E., & Okimoto, T. G. (2007). Why are women penalized for success at male tasks? The implied communality deficit. *Journal of Applied Psychology, 92*, 81–92.

Heilman, M. E., & Okimoto, T. G. (2008). Motherhood: A potential source of bias in employment decisions. *Journal of Applied Psychology, 93*, 189–198.

Heiss, G., et al. (2008). Health risks and benefits 3 years after stopping randomized treatment with estrogen and progestin. *Journal of the American Medical Association, 299,* 1036–1045.

Hellerstedt, W., Rhodes, K., Peterson-Hickey, M., & Garwick, A. (2006). Environmental, social, and personal correlates of having ever had sexual intercourse among American Indian youths. *American Journal of Public Health, 96,* 2228–2234.

HELP Network. (2003). *Guns and domestic violence: A deadly combination.* Chicago: Author.

Helping the patient by helping the caretaker. (2000). *Health after 50: The John Hopkins Medical Letter, 12,* 3.

Helson, R. (1992). Women's difficult times and the rewriting of the life story. *Psychology of Women Quarterly, 16,* 331–347.

Helson, R., & Srivastava, S. (2001). Three paths of adults development: Conservers, seekers, and achievers. *Journal of Personality and Social Psychology, 80,* 995–1010.

Helton, M. R. (2000). Prenatal care. In M. A. Smith & L. A. Shimp (Eds.), *20 common problems in women's health care* (pp. 65–89). New York: McGraw-Hill.

Helwig, A. A. (1998). Gender-role stereotyping: Testing theory with a longitudinal sample. *Sex Roles, 38,* 403–423.

Henderson-King, D., & Zhermer, N. (2003). Feminist consciousness among Russians and Americans. *Sex Roles, 48,* 143–155.

Hendrick, C. L., & Reddy, D. M. (2007, May). *Predictors of sexual risk behavior in women.* Poster presented at the annual meeting of the Midwestern Psychological Association, Chicago.

Hendy, H. M., et al. (2003). Comparison of six models for violent romantic relationships in college men and women. *Journal of Interpersonal Violence, 18,* 645–665.

Henehan, D., Rothblum, E. D., Solomon, S. E., & Balsam, K. F. (2008). Social and demographic characteristics of lesbian, gay, and heterosexual adults with and without children. *Journal of GLBT Family Studies, 3,* 35–79.

Henig, R. M. (2004a, June 6). Sex without estrogen: Remedies for the midlife mind and body. *New York Times,* p. WH12.

Henig, R. M. (2004b, November 30). Sorry. Your eating disorder doesn't meet our criteria. *New York Times,* pp. D1, D9.

Henley, N. M. (1995). Body politics revisited: What do we know today? In P. J. Kalbfleisch & M. J. Cody (Eds.), *Gender, power, and communication in human relationships* (pp. 27–61). Hillsdale, NJ: Erlbaum.

Henley, N. M., Meng, K., O'Brien, D., McCarthy, W. J., & Sockloskie, R. J. (1998). Developing a scale to measure the diversity of feminist attitudes. *Psychology of Women Quarterly, 22,* 317–348.

Henningfield, J. E., Santera, P. B., & Stillman, F. A. (2005). Exploitation by design—could tobacco industry documents guide more effective smoking prevention and cessation in women? *Addiction, 100,* 735–736.

Henningsen, D. D. (2004). Flirting with meaning: An examination of miscommunication in flirting interactions. *Sex Roles, 50,* 481–489.

Henningsen, D. D., Henningsen, M. L. M., & Valde, K. S. (2006). Gender differences in perceptions of women's sexual interest during cross-sex interactions: An application and extension of cognitive valence theory. *Sex Roles, 54,* 821–829.

Henry, A. (2004). *Not my mother's sister: Generational conflict and third-wave feminism.* Bloomington, IN: Indiana University Press.

Henry, D. B., Schoeny, M. E., Deptula, D. P., & Slavick, J. T. (2007). Peer selection and socialization effects on adolescent intercourse without a condom and attitudes about the costs of sex. *Child Development, 78,* 825–838.

Henry, J. G. A. (2000). Depression and anxiety. In M. A. Smith & L. A. Shimp (Eds.), *20 common problems in women's health care* (pp. 263–301). New York: McGraw-Hill.

Heppner, M. J., & O'Brien, K. M. (2006). Women and poverty: A holistic approach to vocational interventions. In W. B. Walsh & M. J. Heppner (Eds.), *Handbook of career counseling for women* (2nd ed., pp. 75–102). Mahwah, NJ: Erlbaum.

Herbert, S. E., & Bachanas, P. (2002). HIV/AIDS. In S. G. Kornstein & A. H. Clayton (Eds.), *Women's mental health: A comprehensive textbook* (pp. 453–466). New York: Guilford.

Herdt, G. H., & Davidson, J. (1988). The Sambia "turnim-man": Sociocultural and clinical aspects of gender formation in male pseudohermaphrodites with 5-alpha-reductase deficiency in Papua New Guinea. *Archives of Sexual Behavior, 17,* 33–56.

Herek, G. M. (2000, Summer). Sexual prejudice and gender: Do heterosexuals' attitudes toward lesbians and gay men differ? *Journal of Social Issues, 56,* 251.

Herek, G. M. (2006). Legal recognition of same-sex relationships in the United States. *American Psychologist, 61,* 607–621.

Herek, G. M. (2007). Confronting sexual stigma and prejudice: Theory and practice. *Journal of Social Issues, 63,* 905–925.

Herek, G. M., Cogan, S. C., & Gillis, J. R. (2002). Victim experiences in hate crimes based on sexual orientation. *Journal of Social Issues, 58,* 319–339.

Herek, G. M., et al. (1998). Correlates of internalized homophobia in a community sample of lesbians and gay men. *Journal of the Gay and Lesbian Medical Association, 2,* 17–25.

Herek, G. M., & Garnets, L. (2007). Sexual orientation and mental health. *Annual Review of Clinical Psychology, 3,* 353–375.

Herman, K., & West, S. A. (2003, Fall/Winter). Ensnared children in modern slavery. *AAUW Outlook,* pp. 16–19, 32.

Herman-Giddens, M. E., et al. (1997). Secondary sexual characteristics and menses in young girls seen in office practice: A study from the pediatric research in office settings network. *Pediatrics, 99,* 505–512.

Herman-Giddens, M. E., Kaplowitz, P. B., & Wasserman, R. (2004). Navigating the recent articles on girls' puberty in pediatrics: What do we know and where do we go from here? *Pediatrics, 113,* pp. 911–917.

Herman-Stahl, M., et al. (2007). Serious psychological distress among parenting and nonparenting adults. *American Journal of Public Health, 97,* 2222–2229.

Heron, M. P. (2007). *Deaths: Leading causes for 2004.* National Vital Statistics Reports, 56(5). Hyattsville, MD: National Center for Health Statistics.

Herrenkohl, T. I., McMorris, B. J., Catalano, R. F., Abbott, R. D., Hemphill, S. A., & Toumbourou, J. W. (2007). Risk factors for violence and relational aggression in adolescence. *Journal of Interpersonal Violence, 22,* 386–404.

Herrera, V. M., Koss, M. P., Bailey, J., Yuan, N. P., & Lichter, E. L. (2006). Survivors of male violence: Research and training initiatives to facilitate recovery from depression and post-traumatic stress disorder. In J. Worell & C. D. Goodheart (Eds.), *Handbook of girls' and women's psychological health: Gender and well-being across the lifespan* (pp. 455–466). New York: Oxford University Press.

Hertz, R. (2006). *Single by chance, mothers by choice: How women are choosing parenthood without marriage and creating the new American family.* New York: Oxford University Press.

Hertz, R., & Ferguson, F. I. (1998). Only one pair of hands: Ways that single mothers stretch work and family resources. *Community, Work, & Family, 1,* 13–37.

Heterosexual transmission of HIV—29 states, 1999–2002. (2004). *Morbidity and Mortality Weekly Report, 53,* 125–129.

Hetherington, E. M. (2004, July). *Lessons learned and unlearned in thirty five years of studying families.* Paper presented at the meeting of the American Psychological Association, Honolulu.

Hetherington, E. M., & Kelly, J. (2002). *For better or for worse: Divorce reconsidered.* New York: Norton.

Hewitt Associates. (2008, April 30). *Flexible work arrangements: Do they work?* Retrieved from http://www.hewittassociates.com/Intl/NA/en-US/AboutHewitt/Newsroom/PressRelease Detail.aspx?cid=5074

Hewlett, S. A. (2007). *Off-ramps and on-ramps: Keeping talented women on the road to success.* Boston: Harvard Business School Press.

Hewlett, S. A., Luce, C. B., & Servon, L. J. (2008). Stopping the exodus of women in science. *Harvard Business Review, 86.* doi:10.1225/F0806A

Heyl, A. R. (2004). The transition from career to retirement: Focus on well-being and financial considerations. *Journal of the American Medical Women's Association, 59,* 235–237.

Heyl, A. R. (2005). Climbing the ladder: Making the most of mentoring. *Journal of the American Medical Women's Association, 60,* 11–14.

Heymann, J., Earle, A., & Hayes, J. (2007). *The work, family, and equity index: How does the United States measure up?* Montreal, QC: Project on Global Working Families.

Heymann, J., Earle, A., Simmons, S., Breslow, S. M., & Kuehnhoff, A. (2004). *The work, family, and equity index: Where does the United States stand globally?* Boston: Project on Global Working Families.

Hickman, L. J., Jaycox, L. H., & Aronoff, J. (2004). Dating violence among adolescents: Prevalence, gender distribution, and prevention program effectiveness. *Trauma, Violence, & Abuse, 5,* 123–142.

Higginbotham, E., & Weber, L. (1996). Moving up with kin and community: Upward social mobility for Black and White women. In E. N. Chow, D. Wilkinson, & M. B. Zinn (Eds.), *Race, class, & gender: Common bonds, different voices* (pp. 125–148). Thousand Oaks, CA: Sage.

Hilbrecht, M., Zuzanek, J., & Mannell, R. C. (2008). Time use, time pressure, and gendered behavior in early and late adolescence. *Sex Roles, 58,* 342–357.

Hill, A. L., Degnan, K. A., Calkins, S. D., & Keane, S. P. (2006). Profiles of externalizing behavior problems for boys and girls across preschool: The roles of emotion regulation and inattention. *Developmental Psychology, 42,* 913–928.

Hill, C., & Silva, E. (2005). *Drawing the line: Sexual harassment on campus.* Washington, DC: American Association of University Women Educational Foundation.

Hill, T. D., & Needham, B. L. (2006). Gender-specific trends in educational attainment and self-rated health, 1972–2002. *American Journal of Public Health, 96,* 1288–1292.

Hillis, S. D., et al. (2004). The association between adverse childhood experiences and adolescent pregnancy, long-term psychosocial consequences, and fetal death. *Pediatrics, 113,* 320–327.

Hillman, J. L., & Stricker, G. (1994). A linkage of knowledge and attitudes toward elderly sexuality: Not necessarily a uniform relationship. *Gerontologist, 34,* 256–260.

Hilton, N. Z., & Harris, G. T. (2005). Predicting wife assault: A critical review and implications for policy and practice. *Trauma, Violence, & Abuse, 6,* 3–23.

Hines, D. A., & Saudino, K. J. (2002). Intergenerational transmission of intimate partner violence: A behavioral genetic perspective. *Trauma, Violence, & Abuse, 3,* 210–225.

Hines, M. (2004a). Androgen, estrogen, and gender: Contributions of the early hormone environment to gender-related behavior. In A. H. Eagly, A. E. Beall, & R. J. Sternberg (Eds.), *The psychology of gender* (pp. 9–37). New York: Guilford.

Hines, M. (2004b). *Brain gender.* New York: Oxford University Press.

Hines, M. (2007). Do sex differences in cognition cause the shortage of women in science? In S. J. Ceci & W. M. Williams (Eds.), *Why aren't more women in science? Top researchers debate the evidence* (pp. 101–112). Washington, DC: American Psychological Association.

Hines, M., et al. (2002). Testosterone during pregnancy and gender role behavior of preschool children: A longitudinal population study. *Child Development, 73,* 1678–1687.

Hirshbein, L. D. (2003). Biology and mental illness: A historical perspective. *Journal of the American Medical Women's Association, 58,* 89–94.

Ho, C. K. (1990). An analysis of domestic violence in Asian-American communities: A multicultural approach to counseling. In L. S. Brown & M. P. P. Root (Eds.), *Diversity and complexity in feminist therapy* (pp. 129–150). New York: Haworth Press.

Hochman, A. (2004, June). Don't panic. *Health,* pp. 99–103.

Hoeber, L. (2008). Gender equity for athletes: Multiple understandings of an organizational value. *Sex Roles, 58,* 58–71.

Hofferth, S. L., & Reid, L. (2002). Early childbearing and children's achievement and behavior over time. *Perspectives on Sexual and Reproductive Health, 34,* 41–49.

Hoffman, E. (2002, June). When couples clam up. *AARP Bulletin,* pp. 24–25.

Hoffman, L. W., & Youngblade, L. M. (2001, April). *Mothers' employment: Effects on families and children*. Paper presented at the meeting of the Society for Research in Child Development, Minneapolis, MN.

Hoffmann, M. L., Powlishta, K. K., & White, K. J. (2004). An examination of gender differences in adolescent adjustment: The effect of competence on gender role differences in symptoms of psychopathology. *Sex Roles, 50*, 795–810.

Hoffnung, M. (2004). Wanting it all: Career, marriage, and motherhood during college-educated women's 20s. *Sex Roles, 50*, 711–723.

Hogan, J. D., & Sexton, V. S. (1991). Women and the American Psychological Association. *Psychology of Women Quarterly, 15*, 623–634.

Hoge, W. (2002, December 7). Britain announces proposal for same-sex partnerships. *New York Times*, p. A8.

Hoggard, L. (2005, January 9). Why we're all beautiful now. *Observer (London)*, p. 4.

Hoglund, W. L., & Leadbeater, B. J. (2004). The effects of family, school, and classroom ecologies on changes in children's social competence and emotional and behavioral problems in first grade. *Developmental Psychology, 40*, 533–544.

Hogue, M., & Yoder, J. D. (2003). The role of status in producing depressed entitlement in women's and men's pay allocations. *Psychology of Women Quarterly, 27*, 330–337.

Hogue, M., Yoder, J. D., & Singleton, S. B. (2007). The gender wage gap: An explanation of men's elevated wage entitlement. *Sex Roles, 56*, 573–579.

Holahan, C. K., & Sears, R. R. (1995). *The gifted group in later maturity*. Stanford, CA: Stanford University Press.

Holcomb, B. (1998). *Not guilty: The good news about working mothers*. New York: Scribner.

Holcomb, L. P., & Giesen, C. B. (1995). Coping with challenges: College experiences of older women and women with disabilities. In J. C. Chrisler & A. H. Hemstreet (Eds.), *Variations on a theme: Diversity and the psychology of women*. Albany, NY: SUNY.

Holick, M. F. (2007). Vitamin D deficiency. *New England Journal of Medicine, 357*, 266–281.

Holland, A., & Andre, T. (1992). College students' attitudes toward women: A three-dimensional approach. *College Student Journal, 26*, 253–259.

Hollingsworth, M. A., Tomlinson, M. J., & Fassinger, R. E. (1997, August). *Working it out: Career development among prominent lesbian women*. Paper presented at the meeting of the American Psychological Association, Chicago.

Holmes, S. E., & Cahill, S. (2004). School experiences of gay, lesbian, bisexual and transgender youth. *Journal of Gay & Lesbian Issues in Education, 1*, 53–66.

Holroyd, S. (2002). Aging and elderly women. In S. G. Kornstein & A. H. Clayton (Eds.), *Women's mental health: A comprehensive textbook* (pp. 584–593). New York: Guilford.

Holroyd-Leduc, J. M., & Straus, S. E. (2004). Management of urinary incontinence in women. *Journal of the American Medical Association, 291*, 986–999.

Holt-Lunstad, J., et al. (2008, May). *Social support and mortality: A meta-analysis*. Poster presented at the meeting of the Association for Psychological Science, Chicago.

Hong, S., Friedman, J., & Alt, S. (2003). Modifiable risk factors for the primary prevention of heart disease in women. *Journal of the American Medical Women's Association, 58*, 278–284.

Hook, J. L. (2004). Reconsidering the division of household labor: Incorporating volunteer work and informal support. *Journal of Marriage and Family, 66*, 101–117.

Hook, J. L. (2006). Care in context: Men's unpaid work in 20 countries, 1965–2003. *American Sociological Review, 71*, 639–660.

Hook, M. K., & Bowman, S. (2008). Working for a living: The vocational decision making of lesbians. *Journal of Lesbian Studies, 12*, 85–95.

hooks, b. (1990). Feminism: A transformational politic. In D. L. Rhode (Ed.), *Theoretical perspectives in sexual difference* (pp. 185–193). New Haven, CT: Yale University Press.

Hopkins, A. B. (1996). *So ordered: Making partner the hard way*. Amherst: University of Massachusetts Press.

Hopkins, A. B. (2007). Opposing views, strongly held. In F. J. Crosby, M. S. Stockdale, & S. A. Ropp (Eds.), *Sex discrimination in the workplace* (pp. 59–68). Malden, MA: Blackwell.

Horgan, T. G., Schmid Mast, M., Hall, J. A., & Carter, J. D. (2004). Gender differences in memory for the appearance of others. *Journal of Personality and Social Psychology Bulletin, 30*, 185–196.

Hornbacher, M. (1998). *Wasted: A memoir of anorexia and bulimia*. New York: Harper Perennial.

Horner, M. S. (1972). Toward an understanding of achievement-related conflicts in women. *Journal of Social Issues, 28*, 157–176.

Horney, K. (1926/1974). The flight from womanhood: The masculinity-complex in women as viewed by men and women. In J. Strouse (Ed.), *Women and analysis: Dialogues on psychoanalytic views of femininity* (pp. 171–186). New York: Viking.

Horn-Ross, P. L., et al. (2004). Patterns of alcohol consumption and breast cancer risk in the California teachers study cohort. *Cancer Epidemiology Biomarkers & Prevention, 13*, 405–411.

Hounsell, C. (2008). *The female factor 2008: Why women are at greater financial risk in retirement and how annuities can help*. Washington, DC: Americans for Secure Retirement.

Houppert, K. (2007, July 17). Final period. *New York Times*, p. A21.

Hourani, L. L., Yuan, H., & Bray, R. M. (2004). Psychosocial and lifestyle correlates of premenstrual symptoms among military women. *Journal of Women's Health, 13*, 812–821.

Houston, D. K., et al. (2007). Association between vitamin D status and physical performance: The InCHIANTI study. *Journal of Gerontology, 62A*, 440–446.

Howard, J. A., & Hollander, J. (1997). *Gendered situations, gendered selves: A gender lens on social psychology*. Thousand Oaks, CA: Sage.

How healthy are American women? (2003). *Women's Health in Primary Care, 6*, 452.

Hoyert, D. L., Kung, H.-C., & Smith, B. L. (2005). *Deaths: Preliminary data for 2003*. National Vital Statitistics Reports, 53, No. 15.

HSBC Insurance. (2007). *The future of retirement: The new old age*. London: Author.

Hu, F. B., et al. (2002). Fish and omega-3 fatty acid intake and risk of coronary heart disease in women. *Journal of the American Medical Association, 287*, 1815–1821.

Huddy, L., Neely, F. K., & Lafay, M. R. (2000). The polls—trends: Support for the women's movement. *Public Opinion Quarterly, 64*, 309–350.

Hudson, V. M., & den Boer, A. M. (2004). *Bare branches: Security implications of Asia's surplus male population*. Cambridge, MA: MIT Press.

Huffman, T., Chang, K., Rausch, P., & Schaffer, N. (1994). Gender differences and factors related to the disposition toward cohabitation. *Family Therapy, 21*, 171–184.

Hughes, I. A. (2004). Female development—all by default? *New England Journal of Medicine, 351*, 748–750.

Huguet, P., & Régner, I. (2007). Stereotype threat among schoolgirls in quasi-ordinary classroom circumstances. *Journal of Educational Psychology, 99*, 545–560.

Hulme, P. A., & Agrawal, S. (2004). Patterns of childhood sexual abuse characteristics and their relationships to other childhood abuse and adult health. *Journal of Interpersonal Violence, 19*, 389–405.

Hurd, L. C. (2000). Older women's body image and embodied experience: An exploration. *Journal of Women & Aging, 12*, 77–97.

Hurley, D. (2005, April 19). Divorce rate: It's not as high as you think. *New York Times*, p. D7.

Hurme, S. B. (2002). *Perspectives on elder abuse*. Washington, DC: AARP.

Hutchinson, M. K., et al. (2003, August). The role of mother–daughter sexual risk communication in reducing sexual risk behaviors among urban adolescent females: A prospective study. *Journal of Adolescent Health, 33*, 98–107.

Hutson-Comeaux, S. L., Westerhaus, E. K., & Snyder, R. (2002, June). *Personality, characteristics of women in male- and female-dominated occupations*. Poster presented at the meeting of the American Psychological Society, New Orleans.

Huyck, M. H. (1995). Marriage and close relationships of the marital kind. In R. Blieszner & V. H. Bedford (Eds.), *Handbook of aging and the family* (pp. 181–200). Westport, CT: Greenwood.

Hwang, K. (1997). Living with a disability: A woman's perspective. In M. L. Sipski & C. J. Alexander (Eds.), *Sexual function in people with disability and chronic illness: A health practitioner's guide* (pp. 119–130). Gaithersburg, MD: Aspen Publishers.

Hyde, J. S. (2003). Issues for women in middle age. In L. Slater, J. H. Daniel, & A. E. Banks (Eds.), *The complete guide to mental health for women* (pp. 48–50). Boston: Beacon Press.

Hyde, J. S. (2005). The gender similarities hypothesis. *American Psychologist, 60*, 581–592.

Hyde, J. S. (2007). Women in science: Gender similarities in abilities and sociocultural forces. In S. J. Ceci & W. M. Williams (Eds.), *Why aren't more women in science? Top researchers debate the evidence* (pp. 131–145). Washington, DC: American Psychological Association.

Hyde, J. S., DeLamater, J. D., & Durik, A. M. (2001). Sexuality and the dual-earner couple. Part II: Beyond the baby years. *The Journal of Sex Research, 38*, 10–23.

Hyde, J. S., & Durik, A. M. (2000). Gender differences in erotic plasticity—evolutionary or sociocultural forces? Comment on Baumeister (2000). *Psychological Bulletin, 126*, 375–379.

Hyde, J. S., Fennema, E., & Lamon, S. J. (1990). Gender differences in mathematics performance: A meta-analysis. *Psychological Bulletin, 107*, 139–155.

Hyde, J. S., & Grabe, S. (2008). Meta-analysis in the psychology of women. In F. L. Denmark & M. A. Paludi (Eds.), *Psychology of women: A handbook of issues and theories* (2nd ed., pp. 142–173). Westport, CT: Praeger.

Hyde, J. S., & Jaffee, S. R. (2000, Summer). Becoming a heterosexual adult: The experiences of young women. *Journal of Social Issues, 56*, 283.

Hyde, J. S., & Kling, K. C. (2001). Women, motivation, and achievement. *Psychology of Women Quarterly, 25*, 364–378.

Hyde, J. S., & Linn, M. C. (1988). Gender differences in verbal ability: A meta-analysis. *Psychological Bulletin, 104*, 53–69.

Hyde, J. S., & Mezulis, A. H. (2001). Gender difference research: Issues and outcome. In J. Worell (Ed.), *Encyclopedia of women and gender* (pp. 551–559). San Diego: Academic Press.

Ibrahim, H. (Fall 2004/Winter 2005). Human rights, education, and women in northern Nigeria. *On Campus with Women, 34*, 7–9.

Iervolino, A. C., Hines, M., Golombok, S. E., Rust, J., & Plomin, R. (2005). Genetic and environmental influences on sex-typed behavior during the preschool years. *Child Development, 76*, 826–840.

Iglehart, J. K. (2002). Medicare's declining payments to physicans. *New England Journal of Medicine, 346*, 1924–1930.

Iglehart, J. K. (2003). The dilemma of Medicaid. *New England Journal of Medicine, 348*, 2140–2148.

Ilies, R., Hauserman, N., Schwochau, S., & Stibal, J. (2003). Reported incidence rates of work-related sexual harassment in the United States: Using meta-analysis to explain reported rate disparities. *Personnel Psychology, 56*, 607–631.

Impett, E. A., Sorsoli, L., Schooler, D., Henson, J. M., & Tolman, D. L. (2008). Girls' relationship authenticity and self-esteem across adolescence. *Developmental Psychology, 44*, 722–733.

Impett, E. A., & Tolman, D. L. (2006). Late adolescent girls' sexual experiences and sexual satisfaction. *Journal of Adolescent Research, 21*, 628–646.

The inadequacy of civil unions. (2007, June 7). *New York Times*, p. A34.

Infertility: A guy thing. (2002, March 25). *Newsweek*, pp. 60–61.

Institute for Women's Policy Research. (2005, March). *Who are Social Security beneficiaries?* Washington, DC: Author.

Institute for Women's Policy Research. (2007, February). *Women and paid sick days: Crucial for family well-being* [Fact sheet]. Washington, DC: Author.

Institute for Women's Policy Research. (2007, April). *The gender wage ratio: Women's and men's earnings* [Fact sheet]. Washington, DC: Author.

Institute for Women's Policy Research. (2007, November). *The economic security of older women and men in the United States.* Washington, DC: Author.

Institute for Women's Policy Research. (2008, February). *The gender wage ratio: Women's and men's earnings* [Fact sheet]. Washington, DC: Author.

Integrated Regional Information Networks. (2007). *The shame of war: Sexual violence against women and girls in conflict.* Kenya: Author.

International Labour Organization. (2004). *Helping hands or shackled lives? Understanding child domestic labour and responses to it.* Geneva: Author.

Inter-Parliamentary Union. (2007). *Women in national parliaments.* Retrieved from http://www.ipu.org/ wmn-eclassif.htm

Irvine, M. (2005, May 31). Anorexics seeking "skinny solidarity." *Peoria Journal Star,* pp. A1, A7.

Isbell, L. M., Swedish, K., & Gazan, D. B. (2005). Who says it's sexual harassment? The effects of gender and likelihood to sexually harass on legal judgments of sexual harassment. *Journal of Applied Social Psychology, 35,* 745–772.

Iwamasa, G. Y., Sorocco, K. H., & Koonce, D. A. (2002). Ethnicity and clinical psychology: A content analysis of the literature. *Clinical Psychology Review, 22,* 931–944.

Iyengar, R. (2007, August 7). The protection battered spouses don't need. *New York Times,* p. A23.

Jack, D. C. (2003). The anger of hope and the anger of despair: How anger relates to women's depression. In J. M. Stoppard & L. M. McMullen (Eds.), *Situating sadness: Women and depression in social context* (pp. 62–87). New York: New York University Press.

Jackson, D., Engstrom, E., & Emmers-Sommer, T. (2007). Think leader, think male and female: Sex vs. seating arrangement as leadership cues. *Sex Roles, 57,* 713–723.

Jackson, L. A., Ervin, K. S., Gardner, P. D., & Schmitt, N. (2001). Gender and the Internet: Women communicating and men searching. *Sex Roles, 44,* 363–379.

Jackson, L. A., Fleury, R. E., & Lewandowski, D. A. (1996). Feminism: Definitions, support, and correlates of support among female and male college students. *Sex Roles, 34,* 687–693.

Jackson, L. A., Gardner, P. D., Sullivan, L. A. (1992). Explaining gender differences in self-pay expectations: Social comparison standards and perceptions of fair pay. *Journal of Applied Psychology, 77,* 651–661.

Jackson, R. A., et al. (2004). Perinatal outcomes in singletons following in vitro fertilization: A meta-analysis. *Obstetrics & Gynecology, 103,* 551–563.

Jackson, Y., & Warren, J. S. (2000). Appraisal, social support, and life events: Predicting outcome behavior in school-age children. *Child Development, 71,* 1441–1457.

Jacobi, C., et al. (2004). Coming to terms with risk factors for eating disorders: Application of risk terminology and suggestions for a general taxonomy. *Psychological Bulletin, 130,* 19–65.

Jacobs, E. A., Karavolos, K., Rathouz, P. J., Ferris, T. G., & Powell, L. H. (2005). Limited English proficiency and breast and cervical cancer screening in a multiethnic population. *American Journal of Public Health, 95,* 1410–1416.

Jacobs, J. E., Lanza, S., Osgood, D. W., Eccles, J. S., & Wigfield, A. (2002). Changes in children's self-competence and values: Gender and domain differences across grades one through twelve. *Child Development, 73,* 509–527.

Jacobs, R. H. (1997). *Be an outrageous older woman.* New York: HarperCollins.

Jacobson, J. (2006, July 7). Report disputes notion that boys' academic performance is in decline. *The Chronicle of Higher Education,* p. A35.

Jacobsson, B., Ladfors, L., & Milsom, I. (2004). Advanced maternal age and adverse perinatal outcome. *Obstetrics & Gynecology, 104,* 727–733.

Jacoby, S. (2002, May). Are Medicare docs taking off? *AARP Bulletin Online.*

Jadva, V., et al. (2003). Surrogacy: The experiences of surrogate mothers. *Human Reproduction, 18,* 2196–2204.

Jaffe, E. (2004, January). Steele and Markus on "stereotype threat and black college students." *APS Observer,* pp. 22, 29.

Jaffe, M. L. (1998). *Adolescence.* New York: Wiley.

Jaffee, S., & Hyde, J. S. (2000). Gender differences in moral orientation: A meta-analysis. *Psychological Bulletin, 126,* 703–726.

Jain, T., & Gupta, R. (2007). Trends in the use of intracytoplasmic sperm injection in the United States. *New England Journal of Medicine, 357,* 251–257.

James, S. D. (2007, December 13). *World's oldest mom says she is 'seriously ill'.* Retrieved on May 16, 2008 from http:// abcnews.go.com/pring?id=3991578

Janofsky, M., & Schemo, D. J. (2003, March 16). The cadet life for many women: Sexual ordeals and internal rage. *New York Times,* pp. YT1, YT9.

Janssen, I., Craig, W. M., Boyce, W. F., & Pickett, W. (2004). Association between overweight and obesity with bullying behaviors in school-aged children. *Pediatrics, 113,* 1187–1194.

Jansz, J., & Martis, R. G. (2007). The Lara phenomenon: Powerful female characters in video games. *Sex Roles, 56,* 141–148.

Jarrell, A. (2000, April 3). The face of teenage sex grows younger. *New York Times,* pp. B1, B8.

Jarviluoma, H., Moisala, P., & Vilkko, A. (2003). *Gender and qualitative methods.* Thousand Oaks, CA: Sage.

Jenkins, C. L. (2003). Widows and divorcees in later life. *Journal of Women & Aging, 15,* 1–6.

Jennings, A. (2007, July 14). Nest eggs emptying, not the nests. *New York Times,* pp. B1, B6.

Jernigan, D. H., Ostroff, J., Ross, C., & O'Hara, J. A. (2004). Sex differences in adolescent exposure to alcohol advertising in magazines. *Archives of Pediatrics & Adolescent Medicine, 158,* 629–634.

Jersild, D. (2002, May 31). Alcohol in the vulnerable lives of college women. *Chronicle of Higher Education,* pp. B10, B11.

Jessell, J. C., & Beymer, L. (1992). The effects of job title vs. job description on occupational sex typing. *Sex Roles, 27,* 73–83.

Jeter, R. F. (2000). Intimate relationships. In M. Biaggio & M. Hersen (Eds.), *Issues in the psychology of women* (pp. 173–198). New York: Kluwer.

Jha, A. K., et al. (2003). Differences in medical care and disease outcomes among Black and White women with heart disease. *Circulation, 110,* 1089–1094.

Jha, P., Kumar, R., Vasa, P., Dhingra, N., Thiruchelvam, D., & Moineddin, R. (2006). Low male-to-female sex ratio of children born in India: National survey of 1.1 million households. *Lancet, 367,* 211–218.

Jin, L., & Christakis, N. A. (2007, August). *Investigating the mechanism of marital mortality reduction: The transition to widowhood and quality of health care.* Paper presented at the meeting of the American Sociological Association, New York.

John, R., Blanchard, P. H., & Hennessy, C. H. (2001). In J. M. Coyle (Ed.), *Handbook on women and aging* (pp. 290–325). Westport, CT: Praeger.

Johns, M., Schmader, T., & Martens, A. (2005). Knowing is half the battle: Teaching stereotype threat as a means of improving women's math performance. *Psychological Science, 16,* 175–179.

Johnson, A. B., & Rodgers, J. L. (2006). The impact of having children on the lives of women: The Effects of Children Questionnaire. *Journal of Applied Social Psychology, 36,* 2685–2714.

Johnson, A. G. (1997). *The gender knot: Unraveling our patriarchal legacy.* Philadelphia: Temple University Press.

Johnson, B. E., Kuck, D. L., & Schander, P. R. (1997). Rape myth acceptance and sociodemographic characteristics: A multidimensional analysis. *Sex Roles, 36,* 693–707.

Johnson, C. L. (1994). Differential expectations and realities: Race, socioeconomic status, and health of the oldest old. *International Journal of Aging and Human Development, 38,* 13–27.

Johnson, D. (2002, March 25). Until dust do us part. *Newsweek,* p. 41.

Johnson, D., et al. (2003). Studying the effects of early child care experiences on the development of children of color in the United States: Toward a more inclusive research agenda. *Child Development, 74,* 1227–1244.

Johnson, D., & Rust, C. (2005, January 17). Who's babysitting the kids? A strange turn in the Andrea Yates saga. *Newsweek,* p. 37.

Johnson, D., & Scelfo, J. (2003, December 15). Sex, love and nursing homes. *Newsweek,* pp. 54–55.

Johnson, D. R., & Scheuble, L. K. (1995). Women's marital naming in two generations: A national study. *Journal of Marriage and the Family, 57,* 724–732.

Johnson, J. O., & Downs, B. (2005). *Maternity leave and employment patterns: 1961–2000.* Current Population Reports, P70–103. Washington, DC: U.S. Census Bureau.

Johnson, L. A. (2004, October 14). Study links growth, breast cancer risk. *New York Times,* p. A3.

Johnson, M. A. (2004). Nutrition and aging—practical advice for healthy eating. *Journal of the American Medical Women's Association, 59,* 262–269.

Johnson, R. D., Stone, D. L., & Phillips, T. N. (2008). Relations among ethnicity, gender, beliefs, attitudes, and intention to pursue a career in information technology. *Journal of Applied Social Psychology, 38,* 999–1022.

Johnson, S. M., & O'Connor, E. (2002). *The gay baby boom: The psychology of gay parenthood.* New York: New York University Press.

Johnson, W., McGue, M., Krueger, R. F., & Bouchard Jr., T. J. (2004). Marriage and personality: A genetic analysis. *Journal of Personality and Social Psychology, 86,* 285–294.

Johnston, D., & Swanson, D. (2003). Undermining mothers: A content analysis of the representations of mothers in magazines. *Mass Communication and Society, 6,* 243–265.

Johnston, D. D., & Swanson, D. H. (2006). Constructing the "good mother": The experience of mothering ideologies by work status. *Sex Roles, 54,* 509–519.

Johnston, D. D., & Swanson, D. H. (2007). Cognitive acrobatics in the construction of worker-mother identity. *Sex Roles, 57,* 447–459.

Johnston, L. D., O'Malley, P. M., Bachman, J. G., & Schulenberg, J. E. (2007). *Demographic subgroup trends for various licit and illicit drugs, 1975–2006.* Monitoring the Future Occasional Paper No. 67. Ann Arbor: Institute for Social Research. Retrieved from http://www.monitoringthefuture.org/

Jones, B. E. (2001). Is having the luck of growing old in the gay, lesbian, bisexual, transgender community good or bad luck? *Journal of Gay & Lesbian Social Services, 13,* 13–14.

Jones, C. J., & Meredith, W. (2000). Developmental paths of psychological health from early adolescence to later adulthood. *Psychology and Aging, 15,* 351–360.

Jones, D. C. (2004). Body image among adolescent girls and boys: A longitudinal study. *Developmental Psychology, 40,* 823–835.

Jones, D. J., O'Connel, C., Gound, M., Heller, L., & Forehand, R. (2004). Predictors of self-reported physical symptoms in low income, inner-city African American women: The role of optimism, depressive symptoms, and chronic illness. *Psychology of Women Quarterly, 28,* 112–121.

Jones, M. (2003, March 16). The weaker sex. *New York Times Magazine,* p. 56.

Jones, S. M., & Dindia, K. (2004). A meta-analytic perspective on sex equity in the classroom. *Review of Educational Research, 74,* 443–471.

Jordan, J. V. (Ed.). (1997). *Women's growth in diversity: More writings from the Stone Center.* New York: Guilford.

Jordan, J. V., Banks, A. E., & Walker, M. (2003). Growth in connection: A relational-cultural model of growth. In L. Slater, J. H. Daniel, & A. E. Banks (Eds.), *The complete guide to mental health for women* (pp. 92–99). Boston: Beacon Press.

Jordan, S. J., Whiteman, D. C., Purdie, D. M., Green, A. C., & Webb, P. M. (2006). Does smoking increase risk of ovarian cancer? A systematic review. *Gynecologic Oncology, 103,* 1122–1129.

Josselson, R. (1994). Identity and relatedness in the life cycle. In H. A. Bosma, T. L. G. Graafsma, H. D. Groterant, &

D. J. de Levita (Eds.), *Identity and development: An interdisciplinary approach* (pp. 81–102). Thousand Oaks, CA: Sage.

Josselson, R. (1996). *Revising herself: The story of women's identity from college to midlife*. New York: Oxford University Press.

Joutsenniemi, K., Martelin, T., Martikainen, P., Pirkola, S., & Koskinen, S. (2006). Living arrangements and mental health in Finland. *Journal of Epidemiology and Community Health, 60*, 468–475.

Jovanovic, J., & Dreves, C. (1997, April). *Sex differences in students competency perceptions in science: Do classroom interactions play a role?* Paper presented at the meeting of the Society for Research in Child Development, Washington, DC.

June, A. W. (2007, February 16). Presidents: Same look, different decade. *The Chronicle of Higher Education*, pp. A33–A35.

Juntunen, C. L., Barraclough, D. J., Broneck, C. L., Seibel, G. A., Winlow, S. A., & Morin, P. M. (2001). American Indian perspectives on the career journey. *Journal of Counseling Psychology, 48*, 274–285.

Kagay, C. R., Quale, C., & Smith-Bindman, R. (2006). Screening mammography in the American elderly. *American Journal of Preventive Medicine, 31*, 142–149.

Kahlenborn, C., Modugno, F., Potter, D. M., & Severs, W. B. (2006). Oral contraceptive use as a risk factor for premenopausal breast cancer: A meta-analysis. *Mayo Clinic Proceedings, 81*, 1290–1302.

Kahn, A. S. (2004). 2003 Carolyn Sherif Award address: What college women do and do not experience as rape. *Psychology of Women Quarterly, 28*, 9–15.

Kahn, J. (2004, May 30). The most populous nation faces a population crisis. *New York Times*, pp. WK1, WK5.

Kainen, A. (1995). Only your regrets. In B. Benatovich (Ed.), *What we know so far: Wisdom among women*. New York: St. Martin's Griffin.

Kaiser Family Foundation. (2001). *Inside-OUT: A report on the experiences of lesbians, gays, and bisexuals in America and the public's views on issues related to sexual orientation*. Menlo Park, CA: Author.

Kajantie, E. (2008). Physiological stress response, estrogen, and the male-female mortality gap. *Current Directions in Psychological Science, 17*, 348–352.

Kalb, C. (2004a, August 2). Fertility and the freezer. *Newsweek*, p. 52.

Kalb, C. (2004b, May 24). A shocking diagnosis. *Newsweek*, p. 57.

Kalb, C., & Murr, A. (2006, May 15). Battling a black epidemic. *Newsweek*, pp. 42–48.

Kalev, H. D. (2004). Cultural rights or human rights: The case of female genital mutilation. *Sex Roles, 51*, 339–348.

Kalil, A., & Kunz, J. (2002). Teenage childbearing, marital status, and depressive symptoms in later life. *Child Development, 73*, 1748–1760.

Kane, E. W. (2000). Racial and ethnic variations in gender-related attitudes. *Annual Review of Sociology, 26*, 419–439.

Kantrowitz, B. (2005, January 31). Sex and science. *Newsweek*, pp. 36–38.

Kantrowitz, B. (2006a, February 27). Building strong bones. *Newsweek*, pp. 59–60.

Kantrowitz, B. (2006b, February 20). Sex & love: The new world. *Newsweek*, pp. 51–54, 58–60.

Kantrowitz, B. (2007a, December 10). Bones of invention. *Newsweek*, p. 88.

Kantrowitz, B. (2007b, July 2/July 9). What kills one woman every minute of every day? *Newsweek*, pp. 56–57.

Kaplan, G. A. (1992). Health and aging in the Alameda County study. In K. W. Schaie, D. Balzer, & J. S. House (Eds.), *Aging health behaviors and health outcomes* (pp. 69–88). Hillsdale, NJ: Erlbaum.

Karch, D. L., Lubell, K. M., Friday, J., Patel, N., & Williams, D. D. (2008). Surveillance for violent deaths—National Violent Death Reporting System, 16 states, 2005. *Morbidity and Mortality Weekly Report, Surveillance Summaries, 57* (SS-3), 1–44.

Karpiak, C. P., Buchanan, J. P., Hosey, M., & Smith, A. (2007). University students from single-sex and coeducational high schools: Differences in majors and attitudes at a Catholic university. *Psychology of Women Quarterly, 31*, 282–289.

Karpiak, S. E., Shippy, R. A., & Cantor, M. H. (2006). *Research on older adults with HIV*. New York: AIDS Community Research Initiative of America.

Karraker, K., & Hartley, J. (2007, March). *Mothers' toy choices for their male and female toddlers*. Poster presented at the meeting of the Society for Research in Child Development, Boston.

Karraker, K. H., Vogel, D. A., & Lake, M. A. (1995). Parents' gender-stereotyped perceptions of newborns: The eye of the beholder revisited. *Sex Roles, 33*, 687–701.

Karrass, J., Braungart-Rieker, J. M., Mullins, J., & Lefever, J. B. (2002). Processes in language acquisition: The roles of gender, attention, and maternal encouragement of attention over time. *Journal of Child Language, 29*, 519–543.

Kasen, S., Chen, H., Sneed, J., Crawford, T., & Cohen, P. (2006). Social role and birth cohort influences on gender-linked personality traits in women: A 20-year longitudinal analysis. *Journal of Personality and Social Psychology, 91*, 944–958.

Kasen, S., Cohen, P., Chen, H., & Castille, D. (2003). Depression in adult women: Age changes and cohort effects. *American Journal of Public Health, 93*, 2061–2066.

Kashubeck-West, S., Mintz, L. B., & Weigold, I. (2005). Separating the effects of gender and weight-loss desire on body satisfaction and disordered eating behavior. *Sex Roles, 53*, 505–518.

Kasturirangan, A., Krishnan, S., & Riger, S. (2004). The impact of culture and minority status on women's experience of domestic violence. *Trauma, Violence, & Abuse, 5*, 318–332.

Kates, E. (1996). Educational pathways out of poverty: Responding to the realities of women's lives. *American Journal of Orthopsychiatry, 66*, 548–556.

Katz, D. S., & Andronici, J. F. (2006, Fall). No more excuses! *Ms.*, pp. 63–64.

Katz, J., Swindell, S., & Farrow, S. (2004). Effects of participation in a first women's studies course on collective self-esteem, gender-related attitudes, and emotional well-being. *Journal of Applied Social Psychology, 34*, 2179–2199.

Katz, P. A. (1987). Variations in family constellation: Effects on gender schemata. In L. S. Liben & M. L. Signorella (Eds.), *Children's gender schemata: New directions for child development* (Vol. 38, pp. 39–56). San Francisco: Jossey-Bass.

Katz, P. A. (1996). Raising feminists. *Psychology of Women Quarterly, 20,* 323–340.

Katz, P. A. (2008). Theories of female personality. In F. L. Denmark & M. A. Paludi (Eds.), *Psychology of women: A handbook of issues and theories* (2nd ed., pp. 303–331). Westport, CT: Praeger.

Katz, P. A., & Walsh, V. (1991). Modification of children's gender-stereotyped behavior. *Child Development, 62,* 338–351.

Katz, S. J., Kabeto, M., & Langa, K. M. (2000). Gender disparities in the receipt of home care for elderly people with disability in the United States. *Journal of the American Medical Association, 284,* 3022–3027.

Katzenstein, L. (1999, June 13). Beyond the horror stories, good news about managed care. *New York Times,* p. WH6.

Kaufman, G., & Goldscheider, F. (2007). Do men "need" a spouse more than women? Perceptions of the importance of marriage for men and women. *The Sociological Quarterly, 48,* 29–46.

Kaufmann, J. A. (1996). Teenage parents and their offspring. Women and mental health. *Annals of the New York Academy of Sciences, 789,* 17–30.

Kawamura, S., & Brown, S. L. (2007, August). *Mattering and wives' perceived fairness of the division of household labor.* Paper presented at the meeting of the American Sociological Association, New York.

Keel, P. K. (2005). *Eating disorders.* Upper Saddle River, NJ: Pearson Prentice Hall.

Keel, P. K., & Haedt, A. (2008). Evidence-based psychosocial treatments for eating problems and eating disorders. *Journal of Clinical Child & Adolescent Psychology, 37,* 39–61.

Keller, J. (2002). Blatant stereotype threat and women's math performance: Self-handicapping as a strategic means to cope with obtrusive negative performance expectations. *Sex Roles, 47,* 193–198.

Keller, J., & Dauenheimer, D. (2003). Stereotype threat in the classroom: Dejection mediates the disrupting threat effect on women's math performance. *Personality and Social Psychology Bulletin, 29,* 371–381.

Kelley, T. (2000, February 13). On campuses, warnings about violence in relationships. *New York Times,* p. L40.

Kelley-Moore, J. A., & Ferraro, K. F. (2004). The Black/White disability gap: Persistent inequality in later life? *Journals of Gerontology, 59,* S34–S43.

Kelly, A. M., et al. (2004). High body satisfaction in adolescent girls: Association with demographic, socio-environmental, personal, and behavioral factors. *Journal of Adolescent Health, 34,* 129.

Kendall-Tackett, K., Marshall, R., & Ness, K. (2003). Chronic pain syndromes and violence against women. *Women & Therapy, 26,* 45–56.

Kendler, K. S., Myers, J., & Prescott, C. A. (2005). Sex differences in the relationship between social support and risk for major depression: A longitudinal study of opposite-sex twin pairs. *American Journal of Psychiatry, 162,* 250–256.

Kenfield, S. A., Stampfer, M. J., Rosner, B. A., & Colditz, G. A. (2008). Smoking and smoking cessation in relation to mortality in women. *Journal of the American Medical Association, 299,* 2037–2047.

Kennedy, D. (2002, June 2). An impatient sisterhood. *New York Times,* pp. AR9, AR22.

Kennedy, M. (2004, Spring). Cheaper than a cow. *Ms.,* pp. 50–53.

Kennedy, M. A., & Gorzalka, B. B. (2002). Asian and non-Asian attitudes toward rape, sexual harassment, and sexuality. *Sex Roles, 46,* 227–238.

Kenney-Benson, G. A., Pomerantz, E. M., Ryan, A. M., & Patrick, H. (2006). Sex differences in math performance: The role of children's approach to schoolwork. *Developmental Psychology, 42,* 11–26.

Kerr, B. (1999, March 5). When dreams differ: Male–female relations on campus. *Chronicle of Higher Education,* pp. 87, 88.

Kersting, K. (2003a, May). Cognitive sex differences: A "political minefield." *Monitor on Psychology,* pp. 54–55.

Kersting, K. (2003b, October). Countering insidious stereotypes. *Monitor on Psychology,* pp. 34–35.

Keshavarz, H., et al. (2002). Hysterectomy surveillance—United States, 1994–1999. *Morbidity and Mortality Weekly Reports, Surveillance Summaries, 51* (SS05), 1–8.

Kessler, R. C., et al. (2004). Age and depression in the MIDUS survey. In O. G. Brim, C. D. Ryff, & R. C. Kessler (Eds.), *How healthy are we? A national study of well-being at midlife* (pp. 227–251). Chicago: University of Chicago Press.

Kessler, R. C., Berglund, P., Demler, O., Jin, R., & Walters, E. E. (2005). Lifetime prevalence and age-of-onset distributions of *DSM-IV* disorders in the National Comorbidity Survey Replication. *Archives of General Psychiatry, 62,* 593–602.

Khor, D. (2007). "Doing gender": A critical review and an exploration of lesbigay domestic arrangements. *Journal of GLBT Family Studies, 3,* 35–73.

Khosla, S., & Melton, L. J., III. (2007). Osteopenia. *New England Journal of Medicine, 356,* 2293–2300.

Kiang, L., Moreno, A. J., & Robinson, J. L. (2004). Maternal preconceptions about parenting predict child temperament, maternal sensitivity, and children's empathy. *Developmental Psychology, 40,* 1081–1092.

Kiecolt-Glaser, J. K., & Newton, T. L. (2001). Marriage and health: His and hers. *Psychological Bulletin, 127,* 472–503.

Kiefer, A. K., & Sekaquaptewa, D. (2007). Implicit stereotypes, gender identification, and math-related outcomes: A prospective study of female college students. *Psychological Science, 18,* 13–18.

Kiefer, A. K., & Shih, M. J. (2004, May). *Stereotype relevance and gender differences in performance attributions.* Poster presented at the meeting of American Psychological Society, Chicago.

Kilborn, P. T. (2004, May 2). An all-American town, a sky-high divorce rate: Economic woes strain Roanoke's marriages. *New York Times,* p. YT20.

Kilbourne, A., Switzer, G., Hyman, K., Crowley-Matoka, M., & Fine, M. (2006). Advancing health disparities research within the health care system: A conceptual framework. *American Journal of Public Health, 96,* 2113–2121.

Kim, J. E., & Moen, P. (2001a). Is retirement good or bad for subjective well-being? *Current Directions in Psychological Science, 10,* 83–86.

Kim, J. E., & Moen, P. (2001b). Moving into retirement: Preparation and transitions in late midlife. In M. Lachman (Ed.), *Handbook of midlife development* (pp. 487–527). New York: Wiley.

Kim, J.-Y., McHale, S. M., Crouter, A. C., & Osgood, D. W. (2007). Longitudinal linkages between sibling relationships and adjustment from middle childhood through adolescence. *Developmental Psychology, 43,* 960–973.

Kim, J.-Y., McHale, S. M., Osgood, D. W., & Crouter, A. C. (2006). Longitudinal course and family correlates of sibling relationships from childhood through adolescence. *Child Development, 77,* 1746–1761.

Kim, W. J., & Singh, T. (2004). Trends and dynamics of youth suicides in developing countries. *Lancet, 363,* 1090.

Kimerling, R., Alvarez, J., Pavao, J., Kaminski, A., & Baumrind, N. (2007). Epidemiology and consequences of women's revictimization. *Women's Health Issues, 17,* 101–106.

Kimmel, D. G. (2002, August). *Ageism and implications for sexual orientation.* Paper presented at the American Psychological Association, Chicago.

Kimmel, E. B., & Crawford, M. (2001). Methods for studying gender. In J. Worell (Ed.), *Encyclopedia of women and gender* (pp. 749–758). San Diego: Academic Press.

Kimmel, M. (2001). Real men join the movement. In S. M. Shaw & J. Lee (Eds.), *Women's voices, feminist visions* (pp. 536–540). Mountain View, CA: Mayfield.

Kimura, D. (2007). "Underrepresentation" or misrepresentation? In S. J. Ceci & W. M. Williams (Eds.), *Why aren't more women in science? Top researchers debate the evidence* (pp. 39–46). Washington, DC: American Psychological Association.

King, A. C., Bernardy, N. C., & Hauner, K. (2003). Stressful events, personality, and mood disturbance: Gender differences in alcoholics and problem drinkers. *Addictive Behaviors, 28,* 171–187.

King, C., & Olsen, P. R. (2002, August 18). Follow the herd? Not her. *New York Times,* p. BU13.

King, D. E., Mainous, A. G., III, & Geesey, M. E. (2008). Adopting moderate alcohol consumption in middle age: Subsequent cardiovascular events. *The American Journal of Medicine, 121,* 201–206.

King, J. E. (2006). *Gender equity in higher education: 2006.* Washington, DC: American Council on Education.

King, L. A., & King, D. W. (1990). Abbreviated measures of sex role egalitarian attitudes. *Sex Roles, 23,* 659–673.

King, M., et al. (2003). Mental health and quality of life of gay men and lesbians in England and Wales. *British Journal of Psychiatry, 183,* 552–558.

Kinsella, K., & Velkoff, V. A. (2001). *An aging world: 2001.* U.S. Census Bureau, Series P95/01-1. Washington, DC: U.S. Government Printing Office.

Kinsey, A. C., Pomeroy, W. B., Martin, C. E., & Gebhard, P. H. (1953). *Sexual behavior in the human female.* Philadelphia: Saunders.

Kinsler, K., & Zalk, S. R. (1996). Teaching is a political act: Contextualizing gender and ethnic voices. In K. F. Wyche & F. J. Crosby (Eds.), *Women's ethnicities: Journeys through psychology* (pp. 27–48). Boulder, CO: Westview.

Kinzer, S. (2003, November 6). Dolls as role models, neither Barbie nor Britney. *New York Times,* pp. B1, B5.

Kinzie, J., Thomas, A. D., Palmer, M. M., Umbach, P. D., & Kuh, G. D. (2007). Women students at coeducational and women's colleges: How do their experiences compare? *Journal of College Student Development, 48,* 145–165.

Kirk, G., & Okazawa-Rey, M. (2001). *Women's lives: Multicultural perspectives* (2nd ed.). Mountain View, CA: Mayfield.

Kissling, E. A. (2006). *Capitalizing on the curse: The business of menstruation.* Boulder, CO: Lynne Rienner.

Kitano, M. K. (1998). Gifted Latina women. *Journal for the Education of the Gifted, 21,* 131–159.

Kite, M. E. (2001). Changing times, changing gender roles: Who do we want women and men to be? In R. K. Unger (Ed.), *Handbook of the psychology of women and gender* (pp. 215–227). New York: Wiley.

Kite, M. E., Deaux, K., & Haines, E. L. (2008). Gender stereotypes. In F. L. Denmark & M. A. Paludi (Eds.), *Psychology of women: A handbook of issues and theories* (2nd ed., pp. 205–236). Westport, CT: Praeger.

Kite, M. E., et al. (2001). Women psychologists in academe: Mixed progress, unwarranted complacency. *American Psychologist, 56,* 1080–1098.

Kite, M. E., Stockdale, G. D., Whitely, B. E., Jr., & Johnson, B. T. (2005). Attitudes toward younger and older adults: An updated meta-analytic review. *Journal of Social Issues, 61,* 241–266.

Kite, M. E., & Wagner, L. S. (2002). Attitudes toward older adults. In T. D. Nelson (Ed.), *Ageism: Stereotyping and prejudice against older persons* (pp. 129–161). Cambridge, MA: MIT Press.

Kitto, J. (1989). Gender reference terms: Separating the women from the girls. *British Journal of Social Psychology, 28,* 185–187.

Kitzinger, C. (1999). Researching subjectivity and diversity: Q-methodology in feminist psychology. *Psychology of Women Quarterly, 23,* 267–276.

Kivimäki, M., et al. (2007). Socioeconomic position, co-occurrence of behavior-related risk factors, and coronary heart disease: The Finnish Public Sector Study. *American Journal of Public Health, 97,* 874–879.

Kivimäki, M., Vahtera, J., Elovainio, M., Helenius, H., Singh-Manoux, A., & Pentti, J. (2005). Optimism and pessimism as predictors of change in health after death or onset of severe illness in family. *Health Psychology, 24,* 413–421.

Klaczynski, P. A., & Aneja, A. (2002). Development of quantitative reasoning and gender biases. *Developmental Psychology, 38,* 208–221.

Klein, A. A., & Larson, K. (2004, July). *Is "he" male? Interpretive and memory bias for pronouns.* Paper presented at the meeting of the American Psychological Association, Honolulu.

Klein, M. H., Hyde, J. S., Essex, M. J., & Clark, R. (1998). Maternity leave, role quality, work involvement, and mental health one year after delivery. *Psychology of Women Quarterly, 22,* 239–266.

Kleinfield, N. R. (2004, December 12). Bowed by age, battered by an addicted nephew and forced into begging and despair. *New York Times,* pp. 1, 56–57.

Kleyman, K. S., Stasson, M. F., Souza, J. G., Jr., & Gjerswold, K. L. (2004, May). *The effects of gender stereotypes on occupational judgments.* Poster presented at the meeting of American Psychological Society, Chicago.

Kline, G. H., et al. (2004). Timing is everything: Pre-engagement cohabitation and increased risk for poor marital outcomes. *Journal of Family Psychology, 18,* 311–318.

Kling, K. C., Hyde, J. S., Showers, C. J., & Buswell, B. N. (1999). Gender differences in self-esteem: A meta-analysis. *Psychological Bulletin, 125,* 470–500.

Klohnen, E. C., & Luo, S. (2003). Interpersonal attraction and personality: What is attractive—self similarity, ideal similarity, complementarity, or attachment security? *Journal of Personality and Social Psychology, 85,* 709–722.

Klomsten, A. T., Skaalvik, E. M., & Espnes, G. A. (2004). Physical self-concept and sports: Do gender differences still exist? *Sex Roles, 50,* 119–127.

Klonoff, E. A., & Landrine, H. (1995). The schedule of sexist events: A measure of lifetime and recent sexist discrimination in women's lives. *Psychology of Women Quarterly, 19,* 439–472.

Klumb, P. L., & Lampert, T. (2004). Women, work, and well-being 1950–2000: A review and methodological critique. *Social Science and Medicine, 58,* 1007–1024.

Klump, K. L., Burt, S. A., McGue, M., & Iacono, W. G. (2007). Changes in genetic and environmental influences on disordered eating across adolescence. *Archives of General Psychiatry, 64,* 1409–1415.

Klump, K. L., & Culbert, K. M. (2007). Molecular genetic studies of eating disorders: Current status and future directions. *Current Directions in Psychological Science, 16,* 37–41.

Kmiec, J., Crosby, J. F., & Worell, J. (1996). Walking the talk: On stage and behind the scenes. In K. F. Wyche & F. J. Crosby (Eds.), *Women's ethnicities: Journeys through psychology* (pp. 49–61). Boulder, CO: Westview.

Knafo, A., & Plomin, R. (2006). Prosocial behavior from early to middle childhood: Genetic and environmental influences on stability and change. *Developmental Psychology, 42,* 771–786.

Knickmeyer, N., Sexton, K., & Nishimura, N. (2002). The impact of same-sex friendships on the well-being of women: A review of the literature. *Women & Therapy, 25,* 37–59.

Knight, J. L., & Giuliano, T. A. (2001). He's a Laker; she's a "looker": The consequences of gender-stereotypical portrayals of male and female athletes by the print media. *Sex Roles, 45,* 217–229.

Knightley, P. (1999, September 20). Grandma led two lives. *New York Times,* p. A21.

Knodel, J., Watkins, S., & VanLandingham, M. (2003). AIDS and older persons: An international perspective. *Journal of Acquired Immune Deficiency Syndromes, 33,* S153–S165.

Kobrynowicz, D., & Branscombe, N. R. (1997). Who considers themselves victims of discrimination? Individual difference predictors of perceived gender discrimination in women and men. *Psychology of Women Quarterly, 21,* 347–363.

Koenig, L. J., Doll, L. S., O'Leary, A., & Pequegnat, W. (Eds.) (2004). *From child sexual abuse to adult sexual risk: Trauma, revictimization, and intervention.* Washington, DC: American Psychological Association.

Koepsell, J. K., Kernic, M. A., & Holt, V. L. (2006). Factors that influence battered women to leave their abusive relationships. *Violence and Victims, 21,* 131–147.

Kohlberg, L. (1966). A cognitive-developmental analysis of children's sex-role concepts and attitudes. In E. E. Maccoby (Ed.), *The development of sex differences* (pp. 82–173). Stanford, CA: Stanford University Press.

Kohlberg, L. (1985). *The psychology of moral development.* San Francisco: Harper & Row.

Kolata, G. (2002, September 25). Abortion pill slow to win users among women and their doctors. *New York Times,* p. A1.

Kolata, G. (2003, September 24). Death at 18 spurs debate over a pill for abortion. *New York Times,* p. A18.

Kolata, G. (2004a, May 11). The heart's desire. *New York Times,* pp. D1, D6.

Kolata, G. (2004b, March 9). Up in the air on hormones: Women under 50. *New York Times,* pp. D5, D8.

Kolata, G., & Moss, M. (2002, February 11). X-ray vision in hindsight: Science, politics and the mammogram. *New York Times,* p. A23.

Kolchakian, M. R., & Fassinger, R. E. (2003, January). Roles of identity in relationship functioning for diverse same-sex couples. In R. E. Fassinger (Chair), *Results of the National Gay and Lesbian Experiences Study.* Symposium presented at the meeting of the American Psychological Association Multicultural Summit, Los Angeles.

Konek, C. W., Kitch, S. L., & Shore, E. R. (1994). The future of women and careers: Issues and challenges. In C. W. Konek & S. L. Kitch (Eds.), *Women and careers: Issues and challenges* (pp. 234–248). Thousand Oaks, CA: Sage.

Konrad, A. M. (2003). Family demands and job attribute preferences: A 4-year longitudinal study of women and men. *Sex Roles, 49,* 35–46.

Konrad, A. M., Ritchie, J. E., Lieb, P., & Corrigall, E. (2000). Sex differences and similarities in job attribute preferences: A meta-analysis. *Psychological Bulletin, 126,* 593–641.

Konrad, A. M., Yang, Y., Goldberg, C., & Sullivan, S. E. (2005). Preferences for job attributes associated with work and family: A longitudinal study of career outcomes. *Sex Roles, 53,* 303–315.

Kornblut, A. E. (2006, June 11). The ascent of a woman. *New York Times,* pp. ST1, ST6.

Koropeckyj-Cox, T., Romano, V., & Moras, A. (2007). Through the lenses of gender, race, and class: Students' perceptions of childless/childfree individuals and couples. *Sex Roles, 56,* 415–428.

Kosiak, B., Sangl, J., & Correa-de-Araujo, R. (2006). Quality of health care for older women: What do we know? *Women's Health Issues, 16,* 89–99.

Koss, M. P., & Cleveland, H. H. (1997). Stepping on toes: Social roots of date rape lead to intractability and politicization. In M. D. Schwartz (Ed.), *Researching sexual violence against women: Methodological and personal perspectives* (pp. 4–21). Thousand Oaks, CA: Sage.

Koss, M. P., & Figueredo, A. J. (2004). Cognitive mediation of rape's mental health impact: Constructive replication of a cross-sectional model in longitudinal data. *Psychology of Women Quarterly, 28,* 273–286.

Koss, M. P., Goodman, L. A., Browne, A., Fitzgerald, L. F., Keita, G. P., & Russo, N. F. (1994). *No safe haven: Male violence against women at home, at work, and in the community.* Washington, DC: American Psychological Association.

Koss, M. P., & Hoffman, K. (2000). Survivors of violence by male partners: Gender and cultural considerations. In R. M. Eisler & M. Hersen (Eds.), *Handbook of gender, culture, and health* (pp. 471–490). Mahwah, NJ: Erlbaum.

Kossek, E. E., & Ozeki, C. (1998). Work-family conflict, policies, and the job-life satisfaction relationship: A review and directions for organizational behavior-human resources research. *Journal of Applied Psychology, 83,* 139–149.

Kowalski, R. M., & Chapple, T. (2000). The social stigma of menstruation: Fact or fiction? *Psychology of Women Quarterly, 24,* 74–80.

Krahé, B., Bieneck, S., & Möller, I. (2005). Understanding gender and intimate partner violence from an international perspective. *Sex Roles, 52,* 807–827.

Krakauer, H. D., & Rose, S. M. (2000). The impact of group membership on lesbians' physical appearance. *Journal of Lesbian Studies, 6*(1), 31–43.

Krakovsky, M. (2006, September). Private loss visible. *Monitor on Psychology, 37,* 50–51.

Kramarae, C. (2001). *The third shift: Women learning online.* Washington, DC: American Association of University Women.

Kramer, A., Lorenzon, D., & Mueller, G. (2004, January/February). Prevalence of intimate partner violence and health implications for women using emergency departments and primary care clinics. *Women's Health Issues, 14,* 19–29.

Krause, N. (1993). Race differences in life satisfaction among aged men and women. *Journal of Gerontology: Social Sciences, 48,* S235–S244.

Krebs, E. E., Ensrud, K. E., MacDonald, R., & Wilt, T. J. (2004). Phytoestrogens for treatment of menopausal symptoms: A systematic review. *Obstetrics & Gynecology, 104,* 824–836.

Kreider, R. (2007, August). *Young adults living in their parents' home.* Paper presented at the meeting of the American Sociological Association, New York.

Kreider, R. M., & Simmons, T. (2003). *Marital status: 2000. Census 2000 brief.* Washington, DC: U.S. Census Bureau.

Kreiger, T. C. (2005, April). *Gender-atypical behavior in young children and its relation to social adjustment.* Poster presented at the meeting of the Society for Research in Child Development, Atlanta, GA.

Kristof, N. D. (2002, June 18). Women's rights: Why not? *New York Times,* p. A25.

Kristof, N. D. (2004a, February 14). Afghan women, still in chains. *New York Times,* p. A29.

Kristof, N. D. (2004b, October 6). Beaten Afghan brides. *New York Times,* p. A29.

Kristof, N. D. (2005, January 26). After the brothel. *New York Times,* p. A17.

Kristof, N. D. (2006, May 28). At 12, a mother of two. *New York Times,* p. WK11.

Kroenke, C. H., et al. (2004). Functional impact of breast cancer by age at diagnosis. *Journal of Clinical Oncology, 22,* 1849–1856.

Kroenke, C. H., Kubzansky, L. D., Schernhammer, E. S., Holmes, M. D., & Kawachi, I. (2006). Social networks, social support, and survival after breast cancer diagnosis. *Journal of Clinical Oncology, 24,* 1105–1111.

Kruger, J., Ham, S. A., & Kohl, H. W., III. (2005). Trends in leisure-time physical inactivity by age, sex, and race/ethnicity—United States, 1994–2004. *Morbidity and Mortality Weekly Report, 54,* 991–994.

Krumrei, E., Coit, C., Martin, S., Fogo, W., & Mahoney, A. (2007). Post-divorce adjustment and social relationships: A meta-analytic review. *Journal of Divorce and Remarriage, 46,* 145–166.

Krupp, C. (2008). *How not to look old.* New York: Springboard Press.

Kubany, E. S., et al. (2004). Cognitive trauma therapy for battered women with PTSD (CTT-BW). *Journal of Consulting and Clinical Psychology, 72,* 3–18.

Kuchment, A. (2006, January 30). Beating back the blues. *Newsweek,* p. 62.

Kuehn, B. M. (2008). Time for "the talk"—again. *Journal of the American Medical Association, 300,* 1285–1287.

Kuhn, J. (2005, Winter). Feminism and childbirth (part 2 of 2). *The Feminist Psychologist,* p. 5.

Kuhn, M. (1991). *No stone unturned.* New York: Ballatine Books.

Kulig, K., Brener, N. D., & McManus, T. (2003). Sexual activity and substance use among adolescents by category of physical activity plus team sports participation. *Archives of Pediatrics and Adolescent Medicine, 157,* 905–912.

Kumra, S., & Vinnicombe, S. (2008). A study of the promotion to partner process in a professional services firm: How women are disadvantaged. *British Journal of Management, 19,* S65–S74.

Kung, H.-C., Hoyert, D. L., Xu, J., & Murphy, S. L. (2008). *Deaths: Final data for 2005.* National Vital Statistics Reports, 56(10). Hyattsville, MD: National Center for Health Statistics.

Kuppermann, M., et al. (2004). Effect of hysterectomy vs. medical treatment on health-related quality of life and sexual functioning. The medicine or surgery (Ms) randomized trial. *Journal of the American Medical Association, 291,* 1447–1455.

Kurdek, L. A. (2005). What do we know about gay and lesbian couples? *Current Directions in Psychological Science, 14,* 251–254.

Kurman, J. (2004). Gender, self-enhancement, and self-regulation of learning behaviors in junior high school. *Sex Roles, 50,* 725–735.

Kvigne, V. L., et al. (2004). Characteristics of children who have full or incomplete fetal alcohol syndrome. *Journal of Pediatrics, 145,* 635–640.

Labaton, V., & Martin, D. L. (2004). Introduction: Making what will become. In V. Labaton & D. L. Martin (Eds.), *The fire this time* (pp. xxi–xxxvii). New York: Anchor Books.

Laber, E. (2001, January 11). Men are from Quake, women are from Ultima. *New York Times*, pp. D1, D4.

Lacasse, A., & Mendelson, M. J. (2007). Sexual coercion among adolescents: Victims and perpetrators. *Journal of Interpersonal Violence, 22*, 424–437.

Lacey, J. V., Jr., et al. (2006). Menopausal hormone therapy and ovarian cancer risk in the National Institutes of Health-AARP Diet and Health Study Cohort. *Journal of the National Cancer Institute, 98*, 1397–1405.

Laditka, J. N., & Laditka, S. B. (2003). Increased hospitalization risk for recently widowed older women and protective effects of social contacts. *Journal of Women & Aging, 15*, 7–28.

Laflamme, D., Pomerleau, A., & Malcuit, G. (2002). A comparison of fathers' and mothers' involvement in childcare and stimulation behaviors during free-play with their infants at 9 and 15 months. *Sex Roles, 47*, 507–518.

LaFrance, M. (2001a). Gender and social interaction. In R. K. Unger (Ed.), *Handbook of the psychology of women and gender* (pp. 245–255). New York: Wiley.

LaFrance, M. (2001b). Is rape natural? A review of "A natural history of rape: Biological bases of sexual coercion." *Contemporary Psychology, 46*, 377–379.

LaFrance, M., Hecht, M. A., & Paluck, E. L. (2003). The contingent smile: A meta-analysis of sex differences in smiling. *Psychological Bulletin, 129*, 305–334.

LaFraniere, S. (2005a, February 18). AIDS and custom leave African families nothing. *New York Times*, pp. A1, A6.

LaFraniere, S. (2005b). Entrenched epidemic: Wife-beating in Africa. *New York Times*, pp. A1, A8.

LaFromboise, T. D., Heyde, A. M., & Ozer, E. J. (1990). Changing and diverse roles of women in American Indian cultures. *Sex Roles, 22*, 455–476.

LaFromboise, T. D., Heyle, A. N., & Ozer, E. M. (1999). Changing and diverse roles of women in American Indian cultures. In L. A. Peplau, S. C. DeBro, R. C. Veniegas, & P. L. Taylor (Eds.), *Gender, culture and ethnicity: Current research about women and men* (pp. 48–61). Mountain View, CA: Mayfield.

Lakkis, J., Ricciardelli, L. A., & Williams, R. J. (1999). Role of sexual orientation and gender-related traits in disordered eating. *Sex Roles, 41*, 1–16.

Lakoff, R. T. (1990). *Talking power: The politics of language.* New York: Basic Books.

Lalumiere, M. L., Blanchard, R., & Zucker, K. J. (2000). Sexual orientation and handedness in men and women: A meta-analysis. *Psychological Bulletin, 126*, 575–592.

Lamb, S. (2006). *Packaging girlhood: Rescuing our daughters from marketers' schemes.* New York: St. Martin's Press.

Lambdin, J. R., et al. (2003). The animal 5 male hypothesis: Children's and adults' beliefs about the sex of non-sex specific stuffed animals. *Sex Roles, 48*, 471–482.

Lamberg, L. (2002). Younger children, more girls commit acts of violence. *Journal of the American Medical Association, 288*, 566–567.

Lamberg, L. (2007). Menopause not always to blame for sleep problems in midlife women. *Journal of the American Medical Association, 297*, 1865–1866.

Landesman, P. (2004, January 25). The girls next door. *New York Times Magazine*, pp. 30–39, 66–67, 72–75.

Lane, C., & Pool, G. J. (2005, August). *Gender stereotypical first-date norms persist in our egalitarian society.* Paper presented at the annual meeting of the American Psychological Association, Washington, DC.

Lane, M., & Etaugh, C. (2001, July). *Is stereotyping of females declining in children's books? It depends on the measure you use.* Poster presented at the meeting of the Seventh European Congress of Psychology, London.

Laner, M. R., & Ventrone, N. A. (1998). Egalitarian daters/traditionalist dates. *Journal of Family Issues, 19*, 468–477.

Lang, M. M., & Risman, B. J. (2006). Blending into equality: Family diversity and gender convergence. In K. Davis, M. Evans, & J. Lorber (Eds.), *Handbook of gender and women's studies* (pp. 287–303). London: SAGE Publications.

Langhout, R. D., Bergman, M. E., Cortina, L. M., Fitzgerald, L. F., Drasgow, F., & Williams, J. H. (2005). Sexual harassment severity: Assessing situational and personal determinants and outcomes. *Journal of Applied Social Psychology, 35*, 975–1007.

Lanham-New, S. A. (2006). Fruit and vegetables: The unexpected natural answer to the question of osteoporosis prevention? *American Journal of Clinical Nutrition, 83*, 1254–1255.

Lannin, D. R., et al. (1998). Influence of socioeconomic and cultural factors on racial differences in late-stage presentation of breast cancer. *Journal of the American Medical Association, 279*, 1801–1807.

Lansky, A. J., et al. (2005). Gender differences in outcomes after primary angioplasty versus primary stenting with and without abciximals for acute myocardial infarction. *Circulation, 111*, 1611–1618.

Lapierre, L. M., Spector, P. E., & Leek, J. D. (2005). Sexual versus nonsexual workplace aggression and victims' overall job satisfaction: A meta-analysis. *Journal of Occupational Health Psychology, 10*, 155–169.

L'Armand, K., et al. (2002, June). *Faculty-student romances: Effects of respondent gender and student status on judgments.* Poster presented at the meeting of the American Psychological Society, New Orleans.

Larose, S., Ratelle, C. F., Guay, F., Senécal, C., Harvey, M., & Drouin, E. (2008). A saciomotivational analysis of gender effects on persistence in science and technology: A 5-year longitudinal study. In H. M. G. Watt & J. S. Eccles (Eds.), *Gender and occupational outcomes: Longitudinal assessments of individual, social, and cultural influences* (pp. 171–192). Washington, DC: American Psychological Association.

LaRossa, R., Jaret, C., Gadgil, M., & Wynn, G. R. (2001). Gender disparities in Mother's Day and Father's Day comic strips: A 55-year history. *Sex Roles, 44*, 693–718.

Larson, R., & Wilson, S. (2004). Adolescence across place and time. Globalization and the changing pathways to adulthood. In R. M. Lerner & L. Steinberg (Eds.), *Handbook of adolescent psychology* (2nd ed., pp. 299–330). Hoboken, NJ: Wiley.

Larson, R. W., & Verma, S. (1999). How children and adolescents spend time across the world: Work, play, and developmental opportunities. *Psychological Bulletin, 125*, 701–736.

Lasswell, M. (2002). Marriage and family. In S. G. Kornstein & A. H. Clayton (Eds.), *Women's mental health: A comprehensive textbook* (pp. 515–526). New York: Guilford.

Laumann, E. O., et al. (2004). *The sexual organization of the city.* Chicago: University of Chicago Press.

Laumann, E. O., Gagnon, J. H., Michael, R. T., & Michaels, S. (1994). *The social organization of sexuality: Sexual practices in the United States.* Chicago: University of Chicago Press.

Laumann, E. O., & Mahay, J. (2002). The social organization of women's sexuality. In G. M. Wingood & R. J. DiClemente (Eds.), *Handbook of women's sexual and reproductive health* (pp. 43–70). New York: Kluwer Academic/Plenum.

Laumann, E. O., Paik, A., & Rosen, R. C. (1999). Sexual dysfunction in the United States: Prevalence and predictors. *Journal of the American Medical Association, 281*, 537–544.

Lauzen, M. M. (2003). *The celluloid ceiling: Behind-the-scenes and on-screen employment of women in the top 250 films of 2002.* MoviesByWomen.com

Lauzen, M. M., & Dozier, D. M. (2002). You look mahvelous: An examination of gender and appearance comments in the 1999–2000 prime-time season. *Sex Roles, 46*, 429–437.

Law, B. M. (2007). Women need sustained exercise programs after heart surgery. *Monitor on Psychology, 38*, 15.

Lawler, A. (2002). Engineers marginalized, MIT report concludes. *Science, 295*, 2192.

Lawlor, D. A., Ronalds, G., Leon, D. A., Macintyre, S., & Clark, H. (2006). Family socioeconomic position at birth and future cardiovascular disease risk: Findings from the Aberdeen Children of the 1950s cohort study. *American Journal of Public Health, 96*, 1271–1277.

Lawlor, D. A., & Sterne, J. A. (2007). Socioeconomic inequalities in health are important but the effects of age and sex may be overlooked. *BMJ, 334*, 963–964.

Lawrence, E., Nylen, K., & Cobb, R. J. (2007). Prenatal expectations and marital satisfaction over the transition to parenthood. *Journal of Family Psychology, 21*, 155–164.

Lawton, C. A., Blakemore, J. E. O., & Vartanian, L. R. (2003). The new meaning of Ms.: Single, but too old for miss. *Psychology of Women Quarterly, 27*, 215–220.

Leach, P., et al. (2006). Child care before 6 months of age: A qualitative study of mothers' decisions and feelings about employment and non-maternal care. *Infant and Child Development, 15*, 471–502.

Leahy, E., & Guo, G. (2001). Gender differences in mathematical trajectories. *Social Forces, 80*, 713–732.

Leaper, C. (2000). The social construction and socialization of gender during development. In P. H. Miller & E. K. Scholnick (Eds.), *Toward a feminist developmental psychology* (pp. 127–152). Florence, KY: Taylor & Francis/Routledge.

Leaper, C. (2002). Parenting girls and boys. In M. H. Bornstein (Ed.), *Handbook of parenting* (2nd ed., pp. 189–225). Mahwah, NJ: Erlbaum.

Leaper, C. (2004, July). *Gender-related variations in affiliative and assertive speech: Meta-analyses.* Paper presented at the American Psychological Association Convention, Honolulu.

Leaper, C., & Brown, C. S. (2008). Perceived experiences with sexism among adolescent girls. *Child Development, 79*, 685–704.

Leaper, C., & Friedman, C. K. (2007). The socialization of gender. In J. E. Grusec & P. D. Hastings (Eds.), *Handbook of socialization: Theory and research* (pp. 561–587). New York: Guilford.

Leaper, C., & Smith, T. E. (2004). A meta-analytic review of gender variations in children's language use: Talkativeness, affiliative speech, and assertive speech. *Developmental Psychology, 40*, 993–1027.

Leary, W. E. (1998, September 29). Older people enjoy sex, survey says. *New York Times,* p. B16.

Lee, C., & Gramotnev, H. (2007). Life transitions and mental health in a national cohort of young Australian women. *Developmental Psychology, 43*, 877–888.

Lee, F. R. (2004, July 3). Engineering more sons than daughters: Will it tip the scales toward war? *New York Times,* pp. A17, A19.

Lee, I. (2007). Dose-response relation between physical activity and fitness. *Journal of the American Medical Association, 297*, 2137–2138.

Lee, J. 8. (2007, May 10). The incredible flying granny nanny. *New York Times,* pp. El, E7.

Lee, J. M., Appugliese, D., Kaciroti, N., Corwyn, R. F., Bradley, R. H., & Lumeng, J. C. (2007). Weight status in young girls and the onset of puberty. *Pediatrics, 119*, e624–e630.

Lee, P. A., Houk, C. P., Ahmed, S. F., & Hughes, I. A. (2006). Consensus statement on management of intersex disorders. *Pediatrics, 118*, e488–e500.

Lee, S. (2002). Health and sickness: The meaning of menstruation and premenstrual syndrome in women's lives. *Sex Roles, 46*, 25–35.

Lee, S. (2004). The new girls network: Women, technology, and feminism. In V. Labaton & D. L. Martin (Eds.), *The fire this time* (pp. 84–104). New York: Anchor Books.

Lee, S., Colditz, G., Berkman, L., & Kawachi, I. (2003). Caregiving to children and grandchildren and risk of coronary heart disease in women. *American Journal of Public Health, 93*, 1939–1944.

Lee, S., & Shaw, L. (2008). *From work to retirement: Tracking changes in women's poverty status.* Washington, DC: AARP.

Lee Badgett, M. V. (2003, September). *Variations on an equitable theme: Explaining international same-sex partner recognition laws.* Paper presented at the meeting "Same-sex couples, same-sex partnerships, and homosexual marriages," Stockholm University.

Leeb, R. T., & Rejskind, F. G. (2004). Here's looking at you, kid! A longitudinal study of perceived gender differences in mutual gaze behavior in young infants. *Sex Roles, 50*, 1–14.

Lefkowitz, E. S., & Fingerman, K. L. (2003). Positive and negative emotional feelings and behaviors in mother–daughter ties in late life. *Journal of Family Psychology, 17*(4), 607–617.

le Grange, D., et al. (2004). Bulimia nervosa in adolescents. A disorder in evolution? *Archives of Pediatrics and Adolescent Medicine, 158*, 478–482.

Lehr, S. (2001). The anomalous female and the ubiquitous male. In S. Lehr (Ed.), *Beauty, brains, and brawn: The construction of gender in children's literature* (pp. 193–207). Portsmouth, NH: Heinemann.

Leiblum, S., & Sachs, J. (2002). *Getting the sex you want: A woman's guide to becoming proud, passionate, and pleased in bed.* New York: Crown.

Leibson-Hawkins, B. (2004). *I'm too young to have breast cancer.* Washington, DC: Regnery Publishing.

Leitner, M. J., & Leitner, S. F. (2004). *Leisure in later life* (3rd ed.). Binghamton, NY: Haworth.

Leland, J. (2000, March 20). Shades of gays. *Newsweek,* pp. 46–49.

Leland, J. (2004, March 23). He's retired, she's working, they're not happy. *New York Times,* pp. A1, A18.

Leman, P. J., Ahmed, S., & Ozarow, L. (2005). Gender, gender relations, and the social dynamics of children's conversations. *Developmental Psychology, 41*, 64–74.

Lemieux, S. R., & Byers, E. S. (2008). The sexual well-being of women who have experienced child sexual abuse. *The Psychology of Women Quarterly, 32*, 126–144.

Lengua, L. J., & Stormshok, E. A. (2000). Gender, gender roles, and personality: Gender differences in the prediction of coping and psychological symptoms. *Sex Roles, 42*, 787–819.

Lennon, M. C., Blome, J., & English, K. (2002). Depression among women on welfare: A review of the literature. *Journal of the Medical Women's Association, 57*, 27–32.

Leon, I. G. (2001). Perinatal loss. In N. L. Stotland and D. E. Stewart (Eds.), *Psychological aspects of women's health care* (2nd ed., pp. 141–173). Washington, DC: American Psychiatric Press.

Leonard, D., & Jiang, J. (1999). Gender bias and the college predictions of the SATs: A cry of despair. *Research in Higher Education, 40*, 375.

LePage-Lees, P. (1997). Struggling with a nontraditional past: Academically successful women from disadvantaged backgrounds discuss their relationship with "disadvantage." *Psychology of Women Quarterly, 21*, 365–385.

Lerner, B. H. (2003, May 27). If biology is destiny, when shouldn't it be? *New York Times,* p. D7.

Lerner, J. S., Castellino, D. R., Lolli, E., & Wan, S. (2002). Children, families and work: Research findings and implications for policies and programs. In R. M. Lerner, F. Jacobs, & D. Wertlieb (Eds.), *Handbook of applied developmental science* (Vol. 1, pp. 281–304). Thousand Oaks, CA: Sage.

Lerner, S. (2002, October 22). Good and bad marriage, boon and bane to health. *New York Times,* pp. D5, D8.

Lesbian community assesses health issues. (2004, June 20). *Associated Press.*

Lescano, C. M., Vazquez, E. A., Brown, L. K., Litwin, E. B., Pugatch, D., & Project SHETLD Study Group. (2006). Condom use with "casual" and "main" partners: What's in a name? *Journal of Adolescent Health, 39*, 443.e1–443.e7.

Lesko, A. C., & Corpus, J. H. (2006). Discounting the difficult: How high math-identified women respond to stereotype threat. *Sex Roles, 54*, 113–125.

Lester, D., & Yang, B. (1998). *Suicide and homicide in the twentieth century: Changes over time.* Commack, AL: Nova Science.

Letourneau, E. J., Schoenwald, S. K., & Sheidow, A. J. (2004). Children and adolescents with sexual behavior problems. *Child Maltreatment, 9*, 49–61.

Leung, S. A., Ivey, D., & Suzuki, L. (1994). Factors affecting the career aspirations of Asian Americans. *Journal of Counseling & Development, 72*, 404–410.

Levant, R., Richmond, K., Cook, S., House, A. T., & Aupont, M. (2007). The femininity ideology scale: Factor structure, reliability, convergent and discriminant validity, and social contextual variation. *Sex Roles, 57*, 373–383.

Levant, R. F. (1997, August). *Deconstructing Disney: Gender socialization through the lens of the cinema.* Paper presented at the meeting of the American Psychological Association, Chicago.

Leventhal, E. A. (1994). Gender and aging: Women and their aging. In V. J. Adesso, D. M. Reddy, & R. Flemming (Eds.), *Psychological perspectives on women's health* (pp. 11–35). Washington, DC: Taylor & Francis.

Levesque, K. (2003). Public high school graduates who participated in vocational/technical education: 1982–1998. *Education Statistics Quarterly, 5*(3), 33–39.

Levesque, M. J., Nave, C. S., & Lowe, C. A. (2006). Toward and understanding of gender differences in inferring sexual interest. *Psychology of Women Quarterly, 30*, 150–158.

Levine, M. (2004, June 1). Tell the doctor all your problems, but keep it to less than a minute. *New York Times,* p. F6.

Levine, S. C., Huttenlocher, J., Taylor, A., & Langrock, A. (1999). Early sex differences in spatial skill. *Developmental Psychology, 35*, 940–949.

Levison, S. P., & Straumanis, J. (2002 September/October). FIPSE: Changing medical education forever. *Change,* pp. 19–26.

Levitt, H. M., & Hiestand, K. R. (2004). A quest for authenticity: Contemporary butch gender. *Sex Roles, 50*, 605–621.

Levy, G. D., Zimmerman, B., Barber, J., Martin, N., & Malone, C. (1998, May). *Preverbal awareness of gender roles in toddlers.* Poster presented at the meeting of the American Psychological Society, Washington, DC.

Levy, J. A., Ory, M. G., & Crystal, S. (2003, June 1). HIV/AIDS interventions for midlife and older adults: Current status and challenges. *Journal of Acquired Immune Deficiency Syndromes, 33*, S59–S67.

Lew, A. S., Allen, R., Papouchis, N., & Ritzler, B. (1998). Achievement orientation and fear of success in Asian American college students. *Journal of Clinical Psychology, 54*, 97–108.

Lewin, T. (1997, September 30). Little talk on sexual diseases. *New York Times,* p. B15.

Lewin, T. (2001a, May 30). Program finds success in reducing teenage pregnancy. *New York Times,* p. A15.

Lewin, T. (2001b, September 10). Study finds little change in working mothers debate. *New York Times,* p. A26.

Lewin, T. (2002, May 30). U.S. defends anti-bias law on college sports. *New York Times*, p. A14.

Lewis, J. M. (2007, August). *Maternal influence on adolescents' formation of work-family gender ideology: Variation by gender, race, and ethnicity*. Paper presented at the meeting of the American Sociological Association, New York.

Lewis, J. R., & Hounsell, C. (2007). *What women need to know about retirement*. Washington, DC: The Women's Institute for a Secure Retirement.

Lewis, M. A., Lee, C. M., Patrick, M. E., & Fossos, N. (2007). Gender-specific normative misperceptions of risky sexual behavior and alcohol-related risky sexual behavior. *Sex Roles*, *57*, 81–90.

Lewis Claar, R., & Blumenthal, J. A. (2003). The value of stress-management interventions in life-threatening medical conditions. *Current Directions in Psychological Science*, *12*(4), 133–137.

Lex, B. W. (2000). Gender and cultural influences on substance abuse. In R. M. Eisler & M. Hersen (Eds.), *Handbook of gender, culture, and health* (pp. 255–297). Mahwah, NJ: Erlbaum.

Li, C., & Kerpelman, J. (2007). Parental influences on young women's certainty about their career aspirations. *Sex Roles*, *56*, 105–115.

Li, N. P., & Kenrick, D. T. (2006). Sex similarities and differences in preference for short-term mates: what, whether, and why. *Journal of Personality and Social Psychology*, *90*, 468–489.

Li, Q. (1999). Teachers' beliefs and gender differences in mathematics: A review. *Educational Research*, *41*(1), 63–76.

Liao, L. M., & Creighton, S. M. (2007). Requests for cosmetic genitoplasty: How should healthcare providers respond? *BMJ*, *334*, 1090–1092.

Liben, L. S., & Bigler, R. S. (2002). The developmental course of gender differentiation. *Monographs of the Society for Research in Child Development*, *67* (2, Serial No. 269).

Liben, L. S., Bigler, R. S., & Krogh, H. R. (2001). Pink and blue collar jobs: Children's judgments of job status and job aspirations in relation to sex of worker. *Journal of Experimental Child Psychology*, *79*, 346–363.

Liben, L. S., et al. (2002). The effects of sex steroids on spatial performance: A review and an experimental clinical investigation. *Developmental Psychology*, *38*, 236–253.

Lichtenstein, A. H., Rasmussen, H., Yu, W. W., Epstein, S. R., & Russell, R. M. (2008). Modified MyPyramid for older adults. *Journal of Nutrition*, *138*, 78–82.

Lichter, E. L., & McCloskey, L. A. (2004). The effects of childhood exposure to marital violence on adolescent gender-role beliefs and dating violence. *Psychology of Women Quarterly*, *28*, 344–357.

Liljestrand, J., & Gryboski, K. (2002). Women at risk of maternal mortality. In E. Murphy (Ed.), *Reproductive health and rights: Reaching the hardly reached* (pp. 121–128). Washington, DC: Program for Appropriate Technology in Health.

Lim, S., & Cortina, L. M. (2005). Interpersonal mistreatment in the workplace: The interface and impact of general incivility and sexual harassment. *Journal of Applied Psychology*, *90*, 483–496.

Lin, J., Manson, J. E., Lee, I.-M., Cook, N. R., Buring, J. E., & Shumin, M. Z. (2007). Intakes of calcium and vitamin D and breast cancer risk in women. *Archives of Internal Medicine*, *167*, 1050–1059.

Lindau, S. T., Schumm, L. P., Laumann, E. O., Levinson, W., O'Muircheartaigh, C. A., & Waite, L. J. (2007). A study of sexuality and health among older adults in the United States. *New England Journal of Medicine*, *357*, 762–774.

Lindberg, L. D., Santelli, J. S., & Singh, S. (2006). Changes in formal sex education: 1995–2002. *Perspectives on Sexual and Reproductive Health*, *38*, 182–189.

Lindberg, S. M., Grabe, S., & Hyde, J. S. (2007). Gender, pubertal development, and peer sexual harassment predict objectified body consciousness in early adolescence. *Journal of Research on Adolescence*, *17*, 723–742.

Lindgren, K. P., Shoda, Y., & George, W. H. (2007). Sexual or friendly? Associations about women, men, and self. *Psychology of Women Quarterly*, *31*, 190–201.

Lindner, K. (2004). Images of women in general interest and fashion magazine advertisements from 1955 to 2002. *Sex Roles*, *51*, 409–421.

Lindsey, E. W., & Mize, J. (2001). Contextual differences in parent–child play: Implications for children's gender role development. *Sex Roles*, *44*, 155–176.

Linn, M. C., & Kessel, C. (2006). Assessment and gender. In J. Worell & C. D. Goodheart (Eds.), *Handbook of girls' and women's psychological health: Gender and well-being across the life-span* (pp. 40–50). New York: Oxford University Press.

Linn, M. C., & Petersen, A. C. (1985). Emergence and characterization of sex differences in spatial ability: A meta-analysis. *Child Development*, *56*, 1479–1498.

Lipka, S. (2007, April 2). At 35th-anniversary conference, backer of Title IX discuss challenges to women's sports. *The Chronicle of Higher Education Today's News*. Retrieved from http://chronicle.com/daily/2007/04/2007040203n.htm

Lippa, R. A. (2005). *Gender, nature, and nurture* (2nd ed.). Mahwah, NJ: Erlbaum.

Lippa, R. A. (2008). Sex differences and sexual orientation differences in personality: Findings from the BBC Internet survey. *Archives of Sexual Behavior*, *37*, 173–187.

Lippert, J. (2008, February). As only a woman's heart can be. *Heart Insight*, pp. 20–21.

Lips, H. M. (1997). *Sex and gender: An introduction* (3rd ed.). Mountain View, CA: Mayfield.

Lips, H. M. (2004). The gender gap in possible selves: Divergence of academic self-views among high school and university students. *Sex Roles*, *50*, 357–371.

Lipson, J. (2001, Fall). Pay equity: Fact or fiction? *Outlook*, pp. 14–18.

Liptak, A. (2005, August 23). California ruling expands same-sex parental rights. *New York Times*, p. A10.

Liptak, A. (2008, May 16). California court overturns a ban on gay marriage. *New York Times*, pp. Al, A19.

Lisi, D. (1993). Found voices: Women, disability, and cultural transformation. *Women & Therapy*, *14*, 195–209.

Liss, M., Crawford, M., & Popp, D. (2004). Predictors and correlates of collective action. *Sex Roles*, *50*, 771–779.

Liss, M., O'Connor, C., Morosky, E., & Crawford, M. (2001). What makes a feminist? Predictors and correlates of feminist social identity in college women. *Psychology of Women Quarterly, 25,* 124–133.

Little, M. V. (2005). Getting your financial priorities straight. *Journal of the American Medical Women's Association, 60,* 9–10.

Littlefield, G. D., et al. (2000). Common themes in long-term lesbian relationships. *Family Therapy, 27,* 71–79.

Littleton, H. L., & Axsom, D. (2003). Rape and seduction scripts of university students: Implications for rape attributions and unacknowledged rape. *Sex Roles, 49,* 465–475.

Livingston, J. A., Hequembourg, A., Testa, M., & VanZile-Tamsen, C. (2007). Unique aspects of adolescent sexual victimization experiences. *Psychology of Women Quarterly, 31,* 331–343.

Livosky, M., Pettijohn, T. F., II, & Capo, J. R. (2008). *Reducing sexist attitudes by completing a psychology of gender course.* Poster presented at the meeting of the Association for Psychological Science, Chicago.

Llabre, M. M., & Hadi, F. (1997). Social support and psychological distress in Kuwaiti boys and girls exposed to the Gulf crisis. *Journal of Clinical Child Psychology, 26,* 247–255.

Lloyd, C. B., Grant, M., & Ritchie, A. (2008). Gender differences in time use among adolescents in developing countries: Implication of rising school enrollment rates. *Journal of Research on Adolescence, 18,* 99–120.

Lloyd-Jones, D. M., et al. (2004). Parental cardiovascular disease as a risk factor for cardiovascular disease in middle-aged adults. *Journal of the American Medical Association, 291,* 2204–2211.

Loeb, S., Fuller, B., Kagan, S. L., & Carrol, B. (2004). Child care in poor communities: Early learning effects of type, quality, and stability. *Child Development, 75,* 47–65.

Lonborg, S. D., & Hackett, G. (2006). Career assessment and counseling for women. In W. B. Walsh & M. J. Heppner (Eds.), *Handbook of career counseling for women* (2nd ed., pp. 103–166). Mahwah, NJ: Erlbaum.

London, K., Bruck, M., Ceci, S. J., & Shuman, D. W. (2007). Disclosure of child sexual abuse: A review of the contemporary empirical literature. In M.-E. Pipe, M. E. Lamb, Y. Orbach, & A.-C. Cederborg (Eds.), *Child sexual abuse: Disclosure, delay, and denial* (pp. 11–40). Mahwah, NJ: Erlbaum.

Long, P. J., Borja, S., Voller, E. K., Aosved, A. C., Carlozzi, N., & Burlingame, S. E. (2005, August). *Gender differences in the experience of childhood sexual abuse.* Paper presented at the annual meeting of the American Psychological Association, Washington, DC.

Longman, J. (2007, February 8). Female athletes embrace size, spurring debate over weight. *New York Times,* pp. A1, C17.

Lonsway, K. A., Cortina, L. M., & Magley, V. J. (2008). Sexual harassment mythology: Definition, conceptualization, and measurement. *Sex Roles, 58,* 599–615.

Lorber, J. (2005). *Breaking the bowls: Degendering and feminist change.* New York: W. W. Norton.

Lorch, E. P. (2007). Health, drugs, and values. In N. Pecora, J. P. Murray, & E. A. Wartella (Eds.), *Children and television: Fifty years of research* (pp. 205–231). Mahwah, NJ: Erlbaum.

Lott, B. (2002). Cognitive and behavioral distancing from the poor. *American Psychologist, 57,* 100–110.

Lott, B., & Bullock, H. E. (2001, Summer). Who are the poor? *Journal of Social Issues, 57,* 189–206.

Lott, B., & Bullock, H. E. (Eds.). (2007). Listening to the voices of poor women. *Journal of Social Issues, 57.*

Lott, B., & Maluso, D. (2001). Gender development: Social learning. In J. Worell (Ed.), *Encyclopedia of women and gender* (pp. 537–549). San Diego: Academic Press.

Lott, B., & Saxon, S. (2002). The influence of ethnicity, social class and context on judgments about American women. *Journal of Social Psychology, 142,* 481–499.

Lottes, I. L., & Kuriloff, P. J. (1992). The effects of gender, race, religion, and political orientation on the sex role attitudes of college freshmen. *Adolescence, 27,* 675–688.

Louie, B. (2001). Why gender stereotypes still persist in contemporary children's literature. In S. Lehr (Ed.), *Beauty, brains, and brawn* (pp. 142–151). Portsmouth, NH: Heinemann.

Lovas, G. S. (2005). Gender and patterns of emotional availability in mother-toddler and father-toddler dyads. *Infant Mental Health Journal, 26,* 327–353.

Lovejoy, M. (1998). "You can't go home again": The impact of women's studies on intellectual and personal development. *NWSA Journal, 10*(1), 119.

Lovell, V., Hartmann, H., & Williams, C. (2008). *Women at greater risk of economic insecurity: A gender analysis of the Rockefeller Foundation's American Worker Survey.* Washington, DC: Institute for Women's Policy Research.

Lovell, V., O'Neill, E., & Olsen, S. (2007, August). *Maternity leave in the United States: Paid parental leave is still not standard, even among the best U.S. employers* [Fact sheet]. Washington, DC: Institute for Women's Policy Research.

Lowell, J. (2004, June 28). Have experience and wisdom, will travel. *Newsweek,* p. 14.

Lown, E. A., Schmidt, L. A., & Wiley, J. (2006). Interpersonal violence among women seeking welfare: Unraveling lives. *American Journal of Public Health, 96,* 1409–1415.

Lubinski, D., & Benbow, C. P. (1992). Gender differences in abilities and preferences among the gifted: Implications for the math-science pipeline. *Current Directions in Psychological Science, 1,* 61–66.

Lubinski, D. S., & Benbow, C. P. (2007). Sex differences in personal attributes for the development of scientific expertise. In S. J. Ceci & W. M. Williams (Eds.), *Why aren't more women in science? Top researchers debate the evidence* (pp. 79–100). Washington, DC: American Psychological Association.

Lucas, R. E., Clark, A. E., Georgellis, Y., & Diener, E. (2003). Reexamining adaptation and the set point model of happiness: Reactions to changes in marital status. *Journal of Personality and Social Psychology, 84,* 527–539.

Luciano, L. (2003). The economics of young women today. In C. B. Costello, V. R. Wight, & A. J. Stone (Eds.), *The American woman 2003–2004: Daughters of a revolution—young women today* (pp. 143–163). New York: Palgrave Macmillan.

Lummis, M., & Stevenson, H. W. (1990). Gender differences in beliefs and achievement: A cross-cultural study. *Developmental Psychology, 26,* 254–563.

Luthar, S. S., & Sexton, C. C. (2004). The high price of affluence. In R. V. Kail (Ed.), *Advances in child development and behavior* (pp. 125–162). San Diego, CA: Elsevier.

Lutzker, J. R., Bigelow, K. M., Swenson, C. C., Doctor, R. M., & Kessler, M. L. (1999). Problems related to child abuse and neglect. In S. D. Netherton, D. Holmes, & C. E. Walker (Eds.), *Child and adolescent psychological disorders: A comprehensive textbook* (pp. 520–548). New York: Oxford University Press.

Lyall, S. (2005, February 22). New course by Royal Navy: A campaign to recruit gays. *New York Times,* p. A1.

Lydon-Rochelle, M. T. (2004). Minimal intervention—nurse-midwives in the United States. *New England Journal of Medicine, 351,* 1929–1931.

Lynch, S. A. (1998). Who supports whom: How age and gender affect the perceived quality of support from family and friends. *Gerontologist, 38,* 231–238.

Lyness, J. M. (2004). Treatment of depressive conditions in later life: Real-world light for dark (or dim) tunnels. *Journal of the American Medical Association, 291,* 1626–1628.

Lyness, K. S., & Thompson, D. E. (1997). Above the glass ceiling? A comparison of matched samples of female and male executives. *Journal of Applied Psychology, 82,* 359–375.

Lyness, K. S., Thompson, C. A., Francesco, A. M., & Judiesch, M. K. (1999). Work and pregnancy: Individual and organizational factors influencing organizational commitment, timing of maternity leave, and return to work. *Sex Roles, 41,* 485–508.

Macalister, H. E. (2003). In defense of ambiguity: Understanding bisexuality's invisibility through cognitive psychology. *Journal of Bisexuality, 3,* 25–32.

MacCallum, F., & Golombok, S. (2002, July). *Families through surrogacy: Psychological implications.* Paper presented at European Society of Human Reproduction and Embryology, Vienna.

Maccoby, E. E. (1998). *The two sexes: Growing up apart, coming together.* Cambridge, MA: Harvard University Press.

Maccoby, E. E. (2002). Gender and group process: A developmental perspective. *Current Directions in Psychological Science, 11,* 54–58.

Maccoby, E. E., & Jacklin, C. N. (1974). *The psychology of sex differences.* Stanford, CA: Stanford University Press.

MacGeorge, E. L., et al. (2004). The myth of gender cultures: Similarities outweigh differences in men's and women's provision of and responses to supportive communication. *Sex Roles, 50,* 143–175.

Mack, K. A., et al. (2004). Health and sociodemographic factors associated with body weight and weight objectives for women: 2000 Behavioral Risk Factor Surveillance System. *Journal of Women's Health, 13,* 1019–1032.

MacMahon, K. M. A., & Lip, G. Y. H. (2002). Psychological factors in heart failure. *Archives of Internal Medicine, 162,* 509–516.

MacWilliams, B. (2003, October 3). Forced into prostitution. *Chronicle of Higher Education,* pp. A34–A36.

Madkan, V. K., Giancola, A. A., Sra, K. K., & Tyring, S. K. (2006). Anatomical and hormonal influences on women's dermatologic health. *Journal of the American Medical Association, 296,* 1443–1445.

Maestripieri, D. (2002, January). Developmental and evolutionary aspects of female attraction to babies. *Psychological Science Agenda, 18*(1). www.apa.org/science/psa

Magai, C., Consedine, N., Neugut, A. I., & Hershman, D. L. (2007). Common psychosocial factors underlying breast cancer screening and breast cancer treatment adherence: A conceptual review and synthesis. *Journal of Women's Health, 16,* 11–23.

Magley, V. J., Hulin, C. L., Fitzgerald, L. F., & DeNardo, M. (1999). Outcomes of self-labeling sexual harassment. *Journal of Applied Psychology, 84,* 390–402.

Magley, V. J., & Shupe, E. I. (2005). Self-labeling sexual harassment. *Sex Roles, 53,* 173–189.

Mahaffy, K. A., & Ward, S. K. (2002). The gendering of adolescents' childbearing and educational plan: Reciprocal effects and the influence of social context. *Sex Roles, 46,* 403–417.

Mahalingam, R. (2003). Essentialism, culture, and beliefs about gender among the Aravanis of Tamil Nadu, India. *Sex Roles, 49,* 489–496.

Mahler, S. (2003). Anxiety disorders. In L. Slater, J. H. Daniel, & A. E. Banks (Eds.), *The complete guide to mental health for women* (pp. 197–203). Boston: Beacon Press.

Mahoney, S. (2003, November/December). Seeking love. *AARP Magazine,* pp. 1–3.

Maine, D., & Chavkin, W. (2002, Summer). Maternal mortality: Global similarities and differences. *Journal of the Medical Women's Association, 57,* 127–130.

Mainiero, L. A., Gibson, D. E., & Sullivan, S. E. (2008). Retrospective analysis of gender differences in reaction to media coverage of crisis events: New insights on the justice and care orientations. *Sex Roles, 58,* 556–566.

Majerovitz, S. D. (2006). Physical health and illness in older women. In J. Worell & C. D. Goodheart (Eds.), *Handbook of girls' and women's psychological health: Gender and well-being across the lifespan* (pp. 379–387). New York: Oxford University Press.

Major, B., Barr, L., Zubek, J., & Babey, S. H. (1999). Gender and self-esteem: A meta-analysis. In W. B. Swann, J. H. Langlois, & L. A. Gilbert (Eds.), *Sexism and stereotypes in modern society* (pp. 223–254). Washington, DC: American Psychological Association.

Major, B., Cozzarelli, C., Cooper, L., Zubek, J., Richards, C., Wilhite, M., & Gramzow, R. H. (2000). Psychological responses of women after first-trimester abortion. *Archives of General Psychiatry, 57,* 777–784.

Major, B., Richards, C., Cooper, M. L., Cozzarelli, C., & Zubek, J. (1998). Personal resilience, cognitive appraisals, and coping: An integrative model of adjustment to abortion. *Journal of Personality and Social Psychology, 74,* 735–752.

Major companies accused of sex discrimination. (2004, Fall/Winter). *AAUW Outlook,* p. 5.

Making the grade on women's health: A national and state report card, 2004. (2004, June). Washington, DC and Portland,

OR: National Women's Law Center and Oregon Health & Science University.

Malamuth, N. M., Sockloskie, R. J., Koss, M. P., & Tanaka, J. S. (1991). Characteristics of aggressors against women: Testing a model using a national sample of college students. *Journal of Consulting and Clinical Psychology, 59*, 670–681.

Malanchuk, O., & Eccles, J. S. (2006). Self-esteem. In J. Worell & C. D. Goodheart (Eds.), *Handbook of girls' and women's psychological health: Gender and well-being across the lifespan* (pp. 149–156). New York: Oxford University Press.

Malatesta, V. J. (2007). Sexual problems, women and aging: An overview. *Journal of Women & Aging, 19*, 139–154.

Malcolmson, K. A., & Sinclair, L. (2007). The Ms. stereotype revisited: Implicit and explicit facets. *Psychology of Women Quarterly, 31*, 305–310.

Maldonado-Molina, M. M., Komro, K. A., & Prado, G. (2007). Prospective association between dieting and smoking initiation among adolescents. *American Journal of Health Promotion, 22*, 25–32.

Maliti, T. (2004, October 9). Kenyan awarded Nobel Peace Prize. *Peoria Journal Star*, p. A3.

Malley-Morrison, K. (Ed.). (2004). *International perspectives on family violence and abuse*. Mahwah, NJ: Erlbaum.

Mangweth-Matzek, B., et al. (2006). Never too old for eating disorders or body dissatisfaction: A community study of elderly women. *International Journal of Eating Disorders, 39*, 583–586.

Mankiller, W. (2004). Coda. In V. Labaton & D. L. Martin (Eds.), *The fire this time* (pp. 291–293). New York: Anchor Books.

Manlove, J., Ryan, S., & Franzetta, K. (2003). Patterns of contraceptive use within teenagers' first sexual relationships. *Perspectives on Sexual and Reproductive Health, 35*, 246–255.

Mannheim Research Institute for the Economics of Aging. (2005). *Health, ageing, and retirement in Europe*. Mannheim, Germany: Author.

Manning, W. D., Longmore, M. A., & Giordano, P. C. (2007). The changing institution of marriage: Adolescents' expectation to cohabit and to marry. *Journal of Marriage and Family, 69*, 559–575.

Mannino, C. A., & Deutsch, F. M. (2007). Changing the division of household labor: A negotiated process between partners. *Sex Roles, 56*, 309–324.

Mansfield, P. K., et al. (1991). The job climate for women in traditionally male blue-collar occupations. *Sex Roles, 25*, 63–79.

Mansfield, P. K., Koch, P. B., & Voda, A. M. (1998). Qualities midlife women desire in their sexual relationships and their changing sexual response. *Psychology of Women Quarterly, 22*, 285–303.

Mansfield, P. K., Koch, P. B., & Voda, A. M. (2000). Midlife women's attributions for their sexual response changes. *Health Care for Women International, 21*, 543–559.

Manson, J. E., & Bassuk, S. S. (2007, January 22). Hot flashes and hormones. *Newsweek*, pp. 44–45.

Manzoli, L., Villari, P., Pirone, G. M., & Boccia, A. (2007). Marital status and mortality in the elderly: A systematic review and meta-analysis. *Social Science & Medicine, 64*, 77–94.

Marano, H. E. (1997, July 1). Puberty may start at 6 as hormones surge. *New York Times*, pp. B9, B12.

Marchbanks, P. A., et al. (2002). Oral contraceptives and the risk of breast cancer. *New England Journal of Medicine, 346*, 2025–2032.

Marcia, J. E. (1993). The relational roots of identity. In J. Krogers (Ed.), *Discussion on ego identity* (pp. 101–120). Hillsdale, NJ: Erlbaum.

Marcus, E. N. (2008, May 20). Screening for abuse may be key to ending it. *New York Times*, p. F5.

Marecek, J. (2001). Disorderly constructs: Feminist frameworks for clinical psychology. In R. K. Unger (Ed.), *Handbook of the psychology of women and gender* (pp. 303–316). New York: Wiley.

Marecek, J., Crawford, M., & Popp, D. (2004). On the construction of gender, sex, and sexualities. In A. H. Eagly, A. E. Beall, and R. J. Sternberg (Eds.), *The psychology of gender* (2nd ed., pp. 192–216). New York: Guilford.

Marecek, J., & Hare-Mustin, R. T. (1998). A short history of the future: Feminism and clinical psychology. In D. L. Anselmi and A. L. Law (Eds.), *Questions of gender: Perspectives and paradoxes* (pp. 748–758). Boston: McGraw-Hill.

Mares, M.-L., & Fitzpatrick, M. A. (2004). Communication in close relationships of older people. In J. F. Nussbaum & J. Coupland (Eds.), *Handbook of communication and aging research* (2nd ed., pp. 231–250). Mahwah, NJ: Erlbaum.

Margolin, G., & Gordis, E. B. (2004). Children's exposure to violence in the family and community. *Current Directions in Psychological Science, 13*, 152–155.

Markens, S. (2007). *Surrogate motherhood and the politics of reproduction*. Berkeley, CA: University of California Press.

Markey, C. N., & Markey, P. M. (2005). Relations between body image and dieting behaviors: An examination of gender differences. *Sex Roles, 53*, 519–530.

Markey, C. N., Markey, P. M., & Birch, L. L. (2004). Understanding women's body satisfaction: The role of husbands. *Sex Roles, 51*, 209–216.

Markham, B. (2006). Older women and security. In J. Worell & C. D. Goodheart (Eds.), *Handbook of girls' and women's psychological health: Gender and well-being across the lifespan* (pp. 388–396). New York: Oxford University Press.

Markovic, M., Manderson, L., & Warren, N. (2008). Pragmatic narratives of hysterectomy among Australian women. *Sex Roles, 58*, 467–476.

Markowe, L. A. (2002). Coming out as a lesbian. In A. Coyle & C. Kitzinger (Eds.), *Lesbian and gay psychology: New perspectives* (pp. 63–80). Oxford, UK: BPS Blackwell.

Markson, E. W. (2001). Sagacious, sinful or superfluous? The social construction of older women. In J. M. Coyle (Ed.), *Handbook on women and aging* (pp. 53–71). Westport, CT: Greenwood.

Markson, E. W., & Taylor, C. A. (1993). Real versus reel world: Older women and the Academy Awards. In N. D. Davis, E. Cole, & E. Rothblum (Eds.), *Faces of women and aging* (pp. 157–175). New York: Harrington Park Press.

Marler, J. H., & Moen, P. (2005). Alternative employment arrangements: A gender perspective. *Sex Roles, 52*, 337–349.

Marlino, D., & Wilson, F. (2006). Career expectations and goals of Latina adolescents: Results from a nationwide study. In

J. Denner & B. L. Guzmán (Eds.), *Latina girls: Voices of adolescent strength in the United States* (pp. 123–137). New York: New York University Press.

Marmot, M. (2003). Social resources and health. In F. Kessel, P. L. Rosenfield, & N. B. Anderson (Eds.), *Expanding the boundaries of health and social science* (pp. 259–285). New York: Oxford University Press.

Marrazzo, J. M. (2004). Barriers to infectious disease care among lesbians. *Emerging Infectious Diseases, 10,* 1974–1978.

Marrazzo, J. M., Coffey, P., & Bingham, A. (2005). Sexual practices, risk perception and knowledge of sexually transmitted disease risk among lesbian and bisexual women. *Perspectives on Sexual and Reproductive Health, 37,* 6–12.

Marriott, M. (2003, May 15). Fighting women enter the arena, no holds barred. *New York Times,* pp. E1, E7.

Marsh, D. T. (2006). Serious emotional disturbance and serious mental illness. In J. Worell & C. D. Goodheart (Eds.), *Handbook of girls' and women's psychological health: Gender and well-being across the lifespan* (pp. 77–84). New York: Oxford University Press.

Marsh, H. W., Ellis, L. A., & Craven, R. G. (2002). How do preschool children feel about themselves? Unraveling measurement and multidimensional self-concept structure. *Developmental Psychology, 38,* 376–393.

Marsh, H. W., Trautwein, U., Lüdtke, O., Köller, O., & Baumert, J. (2005). Academic self-concept, interest, grades, and standardized test scores: Reciprocal effects models of casual ordering. *Child Development, 76,* 397–416.

Marshall, N. L. (1998). *Work and family today: Recent research at the Center for Research on Women* (pp. 102–105). Wellesley, MA: Wellesley College Center for Research on Women.

Marshall, N. L. (2004). The quality of early child care and children's development. *Current Directions in Psychological Science, 13,* 165–168.

Marshall, N. L., & Barnett, R. C. (1993). Work-family strains and gains among two-earner couples. *Journal of Community Psychology, 21,* 64–78.

Martens, A., Goldenberg, J. L., & Greenberg, J. (2005). A terror management perspective on ageism. *Journal of Social Issues, 61,* 223–239.

Martin, C. L. (1995). Stereotypes about children with traditional and nontraditional gender roles. *Sex Roles, 33,* 727–751.

Martin, C. L. (1999). A developmental perspective on gender effects and gender concepts. In W. B. Swann, J. H. Langlois, & L. A. Gilbert (Eds.), *Sexism and stereotypes in modern society* (pp. 45–74). Washington, DC: American Psychological Association.

Martin, C. L., & Dinella, L. M. (2001). Gender development: Gender schema theory. In J. Worell (Ed.), *Encyclopedia of women and gender* (pp. 507–521). San Diego: Academic Press.

Martin, C. L., & Fabes, R. A. (2001). The stability and consequences of young children's same-sex peer interactions. *Developmental Psychology, 37,* 431–446.

Martin, C. L., & Little, J. K. (1990). The relation of gender understanding to children's sex-typed preferences and gender stereotypes. *Child Development, 61,* 1327–1439.

Martin, C. L., & Ruble, D. (2004). Children's search for gender cues: Cognitive perspectives on gender development. *Current Directions in Psychological Science, 13,* 67–70.

Martin, C. L., Ruble, D. N., & Szkrybalo, J. (2002). Cognitive theories of early gender development. *Psychological Bulletin, 128,* 903–933.

Martin, J. A., et al. (2007). *Births: Final data for 2005.* National Vital Statistics Reports, 56(6). Hyattsville, MD: National Center for Health Statistics.

Martin, J. L., & Ross, H. S. (2005). Sibling aggression: Sex differences and parents' reactions. *International Journal of Behavioral Development, 29,* 129–138.

Martin, M. O., Mullis, I. V. S., Gonzalez, E. J., & Chrostowski, S. J. (2004). *TIMSS 2003 international science report.* Boston: Boston College.

Martin, S. (2007, July/August). The labyrinth to leadership. *Monitor on Psychology, 38,* 90–91.

Martin, S. L., et al. (2004, July). *Assault of women with disabilities: Research findings and clinical implications.* Paper presented at the meeting of the American Psychological Association, Honolulu.

Martin, S. L., et al. (2006). Physical and sexual assault of women with disabilities. *Violence against Women, 12,* 823–838.

Martinez, S. (2005). Women's intrinsic and extrinsic motivations for working. In B. Schneider & L. J. Waite (Eds.), *Being together, working apart: Dual-career families and the work-life balance* (pp. 79–101). Cambridge: Cambridge University Press.

Martino, S. C., Collins, R. L., Elliott, M. N., Strachman, A., Kanouse, D. E., & Berry, S. H. (2006). Exposure to degrading versus nondegrading music lyrics and sexual behavior among youth. *Pediatrics, 118,* 430–441.

Martire, L. M., & Parris Stephens, M. A. (2003). Juggling parent care and employment responsibilities: The dilemmas of adult daughter caregivers in the workforce. *Sex Roles, 48,* 167–173.

Marton, K. (2004, May 10). A worldwide gender gap. *Newsweek,* p. 94.

Marulis, L., Warren, D., Uttal, D., & Newcombe, N. (2005, October). *A meta-analysis: The effects of training on spatial cognition in children.* Paper presented at the meeting of the Cognitive Development Society, San Diego, CA.

Maruti, S. S., Willett, W. C., Feskanich, D., Rosner, B., & Colditz, G. A. (2008). A prospective study of age-specific physical activity and premenopausal breast cancer. *Journal of the National Cancer Institute, 100,* 728–737.

Marx, D. M., & Roman, J. S. (2002). Female role models: Protecting women's math test performance. *Personality and Social Psychology Bulletin, 28,* 1183–1193.

Mason, G. (2002). *The spectacle of violence: Homophobia, gender, and knowledge.* London: Routledge.

Masser, B., Grass, K., & Nesic, M. (2007). 'We like you, but we don't want you'—the impact of pregnancy in the workplace. *Sex Roles, 57,* 703–712.

Masser, B. M., & Abrams, D. (2004). Reinforcing the glass ceiling: The consequences of hostile sexism for female managerial candidates. *Sex Roles, 51,* 609–615.

Massoni, K. (2004). Modeling work: Occupational messages in Seventeen magazine. *Gender & Society, 18,* 47–65.

Masters, W. H., & Johnson, V. E. (1966). *Human sexual response*. Boston: Little, Brown.

Mastro, D. E., & Greenberg, B. S. (2000, Fall). The portrayal of racial minorities on prime time television. *Journal of Broadcasting & Electronic Media*, 690–703.

Mathers, C. D., et al. (2002). Global patterns of healthy life expectancy for older women. *Journal of Women & Aging, 14*, 99–117.

Matire, L. M., Stephens, M. A. P., & Townsend, A. L. (1998). Emotional support and well-being of midlife women: Role-specific mastery as a mediational mechanism. *Psychology and Aging, 13*, 396–404.

Matlin, M. W. (2001, May). *Wise and wonderful . . . or wrinkled and wretched: How psychologists and the rest of the world view older women*. Invited address presented at the Midwestern Psychological Association, Chicago.

Matlin, M. W. (2003). From menarche to menopause: Misconceptions about women's reproductive lives. *Psychology Science, 45*, 106–122.

Matthews, K. A., et al. (2004). Optimistic attitudes protect against progression of carotid atherosclerosis in healthy middle-aged women. *Psychosomatic Medicine, 66*, 640–644.

Mattingly, M. J., & Bianchi, S. M. (2003). Gender differences in the quantity and quality of free time: The U.S. experience. *Social Forces, 81*, 999–1030.

Mattis, J. S. (2002). Religion and spirituality in the meaning-making and coping experiences of African American women: A qualitative analysis. *Psychology of Women Quarterly, 26*, 309–321.

Maume, D. J. (2007, August). *Gender differences in providing urgent child care among dual-earner parents*. Paper presented at the meeting of the American Sociological Association, New York.

Mauthner, N. S. (2002). *The darkest days of my life: Stories of postpartum depression*. Cambridge, MA and London: Harvard University Press.

Mauthner, N. S. (2003). Imprisoned in my own prison: A relational understanding of Sonya's story of postpartum depression. In J. M. Stoppard & L. M. McMullen (Eds.), *Situating sadness. Women and depression in social context* (pp. 88–112). New York: New York University Press.

Mavin, S. (2008). Queen bees, wannabees and afraid to bees: No more 'best enemies' for women in management? *British Journal of Management, 19*, S75–S84.

Mayer, K. H., Bradford, J. B., Makadon, H. J., Stall, R., Goldhammer, H., & Landers, S. (2008). Sexual and gender minority health: What we know and what needs to be done. *American Journal of Public Health, 98*, 989–995.

McCabe, M. P., Ricciardelli, L. A., & Ridge, D. (2006). "Who thinks I need a perfect body?" Perceptions and internal dialogue among adolescents about their bodies. *Sex Roles, 55*, 409–419.

McCann, T. (2004, July). 2004 diversity survey: Women struggle to reach the top. *Chicago Lawyer*, pp. 8–17, 76–77.

McCloskey, C., & Mintz, L. (2006). A culturally oriented approach for career counseling with Native American women. In W. B. Walsh & M. J. Heppner (Eds.), *Handbook of career counseling with women* (2nd ed., pp. 315–350). Mahwah, NJ: Erlbaum.

McCloud, A., et al. (2004). Relationship between alcohol use disorders and suicidality in a psychiatric population. *British Journal of Psychiatry, 184*, 439–445.

McClure, E. B. (2000). A meta-analytic review of sex differences in facial expression processing and their development in infants, children, and adolescents. *Psychological Bulletin, 126*, 424–453.

McConnell, A. R., & Fazio, R. H. (1996). Women as men and people: Effects of gender-marked language. *Personality & Social Psychology Bulletin, 22*, 1004–1013.

McCoy, W. D. (2002, June 11). Abundance of "cures" brings ills. *New York Times*, p. D6.

McCreary, D. R. (1994). The male role and avoiding femininity. *Sex Roles, 31*, 517–531.

McDonough, V. T. (2002, June 6). Between the lines. *Missoula Independent, 13*, 1–2.

McDowell, M. A., Brody, D. J., & Hughes, J. P. (2007). Has age at menarche changed? Results from the National Health and Nutrition Examination Survey (NHANES) 1999–2004. *Journal of Adolescent Health, 40*, 227–231.

McFadden, D. (2002). Masculinization effects in the auditory system. *Archives of Sexual Behavior, 31*, 99–111.

McFadden, R. D. (2008, October 11). Gay marriage is ruled legal in Connecticut. *New York Times*, p. A1.

McGarry, K., & Schoeni, R. F. (2003, December). *Widow poverty and out-of-pocket medical expenditures at the end of life*. PSC Research Report, Report No. 03-547. PSC Population Studies Center at the Institute for Social Research, University of Michigan.

McGinn, D. (2004, October 4). Mating behavior 101. *Newsweek*, pp. 44–45.

McGinn, D., & Skipp, C. (2002, June 3). Does Gran get it on? *Newsweek*, p. 10.

McGinnis, J. M., & Foege, W. H. (2004). The immediate vs the important. *Journal of the American Medical Association, 291*, 1263–1264.

McGlone, M. S., & Aronson, J. (2006). Stereotype threat, identity salience, and spatial reasoning. *Journal of Applied Developmental Psychology, 27*, 486–493.

McGorty, E. K., Iyer, S. N., & Hunt, J. S. (2003, May). *The effect of patient sex on medical decision-making: A meta-analysis*. Paper presented at the meeting of the Midwestern Psychological Association, Chicago.

McGuire, L. C., Strine, T. W., Vachirasudlekha, S., Mokdad, A. H., & Anderson, L. A. (2008). The prevalence of depression in older U.S. women: 2006 behavioral risk factor surveillance system. *Journal of Women's Health, 17*, 501–507.

McHale, S. M., Corneal, D. A., Crouter, A. C., & Birch, L. L. (2001). Gender and weight concerns in early and middle adolescence: Links with well-being and family characteristics. *Journal of Clinical Child Psychology, 30*, 338–348.

McHale, S. M., Crouter, A. C., & Tucker, C. J. (1999). Family context and gender role socialization in middle childhood comparing girls to boys and sisters to brothers. *Child Development, 70*, 990–1004.

McHale, S. M., Crouter, A. C., & Tucker, C. J. (2001). Free-time activities in middle childhood: Links with adjustment in early adolescence. *Child Development, 72*, 1764–1778.

McHale, S. M., Crouter, A. C., & Whiteman, S. (2003). The family contexts of gender development in childhood and adolescence. *Social Development, 12*, 126–148.

McHale, S. M., Kim, J. Y., Whiteman, S., & Crouter, A. C. (2004). Links between sex-typed time use in middle childhood and gender development in early adolescence. *Developmental Psychology, 40*, 868–881.

McHale, S. M., Shanahan, L., Updegraff, K. A., Crouter, A. C., & Booth, A. (2004). Developmental and individual differences in girls' sex-typed activities in middle childhood and adolescence. *Child Development, 75*, 1575–1593.

McHugh, M. C. (2005). Understanding gender and intimate partner abuse. *Sex Roles, 52*, 717–724.

McHugh, M. C. (2006). What do women want? A new view of women's sexual problems. *Sex Roles, 54*, 361–369.

McHugh, M. C. (2007). Women and sex at midlife: Desire, dysfunction, and diversity. In V. Muhlbauer & J. C. Chrisler (Eds.), *Women over 50: Psychological perspectives* (pp. 26–52). New York: Springer.

McHugh, M. C. (2008). A feminist approach to agoraphobia: Challenging traditional views of women at home. In J. C. Chrisler, C. Golden, & P. D. Rozee (Eds.), *Lectures on the psychology of women* (pp. 392–417). New York: McGraw-Hill.

McHugh, M. C., Livingston, N., & Frieze, I. H. (2008). Intimate partner violence: Perspectives on research and intervention. In F. L. Denmark & M. A. Paludi (Eds.), *Psychology of women: A handbook of issues and theories* (2nd ed., pp. 555–589). Westport, CT: Praeger.

McKelvey, M. W., & McKenry, P. C. (2000). The psychosocial well-being of black and white mothers following marital dissolution. *Psychology of Women Quarterly, 24*, 4–14.

McKinley, N. M. (2006). The developmental and cultural contexts of objectified body consciousness: A longitudinal analysis of two cohorts of women. *Developmental Psychology, 42*, 679–687.

McLean, R. (2005, April 22). Spanish parliament gives approval to bill to legalize same-sex marriages. *New York Times*, p. A12.

McLoyd, V. C. (1993). Employment among African-American mothers in dual-earner families: Antecedents and consequences for family life and child development. In J. Frankel (Ed.), *The employed mother and the family context* (pp. 180–226). New York: Springer.

McMunn, A., Bartley, M., Hardy, R., & Kuh, D. (2006). Life course social roles and women's health in mid-life: Causation or selection? *Journal of Epidemiology and Community Health, 60*, 484–489.

McNamara, M. P. (2004, January 20). In fighting stereotypes, students lift test scores. *New York Times*, p. D7.

McNeely, C., et al. (2002). Mothers' influence on the timing of first sex among 14- and 15-year-olds. *Journal of Adolescent Medicine, 31*, 256–265.

McNeil, Jr., D. G. (2004, August 17). Facing middle age and AIDS. *New York Times*, pp. D1, D6.

McNeil, D. G., Jr. (2007, August 1). Sex slaves returning home raise AIDS risks, study says. *New York Times*, p. A7.

McPherson, B. J., Fitzpatrick, M. J., Armenta, M. I., Dale, J. A., & Miller, T. E. (2007, August). *Coloring within the lines: Gender stereotypes in children's coloring books*. Poster presented at the annual meeting of the American Psychological Association, San Francisco.

McQuaide, S. (1998). Women at midlife. *Social Work, 43*, 21–31.

McSweeney, J. C., et al. (2003). Women's early warning symptoms of acute myocardial infarction. *Circulation*, pp. 2619–2623.

Mead, S. (2006). *The evidence suggests otherwise: The truth about boys and girls*. Washington, DC: Education Sector.

Medicine, B. (1988). Native American (Indian) women: A call for research. *Anthropology & Education Quarterly, 19*, 86–92.

Mednick, M., & Thomas, V. (2008). Women and achievement. In F. L. Denmark & M. A. Paludi (Eds.), *Psychology of women: A handbook of issues and theories* (2nd ed., pp. 625–651). Westport, CT: Praeger.

Meece, J. L., & Scantlebury, K. (2006). Gender and schooling: Progress and persistent barriers. In J. Worell & C. D. Goodheart (Eds.), *Handbook of girls' and women's psychological health: Gender and well-being across the lifespan* (pp. 283–291). New York: Oxford University Press.

Meier, A. M. (2007). Adolescent first sex and subsequent mental health. *American Journal of Sociology, 112*, 1811–1847.

Mello, Z. R. (2008). Gender variation in development trajectories of educational and occupational expectations and attainment from adolescence to adulthood. *Developmental Psychology, 44*, 1069–1080.

Ménard, K. S., et al. (2003). Gender differences in sexual harassment and coercion in college students: Developmental, individual, and situational determinants. *Journal of Interpersonal Violence, 18*, 1222–1239.

Mendelsohn, D. M., & Perry-Jenkins, M. (2007, March). *Relationship between parental sex-role ideologies and children's gender-typed attitudes*. Poster presented at the meeting of the Society for Research in Child Development, Boston.

Mendle, J., et al. (2006). Family structure and age at menarche: A children-of-twins approach. *Developmental Psychology, 42*, 533–542.

Menec, V. H. (2003). The relation between everyday activities and successful aging: A 6-year longitudinal study. *Journals of Gerontology, 58*, S74–S82.

Menendez, J. A., Vellon, L., Colomer, R., & Lupu, R. (2005, January 10). Oleic acid, the main monounsaturated fatty acid of olive oil, suppresses Her-2/*neu* (*erb* B-2) expression and synergistically enhances the growth inhibitory effects of trastuzumab (Herceptin™) in breast cancer cells with Her-2/*neu* oncogene amplification. *Annals of Oncology*, pp. 1–14.

Menopause herb garden. (2008, April). *Menopause Flashes*. Mayfield Heights, OH: North American Menopause Society.

Mensinger, J. L., Bonifazi, D. Z., & LaRosa, J. (2007). Perceived gender role prescriptions in schools, the superwoman ideal, and disordered eating among adolescent girls. *Sex Roles, 57*, 557–568.

Mercer, C., et al. (2007). Women who report having sex with women: British national probability data on prevalence, sexual behaviors, and health outcomes. *American Journal of Public Health, 97*, 1126–1133.

Mercer, S. O., Garner, J. D., & Findley, J. (2001). Older women: A global view. In J. D. Garner & S. O. Mercer (Eds.), *Women as they age* (2nd ed., pp. 13–32). New York: Haworth.

Mercurio, A. E., & Landry, L. J. (2008). Self-objectification and well-being: The impact of self-objectification on women's overall sense of self-worth and life satisfaction. *Sex Roles, 58,* 458–466.

Merkin, D. (2004, May 2). Keeping the forces of decrepitude at bay. *New York Times Magazine,* pp. 64–67, 96–98.

Merline, A. C., et al. (2004). Substance use among adults 35 years of age: Prevalence, adulthood predictors, and impact of adolescent substance use. *American Journal of Public Health, 94,* 95–103.

Merrick, E. L., et al. (2008). Unhealthy drinking patterns in older adults: Prevalence and associated characteristics. *Journal of the American Geriatrics Society, 56,* 214–223.

Messman-Moore, T. L., & Long, P. J. (2003). The role of childhood sexual abuse sequelae in the sexual revictimization of women: An empirical review and theoretical reformulation. *Clinical Psychology Review, 23,* 537–571.

Messner, M. A., Duncan, M. C., & Jensen, K. (1993). Separating the men from the girls: The gendered language of televised sports. *Gender & Society, 7,* 121–137.

Mestel, R. (2000, May 1). Sex in the shadow of illness and disability. *Los Angeles Times,* p. 1.

Metzl, J. M. (2003, Fall). Selling sanity through gender. *Ms.,* pp. 40–45.

Meyer, I. H. (2003). Prejudice, social stress, and mental health in lesbian, gay, and bisexual populations: Conceptual issues and research evidence. *Psychological Bulletin, 129,* 674–697.

Meyer, M. H., & Bellas, M. L. (1995). U.S. old-age policy and the family. In R. Bleiszner & V. H. Bedford (Eds.), *Handbook of aging and the family* (pp. 263–283). Westport, CT: Greenwood.

Mezulis, A. H., Abramson, L. Y., Hyde, J. S., & Hankin, B. L. (2004). Is there a universal positivity bias in attributions? A meta-analytic review of individual, developmental, and cultural differences in the self-serving attributional bias. *Psychological Bulletin, 130,* 711–747.

Michael, S. T., Crowther, M. R., Schmid, B., & Allen, R. S. (2003). Widowhood and spirituality: Coping responses. *Journal of Women & Aging, 15,* 145–166.

Michael, Y. L., Berkman, L. F., Colditz, G. A., & Kawachi, I. (2001). Living arrangements, social integration, and change in functional health status. *American Journal of Epidemiology, 153,* 123–131.

Michaud, S. L., & Warner, R. M. (1997). Gender differences in self-reported response to troubles talk. *Sex Roles, 37,* 527–540.

Michels, K. B., & Willett, W. C. (2004). Breast cancer—early life matters. *New England Journal of Medicine, 351,* 1679–1681.

Michelson, W., & Tepperman, L. (2003). Focus on home: What time-use data can tell about caregiving to adults. *Journal of Social Issues, 59,* 591–610.

Mikhail, G. W. (2005). Coronary heart disease in women. *BMJ, 331,* 467–468.

Mikkelsen, T. F., Graff-Iversen, S., Sundby, J., & Bjertness, E. (2007). Early menopause, association with tobacco smoking, coffee consumption and other lifestyle factors: A cross-sectional study. *BMC Public Health, 7,* 149.

Milar, K. S. (2000). The first generation of women psychologists and the psychology of women. *American Psychologist, 55,* 616–620.

Milburn, S. S., Carney, D. R., & Ramirez, A. M. (2001). Even in modern media the picture is still the same: A content analysis of clipart images. *Sex Roles, 44,* 277–294.

Milcent, C., Dormont, B., Durand-Zaleski, I., & Steg, P. G. (2007). Gender differences in hospital mortality and use of percutaneous coronary intervention in acute myocardial infarction: Microsimulation analysis of the 1999 nationwide French hospitals database. *Circulation, 115,* 833–839.

Milkie, M. A., Bianchi, S. M., Mattingly, M. J., & Robinson, J. P. (2002). Gendered division of childrearing: Ideals, realities, and the relationship to parental well-being. *Sex Roles, 47,* 21–38.

Miller, B. A., & Downs, W. R. (2000). Violence against women. In M. B. Goldman & M. C. Hatch (Eds.), *Women & health* (pp. 529–540). San Diego: Academic Press.

Miller, B. C., & Moore, K. A. (1990). Adolescent sexual behavior, pregnancy, and parenting: Research through the 1980s. *Journal of Marriage and the Family, 52,* 1025–1044.

Miller, C., & Swift, K. (1991). *Words and women: Updated.* New York: HarperCollins.

Miller, C. F., Trautner, H. M., & Ruble, D. N. (2006). The role of gender stereotypes in children's preferences and behavior. In L. Batter & C. S. Tamis-LeMonda (Eds.), *Child psychology: A handbook of contemporary Issues* (2nd ed., pp. 293–323). New York: Psychology Press.

Miller-Day, M. A. (2004). *Communication among grandmothers, mothers, and adult daughters.* Mahwah, NJ: Erlbaum.

Miller, J. B., & Stiver, I. P. (1997). *The healing connection.* Boston: Beacon Press.

Miller, K. K., et al. (2005). Medical findings in outpatients with anorexia nervosa. *Archives of Internal Medicine, 165,* 561–566.

Miller, K. S., Levin, M. L., Whittaker, D. J., & Xu, X. (1998). Patterns of condom use among adolescents: The impact of mother-adolescent communication. *American Journal of Public Health, 88,* 1542–1544.

Miller, M. K., & Summers, A. (2007). Gender differences in video game characters' roles, appearances, and attire as portrayed in video game magazines. *Sex Roles, 57,* 733–742.

Miller, P. (2004, Spring). Aborted rights. *Ms.,* pp. 14–15.

Miller, W. C., et al. (2004, May 12). Prevalence of chlamydial and gonococcal infections among young adults in the United States. *Journal of the American Medical Association, 291,* 2229–2236.

Miner, J. L., & Clarke-Stewart, K. A. (2008). Trajectories of externalizing behavior from age 2 to age 9: Relations with gender, temperament, ethnicity, parenting, and rater. *Developmental Psychology, 44,* 771–786.

Miner-Rubino, K., & Cortina, L. M. (2004). Working in a context of hostility toward women: Implications for employees' well-being. *Journal of Occupational Health Psychology, 9,* 107–122.

Miniño, A. M., Heron, M. P., Murphy, S. L., & Kochanek, K. D. (2007). Deaths: Final data for 2004. (National Vital

Statistics Reports, 55, No. 19). Hyattsville, MD: National Center for Health Statistics.

Minkler, M., Fuller-Thomson, E., & Guralnik, J. M. (2006). Gradient of disability across the socioeconomic spectrum in the United States. *New England Journal of Medicine, 355*, 695–703.

Minto, C., Woodhouse, C., Ransley, P., & Creighton, S. (2003). The effect of clitoral surgery on sexual outcome in individuals who have intersex conditions with ambiguous genitalia: A cross-sectional study. *Lancet, 361*, 1252–1257.

Mischel, W. (1966). A social-learning view of sex differences in behavior. In E. E. Maccoby (Ed.), *The development of sex differences* (pp. 56–81). Stanford, CA: Stanford University Press.

Misra, D. (Ed.). (2001). *Women's health data book: A profile of women's health in the United States* (3rd ed.). Washington, DC: Jacobs Institute of Women's Health and The Henry J. Kaiser Family Foundation.

Misra, M., et al. (2004). Effects of anorexia nervosa on clinical, hematologic, biochemical, and bone density parameters in community-dwelling adolescent girls. *Pediatrics, 114*, 1574–1583.

Mitchell, B. S., & Stricker, G. (1998, August). *The quality of the grandparent-young adult relationship: How does it relate to attitudes toward older persons and personal anxiety towards aging?* Paper presented at the meeting of the American Psychological Association, San Francisco.

Mitchell, J. E., Agras, S., & Wonderlich, S. (2007). Treatment of bulimia nervosa: Where are we and where are we going? *International Journal of Eating Disorders, 40*, 95–101.

Mitchell, V., & Green, R.-J. (2008). Different storks for different folks: Gay and lesbian parents' experiences with alternative insemination and surrogacy. *Journal of GLBT Family Studies, 3*, 81–104.

Mitka, M. (2007). A change of heart guidelines for women. *Journal of the American Medical Association, 297*, 1421–1422.

Mobily, K. E. (1992). Leisure, lifestyle, and lifespan. In M. L. Teague & R. D. MacNeil (Eds.), *Aging and leisure: Vitality in later life* (2nd ed., pp. 179–206). Dubuque, IA: Brown & Benchmark.

Moen, P., Kim, J. E., & Hofmeister, H. (2001). Couples' work/retirement transitions, gender, and mental quality. *Social Psychology Quarterly, 64*, 55–71.

Moffat, S. C., & Hampson, E. (1996). A curvilinear relationship between testosterone and spatial cognition in humans: Possible influence of hand preference. *Psychoneuroendocrinology, 21*, 323–337.

Mohler-Kuo, M., Dowdall, G. W., Koss, M. P., & Wechsler, H. (2004). Correlates of rape while intoxicated in a national sample of college women. *Journal of Studies on Alcohol, 65*, 37–45.

Mollen, D. (2005, August). *Voluntarily childfree women: Experiences and counseling consideration.* Paper presented at the annual meeting of the American Psychological Association, Washington, DC.

Molnar, B. E., Browne, A., Cerda, M., & Buka, S. L. (2005). Violent behavior by girls reporting violent victimization. *Archives of Pediatrics & Adolescent Medicine, 159*, 731–739.

Mondschein, E. R., Adolph, K. E., & Tamis-LeMonda, C. S. (2000). Gender bias in mothers' expectations about infant crawling. *Journal of Experimental Child Psychology, 77*, 304–316.

Mongeau, P. A., Carey, C. M., & Williams, M. L. M. (1998). First date initiation and enactment: An expectancy violation approach. In D. J. Canary & K. Dindia (Eds.), *Sex differences and similarities in communication: Critical essays and empirical investigations of sex and gender in interaction* (pp. 413–426). Mahwah, NJ: Erlbaum.

Monsour, M. (2002). *Women and men as friends: Relationships across the life span in the 21st century.* Mahwah, NJ: Erlbaum.

Montepare, J. M., & Zebrowitz, L. A. (2002). A social-developmental view of ageism. In T. D. Nelson (Ed.), *Ageism: Stereotyping and prejudice against older persons* (pp. 77–125). Cambridge, MA: MIT Press.

Montes, G., Hightower, A. D., Brugger, L., & Moustafa, E. (2005). Quality child care and socio-emotional risk factors: No evidence of diminishing returns for urban children. *Early Childhood Research Quarterly, 20*, 361–372.

Moore, A. (2007). Breast-cancer therapy—looking back to the future. *New England Journal of Medicine, 357*, 1547–1549.

Moore, A. A., et al. (2005). Longitudinal patterns and predictors of alcohol consumption in the United States. *American Journal of Public Health, 95*, 458–464.

Moore, D. (2007). Self perceptions and social misconceptions: The implications of gender traits for locus of control and life satisfaction. *Sex Roles, 56*, 767–780.

Moore, S. E. H. (2008). Gender and the 'new paradigm' of health. *Sociology Compass, 2*, 268–280.

Moos, R. (1985). *Perimenstrual symptoms: A manual and overview of research with the Menstrual Distress Questionnaire.* Stanford, CA: Stanford University.

Mor, N., & Winquist, J. (2002). Self-focused attention and negative affect: A meta-analysis. *Psychological Bulletin, 128*, 638–662.

Mora, S., Lee, I., Buring, J. E., & Ridker, P. M. (2006). Association of physical activity and body mass index with novel and tradition cardiovascular biomarkers in women. *Journal of the American Medical Association, 295*, 1412–1419.

Moracco, K. E., Runyan, C. W., Bowling, J. M., & Earp, J. A. L. (2007). Women's experiences with violence: A national study. *Women's Health Issues, 17*, 3–12.

Moracco, K. E., Runyan, C. W., & Butts, J. D. (2003). Female intimate partner homicide: A population-based study. *Journal of the American Medical Women's Association, 58*, 20–25.

Morahan-Martin J., & Schumacher, P. (1998, August). *Are Internet and computer experiences and attitudes related? Gender differences.* Paper presented at the meeting of the American Psychological Association, San Francisco.

More women seemingly choosing c-sections. (2004, June 29). *Associated Press.*

Moreau, R., & Yousafzai, S. (2004, October 11). "Living dead" no more. *Newsweek*, p. 37.

Moreau, R., & Yousafzai, S. (2006, June 26). A war on schoolgirls. *Newsweek*, pp. 34–35.

Moreman, R. D. (2008). Best friends: The role of confidants in older women's health. *Journal of Women & Aging, 20,* 149–167.

Morgan, B. L. (1996). Putting the feminism into feminism scales: Introduction of a liberal feminist attitude and ideology scale (LFAIS). *Sex Roles, 34,* 359–390.

Morgan, L., & Kunkel, S. (2001). *Aging: The social context* (2nd ed.). Thousand Oaks, CA: Pine Forge Press.

Morgan, R. (2002, November 29). Bisexual students face tension with gay groups. *Chronicle of Higher Education,* p. A31.

Mori, L., Bernat, J. A., Glenn, P. A., Selle, L. L., & Zarate, M. G. (1995). Attitudes toward rape: Gender and ethnic differences across Asian and caucasian college students. *Sex Roles, 32,* 457–467.

Morrice, P. (2007, April 22). Children on demand. *New York Times Book Review,* p. 16.

Morris, B. R. (2002, June 23). A disturbing growth industry: Web sites that espouse anorexia. *New York Times,* p. 8.

Morris, B. R. (2004a, June 6). Fighting dryness, with pills, gels and rings. *New York Times,* p. WH12.

Morris, B. R. (2004b, July 6). Older women, too, struggle with a dangerous secret. *New York Times,* pp. D5, D8.

Morris, E. W. (2007). "Ladies" or "loudies"? Perceptions and experiences of Black girls in classrooms. *Youth & Society, 38,* 490–515.

Morris, J. F. (1998, August). *Use of therapy by lesbian and bisexual women of color.* Paper presented at the meeting of the American Psychological Association, San Francisco.

Morris, J. F., Waldo, C. R., & Rothblum, E. D. (2001). A model of predictors and outcomes of outness among lesbian and bisexual women. *American Journal of Orthopsychiatry, 71,* 61–71.

Morrison, M. A., Morrison, T. G., & Sager, C. L. (2004, May). Does body satisfaction differ between gay men and lesbian women and heterosexual men and women? *Body Image, 1,* 127–138.

Morrongiello, B. A., & Dawber, T. (2000). Mothers' responses to sons and daughters engaging in injury-risk behaviors on a playground: Implications for sex differences in injury rates. *Journal of Experimental Child Psychology, 76,* 89–103.

Morrongiello, B. A., & Hogg, K. (2004). Mothers' reactions to children misbehaving in ways that can lead to injury: Implications for gender differences in children's risk taking and injuries. *Sex Roles, 50,* 103–118.

Morrow, M. (2002). Rational local therapy for breast cancer. *New England Journal of Medicine, 347,* 1270–1271.

Morrow-Howell, N., et al. (2003). Effects of volunteering on the well-being of older adults. *Journals of Gerontology, 58,* S137–S145.

Mortola, J. F. (2000). Premenstrual syndrome. In M. B. Goldman & M. C. Hatch (Eds.), *Women & health* (pp. 114–125). San Diego: Academic Press.

Mosca, L., et al. (2007). Evidence-based guidelines for cardiovascular disease prevention in women: 2007 update. *Circulation, 115,* 1481–1501.

Mosca, L., Ferris, A., Fabunmi, R., & Robertson, R. M. (2004). Tracking women's awareness of heart disease: An American Heart Association national study. *Circulation, 109,* 573–579.

Mosher, C. E., & Danoff-Burg, S. (2005). Agentic and communal personality traits: Relations to attitudes toward sex and sexual experiences. *Sex Roles, 52,* 121–129.

Mosher, W. D., Chandra, A., & Jones, J. (2005). *Sexual behavior and selected health measures: Men and women 15–44 years of age, United States, 2002.* Advance Data from Vital and Health Statistics No. 362. Hyattsville, MD: National Center for Health Statistics.

Moss, N. W. (2008, October 21). A planet of pain, where no words are quite right. *New York Times,* p. D5

Mroczek, D. K. (2000). Age and emotion in adulthood. *Current Directions in Psychological Science, 10,* 87–90.

Muehlenhard, C. L., & Rodgers, C. S. (1998). Token resistance to sex: New perspectives on an old stereotype. *Psychology of Women Quarterly, 22,* 443–463.

Muehlenkamp, J. J., Swanson, J. D., & Brausch, A. M. (2005). Self-objectification, risk taking, and self-harm in college women. *Psychology of Women Quarterly, 29,* 24–32.

Mueller, K. A., & Yoder, J. D. (1997). Gendered norms for family size, employment, and occupation: Are there personal costs for violating them? *Sex Roles, 36,* 207–220.

Muennig, P., Lubetkin, E., Jia, H., & Franks, P. (2006). Gender and the burden of disease attributable to obesity. *American Journal of Public Health, 96,* 1662–1668.

Mulac, A. (1998). The gender-linked language effect: Do language differences really make a difference? In D. J. Canary & K. Dindia (Eds.), *Sex differences and similarities in communication: Critical essays and empirical investigations of sex and gender in interaction* (pp. 127–153). Mahwah, NJ: Erlbaum.

Mulac, A., Bradac, J. J., & Gibbons, P. (2001). Empirical support for the gender-as-culture hypothesis: An intercultural analysis of male/female language differences. *Human Communication Research, 27,* 121–152.

Mulac, A., et al. (1998). "Uh-huh. What's that all about?" Differing interpretations of conversational backchannels and questions as sources of miscommunication across gender boundaries. *Communication Research, 25,* 641–668.

Mulick, P. S., & Wright, L. W. (2002). Examining the existence of biphobia in the heterosexual and homosexual populations. *Journal of Bisexuality, 2,* 47–64.

Mullis, I. V. S., Martin, M. O., Gonzalez, E. J., & Chrostowski, S. J. (2004). *TIMSS 2003 International Mathematics Report.* Boston: Boston College.

Mullis, I. V. S., Martin, M. O., Kennedy, A. M., & Foy, P. (2007). *IEA's Progress in International Reading Literacy Study in primary schools in 40 countries.* Boston: Boston College.

Mundy, L. (2007). *Everything conceivable: How assisted reproduction is changing men, women, and the world.* New York: Alfred A. Knopf.

Munson, L. J., Miner, A. G., & Hulin, C. (2001). Labeling sexual harassment in the military: An extension and replication. *Journal of Applied Psychology, 86,* 293–303.

Murnen, S. K., & Kohlman, M. H. (2007). Athletic participation, fraternity membership, and sexual aggression among college men: A meta-analytic review. *Sex Roles, 57,* 145–157.

Murnen, S. K., & Smolak, L. (2000). The experience of sexual harassment among grade-school students: Early socialization of female subordination? *Sex Roles, 43,* 1–7.

Murnen, S. K., Wright, C., & Kaluzny, G. (2002). If "boys will be boys," then girls will be victims? A meta-analytic review of the research that relates masculine ideology to sexual aggression. *Sex Roles, 46,* 359–375.

Murphy, E. M. (2003). Being born female is dangerous for your health. *American Psychologist, 58,* 205–210.

Murray, B. (1998, October). Survey reveals concerns of today's girls. *APA Monitor, 29,* 12.

Murray, L. R. (2003). Sick and tired of being sick and tired: Scientific evidence, methods, and research implications for racial and ethnic disparities in occupational health. *American Journal of Public Health, 93,* 221–226.

Murray, T., & Steil, J. (2000, August). *Construction of gender: Comparing children of traditional vs. egalitarian families.* Poster presented at the meeting of the American Psychological Association, Washington, DC.

Murrell, A. J. (1996). Sexual harassment and women of color: Issues, challenges, and future directions. In M. S. Stockdale (Ed.), *Sexual harassment in the workplace: Perspectives, frontiers, and response strategies* (pp. 51–66). Thousand Oaks, CA: Sage.

Murrell, A. J., Frieze, I. H., & Frost, J. L. (1991). Aspiring to careers in male- and female-dominated professions: A study of black and white college women. *Psychology of Women Quarterly, 15,* 103–126.

Murrell, A. J., & Jones, R. (1996). Assessing affirmative action: Past, present, and future. *Journal of Social Issues, 52,* 77–92.

Murthy, V. H., Krumholz, H. M., & Gross, C. P. (2004). Participation in cancer clinical trials: Race-, sex-, and age-based disparities. *Journal of the American Medical Association, 291,* 2720–2726.

Musick, M. A., & Wilson, J. (2003). Volunteering and depression: The role of psychological and social resources in different age groups. *Social Science & Medicine, 56,* 259–269.

Mustanski, B. S., et al. (2004). Genetic and environmental influences on pubertal development: Longitudinal data from Finnish twins at ages 11 and 14. *Developmental Psychology, 40,* 1188–1198.

Muzio, C. (1996). Lesbians choosing children: Creating families, creating narratives. In J. Laird & R.-J. Green (Eds.), *Lesbians and gays in couples and families* (pp. 358–369). San Francisco: Jossey-Bass.

Muzzatti, B., & Agnoli, F. (2007). Gender and mathematics: Attitudes and stereotype threat susceptibility in Italian children. *Developmental Psychology, 43,* 747–759.

Myaskovsky, L., & Wittig, M. A. (1997). Predictors of feminist social identity among college women. *Sex Roles, 37,* 861–883.

Myers, D. J., & Dugan, K. B. (1996). Sexism in graduate school classrooms: Consequences for students and faculty. *Gender & Society, 10,* 330–350.

Nabel, E. G. (2000). Coronary heart disease—an ounce of prevention. *New England Journal of Medicine, 343,* 572–574.

Nagoshi, J. L., Adams, K. A., Terrell, H. K., Hill, E. D., Brzuzy, S., & Nagoshi, C. T. (2008). Gender differences in correlates of homophobia and transphobia. *Sex Roles, 59,* 521–531.

Nagourney, A., & Thee, M. C. (2007, July 27). Young Americans are leaning left, new poll finds. *New York Times,* pp. A1, A20.

Nagourney, E. (2004, September 28). Therapies; Mental, if not physical, benefits. *New York Times,* p. F6.

Nagourney, E. (2005, June 7). Web sites celebrate a deadly thinness. *New York Times,* pp. D6, D8.

Nagourney, E. (2006, May 9). Patterns of deceit raise concerns about teenage sex surveys. *New York Times,* p. F5.

Nagourney, E. (2007, May 15). Moderate drinking may ease effects of 'bad' cholesterol. *New York Times,* p. D7.

Nagy, G., Garrett, J., Trautwein, U., Cortina., K. S., Baumert, J., & Eccles, J. S. (2008). Gendered high school course selection as a precursor of gendered careers: The mediating role of self-concept and intrinsic value. In H. M. G. Watt & J. S. Eccles (Eds.), *Gender and occupational outcomes: Longitudinal assessments of individual, social, and cultural influences* (pp. 115–144). Washington, DC: American Psychological Association.

Naples, N. A. (2003). *Feminism and method: Ethnography, discourse analysis and activist research.* New York: Routledge.

Nation: Faculty and staff. (2004, August 27). *Chronicle of Higher Education,* pp. 24–29.

The Nation: Students. (2007, August 31). *The Chronicle of Higher Education,* pp. 13–20.

National Academies of Sciences Committee on Science, Engineering and Public Policy (COSEPUP) and Policy and Global Affairs (PGA). (2007). *Beyond bias and barriers: Fulfilling the potential of women in academic science and engineering.* Washington, DC: National Academies of Sciences.

National Alliance for Caregiving and AARP. (2004). *Caregiving in the U.S.* Bethesda, MD: Author.

National Campaign to Prevent Teen Pregnancy. (2003). *With one voice 2003: America's adults and teens sound off about teen pregnancy.* Washington, DC: Author.

National Center for Health Statistics. (2004). *Health, United States, 2004 with chartbook on trends in the health of Americans.* Hysttsville, MD: Author.

National Center for Health Statistics. (2007). *Health, United States, 2007.* Hyattsville, MD: Author.

National Center for Injury Prevention and Control. (2005). *Sexual violence: Fact sheet.* Washington, DC: Author.

National Institute of Allergy and Infectious Diseases. (2007). *Sexually transmitted infections.* Washington, DC: Author.

National Institute of Child Health and Human Development. (2007). *Sexually transmitted diseases.* Washington, DC: Author.

National Institute of Child Health and Human Development (NICHD) Early Child Care Research Network. (2004). Type of child care and children's development at 54 months. *Early Childhood Research Quarterly, 19,* 203–230.

National Institute of Child Health and Human Development (NICHD) Early Child Care Research Network. (2006). Child-care effect sizes for the NICHD Study of Early Child Care and Youth Development. *American Psychologist, 61,* 99–116.

National Institute of Mental Health. (2008). *Women and depression.* Washington, DC Author.

National Institute on Alcohol Abuse and Alcoholism. (2003, July). The genetics of alcoholism. *Alcohol Alert, 60.*

National Institute on Drug Abuse. (2007). *NIDA InfoFacts: Steroids (anabolic-androgenic)*. Washington, DC: Author.

National Institutes of Health. (2005). *Alcohol: A women's issue*. NIH Publication No. 04-4956, pp. 1–20. Washington, DC: U.S. Department of Health and Human Services.

National Institutes of Health. (2004). *Women's health in the U.S. Research on health issues affecting women*. NIH Publication No. 04-4697, pp. 1–29. Washington, DC: U.S. Department of Health and Human Services.

National Osteoporosis Foundation. (2002). *The physician's guide to prevention and treatment of osteoporosis*. Washington, DC: Author.

National Osteoporosis Foundation. (2004, Spring). Risk factors for osteoporosis. *Osteoporosis Clinical Updates, V*(1), 6.

National Osteoporosis Foundation. (2008a). *Clinician's guide to prevention and treatment of osteoporosis*. Washington, DC: Author.

National Osteoporosis Foundation. (2008b). *Fast facts*. Washington, DC: Author.

National Partnership for Women & Families. (1998). *Balancing acts: Work/family issues on prime-time TV*. Washington, DC: Author.

National Science Foundation. (2008). *Science and engineering indications 2008*. Washington, DC: Author.

National Women and Girls HIV/AIDS Awareness Day—March 10, 2008. (2008). *Morbidity and Mortality Weekly Report, 57*, 236.

Navarro, M. (2002, May 16). Trying to get beyond the role of the maid. *New York Times*, pp. B1, B4.

Navarro, M. (2004, September 19). When gender isn't a given. *New York Times*, p. 1.

Navarro, M. (2006, May 25). Families add 3rd generation to households. *New York Times*, pp. A1, A22.

Nayak, M. B., Byrne, C. A., Martin, M. K., & Abraham, A. G. (2003). Attitudes toward violence against women: A cross-nation study. *Sex Roles, 49*, 333–342.

Neff, K. D., & Terry-Schmitt, L. N. (2002). Youths' attributions for power-related gender attributes: Nature, nurture, or God? *Cognitive Development, 17*, 1185–1202.

Neff, L. A., & Karney, B. R. (2005). Gender differences in social support: A question of skill or responsiveness? *Journal of Personality & Social Psychology, 88*, 79–90.

Neiterman, E. (2007, August). *When pregnant body becomes visible...* Paper presented at the meeting of the American Sociological Association, New York.

Nelson, D. L., Burke, R. J., & Michie, S. (2002). New directions for studying gender, work stress, and health. In D. L. Nelson & R. J. Burke (Eds.), *Gender, work stress, and health* (pp. 229–242). Washington, DC: American Psychological Association.

Nelson, J. A., et al. (2008). Identity in action: Predictors of feminist self-identification and collective action. *Sex Roles, 58*, 721–728.

Nelson, L. J., Shanahan, S. B., & Olivetti, J. (1997). Power, empowerment, and equality: Evidence for the motives of feminists, nonfeminists, and antifeminists. *Sex Roles, 37*, 227–249.

Nelson, M. R., & Paek, H.-J. (2005). Cross-cultural differences in sexual advertising content in a transnational women's magazine. *Sex Roles, 53*, 371–383.

Nelson, T. D. (2005). Ageism: Prejudice against our feared future self. *Journal of Social Issues, 61*, 207–221.

Nesbitt, M. N., & Penn, N. E. (2000). Gender stereotypes after thirty years: A replication of Rosencrantz et al. (1968). *Psychological Reports, 87*, 493–511.

Netburn, D. (2002, May 26). Young, carefree, and hooked on sunlamps. *New York Times*, pp. ST1, ST7.

Netz, W. M., Becker, B. J., & Tenenbaum, G. (2005). Physical activity and psychological well-being in advanced age: A meta-analysis of intervention studies. *Psychology and Aging, 20*, 272–284.

Neumark-Sztainer, D., Paxton, S., Hannan, P., Haines, J., & Story, M. (2006). Does body satisfaction matter? Five-year longitudinal associations between body satisfaction and health behaviors in adolescent females and males. *Journal of Adolescent Health, 39*, 244–251.

Newcombe, N. S. (2002, August). *Some unanswered questions about a sociobiological theory of sex differences in spatial ability*. Paper presented at the meeting of the American Psychological Association, Chicago.

Newcombe, N. S. (2007a). Taking science seriously: Straight thinking about spatial sex differences. In S. J. Ceci & W. M. Williams (Eds.), *Why aren't more women in science? Top researchers debate the evidence* (pp. 69–77). Washington, DC: American Psychological Association.

Newcombe, N. S. (2007b, October 19). The truth of the mommy wars. *The Chronicle of Higher Education, 54*, B20.

Newman, A. A. (2007, December 31). A guide to embracing life as a single (without the resignation, that is). *New York Times*, p. C4.

Newman, J. (2000, April). How old is too old to have a baby? *Discover*, pp. 60–67.

New risks tied to hormone therapy. (2004, June 29). *New York Times*, p. A20.

Newtson, R. L., & Keith, P. M. (2001). Single women in later life. In J. M. Coyle (Ed.), *Handbook on women and aging* (pp. 385–399). Westport, CT: Greenwood.

NICHD Early Child Care Research Network. (2002). Child-care structure → process → outcome: Direct and indirect effects of child-care quality on young children's development. *Psychological Science, 13*, 199–206.

NICHD Early Child Care Research Network. (2003). Does quality of child care affect child outcomes at age 41/2? *Developmental Psychology, 39*, 451–469.

NICHD Early Child Care Research Network. (2004). Trajectories of physical aggression from toddlerhood to middle childhood. *Monographs of the Society for Research in Child Development, 69*, 1–146.

Niemann, Y. F., Jennings, L., Rozelle, R. M., Baxter, J. C., & Sullivan, E. (1994). Use of free responses and cluster analysis to determine stereotypes of eight groups. *Personality and Social Psychology Bulletin, 20*, 379–390.

Nierman, A. J., Thompson, S. C., Bryan, A., & Mahaffey, A. L. (2007). Gender role beliefs and attitudes toward lesbians and gay men in Chile and the U.S. *Sex Roles, 57,* 61–67.

Nishina, A., & Juvonen, J. (2005). Daily sports of witnessing and experiencing peer harassment in middle school. *Child Development, 76,* 435–450.

Nock, S. L. (1995). A comparison of marriages and cohabiting relationships. *Journal of Family Issues, 16,* 53–76.

Nock, S. L. (2005). Marriage as a public issue. *The Future of Children, 15,* 2, 13–32.

Nolan, S. A., Buckner, J. P., Marzabadi, C. H., & Kuck, V. J. (2008). Training and mentoring of chemists: A study of gender disparity. *Sex Roles, 58,* 235–250.

Noland, V. J., et al. (2004). Is adolescent sibling violence a precursor to college dating violence? *American Journal of Health Behavior, 28,* S13–S23.

Nolen-Hoeksema, S. (2002). Gender differences in depression. In I. Gotlib, & C. Hammen (Eds.), *Handbook of depression* (pp. 492–509). New York: Guilford.

Nolen-Hoeksema, S. (2007, May). *Lost in thought: Rumination and depression.* Poster presented at the annual meeting of the Association for Psychological Science, Washington, DC.

Nolen-Hoeksema, S., & Keita, G. P. (2003). Women and depression: Introduction. *Psychology of Women Quarterly, 27,* 89–90.

Nolen-Hoeksema, S., Larson, J., & Grayson, C. (1999). Explaining the gender difference in depressive symptoms. *Journal of Personality and Social Psychology, 77,* 1061–1072.

Nolen-Hoeksema, S., Wisco, B. E., & Lyubomirsky, S. (2008). Rethinking rumination. *Perspectives on Psychological Science, 3,* 400–424.

Noll, J. G., Trickett, P. K., & Putnam, F. W. (2003). A prospective investigation of the impact of childhood sexual abuse on the development of sexuality. *Journal of Consulting and Clinical Psychology, 71,* 575–586.

Noller, P. (2005). Sibling relationships in adolescence: Learning and growing together. *Personal Relationships, 12,* 1–22.

Nomaguchi, K. M. (2006). Maternal employment, nonparental care, mother–child interactions, and child outcomes during preschool years. *Journal of Marriage and Family, 68,* 1341–1369.

Nordenmark, M. (2004). Does gender ideology explain differences between countries regarding the involvement of women and of men in paid and unpaid work? *International Journal of Social Welfare, 13,* 233–243.

Norris, M. L., Boydell, K. M., Pinhas, L., & Katzman, D. K. (2006). Ana and the Internet: A review of pro-anorexia websites. *International Journal of Eating Disorders, 39,* 443–447.

Norris, P., & Inglehart, R. (2004, Spring). It's the *women,* stupid. *Ms.,* pp. 47–49.

North American Menopause Society. (2003). *Menopause guidebook.* Cleveland, OH: Author.

Nosek, M. A., Hughes, R. B., & Robinson-Whelen, S. (2006, August). *The complex array of antecedents of depression in women with physical disabilities: Implications for clinicians.* Paper presented at the annual meeting of the American Psychological Association, New Orleans, LA.

Not near the top. (2003, Fall/Winter). *AAUW Outlook,* p. 4.

Novack, L. L., & Novack, D. R. (1996). Being female in the eighties and nineties: Conflicts between new opportunities and traditional expectations among white, middle class, heterosexual college women. *Sex Roles, 35,* 57–77.

Nowell, A., & Hedges, L. V. (1998). Trends in gender differences in academic achievement from 1960 to 1994: An analysis of differences in mean, variance, and extreme scores. *Sex Roles, 39,* 21–43.

Nunes, K. L., de Bellefeuille-Percy, K., & Dowden, C. (2004, August). *Factors associated with attributions of blame, fault, responsibility, and causality to victims of sexual assault: A meta-analysis.* Poster presented at the meeting of the American Psychological Association, Honolulu.

Nussbaum, J. F., Pitts, M. J., Huber, F. N., Krieger, J. L. R., & Ohs, J. E. (2005). Ageism and ageist language across the life span: Intimate relationships and non-intimate interactions. *Journal of Social Issues, 61,* 287–305.

Nyad, D. (2004, August 15). The rise of the buff bunny. *New York Times,* p. ST7.

Nygaard, I., Girts, T., Fultz, N. H., Kinchen, K., Pohl, G., & Sternfeld, B. (2005). Is urinary incontinence a barrier to exercise in women? *Obstetrics & Gynecology, 106,* 307–314.

Oates, M. R., et al. (2004). Postnatal depression across countries and cultures: A qualitative study. *British Journal of Psychiatry, 184,* S10–S16.

Obeidallah, D. A., McHale, S. M., & Silbereisen, R. K. (1996). Gender role socialization and adolescents reports of depression: Why some girls and not others? *Journal of Youth and Adolescence, 25,* 776–786.

Oberman, Y., & Josselson, R. (1996). Matrix of tensions: A model of mothering. *Psychology of Women Quarterly, 20,* 341–359.

O'Brien, K., Friedman, S. C., Tipton, L. C., & Linn, S. G. (2000). Attachment, separation, and women's vocational development: A longitudinal analysis. *Journal of Counseling Psychology, 47,* 301–315.

O'Brien, T. L. (2006, March 19). Why do so few women reach the top of big law firms? *New York Times,* pp. BU1, BU4.

Oburu, P. O. (2005). Caregiving stress and adjustment problems of Kenyan orphans raised by grandmothers. *Infant and Child Development, 14,* 199–210.

O'Callaghan, F. V., O'Callaghan, M., Najman, J. M., Williams, G. M., & Bor, W. (2007). Prenatal alcohol exposure and attention, learning, and intellectual ability at 14 years: A prospective longitudinal study. *Early Human Development, 83,* 115–123.

Ofstedal, M. B., Reidy, E., & Knodel, J. (2003, November). *Gender differences in economic support and well-being of older Asians.* Report No. 03-540. Population Studies Center at the Institute for Social Research, University of Michigan.

Ogilvie, D., et al. (2007). Interventions to promote walking: Systematic review. *BMJ, 334,* 1204–1207.

Ogletree, S. M., & Drake, R. (2007). College students' video game participation and perceptions: Gender differences and implications. *Sex Roles, 56*, 537–542.

Ohye, B., Moore, C. W., & Braaten, E. (2003). Becoming a mother: A psychobiosocial transition in a woman's life. In L. Slater, J. H. Daniel, & A. E. Banks (Eds.), *The complete guide to mental health for women* (pp. 18–30). Boston: Beacon Press.

Older Women's League. (1998). *Women, work, and pensions: Improving the odds for a secure retirement.* Washington, DC: Author.

Older Women's League. (2000). *Prescription for change: Why women need a Medicare drug benefit.* Washington, DC: Author.

Older Women's League. (2001). *State of older women in America.* Washington, DC: Author.

Older Women's League. (2002). *Social security privatization and women.* Washington, DC: Author.

Older Women's League. (2004). *A poor prognosis: Healthcare costs and aging.* Washington, DC: Author.

Older Women's League. (2006). *Women and long-term care: Where will I live, and who will take care of me?* Washington, DC: Author.

Older Women's League. (2007). *Give 'em health revisited: Medicare for all.* Washington, DC: Author.

O'Leary, V. E., & Flanagan, E. H. (2001). Leadership. In J. Worell (Ed.), *Encyclopedia of women and gender* (pp. 645–656). San Diego: Academic Press.

Olff, M., Langeland, W., Draijer, N., & Gersons, B. P. R. (2007). Gender differences in posttraumatic stress disorder. *Psychological Bulletin, 133*, 183–204.

Oliver, M. B., & Hyde, J. S. (1993). Gender differences in sexuality: A meta-analysis. *Psychological Bulletin, 114*, 29–51.

Olkin, R. (2003). Women with physical disabilities who want to leave their partners: A feminist and disability-affirmative perspective. *Women & Therapy, 26*, 237–246.

Olkin, R. (2006). Physical or systemic disabilities. In J. Worell & C. D. Goodheart (Eds.), *Handbook of girls' and women's psychological health: Gender and well-being across the lifespan* (pp. 94–102). New York: Oxford University Press.

Olkin, R. (2008). Women with disabilities. In J. C. Chrisler, C. Golden, & P. D. Rozee (Eds.), *Lectures on the psychology of women* (pp. 190–203). New York: McGraw-Hill.

Olshen, E., McVeigh, K. H., Wunsch-Hitzig, R. A., & Rickert, V. I. (2007). Dating violence, sexual assault, and suicide attempts among urban teenagers. *Archives of Pediatrics and Adolescent Medicine, 161*, 539–545.

Olson, E. (2006, June 1). Widowers are eager for another whirl. *New York Times*, p. E2.

Olson, J. E., et al. (2007). Beliefs in equality for women and men as related to economic factors in Central and Eastern Europe and the United States. *Sex Roles, 56*, 297–308.

Olson, K. R., & Dweck, C. S. (2008). A blueprint for social cognitive development. *Perspectives on Psychological Science, 3*, 193–202.

Olson, S. L., & Ceballo, R. E. (1996). Emotional well-being and parenting behavior among low-income single mothers: Social support and ethnicity as contexts of adjustment. In

K. F. Wyche & F. J. Crosby (Eds.), *Women's ethnicities: Journeys through psychology* (pp. 105–123). Boulder, CO: Westview.

Omari, S. R., & Mitchell, J. (2003). The real deal: A qualitative analysis of body image attitudes of African American women in Mississippi. *The Researcher, 19*(1), 126–139.

Ompad, D. C., et al. (2005). Childhood sexual abuse and age at initiation of injection drug use. *American Journal of Public Health, 95*, 703–709.

O'Neil, J. (2003, September 23). Finding just the right cast, as fractures increase. *New York Times*, p. D6.

Onishi, N. (2002, October 3). Globalization of beauty makes slimness trendy. *New York Times*, p. A4.

Orbuch, T. L., & Custer, L. (1995). The social context of married women's work and its impact on black husbands and white husbands. *Journal of Marriage and the Family, 57*, 333–345.

Orenstein, C. (2004, June 9). Stepford is us. *New York Times*, p. A25.

Orenstein, P. (2007, July 15). Your gamete, myself. *New York Times Magazine*, pp. 34–41, 58, 63.

Orman, S. (2001). *The road to wealth: A comprehensive guide to your money—everything you need to know in good and bad times.* New York: Riverhead Books.

Ormerod, A. J., Collinsworth, L. L., & Perry, L. A. (2008). Critical climate: Relations among sexual harassment, climate, and outcomes for high school girls and boys. *Psychology of Women Quarterly, 32*, 113–125.

Ostenson, R. S. (2008). Who's in and who's out: The results of oppression. In J. C. Chrisler, C. Golden, & P. D. Rozee (Eds.), *Lectures on the psychology of women* (pp. 16–25). New York: McGraw-Hill.

O'Sullivan, L. F., McCrudden, M. C., & Tolman, D. L. (2006). To your sexual health! Incorporating sexuality into the health perspective. In J. Worell & C. D. Goodheart (Eds.), *Handbook of girls' and women's psychological health: Gender and well-being across the lifespan* (pp. 192–199). New York: Oxford University Press.

Oswald, D. L., & Harvey, R. D. (2003). A q-methodological study of women's subjective perspectives on mathematics. *Sex Roles, 49*, 133–142.

Otis, M. D., Riggle, E. D. B., & Rostosky, S. S. (2006). Impact of mental health on perceptions of relationship satisfaction and quality among female same-sex couples. *Journal of Lesbian Studies, 10*, 267–283.

O'Toole, C., & Bregante, J. (1993). Disabled lesbians: Multicultural realities. In M. Nagler (Ed.), *Perspectives on disability: Text and readings on disability* (pp. 261–271). Palo Alto, CA: Health Markets Research.

Ott, M. A., Millstein, S. G., Other, S., & Halpern-Felsher, B. L. (2006). Greater expectations: Adolescents' positive motivations for sex. *Perspectives on Sexual and Reproductive Health, 38*, 84–89.

Ozer, E. M. (1995). The impact of childcare responsibility and self-efficacy on the psychological health of professional working mothers. *Psychology of Women Quarterly, 19*, 315–335.

Pacheco, S., & Hurtado, A. (2001). Media stereotypes. In J. Worell (Ed.), *Encyclopedia of women and gender* (pp. 703–708). San Diego: Academic Press.

Packard, E. (2005, December). From basic research to health-care messages. *Monitor on Psychology, 36*, 84–85.

Padavic, I., & Reskin, B. F. (2002). *Women and men at work* (2nd ed.). Thousand Oaks, CA: Sage.

Padgett, D. (1999). Aging minority women. In L. A. Peplau, S. C. DeBro., R. C. Veniegas, & P. L. Taylor (Eds.), *Gender, culture and ethnicity: Current research about women and men* (pp. 173–181). Mountain View, CA: Mayfield.

Palmore, E. B. (2001). Sexism and ageism. In J. M. Coyle (Ed.), *Handbook on women and aging* (pp. 3–13). Westport, CT: Praeger.

Paludi, M. A. (1996). Sexual harassment in college and university settings. In J. C. Chrisler, C. Golden, & P. D. Rozee (Eds.), *Lectures on the psychology of women* (pp. 325–337). New York: McGraw-Hill.

Paludi, M. A., Dillon, L., Stern, T., Martin, J., DeFour, D., & White, C. (2008). Courses in the psychology of women: Catalysts for change. In F. L. Denmark & M. A. Paludi (Eds.), *Psychology of women: A handbook of issues and theories* (2nd ed., pp. 174–204). Westport, CT: Praeger.

Panchanadeswaran, S., & McCloskey, L. A. (2007). Predicting the timing of women's departure from abusive relationships. *Journal of Interpersonal Violence, 22*, 50–64.

Papalia, D. (2005). *A child's world: Infancy through adolescence* (10th ed.). New York: McGraw-Hill.

Pappert, A. (2000, June/July). What price pregnancy? *Ms.*, pp. 43–49.

Paradise, S. A. (1993). Older never married women: A cross cultural investigation. In N. D. Davis, E. Cole, & E. Rothblum (Eds.), *Faces of women and aging* (pp. 129–139). New York: Harrington Park Press.

Paranjape, A., Heron, S., Thompson, M., Bethea, K., Wallace, T., & Kaslow, N. (2007). Are alcohol problems linked with an increase in depressive symptoms in abused, inner-city African American women? *Women's Health Issues, 17*, 37–43.

Parent-Stevens, L., & Burns, E. A. (2000). Menstrual disorders. In M. A. Smith & L. A. Shimp (Eds.), *20 common problems in women's health care* (pp. 381–413). New York: McGraw-Hill.

Parera, N., & Surís, J. C. (2004). Having a good relationship with their mother: A protective factor against sexual risk behavior among adolescent females? *Journal of Pediatric and Adolescent Gynecology, 17*, 267–271.

Park, K. (2005). Choosing childlessness: Weber's typology of action and motives of the voluntarily childless. *Sociological Inquiry, 75*, 372–402.

Parke, R. D., & Buriel, R. (2006). Socialization in the family: Ethnic and ecological perspectives. In W. Damon, R. M. Lerner (Series Eds.) & N. Eisenberg (Vol. Ed.), *Handbook of child psychology: Vol. 3. Social, emotional, and personality development* (6th ed., pp. 429–504). Hoboken, NJ: Wiley.

Parker, H. M., & Fink, J. S. (2008). The effect of sport commentator framing on viewer attitudes. *Sex Roles, 58*, 116–126.

Parker, R. G. (2007). Sexuality, health, and human rights. *American Journal of Public Health, 97*, 972–973.

Parker-Pope, T. (2007, October 9). Antidepressants emerge as coolant for hot flashes. *New York Times*, p. D5.

Parks, C. A., Hughes, T. L., & Matthews, A. K. (2004). Race/ethnicity and sexual orientation: Intersecting identities. *Cultural Diversity and Ethnic Minority Psychology, 10*, 241–254.

Parks, J. B., & Robertson, M. A. (2004). Attitudes toward women mediate the gender effect on attitudes toward sexist language. *Psychology of Women Quarterly, 28*, 233–239.

Parmley, M., & Cunningham, J. G. (2008). Children's gender-emotion stereotypes in the relationship of anger to sadness and fear. *Sex Roles, 58*, 358–370.

Parra, E. B., Arkowitz, H., Hannah, M. T., & Vasquez, A. M. (1995). Coping strategies and emotional reactions to separation and divorce in Anglo, Chicana, and Mexicana women. *Journal of Divorce & Remarriage, 23*, 117–129.

Parsons, E. M., & Betz, N. E. (2001). The relationship of participation in sports and physical activity to body objectification, instrumentality, and focus of control among young women. *Psychology of Women Quarterly, 25*, 209–222.

Pate, R. R., Trost, S. G., Levin, S., & Dowda, M. (2000). Sports participation and health-related behaviors among U.S. youth. *Archives of Pediatric and Adolescent Medicine, 154*, 904–911.

Patel, J. D., Bach, P. B., & Kris, M. G. (2004). Lung cancer in U.S. women. *Journal of the American Medical Association, 291*, 1763–1768.

Patterson, C. J. (2000). Family relationships of lesbians and gay men. *Journal of Marriage and the Family, 62*, 1052–1069.

Patterson, C. J. (2006). Children of lesbian and gay parents. *Current Directions in Psychological Science, 15*, 241–244.

Patterson, C. J., & Friel, L. V. (2000). Sexual orientation and fertility. In G. Bentley & N. Mascie-Taylor (Eds.), *Infertility in the modern world: Biosocial perspectives* (pp. 238–260). Cambridge: Cambridge University Press.

Patterson, C. J., Sutfin, E. L., & Fulcher, M. (2004). Division of labor among lesbian and heterosexual parenting couples: Correlates of specialized versus shared patterns. *Journal of Adult Development, 11*, 179–189.

Paul, E. L., & Hayes, K. A. (2002). The casualties of "casual" sex: A qualitative exploration of the phenomenology of college students' hookups. *Journal of Social and Personal Relationships, 19*, 639–661.

Pawelski, J. G., et al. (2006). The effects of marriage, civil union, and domestic partnership laws on the health and well-being of children. *Pediatrics, 118*, 349–364.

Paxton, P., Hughes, M. M., & Green, J. L. (2006). The international women's movement and women's political representation, 1893–2003. *American Sociological Review, 71*, 898–920.

Paxton, S. J., Eisenberg, M. E., & Neumark-Sztainer, D. (2006). Prospective predictors of body dissatisfaction in adolescent girls and boys: A five-year longitudinal study. *Developmental Psychology, 42*, 888–899.

Paxton, S. J., Norris, M., Wertheim, E. H., Durkin, S. J., & Anderson, J. (2005). Body dissatisfaction, dating, and importance of thinness to attractiveness in adolescent girls. *Sex Roles, 53*, 663–675.

Paynter, N., et al. (2004, January 16). Declining prevalence of no known major risk factors for heart disease and stroke among adults—United States, 1991–2001. *Morbidity and Mortality Weekly Report, 53*, 4–7.

Peacock, P. (1998). Marital rape. In R. K. Bergen (Ed.), *Issues in intimate violence* (pp. 225–235). Thousand Oaks, CA: Sage.

Pearson, S. M., & Bieschke, K. J. (2001). Succeeding against the odds: An examination of familial influences on the career development of professional African American women. *Journal of Counseling Psychology, 48,* 301–309.

Pecora, N., Murray, J. P., & Wartella, E. A. (2007). *Children and television: Fifty years of research.* Mahwah, NJ: Erlbaum.

Peirce, K. (1997). Women's magazine fiction: A content analysis of the roles, attributes, and occupations of main characters. *Sex Roles, 37,* 581–593.

Pellegrini, A. D. (2001). A longitudinal study of heterosexual relationships, aggression, and sexual harassment during the transition from primary school through middle school. *Applied Developmental Psychology, 22,* 119–133.

Pellegrini, A. D., Kato, K., Blatchford, P., & Baines, E. (2002). A short-term longitudinal study of children's playground games across the first year of school: Implications for social competence and adjustment to school. *American Educational Research Journal, 39,* 991–1015.

Penn, N. E., et al. (2000). Health practices and health-care systems among cultural groups. In R. M. Eisler & M. Hersen (Eds.), *Handbook of gender, culture, and health* (pp. 105–137). Mahwah, NJ: Erlbaum.

Pennebaker, J. W., Mehl, M. R., & Niederhoffer, K. G. (2003). Psychological aspects of natural language use: Our words, our selves. *Annual Review of Psychology, 54,* 547–577.

Penner, A. M. (2003). International gender x item difficulty interactions in mathematics and science achievement tests. *Journal of Educational Psychology, 95,* 650–655.

Peplau, L. A. (1998). Lesbian and gay relationships. In D. L. Anselmi & A. L. Law (Eds.), *Questions of gender: Perspectives & paradoxes* (pp. 505–519). Boston: McGraw-Hill.

Peplau, L. A. (2002, August). *Venus and Mars in the laboratory: Current research on gender and sexuality.* Paper presented at the meeting of the American Psychological Association, Chicago.

Peplau, L. A., & Beals, C. P. (2001). Lesbians, gay men, and bisexuals in relationships. In J. Worell (Ed.), *Encyclopedia of women and gender* (pp. 657–666). San Diego: Academic Press.

Peplau, L. A., & Fingerhut, A. W. (2004). The paradox of the lesbian worker. *Journal of Social Issues, 60,* 719–735.

Peplau, L. A., & Fingerhut, A. W. (2007). The close relationships of lesbians and gay men. *Annual Review of Psychology, 58,* 405–424.

Pepler, D., Jiang, D., Craig, W., & Connolly, J. (2008). Developmental trajectories of bullying and associated factors. *Child Development, 79,* 325–338.

Percheski, C. (2008). Opting out? Cohort differences in professional women's employment rates from 1960–2005. *American Sociological Review, 73,* 497–517.

Pérez-Peña, R. (2004, March 15). Use of midwives, a childbirth phenomenon, fades in city. *New York Times,* p. A21.

Perkins, K. P. (1992). Psychosocial implications of women and retirement. *Social Work, 37,* 526–532.

Perkins, K. P. (1995). Social (in)security: Retirement planning for women. *Journal of Women & Aging, 7,* 37–53.

Perkins, K. R. (1996). The influence of television images on black females' self-perceptions of physical attractiveness. *Journal of Black Psychology, 22,* 453–469.

Perlez, J. (2003, July 14). For these transvestites, still more role changes. *New York Times,* p. A4.

Perlez, J. (2004, June 22). Asian maids often find abuse, not riches, abroad. *New York Times,* p. A3.

Perlmutter, C., Hanlon, T., & Sangiorgio, M. (1994, August). Triumph over menopause. *Prevention,* pp. 78–87, 142.

Perls, T. T., & Fretts, R. C. (1998, June). Why women live longer than men. *Scientific American,* pp. 100–103.

Perry, S. (2002, July/August). Not-so-cosmic gender differences. *APS Observer, 15,* 24.

Perry-Jenkins, M., Seery, B., & Crouter, A. C. (1992). Linkages between women's provider-role attitudes, psychological well-being, and family relationships. *Psychology of Women Quarterly, 16,* 311–329.

Peterman, L. M., & Dixon, C. G. (2003). Domestic violence between same-sex partners: Implications for counseling. *Journal of Counseling and Development, 81,* 40–47.

Petersen, A. (2006, April 9). Paying to treat infertility. *The Wall Street Journal,* p. E4.

Petersen, J. L., & Hyde, J. S. (2008). Parental leave. In M. M. Haith & J. B. Benson (Eds.), *Encyclopedia of infant and early childhood development* (Vol. 2, pp. 490–496). San Diego, CA: Academic Press.

Peterson, K. A., Paulson, S. E., & Williams, K. K. (2007). Relations of eating disorder symptomology with perceptions of pressures from mother, peers, and media in adolescent girls and boys. *Sex Roles, 57,* 629–639.

Peterson, Z. D., & Muehlenhard, C. L. (2004). Was it rape? The function of women's rape myth acceptance and definitions of sex in labeling their own experiences. *Sex Roles, 51,* 129–144.

Petitti, D. B. (2003). Combination estrogen-progestin oral contraceptives. *New England Journal of Medicine, 349,* 1443–1450.

Pettifor, A. E., Measham, D. M., Rees, H. V., & Padian, N. S. (2004, November). *Sexual power and HIV risk, South Africa.* Emerging Infectious Diseases [serial on the Internet]. Available from http://www.cdc.gov/ncidod/EID/vol10no11/04–0252. htm

Pew Research Center. (2003). *Religious beliefs underpin opposition to homosexuality.* Washington, DC: Author.

Pfaff, L. A. and Associates. (1999). *Five-year study shows gender differences in leadership skills.* Kalamazoo, MI: Authors.

Phares, T. M., et al. (2004, July). Surveillance for disparities in maternal health-related behaviors—selected states, pregnancy risk assessment monitoring system (PRAMS), 2000–2001. *Surveillance Summaries. Morbidity and Mortality Weekly Report, 53* (SS-4), 1–13.

Phillips, D., & Adams, G. (2001). Child care and our youngest children. *The Future of Children, 11*(1), 35–51.

Phillips, L. (2000). *Flirting with danger: Sexuality and violence in young women's hetero-relations.* New York: New York University Press.

Phipps, B. J. (1995). Career dreams of preadolescent students. *Journal of Career Development, 22,* 19–32.

Phipps, M. G., et al. (2002). Young maternal age associated with increased risk of neonatal death. *Obstetrics & Gynecology, 100,* 481–486.

Pierce, W. D., Sydie, R.A., Stratkotter, R., & Krull, C. (2003). Social concepts and judgments: A semantic differential analysis of the concepts feminist, man, and woman. *Psychology of Women Quarterly, 27,* 338–346.

Pietsch, J., Walker, R., & Chapman, E. (2003). The relationship among self-concept, self-efficacy, and performance in mathematics during secondary school. *Journal of Educational Psychology, 95,* 589–603.

Pigott, T. A. (2002). Anxiety disorders. In S. G. Kornstein & A. H. Clayton (Eds.), *Women's mental health: A comprehensive textbook* (pp. 195–221). New York: Guilford.

Pike, K. M., et al. (2001). A comparison of black and white women with binge eating disorder. *American Journal of Psychiatry, 158,* 1455–1460.

Piller, C. (1998, September). Women avoiding computer field as gender gap goes high tech. *Hartford Courant,* pp. A12–A13.

Pimlott-Kubiak, S., & Cortina, L. M. (2003). Gender, victimization, and outcomes: Reconceptualizing risk. *Journal of Consulting and Clinical Psychology, 71,* 528–539.

Pinheiro, P. S. (2006). *World report on violence against children, 2006.* Geneva, Switzerland: United Nations.

Pinholster, G. (2005, February 18). New research casts doubt on surgery for infants born with male and female traits. *AAAS News Archives.* Available from http://www.aaas.org/news/releases/2005/0218gender.shtml

Pinn, V. W. (2003). Sex and gender factors in medical studies: Implications for health and clinical practice. *Journal of the American Medical Association, 289,* 397–400.

Pinquart, M. (2003). Loneliness in married, widowed, divorced, and never-married older adults. *Journal of Social and Personal Relationships, 20,* 31–53.

Pinquart, M., & Sörensen, S. (2006). Gender differences in caregiver stressors, social resources, and health: An updated meta-analysis. *Journal of Gerontology, 61B*(1), 33–45.

Piran, N. (2001). Eating disorders and disordered eating. In J. Worell (Ed.), *Encyclopedia of women and gender* (pp. 369–378). San Diego: Academic Press.

Pittman, L. D. (2007). Grandmothers' involvement among young adolescents growing up in poverty. *Journal of Research on Adolescence, 17,* 89–116.

Plant, E. A., Kling, K. C., & Smith, G. L. (2004). The influence of gender and social role on the interpretation of facial expressions. *Sex Roles, 51,* 187–196.

Planty, M., Provasnik, S., & Daniel, B. (2007). *High school coursetaking: Findings from The Condition of Education 2007* (NOES 2007-065). Washington, DC: National Center for Educational Statistics.

Plichta, S. B. (1996). Violence and abuse: Implications for women's health. In M. M. Falik & K. S. Collins (Eds.), *Women's health: The commonwealth fund survey* (pp. 237–270). Baltimore: Johns Hopkins University Press.

Plucker, J. A. (1996). Secondary science and mathematics teachers and gender equity: Attitudes and attempted interventions. *Journal of Research in Science Teaching, 33*(7), 737–751.

Polce-Lynch, M., Myers, B. J., Kilmartin, C. T., Forssmann-Falck, R., & Kliewer, W. (1998). Gender and age patterns in emotional expression, body image, and self-esteem: A qualitative analysis. *Sex Roles, 38,* 1025–1048.

Pollack, A. (2007, June 12). Cancer drug may elude many women who need it. *New York Times,* p. F5.

Polusny, M. A., & Arbisi, P. A. (2006). Assessment of psychological distress and disability after sexual assault in adults. In G. Young, A. W. Kane, & K. Nicholson (Eds.), *Psychological Knowledge in Court* (pp. 97–128). New York: Springer.

Pomerantz, E. M., & Ruble, D. N. (1998). The role of maternal control in the development of sex differences in child self-evaluative factors. *Child Development, 69,* 458–478.

Pomerleau, A., Bolduc, D., Malcuit, G., & Cossette, L. (1990). Pink or blue: Environmental gender stereotypes in the first two years of life. *Sex Roles, 22,* 359–367.

Poo, A. J., & Tang, E. (2004). Domestic workers organize in the global city. In V. Labaton & D. L. Martin (Eds.), *The fire this time* (pp. 150–165). New York: Anchor Books.

Popenoe, D. (2008). *Cohabitation, marriage, and wellbeing: A cross-national perspective.* Piscataway, NJ: The National Marriage Project at Rutgers.

Popenoe, D., & Whitehead, B. D. (1999). *The state of our unions: The social health of marriage in America.* New Brunswick, NJ: National Marriage Project at Rutgers University.

Popescu, R., & Carmichael, M. (2008, January 21). A guide to predicting your medical future. *Newsweek,* pp. 59–62.

Popp, D., et al. (2003). Gender, race, and speech style stereotypes. *Sex Roles, 48,* 317–325.

Population Action International. (1998). *Educating girls: Gender gaps and gains.* Washington, DC: Author.

Poran, M. A. (2002). Denying diversity: Perceptions of beauty and social comparison processes among Latina, black, and white women. *Sex Roles, 47,* 65–81.

Porter, P. (2008). "Westernizing" women's risks? Breast cancer in lower-income countries. *New England Journal of Medicine, 358,* 213–216.

Posner, R. B. (2006). Early menarche: A review of research on trends in timing, racial differences, etiology and psychosocial consequences. *Sex Roles, 54,* 315–322.

Poteat, V. P., & Espelage, D. L. (2007). Predicting psychosocial consequences of homophobic victimization in middle school students. *Journal of Early Adolescence, 27,* 175–191.

Potoczniak, M. J., et al. (2003). Legal and psychological perspectives on same-sex domestic violence: A multisystemic approach. *Journal of Family Psychology, 17*(2), 252–259.

Poulin, F., & Pedersen, S. (2007). Developmental changes in gender composition of friendship networks in adolescent girls and boys. *Developmental Psychology, 43,* 1484–1496.

Poulin-Dubois, D., Serbin, L. A., & Derbyshire, A. (1998). Toddlers' intermodal and verbal knowledge about gender. *Merrill-Palmer Quarterly, 44,* 338–354.

Poulin-Dubois, D., Serbin, L. A., Eichstedt, J. A., Sen, M. G., & Beissel, C. F. (2002). Men don't put on make-up: Toddlers' knowledge of the gender stereotyping of household activities. *Social Development, 11,* 166–181.

Powell, L. M., Slater, S., Chaloupka, F. J., & Harper, D. (2006). Availability of physical activity—related facilities and neighborhood demographic and socioeconomic characteristics: A national study. *American Journal of Public Health, 96,* 1676–1680.

Powell, S. R., & Yanico, B. J. (1991). A multimethod attitude study about women's roles and issues. *Psychology of Women Quarterly, 15,* 97–101.

Powers, P. S. (2002). Eating disorders. In S. G. Kornstein & A. H. Clayton (Eds.), *Women's mental health: A comprehensive textbook* (pp. 244–262). New York: Guilford.

Powlishta, K. K. (2001, April). *Own-sex favoritism and gender-role development.* Poster presented at the meeting of the Society for Research in Child Development, Minneapolis, MN.

Powlishta, K. K., Sen, M. G., Serbin, L. A., Poulin-Dubois, D., & Eichstedt, J. A. (2001). From infancy through middle childhood: The role of cognitive and social factors in becoming gendered. In R. K. Unger (Ed.), *Handbook of the psychology of women and gender* (pp. 116–132). New York: Wiley.

Pozner, J. L. (2004, Fall). The unreal world. *Ms.,* pp. 50–53.

Pratto, F., & Walker, A. (2004). The bases of gendered power. In A. H. Eagly, A. E. Beall, & R. J. Sternberg (Eds.), *The psychology of gender* (pp. 242–268). New York: Guilford.

Prejean, J., Satcher, A. J., Durant, T., Hu, X., & Lee, L. M. (2006). Racial/ethnic disparities in diagnosis of HIV/AIDS—33 states, 2001–2004. *Morbidity and Mortality Weekly Report, 55,* 121–125.

Prendergast, M. A. (2004). Do women possess a unique susceptibility to the neurotoxic effects of alcohol? *Journal of the American Medical Women's Association, 59,* 225–227.

Prentice, D. A., & Miller, D. T. (2006). Essentializing differences between women and men. *Psychological Science, 17,* 129–135.

Prentice, K. (2008, February). When a caregiver needs care. *Heart Insight,* pp. 17–19.

Prentice, R. L., et al. (2007). Low-fat dietary pattern and cancer incidence in the women's health initiative dietary modification randomized controlled trial. *Journal of the National Cancer Institute, 99,* 1534–1543.

Press, J., Fagan, J., & Bernd, E. (2006). Child care, work, and depressive symptoms among low-income mothers. *Journal of Family Issues, 27,* 609–632.

Presser, H. B. (2004). Employment in a 24/7 economy: Challenges for the family. In A. C. Crouter and A. Booth (Eds.), *Work-family challenges for low-income parents and their children* (pp. 83–105). Mahwah, NJ: Erlbaum.

Prevalence of regular physical activity among adults—United States, 2001 and 2005. (2007). *Morbidity and Mortality Weekly Report, 56,* 1209–1212.

Price, J. L., Hilsenroth, M. J., Petretic-Jackson, P. A., & Bonge, D. (2001). A review of individual psychotherapy outcomes for adult survivors of childhood sexual abuse. *Clinical Psychology Review, 21,* 1095–1121.

Prinstein, M. J., & La Greca, A. M. (2004). Childhood peer rejection and aggression as predictors of adolescent girls' externalizing and health risk behaviors: A 6-year longitudinal study. *Journal of Consulting and Clinical Psychology, 72,* 103–112.

Procopio, C. A., Holm-Denoma, J. M., Gordon, K. H., & Joiner, T. E. (2006). Two—three-year stability and interrelations of bulimotypic indicators and depressive and anxious Symptoms in middle-aged women. *International Journal of Eating Disorders, 39,* 312–319.

Proctor, B. D., & Dalaker, J. (2002). *Poverty in the United States: 2001.* Current Population Reports, P60–219. Washington, DC: U.S. Census Bureau.

Proctor, B. D., & Dalaker, J. (2003). *Poverty in the United States: 2002.* U.S. Census Bureau, Current Population Reports, P60–222. Washington, DC: U. S. Government Printing Office.

Programme for International Student Assessment. (2004). *First results from PISA 2003.* London: Organization for Economic Cooperation and Development.

Propp, K. (2003). Pregnancy as a life passage. In L. Slater, J. H. Daniel, & A. E. Banks (Eds.), *The complete guide to mental health for women* (pp. 6–9). Boston: Beacon Press.

Proulx, C. M., Helms, H. M., & Buehler, C. (2007). Marital quality and personal well-being: A Meta-analysis. *Journal of Marriage and Family, 69,* 576–593.

Pruchno, R. A. (1999). Raising grandchildren: The experiences of Black and White grandmothers. *The Gerontologist, 39,* 209–221.

Pryor, J. B., & Whalen, N. J. (1997). A typology of sexual harassment: Characteristics of harassers and the social circumstances under which sexual harassment occurs. In W. O'Donohue (Ed.), *Sexual harassment: Theory, research, and treatment* (pp. 129–151). Boston: Allyn & Bacon.

Pryor, J. H., Hurtado, S., Saenz, V. B., Lindholm, J. A., Korn, W. S., & Mahoney, K. M. (2005). *The American freshman: National norms for fall 2005.* Los Angeles: Higher Education Research Institute, UCLA.

Puhl, R. M., & Latner, J. D. (2007). Stigma, obesity, and the health of the nation's children. *Psychological Bulletin, 133,* 557–580.

Punglia, R. S., Morrow, M., Winer, E. P., & Harris, J. R. (2007). Local therapy and survival in breast cancer. *New England Journal of Medicine, 356,* 2399–2405.

Purcell, P., & Stewart, L. (1990). Dick and Jane in 1989. *Sex Roles, 22,* 177–185.

Putting the sex trade on notice. (2004, January 9). *New York Times,* p. A18.

Quail, J. M., Addona, V., Wolfson, C., Podoba, J. E., Lévesque, L. Y., & Dupuis, J. (2007). Association of unmet need with self-rated health in a community dwelling cohort of disabled seniors 75 years of age and over. *European Journal of Ageing, 4,* 45–55.

QuickStats: Percentage of women aged >25 years who had a Papanitolaou (Pap) smear test during the preceding 3 years, by age group and education level—National Health Interview Survey, United States, 2005. (2008). *Morbidity and Mortality Weekly Report, 57,* 529.

Quindlen, A. (2007, October 1). Killing the consumer. *Newsweek,* p. 92.

Quinn, D. M., & Spencer, S. J. (2001, Spring). The interference of stereotype threat with women's generation of mathematical problem-solving strategies. *Journal of Social Issues,* pp. 55–72.

Quinn, J. B. (2001, February 17). Investing women aren't emotionally impaired. *Peoria Journal Star*, p. C2.

Quinn, J. E. A., & Radtke, H. L. (2006). Dilemmatic negotiations: The (un)tenability of feminist identity. *Psychology of Women Quarterly, 30*, 187–198.

Quinn, P. C. (2002). Beyond prototypes: Asymmetries in infant categorization and what they teach us about the mechanisms guiding early knowledge acquisition. In R. V. Kail & H. W. Reese (Eds.), *Advances in child development and behavior* (Vol. 29, pp. 161–193). San Diego: Academic Press.

Raag, T., & Rackliff, C. L. (1998). Preschoolers' awareness of social expectations of gender: Relationships to toy choices. *Sex Roles, 38*, 685–700.

Rabasca, L. (2000, October). The Internet and computer games reinforce the gender gap. *Monitor on Psychology*, pp. 32–33.

Rabin, R. C. (2006, November 14). Health disparities persist for men, and doctors ask why. *New York Times*, pp. D1, D6.

Rabin, R. C. (2007a, May 15). As demand for donor eggs soars, high prices stir ethical concerns. *New York Times*, p. D6.

Rabin, R. C. (2007b, August 28). For a low-dose hormone, take your pick. *New York Times*, p. D5.

Rader, J., & Gilbert, L. A. (2005). The egalitarian relationship in feminist therapy. *Psychology of Women Quarterly, 29*, 427–435.

Radner, G. (1990). *It's always something*. New York: Avon.

Raffaelli, M., & Ontai, L. L. (2004). Gender socialization in Latino/a families: Results from two retrospective studies. *Sex Roles, 50*, 287–299.

Rafferty, Y. (2008). The impact of trafficking on children: Psychological and social policy perspectives. *Child Development Perspectives, 2*, 13–18.

Ragins, B. R., & Scandura, T. A. (1995). Antecedents and work-related correlates of reported sexual harassment: An empirical investigation of competing hypotheses. *Sex Roles, 32*, 429–455.

Rahman, Q., Kumari, V., & Wilson, G. D. (2003). Sexual orientation-related differences in prepulse inhibition of the human startle response. *Behavioral Neuroscience, 117*, 1096–1102.

Raiford, J. L., Wingood, G. M., & Diclemente, R. J. (2007). Prevalence, incidence, and predictors of dating violence: A longitudinal study of African American female adolescents. *Journal of Women's Health, 16*, 822–832.

Raj, A., Gomez, C., & Silverman, J.G. (2008). Driven to a fiery death—the tragedy of self-immolation in Afghanistan. *New England Journal of Medicine, 358*, 2201–2203.

Raley, R. K., & Wildsmith, E. (2004). Cohabitation and children's family instability. *Journal of Marriage and Family, 66*, 210–219.

Ramirez, J. M. (2003). Hormones and aggression in childhood and adolescence. *Aggression and Violent Behavior, 8*, 621–644.

Ramisetty-Mikler, S., Caetano, R., & McGrath, C. (2007). Sexual aggression among white, black, and Hispanic couples in the U.S.: Alcohol use, physical assault and psychological aggression as its correlates. *The American Journal of Drug and Alcohol Abuse, 33*, 31–43.

Ramsey, L. R., et al. (2007). Thinking of others: Feminist identification and the perception of others' beliefs. *Sex Roles, 56*, 611–616.

Randolph, S. M. (1995). African American children in single-mother families. In B. J. Dickerson (Ed.), *African American single mothers: Understanding their lives and families* (pp. 117–145). Thousand Oaks, CA: Sage.

Range, L. M. (2006). Women and suicide. In J. Worell & C. D. Goodheart (Eds.), *Handbook of girls' and women's psychological health: Gender and well-being across the lifespan* (pp. 129–136). New York: Oxford University Press.

Rani, M., & Lule, E. (2004). Exploring the socioeconomic dimension of adolescent reproductive health: A multicountry analysis. *International Family Planning Perspectives, 30*, 110–117.

Raschick, M., & Ingersoll-Dayton, B. (2004). The costs and rewards of caregiving among aging spouses and adult children. *Family Relations, 53*, 317–325.

Rathus, S., Nevid, J., & Fichner-Rathus, L. (2008). *Human sexuality in a world of diversity* (6th ed.). Boston: Allyn & Bacon.

Ratner, E. (1999). *The feisty woman's breast cancer book*. New York: Hunter House.

Räty, H., & Kasanen, K. (2007). Gendered view of ability in parents' perceptions of their children's academic competencies. *Sex Roles, 56*, 117–124.

Räty, H., Kasanen, K., & Honkalampi, K. (2006). Three years later: A follow-up study of parents' assessments of their children's competencies. *Journal of Applied Social Psychology, 36*, 2079–2099.

Rawlins, W. K. (2004). Friendships in later life. In J. F. Nussbaum & J. Coupland (Eds.), *Handbook of communication and aging research* (2nd ed., pp. 273–304). Mahwah, NJ: Erlbaum.

Ray, O. (2004). How the mind hurts and heals the body. *American Psychologist, 59*, 29–40.

Read, J. (2004). Sexual problems associated with infertility, pregnancy, and ageing. *BMJ, 329*, 559–561.

Ream, G. L., & Savin-Williams, R. C. (2002, August). *Development of religion-based homophobia among sexual-minority and heterosexual adolescents and young children*. Paper presented at the meeting of the American Psychological Association, Chicago.

Rebar, R. W., & DeCherney, A. H. (2004). Assisted reproductive technology in the United States. *New England Journal of Medicine, 350*, 1603–1604.

Redberg, R. F. (2007). Disparities in use of implantable cardioverter-defibrillators: Moving beyond process measures to outcomes data. *Journal of the American Medical Association, 298*, 1564–1566.

Reed, M. E., Collinsworth, L. L., & Fitzgerald, L. F. (2005). There's no place like home: Sexual harassment of low income women in housing. *Psychology, Public Policy, and the Law, 11*.

Reeder, H. M. (2003). The effect of gender role orientation on same- and cross-sex friendship formation. *Sex Roles, 49*, 143–152.

Reeves, J. B., & Darville, R. L. (1994). Social contact patterns and satisfaction with retirement of women in dual-career/earner families. *International Journal of Aging and Human Development, 39*, 163–175.

Regan, P. C., & Cachelin, F. M. (2006). Binge eating and purging in a multi-ethnic community sample. *International Journal of Eating Disorders, 39*, 523–526.

Reichert, F. F., Barros, A. J. D., Domingues, M. R., & Hallal, P. C. (2007). The role of perceived personal barriers to engagement in leisure-time physical activity. *American Journal of Public Health, 97*, 515–519.

Reichert, T., & Carpenter, C. (2004). An update on sex in magazine advertising: 1983–2003. *Journalism and Mass Communication Quarterly, 81*, 823–837.

Reichert, T., & Lambiase, J. J. (Eds.). (2005). *Sex in consumer culture: The erotic content of media and marketing.* Mahwah, NJ: Erlbaum.

Reichman, N. E., & McLanahan, S. S. (2001). Self-sufficiency programs and parenting interventions: Lessons from new chance and the teenage parent demonstration. *Social Policy Report, 15*(2), 3–13.

Reid, A., & Purcell, N. (2004). Pathways to feminist identification. *Sex Roles, 50*, 759–769.

Reid, P. T. (1999). Poor women in psychological research: Shut up and shut out. In L. A. Peplau, S. C. DeBro, R. C. Veniegas, & P. L. Taylor (Eds.), *Gender, culture and ethnicity: Current research about women and men* (pp. 336–352). Mountain View, CA: Mayfield.

Reid, P. T., Cooper, S. M., & Banks, K. H. (2008). Girls to women: Developmental theory, research, and issues. In F. L. Denmark & M. A. Paludi (Eds.), *Psychology of women: A handbook of issues and theories* (2nd ed., pp. 237–270). Westport, CT: Praeger.

Reid, P. T., & Kelly, E. (1994). Research on women of color: From ignorance to awareness. *Psychology of Women Quarterly, 18*, 477–486.

Reid, P. T., & Zalk, S. R. (2001). Academic environments: Gender and ethnicity in higher education. In J. Worell (Ed.), *Encyclopedia of women and gender* (pp. 29–42). San Diego: Academic Press.

Reiner, W. G., & Gearhart, J. P. (2004). Discordant sexual identity in some genetic males with cloacal exstrophy assigned to female sex at birth. *New England Journal of Medicine, 350*, 333–341.

Reinhardt, R. (2002). Bisexual women in heterosexual relationships. *Journal of Bisexuality, 2*, 161–169.

Remer, P., & Oakley, D. (2005, Winter). Counselor self-disclosure. *The Feminist Psychologist*, pp. 8–10.

Remez, L. (2003). Few U.S. school-based health centers offer contraceptives on-site. *Perspectives on Sexual and Reproductive Health, 35*, 239–240.

Renk, K., et al. (2003). Mothers, fathers, gender role, and time parents spend with their children. *Sex Roles, 48*, 305–315.

Revenson, T. A. (2001). Chronic illness adjustment. In J. Worell (Ed.), *Encyclopedia of women and gender* (pp. 245–255). San Diego: Academic Press.

Reynolds, A. J., et al. (2007). Effects of a school-based, early childhood intervention on adult health and well-being. *Archives of Pediatrics and Adolescent Medicine, 161*, 730–739.

Reynolds, B. M., & Repetti, R. L. (2006). Adolescent girls' health in the context of peer and community relationships. In J. Worell & C. D. Goodheart (Eds.), *Handbook of girls' and women's psychological health: Gender and well-being across the lifespan* (pp. 292–300). New York: Oxford University Press.

Reynolds, J., Wetherell, M., & Taylor, S. (2007). Choice and chance: Negotiating agency in narrative of singleness. *The Sociological Review, 55*, 331–351.

Rhoades, G. K., Stanley, S. M., & Markman, H. J. (2006). Pre-engagement cohabitation and gender asymmetry in marital commitment. *Journal of Family Psychology, 20*, 553–560.

Rhode, D. L., & Williams, J. C. (2007). Legal perspectives on employment discrimination. In F. J. Crosby, M. S. Stockdale, & S. A. Ropp (Eds.), *Sex discrimination in the workplace* (pp. 235–270). Malden, MA: Blackwell.

Rhodes, J. E., Davis, A. A., Prescott, L. R., & Spencer, R. (2007). Caring connections: Mentoring relationships in the lives of urban girls. In B. J. R. Leadbeater & N. Way (Eds.), *Urban girls revisited: Building strengths* (pp. 142–156). New York: New York University Press.

Ricciardelli, L. A., & McCabe, M. P. (2001). Children's body image concerns and eating disturbance: A review of the literature. *Clinical Psychology Review, 21*, 325–344.

Ricciuti, H. (2004a). On Mother's Day, a hopeful finding for single mothers and their children from a Cornell researcher. *The Journal of Educational Research, 97*, 5.

Ricciuti, H. (2004b). Single parenthood, achievement, and problem behavior in white, black, and hispanic children. *The Journal of Educational Research, 97*, 196–206.

Rice, J. K., & Else-Quest, N. (2006). The mixed messages of motherhood. In J. Worell & C. D. Goodheart (Eds.), *Handbook of girls' and women's psychological health: Gender and well-being across the lifespan* (pp. 339–349). New York: Oxford University Press.

Rice, S. (2001). Sexuality and intimacy for aging women: A changing perspective. In J. D. Garner & S. O. Mercer (Eds.), *Women as they age* (2nd ed., pp. 147–164). New York: Haworth.

Richards, H. M., Reid, M. E., & Watt, G. C. M. (2002). Why do men and women respond differently to chest pain? A qualitative study. *Journal of the American Medical Women's Association, 57*, 79–81.

Richardson, P., & Lazur, A. (1995). Sexuality in the nursing home patient. *American Family Physician, 51*, 121–124.

Richardson, V. E. (2001). Mental health of elderly women. In J. D. Garner & S. O. Mercer (Eds.), *Women as they age* (2nd ed., pp. 85–96). New York: Haworth.

Richie, B. S., et al. (1997). Persistence, connection, and passion: A qualitative study of the career development of highly achieving African American-Black and White women. *Journal of Counseling Psychology, 44*, 133–148.

Richmond, T. K., Hayward, R. A., Gahagan, S., Field, A. E., & Heisler, M. (2006). Can school income and racial/ethnic composition explain the racial/ethnic disparity in adolescent physical activity participation? *Pediatrics, 117*, 2158–2166.

Riddick, C. C. (1993). Older women's leisure activity and quality of life. In J. R. Kelly (Ed.), *Activity and aging: Staying involved in later life* (pp. 86–98). Newbury Park, CA: Sage.

Ridgeway, C. L. (2006). Gender as an organizing force in social relations: Implications for the future of inequality. In F. D. Blau & M. C. Brinton (Eds.), *The declining significance of gender?* (pp. 248–287). New York: Russell Sage Foundation.

Ridgeway, C. L., & England, P. (2007). Sociological approaches to sex discrimination in employment. In F. J. Crosby, M. S. Stockdale, & S. A. Ropp (Eds.), *Sex discrimination in the workplace* (pp. 189–212). Malden, MA: Blackwell.

Riegle-Crumb, C. (2000). *International gender inequality in math and science education.* Unpublished doctoral dissertation, University of Chicago.

Rife, J. C. (2001). Middle-aged and older women in the work force. In J. M. Coyle (Ed.), *Handbook on women and aging* (pp. 93–111). Westport, CT: Greenwood.

Riger, S., & Staggs, S. L. (2004). Welfare reform, domestic violence and employment: What do we know, and what do we need to know? *Violence against Women, 10,* 1–30.

Riggio, H. R., & Desrochers, S. (2005). The influence of maternal employment on the work and family attitudes of young adults. In D. F. Halpern & S. E. Murphy (Eds.), *From work-family balance to work-family interaction: Changing the metaphor* (pp. 177–196). Mahwah, NJ: Erlbaum.

Riggio, H. R., & Desrochers, S. J. (2006). Relations with young adults' work and family expectations and self-efficacy. *American Behavioral Scientist, 49,* 1328–1353.

Riggs, J. M. (1997). Mandates for mothers and fathers: Perceptions of breadwinners and care givers. *Sex Roles, 37,* 565–580.

Riley, G. F., et al. (1999). Stage at diagnosis and treatment patterns among older women and breast cancer: An HMO and fee-for-service comparison. *Journal of the American Medical Association, 281,* 720–726.

Rimer, S. (1999, September 5). Gaps seen in treatment of depression in elderly. *New York Times,* pp. Y1, Y16.

Rimer, S. (2005, April 15). For women in sciences, slow progress in academia. *New York Times,* pp. Al, A15.

Rintala, D. H., et al. (1997). Dating issues for women with physical disabilities. *Sexuality and Disability, 15,* 219–242.

Risman, B., & Schwartz, P. (2002, Spring). After the sexual revolution: Gender politics in teen dating. *Contexts,* pp. 16–24.

Rivers, I. (2002). Developmental issues for lesbian and gay youth. In A. Coyle & C. Kitzinger (Eds.), *Lesbian and gay psychology: New perspectives* (pp. 30–44). Oxford, UK: BPS Blackwell.

Rivers, I., Poteat, V. P., & Noret, N. (2008). Victimization, social support, and psychosocial functioning among children of same-sex and opposite-sex couples in the United Kingdom. *Developmental Psychology, 44,* 127–134.

Rix, Sara E. (1990). Who pays for what? Ensuring financial security in retirement. In C. L. Hayes & J. M. Deren (Eds.), *Preretirement planning for women: Program design and research* (pp. 5–26). New York: Springer.

Robbins, C. L., & Padavic, I. (2007). Structural influences on racial and ethnic disparities in women's health care. *Sociology Compass, 1,* 682–700.

Robert, M., & Héroux, G. (2004). Visuo-spatial play experience: Forerunner of visuo-spatial achievement in preadolescent and adolescent boys and girls? *Infant and Child Development, 13,* 49–78.

Roberto, K. A. (2001). Older women's relationships: Weaving lives together. In J. D. Garner & S. O. Mercer (Eds.), *Women as they age* (2nd ed., pp. 115–129). New York: Haworth.

Roberts, B. W., Helson, R., & Klohnen, E. C. (2002). Personality development and growth in women across 30 years: Three perspectives. *Journal of Personality, 70,* 79–102.

Roberts, H. (2007). Managing the menopause. *BMJ, 334,* 736–741.

Roberts, S. (2007, July 1). The shelf life of bliss. *New York Times,* pp. ST1, ST9.

Roberts, S. T., & Kennedy, B. L. (2006). Why are young college women not using condoms? Their perceived risk, drug use, and developmental vulnerability may provide important clues to sexual risk. *Archives of Psychiatric Nursing, 20,* 32–40.

Roberts, T. A. (2004). Female trouble: The menstrual self-evaluation scale and women's self-objectification. *Psychology of Women Quarterly, 28,* 22–26.

Roberts, T. A., Auinger, P., & Klein, J. D. (2006). Predictors of partner abuse in a nationally representative sample of adolescents involved in heterosexual dating relationships. *Violence and Victims, 21,* 81–89.

Robertson, J., & Fitzgerald, L. F. (1990). The (mis)treatment of men: Effects of client gender role and life-style on diagnosis and attribution of pathology. *Journal of Counseling Psychology, 37,* 3–9.

Robertson, R. M. (2001). Women and cardiovascular disease: The risks of misperception and the need for action. *Circulation, 103,* 2318–2320.

Robin, L., et al. (2004, January). Behavioral interventions to reduce incidence of HIV, STD, and pregnancy among adolescents: A decade in review. *Journal of Adolescent Health, 34,* 3–26.

Robins, R. W., & Trzesniewski, K. H. (2005). Self-esteem development across the lifespan. *Current Directions in Psychological Science, 14,* 158–162.

Robinson, B. K., & Hunter, E. (2008). Is mom still doing it all? Reexamining depictions of family work in popular advertising. *Journal of Family Issues, 29,* 465–486.

Robinson, D. T., Gibson-Beverly, G., & Schwartz, J. P. (2004). Sorority and fraternity membership and religious behaviors: Relation to gender attitudes. *Sex Roles, 50,* 871–877.

Robinson, G. (2007). Helping the world's endangered children. In *Great Decisions* (pp. 89–93). New York: Foreign Policy Institute.

Robinson, J. D., Skill, T., & Turner, J. W. (2004). Media usage patterns and portrayals of seniors. In J. F. Nussbaum & J. Coupland (Eds.), *Handbook of communication and aging research* (2nd ed., pp. 423–450). Mahwah, NJ: Erlbaum.

Roche, K. M., et al. (2005). Parenting influences on early sex initiation among adolescents. *Journal of Family Issues, 26,* 32–54.

Rogers, S. J., & DeBoer, D. D. (2001). Changes in wives' income: Effects in marital happiness, psychological well-being, and the risk of divorce. *Journal of Marriage and Family, 63,* 458–472.

Rohde, D. (2002, October 31). Attacks on schools for girls hint at lingering split in Afghanistan. *New York Times,* p. A1.

Rohrbaugh, J. B. (2004, November). Power and control dynamics in same-gender relationships. *AFCC Newsletter,* pp. 7–12.

Roisman, G. I., Clausell, E., Holland, A., Fortuna, K., & Elieff, C. (2008). Adult romantic relationships as contexts of human development: A multimethod comparison of same-sex couples with opposite-sex dating, engaged, and married dyads. *Developmental Psychology, 44*, 91–101.

Romaine, S. (1999). *Communicating gender.* Mahwah, NJ: Erlbaum.

Romieu, I., et al. (2004). Carbohydrates and the risk of breast cancer among Mexican women. *Cancer Epidemiology Biomarkers & Prevention, 13*, 1283–1289.

Roovers, J. P. W. R., et al. (2003). Hysterectomy and sexual wellbeing: Prospective observational study of vaginal hysterectomy, subtotal abdominal hysterectomy, and total abdominal hysterectomy. *BMJ, 327*, 774–778.

Roper, E. A., & Halloran, E. (2007). Attitudes toward gay men and lesbians among heterosexual male and female student-athletes. *Sex Roles, 57*, 919–928.

Roscoe, L. A., Malphurs, J. E., Dragovic, L. J., & Cohen, D. (2003). Antecedents of euthanasia and suicide among older women. *Journal of the American Medical Women's Association, 58*, 44–48.

Rose, A. J. (2002). Co-rumination in the friendships of girls and boys. *Child Development, 73*, 1830–1843.

Rose, A. J., & Rudolph, K. D. (2006). A review of sex differences in peer relationship processes: Potential trade-offs for the emotional and behavioral development of girls and boys. *Psychological Bulletin, 132*, 98–131.

Rose, A. J., Swenson, L. P., & Waller, E. M. (2004). Overt and relational aggression and perceived popularity: Developmental differences in concurrent and prospective relations. *Developmental Psychology, 40*, 378–387.

Rose, S. (2000, Summer). Heterosexism and the study of women's romantic and friend relationships. *Journal of Social Issues, 56*, 315–328.

Rose, S., & Frieze, I. H. (1993). Young singles contemporary dating scripts. *Sex Roles, 28*, 499–509.

Rose, S. M. (2002). Introduction: Lesbian love and relationships. In S. M. Rose (Ed.), *Lesbian love and relationships* (pp. 1–3). Binghamton, NY: Harrington Park Press.

Rose, S. M. (2007). Enjoying the returns: Women's friendships after 50. In V. Muhlbauer & J. C. Chrisler (Eds.), *Women over 50: Psychological perspectives* (pp. 112–130). New York: Springer.

Rose, S. M., & Zand, D. (2002). Lesbian dating and courtship from young adulthood to midlife. In S. M. Rose (Ed.), *Lesbian love and relationships* (pp. 85–109). Binghamton, NY: Harrington Park Press.

Rosen, E. (2007, April 6). Female lawyers set sights on yet one more goal: A seat on a board. *New York Times*, p. C8.

Rosenberg, D. (2007, May 21). Rethinking gender. *Newsweek*, pp. 50–57.

Rosenberg, D., & Wingert, P. (2006, December 4). First comes junior in a baby carriage. *Newsweek*, pp. 56–57.

Rosenberg, T. (2004, July 5). Mutilating Africa's daughters: Laws unenforced, practices unchanged. *New York Times*, p. A18.

Rosenblum C. (1991, October 31). Yipes! An eery metamorphosis is turning girls into turtles. *New York Times*, p. B1.

Rosenfeld, A. G. (2006). State of the heart: Building science to improve women's cardiovascular health. *American Journal of Critical Care, 15*, 556–566.

Rosenthal, E. (2003, July 20). Bias for boys leads to sale of baby girls in China. *New York Times*, p. YT6.

Rosenthal, E. (2007, October 12). Legal or not, abortion rates compare. *New York Times*, p. A8.

Ross, L. E., & Davis, A. C. (1996). Black-White college students' attitudes and expectations in paying for dates. *Sex Roles, 35*, 43–56.

Rossi, A. S. (2004). The menopausal transition and aging processes. In O. G. Brim, C. D. Ryff, & R. C. Kessler (Eds.), *How healthy are we? A national study of well-being at midlife* (pp. 153–201). Chicago: University of Chicago Press.

Rostosky, S. S., et al. (2004). Same-sex couple perceptions of family support: A consensual qualitative study. *Family Process, 43*, 43–57.

Roter, D. L., Hall, J. A., & Aoki, Y. (2002). Physician gender effects in medical communication. *Journal of the American Medical Association, 288*, 756–764.

Roth, R. (2003). Sexual and reproductive life of women: Gender equality in women's reproductive health in Western Europe and the U.S. *Psychology Science, 45*, 123–143.

Rothblum, E. D. (2002). Gay and lesbian body images. In T. F. Cash & T. Pruzinsky (Eds.), *Body images: A handbook of theory, research, and clinical practice* (pp. 257–265). New York: Guilford Publications.

Rothblum, E. D. (2007, May). *Same-sex couples in legalized relationships: I do, or do I?* Paper presented at the annual meeting of the Association for Psychological Science, Washington, DC.

Rothblum, E. D., & Factor, R. (2001). Lesbians and their sisters as a control group: Demographic and mental health factors. *Psychological Science, 12*, 63–69.

Rothman, E. F., Hemenway, D., Miller, M., & Azrael, D. (2005). Batterers' use of guns to threaten intimate partners. *Journal of the American Medical Women's Association, 60*, 62–68.

Rotundo, M., Nguyen, D., & Sackett, P. R. (2001). A meta-analytic review of gender differences in perceptions of sexual harassment. *Journal of Applied Psychology, 86*, 914–922.

Rowley, L. M. C. (1999, August). *Women in dual-earner marriages: The impact of religious commitment on household task and management performance.* Paper presented at the meeting of the American Psychological Association, Boston.

Roy, R. E., Weibust, K. S., & Miller, C. T. (2007). Effects of stereotypes about feminists on feminist self-identification. *Psychology of Women Quarterly, 31*, 146–156.

Royak-Schaler, R., Lemkau, J. P., & Ahmed, S. M. (2002). Discussing breast cancer risk in primary care. *Journal of the American Medical Women's Association, 57*, 115–116.

Royo-Vela, M., Aldas-Manzano, J., Küster, I., & Vila, N. (2008). Adaptation of marketing activities to cultural and social context: Gender role portrayals and sexism in Spanish commercials. *Sex Roles, 58*, 379–390.

Rozee, P. D. (2008). Women's fear of rape: Cause, consequences, and coping. In J. C. Chrisler, C. Golden, & P. D. Rozee (Eds.), *Lectures on the psychology of women* (pp. 322–337). New York: McGraw-Hill.

Rozee, P. D., & Koss, M. P. (2001). Rape: A century of resistance. *Psychology of Women Quarterly, 25,* 295–311.

Rubin, K. H., Bukowski, W. M., & Parker, J. G. (2006). Peer interactions, relationships, and groups. In W. Damon, R. M. Lerner (Series Eds.) & N. Eisenberg (Vol. Ed.), *Handbook of child psychology: Vol. 3. Social, emotional, and personality development* (6th ed., pp. 571–645). Hoboken, NJ: Wiley.

Rubin, L. R., Nemeroff, C. J., & Russo, N. F. (2004). Exploring feminist women's body consciousness. *Psychology of Women Quarterly, 28,* 27–37.

Rubinstein, R. L. (1994). Adaptation to retirement among the never married, childless, divorced, gay and lesbian, and widowed. In A. Monk (Ed.), *The Columbia retirement handbook* (pp. 448–461). New York: Columbia University Press.

Rubinstein, S., & Caballero, B. (2000). Is Miss America an undernourished role model? *Journal of the American Medical Association, 283,* 1569.

Ruble, D. N., & Martin, C. L. (1998). Gender development. In W. Damon (Series Ed.) & N. Eisenberg (Vol. Ed.), *Handbook of child psychology. Vol. 3. Social, emotional and personality development* (5th ed., pp. 933–1016). New York: Wiley.

Ruble, D. N., Martin, C. L., & Berenbaum, S. A. (2006). Gender development. In W. Damon, R. M. Lerner (Series Eds.) & N. Eisenberg (Vol. Ed.), *Handbook of child psychology: Vol. 3. Social, emotional, and personality development* (6th ed., pp. 858–932). Hoboken, NJ: Wiley.

Ruble, D. N., Taylor, L. J., Cyphers, L., Greulich, F. K., Lurye, L. E., & Shrout, P. E. (2007). The role of gender constancy in early gender development. *Child Development, 78,* 1121–1136.

Rudman, L. A., & Fairchild, K. (2004). Reactions to counterstereotypic behavior: The role of backlash in cultural stereotype maintenance. *Journal of Personality and Social Psychology, 87,* 157–176.

Rudman, L. A., & Fairchild, K. (2007). The *F* word: Is feminism incompatible with beauty and romance? *Psychology of Women Quarterly, 31,* 125–136.

Rudman, L. A., & Phelan, J. E. (2007). The interpersonal power of feminism: Is feminism good for romantic relationships? *Sex Roles, 57,* 787–799.

Rudolph, K. D., & Hammen, C. (1999). Age and gender as determinants of stress exposure, generation, and reactions in youngsters: A transactional perspective. *Child Development, 70,* 660–677.

Rudolph, M. L., & Burt, V. K. (2003). Suicide in elderly women: Addressing this growing concern. *Women's Health in Primary Care, 6,* 281–289.

Ruiz, D. S., Zhu, C. W., & Crowther, M. R. (2003). *Not on their own again*: Psychological, social, and health characteristics of custodial African American grandmothers. *Journal of Women & Aging, 15,* 167–184.

Ruiz, S. A., & Silverstein, M. (2007). Relationships with grandparents and the emotional well-being of late adolescent and young adult grandchildren. *Journal of Social Issues, 63,* 793–808.

Ruling allows legal status for partners of same-sex. (2008, February 3). *New York Times,* p. A14.

Runowicz, C. D. (2007). Molecular screening for cervical cancer—time to give up Pap tests? *New England Journal of Medicine, 357,* 1650–1653.

Runyon, M. K., Kenny, M. C., Berry, E. J., Deblinger, E., & Brown, E. J. (2006). Etiology and surveillance in child maltreatment. In J. R. Lutzker (Ed.), *Preventing violence: Research and evidence-based intervention strategies* (pp. 23–48). Washington, DC: American Psychological Association.

Russell, D. E. H. (2001). Femicide: An international speakout. In D. E. H. Russell & R. A. Harmes (Eds.), *Femicide in global perspective* (pp. 128–137). New York: Teachers College Press.

Russell, J. E. A. (2006). Career counseling for women in management: Career counseling with lesbian clients. In W. B. Walsh & M. J. Heppner (Eds.), *Handbook of career counseling for women* (2nd ed., pp. 453–512). Mahwah, NJ: Erlbaum.

Russell, M., & Carr, P. L. (2003). How to address eating disorders: An overview of screening and treatment in primary care. *Women's Health in Primary Care, 6,* 75–81.

Russell, S. T., & Seif, H. (2002). Bisexual female adolescents: A critical analysis of past research, and results from a national survey. *Journal of Bisexuality, 2,* 73–94.

Russo, N. F. (1979). Overview: Roles, fertility and the motherhood mandate. *Psychology of Women Quarterly, 4,* 7–15.

Russo, N. F. (2008). Understanding emotional responses after abortion. In J. C. Chrisler, C. Golden, & P. D. Rozee (Eds.), *Lectures on the psychology of women* (pp. 172–189). New York: McGraw-Hill.

Russo, N. F., & Tartaro, J. (2008). Women and mental health. In F. L. Denmark & M. A. Paludi (Eds.), *Psychology of women: A handbook of issues and theories* (2nd ed., pp. 440–483). Westport, CT: Praeger.

Russo, N. F., & Vaz, K. (2001). Addressing diversity in the decade of behavior: Focus on women of color. *Psychology of Women Quarterly, 25,* 280–294.

Rust, J., et al. (2000). The role of brothers and sisters in the development of preschool children. *Journal of Experimental Child Psychology, 77,* 292–303.

Rust, P. C. (2000). Bisexuality: A contemporary paradox for women. *Journal of Social Issues, 56,* 205–221.

Rust, P. C. (2001). Too many and not enough: The meanings of bisexual identities. *Journal of Bisexuality, 1,* 33–68.

Rutenberg, J. (2002, June 3). News anchors and the cathode-ray ceiling. *New York Times,* pp. C1, C8.

Rutter, M., et al. (2004). Sex differences in developmental reading disability. *Journal of the American Medical Association, 291,* 2007–2012.

Ryan, M. K., David, B., & Reynolds, K. J. (2004). Who cares? The effect of gender and context on the self and moral reasoning. *Psychology of Women Quarterly, 28,* 246–255.

Ryan, M. K., & Haslam, S. A. (2007). The glass cliff: Exploring the dynamics surrounding women's appointment to precarious leadership positions. *Academy of Management Review, 32,* 549–572.

Sachs-Ericsson, N., Blazer, D., Plant, E. A., & Arnow, B. (2005). Childhood sexual and physical abuse and the 1-year prevalence of medical problems in the national comorbidity survey. *Health Psychology, 24*, 32–40.

Sachs-Ericsson, N., & Ciarlo, J. A. (2000). Gender, social roles, and mental health: An epidemiological perspective. *Sex Roles, 43*, 605–628.

Sack, K. (2008, April 27). The short end of the longer life. *New York Times*, pp. WK1, WK4.

Sadker, M., & Sadker, D. (1994). *Failing at fairness: How America's schools cheat girls*. New York: Scribner.

Sadler, A. G., Booth, B. M., & Doebbeling, B. N. (2005). Gang and multiple rapes during military service: Health consequences and health care. *Journal of the American Medical Women's Association, 60*, 33–41.

Sadler, A. G., Booth, B. M., Mengeling, M. A., & Doebbeling, B. N. (2004). Life span and repeated violence against women during military service: Effects on health status and outpatient utilization. *Journal of Women's Health, 13*, 799–811.

Saewyc, E., Skay, C., Richens, K., Reis, E., Poon, C., & Murphy, A. (2006). Sexual orientation, sexual abuse, and HIV-risk behaviors among adolescents in the Pacific Northwest. *American Journal of Public Health, 96*, 1104–1110.

Saewyc, E. M., Pettingell, S. L., & Skay, C. L. (2004). Hazards of stigma: The sexual and physical abuse of gay, lesbian, and bisexual adolescents in the U.S. and Canada. *Journal of Adolescent Health, 34*, 115–116.

Saftlas, A. F., et al. (2000). Racial disparity in pregnancy-related mortality associated with live birth: Can established risk factors explain it? *American Journal of Epidemiology, 152*, 413–419.

Sahyoun, N. R., Pratt, L. A., Lentzner, H., Dey, A., & Robinson, K. N. (2001). *The changing profile of nursing home residents: 1985–1997: Aging trends, No. 4*. Hyattsville, MD: National Center for Health Statistics.

St. John, W. (2002, May 20). The talk of the book world still can't sell. *New York Times*, pp. A1, A16.

Salganicoff, A., Wentworth, B., & Greene, L. (2003). Baby boom to generation X: Progress in young women's health. In C. B. Costello, V. R. Wight, & A. J. Stone (Eds.), *The American woman 2003–2004: Daughters of a revolution—young women today* (pp. 93–126). New York: Palgrave Macmillan.

Salomone, R. (2007, February 16). A place for women's colleges. *The Chronicle of Higher Education*, p. B20.

Samuels, A. (2004, July 5). Smooth operations. *Newsweek*, pp. 48–49.

Sanchez, P., Hucles, P., Sanchez-Hucles, J., & Mehta, S. C. (2007). Increasing diverse women leadership in corporate America: Climbing concrete walls and shattering glass ceilings! In J. L. Chin, B. Lott, J. K. Rice & J. Sanchez-Hucles (Eds.), *Women and leadership: Transforming visions and diverse voices* (pp. 228–244). Malden, MA: Blackwell Publishing.

Sanchez-Hucles, J. V. (2003). Intimate relationships. In L. Slater, J. H. Daniel, & A. E. Banks (Eds.), *The complete guide to mental health for women* (pp. 104–120). Boston: Beacon Press.

Sanci, L., et al. (2008). Childhood sexual abuse and eating disorders in females. *Archives of Pediatrics and Adolescent Medicine, 162*, 261–267.

Sanderson, C. A. (2004). *Health psychology*. New York: Wiley.

Sanderson, S., & Thompson, V. L. S. (2002). Factors associated with perceived paternal involvement in childrearing. *Sex Roles, 46*, 99–111.

Sandfort, T., Bakker, F., Vanwesenbeeck, I., & Schellevis, F. (2006). Sexual orientation and mental and physical health status: Finding from a Dutch population survey. *American Journal of Public Health, 96*, 1119–1125.

Sandler, B., Silverberg, L. A,, & Hall, R. M. (1996). *The chilly classroom climate: A guide to improve the education of women*. Washington, DC: National Association for Women in Education.

Sandnabba, N. K., & Ahlberg, C. (1999). Parents' attitudes and expectations about children's cross-gender behavior. *Sex Roles, 40*, 249–263.

Sang-Hun, C. (2007, December 23). South Korea, where boys were kings, revalues its girls. *New York Times*, pp. YT1, YT16.

Sanmartin, C., et al. (2004). *Joint Canada/United States survey of health, 2002–03*. Centers for Disease Control and Prevention and *Statistics Canada*. Catalogue 82M0022-XIE.

Santelli, J. S., et al. (2003). Reproductive health in school-based health centers: Findings from the 1998–99 census of school-based health centers. *Journal of Adolescent Health, 32*, 443–451.

Santelli, J. S., et al. (2004). Initiation of sexual intercourse among middle school adolescents: The influence of psychosocial factors. *Journal of Adolescent Health, 34*, 200–208.

Santelli, J. S. Lindberg, L., Finer, L., & Singh, S. (2007). Explaining recent declines in adolescent pregnancy in the United States: The contribution of abstinence and improved contraceptive use. *American Journal of Public Health, 97*, 150–156.

Santelli, J. S., Morrow, B., & Carter, M. (2004). Trends in contraceptive use among U.S. high school students in the 1990s. *Journal of Adolescent Health, 34*, 140.

Santora, M. (2005, January 30). U.S. is close to eliminating AIDS in infants, officials say. *New York Times*, pp. YT1, YT22.

Sanz de Acedo Lizarraga, M. L., & García Ganuza, J. M. (2003). Improvement of mental rotation in girls and boys. *Sex Roles, 49*, 277–286.

Saraiya, M., Ahmed, F., Krishnan, S., Richards, T. B., Unger, E. R., & Lawson, H. W. (2007). Cervical cancer incidence in a prevaccine era in the United States, 1998–2002. *Obstetrics & Gynecology, 109*, 360–370.

Sarto, G. E. (2004). The gender gap: New challenges in women's health. *Sexuality, Reproduction & Menopause, 2*, 9–14.

Sarwer, D. B., et al. (2005). Female college students and cosmetic surgery: An investigation of experiences, attitudes, and body image. *Plastic and Reconstructive Surgery, 115*, 931–938.

Sassi, F., Luft, H., & Guadagnoli, E. (2006). Reducing racial/ethnic disparities in female breast cancer: Screening rates and stage at diagnosis. *American Journal of Public Health, 96*, 2165–2172.

Sassler, S. (2004). The process of entering into cohabiting unions. *Journal of Marriage and Family, 66*, 491–505.

Saunders, K., & Kashubeck, S. (2002, August). *The relations among feminism, gender-role orientation, and psychological well-being in women.* Paper presented at the meeting of the American Psychological Association, Chicago.

Saunders, K. J., & Kashubeck-West, S. (2006). The relations among feminist identity development, gender-role orientation, and psychological well-being in women. *Psychology of Women Quarterly, 30,* 199–211.

Save the Children. (2006). *State of the world's mothers 2006.* Westport, CT: Author.

Save the Children. (2007). *State of the world's mothers 2007.* Westport, CT: Author.

Savin-Williams, R. C. (2006). Who's gay? Does it matter? *Current Directions in Psychological Science, 15,* 40–44.

Savin-Williams, R. C. (2007). Girl-on-girl sexuality. In B. J. R. Leadbeater & N. Way (Eds.), *Urban girls revisited: Building strengths* (pp. 301–318). New York: New York University Press.

Savin-Williams, R. C., & Diamond, L. M. (2004). Sex. In R. M. Lerner & L. Steinberg (Eds.), *Handbook of adolescent psychology* (2nd ed., pp. 189–231). Hoboken, NJ: Wiley.

Savin-Williams, R. C., & Ream, G. L. (2003). Sex variations in the disclosure to parents of same-sex attractions. *Journal of Family Psychology, 17,* 429–438.

Sawaya, G. F., et al. (2003). Risk of cervical cancer associated with extending the interval between cervical-cancer screenings. *New England Journal of Medicine, 349,* 1501–1509.

Saxbe, D. E., Repetti, R. L., & Nishina, A. (2008). Marital satisfaction, recovery from work, and diurnal cortisol among men and women. *Health Psychology, 27,* 15–25.

Sayal, K., Heron, J., Golding, J., & Emond, A. (2007). Prenatal alcohol exposure and gender differences in childhood mental health problems: A longitudinal population-based study. *Pediatrics, 119,* 426–434.

Sayer, L. C., & Bianchi, S. M. (2000). Women's economic independence and the probability of divorce: A review and reexamination. *Journal of Family Issues, 21,* 906–943.

Scarborough, E. (2005, Winter). Constructing a women's history of psychology. *The Feminist Psychologist,* p. 6.

Schafer, J., Caetano, R., & Cunradi, C. B. (2004). A path model of risk factors for intimate partner violence among couples in the United States. *Journal of Interpersonal Violence, 19,* 127–142.

Schaidle, C. (2003, December 4). Manufacturers are playing makeup in creating more toys that appeal to both girls and boys. *Peoria Journal Star,* pp. C9–C10.

Scharf, M., Shulman, S., & Avigad-Spitz, L. (2005). Sibling relationships in emerging adulthood and in adolescence. *Journal of Adolescent Research, 20,* 64–90.

Schein, V. E. (2001). A global look at psychological barriers to women's progress in management. *Journal of Social Issues, 57,* 675–688.

Schemo, D. J. (2000a, December 28). Sex education with just one lesson: No sex. *New York Times,* pp. A1, A18.

Schemo, D. J. (2000b, October 4). Survey finds parents favor more detailed sex education. *New York Times,* pp. A1, A23.

Scherzer, L. (2002, Fall). Older & bolder. *Barnard Alumnae Magazine,* pp. 20–22.

Schewe, P. A. (Ed.). (2002). *Preventing violence in relationships: Interventions across the life span.* Washington, DC: American Psychological Association.

Schiffman, J. B., DeLucia-Waack, J. L., & Gerrity, D. A. (2005). An examination of the construct of homophobia: Prejudice or phobia? *Journal of LGBT Issues in Counseling, 1,* 75–93.

Schlenker, J. A., Caron, S. L., & Halteman, W. A. (1998). A feminist analysis of *Seventeen* magazine: Content analysis from 1945 to 1995. *Sex Roles, 38,* 135–150.

Schmader, T., Johns, M., & Barquissau, M. (2004). The costs of accepting gender differences: The role of stereotype endorsement in women's experience in the math domain. *Sex Roles, 50,* 835–850.

Schmaling, K. B. (2000). Poorly understood conditions. In M. B. Goldman & M. C. Hatch (Eds.), *Women & Health* (pp. 1055–1057). San Diego: Academic Press.

Schmitt, E. (2004, February 26). Rapes reported by servicewomen in the Persian Gulf and elsewhere. *New York Times,* pp. A1, A16.

Schmitt, M. T., Branscombe, N. R., Kobrynowicz, D., & Owen, S. (2002). Perceiving discrimination against one's gender group has different implications for well-being in women and men. *Personality and Social Psychology Bulletin, 28,* 197–210.

Schneider, L. S. (2004). Estrogen and dementia. Insights from the women's health initiative memory study. *Journal of the American Medical Association, 291,* 3005–3007.

Schnieder, S. L. (2001). In search of realistic optimism: Meaning, knowledge, and warm fuzziness. *American Psychologist, 56,* 250–263.

Schnittker, J. (2007). Working more and feeling better: Women's health, employment, and family life, 1974–2004. *American Sociological Review, 72,* 221–238.

Schoen, R., et al. (2002). Women's employment, marital happiness, and divorce. *Social Forces, 81,* 643–662.

Schoenberg, N. E., Peters, J. C., & Drew, E. M. (2003). Unraveling the mysteries of timing: Women's perceptions about time to treatment for cardiac symptoms. *Social Science & Medicine, 56,* 271–284.

Scholler, D. (2008) Real women have curves: A longitudinal investigation of TV and the body image development of Latina adolescents. *Journal of Adolescent Research, 23,* 132–153.

Schooler, D., Ward, L. M., Merriwether, A., & Caruthers, A. (2004). Who's that girl: Television's role in the body image development of young White and Black women. *Psychology of Women Quarterly, 28,* 38–47.

Schoolgirls under fire. (2007, July 12). *New York Times,* p. A22.

Schroeder, K. A., Blood, L. L., & Maluso, D. (1992). An intergenerational analysis of expectations for women's career and family roles. *Sex Roles, 26,* 273–291.

Schulman, A. (2003). Female sexuality. In L. Slater, J. H. Daniel, & A. E. Banks (Eds.), *The complete guide to mental health for women* (pp. 82–91). Boston: Beacon Press.

Schulz, A. J., Israel, B. A., Gravlee, C. C., Mentz, G., Williams, D. R., & Rowe, Z. (2006). Discrimination, symptoms of depression, and self-rated health among African American women in Detroit: Results for a longitudinal analysis. *American Journal of Public Health, 96*, 1265–1270.

Schulz, R., et al. (2003). End-of-life care and the effects of bereavement on family caregivers of persons with dementia. *New England Journal of Medicine, 349*, 1936–1942.

Schumacher, J. A., & Leonard, K. E. (2005). Husbands' and wives' adjustment, verbal aggression, and physical aggression as longitudinal predictors of physical aggression in early marriage. *Journal of Consulting Psychology, 73*, 28–37.

Schwartz, L. M., Woloshin, S., Fowler, Jr., F. J., & Welch, H. G. (2004). Enthusiasm for cancer screening in the United States. *Journal of the American Medical Association, 291*, 71–78.

Schwartz, P. (2007). *Prime: Adventures and advice on sex, love, and the sensual years.* New York: HarperCollins.

Sciolino, E. (2003, October 10). A prize, laureate says, "good for democracy." *New York Times*, p. A6.

Sears, D. O. (1997). College sophomores in the laboratory: Influences of a narrow data base on psychology's view of human nature. In L. A. Peplau & S. E. Taylor (Eds.), *Sociocultural perspectives in social psychology: Current readings* (pp. 20–51). Upper Saddle River, NJ: Prentice Hall.

Sears-Roberts Alterovitz, S., & Mendelsohn, G. A. (2008, May). *Online dating by older adults: What is sought? What is offered?* Poster presented at the meeting of the Association for Psychological Science, Chicago.

Seaver, M. R., Freund, K. M., Wright, L. M., Tjia, J., & Frayne, S. M. (2008). Healthcare preferences among lesbians: A focus group analysis. *Journal of Women's Health, 17*, 215–225.

Sechzer, J., & Rabinowitz, V. C. (2008). Feminist perspectives on research methods. In F. L. Denmark & M. A. Paludi (Eds.), *Psychology of women: A handbook of issues and theories* (2nd ed., pp. 93–141). Westport, CT: Praeger.

Sedgh, G., Henshaw, S., Singh, S., Åhman, E., & Shah, I. H. (2007). Induced abortion: Estimated rates and trends worldwide. *Lancet, 370*, 1338–1345.

Seem, S. R., & Clark, M. D. (2006). Healthy women, healthy men, and healthy adults: An evaluation of gender role stereotypes in the twenty-first century. *Sex Roles, 55*, 247–258.

Seibring, A. (2003). Living with infertility. In L. Slater, J. H. Daniel, & A. E. Banks (Eds.), *The complete guide to mental health for women* (pp. 10–17). Boston: Beacon Press.

Seitz, V. (1996). Adolescent pregnancy and parenting. In E. F. Ziegler, L. Kagen, & N. W. Hall (Eds.), *Children, families and government* (pp. 268–287). New York: Cambridge University Press.

Selingo, J. (1998, February 20). Science-oriented campuses strive to attract more women. *Chronicle of Higher Education*, pp. A53–A54.

Sellers, N., Satcher, J., & Comas, R. (1999). Children's occupational aspirations: Comparisons by gender, gender role identity, and socioeconomic status. *Professional School Counseling, 2*, 314–317.

Selwyn, N. (2007). Hi-tech = Guy-tech? An exploration of undergraduate students' gendered perceptions of information and communication technologies. *Sex Roles, 56*, 525–536.

Sengupta, R. (2006). Reading representations of Black, East Asian, and White women in magazines for adolescent girls. *Sex Roles, 54*, 799–808.

Serbin, L. A., Powlishta, K. K., & Gulko, J. (1993). The development of sex-typing in middle childhood. *Monographs of the Society for Research in Child Development, 58* (Serial No. 232), 1–95.

Serbin, L. A., et al. (2001). Gender stereotyping in infancy: Visual preferences for knowledge of gender-stereotyped toys in the second year. *International Journal of Behavioral Development, 25*, 7–15.

Serbin, L. A., et al. (2004). When aggressive girls become mothers: Problems in parenting, health, and development across two generations. In M. Putallaz & K. L. Bierman (Eds.), *Aggression, antisocial behavior, and violence among girls: A developmental perspective* (pp. 262–288). New York: Guilford.

Serewicz, M. C. M., & Gale, E. (2007). First-date scripts: Gender roles, context, and relationship. *Sex Roles, 58*, 149–164.

Serran, G., & Firestone, P. (2004). Intimate partner homicide: A review of the male proprietariness and the self-defense theories. *Aggression and Violent Behavior, 9*, 1–15.

Settles, I. H., Cortina, L. M., Stewart, A. J., & Malley, J. (2007). Voice matters: Buffering the impact of a negative climate for women in science. *Psychology of Women Quarterly, 31*, 270–281.

Sexual Assault Awareness Month—April 2005. *Morbidity and Mortality Weekly Report, 54*, 311.

Shaffer, D. R., & Wittes, E. (2006). Women's precollege sports participation, enjoyment of sports, and self-esteem. *Sex Roles, 55*, 225–232.

Shakin, M., Shakin, D., & Sternglanz, S. H. (1985). Infant clothing: Sex labeling for strangers. *Sex Roles, 12*, 955–964.

Shanok, A. F., & Miller, L. (2007). Stepping up to motherhood among inner-city teens. *Psychology of Women Quarterly, 31*, 252–261.

Shapiro, J. R., Berkman, N. D., Brownley, K. A., Sedway, J. A., Lohr, K. N., & Bulik, C. M. (2007). Bulimia nervosa treatment: A systematic review of randomized controlled trials. *International Journal of Eating Disorders, 40*, 321–336.

Shapka, J. D., Domene, J. F., & Keating, D. P. (2008). Gender, mathematics achievement, and the educational and occupational aspirations of Canadian youth. In H. M. G. Watt & J. S. Eccles (Eds.), *Gender and occupational outcomes: Longitudinal assessments of individual, social, and cultural influences* (pp. 27–54). Washington, DC: American Psychological Association.

Share, T. L., & Mintz, L. B. (2002). Differences between lesbians and heterosexual women in disordered eating and related attitudes. *Journal of Homosexuality, 42*, 89–106.

Sharp, E. A., & Ganong, L. (2007). Living in the gray: Women's experiences of missing the marital transition. *Journal of Marriage and Family, 69*, 831–844.

Sheehy, G. (1991). *The silent passage.* New York: Random House.

Sheehy, G. (2002, May 12). It's about pure love. *Parade Magazine*, pp. 6–8.

Sheehy, G. (2007). *Sex and the seasoned woman: Pursuing the passionate life*. New York: Ballantine.

Sheeran, P., Abraham, C., & Orbell, S. (1999). Psychosocial correlates of heterosexual condom use: A meta-analysis. *Psychological Bulletin, 125*, 90–132.

Sheldon, J. P. (2004). Gender stereotypes in educational software for young children. *Sex Roles, 51*, 433–444.

Sheldon, K. M. (2007). Gender differences in preferences for singles ads that proclaim extrinsic versus intrinsic values. *Sex Roles, 57*, 119–129.

Shellenbarger, S. (2004). *The breaking point: How female midlife crisis is transforming today's women*. New York: Holt.

Shellenbarger, S. (2008, March 20). In search of wedded bliss: What research can tell us. *The Wall Street Journal*, p. D1.

Shelton, J. N., & Stewart, R. E. (2004). Confronting perpetrators of prejudice: The inhibitory effects of social costs. *Psychology of Women Quarterly, 28*, 215–223.

Shepela, S. T., & Levesque, L. L. (1998). Poisoned waters: Sexual harassment and the college climate. *Sex Roles, 38*, 589–611.

Sherman, S. R. (2001). Images of middle-aged and older women: Historical, cultural, and personal. In J. M. Coyle (Ed.), *Handbook on women and aging* (pp. 14–28). Westport, CT: Greenwood.

Sherry, B., et al. (2004). Attitudes, practices, and concerns about child feeding and child weight status among socioeconomically diverse White, Hispanic, and African-American mothers. *Journal of the American Dietetic Association, 104*, 215–221.

Sherwin, B. B. (2001). Menopause: Myths and realities. In N. L. Stotland & D. E. Stewart (Eds.), *Psychological aspects of women's health care* (pp. 241–259). Washington, DC: American Psychiatric Press.

Sherwin, B. B. (2007). Does estrogen protect against cognitive aging in women? *Current Directions in Psychological Science, 16*, 275–279.

Sheth, S. S. (2006). Missing female births in India. *Lancet, 367*, 185–186.

Shorter-Gooden, K., & Washington, N. C. (1996). Young, black and female: The challenge of weaving an identity. *Journal of Adolescence, 19*, 465–475.

Shupe, E. I., Cortina, L. M., Ramas, A., Fitzgerald, L. F., & Salisbury, J. (2002). The incidence and outcomes of sexual harassment among Hispanic and non-Hispanic White women: A comparison across levels of cultural affiliation. *Psychology of Women Quarterly, 26*, 298–308.

Shute, R., Owens, L., & Slee, P. (2008). Everyday victimization of adolescent girls by boys: Sexual harassment, bullying or aggression? *Sex Roles, 58*, 477–489.

Sices, L., et al. (2004). How do primary care physicians manage children with possible developmental delays? A national survey with an experimental design. *Pediatrics, 113*, 274–282.

Sidener, J. (2004, September 27). Digital dating: A growing number of seniors are looking for love online. *Peoria Journal Star*, pp. C5, C6.

Siebenbruner, J., Zimmer-Gembeck, M. J., & Egeland, B. (2007). Sexual partners and contraceptive use: A 16-year prospective study predicting abstinence and risk behavior. *Journal of Research on Adolescence, 17*, 179–206.

Siegel, J. M. (2002, January). Body image change and adolescent depressive symptoms. *Journal of Adolescent Research, 17*, 27–41.

Sieving, R. E., Eisenberg, M. E., Pettingell, S., & Skay, C. (2006). Friends' influence on adolescents' first sexual intercourse. *Perspectives on Sexual and Reproductive Health, 38*, 13–19.

Sigal, J., et al. (2005). Cross-cultural reactions to academic sexual harassment: Effects of individualist vs. collectivist culture and gender of participants. *Sex Roles, 52*, 201–215.

Sigal, J., & Annan, V., Jr. (2008). Violence against women: International workplace sexual harassment and domestic violence. In F. L. Denmark & M. A. Paludi (Eds.), *Psychology of women: A handbook of issues and theories* (2nd ed., pp. 590–622). Westport, CT: Praeger.

Signorella, M. L., & Frieze, I. H. (1989). Gender schemes in college students. *Psychology: A Journal of Human Behavior, 26*, 16–23.

Signorielli, N. (1997, April). *A content analysis: Reflections of girls in the media*. Menlo Park, CA: Children Now and the Henry J. Kaiser Family Foundation.

Signorielli, N., & Bacue, A. (1999). Recognition and respect: A content analysis of prime-time television characters across the decades. *Sex Roles, 40*, 527–544.

Sikkema, K. J., Wagner, L. I., & Bogart, L. M. (2000). Gender and cultural factors in the prevention of HIV infection among women. In R. M. Eisler & M. Hersen (Eds.), *Handbook of gender, culture, and health* (pp. 299–320). Mahwah, NJ: Erlbaum.

Silenzio, V. M. B., Pena, J. B., Duberstein, P. R., Cerel, J., & Knox, K. L. (2007). Sexual orientation and risk factors for suicidal ideation and suicide attempts among adolescents and young adults. *American Journal of Public Health, 97*, 2017–2019.

Silver, R. B., Measelle, J. R., & Stice, E. (2007, March). *Developmental trajectories of antisocial behavior in adolescent females: Trajectory classes, predictors, and outcomes*. Poster presented at the meeting of the Society for Research in Child Development, Boston.

Silverman, W. K., & Carter, R. (2006). Anxiety disturbance in girls and women. In J. Worell & C. D. Goodheart (Eds.), *Handbook of girls' and women's psychological health: Gender and well-being across the lifespan* (pp. 60–68). New York: Oxford University Press.

Silverschanz, P., Cortina, L. M., Konik, J., & Magley, V. J. (2008). Slurs, snubs, and queer jokes: Incidence and impact of heterosexist harassment in academia. *Sex Roles, 58*, 179–191.

Simmons, R. G., & Blyth, D. A. (1987). *Moving into adolescence: The impact of pubertal change and school context*. Hawthorne, NY: Aldine de Gruyter.

Simmons, T., & Dye, J. L. (2003). *Grandparents living with grandchildren: 2000*. Census 2000 Brief. Washington, DC: U.S. Census Bureau.

Simon, H. B. (2004, June). Longevity: The ultimate gender gap. *Science*, pp. 18–23.

Simon, R. J. (1998, October 2). What are the most pressing issues today in relations between men and women? Race and class drive most conflict now. *Chronicle of Higher Education*, p. B6.

Simon, R. W. (1995). Gender, multiple roles, role meaning, and mental health. *Journal of Health and Social Behavior, 36*, 182–194.

Simon, R. W., & Nath, L. E. (2004). Gender and emotion in the United States: Do men and women differ in self-reports of feelings and expressive behavior? *American Journal of Sociology, 109*, 1137–1176.

Simon, V. R., et al. (2005). *National Institutes of Health: Intramural and extramural support for research on sex differences, 2000–2003.* Washington, DC: Society for Women's Health Research.

Simons, R. L. (1996). The effect of divorce on adult and child adjustment. In R. L. Simons & Associates, *Understanding differences between divorced and intact families: Stress, interaction, and child outcome* (pp. 3–20). Thousand Oaks, CA: Sage.

Simpkins, S. D., Davis-Kean, P. E., & Eccles, J. S. (2005). Parents' socializing behavior and children's participation in math, science, and computer out-of-school activities. *Applied Developmental Science, 9*, 14–30.

Simpkins, S. D., Davis-Kean, P. E., & Eccles, J. S. (2006). Math and science motivation: A longitudinal examination of the links between choices and beliefs. *Developmental Psychology, 42*, 70–83.

Simpson, G. (1996). Factors influencing the choice of law as a career by Black women. *Journal of Career Development, 22*, 197–209.

Sims, M., Hutchins, T., & Taylor, M. (1998). Gender segregation in young children's conflict behavior in child care settings. *Child Study Journal, 28*(1), 1–16.

Singer, N. (2006, March 30). Does the sex of the surgeon matter? *New York Times*, p. E3.

Singer, N. (2007, October 4). Is the 'mom job' really necessary? *New York Times*, pp. E1, E3.

Singh, G. K., & Siahpush, M. (2006). Widening socioeconomic inequalities in US life expectancy, 1980–2000. *International Journal of Epidemiology, 35*, 969–979.

Singh, S., Darroch, J. E., Vlassoff, M., & Nadeau, J. (2003). *Adding it up: The benefits of investing in sexual and reproductive health care.* New York & Washington, DC: Alan Guttmacher Institute.

Singh-Manoux, A., Hillsdon, M., Brunner, E., & Marmot, M. (2005). Effects of physical activity on cognitive functioning in middle age: Evidence from the Whitehall II prospective cohort study. *American Journal of Public Health, 95*, 2252–2258.

Sit, D. (2004). Women and bipolar disorder across the life span. *Journal of the American Medical Women's Association, 59*, 91–100.

Sit, D., Rothschild, A. J., & Wisner, K. L. (2006). A review of postpartum psychosis. *Journal of Women's Health, 15*, 352–368.

Skaalvik, S. (2004). Gender differences in math and verbal self-concept, performance expectations, and motivation. *Sex Roles, 50*, 241–252.

Skerrett, P. J., & Leopold, J. A. (2008, January 21). How to solve three problems: Heart disease in women. *Newsweek*, p. 66.

Sklar, J. B. (2000). Elder and dependent adult fraud: A sampler of actual cases to profile the offenders and the crimes they perpetrate. *Journal of Elder Abuse & Neglect, 12*, 19–32.

Skoe, E. E. A., Cumberland, A., Eisenberg, N., Hansen, K., & Perry, J. (2002). The influences of sex and gender-idle identity on moral cognition and prosocial personality traits. *Sex Roles, 46*, 295–309.

Slaughter-Defoe, D. T., Addae, W. A., & Bell, C. (2002). Toward the future schooling of girls: Global status, issues, and prospects. *Human Development, 45*, 34–53.

Small, F. L., & Schultz, R. W. (1990). Quantifying gender differences in physical performance: A developmental perspective. *Developmental Psychology, 26*, 360–369.

Smallwood, S. (2002, April 5). Women still feel marginalized at MIT, study finds. *Chronicle of Higher Education*, p. A9.

Smetana, J. G., & Daddis, C. (2002). Domain-specific antecedents of parental psychological control and monitoring: The role of parenting beliefs and practices. *Child Development, 73*, 563–580.

Smetana, J. G., Metzger, A., & Campione-Barr, N. (2004). African American late adolescents' relationships with parents: Developmental transitions and longitudinal patterns. *Child Development, 75*, 932–947.

Smirles, K. E. (2004). Attributions of responsibility in cases of sexual harassment: The person and the situation. *Journal of Applied Social Psychology, 34*, 342–365.

Smith, C. A. (2008). Women, weight, and body image. In J. C. Chrisler, C. Golden, & P. D. Rozee (Eds.), *Lectures on the psychology of women* (pp. 116–135). New York: McGraw-Hill.

Smith, C. A., & Stillman, S. (2002a). Butch/femme in the personal advertisements of lesbians. *Journal of Lesbian Studies, 6*(1), 45–51.

Smith, C. A., & Stillman, S. (2002b). What do women want? The effects of gender and sexual orientation on the desirability of physical attributes in the personal ads of women. *Sex Roles, 46*, 337–342.

Smith, D. (2002, May). Studies garner groundbreaking data. *Monitor on Psychology*, pp. 44–45.

Smith, D. (2005, January 16). Brown: Let women lead Africa out of poverty. *Sunday Times (London)*, p. 8.

Smith, G., Mysak, K., & Michael, S. (2008). Sexual double standards and sexually transmitted illnesses: Social rejection and stigmatization of women. *Sex Roles, 58*, 391–401.

Smith, J. L. (2006). The interplay among stereotypes, performance-avoidance goals, and women's math performance expectations. *Sex Roles, 54*, 287–296.

Smith, K. (2002). *Who's minding the kids? Child care arrangements: Spring 1997.* Current Population Reports, P70–86. Washington, DC: U.S. Census Bureau.

Smith, L. (2005). Psychotherapy, classism, and the poor: Conspicuous by their absence. *American Psychologist, 60*, 687–696.

Smith, L. (2007, June 29). Black female participation languishes outside basketball and track. *The Chronicle of Higher Education*, p. A34.

Smith, M. (1980). Sex bias in counseling and psychotherapy. *Psychological Bulletin, 87*, 392–407.

Smith, M. A., Boyd, L., Osuch, J. R., & Schwartz, K. (2000). Breast disorders. In M. A. Smith & L. A. Shimp (Eds.), *20 common problems in women's health care* (pp. 473–477). New York: McGraw-Hill.

Smith, R. A., & Saslow, D. (2002). Breast cancer. In G. M. Wingood & R. J. DiClemente (Eds.), *Handbook of women's sexual and reproductive health* (pp. 345–365). New York: Kluwer Academic/Plenum.

Smith, T. W. (1994). Attitudes toward sexual permissiveness: Trends, correlates, and behavioral connections. In A. S. Rossi (Ed.), *Sexuality across the life course* (pp. 63–97). Chicago: University of Chicago Press.

Smith, T. W. (1999). *The emerging 21st century American family*. Chicago: University of Chicago, National Opinion Research Center.

Smith, T. W. (2003). *American sexual behavior: Trends, sociodemographic differences, and risk behavior*. Chicago: National Opinion Research Center, University of Chicago.

Smock, P. J., & Manning, W. D. (2004). *Living together unmarried in the United States: Demographic perspectives and implications for family policy*. PSC Research Report No. 04-555, Institute for Social Research, University of Michigan.

Smolak, L. (2006). Body image. In J. Worell & C. D. Goodheart (Eds.), *Handbook of girls' and women's psychological health: Gender and well-being across the lifespan* (pp. 69–76). New York: Oxford University Press.

Smolak, L., & Munstertieger, B. F. (2002). The relationship of gender and voice to depression and eating disorders. *Psychology of Women Quarterly, 26*, 234–241.

Smolak, L., Murnen S. K., & Ruble, A. E. (2000). Female athletes and eating problems: A meta-analysis. *Eating Disorders, 27*, 371–380.

Smolak, L., & Striegel-Moore, R. (2001). Body image concerns. In J. Worell (Ed.), *Encyclopedia of women and gender* (pp. 201–210). San Diego: Academic Press.

Snell, M. B. (2002, November/December). Good going. *Sierra*, pp. 26–27.

Snow, D. L., Sullivan, T. P., Swan, S. C., Tate, D. C., & Klein, I. (2006). The role of coping and problem drinking in men's abuse of female partners: Test of a path model. *Violence and Victims, 21*, 267–285.

Snyder, N. M. (1994). Career women and motherhood: Child care dilemmas and choices. In C. W. Konek & S. L. Kitch (Eds.), *Women and careers: Issues and challenges* (pp. 155–172). Thousand Oaks, CA: Sage.

Söchting, I., Fairbrother, N., & Koch, W. J. (2004). Sexual assault of women. *Violence against Women, 10*, 73–92.

Social Security Administration. (2007). *Retirement benefits* SSA Publication No. 05-10035. Washington, DC: U.S. Government Printing Office.

Society for Women's Health Research. (2005). *Women's fear of heart disease has almost doubled, but breast cancer remains the single most feared disease*. Washington, DC: Author.

Solarz, A. L. (Ed.). (1999). *Lesbian health: Current assessment and directions for the future*. Washington, DC: National Academy Press.

Solomon, C. (2005, July 17). Mean girls. *New York Times*, p. AR4.

Sommer, B., et al. (1999). Attitudes toward menopause and aging across ethnic/racial groups. *Psychosomatic Medicine, 61*, 868–875.

Sommers, C. H. (2000). *The war against boys: How misguided feminism is harming our young men*. New York: Simon & Schuster.

Sonnert, G., & Holton, G. (1996). Career patterns of women and men in the sciences. *American Scientist, 84*, 63–71.

Sontag, S. (1979). The double standard of aging. In J. H. Williams (Ed.), *Psychology of women: Selected readings* (pp. 462–478). New York: Norton.

Sorenson, S. B. (1996). Violence against women: Examining ethnic differences and commonalities. *Evaluation Review, 20*, 123–145.

Sowers, M. R. (2000). Menopause: Its epidemiology. In M. B. Goldman & M. C. Hatch (Eds.), *Women & health* (pp. 1155–1168). New York: Academic Press.

Spanier, B. B. (1997). Sexism and scientific research. *National Forum, 77*(2), 26–30.

Spar, D. (2007). The egg trade—making sense of the market for human oocytes. *New England Journal of Medicine, 356*, 1289–1291.

Spataro, J., et al. (2004). Impact of child sexual abuse on mental health. *British Journal of Psychiatry, 184*, 416–421.

Speiser, P. W., & White, P. C. (2003). Congenital adrenal hyperplasia. *New England Journal of Medicine, 349*, 776–788.

Spelke, E. S. (2005). Sex differences in intrinsic aptitude for mathematics and science? A critical review. *American Psychologist, 60*, 950–958.

Spence, J. T., & Buckner, C. E. (2000). Instrumental and expressive traits, trait stereotypes, and sexist attitudes: What do they signify? *Psychology of Women Quarterly, 24*, 44–62.

Spence, J. T., & Helmreich, R. L. (1978). *Masculinity & femininity: Their psychological dimensions, correlates, & antecedents*. Austin: University of Texas Press.

Spence, J. T., Helmreich, R. L., & Stapp, J. (1974). The Personal Attributes Questionnaire: A measure of sex-role stereotypes and masculinity-femininity. *JSAS Catalog of Selected Documents in Psychology, 4* (Ms. No. 617).

Spencer, J. M., et al. (2002). Self-esteem as a predictor of initiation of coitus in early adolescents. *Pediatrics, 109*, 581–584.

Spencer, S. J., Steele, C. M., & Quinn, D. M. (1999). Stereotype threat and women's math performance. *Journal of Experimental Social Psychology, 35*, 4–28.

Spicher, C. H., & Hudak, M. A. (1997, August). *Gender role portrayal on Saturday morning cartoons: An update*. Paper presented at the meeting of the American Psychological Association, Chicago.

Spiegel, D. (1998). Getting there is half the fun: Relating happiness to health. *Psychological Inquiry, 9*, 66–68.

Spiegel, D., Bloom, J. R., Kraemer, H. C., & Gottheil, E. (1989). Effect of psychosocial treatment on survival of patients with metastatic breast cancer. *Lancet, 2*, 888–891.

Spitze, G., & Trent, K. (2006). Gender differences in adult sibling relations in two-child families. *Journal of Marriage and Family, 68*, 977–992.

Spitzer, B. L., Henderson, K. A., & Zivian, M. T. (1999). Gender differences in population versus media body sizes: A comparison over four decades. *Sex Roles, 40,* 545–565.

Spitzer, R. L., et al. (Eds.). (1994). *DSM-IV casebook.* Washington, DC: American Psychiatric Association.

Spraggins, R. E. (2003). *Women and men in the United States: March 2002.* Current Population Reports, P20–544. Washington, DC: U.S. Census Bureau.

Sprecher, S., Fehr, B., & Zimmerman, C. (2007). Expectation for mood enhancement as a result of helping: The effects of gender and compassionate love. *Sex Roles, 56,* 543–549.

Sprecher, S., & Felmlee, D. (1997). The balance of power in romantic heterosexual couples over time from "his" and "her" perspectives. *Sex Roles, 37,* 361–379.

Springen, K. (2000, December 4). The right to choose. *Newsweek,* pp. 73–74.

Springen, K. (2005, February 7). The miscarriage maze. *Newsweek,* pp. 63–64.

Springen, K. (2007, August 6). Be good to your bones. *Newsweek,* pp. 62–63.

Springen, K., & Fragala, K. (2002, October 14). New hope in the war against breast cancer. *Newsweek,* p. 10.

Springen, K., & Kantrowitz, B. (2004, May 10). Alcohol's deadly triple threat. *Newsweek,* pp. 90–92.

Springen, K., & Seibert, S. (2005, January 17). Artful aging. *Newsweek,* pp. 57–65.

Spurgeon, D. (2007). Gender gap persists in treatment of Canadians after heart attack and stroke. *BMJ, 334,* 280.

Srivastava, S., John, O. P., Gosling, S. D., & Potter, J. (2003). Development of personality in early and middle adulthood: Set like plaster or persistent change? *Journal of Personality and Social Psychology, 84,* 1041–1053.

Sroufe, L. A., Bennett, C., Englund, M., Urban, J., & Shulman, S. (1993). The significance of gender boundaries in preadolescence: Contemporary correlates and antecedents of boundary violation and maintenance. *Child Development, 64,* 455–466.

Stabiner, K. (2003, January 12). Where the girls aren't. They're not in computer science. Is it nature or conditioning? *New York Times Education Life,* p. 35.

Stacey, J., & Biblarz, T. J. (2001). (How) does the sexual orientation of parents matter? *American Sociological Review, 66,* 159–183.

Stack, S., & Eshleman, J. R. (1998). Marital status and happiness: A 17-nation study. *Journal of Marriage and the Family, 60,* 527–536.

Stahly, G. B. (2008). Battered women: Why don't they just leave? In J. C. Chrisler, C. Golden, & P. D. Rozee (Eds.), *Lectures on the psychology of women* (pp. 356–375). New York: McGraw-Hill.

Stake, J. E. (1997). Integrating expressiveness and instrumentality in real-life settings: A new perspective on the benefits of androgyny. *Sex Roles, 37,* 541–564.

Stake, J. E. (2007). Predictors of change in feminist activism through women's and gender studies. *Sex Roles, 57,* 43–54.

Stake, J. E., & Malkin, C. (2003). Students' quality of experience and perceptions of intolerance and bias in the women's and gender studies classroom. *Psychology of Women Quarterly, 27,* 174–185.

Stake, J. E., Roades, L., Rose, S., Ellis, L., & West, C. (1994). The women's studies experience: Impetus for feminist activism. *Sex Roles, 18,* 17–24.

Stake, J. E., & Rose, S. (1994). The long-term impact of women's studies on students' personal lives and political activism. *Psychology of Women Quarterly, 18,* 403–412.

Stankiewicz, J. M., & Rosselli, F. (2008). Women as sex objects and victims in print advertisements. *Sex Roles, 58,* 579–589.

Stanley, A. (2002, January 13). For women, to soar is rare, to fall is human. *New York Times,* pp. BU1, BU10.

Stanley, A. (2004, January 16). Women having sex, hoping men tune in. *New York Times,* pp. B1, B28.

Stanley, D., & Freysinger, V. J. (1995). The impact of age, health, and sex on the frequency of older adult's leisure activity participation: A longitudinal study. *Activities, Adaptation & Aging, 19,* 31–42.

Stanley, J. L. (2002). Young sexual minority women's perceptions of cross-generational friendships with older lesbians. In S. M. Rose (Ed.), *Lesbian love and relationships* (pp. 139–148). Binghamton, NY: Harrington Park Press.

Stanley, S. M., Rhoades, G. K., & Markman, H. J. (2006). Sliding versus deciding: Inertia and the premarital cohabitation effect. *Family Relations, 55,* 499–509.

Stanton, A. L. (1995). Psychology of women's health: Barriers and pathways to knowledge. In A. L. Stanton & S. J. Gallant (Eds.), *The psychology of women's health: Progress and challenges in research and application* (pp. 3–21). Washington, DC: American Psychological Association.

Stark-Wroblewski, K., Yanico, B. J., & Lupe, S. (2005). Acculturation, internalization of Western appearance norms, and eating pathology among Japanese and Chinese international student women. *Psychology of Women Quarterly, 29,* 38–46.

Statistics Canada. (2006, November 27). *Readiness to learn at school among five-year-old children in Canada.* Retrieved from http://www.statcan.ca/english/research/89-599-MIE/89-599-MIE2006004.pdf

Steele, C. M., Spencer, S. J., & Aronson, J. (2002). Contending with group image: The psychology of stereotype and social identity threat. In M. P. Zanna (Ed.), *Advances in experimental social psychology, 34,* 379–440.

Steele, J., James, J. B., & Barnett, R. C. (2002). Learning in a man's world: Examining the perceptions of undergraduate women in male-dominated academic areas. *Psychology of Women Quarterly, 26,* 46–50.

Stefanick, M. L. (2006). Risk-benefit profiles of raloxifene for women. *New England Journal of Medicine, 355,* 190–192.

Stefanick, et al. (2006). Effects of conjugated equine estrogens on breast cancer and mammography screening in postmenopausal women with hysterectomy. *Journal of the American Medical Association, 295,* 1647–1657.

Steffens, D. C., et al. (2000). Prevalence of depression and its treatment in an elderly population: The Cache County study. *Archives of General Psychiatry, 57,* 601–607.

Steil, J. M. (2001). Family forms and member well-being: A research agenda for the decade of behavior. *Psychology of Women Quarterly, 25,* 344–363.

Steinberg, J. R., True, M., & Russo, N. F. (2008). Work and family roles: Selected issues. In F. L. Denmark & M. A. Paludi (Eds.), *Psychology of women: A handbook of issues and theories* (2nd ed., pp. 652–700). Westport, CT: Praeger.

Steinbrook, R. (2007). HIV in India—a complex epidemic. *New England Journal of Medicine, 356,* 1089–1093.

Steiner, M., & Born, L. (2002). Psychiatric aspects of the menstrual cycle. In S. G. Kornstein & A. H. Clayton (Eds.), *Women's mental health: A comprehensive textbook* (pp. 48–69). New York: Guilford.

Steiner, M., Dunn, E., & Born, L. (2003). Hormones and mood: From menarche to menopause and beyond. *Journal of Affective Disorders, 74,* 67–83.

Steiner, M. J., & Cates, W., Jr. (2006). Condoms and sexually-transmitted infections. *New England Journal of Medicine, 354,* 2642–2643.

Steinhauer, J. (1999, March 1). For women in medicine, a road to compromise, not perks. *New York Times,* pp. A1, A21.

Steinkamp, M. W., Harnisch, D. L., Walberg, H. J., & Tsai, S. (1985). Cross-national gender differences in mathematics attitude and achievement among 13-year-olds. *The Journal of Mathematical Behavior, 4,* 259–277.

Steinpreis, R. E., Anders, K. A., & Ritzke, D. (1999). The impact of gender on the review of the curricula vitae of job applicants and tenure candidates: A national empirical study. *Sex Roles, 41,* 509–528.

Stephens, J., Moore, B., Galyon, A., Wright, C., & Brinthaupt, T. (2007, May). *BMI, fitness, and body image dissatisfaction in young children.* Poster presented at the annual meeting of the Midwestern Psychological Association, Chicago.

Stephens, M. A. P., Franks, M. M., Martire, L. M., Norton, T. R., & Atienza, A. A. (2009). Women at midlife: Stress and rewards of balancing parent care with employment and other family roles. In K. Shifren (Ed.), *How caregiving affects development: Psychological implications for child, adolescent, and adult caregivers* (pp. 147–167). Washington, DC: American Psychological Association.

Stern, M., & Karraker, K. H. (1989). Sex stereotyping of infants: A review of gender labeling studies. *Sex Roles, 20,* 501–521.

Sternberg, S. (2004, February 25). USA's youth at high risk for venereal diseases. *USA Today,* p. 6D.

Stevens, J. A., et al. (2008). Self-reported falls and fall-related injuries among persons aged ≥65 years—United States, 2006. *Morbidity and Mortality Weekly Report, 57,* 225–229.

Stevens, P., & Galvao, L. (2007). He won't use condoms: HIV-infected women's struggles in primary relationships with serodiscordant partners. *American Journal of Public Health, 97,* 1015–1022.

Stevenson, M. R. (2005, August). *Uncle Sam needs you: Public policy and LGBT psychology.* Address presented at the meeting of the American Psychological Association, Washington, DC.

Stewart, A. J., & Ostrove, J. M. (1998). Women's personality in middle age: Gender history, and midcourse corrections. *American Psychologist, 53,* 1185–1194.

Stewart, A. J., & Vandewater, E. A. (1999). "If I had it to do over again . . .": Midlife review, midcourse corrections, and

women's well-being in midlife. *Journal of Personality and Social Psychology, 76,* 270–283.

Stewart, S. L., et al. (2004, June 4). Cancer mortality surveillance—United States, 1990–2000. *Surveil lance Summaries, Morbidity and Mortality Weekly Report 2004, 53*(SS-3), 1–108.

Stice, E. (2002). Risk and maintenance factors for eating pathology: A meta-analytic review. *Psychological Bulletin, 128,* 825–848.

Stice, E., Burton, E. M., & Shaw, H. (2004). Prospective relations between bulimic pathology, depression, and substance abuse: Unpacking comorbidity in adolescent girls. *Journal of Consulting and Clinical Psychology, 72,* 62–71.

Stier, J. J. (2000, November). The easy lives of working moms. *Working Mother,* pp. 21–27.

Stinson, D. A., et al. (2008). The cost of lower self-esteem: Testing a self- and social-bonds model of health. *Journal of Personality and Social Psychology, 94,* 412–428.

Stith, S. M., et al. (2004, November/December). Intimate partner physical abuse perpetration and victimization risk factors: A meta-analytic review. *Aggression and Violent Behavior, 10,* 65–98.

Stohs, J. H. (2000). Multicultural women's experience of household labor, conflicts, and equity. *Sex Roles, 42,* 339–361.

Stolberg, S. G. (1998). Quandary on donor eggs: What to tell the children. *New York Times,* pp. Y1, Y14.

Stoner, C. C., Gallatti, N., Dugan, A. E., & Cole, P. M. (2005, April). *Anger expression, expressive language & gender in 18-month-olds.* Poster presented at the meeting of the Society for Research in Child Development, Atlanta, GA.

Stoppard, J. M., & McMullen, L. M. (Eds.). (2003). *Situating sadness: Women's depression in social context.* New York: New York University Press.

Straus, M. A., & Smith, C. (1990). Violence in Hispanic families in the United States: Incidence rates and structural interpretations. In M. A. Straus & R. J. Gelles (Eds.), *Physical violence in American families: Risk factors and adaptations to violence in 8,145 families* (pp. 341–367). New Brunswick, NJ: Transaction.

Strauss, L. T., et al. (2004). Abortion surveillance—United States, 2001. *Morbidity and Mortality Weekly Report, 53*(SS09), 1–32.

Strauss, L. T., Gamble, S. B., Parker, W. Y., Cook, D. A., Zane, S. B., & Hamdan, S. (2006). Abortion surveillance—United States, 2003. *Morbidity and Mortality Weekly Report, Surveillance Summaries, 55*(SS11), 1–32.

Strauss, L. T., Gamble, S. B., Parker, W. Y., Cook, D. A., Zane, S. B., & Hamdan, S. (2007). Abortion surveillance—United States, 2004. *Morbidity and Mortality Weekly Report, Surveillance Summaries, 56*(SS09), 1–33.

Strauss, R. S. (2000). Childhood obesity and self-esteem. *Pediatrics, 105*(1), e15.

Street, A. E., Stafford, J., & Bruce, T. A. (2003, Winter). Sexual harassment. *PTSD Research Quarterly, 14,* 1–7.

Street, R. L., Jr. (2002). Gender differences in health care provider–patient communication: Are they due to style, stereotypes, or accommodation? *Patient Education and Counseling, 48,* 201–206.

Street, S., Kimmel, E. B., & Kromrey, J. D. (1995). Revisiting university student gender role perceptions. *Sex Roles, 33,* 183–201.

Street, S., Kromrey, J. D., & Kimmel, E. (1995). University faculty gender roles perceptions. *Sex Roles, 32,* 407–422.

Streppel, M. T., et al. (2005). Dietary fiber and blood pressure. *Archives of Internal Medicine, 165,* 150–156.

Strickland, B. R. (2000). Misassumptions, misadventures, and the misuse of psychology. *American Psychologist, 55,* 331–338.

Striegel-Moore, R. H., & Bulik, C. M. (2007). Risk factors for eating disorders. *American Psychologist, 62,* 181–198.

Strine, T. W., Chapman, D. P., & Ahluwalia, I. B. (2005). Menstrual-related problems and psychological distress among women in the United States. *Journal of Women's Health, 14,* 316–323.

Stroebe, M. S., & Stroebe, W. (1993). The mortality of bereavement: A review. In M. S. Stroebe, W. Stroebe, & R. D. Hanson (Eds.), *Handbook of bereavement* (pp. 208–226). London: Cambridge University Press.

Strong, T. H. (2000). *Expecting trouble: The myth of prenatal care in America.* New York: New York University Press.

Stuenkel, C. P. (2005). A strategy for working families: High-level commodification of household services. In B. Schneider & L. J. Waite (Eds.), *Being together, working apart: Dual-career families and the work-life balance* (pp. 252–272). Cambridge: Cambridge University Press.

Stueve, A., & O'Donnell, L. N. (2005). Early alcohol initiation and subsequent sexual and alcohol risk behaviors among urban youths. *American Journal of Public Health, 95,* 887–893.

Sturza, M. L., & Campbell, R. (2005). An exploratory study of rape survivors' prescription drug use as a means of coping with sexual assault. *Psychology of Women Quarterly, 29,* 353–363.

Sue, D. (2000). Health risk factors in diverse cultural groups. In R. M. Eisler & M. Hersen (Eds.), *Handbook of gender, culture, and health* (pp. 85–103). Mahwah, NJ: Erlbaum.

Sue, D. W., Bingham, R. P., Porché-Burke, L., & Vasquez, M. (1999). The diversification of psychology: A multicultural revolution. *American Psychologist, 54,* 1061–1069.

Suggs, W. (2005a, April 8). Faces in a mostly white, male crowd. *Chronicle of Higher Education,* pp. A34–A36.

Suggs, W. (2005b, June 3). College sports hire more female but fewer minority coaches and officials, report says. *The Chronicle of Higher Education Today's News.* Retrieved from http://chronicle.com/daily/2005/06/2005060302n.htm

Suggs, W. (2005c, July 1). Gender quotas? Not in college sports. *The Chronicle of Higher Education,* pp. A24–A26.

Sui, X., et al. (2007). Cardiorespiratory fitness and adiposity as mortality predictors in older adults. *Journal of the American Medical Association, 298,* 2507–2516.

Suicide and attempted suicide—China, 1990–2002. (2004). *Morbidity and Mortality Weekly Report, 53,* 481–483.

Suicide trends among youths and young adults aged 10–24 years—United States, 1990–2004. (2007). *Morbidity and Mortality Weekly Report, 56,* 905–908.

Sullivan, C. M. (2006). Interventions to address intimate partner violence: The current state of the field. In J. R. Lutzker (Ed.), *Preventing violence: Research and evidence-based intervention strategies* (pp. 195–212). Washington, DC: American Psychological Association.

Sumberg, E. (2007, January 21). Starting over: Many grandparents raising children for second time. *Peoria Journal Star,* pp. A1, A14.

Summers-Effler, E. (2004). Little girls in women's bodies: Social interaction and the strategizing of early breast development. *Sex Roles, 51,* 29–44.

Sumner, K. E., & Brown, T. J. (1996). Men, women, and money: Exploring the role of gender, gender-linkage of college major and career-information sources in salary expectations. *Sex Roles, 34,* 823–839.

Surgeon General's Advisory on Alcohol Use in Pregnancy. (2005, March 11). *Morbidity and Mortality Weekly Report, 84,* 229.

Susan G. Komen for the Cure. (2008). *About breast cancer: Emerging areas in early detection* [Brochure]. Retrieved from http://cms.komen.org/Komen/AboutBreastCancer/EarlyDetectionScreening/ED3-3-5

Susman, E. J., Dockray, S., Schiefelbein, V. L., Herwehe, S., Heaton, J. A., & Dorn, L. D. (2007). Morningness/eveningness, morning-to-afternoon cortisol ratio, and antisocial behavior problems during puberty. *Developmental Psychology, 43,* 811–822.

Susman, E. J., & Rogol, A. (2004). Puberty and psychological development. In R. M. Lerner & L. Steinberg (Eds.), *Handbook of adolescent psychology,* 2nd ed. (pp. 15–44). Hoboken, NJ: Wiley.

Susskind, J. E. (2003). Children's perception of gender-based illusory correlations: Enhancing preexisting relationships between gender and behavior. *Sex Roles, 48,* 483–494.

Susskind, J. E., Hodges, C., Carter, B., & Witmack, C. (2005, April). *Cooties: Distinguishing gender-based in-group favoritism from out-group derogation.* Poster presented at the meeting of the Society for Research in Child Development, Atlanta, GA.

Sutfin, E. L., Fulcher, M., Bowles, R. P., & Patterson, C. J. (2008). How lesbian and heterosexual parents convey attitudes about gender to their children: The role of gendered environments. *Sex Roles, 58,* 501–513.

Swearingen-Hilker, N., & Yoder, J. D. (2002). Understanding the context of unbalanced domestic contributions: The influence of perceiver's attitudes, target's gender, and presentational format. *Sex Roles, 46,* 91–98.

Sweedyk, E., & de Laet, M. (2005). Women, games, and women's games. *Phi Kappa Phi Forum, 85,* 25–28.

Sweeney, C. (2008, February 28). Skin deep: Never too young for that first pedicure. *New York Times,* p. G3.

Swim, J. K., Aikin, K. J., Hall, W. S., & Hunter, B. A. (1995). Sexism and racism: Old-fashioned and modern prejudices. *Journal of Personality and Social Psychology, 68,* 199–214.

Swim, J. K., Mallett, R., Russo-Devosa, Y., & Stangor, C. (2005). Judgments of sexism: A comparison of the subtlety of sexism measures and sources of variability in judgments of sexism. *Psychology of Women Quarterly, 29,* 406–411.

Swim, J. K., Mallett, R., & Stangor, C. (2004). Understanding subtle sexism: Detection and use of sexist language. *Sex Roles, 51,* 117–128.

Swim, J. K., Scott, E., Sechrist, G. B., Campbell, B., & Stangor, C. (2003). The role of intent and harm in judgments of prejudice. *Journal of Personality and Social Psychology, 84,* 944–959.

Switzer, J. Y. (1990). The impact of generic word choices: An empirical investigation of age- and sex-related differences. *Sex Roles, 22,* 69–82.

Sybert, V. P., & McCauley, E. (2004). Turner's syndrome. *New England Journal of Medicine, 351,* 1227–1238.

Sylvester, K. (2001). Caring for our youngest: Public attitudes in the United States. *The Future of Children, 11*(1), 53–61.

Symptoms and ovarian cancer. (2007, June 19). *New York Times,* p. A22.

Szinovacz, M. (1991). Women and retirement. In B. B. Hess & E. W. Markson (Eds.), *Growing old in America* (4th ed., pp. 293–303). New Brunswick, NJ: Transaction.

Szinovacz, M., & Washo, C. (1992). Gender differences in exposure to life events and adaptation to retirement. *Journal of Gerontology: Social Science, 47,* S191–S196.

Szymanski, D. M. (2003). The feminist supervision scale: A rational/theoretical approach. *Psychology of Women Quarterly, 27,* 221–232.

Szymanski, D. M. (2005). Heterosexism and sexism as correlates of psychological distress in lesbians. *Journal of Counseling and Development, 83,* 355–360.

Szymanski, D. M., & Owens, G. P. (2008). Do coping styles moderate or mediate the relationship between internalized heterosexism and sexual minority women's psychological distress? *Psychology of Women Quarterly, 32,* 95–104.

Tafalla, R. J. (2007). Gender differences in cardiovascular reactivity and game performance relate to sensory modality in violent video game play. *Journal of Applied Social Psychology, 37,* 2008–2023.

Taft, C. T., et al. (2006). Examining the correlates of psychological aggression among a community sample of couples. *Journal of Family Psychology, 20,* 581–588.

Taft, C. T., Vogt, D. S., Mechanic, M. B., & Resick, P. A. (2007). Posttraumatic stress disorder and physical health symptoms among women seeking help for relationship aggression. *Journal of Family Psychology, 21,* 354–362.

Tai, Y. (2004, March 15). Shortage of females in China grows grave. *Washington Times,* p. 24.

Tai-Seale, M., McGuire, T., Colenda, C., Rosen, D., & Cook, M. A. (2007). Two-minute mental health care for elderly patients: Inside primary care visits. *Journal of the American Geriatrics Society, 55,* 1903–1911.

Talaga, J. A., & Beehr, T. A. (1995). Are there gender differences in predicting retirement decisions? *Journal of Applied Psychology, 80,* 16–28.

Talbot, M. (2002, February 24). Girls just want to be mean. *New York Times Magazine,* pp. 24–29, 40, 58, 64–65.

Tamis-LeMonda, C. S., Shannon, J. D., Cabrera, N. J., & Lamb, M. E. (2004). Fathers and mothers at play with their

2- and 3-year olds: Contributions to language and cognitive development. *Child Development, 75,* 1806–1819.

Tang, B. M. P., Eslick, G. D., Nowson, C., Smith, C., & Bensoussan, A. (2007). Use of calcium or calcium in combination with vitamin D supplementation to prevent fractures and bone loss in people aged 50 years and older: A meta-analysis. *Lancet, 370,* 657–666.

Tanofsky-Kraff, M., et al. (2004). Eating-disordered behaviors, body fat, and psychopathology in overweight and normal-weight children. *Journal of Consulting and Clinical Psychology, 72,* 53–61.

Tapia, A. (2008). *Women in leadership at a crossroads: Why current best practices will not be enough to shatter the glass ceiling.* Lincolnshire, IL: Hewitt Associates.

Tariq, S. H., & Morley, J. E. (2003). Maintaining sexual function in older women: Physical impediments and psychosocial issues. *Women's Health in Primary Care, 6,* 157–162.

Tarkan, L. (2002, February 26). In many delivery rooms, a routine becomes less routine. *New York Times,* pp. D6, D8.

Tarris, C. (2002, July 5). Are girls really as mean as books say they are? *Chronicle of Higher Education,* pp. B7–B9.

Tasker, F. L. (2005). Lesbian mothers, gay fathers, and their children: A review. *Journal of Developmental and Behavioral Pediatrics, 26,* 224–240.

Tasker, F. L., & Golombok, S. (1997). *Growing up in a lesbian family.* New York: Guilford.

Taylor, A. K., Larson, S., & Correa-de-Araujo, R. (2006). Women's health care utilization and expenditures. *Women's Health Issues, 16,* 66–79.

Taylor, C. R., Lee, J. Y., & Stern, B. B. (1995). Portrayals of African, Hispanic, and Asian Americans in magazine advertising. *American Behavioral Scientist, 38,* 608–621.

Taylor, K. (2001). How far can you flex? *Association Management, 53*(3), 58–64.

Taylor, K. L., et al. (2003). Psychological adjustment among African American breast cancer patients: One-year follow-up results of a randomized psychoeducational group intervention. *Health Psychology, 22,* 316–323.

Taylor, P. L., Tucker, M. B., & Mitchell-Kernan, C. (1999). Ethnic variations in perceptions of men's provider role. *Psychology of Women Quarterly, 23,* 741–761.

Taylor, S. (2004, Summer). Being raised by my grandparents will help make me successful in life. *AARP, The GIC Voice,* p. 11.

Taylor, S. E. (2003). *The tending instinct.* New York: Henry Holt.

Taylor, S. E., et al. (2000). Biobehavioral responses to stress in females: Tend-and-befriend, not fight-or-flight. *Psychological Review, 107,* 411–429.

Taylor, S. E., et al. (2002). Sex differences in biobehavioral responses to threat: Reply to Geary and Flinn. *Psychological Review, 109,* 751–753.

Tedeschi, R. G., & Calhoun, L. G. (2004). Posttraumatic growth: Conceptual foundations and empirical evidence. *Psychological Inquiry, 15,* 1–18.

Tenenbaum, H. R., & Leaper, C. (2002). Are parents' gender schemas related to their children's gender-related cognitions? A meta-analysis. *Developmental Psychology, 38,* 615–630.

Tenenbaum, H. R., & Leaper, C. (2003). Parent–child conversations about science: The socialization of gender inequities. *Developmental Psychology, 39,* 34–47.

Tenenbaum, H. R., Snow, C. E., Roach, K. A., & Kurland, B. (2005). Talking and reading science: Longitudinal data on sex differences in mother–child conversations in low-income families. *Applied Developmental Psychology, 26,* 1–19.

Terlecki, M. S., & Newcombe, N. S. (2005). How important is the digital divide? The relation of computer and videogame usage to gender differences in mental rotation ability. *Sex Roles, 53,* 433–441.

Thébaud, S. (2007, August). *Masculinity, bargaining and breadwinning: A study of men's household labor in 22 countries.* Paper presented at the annual meeting of the American Sociological Association, New York.

Theriault, S. W., & Holmberg, D. (1998). The new old-fashioned girl: Effects of gender and social desirability on reported gender-role ideology. *Sex Roles, 39,* 97–112.

Thiebaut, A. C., et al. (2007). Dietary fat and postmenopausal invasive breast cancer in the National Institutes of Health-AARP Diet and Health Study cohort. *Journal of National Cancer Institute, 99,* 451–462.

This year's freshmen at 4-year colleges: A statistical profile. (2005, February 4). *Chronicle of Higher Education,* p. A33.

This year's freshmen at 4-year colleges: A statistical profile. (2007, January 26). *The Chronicle of Higher Education,* p. 36.

This year's freshmen at 4-year colleges: A statistical profile. (2008, February 1). *The Chronicle of Higher Education,* p. A23.

Thomas, J. J., & Daubman, K. A. (2001). The relationship between friendship quality and self-esteem in adolescent girls and boys. *Sex Roles, 45,* 53–65.

Thomas, J. L., Sperry, L., & Yarbrough, M. S. (2000). Grandparents as parents: Research findings and policy recommendations. *Child Psychiatry and Human Development, 31,* 3–22.

Thomas, J. R., & French, K. E. (1985). Gender differences across age in motor performance: A meta-analysis. *Psychological Bulletin, 98,* 260–282.

Thomas, T. (2005, January 16). So when is a woman too old to give birth? *Sunday Express (London),* pp. 55–57.

Thompson, E. M., & Morgan, E. M. (2008). "Mostly straight" young women: Variations in sexual behavior and identity development. *Developmental Psychology, 44,* 15–21.

Thompson, G. (1999, March 30). New clinics seek patients among lesbians, who often shun health care. *New York Times,* p. 25.

Thompson, R. S., et al. (2006). Intimate partner violence: Prevalence, types, and chronicity in adult women. *American Journal of Preventive Medicine, 30,* 447–457.

Thompson, S. J., & Johnston, L. (2004). Risk factors of gay, lesbian, and bisexual adolescents: Review of empirical literature and practice implications. *Journal of Human Behavior in the Social Environment, 8,* 111–128.

Thorne, B. (1993). *Gender play: Girls and boys in school.* New Brunswick, NJ: Rutgers University Press.

Thornhill, R., & Palmer, C. T. (2000). *A natural history of rape: Biological bases of sexual coercion.* Cambridge, MA: MIT Press.

Tice, J. A., & Grady, D. (2006). Alternatives to estrogen for treatment of hot flashes: Are they effective and safe? *Journal of the American Medical Association, 295,* 2076–2078.

Tichenor, V. (2005). Maintaining men's dominance: Negotiating identity and power when she earns more. *Sex Roles, 53,* 191–205.

Tiedemann, J. (2000). Parents' gender stereotypes and teachers' beliefs as predictors of children's concept of their mathematical ability in elementary school. *Journal of Educational Psychology, 92,* 144–151.

Tiefer, L. (2001). A new view of women's sexual problems: Why new? Why now? *Journal of Sex Research, 38,* 89–96.

Tiefer, L. (2006). Sex therapy as a humanistic enterprise. *Sex & Relationship Therapy, 21,* 359–375.

Tiegs, T. J., Perrin, P. B., Kaly, P. W., & Heesacker, M. (2007). My place or yours? An inductive approach to sexuality and gender role conformity. *Sex Roles, 56,* 449–456.

Tilberis, L. (1998). *No time to die.* London: Little, Brown.

Timmerman, G. (2003). Sexual harassment of adolescents perpetrated by teachers and by peers: An exploration of the dynamics of power, culture, and gender in secondary schools. *Sex Roles, 48,* 231–244.

Tobach, E. (2001). Development of sex and gender: Biochemistry, physiology, and experience. In J. Worell (Ed.), *Encyclopedia of women and gender* (pp. 315–332). San Diego: Academic Press.

Tolan, P., Gorman-Smith, D., & Henry, D. (2006). Family violence. *Annual Review of Psychology, 57,* 557–583.

Tolin, D. F., & Foa, E. B. (2006). Sex differences in trauma and posttraumatic stress disorder: A quantitative review of 25 years of research. *Psychological Bulletin, 132,* 959–992.

Toller, P. W., Suter, E. A., & Trautman, T. C. (2004). Gender role identity and attitudes toward feminism. *Sex Roles, 51,* 85–90.

Tolman, D. L. (2002). *Dilemmas of desire: Teenage girls talk about sexuality.* Cambridge, MA: Harvard University Press.

Tolman, D. L., Striepe, M. I., & O'Sullivan, L. F. (2003). How do we define sexual health for women? In L. Slater, J. H. Daniel, & A. E. Banks (Eds.), *The complete guide to mental health for women.* Boston: Beacon Press.

Tonks, A. (2007). Dark chocolate lowers blood pressure. *BJM, 335,* 68.

Torpy, J. M. (2002). Birth labor. *Journal of the American Medical Association, 288,* 1432.

Torpy, J. M. (2004). Hysterectomy. *Journal of the American Medical Association, 291,* 1526.

Torpy, J. M. (2006). Women's health. *Journal of the American Medical Association, 295,* 1474.

Torpy, J. M. (2007a). Health care insurance: The basics. *Journal of the American Medical Association, 297,* 1154.

Torpy, J. M. (2007b). Polycystic ovary syndrome. *Journal of the American Medical Association, 297,* 554.

Torpy, J. M. (2007c). Women's sexual concerns after menopause. *Journal of the American Medical Association, 297,* 664.

Torres, S. (1987). Hispanic-American battered women: Why consider cultural differences? *Response to the Victimization of Women and Children, 10,* 20–21.

Torres, S. (1991). A comparison of wife abuse between two cultures: Perception, attitudes, nature, and extent. *Issues in mental health nursing: Psychiatric nursing for the 90's: New concepts, new therapies, 12,* 113–131.

Torrez, D. J. (2001). The health of older women: A diverse experience. In J. M. Coyle (Ed.), *Handbook on women and aging* (pp. 131–148). Westport, CT: Greenwood.

Tougas, F., Brown, R., Beaton, A. M., & Joly, S. (1995). Neosexism: Plus ça change, plus c'est pareil. *Personality and Social Psychology Bulletin, 21,* 842–849.

Toussaint, D. (2003, September/October). Outward bound. *Bride's,* p. 346.

Townsend, T. G. (2002). The impact of self-components on attitudes toward sex among African-American preadolescent girls: The moderating role of menarche. *Sex Roles, 47,* 11–20.

Tracy, J. K., & Junginger, J. (2007). Correlates of lesbian sexual functioning. *Journal of Women's Health, 16,* 499–509.

Tran, H., & Weinraub, M. (2006). Child care effects in context: Quality, stability, and multiplicity in nonmaternal child care arrangements during the first 15 months of life. *Developmental Psychology, 42,* 566–582.

Trautner, H. M., Ruble, D. N., Cyphers, L., Kirsten, B., Behrendt, R., & Hartmann, P. (2005). Rigidity and flexibility of gender stereotypes in childhood: Developmental or differential? *Infant and Child Development, 14,* 365–381.

Travis, C. B., & Compton, J. D. (2001). Feminism and health in the decade of behavior. *Psychology of Women Quarterly, 25,* 312–323.

Travis, C. B., & Meltzer, A. L. (2008). Women's health: Biological and social systems. In F. L. Denmark & M. A. Paludi (Eds.), *Psychology of women: A handbook of issues and theories* (2nd ed., pp. 353–399). Westport, CT: Praeger.

Treas, J., & Tai, T.-O. (2007, August). *Long apron strings of working mothers: Maternal employment, occupational attainments, and housework in cross-national perspective.* Paper presented at the meeting of the American Sociological Association, New York.

Treas, J., & Widmer, E. D. (2000). Married women's employment over the life course: Attitudes in cross-national perspective. *Social Forces, 78,* 1409–1436.

Trebay, G. (2003, September 2). The skin wars start earlier & earlier. *New York Times,* p. C12.

Trenholm, C., Devaney, B., Fortson, K., Quay, L., Wheeler, J., & Clark, M. (2007, April). *Impacts of four Title V, Section 510 abstinence education programs.* Princeton, NJ: Mathematica Policy Research.

Trice, A. D., Hughes, M. A., Odom, C., Woods, K., & McClellan, N. C. (1995). The origins of children's career aspirations: IV. Testing hypotheses from four theories. *Career Development Quarterly, 43,* 307–322.

Trickett, P. K., & Gordis, E. B. (2004). Aggression and antisocial behavior in sexually abused females. In M. Putallaz & K. L. Bierman (Eds.), *Aggression, antisocial behavior, and violence among girls: A developmental perspective* (pp. 162–185). New York: Guilford.

Trimberger, E. K. (2005). *The new single woman.* Boston: Beacon Press.

Trivits, L. C., & Repucci, N. D. (2002). Application of Megan's Law to juveniles. *American Psychologist, 57,* 690–704.

Troutman, K. P., & Dufur, M. J. (2007). From high school jocks to college grads: Assessing the long-term effects of high school sport participation on females' educational attainment. *Youth & Society, 38,* 443–462.

Troxel, W. M., Matthews, K. A., Gallo, L. C., & Kuller, L. H. (2005). Marital quality and occurrence of the metabolic syndrome in women. *Archives of Internal Medicine, 165,* 1022–1027.

Trzesniewski, K. H., Donnellan, M. B., Moffitt, T. E., Robins, R. W., Poulton, R., & Caspi, A. (2006). Low self-esteem during adolescence predicts poor health, criminal behavior, and limited economic prospects during adulthood. *Developmental Psychology, 42,* 381–390.

Tucker, C. M., & Herman, K. C. (2002). Using culturally sensitive theories and research to meet the academic needs of low-income African-American children. *American Psychologist, 57,* 762–773.

Tucker, J. S., Ellickson, P. L., Orlando, M., & Klein, D. J. (2006). Cigarette smoking from adolescence to young adulthood: Women's developmental trajectories and associates outcomes. *Women's Health Issues, 16,* 30–37.

Tucker, M. B., & Mitchell-Kernan, C. (1995). *The decline in marriage among African Americans: Causes, consequences, and policy implications.* New York: Russell Sage.

Tuggle, C. A., Huffman, S., & Rosengard, D. S. (2002). A descriptive analysis of NBC's coverage of the 2000 Summer Olympics. *Mass Communication & Society, 5,* 361–375.

Turiel, E. (2006). The development of morality. In W. Damon, R. M. Lerner (Series Eds.) & N. Eisenberg (Vol. Ed.), *Handbook of child psychology: Vol. 3. Social, emotional, and personality development* (6th ed., pp. 789–857). Hoboken, NJ: Wiley.

Turkle, S. (2002, March 7). Lord of the hackers. *New York Times,* p. A27.

Twenge, J. M. (1997a). Attitudes toward women, 1970–1995: A meta-analysis. *Psychology of Women Quarterly, 21,* 35–51.

Twenge, J. M. (1997b). Changes in masculine and feminine traits over time: A meta-analysis. *Sex Roles, 36,* 305–325.

Twenge, J. M. (2001). Changes in women's assertiveness in response to status and roles: A cross-temporal meta-analysis, 1931–1993. *Journal of Personality and Social Psychology, 81,* 133–145.

Twenge, J. M., Campbell, W. K., & Foster, C. A. (2003). Parenthood and marital satisfaction: A meta-analytic review. *Journal of Marriage and Family, 65,* 574–583.

Twenge, J. M., & Crocker, J. (2002). Race and self-esteem: Meta-analyses comparing Whites, Blacks, Hispanics, Asians and American Indians and comment on Gray-Little and Hafdahl (2000). *Psychological Bulletin, 128,* 371–408.

Twins for surrogate grandmother. (2004, January 30). Retrieved on May 16, 2008 from http://news.bbc.co.uk/go/pr/fr/-/2/hi/health/3441939.stm

Tyler, K. A. (2002). Social and emotional outcomes of childhood sexual abuse: A review of recent research. *Agression and Violent Behavior, 7,* 567–589.

Tyler, K. A., & Johnson, K. A. (2006). A longitudinal study of the effects of early abuse on later victimization among high-risk adolescents. *Violence and Victims, 21,* 287–306.

Tyre, P. (2002, June 10). "R" is for retirement. *Newsweek,* p. 48.

Tyre, P. (2005, December 5). No one to blame. *Newsweek*, pp. 50–59.

Tyre, P. (2006, January 30). The trouble with boys. *Newsweek*, pp. 44–52.

Tyre, P., & Pierce, E. (2003, September 14). Ma, I'll be at the spa. *Newsweek*, p. 10.

Uchitelle, L. (2001, June 26). Women forced to delay retirement. *New York Times*, p. A1.

UCLA study looks at women in treatment. (2000, March). *Research Findings: National Institute on Drug Abuse*, *14*, 58.

Uggen, C., & Blackstone, A. (2004). Sexual harassment as a gendered expression of power. *American Sociological Review*, *69*, 64–92.

Uhlmann, E. L., & Cohen, G. L. (2005). Constructed criteria: Redefining merit to justify discrimination. *Psychological Science*, *16*, 474–480.

Ui, M., & Matsui, Y. (2008). Japanese adults' sex role attitudes and judgment criteria concerning gender equality: The diversity of gender egalitarianism. *Sex Roles*, *58*, 412–422.

Ullman, S. E. (2004). Sexual assault victimization and suicidal behavior in women: A review of the literature. *Aggression and Violent Behavior*, *9*, 331–351.

Ullman, S. E., & Brecklin, L. R. (2003). Sexual assault history and health-related outcomes in a national sample of women. *Psychology of Women Quarterly*, *27*, 46–57.

Umbach, P. D., et al. (2004). *Women students at coeducational and women's colleges: How do their experiences compare?* Bloomington, IN: Indiana University Center for Postsecondary Research.

U.N. offers action plan for a world aging rapidly. (2002, April 14). *New York Times*, p. YNE5.

UNAIDS. (2004). *2004 report on the global AIDS epidemic*. Geneva: Author.

UNAIDS. (2006). *AIDS epidemic update: December 2006*. Geneva, Switzerland: Author.

UNAIDS. (2007). *AIDS epidemic update: December 2007*. Geneva, Switzerland: Author.

Unger, J. B., & Seeman, T. E. (2000). Successful aging. In M. B. Goldman & M. C. Hatch (Eds.), *Women & health* (pp. 1238–1251). New York: Academic Press.

Unger, R. K. (2001). Women as subjects, actors, and agents in the history of psychology. In R. K. Unger (Ed.), *Handbook of the psychology of women and gender* (pp. 3–16). New York: Wiley.

UNICEF. (2000). Domestic violence against women and girls. *Innocenti Digest*, No. 6, 1–29.

UNICEF. (2004). *Afghanistan—progress of provinces*. Multiple indicator cluster survey 2003. Afghanistan: Author.

UNIFEM. (2003). *Not a minute more: Ending violence against women*. New York: Author.

UNIFEM. (2008). *Who answers to women? Gender and accountability*. New York: United Nations.

United Nations. (2007, March). *Ending impunity for violence against women and girls*. New York: Author.

United Nations Children's Fund. (2007). *Children and the Millennium Development Goals*. New York: Author.

United Nations Children's Fund. (2007). *The Millennium Development Goals report 2007*. New York: United Nations.

United Nations Population Fund. (2004). *UNFPA state of world population 2004. The Cairo consensus at ten: Population, reproductive health and the global effort to end poverty*. New York: Author.

Unützer, J. (2007). Late-life depression. *New England Journal of Medicine*, *357*, 2269–2276.

Upchurch, D. M., et al. (2004). Social and behavioral determinants of self-reported STD among adolescents. *Perspectives on Sexual and Reproductive Health*, *36*, 276–287.

U.S. Bureau of Labor Statistics. (2005). *Women in the labor force: A data book*. Washington, DC: Author.

U.S. Census Bureau, International Database. (1997, 1995). http://www.census.gov/International/Aging Statistics.htm

U.S. Census Bureau. (2003a). *Custodial mothers and fathers and their child support: 2001*. Current Population Reports, pp. 60–225. Washington, DC: Author.

U.S. Census Bureau. (2003b). *Educational attainment in the United States: March 2001 and March 2002*. Current Population Reports. Washington, DC: Author.

U.S. Census Bureau. (2003c). *Statistical profile of the United States* (123rd ed.). Washington, DC: U.S. Government Printing Office.

U.S. Census Bureau. (2005). *Educational attainment in the United States: 2004*. Current Population Reports. Washington, DC: Author.

U.S. Census Bureau. (2007a, July 9). *Grandparents Day 2007: Sept. 9* (CB07-FF.12). Washington, DC: Author.

U.S. Census Bureau. (2007b). *Marriage and divorce: 2004*. Washington, DC: Author.

U.S. Census Bureau. (2007c). *Statistical abstract of the United States: 2007* (126th ed.). Washington, DC: U.S. Government Printing Office.

U.S. Census Bureau. (2008, January 2). *Women's history month: March 2008* (CB08-FF.03). Washington, DC: Author.

Usdansky, M. L. (2000, March 8). Numbers show families growing closer as they pull apart. *New York Times*, p.10.

U.S. Department of Education. (2007a). *The condition of education 2007*. Washington, DC: Author.

U.S. Department of Education. (2007b). *The nation's report card: Writing 2007*. Washington, DC: Author.

U.S. Department of Health and Human Services (USDHHS). (1999). *1998 national household survey on drug abuse*. Washington, DC: U.S. Government Printing Office.

U.S. Department of Health and Human Services. (2004a). *2002 National survey of family growth (NSFG)*. Washington, DC: Author.

U.S. Department of Health and Human Services. (2004b). *Bone health and osteoporosis: A report of the Surgeon General*. Rockville, MD: Author.

U.S. Department of Labor. (n.d.). *Affirmative action at OFCCP: A sound policy and a good investment*. Employment Standards Administration, Office of Federal Contract Compliance Programs. Washington, DC: Author.

Utter, J., Neumark-Sztainer, D., Wall, M., & Story, M. (2003). Reading magazine articles about dieting and associated weight control behaviors among adolescents. *Journal of Adolescent Health, 32,* 78–82.

Väänänen, A., Buunk, B., Kivimäki, M., Pentti, J., & Vahtera, J. (2005). When it is better to give than to receive: Long-term health effects of perceived reciprocity in support exchange. *Journal of Personality and Social Psychology, 89,* 176–193.

Vaccarino, V., et al. (2005). Sex and racial differences in the management of acute myocardial infarction, 1994 through 2002. *New England Journal of Medicine, 353,* 671–681.

Valian, V. (2007). Women at the top in science—and elsewhere. In S. J. Ceci & W. M. Williams (Eds.), *Why aren't more women in science? Top researchers debate the evidence* (pp. 27–37). Washington, DC: American Psychological Association.

Valkenburg, P. M., & Peter, J. (2007). Preadolescents' and adolescents' online communication and their closeness to friends. *Developmental Psychology, 43,* 267–277.

Valls-Fernández, F., & Martinez-Vicente, J. M. (2007). Gender stereotypes in Spanish television commercials. *Sex Roles, 56,* 691–699.

Vandello, J. A., & Cohen, D. (2004). When believing is seeing: Sustaining norms of violence in cultures of honor. In M. Schaller & C. Crandall (Eds.), *The psychological foundations of culture* (pp. 281–304). New York: Erlbaum.

Van den Berg, P., Neumark-Sztainer, D., Hannan, P. J., & Haines, J. (2007). Is dieting advice from magazines helpful or harmful? Five-year associations with weight-control behaviors and psychological outcomes in adolescents. *Pediatrics, 119,* e30–e37.

Vandewater, E. A., Ostrove, J. M., & Stewart, A. J. (1997). Predicting women's well-being in midlife: The importance of personality development and social role involvements. *Journal of Personality and Social Psychology, 72,* 1147–1160.

Vandewater, E. A., & Stewart, A. J. (1997). Women's career commitment patterns and personality development. In M. E. Lachman & J. B. James (Eds.), *Multiple paths of midlife development* (pp. 375–410). Chicago: University of Chicago Press.

Van Evra, J. (2004). *Television and child development* (3rd ed.). Mahwah, NJ: Erlbaum.

Vanfraussen, K., Ponjaert-Kristoffersen, I., & Brewaeys, A. (2003). Family functioning in lesbian families created by donor insemination. *American Journal of Orthopsychiatry, 73,* 78–90.

Van Gaalen, R. I., & Dykstra, P. A. (2006). Solidarity and conflict between adult children and parents: A latent class analysis. *Journal of Marriage and Family, 68,* 947–960.

Vangelisti, A. L., & Daly, J. A. (1997). Gender differences in standards for romantic relationships: Different cultures or different experiences? *Personal Relationships, 4,* 203–219.

Van Gool, C. H., Kempen, G. I. J. M., Bosma, H., van Boxtel, M. P. J., Jolles, J., & van Eijk, J. T. M. (2006). Associations between lifestyle and depressed mood: Longitudinal results from the Maastricht Aging Study. *American Journal of Public Health, 97,* 887–894.

VanLeuvan, P. (2004). Young women's science/ mathematics career goals from seventh grade to high school graduation. *Journal of Educational Research, 97,* 248–267.

Van Son, G. E., van Hoeken, D., Bartelds, A. I. M., van, Furth, E. F., & Hoek, H. W. (2006). Time trends in the incidence of eating disorders: A primary care study in the Netherlands. *International Journal of Eating Disorders, 39,* 565–596.

Van Willigen, M., & Drentea, P. (2001). Benefits of equitable relationships: The impact of sense of fairness, household division of labor, and decision making power on perceived social support. *Sex Roles, 44,* 571–597.

Vasquez, M. J. T., & de las Fuentes, C. (1999). American-born Asian, African, Latina, and American Indian adolescent girls: Challenges and strengths. In N. G. Johnson, M. C. Roberts, & J. Worell (Eds.), *Beyond appearance: A new look at adolescent girls* (pp. 151–173). Washington, DC: American Psychological Association.

Vasta, R., Knott, J. A., & Gaze, C. E. (1996). Can spatial training erase the gender differences on the water-level task? *Psychology of Women Quarterly, 20,* 549–567.

Vastag, B. (2001). CDC says rates are up for gonorrhea, down for syphilis. *Journal of the American Medical Association, 285,* 155.

Vastag, B. (2002). Hormone replacement therapy falls out of favor with expert committee. *Journal of the American Medical Association, 287,* 1923–1924.

Vastag, B. (2003). Breast cancer racial gap examined: No easy answers to explain disparities in survival. *Journal of the American Medical Association, 290,* 1838–1842.

Vaughan, K. K., & Fouts, G. T. (2003). Changes in television and magazine exposure and eating disorder symptomatology. *Sex Roles, 49,* 313–320.

Veniegas, R. C., & Conley, T. D. (2000). Biological research on women's sexual orientations: Evaluating the scientific evidence. *Journal of Social Issues, 56,* 267–282.

Ventura, S. J., Abma, J. C., Mosher, W. D., & Henshaw, S. (2003). *Revised pregnancy rates, 1990–97, and new rates for 1998–99: United States.* National Vital Statistics Reports, 52(7). Hyattsville, MD: National Center for Health Statistics.

Verni, R., & Rinsky, K. (2006, August). *Same-sex domestic violence: The paradigm of power.* Paper presented at the annual convention of the American Psychological Association, New Orleans, LA.

Vescio, T. K., et al. (2005). Power and the creation of patronizing environments: The stereotype-based behaviors of the powerful and their effects on female performance in masculine domains. *Journal of Personality and Social Psychology, 88,* 658–672.

Vesely, S. K., et al. (2004). The potential protective effects of youth assets from adolescent sexual risk behaviors. *Journal of Adolescent Health, 34,* 356–365.

Vézina, J., & Hébert, M. (2007). Risk factors for victimization in romantic relationships of young women: A review of empirical studies and implications for prevention. *Trauma, Violence, & Abuse, 8,* 33–66.

Vickers, M. R., et al. (2007). Main morbidities recorded in the women's international study of long duration oestrogen after menopause (WISDOM): A randomized controlled trial of hormone replacement therapy in postmenopausal women. *BMJ, 335,* 239–244.

Vigil, J. M., Geary, D. C., & Byrd-Craven, J. (2005). A life history assessment of early childhood sexual abuse in women. *Developmental Psychology, 41*, 553–561.

Viki, G. T., Abrams, D., & Hutchison, P. (2003). The "true" romantic: Benevolent sexism and paternalistic chivalry. *Sex Roles, 49*, 533–537.

Vilhjalmsson, R., & Kristjansdottir, G. (2003). Gender differences in physical activity in older children and adolescents: The central role of organized sport. *Social Science & Medicine, 56*, 363–374.

Villarosa, L. (2002, June 4). At elders' home, each day is Valentine's Day. *New York Times*, pp. D6, D10.

Villarosa, L. (2003, December 23). More teenagers say no to sex, but experts aren't sure why. *New York Times*, pp. D6, D8.

Villarosa, L. (2004, April 5). AIDS fears grow for Black women. *New York Times*, pp. A1, A13.

Viswanathan, A. K., et al. (2005). Smoking and the risk of endometrial cancer: Results from the Nurses' Health Study. *International Journal of Cancer, 114*, 996–1001.

Vitaliano, P. P., Young, H. M., & Zhang, J. (2004). Is caregiving a risk factor for illness? *Psychological Science, 13*, 13–16.

Voda, A. M., & Ashton, C. A. (2006). Fallout from the Women's Health Study: A short-lived vindication for feminists and the resurrection of hormone therapies. *Sex Roles, 54*, 401–411.

Voelker, R. (2002). Elder abuse and neglect a new research topic. *Journal of the American Medical Association, 288*, 2254–2256.

Vogt, A. (1997, August 24). Even in virtual reality, it is still a man's world. *Chicago Tribune*, Sec. 13, pp. 1, 6.

Voracek, M., & Fisher, M. L. (2002). Shapely centrefolds? Temporal changes in body measures: Trend analysis. *BMJ, 325*, 1447–1448.

Votruba-Drzal, E., Coley, R. L., & Chase-Lansdale, P. L. (2004). Child care and low-income children's development: Direct and moderated effects. *Child Development, 75*, 296–312.

Voyer, D., Nolan, C., & Voyer, S. (2000). The relation between experience and spatial performance in men and women. *Sex Roles, 43*, 891–915.

Voyer, D., Voyer, S., & Bryden, M. P. (1995). Magnitude of sex differences in spatial abilities: A meta-analysis and consideration of critical variables. *Psychological Bulletin, 117*, 250–270.

Vyrostek, S. B., Annest, J. L., & Ryan, G. W. (2004). Surveillance for fatal and nonfatal injuries—United States, 2001. *Morbidity and Mortality Weekly Report.* Surveillance Summaries 53 (SS-7).

W/F balance becomes the major job concern; telework a potential solution. (1999, March 23). *National Report on Work & Family, 12*, 45.

Wagner, M. (1992, April). *Being female—a secondary disability? Gender differences in the transition experiences of young people with disabilities.* Paper presented at the meeting of the American Educational Research Association, San Francisco.

Wainer, H., & Steinberg, L. S. (1992). Sex differences in performance in the mathematics section of the scholastic aptitude test: A bidirectional validity test. *Harvard Educational Review, 62*, 323–336.

Wainright, J. L., & Patterson, C. J. (2006). Delinquency, victimization, and substance use among adolescents with female same-sex parents. *Journal of Family Psychology, 20*, 526–530.

Wainright, J. L., & Patterson, C. J. (2008). Peer relations among adolescents with female same-sex parents. *Developmental Psychology, 44*, 117–126.

Waisberg, J., & Page, S. (1988). Gender role nonconformity and perceptions of mental illness. *Women & Health, 14*, 3–16.

Waldfogel, J. (2001). International policies toward parental leave and child care. *The Future of Children, 11*(1), 99–111.

Waldrop, D. P. (2004). Caregiving issues for grandmothers raising their grandchildren. *Journal of Human Behavior in the Social Environment, 7*, 201–223.

Walia, A. (2005, August 9). Female foeticide in Punjab: Exploring the socio-economic and cultural dimensions. *Idea: A Journal of Social Issues, 10*(1). Retrieved from http://www.ideajournal.com/articles.php?id=37

Walker, L. J. (1991). Sex differences in moral reasoning. In W. M. Kurtines & J. L. Gewirtz (Eds.), *Handbook of moral behavior and development. Vol. 2. Research* (pp. 333–367). Hillsdale, NJ: Erlbaum.

Walker, T. (2005, February 28). Parents. Again. Some grandparents who raised their grandchildren are now raising their great-grandchildren. *Peoria Journal Star*, p. C6.

Walsh, W. B., & Heppner, M. J. (Eds.). (2006). *Handbook of career counseling for women* (2nd ed.). Mahwah, NJ: Erlbaum.

Walsh-Bowers, R. (1999). Fundamentalism in psychological science: The publication manual as bible. *Psychology of Women Quarterly, 23*, 375–392.

Walter, C. A. (2003). *The loss of a life partner: Narratives of the bereaved.* New York: Columbia University Press.

Walters, K. L., Evans-Campbell, T., Simoni, J. M., Ronquillo, T., & Bhuyan, R. (2006). "My spirit in my heart": Identity experiences and challenges among American Indian two-spirit women. *Journal of Lesbian Studies, 10*, 125–149.

Walther-Lee, D., & Stricker, G. (1998, August). *The basis of closeness between grandchildren and grandparents.* Paper presented at the meeting of the American Psychological Association, San Francisco.

Wang, L., et al. (2004). Stress and dysmenorrhoea: A population based perspective study. *Occupational and Environmental Medicine, 61*, 1021–1026.

Wang, P., & Walumbwa, F. O. (2007). Family-friendly programs, organizational commitment, and work withdrawal: The moderating role of transformational leadership. *Personnel Psychology, 60*, 397–427.

Wang, P. S., Lane, M., Olfson, M., Pincus, H. A., Wells, K. B., & Kessler, R. C. (2005). Twelve-month use of mental health services in the United States. *Archives of General Psychiatry, 62*, 629–640.

Wang, Y., & Marcotte, D. E. (2007). Golden years? The labor market effects of caring for grandchildren. *Journal of Marriage and Family, 69*, 1283–1296.

Wangby, M., Bergman, L. R., & Magnusson, D. (1999). Development of adjustment problems in girls: What syndromes emerge? *Child Development, 70*, 678–699.

Ward, C. A. (2000). Models and measurements of psychological androgyny: A cross-cultural extension and theory and research. *Sex Roles, 43,* 529–552.

Ward, J. V. (2007). Uncovering truths, recovering lives: Lessons of resistance in the socialization of Black girls. In B. J. R. Leadbeater & N. Way (Eds.), *Urban girls revisited: Building strengths* (pp. 243–260). New York: New York University Press.

Ward, J., & Winstanley, D. (2005). Coming out at work: Performativity and the recognition and renegotiation of identity. *The Sociological Review, 53,* 447–475.

Ward, L. M. (2002). Does television exposure affect emerging adults' attitudes and assumptions about sexual relationships? Correlational and experimental confirmation. *Journal of Youth and Adolescence, 31,* 1–15.

Ward, L. M. (2007, March). A longitudinal study of media use and gender role beliefs among Black and White 6th graders. In L. M. Ward (Chair), *Television's role in the gender and sexual socialization of Black adolescents.* Paper symposium conducted at the meeting of the Society for Research in Child Development, Boston.

Ward, L. M., & Caruthers, A. (2001). Media influences. In J. Worell (Ed.), *Encyclopedia of women and gender* (pp. 687–701). San Diego: Academic Press.

Ward, L. M., Hansbrough, E., & Walker, E. (2005). Contributions of music video exposure to black adolescents' gender and sexual schemas. *Journal of Adolescent Research, 20,* 143–166.

Ward, L. M., & Harrison, K. (2005). The impact of media use on girls' beliefs about gender roles, their bodies, and sexual relationships: A research synthesis. In E. Cole & J. H. Daniel (Eds.), *Featuring females: Feminist analyses of media* (pp. 3–24). Washington, DC: American Psychological Association.

Wardle, J., et al. (2004). Socioeconomic variation in attitudes to eating and weight in female adolescents. *Health Psychology, 23,* 275–282.

Wareham, S., Fowler, K., & Pike, A. (2007). Determinants of depression severity and duration in Canadian adults: The moderating effects of gender and social support. *Journal of Applied Social Psychology, 37,* 2951–2979.

Wargo, E. (2007, August). Vive la difference (not la deficit). *Observer, 20,* 17–19.

Warkentin, J. B., & Gidycz, C. A. (2007). The use and acceptance of sexually aggressive tactics in college men. *Journal of Interpersonal Violence, 22,* 829–850.

Warner, J. (2005). *Perfect madness: Motherhood in the age of anxiety.* New York: Riverhead books.

Warner, J. (2006, July 3). What boy crisis? *New York Times,* p. A14.

Warner, J. (2007, July 24). The full-time blues. *New York Times,* p. A23.

Warner, J., et al. (2004). Rates and predictors of mental illness in gay men, lesbians and bisexual men and women. *British Journal of Psychiatry, 185,* 479–485.

Warshaw, R. (1988). *I never called it rape: The Ms. report on recognizing, fighting, and surviving date and acquaintance rape.* New York: Harper & Row.

Wartella, E., Caplovitz, A. G., & Lee, J. H. (2004). From Baby Einstein to Leapfrog, from Doom to The Sims, from instant messaging to Internet chat rooms: Public interest in the role of interactive media in children's lives. *Social Policy Report, 18*(4), 3, 5–11, 13–14, 16–19.

Wartik, N. (2001, June 24). Paying a price for drinking men under the table. *New York Times,* p. WH4.

Wartik, N. (2002, June 23). Hurting more, helped less? *New York Times,* pp. WH1, WH6, WH7.

Washington, D. L., & Bird, C. E. (2002). Sex differences in disease presentation in the emergency department. *Annuals of Emergency Medicine, 40,* 461–463.

Wasserman, G. A., McReynolds, L. S., Ko, S. J., Katz, L. M., & Carpenter, J. R. (2005). Gender differences in psychiatric disorders at juvenile probation intake. *American Journal of Public Health, 95,* 131–137.

Wasti, S. A., & Cortina, L. M. (2002). Coping in context: Sociocultural determinants of responses to sexual harassment. *Journal of Personality and Social Psychology, 83,* 394–405.

Wathen, C. N., & MacMillan, H. L. (2003). Interventions for violence against women. *Journal of the American Medical Association, 289,* 589–600.

Watkins, P. L., & Whaley, D. (2000). Gender role stressors and women's health. In R. M. Eisler & M. Hersen (Eds.), *Handbook of gender, culture, and health* (pp. 43–62). Mahwah, NJ: Erlbaum.

Watson, C. M., Quatman, T., & Edler, E. (2002). Career aspirations of adolescent girls: Effects of achievement level, grade, and single-sex school environment. *Sex Roles, 46,* 323–335.

Watson, E. (1995). Comfort. In B. Benatovich (Ed.). *What we know so far: Wisdom among women.* New York: St. Martin's Griffin.

Watt, H. M. G. (2004). Development of adolescents' self-perceptions, values, and task perceptions according to gender and domain in 7th-through 11th-grade Australian students. *Child Development, 75,* 1556–1574.

Watt, H. M. G. (2008a). Gender and occupational outcomes: An introduction. In H. M. G. Watt & J. S. Eccles (Eds.), *Gender and occupational outcomes: Longitudinal assessments of individual, social, and cultural influences* (pp. 3–24). Washington, DC: American Psychological Association.

Watt, H. M. G. (2008b). What motivates females and males to pursue sex-stereotyped careers? In H. M. G. Watt & J. S. Eccles (Eds.), *Gender and occupational outcomes: Longitudinal assessments of individual, social, and cultural influences* (pp. 87–114). Washington, DC: American Psychological Association.

Waxman, S. (2005, February 21). "Simpsons" animates gay nuptials, and a debate. *New York Times,* p. A17.

Way, N. (1995). "Can't you see the courage, the strength that I have?" Listening to urban adolescent girls speak about their relationships. *Psychology of Women Quarterly, 19,* 107–128.

Wayne, J. H., & Cordeiro, B. L. (2003). Who is a good organizational citizen? Social perception of male and female employees who use family leave. *Sex Roles, 49,* 233–246.

Weatherall, A. (1999). Exploring a teaching/research nexus as a possible site for feminist methodological innovation in psychology. *Psychology of Women Quarterly, 23,* 199–214.

Weatherall, A. (2002). *Gender, language, and discourse.* London: Routledge.

Weber, L., & Higginbotham, E. (1997). Black and white professional-managerial women's perceptions of racism and sexism in the workplace. In E. Higginbotham & M. Romero (Eds.), *Women and work: Exploring race, ethnicity, and class* (pp. 153–175). Thousand Oaks, CA: Sage.

Wechsler, H., Lee, J. E., Kuo, M., Seibring, M., Nelson, T. F., & Lee, H. (2002). Trends in college binge drinking during a period of increased prevention efforts. *Journal of American College Health, 50*, 203–217.

Wei, G. S., & Herbers, J. E., Jr. (2004). Reporting elder abuse: A medical, legal, and ethical overview. *Journal of the American Medical Women's Association, 59*, 248–254.

Weichold, K., Silbereisen, R. K., & Schmitt-Rodermund, E. (2003). Short-term and long-term consequences of early versus late physical maturation in adolescents. In C. Hayward (Ed.), *Gender differences at puberty* (pp. 241–276). Cambridge: Cambridge University Press.

Weinberg, D. H. (2004). *Evidence from census 2000 about earnings by detailed occupation for men and women*. Washington, DC: U. S. Census Bureau.

Weinberg, M. S., Williams, C. J., & Pryor, D. W. (1994). *Dual attraction: Understanding bisexuality*. New York: Oxford University Press.

Weinberger, N., & Stein, K. (2007, March). *The role of gender and gender composition on early competitive game playing*. Poster presented at the meeting of the Society for Research in Child Development, Boston.

Weinraub, B., & Rutenberg, J. (2003, July 29). Gay-themed TV gains a wider audience. *New York Times*, pp. A1, C5.

Weinstein, A. R., et al. (2008). The joint effects of physical activity and body mass index on coronary heart disease risk in women. *Archives of Internal Medicine, 168*, 884–890.

Weisgram, E. S., & Bigler, R. S. (2006). Girls and science careers: The role of altruistic values and attitudes about scientific tasks. *Journal of Applied Developmental Psychology, 27*, 326–348.

Weitzel, J. N., et al. (2007). Limited family structure and *BRCA* gene mutation status in single cases of breast cancer. *Journal of the American Medical Association, 297*, 2587–2595.

Welch, J., & Mason, F. (2007). Rape and sexual assault. *BMJ, 334*, 1154–1158.

Wellman, N. S., Kamp, B., Kirk-Sanchez, N. J., & Johnson, P. M. (2007). Eat better & move more: A community-based program designed to improve diets and increase physical activity among older Americans. *American Journal of Public Health, 97*, 710–717.

Welty, F. K. (2001). Cardiovascular disease and dyslipidemia in women. *Archives of Internal Medicine, 161*, 514–522.

Welty, F. K., Lee, K. S., Lew, N. S., Nasca, M., & Zhou, J.-R. (2007a). The association between soy nut consumption and decreased menopausal symptoms. *Journal of Women's Health, 16*, 361–310.

Welty, F. K., Lee, K. S., Lew, N. S., & Zhou, J.-R. (2007b). Effect of soy nuts on blood pressure and lipid levels in hypertensive, prehypertensive, and normotensive postmenopausal women. *Archives of Internal Medicine, 167*, 1060–1067.

Wentz, E., Gillberg, C., Gillberg, I. C., & Rastam, M. (2001). Ten-year follow-up of adolescent-onset anorexia nervosa: Psychiatric disorders and overall functioning scales. *Journal of Child Psychology and Psychiatry, 42*, 613–622.

Wentzel, K. R., Filisetti, L., & Looney, L. (2007). Adolescent prosocial behavior: The role of self-processes and contextual cues. *Child Development, 78*, 895–910.

Wenzel, A., Jackson, L. C., & Brendle, J. R. (2004). Psychopathology, sexuality, and the partner relationship. In J. H. Harvey, A. Wenzel, & S. Sprecher (Eds.), *The handbook of sexuality in close relationships* (pp. 545–571). Mahwah, NJ: Erlbaum.

Werner, E. E. (2004). What can we learn about resilience from large-scale longitudinal studies? In S. Goldstein & R. Brooks (Eds.), *Handbook of resilience in children*, Chapter 7. New York: Kluwer.

Werner, E. E., & Smith, R. S. (2001). *Journeys from childhood to midlife: Risk, resilience and recovery*. Ithaca, NY: Cornell University Press.

Werner-Wilson, R. J. (1998). Gender differences in adolescent sexual attitudes: The influence of individual and family factors. *Adolescence, 33*, 519–531.

Wessler, S. L., & De Andrade, L. L. (2006). Slurs, sterotypes, and student interventions: Examining the dynamics, impact, and prevention of harassment in middle and high school. *Journal of Social Issues, 62*, 511–532.

West, C. M. (2002). Black battered women: New directions for research and black feminist theory. In L. H. Collins, M. R. Dunlap, & J. C. Chrisler (Eds.), *Charting a new course for feminist psychology* (pp. 216–237). Westport, CT: Praeger.

West, C. M. (2002). Lesbian intimate partner violence: Prevalence and dynamics. In S. M. Rose (Ed.), *Lesbian love and relationships* (pp. 121–127). Binghamton, NY: Harrington Park Press.

Westcott, K. (2006, March 31). The rise of the 'childfree'. *BBC News*. Retrieved October 27, 2006 from http://news.bbc.co.uk/2/hi/Europe/4813590.stm

Weston, R., Temple, J. R., & Marshall, L. L. (2005). Gender symmetry and asymmetry in violent relationships: Patterns of mutuality among racially diverse women. *Sex Roles, 53*, 553–571.

Weuve, J., et al. (2004). Physical activity, including walking, and cognitive function in older women. *Journal of the American Medical Association, 292*, 1454–1461.

Whaley, R. B. (2001). The paradoxical relationship between gender inequality and rape: Toward a refined theory. *Gender & Society, 15*, 529–553.

Whelehan, P. (2001). Cross-cultural sexual practices. In J. Worell (Ed.), *Encyclopedia of women and gender* (pp. 291–302). San Diego: Academic Press.

Whiffen, V. E. (2001). Depression. In J. Worell (Ed.), *Encyclopedia of women and gender* (pp. 303–314). San Diego: Academic Press.

Whiffen, V. E., & MacIntosh, H. B. (2005). Mediators of the link between childhood sexual abuse and emotional distress. *Trauma, Violence, & Abuse, 6*, 24–39.

Whipple, V. (2005). Addressing the needs of lesbian widows. *Journal of LGBT Issues in Counseling, 1*, 61–74.

Whisman, M. A. (2006). Childhood trauma and marital outcomes in adulthood. *Personal Relationships, 13*, 375–386.

Whiston, S. C., & Keller, B. K. (2004). The influences of the family of origin on career development: A review and analysis. *The Counseling Psychologist, 32*, 493–568.

Whitbourne, S. K., & Skultety, K. M. (2006). Aging and identity: How women face later life transitions. In J. Worell & C. D. Goodheart (Eds.), *Handbook of girls' and women's psychological health: Gender and well-being across the lifespan* (pp. 370–378). New York: Oxford University Press.

White, B. H., & Robinson Kurpius, S. E. (2002). Effects of victim sex and sexual orientation on perceptions of rape. *Sex Roles, 46*, 191–200.

White, J. W. (2001). Aggression and gender. In J. Worell (Ed.), *Encyclopedia of women and gender* (pp. 81–93). San Diego: Academic Press.

White, J. W., Donat, P. L. N., & Bondurant, B. (2001). A developmental examination of violence against girls and women. In R. K. Unger (Ed.), *Handbook of the psychology women and gender* (pp. 343–357). New York: Wiley.

White, J. W., & Frabutt, J. M. (2006). Violence against girls and women: An integrative developmental prespective. In J. Worell & C. D. Goodheart (Eds.), *Handbook of girls' and women's psychological health: Gender and well-being across the lifespan* (pp. 85–93). New York: Oxford University Press.

White, J. W., & Kowalski, R. M. (1994). Deconstructing the myth of the nonaggressive woman: A feminist analysis. *Psychology of Women Quarterly, 18*, 487–508.

White, J. W., Russo, N. F., & Travis, C. B. (2001). Feminism and the decade of behavior. *Psychology of Women Quarterly, 25*, 267–279.

Whitley, B. E. (2001a, May). *Gender-role beliefs and attitudes toward homosexuality*. Paper presented at the meeting of the Midwestern Psychological Association, Chicago.

Whitley, B. E. (2001b, August). *Racial/ethnic differences in attitudes toward homosexuality: A meta-analysis*. Paper presented at the meeting of the American Psychological Association, San Francisco.

Whitley, B. E. (2002, August). *Authoritarianism and social dominance orientation as predictors of heterosexist and racial attitudes*. Paper presented at the meeting of the American Psychological Association, Chicago.

Whitley, B. E., Jr. (2007, May). *Religiosity and anti-gay prejudice: A meta-analysis*. Poster presented at the annual meeting of the Association for Psychological Science, Washington, DC.

Whitmire, R. (2007, July 20). The latest way to discriminate against women. *The Chronicle of Higher Education*, p. B16.

Widom, C. S., DuMont, K., & Czaja, S. J. (2007). A prospective investigation of major depressive disorder and comorbidity in abused and neglected children grown up. *Archives of General Psychiatry, 64*, 49–56.

Widom, C. S., Schuck, A. M., & White, H. R. (2006). An examination of pathways from childhood victimization to violence: The role of early aggression and problematic alcohol use. *Violence and Victims, 21*, 675–690.

Wigfield, A., & Eccles, J. S. (2002). The development of competence beliefs, expectancies for success, and achievement values from childhood through adolescence. In A. Wigfield & J. S. Eccles (Eds.), *Development of achievement motivation* (pp. 91–120). San Diego: Academic Press.

Wigfield, A., Eccles, J. S., Schiefele, U., Roeser, R. W., & Davis-Kean, P. (2006). Development of achievement motivation. In W. Damon, R. M. Lerner (Series Eds.) & N. Eisenberg (Vol. Ed.), *Handbook of child psychology: Vol. 3. Social, emotional, and personality development* (6th ed., pp. 933–1002). Hoboken, NJ: Wiley.

Wilcox, S., et al. (2003). Psychosocial and perceived environmental correlates of physical activity in rural and older African American and white women. *The Journals of Gerontology, 58*, P329–P337.

Wilcox, S., et al. (2003). The effects of widowhood on physical and mental health, health behaviors, and health outcomes: The women's health initiative. *Health Psychology, 22*, 513–522.

Wilcox, S., et al. (2006). Results of the first year of Active for Life: Translation of 2 evidence-based activity programs for older adults into community settings. *American Journal of Public Health, 96*, 1201–1209.

Wilcox, W. B., & Nock, S. L. (2007). "Her" marriage after the revolutions. *Sociological Forum, 22*, 104–111.

Wilgoren, J. (2005, September 25). 'Mothering the mother' with childbirth support. *New York Times*, p. YT11.

Wilkinson, J. A., & Ferraro, K. F. (2002). Thirty years of ageism research. In T. D. Nelson (Ed.), *Ageism: Stereotyping and prejudice against older persons* (pp. 339–358). Cambridge, MA: MIT Press.

Wilkinson, S. (2002). Lesbian health. In A. Coyle & C. Kitzinger (Eds.), *Lesbian and gay psychology: New perspectives* (pp. 117–134). Oxford, UK: BPS Blackwell.

Willetts-Bloom, M. C., & Nock, S. L. (1994). The influence of maternal employment on gender role attitudes of men and women. *Sex Roles, 30*, 371–389.

Williams, A. (2004). E-dating bubble springs a leak. *New York Times*, pp. ST1, ST6.

Williams, A. (2005, April 3). Casual relationships, yes—casual sex, not really. *New York Times*, pp. 1, 12.

Williams, D. R., et al. (2007). Prevalence and distribution of major depressive disorder in African Americans, Caribbean blacks, and non-Hispanic whites: Results from the National Survey of American Life. *Archives of General Psychiatry, 64*, 305–315.

Williams, J. (2002, June 17). How academe treats mothers. *Chronicle of Higher Education*. http://careernetwork.com

Williams, J. E., & Best, D. L. (1990). *Measuring sex stereotypes: A multination study*. Newbury Park, CA: Sage.

Williams, M. K., McCandies, T., & Dunlap, M. R. (2002). Women of color and feminist psychology: Moving from criticism and critique to integration and application. In L. H. Collins, M. R. Dunlap, & J. C. Chrisler (Eds.), *Charting a new course for feminist psychology* (pp. 65–89). Westport, CT: Praeger.

Williams, N., & Leiblum, S. L. (2002). Sexual dysfunction. In G. M. Wingood & R. J. DiClemente (Eds.), *Handbook of women's sexual and reproductive health* (pp. 303–328). New York: Kluwer Academic/Plenum.

Williams, R., & Wittig, M. A. (1997). "I'm not a feminist, but . . ." Factors contibuting to the discrepancy between pro-feminist orientation and feminist social identity. *Sex Roles, 37,* 885–904.

Williams, S. L., & Frieze, I. H. (2005). Patterns of violent relationships, psychological distress, and marital satisfaction in a national sample of men and women. *Sex Roles, 52,* 771–784.

Williams, T. J., et al. (2000). Finger-length ratios and sexual orientation. *Nature, 404,* 455–456.

Williams-Nickelson, C. (2007, July/August). Women and money. *Monitor on Psychology, 38,* 46.

Williamson, J., Softas-Nall, B., & Miller, J. (2001, August). *Grandmothers raising grandchildren: Challenges and rewards.* Paper presented at the meeting of the American Psychological Association, San Francisco.

Willis, F. N., & Carlson, R. A. (1993). Singles ads: Gender, social class, and time. *Sex Roles, 29,* 387–404.

Willness, C. R., Steel, P., & Lee, K. (2007). A meta-analysis of the antecedents and consequences of workplace sexual harassment. *Personnel Psychology, 60,* 127–162.

Willoughby, T. (2008). A short-term longitudinal study of internet and computer game use by adolescent boys and girls: Prevalence, frequency of use, and psychosocial predictors. *Developmental Psychology, 44,* 195–204.

Willson, A. E., & Hardy, M. A. (2002). Racial disparities in income security for a cohort of aging American women. *Social Forces, 80,* 1283–1306.

Wilson, G. T., Grilo, C. M., & Vitousek, K. M. (2007). Psychological treatment of eating disorders. *American Psychologist, 62,* 199–216.

Wilson, H. W., & Widom, C. S. (2008). An examination of risky sexual behavior and HIV in victims of child abuse and neglect: A 30-year follow-up. *Health Psychology, 27,* 149–158.

Wilson, J. F. (1997). Changes in female students' attitudes toward women's lifestyles and career choices during a psychology of women course. *Teaching of Psychology, 24,* 50–52.

Wilson, R. (2004a, January 23). Louts in the lab. *Chronicle of Higher Education,* pp. A7–A9.

Wilson, R. (2004b, December 3). Where the elite teach, it's still a man's world. *Chronicle of Higher Education,* pp. A8–A14.

Wilson, R. (2007a, January 27). The new gender divide. *The Chronicle of Higher Education,* pp. A36–A39.

Wilson, R. (2007b, May 4). Where have all the women gone? *The Chronicle of Higher Education,* pp. A40–A44.

Wilson, R. T., Chase, G. A., Chrischilles, E. A., & Wallace, R. B. (2006). Hip fracture risk among community-dwelling elderly people in the United States: A prospective study of physical, cognitive, and socioeconomic indicators. *American Journal of Public Health, 96,* 1210–1218.

Windle, M., & Windle, R. C. (2002). Alcohol use and women's sexual and reproductive health. In G. M. Wingood & R. J. DiClemente (Eds.), *Handbook of women's sexual and reproductive health* (pp. 153–171). New York: Kluwer Academic/Plenum.

Winerman, L. (2006, September). Body dissatisfaction affects ethnic-minority and white women alike. *Monitor on Psychology, 37,* 16.

Wingert, P., & Kantrowitz, B. (2007, January 22). The new prime time. *Newsweek,* pp. 33–43.

Wingood, G. M., & DiClemente, R. J. (2002). HIV/AIDS. In G. M. Wingood & R. J. DiClemente (Eds.), *Handbook of women's sexual and reproductive health* (pp. 281–301). New York: Kluwer Academic/Plenum.

Winston, C. A. (2003). African American grandmothers parenting AIDS orphans: Concomitant grief and loss. *American Journal of Orthopsychiatry, 73,* 91–100.

Winterich, J. (2007, August). *Medicine, gender and the body at menopause: How biology and culture influence women's experiences with menopause.* Paper presented at the meeting of the American Sociological Association, New York.

Winterich, J. A. (2003). Sex, menopause, and culture: Sexual orientation and the meaning of menopause for women's sex lives. *Gender & Society, 17,* 627–642.

WISER. (2002). *Widowhood: Why women need to talk about this issue.* Washington, DC: Women's Institute for a Secure Retirement.

Wisocki, P. A., & Skowron, J. (2000). The effects of gender and culture on adjustment to widowhood. In R. M. Eisler & M. Hersen (Eds.), *Handbook of gender, culture, and health* (pp. 429–448). Mahwah, NJ: Erlbaum.

Wloszczyna, S. (2003, June 2). It's in to be out in pop culture. *USA Today,* pp. 9B, 10B.

Wolchik, S. A., et al. (2002). Six-year follow-up of preventive interventions for children of divorce. *Journal of the American Medical Association, 288,* 1874–1881.

Wolf, R. S. (2001). Support groups for older victims of domestic violence. *Journal of Women & Aging, 13,* 71–83.

Wolfe, V. (2002, August). *Similarities and differences between heterosexual and same-sex domestic violence.* Paper presented at the meeting of the American Psychological Association, Chicago.

Wolf-Wendel, L. E., Baker, B., & Morphew, C. (2000). Dollars and $ense: Institutional resources and the baccalaureate origins of women doctorates. *Journal of Higher Education, 71,* 165–189.

Wolk, A., et al. (1998). A prospective study of association of monounsaturated fat and other types of fat with risk of breast cancer. *Archives of Internal Medicine, 158,* 41–45.

Wolverton, B. (2006, July 28). Crying foul over postseason opportunities. *The Chronicle of Higher Education,* pp. A26–A27.

Women and disability. (2004, July). *Women's Psych-E, 3*(5), 1.

Women and heart health: From prevention to intervention. (2005, February). *National Women's Health Report, 27*(1), 1–4.

Women can have multiple orgasms. (2007, April 10). *New York Times,* p. D6.

Women heed warnings about stroke better than men do. (1998, March). *APA Monitor,* p. 9.

Women's Institute for a Secure Retirement. (2006a). *The pay gap's connected to the retirement gap.* Washington, DC: Author.

Women's Institute for a Secure Retirement. (2006b). *Social Security reform.* Washington, DC: Author.

Women's Institute for a Secure Retirement. (2007). *What today's woman needs to know: A retirement journey.* Washington, DC: Author.

Women's Sports Foundation. (2007). *Who's playing college sports? Trends in participation.* East Meadow, NY: Author.

Wonderlich, S. A., Joiner, T. E., Jr., Keel, P. K., Williamson, D. A., & Crosby, R. D. (2007). Eating disorder diagnoses: Empirical approaches to classification. *American Psychologist, 62,* 167–180.

Wood, E., Desmarais, S., & Gugula, S. (2002). The impact of parenting experience on gender stereotyped toy play of children. *Sex Roles, 47,* 39–49.

Wood, J. T. (1994). *Gendered lives: Communication, gender, and culture.* Belmont, CA: Wadsworth.

Wood, W., & Eagly, A. H. (2002). A cross-cultural analysis of the behavior of women and men: Implications for the origins of sex differences. *Psychological Bulletin, 128,* 699–727.

Woodhill, B. M., & Samuels, C. A. (2003). Positive and negative androgyny and their relationship with psychological health and well-being. *Sex Roles, 48,* 555–565.

Woodward, L. J., Fergusson, D. M., & Horwood, L. J. (2006). Gender differences in the transition to early parenthood. *Development and Psychopathology, 18,* 275–294.

Woodzicka, J. A., & LaFrance, M. (2005). The effects of subtle sexual harassment on women's performance in a job interview. *Sex Roles, 53,* 67–77.

Woolf, S. E., & Maisto, S. A. (2008). Gender differences in condom use behavior? The role of power and partner type. *Sex Roles, 58,* 689–701.

Worell, J. (1996). Opening doors to feminist research. *Psychology of Women Quarterly, 20,* 469–485.

Worell, J. (2001). Feminist interventions: Accountability beyond symptom reduction. *Psychology of Women Quarterly, 25,* 335–343.

Worell, J. (2006). Pathways to healthy development: Sources of strength and empowerment. In J. Worell & C. D. Goodheart (Eds.), *Handbook of girls' and women's psychological health: Gender and well-being across the lifespan* (pp. 25–35). New York: Oxford University Press.

Worell, J., & Etaugh, C. (1994). Transforming theory and research with women: Themes and variations. *Psychology of Women Quarterly, 18,* 443–450.

Worell, J., & Johnson, D. M. (2001). Feminist approaches to psychotherapy. In J. Worell (Ed.), *Encyclopedia of women and gender* (pp. 425–437). San Diego: Academic Press.

Worell, J., & Remer, P. (2003). *Feminist perspectives in therapy: Empowering diverse women.* Hoboken, NJ: Wiley.

World Health Day—April 7, 2005. (2005). *Morbidity and Mortality Weekly Report, 54,* 309.

World Health Organization. (2002). *World report on violence and health.* Geneva: Author.

World Health Organization. (2004). *World report on knowledge for better health.* Geneva: Author.

World Health Organization. (2007). *Maternal mortality in 2005.* Geneva, Switzerland: Author.

Wortman, C. M., Wolff, K., & Bonanno, G. A. (2004). Loss of an intimate partner through death. In D. J. Mashek & A. Aron (Eds.), *Handbook of closeness and intimacy* (pp. 305–320). Mahwah, NJ: Erlbaum.

Wright, V. C., Chang, J., Jeng, G., Chen, M., & Macaluso, M. (2007). Assisted reproductive technology surveillance—

United States, 2004. *Morbidity and Mortality Weekly Reports, Surveillance Summaries, 56* (SS06), 1–22.

Wrosch, C., Schulz, R., & Heckhausen, J. (2004). Health stresses and depressive symptomatology in the elderly: A control-process approach. *Current Directions in Psychological Science, 13,* 17–20.

Wu, C.-H., et al. (2002). Epidemiological evidence of increased bone mineral density in habitual tea drinkers. *Journal of the American Medical Association, 162,* 1001–1006.

Wyche, K. F., & Crosby, F. J. (Eds.). (1996). *Women's ethnicities: Journeys through psychology.* Boulder, CO: Westview.

Wylie, K. (2004). Gender related disorders. *BMJ, 329,* 615–617.

Yabroff, J. (2007, October 1). Mothers to blame. *Newsweek,* p. 86.

Yabroff, J. (2008, January 28). Birth, the American way. *Newsweek,* p. 46.

Yagil, D., Karnieli-Miller, O., Eisikovits, Z., & Enosh, G. (2006). Is that a "no"? The interpretation of responses to unwanted sexual attention. *Sex Roles, 54,* 251–260.

Yakushko, O. (2007). Do feminist women feel better about their lives? Examining patterns of feminist identity development and women's subjective well-being. *Sex Roles, 57,* 223–234.

Yang, Q., Greenland, S., & Flanders, W. D. (2006). Associations of maternal age- and parity-related factors with trends in low-birthweight rates: United States, 1980 through 2000. *American Journal of Public Health, 96,* 856–861.

Yardley, J. (2004, December 21). Rural exodus for work fractures Chinese family. *New York Times,* pp. A1–A8.

Yardley, J. (2005, January 31). Fearing future, China starts to give girls their due. *New York Times,* p. A3.

Yates, A., Edman, J., & Aruguete, M. (2004). Ethnic differences in BMI and body/self-dissatisfaction among whites, Asian subgroups, Pacific Islanders, and African-Americans. *Journal of Adolescent Health, 34,* 300–307.

Yeung, D. Y. L., Tang, C. S., & Lee, A. (2005). Psychosocial and cultural factors influencing expectations of menarche: A study on Chinese premenarcheal teenage girls. *Journal of Adolescent Research, 20,* 118–135.

Yoder, J. (2005, Summer). Reflections on the place of the *Psychology of Women* course in psychology's curriculum. *The Feminist Psychologist,* pp. 18–19.

Yoder, J. D. (2000). Women and work. In M. Biaggio & M. Hersen (Eds.), *Issues in the psychology of women* (pp. 71–91). New York: Kluwer.

Yoder, J. D., & Aniakudo, P. (1999). "Outsider within" the firehouse: Subordination and difference in the social interactions of African American women firefighters. In L. A. Peplau, S. C. DeBro, R. C. Veniegas, & P. L. Taylor (Eds.), *Gender, culture and ethnicity: Current research about women and men* (pp. 135–152). Mountain View, CA: Mayfield.

Yoder, J. D., Fischer, A. R., Kahn, A. S., & Groden, J. (2007). Changes in students' explanations for gender differences after taking a psychology of women class: More constructionist and less essentialist. *Psychology of Women Quarterly, 31,* 415–425.

Yoon, D. P., & Lee, E. O. (2004). Religiousness/spirituality and subjective well-being among rural elderly Whites, African

Americans, and Native Americans. *Journal of Human Behavior in the Social Environment, 10*, 191–211.

Young, J. R. (2003, September 12). Sexual assault of female Air Force Academy cadets is much more common than reported, survey finds. *Chronicle of Higher Education, 50*, A31.

Yuan, A. S. V. (2007). Gender differences in the relationship of puberty with adolescents' depressive symptoms: Do body perceptions matter? *Sex Roles, 57*, 69–80.

Yunger, J. L., Carver, P. R., & Perry, D. G. (2004). Does gender identity influence children's psychological well-being? *Developmental Psychology, 40*, 572–582.

Zabin, L. S., & Cardona, K. M. (2002). Adolescent pregnancy. In G. M. Wingood & R. J. DiClemente (Eds.), *Handbook of women's sexual and reproductive health* (pp. 231–253). New York: Kluwer Academic/Plenum.

Zablotsky, D., & Kennedy, M. (2003, June 1). Risk factors and HIV transmission to midlife and older women: Knowledge, options, and the initiation of safer sexual practices. *Journal of Acquired Immune Deficiency Syndromes, 33*, S122–S130.

Zack, N. (2005). *Inclusive feminism: A third wave theory of women's commonality*. Lanham, MD: Rowman & Littlefield.

Zager, K., & Rubenstein, A. (2002). *The inside story on teen girls*. Washington, DC: American Psychological Association.

Zahn-Waxler, C., & Polanichka, N. (2004). All things interpersonal: Socialization and female aggression. In M. Putallaz & K. L. Bierman (Eds.), *Aggression, antisocial behavior, and violence among girls: A developmental perspective* (pp. 48–68). New York: Guilford.

Zakriski, A. L., Wright, J. C., & Underwood, M. K. (2005). Gender similarities and differences in children's social behavior: Finding personality in contextualized patterns of adaptation. *Journal of Personality and Social Psychology, 88*, 844–855.

Zalk, S. R. (1991, Fall). Task force report response of mainstream journals to feminist submissions. *Psychology of Women: Newsletter*, pp. 10–12.

Zebrowitz, L. A., & Montepare, J. M. (2000). Too young, too old: Stigmatizing adolescents and elders. In T. F. Heatherton, R. E. Kleck, M. R. Hebl, & J. G. Hull (Eds.), *The social psychology of stigma* (pp. 334–373). New York: Guilford.

Zeller, J. L. (2007). Hip fractures. *Journal of the American Medical Association, 298*, 2442.

Zernike, K. (2001, April 8). The reluctant feminist. *New York Times*, pp. ED34–ED35.

Zernike, K. (2003a, November 30). Just saying no to the dating industry. *New York Times*, pp. ST1, ST12.

Zernike, K. (2003b, December 16). Teenagers want more advice from parents on sex, study says. *New York Times*, p. A32.

Zettel, L. A., & Rook, K. S. (2004). Substitution and compensation in the social networks of older widowed women. *Psychology and Aging, 19*, 433–443.

Zhou, Q., et al. (2002). The relations of parental warmth and positive expressiveness to children's empathy-related responding and social functioning: A longitudinal study. *Child Development, 73*, 893–915.

Zhou, Q., Hofer, C., Eisenberg, N., Reiser, M., Spinrad, T. L., & Fabes, R. A. (2007). The developmental trajectories of attention focusing, attentional and behavioral persistence, and externalizing problems during school-age years. *Developmental Psychology, 43*, 369–385.

Zill, D. G., Toussaint, L. A., & Pittman, D. R. (2004, May). *Portrayal of female and minority athletes in Sports Illustrated: 1988–2002*. Poster presented at the meeting of American Psychological Society, Chicago.

Zink, T., Jacobson, C. J., Regan, S., & Pabst, S. (2004). Hidden victims: The healthcare needs and experiences of older women in abusive relationships. *Journal of Women's Health, 13*, 898–908.

Zink, T., & Sill, M. (2004). Intimate partner violence and job instability. *Journal of the American Medical Women's Association, 59*, 32–35.

Zosuls, K. M., Lurye, L. E., & Ruble, D. N. (2008). Gender: Identity, awareness, and stereotyping. In M. M. Haith & J. B. Benson (Eds.), *Encyclopedia of infant and early childhood development* (Vol. 2, pp. 1–12). San Diego, CA: Academic Press.

Zubenko, G. S., et al. (2002). Genome survey susceptibility loci for recurrent, early-onset major depression: Results at 10 cM resolution. *American Journal of Medical Genetics, 114*, 413–422.

Zucker, A. N. (2004). Disavowing social identities: What it means when women say, "I'm not a feminist, but . . ." *Psychology of Women Quarterly, 28*, 423–435.

Zucker, A. N., Ostrove, J. M., & Stewart, A. (2002). College-educated women's personality development in adulthood: Perceptions and age differences. *Psychology and Aging, 17*, 236–244.

Zucker, A. N., & Stewart, A. J. (2007). Growing up and growing older: Feminism as a context for women's lives. *Psychology of Women Quarterly, 31*, 137–145.

Zucker, K. J. (2001). Biological influences on psychosocial differentiation. In R. K. Unger (Ed.), *Handbook of the psychology of women and gender* (pp. 101–115). New York: Wiley.

Zucker, K. J., Bradley, S. J., Oliver, G., & Blake, J. (1996). Psychosexual development of women with congenital adrenal hyperplasia. *Hormones and Behavior, 30*, 300–318.

Zucker, N. L., Losh, M., Bulik, C. M., LaBar, K. S., Piven, J., & Pelphrey, K. A. (2007). Anorexia nervosa and autism spectrum disorders: Guided investigation of social cognitive endophenotypes. *Psychological Bulletin, 133*, 976–1006.

NAME INDEX

Aaron, R., 410
AARP, 158, 160, 174, 176, 227, 235, 248, 249, 253, 314, 318, 359, 360, 388
Abbey, A., 440
Abele, A. E., 28
Aber, C. S., 356
Abma, J. C., 171
Abrams, D., 28, 291
Abramson, L. Y., 406
Acosta, R. V., 98
Adams, G., 340
Adams, L. L., 412
Adams, P. F., 385, 386, 388, 402
Adams, R. G., 219
Adelmann, P. K., 310
Ader, D. N., 12
Adler, J., 191, 404
Adler, N. E., 192
AFL–CIO, 285, 295, 296
Agam, G., 406
Agnoli, F., 150
Agrawal, S., 434
Ahlberg, C., 107
Ahmed, S. B., 356, 367
Ahnert, L., 340
Ahrens, C. E., 439, 440, 443, 445, 447
Ahrens, J. A., 86
Akers, A., 366
Alan Guttmacher Institute, 189, 193, 198, 199
Al-Delaimy, W. K., 377
Alexander, E. A., 399
Alexander, K., 250
Alfieri, T., 95
Ali, L., 158, 200, 206, 207
Alink, L. R. A., 128
Allan, E. J., 263
Allen, B. A., 265
Allen, K. R., 311, 312
Allen, M. W., 290
Allen, P. G., 449
Allison, P. D., 237
Altman, L. K., 252, 360, 361
Altschuler, J., 364
Alvarez, L., 467
Amaro, H., 166
Amato, P. R., 233, 234
American Academy of Pediatrics, 188
American Association of University Women, 108, 117, 147, 148, 149, 150, 260, 261, 269, 286, 290, 294, 295, 297, 298, 304, 314, 317, 318, 343, 423, 424
American Cancer Society, 174, 211, 357, 367, 368, 376, 377, 378, 380, 383
American Heart Association, 373

American Psychiatric Association, 159, 411
American Psychological Association, 10, 17, 31, 32, 113, 117, 205, 286, 324, 343, 397, 402, 403, 405, 408, 412, 414, 415, 416
American Psychological Association Task Force on the Sexualization of Girls, 42, 48, 49, 51, 121, 122, 157, 172, 466, 468
Amowitz, L. L., 450
Ananth, C. V., 202
Andersen, B. L., 381
Anderson, G. D., 355
Anderson, G. M., 167
Anderson, J., 290
Anderson, L. A., 445
Anderson, R. N., 363
Anderson, S. J., 83
Anderson, V. N., 441
Andre, T., 83
Andreasen, N. C., 397
Andronici, J. F., 297
Angell, M., 204
Angier, N., 144, 147, 157, 302, 446
Aniakudo, P., 428
Anleu, S. R., 190, 201, 209
Annan, V. Jr., 427, 450
Annas, G. J., 191
Annie E. Casey Foundation, 200
Antonucci, T., 237
Aosved, A. C., 83, 441
Apparala, M. L., 86
Appling, S., 209
Arber, S., 315
Arbisi, P. A., 219, 443
Archer, J., 128
Archer, S. L., 116
Arias, E., 382
Arias, I., 448, 449, 450
Armstrong, M. J., 248
Arnett, J. J., 49
Arney, H. T., 236
Arnold, K. D., 400
Aronson, P., 473
Arseneau, J. R., 143, 156, 158, 159, 168
Arsu, S., 443
Arvey, R. D., 303
Asay, P. A., 270
Ashcraft, M. H., 144, 145
Ashkinaze, C., 288
Ashton, C. A., 209
Ata, R. N., 121
Athenstaedt, U., 134, 135
Atwater, L., 291
Aube, J., 339

Aubeeluck, A., 185
Aubin, S., 176
Auster, E. R., 289, 300, 338, 427
Axsom, D., 440
Ayala, C., 375
Ayoola, A. B., 189
Ayoub, N. C., 368
Azar, B., 395
Azari, R., 356, 404

Babcock, J. C., 452
Babcock, L., 297
Bachanas, P. J., 364
Bachar, K., 439
Bacue, A., 31, 42, 44, 47
Badger, K., 118
Baer, J. S., 403
Baghdadi, G., 436
Bailey, J. M., 169
Baillargeon, J.-P., 373
Baillargeon, R. H., 128
Baker, B., 370
Baker, C. N., 50
Baker, D. M., 208
Baker, D. P., 144
Baker, N. L., 34
Baker-Sperry, L., 49
Baldi, S., 143
Balsam, K. F., 65, 232, 412
Bancroft, J., 160
Bancroft, J. H. J., 176
Bandura, A., 71
Banerjee, N., 288, 291, 433
Bang, E., 85
Bank, B. J., 260
Banks, A., 68
Banyard, V. L., 426
Barash, D. P., 239
Barefoot, J. C., 413
Barford, A., 381
Barker, E. T., 117
Barnard, N. D., 184
Barnett, O., 432, 434, 437, 449, 451, 452, 454
Barnett, R. C., 38, 325, 337, 339
Barnett-Connor, E., 212
Barongan, C., 447
Barrett, J., 201
Barry, C. M., 130
Bartini, M., 118
Bartlett, T., 426
Barton, L., 120
Bartsh, R. A., 42, 48
Basow, S. A., 4, 48, 55, 103, 104, 118, 260, 261
Bass, E., 434

Bassuk, S. S., 212
Bauer, G. R., 358
Bauer, P. J., 95
Baumeister, R. F., 117, 158
Bauserman, R., 233
Bay-Cheng, L. Y., 473
Bazargan, M., 407
Bazzini, D. G., 44
Beach, S. R. H., 228
Beadnell, B., 171, 172
Beals, C. P., 230, 231, 232
Beals, K. P., 412
Bean-Mayberry, B. A., 356
Bearman, P., 189
Bearman, P. S., 410
Becker, A. E., 400, 401
Becker, S. W., 130
Beckman, L. J., 190, 205, 206, 207
Bedford, V. H., 246, 247
Bee, H. L., 385
Beehr, T. A., 309
Beemyn, B. G., 168
Beers, M. H., 177, 236, 312, 359, 373, 385, 411, 453
Behbakht, K., 357
Beil, L., 189, 200
Beilock, S., 147
Beiner, T. M., 431, 432
Belansky, E. S., 96
Bell, L. C., 70
Bell, M. P., 427, 428
Bellafante, G., 230
Bellamy, C., 362
Bellas, M. L., 359
Belluck, P., 168, 231
Belmaker, R. H., 406
Belohlavck, 434
Belsky, J., 112
Belsky, J. K., 176
Beltran, A., 252
Bem, S. L., 9, 54, 70, 74, 75, 77, 79, 80, 88
Benbow, C. P., 16, 143
Ben-David, S., 441
Benenson, J. F., 132
Bennice, J. A., 440
Bentley, C. G., 438
Berdahl, J. L., 428, 429
Berenbaum, S. A., 64, 67, 68, 142
Berger, L., 122, 206
Berger, P. S., 338, 339
Berglund, H., 169
Bergman, M. E., 429
Bergmann, B. R., 295, 297
Berk, L. E., 46, 94
Berkman, N. D., 398, 399, 400
Berkowitz, R. L., 202
Bernard, M., 331
Bernstein, N., 170, 252
Berry, G. L., 43
Bersamin, M., 172
Bertakis, K. D., 356, 404
Bertone-Johnson, E. R., 188
Bessenoff, G. R., 44

Best, D. L., 18, 29, 83, 95, 97, 443
Betts, K., 121
Betz, N. E., 96, 145, 263, 268, 269, 270, 276, 277, 400
Beumont, P., 45
Beyer, S., 145, 148, 269, 275
Beymer, L., 96
Bianchi, S. M., 247, 331, 341
Biason-Lauber, A., 63
Biblarz, T. J., 243
Biehl, M. C., 114
Bierman, K. L., 397
Bieschke, K. J., 277
Bigger, J. T. Jr., 374
Bigler, R. S., 95, 268
Bilefsky, D., 443
Billings, A. C., 49
Bingham, C. R., 223
Binion, V. J., 84
Birchler, G., 229
Bird, C. E., 337, 375
Birenbaum, M., 275
Birkeland, R., 121
Birnbaum, G. E., 173
Bisagni, G. M., 234
Bittman, M., 331
Black, M. C., 438, 448, 449
Black, M. M., 250
Blackstone, A., 431
Blake, S. M., 189
Blakemore, J. E. O., 95, 100, 104, 107
Blanchard, L. T., 396
Blanchard-Fields, F., 382, 384, 452
Bleeker, M. M., 147
Blehar, M.C., 414
Blieszner, R., 247
Bly, R., 475
Blyth, D. A., 49, 115
Boduroglu, A., 32
Bogg, T., 382
Bohan, J. S., 3, 10
Boisnier, A. D., 5
Bolen, J., 357, 367, 378, 379
Boles, S. M., 449
Bond, J. T., 337, 344, 430
Bond, M. A., 290, 300
Bondurant, B., 441
Bonell, C., 172
Bongaarts, J., 248
Bonner, R., 436
Bono, J. E., 291
Bonomi, A. E., 450
Bönte, M., 374
Book, A. S., 129
Boonstra, H., 191, 198, 199
Booth, A., 230
Boothroyd, R. A., 407
Boraas, S., 285
Bordo, S., 44, 121
Borkhoff, C. M., 356
Born, L., 188
Bornstein, M. H., 104, 117
Bornstein, R. F., 451

Bos, H. M. W., 242, 243, 412
Bosacki, S. L., 132
Boston Women's Health Book Collective, 164, 182, 185, 196, 201, 205, 235, 239, 354, 434, 447
Bosworth, B., 294
Bottoms, B. L., 433
Bouchard, T. J., 403
Bould, S., 247
Bound, J., 308
Bourgrois, M. J., 431
Boushey, H., 325
Bowker, A., 119
Bowleg, L., 189, 355, 357, 363, 412, 429
Bowman, S., 270, 277
Boxer, S., 467, 470
Boynton, P., 224
Boysen, G. A., 166
Brabant, S., 47
Brabeck, K. M., 221, 239
Brabeck, M. M., 221, 239
Bradford, J., 359
Bradshaw, Z., 192
Bradsher, J. E., 237
Bragger, J. D., 197
Brandsma, L., 398
Brandt-Rauf, S., 376
Branscombe, N. R., 40
Brazile, D., 42
Brecklin, L. R., 434
Breen, A. B., 473
Bregante, J., 232
Brehm, S. S., 7
Breiding, M. J., 448, 449
Breitkopf, C. R., 122
Brender, E., 371
Brendgen, M., 129
Brener, N. D., 148, 382, 388
Brescoll, V. L., 16, 291
Breslow, L., 387
Breslow, N., 387
Brett, K., 205
Brewster, K. L., 86
Bridges, J. S., 15, 52, 84, 217, 245, 270, 271, 273, 324, 326, 328, 335, 336, 339
Bridges, L. J., 249
Bridges, M., 240, 313, 467
Bridges, S. K., 35
Brier, N., 197
Brill, M., 160
Broadbridge, A., 288, 330
Broderick, P. C., 396
Brodey, D., 122, 398
Brody, J. E., 115, 137, 174, 188, 189, 196, 197, 202, 212, 371, 372, 373, 375, 376, 387, 389, 408, 411
Bronstein, P., 104, 330
Brooks, M. G., 287
Brooks-Gunn, J., 111, 112, 113, 114, 139
Broverman, I. K., 414
Brown, C. S., 40
Brown, E. R., 404
Brown, J. S., 121, 406

Brown, L. M., 218, 330
Brown, S. L., 230, 332, 395
Brown, T. J., 273
Brown, W. M., 169
Brownlow, S., 135, 143
Brownridge, D. A., 448
Bruce, T. A., 431
Brukner, H., 356
Brumberg, J. J., 121
Bryant, A. N., 86, 474
Bryant, R. M., 416
Bryant-Davis, T., 441
Bryk, K. L. K., 67, 68
Buchanan, N. T., 431
Buckley, T. R., 77, 117
Buckner, C. E., 78
Buckner, J. C., 287
Budd, K., 204
Buddie, A. M., 439, 440
Budig, M. J., 298
Bugental, D. B., 31, 452
Bukatko, D., 96, 134, 135
Bulik, C. M., 398, 399, 400, 402
Bullock, H. E., 13, 33, 357, 473
Burchinal, M. R., 340
Bureau of Labor Statistics, 329, 330, 331
Burgess, C., 148, 380
Burgess, E. O., 175, 176, 177
Burgess, M. C. R., 42
Burggraf, K., 44, 50
Buriel, R., 108, 340
Burke, M. J., 280
Burlingame-Lee, L. J., 149
Burn, S. M., 165, 166, 194, 241, 298,
    299, 332, 333, 365, 431, 436, 443,
    450, 469
Burns, A., 347, 413
Burns, E. A., 184, 185
Burns-Glover, A. L., 217, 218, 219
Bursik, K., 424
Busch-Rossnagal, N. A., 218
Buss, D. M., 222
Busseri, M. A., 412
Bussey, K., 71
Butler, L. D., 408
Butler, R., 174, 175, 176, 178
Butler, S. S., 232
Butrica, B., 308
Button, S. B., 301
Buysse, J. M., 48
Byars-Winston, A. M., 268
Byers, E. S., 434
Bylsma, W. H., 296
Byrne, A., 235
Byrne, B. M., 276

Caballero, B., 121
Cachelin, F. M., 122
Cadinu, M., 147
Cahill, L., 406
Cahill, S., 168
Caine, E. D., 408, 410
Cairoli, M. Z., 299

Caldera, Y. M., 142
Calhoun, K. S., 440
Calhoun, L. G., 446
Calis, K. A., 370
Calvert, S. L., 48
Cambron, M. J., 117
Cameron, D., 134
Campbell, A., 95, 99, 100
Campbell, J. C., 442, 448
Campbell, P. B., 145, 147
Campbell, R., 445
Canabal, M. E., 266
Canetto, S. S., 149, 219, 237, 308,
    315, 355, 356, 386, 413
Cann, A., 87
Canterbury, R. J., 404
Caplan, J. B., 9, 17
Caplan, P. J., 9, 17, 186
Caprara, G. V., 130
Card, N. A., 128
Cardona, K. M., 171, 172, 198, 200
Carey, B., 253
Carli, L. L., 131, 134, 135, 289, 290,
    291, 293, 297, 329, 430
Carlisle, W., 337
Carlson, K. J., 196, 197, 205, 368, 369,
    373, 375, 385, 386, 389, 405
Carlson, R. A., 221
Carmichael, M., 202, 367, 388, 435
Carney, S., 449
Caron, S. L., 232
Carp, F. M., 308, 310
Carpenter, C., 49
Carpenter, C. M., 383
Carpenter, L. J., 98
Carr, C. L., 100, 118
Carr, D., 235, 237, 238, 246, 347, 348
Carr, P. L., 402
Carrington, C., 242
Carroll, M. H., 441
Carter, B., 47
Carter, R., 394, 405
Carter, R. T., 77, 117
Carvajal, D., 398
Carver, P. R., 118, 169
Case, K. A., 463, 474
Case, P., 358, 412
Casey, M. B., 70, 76
Cash, T. F., 120, 122
Cashdan, E., 134
Casper, L. M., 237, 285
Cassetta, J. A., 388
Castañeda, D., 84, 166, 217, 218, 219,
    449
Castro, I. L., 295
Catalyst, 291, 301
Cates, W. Jr., 364
Catsambis, S., 145
Cattaneo, L. B., 452
Cavanaugh, J. C., 382, 384, 452
Ceballo, R., 241, 449
Center for American Women and
    Politics, 288

Centers for Disease Control and
    Prevention, 119, 190, 206, 382, 383,
    403, 452, 453
Centers, R. E., 100
Cerhan, J. R., 377
Cermele, J. A., 415
Chaffin, M., 435
Chamberlin, J., 363
Chan, A. T., 373
Chan, K. S., 404
Chang, J. T., 387
Chang, K., 144, 147
Chang, Z., 122
Chantler, K., 451
Chapleau, K. M., 441
Chaplin, T. M., 130
Chapman, C., 148
Chapple, C. L., 441
Chapple, T., 184
Chase-Lansdale, P. L., 198, 200
Chasteen, A. L., 32
Chaudron, L. H., 408, 410
Chavez, M., 401, 402
Chavkin, W., 195
Cherlin, A. J., 227, 326, 331, 338
Cherney, I. D., 76, 99, 139, 140, 142, 148
Cherry, F., 275
Chesley, E. B., 383
Chevarley, F. M., 386
Childress, S., 451
Chin-Sang, V., 311, 312
Chira, S., 200
Chisholm, J., 33
Chiu, C., 300
Cho, L., 375
Chodorow, N. J., 3
Choi, N. G., 302, 307
Chou, A. F., 356
Chrisler, J. C., 22, 31, 44, 112, 113, 119,
    182, 183, 184, 185, 186, 187, 208, 209,
    210, 239, 346, 428
Christakis, N. A., 229, 237
Christian, A. H., 372
Ciambrone, D., 364, 366
Ciarlo, J. A., 338
Cichy, K. E., 86
Ciechanowski, P., 408
Cillessen, A. H. N., 129
Cinamon, R. G., 329
Cincotta, R. P., 262
Clampet-Lundquist, S., 287
Clancy, C. M., 356
Clapp, S. K., 428
Clark, M. A., 358
Clark, M. D., 414, 441
Clark, R. A., 135, 364
Clarke-Stewart, K. A., 128, 340
Clarren, R., 299, 427
Classen, C. C., 230, 434
Clay, R. A., 205, 206
Clearfield, M. W., 104, 139
Cleary-Goldman, J., 202
Clemetson, L., 357

Cleveland, H. H., 440
Cleveland, J. N., 286, 291, 427, 430
Clewell, B. C., 145, 147
Clunis, D. M., 218, 230
Cochran, S. D., 412
Cognard-Black, J., 221
Cohen, D., 443
Cohen, D. L., 400
Cohen, G. L., 291
Cohen, J. A., 435
Cohen, P., 235
Cohen, P. N., 297
Cohen, S. A., 191
Cohen-Bendahan, C. C. C., 67
Coie, J. D., 130
Coker, A. L., 450
Colcombe, S., 388
Cole, E. R., 130, 474, 475
Cole, J. B., 166
Cole, T. B., 403, 439, 440, 442, 443, 445
Cole, W., 64
Coley, R. L., 198, 200
Colgan, F., 277
Coll, C. G., 241
Collaer, M. L., 140
Colley, A., 97
Collins, A., 210
Collins, K. A., 452, 453
Collins, K. S., 360
Collins, W. A., 171, 172, 217, 224
Colón-Emeric, C. S., 371
Colton, P. A., 119
Coltrane, S., 43, 329, 332, 333
Commonwealth Fund, 112, 121, 218, 312, 356
Compas, B. E., 381
Compian, L., 223
Compton, J. D., 191, 388, 389
Conkright, L., 54
Conley, T. D., 169
Conrad, M., 36
Consedine, N. S., 379
Coontz, S., 228
Coovadia, H., 364
Corbett, S., 194
Cordeiro, B. L., 335
Corliss, H. L., 358
Corneal, D. A., 120
Cornelius, N., 336
Corpus, J. H., 150
Correa-de-Araujo, R., 355, 356, 375
Correll, S. J., 280, 298
Corrigall, E. A., 83, 279
Cortina, L. M., 430, 432, 450
Cosgrove, L., 186
Costello, C. B., 287, 318, 461
Costello, E. J., 396
Costigan, C. L., 117
Costos, D., 184
Coulter, I., 356
Cowan, G., 441
Cowley, G., 364
Cox, D. L., 122

Coyle, A., 329
Coyle, K., 188
Cozzarelli, C., 33
Crawford, D., 157, 221
Crawford, M., 6, 10, 11, 17, 19, 54, 57, 265, 275
Creighton, J. V., 264
Creighton, S. M., 221
Creswell, J., 288
Crocker, J., 117
Crockett, L. J., 119
Crofford, L. J., 445
Crombie, G., 145
Crosby, F. J., 280, 286, 304, 305, 338, 339, 343, 427, 460
Crouter, A. C., 95, 100, 108, 118
Crow, S. J., 402
Crowley, K., 147
Cuddy, A. J. C., 28, 31, 298
Cuijpers, P., 205
Culbert, K. M., 400
Culp, L. N., 228
Cummings, A. L., 10, 129
Cunningham, G. B., 98
Cunningham, J., 197
Cunningham, J. G., 95, 132
Cunningham, M., 104, 276, 340
Curtis, L. H., 196, 355
Custer, L., 342
Cynkar, A., 10

D'Amico, M., 147
D'Arcy, J., 259
D'Erasmo, S., 45
Daddis, C., 106
Dailard, C., 198, 200
Dalaker, J., 188, 286
Daly, J. A., 228
Daly, K., 197, 344
Dambrun, M., 407
Daniels, E., 98
Daniluk, J. C., 122, 175, 200
Danner, F., 97
Danoff-Burg, S., 441
Dardenne, B., 38
Dar-Nimrod, I., 147
Darroch, J. E., 199
Darville, R. L., 310
Daubman, K. A., 217, 276
Dauenheimer, D., 150
Davey, E. H., 271, 309, 326
David, H. P., 192, 193
David, S., 412
Davidson, J., 67
Davidson, P., 372
Davies, P. G., 150
Davila, J., 406
Davis, A. C., 223
Davis, L., 434
Davis, L. G., 183, 201
Davis, M. K., 435
Davis, P. J., 132
Davison, H. K., 280

Daw, J., 186, 188
Dawber, T., 106
Day, J. C., 294, 295
De Andrade, L. L., 423
de Guzman, M. R. T., 218
de Laet, M., 148
de las Fuentes, C., 116
de Waal, F. B. M., 447
Deal, J. J., 291
DeAngelis, C. D., 360, 394
DeAngelis, T., 122, 132
Deaux, K., 67, 275
DeBell, M., 148
DeBoer, D. D., 342
DeCherney, A. H., 206
Declercq, E., 201
DeGroot, J., 336
DeKlyen, M., 230
Del Priore, R. E., 44
Delaney, J., 187
DeLisi, R., 29
DeLoach, C. P., 268
DeLoache, J. S., 99
DeNavas-Walt, C., 294, 357
denBoer, A. M., 435, 436
Denissen, J. J. A., 145
Denizet-Lewis, B., 171
Denmark, F. L., 8, 9, 10, 22, 70, 116, 337
Denner, J., 188
Dennerstein, L., 209
DePaulo, B. M., 235
DeRose, L. M., 111, 112, 113, 114
Derry, P. S., 188, 209
Désert, M., 28
DeSouza, E. R., 423
Desrochers, S. J., 83, 106, 340
DeUgarte, C. M., 160
Deutsch, F. M., 330, 332, 333, 345
Dey, J. G., 144
DeZolt, D. M., 108
Diamond, D., 197
Diamond, L. M., 158, 163, 168, 170, 171, 172
Diamond, M., 67
Dickert, J., 104
DiClemente, R. J., 200, 361, 363, 364
Diekman, A. B., 35, 37, 83, 291, 292
Diener, E., 228, 395
Dierbeck, L., 208
Dill, K. E., 148
Dillaway, H. E., 209, 210
Dillon, S., 433
DiMatteo, M. R., 200, 229
DiNatale, M., 285
Dindia, K., 108
Dinella, L. M., 76
Dingfelder, S. F., 242
Dittmann, M., 122, 132, 381
Dixon, C. G., 448
Dodge, K. A., 128, 130
Dodson, L., 104
Doering, L. V., 375
Dogar, R., 361

Dohnt, H., 120, 121
Dominus, S., 242, 243, 263
Donaghue, N., 221
Donat, P. L. N., 438, 441
Donatelle, R. J., 183, 201, 388
Done, R. S., 429, 430
Donohoe, M., 191, 192
Donovan, R. A., 33
Doress-Worters, P. B., 154, 175, 176, 178, 236, 238, 247, 253, 313, 314
Dorfman, L. T., 310
Döring, N., 171
Dorn, J. M., 373
Dotson, L. A., 157
Douglas, S. J., 239, 240
Dowd, J. J., 47
Dowling, W., 313
Downing, R. A., 150
Downs, B., 285, 334
Dozier, D. M., 49
Drake, R., 148
Draper, B., 433
Drasgow, F., 429
Drentea, P., 332
Dreves, C., 147
Driscoll, M., 160
Dube, K., 4
Duehr, E. E., 291
Duenwald, M., 308
Duff, J. L., 218
Duffy, J., 423
Dufur, M. J., 98
Dugan, K. B., 263
Dugger, C. W., 84
Duits, T., 94
Duncan, L. E., 86
Dunham, K. J., 335
Dunifon, R., 251
Dunivin, D. L., 208, 354
Dunkle, K. L., 365
Dunne, E. F., 361
Durden, E. D., 395
Durik, A. M., 172
Durkin, S. J., 121
Duxbury, L., 338
Dweck, C. S., 71
Dye, J. L., 207, 250
Dyke, L. S., 279
Dykstra, P. A., 247

Eagly, A. H., 3, 18, 35, 37, 83, 130, 131, 222, 289, 290, 291, 293, 297, 329, 430
East, P. L., 171, 172
Eastman, V. J., 197
Eastwick, P. W., 221, 222
Eaton, D. K., 122, 170, 388, 402, 403, 404, 406, 408, 437, 438
Eberhardt, J. L., 304
Eccles, J. S., 98, 117, 145, 147, 150, 406
Eckenrode, J., 234
Ecker, J. L., 201
Eckert, P., 134
Eddleman, J., 290, 297

Edwards, C. P., 100
Edwards, M., 452, 453, 454
Ehrenreich, B., 436
Ehrlich, S. B., 140
Eisele, H., 475
Eisenberg, N., 94, 95, 103, 104, 109, 122, 130, 132
Ekstrom, B., 210
Elder, J., 207, 361, 383
Ellin, A., 252, 297, 298
Elliot, D. L., 404
Elliot, S., 47
Elliott, G. C., 172
Elliott, K., 433
Ellis, B. J., 112, 114
Ellis, J. A., 395
Ellis, S. J., 166
Elmore, J. G., 378
Elmusharaf, S., 194
Else-Quest, N. W., 143, 144, 208, 234, 239, 240
Elson, J., 368
Elwert, F., 237
Ely, R., 104, 132, 134
Embrick, D. G., 301
Embser-Herbert, M. S., 48
Emery, C., 381
England, P., 286, 291, 298
Enns, C. Z., 463
Ens, L. Z., 4, 5
Epstein, C. F., 22, 262, 286, 292, 404, 443
Epstein, E. E., 403
Erel, O., 340
Erikson, E. H., 116
Eshleman, J. R., 230
Espelage, D. L., 412
Espey, D. K., 383
Espin, O. M., 84
Espinoza, L., 363, 364
Essex, M. J., 112
Etaugh, C., 8, 19, 35, 36, 42, 44, 48, 84, 94, 95, 96, 97, 99, 104, 106, 107, 142, 163, 173, 174, 202, 233, 234, 235, 237, 238, 243, 245, 248, 250, 270, 271, 273, 302, 303, 304, 308, 309, 310, 326, 327, 335, 336, 347, 348
Evans, E. M., 144
Evans, M. A., 74
Evans-Campbell, T., 439
Evenson, R. J., 337
Ewart, C. K., 407

Fabes, R. A., 100, 104, 109
Facio, B. I., 250
Fagot, B. I., 95, 107
Fairchild, K., 37, 471, 473
Fairweather, D., 385
Fals-Stewart, W., 229
Faludi, S., 471
Family Caregiver Alliance, 248, 330, 331
Fang, B., 263
Fang, J., 372
Faria, G., 434

Farmer, H. S., 269, 271
Farris, C., 223, 441
Fassinger, R. E., 156, 158, 159, 168, 259, 270, 277, 285, 288, 290, 301, 338, 428
Fausto-Sterling, A., 2, 65, 446
Fazio, R. H., 54
Federal Bureau of Investigation, 166
Federal Glass Ceiling Commission, 292, 295, 305
Federal Interagency Forum on Aging, 248
Federal Interagency Forum on Child and Family Statistics, 170
Feingold, A., 120, 139, 140
Feiring, C., 434
Feist-Price, S., 364
Felder, S., 228
Feldman, R. S., 10, 21, 210
Feldman, S., 237, 238
Feldstein, K., 317, 318
Felix, E. D., 423
Felmlee, D. H., 226
Feng, J., 142
Fergus, S., 170
Ferguson, F. I., 241
Fergusson, D. M., 397
Fernald, J. C., 473
Ferraro, K. F., 31, 355, 386
Ferraro, S., 377
Ferris, L. E., 452
Fiatarone, M. A., 387
Fichter, M. M., 402
Field, D., 229
Fielding, E. N., 192
Fields, J., 228, 237, 240, 241, 249
Figueredo, A. J., 443
Fine, J., 336
Fine, M., 449
Finer, L. B., 192
Fingeret, M. C., 117, 119
Fingerhut, A. W., 230, 232, 242, 277
Fingerman, K. L., 217, 247
Fingerson, L., 112, 184,
Fink, J. S., 48, 49
Finkel, E. J., 221
Finkelhor, D., 433
Finkelstein, J. S., 389
Firestone, J. M., 84
Firestone, P., 448
Fisher, M. L., 121
Fisher, S. Y., 316
Fisher, T. A., 277
Fisher, T. D., 171
Fisher-Thompson, D., 104
Fiske, S. T., 28, 37, 38, 39, 304, 431
Fitzgerald, L., 427, 431
Fitzgerald, L. F., 414, 426
Fitzgerald, M. H., 187
Fitzpatrick, M. A., 174, 309
Fitzpatrick, M. K., 438
Fitzpatrick, T. R., 309
Fivush, R., 132
Flack, W. F., 440, 443

Flanagan, C., 278
Flannagan, D., 72
Fleck, C., 314
Flegal, K. M., 373
Fleming, L. M., 239
Fletcher, V., 402
Flores, G., 357
Flores, L., 278
Flouri, E., 277
Foa, E. B., 433, 434
Foege, W. H., 383
Fogg, P., 284, 297
Folger, D., 327
Follette, V. M., 434
Forbes, G. B., 122, 184
Ford, E. S., 372
Ford, T. E., 150
Forrest, L., 463
Foshee, V. A., 438
Foster, M. D., 473
Fouad, N. A., 268
Foust-Cummings, H., 289, 290
Fouts, G., 44, 50, 121
Fowers, B. J., 415
Fowler, J. P., 366
Frabutt, J. M., 433, 435, 438, 448, 449, 454
Franco, M., 450
Frank, A., 109, 110
Frankel, L. P., 298
Franklin, K., 168
Franko, D. L., 122, 398
Frankowski, B. L., 163
Frantz, D., 410
Franzoi, S. L., 122
Fraser, A. S., 469
Frasure-Smith, N., 374
Frederick, D. A., 119, 122
Fredricks, J. A., 98
Freeman, E. W., 413
French, D. C., 129
French, K. E., 97
Fretts, R. C., 382
Freud, S., 156, 168
Freyd, J. J., 433, 434
Freysinger, V. J., 311, 312
Fried, L. P., 312
Friedan, B., 9, 475
Friedman, C. K., 95, 99, 100, 106
Friedman, D. E., 343
Friedman, S. R., 270
Frieze, I. H., 128, 129, 130, 143, 225, 295, 434, 435, 447, 448, 450, 452
Frigoletto, F. D. Jr., 201
Frith, K. T., 49
Frome, P. M., 268, 280
Frone, M. R., 343
Frost, J., 117
Frye, J. C., 299
Fuegen, K., 327
Fukkink, R. G., 340
Fulcher, M., 96, 243, 268
Fuller-Thomson, E., 262, 285
Fulton, A., 163
Furman, W., 438

Furnham, A., 47, 147, 275
Fuwa, M., 329

Gadbois, S., 119
Gajendran, R. S., 343
Galambos, N. L., 118, 406
Gale, E., 225
Galinsky, E., 337, 340, 344
Gall, C., 263
Gallagher, C., 218
Gallagher, W., 223
Gallant, S. J., 188
Galliher, R. V., 226
Gallor, S., 301
Galupo, M. P., 218
Galvao, L., 189
Ganahl, D. J., 44
Gangestad, S. W., 221
Gannon, L., 210
Ganong, L. H., 235, 268, 272
Ganske, K. H., 76
Garavalia, L. S., 375
Garbers, S., 357
Garfinkel, P., 47
Garnets, L. D., 13, 168, 412
Garrow, D. J., 168
Gartrell, N. K., 68, 242
Gavey, N., 189
Gaylord, S., 382
Gearhart, J. P., 67
Gearon, C. J., 364
Geary, D. C., 146
Geipert, N., 373
Gelman, S. A., 75, 104
Gennetian, L. A., 200
Genzlinger, N., 44
George, D., 218
George, W. H., 439
Gergen, K. J., 219
Gergen, M., 13
Gergen, M. M., 219
Gerson, K., 328
Gibbons, J. L., 18, 252
Gibbs, N., 202
Gibson, H. B., 175
Gidycz, C. A., 435, 441
Giesbrecht, N., 116
Giesen, C., 267
Gilbert, L. A., 17, 110, 344, 416, 417
Gilbert, S., 202
Giles, J. W., 129
Giles, L. C., 383
Gillen, M. M., 119
Gillespie, R., 208
Gilligan, C., 3, 4, 116, 117, 133
Giltau E. J., 396
Ginorio, A. B., 250
Ginsberg, R. L., 50
Ginty, M. M., 362, 363
Giuliano, T. A., 49
Glass, N., 449
Glass, R. M., 394
Glass, T. A., 387
Glassman, A. H., 374

Glauber, R., 298
Gleason, J. B., 104, 132, 134
Gleaves, D. H., 117, 119
Glenn, D., 435
Glick, P., 37, 38, 39, 431
Glied, S., 408
Godbey, J. K., 434
Godfrey, J. R., 210, 402
Gold, E. B., 184, 188, 190, 209
Goldberg, A. E., 330
Goldberg, C., 203, 268
Goldberg, N., 211, 212, 364, 367, 368, 387
Goldberg, W. A., 340, 341
Golden, C., 2, 64
Goldin, C., 325
Goldman, M. B., 381
Goldscheider, F., 227, 228
Goldshmidt, O. T., 134, 137
Goldstein, A., 329
Goldston, D. B., 408, 410
Golombok, S., 207, 242, 244
Gomez, M. J., 278
Gondolf, E. W., 452
Gonzalez, F. J., 84
Gonzalez, M. H., 221
Good, C., 150
Goodchilds, J. D., 174
Goode, E., 122, 395
Gooden, A. M., 42
Gooden, M. A., 42
Goodman, L. A., 452
Goodman, M., 412
Goodwin, P. J., 381
Goodwin, S. A., 38
Gordis, E. B., 434
Gordon, R. A., 251, 303
Gorman, C., 64
Gorzalka, B. B., 156, 441
Gostin, L. O., 360
Gottlieb, N., 235
Gould, S. J., 9
Goyer, A., 251
Grabe, S., 20, 49, 119, 121, 122, 407
Graber, J. A., 114, 397, 406
Grady, D., 197, 203, 209, 212, 374, 376, 377, 436
Gramotnev, H., 228, 233
Granrose, C. S., 338
Grauerholz, L., 49
Gray, J., 133, 135, 137
Gray, J. J., 50
Gray-Little, B., 117
Green, E. R., 468
Green, R. J., 218
Green, R.-J., 242
Green, V. A., 99
Greenberg, B. S., 43, 50
Greene, B., 33, 166
Greene, M. L., 117
Greenfield, S. F., 402
Greenhaus, J. H., 338
Greenhouse, S., 290
Greenwood, D. N., 48
Grimberg, A., 356

Grimmell, D., 79, 86
Grodstein, F., 211
Groskop, V., 160
Gross, J., 264, 308, 312, 343
Gross, J. J., 413
Gross, S. M., 398
Grossman, A. H., 220, 231
Grossman, A. J., 36
Grossman, A. L., 57
Grossman, S. E., 452
Grunbaum, J. A., 122, 188, 382, 439
Gryboski, K., 195
Guastello, D. D., 79
Guestello, S. J., 79
Guiaux, M., 237
Guo, G., 145
Gupta, S., 206, 333
Gutek, B. A., 296, 429, 430
Gutman, L. M., 37, 117, 406
Guy-Sheftall, B., 166

Ha, J.-H., 237, 238, 246
Haag, P., 169, 198
Hackett, G., 265, 270
Haddock, S., 262
Hadi, F., 395
Haedt, A., 401, 402
Hafdahl, A. R., 117
Hafner, K., 148, 284
Hagekull, B., 397
Haj-Yahia, M. M., 450
Halbreich, U., 196
Hall, D. M., 208, 239
Hall, G. C. N., 447
Hall, J. A., 137, 138
Hall, R. E., 13
Hall, R. L., 98, 166, 220, 387, 389
Hall, R. M., 97
Halloran, E., 167
Halmi, K. A., 400
Halpern, D., 285
Halpern, D. F., 20, 138, 139, 140, 141,
    142, 143, 144, 146, 147
Halpern, D. L., 343
Halpern, M. T., 357, 376
Hamby, S. L., 433, 439
Hamilton, B. E., 198
Hamilton, E. A., 121, 201
Hamilton, M. C., 53
Hammarberg, A., 397
Hammen, C., 406
Hammond, C. B., 440
Hampson, E., 142
Hampton, T., 190
Hanisch, L. J., 405
Hankin, B. L., 406
Hankin, S., 160
Hannaford, P. C., 368
Hanratty, B., 330
Hanson, K., 311
Hardin, M., 49
Hare-Mustin, R. T., 3, 8, 404, 416
Harm, N. J., 252
Harmetz, A., 44

Harmon, A., 226
Harper, B., 121
Harper, G. W., 165, 301
Harper, M., 78
Harris, A. C., 30
Harris, G., 190, 192
Harris, G. T., 449
Harris, K. L., 474
Harris, M. B., 15, 32
Harris, R. J., 84
Harrison, D. A., 343
Harrison, K., 109
Harter, S., 114, 115, 117, 118
Hartley, H., 159, 162
Hartley, J., 104
Hartman, H., 150, 160, 343
Hartman, M., 150, 268
Hartmann, K. E., 174
Harvey, R., 146
Harville, M. L., 85
Hasin, D. S., 402
Haskell, K., 252
Haskell, M., 44
Haslam, S. A., 291
Hassan, M. A. M., 206
Hatala, M. N., 221
Hatch, M. C., 381
Hattery, A., 324, 335, 337
Hawkes, D., 277
Hawkins, D. N., 287, 344
Hawkins, J. W., 356
Hawthorne, F., 308
Hay, D. F., 100
Hayes, K. A., 171
Hayes, S. N., 355
Haynes, M. C., 291
Hayward, C., 223
He, W., 229, 235, 236, 249, 314, 315, 385,
    386, 411
Headlam, B., 148
Hearn, J., 288, 330
Heatherington, L., 276
Hébert, M., 438
Hebl, M. R., 76
Heck, J., 358
Heckert, T. M., 273, 279
Hedges, L. V., 139
Hedley, M., 48
Hefferman, K., 123
Heffner, L. J., 206
Hehman, J. A., 31, 452
Heilman, M. E., 291, 298
Heiman, S. R., 176
Heine, S. J., 147
Heiss, G., 211
Helgeson, V. S., 410
Hellerstedt, W., 171
Helmreich, R. L., 77, 78
Help Network, 450
Helson, R., 347
Helwig, A. A., 96
Henderson-King, D., 473
Hendrick, C. L., 172, 434
Hendy, H. M., 438

Henig, R. M., 174, 175, 398, 399
Henley, N. M., 4, 5, 138
Henningfield, J. E., 383
Henningsen, D. D., 223
Henry, A., 468
Henry, D. B., 189
Henshaw, S. K., 192
Heppner, M. J., 13, 305
Herbers, J. E., 453, 454
Herbert, S. E., 364
Herdt, G. H., 67
Herek, G. M., 166, 167, 168, 220, 231,
    232, 412
Herman, K., 436
Herman, K. C., 10
Herman-Giddens, M. E., 112
Herman-Stahl, M., 413, 416
Heron, M. P., 384, 385
Héroux, G., 142
Herrenkohl, T. I., 128, 129
Herrera, V. M., 432, 434, 439
Hertz, R., 241
Hetherington, E. M., 233, 234
Hewitt Associates, 343
Hewlett, S. A., 292, 325, 345, 346
Heyl, A. R., 289, 308
Heyman, G. D., 129
Heymann, J., 334
Hickman, L. J., 437, 438
Hiestand, K. R., 230
Higginbotham, E., 271, 277, 278, 280
Higgins, C., 338
Hilbrecht, M., 119, 148
Hill, A. L., 397
Hill, C., 104, 107, 144, 423, 426
Hill, T. D., 384
Hillis, S. D., 172
Hillman, J. L., 178
Hilton, N. Z., 449
Hines, D. A., 449
Hines, M., 9, 16, 62, 64, 65, 67, 128, 138,
    139, 140, 141, 142
Hirshbein, L. D., 186
Ho, C. K., 449
Hochman, A., 394
Hochschild, A. K., 436
Hoeber, L., 98
Hofferth, S. L., 198, 200
Hoffman, E., 319
Hoffman, L.W., 80, 106, 341
Hoffman, M. L., 117, 397
Hoffnung, M., 268, 270, 272
Hogan, J. D., 6, 7
Hoge, W., 168
Hogg, K., 106
Hoggard, L., 51
Hoglund, W. L., 397
Hogue, M., 296, 297
Holcomb, B., 240, 256
Holcomb, L. P., 267
Holland, A., 83
Hollander, J., 462
Holmes, S. E., 168, 377
Holroyd-Leduc, J. M., 385

Holt-Lunstad, J., 228, 383
Holton, G., 276
Hong, S., 372, 373
Hook, J. L., 329, 332, 333
Hook, M. K., 270, 277
hooks, b., 22, 148, 468
Hopkins, A. B., 37
Horgan, T. G., 137
Hornbacher, M., 399
Horner, M. S., 274
Horney, K., 3
Hounsell, C., 317, 318
Houppert, K., 113
Hourani, L. L., 184
Houston, D. K., 389
Howard, J. A., 462
HSBC Insurance, 381
Hudak, M. A., 48
Huddy, L., 471
Hudson, V. M., 435, 436
Huffman, M. L., 297
Huffman, T., 230
Hughes, I. A., 63
Huguet, P., 147
Hull, S. H., 108
Hulme, P. A., 434
Hunter, E., 47
Hurley, D., 232
Hurme, S. B., 453, 454
Hurtado, M., 50
Hutchinson, M. K., 171
Hutchinson, S. A., 434
Hutson-Comeaux, S. L., 276
Huyck, M. H., 229, 231
Hyde, J. S., 16, 20, 122, 133, 139, 143,
    144, 156, 158, 159, 172, 274, 275,
    308, 335, 342

Ibrahim, H., 262
Iervolino, A. C., 107
Iglehart, J. K., 359
Ikeda, R. M., 448, 449, 450
Ilies, R., 427
Impett, E. A., 170
Ingersoll-Dayton, B., 331
Inglehart, R., 83
Insel, T. R., 401, 402
Institute for Women's Policy Research,
    259, 295, 296, 318, 330, 332, 343
International Labour Organization, 299
Inter-Parliamentary Union, 288
Irvine, M., 398
Isbell, L. M., 424
Iwamasa, G. Y., 416
Iyengar, R., 451

Jack, D. C., 407
Jacklin, C. N., 18
Jackson, D., 291
Jackson, L. A., 273, 296, 473
Jackson, R. A., 206
Jackson, Y., 395
Jacobi, C., 398, 400

Jacobs, E. A., 357
Jacobs, J. E., 276
Jacobson, J., 261
Jacobsson, B., 202
Jacoby, S., 359
Jadva, V., 207
Jaffe, E., 148
Jaffe, M. L., 116
Jaffe, S., 133
Jain, T., 206
James, S. D., 203, 204
Janofsky, M., 428, 429
Janssen, I., 121
Jansz, J., 148
Jarrell, A., 223
Jarviluoma, H., 17
Jenkins, C. L., 234
Jennings, A., 245
Jernigan, P. H., 403
Jersild, D., 403
Jessell, J. C., 96
Jha, A. K., 372
Jha, P., 436
Jiang, J., 144
Jin, L., 229
Johannesen-Schmidt, M. C., 293
John, R., 250
Johns, M., 150
Johnson, A. B., 239
Johnson, A. G., 471
Johnson, B. E., 441
Johnson, C. L., 413
Johnson, D., 177, 205, 250, 329
Johnson, D. M., 415
Johnson, D. R., 37
Johnson, J. O., 334
Johnson, J. T., 83
Johnson, K. A., 172, 434
Johnson, M. A., 389
Johnson, R. D., 148
Johnson, S. B., 12
Johnson, S. M., 242
Johnson, V. E., 155, 156
Johnson, W., 228, 229
Johnston, D. D., 240
Johnston, L., 168
Johnston, L. D., 402, 404
Jones, B. E., 232
Jones, C. J., 413
Jones, D. C., 122
Jones, D. J., 396
Jones, D. P., 144
Jones, M., 382
Jones, R., 305
Jones, S. M., 108
Jones, T. C., 252
Jones, T. V., 177, 236, 312, 359, 373, 385,
    411, 453
Jordan, J. V., 3, 117
Jordan, V. B., 412
Josselson, R., 116, 239
Joutsenniemi, K., 228
Jovanovic, J., 147

June, A. W., 288
Junginger, J., 173
Juntunen, C. L., 277
Juvonen, J., 423

Kagay, C. R., 357
Kahlenborn, C., 377
Kahn, A. S., 440
Kahn, K. L., 200
Kaiser Family Foundation, 166, 168
Kajantie, E., 382
Kalb, C., 203, 363, 364
Kalil, A., 198
Kane, E. W., 30, 83
Kantrowitz, B., 147, 173, 195, 365,
    369, 371, 372, 373, 403
Kaplan, E. E., 338
Kaplan, G. A., 387
Karass, J., 139
Karney, B. R., 228
Karpiak, C. P., 86
Karpiak, S. E., 366
Karpinski, A., 473
Karraker, K. H., 34, 104
Kasanen, K., 140, 147
Kasen, S., 413
Kashubeck, S., 79
Kashubeck-West, S., 120, 475
Kasturirangan, A., 451
Kates, E., 266
Katz, D. S., 297
Katz, J., 474
Katz, P. A., 96, 107, 396, 462, 464, 465
Katz, S. J., 253
Katzenstein, L., 360
Kaufman, G., 227, 228
Kaufmann, J. A., 200
Kawamura, S., 332
Kearney, L. K., 344, 416, 417
Keel, P. K., 399, 400, 401, 402
Keita, G. P., 406
Keith, P. M., 235, 236
Keller, B. K., 277
Keller, J., 150
Kelley, R., 206, 207
Kelley, T., 438
Kelley-Moore, J. A., 386
Kelly, A. M., 120, 122
Kelly, E., 11, 13
Kelly, J., 233, 234
Kendler, K. S., 395, 406
Kenfield, S. A., 373
Kennedy, B. L., 361
Kennedy, M., 365, 436
Kennedy, M. A., 156, 441
Kenney-Benson, G. A., 143
Kenrick, D. T., 221
Kensicki, L. J., 48, 49
Kerpelman, J., 277
Kerr, B., 471
Kersting, K., 138, 148
Keshavarz, H., 368
Kessel, C., 374

Kessler, R. C., 405, 413
Khor, D., 230
Khosla, S., 370, 371
Kiang, L., 130
Kiecolt-Glaser, J. K., 228, 337, 338
Kiefer, A. K., 145, 275
Kilbourne, A., 357
Killick, S. R., 206
Kim, J. E., 307, 309
Kim, J.-Y., 108, 246
Kim, W. J., 99, 410
Kimerling, R., 434
Kimmel, D. G., 65, 221, 232
Kimmel, E., 6, 10, 12, 19, 30
Kimmel, M., 475
Kimura, D., 146
King, A. C., 403
King, C., 284
King, D. E., 373
King, D. W., 82
King, J. E., 261
King, L. A., 82
King, M., 412
King, R. B., 285
Kinsella, K., 229, 236, 248, 316, 318, 384
Kinsey, A. C., 156
Kinsler, K., 460
Kinzie, J., 264
Kissling, E. A., 112, 185
Kitano, M. K., 278
Kite, M. E., 28, 31, 35, 88, 304
Kitto, J., 56
Kitzinger, C., 146
Kivimäki, M., 384, 396
Klara, M. D., 22
Klein, A. A., 54
Klein, M. H., 335
Kleinfield, N. R., 452
Kleyman, K. S., 280
Kline, G. H., 230
Kling, K. C., 117, 274, 275
Klohnen, E. C., 220
Klomsten, A. T., 117
Klonoff, E. A., 40
Klumb, P. L., 347
Klump, K. L., 400
Kmiec, J., 468
Knafo, A., 130
Knickmeyer, N., 220
Knight, B., 412
Knight, J. L., 49
Knight-Bohnhoff, K., 15
Knightley, P., 54
Knodel, J., 252
Kobrynowicz, D., 40
Koenig, L. J., 434
Koepsell, J. K., 451
Kohlberg, L., 72, 73, 74, 76, 132
Kohlman, M. H., 441
Kolata, G., 192
Kolchakian, M. R., 301
Konek, C. W., 306, 467
Konrad, A. M., 83, 270, 279, 280

Kornblut, A. E., 288
Koropeckyj-Cox, T., 207
Korteland, C., 396
Kosiak, B., 357, 379
Koss, M. P., 439, 440, 443, 450, 466
Kossek, E. E., 337
Kowaleski-Jones, L., 251
Kowalski, R. M., 130, 184
Kraemer, R., 275
Krahé, B., 450
Krakovsky, M., 197
Kramarae, C., 134
Kramer, A., 388, 448
Krantz, M. J., 375
Krause, N., 309
Krebs, E. E., 212
Kreider, R., 245
Kreider, R. M., 233
Kreiger, T. C., 109
Krishnamurthy, P., 331, 338
Kristjansdottir, G., 97
Kristof, N. D., 263, 365, 410, 435, 436
Kroenke, C. H., 381
Kromrey, J. D., 30
Kruger, J., 388
Krumrei, E., 234
Krupp, C., 221
Kubany, E. S., 452
Kuchment, A., 407
Kuhn, J., 202
Kuhn, M., 411
Kulig, K., 98
Kumra, S., 291
Kung, H.-C., 382
Kunz, J., 198
Kuppermann, M., 368
Kurdek, L. A., 230, 231, 232
Kuriloff, P. J., 85
Kurman, J., 145
Kvigne, V. L., 403

L'Armand, K., 426
Labaton, V., 470
Lacasse, A., 442
Lacey, J. V. Jr., 368
Laditka, J. N., 237
Laditka, S. B., 237
Laflamme, D., 330
LaFrance, M., 16, 135, 137, 430, 446, 447
LaFraniere, F., 316
LaFraniere, S., 450
LaFromboise, T. D., 84, 85, 266, 272, 278
LaGreca, A. M., 397
Lakkis, J., 122
Lakoff, R., 16, 36, 134
Lalumiére, M. L., 169
Lamb, S., 42
Lambdin, J. R., 53
Lamberg, L., 209, 211, 397
Lambiase, J. J., 51
Lampert, T., 347
Landesmon, P., 436
Landrine, H., 40

Landry, L. J., 117
Lane, C., 225
Lane, M., 42
Laner, M. R., 226
Lang, M. M., 329
Langhout, R. D., 430
Lanham-New, S. A., 371
Lapierre, L. M., 430
Larose, S., 276
LaRossa, R., 47
Larson, K., 54
Larson, R. W., 104, 262
Laschever, S., 297
Lasswell, M., 228, 233
Latner, J. D., 121
Laumann, E. O., 157, 158, 159, 164, 226
Lauzen, M. M., 42, 43, 47, 49
Lawlor, D. A., 384, 385, 413
Lawrence, E., 239
Lawton, C. A., 36
Lazur, A., 178
Leach, P., 337
Leadbeater, B. J., 397
Leahy, E., 145
Leaper, C., 30, 40, 75, 95, 98, 99, 100,
    103, 106, 107, 134, 135, 139, 147
Leary, W. E., 176
Lee, A., 113
Lee, C., 228, 233
Lee, E., 192, 193
Lee, E. O., 414
Lee, F. R., 435
Lee, J., 250, 371
Lee, J. M., 112
Lee, P. A., 64
Lee, S., 185, 252, 315, 470
Leeb, R. T., 137
Lefkowitz, E. S., 119, 247
Lehr, S., 48, 49
Leiblum, S. L., 159, 174
Leibson-Hawkins, B., 379
Leinbach, M. D., 107
Leitner, M. J., 175, 176, 178, 312, 313
Leitner, S. F., 175, 176, 178, 312, 313
Leland, J., 308
Leman, P. J., 134
Lemieux, S. R., 434
Lengua, L. J., 407
Lennon, M. C., 407
Leon, L. G., 197
Leonard, D., 144
Leonard, K. E., 438
Leonard, R., 347, 413
Leopold, J. A., 374
LePage-Lees, P., 266
Lerner, B. H., 64
Lerner, J. S., 64
Lerner, S., 228, 341
Lescano, C. M., 228
Leschied, A. W., 10, 129
Lesko, A. C., 150
Lespérance, F., 374
Lester, D., 410

LeTourneau, E. J., 434
Leung, S. A., 268
Levant, R. F., 48, 83
Leventhal, T., 139
Levesque, K., 148
Levesque, L. L., 263, 425
Levesque, M. J., 223
Levine, M., 383
Levine, S. C., 32, 140
Levison, S. P., 356
Levitt, H. M., 230
Levy, G. D., 95
Levy, J. A., 364
Lew, A. S., 266
Lewin, T., 200, 326, 363
Lewis, J. M., 106
Lewis, J. R., 317
Lewis, M. I., 174, 175, 176, 178
Leyens, J.-P., 28
Li, C., 277
Li, Q., 147
Liao, L. M., 221
Liben, L. S., 95, 142
Lichtenstein, A. H., 389
Lichter, E. L., 437, 438
Liljestrand, J., 195
Lim, S., 430
Lin, J., 377
Lindau, S. T., 176
Lindberg, L. D., 114, 200
Lindgren, K. P., 223, 441
Lindner, K., 48
Lindsey, E. W., 100, 104
Linn, M. C., 139, 140, 141, 374
Lipka, S., 98
Lippa, R. A., 66, 67, 277
Lippert, J., 373
Lips, H. M., 145, 197, 268
Lipson, J., 273, 297
Liptak, A., 168, 231
Lisi, D., 157
Liss, M. B., 96, 99, 104, 106
Little, M. V., 319
Littlefield, G. D., 231
Littleton, H. L., 440
Livingston, J. A., 442
Livosky, M., 475
Llabre, M. M., 395
Lloyd-Jones, D. M., 372
Loeb, S., 340
Lonborg, S. D., 270
London, K., 99, 139, 142, 148, 433
Long, P. J., 433, 434, 441
Longino, C. F., 247
Longman, J., 400
Lonsway, K. A., 424, 430
Lont, A., 340
Lorber, J., 463
Lorch, E. P., 49
Lott, B., 13, 33, 109, 357
Lottes, I. L., 85
Louie, B., 48
Lovas, G. S., 104
Lovejoy, M., 474

Lovell, V., 314, 334
Low Dog, T., 210
Lowell, J., 312
Lown, E. A., 449
Lubinski, D. S., 143
Lucas, R. E., 228, 237
Lucas-Thompson, R., 340, 341
Luciano, L., 294
Luecken, L., 380
Lule, E., 194, 262
Lummis, M., 140, 147
Lundy, M., 452
Luo, S., 220
Lupton, M. J., 187
Luthar, S. S., 337
Lutzker, J. R., 435
Lyall, S., 168
Lydon-Rochelle, M. T., 202
Lynch, S. A., 228
Lyness, K. S., 300, 334, 407

Macalister, H. E., 164
Macan, T., 197
Maccoby, E. E., 18, 100, 119, 224
MacGeorge, E. L., 135, 137
MacIntosh, H. B., 434
Mack, K. A., 122
MacLeod, M., 265, 275
MacMillan, H. L., 452
MacWilliams, B., 436
Madden, M., 263
Madkan, V. K., 360
Magai, C., 379
Magley, V. J., 429, 430, 432
Maguire, M., 185
Mahaffy, K. A., 270
Mahalingam, R., 65
Mahay, J., 158
Mahler, S., 405
Mahoney, S., 226
Maine, D., 195
Mainiero, L. A., 133
Maisto, S. A., 189
Majerovitz, S. D., 375, 386, 388
Major, B., 117
Major, B., 117, 192, 296
Malamuth, N. M., 447
Malanchuk, O., 117
Malatesta, V. J., 175
Malcolmson, K. A., 36
Maldonado-Molina, M. M., 383
Maliti, T., 467
Malkin, C., 474
Malley-Morrison, K., 450, 453
Maluso, D., 109
Mangweth-Matzek, B., 398
Mankiller, W., 468
Manlove, J., 189
Mannarino, A. P., 435
Mannheim Research Institute, 384, 385,
    406, 408
Manning, W. D., 229, 230
Mannino, C. A., 330, 332, 333
Mansfield, P. K., 173, 428

Manson, J. E., 212
Manzoli, L., 237
Marano, H. E., 111
Marcia, J. E., 116
Marcotte, D. E., 251, 252
Marcus, E. N., 448
Marecek, J., 3, 8, 404, 416, 417
Mares, M. L., 174, 309
Margolin, G., 434
Markens, S., 206
Markey, C. N., 119, 120
Markey, P. M., 119
Markham, B., 389
Markovic, M., 368
Markowe, L. A., 168
Markson, E. W., 31, 44
Marler, J. H., 286
Marlino, D., 278
Marrazzo, J. M., 358, 361
Marriott, M., 148
Marsh, D. T., 168, 205, 394, 412
Marsh, H. W., 119, 145
Marshall, N. L., 335, 339, 340
Martens, A., 31
Martin, C. L., 34, 72, 74, 76, 88, 94, 95,
    100, 109, 140
Martin, D. L., 470
Martin, J. A., 198, 201, 202, 240
Martin, J. L., 130
Martin, M. O., 143
Martin, S. L., 144, 439
Martinez, L. J., 439
Martinez, S., 300
Martínez-Vicente, J. M., 47, 48
Martino, S. C., 49
Martire, L. M., 339
Martis, R. G., 148
Marton, K., 365
Marulis, L., 142
Maruti, S. S., 377
Mason, F., 442, 443, 445
Mason, G., 166
Masser, B., 197
Masser, B. M., 28, 291
Massoni, K., 48
Masters, W. H., 155, 156
Mastro, D. E., 43
Mathers, C. D., 385
Matire, L. M., 344
Matlin, M. W., 32, 185
Matsui, Y., 83
Matthews, K., 396
Mattingly, M. J., 331
Mattis, J. S., 414
Maume, D. J., 330
Mauthner, N. S., 205
Mavin, S., 291
Mayer, K. H., 359
Mayeux, L., 129
Mays, V. M., 412
Mazzella, R., 120
McCabe, M. P., 121
McCann, T., 289
McCauley, E., 64, 67

McCloskey, C., 278
McCloskey, L. A., 437, 438, 451
McClosky, L. A., 451
McClure, E. B., 137
McConnell, A. R., 54
McConnell-Ginet, S., 134
McCoy, W. D., 408
McCreary, D. R., 88
McDowell, M. A., 112
McFadden, D., 169
McGarry, K., 237
McGinn, D., 171, 177
McGinnis, J. M., 383
McGlone, M. S., 143
McGorty, E. K., 415
McGuire, L. C., 407
McHale, S. M., 97, 98, 99, 100, 104, 108, 120
McHugh, M. C., 161, 176, 405, 448, 449, 451, 452
McKelvey, M. W., 234
McKelvie, S., 117
McKenry, P. C., 234
McKinley, N. M., 398
McLanahan, S. S., 200
McLean, R., 168
McLoyd, V. C., 338
McMahon, S. D., 423
McMullen, L. M., 407
McMunn, A., 338
McNeely, C., 171
McNeil, D. G., 364, 366, 436
McPherson, B. J., 48
McPhillips, K., 189
McQuaide, S., 347
Mead, S., 260, 261
Medicine, B., 272
Mednick, M. T., 274, 275
Meece, J. L., 42, 108, 264
Meier, A. M., 172
Mello, Z. R., 260
Melton, L. J. III., 370, 371
Meltzer, A. L., 354, 355, 357, 372, 374, 377
Ménard, K. S., 429, 430
Mendelsohn, D. M., 103
Mendelsohn, G. A., 221
Mendelson, M. J., 442
Mendle, J., 112
Menec, V. H., 388
Menendez, J. A., 377
Mensinger, J. L., 400
Mercer, C., 358, 412
Mercer, S. O., 249, 316, 384
Mercurio, A. E., 117
Meredith, W., 413
Merline, A. C., 404
Merrick, E. L., 402
Merskin, D., 221
Messineo, M., 43
Messman-Moore, T. L., 434
Messner, M. A., 55
Mestel, R., 157
Metzl, J. M., 356

Meyer, I. H., 412
Meyer, M. H., 359
Meyers, S. A., 221
Mezulis, A. H., 16, 275
Michael, S. T., 237
Michael, Y. L., 248
Michaels, M., 239, 240
Michaud, S., 135, 136
Michelson, W., 331
Mikhail, G. W., 355, 372, 373
Mikkelsen, T. F., 208
Milar, K. S., 6
Milburn, S. S., 42
Milcent, C., 372
Milkie, M. A., 330
Miller, A. G., 439, 440
Miller, B. C., 223
Miller, C., 200
Miller, C. F., 95
Miller, D. T., 3
Miller, J. B., 3
Miller, K. K., 398
Miller, K. S., 189
Miller, L., 158, 241
Miller, M. K., 148
Miller, P., 191
Miller-Day, M. A., 239, 247
Miner, J. L., 128, 340
Miner-Rubino, K., 430
Miniño, A. M., 382
Minkler, M., 262, 285, 386
Minto, C., 64
Mintz, L., 122, 278
Miotto, K., 449
Mischel, W., 70
Misra, D., 403
Misra, M., 398
Mitchell, B. S., 32
Mitchell, J., 122
Mitchell, J. E., 401
Mitchell, V., 242
Mitchell-Kernan, C., 227
Mitka, M., 372
Mize, J., 100, 104
Mobily, K. E., 311
Moen, P., 286, 307, 309
Moffat, S. C., 142
Mohler-Kuo, M., 402
Mollen, D., 208
Molnar, B. E., 397
Mondschein, E. R., 97
Mongeau, P. A., 223
Monsour, M., 219
Montepare, J. M., 31
Montes, G., 340
Moody, J., 410
Mooney, L. A., 47
Moore, A., 380
Moore, C., 132, 429
Moore, D., 79
Moore, K. A., 223
Moore, S. E. H., 354
Mor, N., 407
Mora, S., 207, 373

Moracco, K. E., 168
Morahan-Martin, J., 148
Mor-Barak, M. E., 309
Moreau, R., 263, 410
Moreman, R. D., 219
Morgan, B. L., 6, 14, 472
Morgan, E. M., 163
Mori, L., 441
Morley, J. E., 174, 176
Morris, A. S., 130
Morris, B. R., 132, 398
Morris, E. W., 108
Morris, J. F., 412
Morris, W. L., 235
Morrison, M. A., 122
Morrongiello, B. A., 106
Morrow-Howell, N., 312
Mortola, J. F., 186, 188
Mosca, L., 355, 373
Mosher, C. E., 158, 165, 441
Moss, C., 327
Moss, N. W., 197
Mroczek, D. K., 413
Muehlenhard, C. L., 440, 441
Muehlenkamp, J. S., 119
Mueller, K. A., 35
Muennig, P., 373
Mulac, A., 134, 135
Mulick, P. S., 164
Mullis, I. V. S., 139, 143
Mundy, L., 206
Munson, L. J., 430
Munstertieger, B. F., 118
Murnen, S. K., 423, 441
Murphy, E. M., 195
Murphy, S. A., 279
Murr, A., 363, 364
Murray, B., 116
Murray, L. R., 290
Murray, T., 106
Murrell, A. J., 270, 271, 273, 305
Murthy, V. M., 355
Mustanski, B. S., 112
Muzio, C., 217
Muzzatti, B., 150
Myaskovsky, L., 473
Myers, D. J., 263

Nagoshi, J. L., 167
Nagourney, A., 166, 191
Nagourney, E., 373, 381, 388, 398
Nagy, G., 145, 276
Naples, N. A., 17
Nath, L. E., 132
National Alliance for Caregiving, 253, 330, 331
National Campaign to Prevent Teen Pregnancy, 171, 199
National Center for Health Statistics, 357, 383, 384, 385
National Center for Injury Prevention and Control, 439
National Institute of Allergy and Infectious Diseases, 360, 361

National Institute of Child Health and Human Development, 360, 361
National Institute of Mental Health, 407
National Institute on Alcohol Abuse and Alcoholism, 403
National Institute on Drug Abuse, 404
National Institutes of Health, 360, 384, 403, 404
National Osteoporosis Foundation, 369, 370, 371
National Partnership for Women & Families, 47
National Science Foundation, 144
Navarro, M., 43, 64, 251
Nayak, M. B., 443
Needham, B. L., 384
Neff, K. D., 86
Neff, L. A., 228
Neiterman, E., 197
Nekolny, K., 35
Nelson, D. L., 13
Nelson, J. A., 474, 475
Nelson, L. J., 473
Nelson, M. R., 49
Nelson, N. M., 104, 139
Nelson, T. D., 31
Nesbitt, M. N., 28
Netburn, D., 121
Netz, Y., 388
Neumark-Sztainer, D., 397
Newburger, E. C., 294, 295
Newcombe, N. S., 141, 142, 146, 341
Newman, A. A., 235
Newman, J., 204
Newton, T. L., 228, 337, 338
Newtson, R. L., 235, 236
NICHD Early Child Care Research Network, 128, 340
Niemann, Y. F., 33
Nierman, A. J., 83, 167
Nishina, A., 423
Nock, S. L., 85, 227, 228, 230, 331
Nolan, S. A., 289
Noland, V. J., 437, 438
Nolen-Hoeksema, S., 406, 407, 409
Noll, J. G., 434
Noller, P., 246
Nomaguchi, K. M., 340
Nordenmark, M., 329
Norquist, G., 414
Norris, M. L., 398
Norris, P., 83
North American Menopause Society, 212, 389
Nosek, M. A., 157, 386
Novack, D. R., 326, 327
Novack, L. L., 326, 327
Nowell, A., 139
Nunes, K. L., 441

Nussbaum, J. F., 357
Nyad, D., 404
Nygaard, I., 389

O'Brien, E., 106
O'Brien, K., 277
O'Brien, K. M., 13, 86
O'Brien, T. L., 288, 289
O'Callaghan, F. V., 403
O'Connor, E., 242
O'Connor, M., 431, 432
O'Donnell, L. N., 171
O'Neil, J., 371
Oakley, D., 417
Oates, M. R., 205
Obeidallah, D. A., 407
Oburu, P. O., 252
Ofstedal, M. B., 249
Ogilvie, D., 373, 387
Ogletree, S. M., 148
Ohye, B., 196
Okimoto, T. G., 291, 298
Older Women's League, 247, 248, 253, 313, 317, 319, 330, 359, 360
Olff, M., 433, 434
Oliver, M. B., 156, 158, 159
Olkin, R., 13, 33, 157, 221, 228, 233, 235, 243, 262, 285, 406, 433, 448, 451
Olsen, P. R., 284
Olshen, E., 438
Olson, E., 236
Olson, J. E., 83
Olson, K. R., 71
Olson, S. L., 241
Omari, S. R., 122
Ompad, D. C., 434
Onishi, N., 401
Ontai, L. L., 119
Orbuch, T. L., 342
Orenstein, C., 49
Orenstein, P., 206
Orman, S., 316
Ormerod, A. J., 423
Orza, A. M., 328, 339
Ostenson, R. S., 22
Ostrove, J. M., 157, 221, 349
O'Sullivan, L. F., 156, 161, 173
Oswald, D., 146
O'Toole, C., 232
Ott, M. A., 172
Owens, G. P., 165
Ozeki, C., 337
Ozer, E. M., 344

Pacheco, S., 50
Packard, E., 375
Padavic, I., 86, 284, 286, 296, 297, 298, 354, 357
Padgett, D., 248, 414
Padmawidjaja, L., 277
Paek, H.-J., 49
Page, S., 414
Palmer, C. T., 11, 445

Palmore, E. B., 31
Paludi, M. A., 427, 463, 474
Panchanadeswaran, S., 451
Papalia, D., 199
Paradise, S. A., 236
Paranjape, A., 407
Parent-Stevens, L., 184, 185
Parera, N., 171
Park, K., 208
Parke, R. D., 108, 340
Parker, H. M., 48
Parker, R. G., 65
Parker-Pope, T., 212
Parks, C. A., 166
Parmley, M., 95, 132
Parra, E. B., 233
Parsons, E. M., 400
Pate, R. R., 98
Patel, J. D., 383
Patterson, C. J., 231, 232, 242
Paul, E. L., 171
Pawelski, J. G., 242
Paxton, P., 119, 469
Peacock, P., 439
Pearson, S. M., 277
Pecora, N., 51
Pedersen, S., 114
Peirce, K., 44, 49
Pellegrini, A. D., 100
Penn, N. E., 28
Pennebaker, J. W., 134
Penner, A. M., 144
Peplau, L. A., 158, 230, 231, 232, 242, 256, 277, 412
Pepler, D., 129
Percheski, C., 325
Pérez-Pêna, R., 202
Perkins, J., 431
Perkins, K. P., 302
Perkins, K. R., 51
Perlez, J., 65, 436
Perlmutter, C., 32
Perls, T. T., 382
Perry-Jenkins, M., 103, 330, 342
Peter, J., 217
Peterman, L. M., 448
Petersen, A. C., 140, 141, 206
Peterson, J. L., 335
Peterson, K. A., 119, 121
Peterson, Z. D., 440
Petrie, T. A., 400
Pettifor, A. E., 361
Pew Research Center, 166, 167
Pfaff, L. A., 293
Phares, V., 198
Phelan, J. E., 474
Phillips, D., 340
Phillips, L., 440
Phillipson, C., 331
Phipps, B. J., 96
Pierce, W. D., 28, 122
Pietsch, J., 145
Pigott, T. A., 405

Piller, C., 422
Pimlott-Kubiak, S., 450
Pinheiro, P. S., 436
Pinholster, G., 64
Pinn, V. W., 355
Pinquart, M., 234, 235, 237, 331
Piran, N., 400
Pittman, L. D., 250, 251
Plant, E. A., 132
Planty, M., 144
Plomin, R., 130
Plucker, J. A., 147
Poertner, P., 35
Polce-Lynch, M., 132
Pollack, A., 380
Polusny, M., 443
Pomerantz, E. M., 106
Pomerleau, A., 103
Poo, A. J., 468
Pool, G. J., 225
Popanoe, D., 116, 229
Popescu, R., 367
Popp, D., 133
Porter, P., 377
Posner, R. B., 112, 114
Poteat, V. P., 412
Potoczniak, M. J., 448
Poulin, F., 114
Poulin-Dubois, D., 95
Powell, G. N., 338
Powell, L. M., 388
Powell, S. R., 83
Powers, P. S., 400
Powlishta, K. K., 74, 95
Pozner, J. L., 49, 50
Pratto, F., 21
Prehodka, J., 221
Prejean, J., 364
Prendergast, K. A., 403
Prentice, D. A., 3
Prentice, K., 375
Prentice, R. L., 368
Press, J., 337
Presser, H. B., 344
Price, J. L., 434
Prinstein, M. J., 397
Procopio, C. A., 398
Proctor, B. D., 286
Programme for International Student
   Assessment, 139, 144, 145
Propp, K., 195
Proulx, C. M., 228
Pruchno, R. A., 252
Pruzinsky, T., 122
Pucino, F., 370
Puhl, R. M., 121
Punglia, R. S., 380
Purcell, N., 471, 474
Purcell, P., 48

Quail, J. M., 385
Quindlen, A., 383
Quinn, D. M., 148

Quinn, J. B., 319
Quinn, J. E. A., 473

Raag, T., 107
Rabasca, L., 148
Rabin, R. C., 206, 212, 383
Rabinowitz, V. C., 10, 17, 19
Rackliff, C. L., 107
Rader, J., 417
Radner, G., 368
Radtke, H. L., 473
Raffaelli, M., 119
Rafferty, Y., 436
Ragins, B. R., 430
Rahman, Q., 169
Raiford, J. L., 438
Raj, A., 410
Raley, R. K., 229
Ramirez, J. M., 129
Ramisetty-Mikler, S., 440
Ramsey, L. R., 473
Randolph, S. M., 241
Range, L. M., 408, 410
Rani, M., 194, 262
Rankin, S. R., 168
Raschick, M., 331
Rathus, S., 33, 64, 96, 97, 104, 107,
   110, 111, 142, 154, 155, 157, 158, 159, 173,
   175, 176, 190, 191, 201, 362, 364, 432,
   433, 435
Ratner, E., 376
Räty, H., 140, 147
Rawlins, W. K., 219
Ray, O., 237, 381, 383
Read, J., 177, 178, 196
Ream, G. L., 168
Rebar, R. W., 206
Redberg, R. F., 375
Reddy, D. M., 172, 434
Reed, M. E., 13
Reeder, H. M., 219
Reeves, J. B., 310
Regan, P. C., 122
Régner, I., 147
Reichert, F. F., 388
Reichert, T., 49, 51
Reichman, N. E., 200
Reid, A., 471, 474
Reid, L., 198, 200
Reid, P. T., 11, 13, 103, 113, 264, 265,
   301, 423
Reiner, W. G., 67
Reinhardt, R., 164
Rejeskind, F. G., 137
Remer, P., 416, 417
Renk, K., 330
Repetti, R. L., 172, 217
Repucci, N. D., 435
Resick, P. A., 440
Reskin, B. F., 284, 286, 296, 297, 298
Resnick, S., 64, 67, 142
Revenson, T. A., 381
Reynolds, A. J., 340

Reynolds, B. M., 172, 217
Reynolds, J., 235
Rhoades, G. K., 230
Rhode, D. L., 117, 289, 334, 427
Ricciuti, H., 242
Rice, J. K., 234, 239, 240
Rich, Y., 329
Richards, H. M., 375
Richardson, P., 178
Richie, B. S., 277, 278, 280
Richmond, T. K., 388
Riddick, C. C., 312
Riddle, B., 186
Ridgeway, C. L., 286, 291, 298
Riegle-Crumb, C., 144
Rienzi, B. M., 85
Rife, J. C., 304
Riger, S., 450
Riggio, H. R., 83, 106, 340
Riggs, J. M., 35
Riley, G. F., 360
Rimer, S., 290
Rinsky, K., 448
Rintala, D. H., 224
Risman, B., 170, 200
Risman, B. J., 329
Rivers, I., 168, 169, 242
Robbins, C. L., 354, 357
Robert, M., 142
Roberto, K. A., 219, 232, 249
Roberts, B. W., 382
Roberts, H., 209, 212
Roberts, S., 212, 229, 235
Roberts, S. T., 361
Roberts, T. A., 113, 438
Robertson, J., 414
Robin, L., 200
Robins, R. W., 413
Robinson, B. K., 47
Robinson, D. T., 44, 83, 85
Robinson, G., 436
Robinson Kurpius, S. E., 441
Roche, K. M., 171
Rodgers, C. S., 441
Rodgers, J. L., 239
Roe, L., 36
Roeser, R. W., 150
Rogers, M. L., 337
Rogers, S. J., 342
Rogol, A., 113
Rohde, D., 263
Rohrbaugh, J. B., 448
Roisman, G. I., 232
Romaine, S., 54, 55, 207
Romeu, I., 377
Rook, K. S., 237
Roovers, J. P. W. R., 174
Roper, E. A., 167
Roscoe, L. A., 410
Rose, A. J., 100, 129, 217, 395, 396
Rose, N. R., 385
Rose, S., 224, 225
Rose, S. M., 218, 220, 225, 407

Rosen, E., 288
Rosenberg, D., 61
Rosenberg, T., 194
Rosenblum C., 100
Rosenfeld, A. G., 355, 372, 374, 375
Rosenthal, E., 192, 436
Ross, H. S., 130
Ross, L. E., 223
Rosselli, F., 49
Rossi, A. S., 208, 209, 210
Rostosky, S. S., 168
Roter, D. L., 356
Roth, R., 199, 354
Rothblum, E. D., 122, 230, 231
Rothman, E. F., 448
Rotundo, M., 424
Roy, R. E., 475
Royo-Vela, M., 47
Rozee, P. D., 439
Rubenstein, A., 169
Rubenstein, L. M., 310
Rubin, K. H., 109, 217, 223
Rubin, L. R., 4, 121
Rubinstein, S., 121
Ruble, D. N., 74, 88, 95, 100, 106, 140,
    217
Rudman, K. D., 217
Rudman, L. A., 37, 471, 473, 474
Rudolph, K. D., 100, 395, 395, 406
Ruiz, O. S., 252
Ruiz, S. A., 250
Runowicz, C. D., 360, 367
Runyon, M. K., 433, 434
Russell, D. E. H., 422
Russell, J. E. A., 288, 305
Russell, M., 402
Russell, S. T., 164
Russo, N. F., 2, 13, 79, 191, 192, 240, 399,
    402, 404, 405, 406, 407, 414, 416, 433
Rust, C., 205
Rust, J., 108
Rust, P. C., 164, 165
Rutenberg, J., 45
Rutter, M., 139
Ryalls, B. O., 76
Ryan, M. K., 133, 291

Saar, A., 47
Sabattini, L., 338, 339, 343
Sachs, J., 174
Sachs-Ericsson, N., 338, 433
Sack, K., 384
Sadker, D., 108, 117
Sadker, M., 108, 117
Sadler, A. G., 428, 443
Saewyc, E., 168, 412
Saftlas, A. F., 195
Salganicoff, A., 363
Salomone, R., 264
Samuels, A., 122
Samuels, C. A., 79
Sanchez, P., 289
Sanchez-Hucles, J., 218, 219, 223

Sanci, L., 400
Sanderson, C. A., 197
Sanderson, S., 329
Sandfort, T., 358, 412
Sandler, B., 263
Sandnabba, N. K., 107
Sang-Hun, C., 436
Sanmartin, C., 385
Santelli, J. S., 171, 188, 189, 198
Santora, M., 364
Sarto, G. E., 355
Sarwer, D. B., 120
Saslow, D., 377, 381
Sassi, F., 357
Sassler, S., 229
Saudino, K. J., 449
Saunders, K., 79
Saunders, K. J., 475
Save the Children, 195
Savin-Williams, R. C., 163, 165, 168, 170,
    171
Saxbe, D. E., 228
Saxon, S. E., 33, 345
Sayal, K., 403
Sayer, L. C., 341
Scandura, T. A., 430
Scantlebury, K., 42, 108, 264
Scarborough, E., 8
Scelfo, J., 177, 200
Schafer, J., 449
Scharf, M., 246
Schein, V. E., 291
Schemo, D. J., 200, 428, 429
Scher, M., 110
Scheuble, L. K., 37
Schewe, P. A., 454
Schiffman, J. B., 166
Schlenker, J. A., 48
Schmader, T., 145
Schmidt, S., 435
Schmitt, E., 428
Schmitt, M. T., 290
Schneider, L. S., 211
Schneider, O., 441
Schnieder, S. L., 396
Schnittker, J., 324, 384
Schoeman, W. J., 78
Schoen, R., 341, 342
Schoenberg, N. E., 375
Schoenborn, C. A., 388, 402
Schoeni, R. F., 237
Schuler, J., 196
Schulman, A., 155, 196
Schultz, R. W., 97
Schulz, A. J., 407
Schumacher, J. A., 438
Schumacher, P., 148, 170
Schwartz, P., 174, 200
Sciolino, E., 467
Sears, D. O., 13
Sears-Roberts Alterovitz, S., 221
Seaver, M. R., 358, 359
Sechzer, J., 10, 17, 19

Sedgh, G., 191
Seem, S. R., 414
Seeman, T. E., 386
Seif, H., 164
Seitz, V., 200
Sekaquaptewa, D., 145
Seligman, M. E. P., 395
Selingo, J., 268
Selwyn, N., 269
Sengupta, R., 44
Serbin, L. A., 95, 99, 106, 397
Serewicz, M. C. M., 225
Serran, G., 448
Settles, I. H., 289, 300
Sexton, C. C., 337
Sexton, V. S., 6, 7
Shaffer, D. R., 98
Shakin, D., 103
Shanahan, L., 97, 99
Shanok, A. F., 241
Shapiro, J. R., 398, 399
Shapka, J. D., 144
Share, T. L., 122
Sharp, E. A., 235
Shaw, L., 315
Shedd, J., 96
Sheehy, G., 173, 248
Sheeran, P., 189
Sheldon, K. M., 149, 221
Shellenbarger, S., 233, 341, 347
Shelly, S., 316
Shelton, J. N., 431
Shepela, S. T., 263, 425
Sherman, S. R., 31, 304
Sherry, B., 122
Sherwin, B. B., 208, 210, 212
Sheth, S. S., 436
Shih, M. J., 275
Shorter-Gooden, K., 117
Shupe, E. I., 430
Shute, R., 423
Siahpush, M., 384
Sices, L., 139
Sidener, J., 227
Siebenbruner, J., 172
Siebert, S., 308
Siegal, D. L., 154, 175, 176, 178, 236,
    238, 247, 253, 309, 313, 314
Siegel, J. M., 120
Sieving, R. E., 172
Sigal, J., 424, 427, 450
Signorella, M. L., 143
Signorelli, N., 31, 43, 44, 47, 49
Silenzio, V. M. B., 412
Sill, M., 448
Silva, E., 423, 426
Silver, R. B., 397
Silverman, W. K., 394, 405
Silverschanz, P., 412, 429
Silverstein, M., 250
Simmons, R. G., 115
Simmons, T., 233, 251
Simon, L. J., 360

Simon, R. J., 427
Simon, R. W., 132, 337, 338
Simon, V. R., 355
Simpkins, S. D., 145, 147
Simpson, G., 277
Sims, M., 100
Sinacore, A., 4, 5
Sinclair, L., 36
Singer, N., 221
Singh, G. K., 384
Singh, S., 193
Singh, T., 410
Singh-Manoux, A., 388
Sit, D., 205
Skerrett, P. J., 374
Skinner, D., 336
Skipp, C., 177
Sklar, J. B., 452
Skoe, E. E. A., 133
Skowron, J., 237
Skultety, K. M., 236, 243
Slade, P., 192
Slaughter-Defoe, D. T., 262
Small, F. L., 97
Smallwood, S., 290
Smetana, J. G., 106, 247
Smirles, K. E., 424
Smith, B. L., 363
Smith, C. A., 119, 121, 221, 230
Smith, D., 158
Smith, G., 156
Smith, J. L., 275
Smith, K., 250
Smith, L., 98, 416
Smith, L. B., 192
Smith, M., 414
Smith, M. A., 376
Smith, N., 221
Smith, R. A., 377, 381
Smith, R. S., 250
Smith, T. E., 134, 139
Smith, T. W., 157, 326, 333, 364
Smock, P., 229, 230
Smolak, L., 98, 118, 119, 121, 401, 423
Snell, M. B., 385
Snow, D. L., 449
Snyder, N. M., 337
Söchting, I., 442, 445
Social Security Administration, 318
Society for Women's Health Research, 372
Solarz, A. L., 412
Solomon, C., 48
Sommer, B., 210
Sommers, C. H., 260
Sonnert, G., 276
Sontag, S., 44
Sörensen, S., 331
Sorenson, S. B., 451
Soundranayagam, L., 29
Sowers, M. R., 210
Spanier, B. B., 9
Spar, D., 206
Spataro, J., 434

Spelke, E. S., 146
Spence, J. T., 77, 78
Spencer, J. M., 172
Spencer, S. J., 148, 149
Spicher, C. H., 48
Spiegel, D., 381
Spitze, G., 246
Spitzer, B. L., 50, 121, 415
Sprecher, S., 130, 226
Springen, K., 198, 212, 308, 370, 371, 403
Spurgeon, D., 374, 375
Srivastava, S., 413
Sroufe, L. A., 102
St. John, W., 202
Stabiner, K., 148
Stacey, J., 243
Stack, S., 230
Staggs S., 450
Stahly, G. B., 449, 451
Stake, J. E., 81, 474, 475, 476
Stamler, B., 308
Stankiewicz, J. M., 49
Stanley, A., 45, 218, 284
Stanley, D., 311, 312
Stanley, J. C., 16
Stanley, S. M., 229, 230
Stanton, A. L., 354
Stapp, J., 77
Stark-Wroblewski, K., 122
Statistics Canada, 139
Steele, C. M., 148, 149, 265
Steele, J., 268, 269
Stefanick, M. L., 211, 380
Steffens, D. C., 413
Steil, J. M., 106, 228, 234
Stein, K., 100
Steinberg, J. R., 28, 318, 324, 338, 343
Steinberg, L., 114, 171, 172, 217
Steinberg, L. S., 144
Steinbrook, R., 365
Steiner, M., 188, 205, 210
Steiner, M. J., 364
Steinhauer, J., 356
Steinpreis, R. E., 280
Stephens, J., 120, 330, 331
Stephens, M. A. P., 337, 339
Stern, G. S., 79, 86
Stern, M., 104
Sterne, J. A., 384, 385, 413
Stevens, P., 189
Stevenson, H. W., 140, 147
Stevenson, M. A., 291
Stevenson, M. R., 412
Stewart, A. J., 67, 347, 348, 349
Stewart, L., 48
Stewart, R. E., 431
Stewart, S. L., 382
Stice, E., 120
Stier, J. J., 343
Stillman, S., 221, 230
Stinson, D. A., 117
Stith, J. J., 449
Stiver, I. P., 3

Stohs, J. H., 332
Stoner, C. C., 139
Stoppard, J. M., 407
Stormshok, E. A., 407
Straumanis, J., 356
Straus, S. E., 384
Strauss, L. T., 191, 192
Strauss, R. S., 117
Street, A. E., 427, 429
Street, R. L. Jr., 356
Street, S., 30
Streppel, M. T., 373
Stricker, G., 32, 178, 249
Strickland, B. R., 3
Striegel-Moore, R. H., 398, 399, 400
Strine, T. W., 184
Strong, T. H., 202
Stuenkel, C. P., 343
Stueve, A., 171
Sturza, M. L., 445
Suchday, S., 407
Sue, D. W., 464
Suggs, W., 98
Sui, X., 387
Sullivan, C. M., 452
Sumberg, E., 252
Summers, A., 148
Summers-Effler, E., 114
Sumner, K. E., 273
Suris, J. C., 171
Susan G. Komen for the Cure, 379
Susman, E. J., 113, 129
Susskind, J. E., 76, 95
Sutfin, E. L., 106, 242
Sved, M. S., 359
Swanson, D. H., 240
Swearingen-Hilker, N., 333
Sweeney, C., 122
Swim, J. K., 40, 41, 57
Switzer, J. Y., 54
Sybert, V. P., 64, 67
Sylvester, K., 326
Szinovacz, M. E., 309, 310

Szymanski, D. M., 165, 417
Tafalla, R. J., 148
Taft, C. T., 449, 450
Tai, T.-O., 329, 340
Tai, V., 436
Tai-Seale, M., 408
Talaga, J. A., 309
Tamis-Lemonda, C. S., 139
Tang, B. M. P., 370, 371
Tang, C. S., 113
Tang, E., 468
Tapia, A., 291
Tariq, S. H., 174, 176
Tarkan, L., 202
Tartaro, J., 2, 79, 191, 399, 402, 404, 405, 406, 407, 414, 416, 433
Tasker, F. L., 243, 244
Taylor, A. K., 357

Taylor, C. A., 44
Taylor, C. R., 44
Taylor, K., 343
Taylor, K. L., 381
Taylor, P. L., 326
Taylor, S. E., 395
Tedeschi, R. G., 446
Tenenbaum, H. R., 103, 147
Tepperman, L., 331
Terlecki, M. S., 142
Terry-Schmitt, L. N., 86
Thébaud, S., 329
Thee, M. C., 166, 191
Thiebaut, A. C., 377
Thill, K. P., 148
Thomas, J. J., 18, 83, 97, 217
Thomas, J. L., 252
Thomas, J. R., 97
Thomas, T., 204
Thomas, V., 274, 275
Thompson, D. E., 300
Thompson, E. M., 163
Thompson, G., 358
Thompson, R. S., 449
Thompson, S. J., 168
Thompson, V. L. S., 329
Thorne, B., 100
Thornhill, R., 11, 445
Tice, J. A., 209, 212
Tichenor, V., 333
Tiedemann, J., 147
Tiefer, L., 159, 160, 161, 162
Tiegs, T. J., 157, 172
Tiggemann, M., 120, 121
Tilberis, L., 368
Timmerman, G., 423
Tinker, I., 469
Tobach, E., 62, 63
Tobin, D. J., 239
Toepfer-Hendey, E., 277
Tolan, P., 454
Tolin, D. F., 433, 434
Toller, P. W., 473
Tolman, D. L., 117, 159, 170, 172
Tonks, A., 373
Torpy, J. M., 173, 174, 201, 206, 209, 360, 368, 389
Torrez, D. J., 384
Toth, E., 187
Tougas, F., 41
Toussaint, D., 47
Towill, K., 200
Townsend, T. G., 172
Tracy, J. K., 173
Tran, H., 340
Trautner, H. M., 95
Travis, C. B., 192, 354, 355, 357, 372, 374, 377, 388, 389
Treas, J., 327, 329, 340
Trebay, G., 122
Trenholm, C., 189, 200
Trent, K., 246
Trice, A. D., 96

Trickett, P. K., 434
Trimberger, E. K., 235
Trivits, L. C., 435
Troutman, K. P., 98
Troxel, W. M., 374
Trzesniewski, K. H., 117, 413
Tucker, C. J., 100
Tucker, C. M., 10
Tucker, J. S., 57, 171
Tucker, M. B., 227
Tuggle, C. A., 48
Turiel, E., 133
Twenge, J. M., 38, 77, 78, 79, 117, 239
Tyler, K. A., 172, 434
Tynan, M., 309
Tyre, P., 122, 260, 312, 398

U.S. Bureau of Labor Statistics, 294
U.S. Census Bureau, 28, 47, 227, 228, 232, 233, 234, 249, 250, 251, 260, 285, 286, 294, 295, 302, 333, 373, 382, 388
U.S. Department of Education, 139, 269
U.S. Department of Health and Human Services (USDHHS), 171, 371
Uccello, C., 308
Uchitelle, L., 319
Uggen, C., 431
Uhlmann, E. L., 291
Ui, M., 83
Ulin, M., 232
Ullman, S. E., 434
Umbach, P. D., 264
UNAIDS, 252, 365
Unger, J. B., 386
Unger, R. K., 12
UNICEF, 263
UNIFEM, 195, 450
United Nations, 475
United Nations Children's Fund, 262
United Nations Population Fund, 195, 365
Unützer, J, 408
Urquiza, A., 433
Usdansky, M. L., 248
Utley, M. E., 197
Utter, J., 121

Väänänen, A., 395
Vaccarino, U., 374
Valian, V., 143, 144
Valkenburg, P. M., 217
Valls-Fernández, F., 48
Van den Berg, P., 121
Van Evra, J., 43, 47, 49, 51, 109, 148
Van Gaalen, R. I., 247
Van Gool, C. H., 388
Van Son, G. E., 397
Van Willigen, M., 332
Vandello, J. A., 443
Vandewater, E. A., 339, 347, 348
Vanfraussen, K., 242
Vangelisti, A. L., 228
VanLeuvan, P., 268, 269

Vann, E. D., 87
Vasquez, M. J. T., 116
Vasta, R., 142
Vastag, B., 362
Vaughan, K. K., 121
Vaz, K., 13
Veccia, E. M., 138
Velkoff, V. A., 229, 236, 248, 316, 318, 384
Veniegas, R. C., 169
Ventrone, N. A., 226
Ventura, S. J., 198
Verma, S., 104
Verni, R., 448
Vescio, T. K., 290
Vesely, S. K., 171
Vézina, J., 438
Vickers, M. R., 211
Vigil, J. M., 434
Viki, G. T., 38
Vilhjalmsson, N., 97
Villarosa, L., 170, 177, 363, 433
Vinick, B., 309
Vinnicombe, S., 291
Viswanathan, L., 367
Vitaliano, P. P., 253
Voda, A. M., 209
Voelker, R., 452, 454
Vogel, D. L., 166
Vogt, A., 148
Voracek, M., 121
Votruba-Drzal, E., 340
Voyer, D., 139, 140, 142
Vyrostek, S. B., 382

Wagner, L. S., 304
Wagner, M., 262
Wainer, H., 144
Wainright, J. L., 242
Waisberg, J., 414
Wajeman, J., 331
Waldfogel, J., 334
Waldrop, D. P., 252
Walia, A., 435
Walker, A., 21
Walker, L. J., 133
Walsh, V., 96
Walsh, W. B., 305
Walsh-Bowers, R., 8
Walter, C. A., 236, 238
Walters, K. L., 65
Walther-Lee, D., 249
Walumbwa, F. O., 343
Wang, L., 184
Wang, P., 343
Wang, P. S., 416
Wang, Y., 251, 252
Wangby, M., 397
Wapner, S., 311
Ward, C. A., 79
Ward, J., 301
Ward, L. M., 51, 109, 117
Ward, S. K., 270

Wardle, J., 122
Wareham, S., 395
Wargo, E., 16
Warkentin, J. B., 441
Warner, J., 239, 261, 318, 412
Warner, R., 135, 136
Warren, J. S., 395
Warshaw, R., 443
Wartella, E., 148
Wartik, N., 355, 404
Washington, D. L., 375
Washington, N. C., 117
Washo, C., 310
Wasserman, G. A., 397
Wasti, S. A., 432
Wathen, C. N., 452
Watson, C. M., 264, 268
Watt, H. M. G., 144, 145, 276
Waxman, S., 47
Way, N., 117
Wayne, J. H., 335
Wayne, L. D., 358
Weatherall, A., 19, 134, 135
Weber, L., 271, 277, 278, 280
Wechsler, H., 402
Wei, G. S., 453, 454
Weichold, K., 115
Weinberg, D. H., 286, 292, 297
Weinberg, M. S., 231
Weinberger, N., 100
Weinraub, B., 45
Weinraub, M., 340
Weinstein, A. R., 373, 387
Weisgram, E. S., 268
Weishaus, S., 229
Weissbrod, C. S., 270
Weitzel, J. N., 376
Welch, J., 442, 443, 445
Weller, L., 134, 137
Wellman, N. S., 389
Welty, F. K., 212, 373
Wentz, E., 402
Wentzel, K. R., 130, 132
Wenzel, A., 160
Werner, E. E., 250
Werner-Wilson, R. J., 172
Wessler, S. L., 423
West, S. A., 436, 449
Westcott, K., 208
Weston, R., 449
Weuve, J., 388
Whaley, R. B., 11, 447
Whelehan, P., 65
Whiffen, V. E., 205, 434
Whisman, M. A., 434
Whiston, S. C., 277, 445
Whitbourne, S. K., 236, 243
White, B. H., 441

White, J. C., 359
White, J. W., 130, 397, 433, 435, 438,
    448, 449, 467, 468
Whitehead, B. D., 116
Whiteman, S. D., 287, 344
Whitley, B. E. Jr., 165, 166, 167
Whitmire, R., 260
Widmer, E., 327
Widom, C. S., 434
Wigfield, A., 145, 275, 276
Wight, V. R., 318, 461
Wilcox, S., 237, 388, 389
Wilcox, W. B., 228, 331
Wildsmith, E., 229
Wilgoren, J., 201
Wilkinson, J. A., 31, 355
Willetts-Bloom, M., 85
Williams, A., 171, 226
Williams, D. R., 406
Williams, J., 264
Williams, J. C., 289, 334, 427
Williams, J. E., 29, 95, 97
Williams, M. K., 13
Williams, N., 159
Williams, R., 473
Williams, S. L., 450
Williams, T. J., 169
Williams-Nickelson, C., 297, 298
Williamson, J., 252
Willis, F. N., 221
Willness, C. R., 430
Willoughby, T., 148
Wilson, F., 278
Wilson, G. T., 401, 402
Wilson, H. W., 434
Wilson, J. F., 474
Wilson, R., 260, 262, 290
Wilson, R. T., 370
Wilson, S., 262
Windle, M., 404
Windle, R. C., 404
Wingert, P., 173, 372, 373
Wingood, G. M., 361, 363, 364
Winquist, J., 407
Winstanley, D., 301
Winterich, J., 173, 210
WISER, 314, 315, 316, 319
Wisocki, P. A., 237
Wittes, E., 98
Wittig, M. A., 473
Wloszczyna, S., 45
Wojciszke, B., 28
Wolchik, S. A., 233
Wolf, R. S., 454
Wolf-Wendel, L. E., 265
Wolk, A., 377
Wolverton, B., 98
Women's Sports Foundation, 98
Wonderlich, S. A., 398

Wood, E., 99
Wood, J. T., 16, 53
Wood, W., 3
Woodhill, B. M., 79
Woodward, L. J., 171, 397
Woodzicka, J. A., 430
Woolf, S. E., 189
Worell, J., 4, 10, 19, 217, 415, 416, 417,
    467, 470
World Health Organization, 194, 354,
    384, 450, 453
Wortman, C. M., 236
Wright, L. B., 364
Wright, L. W., 164
Wright, V. C., 206
Wright, V. R., 287
Wrosch, C., 408
Wu, C. H., 371
Wyche, K. F., 460
Yabroff, J., 201, 240
Yagil, D., 431
Yakushko, O., 475

Yang, B., 410
Yang, Q., 202
Yanico, B. J., 83
Yardley, J., 252, 435, 436
Yates, A., 119
Yeung, D. Y. L., 113
Yoder, J., 474
Yoder, J. D., 35, 273, 294, 296, 333, 428,
    474
Yoon, D. P., 414
Young, J. R., 428
Youngblade, L. M., 80, 106, 341
Yousafzai, S., 263, 410
Yuan, A. S. V., 114, 120
Yunger, J. L., 109, 118

Zabin, L. S., 171, 172, 198, 200
Zablotsky, D., 365
Zack, N., 463
Zager, K., 169
Zakriski, A. L., 130
Zalk, S. R., 12, 264, 265, 301, 423, 460
Zand, D., 225
Zebrowitz, L. A., 31
Zeller, J. L., 369, 370
Zernike, K., 227, 235, 290
Zettel, L. A., 237
Zhermer, N., 473
Zhou, Q., 104, 397
Zill, D. G., 48
Zimmer, Z., 248
Zink, T., 448, 451
Zosuls, K. M., 94, 95, 103
Zucker, A. N., 473, 475
Zucker, K. J., 62, 66, 67
Zucker, N. L., 398

SUBJECT INDEX

A

Ableism, 33
Acquired immunodeficiency syndrome
      (AIDS), 362–366
Abortion, 191–193
   attitudes toward, 191
   consequences of, 192–193
   incidence, 191–192
   methods, 192
Abuse of children, *See* Child sexual abuse
Abuse of women
   dating violence, 437–438
   intimate partner violence, 448–451
   elder abuse, 452–454
Achievement level, 273–276
Achievement motivation
   attributions for own success
      or failure, 275
   confidence in own achievement,
      275–276
   definition of, 274
   fear of success, 274
Activities of daily living (ADLs),
      386
Adolescence
   body image and, 119–123
   contraception, 188–189
   dating, 223–224
   eating disorders, 397–402
   friendship during, 217–218
   growth spurt, 113
   identity formation in, 115–116
   maturation, 114–115
   menarche, 112–113
   mental health, 397–398
   motherhood and, 199–200
   pregnancy, 198–200
   psychosocial development, 115–123
   puberty, 109–115
   self-esteem, 116–118
   sexual activity during, 169–173
   sexually transmitted infections,
      360–366
   substance abuse, 402–404
   suicide, 408–410
Advocate, 313
Affiliative interruption, 134
Age
   breast cancer and, 375–376
   heart disease and, 372
Ageism, 31–32
Agency, 28
   stereotypes in the media, 48–49
Affirmative action, 304–305
Agoraphobia, 405
Aggression, 128–129

Alcohol
   abuse, 402–404
   breast cancer and, 376
   consequences, 403
   ethnicity, 402
   heart disease and, 373
   incidence, 402–403
   intimate partner violence, and, 449
   osteoporosis and, 370–371
   rape and, 442–443
   risk factors, 403–404
   sexual activity and, 170
   treatment, 404
Alendronate, 371
Alpha bias, 3
Ambivalent sexism, 38
American Psychological Association,
      women in leadership roles, 7–8
Androgen-insensitivity syndrome, 65
Androgens, 63
Androgyny
   definition, 77
   evaluation of concept, 80, 81
   psychological adjustment, 79–80
Anorexia nervosa, 398–402
Anxiety disorders, 405
Aromatase inhibitors, 380
Asian Americans
   alcohol use, 402
   body image and, 122
   career aspirations and, 268
   divorce, 233
   elder caregiving, 253
   gender stereotypes, 33
   heart disease, 372
   high blood pressure, 373
   higher education and,
      266, 272
   illegal drug use, 404
   intimate partner violence, 449
   living with relatives, 248
   menopause attitudes, and, 210
   mortality rates for, 384–385
   perception of family and employment
      roles, 331–332
   poverty, 315
   raising grandchildren, 250–251
   sexual harassment and, 427–429
   single mothers, 240–242
   teen pregnancy, 198
Association for Women in Psychology,
      9–10
Attractiveness
   disabilities and, 221
   media emphasis on, 49–50
   in romantic relationships, 220–221

Augmented families, 241
Authoritarianism and gender attitudes, 86

B

Backlash effect, 37
Balancing family and work, 323–349
Barriers hindering women's advancement,
      289–302
Battering, *See* Domestic violence.
BEM Sex Role Inventory (BSRI), 77
Benevolent sexism, 38
Beta bias, 3
Biases
   in research, 10–18
   publications, 16
Binge drinking, 402–403
Binge eating disorder, 402
Birth control pills, 367, 373, 377
Bisexual women, 163–165
Bisphosphonates, 371
Blacks
   abortion, 191–192
   adolescent friendships, 218
   AIDS and, 363–364
   alcohol use by, 402
   body image and, 122
   breast cancer, 376
   career aspirations, 277–279
   cervical cancer, 367
   divorce and, 233
   elder caregiving, 253
   employment rates, 285
   fibroid tumors, 366
   gender attitudes, 82
   gender stereotypes and, 31–33
   healthcare and, 357
   heart disease, 372
   high blood pressure, 373
   higher education, and, 264, 270–271
   illegal drugs and, 404
   intimate partner violence, 449
   lesbian women of color, 166
   living with relatives, 248
   marriage of, 227–228
   menopause attitudes and, 210
   mortality rates for, 384–385
   occupational choices, 286
   older women, 436
   osteoporosis and, 370
   pension income, 318
   perception of family and employment
      roles, 315, 332, 339
   poverty, 240–241, 315
   raising grandchildren, 250–251
   rape, 439
   retirement, 309–310

self-esteem in adolescence, 117
sexual harassment and, 427–429
sexually transmitted diseases and,
363–364
sexual problems, 160
single motherhood, 240–242
teen pregnancy, 198
wages, 294
Body image, 119–123
ethnic differences in, 122
gender differences in, 120
lesbians and, 122
Brain differentiation, 64
Brain size, 9
BRCA-1 and BRCA-2 genes, 376
Breast cancer, 375–379
Bulimia nervosa, 398–402

C
Calcium, 370–371
Career aspirations, 268–269
Career counseling, 269–270
Cancer
breast, 375–379
cervical, 367
endometrial (uterine), 367
lung, 375, 383
ovarian, 368
Caregiving
by elderly women, 248–252
by mid-life women, 329–330
Castration anxiety, 70
Cervical cancer, 367
Child sexual abuse, 432–435
consequences of, 433–434
incidence of, 432–433
prevention, 435
treatment, 434–435
Childbirth. *See also* Pregnancy.
after age 40, 202–203
cesarean section, 201
doula, 201
family-centered approach to, 202
Lamaze method, 201
in later life, 203
methods of, 201–202
nurse-midwives, 202
and postpartum distress, 205
stages of, 200–201
Children
adult, 247–248
effects of mother's employment on,
340–341
feminist socialization of, 464
Children's literature
sexist stereotypes in, 48, 49
underrepresentation of females, 42
Chilly campus climate, 263–264
Chlamydia, 360, 362
Chromosomes, 63
Classism, 5
Clitoral orgasms, 156
Clitoris, 155

Cognitive abilities, 138–150
Cognitive developmental theory, 72–74
Cohabitation, 229–230
Communication style, 133–138
Communion, 28, 48
Communal orientation, 135
Computers, 148–149
Congenital adrenal hyperplasia (CAH),
64, 65, 67, 68, 142
Contraception, 188–191
adolescents and, 188–189
methods, 189–190
Corpus callosum, 9
Cosmetic surgery, 221
Counselor self-disclosure, 417
Cybersex, 171

D
Dating
during adolescence, 223–224
gender-related behaviors and, 223–224
online sites, 226
recent trends in, 226–227
scripts, 225–226
violence, 437–438
women with disabilities and, 224
Depression
gender differences in, 406–408
heart disease and, 375
in adolescence, 406
in adulthood, 406–407
in older adults, 407–408
postpartum, 205
theories of, 406–407
in widows, 236
Diabetes, 392
Diet. *See* Nutrition.
Differences approach, 3
Disabilities, women with
ableism, 33
career aspirations and, 267
dating issues for women with, 224
divorce, 233
higher education and, 261, 266
in later life, 385–386
perceived attractiveness,
221–223
physical campus environment and, 266
research on, 12–13
sexuality and, 157
stereotypes of, 33
Discrimination
against lesbians, 166
age, 303–304
in hiring patterns, 280
in the workplace, 290, 298–299,
303–304
Division of household labor, 329–335
Divorce, 232–234
Domestic violence
definition of, 448
disability and, 448–449
effects of, 450–451

ethnic and global comparisons, 450
incidence, 448
intervention, 451–452
risk factors, 449–450
theories of, 451
Double standard
of aging, 44, 47
sexual, 156–157, 172
Doula, 201
Drawing conclusions
meta-analysis, 18–20
narrative approach, 18
Dual entitlement, 318
Durable power of attorney, 316
Dysmenorrhea, 184
Dyspareunia, 159

E
Eating disorders, 397–402
anorexia nervosa, 398
binge eating disorder, 399
bulimia nervosa, 398–399
causes of, 400–401
female athlete triad and, 400–401
treatment, 401–402
Economic issues in later life, 314–319
Education
attainment of, 260–261
campus climate, 263–266
environment, 150
level, and gender attitudes, 86
sexual harassment in school, 423–426
single-gender compared to
mixed-gender institutions,
263–264
values, 260
Effect size, 20
Egalitarian gender attitude, 80
Elder abuse, 452–454
Electra complex, 70
Emotionality, 131–132
Emotions
divorce and, 233–234
during motherhood, 239
expression of, and marital satisfaction,
228–229
in pregnancy, 196
Empathy, 132
Employment, 284–319. *See also* Work.
Empty nest period, 243, 245–246
Endometriosis, 206, 367
Enhancement hypothesis of multiple
roles, 338
Equal Pay Act, 9
Eriksen, Erik, 119
Essentialism, 3
Estrogen, 63, 182, 201, 205, 208, 209.
See also Hormone replacement
therapy, Progesterone.
Ethnicity
abortion and, 191–192
AIDS and, 364
and alcohol, 402

Ethnicity (*cont.*)
  attitudes toward menopause and, 210
  body image and, 122
  breast cancer and, 376–377
  career aspirations and, 268
  cervical cancer and, 367
  collectivistic values and, 266
  defined, 21
  feminism and, 473
  gender attitudes and, 80–88
  gender stereotypes and, 30–33
  and health care, 357
  higher education and, 264–265
  intimate partner violence, 448–449
  and lesbianism, 166
  mental health therapy issues and, 416
  mortality rates and, 384–385
  occupational choices, 286
  rape and, 439
  self-esteem and, 117
  sexual dysfunction and, 149
  sexual harassment and, 429, 433
  sexually transmitted infections, 365, 367
  single motherhood and, 234–235
  wage differentials and, 294
  workplace segregation and, 291
Evolutionary theory of rape, 445
Exercise. *See* Physical activity.
Excitement phase, of sexual response cycle, 155
Extended families, 241
Externalizing disorders, 402
External female anatomy, 154–155

F
Family
  augmented, 241
  coordinating work and, 333–346
  division of household labor, 329–333
  extended, 241
  midlife transition in roles, 347–349
  solutions to family-work balancing difficulties, 342–347
Father. *See also* Family.
  household responsibilities, 329–330
Fear of success, 274
Fee-for-service insurance, 359
Female
  athlete triad, 400–401
  genital mutilation, 194
  orgasmic disorder, 159
Feminism
  beliefs, 4–5, 470–474
  definition, 4–5
  liberal feminism, 4
  cultural feminism, 3, 5
  goals of, 460–470
  men and, 475
  socialist feminism, 5
  radical feminism, 5
  women of color feminism, 5
  women's studies courses and, 474–475

Feminist belief system, 20
Feminist identification, 471–474
Feminist research methods, 17–18
Feminist theory
  of intimate partner violence, 451
  of rape, 447
Feminist therapy, 416
Femininity, 77
Feminization of poverty, 241
Fetal alcohol effect, 403
Fetal alcohol syndrome, 403
Fibroid embolization, 368
Fibroid tumors, 367
5 alpha-reductase deficiency, 66–67
Field dependence and independence, 16
Flextime, 343
Follicular phase, 182
Freud, Sigmund, 3, 9, 68–70
  psychosexual stages of development, 68–70
Friendships
  in adolescence, 217–218
  in adulthood, 218–219
  gender differences in, 217–219
  lesbian, 218–219
  of older women, 219–220

G
Gall bladder disease, 210
Gay male, 163
Gender
  attitudes, 62, 82–88
  children's knowledge of, 93–96
  constancy, 73
  definition of, 2
  distinction between sex and, 2
  in English language, 51–57
  flexibility in construction of, 461–462
  identity, 61
  in the media, 41–51
  self concept, 61–62
  social construction of, 22–23
Gender bias
  in diagnosis of psychological disorders, 414–415
  in psychotherapy, 415–416
Gender-biased language, 17
Gender comparisons. *See also* Gender differences.
  aggression, 128–129
  alcohol abuse, 402
  attitudes, 86–88
  attribution patterns, 275
  brain, 9
  cognitive abilities, 138–150
  communication style, 133–138
  computer usage, 148–149
  depression, 406–407
  double standard of sexuality, 156–157, 172
  educational attainment and, 260–261
  educational values, 260
  emotionality, 131–132

  empathy, 132
  exercise, 386–388
  friendships, 217–219
  health care and health services, 356–357
  health insurance, 359–360
  importance of physical attractiveness, 220–221
  influenceability, 130–131
  leisure activities, 311–314
  mathematics ability, 143–150
  mental health, 394
  moral reasoning, 4, 132–133
  motor skills, 97–98
  physical performance and sports, 97–98
  prosocial behavior, 129–130
  retirement, 311–312
  salary expectations, 273
  self-esteem during adolescence, 116–118
  substance abuse, 404
  verbal ability, 139
  video game usage, 148–149
  visual-spatial ability, 140–143
Gender development, influences on, 103–109
  media, 109
  parents, 103–105
  peers, 109
  school, 108
  siblings, 108
Gender differences. *See also* Gender comparisons.
  body image and, 119–123
  division of household labor, 329–333
  friendships, 217–219
  heart disease and, 372
  in illness, 385
  job satisfaction, 299–300
  in leadership and job advancement, 288–293
  in mortality, 381–383
  nonverbal communication, 137–138
  in occupational distribution, 286
  in power, 21–22
  in puberty, 113
  in salaries, 293–299
  sexual activity and, 158–159
  sexual attitudes and, 156–157
  in suicide, 408, 410
  verbal communication, 133–137
Gender harassment, 427
Gender identity, 94–95
Gender intensification, 118–119
Gender paradox, 381
Gender-related activities and interests, 96–100
Gender-related traits, 76–80
  changes in, over time, 77–79
  psychological adjustment and, 79–80
  social behaviors and personality traits, 128–133

Gender representation in media, 41–51
  in English language, 51–57
Gender roles, 2
Gender schema theory, 74–75
Gender segregation, 100–103
Gender stereotypes
  as a barrier to advancement, 291
  of children, 34
  of children in single parent
      homes, 107
  children's knowledge of, 95–96
  content of, 28, 30
  dating and, 223–224
  definition, 28
  development of, 94–96
  in English language, 51–57
  and ethnicity, 30–31
  of occupations, 96
  portrayed by media, 41–51
Gender typing
  definition of, 68
  media and, 41–51
  theories of, 68–76
Genital herpes, 362
Genital warts, 362
Glass ceiling, 288
Global perspectives
  AIDS epidemic, 365
  benevolent sexism, 38
  economic status of older women, 329
  education, gender differences in, 261
  educational climate under Taliban, 263
  elder abuse, 453
  employment of married women,
      attitudes toward, 339
  female genital mutilation, 194
  gender attitudes, 73
  gender stereotype, development of,
      95–96
  grandmothers, 250
  health of women, 384
  human trafficking, 436
  infanticide, 435–436
  intimate partner violence, 450
  lesbianism, 165–166
  living arrangements, older
      women, 249
  mate selection, 222
  mathematics achievement, 144–145
  menopause, 210
  multiple genders, 65
  parental leave policies, 334
  pregnancy-related deaths, 195
  rape victims, attitudes toward, 440
  reproductive lives, 193–194
  research on gender, 18, 20
  suicide, gender differences in, 410
  thinness, cultural pressure for, 401
  women's movements, 469
  working conditions, girls and women,
      299
Gonadal development, 63
Gonorrhea, 360–362

Grandmothers, 248–254
Group pressure conformity studies, 131

H
Harassment. *See* Sexual harassment.
Health insurance, 359–360
Health services and care
  for lesbians, 358–359
  physician-patient relationship,
      355–356
  type and quality, 356–357, 374–375
  women of color, 356–357
Heart disease, 372–375
Herceptin, 380
Heterosexism, 165
High blood pressure. *See* Hypertension.
Higher education
  campus climate, 263–266
  degrees received by women, 260–261,
      268
  ethnicity and, 266
  poor and working class women and,
      265
Homeless mothers, 287
Homophobia, 165–167
Hook-up, 171
Hopkins vs. Price Waterhouse, 37, 291–292
Hormone replacement therapy,
      210–212
  alternatives to standard, 212
  definition of, 210
  benefits, 211
  risks and side effects, 212
Hostile environment, 427
Hostile sexism, 38
Hot flashes, 209
Household labor, division of
  gender differences in, 329–331
  explanations of, 332–333
  women's perceptions of, 331–332
Human capital perspective, 295–297
Human papilloma virus, 361, 367
Human trafficking, 436
HIV, 362–366
Hypertension, 372–373
Hysterectomy, 368–369

I
Identification, 70
Identity formation
  in adolescence, 115
Identity labels, 36–37
In vitro fertilization, 206
Incest, 432
Individuation, 116
Infanticide, 435–436
Infertility, 205–206
Infibulation, 194
Influenceability, 130–131
Inhibited sexual desire, 159
Instrumental activities of daily living
      (IADLs), 386
Insurance. *See* Health insurance.

Intellectual ability, 138–139
Internalizing disorders, 397
Interrole conflict, 337
Interruption of speech
  affiliative, 134
  intrusive, 134
Intersexuality, 64
Intimate partner violence. *See* Domestic
      violence.

J
Job satisfaction, 299–301
Job ladder, 289
Job-related characteristics and career
      choice, 279–280

L
Labia majora, 154
Labia minora, 154
Labor force participation rates of
      women, 285
Laissez-faire leadership, 293
Lamaze method, 201
Language
  gender representation in,
      50–57
  practices based on normative male,
      52–55
  negative female terms, 55–57
Lateralization, 142
Latinas
  AIDS and, 364
  alcohol use by, 402
  body image and, 122
  career aspirations, 277–279
  cervical cancer, 367
  divorce and, 233
  elder caregiving, 253
  gender attitudes, 80, 82
  gender stereotypes, 30–31
  healthcare and, 357
  heart disease, 372
  high blood pressure, 373
  higher education and, 266
  illegal drugs and, 404
  intimate partner violence, 449
  living with relatives, 248
  marriage of, 227–228
  media and, 44
  menopause attitudes and, 210
  mortality rates for, 384–385
  perception of work and family roles,
      315, 332, 339
  pension income, 318
  poverty, 240–241, 315
  raising grandchildren, 250–251
  rape, 439
  self-esteem in adolescence, 117
  sexual harassment, 427–429
  sexual problems, 160
  single motherhood, 240–242
  teen pregnancy, 198
  wages, 294

Leadership
  discrimination, 290–292
  effectiveness, 293
  glass ceiling, 288
  job ladder, 288
  mentors, 289–290
  positions, 288
Leadership style
  laissez-faire, 293
  transformational vs. transactional
    style, 293
Leisure activities in retirement, 311–314
Leisure time, 332
Lesbians
  around the world 165
  attitudes toward, 165–168
  body image and, 122
  career selection, 277
  definition of, 163
  discrimination against, 166
  friendships, 218, 219
  health and healthcare, 358–359
  intimate partner violence, 448
  job satisfaction, 301
  in later life, 232
  loss of partner, 238
  in media, 45–46
  mental health of, 411–412
  as mothers, 242–243, 244
  relationships, 230–232
  research on, 13
  same-sex spousal rights, 168, 230
  sexual harassment and, 426
  women of color, 166
Living arrangements of elderly, 249
Loss of voice, 118
Lumpectomy, 386
Luteal phase, 183

M
Male as normative, 52–55
Mammogram, 357, 378–379
Managed care, 359
Marriage
  division of household labor and,
    329–335
  in later life, 229
  rates, 227–228
  same sex, 168, 230–232
  satisfaction with, 228–229
Masculine generic language, 54
Masculinity, 77
Mastectomy, 380–381
Mate selection across cultures, 221
Maternal employment
  attitudes toward, 326–328
  effects on children, 340–341
  effects on marital relationship, 341–342
Maternal wall, 289
Maternity blues, 205
Mathematics ability, 143–150
  achievment, 144–145
  attitudes toward mathematics, 145–146

gender comparisons, 143–144
  and mathematics self-efficacy, 145
  parents' influence on, 147
  stereotype threat, 147–150
  teachers' influence on, 147
Matriarch stereotype, 242
Maturation, effects of early and late,
    114–115
Media
  attractiveness emphasized in, 49–51
  ethnic women in, 43–44
  gender representation in, 41–51
  invisibility of older women in, 43–44
  lesbians and gays in, 45–46
  sexuality in, 49–51
  thinness emphasized in, 50
Medicaid, 357, 359–360
Medicare, 359–360
Menarche, 112–113
Menopause
  attitudes toward, 209–210
  definition of, 208
  hormone replacement and, 210, 212
  media portrayal of, 210
  physical symptoms, 209
  psychological reaction to, 209
Menstrual Distress Questionnaire
    (MDQ), 187
Menstrual joy, 185
Menstrual Joy Questionnaire (MJQ), 187
Menstruation, 9, 182–188
  menarche, 112–113
  attitudes toward, 184
  menstrual cycle, 182–184
  menstrual pain, 184, 185
Mental health
  childhood and adolescence, 397–398
  gender differences in, 394
  late adulthood, 412–414
  of lesbians, 411–412
  and optimism, 395–396
  and social support, 395
Mental rotation, 132–133
Meta-analysis, 18
Mentoring, 282–283
Midlife
  double standard of aging, 44, 46
  menopause, 208–212
  satisfaction with life roles, 347–348
  sexuality and, 173–174
  transitions, 341–342
Miscarriage 197–198
Modeling. *See* Observational learning.
Modern sexism, 38–40
Modified radical mastectomy, 380
Mons pubis, 154
Moral reasoning, 4, 132–133
Morbidity, 381, 385
Mortality, 381–383
  female-male gap, 381–383
  leading causes of death, 383
  social class and ethnic differences,
    384–385

Motherhood
  empty nest period, 244, 246
  lesbians and, 242–243, 244
  mandate, 240
  penalty, 398
  stereotypes of, 239–240
  surrogate, 206
  teenage, 198–200
  women with disabilities and, 243
Motor skills, 97–98
Mullerian ducts, 63
Mullerian inhibiting substance, 63
Multiple genders, 65
Multiple orgasms, 156

N
Narrative approach, 18
Native Americans
  academic environment and, 265
  achievement, 260
  alcohol use, 402
  body image and, 122
  cervical cancer, 367
  divorce, 233
  gender attitudes, 80–82
  heart disease, 372
  higher education, 260
  illegal drug use, 404
  intimate partner violence, 449
  mortality rates for, 384–385
  raising grandchildren, 250–251
  rape, 439
  sexual harassment and, 429
  single motherhood, 240
  teen pregnancy, 198
  wages, 294
Negative terms for females, 55–57
Never-married women. *See* Single women.
Nonportability, 318
Nonsexist therapy, 439
Nontraditional gender attitude, 80
Nonverbal communication
  gender comparisons, 137–138
Nurse-midwives, 202
Nutrition
  in breast cancer, 376–377
  in heart disease, 372–373
  needs throughout life, 389
  in osteoporosis, 370–371

O
Observational learning, 70–71
Occupational choices, 286
Occupations. *See also* Employment, Work.
Oedipus complex, 68
Older women
  adult children and, 246–247
  advocate/activist, 313–314
  and AIDS, 364–366
  attitudes toward, 31–32
  earnings of, 302
  exercise, 386–388
  friendships, 219–220

as grandmothers, 248–254
health services, 355–357
health insurance, 359–360
leisure activities of, 311–314
living arrangements of, 249
in media, 44
mental health of, 412–414
mortality of, 381–383
pensions, 318–319
in poverty, 314–315
retirement, 307–314
sexuality of, 173–176
siblings of, 246
Social Security benefits, 317–318
underrepresentation in media, 43–44
vital older women, 413–414
as volunteers, 312
widowhood, 236–238
work and, 302–304
Optimism, 395
Organizational tolerance, 431
Orgasm, 155–156
Orgasmic phase, of sexual response cycle, 155
Orgasmic platform, 155
Osteoporosis, 369–371
Ovarian cancer, 368
Ovulatory phase, 183

P
Panic disorder, 405
Pap smear, 357, 360, 367
Parallel terms, 55
Parental leave, 330–332
Patriarchy, 5
Patronizing behavior, 290
Pay equity, 304
Penis envy, 70
Pension plans, 318–319
Perimenopause, 208
Personal Attributes Questionnaire (PAQ), 77–78
Persuasion studies, 131
Phobias, 405
Physical activity, 371, 372–373, 386–389
Physical attractiveness. See Attractiveness.
Physical health
in later life, 381–383
Phyto-estrogens, 212
Plateau phase, of sexual response cycle, 155
Play
gender differences, 98–100
parental influence on, 103–105
rough-and-tumble, 100
Population, 11
Postpartum depression, 205
Postpartum psychosis, 205
Poverty, 314–315
Power
dating and, 226
interpersonal, 21
in lesbian relationships, 231

organizational, 21, 461
power-over, 22
power-to, 22
rape and, 446–447
in relationships, 461
sexual harassment and, 453
theory of, 431
touch and, 123–124
in the workplace, 297
Pregnancy. See also Abortion, Childbirth.
death related to, 195
physical changes during, 196
psychological changes during, 196
reactions to pregnant women, 197
teen pregnancies, 198–200
Premenstrual dysphoric disorder, 186–188
Premenstrual syndrome (PMS), 185–188
cultural factors in, 187–188
definition of, 186
treatment, 188
Prenatal development
androgens, 63
brain differentiation, 64
estrogens, 63
external genitalia, 63
gonadal development, 63
internal reproductive organs, 63
sex differentiation, 62
Primary sex characteristics, 110
Progesterone/progestin, 182, 183, 208, 211
Prostaglandins, 184
Prosocial behavior, 130
Psychoanalytic theory, 68–70
Psychological disorders, diagnosis and treatment, 414–416
Psychology of women
association for, 9
history of, 8–10
research and teaching, 462–464
Psychosocial development, 115–123
Psychotherapy
feminist therapy, 416
gender bias, 415–416
nonsexist therapy, 416–417
poor women and women of color, issues for, 416
traditional therapies, 416
Puberty, 109–115
early and late maturation, 114–115
gender differences in, 113

timing of, 110–112
Q
Quid pro quo harassment, 427
R
Race
defined, 21
Racism, 5

Radical mastectomy, 380
Raloxifene, 223, 371
Rape
acquaintance rape, 439–443
alcohol consumption and, 442–443
attitudes toward, 443
characteristics of rapists, 441
characteristics of victims, 442
definition of, 439
effects of, 443–445
evolutionary theory of, 445
feminist theory of, 447
incidence, 439
myths, 441–442
prevention of, 445
Reach to Recovery program, 174
social learning theory of, 447
Reinforcement and punishment, 71
Relational aggression, 129
Relationships in later life, 246–253
Relationship power equality of, 461
Religious beliefs and gender attitudes, 84
Reproductive functioning in midlife, 208–212
Reproductive health of women globally, 193–194
Reproductive system disorders, 365–366
Research
bias in, 10–18
feminist methods, 17
women's contribution, 8
Resolution phase, of sexual response cycle, 155
Retirement, 307–314
adjustment to, 309–311
decision to retire, 307–309
economic planning for, 315–319
Roe vs. Wade, 191
Role models, 71
Role overload, 337
Role strain, 337
Romantic relationships, 220–223
Rough-and-tumble play, 100

S
Salary
discrimination in, 298–299
expectations, 273
negotiations, 297–298
reasons for differences in, 295–299
gender differences in, 293–296
motherhood penalty, 298
women's perceptions of their, 296
Sample, 11
Savings and investments, 319
Scarcity hypothesis of multiple roles, 337
Secondary sex characteristics, 110
Secular trend, 112
Selection effect, 230
Self-efficacy, 145, 276

Self-esteem
    in adolescence, 116–118
    and ethnicity, 117
    Self-objectification, 119
Self-serving attributional bias, 275
Sex. *See also* Gender.
    definition of, 2
    distinction between gender
       and, 2
Sexism. *See also* Discrimination.
    ambivalent sexism, 38
    attitude changes, 38
    benevolent sexism, 38–39
    definition of, 5
    experiences with, 40–41
    hostile sexism, 38
    modern sexism, 38–40
Sex roles, 2
Sex Role Egalitarianism Scale, 82
Sex-role spillover theory, 430
Sexual abuse of children, 432–433
Sexual attitudes, 156–157, 337
    double standard, 156–157, 172
Sexual behaviors, 157–159
Sexual desire, 172
Sexual harassment
    in blue-collar occupations, 428–429
    college students and, 423–426
    consequences of, 430
    explanations of, 430–431
    hostile environment, 449
    incidence, 423–427
    in elementary and secondary school,
       423
    in the military, 429
    offender characteristics, 430
    quid pro quo harassment, 427
    target characteristics related to, 429
    women's responses to, 426, 431
    in the workplace, 426–427
Sexual interest, perception of, 233
Sexuality
    adolescent sexual behavior,
       169–172
    female sexual anatomy, 154–155
    gender differences, 158–159
    in later life, 173–176
    media portrayal of, 32–34
    midlife and, 173–174
    orgasm, 155–156
    sexual response cycle, 155–156
    wive's employment and sexual
       satisfaction, 342
Sexually transmitted infections (STIs),
       360–366
    acquired immunodeficiency
       syndrome, 362–366
    chlamy dia, 360, 362
    gender differences, 360, 362
    gonorrhea, 360, 362
    HIV, 362–366
    human papillo mavirus, 360, 362, 367
    risk factors in, 361

Sexual orientation, 62, 163–168
    and career development, 277
    explanations of, 168–169
    and gender stereotypes, 34–36
Sexual orientation hypothesis, 88
Sexual problems/dysfunction,
       159–162
    female orgasmic disorder, 159
    inhibited sexual desire, 159
    New view, 160–162
    painful intercourse, 159
    sexual arousal disorder, 159
    vaginismus, 159
Sexual response cycle, 155–156
Sexual script, 440–441
Siblings, 108, 246–247
Similarities approach, 3
Simple mastectomy, 380
Single-gender schools, 264–265
Single women
    attitudes toward, 235–236
    employment and single mothers, 234,
       287
    as mothers, 233–234
    never-married, 235–236
Skip-generation parent, 242
Slimness, emphasis on, 119–122
Smoking, 358, 370, 373, 382–383
Social categorization, 34
Social class. *See also* Ethnicity.
    and academic environment, 265
    and breast cancer, 376–377
    and friendships, 215–216
    and gender attitudes, 86
    and gender stereotypes, 32
    and mortality, 384
    and postpartum depression, 205
    and sexual dysfunction, 159–162
    and therapy, 416
Social cognitive theory, 71
Social construction of gender, 24
Socialization, 103
Social learning theory, 70–72
    of rape, 447
Social role theory, 35–36
Social Security, 317–318
Social status hypothesis, 88
Social support and mental health, 395
Soy products, 213
Specific phobia, 405
Spending down, 359
Sports, 97–98
Spotlighting, 54–55
Statistical significance, 15
Stereotypes
    and employment, 291–292
    of disabled women, 33
    of employed women, 291–292
    of ethnic minority women, 30–33
    of females and males, 28–30
    of girls and boys, 34
    of lesbians, 33
    of older women, 32

Stereotype threat, 147–150, 265
Sticky floor, 288
Substance abuse, 402–404
Suicide, 408–411
Surname choice, 36–37
Surrogate motherhood, 206
Syphilis, 360–362
Superwoman stereotype, 233
Sweatshops, 299

T
Tamoxifen, 380
Teenage pregnancy, 198–200
    consequences of, 198, 199
    prevention of, 200
    rate of, 199
    support for, 200
    Telescoping, 402
Television, as gender-typed socializing
       agent, 41–51
Tend and befriend, 395
Testosterone, 63
Therapy. *See* Psychotherapy.
Title of address, stereotypes based on, 36
Title IX of the Education Amendments
       Act, 98
Toys. *See also* Play.
    gender differences in preferences,
       98–100
    visual spatial skills and, 142
Traditional couples, 323
Traditional gender attitude, 80
Transformational leader, 293
Transactional leader, 293
Transgendered individuals, 61
Trichimoniasis, 362
Turner syndrome, 64, 67
Type A personality, 373

U
Unattached lifestyles, 230–239
Undifferentiation, 77
Unwanted sexual attention, 427
Uterine cancer, 367–368

V
Vacuum aspiration, 192
Vagina, 155
Vaginal orgasms, 156
Vaginismus, 159
Value free, 10
Vasocongestion, 155
Verbal ability, 139
Verbal communication
    language style, 133–137
Vesting, 318
Violence. *See* Abuse of women, Child
       sexual abuse, Dating.
Visual-spatial abilities, 140–143
    explanations of, 140–143
    mental rotation, 140–141
    spatial perception, 140–141
    spatial visualization, 140–141

Vital older women, 222–223
Vitamin D, 369–370, 390
Vulva, 154

W
Wages. *See* Salary.
Wage discrimination, 298
Welfare mother stereotype, 233
Welfare reforms, 287
White Ribbon Campaign, 475
Whites
    abortion, 191–192
    AIDS and, 363
    adolescent friendships, 219
    alcohol use, 402
    breast cancer and, 376
    career aspirations, 277–279
    elder caregiving, 253
    employment rates, 285
    healthcare and, 357
    heart disease, 372
    higher education and, 266
    illegal drugs and, 404
    intimate partner violence, 449
    living with relatives, 248
    marriage rates of, 227–228
    menopause attitudes, 210

mortality rates for, 384–385
occupational choices, 286
pension income, 318
perception of family and employment
    roles, 315, 332, 339
poverty, 240–241, 315
raising grandchildren, 250–251
rape, 439
single motherhood, 240–242
suicide, 409
teen pregnancy, 198
wages, 294
Widowhood, 236–238
Wolffian ducts, 63
Women-as-problem bias, 185
Women of color. *See also* Ethnicity.
    academic environment for, 265–266
    eating disorders, 420
    feminism, 4–5
    and health care, 356–357
    research on, 13–14
    therapy issues, 416
    underrepresentation in media, 43
Women psychologists, 6–10
Women's magazines
    emphasis on appearance, 49–50
    older women in, 44

women of color in, 43
Women's movements, 467–470
Women's studies courses, 474–475
Work. *See also* Employment, Jobs,
    Maternal Employment,
    Occupations.
    balancing family and, 324–347
    career counseling of women,
        269–270
    discrimination in hiring, 280
    discrimination in advancement, 290
    employment rates, 285
    entering the workplace, 280
    family expectations and, 270–271
    in later life, 302–304
    parental leave, 330–332
    salaries, 293–299
    work-related goals, 267–273
Working-class and poor women.
    See also Social class.
    academic environment for, 265
    employment of, 287
    research on, 13
    stereotypes of, 34–35
    therapy issues for, 416

PHOTO CREDITS